7/10

P9-CJJ-042

CAMBRIDGE LIBRARY COLLECTION

Books of enduring scholarly value

Linguistics

From the earliest surviving glossaries and translations to nineteenth-century academic philology and the growth of linguistics during the twentieth century, language has been the subject both of scholarly investigation and of practical handbooks produced for the upwardly mobile, as well as for travellers, traders, soldiers, missionaries and explorers. This collection will reissue a wide range of texts pertaining to language, including the work of Latin grammarians, groundbreaking early publications in Indo-European studies, accounts of indigenous languages, many of them now extinct, and texts by pioneering figures such as Jacob Grimm, Wilhelm von Humboldt and Ferdinand de Saussure.

A Sanskrit-English Dictionary

This one-volume Sanskrit–English dictionary, first published in 1891, is an English version of the seven-volume Sanskrit-Worterbuch, published at St Petersburg between 1852 and 1875, and contains about 50,000 entries. The aim of the editor, Carl Cappeller, was to provide a glossary for Sanskrit texts which were at the time becoming available in printed editions in Europe, particularly 'such works as are most appreciated and studied by every friend of Sanskrit literature'. He hoped that it would provide 'not only a handbook for the beginner in Sanskrit, who wants to have as many words as possible explained to him, but also to serve the purposes of the linguistic student, whose interest is limited to the old stock of words and their relations to other languages'. The dictionary has stood the test of time and is still consulted by students of Sanskrit.

Cambridge University Press has long been a pioneer in the reissuing of out-of-print titles from its own backlist, producing digital reprints of books that are still sought after by scholars and students but could not be reprinted economically using traditional technology. The Cambridge Library Collection extends this activity to a wider range of books which are still of importance to researchers and professionals, either for the source material they contain, or as landmarks in the history of their academic discipline.

Drawing from the world-renowned collections in the Cambridge University Library, and guided by the advice of experts in each subject area, Cambridge University Press is using state-of-the-art scanning machines in its own Printing House to capture the content of each book selected for inclusion. The files are processed to give a consistently clear, crisp image, and the books finished to the high quality standard for which the Press is recognised around the world. The latest print-on-demand technology ensures that the books will remain available indefinitely, and that orders for single or multiple copies can quickly be supplied.

The Cambridge Library Collection will bring back to life books of enduring scholarly value (including out-of-copyright works originally issued by other publishers) across a wide range of disciplines in the humanities and social sciences and in science and technology.

A Sanskrit-English Dictionary

Based upon the St Petersburg Lexicons

Carl Cappeller

Cambridge
University Press

CAMBRIDGE UNIVERSITY PRESS

Cambridge, New York, Melbourne, Madrid, Cape Town, Singapore,
São Paolo, Delhi, Dubai, Tokyo

Published in the United States of America by Cambridge University Press, New York

www.cambridge.org
Information on this title: www.cambridge.org/9781108007306

© in this compilation Cambridge University Press 2009

This edition first published 1891
This digitally printed version 2009

ISBN 978-1-108-00730-6 Paperback

This book reproduces the text of the original edition. The content and language reflect the beliefs, practices and terminology of their time, and have not been updated.

Cambridge University Press wishes to make clear that the book, unless originally published by Cambridge, is not being republished by, in association or collaboration with, or with the endorsement or approval of, the original publisher or its successors in title.

A SANSKRIT-ENGLISH DICTIONARY

BASED UPON THE ST PETERSBURG LEXICONS

BY

CARL CAPPELLER

PROFESSOR AT THE UNIVERSITY OF JENA

LONDON
LUZAC & CO. GREAT RUSSELL STREET WC
STRASSBURG: K. I. TRÜBNER
1891
[*ALL RIGHTS RESERVED*]

TO

WILLIAM DWIGHT WHITNEY

THE CHIEF INTERPRETER

OF THE EASTERN TO THE WESTERN ARYANS

DEDICATED

BY

THE AUTHOR.

Preface.

This English edition of my Sanskrit Dictionary differs from its German original not only in that it covers a much wider range of texts, but also in some minor particulars of its plan and arrangement. A few remarks will suffice to give the reader an idea of the whole.

As to the texts for which this work was designed to serve as a special glossary, I had originally only in view those of the second edition of BÖHTLINGK's Sanskrit-Chrestomathie, the hymns translated by GELDNER and KAEGI, those edited by WINDISCH, the Brāhmaṇa pieces translated by WEBER in Vol. I of the Indische Streifen, Nala, and the plays of Kālidāsa. To render my book more useful to the English student of Sanskrit, I have now added to the texts just mentioned the Marut hymns translated by F. MAX MÜLLER, the Kaṭhopaniṣad, Manu, Bhagavadgītā, Hitopadeça, Meghadūta, Mṛcchakatikā, and Mālatīmādhava. I have abstained from taking in more words from Brāhmaṇa and Sūtra texts, as these will always be least and last of all studied by beginners, thinking it better to enlarge, as much as possible, the Postvedic or classical vocabulary. From the later literature, therefore, a great many words that have not been received into the Petersburg Dictionaries (e.g. those translated from Prākṛt and many compounds) are to be found in my book, which, I believe, will furnish the reader sufficient help to understand also easier texts not particularly held in view by the author, e.g. the most beautiful episodes of the Mahābhārata and the Rāmāyaṇa, the epics of Kālidāsa, the other two plays of Bhavabhūti, and in general such works as are most appreciated and studied by every friend of Sanskrit literature. For while enlarging the number of compounds, I made it no less a rule to incorporate into this Dictionary *all primary words of well-settled meaning*, and so in all essentials to preserve its double character, to be not only a handbook for the beginner in Sanskrit, who wants to have as *many* words as possible explained to him, but also to serve the purposes of the linguistic student, whose interest is limited to the *old* stock of words and their relations to other languages.

With regard to the contents and arrangement of this book I have but little to add. At first sight it appears to be nothing but a list of Sanskrit words put in alphabetical order and confronted with their English equivalents. Such a compilation, little as it may seem, would be much, if it were made with the correctness and accuracy required by the matter. Whether I have succeeded in attaining this aim and rendering my book at least from this point of view useful to the class of readers for which it is destined, actual experience must show. I hope, however, it will be acknowledged that I have always endeavoured not only to put together words with words, but also to give the full development and connection of meanings from their first radical origin up to the various ramifications which appear in the texts enumerated above or are of universal interest. Here we must, of course, distinguish between the old simple words and the comparatively younger derivatives and compounds, which generally are easy and transparent enough to admit of an insight into their origin and growth even by the help of a simple translation. This is also the reason why I abstained from giving a formal analysis of words, such as would, in each individual case, trace the compound back to its constituent parts and the simple word to its root or stem. In the first place, nine tenth of all cases are so clear in themselves, that even for the beginner, if he only has worked his way through the euphonic rules and the elements of word-formation, they need no explanation whatever. The last tenth, on the other hand, offers numerous difficulties, which it would be impossible to remove without altogether changing the elementary character of this book. There are, moreover, two excellent guides through this domain of studies, WHITNEY's Roots and LANMAN's Reader, of which the one furnishes ample material for Sanskrit and the other for comparative etymology, so that a book, which in a certain degree is intended to be a completion or continuation of both, may well be for the most part restricted to purely lexicographic matter.

There are still a few remarks to be made about some particulars of the outer plan and arrangement of this dictionary. On the whole, it offers only *authenticated matter*, i.e. such words, word-forms, genders, accents etc. as are actually *found* in the works of Sanskrit writers, but not such as are merely *taught* by grammarians and lexicographers (with a few exceptions, which are always recognizable as such; cf. p. VIII). To accommodate myself to the English custom, and to be in accordance with WHITNEY's system, roots and stems are throughout given with *ṛ* (instead of *ar* or *ṝ*), e.g. 1 & 3कृ (instead of कर् & कृ). The adjective generally shows only the masculine stem, the regular feminine and neuter being always omitted, except where they have developed a specific signification; *ī* is always treated as the irregular feminine to *a*. Of verbal forms only the present stems are completely enumerated (including the secondary conjugation, causative, desiderative etc.). The so-called past participle is usually put immediately after the present, with which it forms as it were a kind of a-verbo and serves to keep the homonymous roots apart. In a great many cases, however, I have treated this verbal form as a separate word, first because it is no doubt the most frequent of all forms, which the beginner will most particularly like to find sub voce, secondly, because it has very often developed a pregnant meaning, and thirdly because it frequently forms the first part of compounds, at the head of which it is most properly sought and found. Wherever this principle has been carried out, reference has been made at the end of the root to the participles in question. No less have the forms in *anīya*, *tavya* etc., a great many infinitives and gerunds, and in general such forms as belong to the verb only systematically, but actually are felt as separate words, found a separate treatment according to their alphabetical order. Brevity has always conscientiously been striven after; I trust, however, that I have not gone too far in this respect and proposed riddles instead of solving them. If, for instance, I say ‚कत्थन a. & n. boasting', everybody will understand that the word ‚boasting' is to be taken in the one case as an adjective and in the other as a noun of action. Likewise an article such as ,क्ष्माधर m. mountain (earth-holder)' will be in itself clear enough and save the student the trouble of looking up क्ष्मा & धर. By the word *abstract* I understand chiefly the substantives in *tā* and *tva*, by the word *possessive* the adjectives in *vant*, *mant*, etc. In a great many instances merely the formation of such words is given, because their special meaning is easily suggested by the groundword and the passage where the derivative occurs. Of brackets a very frequent and various use has been made, which, I suppose, will be clear by itself in each single case. For all these things I call the attention of the reader to the list of abbreviations on the next page.

How far I have relied on my authorities or followed my own judgment, others may decide. I can only say that I have always tried to keep the mean between blindly following and thougthlessly abandoning the path of my great predecessors. Most difficulties arose from the Rigveda vocabulary, a great part of which has been incorporated into this book. But even on this hotly debated ground I rarely have had occasion to differ from the acknowledged chief of Vedic interpretation.

Before I conclude, I must express my profound gratitude first to the venerable editor of the great work whose treasures I was once more allowed to change into small coin and make accessible to a larger circle; next to his numerous collaborators, one of whom, I hope, will see in the liberty that I have taken of putting his name on the front page of this book, a small but well-meant token of my sincere homage to his incomparable achievements in more than one branch of Sanskrit and linguistic research. Among those who took a kind interest in the undertaking of this English edition. I have to name, in the first place, Professor Ch. R. Lanman, who during his stay in Europe, three years ago, lent me his valuable aid, and did so much by word and deed that I shall always feel myself his debtor. I can only wish that this book may not fall too short of his expectations. Finally I have to thank all those who kindly assisted me in looking over the proof-sheets, and while doing so favoured me with many a useful suggestion.

Jena, March 1891.

C. Cappeller.

List of Abbreviations.

A(ctive).
a(djective).
abl(ative).
absol(utely).
abstr(act), v. pref.
acc(usative).
add(itions).
adv(erb).
C(ausative).
cert(ain).
cf. = compare.
comp(arative).
conj(unctive).
correl(ative).
D(esiderative).
(d.) = drama.
dat(ive).
den(ominative).
du(al).
E(pithet).
e.g. = for example.
encl(itic).
esp(ecially).
excl(amation).
f(eminine).
fig(uratively).
fut(ure).
(g.) = grammar.
gen(etive).
ger(und).
I(ntensive).
i.e. = that is.
i.g. = in general.
imper(ative).
impers(onally).
indecl(inable).
inf(initive).
instr(umental).
interr(ogative).
intr(ansitive).
(j.) = jurisprudence.
l. & f. = literally and figuratively.
lit(erally).
l. l. = later language.
loc(ative).
m(asculine).
M(iddle).
m(eanin)g.
N(ame).
n(euter).
nom(inative).
num(eral).
o(ften).
opp(osed).
opt(ative).
orig(inally).
P(assive).
p(ossessive), v. pref.
part(icle).
perf(ect).
pers(on or personal).
pers(on) & th(ing).
pl(ural).
prec(eding).
pp. = participle.
pref(ix).
prep(osition).
pres(ent).
pron(oun).
q.v. = which see.
r(arely).
(r.) ritual or religion.
(rh.) rhetoric.
S(imple).
s(ubstantive).
sc(ilicet).
seq. = following.
sev(eral).
sgl. = singular.
sp(ace) & t(ime).
superl(ative).
s.v. = sub voce.
trans(itive).
voc(ative).
w(ith).

..́.. the Udātta accent.
..̂.. the proper Svarita.
± with or without.
°— the principal word of an article to be supplied at the beginning of a compound.
—° the same supplied at the end of a compound.
*.... a word taught only by grammarians or lexicographers.
....* a word which occurs only in a translation from Prākrit.
.... the same, if also taught by grammarians or lexicographers.
†.... a word which, although not accented, occurs in an otherwise accented text.
....† a word for which a previously given accent is not to be supplied.

अ

1अ pron. stem of 3^d pers.

2अ, अन् neg. prefix, corresponding to Gr. ἀ ἀν, Lat. in, Germ. un, etc.

अंश m. portion, share, part, party; N. of a god.

अंशकल्पना & °प्रकल्पना f. allotment of shares.

अंशप्रदान n. granting of a share; abl. °तस्.

अंशभागिन् & °भाज् a. having a share, partaking of (gen. or —°).

अंशभूत a. forming part of (gen.).

अंशु m. stem or juice of the Soma plant; ray of light.

अंशुक n. garment, cloth.

अंशुकान्त m. the edge of a garment.

अंशुपट्ट n. a kind of cloth.

अंशुमन्त् a. rich in Soma or rays, m. the sun.

अंस m. shoulder.

अंसकूट m., °पृष्ठ n. the same (lit. top & back of the shoulder).

अंसत्र n. armour, mail.

अंसल a. strong, stout.

अंसवर्तिन् a. being on the shoulder.

अंसव्यापिन् a. reaching up to the shoulder.

अंह्, अंहते walk. C. अंहयति send.

अंहति f., अंहस्, अंहु n. pressure, distress.

अंहीयंस् (comp.) narrower.

अंहुर a. pressed, distressed.

अंहूरण a. pressed, n. pressure.

अंह्रि m. foot.

अक n. not-joy, i.e. sorrow, woe.

अकठोर a. not hard; soft, tender.

अकण्टक a. free from thorns or enemies, untroubled.

अकथित a. not spoken of, unmentioned.

अकनिष्ठ a. pl. having no youngest (brother). equal in age or strength.

अकन्दसमुत्थित a. not grown from a bulb.*

अकन्या f. no (more a) maid.

अकम्पित a. not trembling, unshaken.

अकरण n. non-doing, omission.

अकरुण a. pitiless, cruel.

अकर्ण a. earless, deaf.

अकर्तव्य a. not to be done; n. misdeed.

अकर्तृ a. not acting, m. no agent.

अकर्मक a. having no object, intransitive.

अकर्मकृत् a. performing no action.

1अकर्मन् n. inactivity.

2अकर्मन् a. inactive, lazy.

अकलह a. without quarrel.

अकलित a. unconceived, undefined; °महिमन् a. of immeasurable greatness.

अकल्प a. unfit for (acc.); unable to, incapable of (loc., inf., or — °).

अकल्मष a. stainless.

अकल्य a. unhealthy, sick.

अकव a. abundant, liberal.

अकवि a. unwise.

अकस्मात् adv. abruptly, unexpectedly, at once; (lit. without a why, i.e. without any apparent cause).

अकाण्ड a. immediate, sudden (lit. without any joint, i.e. connection or intervening cause); loc. = prec.

अकाम a. free from love or desire, unwilling, involuntary; adv. °तस्†, abstr. °ता† f.

अकार m. the sound or letter अ.

अकारक a. ineffective, unsuccessful.

अकारण a. causeless; n. no cause.

अकारणबन्धु m. a disinterested friend.

अकारणमारक m. murderer without cause.*

अकार्य a. & n. = अकर्तव्य.

अकार्यकारिन् a. committing a bad action; m. an evil-doer, offender.
अकाल m. not the (right) time; °—, loc., & °तस् untimely, out of time.
अकालक्षेपम् adv. without delay, immediately.
अकालदुर्दिन n. unseasonable or bad weather.
अकालहीनम् adv. without loss of time; at once, suddenly.
अकिंचन a. without anything, poor, indigent; abstr. °ता f., °त्व n.
अकिंचित्कुर्वाण a. not doing anything, inactive.
अकीर्ति f. infamy, disgrace; °कर a. disgracing.
अकीर्तित a. unmentioned.
अकुतोभय a. fearless (lit. not afraid from any quarter).
अकुत्सयन्त् a. not contemning.
अकुर्वन्त् & अकुर्वाण a. not doing, omitting.
अकुल & °लीन a. of low (lit. of no) family; low-born, base.
अकुलता f. lowness of family.
अकुशल a. inauspicious, unlucky; incapable, awkward, clumsy.
अकुसुमित a. not having blossomed.
अकूपार a. boundless; m. the ocean.
अकृत a. undone, unmade, unwrought, unprepared, imperfect, unappointed; often °— not having done or got.
अकृतचूड a. whose tonsure has not been performed.
अकृतज्ञ a. unthankful (lit. not knowing or recognising things done).
अकृतपुण्य a. not having acquired merit; sinful, miserable.
अकृतपूर्व a. never before done.
अकृतप्रसाद a. not having got mercy, unpardoned.*
अकृतबुद्धि a. of imperfect knowledge, dull, stupid; abstr. °त्व n.
अकृतवैर a. unoffended.
अकृतसत्कार a. unaccommodated, not hospitably received.
अकृतात्मन् a. of uncultivated mind, rude.
अकृतान्न n. uncooked food.
अकृतार्थ a. not having attained the (desired) object, unsatisfied.
अकृताह्निक a. not performing the daily rites.
अकृत्य a. = अकर्तव्य.
अकृत्स्न a. not whole, incomplete.
अकृत्स्नविद् a. not omniscient.
अकृपण a. unquerulous, cheerful.
अकृषीवल a. not cultivating the field.
अकृष्ट a. untilled; n. untilled soil.
अकेतु a. without light or shape.
अकैतव a. unfeigned, sincere.
अकोपयन्त् a. not irritating.
अक्ता f. night (cf. seq.).
अक्तु m. ointment; light or night (lit. what is anointed, i.e. tinged bright or dark); instr. pl. o. = by night.
1अक्र a. inactive.
2अक्र m. banner, flag.
अक्रतु a. powerless, unwise, free from desire.
अक्रम m. want of order; °— confusedly.
अक्रव्याद् & °द a. not eating flesh.
अक्रिया f. inactivity, omission.
अक्रीत a. unbought.
अक्रूर a. not cruel or harsh.
1अक्रोध m. abstr. to seq.
2अक्रोध a. free from anger, impassionate.
अक्रोधन a. the same.
अक्लिष्ट a. unvexed, unimpaired; °कर्मन् & °कारिन् a. of unwearied activity.
अक्लेश m. non-affliction.
अक्ष्, pp. अष्ट reach, obtain.
1अक्ष m. die for playing; pl. game at dice.
2अक्ष m. axle.
3अक्ष (adj. —° f. ई) = अक्षन्.
अक्षण्वन्त् a. having eyes.
अक्षत a. unhurt, unbroken, unhusked (grain).
अक्षतयोनि a. virginal (lit. vulvam integram habens), °पत्नी a wife wedded as a virgin.
अक्षत्र a. without the warrior caste.
अक्षद्यूत n. game at dice.
अक्षन् n. eye.
अक्षनैपुण n. skill in playing at dice.
अक्षप्रिय m. friend of, i.e. lucky with the dice.
अक्षभङ्ग m. breaking of an axle.
अक्षम a. unable to bear, no match or unfit for (loc., inf., or —°); f. आ intolerance, impatience, envy.
अक्षमाला f. rosary, string of beads (also °लिका f.); E. of Arundhatī.

अक्षय a. imperishable; abstr. °ता f., °त्व n.
अक्षयफल a. yielding imperishable fruit.
अक्षय्य a. inexhaustible, imperishable.
अक्षर a. the same; n. sound, word, syllable, esp. the sacred Om; record, writing.
अक्षरच्छन्दस् n. a syllabic metre (i. e. a metre regulated by syllables).
अक्षरपङ्क्ति f. N. of a metre.
अक्षरपद n. a word consisting of syllables.*
अक्षरा f. speech.
अक्षवती f. game at dice.
अक्षहृदय n. the art (lit. heart) of playing at dice.
अक्षारलवण n. anything not pungent or salted; °णान्न & °णाशिन् eating such food.
अक्षि n. eye.
अक्षिण्वन्त् a. not hurting.
अक्षित, अक्षीण & अक्षीयमाण a. unhurt, unbroken, imperishable.
अक्षिति a. the same; f. imperishableness.
अक्षिपत् adv. a bit (lit. what flies into the eye).
अक्षिरोग m. disease of the eyes.
अक्षिशिरोमुख (n. sgl.) eye, head, and mouth.
अक्षी f. eye.
अक्षु m. a kind of net.
अक्षुण्ण a. unhurt, uninjured; fresh, new, strange.
1अक्षेत्र n. no field, barren ground.
2अक्षेत्र a. uncultivated, uninhabitable, comp. °तर.
अक्षेत्रिन् a. having no field.
अक्षौहिणी f. a (complete) army.
अक्ष्णया adv. athwart, obliquely, in the wrong way.
अक्ष्णयावन् a. going athwart.
अखण्ड a. undivided, indivisible; whole, entire.
अखण्डकल a. having its digits complete, full (the moon).
अखण्डित a. unbroken, uninterrupted, undisturbed.
अखण्डितचारित्र a. of unbroken (good) conduct.*
अखर्व a. unmutilated, entire, complete.
अखादित a. unchewed.*
अखिद्र a. unwearied.
अखिद्रयामन् a. of unwearied course.
अखिल a. having no gap or void, whole, entire; instr. wholly, completely. n. all, everything.
अखेद m. unweariedness, freshness.
†अखखली exclam. of joy or surprise, °कृ utter this sound.
अग (*a. not moving;) m. tree or mountain.
अगणयन्त् a., °यित्वा ger. not reckoning or heeding; not caring for (acc.).
अगत a. not gone; n. untrodden ground.
अगतासु a. alive (lit. whose breath is not yet gone).
1अगद m. not-disease, health.
2अगद a. free from disease, well, healthy; m. medicine, drug.
अगन्ध & अगन्धवन्त् a. without smell.
अगम a. immovable, inaccessible; m. tree.
अगम्य a. inaccessible, unintelligible; f. आ (a woman) not to be approached.
अगम्यागमन n. approaching an unapproachable (female), illicit sexual intercourse; °नीय a. relating to it.
अगर्हित a. unblamed, blameless.
अगस्ति & अगस्त्य m. N. of a sage.
अगाग्र n. mountain-top.
अगाध a. bottomless, deep; °सत्त्व a. of an unfathomable character.
अगार n. (m.) house. °दाहिन् burning a house, incendiary.
अगु a. having no cows, poor.
अगुण a. having no qualities or virtues, worthless; m. bad quality, vice.
अगुणीभूत a. not being subordinate or secondary.
अगुप्त a. unguarded.
अगुरु a. not heavy; light, short (prosod.); m. n. aloe wood.
अगृभीत a. untaken, unconceived; °शोचिस् having inconceivable splendour.
अगृहीत a. = अगृभीत.
अगृहीत्वा ger. without (taking).*
अगृह्णन्त् a. not taking or conceiving.
अगृह्य a. not to be taken or conceived.
अगोचर a. not being within the reach of, inaccessible to (gen. or —°); abstr. °ता f.
अगोपा a. without a cowherd, unguarded.
अगोपाल a. the same; m. no cowherd.

अगोह्य a. not to be hidden.
अग्नायी f. N. of Agni's wife.
अग्नि m. fire, or Agni (the god of fire).
अग्निकर्मन् n. action of Agni or action pertaining to fire, esp. the arranging or kindling of the sacrificial fire.
अग्निकल्प a. fire-like, fiery.
अग्निकाम m. wish for fire.
अग्निकार्य n., **°क्रिया** f. = **अग्निकर्मन्**.
अग्निगृह n. the place of the sacred fire.
अग्निचय m., **°चयन** n. the arranging of the fire-place.
अग्निजिह्व a. fire-tongued.
अग्निज्वलिततेजन a. having a point blazing with fire.
अग्नित्रय n., **°त्रेता** f. the three sacred fires.
अग्निद m. incendiary.
अग्निदग्ध or **अग्निदग्ध** a. burned with fire; m. pl. a class of Manes.
अग्निदूत a. having Agni as messenger, carried or brought by Agni.
अग्निदूषित a. hurt by fire, branded.
अग्निध् m. (the priest) who kindles the fire.
अग्निपक्व a. cooked with fire; **°पक्वाशन** eating cooked food.
अग्निपरिक्रिया f. care of the sacred fire.
अग्निपरिच्छद m. the implements required for a fire-sacrifice.
अग्निपुराण n. T. of a Purāṇa.
अग्निप्रवेश m., **°प्रस्कन्दन** n. (self-immolation by) entering the fire.
अग्निभ्राजस् a. having fiery splendour.
अग्निमन्त् a. maintaining the sacred fire, also = **अग्निवन्त्**.
अग्निमित्र m. N. of a king.
अग्निवन्त् a. standing at the sacred fire.
अग्निवर्ण a. fire-coloured, boiling hot.
अग्निशरण n. = **अग्निगृह**.
अग्निशिख a. having a fiery or burning point (arrow); f. **आ** fire-flame.
अग्निशुद्धि f. purification by fire.
अग्निशुश्रूषा f. attention to the sacred fire.
अग्निष्टुत् m. the first day of the Agniṣṭoma (v. seq.).
अग्निष्टोम m. a cert. ceremony (lit. praise of Agni).
अग्निष्वात्त m. pl. a class of the Manes (lit. eaten by fire).
अग्निसंस्कार m. rite performed by fire, esp. the burning of the dead body.
अग्निसात् adv. into fire; **°कृ** burn.
अग्निस्वामिन् m. N. of man.
1**अग्निहोत्र** n. fire-sacrifice.
2**अग्निहोत्र** a. sacrificing to Agni.
अग्निहोत्रहवणी f. ladle for a fire-sacrifice.
अग्निहोत्रिन् a. performing the fire-sacrifice.
अग्नीन्द्र m. du. Agni and Indra.
अग्नीध् m. = **अग्निध्**.
अग्नीन्धन n. kindling of the fire.
अग्नीषोम m. du. Agni and Soma.
अग्न्यागार m. = **अग्निगृह**.
अग्न्याधान & **°धेय** n. setting up the fire.
अग्न्याहित a. who has set up the fire.
अग्र n. front, top, summit, tip, point, upper part, surface; outbreak, beginning; the highest or best of anything. — **अग्रम्** in front or in presence of, (gen. or —°); **अग्रे** the same + from (to = **आ**), before (abl.); absol. at first, in the beginning; w. **भू** precede.
अग्रकर m. finger and first ray.
अग्रज a. first-born (also **°जा**); m. eldest brother.
अग्रजन्मन् m. a Brahman (lit. = prec.).
अग्रणी a. leading; m. chief, principal.
अग्रतस् = **अग्रे**; **°कृ** place in front, send before.
अग्रभाग m., **°भूमि** f. uppermost part, top.
अग्रमुख n. bill, beak.
अग्रयायिन् a. marching foremost.
अग्रहस्त m. tip of the hand (i. e. finger) or of an elephant's trunk.
अग्रहार m. a piece of land held by Brahmans under special grants.
अग्रानीक n. front of an army, vanguard.
अग्राहयित्वा ger. without making a person accept a thing (2 acc.).
अग्राहिन् a. not catching or biting (leech).
अग्राह्य a. = **अगृह्य**.
अग्रिम a. preceding, foremost, first.
अग्रिय a. the same, principal, best, excellent; n. the best.
अग्रु, f. **अग्रू** single, unmarried.
अग्रेग, **°गा**, & **°गु** a. first-going.
अग्रेदिधिषु m. a man married at his first

marriage with a widow; f. (also °षू) a younger sister married before her elder.
अग्रेपा & °पू a. first-drinking.
अग्रेसर f. ई preceding, going first.
अग्र्य a. foremost, first, best.
अघ a. evil, bad, sinful (also **अघल**); n. evil, sin, harm, impurity.
अघमर्षण a. forgiving sin; n. N. of a certain Vedic hymn.
अघविघातकर्तृ m. destroyer of evil.
अघशंस a. meditating evil, wicked.
अघाय्, °यति be wicked, a. °युं.
अघाहन् n. day of sin, ill-luck, or impurity.
अघृण a. pitiless, cruel, unkind.
अघोरघण्ट m. N. of a man.
अघ्न्य or **अघ्न्यं** m. bull, f. **आ** cow (lit. not to be slain).
अघ्रेय a. not to be smelled at.
अङ्क m. hook (poss. **अङ्किन्**), bend, flank, esp. of the body, groin, lap, side, proximity; mark, sign; act of a play.
अङ्कपाली f. an embrace.
अङ्कय्, °यति, pp. **अङ्कित** mark, stamp, brand (a criminal).
अङ्कयष्टि f. a slender (lit. stalk of a) body.
अङ्कशायिन् a. lying in the lap.
अंङ्कस् n. bend, curve.
अङ्कसं s. side, flank (of a horse).
अङ्कस्थ a. = **अङ्कशायिन्**.
अङ्कुर m. shoot, sprout; poss. °रित or °रवन्त्.
अङ्कुरय & °राय्, यते to sprout.
अङ्कुश m. hook, esp. for driving an elephant.
अङ्कुशिन् a. hooked, crooked, deceiving.
अङ्क्य्, °यन्त् grapple. — **परि** M. embrace.
अङ्क्य a. to be branded.
अङ्ग्, **अङ्गति** move.
1**अङ्ग** a particle implying sollicitation, confirmation, or stress.
2**अङ्ग** m. N. of sev. men & of a country (Bengal), pl. its inhabitants.
3**अङ्ग** (adj. —° f. ई) limb, member, body (also **अङ्गक** n.); part, means requisite, supplement (cf. **वेदाङ्ग**), theme (g.).
अङ्गण n. court.
अङ्गद m. a man's name; n. bracelet, poss. °दिन्.
अङ्गन n. = **अङ्गण**.
अङ्गना f. woman, female.
अङ्गभङ्ग m. distortion of the limbs.*
अङ्गराग m. paint, ointment, perfume (applied to the body).
अङ्गराज m. the king of Aṅga, i.e. Karṇa.
अङ्गविकार m. disease (lit. alteration of the body).
अङ्गविद्या f. knowledge of the (lucky and unlucky marks of the) body.
अङ्गसंस्कार m. embellishment of the body.
अङ्गसंताप m. bodily pain.*
अङ्गस्पर्श m. bodily contact.
अङ्गहीन a. deficient in limbs; abstr. °त्व n.
अंङ्गार m. n. coal; °क† m. the same; the planet Mars.
अङ्गावपीडन n. injuring of a limb.
अंङ्गिरस् m. a kind of mythol. beings with Agni at their head; N. of an old Rishi, pl. his descendants or their hymns, i.e. the Atharvaveda. — °रस्तम (superl.) quite an A., **अङ्गिरस्वत्** adv. like an A.
अङ्गिन् a. poss. to 3**अङ्ग**; m. a. limbed or living creature.
अङ्गी w. **कृ** appropriate, conquer, subdue (lit. make part of one's self, cf. 3. **अङ्ग**); consent to, promise, grant; abstr. °करण n., °कार m.
अङ्गुरि f. finger, toe.
अङ्गुरीयक n. finger-ring.
अङ्गुल m. n. a thumb's breadth.
अङ्गुलि or °ली f. finger or toe.
अङ्गुलित्र & °त्राण n. finger-protector, i.e. a kind of leather thimble worn by archers.
अङ्गुलित्रवन्त् a. poss. to **अङ्गुलित्र**.
अङ्गुलिमुद्रा f. seal-ring (lit. finger-seal)
अङ्गुलिमूल n. the root of a finger.
अङ्गुलीय & °क n. finger-ring.
अङ्गुष्ठ m. thumb or great toe; °मात्र† & **मात्रक**† a. having the length of a thumb.
अङ्गुष्ठमूल n. the root of the thumb.
अंङ्घ्रि m. foot, root; °पद्म† s. lotus-(like) foot.
अच्, **अंचति**, °ते & **अंच्चति**; **ते**, pp. **अक्त** (**अक्त**)

अचित & अञ्चित (q.v.) bend, move, go; exalt, honour. C. अञ्चयति rouse, excite. — अप push off, remove. आ bend, curve. उद् lift up, raise. नि bend down; drop, sink. परि turn. वि bend asunder, spread, extend. सम् bend or press together.

अचक्षुर्विषय a. not being within the reach of sight, invisible; m. a far distance.

अचक्षुस् a. eyeless, blind.

अचन्दन a. not being sandal.

अचर a. immovable, firm.

अचरम a. having no hindmost, i.e. having innumerable followers.

अचल a. the same; m. mountain, f. आ the earth.

अचलन n. immobility; inflexibility from (abl.).

अचलप्रतिष्ठ a. of firm standing.

अचापल n. non-unsteadiness; firmness, constancy.

अचित् a. unthinking, foolish.

अचित्त a. unconceived, inconceivable.

अचित्ति f. want of intellect, folly.

अचिन्तनीय a. inconceivable.

अचिन्ता f. thoughtlessness, disregard.

अचिन्तित a. unthought of, unexpected.

अचिन्त्य a. incomprehensible.

अचिन्त्यपराक्रम a. of inconceivable power.

अचिन्त्यरूप a. of incomprehensible form.

अचिर a. not long (time); short, brief. °— not long ago, recently, just (esp. before pp.); °रम्, °रेण, & °रात् in a short time, soon, directly.

अचिरद्युति, °प्रभा & °प्रभास् f. lightning (lit. having brief splendour).

अचिरप्रव्रजित a. recently become a religious mendicant.

अचिरस्थित a. not having been kept (lit. not h. stood) a long time.

अचिरोदित a. just risen.

अचेतन a. reasonless, unconscious.

अचेतस् a. the same.

अचेष्ट a. motionless; abstr. °ता f.

अचोदित & **अचोद्यमान** a. not compelled, spontaneous.

अचौर m. no thief.*

1**अच्छ** or **अच्छा** adv. close by, here; prep. to, towards (acc.); often °— in verbs.

2**अच्छ** a. clear, transparent, clean, pure.

अच्छल n. no fraud or artifice; instr. adv.

अच्छिद्र a. unbroken, uninterrupted, complete.

अच्छिन्न a. uncut, unbroken, unhurt.

अच्छेद्य a. not to be cut off.

अच्छोक्ति f. invocation, invitation.

अच्युत or **अच्युत** a. unshaken, firm, imperishable; m. N. of Viṣṇu.

अच्युतच्युत् a. shaking what is firm.

अज्, अजति, °ते drive. — अप drive away. अभि drive near or together, join. अव drive down. आ bring near, fetch; approach. उद् M. drive out, take off. उप drive near or hither. निस् drive out. वि drive asunder, rush through (acc.). सम् drive together, unite; overthrow.

1**अज** m. drift, rush; driver, mover (often w. एकपद् q.v.); he-goat, f. आ she-goat.

2**अज** a. unborn; f. आ nature (ph.).

अजगर m. large serpent, boa.

अजड a. not stupid, wise.

अजन unpeopled; n. solitude.

अजप & °पाल m. goat-herd.

अजमायु a. bleating like a goat.

अजमीढ (°ळ्ह) m. N. of a man.

अजय्य a. invincible.

अजर a. not aging, ageless, undecaying.

अजरन्त् & **अजर्य** a. the same.

अजरामर a. free from age and death; °वत् adv., °त्व n. abstr.

अजल्पन्त् a. not saying.

अजस्र a. unexhausted, incessant; n. adv.

अजहल्लक्षणा f. opp. of जहल्लक्षणा q.v.

अजात a. unborn, not existent.

अजातपक्ष a. having no wings (grown).

अजातशत्रु a. having no enemies (existent), E. of Yudhiṣṭhira etc.

अजानन्त् a. not knowing.

अजामि a. not of kin; not becoming among kindred.

अजावि (m. pl.), **अजाविक** (n. sgl.) goats and sheep.

अजित a. unconquered, unsubdued.

अजितात्मन् a. having an unsubdued soul.

अजितेन्द्रिय a. having unconquered senses, passionate.

अजिन n. hide, esp. of a goat or antelope.
अजिर a. agile, swift; n. adv., as subst. area, court.
†अजिराय्, ॰यते be quick.
अजिह्म a. not crooked; straight, upright.
अजिह्मग a. going straight; m. arrow.
अजिह्विका f. Tongueless, N. of a Rākṣasī.
अजीगर्त m. N. of a Rishi.
अजीत a. unfaded, fresh; abstr. अजीति f.
अजीर्ण n. indigestion.
अजीर्यता f. indestructibleness.
अजीव a. lifeless.
अजीवन्त् a. not living, unable to subsist.
अजीवित n. not-life, death.
अजुर् & अजुर्य a. not aging, imperishable.
अजुष्ट a. unpleasant, disagreeable.
अजेय a. unconquerable.
अज्जुका f. a courtesan.
अज्ञ a. not knowing, ignorant; m. fool.
अज्ञता f. ignorance.
अज्ञात a. unknown; n. adv. without the knowledge of (gen.).
अज्ञाति m. not a kinsman.
अज्ञान a. ignorant. n. ignorance; ॰नात् & ॰नतस् unknowingly, unawares.
अज्ञानज a. born of ignorance.
अज्ञास् a. having no relations.
अज्ञेय a. inconceivable, incomprehensible.
अज्म m., अज्मन् n. course, way, train.
अज्येष्ठ a. not the eldest or the best, pl. having no eldest brother; ॰वृत्ति† a. not behaving like an eldest brother.
अज्र m. acre, field, plain; a. अज्र्य.
अञ्चिन् a. active, agile.
अञ्चल m. end or border of a cloth.
अञ्चित a. bent, crooked; raised, honoured, excellent, extraordinary, beautiful.
अञ्ज्, अनक्ति, अङ्क्ते pp. अक्त smear, anoint, adorn (M. refl.); glorify, extol; make clear, manifest. C. अञ्जयति smear, anoint. — अनु anoint. अभि smear, anoint (M. refl.), adorn. आ anoint, smooth, embellish, glorify. नि smear, anoint; M. slip into, hide among (अन्तर्). प्रति anoint, adorn. वि M. anoint throughout; anoint or adorn one's self with (instr. or acc.); make clear, bring to notice, betray. C. cause to become clear, reveal. अभिवि P. become clear, appear. सम् anoint, adorn, embellish, honour; join, unite; lick, devour; M. feed on (instr.). — Cf. अभिव्यक्त, अभ्यक्त, व्यक्त.
अञ्जन n. smearing, anointing; suggesting (rh.); ointment, paint, esp. a collyrium made of antimony.
अञ्जलि m. the two hollowed hands put together (as a measure or a token of reverence). ॰लिं कृ or बन्ध् put the hands together and raise them to the forehead.
अञ्जस् n. ointment; instr. & acc. quickly, suddenly (lit. in a slippery way or with gliding motion).
अञ्जःसव m. rapid preparation of Soma.
अञ्जि a. smearing, slippery (also अञ्जिव); m. n. ointment, paint, colour, ornament.
अञ्जिमन्त् a. anointed, adorned.
अट्, अटति, ॰ते (± परि) walk about, roam.
अटन n. roaming, wandering.
अटनि or ॰नी f. the notched end of a bow.
अटवी f. forest.
अट्ट m. tower, buttress, also अट्टाल m.
अट्टहास m. loud laughter.
अट्या f. roaming.
अणिष्ठ & अणीयंस् superl. & compar. to अणु.
1अणिमन् m. subtility, minuteness (also considered as a superhuman faculty).
2अणिमन् n. the smallest piece or part.
अणु f. अण्वी small, minute, tiny, atomic; m. atom, f. finger.
अणुमात्रिक a. containing minute particles.
अणुमुख, f. ई small-mouthed.
अण्ड n. egg, testicle; ॰गत a. being in the egg.
अण्डज a. egg-born; m. bird.
अण्व n. a fine hole in the Soma strainer.
अत्, अतति, ॰ते walk about, wander, run. — सम् go or come to (acc.).
अतत्त्व n. untruth, unreality; ॰तस् not really.
अतत्त्वार्थवन्त् a. not answering to the nature of truth.
अतट m. precipice (lit. having no slope)

अतथाभाव m. unreality (lit. the not being so).
अतथोचित a. not used to this (gen.).
अतद्विद् a. not knowing that.
अतनु a. not small, large.
अतन्द्र, अतन्द्रित, & °द्रिन् a. unwearied.
अतपस्, अतपस्क, & अतपस्य a. impious (lit. excercising no austerities).
अतर्कित a. unconsidered, unexpected.
अतल n. N. of a cert. hell (lit. bottomless).
अतस् adv. hence, afterwards, then, from now (± **ऊर्ध्वम्** & **परम्**); therefore, consequently. Also = abl. of 1**अ**.
अतस n. thicket, copse.
अतसि m. wanderer, beggar.
अति adv. (mostly °—) across, beyond, past, over, excessively, quite, most; as prep. beyond, over (w. acc., r. gen.).
अतिकरुण a. too piteous or miserable, n. adv.
अतिकल्यम् adv. too early.
अतिकल्याण, f. **ई** exceedingly beautiful.
अतिकातर a. too timid or shy.
अतिकाय a. very big or tall.
अतिकुपित a. very angry, wrathful.
अतिकृच्छ्र m. a certain penance (lit. too painful).
अतिकृत a. overdone, extraordinary.
अतिकोप m. great anger, wrath.
अतिकोपन a. too angry.
अतिक्रम m. going over, passing; transgression, disregard; mistake, blunder.
अतिक्रमण n. going over, passing, transgressing; irreverence towards (—°).
अतिक्रूर a. too cruel or dreadful.
अतिक्लामित a. very depressed.*
अतिग (—°) exceeding, transgressing.
अतिचतुर a. very quick.
अतिचार m. transgression.
अतिचिरम् adv. very long.
अतिच्छन्दस् a. free from desires; f. a hypermetrical verse.
अतिजगती f. N. of a metre.
अतिजीवन्मृतक a. more dead than living.
अतितपस्विन् a. very ascetic.
अतितराम् adv. more, in a higher degree; much, exceedingly, absolutely.
अतितारिन् a. crossing, getting over.
अतितृष्ण a. very thirsty.
अतितृष्णा f. excessive greediness.
अतितेजस् & °जस्विन् a. very splendid or powerful.
अतिथि m. guest; **°त्व**† n. hospitality.
अतिथिपूजन n., **°पूजा** f. honourable reception of a guest.
अतिदक्षिणता f. too much courtesy.*
अतिदारुण a. too hard or cruel.
अतिदाह m. violent burning or heat.
अतिदीप्त a. blazing violently.
अतिदीर्घ a. too long.
अतिदीर्घकोपनता f. too long lasting anger.*
अतिदुःखान्वित & °दुःखित a. greatly afflicted.
अतिदुर्वृत्त a. of very bad conduct.
अतिदुष्कर a. very difficult.
अतिदुष्ट a. too wicked or cruel.
अतिदुस्तर a. very difficult to be crossed.
अतिदून a. too shaken or troubled.*
अतिदूर a. very or too far.
अतिदृढ a. too firm, close, or tight.
अतिदेश m. transfer, extended application, analogy.
अतिधीर a. quite constant.
अतिधृति f. N. of a class of metres.
अतिनाष्ट्र a. past danger.
अतिनिद्रालु a. too sleepy.
अतिनिर्घृण a. quite pitiless.*
अतिनिर्बन्ध m. too much eagerness; instr. & **°तस्** adv.
अतिनिर्विण्ण a. too despondent or humble.*
अतिनिष्करुण a. too merciless.
अतिनिष्ठुर a. too rude or harsh; abstr. **°ता** f., **°त्व** n.
अतिनृशंस a. too wicked.
अतिपरिक्षत a. grievously wounded.
अतिपात m. passing away; disregard, neglect.
अतिपातिन् a. going beyond, passing, overtaking, neglecting.
अतिपिनद्ध a. too tightly fastened.*
अतिप्रकाश a. very manifest; abstr. **°कत्व** n.
अतिप्रगे adv. too early.
अतिप्रबन्ध m. uninterruptedness, continuance
अतिप्रमाण a. of extraordinary size, huge.
अतिप्रयुक्त a. very much used or common.
अतिप्रवृत्त a. very zealous or active.

अतिप्रवृद्ध a. full-grown, advanced (age); too haughty or arrogant.
अतिप्रशान्त a. quite abated or calm.
अतिप्रसक्ति f., °**प्रसङ्ग** m. excessive attachment to (gen. or —°); abl. °**प्रसङ्गतस्**.
अतिप्रसन्न n. (imp.) too kind of (instr.).
अतिप्राकृत a. quite vulgar or uneducated.
अतिप्रौढयौवन a. in the full bloom of youth.
अतिबल, °**लवन्त्** & °**लिन्** a. very strong.
अतिबाल a. very young.
अतिबीभत्स a. quite disgusting.
अतिबोधिसत्त्व a. exceeding the saints.
अतिभक्ति f. excessive devotion.
अतिभार m. heavy burden.
अतिभीषण a. quite dreadful.
अतिभुक्त n. (imp.) too much eaten.
अतिभूमि f. culmination, high degree; (°**लङ्घिन्** going too far*).
अतिभूरि a. very much; °**पयस्** a. yielding very much milk.
अतिभैरव a. most terrific.
अतिमध्यंदिन n. the very midday.
अतिभोजन n. too much eating.
अतिमधुरम् adv. very sweetly.*
अतिमलिन a. very dirty or mean.
अतिमात्र a. exceeding the measure, excessive; °— & n. adv.
अतिमान m. high opinion, arrogance.
अतिमानिन् a. haughty, arrogant.
अतिमानुष a. superhuman.
अतिमुक्त a. escaped (acc.); s. N. of a plant.
अतिमुखर a. very talkative.
अतिमुग्ध a. much perplexed.
अतिमूढ a. quite foolish.
अतियश & °**यशस्** a. very glorious.
अतिरंहस् a. very quick.
अतिरमणीय & °**रम्य** a. quite delightful.
अतिरस्कृत a. unimpaired.
अतिरात्र a. left over from last night.
अतिरिक्त a. excessive, superfluous, too large, too much, surpassing (acc.) by (instr.); having too much or too many (°— or —°); different from (abl. or —°). Abstr. °**ता**† f.
अतिरिक्ताङ्ग a. having redundant limbs.
अतिरुष् a. very angry.
अतिरूप a. most beautiful; n. great beauty.
अतिरेक m. surplus, remainder, rest; excess, high degree.
अतिलज्जनीय a. too shameful or confounding.*
अतिललित a. very pleasant.
अतिलुब्ध a. very covetous or greedy.
अतिलोभ m., °**ता** f. excessive greediness or desire.
अतिलोम a. too hairy.
अतिलोल a. very unsteady or frail.
अतिलोहित, f. °**हिनी** very red.
अतिलौल्य n. too much eagerness or desire.
अतिवर्तन n. escape.
अतिवर्तिन् a. exceeding, transgressing.
अतिवर्ष m. n., °**वर्षण** n. too much rain.
अतिवाद m. excessive language, injury.
अतिवामोरु a. exceedingly beautiful (lit. handsome-thighed).
अतिविधुर a. too miserable.
अतिविसंष्ठुल a. too unsteady or uncertain.
अतिविस्तर a. diffuseness, prolixity; °**तस्** at large, in full detail.
अतिविस्तार m. too great extent.
अतिवीर्यवन्त् a. very powerful.
अतिवृत्त a. passed away; past or beyond (—°).
अतिवृद्ध a. very old, tall, or strong; prominent by (instr.).
अतिवृष्टि f. too much rain, °**द** giving or causing it.
अतिशक्करी f. N. of a metre.
अतिशङ्कित a. much afraid of (abl.)
अतिशय a. excessive, excellent, superior to (abl.); m. excessiveness, excellence, superiority. °— & instr. adv. excessively, very much, more.
अतिशयन, f. **ई** & °**शयिन्** a. excellent.
अतिशयित a. exceeded; exceeding (acc.), extraordinary.
अतिशयोपमा f. an exaggerated comparison.
अतिशायिन् a. surpassing.
अतिशिथिल a. very inconstant.*
अतिशिष्ट a. left, remaining.
अतिशुद्ध a. quite pure or clean.
अतिशौण्डीरता f. too much generosity.*
अतिश्रम m. excessive weariness.
अतिषक्त a. connected with (instr.), attached to (—°).

अतिष्कद् f. leaping over.

अतिष्ठन्त् a. not staying, restless; withdrawing from (loc.).

अतिष्ठा a. surpassing; f. superiority.

अतिसंकट a. very difficult; n. great trouble.

अतिसंक्रुद्ध a. very angry.

अतिसंचय m. too much hoarding.

अतिसंनिधान n. too great nearness.

अतिसंभ्रम m. vehement agitation or confusion.

अतिसरस a. most delicious (also as compar. w. abl.).

अतिसर्ग m. concession, permission, leave.

अतिसहसा (instr. adv.) too suddenly.

अतिसांवत्सर, f. **ई** extending beyond a year.

अतिसाध्वस n. too much shyness.

अतिसायम् adv. very late.

अतिसार m. diarrhoea.

अतिसाहस n. excessive rashness, temerity.

अतिसुख a. most delightful.

अतिसूक्ष्म a. very subtile or minute.

अतिसृष्टि f. a higher creation.

अतिसौहित्य n. too good cheer (lit. over-saturation).

अतिस्वप्नशील a. too much given to sleep.

अतिस्वल्प a. very small or little.

अतीत a. gone away, passed, dead; going beyond, transcending, surpassing (—°).

अतीतशैशव a. who has passed his infancy or minority.

अतीन्द्रिय a. going beyond or unattainable by the senses; n. mind, soul.

अतीन्द्रियग्राह्य a. conceivable (only) by the internal organ.

अतीर्थ n. not the right way or time.

अतीव adv. exceedingly, very much; as prep. above, more than (acc. or abl.).

अतुदन्त् a. not urging.

अतुल a. unequalled, unparalleled.

अतुष्ट a. dissatisfied.

अतुष्टि f. dissatisfaction.

अतुष्टिकर a. causing discontent, disgusting.

अतूतुजि a. not quick; slow.

अतृप्णुवन्त् a. insatiable.

अतृप्त a. unsatiated, unsatisfied; abstr. **°ता** f.

अतैजस a. not made of metal.

अत्क m. garment, veil; lightning.

अत्तव्य a. to be eaten.

__अत्ता__ & __अत्तिका__ f. mother.

अत्ति a. eating, consuming.

अत्तृ m. eater, devourer; f. **अत्त्री**.

अत्य a. hastening, running, swift; m. courser, horse, f. **आ** mare.

अत्यद्भुत a. most wonderful.

अत्यन्त a. reaching to the end, uninterrupted, continual, thorough, complete, absolute. °— & n. to the end, through life, for ever, continually, throughout, thoroughly.

अत्यय m. going beyond, passing away; transgression, offence, sin; distress, pain, danger; end, death.

अत्यर्थ (°—) & **°म्** adv. excessively, very much.

अत्यल्प a. very little.

अत्यल्पबुद्धि a. of very small understanding, stupid.

अत्यशन n. too much eating.

अत्यश्नन्त् a. eating too much.

अत्यष्टि f. N. of a metre.

अत्याकुल a. very confused; n. adv.

अत्यागिन् a. not leaving or renouncing.

अत्यादर m. too much regard or consideration.

अत्यादित्य a. surpassing the sun.

अत्यायत a. very tall.

अत्याश्चर्य a. most wonderful or strange.

अत्याहित a. extraordinary, dreadful; n. calamity, misfortune.

अत्युग्र a. very mighty or strong; awful, dire.

अत्युच्छ्रित a. highest, most exalted.

अत्युदात्त a. prominent.

अत्युदार a. most sublime.

अत्युन्नति f. elevation, high rank.

अत्युष्ण a. very hot.

अत्र & **अत्रा** adv. here, hither; herein, in this case or matter; there, then; also = loc. of 1 **अ**.

अत्रप a. shameless.

अत्रभवन्त्, f. **°वती** his or her reverence (here).

अत्रान्तरे (loc. adv.) meantime.

अत्रि a. eating, devouring. m. N. of a Rishi & star in the Great Bear, pl. the descendants of Atri.

अत्रिज a. born of Atri.

अत्रिन् a. voracious, ravenous.

अत्रिवर्ष a. not yet three years old.
अत्वर & °रन्त् a. not speeding, slow.
अत्वरा f. want of haste, slowness.
अथ & अथा adv. then, now; therefore, accordingly; further, also; however, but (often merely expletive). At the beginning of books or sections of books = now beginneth (opp. इति q.v.). Often followed by अतस् (अथातस्), अपि (अथापि), उ (अथो), घ, तु, पुनर्, etc. — अथ वा (r. अथ alone or वाथ) or, or rather, but, however, or if, even. अथ वा—अथ वा either or. अथ किम् how else?, i.e. of course. अथ किमु so much the more.
अथर्री f. point (of an arrow).
अथर्वन् m. fire-priest, esp. the first fire-priest; pl. his race or = seq. (then also sgl.).
अथर्ववेद m. the Atharvaveda.
अथर्वशिरस् n. T. of an Upanishad.
अथर्वाङ्गिरस् m. pl. the races of Atharvan and Aṅgiras. also = अथर्ववेद.
अद्, अत्ति eat, feed on, consume, devour. C. आदयति, °ते. — आ, प्र, वि, सम् = S.
अदंष्ट्रिन् a. not having tusks.
1अदक्षिण a. left (not right), undexterous.
2अदक्षिण a. giftless, i.e. not bestowing or not accompanied by sacrificial gifts.
अदक्षिणता f. want of courtesy or kindness.*
अदण्डयन्त् a. not punishing.
अदण्ड्य a. unpunishable.
अदत्त a. not given; f. अदत्ता an unmarried girl; n. not-giving, avarice.
अदत्तदायिन् m. thief (lit. who takes what is not given).
अदत्तपूर्वा f. not yet given (in marriage).
अदत्तफल n. reward for avarice.
अददत् n. not giving.
अदन n. eating, food.
अदन्त् a. toothless.
अदब्ध a. unhurt, unbroken; harmless.
अदभ a. harmless, faithful.
अदभ्र a. not scanty, much.
1अदम्भ a. deceitless, honest.
2अदम्भ m. non-deceit, honesty.
अदम्भित्व n. = prec.
अदय a. merciless; n. adv. violently.
अदरिद्र a. not poor.
अदर्प a. having no pride, humble.
अदर्शन a. invisible; n. not-seeing, not-examining or trying, disregard, neglect; not being seen, not appearing, absence.
अदर्शयन्त् a. not showing or producing.
अदर्शयित्वा ger. without showing or paying.
अदस् (n. pron.) that, yonder (also °—); adv. there.
अदातृ a. not giving (esp. in marriage); avaricious, stingy.
1अदान a. being eaten.
2अदान n. not-giving, withholding.
3अदान a. giftless and juiceless (of an elephant).
अदानव m. not a Dānava, i.e. a god.
अदाभ्य a. uninjurable, infallible.
अदायाद, f. ई (आ) not being an heir.
अदारुण a. not harsh, meek, mild.
अदास m. not a slave, a free man.
अदाह्य a. incombustible.
1अदिति f. want, indigence.
2अदिति a. boundless, unlimited. infinite; f. infinity, person. as the mother of the gods.
अदित्सन्त् & अदित्सु a. not willing to give.
अदीन a. not distressed, cheerful.
अदीनमनस्, °नसत्त्व, & °नात्मन् a. of cheerful mind.
अदीयमान a. not being given or married.
अदीर्घ a. not long.
अदुष्ट a. not bad or wicked.
अदुष्टत्व n. goodness, virtue.
अदुष्प्राप a. not difficult to be attained.
अदून a. unharmed, uninjured.
अदूर a. not far, near; °रे, °रात्, & °रतस् adv. near, not far from (abl. or gen.).
अदूषित a. unvitiated, blameless, virtuous.
अदृढ a. not firm, inconstant.
अदृपित & अदृप्त a. not arrogant or proud; prudent, discreet.
अदृश्य a. invisible, insignificant, ugly; abstr. °ता f., °त्व n.
अदृश्यमान a. not being seen, invisible.
अदृष्ट & अदृष्ट a. unseen, invisible, unforeseen, unexpected; unprecedented, unlawful; n. the invisible power, fate, destiny.
अदृष्टपूर्व a. not seen before.

अंदृष्ट्वा ger. without seeing.
अदेय a. not to be given.
अंदेव, f. **ई** not divine, godless, impious; m. not a god, an Asura.
अदेश m. wrong place.
अदेशकाल m. wrong place and time.
अदेश्य a. not on the spot, not present, not a witness.
अदैव a. unconnected with the gods.
अदेाष a. guiltless, sinless; m. no guilt or sin.
अदेाषज्ञ a. not knowing faults.
अदेाषवन्त् a. faultless, unblamable.
अंद्म m. stalk, stem, cane.
अर्द्धा adv. indeed, truly; superl. **अद्धातमाम्** most truly.
अंद्भुत (**अद्भुतं**) a. invisible, secret, mysterious, wonderful; n. wonder, portent.
अंद्भुतैनस् a. in whom no fault is visible.
अद्भुतेापमा f. a kind of comparison.
अंद्मन् n. food.
अद्मसंद् m. commensal, fellow, friend.
अद्य & **अद्या** adv. to-day, now. — **अद्य पूर्वम्** & **°यावत्** till now. **अद्य प्रभृति** & **अद्यारभ्य** from now, from to-day.
अद्यतन, f. **ई** to day's, present.
अद्यदिव n., **°दिवस** m. the present (lit. to-day's) day.
अद्रव्य n. not the (right) thing or person.
अंद्रि m. rock, stone, esp. bruising or hurling stone; mountain, cloud.
अंद्रिदुग्ध a. extracted (lit. milked) with stones.
अद्रिजा a. mountain-born.
अंद्रिबुध्न a. founded on rocks.
†**अद्रिवन्त्** (only voc. **°वस्**) hurler (lit. having a hurling stone).
अद्रुह् (nom. **अध्रुक्**) a. deceitless, artless, true.
अद्रेाघ or **अंद्रेाघ** a. the same.
अंद्रेाघवाच् a. whose word is true.
अद्रेाह a. harmless, kind; m. kindness.
अद्रेाहचेतस् a. of harmless mind.
अद्वय a. without a second, unique.
अद्वयत्व n. non-duality, unity.
अंद्वयन्त् & **अंद्वयस्** a. free from duplicity; simple, sincere.
अद्वयानन्द m. N. of a philosopher, lit. whose joy is the unity (of the divine essence).

अंद्वयाविन् & **अंद्वयु** a. = **अंद्वयन्त्**.
अंद्वार् & **अंद्वार** n. not the door.
अद्विज a. destitute of Brahmans.
अद्वितीय a. = **अद्वय**.
अद्वेषरागिन् a. free from hatred and affection.
अद्वेषंस् a. free from hatred, benevolent.
अद्वेष्टृ m. not an enemy, or friend; abstr. **°त्व** n.
अद्वैत a. = **अद्वय**, n. = **अद्वयत्व**.
अंध & **अंधा** (cf. **अथ**) then, so, and, but, therefore, accordingly (esp. after a rel., temp., or condit. clause). **अध–अध** & **अध–अध वा** either—or.
अधन a. having no wealth, poor.
अधन्य a. the same; miserable, unhappy.
अधन्यता f. misery, misfortune.*
अधमं a. undermost, lowest, worst of (—°).
अधमचेष्ट a. of meanest conduct.
अधमधी a. of weak understanding.
अधमयेानिज a. born of lowest origin.
अधमर्ण & **अधमर्णिक** m. debtor.
अंधर a. lower; **अधरं कृ** subdue, **अधरः पद्** be subdued. m. the lower lip, coll. the lips.
अधरारणि f. the nether Araṇi (v. **अरंणि**).
अधरेात्तर a. lower and higher, inferior and better, losing or winning; confuse, topsy-turvy. n. state of confusion; address and answer.
अधरेाष्ठ & **अधरैाष्ठ** n. (adj. —° f. **ई**) nether-lip, coll. the lips.
अंधर्म m. unrighteousness, injustice, demerit (often personif.).
अधर्मज्ञ a. not knowing the law.
अधर्मदण्डन n. unjust punishment.
अधर्मभीरु a. afraid of injustice.
अधर्मिष्ठ & **अधर्म्य** a. unrighteous, unlawful.
अधश्चरणावपात m. prostration at the feet of a person.
अधःशयं & **अधःशय्य** a lying low, i.e. on the ground.
अधःशय्या f. lying or sleeping on the ground.
अधःशाख a. having the branches below.
अधःशायिन् a. = **अधःशयं**.
अधंस् adv. below, down; **अधेाऽधस्** deeper and deeper. With **कृ** put low, despise; w. **पत्** sink down. As prep. under, below, w. acc. (also **अधेाऽधस्**), gen., abl., & —°.

अधस्तात् adv. down, on the ground, from below; humbly, submissively; prep. underneath, below (gen., abl., or —°).
अधस्पद a. being under the feet; °पदं कृ tread upon, subdue. n. the place under the feet, as adv. under foot.
अधःस्थ a. being below.
अधार्मिक a. unrighteous, unjust.
अधार्य a. not to be borne or kept up.
अधि adv. up, above, over, within, besides, moreover; highly, very much. As prep. w. acc. above, over, on (also doubled); w. instr. along over (only w. स्नुना & स्नुभिस्); w. abl. above, down, from, out of; w. loc. above (*and below, in rank), over, in, on, in behalf of, concerning.
अधिक a. exceeding, extraordinary; superior, more, better than (abl., instr., gen., or —°), by (instr. or —°). °— and n. adv.; abstr. =n., also °ता f. °त्व n.
अधिकगुण a. h. superior qualities; abstr. °ता f.
अधिकण्ठम् adv. at or round the neck.
अधिकरण n. (lit. the putting over, placing at the head, supremacy); substance, something concrete (as the recipient of qualities, actions, etc.); support, receptacle; relation, esp. the relation of the locative (g.); chapter, head (in books); court of justice.
अधिकरणभोज & °क m. judge.
अधिकरणमण्डप s. hall of justice.
अधिकरणिक m. judge or magistrate.
अधिकाङ्ग, f. ई having a redundant member.
अधिकाधिक a. always increasing.
अधिकार m. supremacy, authority, government, dignity, rank, office, service; right, title to (loc.), chapter, head; heading-rule (g.).
अधिकारिता f. °त्व n. superintendence over (loc. or —°).
अधिकारिन् m. having an office, superintendent of (—°); a person being entitled to (—°), or fit for something.
अधिकृत a. placed at the head, appointed; m. superintendent, magistrate, official.
अधिकृत्य ger. concerning, on account of, with reference to (acc.).
अधिगन्तव्य a. attainable, acquirable.
अधिगम m., °गमन n. obtaining, acquiring, going through or over, reading, studying.
अधिगम्य a. attainable, accessible, conceivable, to be read or studied.
अधिगुण a. possessed of high qualities.
अधिगुप्त a. kept, guarded by (—°).
अधिजनन n. birth.
अधिज्य a. having the string up; strung.
अधिज्यकार्मुक a. having the bow strung (v. prec.).
अधिज्यधन्वन् a. the same.
अधिदेव m., °ता f. a. supreme or tutelary god.
अधिदैव n. the divine agent in material objects.
अधिदैवत n. = अधिदेव + अधिदैव.
अधिप, **अधिपति**, & **अधिपा** m. lord, master, ruler.
अधिपुरुष or °पूरुष m. the supreme spirit.
अधिपेषण a. whereon something is ground.
अधिभूत n. the highest being.
अधिमन्थन a. wherewith something is churned; n. the hard piece of wood used in producing fire.
1**अधियज्ञ** m. the supreme sacrifice.
2**अधियज्ञ** a. relating to the sacrifice.
अधिरथ a. being on the chariot; m. charioteer, a man's name; n. a cart-load.
अधिराज् & **अधिराज** m. supreme ruler, sovereign.
अधिराज्य n. supreme sway, sovereignty.
अधिरूढ a. mounted (act. & pass.), sitting upon (acc. or —°).
अधिरोपण n. placing over or on (—°).
अधिरोहण n. ascending (loc. or —°).
अधिलोक m. the supreme world.
अधिवक्तृ m. intercessor, protector.
अधिवाक m. intercession, protection.
अधिवाद m. offence (with words).
1**अधिवास** m. inhabitant, neighbour; dwelling, abode.
2**अधिवास** m. cover, upper garment.
3**अधिवास** m. perfume; abstr. °ता f.
अधिवासन n. perfuming; °सित a. perfumed.
अधिवासिन् a. dwelling in or near (—°).
अधिविन्ना f. superseded (by another wife).

अधिवेत्तव्या & **°वेद्या** f. to be superseded (cf. prec.).
अ॑धिश्रित a. clinging to, hanging or resting on (loc. or acc.), put on (loc.), esp. on the fire; gone to (acc.).
अधिषवंण a. fit for pressing (the Soma); n. the Soma-press.
अधिष्ठातृ superintendent, ruler; f. **°त्री**.
अधिष्ठा॑न n. standing or dwelling-place; residence, capital; high position, power, dignity.
अधिष्ठाय ger. employing, by means of (acc.).
अधिष्ठित or **धिष्ठित** a. standing, sticking; sitting on, being in (loc. or acc.); being above or foremost; placed at the head of, appointed to (loc. or —°), founded on (loc.); inhabited, occupied, seized, taken, filled, lead, managed, exercised (instr. or —°).
अधीकार m. superintendence (w. loc.).
अधीत a. studied, learnt from (abl.); taught, learned; n. learning, study.
अ॑धीति f. recollection; study, perusal.
अधीतिन् a. well-read, versed in (loc.).
अधीन (mostly —°) subject, dependent.
1**अधीर** a. unsteady, abstr. **°ता** f.
2**अ॑धीर** a. unwise.
अधीराक्ष a. having unsteady eyes.
अधीश m. master, lord, king; abstr. **°ता** f.
अधुना॑ adv. now, presently.
अधूमक a. smokeless.
अ॑धृति f. unsteadiness, inconstancy, restlessness.
अ॑धृष्ट a. not bold or impertinent; humble, modest, also = seq.
अधृष्य a. invincible, irresistible.
अ॑धेनु f. a cow yielding no milk, fig. anything sterile.
अधैर्य n. = **अ॑धृति**.
अधोअक्ष॑ a. not reaching to the axle-tree.
*__अधोऽंशुक__ n. under-garment.
अधोगत a. gone down (lit. & fig.).
अधोगति f. going down, going into hell; also as adj., the same.
1**अधोदृष्टि** f. a downcast look.
2**अधोदृष्टि** a. looking down.
अधोभाग m. underpart, bottom, depth.
अधोमुख f. **ई** looking or turned (lit. h. the face turned) downwards.
अधौत a. unwashed.
अ॑ध्यक्ष m. eye-witness or superintendent.
अध्यग्नि indecl. (what is given) over the fire.
अध्यधीन a. wholly dependent.
अध्यन्ते॑न (instr. adv.) close by or to (gen.).
अध्ययन n. studying, reading, taking lessons from (abl.).
अध्ययनादान n. giving instruction, teaching.
अध्यर्ध a. one and a half.
अध्यवसान n., **°साय** m. making up one's mind, resolution.
अध्यवसायिन् a. resolved, determined to (—°).
अध्यवसित a. finished, settled, certain (n. also impers.).
अध्यवहं॑नन a. whereon something is bruised.
अध्याक्रान्त a. occupied, chosen.
अध्यात्म m. concerning one's self, one's own; n. adv. (**°त्मं॑म**), as subst. the supreme soul.
अध्यात्मचेतस् n. the thinking on the supreme soul.
अध्यात्मरति a. delighting in (the contemplation of) the supreme soul.
अध्यात्मिक a. referring to the supreme soul.
अध्यापक m. teacher.
अध्यापन n. teaching, instruction.
अध्याप्य a. to be instructed.
अध्याय m. study, lesson, section of a book, chapter.
अध्यारोप m., **°रोपण** f. transferring erroneously (ph.).
अध्यावाहनिक n. a cert. part of a wife's property (j.).
अध्यास m. putting in or upon; also = **अध्यारोप**.
अध्यासित a. seated or resting upon; inhabited or occupied by (—°).
अध्युषित a. (having) occupied, inhabited, frequented, passed.
अध्येय a. to be read or studied.
अ॑ध्रि a. unrestrained, irresistible.
अ॑ध्रिगु a. of irresistible course.
अ॑ध्रुव a. not fixed, uncertain, inconstant.
अध्वगं॑ & **अध्वन्य** m. traveller.

अ॑ध्वन् m. road, path, travel; length, space.
अध्वर॑ m. religious service, sacrifice, esp. a. greater one.
अध्वरश्री॑ a. beautifying the sacrifice.
अध्वरीय् or अध्वर्य्, °र्य॑ति perform the sacrifice.
अध्वरे॑ष्ठा a. persevering at the sacrifice.
अध्वर्यु॑ m. priest, esp. one performing the actual work of the sacrifice.
अध्वस्म॑न् a. unpolluted.
अन्, अ॑निति, अ॑नति breathe, live. — अप breathe out or away. उद् breathe up, breathe away. प्र breathe in, respire, live. C. revive. वि breathe, breathe through. सम् breathe, live. अनुसम् breathe after.
1अन pron. stem of 3[d] pers.
2अन॑ m. breath, spiration.
अनंश॑ a. getting no share.
1अनग्नि॑ m. non-fire, anything else than fire.
2अनग्नि a. having no fire.
अनग्निदग्ध a. not burnt by fire; m. pl. a class of Manes.
अनघ a. sinless, guiltless, pure.
अनङ्ग॑ a. bodiless; m. the god of love.
अनङ्गक्रीडा f. love-sport.
अनङ्गत्व n. abstr. to अनङ्ग.
अनङ्गरति f. joy of love; a woman's name.
अनडुद् a. giving a bull.
अनडुह m. (—°) = seq. m.; f. ई॑ cow.
अनडु॑ह् m. (nom. °ड्वा॑न्) bull or ox.
अ॑नणु a. not minute or small.
अनतिकृच्छ्रेण (instr. adv.) without too much pain or trouble.
अ॑नतिक्रम m., °ण॑† n. not overstepping.
अनतिक्रमणीय a. not to be overstepped or transgressed, inviolable.
अनतिक्रुद्ध a. not too angry with (gen.).
अ॑नतिदग्ध a. not burnt over.
अनतिपात्य a. not to be transgressed or neglected.
अनतिप्रकाशक n. not very enlightening (ph.); abstr. °त्व n.
अनतिलम्बिन् a. not too much hanging or undulating, rather tight (garment).
अनतिलुलित a. not too much pressed, not too closely adhered to.
अनतीत a. not passed away.

अ॑नदन्त् a. not eating.
अनद्धा॑ adv. not truly or really.
अनद्यतन m. not this day, not to-day or the same day. — भूतान° & भविष्यदन° not the same day in the past or in the future.
अनधिगत a. not attained.
अनधीत्य ger. without studying.
अनधीयन्त् & °धीयान a. not studying.
अनध्ययन n. want of study.
अनध्यात्मविद् a. not knowing the supreme soul.
अनध्याय m. = अनध्ययन.
अननुज्ञात a. not allowed.
अननुज्ञाप्य a. without permission from (acc.).
अननुभूत a. not experienced, unknown.*
अननुरूप a. not fit, ill suited.
अ॑ननुव्रत a. not devoted, disobedient.
अननुष्ठान n. disregard, neglect.
अ॑ननूक्त a. unstudied.
अनन्त॑ a. endless; m. Viṣṇu, a man's name.
अनन्त॑ता f. endlessness, eternity.
अनन्तपाप a. absolutely wicked.
अनन्तबाहु a. having innumerable arms.
अनन्तर॑ a. having nothing within or between, immediately adjoing or following (in time and space), next, esp. in caste. अनन्तरम् adv. close by; thereupon, at once, soon after (gen., abl., or — °).
अनन्तरज a. next born, also = seq.
अनन्तरजात a. born of a woman of lower caste than the man's.
अनन्तराय a. without interval, uninterrupted, unchecked*; n. अ॑नन्तरायम् adv.
अनन्तरूप a. having innumerable forms.
अनन्तविजय m. N. of Yudhiṣṭhira's conch-shell (lit. counting endless victories).
अनन्तवीर्य a. of endless strength.
अनन्त॑शुष्म a. of endless vigour.
अनन्त्य n. endlessness, eternity.
अनन्द॑ m. pl. N. of a cert. world.
अ॑नन्ध a. not blind.
1अनन्य a. not different from (abl.).
2अनन्य॑ a. having no other (object); concentrated in (loc.).
अनन्यचित्त & °चेतस् a. having no other thought, quite absorbed in (loc.).

अनन्यजन्मन् m. E. of the god of love (lit. born from no other).
अनन्यदृष्टि a. having no other sight, looking at nothing else.
अनन्यपर a. devoted to no other person; abstr. °ता f.
अनन्यपरायण a. = prec. adj.
अनन्यभाज् a. cherishing no other.
अनन्यमनस् & °मानस a. thinking of no other person or thing.
अनन्ययोग m. exclusive devotedness.
अनन्यरुचि a. having no other desire.
अनन्यविषय a. relating to nothing else.
अनन्यसम & °सामान्य a. having no equal, unparalleled.
अनन्यसाधारण, f. ई a. belonging to (lit common with) no other.
अनन्विष्यन्त् a. not seeking for (acc.).
अनपकर्मन् n. non-delivery.
अनपकारिन् a. harmless, innocuous.
अनपक्रिया f. non-delivery, non-payment.
अनपच्युत a. not falling off.
अनपत्य a. childless, having no progeny; n. & °ता† f. abstr.
अनपराद्ध a. faultless, having done no harm.
अनपराध & °धिन् a. the same.
अनपसर a. having no escape or excuse.
अनपस्फुर्, °र, & °रन्त् a. not kicking off.
अनपाकृत्य ger. without restoring.
अनपेक्ष a. inconsiderate, careless; n. adv.
अनपेक्षा f., °क्षत्व n. disregard, independence.
अनपेक्षित a. disregarded, unheeded.
अनप्नस् a. having no possession, poor.
अनप्सरस् f. no Apsaras.*
अनभिख्यात a. unknown.
अनभिगमनीय a. inaccessible.
अनभिज्ञ a. unacquainted with, ignorant of (gen., loc., or —°).
अनभिज्ञात a. not recognised.*
अनभिधान n. non-statement.
अनभिभवगन्ध a. showing no (smell of) contempt.
अनभिभाषिन् a. not addressing, silent.
अनभिमत a. unwished for.
अनभिलुलित a. untouched.
अनभिव्यक्त a. not very distinct.
अनभिषङ्ग & अनभिष्वङ्ग m. absence of attachment.
अनभिसंहितम् adv. unintentionally.
अनभिसंधाय ger. having made no agreement; taking no interest in anything.
अनभिसंधि (°—) disinterestedness.
अनभिस्नेह a. desireless.
अनभिहित a. untied, unfastened; not named or designated.
अनभीशु a. reinless, unbridled.
अनभ्यनुज्ञात a. not having been allowed; without permission of (instr.).
अनभ्यन्तर a. uninitiated in (gen.).
अनभ्यर्च्य ger. without worshipping.
अनभ्यर्थनीय a. not to be desired.*
अनभ्यास m. want of study.
अनभ्र a. cloudless.
अनमित्र a. free from enemies; n. as abstr.
अनमित्रलाभ m. the not-getting of enemies.
अनमीव a. having or causing no sickness or pain, healthy, propitious. n. health, weal.
1अनय m. misconduct.
2अनय m. ill-luck, misery.
अनराल a. not crooked, straight.
अनर्गल a. unrestrained, free.
अनर्घ m. wrong (lit. no) value; a. priceless.
अनर्घराघव n. T. of a drama.
अनर्घ्य a. priceless, invaluable.
अनर्चित a. unpraised, unrespected, given without respect.
अनर्थ a. useless, fruitless, unhappy, unlucky, meaningless, nonsensical (also °क); m. non-advantage, disadvantage, damage, ill-luck, nonsense.
अनर्थकारिन् a. doing mischief.*
अनर्थपण्डित a. learned or versed in useless things.
अनर्थान्तर n. not another i.e. the same meaning.
अनर्थ्य a. useless, good for nothing.
अनर्व, °र्वण, & °र्वन् unchecked, unrestrained, irresistible.
अनर्ह a. not deserving, unworthy; too good or too bad for, unfit or unsuitable to (—°). Abstr. °ता f.

अनर्हन्त् a. unworthy, innocent.
अनल m. fire or the god of fire.
अनलंकृत a. unadorned.
अनवक्लृप्त a. irregular, wrong, unfit for (loc.).
अनवगत a. not attained or understood.
अनवगृहीत a. unconceived, unfathomable.*
अनवग्रह a. unrestrained, indomitable.
अनवच्छिन्न a. undiscerned, undefined, indistinct; abstr. °त्व n.
अनवच्छेद m. indistinctness.
अनवद्य a. faultless; abstr. °ता† f., °त्व† n.
अनवद्याङ्ग f. ई having a faultless body.
अनवधान a. inattentive, careless; n. abstr.
अनवपृग्ण a. undivided.
अनवभास m. non-appearance.
अनवभ्रराधस् a. bestowing durable gifts.
अनवम a. not the lowest; —° = seq.
अनवर a. not inferior to (abl.).
अनवरत a. uninterrupted, continual; n. adv.
अनवलम्बन n. not-adhering to (—°).
अनवलेप a. not anointed or not haughty; m. modesty.
अनवलोकयन्त् a. not looking at (acc.).
अनवलोकित a. unsearched.*
अनवस a. not stopping, restless.
अनवसर m. want of opportunity; not the time or place for (gen.).
अनवसित a. = अनवस; f. आ N. of a metre.
अनवस्थ a. unsteady, fleeting.
अनवस्था f. instability, unboundedness, regressus in infinitum (ph.).
अनवस्थान n. unsteadiness.
अनवस्थायिन् a. unsteady.
अनवस्थित a. unsteady, fickle; abstr. °स्थिति f.
अनवाप्त a. not obtained.
अनवाप्ति f. non-obtaining.
अनवाप्य a. not to be obtained; n. imp.
अनवेक्षण n., °क्षा f. want of attention, regardlessness.
अनवेक्ष्य ger. regardless of (acc.).
अनशन n., अनशनता f. fasting.
अनशित a. uneaten.
अनश्नन्त् a. not eating.
अनश्रु a. tearless.
अनश्व a. horseless.
अनश्वदा a. not giving horses.

अनस् n. cart, (heavy) waggon.
अनसूय a. not grumbling or envious; f. आ a woman's name.
अनसूयक (f. °यिका), °सूयन्त्, & °सूयु = अनसूय a.
अनसूया f. freedom from envy.
अनस्थ, अनस्थक & अनस्थन् a. boneless.
अनस्थि a. the same; s. a boneless animal.
अनस्थिक or अनस्थिक a. = prec. a.
अनहंवादिन् a. not talking (only) of one's self, modest.
अनहंकार m. freedom from self-conceit.
अनहंकृत a. not being egoistic.
अना (instr. adv.) certainly, indeed.
अनाकम्प a. unshaken.
अनाकर्णित & °क (d.) n. not hearing.
अनाकुल a. untroubled, unperplexed.
अनाचारित a. not accused before.
अनाख्यात a. untold.
अनाख्याय ger. without telling.
अनाख्येय a. unutterable.
अनागच्छन्त् a. not coming.
अनागत a. not yet come, future.
अनागतविधातृ m. Disposer of the future (N. of a fish).
अनागस् or अनागस् a. harmless, sinless.
अनागास्त्व n. abstr. to prec.
अनाघ्रात a. unsmelt.
अनाचक्षत् a. not telling.
अनाचरन्त् a. not doing or exercising.
अनाज्ञा f. non-leave; instr. adv. without leave or permission.
अनाज्ञात a. unknown, unperceived.
अनातप a. without heat, shady.
अनातिष्ठन्त् a. not resorting to (acc.).
अनातुर a. not ill, well, healthy.
अनात्मज्ञ a. stupid (lit. not knowing one's self).
अनात्मत्व n. not being the soul.
अनात्मन् m. not the soul.
अनात्मवन्त् a. not self-possessed.
1अनाथ a. having no protector, helpless.
2अनाथ n. helplessness.
अनादर m. disrespect, contempt.
अनादातृ m. not a receiver.
अनादि & °मन्त् a. having no beginning.

अनादृत a. not respected, despised.
अनादृत्य ger. without regarding.
अनादेय a. unacceptable, inadmissible.
अनाद्य a. uneatable, unfit for food.
अनाद्यभक्षण n. eating forbidden food.
अनाद्यादन n. the same.
अंनाधृष्ट a. unconquered.
अनाधृष्य a. unconquerable.
अंनानत a. unbent.
अनापद् f. absence of calamity, misfortune, or need.
अंनापि a. having no friends or relations.
अनापूयित a. not stinking.
अंनाप्त a. not reaching or reached, not obtained or obtainable, unskilful, unapt.
अनाप्ति f. non-obtaining, want of success, disappointment.
अनाभ्युदयिक a. inauspicious, unlucky.
अंनामन् a. nameless.
अनामयं a. not unwholesome, healthy (subj. & obj.); not obnoxious to, exempt from (abl.); n. health.
अनामयप्रश्न m. inquiry after one's health.
अनामुक्त a. not yet put on or worn.
अनायक a. without a leader or protector.
अंनायत a. not fastened; not long, short.
अनायतार्गल a. having its bolt not fastened, unlocked (a house).
अनायान्त् a. not arriving.
अनायास a. exempt from pain or difficulty, easy; m. abstr.
अनायुधं a. not having implements or weapons.
अनायुष्य a. not imparting i.e. shortening life.
अनारभ्य a. not to be undertaken, impossible.
अनारम्भ a. unenterprising; m. the not attempting of (gen.).
अनारुह्य ger. without undergoing (lit. ascending).
अनारोग्य a. unwholesome.
अनार्जव n. crookedness, unrighteousness.
अनार्य a. not-Aryan, un-Aryan, dishonourable, unworthy; abstr. °ता f.
अनार्यकर्मिन् a. not acting like an Aryan.
अनार्ष & अंनार्षेय a. not coming from or relating to a Rishi.
अंनाविद्ध a. unpierced, unwounded, unhurt.
अनाविल a. not turbid, clear, pure.
अनाविष्कृत a. not made known.
अनाविष्कृतपाप a. whose sins have not been made known.
अंनावृत् a. not returning.
अंनावृत a. uncovered, unfenced, unlocked; unchecked, unrestrained.
अनावृत्ति f. non-return.
अनावृष्टि f. no rain, drought.
1अनाशिन् a. not eating.
2अनाशिन् a. not perishing.
अनाशु a. not quick, slow.
अनाश्रित a. not resorting to or caring for (acc.).
अंनाश्वंस् a. not having eaten.
अनाष्ट्र a. exempt from danger.
अनासङ्ग m. unsteadiness, uncertainty.*
अनासादयन्त् a. not obtaining.
अनासाद्य a. unobtainable.
अनास्तिक a. unbelieving, sceptic, impious.
अनास्था f. disregard, indifference to (loc.).
अनास्वादित a. not tasted; °पूर्व never before tasted.
अनाहत a. unbeaten (drum); – unhurt*; *unwashed, new (cloth).
अनाहार्य a. not producible.
अंनाहिताग्नि a. not having set up the sacred fire.
अनाहिताग्निता f. abstr. to prec.
अनाह्वान n. non-calling, non-citation.
अनिकेत a. houseless.
अनिक्षिप्त a. not put down.
अनिक्षिप्य ger. without depositing.
अनिक्षेप्तृ m. non-depositor.
अनिगड a. chainless.
अनिच्छन्त् a. not wishing, against one's will.
अनिच्छा f. want of desire, indifference, dislike; instr. without intention.
अनिच्छापूरक a. not fulfilling a wish.*
अंनितभा f. N. of a river.
अनित्य a. not everlasting, perishable, transient, inconstant; abstr. °ता f., °त्व n.
अनिद्र a. sleepless; f. आ want of sleep.
अनिधाय ger. without putting down.
अनिन्दित & अनिन्द्यं a. unblamed, blameless.

अनिन्दितगामिनी f. a woman of blameless walk.

अनिपात m. non-death (lit. non-sinking).

अ॑निबद्ध a. not bound, not appointed; unconnected, incoherent.

अनिभृत a. not fixed, restless, movable.

अनिमित्त a. having no cause, motive, or design; n. no cause etc., also = **दुर्निमित्त**; **°तस्** without reason.

अनिमिष॑ & **अ॑निमिषन्त्** a. not winking, watchful.

अ॑निमिषम् & **अ॑निमिषा** adv. watchfully (cf. prec.).

अनिमिषेक्षण a. whose eyes do not wink.

अनिमेष not-winking (adj. & subst. m.).

अनियत a. unbound, unrestrained, uncertain.

अनियतवेलम् adv. at irregular hours.*

अनियन्तृकर्तृक a. not having the driver as agent (g.).

अनियन्त्रण a. without restraint; **°णानुयोग** to be questioned freely.

अनियम m. want of restriction; **°योपमा** f. a. kind of comparison.

अनियुक्त a. unauthorized, unappointed.

अनियोज्य a. not to be enjoined.

अनिर॑ a. strengthless, weak; abstr. **अ॑निरा** f.

अनिरुक्त a. not spoken out, unexplained, undefined, obscure.

अनिर्जित a. unvanquished.

अनिर्णिक्त a. unpurified.

अनिर्णीत a. unascertained, undetermined.

अनिर्दय (°) adv. not harshly; softly, meekly.

अनिर्दश a. being not out of, i.e. within the ten days (of impurity).

अनिर्दशाह a. the same.

अनिर्दिष्ट a. unspecified, undefined.

अनिर्देश्य a. not to be fixed, settled, or defined.

अनिर्यातयन्त् a. not delivering.*

अनिर्वचनीय a. undefinable.

अनिर्वर्णनीय a. not to be gazed at.

अनिर्वाण a. not extinguished or gone out.

अनिर्वाहनशील a. irresolute, timid (lit. not disposed to accomplish anything).*

अनिर्वाह्य ger. without carrying out.

अनिर्वृति f. discontent, unhappiness.*

अनिर्वृत्त a. not accomplished, imperfect.

अनिर्वेद m. undauntedness, self-confidence.

अनिर्वेदित a. unrevealed or undaunted.

अनिर्ह्रादिन् a. not sounding, low, soft, gentle.

अनिल m. wind (also in the body); the god of wind.

अनिलानल m du. wind and fire.

अनिलाहति f. gale of wind, gust.

अनिवर्तित्व n. abstr. to seq.

अनिवर्तिन् a. not turning back, brave.

अनिवारण n. non-preventing.

अ॑निविशमान a. restless.

अनिवेद्य ger. without mentioning.

अनिश (°—) & **अनिशम्** adv. uninterruptedly, continually.

अ॑निशित a. uninterrupted; n. adv.

अनिश्चय a. irresolute; m. irresolution, suspension.

अनिषव्य॑ a. impenetrable by arrows.

अनिषिद्ध a. unprohibited, unforbidden.

अ॑निष्कृत a. unfinished, unadorned, unsettled.

अनिष्कृतैनस् a. having one's guilt not settled, i.e. unexpiated.

1**अनिष्ट** a. undesired, unpleasant, unlawful, wrong. m. not a favourite; n. ill-luck, evil, misfortune.

2**अ॑निष्ट** a. not sacrificed; not worshipped with a sacrifice.

अनिष्टगन्ध a. ill-scented.

अनिष्टचिन्तन a. thinking of what is undesirable.

अनिष्टैकबुद्धि a. having only thoughts of ill-luck.

अनिष्ट्वा ger. without offering sacrifices.

अनिष्ठुर a. not harsh or rude.

अनिष्पन्न a. not ripened; abstr. **°त्व** n.

अनिसृष्ट a. not having got permission from (instr.).

अ॑नीक n. face, edge, point, front, troop, host.

अनीति f. bad or unwise conduct, want of discretion.

अनीतिज्ञ a. indiscreet (lit. not knowing discreet conduct).

अनीप्सित a. undesired or undesirable.

अनीर्ष्य & **°र्ष्यु** a. not envious or jealous.

अनीश a. not ruling, not independent, not master over (gen.); abstr. **॰शा** f., **॰शत्व** n.

1**अनीश्वर** = prec. adj.; abstr. **॰त्व** n.

2**अ॑नीश्वर** a. having no master; not lordly.

अनीहित a. unwished, disliked.

अनीहमान a. not exerting one's self, quiet.

1**अ॑नु** adv. afterwards, then; as prep. w. acc. after (in all its mgs), towards, along, over; by (distrib.), with regard to, in consequence of.

2**अ॑नु** m. man, esp. non-Aryan; N. of a king.

अनुकच्छम् adv. on the bank (of a river, lake, etc.).

अनुकम्पक a. compassionate towards (—॰).

अनुकम्पन n., **॰कम्पा** f. compassion, pity.

अनुकम्पनीय a. pitiable, deplorable.

अनुकम्पार्थम् adv. from pity for (gen.).

अकुकम्पिन् a. = **अनुकम्पक**.

अनुका॑र a. doing after, imitating; m. assistant, helper.

अनुकरण n. imitation.

अनुकर्ष m., **॰ण** n. drawing on, attracting; inclusion of a preceding in a subsequent rule (g.).

अनुकल्प m. secondary injunction, subsidiary rule (opp. **प्रथमकल्प**).

अनुकाङ्क्षिन् a. striving after (—॰).

1**अनुका॑म** m. wish, desire.

2**अनुका॑म** a. corresponding to a wish; n. adv.

1**अनुकार** m. imitation.

2**अनुकार** a. imitating, resembling.

अनुकारिन् = prec.

अनुकीर्तन n. the mentioning or naming of (—॰).

अनुकूल a. dwelling or lying on the shore; favourable (orig. said of the wind blowing along or toward the shore, opp. **प्रतिकूल**), convenient, pleasant. n. **॰कू॑लम्** adv.

अनुकूलता f., **॰त्व** n. favour, inclination.

अनुकूलय्, **॰यति** favour, flatter, conciliate.

अनुकृत* n., **अनुकृति** f. imitation.

अनुक्त a. unsaid, not spoken of; abstr. **॰त्व** n.

अनुक्रम m. order, turn; instr. & abl. in due order, in turn.

अनुक्रमण n. methodical arrangement; f. **॰णी** & **॰णिका** table of contents.

अनुक्रोश m. compassion, tenderness (p. **॰वन्त्**); **॰शात्मता** f. compassionate disposition.

अनुक्षणम् adv. every moment, perpetually.

अनुग॑ a. going after, following, corresponding to (—॰). m. companion, attendant.

अनुगत a. gone after, followed, visited, occupied, conquered; following, complying with, obedient; equalling, resembling (—॰).

अनुगति f., **॰गम** m., **॰गमन** going after, following.

अनुगर m. request or summons to the reciter (r.).

अनुगर्जित n. roaring echo.

अनुगामिन् a. going behind, following. m. servant, attendant.

अनुगीत n. imitating (lit. after-) song or hum.

अनुगीति f. N. of a metre.

अनुगुण a. congenial, corresponding to, equal to (mostly —॰); abstr. **॰त्व** n.

अनुगुप्त a. kept, guarded, hidden.

अनुगृहीत a. favoured, satisfied, happy.

अनुग्रह m. favour, kindness, service, benefit.

अनुचर॑ f. **ई** going after, following. m. attendant, servant (adj. —॰ f. **आ**); f. **ई॑** maid-servant.

अनुचित a. unwonted; not used to (gen.); not suitable, improper.

अनुचिन्तन n., **॰चिन्ता** f. the thinking of (—॰), recollection.

अनुच्चलन्त् a. not moving from (abl.).

अनुज a. after-born, younger; m. a younger brother; f. **आ॑** a younger sister.

अनुजात a. = prec. a. + born again, invested with the sacred cord (also **॰क***); taking after, resembling (acc.).

अनुजीविन् a. living upon another, dependent. m. servant, f. **॰नी**.

अनुज्ञा f. **॰न** n. leave, permission.

अनुज्ञात a. allowed, permitted, authorized.

अनुतट (॰—) & **अनुतटम्** adv. on the edge or shore.

अनुताप m. repentance, woe, sorrow.

अनुत्खात n. not uneven, i.e. level, ground.

अ॑नुत्त a. unshaken, invincible.

अनुत्तम a. highest (lit. not having a highest), supreme, best, most, excellent.

अनुत्पत्ति f., **॰त्पाद** m. non-arising.

अनुत्पाद्य ger. without having begotten (sons).
अनुत्सुक a. unpresumptuous, modest; abstr. °ता f.
अनुत्सेक m. non-haughtiness, modesty; poss. °किन्.
अनुदक a. waterless.
अनुदय m. not coming forth.
अनुदर्श m. admonition, exhortation.
अनुदर्शन n. regard, consideration.
अनुदात्त a. not elevated or high, low; spoken with the low accent. m. the Anudātta or low accent; °तर m. the lower accent (before an Udātta or a Svarita).
अनुदासीन a. not indifferent.
अनुदित a. unspoken or not risen.
अनुदिन (°—) & अनुदिनम् adv. daily.
अनुदिवसम् adv. the same.
अनुदेश m. instruction, advice; the mutual reference of a latter to a former element (g.).
अनुद्घात m. no jolt or jerk.
अनुद्घाट्य ger. without opening.
अनुद्धत a. not haughty; m. a low place.
अनुद्धृत a. not taken out, not deducted.
अनुद्विग्न a. not perplexed or frightened.
अनुद्वेग m. freedom from anguish, tranquillity, ease.
अनुद्वेगकर a. not causing fright.
अनुद्वेजयन्त् a. not frightening.
अनुधावन n. running after, pursuit.
अनुनय m. conciliatory behaviour, friendliness, prepossession.
अनुनासिक a. nasal (g.).
अनुपकारिन् a. not assisting.
अनुपक्रम्य or °क्राम्य a. incurable.
अनुपघ्नन्त् a. not damaging or impairing.
अनुपथ a. walking along the path.
अनुपदम् adv. upon the foot, immediately after (gen.); at every step, i.e. repeatedly.
अनुपदेष्टव्य a. not to be commended.
अनुपपत्ति f. not taking place, failing, impossibility.
अनुपपन्न a. unsuitable, improper, unworthy of (loc.).
अनुपभोग्य a. unfit to be eaten or drunk.
अनुपम a. incomparable, excellent,
अनुपयन्त् a. not approaching (a wife).
अनुपयुक्त a. useless, unapplicable, unsuitable.
अनुपरोध m. non-hindrance or prejudice; instr. & °तस् without detriment or prejudice to, with the consent of (gen.).
अनुपलब्धि f. °लम्भ m. non-perception.
अनुपसर्ग a. not compounded with a preposition.
अनुपस्कृत a. unprepared, unfinished; simple, plain.
अनुपहित a. unconnected, independent, absolute.
अनुपाकृत a. not consecrated.
अनुपालिन् a. preserving, guarding.
अनुपूर्व a. following in one's turn, successive, orderly, regular. °—, अनुपूर्वम् & °र्वशस् in due order, successively, further.
अनुपृक्त a. mixed with (—°).
अनुपेत a. not yet having gone (to the teacher).
अनुपेतपूर्व the same.
अनुपेय a. not to be married.
अनुप्रमाण a. proportionate, adequate.
*अनुप्रवचन n. the reciting or learning of the Veda; —°नीय a. belonging to the learning of the Veda.
अनुप्रविष्ट a. fled to (acc.), entered (act. & pass.); hidden, concealed.
अनुप्रवेश m. entry, entering.
अनुप्रास m. alliteration.
अनुबन्ध m. binding, attachment, connexion; (also °न n.); continuance, uninterrupted series; consequence, result; cause, motive, intention; appendage, esp. indicatory letter (g.); indispensable element (ph.).
अनुबन्धिन् a. reaching far, lasting long; connected with, resulting in (—°).
अनुबोध m. perception, observation; *reviving a faded scent.
अनुभर्तृ a. supporting or refreshing.
अनुभव m. apprehension, perception.
अनुभाग m. subdivision.
अनुभाव m. power, dignity.
अनुभाविन् a. perceiving, knowing.
अनुमत a. allowed, permitted, approved, liked, agreeable, pleasant; n. assent, permission.

अनुमति f. = prec.; N. of a moon-goddess.
अनुमन्तृ a. consenting, permitting.
अनुमरण n. the dying after, esp. the self-cremation of a widow after her husband's death.
अनुमाद्य a. to be hailed or greeted with acclamation.
अनुमान m. inference (ph.).
अनुमालिनीतीरम् adv. on the bank of the Mālinī.
अनुमित a. thought, conceived, inferred, conjectured from (abl.).
अनुयाज m. after-offering (r.).
अनुयात्र n., °त्रा f., °त्रिक m. pl. retinue, attendance.
अनुयायिन् a. going after, following; pl. = prec.
अनुयुगम् adv. according to the (four) ages.
अनुयोग m. question, censure.
अनुयोज्य a. to be questioned; to be commanded, standing as the command of (—°).
अनुरक्त a. coloured, red; beloved; attached or devoted to, fond of, loving (acc., loc., or —°).
अनुरत a. fond of (loc. or —°), enamoured.
अनुरसित a. cried after; n. echo.
अनुराग m. colouring, redness, affection (poss. °वन्त्); red, affectionate, enamoured (सह or loc.).
अनुरागिन् a. loving or lovely.
अनुरूप a. suitable, adequate, fit, worthy, like, resembling (gen. or —°); able, equal to, a match for (gen.); adv. °तस्†.
अनुरोध m., °रोधन n. compliance, regard, consideration; °रोधतस् out of consideration for (—°).
अनुरोधिन् a. compliant, considerate; observing, having regard for (—°).
अनुलग्न a. following immediately (—°).
अनुलेप m., °न n. unction, unguent, roughcast.
अनुलोम a. with the hair or grain, i.e. natural, regular. अनुलोम (°—) °मम् adv. f. अनुलोमा a woman of a caste inferior to the man's; °मज m. her son.
अनुल्बण a. not excessive; moderate, correct.
अनुवंश m. pedigree, lineage, genealogy; a. of equal race, adv. according to the race.
अनुवचन m. speaking after, repeating, reciting.
अनुवर्तन n. = अनुवृत्ति.
अनुवर्तिन् a. following (acc. or —°); obedient.
अनुवश a. obedient; m. obedience.
अनुवाक m. recital, reading; section, chapter.
अनुवाक्य a. to be repeated or recited; f. °क्या invitatory prayer (r.).
अनुवात m. the wind that blows from behind; °तम् & °ते to windward.
अनुवाद m. repetition, explanation.
अनुवादिन् n. repeating, answering or corresponding to (—°).
अनुवित्त a. found, existing.
अनुविद्ध a. pierced; intertwined or set with, full of (instr. or —°).
अनुविधायिन् a. obedient; conformable (—°).
अनुवृत्त a. round, full; also = अनुवर्तिन्; n. compliance, obedience.
अनुवृत्ति f. sequence, continuance, esp. the continued application of a rule (g.); conformity, compliance with (gen. or —°).
अनुवेलम् adv. hour by hour, continually.
अनुव्यूम् adv. behind, below.
अनुव्याख्यान n. a cert. class of texts.
अनुव्रज्या f. following (a departed guest).
अनुव्रत a. subject to the will of another; obedient, faithful, devoted to (gen. or acc.).
अनुशय m. repentance, regret, rescission of sale or purchase (j).
अनुशासन n. instruction, precept, command.
अनुशासनीय a. to be instructed.
अनुशासितृ m. ruler, commander.
अनुशासिन् a. reprimanding, punishing (—°).
अनुशास्ति f. instruction.
अनुशिष्ट a. taught, bidden, commanded (pers. & th.), inflicted, executed, punished.
अनुषक्त a. clinging to (loc.); connected or endowed with (instr. or —°).
अनुषङ्ग m. connexion, association, necessary consequence.
अनुषङ्गिन् a. attached, connected.
अनुष्टुति f. praise, eulogy.
अनुष्टुभ् a. shouting after. f. shout, praise; N. of a metre.
अनुष्ट्र a. except camels.
अनुष्ठान n. performing, practice.

अनुष्ठित a. following, imitating, practising (acc.); accompanied, assisted, practised, effected, done, begun.
अनुष्ठु, °ष्ठुया, & °ष्ठ्या adv. directly, forthwith.
अनुष्ठेय a. to be done or accomplished.
अनुष्ण a. not hot; lukewarm, chilly, cold; abstr. °ता f.*, °त्व n.
अनुष्वधम् adv. willingly, freely.
अनुसंस्थित a. followed or died after (acc.).
अनुसंचर m. follower.
अनुसंधान n. inquiry, investigation.
अनुसंध्यम् adv. about dusk.*
अनुसर, f. ई going after; m. attendant.
अनुसरण n. following, pursuing.
अनुसार m. the same; rule, legal precept; instr. according to, after (—°).
अनुसारिन् a. following, striving after, according with, seeking for (acc. or —°).
अनुसृत a. following, repaired to (acc.); followed, pursued, gone through.
अनुसृत्य ger. following, i.e. according to (acc).
अनुसेवा f. attendance, service.
अनुसृष्ट a. seen, observed.
अनुस्मृत a. remembered (n. impers.); recorded, taught, enjoined.
अनुस्यूत interwoven with (—°); abstr. °त्व n.
अनुस्वार m. the nasal element of a nasalized vowel and its sign (g.).
अनूक m. n. the spine.
अनूक्त a. recited, studied, heard; addressed (with a sacred verse), named, called; n. = seq.
अनूक्ति f. repeated mention, study.
अनूचान a. learned, esp. in the Veda.
अनूचीन a. following each other, successive.
अनूढा f. unmarried (of a woman).
अनून a. not wanting, complete, full; no less, no inferior to (abl.).
अनूनवस्तुक a. of perfect substance or nature.
अनूप m. a moist country; water-basin; shore.
अनूच्चर a. thornless.
अनृच् & अनृच a. not having or knowing hymns; adv. अनृचम्.
अनृजु a. not straight; crooked, wicked.
अनृण a. free from debt, unindebted to (gen.); abstr. °ता f., °त्व n.
अनृत or अनृत a. untrue, false. m. a liar; n. untruth, falsehood, fraud.
अनृतपूर्वम् adv. untruly, falsely.
अनृतभाषण n. untruth, perjury.
अनृतवादिन् a. speaking untruth, lying.
अनृतात्मक, f. °त्मिका of an untrue character.
अनृतिन् a. the same, m. liar
अनृतु m. no time or season; loc. & adv. °तु out of season.
अनेक a. not one; many or much (also pl.), manifold.
अनेकरूप a. multiform, also = seq.
अनेकवर्ण a. many-coloured, variegated.
अनेकविध a. various, different.
अनेकशस् adv. differently, frequently.
अनेकसंस्थान a. variously disguised.
अनेद्य a. blameless.
अनेन a. deerless.
अनेनस् a. sinless, faultless; a man's name.
अनेवंविद् a. not knowing this.
अनेहस् a. unattainable, incomparable, unaccessible, secure. m. time; n. security, protection.
अनोकह m. tree (lit. not quitting the place).
अनोंकृत a. not preceded by (the syllable) Om.
अनोवाह्य a. to be carried in a cart; n. a cart-load.
अनोशीर a. not being the unguent Auçīra.
अन्त m. (n.) end (in space), limit, border, hem (of a garment), vicinity, proximity; end (in time), issue, event; end of life, death; conclusion, settlement, termination; final letter, syllable, or word, final part in a compound (g.), —° ending with. अन्तम् as far as, till, to, into (—°). अन्ते at last; close by, near, in the presence of, in, within (gen. or —°).
अन्तःकरण n. the interior sense, the heart.
अन्तःपुर n. the king's palace (lit. inner town); stronghold, esp. the inner apartment of it, i.e. the gynaeceum, harem. Sgl., pl. & °जन m. the females of the harem.
अन्तःपुरिका f. a woman of the harem.

अन्तःप्रचलित a. internally moved.

अन्तःप्रमोद m. inner joy.

अन्तःप्राण m. the interior breath.

अन्तक a. ending, destroying; m. death or Yama, the god of death.

अन्तकर a. making an end, destroying (mostly —°).

अन्तकरण a. the same; n. as subst.

अन्तकाल m. time of death.

अन्ततस् adv. from the end or ends, at the end of (gen.); finally, at last.

अन्तपाल m. a guard of the frontiers.

1अन्तम a. nearest, next, intimate, dear; m. neighbour, friend.

2अन्तम a. the last.

अन्तर् adv. inward, within, between; prep. in within (gen., loc., or —°), between, among, amidst (gen., loc., or acc.), from out (gen. or abl.).

1अन्तर a. nearer (cf. 1अन्तम), near, intimate, dear; inner, interior, inmost. Compar. °तर, superl. °तम†. — n. the interior, middle, entry (अन्तरमन्तरम् make room!); distance, interval, start of (gen.); time, period, while; occasion, juncture; abstr. °त्व† n.— अन्तरम् further, onward; among, into (gen. or —°). अन्तरेण in the middle; within, amidst, during, after, without, except, concerning, in behalf of (acc. or —°). अन्तरात् from out, after (—°). अन्तरे meanwhile, midway (cf. अत्रान्तरे & तत्रा°); in, within (also °रेषु) during, after; among, amidst (gen. or —°); on behalf of, concerning (—°).

2अन्तर a. another, different from (abl.); n. difference, distinction, species, sort; kind of, a particular —, often = another (—°).

अन्तरगत a. gone into, being within (gen. or —°).

अन्तरङ्ग a. inner, inmost, essential; near, related. n. m. inner part or organ, esp. the heart.

अन्तरतस् adv. within; as prep. the same (w. gen.), from out (—°).

अन्तरपूरुष m. the soul (lit. the male within the breast).

अन्तरप्रभव a. of mixed origin or caste.

अन्तरय्, °यति step between.

अन्तरागमन n. passing between.

अन्तरस्थ & °स्थित a. being within (gen. or —°).

अन्तरा adv. in the middle, amidst, midway; therein, meanwhile; near, nearly. अन्तरा-अन्तरा sometimes—sometimes, now—then. As prep. between (acc. or loc.); during (acc.); without, except (acc.).

अन्तरात्मन् m. the inward soul, heart.

अन्तरान्वेषिन् a. seeking an opportunity.

अन्तराय m. obstacle, impediment, interval, anything that comes between.

अन्तराराम a. rejoicing in one's self.

अन्तराल n. interval (of sp. & t.), mixed caste; °ले midway, meanwhile.

अन्तरिक्ष n. the intermediate region, i.e. the atmosphere or air.

अन्तरिक्षग a. moving in the air; m. bird.

अन्तरिक्षगत a. = prec. a.

अन्तरिक्षसद् a. dwelling in the air.

अन्तरित a. gone or standing between, being in (—°); interior, hidden, concealed; excluded, disappeared.

अन्तरिन्द्रिय n. = अन्तःकरण.

अन्तरीक्ष n. = अन्तरिक्ष.

अन्तरीक्षस्थ a. standing or being in the air.

अन्तरीय n. under-garment.

†अन्तरुष्य m. station; cf. दशान्तरुष्य.

अन्तर्गत a. gone into, entered, being within (—°); inmost, hidden, secret.

अन्तर्जलचर a. moving in the water.

अन्तर्जलनिवासिन् a. dwelling in the water.

अन्तर्जलौघ m. the quantity of water within.

अन्तर्ज्योतिस् a. having inner light.

अन्तर्दशाह m. an interval of ten days.

अन्तर्दीप v. सान्तर्दीप.

अन्तर्धान n. covering, hiding, disappearance; °नं गम्, इ, व्रज्, etc. disappear.

अन्तर्धि m. = prec.

अन्तर्नगर n. a king's palace (lit. inner town).

अन्तर्निखात a. engraven.

अन्तर्निवेशन n. inner house or apartment.

अन्तर्बाष्प a. containing or suppressing tears, m. suppressed tears; lit. (having) inward tears.

अन्तर्भवन (°—) in or into the house.

अन्तर्भाव m. the being included or comprehended by (loc.).
अन्तर्भिन्न a. cleft or torn inwardly.
अन्तर्भूत a. being within, interior, contained in (—°); abstr. °त्व n.
अन्तर्मन्मथ m. suppressed (lit. inward) love.
अन्तर्मोद m inward joy.
अन्तर्यामिन् m. the inward regulator (ph.).
अन्तर्वक्त्र n. the interior mouth.
अन्तर्वन्त् (f. अन्तर्वती & अन्तर्वत्नी) pregnant.
अन्तर्वृत्ति f. interior condition.
1अन्तर्वेदि m. pl. the inhabitants of Antarvedī.
2अन्तर्वेदि adv. within the sacrificial ground.
अन्तर्वेदी f. the country between the Gangā and Yamunā rivers.
अन्तर्वेश्मन् n. inner house or apartment.
अन्तर्हास m. inward, i.e. suppressed laughter.
अन्तर्हित a. separated, covered, hidden, disappeared.
अन्तवन्त् a. having an end, limited, perishable.
अन्तःशरीरस्थ a. being within the body.
अन्तःशीर्ण a. withered or rotten within.
अन्तःश्लेष m., °श्लेषण n. support, pillar (lit. interlacement, structure).
अन्तस्तप्त a. internally heated.
अन्तस्ताप m. inward heat.
अन्तस्तुषार a. having dew in the interior.
अन्तस्तोय a. containing water.
अन्तस्पथ a. walking within the path.
अन्तःसंज्ञ a. having internal consciousness.
अन्तःसलिल with concealed (lit. inward) water.
अन्तःसार a. having internal essence, i.e. water.
अन्तःसुख a. inwardly happy.
अन्तःस्थ a. being amidst or within (gen. or —°).
अन्ति adv. opposite, in front, before, near. As prep. = near, toward, to (gen. or —°).
अन्तिक n. vicinity. Acc. near to, towards (cf. जनान्तिकम्); abl. from near, from, next, close by; loc. near, in presence of (all with gen. or —°).
अन्तिकचर a. moving near or about (—°).
अन्तितस् adv. from near.
अन्तिम a. the last.
अन्तेवास m. neighbour.
अन्तेवासिन् m., °सिनी f. pupil (lit. living close by).
अन्त्य a. ultimate, last (in sp., t., and order).
अन्त्यकर्मन् n. last, i.e. funeral rite.
अन्त्यज & °जन्मन् a. lowest born.
अन्त्यजाति a. the same; abstr. °ता f.
अन्त्ययोनि a. of lowest origin.
अन्त्यस्त्री f. a very low woman.
अन्त्यावसायिन् m. a man of low caste (lit. living at the end, scil. of the town or village).
अन्त्र n. (mostly pl.) intestines, bowels.
अन्दु s., अन्दू f. chain, esp. for an elephant's foot, or an ornament worn round the ancles.
अन्दोलन n. swinging, oscillating.
अन्दोलय्, °यति swing, pp. अन्दोलित.
अन्दोलाय्, pp. °यमान wavering.*
अन्ध a. blind, dark.
अन्धक a. the same; m. pl. N. of a princely race.
अन्धकार a. dark; m. n. darkness, abstr. °ता f.
अन्धकूप m. a covered (lit. blind) well.
अन्धता f., °त्व n. blindness.
अन्धतामिस्र m. blind or deep darkness (of the soul); n. N. of a hell.
1अन्धस् n. darkness.
2अन्धस् n. herb, juice, esp. of the Soma-plant, juice or food i. g.
अन्धी कृ make blind, °भू become blind.
अन्धु m. a well.
अन्ध्र m. N. of a people and of a caste.
अन्न n. food, esp. boiled rice; p. °वन्त्.
अन्नकाम a. desirous of food.
अन्नद a. giving food.
अन्नदोष m. fault committed by eating forbidden food.
अन्नपक्ति f. cooking of food.
अन्नपति m. lord of food (E. of sev. gods).
अन्नपान n. pl. food and drink.
अन्नपिण्ड s. lump of food.*
अन्नप्राशन n. (first) feeding (of an infant) with rice (r.).
अन्नमय a. consisting of food.
अन्नरस (n. sgl. & m. pl.) food and drink.
अन्नरसमय a. consisting of food and drink.
अन्नविकार m. transformation of food; abstr. °त्व.

अन्नशेष m. leavings of food, offal.
अन्नहर्तृ m. thief of food.
अन्नाद (f. ई & आ) eating food.
अन्नाद्य n. (eating of) food.
अन्नाद्यज a. born or bred in food.
अन्नार्थ a. desiring food, hungry.*
अन्य (n. अन्यद्) another, other, else, different from (abl.). — अन्यच्च and something else, i.e. further, again. अन्य (or एक)—अन्य the one—the other.
अन्यकर्तृक a. having another agent (g.).
अन्यकृत a. done by another or others.
अन्यगत a. relating to some one else.*
अन्यचित्त & °चेतस् a. thinking of some one or something else, of absent mind.
अन्यचिन्ता f. thought or care of some one else.
अन्यजन्मन् n. another birth or existence.
अन्यतःप्लक्षा f. N. of a lotus-pond.
अन्यतम a. one of several, the one or the other of (gen. or —°).
अन्यतर a. one of two; rep. the one—the other; °स्याम्† in either way, optionally (g.).
अन्यतस् adv. from elsewhere, elsewhere, otherwise, else; (only) on one side. Also =abl. & loc. of अन्य m. & f., sgl. & pl. Repeated = on one side—on the other side, here—there.
अन्यता f. the being other, difference.
अन्यत्र adv. elsewhere, else, otherwise, also = loc. of अन्य m. f.; as prep. with abl. (r. —°) = in another place, time, case, or way than, without, except, apart from.
अन्यत्व n. = अन्यता.
अन्यथा adv. otherwise, else, differently, wrongly. °भू suffer change. °कृ act otherwise or wrongly, change, alter; frustrate, undo.
अन्यथादर्शन n. false trial (of a cause).
अन्यथाप्रथा f. the becoming other, change.
अन्यथाभाव m. change, difference.
अन्यथाभिधान n. false statement (j.).
अन्यथावादिन् a. making a false statement or deposition; abstr. °दित्व n.
अन्यथावृत्ति a. changed, altered.
अन्यथासंभावना f. false supposition, distrust.
अन्यथासंभाविन् a. suspicious, distrustful.*
अन्यदा adv. at another time, else, once.
अन्यनिमित्त a. having another cause or motive.
अन्यपर a. having another object.
अन्यपुष्ट & °भृत m. the Indian cuckoo (lit. reared by another, sc. the crow).
अन्यबीजज a. born from another's seed.
अन्यमनस् & °मानस a. thinking of some one (thing) else.
1अन्यरूप n. different shape.
2अन्यरूप & °पिन्† a. of a different shape.
अन्यलोक्य a. destined for another world.
अन्यवादिन् = अन्यथावादिन्.
अन्यविषय a. having another object, relating to something else.
अन्यशङ्कित a. supposing something else, suspicious.*
अन्यसंक्रान्त a. gone over to another.*
अन्यस्त्रीग m. adulterer (lit. going to another's wife).
अन्यादृक्ष, °दृंश्, & °दृश (f. ई) looking different, of another kind or nature.
अन्याय m. unlawfulness, injustice, impropriety. °— & instr. adv. illegally, improperly.
अन्यायवर्तिन् a. acting improperly.
अन्याय्य a. unlawful, unjust.
1अन्यार्थ m. another's cause; another sense or purpose.
2अन्यार्थ a. having another sense or purpose.
अन्यून a. not deficient, entire.
अन्यूनार्थवादिन् a. expressing the whole subject.
अन्येद्युस् adv. on the other or following day; one day, once.
अन्योत्पन्न a. begotten by another.
अन्योऽन्य (only sgl. m. f.) one another, mutual. अन्योन्य (°—) & n. अन्योन्यम् mutually.
अन्योऽन्यकृत्य n. pl. reciprocal friendly acts.
अन्योऽन्यगत a. mutual, reciprocal.
अन्योऽन्यदर्शन n. interview.*
अन्योऽन्यभेद m. mutual division.
अन्योऽन्यस्पर्धा a. mutual emulation; adj. °र्धिन्.
अन्योऽन्यानुराग m. mutual affection.*
अन्योऽन्योपमा f. a kind of comparison.
अन्योपतापिन् a. vexing others.
अन्वञ्च् (f. अनूची or अन्वंची) going behind or along, following (acc.); n. अन्वक् adv. behind, after (acc.).

अन्वय m. posterity, race, family; connexion, relation; °**वत्** adv. before one's eyes, openly (lit. in connexion with).
अन्वयिन् a. related, connected, consecutive.
अन्वर्थ a. answering to the matter, having an obvious sense; °**र्थाभिध** a. having a name of obvious meaning.
अन्वष्टका f. the day after the **अष्टका** (q.v.).
अन्वहम् adv. daily.
अन्वाधेय n. a gift subsequent (j.).
अन्वायत्त a. partaking of, connected with, dependent on, being in or at (loc. or acc.).
अन्वालभन n. handle.
अन्वाहार्य n. a cert. sacrificial gift (lit. to be offered after, sc. the cakes); the monthly funeral repast.
अन्वाहार्यपचन m. one of the sacrificial fires, serving to cook the Anvāhārya (v. prec.).
अन्वित a. followed; accompanied by, endowed, filled, connected with (instr. or —°).
अन्वेष m., °**षण** n., °**षणा** f. searching, investigation.
अन्वेषणीय & °**ष्य** a. to be searched or investigated, questionable, dubious.
अन्वेषिन् & **अन्वेष्टृ** a. searching, seeking.
1**अप्** s. work.
2**अप्** f. pl. (sgl. only in V.) water, waters.
अप adv. away, off (*as prep. w. abl.).
अपकर्ष m. drawing away, taking off, diminution, deterioration; anticipation (ph.).
अपकर्षक a. detracting, diminishing.
अपकर्षण a. the same; n. = **अपकर्ष**.
अपकार m., °**ता** f. injury, mischief.
अपकारिन् a. injuring, hurting.
अपकृत n., °**ति** f., °**त्य** n. = **अपकार**.
अपकृष्ट a. drawn down, inferior, low, mean.
अपक्रम m., **अपक्रमण** n., **अपक्रान्ति** f. going away.
अपक्रुष्ट a. abused, reviled.
1**अपक्ष** a. wingless.
2**अपक्ष** m. a rival, lit. not belonging to the (right) party.
अपक्षय m. diminution, decrease.
अपक्षलोप & °**साद** m. non-loss of the wings.
अपगम m., °**गमन** n. going away, flying, disappearing.
अपघन a. cloudless.
अपघात m. striking or warding off, driving away.
अपघातक a. the same.
अपचमान a. not cooking for one's self.
अपचय m. decrease, decline.
अपचरित n. misconduct, transgression.
अपचार m. absence, want; also = prec.
अपचारिन् a. deviating from (—°); acting improperly; faithless, false, adulterous.
1**अपचित** a. emaciated, thin, slender.
2**अपचित** a. respected, honoured.
अपचिति f. expiation, vengeance for (gen.); awe, honour, respect.
अपच्छेद m. °**न** n. cutting off, interrupting.
अपज्वर a. free from fever, well.
अपञ्चीकृत & °**भूत** n. having not yet become the five, sc. elements (ph.).
अपटीक्षेप m. the not tossing-up the curtain (d.).
अपटु a. not sharp, blunt, awkward, uncouth.
अपण्डित a. unlearned, ignorant.
अपण्य a. not to be sold; n. such an article.
अपतरम् adv. further away.
अपतित a. not fallen or sunk; not degraded or outcast.
अपतिव्रता f. not devoted to her husband.
अपत्य n. offspring, child; poss. °**वन्त्**.
अपत्यविक्रयिन् m. a seller of his offspring.
अपत्यस्नेह m. love of one's own children.
अपथ n. no or the wrong road; fig. a bad course or wrong place.
अपथ्य a. unfit, unsuitable.
अपद् (f. = m. or **अपदी**) & **अपद्** a. footless.
1**अपद** n. no or a wrong place.
2**अपद** a. footless.
अपदान n. a glorious deed.
अपदेश m. statement, designation, name, pretence, pretext, excuse, evasion, refusal.
अपद्म a. having no lotus.
अपधा f. concealment, confinement.
अपध्यान n. grudge, envy.
अपध्वंस m. sinking down, concealment, degradation.
अपध्वंसज a. born in consequence of degradation, i.e. of a mixed marriage.
अपध्वस्त a. brought down, degraded, ruined.

अपध्वान्त a. sounding wrong.
अ॑पनत a. bent out.
1**अपनय** m. taking away, removal.
2**अपनय** m. bad conduct or policy.
अपनयन a. taking away; n. = 1**अपनय.**
अपनीत a. led away, removed from, i.e. opposite of (—°); n. = 2**अपनय.**
अपनुत्ति f. removing, expiation.
अपनुनुत्सु a. desiring to removè or expiate.
अपनेय a. to be removed.
अपनोद m. driving away, repulsion, removal, expiation.
अपनोदन a. removing; n. = prec.
अपपात्र & °**त्रिक** a. excluded from (the common use of) vessels.
अपभय a. fearless.
अपभर्तृ m. remover, destroyer.
अपभ्रंश m. falling down; fallen off, i.e. corrupted or vulgar language.
अपभ्रष्ट a. fallen off, i.e. corrupted, vulgar (cf. prec.).
अपमं a. farthest, remotest, last.
अपमर्श m. contact, touch.
अपमान m. (n.) disrespect, contempt.
1**अपमार्ग** m. by-road, side-way.
2**अपमार्ग** m. wiping off, cleaning.
अपमार्जन the same adj., as n. subst.
अपमृग adj. having no game (wood).
अपयशस् n. disgrace, infamy.
अपयान n. retreat, flight.
1**अ॑पर** a. hinder, farther, later, inferior, posterior, western; following (in sp. & t.); different from, another than (abl. or gen.), foreign (opp. **स्व**), particular, strange, extraordinary. m. **अपर** hind-foot of an elephant. n. **अ॑परम्** adv. in future (also **अप॑रम्**); further, moreover (± **च**); west of (abl.). **अ॑परेण** behind, west of (acc.).
2**अप॑र** n. °**री** f. the future.
अपरक्त a. discoloured, pale; averse from (abl.), unfavourable.
अपरतस् & °**त्र** adv. elsewhere.
अपरपक्ष m. the latter or dark half of a month.
अपररात्र m. the latter half of a night.
अपरवक्त्र n. N. of a metre.
अ॑परशुवृक्ण a. not hewn down with an axe.
अपरस्परसंभूत a. not produced by one another or in regular order.
अपराग m. dislike, aversion.
अपराङ्मुख a. not having an averted face, encountering, facing. (n. adv. frankly, plainly.*)
अपराजय m. invincibleness.
अ॑पराजित a. unconquered, invincible. – f. **आ** w. **दिश्** the northeast (lit. invincible) quarter; N. of a metre and of sev. plants. — n. the castle of Brahman.
अ॑पराद्ध a. sinned; having sinned, guilty. n. impers. it has been sinned by (instr.), against (gen. or loc.); as subst. = seq.
अ॑पराद्धि f. sin, offence, transgression.
अपराध m. the same.
अपराधिन् a. guilty, criminal, offending.
अपरान्त m. last end, death; the farthest west, pl. its inhabitants.
अपरावृत्त a. not turned back. °**भागधेय** to whom fortune does not return, unhappy, miserable.
अपराह्ण m. the afternoon.
अपरिक्रम a. unable to move.
अपरिक्लिष्ट a. not vexed or troubled; °**पूर्व** not vexed before.
अपरिक्षत a. unhurt, untouched.
1**अपरिग्रह** m. non-comprehension, non-acceptance; want of property.
2**अपरिग्रह** a. having no property or no wife.
अपरिचय m. unacquaintedness.
अपरिचित a. unacquainted, unknown.
अपरिच्छद a. having no attendance or luggage.
अपरिच्छिन्न a. uncut, unlimited.
अपरिच्छेद m. inability to decide.
अपरिज्ञात not known.
अपरितुष्ट a. = seq.
1**अपरितोष** a. dissatisfied.
2**अपरितोष** m. dissatisfaction.
अपरित्यक्त a. not abandoned.*
अपरित्याग m. not giving up.
अपरिनिर्वाण a. not quite extinct or ended.
अपरिनिष्ठित a. not quite fixed or settled.
अपरिपन्थिन्, f. **ई** not an opponent, friendly.*

अपरिपूत a. uncleaned, unhusked (corn).
अपरिबाध a. undisturbed.*
अपरिमित a. unmeasured, unlimited.
अपरिमेय a. immeasurable, countless, illimited.
अपरिवाद्य a. not to be blamed.
अपरिवृत a. unfenced, uninclosed.
अपरिश्रान्त a. unwearied.
अपरिस्थान a. improper, n. impropriety.*
अपरिहत a. unrestrained, unlimited.
अपरिहार m. non-avoiding.
अपरिहार्य a. not to be avoided.
अपरिहीयमाण a. unavoided; °नं कृ carry out, accomplish.
अपरिहृत a. unavoided, i.e. carried out.
अपरीक्षित a. inconsiderate (of p. & th.).
अपरीक्ष्य ger. without deliberating.
अपरीक्ष्यकारिन् a. acting inconsiderately.
अपरीत a. unrestrained, irresistible.
अपरीवृत = अपरिवृत.
अपरेद्युस् adv. on the following day.
अपरोक्ष a. not beyond the eye or out of sight, witnessed, testified, perceptible, clear; abstr. °त्व n. -- °क्षम् & °क्षे in the presence of; अपरोक्षात् clearly.
अपरोक्षय्, °यति to witness.
1अपर्तु m. not the right season.
2अपर्तु a. unseasonable.
अपर्यन्त a. unlimited, boundless.
अपर्याप्त a. insufficient, unable.
अपर्याप्ति f. insufficiency, inadequacy.
अपर्वन् n. no joint (Ved. loc. the same form); no Parvan- or holiday (v. पर्वन्).
अपलापिन् a. denying, concealing (—°).
अपलायन n. firmness, valour (lit. non-flight.).
अपवर्ग m. completion, end, final delivery.
अपवाद m. refutation, restriction, exception, censure, blame.
अपवादिन् a. blaming, slandering (—°).
अपवारक s. bed-chamber.*
अपवारित a. covered, hidden. °तम्, °तकेन, & °वार्य apart, aside (d.).
अपविघ्न a. unhindered.
अपविक्षडाकिनी f. a dirty witch.*
अपविद्ध a. pierced, hit; thrown away, rejected, removed, given up, neglected.

अपवृत्त a. turned away, overthrown, inverted, perverse, of bad conduct.
अपवेध m. unskilful piercing (of a pearl).
अपव्रत a. not devout, faithless, disobedient.
अपशब्द m. bad or ill language.
1अपश्चिम a. not the last.
2अपश्चिम a. the last of all (lit. h. no last); n. adv. last of all.
अपश्य a. not seeing.
अपश्यन्त् & अपश्यमान a. the same.
1अपस् n. work, action.
2अपस् a. active, skilful; f. pl. the fingers.
अपसद m. an outcast; a. base-born (of a father inferior to the mother), low, vile (esp. —°).
अपसर m., °ण n. going away.
अपसलवि & °सलैस् adv. to the left.
अपसव्य a. right, southern; n. & instr. adv.
अपसार m. going out, issue, egress.
अपसारण n. removal, expelling (°णं कृ make room, clear the way*).
अपसारिन् a. decreasing, vanishing (abstr. °रिता f.*).
अपस्नान n. water used (previously) for a bath.
अपस्मार m. epilepsy (lit. want of memory).
अपस्मारिन् a. epileptic.
अपस्य्, °स्यति be active; abstr. °स्या f.
अपस्य (f. अपसी) watery.
अपस्यु a. active, zealous.
अपह (—°) a. removing, destroying.
अपहति f. removal, destruction.
अपहन्तृ m. (f. °न्त्री) = अपह.
अपहरण n. taking away, robbing.
अपहर्तृ a. removing; m. ravisher, destroyer.
अपहस्तय्, pp. °हस्तित shake off (hands); throw away.
अपहाय ger. holding off, putting aside, notwithstanding, except, save.
अपहार m. taking away, stealing, robbing, concealing; a. °रक & °रिन्.
अपह्नव m., °ह्नुति f. denial, concealment.
अपाक a. coming from far.
अपाका adv. far; °कात् from far.
अपाङ्क्तेय a. unworthy (of a society); abstr. °त्व n.
अपाङ्क्त्य a. the same, °दान n. giving to some one unworthy.

अपाङ्ग m. (adj. —° f. आ & ई) the outer corner of the eye.

अपाङ्गनेत्रा f. having eyes with beautiful outer corners.

अपाङ्गविशालनेत्र a. having large eyes with beautiful outer corners.

अपाचीन & अपाञ्च् (f. अपाची) turned back, western. n. अपाक् adv. west.

अपाणि a. handless; °पाद् hand and footless.

अपातक n. no crime.

अपात्र n. (m.) an unworthy person (lit. no recipient).

अपात्रकृत्या f. an act rendering unworthy (v. prec.).

अपात्रवर्षिन् a. liberal to (lit. raining on) the unworthy.

अपात्रीकरण n. = अपात्रकृत्या.

अपादान n. ablation (g.).

अपान m. the wind that goes downward (in the body); the anus.

अपाप a. not bad, sinless; °शील a. good-natured.

अपांपति m. the ocean or the god Varuṇa.

अपाय m. departure (a. °यिन्); going astray or missing the aim, i.e. disadvantage, danger, diminution, loss; end, death.

अपार a. unbounded, immeasurable.

अपारयन्त् a. being unable to (inf.).

अपार्थ & °क a. useless, unmeaning.

अपावृत a. unlocked, uncovered; open, manifest.

अपावृत्त a. inverted, turned away; averse from (abl.).

अपाश्रय m. support, refuge; p. °वन्त् & °यिन्.

अपास्य ger. putting aside, i.e. in spite of, except, save (acc.).

अपि (prep. w. loc., or °— in verbs & nouns) close by or to, within, before; adv. further, also, too; even (w. न = Lat. quidem); at least, however, but (between words, clauses and sentences, or after, r. before an emphasized word). Converts an interrog. into an indefinite; after numerals = all; at the beginning of a sent. it is a particle of interrogation, with an optat. it expresses hope, fear, or desire. – अपि च or चापि further, moreover. अपि—अपि (or च) as well—as. अपि च—न चापि rather than. येऽपि—तेऽपि they too—who. यद्यपि however, although. तथापि even so, nevertheless.

अपित् a. barren, dry.

अपितृदेवत्य a. not having the Manes as deity.

अपित्र्य a. not paternal.

अपित्व n. portion, share; p. °त्विन्.

अपिधान n. cover, bar; p. °वन्त्.

अपिनद्ध or पिनद्ध a. tied on, bound under, closed obstructed, covered.

अपिहित or पिहित a. covered, concealed; checked, restrained.

अपीच्य a. secret, hidden.

अपीडयन्त् a. not oppressing.

1अपीत a. entered into, united with (acc.); abstr. °ति f.

2अपीत a. not (having) drunk.

अपुण्यकृत् a. acting wickedly; m. sinner.

1अपुत्र m. not a son.

2अपुत्र & अपुत्रक (f. °त्रिका) sonless.

अपुत्रिन्, °त्रिय, & °त्र्य a. the same.

अपुनरावर्तन n., °वृत्ति f. not returning again (into life).

अपुमंस् m. hermaphrodite (lit. not a man).

अपुष्प a. not flowering.

अपूजित a. unworshipped.

अपूत a. impure.

अपूप m. cake.

अपूपशाला f. a bake- (lit. cake-)house.

अपूर्ण a. not full; less by (instr.).

अपूर्व a. having no predecessor, not having existed before, unknown, unheard of, unprecedented, extraordinary, wonderful, incomparable, strange, new; instr. adv. never before. Abstr. °ता† f., °त्व† n.

अपूर्व्य a. having no predecessor, first, singular, incomparable.

अपृणन्त् a. not munificent (lit. filling), avaricious.

अपृथग्जित a. not conquered singly.

अपृष्ट a. unasked, unquestioned.

अपेक्षा f. regard, attention, expectation, consideration; often adj. —° regarding, expecting, requiring. Instr. with regard or in proportion to (—°).

अपेक्षितत्व n. being expected or required.
अपेक्षिता f. expectation, regard.
अपेक्षिन् a. considering, respecting, expecting.
अपेत a. gone away, fled, departed, ceased; rid of, free from (abl., °—, or —°).
अपेतप्राण a. dead (whose life is gone).
अपेय a. not to be drunk.
अपेशस् a. shapeless.
अपैशुन n. no calumny.
अपोगण्ड a. not a minor (j.).
अपोढ a. carried off, removed.
अपोह m., **°न** n. removal, rejection, negation.
अपौरुषेय a. not produced by man, superhuman.
अप्-चर m. aquatic animal (lit. moving in the water).
अप्तु a. light (lit. not falling), small.
अप्तुर् a. active, zealous.
अप्य a. watery.
अप्नस् n. wealth, property; work.
अप्पति m. the lord of the waters, i.e. Varuṇa.
अप्य, f. **आ** & **ई** born in water; made of or mixed with water.
अप्यय m. the going in, union, junction; absorption, destruction (opp. **प्रभव**).
अप्रकाश a. not bright, dark, secret; **°शं कृ** hide, secrete. m. darkness; n. adv. secretly.
अप्रकाशन्त् a. invisible.
अप्रकाश्य a. not to be shown.
अप्रकेत a. indistinct, shapeless.
अप्रगल्भ a. not bold; timid, modest.
अप्रचेतस् a. unwise.
अप्रच्युत a. unmoved, undeviating from (abl.).
अप्रज a. childless; f. **आ** not bringing forth children.
अप्रजज्ञि a. unprolific; ignorant.
अप्रजस् or **अप्रजस्** a. childless.
अप्रजस्ता f., **°जस्य** & **°जास्त्व** n. childlessness.
अप्रज्ञ a. unknowing, **°ज्ञात** a. unknown.
अप्रणीत a. not carried forth.
अप्रतर्क्य a. incomprehensible.
अप्रति a. irresistible.
अप्रतिकार a. irremediable, helpless (**°गुरु** helplessly oppressive*).
अप्रतिकूल a. not adverse; willing, obedient.
अप्रतिगृह्णन्त् a. not receiving.
अप्रतिग्राहक a. who accepts nothing.
अप्रतिग्राह्य a. unacceptable.
अप्रतिघ a. not to be kept off, irresistible.
अप्रतिपत्ति f. non-perception; irresolution.
अप्रतिपद्यमान a. not being granted or admitted.
अप्रतिपादन n. not giving, withholding.
अप्रतिपूजित a. not (duly) honoured.
अप्रतिबन्ध m. no obstacle; adj. unhindered.
अप्रतिबुद्ध & **°क** a. not enlightened, stupid.
अप्रतिम, **°मान**, & **मेय** a. incomparable.
अप्रतिमप्रभाव a. of unmatched power.
अप्रतिमौजस् a. of unmatched strength.
अप्रतिरथ a. having no antagonist, invincible.
अप्रतिरूप a. of incomparable form, unequalled unfit for (gen.).
अप्रतिवारित a. unprohibited.
अप्रतिषेध m. no prohibition or contradiction.
अप्रतिष्ठ & **°ष्ठित** a. unfixed, unsettled, uncertain.
अप्रतिहत a. unrestrained, unimpaired.
अप्रतिहार्य a. irresistible.
अप्रतीकार a. resistless (act. & pass.), also = **अप्रतिकार**.
अप्रतीत a. not encountered, unattackable; not understood, unintelligible.
अप्रतीति f. unintelligibility; inconclusiveness.
अप्रत्यक्ष a. not being before the eyes, not witnessed, unknown.
अप्रत्यय a. distrustful (loc.), untrustworthy; m. distrust.
अप्रत्याख्यायिन् a. not refusing or turning away.
अप्रधान a. not principal; subordinate or secondary; n. anything subord. or sec. Abstr. **°ता** f., **°त्व** n.
अप्रधृष्य a. invincible, unconquerable.
अप्रबुद्ध a. unawakened (l. & f.).
अप्रमत्त a. not negligent; attentive, vigilant, careful.
अप्रमाण n. no authority.
1**अप्रमाद** m. attention, carefulness.
2**अप्रमाद**, **°दिन्**, & **°द्यन्त्** a. = **अप्रमत्त**.
अप्रमेय a. immeasurable, infinite.
अप्रमोद m. want of joy or pleasure.
अप्रयच्छन्त् a. not giving, withholding.

अप्रयत a. unprepared, impure (r.).
अप्रयत्न m. want of effort, indifference; adj. not endeavouring, indifferent about (loc.).
अ॑प्रयुक्त a. not employed; unusual.
अ॑प्रयुच्छन्त् a. not indolent; watchful, attentive.
अप्रयुज्यमान a. not being applied.
अप्रवृत्ति f. non-activity, indolence.
अप्रशस्त॑ or **अ॑प्रशस्त** a. unpraised or unpraiseworthy; bad, evil.
अप्रसक्ति f. non-attachment to, abstinence from (loc.).
अप्रसन्न a. not calm, uneasy, displeased.
अप्रसिद्ध a. unfinished, unsettled; unknown, unheard of.
अप्रस्तुत a. unpraiseworthy; not being spoken of, not the topic of conversation.
अप्राज्ञ a. unwise, stupid; abstr. **°ता** f.
अप्राण॑, **अ॑प्राणन्त्**, & **अप्राणिन्** a. lifeless, inanimate.
अप्राधान्य n. the being secondary or inferior.
अ॑प्राप्त a. not obtained; not established by a rule, unproved; not arrived, not occurred, not full grown.
अप्रामाण्य n. no authority or proof.
अप्रास्ताविक, f. **ई** not belonging to the matter.
अ॑प्रिय a. unkind, unfriendly, disagreeable.
अप्रियंवद & **°वादिन्** a. speaking unkindly.
अप्रियकर a. causing displeasure.
अप्रीति f. want of love, enmity.
अप्रीतिकर a. not giving joy.
अप्रेक्षणीय a. not worth seeing, ugly.
अप्रेक्ष्य a. invisible.
अप्वा f. a kind of disease.
अप्सर॑स् & **°रा** f. Apsaras (a cert. class of fem. deities).
अ॑प्सस् n. forehead or face.
अफल॑ a. fruitless (l. & f.); emasculated.
अफलप्रेप्सु a. not desirous of any result or recompense.
अफलाकाङ्क्षिन् a. the same.
अफेन & **अफेनिल** a. frothless.
अ॑बद्ध a. untied, unconnected, nonsensical.
अबन्ध्य a. not to be bound.
अबर्ह a. not yet having tail-feathers.
अबल॑ a. weak, feeble; f. **आ** woman, maid.
अ॑बलीयंस् (compar.) weaker.
अबल्य॑ or **अ॑बल्य** n. weakness, disease.
अबहिष्कार्य a. not to be expelled or excluded.
अबाध, **°क**, & **अ॑बाधित** a. unimpeded.
अबान्धव a. having no relatives.
अबान्धवकृत a. not brought about by relatives.
अबालसत्त्व a. having an unchild-like disposition.
अ॑बिभीवंस् & **अ॑बिभ्यत्** a. fearless.
अबीज n. no or bad seed; adj. without seed or manly strength.
अबीजक a. not having (good) seed.
अबुद्धि a. ignorant (also **°मन्त्**); f. ignorance.
अबुध & **अबुध॑**=prec. adj.
अबुध्य॑ a. not to be wakened.
अ॑बुध्यमान a. not awaking.
अबोध m. ignorance; ignorant; **°पूर्वम्** adv.
अब्ज a. born in water; n. a lotus-flower.
अब्जसरस् n. a lotus-pond.
अब्जा॑ a. water-born.
अ॑ब्द m. year (lit. giving water; cf. **वर्ष**).
अब्दपर्यय m. change of the year.
अब्दया॑ (instr.) from desire to give water.
अब्दार्ध a. half-year.
अब्दुर्ग n. a fortress (protected) by water.
अब्दैवत a. having the waters as deity.
अब्धि m. ocean, sea (lit. water-receptacle).
अब्भक्ष a. living (only) on water.
अब्रह्मण्य a. unbrahmanical; n. misdeed, violence.
अ॑ब्रह्मन् m. no Brahman; adj. without Brahmans or prayers.
1**अ॑ब्राह्मण** m. no Brahman.
2**अब्राह्मण॑** a. without Brahmans.
अब्रुवन्त् a. not speaking, silent.
अ॑भक्त a. not imparted; not attached or devout.
अभक्ष्य a. not to be eaten.
अभक्ष्यभक्षिन् a. eating forbidden food.
अभग॑ a. luckless, unfortunate.
अभणित a. unspoken, untold.*
अभणित्वा ger. without saying.*
अभद्र n. inauspicious; n. misfortune, ill-luck.
अ॑भय a. free from fear or danger, safe; n. safety, superl. greatest s.
अभयंकर॑ & **कृ॑त्** a. procuring safety.
अभयद, **°प्रद**, & **°प्रदायिन्** a. giving safety.

अभयदक्षिणा f. promise or gift of safety.

अभव्य a. bad, vicious, ugly, miserable (lit. what ought not to be).

अभाग a. having no portion or share.

अभाग्य a. unfortunate; n. misfortune.

अभाजन n. no object (lit. vessel or recipient) for (gen.), unworthy.

अभान n. non-appearance.

अभार्य a. without a wife.

अभाव m. not being, non-existence, absence, want, failure, destruction, death. — °वं गम् perish, die.*

अभावयन्त् a. unconscious, unwise.

अभाविन् a. what is not to be.

अभि adv. to, unto, near (comp. अभितरम् or °राम् nearer); towards, against; as prep. the same + into, for, for the sake of, over, above, concerning, about (acc.); without, except (abl.).

अभिक a. eager, desirous, libidinous.

अभिकाङ्क्षा f. wish, desire (acc. or —°).

अभिकाङ्क्षिन् a. wishing for, desirous of (acc. or —°).

अभिकाम a. affectionate, loving, desirous of (acc. or —°); m. affection, love, desire.

अभिक्लृप्त a. formed or manifested by (instr.).

अभिक्रम m. approaching (also °मण n.), undertaking, overcoming.

अभिक्षदा a. giving without being asked.

अभिख्या f. sight, glance (subj. & obj.), brightness, clearness, splendour, glory, beauty; name, designation.

अभिख्यात a. known, notorious.

अभिगम m., °न n. coming near, going to, approaching (also of sex. intercourse).

अभिगम्य a. to be approached, accessible.

अभिगर्जन &, °गर्जित n. shout, roar.

अभिगामिन् a. approaching (sexually).

अभिगुप्त a. kept, guarded.

अभिघात m. stroke, attack, affliction.

अभिघातिन् a. striking; m. enemy.

अभिघृत a. sprinkled.

अभिचक्षे (dat. inf.) to view.

अभिचार m. incantation, sorcery.

अभिजन m. origin, race, family, ancestors, °वन्त् = seq. adj.

अभिजात a. well or nobly-born; n. = seq.

अभिजाति f. (noble) birth, nobility.

अभिजित् a. victorious. m. a cert. sacrifice, N. of a lunar mansion.

अभिज्ञ a. knowing, understanding, acquainted with, skilled in (gen. or —°). f. आ remembrance, recollection.

अभिज्ञान n. = prec. f.; recognition or sign of recognition. °शकुन्तल n. T. of a drama (the Token or Ring-Sakuntala).

अभिज्ञु adv. on or up to the knees.

अभितस् adv. & prep. (w. acc.) towards, near; around, behind, before and after.

अभिताप m. heat, pain.

अभिदर्शन n. sight, appearance.

अभिद्यु a. tending heavenward, heavenly.

अभिद्रुह् a. offending, impious.

अभिद्रोह m. offence, wickedness.

अभिधा a. surrounding; f. name, appellation.

अभिधान n. = prec. f. + statement, speech, discourse, word; also = seq; f. °धानी a halter.

अभिधानकोश m. a dictionary.

अभिधेय a. to be named or expressed; n. meaning, signification.

अभिध्यान n. thinking of (gen.), longing for, coveting (loc.).

अभिनन्द m. voluptuousness, desire.

अभिनन्दनीय & °नन्द्य a. to be praised or rejoiced at.

अभिनन्दिन् a. praising, rejoicing at (—°).

अभिनभ्यम् adv. up to the sky.

अभिनय m. pantomime, dramatic representation; °याचार्य m. teacher of this art.

अभिनव a. quite new or fresh; °यौवन & °वयस्क a. of tender youth, very young.

अभिनिविष्ट a. entered, penetrated, fixed, settled, intent upon, attached to (loc., acc. w. प्रति, or —°), endowed with (instr.).

अभिनिवेश m. inclination, attachment to (loc. or —°); intentness, resolution, tenacity.

अभिनिवेशिन् a. inclined, adhering, clinging to (—°).

अभिनिश्चित a. fixed, certain (pers. & thing).

अभिनीत a. brought near, adduced, performed; trained, educated; fit, proper.

अभिन्न a. uncleft, unpierced, unbroken, uninterrupted, whole, entire, continual, undivided, one, the same as, not different from (abl. or —°).

अभिपित्व n. approach, arrival, stopping, esp. of the day, i.e. evening.

अभिपूजित a. honoured, pleasant, dear.

अभिपूर्ण a. filled, full of (instr., gen., or —°).

अभिप्रचक्षे dat. inf. to view.

अभिप्राय m. intention, purpose, goal, object, wish, opinion, meaning; the conception (of a thing) as (—°).

अभिप्रेप्सु a. desirous of, wishing for (acc.).

अभिप्लुत a. visited by, suffering from (instr.).

अभिभव a. predominant, superior. m. predominance, superiority, overthrow, humiliation, defeat (also °न† n.).

अभिभाषिन् a. addressing.

अभिभु & °भू = अभिभव adj.

अभिभूति a. & f. = अभिभव adj. & m.

अभिभूत्योजस् a. having victorious power.

अभिमत a. approved, wished for, dear.

अभिमत्त a. intoxicated.

अभिमन्तु a. self-conscious.

अभिमन्यु m. a man's name.

***अभिमर** m. slaughter, war.

अभिमर्श m. touch, contact.

अभिमाति f. plot, hostility; plotter, adversary, enemy.

अभिमातिन् a. inimical, m. foe.

अभिमान m. = prec. abstr.; self-conceit, arrogance, pride (p. °वन्त्); affection, love; conception, supposition, esp. a false one.

अभिमानित्व n. abstr. to seq.

अभिमानिन् a. self-conceited, arrogant; imagining one's self to have or to be (—°).

अभिमुख, f. ई (आ) having the face towards, facing, turned to (acc., dat., gen., or —°); propitious, favourable to (gen. or instr.); approaching, near; occupied in, going to (—°). n. adv. in front, towards, against, over against (acc., gen. or —°); °खे against, opposite (gen. or —°). °खी भू turn towards, be favourable.

अभियान n. approach, assault.

अभियायिन् a. approaching, assaulting.

अभियुक्त a. assailed, charged, prosecuted (j); intent on (loc. or —°), versed in (loc.), competent.

अभियुत a. contained in (acc.).

अभियोक्तृ assailing; m. enemy, plaintiff, claimant.

अभियोग m. application, endeavour, effort at (loc. or —°); attack, assault, accusation.

अभिरति f. delight in (loc. or —°).

अभिराद्ध a. propitiated, satisfied.

अभिराधन n. propitiation.

अभिराम a. agreeable, pleasing; m. = seq.; abstr. °ता f., (°त्व n.*).

अभिरुचि f. delight in (loc. —°).

अभिरुत a. sounding; n. sound, cry.

अभिरुचित a. pleasing, agreeable (dat. or gen); pleased with, delighting in (—°).

अभिरुषित a. enraged, wrathful.

अभिरूप a. suitable, apt, beautiful (also °वन्त्†); learned, wise.

अभिरूपपति m. a. cert. rite.*

अभिलक्ष्य a. recognisable by (—°).

अभिलक्ष्यम् adv. towards the goal.

अभिलङ्घन n. jumping over, transgression.

अभिलङ्घिन् a. overleaping, transgressing (—°).

अभिलाष m. desire, wish (loc. or —°); poss. °षिन्.

अभिलाषपूरयितृक a. fulfilling a desire.*

अभिलीन a. adhering; occupied by (—°).

अभिलुलित a. touched.

अभिवन्दन n. respectful greeting.

अभिवाञ्छित a. wished for; n. wish.

अभिवात a. tired, languid.

अभिवाद m. salutation; °क a. saluting.

अभिवादन n. = prec. m.; °शील a. respectful, modest.

अभिवाह्य n. being carried, conveyance.

अभिविख्यात a. celebrated; known as, called (इति).

अभिविनीत a. instructed, versed in (loc.).

अभिविश्रुत a. known as, called (nom.).

अभिविष्ट a. penetrated, seized by (—°).

अभिवीत a. sought for, desired.

1**अभिवृत** a. surrounded, covered.

2**अभिवृत** a. chosen, preferred.

अभिवृद्धि f. increase, plenty, success.

अभिव्यक्त a. apparent, clear; n. adv.
अभिव्यक्ति f. manifestation, appearance.
अभिव्याहरण n., °हार m. speaking, utterance.
अभिव्याहृत a. spoken to; said, uttered; n. word.
अभिशंसन n. defamation, accusation.
अभिशङ्का f. distrust (gen.), suspicion; p. °ङ्किन्.
अभिशङ्कित a. suspected of (gen.), suspicious.
अभिशस् f. imprecation.
अभिशस्त a. defamed, cursed, wicked.
अभिशस्ति f. imprecation, curse; censure, blame; misfortune, harm; concr. a slanderer, enemy.
अभिश्री a. closing or closed together; joining or joined.
अभिश्रुत a heard of, known, famous.
अभिषङ्ग m. inclination, attachment, curse, imprecation; defeat, humiliation; a. °ङ्गिन् defeating, humiliating.
अभिषव m. pressing out (of the Soma).
अभिषात a. won, conquered.
अभिषेक m. sprinkling over, bathing, religious, ablation, consecration, inauguration; the consecrated water itself.
अभिषेचनीय a. worthy or destined to be consecrated; m. consecration.
1अभिष्टि a. superior, victorious.
2अभिष्टि f. help, aid.
अभिष्ठित a. trampled or stepped upon.
अभिष्टिशवस् a. granting strong assistance.
अभिष्वङ्ग m. attachment, affection.
अभिसंहत्य ger. jointly.
अभिसंहित a. directed, turned; intended, agreed; connected with (—°).
अभिसंधान n. holding together, union; declaration, statement, speech; aim, purpose, interest; cheating, deceiving.
अभिसंधि m. intention, purpose, interest, condition; °पूर्वकम् adv. with a fixed purpose.
अभिसंबन्ध m. connexion, relation.
अभिसार m. approach, attack; love-visit, appointment.
अभिसारिका f. a woman visiting her lover.
अभिसारिन् a. going to (—°); f. °णी = prec.
अभिसृत a. come, gone to (acc.) or against (—°); turned towards (—°); visited by (instr.).
अभिसृष्ट a. let loose, hastening to (acc.), allowed, granted.
अभिस्वर् f. calling, invocation.
अभिस्वरे prep. behind (gen.), lit. within calling.
अभिस्वर्तृ m. invoker, singer.
अभिहत a. struck, smitten, beaten (drum), broken; visited by, suffering from (instr. or —°).
अभिहस्य a. ridiculous.
अभिहित a. fastened, attached; yoked; said, spoken named, designated, declared, addressed, called.
अभिह्रुत् & अभिह्रुति a. bending, hurting; f. injury, defeat.
अभीक n. encountering, meeting; loc. at the same time or in time; out of or from out (abl.).
अभीक्ष्णम् adv. every moment, frequently.
अभीत a. fearless; °वत् adv. as if not afraid.
अभीति f. assault, attack.
अभीप्सित a. desired, agreeable, dear.
अभीप्सु a. desirous to obtain (acc.).
अभीरु a. fearless or harmless.
अभीवर्ग m. reach, compass.
अभीवर्त a. victorious; m. victory.
अभीशु m. rein; ray.
अभीष्ट a. longed for, wished, pleasant, dear. m. favourite, lover; n. wish.
अभुक्त a. uneaten, not enjoyed.
अभुजिष्य*, f. आ not a slave or a servant; abstr. °त्व n.
अभूत a. not having been; °पूर्व —before.
अभूतलस्पर्श a. not touching the earth; abstr. °ता f.
अभूति f. non-existence, weakness, wretchedness, misfortune.
अभूतोपमा f. a kind of comparison.
अभूमि f. not the right place or object.
अभृत a. not hired or paid.
अभेत्तृ m. observer (lit. not-breaker).
अभेद a. not different, identical; m. undividedness, sameness, identity.

अभेद्य a. not to be divided or pierced.
अभोग m. non-enjoyment.
अभोगघ्नन् a. killing the stingy.
अभोजन a. not eating, fasting.
अभोजयन्त् a. not feeding.
अभोज्य not to be eaten; also = seq.
अभोज्यान्न a. whose food is not to be eaten.
अभ्यक्त a. smeared or anointed with (—°).
अभ्यङ्ग m. smearing, unction, unguent.
अभ्यञ्जन n. the same; also embellishment, ornament.
अभ्यतीत a. passed away, dead.
अभ्यधिक a. excessive, eminent; superior to; greater, stronger, more, dearer than or by (abl., instr., or —°); excellent, extraordinary. n. adv. extraordinarily, very much.
अभ्यनुज्ञा f., °न n. permission, leave.
अभ्यनुज्ञात a. allowed, permitted, authorized.
अभ्यनुज्ञापन n. inducement to approve, corroboration.
अभ्यन्तर a. interior, included by, contained in (loc., gen., or —°), inner, secret, near, intimate (also °क*); initiated in, conversant or familiar with (loc.). n. interior, interval; acc. into, loc. in, within, inside (—°).
अभ्यन्तरचारिन् a. moving within (—°).
अभ्यन्तरी कृ place between, insert; initiate in (loc.).
अभ्यर्कबिम्बम् adv. towards the sun's orb.
अभ्यर्चन n. worship, reverence.
अभ्यर्ण a. near; n. nearness (space & time).
अभ्यर्थन n., °र्थना f. request, begging.
अभ्यर्धयज्वन् a. receiving sacrifices.
अभ्यर्हण n. veneration, honour.
अभ्यर्हणीय a. worthy of honour, venerable.
अभ्यलंकार m. ornament.
अभ्यवहरण n. throwing down or away; also = seq.
अभ्यवहार m. taking food, eating or drinking.
अभ्यवहार्य a. fit for eating or drinking; n. food.
अभ्यसूयक a. envious, m. detractor.
अभ्यसूया f. indignation, envy.
अभ्यस्त a. thrown, shot; exercised, studied, learned; repeated, reduplicated (g.).
अभ्यस्तगुण a. containing studied virtues or merits.
अभ्यागत a. arrived; m. guest.
अभ्यागम m., °न n. approach, arrival.
अभ्याघात m. assault, inroad.
अभ्यात्म a. directed towards one's self; n. °त्मम् adv.
अभ्याधान n. laying on, adding.
अभ्याप्ति f. getting, acquiring.
अभ्यारम् adv. at hand, readily.
अभ्यारम्भ m. beginning.
अभ्यारूढ a. risen, high.
अभ्यारोह m. rising, increasing.
अभ्यावृत्त a. turned towards (acc.), returned.
अभ्याश m. obtaining; result, consequence; vicinity, nearness (sp. & t.); adj. near, proximate. °शम् & °शे adv. near, close by (gen., abl., or —°).
अभ्यास m. addition, repetition; reduplicate (g.), study, reading, exercise, custom.
अभ्युच्छ्रित a. elevated, high, excelling.
अभ्युत्थान n. rising, increasing.
अभ्युत्थित a. risen, high, excellent in (instr.), appearing, going to (acc.), ready.
अभ्युदय m. rising (lit. & fig.), beginning, event, result, success, fortune, welfare, feast, esp. a kind of Çrāddha.
अभ्युद्दृष्ट a. having become visible (of a star); n. as subst.
अभ्युपगम m. consent, agreement, promise.
अभ्युपपत्ति f. assistance, favour; — °निमित्तम् for the sake of (gen.)*.
अभ्युपपन्न a. approached, suppliant.
अभ्युपशान्त a. calmed, allayed.
अभ्युपस्थित a. come, approached; accompanied or attended by (instr.).
अभ्युपाय m. means, expedient.
अभ्युपावृत्त a. returned.
अभ्युपेत a. come to (acc.), joined by (instr.), agreed upon, promised.
अभ्युषित a. having dwelt or passed (acc. of time).
अभ्यूह m. reasoning, inference, conjecture, suspicion.

अभ्र n. (m.) rain-cloud, sky.
अभ्रंलिह a. touching (lit. licking) the clouds.
अभ्रकूट s. a dense mass of clouds.
अभ्रखण्ड s. part (lit. piece) of a cloud.*
अभ्रप्रुष् f. the sprinkling of a cloud.
अभ्रागम m. approach of the clouds, rainy season.
अभ्रातृ (अभ्रातृ) f. brotherless.
अभ्रावकाशिक & °शिन् a. exposing one's self to the rain.
अभ्रि f. shovel, spade.
अभ्रित a. clouded.
अभ्रिय or अभ्रिय a. belonging to or coming from a cloud; m. n. a thunder-cloud.
अभ्व (अभ्व or अभ्व) a. huge, enormous, dreadful; n. enormity, monster, dread, horror.
अम्, अमीति press on, harm (only pp. एमुषम harmful, pernicious). C. आमयति suffer, be sick. — अभि & परि = S.
1अम (pron. st.) this.
2अम m. onset, impetuosity; fear, terror.
अमङ्गल & °ल्य a. inauspicious, unlucky.
अमण्डित a. unadorned.
अमत a. unthought, unexpected, unapproved.
1अमति f. appearance, shape.
2अमति a. poor, f. poverty.
3अमति f. not-knowing; instr. unwittingly.
1अमत्र a. strong, firm.
2अमत्र & °क† n. vessel, cup; p. अमत्रिन्.
अमत्सर a. not egoistic, unselfish. as subst. unselfishness; charity.
अमध्यम a. pl. having no midmost.
1अमनस् n. no mind or intellect.
2अमनस् a. without mind or understanding.
अमन्तु a. unadvised, ignorant, unknowing.
अमन्त्र a. not having or knowing mantras.
अमन्त्रक, f. °न्त्रिका not having, i.e. not accompanied by mantras.
अमन्त्रज्ञ & °विद् a. not knowing mantras.
अमन्द a. not slow or dull; abstr. °ता† f.
अमन्यमान a. unaware.
अमर, f. आ & ई immortal; m. a god.*
अमरपक्षपातिन् m. a. friend of the gods.
अमरप्रभ a. god-like.
अमरलोक m. the world of the immortals; abstr. °ता f.
अमरवर्णिन् a. of divine colour or beauty.
अमरसदस् n. assembly (lit. seat) of the gods.
अमरावती f. N. of Indra's capital.
अमरु m. N. of a poet (also °रू & °रुक); °शतक n. the hundred (stanzas) of Amaru.
अमरेश & °रेश्वर m. lord of the gods, E. of Çiva, Viṣṇu, or Indra.
अमरोपम a. god-like.
अमर्त & अमर्त्य a. undying, immortal.
अमर्धन्त् a. untiring (intr. & tr.).
अमर्ष m. non-endurance, impatience, anger.
अमर्षण a. not enduring, impatient; n. = prec.
अमर्षित & °र्षिन् = prec. adj.
अमल & °लिन a. free from dirt; clean, pure.
अमलान्वय a. of pure or noble race.
अमवन्त् a. impetuous, bold, strong; n. °वत् adv.
अमहात्मन् a. not high-minded.
अमहीयमान a. depressed.
अमा adv. at home, home; with कृ appropiate or keep by one's self.
अमाजुर् f. old maid, spinster (lit. growing old at home).
अमात् (abl. adv.) from home, from near.
अमात्य m. inmate, relative, householder, councillor of a king, minister.
अमानयन्त् a. not honouring.
अमानित्व n. abstr. to seq.
अमानिन् a. not proud; modest, humble.
अमानुष, f. ई not human, un-or superhuman. m. no human being, a beast, brute, f. ई a female animal.
अमाय a. not clever, unwise.
अमाया f. no deceit or guile; instr. without guile.
अमार्जित a. unwashed.
अमावसु m. N. of a king.
अमावासी & °स्या f. (± रात्रि) the night of the new moon (lit. of the cohabitation or conjunction. scil. of sun and moon).
अमित a. unmeasured, unlimited.
अमिततेजस् a. of unmeasured lustre.
अमितबुद्धिमन्त् a. of unmeasured intellect.
अमितविक्रम a. of unmeasured power.
अमितौजस् a. of unmeasured strength.
अमित्र m. (आ f.) enemy; adv. वत्†; abstr. °ता† f.; den. °त्राय्, °यते†.

अमित्रकर्षण a. harassing enemies.
अमित्रघातिन् & °घ्न a. killing enemies.
अमित्रविनिबर्हिन् a. destroying enemies.
अमित्रयन्त् & °यु a. inimical.
अमित्रहन् a. = अमित्रघातिन्.
अमित्रिन् & °त्रिय a. inimical.
अमिथ्या adv. not falsely; °कृ make true, confirm, accomplish.
अमिन a. impetuous, bold.
अमिनन्त् a. not injuring; undisturbed, unfailing.
अमीमांस्य a. not to be reasoned about, unquestionable, certain.
अमीव n. pain, disease, distress, grief; f. अमीवा the same, concr. tormentor, fiend.
अमीवचातन, f. ई dispelling, grief or disease.
अमु pron. st. of 3[d] pers.
अमुक्त a. not loosed or liberated, not given up.
अमुक्तहस्त a. economical (lit. not open-handed).
अमुतस् adv. from, there, thence, further. Also = abl. of अदस्.
अमुत्र adv. there, in the other world; here. Also = loc. of अदस्.
अमुथा & अमुया adv. in that way; w. अस् be away or gone.
अमुर्हि adv. at that time, then.
अमूढ a. not perplexed or troubled.
अमूर a. infallible, sagacious.
अमूल a. having no root (lit. & fig.).
अमूल्य a. priceless, inestimable.
अमृक्त a. unharmed, safe.
अमृत m. immortal. m. a god. n. immortality (also concr. = the gods); the drink of the gods, i.e. nectar; anything sweet, delightful, or wholesome, e.g. water, milk, medicine, the remainder of sacrifice, alms unasked.
अमृतकल्प a. nectar-like.
अमृतत्व n. immortality.
अमृतधायिन् a. sipping nectar.
अमृतप्लवन n. a flood of nectar.
अमृतमय f. ई immortal; nectar-like or consisting of nectar.
अमृतमेघ m. a cloud containing nectar.
अमृतरश्मि m. the moon (lit. having nectar-like rays).
अमृतवर्ति f. a nectar-like unguent.
अमृतांशु m. the same.
अमृतोद्भव a. nectar-born.
अमृतोपम a. nectar-like.
अमृत्यु m. not death; a deathless.
अमृध्र a. incessant, indefatigable.
अमृषा adv. not falsely truly.
अमृष्यमाण a. not enduring.
अमेध्य a. unfit for sacrifice (act. & pass.), impure. n. impurity, ordure.
अमेध्यकुणपाशिन् a. feeding on ordure and carrion.
अमेध्याक्त a. soiled by ordure.
अमेन a. having no wife.
अमेनि a. harmless.
अमेय a. immeasurable, unfathomable.
अमोघ a. infallible, efficacious, auspicious; f. आ N. of a spear.
अमोघदर्शन a. of auspicious sight.
अमोघवचन a. of unfallible speech.
अमोघार्थ a. of infallible purpose.
अमोच्य a. not to be loosed.
अमौक्तिक a. not containing pearls.
अम्णस् or अम्नस् adv. immediately, just.
अम्बर n. garment, (also m.) sky; abl. °तस्.
अम्बरखण्ड m. n. piece of cloud or cloth.
अम्बरीष m. n. a frying-pan; m. a man's name.
अम्बष्ठ m. N. of a caste, also of a people and its country.
अम्बा f. mother (voc. अम्बे or अम्ब, the latter form o. used as a simple exclamation); N. of a princess.
अम्बालिका f. mother, N. of a princess.
अम्बि or अम्बी f. mother, good wife.
अम्बिका f. the same; N. of a princess.
अम्बु n. water.
अम्बुचारिन् moving in water; m. aquatic animal.
अम्बुज a. water-born; n. lotus.
अम्बुद m. rain-cloud (lit. giving water).
अम्बुधारा f. pl. water-drops.
अम्बुधि m. the ocean (lit. water-receptacle).
अम्बुनिवह m. rain-cloud (carrying water).
अम्बुरय m. current of water.
अम्बुराशि m. the ocean (lit. heap of water).
अम्बुरुह n. lotus (lit. grown in water).
अम्बुवाह m. = अम्बुनिवह.

अम्बूकृत a. accompanied by water, i.e. spitting, sputtered (sounds).
अंम्भस् n. water.
अम्भृण a. dreadful; m. tub, vat.
अम्भोगर्भ a. containing water (cloud).
अम्भोज n. lotus (lit. water-born).
अम्भोधि & **अम्भोनिधि** m. = **अम्बुधि**.
अम्भोरुह् & **अम्भोरुह** n. = **अम्बुरुह**.
अम्ल a. sour, acid; m. wood-sorrel.
अम्लान a. unfaded, unimpaired, fresh.
अंय m. walk, course (—°); luck, fortune; die.
अयःपिण्ड m. n. a piece of iron.
अयक्ष्मं a. not sick, healthy; n. health.
1**अंयज्ञ** m. no sacrifice.
2**अयज्ञं** a. = seq.
अंयज्यु & **अंयज्वन्** a. not sacrificing, impious.
अयति m. no ascetic; N. of a man.
अयत्न m. no effort, no pains; °—, **अयत्नेन** & °**त्नतस्** adv. without effort, easily, gently.
अयत्नलभ्य a. easy to be got.
अयंथ n. leg, foot.
अयथातथम् adv. not as it ought to be.
अंयथायथम् adv. the same.
अयथार्थ a. unsuitable to the matter or sense; incorrect, false.
अयथावत् adv. unjustly, erroneously.
अंयन a. going, coming; n. motion, walk, course, esp. the sun's road between the solstitial points, also solstice, half-year; way, manner; refuge, residence.
अंयव & °**वन्** m., °**वस्** n. the dark half-month.
1**अयशस्** n. dishonour, infamy.
2**अयशंस्** a. inglorious.
अयशस्कर, f. **ई** disgraceful, ignominious.
अंयस् n. metal, iron.
अयस्कान्त & °**मणि** m. the loadstone (lit. the beloved of iron).
अयस्मय, **ई** made of iron.
अयां (instr. adv.) thus, in this way.
अयाचन्त् a. not begging or asking.
अंयाचित a. unasked.
अयाज्यं a. what or for whom it is not permitted to sacrifice.
अयाज्ययाजन & **अयाज्यसंयाज्य** n. sacrifice for persons unworthy to offer sacrifices.
अंयातयाम a. vigorous, powerful, fresh, strong (lit. not having gone one's way); n. pl. cert. mantras of the Yajurveda.
अयांस् a. untired, brisk, active.
अयांस्य a. the same; m. N. of a Rishi.
अयि vocat. or interrog. particle.
अंयुक्त not yoked, not harnessed, not joined unconnected, unappointed; not attentive or devout, unsuitable, unfit, improper, wrong; abstr. °**त्व**† n.
अयुगू f. a girl that is the only child of her mother.
अयुग्म, **अंयुङ्ग**, **अयुंज्**, & **अयुजं** a. not paired, uneven, odd.
1**अंयुत** a. unrestrained.
2**अयुंत** m. n. a myriad; adv. °**शस्**†.
अंयुद्ध a. not fought or combated. n. no fight, loc. = seq.
अंयुद्धी abs. without fighting.
अयुध्यमान a. not fighting.
अये a. vocat. particle.
अयेाग m. separation (lit. non-union), inconsistency, impropriety, impossibility; want of devotion (abl. °**तस्**).
अयेागव m. N. of a cert. mixed caste.
अयेागुड m. an iron ball.
अयेाग्य a. unfit, unsuitable, incapable, unqualified. Abstr. °**त्व** n.
अंयेादंष्ट्र a. iron-toothed.
अयेाध्यं a. unconquerable, invincible. f. **आ** N. of a town.
1**अंयेानि** f. not a vulva.
2**अयेानिं** a. without, or of low, origin.
अयेामय, f. **ई** iron.
अंयेामुख a. having an iron mouth, beak, or point.
अंयेाहत a. beaten or forged of iron.
अरं m. spoke of a wheele.
अरक्त a. undyed.
अरक्षन्त् a. not protecting.
अरक्षंस् a. harmless, true.
अरक्षितृ m. non-protector.
अरघट्ट & °**क** m. a wheel for raising water from a well.
अंरंकृत a. prepared, ready; abstr. **अंरंकृति** f.
अरजंस् a. free from dust or impurity, passionless; f. a young girl (cf. **रंजस्**).

अ॑रण, f. ई distant, strange.
अ॑रणि or °णी f. a. piece of wood used for producing fire by attrition.
अ॑रण्य n. wilderness, forest.
अरण्यरुदित n. a useless complaint (lit. weeping in a forest).
अरण्यवास m. residence in a forest, hermitage.
अरण्यवासिन् a. dwelling in a forest; m. deer.
अरण्यानि or °नी f. wilderness and the deity of the wilderness.
अरण्यौकस् m. inhabitant of a forest. a hermit.
1अरति॑ m. assistant, minister, disposer.
2अरति f. discomfort, uneasiness.
अर॑त्नि m. elbow, cubit; angle, corner.
अरथ॑ a. having no chariot.
अ॑रथी m. no charioteer.
अ॑रध्र a. unwilling, disobedient.
अरप॑ & °प॑स् a. unhurt, safe.
अरप॑स् a. the same; harmless, salutary.
अ॑रम् adv. suitably, conveniently, sufficiently, enough; ° कामाय according to one's wish. — °कृ make or get ready, serve (dat.), °भू & °गम् be present or at hand.
अरमणीयत्व n. unpleasantness.*
1अर॑मति f. devotedness, also personif.
2अरमति a. restless.
अरम्य a. unpleasant, disagreeable.
अ॑ररिवंस् & अररु a. envious, unkind.
अरविन्द n. day-lotus; abstr. °त्व n.
अरस॑ a. tasteless, insipid (subj. & obj.).
अरसिक a. having no taste, insensible, dull.
अराक्षस a. free from Rākṣasas.
अरागद्वेषतस् adv. not from passion or anger.
अराज॑क a. having no king; n. anarchy.
अ॑राजन् m. not a king.
अराजन्य॑ a. without the warrior-caste.
अराजन्यप्रसूति a. not born in the warrior caste (abl. °तस्).
अराजि॑न् a. having no splendour.
अराज्यभाज् a. not enjoying dominion.
अ॑राड & अराड्ड a. long-horned.
अ॑राति f. envy, jealousy (lit. the not giving), enmity; concr. enemy, foe.
अरातीय्, °य॑ति be malign; a. °यु॑ = seq.
अरातीव॑न् a. malign, envious.
अराध॑स् a. unkind, stingy, selfish.
1अ॑राय a. niggard, stingy.
2अर॑ाय m., °यी॑ f. a kind of evil spirits.
अराल a. crooked, bowed, curled (hair); m. a kind of resin.
अ॑रावन् a. hostile, adverse (lit. not giving).
1अरि॑ a. eager, devoted, faithful.
2अरि॑ a. greedy (lit. not giving), impious, envious, hostile, adverse. m. enemy.
अरिक्त a. not void or empty; — °पाणि not with empty hands.*
अरिक्थीय a. not entitled to inheritance.
अरि॑त्र or अ॑रित्र m. n. oar.
अरि॑ंदम m. tamer of enemies.
अरिप्र॑ a. stainless, clear, pure.
अ॑रिष्ट a. unharmed, safe, secure. m. N. of a tree; n. good or bad luck.
अरिष्टक m. = prec. m.; n. the fruit of the A. tree.
अ॑रिष्टग्राम a. whose troop is unhurt.
अरिष्ट॑ताति f. unharmedness; welfare.
अरिष्टशय्या f. the lying-in chamber.
अ॑रिष्टि f. unharmedness, safety.
अरिसूदन m. slayer of enemies.
अरिसे॑विन् m. partisan of a foe.
अरिहन् a. slaying enemies.
अ॑रीढ or अ॑रीळ्ह a. unlicked.
अरु (°—) = अरु॑स् n.
अ॑रुग्ण a. unbroken.
अरु॑च् a. lightless.
अरुज् a. free from disease, sound, healthy, well.
अरुज a. the same; m. N. of a demon.
अरुण॑, f. आ (ved. also ई) ruddy, light-brown, yellowish. m. redness, pers. as Aruṇa, the Dawn, conceived as the charioteer of the Sun; the Sun itself; N. of an old teacher etc. f. ई a red cow; the dawn. n. redness, gold, ruby.
अरुण॑प्सु a. of ruddy appearance.
अरुणा॑श्व a. having ruddy horses.
अरुणिमन् m. redness.
अरुणोदय m. sunrise.
अरुं॑तुद a. cutting to the quick (lit. striking a wound.)
अरुन्धती॑ f. cert. plant; N. of the wife of

Vasiṣṭha, conceived as a star in the Great Bear.

अरुष, f. **अरुषी** red, fire-coloured. m. the Sun, day. f. the Dawn; a red mare, pl. flames, conceived as the team of Agni.

अरुस् a. sore, n. wound; **अरुष्कृत** wounded.

अरूढमूलत्व n. the not having firm (lit. grown) roots.

अरूप a. shapeless, ill formed, ugly.

अरूपण n. no metaphorical expression.

अरे a vocat. particle.

अरेणु a. not dusty, not earthly, i.e. heavenly. m. pl. the gods.

अरेपस् a. stainless, pure, bright.

अरोग a. free from disease, healthy (also °गिन्); m. health.

अरोगता f., °गत्व n., °गिता & °ग्यता f.=prec. m.

अरोचकिन् a. having no appetite; critical, dainty.

अरोचमान a. not shining, not pleasing.

अरोषण a. not angry; meek, tender.*

अर्क m. beam, ray; the sun, fire; praise, song, sound, roar; singer; N. of a plant.

अर्किन् a. rich in beams or songs.

अर्गल m. n., **आ** f. bolt, bar, obstacle.

अर्घ्, **अर्घति** to be worth, cost.

अर्घ m. worth, price; gift of honour.

अर्घोदक or **अर्घ्योदक** n. water of honour* (v. seq.).

अर्घ्य n. worth or fit for an honourable reception. n. a reverential offering to gods or venerable men.

अर्चक a. honouring (—°).

अर्चत्रि a. singing, thundering.

अर्चन n., **अर्चना** & **अर्चा** f. praise, worship.

अर्चनीय a. to be honoured.

अर्चार्ह a. worthy of honour or praise.

अर्चि m. beam, flame; p. **अर्चिमन्त्** & °वन्त्.

अर्चित a. honoured, adorned.

अर्चिष्मन्त् a. flaming, brilliant, resplendent; m. fire.

अर्चिस् n. (later also f.) beam, flame.

अर्च्य a. to be honoured.

अर्जक a. gaining, acquiring.

अर्जन n. gain, acquisition.

अर्जुन, f. **ई** silver-white. m. Arjuna, one of the Pāndavas, N. of a tree; f. du. & pl. name of a lunar mansion.

अर्ण m. n. wave, flood, stream; m. letter, syllable.

अर्णव a. waving, undulating, rising. m. (n.) = seq.

अर्णस् n. wave, flood, sea, ocean; sky.

अर्णसाति f. winning of the streams; bustle of the fight, broil.

अर्थ n. m. aim, purpose, meaning, sense, object, profit, advantage of (instr.), wealth, property, money, thing, matter, business, cause, suit, action; o. —° adj. having a thing for object, for the sake of, on accouut of, for; acc., instr., dat. & loc. the same adv.

अर्थकल्यवर्त n. money, (this) paltry thing.*

1**अर्थकाम** (n. sgl., m. du.) wealth and pleasure.

2**अर्थकाम** a. desirous of wealth.

अर्थकिल्बिषिन् m. a sinner for gain.

अर्थकृच्छ्र n. difficulty (of a matter).

अर्थघ्न, f. **ई** wasteful, extravagant.

अर्थजात (n. sgl. & pl.) the whole of or whatever (v. **जात**) money, things, matter, business etc.

अर्थतस् adv. for a purpose, for profit; on account of (—°); indeed, intruth; according to the sense.

अर्थतृष्णा f. desire (lit. thirst) of money.

अर्थद a. useful or munificent.

अर्थदत्त m. a man's name.

अर्थदान n. gift of money, gratuity.

अर्थदूषण n. spoiling or seizure of (another's) property.

अर्थना f. begging, request.

अर्थबन्ध m. text, verse (lit. context of the sense or matter).

अर्थय्, **अर्थयते** (**अर्थति**, **अर्थते**) aim at, strive after, beg or wish for (acc.); ask or entreat (2 acc.). — **अभि** beg a person (acc.) for (acc., dat., loc., or **अर्थम्**). **प्र** entreat, desire, sue for (acc.), beg of (abl.). **सम्** prepare, conclude, reflect, judge, think, consider as (2 acc.), approve, determine.

अर्थरुचि a. avaricious, eager for money.

अर्थवत्ता f., °त्त्व n. significancy, importance, consequence.

अर्थवन्त् a. having sense or meaning, significant; suitable, apt, wealthy, rich. n. **°वत्** according to the purpose.
अर्थवाद m. declaration of purpose or object.
अर्थविद् a. knowing the signification (of words).
अर्थवैकल्य n. deficiency of a transaction.
अर्थशास्त्र n. manual of practical life.
अर्थशौच n. honesty in money-matters.
अर्थसमाहर्तृ m. collector of money.
अर्थसंपादन n. attaining of advantage or arranging of a matter.
अर्थसंबन्धिन् a. connected with or interested in a cause.
अर्थसिद्ध a. self-evident, perfectly clear.
अर्थसिद्धि f. recovering of money; attaining of a purpose, success; evidence (v. prec.).
अर्थानर्थ (m. du.) what is expedient or inexpedient.
अर्थान्तर n. another thing or meaning.
अर्थार्जन n. acquisition of an object.
अर्थार्थिन् a. wanting money, covetous.
अर्थितव्य a. desirable.
अर्थिता f., **°त्व** n. abstr. to seq.
अर्थिन् a. having an object, industrious, eager; wanting, poor, desirous of (instr. or —°), begging, a beggar or petitioner, amorous, wooing, a wooer, suitor, plaintiff.
अर्थिभाव m. condition of a petitioner.
अर्थ्य a. suitable, apt, fit; wealthy.
अर्थ्युक्त a. called by the suitor (j.).
अर्दन (—°) vexing, tormenting.
1**अर्ध** a. half, halved. m. n. half, middle; party.
2**अर्ध** m. side, part, place.
अर्धकृष्ट a. half-drawn.
अर्धकोटी f. half a koṭi, i.e. five millions.
अर्धचन्द्र m. half-moon, crescent.
अर्धदण्ड m. half the fine.
अर्धदेव m. demi-god.
अर्धपञ्चन् & **°पञ्चम** (pl.) four and a half.
अर्धपञ्चाशत् f. twenty-five (lit. half of fifty).
अर्धपण m. half a paṇa.
अर्धपतित a. half decayed.*
अर्धपथ m. half the way, midway.
अर्धपादिक a. half-footed (having the half of one's feet cut off.).
अर्धपीत a. half-drunk or sucked.
अर्धबृगल n. semi-morsel, fragment.
अर्धभक्षित a. half eaten.
अर्धभाज् a. obtaining a half; m. partner, fellow.
अर्धमागधी f. half-Māgadhī (a dialect).
अर्धमार्ग m. = **अर्धपथ**.
अर्धमास m. half a month, a fortnight.
(**अर्धरजनी** f.* &) **अर्धरात्र** m. midnight.
अर्धर्च m. half-stanza.
अर्धर्चशस् adv. by half-verses.
अर्धलिखित a. half-painted.
अर्धवाचित a. half read.*
अर्धशत n. a hundred and a half, i.e. a hundred and fifty.
अर्धसमवृत्त n. a half-equal metre, i.e. a metre the halves of which are equal (pāda 1 = 3, 2 = 4).
अर्धसीरिन् m. = **आर्धिक**.
अर्धहार m. a necklace of 64 strings.
अर्धाक्षि n. side glance.
अर्धावलीढ a. half-licked or chewed.
अर्धिन् a. getting one half.
अर्धेन्दु m. = **अर्धचन्द्र**; **°मौलि** m. E. of Çiva (having the crescent as diadem).
अर्धोक्त a. half spoken.
अर्धोदित a. half risen.
अर्धोरुक n. a short petticoat.
अर्पण, f. **ई** procuring, getting, conferring; n. **अर्पण** throwing, sending, putting in or on, delivering, entrusting, offering, sacrifice; transmission, restitution.
अर्बुद m. a snake, a serpent-demon (**अर्बुद**); N. of a mountain, pl. of a people; n. a hundred millions, cartilage of the ribs.
अर्बुदशिखर m. N. of a mountain.
अर्बुदोदासर्पिणी f. the creeping near of Arbuda (v. **अर्बुद**), N. of a path of the sacrifice.
अर्भ & **अर्भक** a. small, weak, young; m. a child.
अर्म m. pl. rubbish, remnants, ruins.
1**अर्य** (**अर्य्य**) a. faithful, devoted, pious, attached, kind.

2अर्य, f. आ a man or woman of one of the first three castes, esp. a Vaiçya.

अर्यमन् m. intimate, friend, esp. a bridegroom's friend; N. of a god.

अर्यम्य a. intimate.

अर्वन् & अर्वन्त् running, quick. m. a courser, horse, charioteer.

अर्वश or अर्वशं = prec. a.

अर्वाके (loc. adv.) near.

अर्वाक्कालिकता f. posteriority (of time).

अर्वाचीन or °चीन turned towards, being on this side or below, nearer (time). n. as prep. on this side, from, since, less than (abl.).

अर्वाञ्च्, f. अर्वाची turned towards or downwards, coming near; acc. with कृ bring hither. n. अर्वाक् as adv. and prep. hitherwards, down, near (loc.); from, since, before, after (abl. or instr.).

अर्शस् n. haemorrhoids.

अर्शस a. suffering from haemorrhoids.

अर्ह्, अर्हति (अर्हते) deserve, merit, have a right or be worthy to (acc. or inf.), be liable to, capable of (acc.); dare, be obliged or able to (inf.). C. अर्हयति honour or present with (instr.).

अर्ह a. deserving, worthy, entitled to (acc. or inf.); fit or apt for (gen. or —°).

अर्हण a. deserving (—°); f. आ veneration, worship, instr. अर्हणा according to merit. n. merit, worth, also = f.

अर्हणीय a. venerable.

अर्हन्त् a. deserving, entitled to (acc.); worthy, venerable, superl. अर्हत्तम m. an Arhant, i.e. a Jaina saint.

अर्हसे (dat. inf.) to be worthy of (acc.).

अलक m. n. curl. f. आ Kubera's residence.

अलकम् adv. in vain, for nothing.

अलक्त m., अलक्तक m. n. red lac.

अलक्ताङ्क a. marked by a red colour (lit. lac).

1अलक्षण n. inauspicious mark.

2अलक्षण a. unmarked, inauspicious.

अलक्षित a. unmarked, unnoticed.

अलक्ष्य a. invisible, not to be observed, not appearing (thus), insignificant.

अलगर्द m. a kind of snake. f. आ a large black leech.

अलघु a. not light; heavy, slow.

अलंकरण n. adorning, dressing; ornament.

अलंकरणरत्न n. jewel for ornament.

अलंकरिष्णु a. fond of ornament; *adorning (acc.).

*अलंकर्तृ m. ornamenting.

अलंकार & °क† m. ornamenting or ornament (lit. & fig.).

अलंकारकारिन् a. forming the ornament of (—°).*

अलंकारभाण्ड n. jewel-box.

अलंकारिन् a. adorning.

अलंकृति & °क्रिया f. = अलंकार.

अलङ्घनीय a. not to be overtaken; not to be left unnoticed or neglected.*

अलङ्घित a. not reached, untouched.

अलङ्घितपूर्व a. not before violated.*

अलङ्घ्य a. impassable; not to be touched or violated.

अलज m. a kind of bird.

अलजि (°जी†) f. a cert. disease of the eye.

अलज्ज a. shameless; f. आ shamelessness.

अलंधन a. having sufficient money.

अलब्ध a. not obtained or gained. °वन्त् not having obtained.

अलभमान a. not getting.

अलभ्य a. not to be obtained.

अलम् (indecl.) enough, one's fill; sufficient, a match for (dat.); capable of, able to (inf. or loc.). With instr. or absol. enough with, have done with! — °कृ make ready, prepare, adorn (M. also refl.), with gen. violate (M.); °भू suffice.

अलर्क m. a mad dog; a fabulous animal; a plant.

अललाभवन्त् a. dabbling, splashing (water).

अलस a. lazy, indolent, dull, weary.

अलाघव n. not-lightness, heaviness (fig.).

अलाण्डु m. a kind of vermin.

अलात n. a fire-brand.

अलातृण a. stingy, greedy.

अलाबु (°बू) f. the bottle gourd; m. n. a vessel made of the b. g.

अलाभ m. non-acquirement, not getting, loss.

अलायुध m. N. of a Rākṣasa.
अलाव्य m. E. of Indra.
अलि m. bee; **°कुल** n. a flight of bees.
अलिङ्ग a. having no mark or sign, having no gender (g.).
अलिङ्गिन् m. not a student, an impostor.
अलिञ्जर m. a large water-jar.
अलिन् m., **°नी** f. male and female bee.
अलिन्द (& **°क***) m. terrace before a house.
अलिमाला f. a flight of bees.
अलीक a. unpleasing, contrary, false, untrue; n. adversity, falsehood, untruth.
अलीकदाक्षिण्य a. of a feigned courtesy.*
अलीकनिर्बन्ध m. accusing of falsehood.
अलीकपण्डित a. unpleasantly or falsely wise. pedantic.
अलीकसुप्त n. feigned sleep.
अलुब्ध a. not avaricious or covetous.
अलून a. uncut, unplucked, unhurt.
अलेपक a. stainless, pure.
1**अलोक** m. not the world, the end of the world.
2**अलोक** a. finding no place.
अलोकसामान्य a. not common in the world.
अलोक्य a. unusual (lit. unwordly), unallowed; making unfit for the (other) world.
अलोभ a. not greedy; m. absence of greed or cupidity, moderation, content.
अलोमक & **अलोमक** (f. **°मका** & **°मिका**), & **अलोमन्** a. not covered with hair.
अलोलत्व n. steadiness, constancy.
अलौकिक, f. **ई** not common in the world. extraordinary, strange, rare.
अल्गा m. du. the loins, flanks.
अल्प a. small, minute, little. n. little, a trifle. **अल्पेन** and ***अल्पात्** adv. for a little, easily, without pain. Comp. **अल्पीयंस्** less, little; n. a little bit.
अल्पक (f. **अल्पिका**) = prec.; n. little, **°कम्** adv. a little, **°कात्** soon after.
अल्पकालत्व n. shortness of time.
अल्पक्लेश a. causing little pain.
अल्पचेतस् a. weak-minded, stupid.
अल्पच्छद a. scantily clad.
अल्पज्ञ a. knowing little, ignorant; abstr. **°त्व** n.
अल्पता f., **°त्व** n. smallness, minuteness.
अल्पतेजस् a. of little fire or energy; dull, weak.
अल्पदक्षिण a. deficient in fees (sacrifice).
अल्पद्रोह m. little injury.
अल्पधन a. having little wealth.
अल्पधी a. of small understanding, ignorant.
अल्पपायिन् a. little or ill sucking (leech).
अल्पपुण्य a. of small religious merit or virtue, wicked, miserable.
अल्पबुद्ध a. little or sarcely awakened.*
अल्पबुद्धि a. weak-minded, ignorant.
अल्पभाग्य a. of small fortune; unhappy, miserable; abstr. **°त्व** n.
अल्पभुजान्तर a. narrow-breasted.
अल्पमूल्य a. of small value.*
अल्पमेधस् a. of little sense.
अल्पविद्य a. of small learning.
अल्पशंस् adv. to a small degree, little, rarely.
अल्पशेष a. of which little is left; almost finished or gone.
अल्पसार a. having little strength or value; worthless, insignificant.
अल्पाङ्ग a. of small body; abstr. **°त्व** n.
अल्पायास m. little pains;* instr. easily.
अल्पायुस् a. short-lived.
अल्पाल्प a. very little.
अल्पाल्पभास् a. of very little splendour.
अल्पावशिष्ट a. = **अल्पशेष**; abstr. **°त्व** n.
अव्, **अवति**, pp. **ऊत** favour, like, delight in (acc.), accept; further, protect, aid, comfort, satiate. C. **आवयति** enjoy, eat, devour. — **उप** caress, encourage, join (acc. or dat.). **प्र** = S. — Cf. **अवन्त्**.
1**अव** adv. down, off; mostly as pref. in nouns and verbs, rarely as prep. w. abl.
2**अव** m. favour, protection.
1**अवंश** m. low (lit. no) family.
2**अवंश** n. the sky (lit. what has no beams or support).
अवकर m. dust, sweepings, rubbish.
अवकर्त m. piece cut off.
अवकर्तन n. cutting off.
अवकाश m. open place, space, room, free course or scope, interval, while, time, opportunity of (gen.).
अवकाशद a. giving room or shelter.

अ॑वकीर्ण a. who has shed (esp. his sperm); scattered, spread; bestrewn, filled with, seized by (—°).
अवकीर्णिन् a. = prec. act.; unchaste, incontinent.
अवकीर्णिव्रत n. penance for incontinency.
अवकृष्ट a. drawn down, being below or under (—°); remote, inferior, low.
अवकृष्टजाति a. of a low(er) caste.
अवक्रचेतस् a. of upright mind.
अवक्रय m. letting or hiring out; rent, price.
अवक्षाण a. burnt down.
अवक्षुत a. sneezed upon.
अवक्षेप m. derision, scoff, sarcasm.
अवक्षेपण n. throwing down, also = the prec.
अवखाद m. devouring, wasting, destruction.
अवगम m., °न n. understanding, knowledge.
अवगाढ a. entered (act. & pass.), immersed (l. & f.), depressed, deep.
अवगाह m., °न n. submersion, bathing.
अवगुण्ठन n. veiling, a veil. °वन्त् veiled.
अवग्रह m. hindrance, impediment; separation of padas and the pause between them (g.).
†अवच a. lower (only in उच्चावच q.v.).
अवचन a. speechless, silent.
अवचनीय a. not to be spoken, (blameless.*).
अवचय & °चाय m. gathering, plucking.
अवचारण n. application (medic.); °णीय relating to the application of (—°).
अवच्छन्न a. covered over, overspread, filled.
अवच्छात a. emaciated, thin.
अवच्छिन्न a. interrupted, bordered or included by (—°); defined.
अवच्छेद m. cutting off, part cut off, piece; separation, distinction.
अवज्ञा f., °न n. contempt.
अवञ्चक a. not a deceiver.*
अवट॑ m. hole, pit; a. °ट्य being in a pit.
अवटु m. or f. neck.
अवत॑ m. well, cistern.
अवतंस m. garland or ear-ring.
अवतंसक m. the same, as adj. (f. °सिका) crowned with (—°).
अवतंसनीय a. to be made into a garland.*
अवतंसय्, °यति make into a garland.*
अवतंसिनी f. wearing a garland of flowers.*
अवतरण n. descending, alighting.
अवतरम् adv. further away.
अवताडन n. pounding, crushing.
अ॑वतान्त a. faint, feeble.
अवतार m. descent, esp. of a deity from heaven, incarnation, appearance; a. °रिन्.
अवतीर्ण a. come down, descended (cf. prec.) from (abl. or —°), in consequence of or in the shape of (—°), fallen or got into (acc.).
अ॑वत्त a. cut off, divided.
अवत्सल a. not tender, cruel to (loc.).
अवदात a. clean, pure, white, clear.
1अवदा॑न n. cutting off or a part cut off.
2अवदान n. heroic deed, exploit.
अवदार m. breaking, rupture. °ण a. breaking through, tearing; n. as subst.
अवदावद a. undisputed, indisputable.
अवदीर्ण a. perplexed, bewildered.
अवद्य a. blamable, bad. n. imperfection, want, fault; blame, censure, blemish, disgrace.
1अवध m. no murder.
2अवध॑ a. inviolable.
अवधान n. attention, devotion.
अवधारण n. ascertainment, strict determination, restriction.
अवधि॑ m. limit, term, period. अवधि (—°) & °धेस् (gen. or —°) till, as far as.
अवधीरण n., °णा f. disregard, contempt.
अवधीरय्, °यति despise, reject.
अ॑वधूत a. shaken off, removed, rejected, spurned, tossed, trodden upon, unclean.
अवधूनन n. shaking.
अवध्य॑ a. not to be killed, inviolable.
अवध्यता f., °त्व† n. inviolability.
अवध्यभाव m. the same.
अवध्र॑ a. indelible.
अवन n. favour, grace, protection.
अवनत a. bent down, deepened, not projecting.
अवनति f. stooping, setting; humiliation.
अ॑वनि f. bed or course of a river; river, stream; earth, ground, place (also °नी† f.).
अवनिप, °पति, & °पाल m. king.
अवने॑ग्य a. fit for washing.
अवने॑जन, f. ई the same; n. washing, wash-water.

अ॑वन्त् a. favourable, kind; N. of a man.
अवन्ति m. pl. N. of a people.
अवन्ती f. N. of the capital of the Avanti.
अवन्ध्य a. not fruitless or vain; successful, happy. °पात unerring (of an arrow, lit. whose flight is not vain).
अवपतित & °पन्न a. on what something (—°) has fallen.
अवपात m. downfall, descent; a pit for catching game in.
अवपातन n. felling, throwing down.
अवपा॑न n. drinking or giving to drink.
अवबद्ध a. tied on, fettered; fixed by, sticking in (—°); hanging on, concerned about (loc.).
अ॑वबाढ a. uncovered.
अवबो॑ध m. waking; perception, understanding, knowledge.
अवभङ्ग m., °भञ्जन n. breaking, splitting.
अवभास m. splendour, light, manifestation, appearance; °क a. illumining, manifesting; abstr. °त्व n.
अवभासन n. manifestation, appearance; enlightening, illumination.
अवभासिन् a. shining, bright; enlightening, manifesting.
अवभृ॒थ॑ or °भृ॒॑थ m. bathing after a sacrifice; conclusion, end.
अवम॑ a. lowest, vilest; nearest, next; latest, last.
अवमन्तृ m. despiser (w. acc.).
अवमन्यक (—°) a. despising, rejecting.
अवमर्श m. contact, touch; reflection, consideration.
अवमान m., °मानन n., °मानना f. disrespect, contempt.
अवमानिन् a. despising, contemning.
अवयव m. limb, member; p. °विन्.
अवयवधर्म m. the figure of pars pro toto.
अवयवरूपक & अवयवविरूपक n. two kinds of comparison.
अ॑वयातहेळस् a. whose wrath is appeased.
अ॑वर lower, inferior; posterior, following, later, younger; nearer; preceding (w. abl.); western; vile, base, mean; —° at least in adj., n. in adv. — f. अवरा after-birth.
अवरज a. low-born, born after (another). m. a Çūdra or a younger brother; f. आ a younger sister.
अवरवर्ण m. a low caste; °ज m. a Çūdra (cf. prec.).
अ॑वरूढ a. descended; put down or taken off (load).
अ॑वरे॑ण (instr. as prep.) under (acc.).
अवरो॑ध m. hindrance, oppression, investment, siege, imprisonment, confinement; harem, pl. the females of the h.
अवरो॑धन n. the same; interior, sanctuary.
अवरो॑ह m. descent (fig.).
अव॑रो॑हण, f. ई descending; n. descent (l. & f.).
अवरो॑हिन् a. descending (lit. & fig.).
अवर्तमान a. not taking place, not present.
अ॑वर्ति f. want, need (lit. going down).
अवर्त्र॑ a. unchecked.
अवर्ष & °ण n. want of rain, drought.
अवलग्न a. hanging down, hanging on (—°).
अवलम्ब a. hanging down; m. = seq. n.
अवलम्बन, f. ई hanging down; hanging, leaning, depending on; n. the same as subst. hold, support.
अवलम्बित & अवलम्बिन् = prec. adj.
अवलिप्त a. haughty; abstr. °ता f., °त्व n.
अवलेप m., °न n. = prec. abstr. + ointment.
अवलोक m., °न n. sight, seeing.
अवलोकयितृ m. looker on, spectator.
अवलोकिता f. a woman's name.
अवलोकिन् a. seeing, looking at (—°).
अवश॑ a. independent, uncontrolled, free; unwilling, reluctant.
अवशक, f. °शिका the same.*
अवशग a. not subject or submissive to (gen.).
अवशान्त a. extinct.
अवशिन् a. having no (own) will, dependent.
अवशिष्ट a. left, remaining from (gen. or —°), having only (instr. or —°) left.
अवशीर्ण a. decayed, shattered.
अवशेष m. rest, remainder; abstr. °ता f.
अवश्य a. not yielding to another's will; °— & अवश्यम् adv. necessarily, by all means.
अवश्यकता f., अवश्यभाव m. necessity.
अवश्यभाविन् a. what must be.

अवश्याय m. frost, rime.
अवष्टब्ध a. standing firm, reclining, leaned upon (act. & pass.), seized, taken, held.
अवष्टम्भ m. leaning or depending on; confidence, courage.
अवष्टम्भमय a. confident, bold (arrow).
1**अ॑वस्** n. favour, aid, assistance, recreation, relief, comfort, joy, inclination, desire.
2**अ॒वः॑स्** adv. down; as prep. down from (abl. or instr.), under (instr.).
अवस॑ n. refreshment, food.
अवसक्थिका f. a kind of wrapper; °**कां कृ** tie a cloth round one's legs or knees.
अवसन्न a. sunk down, impressed, deep; brought down, exhausted, afflicted.
अवसर m. opportunity, occasion, right moment to (gen. or —°).
अवसर्पण n. descent.
अ॑वसा f. rest, liberation.
अवसातृ॑ m. deliverer.
अवसाद m. sinking, decline, weakness, defeat.
अवसा॑न n. resting-place, rest, end, death.
अवसाय m. stopping, settling down; a. °**यिन्**.
अ॑वसित a. (act.) having stopped, having ceased or desisted from (abl. or —°); (pass.) finished, settled, determined.
अवसितकार्य a. satisfied (lit. who has done his duty).*
अवसितमण्डन a. entirely dressed (lit. whose toilet is completed).*
अवसुप्त a. asleep.
अवसेक m. sprinkling, bleeding.
अवसेचन n. the same; wash-water (cf. **पादावसेचन**).
अवस्कन्द m. assault, attack.
अ॒व॑स्तात् adv. underneath; on this side, before; prep. under, west of (gen).
अवस्तु n. a slight or bad thing; nonentity, unreality. Abstr. °**त्व** n.
अवस्त्र a. unclothed; abstr. °**ता** f.
अवस्थ॑ m. membrum virile. f. **आ॑** (often adj. —°) state, condition, situation, circumstance, appearance in court; vulva.
अवस्थान n. treading upon; staying, abiding; position, situation.
अवस्थान्तर n. altered condition, alteration.*
अवस्थित or **वस्थित** a. standing, posted; contained or remaining in, intent upon (loc. or —°), keeping on, continuing (instr. of an abstr. or nom. of a pp.), ready to (dat.); fixed, settled, firm, steady, true; (thus) situated or circumstanced.
अवस्थिति f. abode, stay.
†**अवस्पर्तृ॑** m. deliverer.
अवस्य॑न्त् & °**स्यु॑** a. seeking favour or help.
अवस्रुत a. flowed down.
अ॑वस्वन्त् a. striving, eager.
अवहनन n. trashing, husking.
अवहार्य a. to be restored; to be made to restore or to pay (acc.).
अवहास m. jest, joke; °**सार्थम्** for jest.
अ॑वहित a. put down, fallen into (esp. the water); absorbed, attentive.
अवाक्शाख a. having the branches downwards.
अवाक्शिरस् a. having the head downwards, headlong.
अवाग्गमनवन्त् a. moving downwards.
अवाङ्मनसगोचर a. not within the reach of language or intellect.
अवाङ्मुख, f. **ई** looking or turned (lit. having the face t.) downwards.
अवाची॑न a. directed downwards, lying under (abl.).
अवाच्य a. unspeakable, not to be spoken to.
अवाच्यवाद m. a forbidden word.
अ॑वाञ्च्, f. **अ॑वाची** directed downwards, lower. n. **अवाक्** downwards, headlong.
1**अ॑वात** a. unconquered, secure.
2**अवात॑** a. not windy. n. calm.
अवान्तर॑ a. included, intermediate (°**रम्** adv. between); always another, different.
अवान्तरदेश॑ m. intermediate region (cf. **दिश्**).
अवाप्त a. (having) reached or obtained.
अवाप्ति f. acquirement, getting.
अवाप्य a. to be obtained; due to (—°).
अवारणीय a. not to be stopped.
अ॑वि a. favourable, kind. m. sheep, f. ewe.
अविकत्थन a. not boastful.
अविकम्प a. unshaken.
अविकल a. not incomplete, full.

अविकार a. not changing; m. no change.
अविकारिन् a. not liable to change (sides), loyal.
अविकार्य a. immutable.
अविकृत a. unaltered, unprepared, undeveloped.
अविकृत्य ger. without detailing.
अविक्रिय a. unchanging; f. **आ** no change, **°यात्मक** a. not subject to change.
अविक्रीत a. who has not sold.
अविक्रेय a. unsalable.
अविक्षत a. unhurt.
अविक्षुब्ध a. undisturbed.
अविगणय्य ger. without reckoning or heeding.
अविघ्न a. unhindered (also **°घ्नित**); n. undisturbedness, quiet.
अविघ्नमङ्गल n. prayer for undisturbedness or quiet.
अविचक्षण a. not sagacious; stupid, ignorant.
अविचल & **°चलित** a. unmoved, constant.
1**अविचार** a. undiscerning, inconsiderate. n. adv.
2**अविचार** m. want of discrimination or reflection (also **°ण** n.); (instr. without much reflecting, quickly*).
अविचारज्ञ a. knowing no reflection, inconsiderate.
अविचारयन्त् a. not reflecting or hesitating.
अविचारित a. inconsiderate, n. adv.
अविचार्य a. not to be reflected upon.
अविजानन्त् a. not knowing, ignorant.
अविज्ञात a. unknown.
1**अविज्ञान** n. want of knowledge.
2**अविज्ञान** a. having no knowledge, unwise.
अविज्ञानवन्त् a. the same.
अविज्ञाय ger. without knowing.
अविज्ञेय a. unknowable, indiscernible.
अवितथ a. not false or vain; real. effective, true; n. adv., as subst. N. of a metre.
अवितृ m. protector, assistant.
अविथुर a. not staggering.
अविद exclam. of surprise or grief; also repeated and with **भेाः** or **मादृके**.*
अविदित a. unknown; n. unknowingly.
अविदूर a. not very far, near; n. nearness, adv. near = **°रे**, **°रात्** & **°रतस्**.
अविद्ध a. unpierced.
अविद्य a. ignorant, without knowledge.
अविद्यमान a. not existent.
अविद्या f. want of knowledge, ignorance.
अविद्वंस् a. not knowing, ignorant.
अविधवा f. not a widow.
अविधान n. non-rule, irregularity; **°तस्** adv. not according to regulation.
अविधाय ger. without having settled.
अविधि m. no rule; instr. against the rule.
अविधिपूर्वकम् adv. not according to the rule.
अविनय m. want of breeding or manners, incivility.
अविनश्यन्त् & **अविनाशिन्** a. imperishable.
अविनीत a. untrained; ill-bred, ill-behaved.
अविनोद m. want of diversion or amusement.
अविन्दन्त् a. not finding.
अविन्ध्य m. N. of the minister of Rāvaṇa.
अविपश्चित् a. ignorant, unwise.
अविपाल m. shepherd.
अविप्लुत a. unbroken, unshaken, unviolated.
अविब्रुवन्त् a. not saying or explaining..
अविभक्त a. undivided, unseparated, joint.
अविभावित a. not clearly perceived, undistinguished, unobserved, unknown or unknowable.
अविभ्रम a. free from coquetry, unfeigned.
अविमर्शितव्य a. not to be thought of, unimportant.
अविमृश्य ger. without reflecting; **°कारिन्** acting inconsiderately.
अवियुक्त a. undivided, unsevered from (abl.).
अविरत a. not deviating from (abl.), uninterrupted, continual. n. adv.
अविरल a. having no interstices, uninterrupted, close, contiguous. n. adv.
अविरह m. non-separation, staying together.*
अविरहित a. unabandoned by (°—), unseparated.
अविरुद्ध a. unimpeded; not opposite or contrary to (instr. or —°); right, proper.
अविरोध m. no conflict with, prejudice to (—°).
अविरोधिन् a. not contradictory or detrimental to (gen. or —°).
अविलम्ब a. not delaying, n. adv. quickly. m. no delay; instr. without delay.

अविलम्बन n. not delaying, quickness.
अविलम्बित a. immediate, prompt, speedy; n. adv.
अविलम्बिन् a. = prec. adj.*
अविलम्ब्य ger. without delaying.
1अविवाद a. undisputed, uncontested.
2अविवाद m. non-dissent, consent.
अविवाह a. not living in matrimony (beasts).
अविवाहिन् & °ह्य a. unfit for matrimonial alliance.
अविविक्त a. undiscriminated.
1अविवेक m. non-discrimination.
2अविवेक a. = seq.; abstr. °ता f.
अविवेकिन् a. undiscriminating, unwise.
अविवेनन्त् a. not turning away, kind.
अविशङ्क & °शङ्कित a. unhesitating, confident.
अविशङ्का f. no fear or hesitation.
अविशद a. not clear, indistinct.
अविशिष्ट a. not different, like, equal; abstr. °ता f., °त्व n.
अविशेष a. the same. m. no difference or distinction. °षेण & °षतस् indiscriminately, in general.
अविशेषित a. unspecified.
अविश्रम, °श्रान्त, & °श्राम a. unwearied, restless.
अविश्वसनीय a. not to be trusted; abstr. °ता f., °त्व n.
1अविश्वास m. mistrust, suspicion.
2अविश्वास a. mistrustful, suspicious.
अविश्वासजनक a. raising suspicion.*
अविश्वासिन् a. = 2अविश्वास.
1अविष n. no poison.
2अविष a. not poisonous.
अविषम a. not unequal; equal, even.
1अविषय m. no province, no sphere; no object for (—°), anything impossible or illicit.
2अविषय a. having no object.
अविषयमनस् a. whose mind has no object, unworldly.
अविषयीकरण n. the not making a thing (gen.) an object.
अविषह्य a. unbearable (lit. & fig.), irresistible, impracticable, inaccessible.
अविषाद m. non-despondency, courage.

अविष्ठ (superl.) deigning to accept.
अविष्यन्त् & °ष्यु a. eager; °ष्या f. eagerness.
अविस्पष्ट a. not clear, indistinct; n. adv.
अविह्रुत a. unbent, calm, composed.
अवीतराग a. whose passions are unsubdued (lit. not gone).*
1अवीर a. unmanly, childless (abstr. °ता f.); weak, impotent; f. आ having no husband.
2अवीर a. devoid of men; n. an unpeopled country.
अवीरजुष्ट a. hateful to (lit. not liked by) men.
अवीर्य a. weak, feeble.
अवृक a. harmless; n. adv. as subst. safety
अवृजिन a. guileless (lit. not crooked).
1अवृत a. unchecked, unimpeded.
2अवृत a. unchosen, uninvited.
अवृत्ति f. want of subsistence.
अवृषण a. having no testicles.
अवृष्टि f. want of rain; drought.
अवेक्षण n. looking to, attention.
अवेक्षा (& °क्षिता*) f. the same; regard, care for (loc. or —°).
अवेदन n. want of knowledge, ignorance.
अवेदयान a. not knowing.
अवेदविद् a. not knowing the Veda.
अवेदविहित a. not enjoined in the Veda.
1अवेद्य a. not to be known.
2अवेद्य a. not to be married.
अवेशहदृश a. not belonging to prostitution.
अवैरिजुष्ट a. not (even) resorted to (lit. liked) by an enemy.
अव्य a. coming from the sheep, made of wool or threads; s. the Soma-strainer.
अव्यक्त a. undisclosed, unmanifested, not clear, indistinct, imperceptible, transcendental; n. adv.
अव्यक्तभाषिन् a. speaking, indistinctly.*
अव्यक्तमूर्ति a. of imperceptible form, invisible.
अव्यग्र a. undistracted, unoccupied, tranquil, steady; n. adv.
अव्यङ्गाङ्ग, f. ई having complete (lit. unmutilated) limbs.
अव्यथि a. not wavering, firm; f. firmness, intrepidity.

अव्यभिचार m. not going astray, non-failure, constancy, fidelity; as adj. = seq.
अव्यभिचारिन् a. steady, constant, faithful.
अव्यभीचार = **अव्यभिचार** a. & m.
1**अव्यय** m. non-expense.
2**अव्यय** a. imperishable, immutable. n. an indeclinable word.
3**अव्यय** (**अव्यय**) a. = **अव्य**.
अव्ययात्मन् a. of imperishable nature.
अव्ययीभाव m. an indeclinable compound.
अव्यवधान a. uninterrupted; n. the not being interrupted by (instr.).
अव्यवसायवन्त् & **°यिन्** a. irresolute.
अव्यसन & **°निन्** a. not vicious.
अव्याकृत a. undivided.
अव्याज m. no fraud; a. artless, natural, °— adv.
अव्यापार m. no (regular) occupation.
अव्याप्त a. not pervaded by or mixed with (instr.).
अव्याहृत n. not speaking, silence.
अव्युच्छिन्न a. uninterrupted.
अव्युष्ट a. not yet risen or shining.
अव्रण a. having no wound, scar, or blemish.
1**अव्रत** n. non-observance of religious precepts.
2**अव्रत** a. lawless, disobedient.
1**अश्**, **अश्नोति**, **अश्नुते** attain, reach, come to, arrive at (acc.); obtain, get, befall, betide; overcome; offer, bring. — **अभि** reach, obtain, overwhelm. **उप** obtain, get. **वि** reach, attain, get; fill, penetrate. **सम्** attain, get, receive; fall to one's share.
2**अश्**, **अश्नाति**, pp. **अशित** partake of, eat, drink, taste, enjoy. C. **आशयति** feed (2 acc.). D. **अशिशिषति** wish to eat. — **अति** eat before (acc.). **उप** = S. **प्र** the same; C. feed. **सम्** = S.
अशक्त a. unable to or incapable of (inf., loc., or dat.).
अशक्ति f. inability.
अशक्नुवन्त् a. not being able.
अशक्य a. impossible to or to be (inf.), impracticable. Abstr. **°ता** f., **°त्व** n.
अशङ्क & **°ङ्कित** a. without fear or doubt; n. adv.; f. **अशङ्का** no fear or hesitation.
अशङ्कनीय a. not to be feared or supposed.
अशठ a. not deceitful, honest.
अश्मन् m. stone, rock, sky.
अशन n. eating, food.
अशना f. = **अशनाया**.
अशनानशन n. eating and fasting.
अशनाया or **अशनाया** f. hunger.
अशनायापिपासा (f. du.) hunger and thirst.
अशनायावन्त् & **अशनायुक** a. hungry.
अशनि f. (m.) thunderbolt, flash of lightning.
अशब्द a. soundless; unvedic.
अशम् (indecl.) ill luck; woe.
अशम m. restlessness.
अशरण a. unprotected; n. want of protection, helplessness.
अशस् a. cursing, hating, foe.
अशस्त्र a. unarmed.
अशस्त्रपूत a. not purified by the sword.
अशान्त a. unsubdued, **°मानस** a. in mind.
†**अशाय्**, **°यते** = 1**अश्**.
अशाश्वत, f. **ई** not eternal, transitory.
अशासन्त् a., **अशासित्वा** ger. not punishing.
अशास्त्रविहित a. not enjoined by the precept books, unscriptural.
अशिक्षित unlearnt, untaught (w. acc. or loc.).
अशितव्य or **°तव्य** a. to be eaten; (n. food*).
अशितृ m. eater.
अशित्र n. food.
अशिरस् & **°स्क** a. headless.
अशिव unlucky, evil. n. ill luck.
अशिवशंसिन् a. announcing ill luck, inauspicious.
अशिशिर a. not cold, hot; abstr. **°ता** f.
अशिष्यवृत्ति a. not behaving like a pupil.
अशीत a. the eightieth.
अशीति f. eighty.
अशीतितम a. the eightieth.
अशीतिभाग m. the eightieth part.
अशीर्य a. indelible.
अशीर्षक & **°र्षन्** headless.
अशुचि a. impure.
अशुचिभक्षण n. eating of impure things.
अशुचिभाव m. impurity.
अशुचिव्रत a. making unholy vows.
अशुद्ध a. impure.
अशुद्धि f. impurity.
अशुभ a. ugly (lit. not shining), unpleasant,

inauspicious, bad, wicked, impure. n. ill luck, woe, evil, sin.
अशुभमति a. evil-minded.
अशुश्रूषा f. disobedience.
अशुश्रूषु a. not willing to learn or to obey.
अशुष a. devouring, voracious.
अशुष्क a. not dry; fresh, green.
अशून्य a. not empty or void, not incomplete, not in vain. °न्यं कृ fulfil, execute.
अशेव a. hateful, odious.
अशेष m. no rest or remainder; adj. entire, whole. °षम्, °षेण, & °षतस् adv. entirely, wholly.
अशोक a. heatless, painless; m. the Açoka tree.
अशोकवनिका f. Açoka wood.
अशोचनीय & अशोच्य a. not to be regretted.
अशोधयित्वा ger. without trying or deciding.
अशौच n. impurity.
अशौण्डीर्य n. want of generosity.
अश्म m. stone; N. of a demon.
अश्मक m., ई f. a man's and a woman's name; m. pl. a tribe of warriors.
अश्मकुट्ट & °क a. grinding with a stone.
अश्मदिद्यु a. having stones for a weapon.
1अश्मन् m. eater.
2अश्मन् m. rock, stone, thunderbolt, sky. अश्मन् loc. in the sky. Du. heaven and earth.
अश्मप्लव m. a boat made of stone.
अश्मन्तक m. a kind of grass.
अश्मन्मय, f. ई of stone, stony.
अश्मन्वन्त् a. stony.
अश्ममय, f. ई the same.
अश्ममूर्धन् a. stony-headed.
अश्रद्ध a. =seq.; f. अश्रद्धा disbelief.
अश्रद्दधान a. unbelieving, having no faith.
अश्रद्धेय a. incredible.
1अश्रम m. absence of fatigue.
2अश्रम & अश्रम a. unwearied, indefatigable.
अश्रवण n. the not being heard, the not occurring (in a text), absence, want (of a word, suffix, etc.).
अश्राद्धिन् a. not performing funeral meals.
अश्रान्त a. indefatigable, n. adv.
अश्रि f. (adj. —° अश्रिक) edge, corner.
अश्रु n. (m.) a tear.
अश्रुकण्ठ a. having tears in the throat.
अश्रुत a. unheard.
अश्रुधारा f. flood of tears.
अश्रेयंस् a. worse; n. ill luck.
अश्रोत्र a. earless.
अश्रोत्रिय a. not knowing the Veda.
अश्लाघ्य a. not praiseworthy, disgraceful.
अश्लील a. inauspicious.
अश्व m. horse, a man's name; f. अश्वा mare.
1अश्वकर्ण m. a horse's ear.
2अश्वकर्ण a. horse-eared; m. N. of a tree.
अश्वखुर m. a horse's hoof; °वत् adv.
अश्वत्थ m. the holy fig-tree.
अश्वत्थामन् m. N. of an ancient warrior.
अश्वद, °दा, & †°दावन् m. giver of horses.
अश्वनदी f. N. of a river.
अश्वप & °पाल m. groom.
अश्वपर्ण a. winged with horses.
अश्वमुख, f. ई having the head of a horse; m. & f. ई = किंनर, ई q.v.
अश्वमेध m. horse-sacrifice.
अश्वयुज् a. yoking or being yoked with horses; f. sg. & du. a lunar mansion.
अश्वराज m. king of the horses.
अश्ववन्त् a. rich in horses.
अश्ववृष m. stallion.
अश्वशाला f. stable for horses.
अश्वसारथ्य n. horsemanship and driving.
अश्वसेन m. N. of a serpent-demon.
अश्वस्तन a. not having a to-morrow.
अश्वस्तनविधान n. care for to-morrow.
अश्वस्तनिक a. not caring for to-morrow.
अश्वहारक m. horse-thief.
अश्वहृदय n. horsemanship (cf. अक्षहृदय).
अश्वाध्यक्ष m. overseer or master of the horse.
अश्वानीक n. cavalry, cavalcade.
अश्वानृत n. a lie about horses.
अश्वारूढ a. mounted, on horseback.
अश्वावन्त् = अश्ववन्त्.
अश्विन् a. horsed. m. horseman; du. the two Açvins; f. अश्विनी their wife or mother.
अश्विय (n. pl.) troops of horses.
अश्वीय n. troop of horses or of horsemen.
1अश्व्य a. equine; n. = अश्विय.
2अश्व्य m. a patr. name.

अषतर (compar.) more acceptable.

अषाढ or **अषाळ्ह** a. unconquerable; m. a man's name.

अष्टक a. eightfold; m. a man's name; f. **आ** the eighth day after full moon.

अष्टगुण a. = prec. adj.

अष्टधा adv. eightfold, eight times.

अष्टन् a. eight.

अष्टपाद् a. eight-legged.

अष्टभाग m. an eighth.

अष्टम, f. **ई** eighth.

अष्टमकालिक a. eating (only) at every eighth meal-time.

अष्टरसाश्रय a. based on the eight sentiments, i.e. dramatic.

अष्टवर्ष a. aged eight years.

अष्टविध a. eightfold, of eight kinds.

अष्टाङ्ग a. eight parts of the body (° –); adj. consisting of eight parts or members.

अष्टादशधा adv. eighteenfold.

अष्टादशन् a. eighteen.

अष्टादश & **अष्टादशम** a. eighteenth.

अष्टापद् (nom. **°पात्**, f. **°पदी**) eight-legged.

अष्टापाद्य a. eightfold.

1**अष्टि** f. reaching.

2**अष्टि** f. N. of a class of metres.

3**अष्टि** f. grain of seed.

अष्टोत्तर a. more eight.

अष्ट्रा f. goad.

अष्ठीला f. globe, ball, round pebble or stone.

अष्ठीव n. (only —°) & **°वन्त्** m. knee-pan.

1**अस्**, **अस्ति** be, exist, happen, become; be present or at hand; fall or belong to (gen. or dat.), be enough for (gen.), be able to (dat.); turn to, serve for (2 dat.). **अस्तु** or **एवमस्तु** well, so be it. With **न** not be, be gone. Pers. or impers. with another fin. verb = I happen to or it happens that I, e.g. **अस्ति पश्यसि** do you happen to see? **अस्मि विक्रीणे** I happen to sell. — **अति** be beyond, surpass (acc.). **अपि** be in or with (loc.), fall or belong to (loc. or dat.); partake of (impers. w. gen. & loc.). **अभि** be above, rule, overcome, conquer. win; *fall to one's (gen.) share. **उप** be in or with, partake of (acc.). **परि** overtake; pass or spend (time). **प्र** be prominent, excel. **प्रति** equal, emulate (acc.). **सम्** equal, reach; be together with (**सह**).

2**अस्**, **अस्यति** (**असति**), pp. **अस्त** (q.v.) throw, cast, shoot at (loc., dat., or gen.), with (instr.). — **अप** throw away, lay down, doff, leave, give up. **अभि** (also **असति**, **°ते**) throw, hurl; throw one's self upon, take to, practise, study, read; repeat, double, reduplicate (g.). **उद्** throw up, lift, throw away; rise from (acc.). **व्युद्** spread, disperse, dismiss, give up. **नि** (also **असति**) throw or put down, lay aside, put or pour in (loc.), apply to (loc.), turn (the eyes) upon (loc.), deposit, commit to (loc), give up, relinquish; bring forward, mention. **उपनि** put down, bring forward, indicate, insinuate. **विनि** (also **असति**) lay asunder, spread; put, place, turn upon or in, apply to (loc.), deposit, commit, entrust to (loc.). **संनि** (also **असति**) put down (together), take off; put or place on (loc.), commit or entrust to (loc. or gen.); abandon, relinquish, give up, esp. the world, i.e. become an ascetic. **निस्** throw out, send away, banish from (abl.); keep of, remove, destroy. **परा** cast away, expose (a child); leave, reject, refute. **परि** cast or turn about, throw down, toss, upset (also C.). put on (M.). **विपरि** overturn, upset, invert, transpose, change. **प्र** cast forwards, hurl, throw or put in (loc.), throw down. **प्रति** throw towards or against; cast away, shake off. **वि** cast asunder, break in pieces, scatter. **सम्** put together, join; P. be composed with (instr.). — Cf. **अपास्त**, **अभ्यस्त**, **उपन्यस्त**, **न्यस्त**, **पर्यस्त**, **विपर्यस्त**, **व्यत्यस्त**, **व्यस्त**, **समस्त**.

असंयत a. unrestrained, uncontrolled.

असंयतात्मन् a. having the soul uncontrolled.

असंयाज्य a. unfit for common sacrifices.

असंवसन्त् a. not living together with (instr.).

असंवीत a. uncovered, unclothed.

असंवृत a. uncovered, bare; n. a cert. hell.

असंशय m. no doubt; a. having no doubt, n. adv.

असंश्रवणे & °श्रवे (loc.) not within hearing of (gen.).
असंसारिन् a. not subject to the mundane existence.
असंसृष्ट a. unconnected, strange, unknown, unmixed with, free from (instr.).
असंस्कार a. unadorned; m. want of ornament, artlessness.
असंस्कार्य a. not to be adorned etc. (v.seq.).
असंस्कृत a. unadorned, uncultivated, unprepared, uninitiated, unmarried.
असंस्तुत a. not harmonizing, refractory; distant, foreign.
असंस्थित a. not standing still, restless, inconstant.
असकल a. incomplete; °व्यक्ति a. not fully appearing.
असकृत् adv. not once; repeatedly, often.
असक्त a. not hanging on or entangled in (loc.); independent, free.
असक्तबुद्धि & असक्तात्मन् a. whose mind is not attached to (loc.).
असक्ति f. non-attachment (to worldly things).
असगोत्र a. not of the same family.
असंकसुक a. not fickle; firm, steady.
असंक्षिप्त a. not laid down*; not concise, extensive, full.
असंख्य, असंख्यात, & असंख्येय a. innumerable.
1असङ्ग m. not sticking to (—°).
2असङ्ग or असङ्ग a. not sticking or hanging, moving freely, independent.
†असचद्विष् a. not hating the followers.
असंगीतकम् adv. without music; ° नृत् dance w. m., i.e. do something absurd or ridiculous.*
असजाति a. belonging to a different caste.
असजात्य a. having no kin.
असज्जन m. a bad man, villain.
असंज्ञ a. insensible; abstr. °त्व n.
असंज्ञा f. dissension, discord.
असंज्वर a. feeling no heat or resentment.
असत्कल्पना f. fabrication of an untruth, lie.
असत्कार्य n. an evil deed.
असत्कार्यपरिग्रह m. commission of evil deeds.
असत्कृत a. ill-done or ill-used; n. injury, wrong.
1असत्त्व a. wanting strength or courage.
2असत्त्व n. non-existence, non-substantiality; non-presence, absence.
असत्त्ववचन a. not signifying anything substantial or material; abstr. °ता f.
असत्पुत्र a. having no son.
असत्य a. untrue, false; n. falsehood, lie.
असत्यवचन a. speaking falsely, lying.
असत्यसंध a. faithless, treacherous.
असदृश a. unlike, dissimilar, incomparable; of unequal birth; unfit, improper.
असद्ग्रह a. bent upon something evil, following a bad caprice; m. bad inclination, caprice, whim.
असद्भाव m. non-presence, absence.
असन् n. blood.
असन n. throwing, hurling; f. असना dart, arrow.
असनाम a. not having the same name.
असन्त् (f. असती) not existing, unreal, untrue, bad, wicked. f. असती an unchaste woman. n. non-existence, untruth, lie, evil.
असंतुष्ट a. dissatisfied.
असंतोष m. dissatisfaction.
असंदित & °दिन a. unbound.
असंधेय a. irreparable.
असंनिधान n., °निधि m. distance, absence.
असंनिवृत्ति f. non-return; dat. never to return.
असंनिहित a. distant, absent.*
असंन्यस्त a. not laid down or given up.
1असपत्न m. no rival.
2असपत्न a. unrivalled; n. peace, quiet.
असपिण्ड a. unconnected by the funeral cake.
1असम a. unlike, uneven.
2असम a. having no equal, incomparable.
असमग्र a. incomplete; not full (moon), °— & n. adv.
असमञ्ज & °ञ्जस् m. N. of a man.
असमञ्जस a. unequal, irregular, false; n. adv.
असमद् f. concord, harmony.
असमय m. wrong time.
असमर्थ a. incapable of, unable to (inf., dat., loc., or —°). Abstr. °त्वा n.
असमस्त a. not compounded (g.).
असमान a. unequal, dissimilar; n. an awkward situation.

असमाप्त a. unfinished.
असमावृत्तक & **°वृत्तिक** a. not yet returned (from the teacher's house).
असमाहित a. not concentrated.
असमिध्य ger. without kindling.
असमीक्ष्य ger. without considering.
असमुद्यम m. no effort, no pain about (loc.).
असमुद्रोत्थित a. not risen from the ocean.
असमृद्ध a. imperfect.
असमृद्धि f. non-success, failure.
असमेत्य ger. without having approached (instr.).
असंपत्ति f. want of success, failure.
असंपाठ्य a. unfit for common instruction.
असंपूर्ण a. incomplete, imperfect.
असंपूर्णमनोरथ a. having one's desire unaccomplished.*
असंप्राप्त a. not arrived, unsuccessful; not arrived at, unfulfilled (desire).
असंबद्ध a. unconnected, incoherent, absurd, foolish.
असंबद्धप्रलाप m. idle talk.
असंबद्धप्रलापिन् (& **°भाषक***) a. talking idly.
असंबद्धमनोरथ a. having absurd wishes.*
1**असंबन्ध** m. no connection or relation.
2**असंबन्ध** a. unconnected, not a relative.
असंबाध a. unlimited, unbounded, unrestrained, spacious, empty.
1**असंभव** m. non-existence, absence, want; impossibility, absurdity.
2**असंभव** a. not existing, absent, wanting, impossible.
असंभावित a. impossible (lit. unconceived).
असंभावितोपमा f. a kind of comparison.
असंभाष्य a. unfit for conversation.
असंभोज्य a. unfit for common meals.
असंभ्रम a. free from agitation, tranquil, calm; n. adv.
असंभ्रान्त a. the same; n. adv.
असंमत a. disapproved, despised; unauthorized by (—°).
असंमूढ a. unconfused, composed, calm.
असंमोह m. abstr. to prec.
असम्यक् adv. not in the right way, wrongly.
असम्यक्कारिन् a. acting improperly.
असर्व a. not whole, incomplete.
असवर्ण a. not belonging to the same caste.
असश्चत् & **असश्चन्त्** (f. **असश्चन्ती**) unceasing, inexhaustible.
असस्नन्त् a. sleepless.
असह a. incapable of bearing (acc. or —°), unable to (infin. or —°), impatient, intolerant.
असहन a. unable to bear (—°); impatient, jealous, envious. n. intolerance, impatience.
असहन्त्, f. **°न्ती** a. not bearing, unable to (infin.).
असहमान a. not bearing, impatient.
असहाय a. friendless, lonely; abstr. **°ता** f.
असहायवन्त् & **°यिन्** a. = prec. a.
असहिष्णु a. unable to bear (acc., loc., or —°); intolerant, jealous; abstr. **°ता** f., **°त्व** n.
असह्य a. intolerable, irresistible, impossible.
असाक्षिक a. unwitnessed, unattested.
असादृश्य n. unequality, dissimilarity.
असाधक a. not accomplishing, not satisfactory.
असाधन n. no means, no requisite; a. without means, impossible.
असाधारण, f. **ई** uncommon, special, singular.
असाधारणोपमा f. a kind of comparison.
असाधु a. not good, bad, wicked; m. a bad man, a villain; n. evil, malice, also adv.
असाधुदर्शिन् a. of little discrimination (lit. seeing not well).
असाधुवृत्त a. of bad conduct.
असाध्य a. not to be overcome, impracticable, incurable, irremediable; not susceptible of proof. Abstr. **°ता** f., **°त्व** n.
असांनिध्य n. non-presence, absence.
असामान्य a. not common, peculiar.
असामि a. not half; whole, entire.
असामिशवस् a. having full strength.
असांप्रत a. unfit, improper; n. adv.
असार a. worthless, vain.
असावधान a. inattentive, inconsiderate.*
असि m. sword, knife; p. **असिमन्त्**.
असिंहासन a. throneless (a reign).
1**असित** a. unbound.
2**असित** (f. **असिता** & **असिक्नी**) a. dark-coloured, black. m. N. of a cert. myth. being & of sev. men; f. **असिक्नी** or **असिक्नी** N. of a river.
असितोत्पल n. a blue lotus-flower.
असितपीतक, f. **°तिका** dark yellow, tawny.

असितेक्षण a. black-eyed.
असिधारा f. the edge of a sword.
असिधाराव्रत n. a vow to stand on the edge of a sword; i.e. a hopeless task.
असिन्वं & **असिन्वन्त्** a. insatiable.
असिपत्त्र n. the blade of a sword.
असिपत्त्रवन n. a cert. hell (lit. a wood whose leaves are sword-blades).
असिपत्त्रव्रत n. = **असिधाराव्रत**.
असिलता f. the blade of a sword.
असु m. (later always pl.) vital spirit, breath, life.
असुख a. unpleasant, painful, unhappy, difficult to (infin.); n. sorrow; pain, grief.
असुखोदय a. having evil results.
असुखोदर्क a. the same.
असुतृप् a. taking away (lit. feeding on) one's life, or insatiable.
असुर a. spiritual, divine. m. spirit, esp. the highest spirit, later a bad spirit, demon f. **†ई** (opp. **सुर** a god).
असुरधर्म m. law or custom of the Asuras.
असुरब्रह्म m. a priest of the Asuras.
असुररक्षस n. a being as well Asura as Rakṣas, pl. the Asuras and Rakṣas.
असुरहन्, f. **असुरघ्नी** killing Asuras.
असुर्य a. spiritual, god- or demonlike; n. godhead, divinity.
असुलभ a. not easy to get, rare; abstr. **॰त्व** n.
असुवर्ण a. not golden.*
असुष्वि a. not pressing Soma; impious.
असुस्थ & **असुस्थित** a. unwell.
असुहृद् m. not friend, foe.
असू f. not bringing forth, barren.
असूय्, **॰यति** & **॰यते** grumble, be impatient or angry with, murmur at (dat., acc., or gen.) C. **असूययति** also = S. — **अभि** = S.
असूय grumbling, displeased, envious. f. **आ** discontent, envy.
असूयक, **॰यितृ** and **॰यु** = prec. adj.
असूत a. untrodden, unknown.
असूर्य a. sunless.
असूर्यग not moving towards the sun.
असृक्पात (m. pl.) drops of blood (lit. the falling of blood).
असृज् n. blood.
असृष्टान्न a. whereat no food is distributed (sacrifice).
असेन्य a. not hurting or wounding.
असेवन n. non-performance of (—°).
असेवा f. non-use, neglect.
असोढ a. unconquered.
1**असोम** m. no Soma-juice or sacrifice.
2**असोम** a. not having Soma-juice.
असोमप a. not drinking Soma.
असौ m. f. (n. **अदस्** q.v.) yonder, that, one so and so; with **एव** the same.
असौवर्ण a. not golden.
असौष्ठव a. not well, ill-disposed.
असौहृद n. enmity.
अस्कन्द m., **॰त्व** n. not spilling.
अस्कन्दयन्त् a. not spilling; not omitting or neglecting.
अस्कन्न a. unspilt.
अस्कृधोयु a. not scarce, abundant.
अस्खलन n. not wavering from (abl.), firmness.
अस्खलित a. not stumbling, firm (gait), unshaken, uninterrupted. n. not stumbling or sticking.
अस्खलितचक्र a. indefatigable (lit. whose chariot never stops).
अस्खलितपद a. safe, secure (lit. where the foot does not stumble).*
1**अस्त** n. home (also **॰क** n.); acc. w. **इ**, **गम्**, **या** etc. go home, go down, set (of the sun); come to an end, die. As m. the mountain behind which the sun and moon are supposed to set (cf. **उदय**), also = **अस्तमय**.
2**अस्त** a. thrown, cast off (mostly °—).
अस्तंयन्त् a. going down, setting.
अस्तकरुण a. pitiless, cruel.
अस्तमय m., **॰मयन** n. setting (of the sun).
अस्तमित a. set (sun); **॰ते** (sc. **सूर्ये**) after sunset.
अस्ता f. dart, bolt, arrow.
अस्तृ m. hurler, archer.
अस्तृत & **अस्तृत** a. not overthrown, invincible.
अस्तेन m. no thief or robber.
अस्तेनमानिन् a. not considering o.'s self as a thief.
अस्तेय n. non-theft, honesty.
अस्तोक a. not small or insignificant.

अस्तोतृ m. not a praiser.
अस्त्र n. (m.) dart; bow, arrow.
अस्त्रग्राम m. collection of weapons.
अस्त्री f. no woman; masculine and neuter (g.).
अस्थन् n. bone; poss. °न्वन्त्†.
अस्था adv. immediately.
अस्थान n. no stay; no place or the wrong place for (gen.). °— & loc. in the wrong place, not in time, without cause.
अस्थि n. bone; poss. °मन्त्†.
अस्थिचूर्ण n. pulverized bone, bone-dust.
अस्थिज a. produced in the bones; m. thunderbolt, marrow.*
अस्थिपञ्जर m. skeleton.
अस्थिभेदक m. bone-breaker.
अस्थिर a. not firm, unsteady, inconstant, dubious, uncertain. Abstr. °त्व† n.
अस्थिसंस्थ a. being on the bone (flesh).
अस्थिस्थूण a. having bones for beams (the body).
अस्थिस्नेह m. marrow.
अस्थूल a. not big or coarse; slender, thin.
अस्नातृ a. not bathing, not wet, dry.
अस्पर्श a. touchless.
अस्पष्ट a. not clear, indistinct.
अस्पृशन्त् a. not touching.
अस्पृष्ट a. untouched.
अस्पृह a. free from desires.
अस्पृहा f. no desire.
अस्फुट a. indistinct, incorrect; n. adv.
1अस्म pron. stem of 1st pers.
2अस्म or अस्म pron. stem of 3d pers.
अस्मत्तस् adv. from us.
अस्मत्रा adv. among or to us; a. °त्राञ्च्.
अस्मद् (°—) = 1अस्म.
अस्मदीय a. our.
अस्मद्र्यञ्च् a. turned towards us; n. °द्र्यक् adv.
अस्मद्विध a. our like.
अस्मयु a. fond of us.
अस्माक a. our, ours.
अस्मादृश a. our like.*
1अस्मृति f. want of memory, oblivion.
2अस्मृति a. forgetful, inattentive.
अस्मेहिति f. commission for us.
1अस्र n. a tear.
2अस्र a. throwing, hurling.
अस्रमुख, f. ई having tears in the face.*
अस्रिध् a. not going wrong; safe, harmless.
अस्रिधान & अस्रेधन्त् a. the same.
अस्रेमन् a. faultless, perfect.
अस्वतन्त्र a. not independent.
अस्वदित a. not tasted.
अस्वप्नज् a. not sleepy, sleepless.
अस्वरित a. not having the Svarita accent; abstr. °त्व n.
अस्वर्गयोग्य a. unworthy of heaven.
अस्वर्ग्य a. not leading to heaven, unheavenly.
अस्वस्थ a. indisposed, unwell; abstr. °ता f.
अस्वस्थचेतस a. of troubled mind.
अस्वस्थशरीर a. sick at body.*
अस्वातन्त्र्य n. want of independence.
अस्वाधीन a. not free, dependent.
अस्वामिविक्रय m. sale without ownership (j.).
अस्वामिन् m. non-owner.
अह् (only pf. आह) say, speak, tell (w. dat. or acc. of pers. & acc. of th.), call, name (2 acc.); state, declare to be (acc.); attribute or adjudge (acc.) to (gen.). — अधि speak or intercede for (dat.). अनु recite, repeat. अभि speak to (acc.), answer, reply; tell (dat. of pers. & acc. of th.). निस् speak out, express. प्र pronounce, deliver; say tell, name, declare (= S.).
1अह indecl. of course, certainly, namely, at least; often only emphasizing the preceding word.
2अह m. n. day (mostly —°).
अहंयु a. selfish, haughty.
अहंकार m. sense of self, egoism, pride, arrogance; poss. °रिन्.
अहंकार्य a. forming the object of the sense of self.
अहंकृत a. conscious of self, egoistic.
अहंकृति f. = अहंकार.
अहत a. not beaten, not washed, new (cloth).
अहतमार्ग a. whose course is unchecked or free.*
अहत्वा abs. without killing.
अहन् & अहर् n. day. — अहन्यहनि & अहरहस् every day, daily. उभे अहनी day and night.
अह्न्य a. daily.

अहम् (pron.) I; सोऽहम् I here.
अहर् & अंहस् n. = अंहन्.
अहरागम m. the approach of day, morning.
अहर्निश n. day and night.
अहर्विद् a. knowing the (right) days.
अहल्या f. N. of the wife of Gautama.
अहःशेष m. the rest of the day.
अहस्त a. handless.
अहह exclam. of joy or sorrow.
अहार्य not to be taken or stolen; unalterable, incorruptible.
अंहि m. serpent, esp. the demon Vṛtra.
अहिंसक & अंहिंसन्त् a. harmless, innocuous.
अंहिंसा f. the not injuring or being injured, harmlessness.
अहिंस्र a. = अहिंसक.
अहिगन्ध m. likeness to (lit. smell of) a serpent.
अंहित a. unfit, improper, bad, wrong, evil, hostile. m. enemy; n. evil, misfortune, ill luck.
†अहिभानु a. shining like serpents.
अहिम a. not cold, warm.
अंहिमन्यु a. having the ire of serpents.
अहिहत्य n. the slaying of the serpent, the fight with Vṛtra.
अही m. serpent, a cert. serpent-demon.
1अहीन a. lasting several days; m. a sacrifice lasting several days.
2अंहीन a. unimpaired, whole, entire, not deficient in (instr.).
अंहुत a. unoffered, unsacrificed; not worshipped with or not attained by sacrifice; m. a muttered prayer, unaccompanied by sacrifices.
अंहृणान a. not being angry.
अहैतुक, f. ई having no cause or motive; n. adv.
अहो exclamation of joy, sorrow or astonishment.
अहोरात्र m. n. day and night; °विद्† a. knowing d. & n.
अह्न m. day (—°); dat. instantly, at once.
अह्यर्षु m. a cert. bird of prey.
अंह्रय, °याण, & अंह्रि a. luxurious, proud.
अंह्रस्व not short.
अंह्रुत not crooked, straight.
अंह्रुतप्सु a. of upright appearance.
अंह्रुला f. not staggering, firmness.

आ

1आ adv. hither, near, towards (esp. as a pref. to verbs of motion); besides, further; quite, entirely, even (often only emphasizing the prec. word). °— a little, slightly, scarcely (in adj. & subst.); reaching to (in adj.); till, as far as, before, from (in adv.). As prep. towards, up to, till, as far as (acc. or abl.); except, but, save (acc.); all the way or time from (abl.); in, at, on (loc.).
2आ excl., esp. of sudden remembrance.
आकर m. scatterer, dispenser, giver; heap, plenty, abundance; mine.
आकर्ण (°—) & आकर्णम् adv. up to the ear.
आकर्णन n. listening, hearing; news.
आकर्णय्, °यति, pp. आकर्णित listen, hear, understand. — उप & सम् = S.
आकर्ष m. drawing towards one's self.
आकर्षण, f. ई the same as adj.; n. = prec., also bending (a bow).
1आकल्प m. ornament.
2आकल्प (°—) = seq.
आकल्पम् & °ल्पान्तम् adv. to the end of the world.
आकाङ्क्ष a. desiring, wanting (esp. a word to complete the sense); f. आ wish, desire, want (of a word to complete the sense).
1आकार m. form, shape, figure; abstr. °ता f.
2आकार m. the sound आ.
आकारवन्त् a. shaped, embodied; well-formed, shapely.
आकारित a. having the shape of (—°).
आकालम् adv. until the same hour (of the next day).

1आकालिक, f. आ & ई a. lasting until the same hour (of the next day).
2आकालिक, f. ई unseasonable.
आकाश m. n. free or open space, sky; esp. the atmosphere or sky as the fifth element. °शे behind the scene or into the air (d.).
आकाशग & °चारिन् moving through the sky; m. bird.
आकाशयान n. moving through the sky.
आकाशवर्त्मन् n. the aerial path.
आकाशशयन n. lying in the open air.
आकाशसंचारिन् m. wanderer in the sky.*
आकाशेश m. ruler of the atmosphere.
आकिंचन्य n. want of anything, poverty.
आकीम् (prep.) from (abl.).
आकीर्ण a. scattered, spread; filled with, surrounded by (instr. or —°).
आकुञ्चित a. contracted, crooked, curled.
आकुटिल a. slightly curved.
आकुल a. confounded, confused, agitated, anxious; overburdened with, full of (instr. or —°).
आकुलय्, °यति confound, confuse, trouble. pp. आकुलित confounded, bewildered, obscured by (—°).
आकुलि m. N. of an Asura priest.
आकुली कृ = आकुलय्; °भू become or be perplexed.
आकुलीयमान a. confused, agitated, frightened.*
आकूत n., आकूति f. intention, purpose.
आकृति f. constituent part; shape, form (poss. °मन्त्†), beauty.
आकृष्टि f. drawing near, attraction.
आके (loc. adv.) near, hither.
आकेकर a. a little squinting or looking aside; °राक्ष a. having such eyes.
आकौशल n. inexpertness, want of skill.
आक्रन्द m. cry, call; friend, protector, esp. the neighbour of a (king's) neighbour.
आक्रन्दन m., °न्दित n. crying, calling.
आक्रम m. approach, attack.
आक्रमण a. approaching; n. = prec.
आक्रान्त a. taken, seized; overcome, ruled by (instr. or —°).
आक्रान्ति f. ascending, rising.
आक्रीड m. n. play-ground, garden,
आक्रुष्ट a. being reviled.
आक्रोश m. crying out, scolding, reviling.
आक्षिक a. relating to the dice, won or lost at dice.
आक्षिप्त a. hit, struck, touched.
आक्षिप्तिका f. song of approach (d.).
आक्षेप m. throwing up, tossing, drawing to one's self, attraction; applying, laying on; casting off, removing, giving up; hint, allusion; objection; abuse, injury.
आक्षेपण n. tossing, impelling; abuse, objection.
आक्षेपरूपक n. = आक्षेपोपमा.
आक्षेपवलन n. tossing to and fro.
आक्षेपिन् a. drawing away; °णी सिद्धि f. the power of flying into the air.
आक्षेपोपमा f. a kind of comparison.
आखण्डल m. E. of Indra (lit. breaker, destroyer).
आखु m. mole, mouse.
आखुकिरि m. a mole-hill.
आखेट m. chase.
आख्या f. appellation, name; instr. with name; adj. —° called, named.
आख्यात n. finite verb (g.).
आख्यातुकाम a. wishing to tell.
आख्यातृ m. relater, speaker.
आख्यान n. telling, relating; tale, legend.
आख्यानक n. a short tale; f. ई N. of a metre.
आख्यानविद् m. knower of (ancient) tales.
आख्यायिका f. = आख्यानक.
आख्यायिन् a. telling, relating (—°).
आख्येय a. to be told or related.
आगत a. come, arrived (acc., loc. or —°), returned (± पुनर्), sprung or descended from (abl.), happened, occurred (gen.); fallen into, having met with (acc.). m. guest.
आगति f. coming, arrival, return.
आगधित a. clasped, held fast.
आगन्तव्य n. veniendum.
आगन्तु a. coming, arriving; m. new-comer, guest.
आगन्तुक a. & m. the same (abstr. °ता*).
आगन्तृ a. venturus.
आगम a. coming to, approaching, being added. m. approach, arrival, going to (—°);

course (of a river), appearance, origin; income, revenue, possession, title; knowledge, science, doctrine; augment (g.).

आगमन n. coming, arrival, appearance.

आगमवन्त् a. approaching sexually.

आगमापायिन् a. coming and going.

आगमिन् a. augmented (g.).

आगर्भनिर्गम (°—) from birth.*

आगस् n. offence, injury, sin.

आगस्त्य a. relating to Agasti; pl. Agasti's descendants.

आगामिन् a. coming, future.

आगामुक a. coming, wont to come to (acc.).

आगार n. room, dwelling, house.

आगुर् f. acclamation (r.).

आग्निक, f. **ई** belonging to fire or to the fire-sacrifice.

आग्नीध्र a. belonging to the Agnīdh. m. = **अग्नीध्**; n. the place for or the function of the A.

आग्नीध्रीय being within the Āgnīdhra (v. prec. n.); m. the fire therein.

आग्नेय, f. **ई** relating to fire or Agni, fiery.

आग्रयण m. firstling (a cert. Soma-libation); f. **ई** & n. oblation of firstlings or first-fruits.

आग्रयणक n. (& adj. —°) = prec. n.

आग्रहायणी f. a cert. day of full moon.

आघर्घरम् adv. growlingly.

आघाट m. & **आघाटि** m. or f. cymbal, rattle (cf. seq.).

आघात m. striking, killing, blow; slaughter-house, place of execution.

आघृणि & †**आघृणीवसु** a. glowing, hot.

आघोषणा f. calling, proclaiming.

आङ्गिरस, f. **ई** relating to or descending from the Aṅgiras.

आङ्गूष m. n. praise, hymn.

आचमन n. rinsing the mouth or sipping water; the water used for rinsing the mouth (also f. **ई**).

आचरण n. approach, arrival; conduct, behaviour; cart, carriage.

आचरित n. arrival, conduct, custom, customary proceeding, usage, way.

आचरितव्य a. to be done; n. impers. (it is) to be acted in the usual way.

आचान्त a. sipped (water); rinsed or having rinsed (the mouth).

आचाम m. the water or foam of boiled rice.

आचार m. conduct, (good) behaviour; custom, usage, ordinance, institute; abl. in **°तस्**.

आचारवन्त् a. of virtuous conduct.

आचारहीन a. defective in conduct.

आचार्य m. teacher, spiritual guide (poss. **°वन्त्**; abstr. **°ता**† f., **°त्व**† n.); a cert. caste.

आचार्यक n. office or art of teaching.

आचार्योपासन n. reverence for the teacher.

आचिख्यासा f. wish to express; a. **°सु**.

आचिख्यासोपमा f. a kind of comparison.

आचित a. heaped, accumulated; filled or covered with (instr. or —°).

आच्छन्न a. covered, clothed.

आच्छाद m. clothing, clothes.

आच्छादक a. concealing, covering.

आच्छादन n. covering, clothing.

आच्छादिन् a. concealing, hiding (—°).

आच्छिन्न a. cut off, split, broken.

आज a. coming from or belonging to goats; n. E. of a cert. lunar mansion.

आजमीढ (°ह्ळ) m. patr. from **अजमीढ**.

आजाति f. birth, origin, existence.

आजान n., **आजानि** f. the same.

आजि m. f. running or fighting match; race, battle, combat; place for running, course.

आजिमुख n. front of battle.

आजीगर्ति m. patron. from **अजीगर्त**.

आजीव m., **°वन** n., (**°विका** f.*) livelihood, subsistence.

आजीवितान्तम् adv. through (lit. to the end of) life.

आजुह्वान a. sacrificed or worshipped with sacrifices.

आज्ञप्ति f. order, command.

आज्ञा f. the same.

आज्ञाकर m., **ई** f. servant; abstr. **°करत्व** n.

आज्ञान n. perceiving, understanding.

आज्ञाभङ्ग m. violation of a command, disobedience.

आज्ञाभङ्गकारिन् a. violating a command, disobedient.

आज्य n. melted or clarified butter, also oil and milk (used for religious purposes).

आज्यपं a. drinking melted butter; pl. a class of Manes.

आञ्छ्, आञ्छति tear, stretch.

आंञ्जन n. ointment. esp. for the eyes.

आंञ्जनगन्धि a. smelling of ointment (v. prec.).

आटविक a. belonging to a wood; n. woodman, forester.

आटोप m. puffing up, pride, self-conceit.

†**आडम्बर** m. a kind of drum, noise. sound, bombast; the non-plus-ultra of (—°).

आढक m. n. (adj. —° f. **ई**) a cert. measure of grain.

आढ्यं a. opulent. wealthy; abstr. °**ता**† f.

आणिं m. the pin of the axle-tree (also *°**अणि**).

आण्डं n. egg; m. du. the testicles; f. **ईं** a t.

आंत् (abl. adv.) from this, afterwards, thereupon, then, further, often correl. to **यद्**, **यदा**, **यदि** and followed by **इत्**.

आतङ्क m. pain, sorrow, anguish.

आतंञ्चन n. rennet.

आंतत a. stretched out, spread, strung (bow), turned to, hung on (loc.); wide, long.

आततायिंन् & °**ताविंन्** a. having a stretched bow; threatening, inimical.

आतपं a. causing pain; m. heat, sunshine.

आतपत्र n. a large umbrella used as a parasol.

आतपवारण n. a parasol.

आंता f. (instr. pl. also **आंतैस्**) frame, border, edge.

आताम्र a. reddish.

आतिं or **आतीं** f. a kind of water-bird.

आतिथेय, f. **ई** hospitable; f. **ई** & n. hospitality.

आतिथ्यं a. = prec. a.; n. hospitality, (hospitable) reception.

आतिरैक्य n. excess, superfluity.

आतुंजे (dat. inf.) to procure or bestow.

आंतुर a. diseased, sick, suffering from (—°).

आंत्त a. seized, assumed, taken. °— having taken or having been robbed of.

आत्तगन्ध a. hurt, insulted (lit. whose smell or breath is taken away).

आत्तदण्ड a. having taken or lifted the sceptre.

आत्तधन्वन् a. having taken or grasped a bow.

आत्तशस्त्र a. having taken a weapon, armed.

आत्म (—°) = **आत्मन्**.

आत्मक, f. **आत्मिका** (—°) having the nature of, consisting of, -like.

आत्मकृत a. done by or against one's self.

आत्मगत a. being connected with or contained in one's self; n. adv. to one's self, i.e. aside (d.).

आत्मगति f. one's own way, course, power; instr. by one's own act or means.

आत्मचिन्ता f. meditation on the soul.

आत्मच्छन्दानुचारिन् a. following one's own will, wilful. wayward.*

आत्मज a. born of one's self; m. son, f. **आ** daughter.

आत्मज्ञ a. knowing one's self or the all-soul.

आत्मज्ञान n. self-knowledge; knowledge of the all-soul.

आत्मता f., °**त्व** n. abstr. to **आत्मंन्**.

आत्मतुल्य a. like one's self.

आत्मतृप्त a. satisfied with one's self.

आत्मत्याग m. suicide (lit. leaving one's self).

आत्मत्यागिन् a. suicide (lit. who leaves himself).

आत्मदान n. gift of self.

आत्मंन् m. breath, life, spirit, soul; the supreme spirit or all-soul; nature, character; self. one's self (as refl. pron.). Often °— one's own; —° = **आत्मक**. Instr. w. an ordin. number v. seq.

आत्मनातृतीय a. (made) the third by one's self; being one's self the third with two others.

आत्मनेपद n. the middle (lit. self-) form of the verb.

आत्मन्वंन्त् & **आत्मन्विंन्** a. having a soul, animated.

आत्मप्रदान n. = **आत्मदान**.

आत्मप्रभ a. shining by one's self, self-illuminated.

आत्मप्रशंसा f. self-applause.

आत्मबोद a. knowing the all-soul; m. knowledge of the all-soul, T. of a philos. work.

1**आत्मभव** m. the existence or being of one's self.

2**आत्मभव** a. existing of one's self.

आत्मभाव m. the being or nature of one's self, one's own personality; °**स्थ** a. remaining in one's own nature.

आत्मभू a. self-existent (E. of sev. gods).
आत्मभूत a. being (another's) self, entirely devoted.
आत्मयाजिन् a. sacrificing (for) one's self.
आत्मयोग m. union with the all-soul.
आत्मरति a. happy in one's self.
आत्मलाभ m. one's own gain or advantage.
आत्मवत् adv. as one's self.
आत्मवत्ता f. self-control.
आत्मवध m., °वध्या f. suicide.
आत्मवन्त् a. having a soul, animated; self-possessed, wise, virtuous.
आत्मवश & °वश्य a. depending on one's self.
आत्मविक्रय m. sale of one's self.
आत्मविद् a. knowing the supreme spirit.
आत्मविद्या f. knowledge of the supreme spirit.
आत्मविनिग्रह m. subduing of one's self.
आत्मश्रेयस् n. the best of the soul.
आत्मसंसिद्धि f. highest perfection of the soul.
आत्मसंस्थ a. staying with or confined to one's own person.
आत्मसंदेह m. personal risk.
आत्मसम a. like one's self, abstr. °ता f.
आत्मसंभव m., आ f. = आत्मज, °जा.
आत्मसंभावित a. self-conceited.
आत्मसात्कृ make one's own, acquire.
आत्मस्तव m. self-praise.
आत्महन् a. killing the soul or one's self.
आत्महित a. good for one's self.
आत्मानपेक्ष a. not considering one's self, disinterested.
आत्मापहार m. concealment of one's self.
आत्मापहारक & °रिन् a. concealing or making away with one's own self.
आत्मार्थम् & °र्थे adv. for one's own sake.
आत्मीय a. one's own.
आत्मोपजीविन् a. living by one's own self (i.e. by labour).
आत्मौपम्य n. likeness or analogy to one's own self.
आत्यन्तिक, f. ई continual, uninterrupted, infinite, absolute.
आत्ययिक, f. ई connected with danger, pressing, urgent.
आत्रेय m., ई f. descendant of Atri; f. also a woman in her courses.
आथर्वण, f. ई belonging to Atharvan; m. descendant of A. or the Atharvaveda.
आदघ्न a. reaching up to the mouth.
आदर m. consideration of, respect to, care about (loc. or —°); reverence, honour. Instr. & abl. respectfully, carefully, eagerly.
आदर्दिर a. crushing.
आदर्श m. looking-glass, mirror; reflected image; illustration, copy, commentary.
आदातृ m. recipient.
आदान n. taking, seizing, acceptance.
आदाननित्य a. who always takes.
आदाय (ger.) having taken, i.e. with (acc.).
आदि m. commencement, beginning, firstling; loc. आदौ in the beginning, first. Often adj. —° (also आदिक) beginning with, and so on. Abstr. आदित्व & आदिकत्व n.
आदिकर्तृ m. the (first) creator.
आदिगुरु m. the first father (Brahman).
आदिग्ध a. anointed or smeared with (—°).
आदितस् adv. from the beginning, from the first.
आदितेय m. son of Aditi.
1आदित्य m. belonging to or coming from Aditi. m. = prec., esp. Sūrya or the sun; pl. the (highest) gods.
2आदित्य a. belonging to the Ādityas or the sun.
आदित्यगत a. being in the sun.
आदित्यचन्द्र m. du. sun and moon.
आदित्यमण्डल n. the orb of the sun.
आदित्यवत् adv. like the sun.
आदित्यवर्चस् a. having the splendour of the sun.
आदित्यवर्ण a. having the colour of the sun.
आदित्यसंकाश a. sun-like.
आदित्सु a. wishing to take or have.
आदिदेव m. first god (Brahma, Viṣṇu, or Çiva).
आदिन् a. eating.
आदिपुरुष or °पूरुष m. the first male or primeval spirit, E. of Viṣṇu.
आदिभूत a. being the first of (gen.).
आदिम a. first.
आदिमूल n. the first cause.
आदिवंश m. primeval race.

आदिश् f. aiming at, design; dat. (as inf.) to aim at, to hit.
आदिष्ट n. instruction, order, command; m. a sort of treaty or alliance.
आदिष्टिन् a. having received instruction; a novice.
आदीप्त a. flaming, glowing, brilliant.
आदृत a. respectful, zealous, intent upon (loc.); esteemed, honoured.
आदेय a. to be taken or employed.
आदेवन n. gambling-place.
आदेश m. account, information, prophecy; instruction, precept, rule, command; substitute (g.).
आदेशिन् a. imparting, ordering (—°).
1आद्य a. eatable, n. food.
2आद्य a. first, preceding, primitive, extraordinary, excellent; n. beginning. °— = आदि.
आद्यन्त n. beginning and end; a. beginning and ending with (—°).
आद्यन्तवन्त् a. having beginning and end.
आद्याद्य a. each preceding (opp. परस्पर).
आद्यून a. voracious.
आधमन n. mortgage.
आधमर्ण्य n. state of being indebted.
आधव m. stirrer or a stirred mass, mixture.
आधवनीय m. a vessel for shaking and cleansing the Soma.
आधातृ m. = अग्न्याहित + giver, imparter, teacher.
आधान n. placing, adding, causing, producing; depositing, deposit, pledge; receptacle, enclosure; also = अग्न्याधान & गर्भाधान q.v.
आधार m. support, basis (l. & f.); receptacle, canal; (g.) province, sphere (of an action).
1आधि m. receptacle, foundation; base (fig.); deposit, pledge, earnest-money.
2आधि m. (mostly pl.) thought, care, woe, sorrow.
आधिकरणिक m. judge.
आधिक्य n. excess, abundance, high degree, superiority.
आधिदैवत & °दैविक a. referring to the gods.
आधिपत्य n. supremacy.
आधिरथि m. patr. from अधिरथ.
आधिराज्य n. sovereignty.
आधिस्तेन m. stealer of a pledge.
आधी f. thought, care.
आधीत a. thought of; n. object, purpose, hope.
आधीति f. reflection, intention.
आधुनिक a. new, recent.
आधूत a. shaken, vexed, tormented.
आधृषे (dat. inf.) to attack or defy.
आधेय a. to be set, placed, deposited, granted; being contained, situated.
आध्मात a. inflated, puffed up by (—°).
आध्यात्मिक (f. ई & आ) referring to the self or the supreme soul.
आध्र a. poor, destitute.
आध्वनिक a. being on a journey.
आध्वर्यव a. belonging to the Adhvaryu priest; n. the office of the A.
आध्वस्त a. veiled, covered.
आन m. mouth, face.
आनक m. a kind of drum.
आनत a. bowed, bent (of a bow); bent inwards, hollowed, flat, level; bowing, stooping.
आनतपर्वन् a. having the knots or joints flatted; smooth, polished (arrow).
आनति f. bowing; salute, submission.
आनद्ध a. bound, tied, costive; overlaid or covered with (instr.).
आनन n. mouth, face.
आननचर, f. ई falling into the mouth of (gen.).
आनन्तर्य n. absence of interval, immediate consequence or succession.
आनन्त्य a. infinite; n. infinity, immortality.
आनन्द m. (n.) joy, pleasure, bliss.
आनन्दन a. delightful.
आनन्दमय, f. ई made up of joy, blissful. Abstr. °त्व n.
आनन्दयितृ n. who gladdens.
आनन्दित a. delighted with (loc.).
आनन्दिन् a. joyful or gladdening.
आनन्दोत्सव m. feast of joy.
आनयन n. bringing towards, back, or about.
आनर्दित n. roaring.
आनव a. kind to men; human; m. foreigner.

आनाय m. net; °यिन् m. fisherman.
आनीति f. leading near.
आनील a. blackish.
आनुपूर्व n., °पूर्वी f., °पूर्व्य n. order, succession; instr. in due order, one after the other.
आनुयात्रिक (± जन) m. follower, attendant.
आनुवेश्य m. the next neighbour but one.
आनुलोम्य n. natural order (cf. अनुलोम).
आनुषक् adv. coherently, uninterruptedly.
आनुषङ्गिक a. connected, adherent.
आनृण्य n. state of not being indebted to (gen.); abstr. °ता f.
आनृशंस n. mildness, kindness.
आनृशंस्य a. mild, kind; n. = prec.
आनेतृ m., °त्री f. bringer.
आन्तर a. interior, inner; °ज्ञ a. knowing the inner state or the heart.
आन्तरिक्ष or आन्तरीक्ष, f. ई aerial, celestial.
आन्त्र n. sgl. & pl. the bowels, entrails.
आन्ध्य n. blindness.
आन्वाहिक, f. ई daily.
आन्वीक्षिकी (± विद्या) f. logic.
आप्, आप्नोति (आप्नुते), pp. आप्त (q.v.) obtain, reach, overtake, meet with, find; acquire, win, get, beget; pervade, occupy; befall, betide. P. become filled. C. आपयति cause to reach or attain, bring to, let a person (acc.) have or feel a thing (acc.). D. ईप्सति, °ते (q.v.) — अनु attain. अभि reach to, attain; C. accomplish. अव reach, get at, meet, acquire, obtain, incur. समव the same. परि reach, acquire, make up, finish. प्र reach, arrive at, come upon (acc.); obtain, win, get, catch, incur; befall, betide, exist, be; result or follow from a rule (also P.). C. cause to arrive at, bring to (2 acc. or dat. of pers. & acc. of th.); announce, bring before the court (j.), obtain, get. अनुप्र reach, attain, meet, follow, imitate; come, arrive. समनुप्र reach, attain, arrive. संप्र reach, arrive at, come upon, obtain, win, catch. अनुसंप्र = समनुप्र. वि pervade, occupy, reach up to (आ). सम् reach, obtain, get, win; finish, accomplish. C. cause to reach or attain; achieve. finish, conclude. परिसम् P. be comprehended in, belong to (loc.). — Cf. अवाप्त, 1आपान, परिसमाप्त, पर्याप्त, प्राप्त, व्याप्त, समाप्त, संप्राप्त.
आपगा f. river, stream.
आपण m. market; merchandise.
आपत्कल्प m. rule for times of need.
आपत्ति f. occurrence of, entering or changing into (—°); also = आपद्.
आपथि a. being on the road.
आपथी m. traveller.
आपद् f. accident, misfortune, distress.
आपद्गत a. fallen into misfortune, unhappy.
आपद्धर्म m. law for times of need.
आपनेय a. to be obtained.
आपन्न a. having got or come to (°— or —°); unfortunate, unhappy.
आपन्नसत्त्वा f. having got a (new) being, i.e. pregnant.
1आपस् n. religious work.
2†आपस् n. water.
1आपस्तम्ब m. N. of a sage.
2आपस्तम्ब, f. ई coming from Āpastamba.
आपाटल a. reddish.
आपाण्डु a. palish, yellowish; abstr. °ता f.
आपाण्डुर a. the same.
आपात m. rushing on, onset, entering into (—°); sudden event. °— or °तस् adv. immediately, at first sight.
1आपान a. reaching, obtaining; successful.
2आपान n. drinking-party, banquet.
आपार्ष्णि adv. up to the heels.
आपि m. friend, ally; abstr. आपित्व n.
आपीड m. pressure, squeeze (also °न n.); crown, garland (lit. head-presser).
1आपीत a. yellowish.
2आपीत a. turgid, swelled, full.
आपीन a. = prec.; n. udder.
आपूरण a. filling; n. as subst.
आपूर्ण a. filled with (instr. or —°), full.
आपूर्णमण्डल a. having a full round (of the moon and the face).
आपृक् adv. in contact with, upon (gen.).
आपृच्छ्य a. to be saluted or revered; praiseworthy.
आपोमय a. consisting of water.

आप्त a. got, begot, attained, accomplished, complete, abundant, apt, fit, able, true, intimate; m. friend.

आप्तकारिन् a. acting properly or faithfully, i.e. trustworthy.

आप्तदक्षिण a. abounding in fees.

आप्तवर्ग m. acquaintance (concr.).

आप्तवाच् a. trustworthy (lit. whose word is true).

आप्ति f. reaching, meeting, gain, acquisition.

आप्त्य m. E. of sev. gods.

1**आप्य** a. watery, aquatic; n. a lunar mansion.

2**आप्य** a. to be got or acquired.

3**आप्य** n. friendship, alliance.

आप्यायन n. filling, satiating (also °ना† f.); strengthening, satisfying.

आप्र a. active, busy.

***आप्रपदम्** adv. up to the feet.

आप्रपदीन a. reaching to the feet.

आप्री f. pl. N. of cert. invocations.

आप्रीत a. glad, merry.

आप्लव m., **आप्लवन** n., & ***आप्लाव** m. bath, bathing.

आप्लुत a. bathed, wetted, sprinkled, covered or filled with, rich in (instr. or —°).

आप्लुष्ट a. a little scorched or singed.

आबद्ध a. bound, joined, fixed; caused, got, manifested (esp. °—).

आबन्ध m. tie or bond.

आबाध m. attack; trouble, pain, sorrow (also f. **आ**).

आबुत्त m. honourable man.*

आब्दिक a. annual, yearly; —° of —years.

आभक्त a. partaking of (loc.).

आभग m. partner of (loc.).

आभरण n. ornament, decoration.

आभरणस्थान n. place for ornament (on the body).*

आभा f. splendour, light; likeness, a. —° resembling, like.

आभात a. shining, bright, appeared, manifest.

आभास m. splendour, light; appearance, phantom.

आभिजाती f., °**जात्य** n. noble birth, generosity.

आभिमुख्य n. direction towards (gen., acc., or —°), intention to (—°); °**करण** n. calling hither.

आभिषेक & °**षेचनिक** (f. **ई**) relating to the inauguration of a king.

आभीक्ष्ण्य n. frequent repetition (g.).

आभीर m. N. of a people & a caste.

आभु a. empty, stingy.

आभुग्न a. bent, curved.

आभू a. present, helpful, ready; m. assistant.

आभूति f. power, might.

आभूषेण्य a. to be honoured or obeyed.

आभृत a. procured, got, caused, filled with (—°).

आभोग m. curve, circuit, extension, fullness, amplitude, abundance.

आभोगय m., °**गि** f. food, enjoyment.

आभ्यन्तर a. interior, inner.

आम् excl. of recollection or assent.

आम a. raw.

आमग्न a. quite immersed in (loc.).

आमन n. benevolence, kindness.

आमनस् a. benevolent, kind.

आमन्त्रण n. addressing, calling to; greeting, taking leave; invitation, consultation.

आमन्त्रणक n. invitation.*

आमन्त्रित n. addressing, the vocative case.

आमन्द्र a. somewhat deep or hollow (of a sound).

आमपात्र n. a raw vessel, i.e. a vessel of unburnt clay.

†**आमय** m. hurt, disease.

आमयाविन् a. sick, esp. dyspeptic; abstr. °**वित्व**† n.

आमरणम् adv. until death.

आमरणान्त & °**णान्तिक** a. lasting till death.

आमर्द m. crushing, squeezing; °**र्दिन्** adj.

आमर्श m. touch.

आमलक m., **ई** f. the Myrobalan tree; n. its fruit.

आमाद् a. eating raw flesh.

आमावास्य a. belonging to the new moon; n. the new-moon oblation.

आमिक्षा f. curds; poss. °**क्षवन्त्**.

आमिश्र a. mixed, mingled.

आमिश्ल a. (readily) mixing.

आमिष n. flesh; °**षाशिन्** a. eating f.

आमिस् m. raw flesh.
आमुक्त a. put on or off, clothed in or with (acc. or —°).
आमुर् & आमुरि m. destroyer.
आमुष्मिक, f. ई belonging to that place, b. to the beyond or the other world.
आमुष्यायण m. the descendant of such and such, born from that race.
आमूल (°—) & आमूलम् a. from the first (lit. the root).
आमृष्ट a. touched, seized, occupied.
आमेष्टका f. an unburnt brick.
आमोटन n. cracking, breaking.
आमोद a. gladdening; m. joy, fragrance.
आमोदित & °दिन् a. fragrant.
*आम्नातिन् a. having quoted (loc.).
आम्नाय m. tradition, sacred text, legend.
आम्नायपर a. honouring the sacred tradition.
आम्र m. the mango tree; n. its fruit.
आम्रेड m. repetition.
आम्रेडित n. the same, reduplication (g.).
आम्लान a. (somewhat) faded.
आय m. approach; income, revenue.
आयजि, °जिन्, & °ज्यु a. procuring (by sacrifices).
आयत a. extended, long; turned towards, put on (arrow); n. & instr. f. °तया adv. directly, forthwith.
आयतन n. foot-hold, support, seat, object of (—°); fire-place, sanctuary; barn.
आयतलोचन a. having long eyes.
आयताक्ष, f. ई the same.
आयति f. extension, length; sequel, future; expectation, hope; offspring, son.
आयतिक्षम a. faithful (lit. bearing the future).
आयतेक्षण a. having long eyes.
आयत्त a. striving, active, ready; being in (loc. or acc.); resting, based, dependent on (loc., gen., or —°); abstr. °ता† f., °त्व† n.
आयदर्शिन् a. seeing i.e. enjoying an income.
आयव्यय m. du. revenues and disbursements.
आयस (f. °सी or आयसी) of iron, metallic.
आयाति f. = seq.; m. N. of a man.
आयान n. coming, arrival.
आयाम m. stretching out, extension, length (poss. °मवन्त् or °मिन्); stopping, restraint (poss. °मिन्).
आयास m. effort, trouble, sorrow; p. °सिन्.
आयासक, °सकर & °सद a. tiring, trying.
आयासयितृ (& °तृक, f. °यिका) causing pain.*
1आयु a. living, lively, active; m. living creature, man, mankind.
2आयु m. the genius of life; n. life.
आयुक्त a. yoked to (loc.), intent upon*, charged with (gen. or loc.); m. (also °क) minister, agent.
आयुत a. connected or endowed with (—°).
आयुध n. weapon, vessel; adj. —° armed with.
आयुधभृत् a. bearing arms; m. warrior.
आयुधागार n. armoury, arsenal.
आयुधिक, आयुधिन् & आयुधीय a. & m. = आयुधभृत्.
आयुर्वेद m. the science of health; T. of a book on medicine.
1आयुःशेष m. rest of life.
2आयुःशेष a. having a rest of life, not yet dead; abstr. °ता f.
आयुष्काम a. wishing for (a long) life.
आयुष्मन्त् a. having life or vitality, healthy, long-lived, old, lasting (for life).
आयुष्य a. giving (long) life; n. vital power, longevity.
आयुस् n. life, vitality, longevity; world (= living creatures).
आयोग m. team or set (of draught-cattle); ornament, decoration; swarm of bees.
आयोगव m. a cert. mixed caste.
आयोद m. patron. of a Rishi.
आयोधन n. war, battle, battle-field.
आर्, आर्यति praise.
आर m. n. ore, metal; n. sting, point, corner, angle.
आरकात् adv. far from (abl.).
आरक्त a. reddish.
आरक्ष m., °क्षा f. protection, guard.
आरक्षक m. watchman, guard.
आरक्षण (f. °णी), °क्षिक, & °क्षिन् (f. °णी) m. the same.
आरङ्गर m. bee.
आरटि s., °त n. roaring, sound.

आरण n. depth, abyss.
आरण्य a. belonging to a forest, forest-born, wild; m. a wild animal.
आरण्यक a. = prec. a.; m. forester, hermit; n. a class of religious writings to be studied in the forest.
आरण्यपशु m. a wild animal.
आरब्ध a. (having) begun.
आरब्धि f. undertaking.
आरभ्य ger. beginning with, i.e. from, since (acc., abl. or —°).
आरम्भ m. undertaking, beginning, abstr. °ता† f.
आरम्भण n. getting hold of, seizing, concr. support, handle.
आरम्भरुचि a. delighting in undertakings; abstr. °ता f.
आरव m. cry, howl, crash, sound.
आरसित a. crying; n. cry.
आरा f. awl, prick.
आरात् (abl. adv.) far, from afar, far from (abl.); immediately, at once.
आरात्तात् (abl. adv.) from afar, from a distance.
आराध m. homage.
आराधन a. propitiating, conciliating, gaining over. n. the same as subst., also adoration, homage.
आराधयितृ m. adorer.
आराध्य a. to be made favourable, to be won.
आराम m. pleasure, pleasure-garden.
आराव m. cry, howl, sound; p. आराविन्.
आरुक a. hurting (acc.).
आरुज्, आरुज, & आरुजत्नु a. breaking.
आरुण & आरुणि m., ई f. descendant of Aruṇa; f. आरुणी also a red mare.
आरुरुक्षु a. wishing to ascend or advance to (acc.).
आरूढ a. mounted, ridden by (—°), got, obtained; act. (having) mounted, riding, sitting or standing on (loc., acc. or —°); come forth, risen; fallen into, got to (acc. or —°).
आरूढि f. mounting, rising (only —°).
आरे (loc. adv.) far, far from (abl.).
आरोग्य a. healthy; n. health.
आरोप m. imposing, laying in or upon; substitution of, identification with (loc.).
आरोपण n. the same; the stringing of a bow.
आरोपणीय a. to be caused to mount (loc.), to be strung (a bow), being substituted or identified.
आरोपित a. raised, elevated, strung (a bow); placed or put upon, brought to (acc.).
आरोप्य a. to be placed upon; to be strung; being substituted or identified.
आरोषित a. angry, wrathful.
आरोह m. mounted on (—°), a rider; mounting, rising, increase, eminence, heap, mountain; a woman's hip.
आरोहण, f. ई a. mounting, ascending; n. the same as subst., also vehicle, carriage, staircase, ladder.
आरोहिन् a. mounting; causing to rise, bringing to (—°).
आर्जव a. straight, honest; n. straightness, rectitude.
आर्जीक & °कीय m. a cert. Soma-vessel.
आर्त a. fallen into (mischief); afflicted, distressed, pained, troubled by (—°), suffering, sick, sore, unhappy; abstr. °ता† f.
आर्तव a. seasonable, menstrual; n. the menstrual discharge.
आर्ति f. mishap, disaster, sorrow, pain, woe; p. °मन्त्†.
आर्तिहर m. remover of pain.*
आर्त्नी f. the end of the bow.
आर्त्विज्य n. office or service of the sacrificing priest.
आर्थ, f. ई based upon advantage; relating to things (not words).
आर्द्र a. wet, moist, succulent, fresh, new, soft, tender. f. आ N. of a lunar mansion.
आर्द्रपाद a. having wet feet.
आर्द्रभाव m. wetness, humidity, softness.
आर्द्रवस्त्र & °वासस् a. wearing wet clothes.
आर्द्रैधाग्नि m. a fire of fresh fuel.
आर्धधातुक a. applicable to the shorter form of the base (g.).
आर्धिक m. a ploughman who gets half the crop.
आर्य (f. आ & आरी) belonging to the faith-

ful or loyal, to one's own race, i.e. Aryan, noble, reverend, honourable. m. (f. आ) an Aryan, a honourable man, esp. one of the first three castes; also one's senior, i.e. grandfather, great-grandfather, or elder brother. f. आ mother (also pl.) or wife of the elder brother; voc. m. & f. often in reverential address = your honour. f. आ also N. of a metre.

आर्यक m. an honourable man; N. of a man, pl. of a people.

आर्यकर्मन् a. acting like an Aryan.

आर्यचेतस् a. of an Aryan or noble mind.

आर्यजात a. born of an Aryan.

आर्यजुष्ट a. liked by decent people, respectable.

आर्यता f., °त्व n. respectability.

आर्यदेश m. country inhabited by Aryans.

आर्यपुत्र m. son of an Aryau or a gentleman (often in respectful address, esp. of a wife to her husband).

आर्यप्राय a. chiefly inhabited by Aryans.

आर्यभट m. N. of two astronomers.

आर्यमिश्र m. honourable etc.

आर्यम्ण m. E. of a lunar mansion.

आर्यरूप a. having the form of an Aryan.

आर्यलिङ्गिन् a. bearing the (external) marks of an Aryan.

आर्यवाच् a. speaking an Aryan language.

आर्यविदग्धमिश्र m. honourable, learned, etc.

1**आर्यवृत्त** n. decent behaviour.

2**आर्यवृत्त** a. behaving decently.

आर्यागीति f. N. of a metre.

आर्याधृता f. honourable lady (lit. daughter of an Aryan wife).*

आर्यावर्त m. the country of the Aryans (between the Himālaya and Vindhya mountains); pl. its inhabitants.

आर्ष, f. ई belonging to or derived from the Rishis, archaic. m. (± विवाह) a cert. form of marriage. n. holy text or Veda; sacred origin.

आर्षभ a. belonging to a bull, a bull's.

आर्षेय a. = आर्ष a; n. sacred origin.

आर्षेयब्राह्मण n. T. of a Brāhmaṇa.

आर्षोढा a. wife married by the Ārsha rite; °ज m. her son.

आर्ष्टिषेण m. patron. of Ṛṣṭisena.

आल n. spawn, venomous matter (of animals).

आलक्ष्य a. (scarcely) visible.

आलग्न a. clinging to (—°).

आलपन n. talk, conversation.

आलपित n. the same.

आलभन n. = आलम्भन.

आलम्ब a. hanging down; m. anything to hang on, support (l. & f.).

आलम्बन n. leaning or depending on; also = prec. m.

आलम्बित a. hanging down from (—°); upheld, supported, seized, taken hold on.

आलम्बिन् (—°) a. hanging from; leaning, resting, depending on; supporting, maintaining.

आलम्भ m. taking hold of, seizing, tearing off (plants), killing (cf. seq.).

आलम्भन n. touching, killing (of animals at the sacrifice).

आलम्भिन् a. touching (—°).

आलय m. (n.) dwelling, house.

आलवाल n. trench for water round the root of a tree.

आलस्य n. sloth, idleness.

आलान n. the post or rope, to or with which an elephant is tied.

आलानस्तम्भ m. the post to which an elephant is tied.*

आलाप m. talk, conversation, singing (of birds); poss. °वन्त् † & °पिन्.

1**आलि** or **आली** f. female friend.

2**आलि** or **आली** f. line, row; swarm (of bees).

आलिखित a. painted.

आलिङ्ग्, °ङ्गति & °ते, also °ङ्गयति embrace. — प्रति embrace in return. सम् = S.

आलिङ्गन n. an embrace.

आलीढ n. licked, touched, smoothed, polished; n. a cert. attitude in shooting.

आलीन a. clinging to (acc.), cowering, hid in (—°).

आलु or **आलू** f. a small water-jar; n. raft, float.

आलुञ्चन n. lacerating.

आलुलित a. gently touched.

आलून a. cut or plucked off.
आलेखन n. scratching, painting.
आलेख्य n. painting, picture.
आलेख्यसमर्पित a. fixed on a picture, painted.
आलेप m., **°न** n. smearing, ointment.
आलोक m. sight, view, glance, aspect.
आलोकन a. looking, viewing; n. = prec.
आलोकपथ & **°मार्ग** m. horizon (lit. path or reach of sight).
आलोकस्थान n. reach of sight.
आलोकनीय a. to be seen or considered, visible; abstr. **°ता** f.
आलोकिन् a. seeing, beholding (—°).
आलोचन n. seing, perceiving; considering, reflecting (also **°ना** f.).
आलोचनीय & **आलोच्य** a. to be considered.
आलोहित a. reddish.
आव pron. st. of 1st pers. du.
आवत् f. proximity (opp. **परावत्**).
आवन्तक & **°न्तिक** a. belonging to or coming from the Avantis.
आवन्त्य a. the same; m. a cert. caste.
आवपन n. throwing or putting down, strewing, scattering, inserting, capacity; (also = f. **°नी**) receptacle, vessel.
आवय n. conception.
आवरण a. covering, concealing; n. the same as subst. + shutting, enclosing; obstruction, hindrance; cover, garment; bolt, lock; guard, protection.
आवर्जन n. conciliating, winning.
आवर्जित a. bent, inclined, poured down, offered, presented; propitiated, won over.
आवर्त m. turning, winding; whirl, vortex (lit. & fig.); tuft of hair on the top of the head or between the eyebrows.
आवर्तन a. turning round (tr. & intr.); n. turn, return.
आवलि & **°ली** f. row, range, series.
आवल्गित & **°ल्गिन्** a. jumping, leaping.
आवश्यक, f. **ई** necessary, inevitable (n. & **°ता** f. abstr.); **°कं कृ** perform the necessities of nature.
आवसति f. resting-place, night (as the time for rest).
आवसथ m. dwelling-place, habitation.
आवह a. bringing, causing (—°).
आवहन n. bringing near.
आवाप m. scattering, sowing, mixing, inserting, adding; receptacle, vessel; also = **हस्तावाप** q.v.
***आवापक** m. a kind of bracelet.
आवार m. guard, protection.
आवास m. dwelling, abode; p. **°सिन्**.
आवाह m., **°न** n. invitation.
आवि or **आवी** f. pain; pl. the pangs of childbirth (adj. —° f. **ई**).
आविक a. sheep's, woolen; n. sheep's skin, woolen cloth.
आविकसौत्रिक a. made of woolen thread.
आविग्न a. perplexed, astounded.
आविद् f. knowledge.
आविद्ध a. thrown (arrow), pierced, broken; wound, crooked.
आविद्वंस् a. knowing.
आविर्भाव m., **°र्भूति** f. coming forth, appearance, notoriety.
आविल a. turbid; disturbed by, covered or mixed with (—°).
आविलय्, **°यति** disturb, trouble.
आविष्करण n., **°ष्कार** m. manifestation, revelation.
आविष्ट a. entered (act. & pass.), inhabited, filled, hit, pierced, seized, overwhelmed with (instr. or —°).
आविष्टित a. covered or clothed with (instr. or —°).
आविष्य a. apparent, manifest.
आविस् adv. openly, before the eyes. With **अस्** & **भू** become visible, appear; w. **कृ** make visible, reveal, show.
आवीत & **°तिन्** v. **प्राचीनावीत** & **°तिन्**.
***आवुक** m. father (d.).*
आवृत् f. turning, stopping, entering (dat. as infin.); way, process, course, direction, order, method; (r.) performance, ceremony (opp. the spoken word).
आवृत a. covered, veiled, hidden, clothed, surrounded, filled with (instr. or —°), fenced, locked; withheld, forbidden; captive, prisoner; m. a cert. mixed caste.
आवृत्त a. turned round, towards, or sidewards,

bent, inverted, averted from (abl.), returned, repeated.
आवृत्ति f. turning, return, repetition, new birth; course, way, direction.
आवेग m. hurry, haste, excitement.
आवेदन n. communication, denunciation, statement of a complaint.
†आवेश m. entrance, access; fit, wrath, anger.
आवेशन n. workshop.
आवेष्ट m., °न n. enclosure, embrace.
1आव्य (f. आवी) sheep's, woolen.
2आव्य ger. by granting.
आव्यथा f. a slight emotion (°थां कृ feel —).
आव्याधिन् a. shooting, striking; f. pl. (scil. सेनास्) a gang of robbers.
आव्रश्चन n. stump of a tree.
1आश m. acquiring (only —°).
2आश m. food.
आशंसन n., आशंसा f. wish, desire, expectation, hope.
आशङ्कनीय a. to be feared.
आशङ्का f. fear, apprehension of (abl.); distrust. — °शल्य n. the dart or thorn of fear.*
आशङ्किन् a. fearing, supposing (—°).
आशय m. resting-place, couch, abode, retreat, seat, esp. of feelings and thoughts, i.e. heart, mind; intention, disposition
आशस् f. wish, expectation, hope.
आशसन n. cutting up a killed animal.
1आशा f. = आशस् (w. gen., loc., or —°).
2आशा f. space, region, quarter (of the sky).
आशाजनन a. awaking hope.
आशातन्तु m. (the thread of) hope.
आशान्वित a. hopeful.
आशापाश m. (the cord of) hope.
आशाप्रतीक्षा f. du. hope and expectation.
आशाबन्ध m. hopefulness (lit. the binding or gathering of hope).
आशामुख n. = 2आशा (lit. front of a region).
आशावन्त् a. hopeful.
आशावासस् n. the sky as garment; acc. w. वस् put on the garment of the sky, i.e. go naked.
आशास्य n. to be wished, desirable; n. wish, desire.
आशि s. eating.
आशिञ्जित a. tinkling; n. as subst.
आशित a. eaten, filled; n. food.
आशिन् a. eating (—°).
आशिन a. aged.
आशिर् f. the milk mixed with the Soma-juice.
आशिष्ठ superl. to आशु.
1आशिस् f. prayer, wish, benediction.
2आशिस् & *आशी f. a serpent's fang.
आशीन a. = आशिन.
आशीयंस् compar. to आशु.
आशीर्मन्त् & °वन्त् a. mixed with milk.
आशीर्वचन n., °र्वाद m. benediction, blessing.
आशीर्वादाभिधानवन्त् a. containing a word of benediction.
आशीविष m. a venomous serpent.
आशीविषोपम a. resembling a venomous serpent, poisoned (an arrow).
आशु a. swift; n. adv.; m. horse.
आशुक्लान्त a. swiftly faded.
आशुग a. swiftly going; m. arrow.
आशुगमन n. swiftly going, speed.
आशुमत् & आशुया adv. quickly.
आशुशुक्षणि a. shining forth; m. fire.
आशृत a. little boiled.
आशौच n. impurity (r.).
आश्चर्य a. strange, miraculous; n. wonder, prodigy.
आश्चुतित a. dripped (intr.).
आश्यान a. coagulated.
आश्रम m. hermitage; one of the (four) orders of religious life (also °पद n.).
आश्रमवासिन् m. inhabitant of a hermitage, hermit, ascetic.
आश्रमिन् a. belonging to one of the orders of religious life.
आश्रय m. leaning, resting, depending on (—°); resting place, dwelling, seat, recipient or subject (of any quality or action); refuge, protection, aid, assistance; adj. —° = seq. a.
आश्रयण, f. ई depending on, relating to (—°); n. going to, seeking, choosing.
आश्रयणीय a. to be approached for protection.
आश्रयभूत a. being the refuge, support, recipient, or subject of (gen. or —°).
आश्रयिन् a. leaning on, attaching to; dwelling in (—°).

आश्रव a. obedient; abstr. °ता f.
आश्रावण n. call (r.).
आश्रित a. leaning, hanging, depending on; resorting, devoted, subject to (acc., gen., loc., or —°), m. dependant. servant; clinging, belonging, relating to (acc. or —°); come to, having got, obtained, or taken to (acc. or —°), dwelling, seating, standing, lying, situate in or on (acc., loc. or —°); visited, approached, assisted, helped, reached, entered, got, obtained, practised, chosen.
आश्रित्य ger. resorting to, taking care of (acc.), often = because or for the sake of.
आश्रुत a. heard, audible, granted, promised; n. calling, exhortation (r.).
आश्रुति f. reach of hearing.
†आश्रुत्कर्ण a. having ears to hear.
आश्रेष m. embracer (a demon).
आश्लिष्ट a. hanging on, clinging to (loc. or —°); embraced, encircled.
आश्लेष m. close contact, embrace. f. आश्लेषा sgl. & pl. N. of a lunar mansion.
आश्व a. belonging to or coming from horses.
आश्वत्थ, f. ई made of (the wood of) the holy fig tree.
आश्वयुज m. = 2आश्विन m.
आश्वश्व a. having quick horses.
आश्वास m. breathing anew, recovery, comfort, confidence in (gen. or loc.).
आश्वासन n., °ना f. consoling, encouraging, refreshment, comfort.
आश्वासनशील a. disposed to encouraging another; abstr. °ता f.*
आश्वासिन् a. reviving, cheering up.
1आश्विन, f. ई a. resembling riders.
2आश्विन a. belonging or consecrated to the Açvins; m. a cert. mouth.
आषाढ m. a cert. mouth.
आष्ट्री f. fire-place, hearth.
1आस् excl. of joy or displeasure.
2आस्, आस्ते (आस्ति, आसति, °ते, आस्यति, °ते), pp. आसित (q.v.) & आसीन sit, seat one's self on (loc.); settle down, keep quiet, rest, lie, dwell, stay, remain; continue, keep on (w. nom of a pp., adj. or subst., also adv. or ger.); belong to (gen.); be or turn to (dat.); also trans. keep, perform, celebrate. C. आसयति cause to sit down. — अधि sit or lie down upon (acc.), inhabit, enter, get into. undergo; preside, rule. अनु sit near or round (acc.), sit down after another (acc.); worship, celebrate. उद् sit apart, be indifferent or passive. उप be seated, esp. sit near or round (acc.); surround, invest; expect, wait for or on, honour, respect; partake of, enjoy, celebrate, perform, execute; get into, inhabit; undergo, take pains, endeavour to (pp.); keep on, continue (pp. or ger.). C. उपासयति cause to sit or to do homage.* पर्युप sit upon or around, surround; revere, worship; partake of, enjoy. समुप be seated; perform, execute; celebrate, revere, wait upon, attend. परि sit or assemble round (acc.), endeavour at (acc.); keep quiet, i.e. do nothing. सम् sit (together), assemble round (acc.), hold a meeting; abide, dwell in (loc.); take to, exercise (acc.); also = प्रतिसम् be a match for, withstand. — Cf. अध्यासित, उदासीन.
3आस् n. mouth, face; only abl. आसस् w. आ by word of mouth, in person; & instr. आसा before one's eyes, near or from near, openly.
1आस m. ashes, dust.
2आस m. seat, proximity; abl. adv. (from) near.
आसक्त a. suspended, hanging on; clinging, attached, or used to; intent on (loc. or —°).
आसक्ति f. adhering, clinging to, pursuit, devotion; as adv. coherently, entirely.
आसङ्ग m. = prec. f.
आसङ्गिन् a. hanging on (—°).
आसंज्ञन n. hanging on, fastening; handle, hook.
आसत्ति f. close connection, union.
आसन् n. mouth, jaws.
आसन or आसन n. sitting, sitting down; the way of sitting (r.); sitting quiet, halting; seat, throne, high position.
आसनस्थ a. being seated.
आसनोदक n. du. seat and water.

आसन्न a. set, put down, reached, got; come to, neared, approached; proximate, near, next, imminent. n. proximity.
आसन्नचर a. moving near (—°).
आसन्नप्रसवा f. near parturition or about to lay eggs.
आसन्नवर्तिन् a. being near.
आसपिण्डक्रियाकर्म adv. before the performance of the Sapiṇḍīkaraṇa.
आसया (instr. adv.) before one's eyes.
1आसव m. spirituous liquor, rum.
2आसव m. excitement, impulse.
आसवकरक m. maker of liquors.*
आसादन n. laying down; meeting with, obtaining.
1आसाद्य a. to be got or obtained.
2आसाद्य ger. having reached or got; often = a prep. on, in, at, with; according to, in consequence of (acc.).
आसार m. shower of rain.
*आसिका f. one's turn to sit.
आसिच् f. dish, vessel.
आसित a. sitting (n. imp. it has been seated); practised, done; n. sitting, being seated, seat, place.
आसिद्ध a. arrested, prisoner.
1आसुति f. decoction, draught.
2आसुति f. = 2आसव.
आसुर, f. ई belonging to the Asuras, divine or demoniacal.
आसुरनिश्चय a. of a demonic state of mind.
आसुरस्व n. property of the Asuras.
आसेक m. wetting, sprinkling.
आसेचन n. the same; cavity, vessel for fluids.
आसेद्धृ m. who arrests another.
आसेध m. arrest, custody.
आसेवन n., आसेवा f. (p. °विन्) practice, cultivation, intercourse, stay in (—°).
आस्कन्द m. ascending; assault, onset.
आसक्त m. joined, united.
आस्तर m., आस्तरण n. spread, couch, carpet, cushion, coverlet.
आस्तार m. spreading, arranged place (for dicing).
आस्ताव m. place for a cert. recitation (r.).
आस्तिक a. pious, faithful; abstr. °क्य n.
आस्तीक m. N. of a saint.
आस्तीर्ण & आस्तृत a. strewed, spread, covered.
आस्था f. consideration, care, wish, interest, inclination (w. loc. or —°).
आस्थातृ m. charioteer, lit. standing on (the chariot).
आस्थान n. stand, station place, basis for operation; also = f. आस्थानी audience or assembly hall.
आस्थित a. standing or sitting on, dwelling in or at, entered or fallen into, arrived at (acc.); proceeded to, ready for (acc. or —°); occurred, happened; damaged, sore, ill; (pass.) entered, occupied, resorted to, undertaken, begun.
आस्पद n. place, seat, station, abode; object for (—°). °दी भू become an object of (—°).
आस्पात्र n. mouth, i.e. drink-vessel.
आस्फालन n. striking on, friction.
आस्फोट m., °न n. moving to and fro, shaking, waving.
आस्य n. mouth, face.
आस्यगर्त m. the mouth-cavity.
आस्या f. sitting.
आस्यूत a. sewn together out of (instr.).
आस्रस्त a. fallen off.
आस्राव m. flowing out, efflux, suppuration, diarrhoea, i.g. disease, bodily pain.
आस्वाद m. tasting, taste (also °न n.).
आस्वादवन्त् a. tasting well, delicious.
आस्वाद्य a. to be tasted; also = prec.; abstr. °त्व n.
आहत a. beaten, struck, hurt, wounded, damaged, injured.
आहति f. blow, hit.
आहनन n. striking, beating, killing.
आहनस् a. luxuriant, lascivious; abstr. °स्य n.
आहरण n. seizing, fetching, bringing, offering, removing.
आहर्तृ the same as adj.
आहव m. challenge, war, fight.
आहवन n. offering, sacrifice.
आहवनीय (± अग्नि) m. sacrificial fire, esp. the eastern of the three s. fires.

आहवनीयागारं a. house or place for the Â.-fire (v. prec.).
आहार, f. ई fetching, procuring, going to fetch (—°); m. taking, seizing, employing; eating, food.
आहारदान n. giving food, feeding.
आहारार्थिन् a. seeking food, hungry.
आहिण्डक m. traveller,* also = seq.
आहिण्डिक m. a cert. mixed caste.
आंहित a. put on (esp. of wood put on fire), placed, deposited, pledged, performed, done; being in, resting on (—°).
आंहिताग्नि m. = अग्न्याहित.
आंहिति f. laying on or what is laid on.
आहिर्बुन्ध & °ध्न्य m. n. E. of a lunar mansion.
आहोन्त m. a man's name.*
आंहुत a. sacrificed or worshipped with sacrifices, put into the fire.
आंहुति f. offering, oblation; p. °मन्त् † & °वन्त्.
आहुती कृ offer as a sacrifice.
आहूं f. invocation.
आहूत a. called, invoked, invited, summoned, challenged.
आहूतप्रपलायिन् m. who absconds when summoned.
आहूति f. = आहूं.
आंहो (indecl.) or; w. स्विद् or perhaps.
आह्निक a. daily, diurnal.
आह्लादं m. refreshment, delight.
आह्लादक a. refreshing, delighting.
आह्लादकर, °कारिन्, & आह्लादिन् a. the same.
आह्वय m. betting; also = seq.
आह्वयन n., आह्वा f. appellation, name.
आह्वान n. calling, invitation, legal summons.
आह्वानय्, °यति summon (j.).

इ

1इ pron. stem of 3^d pers.
2इ, एंति, अंयते, °ति (इंयति), इतें & इयते (only —°), P. ईयते, pp. इतं (mostly —°) go, come (पुनर् again or back); go to or towards, approach (acc.); attain, get; go or come from (abl.); cease, pass away; go on, continue (w. pres. pp.); be engaged in (instr.); w. acc. of an abstr. often = become or get w. a pp. or adj. (cf. गम्); ईंयते, pp. ईयानं (also w. pass. mg), 1. pl. ईमहे move, speed, hasten to (acc., dat. or loc.), approach with prayers, implore, ask, request (w. 2 acc.). — अच्छ go to, approach (acc.). अति go beyond or past; go in, enter; overstep, exceed, overwhelm; leave behind, neglect, escape. अभ्यति go beyond, pass, neglect. व्यति = अभ्यति + overcome, vanquish; cease, deviate, decline from (abl.). अधि perceive, notice, call to mind; repeat, study, learn, recite (esp. M. अधीतें). C. अध्यापयति (°ते) cause to learn, teach (2 acc.). समधि M. study, learn. अनु go along or after, follow, pursue; obey, resemble, imitate (acc.). अन्तर् go within or between; remove, exclude from (abl., r. gen.). अप go away, retire, escape, disappear. व्यप go asunder, part; cease, disappear. अपि enter, dissolve into (acc.); perish, die. अभि come up to, approach, appear; go against or along, enter (acc.); reach, meet, attain, get; betide, befall. अव go down, descend; go to, rush on (acc.); go off, depart; look at, consider, perceive, notice; learn, understand; know that — (2 acc. or acc. & nom. w. इति); w. ईमहे conciliate, beg pardon of (gen.), for (acc.). समव meet in (acc.); consider, regard as (acc. w. इव). आ come, go to (acc. or dat.), fall or get into (acc.); befall, betide; w. ऊर्ध्वम् rise. अभ्या approach, come or go to (acc.), meet with (acc. or instr.); w. भूयस् come back. उदा go up, rise; go out, come forth. उपा come near, approach, betake one's self to or into (acc.), ask or beg for (2 acc.). पर्या walk about, circumambulate (acc.), return. प्रत्या return, come back to (acc.). समा approach together, gather, assemble

at or in (acc. or loc.); meet, encounter (instr. ± समम्); marry (instr.); come near, go to, enter (acc.). उद् go up, rise, mount, increase; spring forth, appear, begin. अपोद् retire, withdraw, abstain from (abl.). अभ्युद् rise, come forth, appear. समुद् rise. उप come near, arrive, enter from (abl.) into (acc.), address one's self to (acc.), approach sex., marry; attain, get, meet with (acc. of an abstr., cf. S.); befall, betide. अभ्युप arrive at, come to, meet, encounter; attain, get undergo, incur (w. acc. of an abstr. = उप); suppose, believe, assent. समुप come together, meet, encounter, approach sex., turn or address one's self to; attain, get; come forth, appear; befall, betide. नि go or fall into (acc.). निस् come forth. परा go away, depart, die. परि walk about, circumambulate, surround; come to, attain, get. विपरि turn about, return; fail. संपरि circumambulate, enclose; ponder on, consider. प्र go onward, set out, advance proceed; go to, attain, get; go on, succeed, prosper; go off, depart, die. अनुप्र go after, seek for, follow. अभिप्र come near, go to, fall to one's (acc.) share; call to mind, think of, understand, consent to (acc.). संप्र come together, meet. प्रति go towards or against, meet, encounter; come near or back; address one's self to (acc.); fall to one's (dat.) share; accept, assume, admit, acknowledge, approve, believe, become or be sure of, trust, confide. P. प्रतीयते be understood, result from, follow. C. प्रत्याययति make understood, show, explain, prove, convince. वि go asunder, disperse, spread over, pervade; cease, disappear, perish. अभिवि come from different parts to (acc.). सम् come together, assemble, meet, encounter, approach sex. (acc. or सार्धम्, सह w. instr.), agree, harmonize with (instr.). अनुसम् = seq. + pass into, enter (acc.). अभिसम् & उपसम् go or come (together) to (acc.). — Cf. अतीत, अधीत, अन्तरित, अन्वित, 1अपीत, अपेत, अभिप्रेत, अभ्यतीत, अभ्युपेत, उदित, उदेतोस्, उपेत, परीत, परेत, प्रतीत, प्राधीत, प्रेत, प्रेत्य, विपरीत, वीत, व्यतीत, व्यपेत, समन्वित, समवेत, संमित, समुपेत, समेत.

इकार m. the sound or letter इ.

इक्षु m. sugar-cane; °मती† f. N. of a river.

इक्ष्वाकु m. N. of a king & his descendants.

इङ्ग्, इङ्गति, °ते stir, move (intr.). — C. इङ्गयति stir, move (tr.); shake, agitate. उद् & सम् C. = S. C.

इङ्ग a. movable.

इङ्गन n. shaking.

इङ्गिड m. N. of a plant.

इङ्गित n. gesture, intention.

इङ्गुद m., ई f. the Inguda tree; n. its nut.

इच्छा f. wish, desire; °— & instr. according to one's wish, voluntarily, intentionally.

इच्छाशक्तिमन्त् a. possessed with the faculty of desire.

इच्छु a. desirous of, willing to (acc., inf., or —°).

इज्य a. to be honoured or worshipped. m. a teacher or a god, esp. Bṛhaspati, the teacher of the gods. f. आ offering, sacrifice.

इट m. cane, grass; also = इटसून n. a mat.

इड् f. refreshing draught; libation; prayer; इडस्पति m. lord of libation, E. of gods.

इड m. E. of Agni; N. of a king.

इडा, इळा, इला f. = इड् + speech, earth, cow; N. of a goddess (personif. of worship and sacrifice), a daughter of Manu or Daksha, E. of Durgā.

इडावन्त् a. refreshing or refreshed.

इण्ड्व n. du. the two hand-plates (r.).

इत n. going, way.

इतर (n. °रम् or °रद्) a. other, different from (abl. or —°); usual, common. इतर–इतर the one — the other. Obs. also द्विजेतर not a Brahman; सुखेतर n. pl. joy and woe; दक्षिणेतर left.

इतरतस् adv. otherwise, elsewhere.

इतरत्र adv. the same, also = loc. of इतर.

इतरथा adv. otherwise, else.

इतरेतर (only °—, n., & in the obl. cases of sgl.) each other, mutual(ly), several(ly).

इतरेतरकाम्या f. mutual inclination.

इतरेतरानुराग m. mutual affection.

इतस् adv. hence, from here (also **इत ऊर्ध्वम्**); from this time, from now, henceforward (also **इतो ऽपरम्**, **इतः परम्**, and **इतः प्रभृति**); here, hither. **इत इतः** hither, hither! **इतः — इतः** here — there; **इतस्ततः** here and there, hither and thither, to and fro. **इतः पूर्वम्** formerly. — Also = abl. or loc. of 1**इ**.

1**इति** adv. thus, so. It refers to something said or thought, which it follows (rarely precedes), and is often = with these words, here endeth (cf. **अथ**), at this thought, as you know etc.; often not to be transl. at all. A nom. before **इति** may have the mg. of an acc. **इतीति**, **इतीव**, **इत्युत**, **इत्येव**, **इत्येवम्**, **इति ह स्म**, & **इति स्म ह** = **इति** alone. **इति तावत्** as much as, the same as (—°). **इति कृत्वा** for this reason. **किमिति** wherefore, why? or = **इति किम्**.

2**इति** or **इति** f. going, pursuing.

इतिकर्तव्य, **°कार्य** & **°कृत्य** a. fit or proper to be done, necessary; abstr. **°कर्तव्यता** etc. necessity, obligation.

इतिथ, f. **ई** such and such.

इतिवत् adv. just so.

इतिवृत्त n. occurrence, event.

इतिहास m. story, legend, tradition.

इतोगत a. relating to this (lit. gone hither).*

इतोमुख a. hither-faced; n. adv. hitherwards.*

इत्थंविध a. so qualified, such.

इत्थंगत a. so circumstanced; loc. under these circumstances.*

इत्थम् adv. thus, in this way.

इत्थंभूत a. being thus, so qualified, of this kind.

इत्था adv. = **इत्थम्** + right, well, really, truly, indeed, even; o. only emphasizing.

इत्यर्थम् adv. for this purpose.

इत्या f. course, way.

इत्यादि & **इत्येवमादि** adj. beginning thus; n. —and so on.

इत्वन् a. (only —°) going, moving.

इत्वर a. the same; low, mean.

इद् (indecl., orig. n. of 1. **इ**) just, exactly, even (lays stress on the prec. word).

इदंरूप a. thus shaped.

इदम् (n. sgl. & °— as stem) this, this here (refers to something following, rarely preceding); this all or this universe (± **विश्वम्**, **सर्वम्**, or **सकलम्**). Obs. also **तदिदम्** even this, this very thing, **किमिदम्** what here? As adv. here; now, thus, even, right. **इदमिदम्** here and there, now and then.

इदा adv. now, this moment; w. **अह्नस्** this very day; w. **ह्यस्** only yesterday.

इदानीम् adv. = prec. (also w. **अह्नस्**); **इदानीमेव** immediately, just; **इदानीमपि** even now, still.

इध् or **इन्ध्**, **इन्द्धे**, pp. **इद्ध** kindle, set on fire, inflame; P. **इध्यते** be lighted. flame. **अनु** kindle. **अभि** surround with flames, set on fire. **आ** kindle, burn (tr. & intr.). **परि** kindle on all sides. **सम्** kindle, burn (tr. & intr.); inflame, rouse, strengthen. — Cf. **प्रेद्ध**.

इध्म (& **इध्मन्**) m. fuel, esp. for the sacred fire, p. **°वन्त्**.

इन a. strong, mighty, fierce; m. a great lord or king, the sun.

इनच्, **इनचति** strive to get. — **उद्** & **सम्** the same.

इन्दीवर m. n. the blue lotus; m. a bee.

इन्दु m. a drop, esp. of Soma; the drop or spark in the sky, i. e. the moon.

इन्दुबिम्ब n. the orb of the moon.

इन्दुमुख (f. **ई**) & **°वदन** a. moon-faced.

इन्दुशेखर m. E. of Çiva (lit. moon-crested).

इन्द्र m. N. of the national god of the Indo-Aryans; later also chief, first, the best of one's kind.

1**इन्द्रगोप** & **°पा** a. having Indra as guard.

2**इन्द्रगोप** & **°गोपक** m. the cochineal insect.

इन्द्रचाप m. Indra's bow, i.e. the rain-bow.

इन्द्रजाल n. Indra's net; a cert. mystic weapon; juggling, magic.

इन्द्रजालिक & **°जालिन्** m. juggler, prestigiator.

इन्द्रजित् m. Indra' conqueror, N. of Rāvaṇa's son etc.

इन्द्रजूत a. sped by Indra.
इन्द्रज्येष्ठ a. having Indra as chief.
इन्द्रतम (superl.) most Indra-like.
इन्द्रत्व n. Indra's might; kingship, sovereignty.
इन्द्रधनुस् n. = इन्द्रचाप.
इन्द्रनील m. sapphire.
इन्द्रपुत्र m. Indra's son*; f. आ I.'s mother (lit. having I. as son).
इन्द्रप्रस्थ n. N. of a town.
इन्द्रमद m. a. cert. disease of leeches.
इन्द्रमह m. Indra's feast; *°कामुक m. dog (lit. fond of Indra's feast).*
इन्द्रय्, °यते long for Indra; a. °यु.
इन्द्रलोक m. Indra's world, heaven.
इन्द्रवंशा f. N. of a metre.
इन्द्रवज्र n. Indra's thunderbolt; f. आ N. of a metre.
इन्द्रवन्त् a. joined with Indra; I.'s comrade.
इन्द्रवह (°वाह्) a. carrying Indra.
1इन्द्रशत्रु m. Indra's conqueror.
1इन्द्रशत्रु a. having Indra as conqueror.
इन्द्रसख or °सखि a. having Indra as friend.
इन्द्रसेन m. a man's name.
इन्द्रसेना f. Indra's weapon, personif. as his bride; a woman's name.
इन्द्राग्नि m. du. Indra and Agni.
इन्द्राणी f. N. of Indra's wife.
इन्द्राबृहस्पति m. du. Indra and Bṛhaspati.
†इन्द्राब्रह्मणस्पति m. du. Indra and Brahmaṇaspati.
†इन्द्रामरुत् m. pl. Indra and the Maruts.
इन्द्रायुध n. Indra's weapon or bow, the rainbow; f. आ a kind of leech.
इन्द्रावरुण m. du. Indra and Varuṇa.
इन्द्राविष्णु m. du. Indra and Viṣṇu.
इन्द्रासोम m. du. Indra and Soma.
इन्द्रिय a. belonging or agreeable to Indra. m. a friend of Indra. — n. Indra's chief quality i. e. strength, might; used also of man's powers, esp. a sense or organ of sense, also the virile power, concr. semen.
इन्द्रियनिग्रह m. restraint of the organs of sense.
इन्द्रियवन्त् (superl. °यवत्तम) a. powerful, vigorous.
इन्द्रियशक्ति f. power of the organs of sense.
इन्द्रियार्थ m. object of the senses, sensual pleasure.
इन्द्रियावन्त् & °याविन् a. = इन्द्रियवन्त्.
इन्द्रियासङ्ग m. non-attachment to sensual objects.
इन्द्रेषित a. sent or impelled by Indra.
इन्ध a. kindling.
इन्धन n. kindling, lighting; fuel, wood, p. °वन्त्.
इन्धन्वन् a. flaming.
इन्व् (इनु, इन्), इन्वति, इनोति send forth, press on, set in motion, give out, utter; further, favour; possess, dispose of (acc.); force, overwhelm, remove, destroy. — अव send down. आ send hither, procure. प्र stir up, raise. प्रति further, speed. वि push off, remove; send forth, spend. सम् impart, restore. — Cf. उपेनित.
इभ m. n. household, family; m. elephant.
*इभदन्ता f. N. of a plant.
इभ्य a. belonging to one's household; m. vassal, rich man.
इम् interj.
इम (pron. stem in some obl. cases) this.
इमथा adv. in this manner.
इयक्ष्, इयक्षति, pp. इयक्षन्त् & इयक्षमाण pray, ask, long for (w. acc. of th. & gen. or acc. of pers.). अभि and प्र strive after, wish or long for (acc.).
इयक्षु a. longing, eager.
इयच्चिरम् adv. so long, till now.
इयत्तक (f. °त्तिका) so small, so little.
इयत्ता f. quantity, number. measure, distance.
इयन्त् a. so large, so much; so small, so little.
इयम् f. this (here), this earth (± पृथिवी).
इयसा f. shrinking, lassitude.
इयस्य्, °स्यते shrink, relax, dwindle; pp. इयसित, as n. = इयसा.
इरज्य्, °ज्यति, °ते direct, lead; dispose of, command over (gen.).
इरज्यु a. preparing (the sacrifice).
इरध्, °धते strive to gain; dat. inf. इरध्यै.
इरस्य्, °स्यति be angry or envious (w. dat.). — अभि the same.
इरस्या f. ill-will, anger.
इरा or इरा f. drink, refreshing draught; comfort, enjoyment.

इरावन्त् a. giving refreshment, gladdening; °वती† f. N. of a river and sev. mythol. women.

इरिण n. water-course, rivulet; a hollow or hole, desert land; gaming board.

इरिणस्थ a. standing on barren soil.

इरिन् a. strong, mighty; m. a despot.

इर्य a. active, vigorous, powerful.

इल् (इलति come), इलयति be quiet, not budge.

इलव m. ploughman, peasant.

इव (encl.) like, as, as it were, so to speak, almost, nearly, about; just, quite, even (o. only explet.).

1इष्, इषति, एषति (—°), इष्यति, इष्णाति (also M.), pp. इषित send, impel, hurl, throw, raise (the voice), utter, proclaim; incite, promote, further; intr. advance, strive; tend towards, aim at (dat. or loc.). — अनु follow, seek, look for (acc.). प्र A. & M. drive forth, send out; call upon, summon, invite. C. प्रेषयति, °ते hurl, cast, send out, dismiss. अनुप्र C. send forth after. संप्र summon, invite; send forth, dismiss.

2इष्, इच्छति, °ते, pp. इष्ट (q.v.) seek, desire, like, choose; acknowledge, state, take for (2 acc.); wish that (acc. & inf. or 2 acc.); ask a thing (acc.) of some one (abl. or loc.); intend, be about or going to (inf.); w. न disagree, decline, refuse to (inf.), object to (acc.). P. इष्यते be liked, wanted, approved, recognised; pass for (nom.). — अनु seek, search, try, strive after, wish for. C. अन्वेषयति seek, wait for (acc.). पर्यनु seek about. समनु search. अभि seek for, strive after, exert one's self at (acc.); intend to (inf.). परि look about for (acc.). प्रति strive towards, seek after (acc.), receive, accept from (gen.); attend to, observe. वि seek. — Cf. अभीष्ट.

3इष् f. drink, refreshment, vigour, strength; w. ऊर्ज् drink and food.

1†इष (—°) a. seeking.

2इष a. vigorous, strong, fat, juicy, fruitful.

इषण्य्, °यते, & इषण्य्, °ण्यति impel, stir up.

इषण्या f. stir, impulse.

इषय्, इषयति, °ते intr. be fresh, active, quick; tr. refresh, strengthen.

इषयु & इषवन्त् a. fresh, vigorous.

इषि f. refreshing (dat. as inf.).

इषिध् f. offering, gift.

इषिर a. refreshing, enlivening; fresh, strong, quick.

इषीका f. reed, stem of grass, arrow.

इषु m. f. arrow; poss. इषुमन्त् (इषुमन्त्).

इषुधि m. quiver (arrow-receptacle).

इषुधिमन्त् a. poss. to prec.

इषुध्य्, °ध्यति implore (acc.); beg for (dat.).

इषुध्या f. imploring, request.

इषुध्यु a. imploring, desirous.

†इषूय्, °यति strive, endeavour.

इष्कर्तृ m. arranger, disposer.

इष्कृत a. arranged, prepared.

इष्कृति f. arrangement, putting right.

1इष्ट a. sought, wished for, desired, liked, pleasant, dear; auspicious, happy; approved, settled, valid. m. favourite, lover, husband; n. wish, desire.

2इष्ट a. sacrificed; m. n. sacrifice.

इष्टका f. brick.

इष्टकामदुह् f. (nom. धुक्) the fabulous wonder-cow granting (all) desires.

इष्टजन m. the beloved person (man or woman).

इष्टनि a. rustling, rushing.

इष्टव्रत a. obtaining a wish.

इष्टसाधन a. fulfilling one's wish.

इष्टापूर्त n. sgl. & du. & इष्टापूर्ति f. sacrifice and charity; poss. °र्तिन्.

1इष्टि f. impulse, furtherance, aid (abstr. & concr.).

2इष्टि f. seeking, request, wish, desire.

3इष्टि f. sacrifice (mostly of a simpler kind).

इष्मिन् a. impetuous, rash.

इष्वसन & इष्वस्त्र n. a bow (arrow-thrower).

इष्वस्त्रकर्मन् n. the practice of archery.

इष्वास m. archer or bow (lit. = इष्वसन).

इस् (= निस्) v. 1कृ.

इह adv. here, hither; here in this world, in

this case, in this system or book, etc.; now, this moment. Also = loc. of 1अ. — इहेह here and there, hence and thence, now and then.

इहलोक m. the world here (below).

इहस्थ a. standing or staying here.

इहार्थ a. useful here (for this world).

इहार्थिन् a. busy here (for this world).

ई

ईक्ष्, ईक्षते (°ति), pp. ईक्षित (q.v.) look, view, behold, perceive, see (l. & f.), consider, regard, expect; *tell fortune to (dat.). C. ईक्षयति cause to look at (acc.). – अप look away, look off to, watch, regard, consider, wait for, expect, require. अभि look at (acc.). अव look at, view, consider, regard, expect, hope. अन्वव regard, consider. प्रत्यव look at, inspect, examine. समव view, regard, consider. उद् look up to, gaze at (acc.), wait, expect. समुद् look up to, gaze at, behold, perceive; think of, consider (acc.). उप look on, behold, observe; overlook, neglect. समुप the same. निस् look at, perceive, contemplate. परि look round, investigate, scrutinize, examine. प्र look at, behold, perceive; overlook, neglect. अभिप्र view, regard. उत्प्र look up to (acc.), regard as (2 acc.), suppose, imagine; transfer, use or call metaphorically (rh.). उपप्र A. disregard, overlook. अभिसंप्र look at (acc.). प्रति look towards, behold, observe; wait, expect; bear with, tolerate (acc.). संप्रति wait, expect. वि regard, behold, deliberate, ponder, consider as (वत्); inquire, perceive, discern. अनुवि look about, behold; examine, try. अभिवि & समभिवि regard, behold, perceive, observe. उद्वि look (up) to, perceive, observe, investigate. सम् look upon, behold, observe, consider; think of, aim at (acc.); try, examine, find out, ascertain. अभिसम् & प्रसम् behold, regard, consider.

ईक्ष, f. ई looking, seeing (—°); f. आ view, consideration.

ईक्षक m. spectator, beholder.

ईक्षण n. look, view, aspect, eye; looking after, caring for (gen.).

ईक्षणपथ m. path of the eyes, horizon.

ईक्षणिक or °णीक m. seer, soothsayer.

ईक्षित a. seen, beheld; n. view, aspect.

ईक्षितृ a. seeing, a beholder of (gen.).

ईक्षेण्य a. worth seeing.

ईङ्ख्, ईङ्खति; C. ईङ्खयति swing, shake. — प्र tremble, shake. C. swing (tr.); M. swing (intr.).

ईङ्खन n. swinging.

ईज्, ईजते, अप drive away. — सम् drive together.

1**ईड्**, ईट्टे, pp. ईळित praise, implore, beg for (acc., gen., or dat.). — प्र, उपप्र, प्रति, सम्, & प्रसम् praise, honour, worship.

2**ईड्** f. praise, veneration.

ईडितृ or **ईळितृ** m. adorer, worshipper.

ईडेन्य or **ईळेन्य** a. to be asked for (dat.); also = seq.

ईड्य a. praiseworthy, venerable.

ईति f. plague, distress.

ईदृक्ष, f. आ, ईदृश् & ईदृश, f. ई of this kind, such like. ईदृश तादृश such and such.*

ईप्स्, ईप्सति & °ते, pp. ईप्सित (q.v.) wish to obtain, desire, long for (acc.). — अभि, परि, & प्र the same.

ईप्सा f. wish, desire.

ईप्सित a. wished, desired; n. = prec.

ईप्सु a. striving to obtain, desirous of (acc., inf., or —°).

ईम् (encl.) used as acc. sg. of 1इ, makes a rel. indef. — य ईम् whoever, after other pron. or conj. emphasizing or only explet.

ईर्, ईर्ते, pp. ईर्ण tr. set in motion, impel, further; intr. stir, move, rise. C. ईरयति, °ते, pp. ईरित = S. tr.; also bring forth, raise (the voice), utter, proclaim, cite; P. be raised, uttered, called. — आ (also C.) procure, get, obtain, raise, utter. न्या

appoint as (2 acc.). उद्द् tr. cause to rise, draw out of (abl.); intr. stir. move, rise. C. = उद्द् tr., also throw, hurl, shoot (lit. & fig.), raise, utter, speak; show, betray; further, strengthen, elevate; rouse up, impel, excite. P. be hurled, raised, excited; be proclaimed or taught, pass for (nom.). अभ्युद्द् C. simpel, further, excite; utter, speak. समुद्द् C. drive out, hurl, cast, raise, utter, proclaim (pp. समुदीरित). प्र stir, move, come forth; rise, sound. C. drive on, send forth; push on, press urge; turn, direct; emit, utter, pronounce. — वि (also C.) split, divide. सम् put together, shape, create, produce. C. the same, also rouse up, impel, revive, instruct with (instr.). — Cf. उदीर्ण, समुदीर्ण.

ईर m. wind.

ईरण a. driving, agitating; m. = prec., n. pressing, sqeezing, uttering.

ईरपाद् m. snake (lit. wind-foot).

ईरिण n. salt and barren soil.

ईरिणस्थ = ईरिणस्थ.

ईर्म m. arm, the fore-quarter of an animal.

ईर्मा (ईर्म) adv. here, on the spot.

ईर्य a. to be stirred or impelled.

ईर्ष्य्, ईर्ष्यति be jealous or envious.

ईर्ष्या f. envy, jealousy.

ईर्ष्यालु, ईर्ष्यावन्त्, & ईर्ष्यु a. envious, jealous.

ईलय्, ईलयति move (tr. & intr.).

ईवन्त् a. so large, so great, so much.

1ईश्, ईष्टे (ईशे) be master, own, possess, reign, rule (gen. or acc.); dispose of, claim at (gen.); have power or be able to (inf. in तुम् or तोस्, loc., or acc.). — Cf. ईशान.

2ईश् m. lord, master, Çiva.

ईश, f. आ owner, disposer of (gen.), able to (inf.). m. lord, sovereign, chief of (gen. or —°); N. of Çiva, Kubera, & Rudra. f. आ = seq.

ईशान n. power, dominion.

ईशान or ईशान a. owning, disposing of (gen. or acc.), able; m. ruler, sovereign; E. of Çiva & other gods. f. ईशाना E. of Durgā.

ईशानकृत् a. acting as a lord.

ईशिता f., °त्व n. omnipotence.

ईशितृ m. lord, master.

ईशिन् m. ruler of (—°); °नी f. supremacy.

ईशोपनिषद् f. N. of an Upanishad.

ईश्वर a. powerful, supreme; able or liable to, capable of (loc. or inf., esp. in तोस्, then often w. nom. sg. m. ईश्वर for all genders & numbers). — m. owner of (gen., loc., or —°); ruler, king, lord, a rich man, husband; E. of Brahman, Çiva, & other gods. f. ईश्वरी mistress, queen.

ईश्वरता f., °त्व n. supremacy, sovereignty.

ईश्वरप्रणिधान n. subjection to the will of god.

ईश्वरभाव m. royalstate, sovereignty.

ईष्, ईषति & °ते move, hasten, flee, retire, deviate from (abl.); leave, abandon (acc.); ईषन्त् assaulting, hurting. — अप withdraw from (abl.). आ (mostly M.) hasten towards; approach with prayers, beseech, assail, attack; strive after, covet. वि stretch (intr.). — Cf. उदीषित, समीषित.

ईषत् adv. nearly, slightly, easily, a little.

ईषत्कर a. easy to be done.

*ईषत्पान a. easy to be drunk.

ईषा f. the pole of a carriage; du. the double or fork-shaped pole, the thills.

ईषीका f. = इषीका.

ईह्, ईहते (°ति), pp. ईहित (q.v.) be eager endeavour, strive after, wish for (acc.); have a mind or intend to (inf.). सम् = S. — Cf. समीहित.

ईह m. attempt, endeavour.

ईहा f. the same + effort, exertion, labour; wish, desire. ईहातस् by labour or exertion.

ईहावन्त् a. zealous, brave, valiant.

ईहित a. wished for, striven after; destined for (loc.); n. = ईहा.

उ

1उ interj.

2उ, ऊ (encl.) and, also, yet, now, soon, again; lays stress on a prec. pron., particle or infin. in तवै (तवा उ); उ षु (= सु) right soon, मो (= माउ) षु never. उ—उ (or उत) on the one hand—on the other hand, as well—as.

3उ, उनोति proclaim.

उकार m. the sound उ.

उक्त a. spoken, said, mentioned, stated, taught (n. impers. w. instr. of pers.); declared as, meant by (instr.); spoken to, addressed, told something (acc.) by (instr.), summoned, called by (—°). n. word, term.

उक्तपूर्व a. said or told before.

उक्तप्रत्युक्त n. speech and reply, conversation.

उक्तमात्र a. just spoken.

उक्तवाक्य a. who has said his say.

†उक्ति f. expression, saying, speech, word, term.

उक्थ n. saying, praise, verse; a cert. recitation (r.).

उक्थिन् a. praising or accompanied by praise.

उक्थ्य a. praiseworthy, also = prec.; m. a cert. libation.

1उच्, उक्षति, °ते, pp. उक्षित sprinkle, besprinkle; drip, drop (M. intr.). — अनु, अभि, अव, आ besprinkle. परि sprinkle round. प्र sprinkle before one's self, consecrate, sacrifice, kill. संप्र besprinkle, M. refl. वि shed, M. besprinkle. सम् besprinkle (l. & f.), pour out.

2उच्, उक्षति, pp. उक्षित grow up, get strong. C. उक्षयते strengthen. — सम् grow up or get strong together.

उक्षण n. sprinkling, consecration.

उक्षण्य्, °ण्यति wish for bulls, a. °ण्यु.

उक्षन् m. bull, ox.

उखा m. pot, boiler (also आ f.); a cert. part of the upper portion of the thigh (v.seq.).

उखच्छिद् a. who has broken the hip.

उख्य a. being in a pot.

उग्र a. mighty, strong, huge, fierce, dire. m. a mighty one, a despot, tyrant, N. of a caste; E. of Çiva or Rudra. f. उग्री a cert. female demon.

उग्रकर्मन् a. performing fierce acts, cruel.

उग्रता f., °त्व n. vehemence, rigour, cruelty.

उग्रपूति a. giving forth a strong stench.

उग्रप्रभाव a. having strong power.

उग्रबाहु a. having strong arms.

उग्ररूप a. of awful appearance.

उग्रशासन a. bearing terrible sway.

उग्रसेन m. N. of sev. princes.

उग्रातप a. dreadfully hot.

उग्रान्न n. food of an Ugra

उच्, उच्यति, pp. उचित (q.v.) be pleased or wont, like. — नि delight in (acc. or loc.). सम् be fond of (instr.). — Cf. समुचित.

उचथ n. verse, praise.

उचथ्य a. praiseworthy.

उचित a. pleased with, wont to (gen., loc., or —°), obliged to (infin.); customary, usual, proper, suitable. Abstr. °त्व† n.

उच्च a. lofty, high (l. & f.) loud; abstr. °ता f., °त्व n. — Cf. उच्चा & उच्चैस्.

उच्चण्ड a. most violent, terrible.

उच्चय m. gathering, picking up; collection, heap, plenty, multitude.

उच्चसंश्रय a. standing above (star).

उच्चा adv. high (esp. in heaven), from above, upwards.

उच्चार a. getting up, rising. m. discharge, excrement, also = seq.

उच्चारण n. utterance, pronunciation.

उच्चावच a. high and low, great and small, various.

उच्चासन n. an elevaled seat.

उच्चित्र a. ornamented.

उच्चैःकुल n. a high family.

उच्चैःपद n. high stand-point.

उच्चैर्घोष a. sounding loud.

उच्चैर्धामन् a. shining above.

उच्चैर्भुज a. with uplifted arms.

उच्चैःशिरस् a. of high rank (lit. carrying the head high).
उच्चैःश्रवस् m. N. of a myth. horse.
उच्चैस् (instr. adv.) above, high, loud; intensely, very much. Often used as an adj., esp. °—. **उच्चैर्भू** rise, get up.
उच्चैस्तर (compar.) higher, very high; **°राम्** adv.
1**उच्चैःस्थान** n. a high place.
2**उच्चैःस्थान** a. of high rank.
उच्छलन्त् & **°लित** a. leaping or leapt up; rising or risen.
उच्छास्त्रवर्तिन् a. transgressing the law.
उच्छिख a. with erected crest or point.
उच्छिखण्ड a. with erected tail (peacock).
उच्छित्ति f. extirpation, destruction.
उच्छिन्न a. cut off, lost, abject, vile.
उच्छिरस् a. carrying the head high.
उच्छिलींध्र a. covered with sprouted (lit. erected) mushrooms.
उच्छिष्ट a. left, rejected, impure (pers. & th.). n. leavings, esp. of the sacrificial food; abstr. **°ता†** f.
उच्छिष्टभोजिन् a. eater of leavings.
उच्छीर्षक a. having the head raised; n. pillow.
उच्छुष्क a. dried up, withered.
उच्छून a. swollen, turgid, increased.
उच्छृङ्खल a. unchained, unrestrained.
उच्छेत्तृ m. extirpator, destroyer.
उच्छेद m., **°न** n. = **उच्छित्ति**.
उच्छेदनीय a. to be cut off.
उच्छेदिन् a. destroying (—°).
उच्छेष m., **उच्छेषण** n. rest, remainder.
उच्छोथ m. swelling, inflation.
उच्छोषण a. drying, burning; n. subst.
उच्छ्रय m., **°ण** n., **उच्छ्राय** m. rising, increase, elevation.
उच्छ्रित a. lifted, raised, high, haughty; proud of (—°); increased, grown, enormous.
उच्छ्रिति f. = **उच्छ्रय** etc.
उच्छ्वसन n. getting loose (girdle).
उच्छ्वसित a. calmed (also **उच्छ्वस्त**), refreshed, lifted, opened, loosed; n. breathing, breath; also = prec.
उच्छ्वास m. = prec. n. + exhaling, expiring, draught (in drinking); sigh, death.
उच्छ्वासिन् a. breathing, expiring, sighing; rising.
उज्जयिनी f. N. of a city.
उज्जिति f. victory.
उज्जिहानजीवित a. whose life is going out.
उज्जृम्भ a. gaping.
उज्जृम्भण a. gaping, expansion.
उज्जृम्भित a. expanded, opened, blown.
उज्जेष a. victorious; m. victory.
उज्ज्य a. having the bow-sinew loosened.
उज्ज्वल a. flaming, beaming, beautiful.
उज्झ्, **उज्झति**, pp. **उज्झित** (q.v.) forsake, leave, give up, avoid, escape. — **प्र** and **सम्** = S.
उज्झ a. having left or forsaken (—°); abstr. **°ता** f.
उज्झटित a. confused, troubled.
उज्झित a. forsaken, left; destitute of, free from (instr. or —°).
उञ्छ्, **उञ्छति** glean, gather.
उञ्छ m., **°न** n. gleaning.
उञ्छवर्तिन् & **°वृत्ति** a. who lives by gleaning; m. a gleaner.
उञ्छशिल n. gleaning (cf. **शिलोञ्छ**).
उटज m. n. a hut made of leaves.
उट्टङ्कित a. stamped or marked with (—°).
उडु f. n. star, lunar mansion.
उडुप m. n. boat; m. = seq.
उडुपति m. the moon (lord of the stars).
उडुमर a. extraordinary, strange, intense.
उड्डयन n. flying up, flying.
उड्डामर a. = **उडुमर**.
उड्डीन & **उड्डीयन** n. = **उड्डयन**.
उणादि m. pl. a cert. class of suffixes.
उत (indecl.) and, also, even; **अप्युत** and also; **उत — उत** (also **उतो**) as well — as, both — and. As interr. particle or in the sec. part of a double interrogation, often w. **वा**, **आहो**, **स्विद्**, & **आहो स्विद्** or also, or even. — Cf. **उ** & **किम्**.
उतथ्य m. N. of a son of Aṅgiras.
उतथ्यतनय m. the son of Utathya, i.e. Gautama.
उताहो & **उतो** v. **उत**.
उतूल m. slave, servant; pl. N. of a people.

उत्क a. longing for, willing to (inf. or —°). n. & °ता f. longing, desire.
उत्कट a. exceedingly great, strong, intense, violent; abounding in, full of (—°); drunken, mad.
उत्कण्ठ्, °ण्ठते, pp. उत्कण्ठित (q.v.) lift the neck, long for (dat.). C. उत्कण्ठयति make a person (acc.) lift his neck; also = seq. — प्र C. excite longing in (acc.). सम् long for, regret, remember.
उत्कण्ठ a. having the neck uplifted, longing for, desirous; n. adv.
उत्कण्ठा f. longing, regret, sorrow.
उत्कण्ठाकारिन् a. causing regret.*
उत्कण्ठानिर्भरम् adv. sorrowfully.*
उत्कण्ठाभागिन् a. having sorrow as one's lot.*
उत्कण्ठित a. = उत्कण्ठ + enamoured.
उत्कम्प a. trembling; m. = seq.
उत्कम्पन & °म्पित n. trembling, agitation.
उत्कम्पिन् a. trembling, shaking (—°).
उत्कर m. what is dug up, rubbish; pile, heap, multitude.
उत्कर्ण a. having the ears erect.
उत्कर्ष a. haughty. m. elevation, increase, eminence, ascendency, superiority, excess, abundance.
उत्कर्षिन् a. superior, better.
उत्कलाप a. having the tail erect and expanded (of a peacock).
उत्कलिका f. longing, ardent desire.
उत्कलित a. let loose, opened, appeared, blown, blossoming, shining with (—°).
उत्कषण n. tearing up.
उत्किर a. piling up (—°).
उत्कीर्ण a. cut out, shaped, engraven.
उत्कुल a. degenerate (from one's race).
उत्कूर्दन n. jumping up.
उत्कृष्ट a. drawn out, lifted, raised, high, eminent by (—°); abstr. °त्व n.
उत्कृष्टवेदन n. marriage with a man of higher caste.
उत्कोच m. bribing, a bribe (lit. crookedness, crooked way).
उत्कोचक a. accessible to bribes (cf. prec.).
उत्क्रम m. going up or out.
उत्क्रमण n., उत्क्रान्ति f. = prec.
उत्कृष्ट v. बीजोत्कृष्ट.
उत्क्रोद m. exultation, a. °दिन्.
उत्क्षिप्ति f., उत्क्षेप m., °ण n. lifting up, raising.
उत्खचित a. mixed, interwoven with (instr. or —°).
उत्खण्डित a. broken, destroyed.*
उत्खात n. undermining, extirpation; uneven soil.
उत्खातिन् a. uneven (soil).
उत्तंस m. crown, wreath of flowers.
उत्तंसय्, °यति, pp. उत्तंसित crown, adorn with a wreath.
उत्तङ्क m. N. of a Rishi.
उत्तप्त a. heated, glowing, red-hot.
उत्तब्ध & उत्तभित a. erected, set up.
उत्तम (superl.) upmost, highest, first or best of (—°); chief, excellent; extreme, last; better than, superior to (abl.); m. the first person (g.).
उत्तमजन m. pl. excellent people.
उत्तमतेजस् a. having excellent splendour or power.
उत्तमपुरुष m. the first person (g.), also = seq.
उत्तमपूरुष m. the supreme spirit.
उत्तमर्ण & °र्णिक m. creditor.
उत्तमवर्ण a. of beautiful colour or high caste.
उत्तमविद् a. having the highest wisdom.
उत्तमसाहस m. the highest fine (j.).
उत्तमाङ्ग n. the head (lit. highest member).
उत्तमौजस् m. N. of a man (lit. of highest strength).
उत्तर (compar.) upper, higher; northern, left (opp. दक्षिण); later, following, subsequent, future, last; being above, victorious, superior, mightier, better. n. surface, cover (mostly adj. —° covered with); the north, hinder or last part, sequel, consequence (—° followed by); answer, reply; defence, rejoinder (j.); superiority, victory, power of (loc. of an abstr.); chief part or characteristic; excess, surplus (only adj. —°).
उत्तरकाल m. future time; a. future, imminent.
उत्तरकुरु m. pl. the northern Kurus.
उत्तरकोसल m. the northern Kosalas.

1उत्तरङ्ग m. a surging wave.
2उत्तरङ्ग a. surging, heaving.
उत्तरङ्गिन् a. = prec.*
उत्तरण a. crossing, passing, over; n. the same as subst., overcoming (—°).
उत्तरणसेतु m. bridge to pass over (gen.).*
उत्तरतस् adv. northward, from north, north or left of (gen.); further.
उत्तरदायक a. giving answer, contradicting.
उत्तरपक्ष m. the northern or left wing (side); reply to an objection, refutation (ph.).
उत्तरपद n. last member of a compound (g.).
उत्तरम् adv. further, later, hereafter.
उत्तरमीमांसा f. the latter part of the Mīmāṅsā, i.e. the Vedānta.
उत्तररामचरित & °त्र n. the further deeds of Rāma, T. of a drama.
उत्तरल a. starting up, trembling; den. °लाय्, °यते.
उत्तरवेदि or °दी f. the northern altar (r.).
उत्तरा adv. northward*; north of (gen. or (abl.).
उत्तरात् (abl. adv.) from the north or from the left.
उत्तराधर a. higher and lower; n. the upper and under lip, the lips.
उत्तरापथ m. the northern path, the north.
उत्तराम् adv. farther off.
उत्तरायण n. the northern progress (of the sun), the winter-solstice.
उत्तरारणि f. the upper Araṇi (v. अरणि).
उत्तरार्थ a. taking place for the sake of what follows.
उत्तरार्ध m. the upper part (esp. of the body); the northern part, the latter half.
उत्तरावन्त् a. superior, victorious.
उत्तरासङ्ग m., उत्तरीय n. upper or outer garment.
उत्तराहि adv. north (of— abl.*).
उत्तरेण (instr. adv.) in the north or in the left side (w. gen., abl., acc., or —°).
उत्तरेद्युस् adv. the next day.
उत्तरोत्तर a. following and following, later and later, higher and higher, more and more. °— & n. adv.; n. as subst. reply, talking, chattering.
उत्तरोत्तरोक्त a. always later mentioned.
उत्तरोष्ठ & °रौष्ठ m. upper lip.
उत्तान a. stretched out (lying); turned upwards, high, straight, upright; being on the surface, open, shallow.
उत्तानहृदय a. open-hearted.*
उत्तानी कृ open wide.
उत्तार m. crossing, passing over (—°); rescue, delivery.
उत्तारण a. saving (Çiva); n. bringing over (—°), delivering from (abl.).
उत्ताल a. vehement, violent; huge, dreadful; abundant, copious.
उत्तीर्ण a. (having) crossed or passed, saved or escaped from (abl. or —°); victorious, fortunate; learned, clever.
उत्तुङ्ग a. lofty, high.
उत्त्रस्त a. frightened.
उत्थ a. standing up, rising; coming from, consisting of, beginning with (—°).
उत्थान n. rising, coming forth, origin, setting out, starting, exertion, endeavour, energy (poss. °वन्त्†); leaving off, conclusion.
उत्थानवीर m. a man of energy or activity.
उत्थापन n. causing to rise, awakening, producing, bringing about, finishing.
उत्थायिन् a. getting up, rising, coming forth; active, energetic.
उत्थित a. risen, high, erect, upright, prominent; sprung or come from (abl. or —°); broken out (fire); occurred, appeared, manifest; come in (money); eager, ready or devoted to (loc. or dat.).
उत्पक्व a. over-ripe, swollen, turgid.
उत्पक्ष्मन् & °क्ष्मल a. upturned-eyelashed (eye).
उत्पतन, f. ई flying up; n. leaping high.
उत्पत्ति f. coming forth, origin, birth (p. °मन्त्); result, produce.
उत्पत्तिव्यञ्जक a. indicating a new birth.
उत्पथ m. wrong way (lit. & fig.).
उत्पन्न a. risen or come from (—°); born of (loc.), begot by (instr. or —°); happened, occurred, existing, present, ready.
उत्पन्नबुद्धि a. judicious, wise (lit. having a ready mind).
उत्पल n. the blue lotus.

उत्पलदृश् f. lotus-eyed.
उत्पलवन n. group of lotus-flowers.
उत्पलिन् a. abounding in lotus flowers; f. °**नी** = prec.
उत्पवन n. cleaning or any implement for cleaning.
उत्पवितृ m. purifier.
उत्पाटन n. pulling up, tearing out.
उत्पाटिन् (—°) the same as adj.
उत्पात m. flying up, jump; sudden and unusual event, portent, phenomenon.
उत्पाद m. coming forth, birth.
उत्पादक a. producing, causing, begetting; m. producer, begetter; abstr. °**त्व** n.
उत्पादन, f. **ई** = prec. adj.; n. as abstr.
उत्पादिन् a. bringing forth (—°); produced, born.
उत्पिष्ट a. crushed, trodden down.
उत्पीड m. pressing out, pressure; stream, flood; gash, wound.
उत्प्रबन्ध a. continual, uninterrupted.
उत्प्रास m., °**न** n. derision, irony.
उत्प्रेक्षण n. foresight; comparison, metaphor (rh.).
उत्प्रेक्षा f. disregard, indifference; also = prec. (rh.).
उत्प्रेक्षितोपमा f. a kind of comparison (rh.).
उत्फाल m. jump, bounding.
उत्फुल्ल a. blown (flower), opened; °**नयन** & °**लोचन** a. having wide opened eyes.
उत्स m. spring, fountain (lit. & fig.).
उत्सङ्ग m. lap, roof, surface; seat, bottom.
उत्सधि m. receptacle of a spring; well.
उत्सन्न a. prominent, projecting; ceased, vanished, lost.
उत्सर्ग m. pouring forth, emission, excretion; laying aside, taking off, loosening, delivering, abandoning, giving up, closing, completion (esp. of the study of the Veda); oblation, present.
उत्सर्जन n. letting loose, giving up, dismission, closing, completion (v. prec.).
उत्सर्पण n. rise (of the sun), coming forth.
उत्सर्पिन् a. leaping up, soaring, rising, appearing.
उत्सव m. enterprise, beginning; feast, joy.
उत्सवप्रिय a. fond of feasts.
उत्सादन n. putting off, interrupting, injuring, destroying; rubbing or chafing the limbs.
उत्साह m. strength, resolution, energy, exertion, endeavour, eagerness, inclination for, delight in (—°).
उत्साहकारण a. causing exertion, painful.*
उत्साहयितृ (°**तृक**) n. instigator.*
उत्साहयोग m. display of energy.
उत्सिक्त a. exuberant, abundant in, swelled by (instr. or —°); overstrained (lit. & fig.); extravagant, haughty, disordered (mind).
उत्सिक्तमनस् a. of disordered mind.
उत्सित a. fettered.
उत्सुक a. restless, uneasy, intent; regretful, sad, anxious about, longing or wishing for (loc., **प्रति**, or —°); *caring about (loc. or instr.). Abstr. °**ता** f.
उत्सुकय्, °**यति** make sad, afflict.
उत्सुकवदन a. having a sad face.*
उत्सृष्टि f. letting out, emission.
उत्सेक m. overflow, excess; extravagance, haughtiness; poss. °**किन्**.
उत्सेध m. eminence, height (lit. & fig.).
उत्स्फुर m. a jump.*
उत्स्वप्नाय्, °**यते** talk in sleep.
उत्स्रस्त a. loosened, fallen down (girdle).
1**उद्** (only °— in nouns and verbs) up, upwards, forth, out, beyond.
2**उद्**, **उन्द्**, **उनत्ति** & **उन्दति** (also M.), pp. **उत्त** & **उन्न** spring (water), bubble up, wet, bathe. — **अनु**, **अभि** & **उप** sprinkle, wet. **नि** immerse. **वि** spring or bubble forth, also = **सम्** sprinkle, wet.
उद (only °— and adj. —°) water.
उदक n. water. — **उदकं दा** or **प्रदा** offer a libation of water to a dead person (gen. or dat.); **उदकं कृ** the same, also = °**कमुपस्पृश्** touch cert. parts of the body with water (r.).
उदककर्मन् n. libation of water (v. prec.).
उदककार्य n. the same, + ablution of the body.
उदकक्रिया f., °**दान** n. = **उदककर्मन्**.
उदकदायिन् a. performing a libation of water.

उदकवन्त् a. furnished with water; f. उदकावती a woman's name.
उदकसेचन n. shower of rain.
उदकाञ्जलि m. a handful of water.
उदकान्त m. margin of water. आोदकान्तात् as far as the water's brink.
उदकार्णव m. the ocean of water.
उदकार्य m. ablution (lit. water-business); °म् to perform an ablution.
उदकुम्भ m. a water-jug; N. of a physician.
उदक्तस & उदक्तात् adv. from above or from the north.
उदक्य a. being in water; f. आ a woman in her courses.
उदगयन n. the (sun's) northern progress; the time from the winter to the summer solstice.
उदग्र a. having the top lifted, i.e. lofty, high, tall, long; increased, excited, roused by (—°); fierce, intense.
उदग्रप्लुत a. making lofty boundings; abstr. °त्व n.
उदङ्मुख a. turned (lit. having the mouth or front) upwards or to the north.
उदज n. lotus flower (water-born).
उदञ्च् (f. उदीची) turned upwards or to the north, northern; n. उदक् adv. northward.
उदञ्चन m. pail or bucket for drawing water out of a well.
उदञ्जलि a. hollowing and raising the palms (cf. अञ्जलि).
उदधि a. containing water. m. receptacle of water (cloud, lake, or river, in l. l. the sea).
उदधीय्, °यति take a thing (acc.) for the sea.
उदन् n. wave, water; p. उदनिमन्त्.
1उदन्त m. end of labour, harvest, feast, quiet; news, intelligence.
2उदन्त a. running over the brim; n. adv. to the end.
उदन्त्य a. living beyond a boundary.
उदन्य्, °न्यति, pp. °न्यन्त pour down on (loc.).
उदन्यु a. fluctuating, watery.
उदन्यु a. seeking water.
उदन्वन्त् a. = उदन्यु; m. the sea.
उदपात्र n. water-jug, ewer.
उदपान m. n. well, cistern.
उदप्लुत् a. swimming in water, splashing.
उदबिन्दु m. a drop of water.
उदमय a. consisting of water.
उदय m. going up, rising (also = seq.); coming forth, appearance, manifestation, origin; result, issue, consequence; success, advantage; income, revenue, interest.
उदयगिरि & °शैल m. the eastern mountain, behind which the sun rises (cf. अस्त).
उदयतट s. slope of the eastern mountain.
उदयन n. going up, rise; issue, end; m. N. of a king.
उदयाचल m. = उदयगिरि.
उदयाधिप m. the lord of rising, i.e. the Sun.*
उदयास्तमय m. du. rising and setting.
उदयिन् a. coming forth.
उदयोर्वीभृत् m. = उदयगिरि.
उदर n. (adj. —° f. आ & ई) belly, womb, cavity, interior, inside; loc. within, amidst (—°).
उदरण n. rising.
उदरंभर & *उदरंभरि* nourishing one's own belly, a glutton.
उदरविस्तार m. expansion of the belly, corpulence.*
उदर्क m. breaking forth, sounding; result, consequence, future; issue, end.
उदर्चिस् a. shining, luminous; m. fire.
उदवास m. dwelling in water; a. °सिन्.
उदवाह a. bringing water.
उदश्रु a. weeping (lit. having one's tears up).
उदहार, f. ई fetching water.
उदाज m. selection, choice (also concr.).
उदात्त a. elevated, high (lit. & fig.), highly or acutely accented, sublime, illustrious, high-minded, generous, haughty, arrogant. m. the high or acute accent.
उदान m. the wind that goes upward (in the body).
उदार a. raising, causing; sublime, noble, excellent. m. rising fog or mist; pl. the spirits of the fog.
उदारता f., °त्व n. sublimity (of style).
उदारचरित a. of noble conduct, acting nobly.

उदारधी a. of noble mind.
उदारशील a. of noble character.
उदासीन a. indifferent, passive, neutral; adv. °वत्.
उदाहरण n. saying, speech; example.
उदाहार a. going to fetch water. m. the fetching water.
उदाहृत a. called, quoted.
1उदित a. risen, high, elevated, haughty; begun, occurred, appeared, manifest, clear.
2उदित a. said, spoken, proclaimed, taught; spoken to, addressed.
उदिति f. rising (of the sun); going away, setting (of the sun); disappearance, end.
उदीक्षा f. looking up, gazing.
उदीचीन a. turned northward.
उदीच्य or उदीच्य a. northern; m. the northern country, pl. its inhabitants.
उदीरण n. throwing, uttering, speaking.
उदीर्ण a. roused, excited, haughty; abstr. °ता f.
उदीषित a. risen, lifted.
उदुम्बर m. the glomerous fig tree, its fruit (also n.); N. of a race of priests.
उदुम्बल a. copper-coloured, brown.
उदूढा f. married, taken to wife.
उदृच् f. issue, end; loc. at last.
उदेतोस् (abl. inf.) go up, rise.
उदोजस् a. of high power.
उद्गत a. come forth, sprung from (abl. or —°), appeared, risen; f. N. of a metre.
उद्गम m. rising, exertion; expansion, fulness; appearance, origin; shoot (of a plant).
उद्गमन n. rising, appearance.
उद्गमनीय n. a clean garment.
उद्गर्जित n. roaring, grunting.
उद्गर्भ a. pregnant.
उद्गाढ a. overflowing with (—°); excessive, vehement.
उद्गातृ m. chanter (of the Sāman-hymns).
उद्गार m. spitting or pouring out, ejecting; spittle, flood; roaring, sound, echo; utterance, tale.
उद्गारिन् a. spitting or pouring out (—°).
उद्गिरण n. spitting, vomiting.
उद्गीत n. song.
उद्गीति f. N. of a metre.
उद्गीथ m. (n.) chanting (of the Sāman-hymns).
उद्गीर्ण a. spit out, ejected, brought forth, caused.
उद्गूर्ण a. lifted, raised.
उद्ग्रहण n. taking away.
उद्ग्राह m. taking up or away, a kind of Saṁdhi.
उद्ग्रीव a. with lifted neck.
उद्घट्टन n. opening, bursting (tr. & intr.), outbreak.
उद्घर्षण n. rubbing, cudgelling.
उद्घाट m. = उद्घाटन n.
उद्घाटक m. opener, key.
उद्घाटन a. opening, pushing away (a bolt); n. opening, laying bare, showing.
उद्घाटिन् a. = prec. adj.
उद्घात m. strike, blow, jerk, jolt; elevation, eminence; rising, beginning.
उद्घातिन् a. jolting, uneven, rough.
उद्घुष्ट a. sounding; n. sound, noise.
उद्घोष m. calling out, proclaiming. °डिण्डिम m. drum for publishing.
उद्घोषण n. announcing, publishing.
उद्दण्ड a. having a raised staff or stalk; raised, extraordinary, sublime.
उद्दाम a. unbound, unrestrained, unlimited, extraordinary, full of (—°). °— & n. adv. beyond measure, wildly, exultingly.
उद्दालक m. N. of a man (lit. Up-tearer).
उद्दाह m. heat, fire.
उद्दिश्य (ger.) aiming at; used as prep. w. acc. = towards, with regard to, for the sake of, concerning, about.
उद्दृष्ट n. the becoming visible (of the moon).
उद्देश m. pointing to, mentioning, statement, rule; place, region. -- Instr. & abl. concerning, with regard to (—°); °तस् briefly, in a few words.
उद्द्योत a. flashing up, shining; m. flash, shine, light, splendour.
उद्धत a. raised, excited, elevated; excessive, vehement, intense; haughty, proud, arrogant; full of, rich in (instr. or —°).
उद्धरण n. taking out or off, removing, destroying, extricating, delivering.

उद्धार m. = prec. (also °धारा† n.); deduction, deducted or selected portion, additional share (j.).

उद्धि m. a cert. part of a carriage.

उद्धित a. set up, erected.

उद्धुत a. shaken, brandished.

उद्धुर a. unrestrained, extravagant, extraordinary (lit. freed from a yoke).

उद्धूत a. = उद्धुत + roused, kindled (fire); n. roaring (of the sea).

उद्धूति f. shaking, brandishing.

उद्धूमाय्, pp. °यित filled with vapour.*

उद्धूलय्, °यति bestrew.

उद्धृत a. drawn up or out, raised, extracted, separated, selected.

उद्धृतस्नेह a. from which the oil or fat has been extracted, skimmed.

उद्धृति f. drawing out, extraction, salvation.

उद्धृत्य ger. excepting, except.

उद्बद्ध a. tied up, suspended, hung; compact, solid.

1**उद्बन्ध** m. hanging one's self.

2**उद्बन्ध** a. untied, loose.

उद्बाष्प a. shedding tears (lit. having one's tears up); abstr. °त्व n.

उद्बुद्ध a. awakened, budded, appeared.

उद्भग्न a. burst, rent.

उद्भट a. eminent, extraordinary.

उद्भव m. origin, coming forth; adj. coming from (—°).

उद्भासिन् a. shining, radiant with; appearing, bursting from (—°).

उद्भिज्ज a. propagated by sprouts or seed (v. seq.).

उद्भिद् a. breaking forth, sprouting, piercing, victorious. m. a kind of sacrifice; f. sprout, plant; spring, fountain.

उद्भिन्न a. burst, openened, blossomed, apparent.

उद्भु (f. उद्भ्वी, n. उद्भु) lasting, perpetual.

उद्भूत a. come forth, born, risen, increased.

उद्भूति f. origin, rise, appearance.

उद्भेद m. breaking forth, becoming visible, appearance; spring, fountain.

उद्भ्रान्त a. started or flown up, risen, fled; agitated, bewildered; wandering, roving. n. rising; waving a sword.

उद्भ्रान्तक n. rising into the air.

उद्मन् n. surging, flooding.

उद्यत a. held up, offered (esp. food); undertaken, begun; prepared, ready, eager; occupied in, endeavouring or going to (inf., dat., loc., or अर्थम्).

उद्यतदण्ड a. ready to strike (lit. having lifted up the stick).

उद्यति f. raising, elevation, offering.

उद्यम m. uplifting, elevation; undertaking, effort, endeavour, exertion at (dat., acc. w. प्रति, inf., or —°).

उद्यमन n. raising, elevation, exertion.

उद्यमभृत् a. bearing or undergoing exertions.

उद्यान n. walking out; garden, park.

उद्यानगहन n. garden-thicket.

उद्यानपाल m., ई f.; °पालक m., °लिका a. gardener.

उद्यानमाला f. a row of gardens.

उद्यानवाट m. garden-fence.

उद्युक्त a. prepared, ready, intent on, going or about to (dat., loc., प्रति w. acc., or —°).

उद्योग m. effort, endeavour, activity.

उद्योगिन् a. taking pains, active, industrious.

उद्र m. a kind of aquatic animal.

उद्रिक्त a. excessive, superfluous, surpassing (—°); highminded, haughty.

उद्रिन् springy, wet.

उद्रेक m. excess, preponderance; p. °किन्.

उद्वत् f. eminence, hill.

उद्वर्तन a. bursting (tr. —°); n. rising, ascending; rubbing, anointing, unguent.

उद्वह a. leading up, carrying away or on, continuing (—°); m. leading home, marriage; son, offspring (—°).

उद्वहन n. lifting up, carrying, drawing; riding on (instr.); leading home, marriage, possession.

उद्वाह m. leading home, marriage.

उद्वाहमङ्गल n. marriage-feast.

उद्विद्ध a. raised, high.

उद्विग्न a. astounded, terrified, afraid of (abl., gen., instr., or —°); dejected, depressed, wearied of (instr.); sorrowful, tired of life.

उद्विग्नोद्विग्न a. quite astounded.*

उद्वीक्षण n. looking up, beholding, sight.
उद्वृत्त a. swollen, turgid, prominent; roused, excited; extravagant, dissolute.
उद्वेग m. trembling, waving, agitation, uneasiness, disgust.
उद्वेगकर (f. ई), °कारक, (°कारण*), & कारिन् a. causing anxiety or agitation.
उद्वेजन a. the same; n. anxiety, agitation.
उद्वेजनकर, f. ई = prec. adj.
उद्वेजनीय a. horrible.
उद्वेल्लित a. tossed up, moving to and fro.
उद्व्यूढ a. dropped from (—°).*
*उन्दर, उन्दुर, & °रु m. mouse, rat.
उन्नत a. raised, high, eminent; n. = seq.
उन्नति f. rising, elevation, height; p. °मन्त्.
उन्नद्ध a. tied up, unbound; haughty, arrogant.
उन्नयन n. lifting up, raising, drawing out (water).
उन्नाल a. having an erected stalk.
उन्नाह m. exuberance, fulness.
उन्निद्र a. sleepless, awake, expanded, budded, blown.
उन्मग्न a. emerged.
उन्मत्त a. excited, intoxicated, drunk, mad, furious; m. the thorn-apple.
उन्मत्तीभूत being mad.*
उन्मथ्य ger. with violence.
उन्मनस् & °स्क a. excited or disturbed in mind, agitated, restless; abstr. °स्कता f.
उन्मर्द m. rubbing in.
उन्मर्दन n. the same; a fragrant essence.
उन्माद a. mad, insane; m. madness, insanity.
उन्मादयितृ (°तृक) a. inebriating.*
उन्मादवन्त् & °दिन् = उन्माद a.
उन्मार्ग m. by-way, evil way; a. = seq.
उन्मार्गगामिन् & °वर्तिन् a. going evil ways.
उन्मिश्र a. mixed with (—°).
उन्मिषित a. opened, budded, blown.
उन्मीलन n. = उन्मेष.
उन्मीलित a. = उन्मिषित + unfolded, manifest.
उन्मुक्त a. destitute of, wanting (—°); taken off, sent forth.
उन्मुख, f. ई looking or turned (lit. having the face) upwards; looking at, desirous of, going or about to, waiting for (—°).
उन्मूल्, °लति be unrooted. C. °लयति unroot, destroy, dethrone. — सम् C. eradicate, destroy.
उन्मूलन n. eradication, destruction.
उन्मृष्ट a. wiped off, blotted out.
उन्मेष m. opening (of the eye), expanding, becoming visible, appearance.
उन्मेषिन् a. starting or flying up.
उप adv. thereto, further, as prep. towards, unto, near, at, in, *below, less than (acc.); near, by, at, upon, at the time of, up to, *above, more than (loc.); together with, according to (instr.). — It is mostly used °— in verbs, adverbs or nouns, denoting approach, vicinity, or inferiority (cf. उपगम्; °गमन, °मूलम्, °पुराण).
उपकक्ष a. reaching to the shoulder.
उपकण्ठ n. nearness, proximity; °ण्ठम् adv. near (—°).
उपकरण n. doing a service, helping, assistance; instrument, supplement, means, expedient; p. °णवन्त्.
उपकर्तृ, f. °र्त्री assisting, befriending, kind.
उपकार m. service, assistance, favour.
उपकारक (f. °रिका) & °रिन् a. serviceable, officious, useful, kind. — *f. °रिका royal tent.
उपकार्य a. to be served or favoured; f. आ royal tent.
उपकृति f. service, kindness.
उपकॢप्त a. being at hand, ready, prepared.
उपक्रम m. approach, arrival; commencement, enterprise; means, expedient.
उपक्रान्त n. commencement, beginning.
उपक्रिया f. service, benefit.
उपक्रुष्ट m. carpenter (lit. blamed, despised).
उपक्षय m. decrease, decay, disappearance.
उपक्षेप m., °ण n. allusion, insinuation (rh.).
उपग a. going to, being in, belonging to, serving for, furnished with (—°).
उपगत a. approached, happened, occurred, fallen into or got at (acc. or —°); n. receipt, acquittance.
उपगति f., °गम m. approach, arrival.
उपगान n. accompanying song.

उपगीत a. (pass.) sung, praised, celebrated by (—°); (act.) having begun to sing.
उपगीति f. N. of a metre.
उपगूढ n. an embrace.
उपग्रह m. taking possession of, annexing, winning over.
उपग्रहण n. holding up, supporting, promoting.
उपग्राह m. gift, present.
उपघात m. stroke, blow, hurt, injury, damage, offence.
उपघातक & **°तिन्** a. damaging, offending (—°).
उपचय m. accumulation, increase, growth; prosperity, advantage.
उपचर a. approaching; m. & **°ण** n. approach, coming near.
उपचरितव्य & **°चर्य** to be treated, served, waited on.
उपचर्या f. service, attendance.
उपचार m. conduct, behaviour, use, practice, dealing with (gen.); civility, kindness, service, attendance, ceremony; ornament (p. **°वन्त्**†), figure of speech.
उपचारक, f. **°रिका** (adj. —°) politeness, kindness.
उपचित a. augmented, strengthened, covered or furnished with, full of (instr. or —°).
उपच्छन्न a. covered. hid.
उपज a. additional, belonging to (gen.); coming from (—°).
उपजाति f. N. of a metre.
उपजाप m. whispering, talking over, persuading, seducing.
उपजापक m. whispering to, conspiring with (—°).
उपजिगमिषु a. approaching (acc.).
उपजिह्वा f. uvula, epiglottis.
उपजीवक a. living, subsisting, dependent upon (instr. or —°); m. subject or dependant.
उपजीवन n. & **उपजीवा** f. livelihood, subsistence.
उपजीवनीय a. affording a livelihood.
उपजीविन् a. = **उपजीवक** (absol. or w. acc., gen., —°).
उपजीव्य a. = **उपजीवनीय**; n. subsistence.
उपतटम् adv. on the slope.
उपतप्त a. hot, warm; sick, unwell.
उपताप m. heat, pain, sickness, trouble, distress, woe, sorrow.
उपतापक a. causing pain, distressing.
उपतापिन् a. the same (—°); ill, diseased.
उपत्यका f. land at the food of a mountain.
उपदा f. offering, present.
उपदिग्ध a. smeared or covered with (—°).
उपदिश् & **°दिशा** f. intermediate region (north-east etc.).
उपदृश् f. sight, view.
उपदेश m. hint, direction, advice, instruction; indicatory or conventional form (g.).
उपदेशन n., **°शना**† f. advice, instruction.
उपदेशिन् a. instructing, teaching; m. teacher, f. **°नी**.
उपद्रव m. misfortune, calamity.
उपद्रष्टृ m. supervisor, witness.
उपधर्म m. minor duty, by-law.
उपधा f. imposition, fraud; penultimate letter (g.).
उपधान a. & n. setting up; n. also = seq.
उपधानीय n. cushion, pillow.
उपधि m. putting to, i.e. adding; imposition, fraud; the part of a wheel between nave and circumference.
उपध्मानीय m. the Visarga before **प** & **फ**.
उपध्वस्त a. brindled, spotted.
उपनत a. bent towards or inwards, brought down, subject, dependent; brought about, existing, present.
उपनति f. abstr. to prec., + inclination, affection.
उपनय m. bringing near, procuring, getting, obtaining, employing; introduction (into a science).
उपनयन n. the same + seq.
उपनायन n. leading to a teacher, initiation.
उपनिधातृ a. setting down.
उपनिधि m. deposit, esp. a sealed one.
उपनिपात m. outbreak, onset, attack.
उपनिपातिन् a. falling into (—°).
उपनिबद्ध a. hanging on, sticking to (—°); written down, composed; abstr. **°त्व** n.

उपनिबन्धन n. writing down, description, literary composition, versification.
__उपनिर्गम__ m. departure from (—°).
उपनिषद् f. secret doctrine (lit. sitting down, sc. to listen); an Upaniṣad, i.e. a class of writings intended to ascertain the secret meaning of the Veda.
उपनेतृ, f. °त्री who brings, bearer of (gen.).
उपन्यस्त a. brought forward, adduced, hinted; n. hint, insinuation.
उपन्यास m. placing near, juxtaposition, addition; utterance, argumentation, also=prec.n.
उपपक्ष m. armpit; a. °पक्ष्य.
उपपति m. paramour, gallant.
उपपत्ति f. happening, appearing, following, resulting; rightness, exactness, fitness, propriety.
उपपद n. a secondary word of any kind (g.).
उपपन्न a. having gone or come to, got at, met with (acc. or —°); endowed with, possessed of (instr. or —°); happened, occurred, born, existing; fit, suited, right, proper, natural.
उपपन्नार्थ a. having good reasons, well founded.
उपपात m. occurrence, accident.
उपपातक n. minor offence; poss. °किन्.
उपपातिन् a. falling into (—°).
उपपादक a. effecting, producing, making; possible.
उपपादन a. producing, mentioning; n. bringing near, presenting, appearing.
उपपार्श्व m. shoulderblade.
उपपीडन n. torture, pang.
उपपुराण n. a secondary or minor Purāṇa.
उपप्लव m. visitation, disturbance, trouble, calamity, any portent, esp. an eclipse.
उपप्लुत a. visited, afflicted.
*__उपबर्ह__ m. cushion, pillow.
उपबृंहित a. strengthened, increased, accompanied by, furnished with (instr. or —°).
उपब्दि & **उपब्दि** m. rattling, noise.
उपभङ्ग m. division of a verse.
उपभोग m. enjoyment, use, pleasure.
उपभोगिन् a. enjoying, using (—°).
उपभोग्य a. to be enjoyed or used.
उपमं a. uppermost, highest; nearest, next; first, best, excellent, chief.
उपमन्त्रन n. inviting, persuading.
1**उपमन्त्रिन्** the same as adj.
2**उपमन्त्रिन्** m. a king's counsellor of second rank.
उपमन्यु a. eager, zealous; m. a man's name.
उपमर्द m. friction, injury, reproach, abuse; also = **उपमर्दन**.
उपमर्दक a. crushing, destroying.
उपमर्दन n. oppression, destruction.
उपमर्दिन् a. = **उपमर्दक**.
1**उपमा** adv. quite, near.
2**उपमा** f. resemblance, similarity; comparison, image (rh.); o. adj. resembling, equal to, -like (—°).
उंपमाति f. address, invocation; fit to be invoked, accessible, kind.
उपमान n. comparison, simile, esp. that with which a thing is compared, opp. **उपमेय** (rh.); adj. —° = **उपमा** adj.
उपमाम् adv. highest.
उपमाव्यतिरेक m. a kind of comparison (rh.).
उपमिति f. resemblance; induction (ph.).
उपमेय a. to be or being compared, comparable with (instr. or —°); n. (rh.) the thing compared with something else (opp. the **उपमान** q.v.).
उपमेयोपमा f. a reciprocal comparison (rh.).
उपयन्तृ m. husband.
उपयम m. wedding, marriage.
उपयमन n. = prec.; f. **ई** any support (for holding fire-wood), a sacrificial ladle.
उपयान n. nearing, approach.
उपयुक्त a. employed, used, consumed; useful, requisite, fit, proper, worthy.
उपयोक्तव्य a. to be employed.
उपयोग m. employment, application; use, enjoyment.
उपयोगिन् a. being employed, conducive, useful, fit, suitable; employing, using (—°).
उपयोज्य a. to be or being used.
उंपर a. placed below, deeper, posterior, later, nearer, neighbouring. m. the lower pressing stone or the lower part of the sacrificial post.

उपरक्त a. coloured, reddened, eclipsed (sun or moon).

उपरति f. ceasing, resting; quietism (ph.).

उपरम m. ceasing, ending, desisting from (—°), death; abstr. °त्व n.

उपरमण & °त्व n. coming to rest.

उपराग m. colour, darkness.

उपरि adv. above, upwards, moreover, further, then; doubled = higher and higher, more and more. As prep. above, over, beyond, upon, up into (acc., gen., abl., loc., °— or —° in an adv.); above in number or order (gen. or —° in an adv.), after (gen. or —°); concerning, as to (gen.); doubled = immediately over (acc.), high over (gen.).

उपरितन, f. **ई** upper.

उपरिष्टात् adv. above, from above, behind, later, afterwards. As prep. over, upon (acc. or gen.), behind; concerning, about, as to (gen.).

उपरुद्ध a. captive, prisoner; n. shut up or inner apartment.

उपरूढ a. ascended; come to, arrived at (acc.), situated on (loc.).

उपरूपक n. a drama of the second rank (rh.).

उपरोध m. hindrance, impediment; locking up, blockading; trouble, disturbance.

उपल m. stone, rock, jewel; f. **उपला** the upper mill-stone.

उपलक्षण n. observation, designation; implicit or elliptical expression.

उपलक्ष्य a. recognisable.

उपलप्रक्षिन्, f. °णी arranging the press or millstones.

उपलब्धि f. acquirement, gain; perception, knowledge, p. °मन्त्.

उपलम्भ m. = prec. f.

उपलेप m. smearing.

उपलेपन n. the same, (painting, colouring*).

उपवक्तृ m. exhorter.

उपवन n. a small wood, grove.

उपवसथ m. a fast-day.

उपवास m. fast.

उपवासिन् a. fasting.

उपविष्ट a. seated; resorted to (acc. or —°).

उपवीत n. investiture with the sacred cord, the sacred cord itself.

उपवीतिन् a. wearing the sacred cord.

उपवेश m., °न† n. sitting down; devoting one's self to (—°).

उपशम m. coming to rest, cessation, tranquillity.

उपशमन, f. **ई** calming, appearing; n. subst.

उपशय a. lying near or at hand.

उपशान्त a. allayed, extinct.

उपशान्ति f. = **उपशम**.

उपशिक्षा f. learning, skill in (gen.).

उपशोभन a. & n. adorning.

उपशोभा f. ornament.

उपशोभिन् a. adorned; shining with (—°).*

उपश्लिष्ट a. clinging to (acc.), come near (loc. or **समीपम्**), contiguous.

उपसंव्यान n. under-garment.

उपसंहार m. drawing towards one's self; winding up, recapitulation, conclusion.

उपसंहित a. connected or endowed with, accompanied or surrounded by (instr. or —°).

उपसक्त a. attached to sensual objects.

उपसंख्यान n. annumeration, addition.

उपसंग्रह m. gathering, taking (esp. of a wife); also = seq.

उपसंग्रहण n. clasping (of a person's feet); deferential greeting.

उपसंग्राह्य a. to be greeted deferentially.

उपसत्तृ m. worshipper (lit. who approaches).

उपसद् a. serving, attending; f. approach, assault, siege; attendance, waiting on; N. of a ceremony (r.).

उपसदन n. going to (a teacher), apprenticeship, also = **उपसंग्रहण**.

उपसद्य a. to be revered or waited on.

उपसन्न a. placed upon (the Vedi), presented, granted; approached (esp. to worship or to seek information or protection).

उपसंपन्न a. furnished or familiar with (instr. or —°); living in the same house.

उपसरण n. approach.

उपसर्ग m. addition (lit. pouring on), accident, ill luck, calamity; preposition.

उपसर्जन n. pouring on; inauspicious phenomenon, esp. an eclipse; a secondary word (g.) or person (j.).

उपसर्पण n. advancing towards, approaching.

उपसर्पणीय a. to be approached.*

उपसर्पिन् a. creeping near, approaching.

उपसिद्ध a. prepared, ready.

उपसृष्ट a. thrown, sent; hit, visited, afflicted by (instr. or —°); eclipsed (sun or moon), having a prefix (g.).

उपसेचन a. pouring or sprinkling upon; n. the same as subst. + juice, broth, condiment; f. **ई** a ladle or cup for pouring.

उपसेवक (—°) a. serving, following.

उपसेवन n., **°सेवा** f. attendance, homage, worship, devotion; enjoyment, use.

उपसेविन् (—°) serving, worshipping; pursuing, practising.

उपस्कर m. (n.) anything subsidiary or complementary, ingredient, condiment, utensil, instrument, esp. of household.

उपस्कृत a. prepared, arranged.

उपस्तम्भ m., **°स्तम्भन** n. stay, support.

उपस्तरण n. pouring under. spreading out; a covering or mattress.

उ॑पस्ति or **उपस्ति॑** m. inferior, a follower, servant.

उपस्ति॑रे (dat. inf.) to spread out.

उपस्तीर्ण a. covered, spread out; poured upon (r.).

उ॑पस्तुत् & **उ॑पस्तुति** f. invocation, praise.

उप॑स्थ m. lap, groin; m. n. the sexual organs, esp. of a woman.

उपस्थातव्य a. to appear (n. impers.); to be waited upon.

उपस्थातृ m. coming near, appearing (in court); m. servant, attendant.

उपस्था॑न n. coming or standing near, appearance, presence, attendance, service, worship; gathering, assembly.

उ॑पस्थित a. approached, arrived at. got to (acc. or loc.); fallen to one's (gen.) lot or share, happened, appeared, present, impending, ready; visited, waited upon, attacked by, furnished with (instr.).

उपस्थेय a. = **उपस्थातव्य**.

उपस्पर्श m., **°न** n. touching, bathing, rinsing the mouth.

उपस्पर्शिन् a. touching, bathing in (—°).

उपस्पृष्ट a. touched; n. impers. or = **स्पर्श**.

उपस्वेद m. moisture.

उपहर्तु॑ a. assailing.

उपहरण n. presenting, offering.

उपहर्तृ m. who presents or offers.

उपहव॑ m. calling near, invitation.

उपहार m. present, gift, offering; abstr. **°ता** f., **°त्व** n.

उपहारक, f. **°रिका** (adj. —°) = **उपहार**.

उपहारी कृ offer as a sacrifice; **°चिकीर्षु** a. going to offer.

उपहार्य a. to be offered; n. offering.

उपहास॑ m. laughter, fun.

उपहासनीयता f. ridiculousness.*

उपहासिन् a. laughing at (—°).

उपहास्य a. laughable, ridiculous; abstr. **°ता** f., **°त्व** n.

उप॑हित a. placed or set upon, connected with, dependent on, preceded by (—°); brought near, procured, got, put, applied, undertaken, begun, set to action, employed, led, seduced.

उ॑पहूत a. called, invoked, invited.

उपह्वर॑ m. bend, curve, slope. n. solitude, proximity, loc. secretly, near.

उपांशु॑ adv. in a low voice, inaudibly; m. an inaudible prayer.

उपांशुव्रत n. an inaudible vow.

उ॑पाक or **उपाक॑** a. neared, joined, close, connected; loc. **°के** close by, at hand, present (w. gen.).

उपाक॑रण n. bringing near. fetching, also = seq.

उपाकर्मन् n. preparation, commencement, esp. to study the Vedas.

उपाख्यान & **°क** n. short narrative, episode.

उपाङ्ग n. minor limb or member, subdivision, supplement.

उपाञ्जन n. smearing, anointing.

उपात्त a. taken, received, got, felt, done.

उपात्तसार a. thoroughly enjoyed (lit. whereof the best has been taken).

उपादान n. taking, acquiring, appropiating; non-exclusion, addition; enumeration, mention; the material cause (ph.).

उपादाय ger. together with (lit. having taken), including, besides, by means of; since, from (acc.).

उपादेय a. to be taken from (abl.); contained in (—°); acceptable, admirable, excellent.

उपाधाय ger. taking, i.e. along with (acc.).

उपाधि m. substitution, substitute; supposition, postulate, cause.

उपाध्याय m. teacher, subteacher; **°ध्यायानी** f. the teacher's wife.

उपानसं a. being on a carriage.

उपानह् f. (nom. **°नत्**) & **उपानह** m. sandal, shoe.

उपान्त n. nearness of the end, edge, margin, immediate proximity; acc. & loc. near (gen. or —°); °— near, neighbouring.

उपान्तिक n. nearness, proximity; acc. & loc. near, abl. (from) near.

उपाप्ति f. getting, acquiring.

उपाय m. approach, way to or of, means, expedient, stratagem; **°येन** & **°यतस्** in a clever way, by stratagem.

उपायन n. approach, going to a teacher, becoming a scholar; undertaking, enterprise, offering, gift.

उपायिन् & **°युं** a. approaching.

उपायोपेय (°—) means and purpose.

उपार m., **उपारण** n. transgression, offence, sin.

उपार्जन n., **आ** f. bringing near, acquiring, obtaining.

उपालब्धव्य a. to be blamed or censured.

उपालम्भ m., **°न** n. censure, reviling.

उपालम्भनीय a. = **उपालब्धव्य**.

उपावृत् & **उपावृत्ति** f. return.

उपावृत्त a. turned round or towards (acc.), come to (acc.); approached, arrived, returned.

उपाश्रित a. leaning or resting on, resorted to, staying in or with (acc. or loc.); intent upon, given to (acc.).

उपाश्रित्य ger. having resorted to, i.e. by means of (acc.).

उपासक a. serving, intent upon (—°); m. a servant or follower, esp. of Buddha (f. **°सिका***).

उपासन n. seat; service, attendance, worship (also **°सा** f.); meditation, practice, exercise.

उपास्थित a. standing on (loc.), intent upon (acc.).

उपास्य a. to be served, worshipped, practised, resorted to.

उपाहित a. set out as a price; caused, produced; s. a conflagration.

उपेक्षण n., **°क्षा** f. overlooking, disregard, neglect.

उपेत a. arrived, present, existing, come or gone to (acc. or —°), come to the teacher i.e. initiated; fallen to one's (gen.) share; being in (loc.); accompanied by, endowed with (instr. or —°).

उपेतपूर्व a. initiated before.

उपेति f. approach.

उपेतृ m. contriver, employer.

उपेनित a. driven or pressed in.

उपेन्द्र m. E. of Viṣṇu (lit. inferior to Indra).

उपेन्द्रवज्रा f. N. of a metre.

उपेय a. being or to be effected, to be gone to or approached; n. aim, object.

उपोढ a. brought near, brought about, begun, caused, attained, got; existing, present.

उपोढतपस् a. rich in penitence.

1**उपोढराग** m. a rising blush.

2**उपोढराग** a. blushing.

उपोढशब्द a. causing a sound, noisy.

उपोत्तम a. last but one.

उपोद्घात m. introduction, beginning, opportunity.

1**उपोषण** a. burning down (—°).

2**उपोषण** n. fasting.

उपोषित a. (having) fasted; n. = prec.

उप्त a. sown, strewn, thrown down, lying; covered or sprinkled with (instr. or —°).

उप्ति f. sowing.

उप्तिविद् a. acquainted with sowing (—°).

उब्ज्, **उब्जति** force, subdue. — **नि** press down, overthrow. **निस्** let loose.

उभ्, **उभ्नति**, **उभ्नाति**, **उनप्ति**, pp. **उब्ध**, **उम्भित** confine, unite, couple. — **नि** keep down. **सम्** keep together, cover, shut up.

उभ du. both.

उभय, f. **ई** (sgl. & pl.) both, of both sorts.
उभयचक्रवर्तिन् m. ruler of both (worlds).
उभयतस् adv. from or on both sides (w. gen. or acc.); in both cases.
उभयतोदन्त्, **°दन्त**, & **उभयदन्त्** a. having a double row of teeth.
उभयत्र adv. in both places, on both sides, in both cases.
उभयथा adv. in both ways or cases.
उभया adv. in both ways.
उभयात्मक a. having a double nature.
उमा f. flax; N. of the daughter of Himavant, the wife of Çiva-Rudra.
उमानाथ, **°पति**, & **उमेश** m. the lord or husband of Umā, i.e. Çiva.
उर m. N. of a Rishi; °— = **उरस्** or **ऊर्णा**.
उरग, **उरंग**, & **°म** m. a snake (lit. going on the breast).
उरण & **उरभ्र** m. a ram (wool-bearer).
उररी कृ = **उरी कृ** q.v.
उरल्लि s. roaring.*
उरस् n. breast; adj. —° **उरस्क**.
***उरःसूत्रिका** f. a kind of necklace.
उरा f. a ewe.
उरी कृ accept, get, show; admit, assent, promise; place at the head, begin with (acc.).
उरु, f. **उर्वी** spacious, extensive, wide, broad, great. — n. adv. widely, far; as subst. space, room, wide scope, freedom, w. **कृ** give room, liberty, opportunity. — f. **उर्वी** the earth, the soil; du. heaven and earth; pl. w. **षष्** the six spaces (the four quarters of the sky with what is above and below).
उरुकृत् a. granting space.
उरुक्रम a. far-stepping; m. the wide step (of Viṣṇu).
उरुगाय a. = prec. a. + far, extending (way); m. E. of Viṣṇu; n. = **उरु** n.
उरुया (instr. adv.) far.
उरुचक्षस् a. far-seeing.
उरुव्यचस् a. capacious, widely extending.
उरुव्यञ्च् a. the same; f. **उरूची** also the earth.
उरुशंस a. praising aloud; far-ruling.
उरुष्य्, **उरुष्यति** seek or grant wide scope, i.e. either turn from (abl.), escape (acc.); or rescue, protect from (abl.), avert.
उरूणस a. broad-nosed.
उरोगत a. being on the breast.
उर्वरा f. fertile soil, land i.g.; the earth.
उर्वरी f. tow, hards.
उर्वशी f. ardour, wish, desire; N. of an Apsaras.
उर्वारु *m., **°रू** f. a kind of cucumber.
उर्वारु & **°क** n. the fruit of prec.
उर्वशीसुत m. the son of Urvaçī, i.e. Āyus.
उर्विया (instr. adv.) far, far off, widely.
उर्वीतल n. the surface of the earth.
उर्वीपति & **°भुज्** m. king (lit. earth-lord).
उर्वीभृत् m. mountain (lit. earth-bearer).
उर्वीश & **°श्वर** m. = **उर्वीपति**.
उर्व्या f. freedom, security.
उल m. a kind of wild animal.
उलप m. shrub, bush.
उलूक m. owl; E. of Indra, pl. N. of a country & people.
उलूखल n. mortar.
उलूखलमुसल n. du. mortar and pestle.
उलूप m. a sort of plant; f. **ई** N. of the wife of Arjuna, orig. a serpent-maid.
उल्का f. meteor, firebrand, flame.
उल्कामुख m. a kind of demon or goblin.
उल्ब n. (m.) the bag enveloping the embryo, womb i.g.
उल्बण a. massy, thick, big, huge, extraordinary; rich in, full of (—°). n. **उल्बण** = **उल्ब**.
उल्मुक n. firebrand.
उल्लङ्घन n. leaping or passing over, transgression.
उल्लङ्घनीय & **उल्लङ्घ्य** a. to be transgressed.
उल्लसित a. shone forth, appeared; joyous, petulant; moving to and fro.
उल्लास m. shining forth, appearing; joy, happiness; prosperity, increase; chapter, section.
उल्लीढ a. ground, polished.
उल्लुञ्चित a. plucked out or off.
उल्लून a. cut, mown.
उल्लेख m. mention, description.

उल्लेखन a. scraping, painting, describing; n. the action of scraping etc.

उल्लेख्य a. to be or being scraped, written, painted, described.

*__उल्लोच__ m. awning, canopy.

उल्लोल a. dangling, swinging.

उशनस् m. (nom. °ना) N. of an old sage.

उशना f. (instr.) with ardour or haste.

उशन्त् & **उशान** a. desirous, eager, striving, willing, ready.

उशिज् a. the same.

उशीनर m. pl. N. of a people or country.

उशीर m. n. a kind of fragrant root.

1**उष्**, **ओषति** & **उष्णाति** burn, consume, destroy, punish. — **उद्** expel by heat. **नि** burn down. **प्रति** & **सम्** burn.

2**उष्** f. dawn, morning.

उष a. desirous, eager.

उषर्बुध् a. early awake.

उषस् f. morning light, dawn (often personif.), also evening light; du. **उषासौ** morning and evening.

उषा f. dawn, morning.

उषासानक्ता (nom. du. f.) dawn and night.

उषित a. passed, spent (day), dwelt (n. imp.); having stopped, stayed, dwelt, lived, passed the night, fasted.

उष्ट or **उष्ट्र** m. plough-bull.

उष्ट्र m. buffalo; camel (f. **उष्ट्री**).

उष्ट्रयान n. carriage drawn by camels.

उष्ण, f. **आ** (**ई**) hot, warm. n. heat, warmth, the hot season.

उष्णकर & **उष्णकिरण** m. the sun (lit. having hot rays).

उष्णता f., °**त्व** n. heat, warmth.

उष्णकटुक a. warm and bad-smelling.*

उष्णदीर्घम् adv. hot and long (breathing).*

उष्णरश्मि & **उष्णरुचि** m. = **उष्णकर**.

उष्णसमय m. the hot season.

उष्णांशु m. = **उष्णकर**.

उष्णालु a. suffering from heat.

उष्णिह् (nom. °क्) N. of a metre.

उष्णी कृ make warm or hot.

उष्णीष m. n. turban, headband, diadem.

उष्णीषपट्ट s. the same.

उष्णोष्ण a. very hot.*

उष्मन् v. **ऊष्मन्**.

उष्य = **उषित्वा**.

उस् f. = **उषस्**.

उस्र a. morning-, bright; m. bull or ray; f. **आ** dawn or cow.

उस्रि f. dawn, morning.

उस्रिय a. reddish, bull-; m. bull, calf; f. **आ** brightness, light; cow, milk.

उह् = 1**ऊह्**.

उह्यमान & °**क** a. carried or borne along.

ऊ

ऊ & **ऊँ** = 2**उ**.

ऊकार m. the sound **ऊ**.

ऊढ a. carried, borne; n. load, prey; f. **आ** bride, wife.

ऊढपूर्वा f. married before.

ऊढि f. carrying.

1**ऊति** f. (m.) furtherance, help, aid, refreshment; helper, furtherer, protector.

2**ऊति** f. weaving, sewing.

ऊधन्, **ऊधर्**, **ऊधस्** n. udder, bosom, lap, the cloudy sky.

ऊधस्य a. milking; n. milk.

ऊन a. wanting, incomplete; inferior to, less than (abl. or —°); less by (instr. or —°); °— in numerals = **एकोन**, i.e. minus one.

ऊनद्विवार्षिक a. less than two years old.

ऊनय्, **ऊनयति** leave unfulfilled (a wish); pp. **ऊनित** lessened by (instr.).

ऊम m. protector, friend, companion.

ऊरु m. thigh (adj. —° f. **ऊरु** or **ऊरू**); N. of an old sage.

ऊरुजन्मन् = 2**और्व** (lit. descending from Ūru).

ऊरुसंभव a. born from the thigh.

ऊरुस्कम्भ m. paralysis of the thigh.

ऊरुस्तम्भ m. the same.

ऊरूद्भव = **ऊरुसंभव**.

ऊर्ज् f. sap, food; vigour, strength.
ऊर्ज a. strong; m. & f. ऊर्जा = prec.
ऊर्जय्, ऊर्जयति, pp. ऊर्जित (q.v.) feed, strengthen; M. be strong or exuberant; ऊर्जयन्त् tr. or intr.
ऊर्जस् n. strength, power, exuberance.
ऊर्जस्वन्त्, °स्वल†, or °स्विन्† poss. to prec.
ऊर्जावन्त् a. giving strength; also = seq.
ऊर्जित a. strong, powerful, n. adv.
ऊर्जिन् a. fertile, exuberant.
ऊर्ण m. N. of a Yakṣa; n. & f. ऊर्णा wool, a spider's thread.
ऊर्णनाभ & °नाभि m. spider (wool-navel).
ऊर्णम्रद & ऊर्णम्रदस् a. soft as wool.
ऊर्णवाभि m. spider (wool-weaver).
ऊर्णामय, f. ई woollen.
ऊर्णामृदु & ऊर्णाम्रदस् a. = ऊर्णम्रद.
ऊर्णायु a. woolly; f. ewe.
ऊर्णावन्त् a. woolly; m. spider.
ऊर्णु, ऊर्णोति & ऊर्णौति, ऊर्णुते cover, veil, hide, M. one's self. — अप uncover, unveil, open; M. also refl. अभि & प्र = S. वि uncover, open.
ऊर्दर m. bushel.
ऊर्ध्व a. going upwards, raised, elevated, upright, erect, high (mostly °—). — n. eminence, height; as adv. & prep. upwards, aloft, in(to) heaven (w. गम् die), above (abl.); in the sequel, afterwards, later; beyond, from, since, after (abl.); later than i.e. after the death of (gen.); in a high tone, aloud. — Cf. अतस् & इतस्.
ऊर्ध्वक a. raised; n. adv. loud.*
ऊर्ध्वकर a. with lifted hands or rising rays.
ऊर्ध्वकर्ण a. having the ears pricked up.
ऊर्ध्वग a. going upwards, ascending.
ऊर्ध्वगति a. the same; f. subst.
ऊर्ध्वगमन n. rising (of stars), also = prec. f.
ऊर्ध्वगमनवन्त् & ऊर्ध्वगामिन् = ऊर्ध्वग.
ऊर्ध्वचूड a. tied up in a tuft (hair).*
ऊर्ध्वजानु & ऊर्ध्वज्ञु a. raising the knees.
ऊर्ध्वतस् & ऊर्ध्वथा adv. upwards.
ऊर्ध्वदृश् & °दृष्टि a. looking upwards.
ऊर्ध्वदेह n. funeral ceremony (lit. the body above).
ऊर्ध्वनभस् a. being above the clouds.
ऊर्ध्वपथ n. the sky (lit. upper path).
ऊर्ध्वपात्र n. a high vessel.
ऊर्ध्वपाद a. having the heels upwards; m. the point of the foot.
ऊर्ध्वपुण्ड्र & °क m. the perpendicular line on the forehead of a Brahman.
ऊर्ध्वबाहु a. having the arms raised.
ऊर्ध्वबृहती f. N. of a metre.
ऊर्ध्वभाग m. the upper part.
ऊर्ध्वमुख a. (having the mouth or opening) turned upwards.
ऊर्ध्वमुण्ड a. shaved or bald on the head.
ऊर्ध्वमूल a. having the roots above.
ऊर्ध्वराजि f. a line running upwards.
ऊर्ध्वरेत & °रेतस्† a. chaste (lit. having the semen above).
ऊर्ध्वलोक m. the upper world, heaven.
ऊर्ध्ववृत a. put on or worn above (i.e. on the shoulder).
ऊर्ध्वसान a. rising.
ऊर्ध्वसानु a. having the neck raised.
ऊर्ध्वाङ्गुलि a. having the fingers raised.
ऊर्मि m. f. wave, current, flood; metaph. of the (six) human infirmities.
ऊर्मिका f. a finger-ring.
ऊर्मिन् & ऊर्मिमन्त् a. undulating.
ऊर्मिमाला f. a wreath or row of waves.
ऊर्मिला f. a woman's name.
ऊर्म्य a. undulating, agitated; f. ऊर्म्या night.
ऊर्व m. receptacle, esp. of water, i.e. cloud; fence, fold, stable, prison; N. of an ancient sage.
ऊर्वष्ठीव n. knee-pan.
ऊर्वस्थ n. thigh-bone.
ऊली f. bulb.
ऊष m., ऊषा & ई f. alkaline earth.
ऊषक n. salt or pepper.
ऊषण n. pepper.
ऊषर a. impregnated with salt; s. = seq.
ऊषरक्षेत्र n. saline or barren soil.*
ऊष्मन् m. heat, steam, ardour, passion.
ऊष्मप a. drinking (only) the steam of food; m. pl. a class of Manes.
1ऊह् (उह्), ऊहति, ऊहते, pp. ऊढ & ऊहित

shift, change. — अधि put on; raise above (loc.). अप push off, remove, destroy; avoid, shun, give up. व्यप dispel, remove, destroy. अभि overlay, cover. अव push down. उद् push upwards, bring forth. अभ्युद् push on, push further. व्युद् push asunder, move away, sweep out. उप push near, insert, produce. समुप bring near, offer. निस् push out, pull out, remove. परि heap or pile round, surround, fortify. प्रति push back, strip off, doff, remove; keep off, detain; reject, refuse; outstrip, surpass, excel; disturb, interrupt. वि push asunder, separate, divide, arrange (esp. in battle-array). प्रतिवि arrange in return. सम् bring together, gather, collect. परिसम् sweep together. — Cf. उद्व्यूढ, उपोढ, निर्व्यूढ, व्यूढ.

2ऊह्, ओहते, ऊहति, °ते mind, mark, watch, wait or lurk for (acc. or loc.); conceive, understand; be regarded as, pass for (nom.). — अपि conceive, comprehend, guess. अभि wait or lurk for (acc.), also = prec. नि mind, notice.

1ऊह m. addition, change, modification.

2ऊह m. consideration, examination.

ऊहन n. the same.

1ऊहनीय & ऊह्य a. to be changed or modified.

2ऊहनीय & ऊह्य a. to be examined or found out.

ऊहवन्त् a. reasoning well, sagacious.

ऋ

ऋ, इयर्ति, ऋणोति, ऋणुते, ऋण्वति, ऋच्छति, °ते, अर्च्छति, अर्ति, pp ऋत (q.v.) move (tr.), raise, excite; move (intr.), rise, hasten, meet with, get at, reach, attain. C. अर्पयति hurl, throw, pierce, send, put, place, fasten or fix in, turn, direct (eyes or mind); offer, deliver, give back, restore. — अनु M. rise after (acc.). अप open, unlock. अभि hasten towards, approach, assail. आ put in, insert, get, procure, reach, fall into (acc.), afflict, distress. उद् rise, raise. C. make to rise or thrive. उप approach, assist; go against, offend, transgress. नि put down, set in; succumb, perish. निस् put asunder, dissolve; be deprived of (abl. or gen.). प्र go forth, advance, also = C. set in motion, stir up. प्रति insert. C. throw against, fasten, fix, put on; deliver, give back, restore. वि open (tr. & intr.). सम् put together, get done; come together, meet (instr.), run together to (acc. or loc.). C. hurl at (acc.) strike, hit; put on, insert, fasten; deliver, restore. — Cf. आर्त.

ऋकार m. the sound ऋ.

ऋक्तस् adv. concerning the Ric (cf. 2ऋच्).

ऋक्क, ऋक्कन्, & ऋक्कन्त् a. praising, m. praiser singer.

1ऋक्ष a. bald, bare.

2ऋक्ष a. hurtful, bad. m. bear, the Seven Stars (pl.); a kind of monkey; a man's name; f. ऋक्षी a. female bear; m. n. star, constellation, lunar mansion.

†ऋक्षर m. thorn (cf. अनृक्षर).

ऋक्षराज m. the king of the bears or monkeys, the king of the stars, i.e. the moon.

ऋक्षवन्त् m. N. of a mountain.

ऋक्षीका f. a kind of evil spirits.

ऋक्षेष्टि f. offering to the lunar mansions.

ऋक्संहिता f. the Riksaṃhitā, i.e. the collection of the Rigveda-hymns.

ऋग्मिन् a. praising.

ऋग्मिय or ऋग्मिय a. deserving praise, laudable.

ऋग्यजुष् n. du. the Rig- and Yajurvedas.

ऋग्विधान n. the application of the Ric, N. of a book.

ऋग्वेद m. the Rigveda (the hymns with or without the Brāhmaṇa and Sūtra works).

ऋघाय्, ऋघायति, °ते tremble, rage, rave.

ऋघावन् & °वन्त् a. raving, storming, impetuous.

1ऋच्, अर्चति beam, shine, sing, praise, honour, adorn. C. अर्चयति, °ते, pp. अर्चित (q.v.) cause to shine; honour, salute. — अभि sing, praise, honour. प्र shine forth, intone, sing, honour. सम् honour, worship, adorn. — Cf. ऋचसे.

2ऋच् f. lustre, beam; hymn, verse; the Rigveda (mostly pl.).

ऋचसे (dat. inf.) to praise.

ऋचीक m. N. of a man.

ऋचीषम a. E. of Indra.

1ऋज्, ऋञ्जति, °ते, ऋज्यति, °ते stretch out (intr.), strive after, long for. — अभि grasp, snatch. आ M. strive after, long for. नि reach, attain. प्र strive towards. सम् strive together. — Cf. इरज्य्, °ज्यति & ऋञ्जसान.

2ऋज्, अर्जति reach, get, obtain. C. अर्जयति, °ते = S. — अति get over, admit or remove. अनु & अव dismiss. उप admit; C. get, acquire.

ऋजिप्य a. striving onwards, hastening.

†ऋजीक a. beaming, shining (only —°).

ऋजीति a. burning, sparkling.

ऋजीयंस् compar. to ऋजु.

ऋजीष a. = seq., m. a cert. hell.

ऋजीषिन् a. hastening, advancing, swift.

ऋजु (f. ऋज्वी) straight, right, upright, honest; n. adv.

ऋजुता f. straightness; also = seq.

ऋजुत्व n. sincerity, honesty.

ऋजूय्, only ऋजूयन्त् honest & ऋजूयमान upright.

ऋजूया (instr. adv.) straightways, directly.

ऋजूयु a. honest.

ऋज्र a. reddish brown, dark red.

ऋञ्जसान a. rushing on, hastening near, striving to (acc.).

ऋण a. guilty; n. guilt, debt, obligation. ऋणं कृ borrow of (gen.), ° धारय् be indebted to (gen.), ° दा, नी, or संनी pay a debt.

ऋणकर्तृ a. indebted (lit. making debts).

ऋणया, °यात् & °यावन् a. prosecuting or punishing guilt.

ऋणवन् & °वन्त् a. guilty, indebted.

ऋणादान n. non-payment of a debt.

ऋणावन् a. = ऋणवन्.

ऋणिन् a. indebted, obliged; m. a debtor.

ऋत a. right, true, honest, fit, proper. n. & instr. ऋतेन adv.; n. as subst. right way, established order, divine law, pious work; righteousness, faith, truth, oath.

ऋतजा & ऋतजात a. right or righteous by nature.

ऋतज्ञा a. knowing the sacred law.

†ऋतद्युम्न a. full of sacred strength.

ऋतधीति a. right or true-minded.

ऋतनी a. leading the right way.

ऋतपा a. observing righteousness.

ऋतप्रजात a. = ऋतजा.

†ऋतप्सु a. of right or good appearance.

ऋतय्, °यते (pp. ऋतयन्त् or ऋतयन्त्) make right.

ऋतया (instr. adv.) in the right way.

ऋतयु a. observing the divine law, pious, holy.

ऋतयुज् a. well harnessed or well allied.

ऋतवाक m. right or pious speech.

ऋतसद् a. dwelling in truth.

ऋतसाप् a. practising righteousness.

ऋतस्पृश् a. loving (lit. touching) righteousness.

ऋताय्, pp. °यन्त् lead or make right, observe the law; be obedient, pious, or honest.

ऋतावन्, f. °वरी lawful, righteous, just, pious.

ऋतावृध् a. rejoicing in the divine law, holy-minded, faithful.

ऋतामृत n. du. truth and nectar.

ऋति or ऋति f. onset, struggle.

ऋतीय्, °यते struggle, quarrel.

ऋतीषह् (°षाह्) a. enduring or defying assault; durable, lasting.

ऋतु m. right or fixed time, period, epoch, season (mostly reckoned as 6, but also 5, 7, 12, & 24); the menses of a woman & coition at that time; fixed order, rule. — ऋतुना & ऋतुभिस् in time, at the appointed time, esp. for sacrifice or a festival; पुरा ऋतोस् before the (right) time, too early.

ऋतुकाल m. the time of the season or the time of menstruation.

ऋतुथा adv. in order, duly, exactly.

ऋतुपर्ण m. N. of a king.

ऋतुपर्यय m. the change of the seasons.

ऋतुमङ्गल n. good omen for the season.*

ऋतुलिङ्ग n. mark of the seasons.

ऋतुमन्त् a. coming at regular times; f. °मती having the menses.

ऋतुशस् adv. orderly, duly.

ऋतुसहार m. collection of the seasons, T. of a poem.

ऋतूत्सव m. feast of the season.*

ऋते (loc. as prep.) except, besides, without (abl. or acc.).

ऋतेजा a. living in truth or in the sacred law.

ऋतोक्ति, f. ऋतोद्य n. true speech.

ऋत्व n. timely seed; the menses.

1ऋत्वन्त m. the end of a season.

2ऋत्वन्त a. forming the end of a season (a day).

ऋत्विज् a. sacrificing at the proper seasons; m. a priest.

1ऋत्विय a. orderly, regular, corresponding to or knowing the sacred rules.

2ऋत्विय, f. आ menstruating; n. menstruation.

ऋद्, ऋदति, अर्दति dissolve (intr.), pass away; stir (tr.), trouble, vex, afflict, hurt, destroy, torment. C. अर्दयति, pp. अर्दित = S. tr. — अभि vex, afflict. वि pass away; C. destroy, annihilate. सम् C. wound.

ऋदूदर a. mild, soft, kind.

ऋद्ध a. thriven, prosperous, wealthy, rich.

ऋद्धि f. success, prosperity, welfare, happiness, perfection.

ऋद्धिमन्त् a. prosperous, considerable, important, wealthy, rich in (—°).

ऋध्, ऋध्नोति, ऋध्यते, °ति, pp. ऋद्ध (q.v.) thrive, succeed, prosper; make prosperous, further, promote, accomplish. C. अर्धयति gratify. — अनु fulfil, execute. वि be deprived of (instr.). C. exclude from, deprive of (instr.). सम् thrive, prosper, be accomplished. C. make succeed, fulfil, furnish with (instr.). — Cf. व्यृद्ध, समृद्ध.

ऋधक् or ऋधक् adv. separately, singly, apart, particularly.

ऋबीस n. gulf, abyss.

ऋभु a. skilful, clever; m. artist, builder, N. of three myth. beings, the Ribhus, esp. the first of them.

ऋभुक्षन् & °क्षा m. N. of the first Ribhu, E. of Indra and the Maruts.

ऋभ्व & ऋभ्वन् a. clever, skilful.

ऋभ्वस् a. the same; skilfully made.

ऋश्य m. the male of a species of antelope.

ऋश्यद a. pit for catching antelopes.

ऋश्यमूक m. N. of a mountain.

ऋश्यशृङ्ग m. a man's name.

1ऋष्, अर्षति flow, glide. — अनु flow after (acc.). अभि flow or let flow towards (acc.). परि flow or let flow round (acc.). वि run through (acc.). सम् meet with (instr.), come together to (acc.).

2ऋष्, ऋषति, pp. ऋष्ट push, thrust. — नि put in, cover, fill.

ऋषभ m. bull, male animal i.g.; the best, first, chief of (—°).

ऋषि m. holy singer, poet, saint, sage, hermit, a Rishi; pl. w. सप्तन् the seven (i.e. many)
7 Rishis of the olden times, or the seven stars of the Great Bear.

ऋषिकल्प a. resembling a Rishi or approaching him in dignity.

ऋषिकुमार m. the boy or son of a Rishi.

ऋषिद्विष् a. hating Rishis.

ऋषिपुत्र m. the son of a Rishi.

ऋषियज्ञ m. offering to the Rishis (i.e. prayer and study of the Veda).

ऋषिवत् adv. like a Rishi.

ऋषु (only gen. pl.) flame, glowing fire.

ऋष्टि f. spear.

ऋष्टिमन्त् a. armed with spears.

ऋष्टिविद्युत् a. shining with spears.

ऋष्यमूक & ऋष्यशृङ्ग m. = ऋश्यमूक & ऋश्यशृङ्ग.

ऋष्व a. high, lofty, sublime.

ऋहन्त् a. small, weak.

ए

ए pron. stem of 3d person.

एक a. one of (gen, abl., or — °); alone, sole, single, solitary; the same, identical, common (esp. °—); in l. l. a certain or = the indef. article; with न and mostly w. चन or अपि no one, none; pl. एके some. — एके—एके (अपरे, अन्ये) some—some (others).

एकक (f. एकका & एकिका) sole, single.

एककाल a. occurring at the same time; abstr. °ता f., °त्व n.

एककालम् & °लिकम् adv. (only) once a day.

एकक्रम (°— & instr.) mutually or at once.*

एकक्रियाविधि m. application of one and the same verb.

एकखुर a. one-hoofed, i.e. whole-hoofed; m. such an animal.

एकग्राम m. the same village; °ग्रामीण a. dwelling in the same village.

एकचक्र a. having (only) one wheel.

एकचर a. going alone, solitary.

1एकचित्त n. one and the same thought.

2एकचित्त a. having one and the same thought, agreeing; abstr. °ता f.

एकच्छत्र n. = एकातपत्र.

एकज a. born or growing alone.

एकजात a. born of the same parents.

एकजाति a. having (only) one birth (cf. द्विजाति) or belonging to the same family.

एकत m. N. of a cert. mythol. being.

एकतम or एकतम a. one of many.

एकतय, f. ई single.

एकतर a. one of two.

एकतस् adv. from or on one side, also = abl. of एक.

एकता f. unity, identity.

एकतोदन्त a. having only one row of teeth.

एकत्र adv. in one or in the same place, together, also = loc. of एक.

एकत्रिंश a. the thirty-first.

एकत्रिंशत् f. thirty-one.

एकत्व n. = एकता, also = singular (g.).

एकदा adv. at once, at the same time, sometimes, at a certain time = once upon a time.

एकदुःख a. having the same sorrow.

एकदेश m. a certain place or spot, one and the same place; a part or portion of a whole, something individual.

1एकधन m. a kind of jug (r.).

2एकधन n. one (part of the) property.

3एकधन a. having something as one's only property or wealth, quite filled with (—°).

एकधर्म & °धर्मिन् a. having the same nature.

एकधा adv. simply, singly; together with (instr.).

एकपञ्चाशत् f. fifty-one.

एकपत्नि a. having (only) one wife.

एकपत्नी f. the wife of one man, a faithful wife; pl. having one and the same man.

एकपद् or एकपद् (°पाद्), f. °पदी a having (only) one foot, limping, lame, imcomplete. f. एकपदी foot-path.

1एकपद n. one and the same spot; one (and the same) word. — °दम् & °दे on the spot, at once, suddenly.

2एकपद a. measuring only one step; having one foot; consisting of one word.

एकपर a. only and solely important or dear.

एकपलाधिक n. one pala more.

एकपातिन् a. being alone, solitary.

1एकपाद m. one foot.

2एकपाद a. one-footed; f. आ N. of a Rākṣasī.

एकपार्थिव m. single ruler, monarch.

एकपीत a. only i.e. quite yellow.

एकपुरुष m. only one man or the one (supreme) spirit.

एकप्रहारिक a. getting (only) one blow; °कं कृ kill with one blow.*

एकफल a. offering the same fruit as (—°).

एकबुद्धि a. having only one thought, unanimous

एकभक्त & °भक्ति a. devoted only to one, faithful.

1एकभाव m. the being one, oneness, simplicity.
2एकभाव a. being or becoming one.
एकभाविन् & °भूत a. the same.
1एकमति f. the mind fixed upon one object.
2एकमति a. unanimous.
एकमनस् a. the same + having the mind fixed upon one thing, thoughtful.
एकमय, f. ई only consisting of or in (—°).
एकमाषक n. one māṣa (a cert. weight).
एकमुख a. having one mouth, head, or chief; having the same aim.
एकमूल a. having but one root.
*एकयष्टि & °का f. a single string of pearls.
एकयोनि a. of the same womb or origin.
1एकरस m. the only inclination or pleasure.
2एकरस a. having only one inclination; finding pleasure only in (—°).
एकराज् & एकराज m. single king, monarch; f. एकराज्ञी single queen.
एकरात्र m. a ceremony lasting one night; n. a night's (day's) duration.
एकरात्रिक a. sufficient for one night or day.
एकरिक्थिन् m. coheir.
1एकरूप n. one form or manner.
2एकरूप a. of one colour, uniform; n. N. of two metres.
एकरूपता f. uniformity, immutability.
एकर्च a. consisting of one verse; n. such a hymn.
एकर्षि m. the only or chief Rishi.
एकल a. one, alone.
एकलोचन a. one-eyed; f. आ N. of a Rākṣasī.
एकवचन n. the singular number.
एकवर्ण a. one-coloured, not brindled.
एकवसन a. having only one garment.
एकवस्त्र (abstr. °ता f.) & °वासस् a. the same.
एकविंश, f. ई the twenty-first or consisting of twenty-one.
एकविंशक, f. °शिका the same.
एकविंशत् f. pl., एकविंशति f. sgl. (& pl.) twenty-one.
एकविध a. of one kind, simple; identical.
एकवीर m. an only, i.e. an incomparable hero.
1एकवेणि or °णी f. a single braid of hair (as a sign of mourning); °णीधरा f. wearing such a one.
2एकवेणी f. consisting of a single braid (hair).
1एकवेद m. only one Veda.
2एकवेद a. knowing only one Veda.
एकवेश्मन् n. one house or stable.
एकव्रत a. commanding alone or devoted only to one, i.e. faithful.
1एकशत n. 101.
2एकशत & एकशततम a. the 101st.
एकशफ a. one i.e. whole-hoofed. m. a whole-hoofed animal; n. the solidungulous class of animals.
एकशस् adv. singly.
एकशेष m. the only rest, only left of (—°); a kind of ellipsis (g.).
एकश्रुति a. monotonous; f. monotony, a kind of accent (g.).
एकषष्ट a. the sixty-first.
एकषष्टि f. sixty-one.
एकसंश्रय a. keeping together; m. as subst.
एकसप्तत a. the seventy-first.
एकसप्तति f. seventy-one.
एकसप्ततिगुण a. multiplied by seventy-one.
एकसहस्र n. 1001; adj. the 1001st.
एकसार a. whose only essence is (—°).
एकस्तम्भ a. resting upon one pillar.
एकस्थ a. standing together, joined, concentrated, assembled. — With भू join, meet.*
एकस्थान n. one or the same place.
एकहायन, f. ई one year old; f. a heifer one year old.
एकांश m. part; °ता f. partnership.
एकाकिन् a. alone, solitary.
1एकाक्ष a. having only one axle.
2एकाक्ष a. one-eyed.
1एकाक्षर n. the only imperishable; only one syllable.
2एकाक्षर a. monosyllable; n. a monosyllabic word.
एकाग्र a. having one point or aim, fixed, concentrated, intent or attentive upon (—°). n. & °तस् adv., abstr. °ता f., °त्व n.
एकाङ्ग n. a single member or part; m. pl. a body guard.
एकाङ्गरूपक n. an incomplete simile.
एकातपत्र a. being under one umbrella (cf. आतपत्र); w. प्रभुत्व n. universal sovereignty.

1एकात्मन् m. the one spirit.
2एकात्मन् a. reduced to one's self, solitary; of the same essence as (gen.), abstr. °त्मता f.
एकादश, f. ई the eleventh.
एकादशगुण a. eleven times as much.
एकादशन् a. eleven.
एकादशम a. the eleventh.
एकादशिन् a. consisting of eleven; f. °शिनी the number eleven.
एकादशद्वार a. having eleven gates.
एकाधिक a. more by one.
एकानर्थ a. suffering the same mischief.
एकानुदिष्ट n. (sc. श्राद्ध) funeral meal in honour of one ancestor.
1एकान्त m. a solitary place, lonelines, exclusiveness, absolute oneness. एकान्त (°—), एकान्तम्, °न्तेन, °न्तात्, & °न्ततस् adv. exclusively, absolutely, wholly, necessarily.
2एकान्त a. quite devoted to or intent upon (loc. or —°); abstr. °ता f.
एकान्तभीरु a. quite afraid or timorous.
एकान्तर a. separated by one intermediate member.
एकान्तशील a. fond of solitude.
एकान्तसाध्य a. quite practicable.
एकान्तहित a. quite good, perfect.
एकान्तिन् a. = 2एकान्त, abstr. °न्तित्व n.
एकान्नादिन् a. eating the food given by one.
एकान्वय a. belonging to the same family, related to (gen.).
एकापाय m. diminution by one (in each).
1एकायन n. a path passable for only one; meeting-place; absolute oneness.
2एकायन a. passable for only one, narrow.
एकार m. the sound ए.
1एकार्थ m. one and the same matter.
2एकार्थ a. having the same object or meaning; abstr. °ता f., °त्व n.
एकावलि or °ली f. a single string of pearls (adj. —° f. ई).
एकाह m. period or ceremony of one day.
एकाहन् n. one single day.
एकिन् a. single, simple.
एकी कृ unite; °भू become one.
एकीभाव m. becoming one.
एकैक a. each single or singly (also pl.); n. adv.
एकैकशस् adv. each singly, one by one.
एकैश्वर्य n. universal sovereignty.
एकोत्तर a. greater or more by one.
एकोदक a. connected by the water-libation (lit. having the same w.-l.); related, kin.
एकोद्दिष्ट n. = एकानुदिष्ट.
एकोन a. less by one.
एज्, एजति stir, move, tremble; C. एजयति, °ते move (tr.). — अप drive away, chase. उद् move, rise. सम् the same.
एजथु m. trembling, shaking (of the earth).
एजन्त् a. moving, alive.
†एजय a. stirring, rousing (only —°).
एज्य a. to be offered.
एड & एडक m. a kind of sheep.
एण m., एणी f. a kind of black antelope.
एणनेत्रा, एणाक्षी, & एणीदृश् f. deer-eyed.
1एत pron. stem, nom. sgl. एष, एषा, एतद् (q.v.) this, this here; refers oftener to the preceding than the following; may be connected with another demonstr., rel. or interr. pron. — Loc. एतस्मिन् in this case.
2एत, f. एनी rushing, quick; m. a deer; f. एता a doe.
3एत a. arrived, come.
एतग्व a. going quickly.
एतत्काल m. this time, i.e. present (opp. तत्काल).
एतत्तुल्य a. like this.
एतद् (n. sgl. of एत) adv. thus, in this manner.
एतदन्त a. ending with this or these.
एतदर्थम् adv. for this purpose, therefore.
एतदवस्थ a. being in this condition, thus situated.
एतद्योनि a. having this origin.
एतद्वश a. depending on this.
एतद्विद् a. knowing this.
एतन्नामक a. having this name.
एतन्निमित्तम् adv. for this reason.*
एतन्मय, f. ई consisting of this, of such a kind or nature.
एतर्हि adv. now, at present, at this time (often correl. to यर्हि).
एतवे & एतवै dat. inf. to 2इ.
एतश & एतश a. swift, quick; m. a horse, esp. of the Sun.

एतादृच, °दृश् & °दृश (f. ई) such, of this or the same kind.
एतावन्त् a. so great, so much, so many, so far; n. adv., loc. एतावति at such a distance, here.
एतावन्मात्र n. so much.*
एति f. arrival.
एतृ a. going (—°).
एद् (= आ + इद्) behold! (w. acc.).
एध्, एधते (°ति), pp. एधित thrive, prosper, grow up, get strong, great, or happy. C. एधयति make thrive or prosper, strengthen, honour, celebrate. — सम् = S.
एध a. kindling (—°); m. sgl. & pl. fuel.
एधतु m. f. prosperity, welfare.
एधवन्त् a. nourished with fuel.
1एधस् (n. sgl. & pl.) fuel.
2एधस् n. prosperity.
एधोदक n. fuel and water.
1एन pron. stem of 3^d pers. (used subst.).
2एन m. deer (only —°).
एनस् n. sin, crime, fault.
एनस्वन्त् & °स्विन् sinful, wicked.
एना (instr. of 1अ adv.) thus, in this way, here, there, then. — एना परः beyond here; परः एना beyond (w. instr.).
एम m., एमन् n. course, way, path.
एरक m. N. of a serpent-demon; f. आ a kind of grass, ई N. of a plant & a river.
एरण्ड m. the castor-oil plant.
एला f. cardamoms.
1एव, एवा adv. so, even so; certainly, really; even, just, exactly, emphasizing the prec. word or only expl., often connected with a pron. or another adv., e.g. स एव, एतदेव, इत्येव, तथैव, नैव, चैव; एव च, एव वा, etc.
2एव a. speedy, quick; m. (mostly pl.) course, way, custom, manner, use.
एवंरूप a. of such a form or kind.
एवंविद् & °विद्वंस् a. knowing (thus).
एवंविध a. of such sort, such.
एवंवृत्त a. behaving thus.
एवंकर्मन् a. having (done) this deed.
एवंगत a. so circumstanced or situated, such; loc. under such circumstances.
एवंगुण & °गुणोपेत a. having such qualities or virtues.
एवंतर्किन् a. so thinking.
एवंदर्शिन् a. so seeing or judging.
एवम् adv. so, in this way (later than एव q.v.), often correl. to यथा. Refers to what precedes or follows. एवं कृत्वा for this reason.
एवमादि a. this (these) and the like, similar (lit. whose beginning is such).
एवंपूर्व a. preceded by this (lit. having such a predecessor).
एवंप्रकार a. of such kind.
एवंप्राय a. the same.
एवंभूत a. (being) such.
एवया & °यावन् a. going quickly, swift.
एवयामरुत् exclamation pertaining in some way to the Maruts.
एवाष m. a cert. small animal.
एष्, एषति creep, slide.
1एष a. rushing on, एष m. as subst.
2एष m. seeking, looking for; wish, desire.
एषण a. seeking, wishing; n. & एषणा f. the same as subst.
एषिन् a. = prec. adj. (mostly —°).
एष्ट a. won by offerings or worship.
एष्टव्य a. to be sought or desired.
एष्टि f. wish, desire.
एष्टृ a. rushing on, advancing.
1एष्य a. to come, future.
2एष्य a. to be sought or searched.
एह a. wishing, desirous.
†एहस् v. अनेहस्.

ऐ

ऐ interj.
ऐकमत्य n. unanimity.
ऐकशफ a. coming from one-hoofed animals.
ऐकश्रुत्य n. monotony.
ऐकाग्र्य n. concentrated attention.
ऐकात्म्य n. unity of essence or nature.

ऐकान्तिक, f. ई exclusive, absolute.
ऐकान्त्य n. exclusiveness.
ऐकार m. the sound ऐ.
ऐकार्थ्य n. unity of purpose, meaning, or notion.
ऐकाहिक, f. ई ephemeral, quotidian; belonging to the Ekāha-ceremony.
ऐक्य n. unity, identity.
ऐक्षव & °क्षूव, f. ई made of or coming from the sugar-cane; n. sugar.
ऐक्ष्वाक, f. ई belonging to Ikṣvāku; m. a descendant of I.
ऐड, f. ई containing refreshment; m. descendant of Iḍā, i.e. Purūravas.
ऐण a. coming from the male black antelope.
ऐणेय a. the same; m. = एण.
ऐतदात्म्य n. the state of being the nature of this (ph.).
ऐतरेय m. N. of an ancient teacher (lit. descendant of Itarā); a. coming from Aitareya.
ऐतरेयक & ऐतरेयब्राह्मण n. the Brāhmaṇa of Aitareya.
ऐतरेयिन् m. pl. the school of Aitareya.
ऐतिहासिक, f. ई relater of old legends.
ऐतिह्य n. oral tradition.
ऐदंपर्य n. chief matter or purpose.
ऐध m. thrift, prosperity.
ऐन्दव, f. ई lunar, belonging to the moon.
ऐन्द्र, f. ई Indra's, belonging to or coming from I.; n. E. of a lunar mansion.
ऐन्द्रजाल n. magic, sorcery.
ऐन्द्रजालिक, f. ई magical; m. a juggler.
ऐन्द्रिय a. sensual, belonging to or perceptible by the senses; n. sensual pleasure.
ऐभ, f. ई belonging to an elephant.
ऐरावण m. N. of Indra's elephant.
ऐरावत m. the same; also N. of a fabulous serpent-demon.
ऐल m. = ऐड m.
ऐलब m. noise, roar.
ऐश a. Çiva's, belonging to Çiva.
ऐशान, f. ई the same + north-eastern; f. ई (sc. दिश्) the north-east (Çiva's quarter).
ऐशि m. son of Īça i.e. Çiva; patr. of Skanda.
ऐश्य n. power, might, sway.
ऐश्वर, f. ई belonging to a sovereign or great lord, majestic; n. sovereignty, supremacy.
ऐश्वर्य n. = prec. n. (w. gen., loc., or —°); reign, realm, dominion; superhuman power; poss. °वन्त्.
ऐश्वर्यमत्त a. intoxicated by power.
ऐषमस् adv. this year.
ऐषीक a. made of stalks or cane.
ऐष्टक a. made of bricks.
ऐष्टिकपौर्तिक a. consisting of sacrifices and charitable works.
ऐहलौकिक a. belonging to this world.
ऐहिक a. the same.

ओ

ओ = 1आ + 2उ.
ओक s. home, house.
ओकस् n. wont, comfort, pleasure; wonted or resting place, refuge, home.
ओकार m. the sound ओ.
ओक्य a. homely; n. = ओकस्.
ओघ m. flood, stream (p. °वन्त्); abundance, heap, multitude of (—°).
ओंकार m. the syllable ओम् (q.v.).
ओगण a. standing alone, an outcast.
ओज a. odd (the first, third, etc.).
ओजस् n. strength, vigour, energy, power, might; instr. ओजसा with might, energetically.
ओजसीन a. showing one's self strong.
ओजस्य & ओजस्वन्त् a. powerful.
ओजस्विता f. (strength, power*); energetic speech.
ओजस्विन् a. strong, energetic, courageous.
ओजाय, °यते employ or show strength.
ओजिष्ठ (superl.) the strongest of (gen.); very strong or mighty.
ओजीयंस् (compar.) stronger or mightier than (abl.); very strong or mighty.

ओजोदा a. giving strength.
ओज्मन् m. strength.
ओड m. N. of a man.
ओड्र m. N. of a country, pl. a people.
ओढ a. brought near, got, procured.
ओणि (m. or f.) a kind of Soma-vessel.
ओण्ड्र m. pl. N. of a people.
ओत a. woven or sewn in, pulled through (loc.), interwoven with (instr.).
ओतवे, ओतवै & ओतुम्, infin. of 2वा.
ओतु m. the woof or cross-threads of a web.
ओद्ती f. flowing forth, rising, waving, swarming.
ओदन m. n. boiled rise, porridge; food i.g.
ओदनपचन m. the southern fire of the altar (lit. rice-boiler).
ओदनपिण्ड m. rice-cake (r.).
ओदनमय a. consisting of boiled rice.*
ओदनवन्त् a. having boiled rice.
ओदनीय्, °यति wish for boiled rice.
ओद्मन् n. waving, flooding; moisture, rain.
ओपश m. lock of hair, top-knot; p. °शिन्.
ओम् (indecl.) the mystic syllable Om (somewhat like Amen!).
†ओम m. = ऊम.
1ओमन् m. protection, favour, assistance.
2ओमन् m. = ओम.
ओमन्वन्त् a. friendly, favourable.
ओमात्रा & ओम्या f. = ओमन्.
ओम्यावन्त् = ओमन्वन्त्.
ओष m. burning, combustion.
ओषधि or °धी f. a herb or plant.
ओषधिपति m. the lord of the plants, i.e. the moon or a physician.
ओषधीमन्त् a. poss. to ओषधी.
ओषम् adv. quickly, at once.
ओष्ठ m. the (down-hanging) upper-lip, lip i.g. (adj. —° f. ई).
ओष्ठ्य a. being at or belonging to the lips, labial; m. labial sound.
ओह m. attention, kindness, service, also = ओहस्.
ओहब्रह्मन् m. a real or true Brahman.
ओहस् n. conception, notion; instr. really.

औ

औकार m. the sound औ.
औक्ष, f. ई coming from an ox, taurine.
औक्षक n. a multitude of oxen.
औक्षण or औक्ष्ण a. the same.
औग्र्य n. fierceness, dreadfulness.
औघ m. a flood.
औचित्य n. fitness, propriety; wont, habit; pleasure at (—°).
औच्चैःश्रवस m. N. of a mythical horse.
औज्ज्वल्य n. brilliancy, brightness.
औडव, f. ई relating to the stars.
औत्कण्ठ्य & औत्क्य n. longing, desire.
औत्तम & °मि m. patr. of the third Manu.
औत्तराधर्य n. state of being above one another.
औत्पत्तिक, f. ई inborn, natural.
औत्पातिक, f. ई prodigious, supernatural.
औत्सुक्य n. longing, desire; p. °वन्त्.
औदक, f. ई belonging to water, grown in water, watery, aquatic.
औदन्य & °न्यव m. patron. of Muṇḍibha.
औदन्वत a. marine.
औदर a. being in the belly.
औदरिक a. voracious, gluttonous.
औदर्य a. being in the belly or womb.
औदात्त्य n. having the high tone (g.).
औदार्य n. sublimity; generosity, liberality (also °ता f.).
औदासीन्य & औदास्य n. indifference.
औदुम्बर, f. ई coming from the Udumbara tree, made of its wood.
औद्गात्र a. relating to the Udgātṛ; n. his office.
औद्दालकि m. patron. to उद्दालक.
औद्धत्य n. haughtiness, arrogance.
औद्धारिक a. belonging to the additional share (j.).
औद्भिद a. springing forth, prevailing, victorious; n. spring-water.
औद्भिद्य n. prevalence, victoriousness.

औद्गात्र & °त्रियⁿ n. = prec.
औद्वाहिक a. relating to marriage, given at marriage.
औन्नत्य n. height.
औन्मुख्य n. longing, ardent desire.
औपकार्य n. or °र्या f. royal tent.
औपच्छन्दसक & °सिक n. N. of a metre.
औपधिक a. deceitful; m. deceiver, extorter of money.
औपनायनिक a. relating to the initiation.
औपनिधिक a. forming a deposit (j.).
औपनिषद, f. ई contained or taught in the Upanishads.
औपमन्यव m. patron. to उपमन्यु.
औपम्य n. likeness, similitude, comparison.
औपयिक, f. ई answering to a purpose, suitable, fit, proper.
औपल a. stony, of stone.
औपवसथिक & °वसथ्य a. belonging to the fast-day.
औपवाह्य a. used for driving or riding (carriage, elephant, etc.).
औपासन m. (sc. अग्नि) the fire used for domestic rites.
औम a. flaxen or relating to Umā.
औरग a. relating to serpents, serpentine.
औरभ्र a. belonging to or coming from a ram or sheep.
औरभ्रिक m. shepherd.
औरस, f. ई produced from the breast or the (own) body; innate, natural, own; self-begotten, legitimate; m. & f. ई a legitimate child.
औरस्य a. = prec. a.
और्ण & और्णिक a. woollen.
और्णासूत्र, f. ई consisting of woollen threads.
और्ध्वदेह n. the future life.
और्ध्वदेहिक a. relating to the future life; n. funeral solemnities.
1और्व, f. ई relating to the earth.
2और्व m. Aurva, patron. of sev. Rishis.
3और्व a. relating to Aurva (v. prec.); m. the submarine fire (supposed to come from A.).
और्वशेय a. descending from Urvaçī.
और्वाग्नि & और्वानल m. = 3और्व m.
और्वाय, °यते be like the Aurva fire.
औलूखल a. belonging to the mortar; m. du. mortar and pestle.
औशनस, f. ई a. & patron. to उशनस्.
औशिज a. eager, zealous.
औशीनर, f. ई belonging to the Uçīnaras; f. N. of the wife of Purūravas.
औशीर a. made of the Uçīra root; n. such an unguent.
औषध a. consisting of herbs. n. a herb or herbs (collect.); simples, medicine.
औषधविक्रयिन् a. selling medicine.
औषस a. early, matutinal; f. ई daybreak.
औष्ट्र a. derived from a buffalo or camel.
औष्ट्रक n. a multitude of camels.
औष्ठ a. lip-shaped.
औष्ण्य n. warmth, heat.

क

1क stem of the interr. pron. (n. कद् older than किम् q.v.) who, what, which? Used as subst. or adj. in direct & indirect questions, often connected w. इव, उ, नाम, नु, वा, स्विद्, also w. a demonstr. pron., e.g. को ऽयमायाति who comes here? किमिदं कुरुषे what are you doing there? Used also as indef. pron. = some, any, whoever, whatever, whichever, esp. after य & मा, before च, चन, चिद्, & (later) अपि; कश्च, कश्चन, etc. w. neg. = nobody, none, n. nothing. कश्चित्-कश्चित् the one-the other; pl. some-others.
2क m. the god Who (E. of Prajāpati, Brahman, etc.); n. joy, water, head.
कंवन्त् a. salutary, pleasant, lovely.
कंस m. a vessel made of metal; metal, brass (also n.); N. of a myth. king slain by Kṛṣṇa.
कंसनिषूदन, कंसशत्रु, & कंसारि m. E. of Kṛṣṇa (v. prec.).
ककार m. the sound क.

ककुत्स्थ m. N. of an ancient king.

ककुद् f. peak of a mountain, hump on the shoulders of the Indian bull; head, chief.

ककुद n. (m.) the same.

ककुद्मन् a. high, lofty.

ककुद्मन्त् a. = prec. & seq.; m. mountain or buffalo.

ककुद्मिन् a. having a hump.

ककुन्मन्त् a. towering, lofty.

ककुभ् f. peak, summit; region, quarter; N. of a metre.

ककुभ a. high, lofty, sublime, eminent. m. a kind of goblin, a cert. musical mode.

ककुह a. = prec. adj.

कक्कोल m. a cert. tree (also ई f.); n. (also °क n.) a perfume made of its berries.

कक्ष m. hiding-place, recess; thicket, weeds; f. आ enclosed court, private apartment; m. & f. आ armpit, region of the girth; girdle, cincture; balance (mostly f.); likeness, similarity; rivalry, emulation (only f.)

कक्षीवन्त् m. N. of a Rishi.

1कक्ष्य a. belonging to a thicket.

2कक्ष्य a. hidden. secret. f. आ girdle, cincture; balance.

कङ्क m. heron; N. of a man, pl. of a people.

कङ्कट m. mail, armour.

कङ्कण n. ring-shaped ornament, bracelet.

कङ्कणाभरण a. adorned with a golden bracelet.*

कङ्कत m., कङ्कतिका f. comb.

1कङ्कपत्त्र n. a heron's feather (on the arrow).

2कङ्कपत्त्र a. furnished with heron's feathers; m. such an arrow.

कङ्कपत्त्रिन् a. = prec. a.

कङ्काल m. n. skeleton.

कङ्केलि or °ल्लि m., °ल्ली f. the Açoka tree.

कङ्कोल m., °ली f. N. of a plant.

कच m. the hair of the head; N. of a son of Bṛhaspati.

कचटतपगजडदब n. specimen of a nonsensical speech.

कचरूपिन् a. wearing the form of Kaca.

कच्चिद् v. कद्.

कच्छ m. the margin of a river or lake; marshy or watery ground.

कच्छप m. tortoise; N. of a serpent-demon.

कज n. a lotus.

कज्जल n., ई f. lampblack, used as ink or a collyrium.

कञ्चुक m. n., ई f. (adj. —° f. आ) coat of mail, bodice, jacket.

कञ्चुकिन् m. chamberlain (poss. to prec.).

1†कट v. विंकट.

2कट m. a straw mat; hip (= कटि); the temples of an elephant; a cert. throw of the dice.

कटक m. a straw mat; m. n. cord, string, bracelet; valley; royal camp; caravan.

कटकटाय्, °यति & °ते gnash, grate (onomat.).

कटकरण n., °क्रिया f. the twisting of a mat.

कटपूतन m., °ना f. a kind of demon.

कटाक्ष m. a sidelong glance.

कटाग्नि m. straw-fire.

कटाह m. (n., & ई f.) a frying pan, anything hollow, e.g. the temples of an elephant.

कटि or कटी f. hip.

कटु a. pungent, biting, sharp, bitter; abstr. °ता f., °त्व n.

कटुक a. = prec. adj.; abstr. °ता† f., °त्व† n.

कटुकित a. irritated (lit. made sharp).*

कटुभाषिन् a. speaking sharply.*

कट्ट्, कट्टयति hill (i.e. heap up the earth about).

कट्फल & कट्वङ्ग m. names of trees.

कठ m. N. of an ancient teacher & his disciples.

कठिन a. hard, violent (abstr. °ता f., °त्व n.); f. ई chalk; n. cooking vessel.

कठिनय्, °यति & कठिनी कृ make hard, harden.

कठोर a. hard, stiff; sharp, cruel; young, buxom.

कठोरचित्त a. hard-hearted; abstr. °ता f.

कठोरय्, यति harden, strengthen, vivify.

कड a. dumb.

कडार a. tawny.

कण m. a small grain or single seed; flake, drop, spark; atom, a bit.

कणवाहिन् a. bearing drops, wet.

कणाद m. N. of the author of the Vaiçeṣika philosophy.

कणान्न a. feeding on grains, abstr. °ता f.
कणिक m. = कण.
कणूकय्, pp. °यन्ती being in distress.
कण्टक m. thorn, prickle, point, sting, fish-bone; erection of the hair of the body; annoyance, vexation, pain; foe, enemy.
कण्टकित a. thorny, covered with erect hairs.
कण्टकिद्रुम & °वृक्ष m. thorn-tree.
कण्टकिन् a. thorny; m. thorn-plant.
कण्ठ m. (adj. —° f. आ & ई) throat, neck (lit. & fig.); sound, voice; —° often = having a thing at or in the throat.
कण्ठग a. reaching up to the throat.
कण्ठगत a. the same, being at or in the throat, cf. कण्ठवर्तिन्.
कण्ठग्रह m., °ण n. an embrace.
कण्ठभूषण n., *°भूषा f. ornament for the neck.
कण्ठवर्तिन् a. being in the throat i.e. ready to escape (life).
कण्ठसज्जन n. hanging down from the neck.
कण्ठाश्लेष m. = कण्ठग्रह.
कण्ठ्य a. being at or in the throat; produced by the throat, guttural.
कण्डन n. thrashing, husking; husk, chaff; f. ई mortar.
कण्डु, mostly कण्डू f. itching, scratching.
कण्डुर & **कण्डुल** a. itching.
कण्डूति f. = कण्डु.
कण्डूय्, °यति, °यते scratch; M. itch (lit. & fig.).
कण्डूयन n. scratching, itching.
कण्व m. N. of an old Rishi, pl. his descendants.
कतक m. the Kataka tree; n. the nut of it (used for clearing water).
कतम a. (pron. interr.) who or which (of many)?
कतर (pron. interr.) who or which (of two)?
कतरतस् (adv. interr.) on which of the two sides?
1**कति** (pron. interr.) how many? w. चिद् & अपि some, several.
2**कति** m. N. of an ancient sage.
कतिथ w. चिद् (pron. indef.) the so and so maniest.
कतिधा (adv. interr.) in how many places or parts? how often? w. चिद् everywhere.
कतिपय, f. ई (आ) some, several. *Instr. & abl. n. adv. with some exertion, hardly.
कतिपयकुसुम a. having few flowers or blossoms.
कतिपयरात्रम् (acc. adv.) some days (lit. nights).
कतिपयाहस्य (gen. adv.) after some days.
कतिविध a. how manifold?
कत्ता f. a die.*
कत्थ्, कत्थते (°ति) boast, praise, flatter; abuse, blame. — वि boast or brag of (instr.), praise, extol; degrade, humble (also C.).
कत्थन a. & n. boasting.
कथंरूप a. of what shape?
कथंवीर्य a. of what power?
कथक a. relating; m. relater, reciter.
कथंजातीयक a. of what kind?
कथन a. telling, tale, story.
कथनीय a. to be told or named.
कथम् adv. how? in what way? whence? interr. & excl.; often followed by नु (= कथम् alone or = how much more, w. neg. how much less); also by इव, नाम, स्विद्. With चन, चिद्, & (later) अपि indef. somehow, in any way, scarcely, hardly, a little (कथम् sometimes doubled); w. a negation (कथं चन also alone) in no way, by no means, not at all. यथा कथं चिद् howsoever, anyhow.
कथंभूत a. how being? of what quality?
कथय्, °यति (°यते), pp. कथित (q.v.) talk, converse with (instr. ± सह); relate, report, denounce, declare, explain, state. P. be called, pass for (nom.). — परि name. प्र announce, report. वि talk idly, chatter. सम् = S.
कथयितव्य a. to be told or mentioned.
1**कथा** adv. how? in what way? whence? In a. l. more frequent than कथम् q.v. — यथा कथा च howsoever.
2**कथा** f. talk, conversation about (loc. or —°); tale, story of (gen. or —°); communication, mention, statement; discussion, dialogue. — का कथा what mention of i.e. to say nothing of (gen., loc., or प्रति w. acc.). कैषा कथा to say nothing of it. कथां कृ talk or think of (gen.).*
कथानक n. a short tale or story.

कथान्तर n. (course of) conversation.
कथावली f. collection of tales.
कथासरित्सागर m. ocean of the rivers of tales, T. of a work of Somadeva.
कथित a. said, mentioned; n. talk, conversation.
कथोदय m. beginning of a tale; mention, statement.
कद् (Ved. n. acc. sgl. of 1क) nonne, num? w. neg. & चन by no means; कच्चिद् & कच्चिन्नु = कद् alone. Often °—, where it marks abnormity or defectiveness.
कदन n. slaughter, destruction.
कदम्ब & °क m. the Kadamba tree (has orange-coloured fragrant blossoms). m. multitude, group.
कदम्बगोल m. Kadamba blossom (lit. globe)*.
कदम्बपुष्पत्व a. state of a Kadamba blossom (v. prec.).
कदर्थ a. having what purpose?
कदर्थन n., °ना f. vexation, annoyance.
कदर्थय्, °यति despise, vex, annoy; *surpass.
कदर्य a. avaricious, stingy; abstr. °ता f.
कदल m., °ली f. N. of a tree.
कदलिका f. the same; flag, banner.
कदलीगृह n. bower of Kadalī trees.
कदा adv. when? at what time? how? With न never; w. चन the same or at some time, once; w. चिद् some time or other, sometimes, perhaps; w. अपि (later) at any time, always, ever. कदा चिद्, कदा चिदपि, & कदापि w. न never.
कद्रु a. tawny, reddish-brown. f. कद्रू a cert. Soma-vessel; N. of the mythol. mother of serpents (also कद्रु).
कधप्रिय & °प्री a. ever kind or friendly.
कन् (only pp. कायमान, aor. अकानिषम्, & perf. or intens.-stem चाकन् or चकान्) be glad, be satisfied with, enjoy (acc., loc., gen., or instr.); be liked, please, (w. gen.); love, wish, desire (acc.). — आ be pleased with (loc.); strive after, long for. — Cf. संचकान.
कनक n. gold; m. N. of sev. plants.
कनकमय, f. ई golden.
कनकरस m. liquid gold.
कनकवलय m. n. a gold bracelet.
कनकशक्ति m. E. of Skanda (lit. Gold-spear).
कनकसूत्र n. a gold cord or chain.
कनकाब्ज n. gold-lotus.
कनकोज्ज्वल a. shining with gold.
कनखल n. N. of a bathing-place.
कना f. a girl.
कनिष्क m. N. of an Indoscythic king.
कनिष्ठ or कनिष्ठ (superl.) the smallest, least, lowest, youngest, younger; f. आ the youngest wife, (± अङ्गुलि) the little finger.
कनिष्ठक, f. °ष्ठिका the smallest; f. कनिष्ठिका the little finger; subordination, obedience.
कनी f. girl, maiden (in a. l. only gen. pl.).
कनीन a. young, youthful.
1कनीनक m. boy, youth; f. आ girl, maiden.
2कनीनक m., °नका, & °निका f. the pupil of the eye.
कनीयंस् (compar.) smaller, less, younger, very little or small; m. a younger son or brother.
कनीयस a. smaller, less, younger.
कन्त्व n. welfare, happiness.
कन्था f. a patched garment.
कन्द m. bulbous root, bulb.
कन्दर n. cave, glen.
कन्दर्प m. the god of love, love.
कन्दर्पजनन, f. ई exciting love.*
कन्दल n. the flower of the Kandalī plant.
कन्दलय्, pp. कन्दलित bring forth abundantly (lit. like Kandalas, v. prec.).
कन्दली f. N. of a plant.
कन्दु s. cooking utensil, boiler or saucepan.
कन्दुक m. the same; playing ball, pillow.
कन्दोत्थ n. blue lotus.
कंधर m. neck (lit. head-bearer).
कन्य a. the smallest; f. कन्या girl, maid, daughter, the Virgo in the zodiac.
कन्यक, f. आ = prec. a. & f.
कन्यकाभाव m. state of maidenhood, virginity.
कन्यकुब्ज n. N. of a town.
कन्यात्व n. virginity.
कन्यादातृ m. who gives his daughter in marriage.
कन्यादान & °प्रदान n. the giving a daughter in marriage.

कन्यादूषक m. defiler of virgins.
कन्यापुर n. gynaeceum.
कन्याभाव m. virginity.
कन्याभैक्ष n. the begging for a maiden.
कप m. pl. a cert. class of gods.
कपट m. n. fraud, deceit; °— feigned, pretended, dissimulated.
कपटकापटिक m. cheat, rogue, sharper; f. आ fraud, deceit.*
कपटनाटक n. the comedy of deceit.*
कपना f. worm, caterpillar.
कपर्द m. a small shell used as a coin; braided or knotted hair (resembling a shell).
कपर्दक m., °र्दिका f. a small shell (v. prec.).
कपर्दिन् a. wearing braided or knotted hair (v. कपर्द), shaggy (of a bull); m. E. of Çiva etc.
कपल n. a half, a part.
कपाट m. n. door or door-panel.
कपाटवक्षस् a. broad-breasted (v. prec.).
कपाल n. cup, jar, cover or lid, shell, potsherd, skull, the cotyla.
कपालक a. formed like a shell; m. a shell, dish, f. °लिका a. potsherd.
कपालकुण्डला f. N. of a sorceress.
कपालमालिन् a. wearing a garland of skulls (Çiva).
कपालिन् a. bearing a cup (for begging) or skulls (Çiva or a cert. Çivaitic sect).
कपि m. ape.
कपिकेतन m. E. of Arjuna.
कपिञ्जल m. a kind of partridge.
कपित्थ m. N. of a tree; n. its fruit.
कपिध्वज m. = कपिकेतन.
कपिपति m. chief of the monkeys.
कपिल a. brown, reddish; m. N. of an ancient sage etc.; f. आ a brown cow or a kind of leech.
कपिलर्षि m. the Rishi Kapila.
कपिलवस्तु s. N. of Buddha's native town.
कपिश a. brown, reddish.
कपिष्ठल m. N. of a Rishi, pl. his descendants.
कपीतन m. N. of sev. plants.
कपीन्द्र & **कपीश्वर** m. = कपिपति.
कपुच्छल n. the hair on the back part of the head; the forepart of a sacrificial ladle.

कपूय a. smelling badly, stinking.
कपृथ् & **कपृथ** m. the membrum virile.
कपोत m. dove, pigeon; f. कपोती a. pigeon-hen.
***कपोतपालिका** f. a dove-cot, pigeon-house.*
कपोल m. cheek.
कफ m. phlegm (one of the three humours of the body).
कंबन्ध & **कबन्धिन्** v. कवन्ध & कवन्धिन्.
कबर a. speckled, brindled; f. ई a braid of hair.
1**कम्** interr. or emphasizing particle, esp. after dat. inf.; encl. after नु, सु, & हि.
2**कम्** (without pres.), pp. कान्त (q.v.) wish, desire, love. C. कामयते (°ति) the same; कामं कामयमान having a wish. — अनु & अभि wish, desire. नि lust after, long for (acc.).
कमठ m. tortoise.
कमण्डलु m. water-jar.
कमण्डलूदक n. water from a jar.
कमल m. n. lotus-flower.
कमलनयन, °नेत्र, & °लोचन a. lotus-eyed.
कमलपत्त्र n. a lotus-leaf; °पत्त्राक्ष a. = prec. a.
कमलमुख, f. ई lotus-faced.
कमलवन n., °लाकर m. a group of lotuses.
कमलाक्ष, f. ई lotus-eyed.
कमलाय्, pp. °यमान resemble a lotus-flower.
कमलिनी f. the lotus-plant; a group or lake of lotuses.
कमलिनीदल n. a lotus-leaf.*
कमलेक्षण a. lotus-eyed.
कमि (± धातु) m. the root कम्.
कम्प्, कम्पते (कम्पति), pp. कम्पित (q.v.) tremble, shake. C. कम्पयति, °ते make tremble or shake, agitate. — अनु sympathize with, commiserate (loc. or acc.); C. the same (w. acc.). अभि & आ = S. उद् tremble, swing upwards. C. shake up, agitate. प्र tremble, quiver, shake, become loose. C. make tremble, swing, agitate. वि tremble, stir, move, cease from (abl.). C. make tremble. सम् = S.
कम्प m. trembling, shaking, esp. earthquake.
कम्पन a. trembling or causing to tremble; n. = prec.

कम्पवन्त् a. trembling.
कम्पित a. trembling; shaken, swung; n. a trembling, tremor.
कम्पिन् a. trembling; —° shaking, swinging.
कम्र a. trembling, agile, quick.
कम्बल॑ m. (n.) woollen cloth or cover; m. also dew-lap.
कम्बु m. a shell or a bracelet made of shells.
कम्बुकण्ठ, f. ई shell-necked (i.e. having a neck with three folds).
कम्बुग्रीव the same; m. N. of a tortoise.
कम्बोज m. pl. N. of a people.
कम्र a. pleasant, beautiful.
कं॑म्वन्त् v. कं॑म्वन्त्.
कं॑य (only gen. sgl. m.) w. चिद् each, every.
कं॑या (instr. adv.) in what manner?
1कर॑, f. ई (आ) making, doing, causing, producing (mostly —°); m. the hand (lit. maker); an elephant's trunk.
2कर m. ray of light, sun-beam; revenue, tax, tribute.
करक m. a water-pot.
करकिसलय n. finger (lit. shoot of the hand).
करग्रह m., °ण n. taking the hand, marriage.
करङ्क m. skull or head.
कं॑रञ्ज m. N. of a tree.
करट m. an elephant's temple or cheek; crow.
करटक m. a kind of musical instrument*; N. of a jackal.
1करण॑ a. active, clever, skilled.
2कं॑रण, f. ई making, causing (—°). m. helper, assistant, N. of a caste (f. ई); complex of sounds, i.e. word. n. making, doing, causing; action, occupation; organ, instrument; instrumentality or the instrumental case (g.); document, bond, evidence (j.).
करणरूप a. having the function of an instrument.
करणीय a. to be done or caused; n. affair, matter, business.
करण्ड n., °ण्डक m., °ण्डिका f. a basket or box.
करतल n. the palm of the hand.
करपत्त्र n. a saw.
करपल्लव m. = करकिसलय.
करपाल m. chief tax-gatherer.
करभ m. the trunk of an elephant; a young elephant or camel.
करभक m. a man's name.
करभूषण n. ornament for the hand, bracelet.
करभोरू f. having round thighs (lit. thighs resembling an elephant's trunk).
करम्भ॑ m. groats, gruel; poss. °म्भि॑न्.
करम्भवालुका f. sgl. & pl. hot sand for groats (a punishment in hell).
करम्भा॑द् a. eating groats.
कररुह m. a finger-nail.
करवाल m. sword; — °पाणि s. in hand.*
करवीर m. fragrant oleander.
करवीरदाम n. a garland of fragrant oleander.*
कं॑रस् n. action, deed.
करस्थ a. being in or on the hand.
करं॑स्न m. fore-part of the arm; finger-nail.
कराङ्गुलि f. finger of the hand.
करार्पण n. marriage (lit. giving the hand, said of a woman).
कराल a. projecting (teeth or eyes), opening wide, gaping, ugly, terrible; f. आ E. of Durgā. Abstr. °ता f.
करालवदन a. having a gaping mouth.
करिदन्त m. ivory.
करिन् m., °णी f. an elephant (lit. having a trunk).
कं॑रिष्ठ (superl.) doing most.
करी॑र m. n. the shoot of a bamboo; m. a cert. thorny plant, n. its fruit.
कं॑रीष n. rubbish, dung, esp. dry cow-dung.
करु॑ण a. pitiable, miserable, n. adv.; f. आ pity, compassion.
करुणध्वनि m. piteous sound, lamentation.
करुणवेदिन् a. compassionate; abstr. °दिता f., °दित्व n.
करे॑णु m. f. an elephant (f. also °का).
करो॑टि f. basin, cup; the skull.
कर्क, f. ई white; m. a white horse (f. आ).
कर्कट & °क m. a crab; the sign Cancer.
कर्कन्धु m. f. the jujube tree, n. its fruit.
कर्कर a. hard, firm.
कर्करि॑ or °री f. a kind of lute; f. °री water-jar.
कर्कश a. rough, hard.

कर्कारु & °क m. a kind of gourd.
कर्कि & कर्किन् m. the Cancer in the zodiac.
कर्केतण, °तन, (& °तरक*) m. the cat's eye (a sort of gem).
कर्कोट m. N. of a serpent-demon, pl. of a people.
कर्कोटक m. N. of sev. plants; pl. = prec. pl.
कर्चूर n. auripigment.
1कर्ण m. (adj. —° f. आ & ई) ear (lit. & fig.), rudder; N. of a hero etc.
2कर्ण or कर्ण a. having (long) ears.
कर्णक m. lateral prominence, tendril, handle; f. कर्णिका earring, the pericarp of a lotus.
कर्णकिसलय n. a blossom (as ornament) for the ear.
कर्णताल m. the flapping of an elephant's ears.
कर्णधार m. helmsman, sailor; abstr. °ता f.
कर्णपथ m. compass (lit. path) of hearing.
कर्णपूर m. n. ornament for the ears, earring; °क m. N. of a servant (Ear-filler).
कर्णभङ्ग m. bending of the ears.
कर्णभूषण n. ornament for the ears.
कर्णमूल n. the root of the ear; °मूले into the ear.
कर्णवन्त् a. having ears or hooks.
कर्णविष् f. ear-wax.
कर्णवेष्ट & °क m. earring.
*कर्णवेष्टन n. the same.
कर्णशिरीष n. a Çirīṣa flower as an ornament for the ears.
कर्णश्रव a. audible to the ears.
कर्णाट m. N. of a people (f. ई).
कर्णाटकलह m. a Karnatic quarrel (v. prec.), i.e. a quarrel about nothing.*
कर्णाभरण n. ornament for the ears.
कर्णालंकरण n.; °कार m., °कृति f. the same.
कर्णिकार m. N. of sev. plants.
कर्णिन् a. having ears; having knots, barbed (weapons).
कर्णोत्पल n. a lotus flower (as an ornament) for the ears; m. N. of a poet and king.
कर्णोपघातिन् a. deafening (lit. beating the ears).*
कर्ण्य a. being in or at the ear.
1कर्त m. division, distinction.
2कर्त m. hole, cavity (cf. गर्त).
कर्तन n. cutting off, excision, destruction.
कर्तरि f. scissors or some other cutting instrument.
कर्तरी f. the same; °फल n. blade of a knife.
कर्तव्य or कर्तव्य a. to be made or done; n. duty, task.
कर्तव्यता f. obligation, necessity.
कर्तुकाम a. desirous to make.
कर्तृ m. doer, accomplisher, creator, author, officiating priest; making, causing, working at (—°); facturus; the agent or spontaneous performer of an action (g.).
कर्तृक (—°) = कर्तृ agent.
कर्तृता f., °त्व n. the being an agent.
कर्तृभूत a. being an agent.
कर्तृरूप a. having the function of an agent.
कर्तोस् gen. inf. of 1कृ.
1कर्तृ m. destroyer.
2कर्तृ m. spinner.
कर्त्र n. spell, charm.
कर्त्व a. = कर्तव्य (also n.).
कर्दम m. slime, mud; as adj. = seq.
कर्दमित a. muddy, dirty.
कर्पट n. rag, patch.
कर्पण s. a kind of lance or spear.
कर्पर m. cup, pot; a turtle's shell.
कर्पूर m. n. camphor.
कर्पूरकेलि m. N. of a flamingo.
कर्पूरतिलक m. N. of an elephant.
कर्पूरपट m. N. of a dyer.
कर्पूरमञ्जरी f. N. of a woman, a flamingo, & a drama.
कर्पूरविलास m. N. of a washer.
कर्बु a. spotted, variegated.
कर्बुर a. the same; f. आ a kind of leech.
कर्मक (—°) = कर्मन्.
कर्मकर, f. ई doing work (for others); servant, artisan.
कर्मकर्तृ m. the object-agent (g.).
कर्मकृत् a. doing work, active, skilful; m. workman, servant.
कर्मकृत्य n. activity, industry.
कर्मचेष्टा f. active exertion, labour.

कर्मचोदना f. impulse to (pious) works.
कर्मज a. sprung from an action.
कर्मजन्यता f. the resulting from an action.
कर्मठ a. capable of, fit for (—°); working or exerting one's self at (loc. or —°); absol. doing religious work, pious.
कर्मणृ a. skilful in work, clever, fit for religious acts, auspicious.
कर्मता f., °त्व n. abstr. to **कर्मन्**.
कर्मदोष m. sinful deed, sin, vice.
कर्मधारय m. a cert. class of compounds (g.).
कर्मन् n. action, deed, work, esp. holy work, sacrifice, rite; result, effect; organ of sense; the direct object (g.); fate, destiny.
कर्मनामन् n. a name given according to an action.
कर्मनिष्ठ & °**निष्ठा** a. diligent in sacred works.
कर्मपाक m. the ripening (i.e. consequence) of actions.
कर्मप्रवचनीय m. term for some prepositions & adverbs under certain conditions (g.).
कर्मफल n. fruit or result of actions.
कर्मबन्ध m. the tie or fetter of actions.
कर्मबन्धन n. the same; a. bound by actions.
कर्ममय, f. **ई** consisting of or resulting from works.
कर्मयोग m. performance of actions, esp. of religious works.
कर्मविधि m. rule of action, observance, practice.
कर्मविपाक m.=**कर्मपाक**.
कर्मसङ्ग m. attachment to action.
कर्मसङ्गिन् a. attached to action.
कर्मसंग्रह m. the totality of acts.
कर्मसंभव a. resulting from acts.
कर्मसाक्षिन् m. witness of acts.
कर्मसिद्धि f. success of an act.
कर्महेतु a. caused by acts.
कर्मात्मन् a. whose nature is action.
कर्मानुबन्धिन् a. involved in action.
कर्मान्त m. end or completion of a work, management of (—°); occupation.
कर्मार m. workman, mechanic, smith.
कर्मिन् a. active; doing, performing (—°); m. workman, labourer.
कर्मेन्द्रिय n. organ of action (opp. **बुद्धीन्द्रिय**).
कर्मोपकरण a. doing service by labour.
कर्वट n. market-place, borough.
कर्वर n. deed, action.
कर्शन a. rendering lean, attenuating; tormenting, vexing (—°).
कर्ष m. drawing, ploughing, agriculture; a cert. weight.
कर्षक a. tearing, vexing (—°); ploughing, cultivating; m. cultivator, husbandman.
कर्षण a. tearing, vexing (—°); n. tearing, drawing near or away; bending (of a bow), vexing, tormenting; ploughing, agriculture.
कर्षिन् a. drawing near, dragging, ploughing; attractive, inviting; m. ploughman, cultivator.
कर्षू f. furrow, trench, incision.
कर्हि adv. when? With **चिद्** & **अपि** at any time, ever; w. **चिद्** & neg. at no time, never.
कल्, **कलयति** (°ते) & **कालयति**, pp. **कलित** (q.v.) drive, impel; carry, bear; do, make, cause, produce, utter; observe, notice; try, examine; suppose, think, regard as (2 acc.). — **आ** shake, agitate, cast, fling; seize, tie, fasten; observe, notice; try, etc. = S. **उद्** drive out, let loose. **उप** drive home. **निस्** drive out, chase away. **परि** follow, pursue, seize, devour; consider or regard as. **प्र** drive out, impel, pursue. **सम्** drive away, put to flight; join, combine, be of opinion. — Cf. **उत्कलित**.
कल a. dumb, indistinct, low, soft (of sounds); n. adv. — f. **कला** q.v.
कलकण्ठ m., **ई** f. N. of sev. birds.
कलकण्ठिका f. the female Indian cuckoo.
कलकण्ठिन् m. the Indian cuckoo.
कलकल m. confused noise, buz, humming.
कलङ्क m. spot, mark (l. & f.); poss. °**किन्**.
कलञ्ज m. tobacco.
कलत्र n. wife or any female being.
कलत्रवन्त् & °**त्रिन्** a. having a wife.
कलधौत n. gold or silver; adj. = seq.
कलन a. causing, producing (—°); f. **आ** driving, impelling, performing, demeanour, gesture; n. shaking, agitating.
कलभ m. a young elephant or camel.

कलभाषिन् a. speaking softly.
कलम m. a kind of rice.
कलमकेदार m. a rice-field.*
कलमोदन s. boiled rice.*
कलविङ्क m. sparrow or the Indian cuckoo.
कलश m., **ई** f. pot, water-jar (adj. —° f. **ई**).
कलशोदक n. the water in the jar.
कलस v. **कलश**.
कलह m. strife, quarrel.
कलहंस m. a kind of duck, goose, or swan (f. **ई**); N. of a man. — Abstr. **°ता** f.
कलहंसगामिनी f. moving like a swan.*
कलहकार, f. **ई** causing quarrel, quarrelsome.
कलहप्रिय a. fond of quarrel, contentious.
कलहवन्त् & **°हिन्** a. having quarrel with (**सह**).
कलहाय्, **°यते** quarrel, contend.
कला f. a small part, esp. a sixteenth of the moon's orb; a cert. small division of time; an art (there are 64).
कलाज्ञ a. knowing the arts; m. an artist.
कलानाथ & **कलानिधि** m. the moon.
कलाप m. band, bundle, quiver (also n.); a peacock's tail, ornament i.g.; totality.
कलापिन् a. having a quiver with arrows or spreading its tail. m. a peacock.
कलाभृत् m. an artist, mechanic.
कलावन्त् m. the moon.
कलाविद् a. = **कलाज्ञ**.
कलाशेष a. forming only a small sickle (moon).
1**कलि** m. the One-side of a die; the last and worst of the 4 ages of the world; quarrel, strife (personified in all mgs).
2**कलि** m. a class of mythic beings; N. of a man, pl. his race.
कलिका f. the sixteenth part of the moon's orb; a cert. small division of time; an unblown flower, blossom.
कलिकाता f. the city of Calcutta.
कलिङ्ग m. N. of a king, pl. of a people.
कलिङ्गदेश m. the country of the Kalingas.
कलित a. furnished with (°— or —°).
कलितकुसुम a. furnished with flowers, budded.
कलिन्दकन्या & **°तनया** f. E. of Yamunā.
कलिल a. covered with, full of (—°); n. confusion, chaos.
कलुष a. unclean, muddy, turbid (lit. & fig.); n. dirt, stain, blemish.
कलुषचेतस् & **°मति** a. having impure thoughts.
कलुषय्, **°यति** make turbid, soil.
कलुषयोनिज a. of impure origin, base born.
कलुषाय्, **°यते** get turbid or troubled.
कलुषी w. **कृ** make turbid, trouble.
कलेवर n. (m.) the body.
कल्क m. dough, paste; dirt, sin.
कल्कि & **कल्किन्** m. N. of a future liberator of the world.
कल्प a. feasible, possible; fit for, able to, capable of (gen., loc., inf., or —°). m. ordinance, rule, esp. for ceremonial or sacrificial acts, practise, custom, manner, way (adj. —° having the manner or way of—, i.e. resembling—, similar to—; after an adj. almost, as it were); a fabulous period of time, a day of Brahman or 1000 yugas. **एतेन कल्पेन** in this way. **प्रथमः कल्पः** or **प्रथमकल्पः** primary rule (opp. **अनुकल्प**), chief matter, main point.
कल्पक a. normal, answering; stating, supposing (—°); m. ordinance, rule, precept.
कल्पक्षय m. the end of a Kalpa.
कल्पतरु & **कल्पद्रुम** m. the (mythic) Wish or Wonder-tree.
कल्पधेनु f. the (mythic) Wish or Wonder-cow.
कल्पन n. forming, imagining, cutting, fashioning; f. **आ** the same + contrivance, arrangement, action, deed; form, shape.
कल्पनीय a. practicable, possible, to be supposed or stated.
कल्पपादप & **कल्पवृक्ष** m. = **कल्पतरु**.
कल्पसूत्र n. a Sūtra work on ritual.
कल्पादि m. the beginning of a Kalpa (v. seq.).
कल्पान्त m. the end of a Kalpa, destruction of the world.
कल्प्य a. to be made of (instr.); to be supposed, imagined, or stated.
कल्मलि s. splendour.
कल्मलीकिन् a. shining, bright.
कल्मष n. dirt, stain, sin.
कल्माष, f. **ई** black spotted. m. N. of a serpent-demon; f. **कल्माषी** a spotted cow; n. spot, stain.

कल्य a. well, healthy, ready, able, capable. n. health; dawn, daybreak; an intoxicating drink. **कल्यम्**, **कल्ये** & **कल्य** (°—) early.

कल्यवर्त (*m.) morning meal, breakfast; n. a trifle, a little.

कल्याण (f. **कल्याणी**) beautiful, lovely, good, excellent, noble, auspicious, fortunate. f. **°णी** a kind of shrub; n. fortune, happiness, virtue (p. **°णिन्**†); festival.

कल्याणकटक s. N. of a place.

कल्याणकृत् a. doing good, virtuous.

कल्याणसूचक a. indicating fortune, auspicious.*

कल्लोल m. wave, billow.

कल्हण m. N. of an author.

†**कव** v. **अकव**, **कवत्नु** & **कवारि**.

कवक n. a mushroom.

कवच m. n. armour, mail, jacket, the bark of a tree.

कवचधर m. a wearer of mail (= a young man).

कवचिन् a. dressed in armour.

कवत्नु a. stingy.

कवन्ध m. n. barrel, cask (metaph. of a cloud or the belly); a headless trunk. m. E. of the demon Danu.

कवन्धिन् a. having casks (of water), driving the rain clouds (the Maruts).

कवल m. mouthful, bit, morsel; — gulf.*

कवलन a. swallowing, devouring; n. the same as subst.

कवलय्, **°यति**, pp. **कवलित** swallow, devour.

कवष् & **कवष** (f. **कपषी**) gaping, opened wide.

कवारि a. stingy.

कवि a. wise, thoughtful; m. a wise man, seer, sage, poet (esp. of artificial poems); N. of sev. men.

कविक्रतु a. = prec. adj. (lit. h. wise understanding).

कविता f. poetry.

कवित्व n. wisdom (also **°त्वन**), poetry, poetic talent.

कविपुत्र m. N. of a dramatic poet.

कविराज m. king of poets; N. of a poet.

कविशस्त or **कविशस्त** a. said or praised by wise men.

कवोष्ण a. lukewarm, tepid.

कव्य a. = **कवि** a.; m. pl. a class of Manes; n. an oblation to the Manes (mostly connected with **हव्य**).

कश m. a kind of gnawing animal, a whip; f. **कशा** whip, rope, rein.

कशावन्त् a. having a whip.

कशिका f. a whip.*

कशिपु m. n. mat, pillow.

कशीका f. a weasel.

कश्यु m. N. of a man.

कश्मल, f. **ई** & **आ** dirty, foul; timid, shy. n. dirt; timidity, shyness (also m.).

कश्मीर m. N. of a country, pl. of a people.

कश्यप a. black-toothed. m. tortoise; a class of divine beings; N. of sev. Rishis.

कष्, **कषति**, **°ते** rub, scratch (M. scratch one's self or being scratched), hurt, destroy. — **अप** scratch off. **उद्** rub in, dye. **नि** rub in or scrape off.

कष a. rubbing, wearing off (—°); as subst. the touchstone.

कषण n. rubbing, scratching.

कषाय a. astringent, sharp (of taste), fragrant, red, dark-red. m. red colour, passion, emotion; decoct, extract, ointment (also n.); n. a yellowish-red garment.

कष्ट a. bad. evil, painful, rough, constrained, affected, unnatural. n. evil, grief, pain, difficulty. °—, abl., & instr. with difficulty, hardly; n. **कष्टम्** the same, as interj. ah! alas! often after **धिक्** or **हा धिक्**.

कष्टतपस् a. doing severe penance.

कष्टता f., **°त्व** n. affectation, unnaturalness.

कस्, **कसति**, pp. **कस्त** w. **उद्** gape, open (intr.). **निस्** C. **निष्कासयति** drive away. **प्र** C. (the same*), cause to expand or bloom. **वि** burst, expand, spread, bloom, blossom, shine, beam. C. cause to blow or shine.

कस्तम्भी f. the prop of a carriage-pole.

(***कस्तुरिका**), **कस्तूरिका** & **कस्तूरी** f. musk.

कस्मात् (abl. of 1**क** as adv.) whence? why?

कहोड m. N. of a man, n. of his work.

कह्लार n. the white water-lily.

1**का** (°—) = **कद्** or **कु** (°—).

2**का** v. **कन्**.

कांशि m. coup, goblet.

कांस्य a. brazen; n. brass.
कांस्यताल m. a cymbal.
कांस्यपात्र n., °त्री f. a brazen vessel.
काक m., ई f. a crow; abstr. °ता f.
काकतालीय a. unexpected, sudden, lit. like the crow (killed by the) palmfruit; n. & °वत् adv.
काकपक्ष m. crow's wing; a side or temple lock (—° also °क m.).
काकपद n. a crow's foot.
काकपदमस्तशीर्षक an abusive word (lit. foot, head, and skull of a crow).*
काकलि or °ली f. a soft sweet sound or song.
काका f. croaking (onom.).
काकाय, °यते make kākā.
काकिणी or °नी f. a cert. small coin.
काकु f. wail, lamentation, emphatic speech.
काकुत्स्थ m. descendant of Kakutstha (E. of Daçaratha, Rāma, Lakṣmaṇa, etc.).
काकुद f. the hollow of the mouth, palate.
काकोल m. raven; n. a cert. poison or hell.
काकोलूक m. pl. crows and owls.
काङ्क्ष्, काङ्क्षति, °ते desire, long for, strive after, expect (acc.), wait (absol.). — अनु M. & अभि wish for, strive after (acc.). आ the same + long for (gen.), turn to (acc.), require as a complement (g.). प्रत्या M. expect, watch. समा, प्र, & प्रति desire, long for.
काङ्क्षा f., काङ्क्षित n., °ता f. wish, desire.
काङ्क्षिन् a. desiring, expecting (acc. or —°).
काच m. glass; pl. glass-pearls.
काचमणि m. crystal or quartz (lit. glass jewel).
काचर a. made of glass.
काचित्कर a. doing many things or serving many purposes.
काज n. a wooden hammer.
1काञ्चन n. gold.
2काञ्चन, f. ई golden; m. & f. N. of sev. plants.
काञ्चनकलश m. a golden jar.*
काञ्चनगिरि m. the golden mountain (Sumeru).
काञ्चनप्रभ a. gold-like; m. N. of a king.
काञ्चनमय, f. ई golden.
काञ्चनमाला f. a woman's name (lit. Gold-garland).
काञ्चनाचल & °नाद्रि m. = काञ्चनगिरि.
काञ्चनीय a. golden.
काञ्चि m. pl. N. of a people.
काञ्ची f. a girdle, esp. a woman's.
काञ्चीगुण m. the same (lit. girdle-band).
काञ्चीगुणस्थान n. a woman's hips (lit. the region of the girdle).
काञ्जिक n. sour gruel.
काट m. n. depth, hole, bottom.
काटयवेम m. N. of a commentator.
काटव n. acidity.
काटवेम m. = काटयवेम.
काट्य a. being in the depth.
काठ a. coming from Kaṭha.
काठक, f. ई belonging to Kaṭha; n. T. of a Veda.
काठकोपनिषद् f. = कठोपनिषद्.
काठिन्य n. hardness, rigidity, firmness, severity.
काण a. one-eyed (*अक्ष्णा blind of one eye); perforated (shell or *eye).
काणत्व n. one-eyedness.
काणेलीमातृ (& काणेलीसुत*) m. a whoreson, bastard.
काण्ड or काण्ड m. n. section, part, internode (of a plant), chapter (of a book); stalk, stem, switch, cane, arrow, long bone.
काण्डपृष्ठ m. a Brahman following the military profession (lit. arrow-backed).
काण्डार m. a cert. mixed caste.
काण्डिन् a. reed-shaped.
काण्डीर a. armed with arrows.
काण्व m. descendant or follower of Kaṇva.
कात् w. कृ insult, deride.
कातन्त्र n. title of a grammar; m. pl. the followers of the Kātantra grammar.
कातर a. cowardly, timid, shy, afraid of (loc., inf., or —°); abstr. °ता f., °त्व n.
कातर्य n. = prec. abstr.
कात्यायन m. N. of an old ancient (descendant of Kati), & sev. authors, f. ई a woman's name; adj. (f. ई) coming from Kātyāyana.
कात्यायनीय m. pl. the followers of Kātyāyana; n. T. of sev. works.
कादम्ब m. a kind of goose; n. the flower of the Kadamba tree.
कादम्बरी f. a cert. spirituous liquor; N. of

the heroine of Bāṇa's novel and the novel itself.

कादम्बरीसग्धिका f. compotation.*

कादम्बिनी f. a thick mass of clouds.

काद्रव a. tawny, reddish-brown.

काद्रवेय m. metron. of sev. serpent-demons.

कानन n. forest; **°नान्त** n. region of the f.; **°नौकस्** m. ape (inhabitant of the f.).

कानीन a. born of a virgin.

कान्त a. desired, loved, lovely, beautiful. m. the beloved man, husband; f. beloved or lovely woman, mistress, wife.

कान्तत्व n. loveliness, beauty.

कान्तार m. n. large forest, wilderness.

कान्तारभव m. inhabitant of a forest, forester.

कान्ति f. (adj. —° f. also **ई**) loveliness, splendour, beauty, esp. womanly beauty, charms.

कान्तिप्रद a. giving splendour.

कान्तिमन्त् a. lovely, charming; abstr. **°मत्ता** f.

कान्यकुब्ज n. N. of a town.

कापट, f. **ई** deceitful.

कापथ m. bad road or course (fig.).

कापाल, f. **ई** pertaining to or made of skulls. m. pl. the followers of a cert. Çivaitic sect (cf. **कापालिन्**).

कापालिक m. pl. = prec. m. pl.; also a cert. mixed caste.

कापालिकत्व n. barbarity, cruelty.

कापालिन् m. N. of Çiva (bearer of skulls); pl. a cert. mixed caste.

कापिल, f. **ई** pertaining to or coming from Kapila; m. a follower of Kapila.

कापिलेय a. & m. the same.

कापिलेयबाभ्रव m. pl. the Kāpileyas and Bābhravas.

कापुरुष m. wretch, coward; adj. cowardly, mean.

कापोत, f. **ई** peculiar to or coming from a pigeon; pigeon-coloured, grey.

काभर्तृ m. a bad lord.

काम (**कामं**) m. wish, desire, longing for (gen., dat., or loc.); love, inclination, lust, pleasure; pers. as the god of desire or of love; adj. —° (esp. after an inf.-stem in **तु**) wishing for, intending to. — **कामाय** or **कामे** according to one's wish, out of love for or for the sake of (gen. or dat.). **कामात्** & **कामतस्** voluntarily, intentionally. **कामया** (instr. f.) only after **ब्रूहि** & **प्रब्रूहि** freely, unreservedly.

कामकानन n. the grove of Kāma.

कामकाम & **°कामिन्** a. wishing wishes.

कामकार a. fulfilling one's (gen.) wishes. m. voluntary or spontaneous action; °—, instr., abl., & adv. in **तस्** voluntarily, intentionally.

कामक्रोध m. du. desire and wrath.

कामग a. going or acting of one's own accord.

कामगति & **°गम** a. moving freely.

कामचर, f. **ई** = **कामग**; abstr. **°त्व** n.

कामचरण n. free motion.

1**कामचार** m. free motion or action. **°चारतस्** adv. intentionally.

2**कामचार** a. moving or acting freely.

कामचारिन् a. the same; sensual, libidinous.

कामज a. born of desire or love.

कामतन्त्र n. the book of love, T. of a work.

कामतस् v. **काम**.

कामद a. granting wishes, abstr. **°त्व** n.

कामदुघ a. the same (lit. milking wishes); successful, fortunate; f. **आ** the fabulous Wish or Wonder-cow.

कामदुह् (nom. **°धुक्**) = **कामद** a. & prec. f.

कामदेव m. the god of love.

कामधेनु f. the fabulous Wonder-cow.

कामन्दकि m. N. of an author.

कामन्दकी f. N. of a town & a Budhhistic priestess.

कामपाल m. E. of Çiva (*& Baladeva).*

कामपूर & **कामप्र** a. fulfilling desires.

कामभाज् a. enjoying desires (**कामानाम्**).

कामम् adv. at will, willingly, freely, easily, by all means, indeed, w. a neg. by no means. **कामम्** (o. w. imper.)—**तु**, **किंतु**, **च**, **पुनर्**, **तथापि** granted, admitted that, although, however—nevertheless. **कामम्**—**न तु** or **न च** rather—than.

काममत a. actuated by love.

कामराग m. the affection of desire.

1**कामरूप** n. a shape changing at will.

2**कामरूप** a. taking any shape at will.

कामरूपिन् a. the same.

कामलुब्ध a. libidinous (lit. greedy of love).
कामवन्त् a. enamoured.
कामवश m. subjection to love, amorousness.
कामवासिन् a. taking any abode at will.
कामविहारिन् a. roaming freely (at will).
कामवृत्त a. indulging desires, licentious.
कामशास्त्र n. manual of pleasure or of love.
कामसमुत्थ a. springing from desire.
कामसूत्र n. the thread of love, also a love-manual.
कामहैतुक a. caused (only) by desire.
कामात्मन् a. whose nature is desire, voluptuous; abstr. °त्मता f.
कामान्ध a. blind from love.
कामाभिष्वङ्ग m. amorous inclination.
कामारि m. the foe of Kāma (E. of Çiva).
कामार्त a. tormented by passion or desire.
कामार्थ m. object or matter of pleasure.
कामाशोक m. N. of a king.
कामिक a. desired, wished for.
कामिजन m. a lover or lovers (cf. जन).
कामित n. wish, desire.
कामिता f. the state of a lover, amorousness.
कामिन् a. wishing, desiring, longing for (acc. or —°); loving, affectionate, enamoured of (acc. or सार्धम्). m. a lover; f. कामिनी a (loving) woman or maiden.
कामुक a. wishing, desiring (acc.), loving, fond of (—°). m. lover. — f. ई mistress of (—°).*
कामेप्सु a. = कामकाम.
कामेश्वर m. E. of Kubera.
काम्पिल & °क m. N. of a tree.
काम्बोज a. coming from Kamboja. m. a king of the Kambojas; pl. N. of a people = कम्बोज.
काम्य a. desirable, precious, lovely, pleasant; voluntary, relating to or sprung from a certain wish, egoistical.
काम्यक m. N. of a wood and a lake.
काम्यता f. loveliness, beauty.
काम्या f. wish, desire, striving after (gen. or —°).
1काय, f. ई relating to the God Ka (Prajāpati); m. the marriage rite of Ka.
2काय m. body, heap, group, multitude.
कायक्लेश m. bodily toil or pain.
कायगत a. dwelling in the body.
कायदण्ड m. control over the body.
कायवन्त् a. bodily, embodied.
कायस्थ m. writer (a mixed caste).
कायिक, f. ई bodily, corporeal.
कायोढज a. born from a wife married by the rite of Ka.
1†कार, f. ई (—°) making, doing, performing, causing; m. maker, author; sound, word.
2कार m. hymn, battle-song.
कारक (f. कारिका) a. = 1कार (—°), *also = facturus (acc., abstr. °त्व n.); absol. who effects anything, successful. m. maker, doer, author of (gen. or —°). f. metrical explanation of a difficult rule (g.). n. the relation of the noun to the verb, the notion of a case (g.).
कारण a. = 1कार (—°). n. (adj. —° f. ई) cause, reason, motive, first or chief matter or element, substance; sign, mark, document, proof; means, instrument, organ. °—, abl., instr., & loc. from some cause or reason; for the sake of (gen.); abl. also instead of (gen.). —* Abstr. ता f., °त्व n.
कारणकोप & °क्रुध् a being angry with cause.
कारणशरीर n. the causal body (ph.).
कारणात्मन् a. whose nature is the cause of (gen.).
कारणान्तर n. a particular occasion.
कारण्डव m. a kind of duck.
कारयितव्य a. to be (caused to be) done.
कारयितृ a causing to act.
कारा f. prison.
कारागार & कारागृह n. prison-house.
कारावर m. N. of a caste.
कारित a. caused, effected by (—°); f. आ (± वृद्धि) stipulated (not legal) interest.
1कारिन् a. doing, making, causing, acting (w. gen., adv., or —°).
2कारिन् a. praising, exulting; m. singer, poet.
1कारु m., °रू f. artisan.
2कारु m. singer, praiser, poet.
कारुक m. = 1कारु.
कारुकान्न n. the food of an artisan.

कारुण्य a. praiseworthy, excellent; n. pity, compassion.
कारुष m. N. of a country and caste.
कारूष m. N. of a son of Manu.
कार्कश्य n. roughness, hardness, severity.
कार्त्तिक m. a cert. month in autumn, also = seq.
कार्त्तिकेय m. metron. of Skanda.
कार्त्स्न्य n. entireness, totality; instr. wholly.
कार्पण्य n. peevishness, wretchedness, niggardliness; pity, compassion.
कार्पास m., **ई** f. cotton; adj. made of cotton.
कार्पासक (f. **°सिका** & **°सिकी**) = prec. adj.
कार्पासतान्तव n. weft of cotton.
कार्पासास्थि n. the seed of the cotton plant.
कार्मण a. pertaining to or sprung from actions; enchanting, bewitching (abstr. **°त्व** n.). n. magic, sorcery.
कार्मणिक a. caused by magical art.
कार्मार m. artisan, smith.
1**कार्मुक** a. effective.
2**कार्मुक**, f. **ई** consisting of wood of the tree Kṛmuka; n. (m.) a bow.
कार्मुकिन् a. armed with a bow.
कार्य a. to be done etc. (v. 1**कृ**). n. affair, duty, business, work, matter; lawsuit, dispute; an operation in grammar; effect, result; purpose, object. **किं कार्यम्** to what purpose? **न कार्यमस्माकम्** we have no business with or need of (instr.).
कार्यकरण n. performing one's duty.
कार्यकारण n. a special cause or motive.
कार्यकाल m. time for acting.
कार्यता f., **°त्व** n. the being an effect or a result.
कार्यदर्शन n. trial of a law-suit.
कार्यदर्शिन् a. sagacious, ingenious (lit. seeing what is to be done).
कार्यध्वंस m. the giving up of a business.
कार्यनिधान, f. **आ** accomplisher or treasure of works.*
कार्यनिर्णय m. decision of a law-suit.
कार्यपद्वी f. way to act.
कार्यरूप a. appearing as a result (ph.).
कार्यवत्ता f. abstr. to seq.
कार्यवन्त् a. having a business, occupied.
कार्यवशात् (abl.) for a certain purpose or business.
कार्यविनिमय m. reciprocity of duty, mutual obligation.
कार्यवृत्तान्त m. matter of fact.
कार्यव्यसन n. the failure of a business.
कार्यशेष m. the rest of a business.
कार्यशेषज्ञ a. knowing what is left to be done (v. prec.).
कार्यसिद्धि f. accomplishment of a business, success.
कार्यहन्तृ m. destroyer of a business.
कार्याकार्य (°—) what is and what is not to be done, right and wrong.
कार्यातिपात m. neglect of a business; a. **°तिन्**.
कार्याधिकारिन् m. minister of politics.
कार्यान्तर n. another business or something else than business, i.e. recreation, pleasure.
कार्यान्तरसचिव m. the companion of a king in his hours of recreation (v. prec.), maître de plaisir.
कार्यार्थ m. an object or business; **°म्** adv. for one's purpose, after one's business.
कार्यार्थिन् a. having an object, business, or law-suit.
कार्यिक & **कार्यिन्** a. the same.
कार्येक्षण a. = **कार्यदर्शन**.
कार्योपरोध m. interruption of a business.
कार्योपेक्षा f. neglect of a duty, carelessness.
कार्श्य n. meagerness, thinness, smallness, decrease.
कार्षापण m. n. a cert. coin or weight.
कार्षि or **कार्षिन्** a. drawing, furrowing.
कार्षिक a. weighing a Karsha.
कार्षीवण m. ploughman.
कार्ष्ण, f. **ई** pertaining to the black antelope, the dark half of the month, or to Kṛṣṇa; n. the skin of the black antelope.
कार्ष्णायस, f. **ई** made of iron; n. iron.
कार्ष्णि m. patron. of Kṛṣṇa.
कार्ष्ण्य n. blackness, darkness.
कार्ष्मन् n. a furrow as the goal in a race-course.
कार्ष्मर्य m. N. of a tree.
1**काल**, f. **ई** dark-blue, black. m. the black part of the eye, E. of Rudra-Çiva; N. of

sev. kings etc., also = कालसर्प q.v.; f. ई E. of Durgā etc.

2काल m. time, esp. the right or proper time (w. gen., dat., loc., inf., or —°); opportunity, case; season, mealtime (twice a day); the half of a day, hour; age, era, measure of time, prosody; time as ruler or destroyer of the world, i.e. destiny, fate; end; death or the god of death. — परः कालः high time (w. inf.). कालं कृ appoint a time for (loc.). कालेन in course of time (also °गच्छता; कालात् or कालतस्), at times; कालेन दीर्घेण, बहुना, or महता (also gen.) after a long time. कस्य चित्कालस्य after some time. काल° & काले in time, at the right or appointed time; (also काले गच्छति) in course of time, little by little. काले काले always in time or at the right time. कस्मिंश्चित्काले one day. — उभौ कालौ morning and evening. षष्ठे काले on the sixth half-day i.e. after three days; पञ्चशते काले after 250 days.

1कालक a. dark-blue, black. m. mole, freckle, a sort of grain. f. कालका a kind of bird; कालिका black spot, E. of Durgā.

2कालक (f. कालिका) monthly.

कालकञ्ज m. pl. N. of a race of Asuras.

कालकण्ठक m. sparrow.

कालकर्मन् n. death (lit. the work of time).

कालकारित a. temporary (lit. caused by time).

कालकूट m. a poison produced at the churning of the ocean; poison i.g.

कालकृत a. temporary, passing (lit. made by time).

कालक्षम a. durable, lasting (lit. bearing time).

कालक्षेप m. loss of time, delay; °क्षेपाय to win time.

कालचक्र n. the time (thought as) a wheel.

कालजिह्व a. black-tongued.

कालज्ञ a. knowing the (proper) times.

कालज्ञान n. knowledge of time or chronology.

कालदण्ड m. the staff of Death.

कालधर्म & °र्मन् m. the law of time, i.e. death.

कालनेमि m. N. of an Asura.

कालपक्क a. ripened by time.

कालपक्कभुज् a. eating things ripened by time.

कालपरशुधार m. executioner (lit. bearer of the axe of Death).*

कालपर्यय & °पर्याय m. the course of time.

कालपाश m. the sling of Death.

कालपाशस्थित a. being in the sling (i.e. on the brink) of death.

कालप्राप्त a. come with or produced by time.

कालयोग m. a connection with or arrangement of time. °तस् according to circumstances.

कालप्रियनाथ m. E. of Çiva.

कालवर्षिन् a. raining in time.

कालवाल a. black-tailed.

कालविद् a. & °विद्या f. = कालज्ञ & °ज्ञान.

कालविभक्ति f. division of time.

कालवृद्धि f. periodical (not legal) interest.

कालशाक m. a kind of pot-herb.

कालसंरोध m. keeping (of a pledge) for a long time.

कालसर्प m. coluber naga.

कालसूत्र n. the cord of the god of death; m. n. N. of a certain hell.

कालहरण n., °हार m. loss of time, delay.

कालागुरु m. a black kind of Agallochum.

कालातिपात m. loss of time, delay.

कालात्यय m. lapse of time, prescription (j.).

कालानुसार्य s. a kind of gum.

कालान्तर n. another time or intermediate time, interval, delay. — Instr. & abl. after some delay.

कालान्तरक्षम a. bearing a delay, patient.

कालायस n. iron, adj. made of iron.

कालायसदृढ a. iron-hard.

कालिक a. relating to time; timely, seasonable; lasting as long as (—°).

कालिङ्ग & °क a. coming from the country of the Kalingas; m. an inhabitant or king of it; f. °ङ्गी princess of the Kalingas.

कालिदास m. N. of several poets.

कालिन्द n. water-melon, f. ई patr. of the Yamunā river; a. coming from this river.

कालिमन् m. blackness.

कालीन a. relating to the time of —°; also = कालिक (—°).

कालीयक m. N. of a serpent-demon; n. a kind of fragrant black wood.

काल्य n. daybreak; loc. & acc. at daybreak, early.

1काव्य a. having the qualities of a sage; wise, inspired; m. patr. of Uçanas.

2काव्य a. the same; n. wisdom, inspiration; poetry, poem; m. pl. a class of Manes.

काव्यकर्तृ m. a poet.

काव्यप्रकाश m. light of poetry, T. of a work.

काव्यबन्ध m. a poem or verse (lit. composition of poetry).*

काव्यरस m. the flavour of poetry.

काव्यशास्त्र n. manual on poetry, T. of a work.

काव्यादर्श m. mirror of poetry, T. of a work.

काव्यालंकार m. ornament of poetry, T. of a work = seq.

काव्यालंकारसूत्र n. a manual on the ornaments of poetry; °वृत्ति f. the commentary to this work.

काश्, काशते (°ति), pp. काशित be visible, appear, shine, be brilliant or pleasant. I. चाकशीति & चाकश्यते shine bright; see clearly, survey. — अभि I. shine bright upon, illumine; look on, survey. अव be visible, lie open. निस् C. निष्काशयति v. कस्. प्र be visible, shine, radiate, appear, become clear or manifest. C. प्रकाशयति (°ते) make visible, cause to appear, show, unveil, explain, declare as (acc.). संप्र & C. the same. वि appear. C. display, spread; illuminate, irradiate. I. pp. विचाकशत् shining, beaming; beholding, perceiving. सम् appear, behold.

काश m. a kind of grass.

काशि m. the clenched hand or a handful; m. N. of a people; काशि or काशी f. the town of Benares.

काशिक a. coming from Kāçi or Benares; f. आ the town of Benares (± वृत्ति T. of a commentary).

काशिन् a. appearing (— °).

काशिराज m. king of the Kāçi.

काश्मरी f., काश्मर्य m. N. of a plant.

काश्मीर, f. ई pertaining to or coming from Kaçmīra; m. = कश्मीर.

काश्मीरज & *°जन्मन् n. saffron.

काश्य m., आ f. king & queen of the Kāçi.

काश्यप, f. ई patron. to Kaçyapa; N. of sev. persons.

काष m. rubbing.

काषाय a. dyed brown-red; f. ई a kind of wasp or bee; n. a brown-red garment.

काष्ठ n. stick of wood, log; a kind of measure.

काष्ठभार m. a load of wood.

काष्ठभृत् a. leading to the goal (cf. काष्ठा).

काष्ठमय, f. ई made of wood, wooden.

काष्ठलोष्टमय a. made of wood or clay.

काष्ठस्तम्भ m. a beam of wood.

काष्ठा f. race-course, course (esp. of the winds and clouds); mark, goal, limit; summit, top, height (fig.); cardinal point or quarter of the heaven; a cert. measure of time.

1कास्, कासते (°ति) to cough.

2कास् f., कास m., †कासा f. cough.

कासवन्त् a. having a cough.

कासार m. pond, lake.

कासिका f. cough.

कासिन् a. having a cough.

काहन् & काहस् n. a day of Brahman, a Kalpa.

काहल a. improper, unbecoming (speech); m. a large drum, f. आ a cert. wind-instrument.

काह्लार a. coming from the white water-lily.

कि interr.-stem in किम् & किस्.

किंयु a. what wishing?

किंरूप a. of what shape or form?

किंवदन्त m. N. of an imp or goblin. f. ई rumour, common saying (lit. what do they say?).

किंवर्ण a. of what colour?

किंव्यापार a. of what occupation?

†किंशुक m. N. of a tree; n. its flower.

किंसखि & किंसुहृद् m. a bad friend.

किंहेतु a. having what reason?

किकिदीवि m. the blue jay.

किंकर m., ई f. servant or slave.

किंकर्तव्यमूढता f. the being at a loss about what is to be done.*

किङ्किणी f. a small bell.

*किङ्किरात m. the Açoka tree.

किंचन्य n. possession (lit. somethingness).
किञ्जल्क s. filament or blossom, esp. of the lotus.
किंज्योतिस् a. having what light?
किटि m. a wild hog.
किट्ट n. secretion, dirt.
किण m. thick hard skin, callosity, scar.
किण्व n. ferment, lees.
कितव m. gambler (f. °वी); cheat, deceiver.
किनाट n. bark of a tree.
किंदैवत a. having what as a deity?
किंदेवत्य a. belonging or consecrated to what deity?
किंनर m. a class of mythical beings (half man half animal).
किंनरकण्ठ, f. **ई** singing like a Kiṃnara (v. prec.).
किंनामक, f. °मिका a. having what name?
किंनामधेय & °नामन् a. the same.
किंनिमित्त a. having what cause or reason? (°तस् adv. wherefore?*).
किम् (n. sgl. of कि to 1क, used also °— as stem o. = कद् q.v.) what? as adv. whence? wherefore? why? also merely interr. = num, an; in all these mgs o. connected with अङ्ग, इति, इव, उ, उत, नु (खलु), वा, स्विद्, in the second clause of a double question किम् alone or w. उत, उ वा, नु वा, वा. also (without किम्) उत, उत वा & वापि, अथ वा or आहो स्विद्. — With चन (च न), चिद् (& अपि*) indef. = something, a little (किमपि also in l. l. rather, much, vehemently); w. all three & a neg. by no means, not at all. किमु how much more, however, still. किं च moreover, further (esp. between two stanzas). किं तु yet, however, nevertheless. किमुत & किं नु how much more or less. किं पुनर् the same + still, yet however. किमुद्दिश्य for what purpose (lit. aiming at what)? किम् w. instr. what is gained by? what is the use of? what is it (instr.) to (gen.)?
किमर्थ a. having what purpose or aim?
किमाख्य a. having what name?
किमाचार a. of what conduct?
किंपर a. having what consequences?
किंपुरुष or °पूरुष m. a class of mythical beings, imp, dwarf (cf. किंनर).
किंपुरुषपर्वत m. the mountain of the Kimpurushas.
किंप्रभु m. a bad master.
किंफल a. bearing what fruit or result?
किंबल a. of what strength? how strong?
किंभृत्य m. a bad servant.
किम्मय a. consisting of what?
किंमात्र a. of what measure?
कियच्चिरम् adv. how long? °रेण how soon?
कियदद्भुत n. no great wonder.
कियद्दूर n. what or some distance (v. seq.); °—, acc., or loc. not far, a little way off (loc also how far?*).
कियन्त् a. how great? how far? how long? what sort of? indef. in a derogatory sense = not great; small, little. कियात्यां (loc. w. 1आ) how long ago? n. कियत् adv. how far? how much? something, a little.
कियन्मात्र a. of small importance.
कियाम्बु n. N. of a cert. water-plant.
किर् a. scattering, spreading (—°).
किरण m. very small dust, a mote, a ray or beam of light.
किराट m. merchant, trader.
किरात m., **ई** f. N. of a barbarous mountain-tribe (appearing also in the service of kings).
किरातार्जुनीय n. (the combat of) Arjuna with (Çiva in the form of) a Kirāta, T. of an epic poem.
†**किरि** v. आखुकिरि.
किरिक a. sparkling.
किरीट n. diadem; m. = किराट.
किरीटिन् a. diademed, crowned (E. of gods and heroes).
किर्मिर, **किर्मीर**, & **किर्मीरित** a. variegated, many-coloured.
किल (**किला**) adv. indeed, of course (lays stress on the preceding word).
किलकिल m. E. of Çiva; f. °ला (onom.) shout of joy.
किलञ्ज m. a mat.
किलास a. leprous; f. **किलासी** a kind of spotted deer; n. leprosy.

किलिञ्ज m. = **किलञ्ज**.
किल्बिष n. fault, guilt, sin against (—°), offence, injury; p. **°षिन्†**.
किल्बिषस्पृत् a. shunning or removing sins.
किशोर m., **ई** f. colt; young animal i.g., also lad, lass.
किष्किन्ध m. N. of a mountain, f. **आ** of a cave in it.
किष्कु m. fore-arm, handle (of an axe).
किस् interr. particle.
किसलय्, **°यति** cause to sprout or germinate (also fig.).
किसलय n. sprout or shoot; **°यित** having sprouts or leaf-buds.
कीकट m. pl. N. of a people.
कीकस m. the spine; f. **कीकसा** vertebre; n. a bone i.g.
कीचक m. reed. sedge; m. N. of an ancient chief, pl. of a people.
कीज m. a cert. instrument.
कीट m. worm, insect; w. **आग्नेय** a fire-worm (applied by a thief for extinguishing a lamp).
कीटक m. = prec.
कीटज n. silk (lit. produced by a worm).
कीदृच् a. of what sort?
कीदृगाकार & **°रूप** a. of what shape?
कीदृग्व्यापारवन्त् a. having what occupation?
कीदृश्, f. **ई** of what sort? what like? Before **च** & after **यावत्** indef.
कीदृश, f. **ई** = prec., also good for what, i.e. useless.
कीनार m. cultivator of the soil.
कीनाश m. plougher, drudge, slave, niggard.
कीर m. parrot; pl. N. of a people.
कीरि m. praiser, poet.
कीरिन् a. praising; m. = prec.
कीर्ण a. scattered, dispersed, spread, strewn, covered. filled.
कीर्तन n., **°ना** f. mentioning, report.
कीर्तय्, **कीर्तयति** (**°ते**) mention, commemorate, tell, report, proclaim, praise (gen. or acc.); mention or declare as, name, call (2 acc.); P. be called, pass for (nom.). — **अनु** remember, mention, report, relate. **परि** tell around, announce, relate, report, praise, commend; w. 2 acc., P. w. 2 nom. = S. **प्र** mention, quote, communicate, relate, divulge, praise, approve; w. 2 acc. etc. = **परि**. **संप्र** mention, declare, name. **सम्** mention, repeat, proclaim, praise.
कीर्ति f. mention, speech, report, renown, glory.
कीर्तिनाशन a. destroying reputation.
कीर्तिभाज् a. enjoying reputation, renowned.
कीर्तिमन्त् & **कीर्तियुत** a. glorious, celebrated (of pers.).
कीर्तेन्य a. deserving praise.
कील & **°क** m., **कीलिका** f. a pointed piece of wood; peg, bolt, wedge, etc.
कीलाल m. a sweet drink, similar to the Amrit; n. blood.
कीलित a. stuck on, fastened; stuck or covered with (—°).
कीवन्त् a. = **कियन्त्**.
कीश m. ape, monkey.
कीस्त m. praiser, singer.
1**कु** (°—) = **कद्**.
2**कु** v. **कू**.
3**कु** f. earth, soil, land.
कुकाव्य n. a bad poem.
कुकुर m. N. of a people.
कुक्कुट m. cock; f. **कुक्कुटी** hen.
कुक्कुटक m. N. of a caste.
कुक्कुर m. dog. f. **ई** bitch.
कुक्षि m. belly, womb (also **कुक्षी** f.); cave, valley.
कुङ्कुम m. saffron.
कुच् or **कुञ्च्**, **कुचति**, **कुञ्चते**, pp. **कुञ्चित** (q.v.) & **कुचित** shrink, curl, contract, draw in (intr.) C. **कुञ्चयति**. — **सम्** A. = S. + close, shut (intr.). C. **संकोचयति** contract, draw in (tr.), close up, lessen, diminish. — Cf. **आकुञ्चित**, **विकुञ्चित**, **संकुचित**.
कुच m. the female breast (mostly du.).
कुचन्दन m. red sanders or saffron.
कुचर a. roving, wandering; behaving ill.
कुचरित्र n., **कुचर्या** f. evil conduct.
कुचेल n. bad garment; a. badly clothed.
कुजीविका f. a wretched life.
कुञ्चन n. contraction.
कुञ्चि m. a cert. measure of quantity.

कुञ्चिका f. a key.
कुञ्चित a. contracted, bent, curled.
कुञ्ची f. cumin.
कुञ्ज्, कुञ्जति murmur.
कुञ्ज m. bush, bower.
कुञ्जर m. elephant (f. ई); chief or best of (—°).
कुटज m. N. of a tree.
कुटरु m. cock.
कुटि f. curve, contraction (—°); hut, cottage.
कुटिल a. crooked, curled; false, deceitful. Abstr. °ता f., °त्व n.
कुटिलक a. bent, curved; f. °लिका a kind of dance.
कुटिलकर्कश a. crooked (false) and hard.
कुटिलकेश, f. ई having curled hair.
कुटिलगामिन् a. going crookedly.
कुटिली w. कृ bend, curve.
कुटी f. = कुटि.
कुटीर s. hut, bower.
कुटुम्ब & °क n. household, family.
कुटुम्बभरण n. support of the family.*
कुटुम्बिन् m. householder, father of a family; member of a household or family, servant. °नी f. housewife, matron; maid-servant.
कुट्ट्, कुट्टयति, pp. कुट्टित sqash, stamp, crush.
कुट्ट & °क a. sqashing, stamping, crushing, hammering.
कुट्टन n. stamping, pounding, beating; f. ई = कुट्टिनी.
कुट्टाक a. tearing, lacerating (—°).
कुट्टिनी f. a bawd, procuress.
कुट्टिनीपुत्र m. son of a bawd.*
कुट्टिम n. plaster-floor, pavement.
कुठार & °क m. axe; °रिका f. a small axe.
कुठारिक m. a wood-cutter (axe-bearer).
कुड्मल a. blossoming; s. blossom (l. & f.), n. a cert. hell.
कुड्मलित a. blossomed or shut like a blossom.
कुड्य n., आ f. wall.
1कुणप n. carcase, corpse.
2कुणप a. rotting, mouldering.
कुणपभुज् m. a Rakṣas (lit. carcase-eater).
कुणारु a. lame in the arm.
कुणि a. = prec. (*w. instr.); abstr. °त्व n.

कुण्ठ्, only pp. कुण्ठित blunted, dulled. — Cf. विकुण्ठित.
कुण्ठ a. blunt, dull; abstr. °ता f., °त्व n.
†कुण्ड n. jar, pitcher (also ई f.); hole in the ground, fire-pit. m. the son of a wife by a paramour.
कुण्डक s. & कुण्डिका f. = कुण्ड n. & ई f.
कुण्डल n. ring, esp. ear-ring.
कुण्डलिन् a. wearing ear-rings; forming a ring, coiled; m. a snake.
कुण्डाशिन् a. eating from a Kuṇḍa.
कुण्डिन m. a man's name; n. = seq.
कुण्डिननगर & °पुर n. N. of a town.
कुतप m n. a blanket of goat-hair; m. Kuça grass.
कुतस् adv. whence? whither? wherefore? why? how? Also = abl. of the inter. pron.; w. अपि, चन, & चिद् from any (side), w. neg. from no side, from nowhere.
कुतुक n. curiosity, eagerness, interest; desire for (—°).
कुतूहल n. the same (also w. प्रति or loc.); anything curious, interesting, or amusing.
कुतूहलवन्त् & °लिन् a. curious, eager, interested in anything.
कुत्र (कुत्रा) adv. where? whither? on what account? for what purpose? With चिद् & अपि indef. anywhere, somewhere. कुत्र चिद् w. neg. nowhere; कुत्र चिद्—कुत्र चिद् here—there, sometimes—sometimes; कुत्र—क्व = क्व—क्व.
कुत्स m. N. of a Rishi etc.
कुत्सन n. reviling, abuse, reproach.
कुत्सय्, °यति, pp. कुत्सित revile, abuse, blame. — अभि & अव = S.
कुत्सा f. = कुत्सन.
कुत्स्य a. blamable.
कुथ्, only pp. कुथित putrid, stinking, & C. कोथयति cause to putrify.
कुथ m., आ f. a dyed woollen blanket.
कुदृष्टि f. bad sight; bad doctrine or system.
कुद्दाल s. hoe, spade.
कुधी a. foolish, stupid; m. a fool.
कुनख & कुनखिन् a. having ugly nails.
कुन्त m. spear, lance.

कुन्तल m. the hair of the head; pl. N. of a people.

कुन्ताप n. cert. organs in the belly; N. of a section of the Atharvaveda.

कुन्ति m. pl. N. of a people; sgl. = seq.

कुन्तिभोज m. a prince of the Kuntis.

कुन्ती f. N. of Pṛthā, one of the two wives of Pāṇḍu, adopted daughter of Kunti.

कुन्तीसुत m. son of Kuntī, E. of the Pāṇḍavas.

कुन्द m. a kind of jasmine; n. its flower.

कुन्दलता f. stalk or twig of jasmine.

कुप्, कुप्यति, °ते, pp. कुपित become moved or agitated, boil up, be angry with (dat. or gen.). C. कोपयति, °ते excite, agitate, make angry. — परि become greatly moved, be very angry. C. excite vehemently, make very angry. प्र = S., C. = S. C. सम् become angry. C. boil up; make angry, excite. — Cf. प्रकुपित.

कुप m. beam of a pair of scales.

कुपय a. moving, restless.

कुपायु a. liable to anger.

कुपुत्र m. a bad son.

कुपुरुष m. bad man, wretch, coward.

कुप्य n. base metal (all metal except silver and gold).

कुप्लव m. a bad raft.

कुबेर m. Kubera, the chief of the spirits of darkness, afterwards the god of riches, the regent of the north.

कुब्ज a. humpbacked, crooked.

कुब्जक m. N. of a plant.

कुब्जकगुल्म m. thicket of Kubjakas (v. prec.).

कुभन्यु a. desirous of water.

कुभा m. N. of a river.

कुभिक्षु m. a wicked beggar.

कुभ्र m. a cert. animal.

1कुमति f. false opinion, folly.

2कुमति a. foolish, stupid.

कुमनस a. displeased, angry.

कुमार m. boy, youth, son, prince (lit. easily dying, frail); E. of Skanda, the god of war. f. °री girl, maiden, daughter; a woman's name.

कुमारक m. child, little boy, youth; f. °रिका girl, maid.

कुमारत्व n. boyhood, youth.

कुमारदेष्ण a. granting perishable gifts.

कुमारब्रह्मचारिन् a. chaste from infancy.

कुमारवन n. Kumāra's grove.*

कुमारव्रत n. vow of chastity.

कुमारसंभव m. the birth of the god of war, T. of a poem.

कुमारिन् a. having or granting children.

कुमारिल, °भट्ट & °स्वामिन् m. N. of a philosophical teacher.

कुमारीभाग m. a daughter's share.

कुमारीभाव m maidenhood, virginity.*

कुमित्र n. a bad friend.

कुमुद n. the flower of the white water-lily.

कुमुदाकर m. a group of Kumudas (v. prec.).

कुमुदिनी f. the Kumuda plant, also = prec.

कुमुद्वन्त् a. abounding in Kumudas; f. कुमुद्वती = prec.

कुम्ब s. a kind of head-dress for women.

कुम्भ m. jar, pot (also कुम्भी), funeral urn; du. the two frontal globes of an elephant, which swell in the time of rutting.

कुम्भक = prec. adj —°; m. n. a cert. religious exercise to suspend the breath.

कुम्भकर्ण m. N. of a Rākṣasa.

कुम्भकार m. a potter (a cert. mixed caste).

कुम्भदासी f. a whore or bawd.

कुम्भधान्य a. having grain enough to fill a jar.

कुम्भाण्ड m. a cert. class of demons.

कुम्भिन् a. having a jar; m. elephant.

कुम्भिल (& °क) m. thief.

कुम्भीधान्यक a. = कुम्भधान्य.

कुम्भीनस m. a kind of serpent.

कुम्भीपाक m. the contents of a cooking vessel; the being cooked in jars (in a cert. hell).

कुम्भीर m. crocodile.

कुम्भील m. the same; thief (also °क m.).

कुम्भीलक m. N. of a servant.

कुयव a. bringing a bad harvest. m. N. of a demon; n. a bad harvest.

कुयवाच् a. speaking ill, abusing.

कुरङ्ग m. a kind of antelope, antelope i.g., f. ई a female antelope.

कुरङ्गक (& °क*) m. = prec. m.

कुरङ्गनयना, °नेत्रा, °लोचना, & °ङ्गाक्षी f. a fawn-eyed woman.

कुरबक m. crimson amaranth; n. its flower.
कुरर m., ई f. osprey.
कुरीर n. a kind of head-band.
कुरु m. N. of an ancient king; pl. his race and people.
कुरुकुराय्, °ते prattle, chatter.*
कुरुक्षेत्र n. N. of a country and celebrated battle-field; m. pl. its inhabitants.
कुरुपञ्चाल m. pl. the Kurus and Pañcālas.
कुरुपाण्डव (m. du. & pl.) the descendants of Kuru and Pāṇḍu.
कुरुवृद्ध m. E. of Bhīṣma.
कुरूप a. ill shaped, ugly; abstr. °ता f.
कुरूरु m. a kind of worm.
कुर्कुर m. dog.
कुल n. herd, flock, swarm, multitude, race, family, esp. good family, nobility; guild, corporation, community, association, caste, tribe; land for one family, abode, residence, house; chief of a corporation (v. कुलभूत). °— often = chief, noble.
कुलक multitude (adj. —°); n. three or more Çlokas forming only one sentence.
कुलकन्यका (& कुमारी*) f. a girl of good family.
कुलक्षय m. ruin of a family.
कुलगुरु m. chief or priest of a family.
कुलगोत्र n. du. family and tribe.
कुलघ्न a. destroying a family.
कुलज a. born of noble race.
कुलतन्तु m. the last (lit. thread) of his race.
कुलत्थ m. a kind of pulse.
कुलदूषण a. disgracing a family.
कुलदेव m., °ता f. family god or deity.
कुलदैव & °त n. the same.
कुलधर्म m. practice, observance, or duty of a family.
कुलनारी f. a noble woman.
कुलनाशक, f. °शिका destroying a family.*
कुलपति & कुलपा m. head of a family.
कुलपांसन, f. ई disgracing a family.
कुलपुत्र m. son of a noble family.
कुलप्रतिष्ठा f. support or prop of a family.
कुलभूत a. being the chief of a corporation.
कुलभूभृत् m. chief mountain; excellent prince.
कुलमित्र n. a friend of the family.
कुलवधू f. a woman of good family.
कुलवर्धन a. propagating a race.
कुलविद्या f. family science.
कुलव्रत n. family vow.
कुलसंख्या f. the being numbered among the (noble) families, respectability.
कुलसंतति f. propagation of the race, posterity.
कुलसंनिधि m. the presence of many; loc. before witnesses.
कुलस्तम्ब m. the grass-tuft (last straw) of a family.
कुलस्त्री f. a woman of good family.
कुलाङ्कुर m. offspring of a family.
कुलान्तकरण n. causing the end of a family.
कुलान्वय m. descent from a noble race.
कुलान्वित a. descended from (lit. possessed of) a noble race.
कुलाय m. n. texture, web, nest, case.
कुलायिन् a. forming a nest, nest-like, homely.
कुलाल m. potter, f. °ली†.
कुलिक m. a kinsman.
कुलिङ्ग m. a kind of mouse or bird.
कुलिज n. a cert. vessel or measure.
कुलिश m. axe, hatchet, a cert. fish; n. thunderbolt, diamond; f. कुलिशी N. of a river in the sky.
कुलिशधर m. the thunderbolt-bearer (Indra).
कुलिशभृत् m. the same.
कुलीकय m. a cert. aquatic animal.
कुलीका f. a kind of bird.
कुलीन a. of noble race or mind; belonging to the family of, related to (—°).
कुलीय (—°) = कुलीन (—°).
कुलीर m. a crab.
कुलूत m. pl. N. of a people.
कुलोद्गत a. sprung from a noble race.
कुलोद्वह a. propagating the race of, descendant of (—°).
कुल्फ m. ankle.
कुल्मल n. neck i.e. the portion between point and shaft (of an arrow).
कुल्माष (m. sgl. & pl.) sour gruel of fruits etc.
कुल्मि s. herd, multitude.
1कुल्य a. belonging to a family; also = कुलीन.
2कुल्य a. belonging to a river.

3कल्य n. place for preserving the bones of a burnt corpse.

कुल्या f river, channel.

कल्लूक m. N. of a celebrated scholiast on Manu.

ल्व a. bald.

कवंय m. a cert. bird.

कुवल n. the fruit of the jujube tree (f. कुवली); also = seq.

कुवलय n. the blue water-lily.

कुवलयदृश् f. a dark-eyed woman (v. prec.).

कुवलयनयना & कुवलयाक्षि f. the same.

कवलयानन्द m. T. of a work.

कुवलयित a. adorned with water-lilies.

कवित्स m. anybody, an unknown person.

कुविद् interr. particle (in direct and indir. questions).

कुविन्द & °क m. weaver.

कुविवाह m. a low marriage.

कुश m. grass, esp. the sacred grass used at cert. rel. ceremonies. — f. कुशा & कुशी a little peg, serving as a mark.

कुशर m. a kind of reed.

कुशल a. in good condition, in order, all right, proper, suitable, well, healthy; equal to, capable of, clever, skilful, versed in (loc., gen., inf., or —°). f. कुशली N. of sev. plants. n. right condition, welfare, health, luck; also = seq.

कुशलता f. ability, skill, cleverness.

कुशलप्रश्न m. inquiry after another's wellfare.

कुशलवन्त् a. healthy, well.

कुशलवाच् a. eloquent.

कुशलावसानता f. happy result.*

कुशलिन् a. = कुशलवन्त्, also auspicious, favourable.

कुशली w. कृ put in order, arrange.

कुशवारि n. water boiled with Kuça grass.

कुशस्तम्ब m. a heap of (Kuça) grass.

कुशावती f. N. of a town.

कुशिक m. N. of an ancient sage; pl. his race, also N. of a people.

कुशीलव m. bard, herald, actor; du. N. of the two sons of Rāma.

कुशूल & °धान्यक m. v. कुसूल & °धान्यक.

कुशेशय a. lying on Kuça grass; n. water-lily.

कुशोदक n. = कुशवारि.

कुशोर्णा f. pl. grass-wool.

कुश्रि or कुश्रि m. N. of a teacher.

कुष्, कुष्णाति & कुषति, pp. कुषित pinch, tear, gnaw, knead. — निस् the same.

कुषवा f. N. of a river or a Rākṣasī.

कुषीतक m. a cert. bird; a man's name.

कुष्ठ m. N. of sev. plants (also n.); f. कुष्ठा point, beak, hind-claw; n. leprosy.

कुष्ठिका f. hind-claw.

कुष्ठित & कुष्ठिन् a. leprous.

कुष्माण्ड m. N. of a plant; pl. a class of demons.

कुसिता, कुसितायी, & कुसिदायी f. a cert. demoniacal being.

कुसिन्ध n. trunk.

कुसीद a. lazy, inert; n. lending money, loan; also = कुसीदपथ & °वृद्धि.

कुसीदपथ m. usury.

कुसीदवृद्धि f. interest on money.

कुसीदिन् m. usurer.

कुसुम n. flower, bud.

कुसुमकोमल a. tender as a flower.

कुसुमचाप m. the god of love (having a bow of flowers).

कुसुमदायिन् a. putting forth buds.*

कुसुमधन्वन् m. = कुसुमचाप.

कुसुममय, f. ई consisting of flowers.

कुसुममाला f. garland of flowers.*

कुसुमय्, °यति, pp. कुसुमित (q.v.) bring forth flowers.

कुसुमशयन n. a couch of flowers.

कुसुमशर having flowers for arrows (abstr. °त्व n.); m. the god of love.

कुसुमाकर m. the spring; — N. of a garden.*

कुसुमाञ्जलि m. two handfuls of flowers, a flower offering.

कुसुमाढ्य a. rich in or adorned with flowers.

कुसुमापीड m. wreath of flowers.*

कुसुमायुध m. = कुसुमशर m.

कुसुमावचय m. gathering flowers.

कुसुमास्तरण n. = कुसुमशयन.

कुसुमित a. budded, flowered; n. blossoming or the time of blossoming.

कुसुमोद्गम m. the coming forth of flowers, blossoming.*

कुसुम्भ m. safflower; pot, water-jar.
कुसुम्भक्षेत्र n. field of safflower.
कुसुम्भवन्त् a. carrying a water-pot.
कुसूल m. a granary.
कुसूलधान्यक a. having enough to fill a granary.
कुस्त्री f. a bad woman.
कुह adv. where (also w. स्विद्). With चिद् wherever, somewhere.
कुहक m. cheat, deceiver, juggler; f. आ and n. juggling, deception.
कुहयां adv. where?
कुहर m. N. of a serpent-demon; n. hole, cave.
कुहरभाज् a. dwelling in dens.
कुहा f. N. of a plant.
कुहू f. the new moon (personif.).
1कू, कुवते, w. आ intend.
2कूं adv. where? w. चिद् anywhere.
कूचो f. pencil, brush.
कूज्, कूजति, °ते make inarticulate sounds, cry, sing (of a bird), coo, caw, hum, moan, groan, etc. — अनु follow in crying etc. अभि, आ, उद्, वि, सम् = S.
कूज m., कूजन & °जित n. crying, singing, etc.
1कूट n. bone of the forehead, horn; peak, point, heap, mass (also m.); trap, snare, fraud, deceit, falsehood.
2कूट a. not horned (ox etc.); false, deceitful.
कूटक a. false; n. eminence, projection.
कूटकर्मन् n. fraud, deceit.
कूटकारक m. forger, false witness.
कूटकृत् m. briber, falsifier.
कूटतापस m. a false (not real) ascetic.
कूटपाल & °क m. fever of the elephant.
कूटवागुरा f. a hidden trap or snare.*
कूटशासन n. a forged edict; °कर्तृ m. forger of an edict or document.
कूटसाक्षिन् m. false witness.
कूटस्थ a. being at the head, highest, supreme; standing amidst (—°); immovable, unchangeable.
कूटाक्ष m. a false die.
कूटागार m. n. upper room, pleasure-house.
कूड्, कूडयति (°ळयति) singe, scorch. — उप roast.
कूण्, कूणति, pp. कूणित contract, close (intr.). — नि & वि = S.
कूर्दो f. fagot, bundle, bunch.
कूप m. hole, cave, well.
कूपखनन n. digging of a well.
कूपचक्र & °यन्त्र n. wheel for drawing water from a well.
†कूपार v. अकूपार.
कूप्य a. being in a hole or well.
कूबर m. or n., कूबरी f. (adj. —° f. आ) the pole of a carriage.
कूर n. boiled rice.
कूर्च m. n. bundle, bunch, brush; n. beard.
कूर्चक m. the same.
कूर्चता f. beardedness.
कूर्चल a. bearded.
कूर्चानत a. long-bearded (lit. bent down by the beard).*
कूर्द्, कूर्दति, °ते leap, jump. — उद् jump up. प्र jump forward.
कूर्द m., °न n. a jump.
कूर्प s. sand.
कूर्पर m. elbow, r. knee.
कूर्पासक m. jacket, bodice.
कूर्म m. tortoise (f. कूर्मी); one of the winds of the body; N. of a serpent-demon & a Rishi.
कूर्मपति m. the king of tortoises (who bears the earth).
†कूर्मि & कूर्मिन् v. तुविकूर्मि & °र्मिन्.
कूल्, कूलयति (cf. कूड्) singe. — अव = S.
कूल n. slope, hill; shore, bank.
कूलंकष a. wearing of the bank (river).
कूलजात a. grown on the shore.
कूलवती & कूलिनी f. river (lit. having banks).
कूल्य a. belonging to a bank or shore.
कूल्व a. bald.
कूश्मं & कूष्मं m. a cert. demoniacal being.
कूष्माण्ड m. a kind of imp or spirit; a cert. spell or magical verse (also f. ई & n.).
1कृ (स्कृ), कृणोति, कृणुते, करोति, कुरुते (करति & कर्ति), pp. कृत (q.v.) make, do, cause or produce anything in or on one's self or others; absol. act, work; bring or help to (dat.); get or procure for (gen.),

M. for one's self; make or begin something (acc., esp. किम्) with something (instr.); make something (acc.) of something (instr. or abl.); make (into), render 2 acc. or acc. & adj. or adv. in ई, ऊ. — With the acc. of an abstr. कृ answers to a verb of kindred mng, e.g. w. प्रवेशम् = enter, w. मरणम् die, w. राज्यम् reign; esp. in the periphr. perf., e.g. विदां चकार he knew. We often use a more special verb, e.g. perform or offer (यज्ञम्), prepare or till (क्षेत्रम्), fix (समयम्), wait (क्षणम्), utter (वाचम् or शब्दम्), exert (वीर्यम्), show, betray, feel (कृपाम्, भावम्, स्नेहम्), enjoy (सुखम्), marry (दारान्), violate, dishonour (कन्याम्) etc.; put, set in or on (पाणौ, स्कन्धे), take to (हृदि), ponder, deliberate (चेतसि, मनसि, हृदये), turn, direct (मनस्, w.loc.), call, name (नाम्ना) etc. Note also द्विधा कृ divide into two, भस्मसात् ° reduce to ashes, तृणवत् ° value like straw. For other phrases cf. the corr. adj. or adv. C. कारयति, °ते cause to act or do (2 acc. or acc. of th. & instr. of pers.), have something put in (loc.), also = S. D. चिकीर्षति, °ते wish to act or do. I. करिक्रति (3 pl.) do repeatedly. — अधि put before or over, place at the head, appoint to (loc.); make a thing the chief matter or main point; be entitled to (A. w. loc., M. w. acc. or inf.). अनु do afterwards, imitate, equal (acc. or gen.). अप put off, remove; injure, offend, do wrong (acc., loc. or gen.). अभि do in behalf of (acc.); effect, make. आ bring or call near; bring about, perform, prepare; serve a god (gen.), sacrifice. C. call near; ask for (2 acc.). अपा keep off, remove, pay (a debt); reject, desist. उदा expel, select. उपा bring near, fetch; grant, present; acquire, get; invite, prepare, undertake, begin (r.). निरा separate, select; push, away, keep off, reject, destroy; refuse, contradict. व्या divide, separate from (instr.), analyse, explain. समा bring together, collect, unite; make ready, prepare. दुस् (= निस्) arrange, make ready, prepare. उप bring near, impart, grant, offer, render a service (gen. or loc. of pers.); further, support; w. स्कृ M. prepare, cultivate (land), adorn, enchase; think of, care for (acc. or *gen.); deform, corrupt. प्रत्युप return a service. तिरस् put aside, remove, cover, conceal; cut out, supplant, surpass; contemn, despise, blame, abuse. नि bring down, humiliate. विनि wrong, injure, offend. निस् bring forth from (abl.); drive away (also w. स्कृ), dispel, exclude; accomplish, arrange, settle, prepare, bring together; restore, requite. परि prepare (food); w. स्कृ make ready, fit out, adorn. पुरस् put before or at the head, place in front, introduce, appoint to (loc.); show, betray. प्र perform, effect, cause, make, render (2 acc.); take, marry; appoint to (loc.); undo, destroy, kill; violate, deflower; M. induce, move, cause to do; direct or turn (मनस्, बुद्धिम्) upon (dat. loc.), resolve; gain, acquire, effect; put before, mention. विप्र hurt, wrong, injure, disappoint (Caus. the same*). प्रति do against, return, repay, revenge (acc. of th., gen., dat., loc. of pers.); counteract, withstand (act. of th. and gen. of pers.); restore, requite, repay. D. wish to requite or revenge (acc. of th., acc. or loc. of pers.). वि make different, change, alter, divide, detail, specify; deform, spoil, destroy; develop, produce; M. (P.) become different, alter, become hostile, unkind, or faithlesss (w. gen. or loc.); contend, fight. सम् (कृ & स्कृ) put together, join, compose, prepare, arrange; consecrate, invest, initiate, marry; refine, embellish, adorn. अभिसम् (स्कृ) arrange, perform. M. render (2 acc.); consecrate, dedicate. उपसम् (स्कृ) prepare, adorn. प्रतिसम् restore, repair. — Cf. अधिकृत, अधिकृत्य, उपस्कृत, निकृत, परिष्कृत, पुरस्कृत, पुरस्कृत्य, प्रकृत, विकृत, संस्कृत.

2कृ, I.-st. चर्कृ (3 sgl. M. चर्कृषे w. act. & pass. mg.) commemorate, mention, extol (gen.).

3कृ (स्कृ), किरति, °ते, pp. कीर्ण pour out, cast forth, scatter, strew, cover, fill. — अनु scatter, strew; cover, fill. अभि sprinkle, cover, fill. अव pour down, scatter, spread, spend (semen); cast off, reject; sprinkle, bestrew, cover, fill. समव bestrew, cover entirely. आ scatter or bestow abundantly, cover over, fill. समा scatter over, cover. उद् whirl up (dust); excavate, engrave. उप scatter or throw down, besprinkle, bestrew. विनि scatter, disperse; throw away, abandon. परि scatter or strew about, surround. प्र scatter forth, throw down; spring forth, issue, rise. वि throw asunder or about, cast, hurl, scatter, disperse, dissolve, split, rend. सम् pour out, bestow richly, cover, fill; mix together, confound. — Cf. अवकीर्ण, आकीर्ण, उत्कीर्ण, प्रकीर्ण, विकीर्ण, विप्रकीर्ण, व्याकीर्ण, संकीर्ण.

कृकर m. a kind of patridge; one of the winds of the body.

कृकलास m. lizard, chameleon.

कृकवाकु m. cock, esp. peacock.

कृकषा f. a cert. bird.

कृकाट n., °टिका† & °टी† f. the joint of the neck.

कृकालिका f. a cert. bird.

कृच्छ्र a. troublesome, painful, difficult, dangerous, bad, miserable. n. adv. — m. n. trouble, pain, difficulty, danger, misery; austerity, expiation, a cert. slight penance. °—, instr., & abl. (*w. pp.), & कृच्छ्रतस् adv. with difficulty, hardly.

कृच्छ्रकर्मन् n. hard work, toil, drudgery.

कृच्छ्रकाल m. the time of distress or danger.

कृच्छ्रगत a. being in trouble or doing a penance.

कृच्छ्रता f. dangerous state (of a disease).

कृच्छ्रपतित a. fallen into trouble.

कृच्छ्रातिकृच्छ्र m. du. the ordinary and extraordinary penance.

1कृत्, कृन्तति, °ते (कर्तति), pp. कृत्त cut, cut off, cleave, split, divide, destroy. C. कर्तयति (कृन्तयति) the same. — अप & अपि cut off. अव cut off, destroy. C. cause to be gashed. उद् cut out or off, carve, tear asunder, destroy. नि cut or hew down, cut or tear off; M. cut one's self (e.g. the nails). C. cause to be cut. परि cut round, clip, cut off, exclude from (abl.). प्र cut off or asunder. वि the same, tear to pieces, lacerate, destroy. C. the same. सम् cut etc. (together).

2कृत्, कृणत्ति twist the thread, spin. C. कर्तयति weave.

3कृत् a. making, doing, causing, effecting; maker, performer, author of (—°) m. a suffix forming nouns from roots, also = कृदन्त m.

कृत a. made, done, prepared, arranged, appointed, got; present, ready, fit, proper, good. Often °— having done, doing, using, showing, betraying etc. — n. it is done, i.e. shall be done instantly; w. instr. (± सह) be it done with, i.e. away with, enough of! n. as subst. act, deed, work, esp. religious work, sacrifice, ceremony, etc.; service, benefit; stake at game; booty in battle; the (lucky) Four-side of the die; the first or golden age. कृतेन because or instead of (gen. or —°); कृते the same, abs. for something.

कृतक a. made, prepared, artificial, unnatural, false. °— & n. adv. — With पुत्र m. an adopted son; abstr. °त्व n.

कृतकर्तव्य a. who has attained his object.

1कृतकार्य a. the same, satisfied.

2कृतकार्य n. an attained object.

1कृतकृत्य a. what has been done and is to be done.

2कृतकृत्य a. who has done his duty or attained his object; abstr. °ता f. satisfaction.

कृतकौतुक a. giving pleasure to (gen.).

कृतक्रिय a. who has performed a religious ceremony, married.

कृतक्षण a. waiting (a moment) for, intent upon (loc., acc. w. प्रति, inf., or —°); impatient.

कृतघ्न a. ungrateful (lit. killing benefits).

कृतचूड a. who has received the tonsure (r.).

कृतज्ञ a. grateful (lit. mindful of benefits).

कृतत्वर a. making haste, being quick.

कृतदार a. married (of a man).
कृतध्वज a. furnished with banners.
कृतनिर्णेजन a. having done penance.
कृतनिश्चय a. convinced, certain, sure; resolute, determined to (dat., loc., infin., or —°).
कृतपुण्य a. blessed, fortunate.
कृतप्रणय a. enamoured.
कृतपूर्व a. done before.
*कृतपूर्विन् a. having made (acc.) before.
कृतबुद्धि a. who has formed his mind, wise, judicious, also = seq.
कृतमति a. who has made up his mind, resolute.
कृतमार्ग a. made accessible.
कृतमाल m. the spotted antelope; N. of a plant & a river.
कृतलक्षण a. marked, branded (cf. कृताङ्क).
कृतवध्यचिह्न a. bearing the mark of death.
कृतवसति a. having fixed one's habitation, dwelling, abiding.
कृतवाप & °वापन a. who has shaven his hair.
कृतविद्य a. having acquired knowledge, learned.
कृतविशेषक a. having made coloured lines on the forehead; painted.*
कृतवैर a. who has become an enemy.
कृतशौच a. who has purified himself.
कृतसंस्कार a. prepared, adorned, initiated.
कृतसंज्ञ a. having signals given or arranged.
कृतसंधान a. brought near, united, fitted, adapted.
कृतस्मित a. smiling.
कृतहस्त a. dexterous, skilled; abstr. °ता f.
कृता f. cleft, abyss.
कृताङ्क a. having got a mark, branded.
कृताकृत a. done and not done, half-done; arbitrary, indifferent; n. sg. & du. what is done and not done.
कृताञ्जलि a. humble, suppliant (cf. अञ्जलि).
कृतानुसार m. established rule, arrangement, stipulation.
कृतान्त a. causing an end, finishing (f. ई perished, vanished*); m. matter, cause, conclusion, dogma; fate, destiny, the god of death.
कृतान्तनगरी f. the city of the god of death.
कृतान्न n. prepared or cooked food.
कृतापराध a. having done wrong, guilty.
कृताभियोग a. taking pains.
कृतार्थ a. who has attained his object, satisfied. Abstr. °ता f., °त्व n.
कृतार्थय्, °यति satisfy, content; fulfil, accomplish.
कृतावगुण्ठन a. veiled.
कृतावस्थ a. brought into court (j.).
कृतावृत्ति a. going to and fro, swinging.
कृतास्त्र a. skilled in arms, esp. in archery.
कृताहारक a. having done eating.
1कृति f. doing, action, production, work.
2कृति m. or f. a cert. weapon.
कृतिन् a. active, clever, wise, skilful in (loc. or —°), also = कृतार्थ.
कृतोपकार a. having (been) rendered a service.
कृतोपनयन a. initiated.
कृतोपवास a. having fasted.
कृत्तावशेष a. broken off (chain).
कृत्तिका f. pl. (later sgl.) the Pleiads, personif. as the nurses of Skanda.
कृत्तिवासस् m. f. clothed in a skin, E. of Çiva & Durgā.
कृत्नु a. active, skilful, clever.
कृत्य a. to be done, fit, proper, right; n. impers. it imports or matters (w. gen. of pers. & instr. of th.). — m. a suffix of the fut. pass. part. f. कृत्या act, action, deed; magic, spell. n. business, task, duty, purpose, end.
कृत्यवन्त् a. having an object or request, active, busy.
कृत्याकृत् a. practising magic, bewitching.
कृत्यारूप a. spectre-like
कृत्याहत a. stricken by spell.
कृत्रिम a. artificial, factitious, adopted (पुत्र); unnatural, accidental; false, feigned.
*कृत्रिमधूपक m. a compound perfume.
कृत्वन् (f. कृत्वरी) causing, producing (—°); active, magical.
कृत्वस् (acc. adv.) —times (in l. l. only —°).
कृत्व्य a. capable, apt, strong.

कृत्स्न a. whole, entire; abstr. °ता f., °त्व† n.; adv. °शस्†.
कृत्स्नकर्मकृत् a. doing all things.
कृत्स्नविद् a. knowing all things, omniscient.
†कृथ v. तनूकृथ & पुत्रकृथ.
कृदन्त a. ending in a Kṛt-suffix; m. such a word (g.).
कृंदर n. store-room, treasury.
कृधु a. shortened, deficient.
कृन्तत्र n. section, cleft, shred.
कृन्तन n. cutting off.
1कृप् f. (only instr. कृपा) shape, appearance, beauty.
2कृप्, कृपते mourn, long for (acc.). — अनु = S.
कृप m., ई f. a man's & woman's name.
1कृपण a. pitiable, miserable, querulous (n. adv.); poor, stingy. m. a poor man or a miser.
2कृपण n. misery, pity.
कृपय्, °यति mourn, grieve, pity.
कृपा f. compassion, pity.
कृपाण m. sword; f. ई scissors, dagger, knife.
कृपाणपाणि a. sword in hand.
कृपाणपात m. fall or stroke of a sword.
कृपाय्, °यते = कृपय्. — अनु M. feel pity for (loc.).
कृपालु a. having pity upon (loc.), compassionate.
कृपावन्त् a. the same.
कृपीट n. underwood, copse, thicket.
कृमि m. worm, esp. silk-worm, mite, spider, insect i.g.; a man's name; f. a woman's name (also कृमी), N. of a river.
कृमिक m. a small worm.
*कृमिकोश m. the cocoon of a silkworm.
*कृमिकोशज & *°कोशोत्थ a. silken (lit. coming from the cocoon, v. prec.).
कृमिज a. produced by a worm.
कृमुक m. a kind of tree.
कृश्, कृश्यति, pp. कृशित become or be lean or feeble. C. कर्शयति, pp. कर्शित (often confounded with the C. of कृष्) make lean, keep short of food, diminish, attenuate, vex, torment. — अनु, अव, परि, वि afflict, vex.

कृश a. lean, thin, slender; weak, feeble; insignificant, poor.
कृशता f., °त्व n. leanness, thinness.
1कृशन n. a pearl.
2कृशन m. the pulsing of the heart.
कृशनावन्त् & °निन् a. wearing pearls.
कृशाङ्ग, f. ई lean (-membered), thin, slender.
कृशानु a. bending the bow, shooting; m. archer, esp. a cert. divine archer, also E. of Agni, in l. l. fire.
कृशी w. कृ & भू make or become thin, weak, or poor.
कृशोदर, f. ई thin-waisted, slender.
कृष्, कर्षति, °ते (कृषति, °ते), pp. कृष्ट (q.v.) drag, draw; pull, tear, bend (a bow); draw furrows, plough (only कृषति); draw to one's self, get possession of, overpower. C. कर्षयति tug, pull, tear, extract; afflict, vex (cf. कृश् C.). I. चर्कृषति plough. — अति draw beyond. अनु draw after one's self; attract from the preceding, supply (g.); quote. अप draw away, take off; reject, remove; bend (a bow); detract, debase, dishonour. व्यप draw away, take off, doff; reject, remove, abandon. अव draw or take off, remove, drag down. आ draw on, attract; bend (a bow); drag away; take off, extract, remove from (abl.). अपा turn away, avert from (abl.). व्या draw to one's self; draw off, remove, avert. समा draw near; extract from (abl.). उद् draw out or up, take off; bend (a bow); raise (fig.); rise, be superior. नि draw down. संनि P. come near, come in contact with (instr.). निस् draw out, extract; tear in pieces, rend asunder. परि draw about, conduct (army); vex afflict; think over, ponder. प्र draw forth, conduct (an army); vex, afflict. विप्र draw away, remove. संप्र the same. वि draw asunder, tear in pieces; draw towards one's self (arrow), bend (bow); turn up (foam), drag about, pull; conduct (army); extract, deprive, withhold. सम् draw together, contract; drag away, carry off. —

Cf. अपकृष्ट, अवकृष्ट, उत्कृष्ट, निकृष्ट, प्रकृष्ट, विकृष्ट, विप्रकृष्ट, संनिकृष्ट.

कृषक m. ploughman, husbandman; f. **कृषिका** agriculture.

कृषि f. ploughing, agriculture, husbandry; field (also **कृषी**); harvest.

कृषिकर m. plougher, husbandman.

कृषिकर्मन् n. ploughing, agriculture.

कृषिकृत् m. = **कृषिकर**.

कृषिजीविन् m. the same (lit. living by agriculture).

†**कृषीवल** m. plougher, husbandman.

कृष्ट s. a ploughed field.

कृष्टज a. grown on tilled ground.

कृष्टि f. (lit. drawing, ploughing) pl. the (ploughing) people, the races of men (supposed to be 5).

†**कृष्ट्योजस्** a. conquering men.

कृष्ण a. black, dark. — m. (± पक्ष) the dark half month, the black antelope (mostly **कृष्ण**); N. of an ancient hero and teacher, later as the god Kṛṣṇa identified with Viṣṇu; du. **कृष्णौ** = Kṛṣṇa and Arjuna. f. **कृष्णा** a black kind of leech. N. of sev. plants, E. of Durgā and Draupadī; f. **कृष्णी** night. n. blackness, darkness.

कृष्णचतुर्दशी f. the fourteenth day of the dark half of the month, i.e. new moon's day.

कृष्णजन्माष्टमी f. the eighth (of a cert. month, thought as) Kṛṣṇa's birth-day.

कृष्णता f., °त्व n. blackness, darkness.

कृष्णनयन & **कृष्णनेत्र** a. black-eyed.

कृष्णपक्ष m. = **कृष्ण** (± पक्ष).

कृष्णभूम m. black soil.

कृष्णमुख, f. **ई** black-mouthed.

कृष्णयजुर्वेद m. the black Yajurveda.

कृष्णल (m.) n. a kind of black berry (used as a weight or a coin).

कृष्णवर्ण a. black-coloured.

कृष्णवर्त्मन् m. fire (lit. having a black way).

कृष्णवाल a. black-tailed.

कृष्णश a. blackish.

कृष्णसर्प m. a very venomous black serpent.

कृष्णसार, f. **ई** essentially black, spotted black; m. (± मृग) the spotted antelope.

कृष्णाजिन n. the skin of the black antelope.

कृष्णाय्, °यति behave like Kṛṣṇa, °यते make black.

कृष्णायस् & °यस n. iron.

कृष्णिमन् m. blackness.

कृसर m. n., **आ** f., a dish of rice and sesamum.

कॢप्, **कल्पते**, pp. **कॢप्त** (q.v.) be in order or right, succeed; answer or correspond to, accord or agree with (instr.); be fit or serve for, help to (dat.); get at, partake of (dat.); fall to the share of, be partaken by (loc., dat., or gen.), become, be (nom. or dat.); happen, occur. C. **कल्पयति**, °ते put in order, arrange, prepare, dispose, distribute; furnish with (instr.), help to (dat. or loc.); bestow on (acc. of th. & gen. of pers.); make, fabricate, compose, perform, accomplish; fix, settle; declare or regard as (2 acc.); put to (loc.), use, employ. — **अभि** answer or correspond, being adequate to (acc.). **अव** be in order or right, answer, serve, be fit for (dat.). C. prepare, arrange, employ. **उप** the same; C. also procure, fetch; assign, destine for or to (dat. or loc.); assume, state. **परि** C. fix, settle, determine, choose, contrive, arrange, distribute (with a num. in धा), invent, imagine, believe, suppose, regard as (acc.). **प्र** proceed well, succeed; be right or in order. C. arrange, prepare, fix, settle, appoint to (loc.); choose for (acc.), contrive, effect. **वि** shift, change; fluctuate, balance; be doubtful or optional (g.). C. make, form, compose, distribute; choose, select; consider as doubtful, state as optional or arbitrary (g.); suppose, imagine, invent. **सम्** be all right, succeed, prosper. C. join together, produce, create; assign, destine, settle, determine, intend, imagine, appoint to (loc.); consider or regard as (acc. w. इव). **उपसम्** put down, appoint, select. — Cf. **अभिकॢप्त**, **उपकॢप्त**, **प्रकॢप्त**, **संकॢप्त**.

कॢप्त a. put in order, arranged, prepared; finished, accomplished; fixed, settled, ready, all right; being, existing.

क्लृप्ति or क्लृप्ति f. coming round, success; exposition, description, definition.
केकय m. N. of a people, f. ई.
केका f. the cry of a peacock.
केकोत्कण्ठ a. fond of crying (peacock).
केत m. desire, intention; abode etc. = केतन.
केतक m., (°कि &) °की f. N. of a tree.
केतककाण्डक s. thorn from the Ketaka tree.*
केतन n. desire, intention, summons, invitation; abode, place of refuge; flag, banner.
केतनजुष् a. desirous of (—°).
केतय्, °यति, pp. केतित summon, invite.
केतु m. brightness, light (pl. beams); apparition, form, shape; sign, mark, flag, banner; chief, leader.
केतुमन्त् a. bright, clear.
केदार m. an irrigated field; °खण्ड n. a hole in such a field.
केदारभट्ट m. N. of an author.
केन (instr. to 1क) by whom? etc.; adv. why? whence? how?
केनिप m. a sage.
केनेषितोपनिषद् or केनोपनिषद् f. T. of an Upanishad (beginning w. केनेषितम्).
केन्द्र n. the centre of a circle.
केपि a. trembling, shaking.
केयूर m. n. a bracelet worn on the upper arm.
केरल m. pl. N. of a people.
†केरु v. मंहिकेरु.
केलि m. f., °ली f. play, sport, esp. amorous sport.
केलिकल a. playing, sporting; *f. आ = prec.*
केलिकलह m. love-quarrel.
केलिगृह n. pleasure-house.
केलित n. playing, sporting.
केलिवन n. pleasure-grove.
केलिशयन n. pleasure-couch.
केवट m. cave, pit.
केवर्त m. a fisherman.
केवल, f. ई (later आ) exclusive, belonging only to (gen. or dat.); alone, simple, pure, mere; whole, entire, each, all. °— & n. adv. only. न केवलम्—अपि not only—but also.
केवलाघ a. alone guilty.
केवलादिन् a. eating alone.
केश m. (adj. —° f. आ & ई) hair (of the head), mane, tail (of the Yak).
केशकल्पना f. arranging of the mane.*
केशग्रह m. pulling of the hair.
केशपाश m. tuft of hair.
केशबन्ध m. hair-band.
केशरचना f. arranging of the hair.
केशव a. having long hair; m. E. of Viṣṇu-Kṛṣṇa.
केशवन्त् = prec. a., also maned.
केशवपन n. cutting of the hair.
केशहस्त m. tuft of hair.
केशाकेशि adv. hair to hair, head to head.
केशाग्र n. the top of a hair.
केशान्त m. end or lock of hair, tuft; tonsure.
केशान्तिक a. reaching the end of the hair (at the forehead).
केशिन् a. = केशवन्त्; m. N. of an Asura & sev. men. f. केशिनी E. of Durgā etc., a woman's name; pl. cert. mythical beings.
केशिनिषूदन, °मथन, °सूदन, °हन्, & °हन्तृ m. slayer of Keçin (Kṛṣṇa).
केसर n. (आ f.) = केश; also filament, esp. of a lotus; m. N. of a plant = बकुल.
केसरगुण्ड m. Kesara pollen.*
केसरमालिका f. a Kesara garland.*
केसरवृक्ष m. the Kesara tree.*
केसराग्र n. the ends of a mane.
केसराल a. rich in filaments.
केसरावली f. = बकुलमाला q.v.*
केसरिन् a. maned; m. lion.
कैकेय m. a king of the Kekayas; f. ई a princess of the K., one of the wives of Daçaratha.
कैंकिरात a. belonging to the Açoka tree.
कैटभ m. N. of an Asura slain by Viṣṇu.
कैतव, f. ई a deceitful; f. ई & n. fraud, deceit, lie.
कैरात a. pertaining to the Kirātas; m. a prince of the Kirātas.
कैरिशि m. patron. of Sutvan.
कैलास m. N. of a mountain, the seat of Çiva and Kubera.
कैवर्त m. fisherman (a mixed caste); f. ई.
कैवल्य n. exclusiveness, absolute oneness, eternal happiness, beatitude.

कैशिक, f. ई as fine as a hair; m. N. of an ancient king, pl. his people (cf. क्रथकैशिक).
कोक m. wolf; cuckoo (f. ई).
कोकिल m., आ f. the Indian cuckoo.
कोङ्कण m. pl. N. of a people.
कोच m. drying, shrinking up.
कोट m. fort, stronghold.
कोटक m. carpenter (a mixed caste).
कोटर n. hollow of a tree.
कोटरवन्त् a. having holes or cavities.
कोटि & °टी f. the curved end of the bow, of claws etc., the horns of the moon; edge or point i.g., utmost degree, highest number (= 10 millions).
कोटिमन्त् a. edged, pointed.
कोण m. corner, angle.
कोथ m. putrefaction. corruption.
कोदण्ड s. a bow.
कोप m. irritation, passion, wrath, anger (w. loc., gen., प्रति, or उपरि).
कोपन a. passionate, angry; irritating, making angry (also as subst. n.).
कोपानुबन्ध m. continuance of anger.
कोपिन् a. angry; making angry, irritating (—°).
कोमल a. tender, soft.
कोम्य a. smooth, lithe.
कोयष्टि & °क m. the lapwing.
कोर m. a movable joint.
कोरक s. bud, unblown flower.
कोल m. boar.
कोलक *m. a cert. perfume.
कोलाहल m. n. confused cry, uproar.
कोविद a. knowing, clever, skilful in (loc., gen., or —°). Abstr. °त्व n.
कोश m. cask, bucket (fig. of a cloud), box, chest, inner part of a carriage, sheath, scabbard, case, cover; ball, globe (—°); bud, seed-cup (esp. of the lotus plant); pod, husk, shell; cocoon, womb, scrotum; store-room, treasury; treasure, dictionary, anthology.
कोशदण्ड m. du. treasury and army.
कोशपेटक s. treasure or jewel-box.
कोशफल n. the scrotum.
कोशरक्षिन् m. guard of the treasury, treasurer.
कोशराष्ट्र n. du. treasury and realm.
कोशल v. कोसल.
कोशवन्त् a. having treasures, rich, wealthy.
कोशहीन a. wanting treasures, poor.
कोशागार m. n. treasure-house, treasury.
कोशाध्यक्ष m. superintendent of the treasury, treasurer.
कोष v. कोश.
कोष्ठ m. the bowels or the belly (also n.), a kind of vessel or pot; n. store-room, surrounding wall.
कोष्ठागार n. store-room, treasury.
कोष्ण a. tepid, warm.
†कोसल m. N. of a country, pl. its people, f. आ its capital (Ayodhyā).
कोसलविदेह m. pl. the Kosala and Videha.
कौक्षेय & °क m. sword, knife.
कौङ्कुम, f. ई consisting of or dyed with saffron.
कौट a. deceitful, false.
कौटसाक्ष्य n. false evidence.
कौटिल्य n. crookedness, deceit, falsehood.
कौटुम्ब n. relation to a family; as adj. = seq. a.
कौटुम्बिक a. belonging to the household or family; m. the father of a family.
कौणकुत्स्य m. N. of a Brahman.
कौणप a. pertaining to corpses; m. a Rakṣas.
कौतुक n. curiosity, interest, eagerness, vehement desire or longing for (loc. or —°), anything curious or interesting, show, festival, ceremony, esp. the marriage-thread ceremony, also the marriage-thread itself; blessing, happiness.
कौतुकक्रिया f. nuptial ceremony.
कौतुकगृह n. wedding-house.
कौतुकरत्नाकर m., °रहस्य & °सर्वस्व n. the jewel-mine, secret, & essence of curiosity (T. of comedies).
कौतुकालंकार m. nuptial ornament.*
कौतूहल n. curiosity, interest, longing after (loc., प्रति, or inf.); feast, ceremony.
कौत्स a. Kutsa's; m. a patr. name (f. ई).
कौनख्य n. disease or ugliness of the nails.
कौन्तेय m. metron. of the Pāṇḍavas.
कौन्द, f. ई jasmine (as adj.).

कौपीन n. the pudenda or a piece of cloth worn over them.

कौबेर, f. ई belonging to Kubera; f. ई (± काष्ठा or दिश्) K.'s region, i.e. the north.

कौमार, f. ई a. juvenile, belonging to a youth or maiden; belonging to Skanda, Skanda's; n. (w. व्रत) = °व्रत (q.v.), as subst. childhood, youth, virginity.

कौमारबन्धकी f. whore.*

कौमारव्रत n. vow of abstinence; °चारिन् a. practising the vow of abstinence.

कौमुद m. a patr. name. f. ई the moonshine (causing the Kumudas to blossom); the full-moon, often —° in the titles of books = elucidation, explanation.

कौमुदिका f. a woman's name.

कौमुदीमह (& °महोत्सव*) m. festival of the full moon.

कौरव, f. ई belonging to the Kurus; m. a descendant of Kuru.

कौरवेय m. pl. the descendants of Kuru.

कौरव्य or कौरव्य m. the same, also N. of a people.

कौर्म a. belonging to a tortoise.

कौल, f. ई relating to a family, ancestral, hereditary; m. a cert. sect.

कौलिक m. = कौल m., also weaver.

कौलितर m. E. of the demon Çambara.

कौलीन a. noble; n. (family-)talk, gossip, rumour.

कौलूत m. pl. N. of a people.

कौलेय & °क m. dog (lit. family or domestic animal).

कौल्य a. of noble race; n. noble race.

कौवेर v. कौबेर.

1कौश, f. ई made of Kuça grass.

2कौश a. silken.

कौशल & °ल्य n. welfare, health; cleverness, skill in (loc. or —°).

कौशाम्बिका f. a woman's name.*

कौशाम्बी f. N. of a town.

कौशाम्बीय a. of or from Kauçāmbī.

1कौशिक a. pertaining to Kuçika; m. patron. of sev. men, E. of Indra, f. कौशिकी E. of Durgā; N. of sev. women & rivers.

2कौशिक n. a silk cloth.

3कौशिक m. owl.

कौशीलव & °लव्य n. the profession of an actor or bard.

कौशेय a. silken; n. silk, a silk cloth.

कौषारव m. a patron. name.

कौषीतक & °कि m. patron. names.

कौषीतकिन् m. pl. N. of a Vedic school.

कौषीतकिब्राह्मण m. T. of a Brāhmaṇa, °णोपनिषद् & कौषीतक्युपनिषद् f. T. of an Upanishad.

कौष्ठ a. being in the belly or in a store room.

कौसल m. pl. N. of a people & a dynasty.

कौसल्य a. belonging to the Kosalas; m. a prince of the Kosalas, f. आ a princess of the Kosalas, esp. one of the wives of Daçaratha.

कौसीद, f. ई connected with a loan.

कौसुम, f. ई made of flowers, flowery.

कौसुम्भ, f. ई made of safflor, dyed with s., orange, red.

कौस्तुभ m. n. N. of a celebrated jewel, the ornament of Viṣṇu.

*क्नथ्, क्नथति hurt, kill.

क्नूय् (*क्नूयते), only C. क्नोपयति (± अभि) wet, moisten.

क्य a. agreeable to Ka (= Prajāpati).

क्याकु n. a mushroom.

क्रकच m. n. a saw.

क्रन्द् only pp. क्रंन्दमाण crashing, roaring.

क्रतु m. power, might, strength (of body or mind); deliberation, insight, wisdom; inspiration, enthusiasm; plan, design, purpose, will; act, deed, work, esp. sacred work, sacrifice, feast; festival (चाक्षुष of the eye); N. of an old sage who appears as a star in the Great Bear.

क्रतुमन्त् a. intelligent, wise, inspired, resolute.

क्रतुमय a full of wisdom.

क्रतुराज् m. the highest sacrifice (lit. king of sacrifices).

क्रतुविक्रयिन् a. who sells (the benefits of) sacrifices.

क्रतूय्, क्रतूयति exert one's self.

क्रथ् (*क्रथति), only C. क्राथयति exult; *hurt, injure (gen.).

क्रथ m. N. of an ancient king, son of Vidarbha (cf. seq.).

क्रथकैशिक m. pl. N. of a people (identif. w. the Vidarbhas).

क्रन्द्, क्रन्दति, °ते roar, neigh, creak, click, cry, lament. C. क्रन्दयति make roar, neigh, etc., also = S. I. कनिक्रन्ति, कनिक्रन्ते, esp. pp. कनिक्रत्, कनिक्रदत् & कनिक्रद्यमान = S. — अभि shout or roar at, call to (also C. & I.). अव roar (also C.). आ call to, invoke, cry, lament. C. the same; also cause to cry or lament. प्र call aloud. वि lament. सम् cry together with (instr.). — Cf. आक्रन्दित.

क्रन्द m., क्रन्दन n. crying, calling.

क्रन्दनध्वनि m. (sound of) lamentation.

क्रन्दनु m. roaring, sounding.

क्रन्दस् n. war-cry; du. the two opposed armies (lit. the two shouting ones).

क्रन्द्य n. neighing.

क्रम्, क्रामति, क्रमते (क्रमति, क्रामते), pp. क्रान्त (mostly —° & w. act. mg) stride, step, walk, go or come to (acc. or loc.); go over, pass, ascend, approach (sex.); surpass, pervade, fill, accomplish; M. proceed well, succeed. C. क्रमयति (क्रामयति) cause to stride. I. चङ्क्रमते, चङ्क्रम्यते, & चङ्क्रमीति step to and fro, wander, walk, pass. — अति step beyond, cross, pass, excel, overcome, pass by, neglect, transgress (abs. or w. acc.); part or escape from, lose, be deprived of (abl.). C. let pass, take no notice of (acc.). अभ्यति step beyond or across, pass, excel, overcome, overstep, neglect, transgress. व्यति & समति the same. अधि ascend, mount up to (acc.) अनु go on or along, follow; go through, enumerate. अप go or pass away; withdraw or fly from (abl.). अभि step near, approach, attack, overwhelm; enter, begin, undertake. समभि come near, approach. अव go away, fly; tread upon, overwhelm (acc.). — आ approach, visit, enter, tread upon (acc. or loc.); cling to, grasp, attack, overpower, take hold or possession of (acc.); undertake, begin (inf.); ascend, mount (mostly M.). अध्या attack, seize, occupy. समा the same + tread upon, overpower, take hold or possession of (acc.). उद् go up or out, depart; escape, fly or withdraw from (abl. or acc.); pass by, neglect. व्युद् go asunder, part, go away; overstep, transgress, disregard. उप come near, approach, enter (acc. or loc.); go against, attack; treat, deal with (acc.); (mostly M.) undertake, begin, be about to (acc., dat., or inf.). समुप come near; undertake, begin (M. w. inf.). नि enter, step, tread down. निस् go out of (abl.), depart, fly, escape. C. cause to step out, expel, lead or take away. अभिनिस्, उपनिस्, & विनिस् go out, come forth from (abl.). परा step forward, advance, exert one's self, excel. परि walk about (esp. on the stage), circumambulate, walk through, visit; overtake, overcome. प्र step forth, set out, go to (acc.), go across, pass; M. deal with (loc.); M. (A.) proceed to, undertake, begin (acc., अर्थम्, or inf.). संप्र M. proceed to, begin (acc. or inf.). प्रति & अनुप्रति come back. वि go asunder, part, separate; walk through, bestride; move on, advance, proceed, exert one's self; content, fight against (acc.). अनुवि M. step after. निर्वि step out. सम् come together, meet, encounter; go to, enter (acc.), pass from (abl.) to (loc.), go through or across, come near, walk along. C. cause to pass, transport, deliver; lead to (2 acc.), cast upon (acc. of th. and loc. of pers.). अनुसम् follow after (acc.), also = उपसम् step towards, come or pass to (acc.). — Cf. अध्याक्रान्त, आक्रान्त, निष्क्रान्त, विक्रान्त, संक्रान्त.

क्रम m. step, course, method, way; regular progress, order, succession; cause or reason of (gen. or —°); also = क्रमपाठ. — क्रम (°—) & क्रमतस् in due order, successively, gradually. क्रमेण & क्रमात् the same + according to (—°).

क्रमगत a. come into the way of (gen.).
क्रमण m. step; n. stepping, walking, crossing.
क्रमदीश्वर m. N. of a grammarian.
क्रमपाठ m. the step-recitation (of the Veda, opp. **संहितापाट** q.v.).
क्रमप्राप्त a. got by succession, hereditary.
क्रमयोग m. regular order, succession.
क्रमशस् adv. step by step, in order, gradually.
क्रमागत & **क्रमायात** a. come in due order, hereditary.
क्रमिक a. successive, hereditary, inherited.
क्रमुक m. the betel-nut tree.
क्रमेल & **°क** m. camel.
क्रय m. purchase, purchase-money.
क्रयण n. buying.
क्रयविक्रय m. buying and selling (sgl. & du.), traffic.
क्रयविक्रयानुशय m. rescission of a bargain (j.).
क्रयविक्रयिन् a. one who buys or sells.
क्रयिक & **क्रयिन्** m. buyer.
क्रय्य a. purchasable.
क्रविष्णु a. greedy for raw flesh.
क्रविस & **क्रव्य** n. raw flesh, carrion.
क्रव्यगन्धिन् a. smelling of raw flesh.
क्रव्यभोजन a. eating raw flesh; m. bird of prey.
क्रव्याद् & **क्रव्याद** a. = prec. adj.; m. beast of prey.
क्रष्टव्य a. to be drawn or extracted.
क्राण a. busy, eager; instr. **°णा** adv.
क्रान्त n. step.
क्रान्ति f. passage.
क्रिमि v. **कृमि**.
क्रिमिज v. **कृमिज**.
क्रिया f. action, performance, occupation, labour, pains; activity, verb; work, esp. religious work, sacrifice, ceremony, worship; argument, document, bond, contract.
क्रियाकुल a. busy (lit. troubled by work).
क्रियात्मक a. whose nature is activity; abstr. **°त्व** n.
क्रियाद्वेषिन् a. rejecting arguments or documents (j.).
क्रियान्तर n. another action.
क्रियाप्रबन्ध m. the uninterrupted continuance of an action.
क्रियाभ्युपगम m. explicit agreement (j.).
क्रियायोग्य a. fit for action or work.
क्रियारम्भ a. undertaking works.
क्रियार्थ a. having the sense of a verb (g.).
क्रियालोप m. omission of (pious) works.
क्रियावन्त् a. active, busy, religious.
क्रियाविधि m. application of a verb, also = **कर्मविधि**.
क्रियाविशेषण n. adverb (lit. that which specifies an action).
क्रियाशक्ति f. capability of acting.
क्रियाशक्तिमन्त् a. poss. to prec.
क्रियाश्रय m. recipient of an action (g.).
क्रिवि m. a leather bag; N. of a people (later the Pañcālas).
क्रिविर्दती f. having teeth like a saw.
क्री, क्रीणाति & **क्रीणीते**, pp. **क्रीत** (q.v.) buy, purchase (w. instr. of price & acc. or gen. of pers.). — **अप** = S. **अभि** buy for a certain purpose. **अव** M. purchase, hire. **आ** & **उप** buy. **निस्** buy off or ransom from (abl.); M. (± **आत्मानम्**) buy off one's self. **परि** purchase, get by exchange; hire, obtain (*w. dat. or instr. of price). **वि** exchange or sell for (instr.). **सम्** = S.
क्रीड्, क्रीडति (**क्रीळति**) & **क्रीडते**, pp. **क्रीडित** (q.v.) play, sport, amuse one's self with (instr. of th. & instr. ± **सह, सार्धम्**, or **समम्** of pers.). C. **क्रीडयति** cause to play. **आ** & **समा** = S. **परि** play about. **प्र** begin to play, also = S. **वि** & **सम्** = S.
क्रीड a. playing, sporting; f. **क्रीडा** play, sport, amusement.
क्रीडन n. playing, play.
क्रीडनक m. plaything, toy.
क्रीडागृह m. n. pleasure-house.
क्रीडामयूर m. a peacock to play with.
क्रीडामर्कटपोत m. a young monkey to play with.
क्रीडामहीध्र m. pleasure-mountain, hillock.
क्रीडामात्र n. only a joke.
क्रीडामुद् f. amorous joy or sport.
क्रीडायोग m. occupation with playing.
क्रीडारस m. delight in playing.

क्रीडावेश्मन् n. pleasure-house.

क्रीडासरस् n. pleasure-lake.

क्रीडिं a. sporting, playful.

क्रीडित n. play, sport.

क्रीडिन्, क्रीडु, & क्रीडुमन्त् a. = क्रीडिं.

क्रीतं a. bought (esp. a son); n. buying.

क्रीतक a. = prec. adj.

क्रुंच् & क्रुंच m. curlew.

1क्रुध्, क्रुध्यति (क्रुध्यते), pp. क्रुद्धं be angry with (dat., gen., or loc.; pp. also w. उपरि or प्रति). C. क्रोधयति make angry, irritate. — अभि be angry with (acc.). प्रति be angry with (acc.) in return. सम् & अभिसम् be angry.

2क्रुध् f. anger, wrath.

क्रुधि & क्रुध्मिन् a. wrathful, irritable.

क्रुमु f. N. of a river.

क्रुमुक m. fire-catcher (r.).

क्रुश्, क्रोशति, °ते. pp. क्रुष्ट (w. act. & pass. mg) cry out, shout, croak, lament; call to (acc). — अनु shout at (acc.); C. show sympathy (lit. follow in lamenting). अभि call or cry at (acc.), lament, mourn. आ call aloud, scold at, revile, defame; challenge, emulate. उद् cry out, call to (acc.). उप show anger or defiance. प्र raise a cry, call at (acc.). वि the same. सम् cry out together, shout angrily at (acc.). — Cf. अपक्रुष्ट, आक्रुष्ट, उपक्रुष्ट.

क्रूड्, क्रूडयति thicken (trans.).

क्रूरं a. bloody, raw, sore; cruel, harsh, dreadful. n. a wound or sore; bloodshedding, slaughter; cruelty, harshness.

क्रूरकर्मकृत् m. a carnivorous animal (lit. = seq. 2.).

1क्रूरकर्मन् n. a bloody or cruel work.

2क्रूरकर्मन् a. doing cruel deeds.

क्रूरता f. cruelty, harshness.

क्रूराचार a. of cruel conduct.

क्रूराचारविहारवन्त् a. whose conduct and delights are cruel.

क्रेतव्य & क्रेय a. to be bought.

क्रेतृ m. buyer.

क्रोडं m. breast, chest, lap; cavity, hollow; a hog.

क्रोडवाल m. a hog's bristle.

क्रोध m. anger, wrath.

क्रोधचक्षुस् n. an angry eye.

क्रोधज a. sprung from anger.

क्रोधन & क्रोधिन् a. irritable, passionate.

1क्रोधवश m. the power of anger.

2क्रोधवश a. subject to anger.

क्रोश m. shout, yell; calling distance.

क्रोशनं a. & n. crying.

क्रोष्टृ & क्रोष्टुक m. a jackal.

क्रोष्टुं a. crying, lamenting; m. = prec.

क्रौञ्च m. curlew (f. ई also the myth. mother of the curlews); N. of a mountain torn asunder by Kārttikeya.

क्रौञ्चरिपु m. E. of Kārttikeya (v. prec.).

क्रौञ्चशत्रु & क्रौञ्चारि m. the same.

क्रौड, f. ई belonging to a hog.

क्रौर्य n. harshness, cruelty.

क्लथ्, क्लथति turn round (intr.).

क्लन्द् v. क्रन्द्.

क्लम्, क्लाम्यति, pp. क्लान्त (q.v.) be weary or languid. C. क्लामयति tire, exhaust. — परि be extremely tired or exhausted. वि M. languish, despond. — Cf. अतिक्लामित, विक्लान्त.

क्लम m. fatigue, weariness.

क्लमापह a. destroying weariness.

क्लान्त a. tired, exhausted, languid, dejected, sad; thin, slender.

क्लान्ति f. = क्लम.

क्लिद्, क्लिद्यति, pp. क्लिन्न (q.v.) be or become wet. C. क्लेदयति wet, moisten, soil. — Cf. क्लिन्दन्त्, परिक्लिन्न, विक्लिन्न.

क्लिन्दन्त् a. wet, dripping.

क्लिन्न a. wet, moist; soft, tender (heart).

क्लिश्, क्लिश्नाति (क्लिश्यति, °ते), pp. क्लिष्ट (q.v) torment, trouble, molest; P. क्लिश्यते (°ति) be distressed, suffer. C. क्लेशयति = S. trans. — अति (क्लिश्यति) have or give too much pains.* सम् press together, sqash; trouble, molest. — Cf. परिक्लिष्ट, विक्लिष्ट.

क्लिष्ट a. distressed, afflicted, sad (n. adv.); hurt, injured, worn, used; painful, difficult; constrained, affected, obscure (rh.).

क्लीबं a. impotent, emasculated, unmanly, timorous. m. eunuch, weakling, coward. n. the neuter gender (g.).

क्लीबता f., **°त्व** n. impotence, weakness.
क्लेद m. moisture, wetness.
क्लेदन a. & n. wetting.
क्लेश m. affliction, pain, distress.
क्लेशिन् a. tormenting, hurting.
क्लैब्य n. impotence, weakness.
क्लोमन् m. n. the right lung.
क्लोश m. cry, calling (cf. **क्रोश**).
क्व adv. where? wither? how? Used also as loc. of 1**क**. Often connected w. **अह, इद्, इव, नु, स्विद्**, w. the latter also = somewhere. — With **चिद्** & (later) **अपि** somewhere, anywhere, at or to a cert. place. **क्व चिद्—क्व चिद्** here—there, now—now. **क्व** w. negation & **अपि, चिद्, च**, or **चन** nowhere, in no place. **क्व—क्व** where is this? where is that? i.e. how distant or different is this from that.
क्वण्, क्वणति, pp. **क्वणित** (q.v.) sound, hum, tinkle. — **उद्** = S.*
क्वणित n. sound, hum, twang.
क्वथ्, क्वथति, °ते, pp. **क्वथित** boil (tr. & intr.).
क्वथ m. decoction, extract.
क्वथन n. boiling, decocting.
क्वयि m. a cert. bird.
क्वल m. pl. a kind of jujube.
क्वस्थ a. where standing or being?
क्वाण m. sound.
क्वाथ m. boiling, decoction.
क्षण m. (n.) instant, moment, little while; suitable time, opportunity of (—°); feast. °—, abl., & instr. instantly, immediately; loc. (also doubled) every moment. — **क्षणं कृ** wait a moment (also **ग्रह्***) or give an opportunity (also **दा**); **क्षणं लभ्** find an opportunity.
क्षणदा f. the night (giving moments or opportunities).
क्षणदाकर m. the moon (night-maker).
क्षणदाचर m. night-walker, a Rakṣas.
क्षणन n. hurt, injury.
क्षणमङ्गल n. good omen for a feast.*
क्षणान्तर n. a moment's interval; loc. immediately.
क्षणिक, f. **ई** momentary, transient; abstr. **°ता** f., **°त्व** n.

क्षत a. hurt, wounded, destroyed, violated. f. **आ** a dishonoured maiden; n. hurt, wound.
क्षति f. hurt, injury, destruction, damage.
क्षत्तृ m. cutter, carver, attendant, charioteer; N. of a caste.
क्षत्तृजाति m. who belongs to the Kṣattṛ caste.
क्षत्र n. rule, dominion, power; the reigning or warrior (second) caste or a member of it.
क्षत्रजात a. born of the warrior caste.
क्षत्रधर्म m. the duty of the warrior caste.
क्षत्रधर्मन् a. fulfilling the duties of the warrior caste.
क्षत्रबन्धु m. who belongs to the warrior caste.
क्षत्रयोनि a. descended from the warrior caste.
क्षत्रविद्या f. the science of the warrior caste.
क्षत्रिय a. reigning, supreme. m. member of the princely (second) caste (f. **आ**); n. supremacy, dominion.
क्षद्, क्षदते cut, carve, distribute; take, eat.
क्षद्मन् n. carving knife.
क्षन्, क्षणोति, pp. **क्षत** (q.v.) hurt, harm, wound, break; M. **क्षणुते** refl. & intr — Cf. **परिक्षत, विक्षत**.
क्षन्तव्य a. to be forgiven (of pers. & th.); n. impers. w. gen. of pers. & abl. of th.
1**क्षप्, क्षपति** & **क्षपते** do penance, be abstinent. — **सम्** the same.
2**क्षप्** f. night; gen. & instr. at night.
1**क्षपण** m. a Buddhist or Jaina mendicant; n. penance, abstinence.
2**क्षपण** a. destroying; m. destroyer; n. destruction, expulsion, omission (of studies), passing away (the time).
क्षपणक m. = 1**क्षपण** m.
क्षपा f. night.
क्षपाकर & **°कृत्** m. the moon (night-maker).
क्षपात्यय m. the end of the night, i.e. morning.
क्षपाचर m. night-walker; night-animal or bird, a Rakṣas or goblin.
क्षपाह n. night and day.
1**क्षम्, क्षमते** (**क्षमति** & **क्षम्यते**), pp. **क्षान्त** (q.v.) be patient or quiet, endure, suffer, bear, pardon, forgive (gen. or dat. of pers. & acc. of th., pp. also **क्षमित**); be able to

(infin.). C. क्षमयति, °ते ask pardon for (2 acc.); endure, put up with (acc.). — अभि be gracious, pardon. सम् suffer, put up with (acc.).

2क्षम् (क्षाम) f. the earth; instr. क्षमा on the earth.

क्षम a. patient; enduring, resisting (—°); propitious, friendly; tolerable; able to, capable of (loc., infin., or —°); suitable, fit, proper for (dat., gen., loc., inf., or —°). f. क्षमा patience, forbearance, indulgence (gen. or प्रति); the earth.

क्षमता f., °त्व n. fitness, capability.

क्षमान्वित a. endowed with patience, enduring, indulgent.

क्षमावन्त्, क्षमाशील, & क्षमिन् a. the same.

क्ष्म्य a. earthly, terrestrial.

1क्षय a. dwelling; m. dwelling-place, abode, seat; tribe, people.

2क्षय m. decrease, waste, loss, destruction, consumption (also as a sickness); decay, ruin, fall, end; क्षयं गम्, इ, or या come to an end, perish; क्षयं नी bring to an end, destroy.

क्षयकर, °कर्तृ, & °कृत् a. making an end, destroying (—°).

क्षयंकर, f. ई the same.

1क्षयण a. ending, destroying.

2क्षयण (क्षयण) a. habitable.

क्षयद्वीर a. ruling over men.

क्षयरोग m. the disease consumption.

क्षयरोगिन् a. consumptive; °गित्व n. = prec.

क्षयिन् a. decreasing, perishable, consumptive; abstr. क्षयिता f., °त्व n.

क्षयिष्णु a. perishable or destroying.

क्षर्, क्षरति (°ते) flow, glide, melt away, perish; flow with, abound in (acc.). C. क्षारयति cause to flow, dismiss. — अभि flow through (acc.); overflow. अनु flow upon or into (acc.) अभि the same, flow about. आ C. cause to flow near, sprinkle, soil; defame, accuse. उप flow near. प्रति flow around or towards. प्र stream forth. वि flow asunder, pour down. सम् flow together.

†क्षर a. melting away, perishable; n. the body.

क्षल्, क्षालयति wash, cleanse. — प्र & अभिप्र = S.

क्षव & क्षवथु m. sneezing.

1क्षा, क्षायति, pp. क्षाण burn, set on fire. C. क्षापयति burn, scorch. — प्र burn (intr.). सम् burn (trans.). — Cf. अवक्षाण.

2क्षा f. (Nom. क्षास्) = क्षम्.

क्षाति f. heat, flame.

क्षात्र, f. ई pertaining to the military tribe; n. dominion, supremacy.

क्षान्त a. borne, pardoned, forgiven (n. impers.); patient, indulgent. n. patience, indulgence.

क्षान्ति f. = prec. n.; poss. °मन्त्.

क्षान्तिशील m. N. of a man.

क्षाम a. burned, scorched, dried; thin, slender, weak.

क्षामक्षाम a. quite emaciated.

क्षामन् n., क्षामि f. the earth.

क्षामाङ्ग, f. ई slender(-limbed).

क्षामी w. कृ shorten.

क्षार a. pungent, saline, sharp; m. (n.) any pungent or saline substance, as caustic alcali, saltpetre, natron, etc.

क्षारलवण n. du. anything pungent and salt.

क्षाल m. washing.

क्षालन a. & n. washing, cleansing.

1क्षि, क्षेति, क्षियति, क्षयति abide, dwell, inhabit; rule, be master of (gen.). C. क्षयय-ति & क्षेपयति pacify. — अधि dwell in, rest on, spread over (acc. or loc.). आ dwell in, inhabit, be or become possessed of (acc.), exist. उप dwell in or near, remain with, rest or depend on (acc.), परि dwell about (acc.). प्रति settle at (acc.). सम् dwell together with (instr.).

2क्षि, क्षिणाति, क्षिणोति (क्षयति), pp. क्षित & क्षीण (q.v.) destroy, injure, exhaust; P. क्षीयते (क्षीयते) be exhausted, perish, cease, wane (moon). C. क्षययति & क्षपयति, °ते = S. tr.; w. कालम् etc. pass, spend. — अप & उप P. = S. P. परि destroy; P. suffer loss, become poor. — प्र, सम् A. & P. = S. — Cf. परिक्षीण, प्रक्षीण.

क्षित् a. & s. dwelling, ruling; inhabitant, ruler.

क्षित pp. exhausted, afflicted, wretched.

1क्षिति f. abode, settlement, the earth; pl. the settlements, i.e. tribes, nations, men, people.

2क्षिति f. destruction, decay, end.

क्षितिकम्प m. earthquake.

क्षितितल n. the surface of the earth.

क्षितिधर m. a mountain (earth-bearer).

क्षितिधरगुरु m. the master of the mountains i.e. the Himālaya.

क्षितिप, °पति, & °भुज् m. a king.

क्षितिभृत् m. a mountain or king.

क्षितिरस m. the sap or juice of the earth.

क्षितीन्द्र, क्षितीश, & क्षितीश्वर m. a king.

1क्षिप्, क्षिपति, °ते, pp. क्षिप्त (q.v.) throw, cast, send; put, place, direct, turn (esp. the eye or mind); hit, hurt; abuse, scold; throw down, cast off, reject; destroy, annihilate; pass, spend (time). C. क्षेपयति cause to (be) cast, make to descend through (instr.) into (loc.). — अधि bespatter, insult, abuse. अप cast off, take away, remove. अभि strike at (acc.). अव throw down, throw into (loc.), hurl at (dat.); take off. आ throw at (loc. or dat.), put in (loc.); strike, hit; draw near, attract; take away, withdraw, cast off; insult, revile. व्या stretch out (the hand), open (the mouth); strike, attract (the mind). समा throw together, pile up; shake, hurl; take away, tear off, expel, destroy; insult, revile. उद् throw, set or take up, lift, raise; extract from (abl.); cast off, get rid of (acc.). समुद् throw up, lift; loosen, deliver of (abl.); annihilate, destroy. उप throw at, hurl against (loc.); strike, hit, esp. w. words, i.e. either insult, mock, revile, or intimate, insinuate, alledge, allude to (acc.). नि throw down, place, put, apply; deposit, grant, deliver, entrust, appoint (2acc. or acc. of pers. & loc. of th.); leave, abandon, give up. उपनि put down. विनि throw or put down, commit, entrust. परि throw beyond, put or lay round, surround, encircle, place or put in (loc.). प्र throw far, set before; fling at, put in (loc.); let down. प्रति hurt, harm, reject, despise. वि throw asunder, scatter, dispel, distribute; extend, stretch out; let loose (the bow-string), shoot off (the bow); *handle, manage. प्रवि toss, harass. सम् throw together, heap up; compress, contract, abbreviate, diminish. — Cf. आक्षिप्त, विक्षिप्त, संक्षिप्त.

2क्षिप् f. (only nom. pl.) finger.

क्षिपणि f. gallop, course.

क्षिपणु m. archer or arrow.

क्षिपा f. (only instr. pl.) finger.

क्षिप्त a. thrown, tossed, hit, afflicted; defamed, despicable; n. a wound caused by shooting or throwing.

क्षिप्र a. darting (bow); quick, fast; n. quickly, immediately.

क्षिप्रनिश्चय a. quick of resolution, resolute.

क्षिप्रेषु a. having quick arrows.

क्षीण a. diminished, wasted, exhausted, broken down, thin, emaciated, feeble; abstr. °ता† f., °त्व† n.

क्षीणकल्मष a. freed from sins.

क्षीणवृत्ति a. whose means of subsistence are exhausted.

क्षीणायुस् a. whose life is (nearly) ended.

क्षीब & क्षीव a. drunk, intoxicated, excited; abstr. °ता f., °त्व n.

क्षीर n. milk (also of plants).

क्षीरक्षय m. the diminution of milk (in the udder).

क्षीरधि & °निधि m. the ocean (lit. milk-receptacle).

क्षीरनीर (°—) milk and water.

क्षीरप a. drinking milk; m. a suckling baby, infant.

क्षीरभृत a. paid with milk.

क्षीरवन्त् a. full of milk.

क्षीरवृक्ष m. milktree (E. of sev. kinds of fig.).

क्षीरसमुद्र & °सागर m. the ocean (of milk).

क्षीरस्निग्ध a. wet with milky juice.

क्षीरस्वामिन् m. N. of a grammarian.

क्षीरान्न n. milk-rice.

क्षीराब्धि, क्षीराम्बुधि, & क्षीरार्णव m. = क्षीरसमुद्र.

क्षीरिन् a. milky, yielding milk; m. N. of sev. plants.

क्षीरोद & °धि m. = क्षीरसमुद्र.

1क्षु, क्षौति sneeze (upon); pp. क्षुत (q.v.) — Cf. अवक्षुत.

2क्षु n. food.

क्षुण्ण a. pounded, bruised, crushed, broken, pierced, violated, interrupted.

क्षुत् f. sneeze, sneezing.

क्षुत a. having sneezed or being sneezed upon; n. = prec.

क्षुद्, क्षोदति, pp. क्षुण्ण (q.v.) pound, shatter, shake, stamp upon, dash to pieces. C. क्षोदयति shake, crush. — अव, प्र, वि, सम् = S.

क्षुद्र a. small, minute (also क्षुद्रक); low, mean.

*क्षुद्रघण्टिका f. a small bell (worn for ornament).

क्षुद्रजन्तु m. a small animal or a mean person.

क्षुद्रबुद्धि m. N. of a jackal (lit. Small-wit).

क्षुद्रशत्रु m. a small enemy.

1क्षुध्, क्षुध्यति, pp. क्षुधित be hungry. — वि = S.

2क्षुध् f. hunger.

क्षुधा f. the same; °कर causing hunger.

क्षुधार्त a. distressed with hunger.

क्षुधालु & क्षुध्मन्त् a. hungry.

क्षुप m., क्षुपक m. & °का f. shrub, bush.

क्षुब्ध v. seq.

1क्षुभ्, क्षुभ्यति, °ते (क्षोभते), pp. क्षुब्ध or क्षुभित tremble, shake, be agitated. C. क्षोभयति (°ते) agitate, impel, set in motion. — प्र वि, & सम् = S. — Cf. प्रक्षोभ्योस्.

2क्षुभ् f. jerk.

क्षुमन्त् a. rich in food, nourishing; strong, brave.

क्षुम्प m. shrub, bush.

क्षुर m. knife, esp. razor.

क्षुरक m. N. of a plant; f. क्षुरिका knife, dagger.

क्षुरकर्मन् & °कृत्य n. the work of shaving.

क्षुरधान n. razor-case.

क्षुल्ल & क्षुल्लक a. minute, small.

क्षेत्र n. dwelling-place, piece of ground, field, place, seat; womb, wife.

क्षेत्रगृह n. field and house.

क्षेत्रज a. growing in fields; m. the wife's son (by another than the husband).

क्षेत्रज्ञ a. knowing (fields or places); m. the soul.

क्षेत्रतर a. fitter for habitation or cultivation.

क्षेत्रप m. protector of the fields.

क्षेत्रपति m. the lord or owner of a field.

क्षेत्रपाल m. = क्षेत्रप.

क्षेत्रविद् a. = क्षेत्रज्ञ; comp. °वित्तर.

क्षेत्रिक m. owner of a field or wife, husbandman.

क्षेत्रिन् m. the same; soul.

क्षेत्रिय a. belonging to a place. m. husband; n. pl. environs.

क्षेप m. throwing, a throw or cast; loss (of time), delay; insult, abuse; accusation.

क्षेपक a. throwing, destroying; inserted, interpolated.

क्षेपण n. darting, throwing, loosing, sending off; passing away (time); also = f. ई a sling.

क्षेपणिक m. mariner, pilot.

क्षेपन् m. a throw; instr. क्षेपणा quickly.

क्षेपिष्ठ & क्षेपीयंस् superl. & comp. to क्षिप्र.

क्षेप्तृ m. thrower, hurler.

क्षेप्नु m. darting (of the bowstring).

क्षेम a. habitable, comfortable, peaceful, tranquil, safe. m. resting place, abode, home; security, tranquillity, comfort, welfare, enjoyment (opp. योग exertion, acquisition). क्षेमं ते hail to thee! Instr. sgl. & pl. safely, at ease.

क्षेमकर, °कृत्, & क्षेमंकर a. causing peace or rest.

क्षेमय्, only pp. क्षेमयन्त् resting or giving rest, harbouring.

क्षेमयोग m. du. rest and exertion.

क्षेमिन् a. safe, secure.

क्षेमीश्वर m. N. of a poet.

क्षेमेन्द्र m. N. of sev. authors.

क्षेम्य or क्षैम्य a. resting or giving rest, secure, comfortable.

क्षेष्णु a. perishable.

क्षैण्य n. perishing.

क्षैत m. chief of a tribe, prince; °वन्त्† princely.

क्षैत्र n. husbandry.

क्षैप्र a. gliding (a kind of Saṁdhi).

क्षोणि or णी f. (nom. °णीस्) woman, wife, fig. the earth; du. heaven and earth.

क्षोणिपति & °पाल m. king (earth-lord).

क्षोणीन्द्र & **क्षोणीपति** m. = prec.
क्षोद m. jolt, blow, pounding, grinding; flour, powder.
क्षोदस् n. swell of water.
क्षोदिष्ठ & **क्षोदीयंस्** superl. & comp. to **क्षुद्र**.
क्षोभ m. shaking, agitation, emotion.
क्षोभण a. shaking, agitating; n. = prec.
क्षौणी f. the earth, land.
क्षौणीधर m. a mountain (earth-bearer).
क्षौणीनाथ m. a king (earth-lord).
क्षौणीभृत् m. = **क्षौणीधर**.
क्षौद्र m. a cert. tree, N. of a caste; n. a species of honey.
क्षौम, f. **ई** made of linen; n. linen garment, linseed.
क्षौमयुगल n. pair of linen garments, under and upper garment of linen.*
क्षौर a. done with a razor. n. (± **कर्मन्**) shaving. **क्षौरं कृ** shave, ° **कारय्** have one's self shaved.
क्षौरकरण & °**कर्मन्** n. = prec. n.
क्ष्णु, **क्ष्णौति** whet, sharpen. — **अव** rub to pieces, crush. **सम्** M. = S.
क्ष्णोत्र n. whet-stone.
क्ष्मा f. the earth; only instr. **क्ष्मया** on the earth.
क्ष्माधर m. a mountain (earth-holder).
क्ष्माप, °**पति**, °**भर्तृ**, & °**भुज्** m. king.
क्ष्माभृत् m. a king or a mountain.
क्ष्विङ्का f. a cert. animal.
क्ष्विड्, **क्ष्वेडति** creak, hum, murmur, whistle.
क्ष्विद्, **क्ष्वेदति**, pp. **क्ष्विण्ण** the same.
क्ष्वेल्, **क्ष्वेलति** leap, jump; play.
क्ष्वेलन & °**लित** n., **क्ष्वेलि** & °**लिका** f. play, sport.

ख

खं n. hole, hollow, aperture, esp. the hole in the nave of a wheel or an aperture of the human body (as eyes, mouth, etc.); organ of sense; void space, sky, air. f. **खा** source, fountain.
खग a. moving in the air, flying; m. bird.
खगपति m. king of birds (E. of Garuḍa).
खगम a. & m. = **खग**.
खगाधिप & **खगेन्द्र** m. = **खगपति**.
खङ्खण a. or s. snarling.*
खच्, **खचति**, pp. **खचन्त्** glimmering, shining, & **खचित** q.v. — Cf. **उत्खचित** & **परिखचित**.
खचर a. & m. = **खग**.
खचित a. glittering, shining; inlaid, adorned with (—°).
खज m. churning; agitation, bustle, esp. of war; f. **खजा** churning stick.
खजल n. mist, dew, rain (lit. water of the sky).
खञ्ज्, **खञ्जति** limp.
खञ्ज a. lame; abstr. °**ता** f., °**त्व** n.
खञ्जन & °**क** m. wagtail.
खञ्जरीट & °**क** m. the same.
खटखटाय्, °**यते** crackle.
खटिका & **खटिनी** f. chalk.
खट्वा f. bedstead, couch.
खट्वाङ्ग m. a club shaped like the food of a bedstead, considered as the weapon of Çiva & worn by his adherents; °**घण्टा** f. a bell fastened to this club.
खट्वाङ्गधर & °**धार** m. E. of Çiva (lit. bearer of the Khaṭvāñga, v. prec.).
खट्वाङ्गभृत् & **खट्वाङ्गिन्** a. bearing the foot of a bedstead, also = prec.
खट्वातल n the place under a bedstead.
खड m. a kind of sour drink.
खड्ग m sword; rhinoceros.
खड्गधर a. bearing a sword; m. a man's name.
खड्गपाणि a. sword in hand.
खड्गप्रहार m. a sword-cut.
खड्गलता f. the blade of a sword.
खड्गविद्या f. the art of the sword, i.e. fencing.
खड्गहस्त a. = **खड्गपाणि**.
खड्गिन् a. armed with a sword.
खण्ड a. broken, crippled, defective, not full (moon). m. n. break, fragment, piece, part, section (of a book), sickle (of the moon); number, multitude.

खण्डक m. piece, part; lump-sugar.
खण्डधारा f. a kind of dance or air.
खण्डन a. breaking to pieces, destroying, removing. n. the act of breaking etc., also wounding, injuring, interrupting, frustrating, refusing, cheating, deceiving.
__खण्डमोदक__ m. a kind of sweetmeats.
खण्डय्, °**यति**, pp. **खण्डित** break or cut to pieces, divide, dispel, hurt, wound, destroy; interrupt, violate, transgress, frustrate, disappoint, refute, cheat, deceive. — **वि** cut to pieces, tear asunder, interrupt, trouble.
खण्डशस् adv. in or to pieces. — With **कृ**, **कल्पय्**, & **परिकल्पय्** cut asunder, divide.
खण्डितवृत्त a. immoral (lit. of broken conduct).
खद्, **खदति** be firm or hard.
खदा f. hut, stable.
खदिर m. N. of a tree (Acacia Catechu).
खद्योत m. a glowing flying insect.
खन्, **खनति**, °**ते**, pp. **खात** dig, dig up, delve, bury. C. **खानयति**. — **अभि** turn up (the soil). **उद्** root up, extract, exterminate, destroy. **प्रोद्** & **समुद्** the same. **नि** bury, inter; dig up, root up; infix. pierce. **निस्** dig out. **परि** dig round, dig up. **प्र** eradicate, overturn. **वि** dig up. — Cf. **अन्तर्निखात**, **उत्खात**.
खन a. digging; m. hollow, pit.
खनक m. digger.
खनन n. digging, burying, burial.
खनि a. digging; f. mine.
खनितृ m. digger.
खनित्र n., **खनित्रा** f. spade, shovel.
खनित्रिम a. produced by digging, dug up.
खन्य a. coming from holes or pits.
खमूर्तिमन्त् a. having an ethereal form.
खर a. harsh, rough, sharp, piercing; n. adv. — m. ass, mule, f. **खरी**.
खरमयूख & **खरांशु** m. the sun (having piercing rays).
खरयान n. a donkey-cart.
खराय्, pp. °**यित** behave like an ass.
खर्गला f. owl or some other night-bird.
खर्ज्, **खर्जति** creak (of a carriage-wheel).
खर्जूर m., **ई** f. the date tree; n. its fruit.
खर्पर n., **ई** f. a cert. mineral.
खर्म n. harshness, rudeness.
खर्व a. mutilated, crippled, imperfect, minute, low, vile.
1**खल** m. threshing floor, granary; oil-cake (also **ई** f.).
2**खल** m. a wicked person, villain, ruffian, f. **आ**.
खलति a. bald-headed; m. baldness.
खलाय्, °**यते** act like a villain.
खली w. **कृ** use ill, hurt, offend.
खलु adv. indeed, verily, truly (also **खलु वै**); now, now then (also **अथ खलु**, **उ खलु**, **वै खलु**), often only expl. — **न खलु** (± **वै**) indeed not; **खल्वपि** further, moreover.
खल्य a. being in the granary.
खल्ल्, **खल्लते**, pp. **खल्लित** be loose, hang down.
खल्ल m. paper-cornet; f. **ई** gouty pain in the extremities.
खल्लिका f. frying-pan.
खल्व m. a cert. grain or leguminous plant.
खल्वाट a. bald-headed.
खशरीरिन् a. = **खमूर्तिमन्त्**.
खस m. a degraded Kshatriya; pl. N. of a people.
खस्थ a. standing in the air.
खाखस m. poppy. °**तिल** m. poppy-seed.
खाञ्ज्य n. limping, lameness.
खाट् w. **कृ** make khāṭ, i.e. clear the throat.
खाण्डव m. a cert. sweetmeat (also n.); N. of a sacred wood.
खात् = **खाट्**.
खात m. n. ditch, well, pond; n. cavity, hole.
खातृ m. digger.
खात्र n. a breach.
खाद्, **खादति** (**खादते**) chew, bite, eat, devour, consume, destroy. C. **खादयति** also = S. — **प्र** & **सम्** chew, eat, devour.
खाद a. eating, devouring (—°); n. eating, food.
खादक m. eater, devourer; debtor; f. °**दिका** eating, devouring of (—°).
खादन n. = prec. f.; also food.
खादनीय a. to be eaten, eatable.
खादि s. bracelet, ring.
खादितव्य a. = **खादनीय**.
खादितृ m. eater, devourer.

1खादिन् a. chewing, eating (—°).
2खादिन् a. wearing bracelets or rings.
खादिर, f. ई made of Khadira wood.
खादिहस्त a. having rings on the hands.
खाद्य a. = खादनीय.
खान n. eating; °पान n. eating and drinking.
खानक a. digging up (—°); m. digger.
खानि f. cave, mine.
खार m., खारी f. a cert. measure of grain.
खार्वा f. the second age of the world.
खालत्य & खालित्य n. baldness.
खिद्, खिदति, pp. खिन्न (q.v.) depress (fig.); P. खिद्यते (°ति) be depressed, languish, suffer pain. C. खेदयति, °ते depress, afflict, vex. — आ snatch. उद् pull out. नि press down. निस् cut off, remove. परि P. = S. P. प्र push away. वि tear asunder. सम् press together; pull out, snatch away. — Cf. परिखिन्न.
खिद्र n. a borer or hammer.
†खिद्वंस् a. pressing.
खिन्न a. depressed, tired, weary, sad.
खिल m. a waste piece of land, desert, vacant space; n. supplement, addition.
खिली w. कृ waste, weaken; w. भू become void of (gen.), be frustrated, fail.
खिल्य m. lump, piece; also = खिल m.
खील m. = कील.
खुद्, खुदति futuere.
खुर m. hoof, claw.
खुरक m. a kind of dance.
खुरिन् m. a hoofed animal.
खृगल m. a crutch.
खेचर, f. ई = खचर.
खेट m. n. a kind of village or small town, shield (also °क); m. phlegm; adj. low, vile, wretched (esp. —°).
खेद m. depression, weariness, distress, sorrow, trouble, anger at (gen.). f. खेदा borer.
खेदन n. weariness, languor.
खेदयितव्य a. to be troubled.
खेदिन् a. tiresome or tired.
खेल्, खेलति move to and fro, swing; C. खेलयति.
खेल a. moving, swinging; N. of a man.
खेलगमन a. of a dallying gait.
खेलन n. swinging, going to and fro (also f. आ) play, sport.
खेलनक m. play, pastime.*
खेलि f. play, sport.
खोट & खोर a. lame, limping.
ख्या (ख्याति), pp. ख्यात (q.v.) see, appear; P. ख्यायते be called or known; C. ख्यापयति, °ते make known, proclaim; show, betray; praise, celebrate. — अति survey, overlook, neglect, abandon. अनु behold, view. अन्तर् descry, find out. अभि behold, look at; favour, protect. C. make known. अव look down, behold. आ behold, view; count, enumerate; show, declare, announce, tell, narrate; name, designate as (2 acc.). C. make known, tell; M. have told to one's self. प्रत्या name singly; turn away, repulse, reject, refute, deny, forbid; outvie, excel, surpass. व्या explain, illustrate; announce, proclaim, tell, call, name. समा enumerate, communicate, declare as (इति). परि look around, behold, consider; overlook, neglect. प्र behold, see; announce, tell; P. be visible or known. प्रति behold, see. वि look about, look at, see, perceive; shine forth, beam; illuminate, make visible, show. C. make visible or known, proclaim, tell, confess. अभिवि look at, behold. सम् appear together with, belong to (instr.); count together, reckon up, estimate. परिसम् reckon up completely, enumerate, calculate. — Cf. अभिख्यात, अभिविख्यात, प्रख्यात, प्रविख्यात, विख्यात.
ख्यात a. named, called, known, celebrated.
ख्यातकीर्ति a. of celebrated renown.
ख्याति f. apprehension, notion, idea, knowledge; renown, name.
ख्यान n. apprehension, knowledge.
ख्यापक a. telling, indicating (—°).
ख्यापन n. declaration, confession.
ख्यापिन् a. making known, showing (—°).
ख्याप्य a. to be related or told.

ग

ग a. going in or to, situate or being in, referring to (—°).

गगण or **गगन** n. sky, heaven, air.

गगनतल n. celestial vault, firmament.

गगनप्रतिष्ठ a. standing or being in the air.

गगनविहारिन् a. walking in the air.

गगनस्पृश् a. touching the sky.

गगनाङ्गन n. the space (lit. court) of heaven.*

गगनाङ्गना f. (nymph of heaven*); N. of a metre.

गगनोज्ज्वल a. beaming like the sky.*

गङ्गा f. the river Ganges (often personif.).

गज m. elephant (f. ई); a man's name.

गजदन्त m. an elephant's tusk, ivory.

गजपुंगव m. a noble elephant (lit. bull, chief of the elephants).

गजपुर n. N. of a town (= हास्तिनपुर).

गजमद m. the rut-juice (flowing from the temples) of an elephant.

गजमान m. N. of a man.*

गजयूथ m. a herd of elephants.

गजयूथप m. chief of the herd of elephants.

गजवधू f. female elephant.

गजसाह्वय & **गजाह्वय** n. = गजपुर.

गजेन्द्र m. a noble elephant (lit. chief of the elephants).

गञ्ज s. treasury; f. आ a tavern; hemp.

गञ्जन a. contemning, outvying (—°).

गडि m. a young bull.

गडु s. excrescence on the body, as goitre, hump, etc.

गणं m. troop, crowd, host, tribe, suit, retinue, flock, number, series, line; a troop deity (esp. pl. the followers of Çiva, ruled by Gaṇeça); company, association; a group of words belonging to the same rule (g.), foot of a verse consisting of 4 instants.

गंणक m. arithmetician, astrologue.

गणच्छन्दस् n. a metre consisting of feet of 4 instants each.

गणदास m. N. of a dancing master.

गणन n., **ना** f. numbering, calculation; taking into account.

गणनाथ & **गणनायक** m. = गणेश.

गणप m. the same, protector or chief of a corporation.

गणंपति m. chief of a troop; the god Ganeça.

गणपाठ m. collection of gaṇas; cf. गणं (g.).

गणय्, °यति (°ते), pp. गणित (q.v.) number, calculate, count among (loc.); esteem, value at (instr.), regard as (2 acc.); care about, take notice of, esp. w. न or बहु (acc.). — अव disregard. परि count over, consider, reflect.

गणवृत्त n. = गणच्छन्दस्.

गणशंस् adv. by troops.

गणश्री a. joined in troops.

गणान्न n. food from a corporation.

गणाभ्यन्तर m. member of a corporation.

गणिका f. a harlot, courtesan.

गणिकादारिका f. daughter of a courtesan.*

गणिकान्न n. food from a courtesan.

गणिकाप्रवहण n. carriage of a courtesan.

गणित a. numbered, reckoned, valued at (instr.); n. reckoning, calculation.

गणिन् a. having adherents; surrounded by (—°).

गणेश m. the god Gaṇeça (lit. the lord of the hosts or troops, cf. गणं), also E. of Çiva.

गण्ड m. cheek, side of the face (adj. —° f. आ & ई), side i.g.; boil, pimple, crop, (pledge*).

गण्डपाली f. the region of the cheeks.

गण्डमाल & °ला (f.) swelling of the glands of the neck.

गण्डमालिन् a. having swollen glands (cf. prec.).

गण्डलेखा f. the region (lit. line) of the cheeks.

गण्डस्थल n., °ली f. (adj. —° f. आ & ई) cheek (lit. place or region of the cheeks).

गण्डु s. a pillow.

गण्डूष m. n. a mouthful of water or any other

liquid (for rinsing the mouth or drinking); draught, gulp. — °पेय a. to be drunk by gulps, to be devoured (fig.).

गण्य a. consisting in lines (a song); to be counted or calculated, to be taken care or notice of.

गत a. gone, come; arrived at, got to, fallen into, situated, contained, or being in (acc., loc. or —°); belonging or relating to (प्रति or —°); spread, celebrated, known as (loc.); departed, gone away to (dat. or inf.); come forth from (abl. or —°); passed away, disappeared, lost, dead, often adj. °— whose— is gone, bereft of—, free from—, -less; entered, frequented, visited; got, acquired. n. going, motion; disappearance, loss of (—°); extension. divulgation; way, manner.

गतक्लम a. rested, refreshed.

गतजीव & °जीवित a. lifeless, dead.

गतपार a. who has reached his goal.

गतपूर्व a. gone before.

गतप्रत्यागत a. gone and come back.

गतप्राण a. breathless, dead.

गतप्राय a. almost gone or perished.

गतमात्र a. scarcely or just gone away.

गतयौवन & °वयस् a. whose youth has passed away, no more young.

गतरस a. flavourless, insipid.

गतव्यथ a. free from pain or anxiety.

गतसङ्ग a. free from attachment.

गतसंदेह a. free from doubt.

गतसार a. worthless, vain.

गतागत a. going and coming; n. sgl. & pl. the same as subst.

गतागति f.=prec. n.

गताध्वन् a. who has gone or made his journey (also of the moon).

गतानुगतिक a. moving always in the same ruts (lit. going after the gone).

गतायुस् a. going to die or dead (lit. whose life is gone).

गतासु a. lifeless, dead.

गति f. going, flying, motion i.g.; going on, progress; course, path, way, manner; getting to, obtaining, acquirement (gen., loc. or —°); going out, event, issue; starting point, origin, root, cause; expedient, means, remedy, refuge; success, happiness; transmigration, metempsychosis; lot, fate, condition.

गतिपथ m. path (to go).*

गतिभङ्ग m. a broken or uncertain gait (lit. interruption of the gait).

गतिभेद m. the same.

गतिमन्त् a. having motion, moving.

गतोदक a. waterless.

†गत्वन् v. पूर्वगत्वन्.

गत्वर, f. ई going to (dat.); perishable.

गद्, गदति (°ते), pp. गदित speak, pronounce, recite, tell (acc. of pers. & th.), enumerate, name, call. — नि=S.; P. be called, pass as (nom.). प्रणि teach, assert. विनि speak to, address (acc.); P. be called.

1गद m., आ f. speech, sentence.

2गद m. disease, sickness.

गदन n. speaking, reciting.

गदा f. mace, club.

गदाधर, गदाभृत्, & गदिन् a. bearing a mace (E. of Kṛṣṇa).

गद्गद a. & n. stammering; abstr. °ता f., °त्व n.

गद्य a. to be spoken; n. speech, prose.

गध्, only गध्य to be taken hold of, to be seized. — Cf. आगधित & परिगधित.

गन्तवे & गन्तवै dat. inf. to go.

गन्तव्य n. to be gone (n. impers. w. instr. of subj.); to be walked (a way), to be approached (esp. sex.); to be undergone or begun; to be reached, got, acquired; to be understood, intelligible.

गन्तु m. way, course.

गन्तुकाम a. willing to go.

गन्तृ going or coming to (acc., loc. or *dat.), used also as fut. pp. (f. गन्त्री).

गन्ध m. (n.) smell, odour, fragrance, fragrant substance, perfume (mostly pl.); the mere smell i.e. a bit of, some likeness with (—°).

गन्धक, f. इका smelling of (—°).

गन्धगज m. scent-elephant (i.e. an elephant in rut).

गन्धगुण m. the quality of smell.

गन्धद्विप & गन्धद्विरद m.=गन्धगज.

गन्धन m. a sort of rice; n. smelling.
गन्धमादन m. N. of a mountain and forest.
गन्धमाल्य n. du. & pl. fragrances and garlands.
गन्धयुक्ति f. preparation or application of perfumes.
गन्धर्व m. N. of a genius, connected with Soma and the Sun; w. **अपाम्** = **गर्भ**; later mostly pl. the heavenly singers.
गन्धर्वराज m. the king of the Gandharvas.
गन्धर्वलोक m. the world of the Gandharvas.
गन्धवन्त् a. smelling, odoriferous.
गन्धवह & **°वाह** m. the wind (bearer of odours).
***गन्धसार** m. sandal-wood.
गन्धाढ्य a. rich in odours, fragrant.
गन्धार & **गन्धारि** m. pl. N. of a people.
गन्धि, **गन्धिक** & **गन्धिन्** a. smelling of, perfumed with; having the mere smell of a thing, being— only by name.
गन्धोद्दाम a. perfumed, odoriferous.
गभ m. vulva.
गभस्तल n. N. of a hell.
गभस्ति m. arm, hand, ray.
गभस्तिमन्त् a. having rays, shining; m. the sun.
गभीर deep, profound, impervious, inscrutable, secret; °— & n. adv.
गम्, **गच्छति**, **°ते**, **गमति**, **गन्ति**, pp. (—° w. act. & pass. mg.) **गत** (q.v.) go, move; go or come to, get at, fall into or upon, undergo, incur, reach, acquire (acc. ± **प्रति**, loc., or dat.); approach sex. (acc.); move on, wander; keep on (with a pp.); approach mentally, perceive (± **मनसा**), guess, understand (P. be understood or meant); go away, pass, set out, depart, die. — With the acc. of an abstr. often = become or be w. adj. or pp., as **हर्षं गच्छति** he becomes glad, **उपालम्भनं गच्छति** he is censured (cf. 2**इ**). C. **गमयति**, **°ते** cause to go or come, lead or bring towards (acc., dat., or loc.); put a person into a condition (2 acc.); grant, impart (gen. of pers. & acc. of th.); cause to go away i.e. send forth; pass, spend; overcome; *cause a person (acc.) through some other (instr.) to go; make understood, explain; convey the idea of (acc.), mean, denote. D. **जिगमिषति** & **जिगांसति** wish to go, be going. I. **गंनीगन्ति** approach, visit. — **अच्छ**, **अच्छा** go to, meet with. **अति** pass away, pass over (acc.). **अधि** get at, meet with, obtain, acquire; commence, undertake, accomplish; approach (sex.), take to wife, marry; find out, invent, discover; perceive, learn, study, read. **समधि** come near, get at, obtain, acquire; learn, study, read. **अनु** go after, follow, accompany (also C.); seek, look for; approach, arrive, visit, enter; observe, obey, imitate, answer to; go out, be extinguished, die. **समनु** go after, follow; penetrate, pervade. **अन्तर्** step between, exclude from (abl.). **अप** go away, depart, cease, disappear. **व्यप** the same. **अपि** go into, join, approach (sex.); get, obtain. **अभि** come near, approach, visit; go after, follow; find, meet; approach (sex.); undertake, take to (acc.), get, acquire; perceive, understand, learn (also C.). **अव** come down, descend; come to, approach, visit; fall into, incur; get, obtain; undergo, undertake; learn from (abl.), perceive, guess, understand; be of opinion, know; take for, consider as (2 acc.). C. bring near, procure; cause to know, make acquainted with, teach (2 acc. or gen. of pers. & acc. of th.). **आ** go near, approach, come to (acc. or loc.), come back (± **पुनर्**); meet with (instr.); reach, obtain, get at, undergo, incur; befall, betide. C. bring near, convey; procure, ascertain (acc.), learn from (abl.). D. wish to come to (acc.). I. approach repeatedly (acc.). **अध्या** meet with, encounter, find. **अन्वा** go after or along. **अभ्या** come near, approach, visit; fall into, incur. **उपा** & **समुपा** the same. **न्या** come down to (acc.). **पर्या** go or come round. **प्रत्या** come back, return from (abl.) to (acc.); return to life, revive, recover. **समा** come together, associate, meet, encounter (instr. ± **सह** or **सार्धम्**); come near, approach, come to (acc. or loc.),

come back; meet with, find. उद् go up, rise, shoot up, grow; come forth, extend, spread. अपोद्, D. अपोज्जिगांसति wish to withdraw from, to avoid (abl.). अभ्युद् rise, go out to meet (acc.), extend, spread; agree, consent to (acc.). प्रत्युद् come forth again; go out to meet or to face (acc.); set out, depart. उप come near, approach, visit; go against, attack; meet, encounter, approach (sex.), undertake; undergo, incur; reach, befall, happen. अभ्युप come near, go to, join, get at; reach, obtain; admit, consent to (acc.). समुप come near, go to, undergo, incur. नि settle down, approach (also sex.), get at, incur, undergo. उपनि & संनि meet with, encounter. निस् go out, depart, proceed from (abl.), appear; go away, disappear; get rid of (abl.); reach, get, fall into (निद्राम् fall asleep). विनिस् go out, depart, set off, cease, vanish; get rid of (abl.). परा go away, depart. परि walk about, circumambulate, surround, inclose, pervade, spread. प्र set out, start, advance, proceed; go to, get at (acc.). प्रति go to meet, come back, return. वि go asunder, go away, pass, cease, vanish. C. pass, spend (time). सम् (mostly M.) meet, encounter, join, approach (sex.); harmonize, agree; be fit, answer, correspond. C. bring together, join with (instr.); lead to (acc.), bestow on (loc.). अभिसम् & उपसम् meet with, come (together) to (acc.). — Cf. अनुगत, अन्तर्गत, अभ्यागत, आगत, उद्गत, उपगत, परिगत, विगत, संगत.

†गम a. going to or in (—°); m. going, march, approach, cohabitation.

गमक a. convincing, conclusive; showing, betraying (—°). Abstr. °ता f., °त्व n.

ग॑मध्यै (dat. inf.) to go or come.

गमन n. going, coming, moving; going to, entering, approaching (प्रति, acc., gen., or —°); intercourse, cohabitation (—°); setting out, departure, march.

गमनीय a. accessible, attainable, assailable by (gen.)

गमागम m. going and coming, going to and fro.

*गमिन् a. intending to go to (acc. or —°).

ग॑मिष्ठ (superl.) coming willingly, ready to enter (—°).

गमिष्णु॑ a. going or willing to go.

ग॑म्भन् s. depth, bottom.

ग॑म्भिष्ठ superl. to गम्भीर.

गम्भीर॑ = गभीर॑.

गम्भीर॑शंस a. reigning secretly.

गम्य a. to be approached or entered, accessible (also for sex. intercourse), attainable to (gen., loc., or —°), possible, fit, proper; to be guessed or understod, perceptible, intelligible. Abstr. °ता f., °त्व n.

ग॑य m. house, household, family, N. of a Rishi etc., pl. N. of a people. f. गया N. of a famous place of pilgrimage.

गयस्फान a. increasing the family wealth.

गर॑ a. devouring (—°); m. drink, fluid, poison (also n.); a man's name. f. devouring, swallowing.

गरद a. giving poison, m. poisoner.

गरल n. poison.

गरिमन् m. heaviness, weight, importance, dignity, power.

गरिष्ठ & ग॑रीयंस् v. गुरु॑.

गरीयस्त्व n. weight, importance.

गरुड m. N. of a mythical bird; also a building or military array of a cert. shape.

गरुत् s. wing.

गरुत्मन्त् a. winged; m. bird, esp. Garuḍa.

गर्ग m. a man's name; f. आ & ई a woman's name.

ग॑र्गर m. whirlpool, eddy; also = f. गर्गरा & °री churn, butter-vat, a kind of water-jar.

गर्ज्, गर्जति (°ते) roar, growl, hum, rave, thunder, chatter (of birds); brag, boast. — अनु roar or rave after. अभि roar at (acc.), shout. प्र begin to roar or thunder. प्रति roar against, answer with roars, shout at (acc.); oppose, resist; emulate or vie with (gen. or instr.). वि roar, shout. सम् shout together (अन्यो ऽन्यम्). — Cf. अभिगर्जित, उद्गर्जित.

गर्ज m., °न n. roar, noise, thunder.

गर्जित n. the same + bragging, boasting.

1गर्त m. high seat, throne; the seat of a war-chariot, carriage i.g.
2गर्त m. n., आ f. hollow, cave, ditch, grave; a water-hole (only m.).
गर्तमित् a. buried in a hole; s. such a post.
गर्तसद् a. sitting in the war-chariot.
गर्तारुह् (nom. °रुक्) mounting the war-chariot.
गर्ताश्रय m. an animal living in holes.
गर्द्, गर्दति exult.
गर्द a. ardent, eager.
गर्दभ m. ass (adj. —° f. आ); f. ई she-ass; N. of sev. plants; (a cert. throw with the dice*).
गर्ध m. eagerness, desire of (—°).
गर्धिन् a. greedy, desirous or fond of (—°).
गर्भ m. womb, inside, interior (adj. —° having in the interior, containing, filled with); fetus, embryo, scion, fruit, offspring, child.
*गर्भक m. kind of garland.
गर्भकाल m. the time of pregnancy.
गर्भगत a. lying in the womb.
गर्भगृह n. a lying-in chamber, also=seq.
गर्भगेह n. sanctuary of a temple.
गर्भग्रह m., °ग्रहण n. conception (of the fetus).
गर्भता f., °त्व n. pregnancy.
गर्भदास m. (ई f.*) a slave by birth.
गर्भध a. impregnating.
गर्भधरा f. bearing a fetus, pregnant.
गर्भधारण n. gestation (of the fetus), pregnancy.
गर्भधि m. breeding place, nest.
गर्भभर्तृद्रुह् f. (a woman) killing her husband and the child in her womb.
गर्भभवन n.=गर्भगेह.
गर्भवती f. pregnant.
गर्भवसति f., °वास m. womb (abode of the fetus).
गर्भवेश्मन् n. inmost apartment, also=गर्भगृह.
गर्भस्थ a.=गर्भगत, also being inside (—°).
गर्भस्राव m. abortion, miscarriage.
गर्भाधान n. impregnation.
गर्भाष्टम m. the eighth year from conception.
गर्भिन् a. pregnant (l. & f., w. acc. or instr.); f. गर्भिणी a pregnant woman.
गर्भेश्वर m. a ruler by birth.
गर्मुत् f. a kind of wild bean.
गर्वगिर् f. pl. arrogant language.
गर्वित a. arrogant, proud of (instr. or —°).
गर्ह्, गर्हते (°ति), गर्हयते (°ति), pp. गर्हित (q.v.) chide, blame, censure, reproach, complain to (dat.) of (acc.). — *नि (गर्हते) find fault with (dat.). वि reproach, blame, abuse, revile. — Cf. विगर्हित.
गर्हण a. reproachful; n. & f. आ=seq.
गर्हा f. reproach, censure.
गर्हित a. blamed, censured, forbidden, bad, worse than (abl.). — n. adv. badly, ill.
गर्हितान्नाशन a. eating forbidden food.
गर्हिन् a. blaming, censuring (—°).
गर्ह्य a. to be blamed, contemptible.
गल्, गलति, pp. गलित (q.v.) drip, drop, fall, vanish, pass away. C. गालयति cause to drop, liquify, melt, filter, wring out. — अव & आ drop down. प्र the same. वि be dissolved or melted, fall down, pass away, perish. प्रवि stream forth, cease, vanish. (सम् come forth, break out, rise.*) — Cf. निर्गलित, परिगलित.
गल m. throat, neck.
गलगुहा f. cavity of the throat, gulf.
गलहस्त m. seizing by the throat, collaring.
गलित a. dropped, lost, omitted (esp. a passage in the Rigveda omitted in the Padapāṭha).
गलितक m. kind of dance or gesticulation.
गल्द a.=गर्द.
गल्ल m. cheek.
गल्लपूरण a. filling or swelling the cheeks.*
गल्वर्क m. crystal, crystal vessel.
1गव (°— & —°, f. ई) bull, cow.
2†गव v. पुरोगव.
गवय m. a species of ox, the Gayal, f. ई.
गवल m. buffalo.
गवाक्ष m. round window (lit. bull's eye).
गवानृत n. untruth concerning cows.
गवांपति m. bull (lit. master of the cows); E. of Agni and the Sun (lord of the rays).
गविष् & गविष a. wishing for cows; fervent, eager i.g.
गविष्टि a. the same; f. passion, desire. esp. for fighting; fight, battle.
गवीधुमत् n. N. of a town.
गवीनिका & गवीनी f. du. the groins.

गवेष्, ॰षते, ॰षयति & ॰ते strive after, look for (acc.).

गवेषण a. eager, desirous, esp. of combat.

गवेषिन् a. seeking (—॰).

गव्य्, only pp. **गव्यन्त्** eager, desirous (orig. & esp. of cattle or combat).

गव्य or **गव्य** a. consisting of, belonging to, coming from cows or cattle; f. **गव्या** desire for cows or milk, ardour of battle; n. **गव्य** cattle, milk, pasture-ground.

गव्यय, f. **ई** = prec. adj.

गव्ययु a. wishing for cattle.

गव्यु = **गव्यन्त्**, v. **गव्य्**.

गव्यूति f. pasture land, district, dwelling place, abode.

गहन a. deep, thick, impenetrable; n. depth, abyss, thicket, impenetrable place or darkness.

गह्वर, f. **आ** & **ई** deep, impenetrable, confused, perplexed; n. = prec. n., also secret, riddle.

गह्वरेष्ठ a. being in the depth or in the secret.

1**गा**, **जिगाति** go, move, come, approach, repair to (acc. or loc.); follow, persecute; undergo, incur, obtain. — **अच्छ** go or come. **अति** step beyond, cross; surpass, overcome, escape; leave unnoticed, neglect; pass away, perish, die. **अधि** fall into, obtain; think of, resolve on (acc.); remember, attend to (gen. or acc.); study (mostly M.), learn from (abl.). **अनु** go after, follow, go along; undergo, incur. **अन्तर्** go between (acc.); separate, exclude from (abl.). **अप** go away; keep or cease from (abl.). **अपि** enter, mix with (acc.). **अभि** come near, approach, get at, obtain. **अव** go away, be lost; go to, join (acc.). **आ** & **अभ्या** come near, approach, get at; befall, visit (acc.). **उपा** come near, approach, come to (acc.). **पर्या** turn round (intr.); carry on, be engaged in (acc.). **उद्** rise. **उप** go to, get at (acc.). **निस्** go out, go away or come forth from (abl.). **परि** go about, surround, pervade, enter, befall, visit; disregard, avoid. **प्र** come forth, proceed; move towards (acc.); go away, withdraw from (abl.). **अपप्र** go away, cease, desist. **वि** the same. **सम्** meet; go to (acc.).

2**गा**, **गायति** (॰ते) & **गाति**, pp. **गीत** (q.v.) sing, chant, recite, praise, proclaim; P. also be called, have the name of (nom.). C. **गापयति**. I. **जेगीयते** (w. act. & pass. mg.). — **अच्छ** call with a song. **अनु** sing after or to (acc.); praise, celebrate. **अभि** sing or call to (acc.), fill or praise with song. **आ** sing to (acc.), gain by singing. **उद्** intonate, begin to sing, chant, recite, fill with song. **उप** sing to or before (dat., loc., acc.), praise, celebrate, fill with song. **नि** accompany with song, sing, proclaim. **प्र** begin to sing; praise, celebrate; sound, resound. **अभिप्र** begin to celebrate. **वि** decry, blame. **सम्** sing together. — Cf. **अनुगीत, उद्गीत, उपगीत, विगीत, संगीत**.

गाङ्ग, f. **ई** being on or in the Ganges, coming from it, etc.; m. metron. of Bhīṣma.

गाङ्गेय & **गाङ्ग्य** a. & m. the same.

गाढ a. dived into, entered; tight, fast, close; vehement, strong; ॰— & n. adv. strongly, extremely, very much.

गाढता f., ॰त्व n. intensity, strongness, excess.

गाढानुरागिन् a. extremely passionate.

गाढोद्विग्न a. extremely anxious.

गाण्डिव or **गाण्डीव** m. n. Arjuna's bow.

गातवे (dat. inf.) to go.

1**गातु** m. (f.) motion, course, way, path; progress, welfare, refuge, abode, space.

2**गातु** m. song or singer.

गातुमन्त् a. capacious, commodious.

गातुय् (**गातूय्**) ॰यति grant free course, further.

गातृ m. singer; a man's name.

गात्र n. (adj. —॰ f. **आ** & **ई**) a limb of the body (lit. means of going); the body.

***गात्रानुलेपनी** f. unguent for the body.

गात्रोत्सादन n. rubbing of the body.

गाथ m. song; f. **गाथा** the same, esp. a kind of rel. verse or stanza; N. of a metre (= **आर्या**).

गाथक m. singer; f. **गाथिका** song, verse.

गाथिन् a. familiar with songs, m. a singer; N.

of the father of Viçvamitra, pl. his descendants.

गाधं a. offering a standing ground, fordable, shallow; n. (m.) a shallow place in water, ford.

गाधि & **गाधिन्** m. = **गाथिन्** m.

गाधिज, **°नन्दन**, **°पुत्र**, **°सूनु**, & **गाधेय** m. patr. names of Viçvamitra.

गान n. singing, song.

गान्धर्व, f. **गान्धर्वी** belonging or peculiar to the Gandharvas, esp. w. **विवाह** or **विधि** m. a marriage without any ceremony; m. a singer, pl. N. of a people; n. the art of the Gandharvas i.e. song, music.

गान्धर्वविधि m. the Gandharva marriage (v. prec.).

गान्धार m., **ई** f. a prince and princess of the Gāndhāris; m. pl. = seq.

गान्धारि m. pl. N. of a people.

गामिन् a. going, moving, going to (adv., *acc. ± **प्रति**); mostly —° going or moving on, in, to, towards, or -like (after an adv.), approaching (sex.); reaching, belonging or relating to, meeting with, obtaining.

गाम्भीर्य n. depth, profundity, dignity, generosity.

1†**गाय** a. moving (only —°).

2**गाय** m. song.

3**गाय** a. belonging to or coming from Gaya.

गायक m., **ई** f. singer.

गायत्र m. n. song, verse, hymn; f. **ई** N. of a metre & a cert. sacred verse.

गायत्रिन् m. chanter of hymns.

गायन m. singer, chanter; n. song.

गारुड & **°रुत्मत** a. pertaining to or resembling the bird Garuḍa.

गार्ग्य m. patr. from **गर्ग**; N. of sev. men, pl. of a people.

गार्ग्यायण m. patr. from **गार्ग्य**.

गार्ध्य n. greediness, desire.

गार्भ a. born from the womb, relating to the fetus or the pregnancy.

गार्भिक a. relating to the womb, maternal.

गार्हपत्य m. (± **अग्नि**) the fire of the householder (r.). m. n. = seq., n. government of a family, household.

गार्हपत्यागार m. house or place for the G.-fire (r.).

गार्हस्थ्य a. pertaining to a householder; n. household.

गार्ह्य a. domestic.

गाल a. produced by the throat.

गालन n. straining, filtering; abusing, reviling.

गालव m. N. of an ancient teacher; pl. his descendants.

गालि f. pl. (& sgl.*) abusive language, insult.

गाह्, **गाहते** (**°ति**), pp. **गाढ** (q.v.) dive or enter into (acc.). — **अति** emerge from, overcome (acc.). **अभि** penetrate into (acc.). **अव** or **व** plunge or enter into, be absorbed in (loc. or acc.). **उद्** emerge, rise. **उप** enter. **प्र** penetrate, pervade. **वि** dive into, bathe in, enter, penetrate (acc. or loc.); get, attain (acc.); w. **कक्षाम्** be equal to (gen.). — Cf. **अवगाढ**, **उद्गाढ**, **परिगाढ**, **प्रगाढ**, **वगाढ**, **विगाढ**.

गाह m. depth, interior.

गाहन n. plunging, bathing.

1**गिर्** v. 1**गृ**.

2**गिर्** a. s. singing, singer; f. song, word, voice, call, verse, praise. **गिरा** by the advice or in the name of (gen. or —°).

3**गिर्** v. 2**गृ**.

4**गिर्** (—°) devouring.

5**गिर्** m. = **गिरि**.

1**गिर** (—°) = 2**गिर्**.

2**गिर** (—°) = seq.

गिरि m. mountain, hill.

गिरिकानन n. mountain-wood.*

गिरिक्षित् a. dwelling on hills.

गिरिचर a. mountain-roving.

गिरिज a. mountain-born, f. **आ** the mountain-daughter (Pārvatī).

गिरिजा a. = prec. a.

गिरिणदी f. mountain-torrent.

गिरित्र a. protecting mountains (Rudra-Çiva).

गिरिदुर्ग a. hill-fort.

गिरिधातु m. pl. the minerals in a mountain; red chalk.

गिरिनदी f. = **गिरिणदी**.

गिरिपति m. chief of the mountains; high mountain or rock.

गिरिपृष्ठ n. hill-top.
गिरिप्रस्थ m. the table-land of a mountain.
गिरिराज् m. = गिरिपति.
गिरिवर m. an excellent mountain.
गिरिश a. dwelling on mountains, m. E. of Rudra-Çiva.
गिरिष्ठा a. being on mountains.
गिरीश m. = गिरिपति.
गिर्वणस् & गिर्वणस्यु a. = seq.
गिर्वन् a. rich in praise.
गीत a. sung, praised, proclaimed, named, called; n. song, verse. f. आ sacred song or poem.
गीतक n. = prec. n.
गीतक्षम a. fit to be sung.
गीतगोविन्द n. T. of a poem (lit. Govinda praised in song).
गीतनृत्य n. song and dance.
गीतवादन n. song and music.
गीताचार्य m. singing master.
गीति f. song; N. of a metre.
गीत्यार्या f. a cert. metre.
गीथा f. song.
गीर्वाण m. a god.
1गु, only I. जोगुवे & जोगुवान sound, praise, proclaim.
2गु a. going, coming (—°).
3गु (adj. —°) = गो.
गुग्गुलु (m.) n. bdellium.
गुङ्गु m. N. of a man, pl. his race. f. गुङ्गू = कुहू.
गुच्छ (& *क) m. bundle, bunch, bush.
गुच्छगुल्म n. sgl. bushes and shrubs.
गुञ्ज्, गुञ्जति buz, hum.
गुञ्ज m., गुञ्जित n. buzzing, humming.
गुञ्जा f. the Guñjā berry (used as a weight).
गुटिका f. globe, pill, pearl, jewel.
गुड m. a globe or ball (also °क m.); treacle, molasses, a pill (also गुडिका f.); pl. N. of a people.
*गुडधाना f. pl. grains of corn with sugar.
गुडमय, f. ई made of sugar.
गुडशर्करा f. sugar.
गुडाकेश m. E. of Arjuna.
गुडोदक n. sugar-water.
गुडौदन n. boiled rice with sugar.
गुण m. thread, cord, rope, string (adj. —° after a num. = -fold or — times, lit. -threaded); division, species, kind; anything secondary or unessential, e.g. the seasoning of a dish (opp. अन्न), (g.) the secondary object (cf. गुणकर्मन्), the articulation (opp. स्थान), the secondary gradation (opp. वृद्धि); (ph.) the quality, peculiarity or attribute (opp. द्रव्य or स्वभाव), one of the five attributes or the three qualities; good quality, virtue, excellence; merit, high degree, pl. the six or four measures of royal policy. Abstr. गुणता f., °त्व n.
गुणक (adj. —°) = गुण.
गुणकर्मन् n. a secondary action (abl. °मतस्) or secondary object (opp. प्रधानं कर्मन्).
गुणकलुष n. confusion of the (three) qualities.
गुणगुरु a. respectable.
गुणगृह्य & °ग्रह a. to be captivated by, i.e. sensible of, virtues or merits.
गुणग्राम m. assemblage of virtues or merits.
गुणग्राहिन् a. = गुणगृह्य.
गुणच्छेद m. the breaking of the cord (loss of merits).
गुणज्ञ a. knowing virtues or merits; abstr. °ता f.
गुणतस् adv. according to the (three) qualities.
गुणत्यागिन् a. abandoning virtue.
गुणदोषज्ञ a. knowing good and evil.
गुणधृत a. supported by virtues (cords).
गुणभद्र m. N. of an author.
गुणभूत a. secondary, subordinate.
गुणभेदतस् adv. according to the difference of quality.
गुणभोक्तृ a. perceiving the qualities.
गुणमय a. consisting of threads; containing the three qualities; virtuous.
गुणय्, °यति, pp. गुणित multiply, increase.
गुणवचन m. n. an attributive or adjective.
गुणवत्ता f., °त्त्व n. abstr. to seq.
गुणवन्त् a. having a thread (virtues); possessed of the five qualities (cf. गुण); virtues, excellent, useful, good. Compar. गुणवत्तर, superl. °त्तम.
गुणसंयुक्त & °संपन्न a. endowed with good qualities or virtues.

गुणसङ्ग m. attachment to the qualities (ph.).
गुणहार्य to be won by virtues.
गुणहीन a. destitute of merit or virtues.
गुणागुण m. pl. virtues or faults.
गुणाढ्य m. N. of a poet (lit. rich in virtue).
गुणातीत a. having overcome the qualities (ph.).
गुणान्तर n. another quality. **°राधान** n. the addition of another quality, i.e. occupation with, care of (gen.).
गुणान्वित a.=**गुणसंयुक्त**, also auspicious, lucky.
गुणाभिलाषिन् a. desirous of virtues.
गुणालय m. the (very) seat of virtues; adj. most virtuous.
गुणाश्रय m. the seat of the qualities, also = prec. (m. & adj.)
गुणिन् a. having a cord (virtues); having parts, qualities, advantages, or merits; auspicious, lucky (day); object, thing, substantive.
गुणी w. **अस्** or **भू** submit, yield to (gen.); pp. **गुणीभूत** subject to (gen.), also=**गुणभूत**.
गुणोज्ज्वल a. shining with virtues.
गुणोत्कर्ष m. superiority of merits.
गुणोत्कृष्ट a. distinguished by merits.
गुणोदय m. rising or development of virtues.
गुण्ठ्, **गुण्ठयति**, pp. **गुण्ठित** veil, conceal, hide, cover. — **अव**, **समव**, **आ**, & **परि**= S.
गुण्ठन n., **°ना** f. veiling, covering with (—°).
***गुत्स** m. a necklace of 32 strings.
***गुत्सार्ध** m. a necklace of 24 strings.
गुद m. (n.) the rectum or anus.
गुन्द्र m., **आ** f. N. of sev. plants.
1**गुप्**, pp. **गुपित** & **गुप्त** (q.v.) keep, protect, guard from (abl.). D. **जुगुप्सते** (**°ति**) beware of, shun, detest; pp. **जुगुप्सित** detested, abominable, or *detesting (w. abl.). — **प्रति** beware of (abl.). **वि** D. fly from, be afraid of (abl.). — Cf. **अधिगुप्त**, **अनुगुप्त**, **अभिगुप्त**, **संगुप्त**.
2**गुप्** (—°) keeping, guarding.
गुप्त a. kept, preserved, guarded, hidden, secret; n. adv. privately, secretly, loc. at a secret place; m. N. of sev. kings, esp. —°.
गुप्ति f. keeping, protection, guard, caution, hiding, concealment, prison.
गुप्तिपालक m. guardian of a prison, jailer.*
गुम्फ्, **गुम्फति** & **गुम्फयति**, pp. **गुम्फित** string together, wreathe, wind.
गुर् (**गुरते** only —°), pp. **गूर्त** (q.v.) & **गूर्ण** (—°) *lift up. — **अप** reject, revile, threaten. **अव** threaten. **आ** approve, agree. **उद्** lift up, raise. — Cf. **उद्गूर्ण**.
गुरु, f. **गुर्वी** a. heavy, weighty (w. abl. also = **गुरुतर**), big, large, great, long (prosod.); strong, vehement; difficult, hard; bad, evil; important, valuable, venerable. Comp. **गुरुतर** & **गरीयंस्** heavier, weightier, etc. than (abl.); very heavy, weighty etc.; superl. **गरिष्ठ** very big or swollen. — m. any venerable person, as father, mother (du. the parents), teacher (also pl.), esp. Bṛhaspati as the teacher of the gods, any elder relative; chief of (—°). f. **गुर्वी** pregnant, a pregnant woman.
गुरुकार्य n. an important matter.
गुरुकुल n. the teacher's house; **°वास** m. the living in it, scholarship.
गुरुगृह n. = prec. n.
गुरुचर्या f. service to the teacher.
गुरुतल्प m. the teacher's bed; violator or violation of it.
गुरुतल्पग, **°गामिन्**, & **गुरुतल्पिन्** a. violating the teacher's bed.
गुरुता f. weight, burden, difficulty, importance, gravity; the office or state of a teacher.
गुरुत्व n. weight, heaviness, severity; prosodical length, importance etc. = prec.
गुरुदक्षिणा f. the teacher's fee.*
गुरुदार m. the teacher's wife.
गुरुधुर् f. pl. hard work.
गुरुपत्नी f. = **गुरुदार**.
गुरुपुत्र m. the teacher's son.
गुरुपूजा & **गुरुभक्ति** f. reverence towards the teacher.
गुरुभार्या f. = **गुरुदार**.
गुरुयोषित् f. = **गुरुदार**.
गुरुलाघव n. great and small, i.e. relative importance or value, prosodical length and shortness.
गुरुवत् adv. like (towards) the teacher.
गुरुवास m. = **गुरुकुलवास**.

गुरुवृत्ति f. the (right) conduct towards the teacher; **°पर** a. behaving properly towards the teacher.

गुरुशुश्रूषा f. obedience to the teacher.

गुरुशुश्रूषु a. obedient to the teacher.

गुरुसुत m. = **गुरुपुत्र**.

गुर्जर m., **°री** f. the district of Guzerat.

गुर्वङ्गना f. the teacher's wife.

गुर्वङ्गनागम m. adultery with the teacher's wife.

गुर्वर्थ m. an important affair; also the teacher's affair or fee; **°र्थम्** adv. for the parents or the teacher.

गुर्विणी f. pregnant, a pregnant woman; N. of a metre.

गुल m. = **गुड**.

गुलिका f. a ball or pill.

गुल्गुलु n. bdellium (cf. **गुग्गुलु**).

गुल्फ m. the ancle.

गुल्फदघ्न a. reaching to the ancles.

गुल्म m. (n.) shrub, bush, thicket; a troop or guard of soldiers.

गुवाक m. the betel-nut tree.

1**गुह्**, **गूहति**, **°ते**, pp. **गूढ** (q.v.) hide, cover, keep secret. — **अप** hide, put away. **अव** cover, conceal; embrace. **उद्** pierce or twist through. **उप** cover, hide, embrace. **नि** & **विनि** cover, conceal, keep secret. — Cf. **उपगूढ**, **निगूढ**, **विगूढ**.

2**गुह्** f. hiding-place.

गुह m. E. of Skanda & Çiva. f. **गुहा** = prec. + cave, pit, mine, fig. the heart. Instr. **गुहा** in secret, secretly; w. **कृ** & **धा** conceal, remove.

गुहाशय a. living in hiding-places or caverns. also = seq.

गुहाहित a. being (laid) in a secret place, in the heart.

गुह्य a. (to be) hidden or covered, secret. n. a secret, mystery, adv. secretly, in silence.

गुह्यक m. a cert. class of demi-gods.

गूढ (**गुळ्हं**) a. hidden, private, secret; n. darkness, a secret, loc. secretly.

गूढज a. secretly born.

गूढागार s. prison (lit. secret house).

गूढार्थ a. & m. (having a) secret meaning.

गूढोत्पन्न a. = **गूढज**.

गूर्त a. approved, welcome, pleasing.

गूर्ति f. praise, applause, flattery.

गूर्द m. a jump.

गृधय्, **गृधयति** praise.

गूहन n. hiding, concealing.

1**गृ**, **गृणाति**, **गृणीते** (also w. pass. mg), **गिरते**, **°ति** (only w. **सम्**) sing, invoke, call, praise, proclaim, relate. — **अनु** join in praising; answer, agree (*dat.); repeat. **अभि** chime in with (acc.); salute, praise, approve, accept. **आ** approve, praise. **प्रत्या** answer, respond. **उप** invoke, call to (acc.). **प्र** proclaim, extol, celebrate. **प्रति** invoke, welcome (acc.); answer, respond (dat.); assent, agree (*dat.). **सम्** chime in, agree, assent, promise, acknowledge, affirm.

2**गृ**, **गिरति** or **गिरति**, **गिरते**, **गिलति** (**गृणाति**), pp. **गीर्ण** swallow, devour. — **अव** swallow down. **उद्** spit out, pour out, discharge, eject, burst out with (acc.). **नि** swallow down, devour, suppress. **निस्** spit out. **सम्** devour. — Cf. **उद्गीर्ण**.

3**गृ**, I. **जागर्ति** (**जागरति**, **जाग्रति**, **°ते**) be awake, wake up, wake or be watchful, have a care for (dat.), rule over (loc. ± **अधि**). C. **जागरयति** wake (trans.), rouse, excite, animate. **प्र** keep watch, wait for (gen.), wake (trans.). **प्रति** watch near or over (acc.). — Cf. **जागृवंस्**.

गृञ्ज m. N. of a plant.

गृञ्जन & **°क** m. a kind of garlic.

गृत्स a. clever, dexterous, wise.

गृत्समद m. N. of a poet; pl. his descendants.

गृद s. the region near the anus (of a horse).

गृद्ध a. eager, desirous of, longing for (loc.).

गृध्, **गृध्यति**, pp. **गृद्ध** (q.v.) be eager or greedy, speed, hasten, strive after, long or wish for (acc. or loc.). — **अनु** & **प्रति** strive after, covet (loc.).

गृध्नु a. rash, eager, greedy, desirous of (loc. or —°).

गृध्नुता f. abstr. to prec.

गृध्य a. to be desired; f. **गृध्या** = prec.
गृध्यिन् a. eager, desirous of (—°).
गृध्र a. the same; m. vulture, f. **ई** female v., the myth. mother of the vultures.
गृध्रकूट m. vulture-peak (N. of a mountain).
गृध्रपति, **गृध्रराज्**, & **°राज** m. the king of the vultures (Jaṭāyu).
गृभ् f. grasping, seizing; dat. **गृभे** as inf.
गृभ m. grasp.
गृभय्, **गृभयति** grasp, seize.
गृभाय्, **°यति** the same. — **अनु** accept, take care of (acc.). **उद्** keep back, stop. **सम्** grasp, seize, keep together.
गृभि a. holding, containing (gen.).
गृष्टि f. heifer.
गृह् (—°) grasping, seizing.
गृह m. a servant (lit. who grasps or lays hold on anything); n. house (as the receiving or containing), mansion, habitation (also m. pl., sgl. only in Veda); temple, bower (mostly —°), sign of the zodiac; m. pl. inhabitants of a house, a family.
गृहकपोत & ***°क** m.* domestic pigeon.
गृहकर्मन् n. domestic work or rite.
गृहकारिन् m. house or mason wasp.
गृहकार्य & **गृहकृत्य** n. domestic work or affair.
गृहज a. born in the house.
गृहजन m. family.
गृहजात a. = **गृहज**.
गृहद m. giver of a house.
गृहदारु n. house-post; **°वत्** adv.
गृहदास m., **ई** f. domestic servant or slave.
गृहदाह m. burning of a house, conflagration.
गृहदीप्ति f. the splendour or ornament of a house (a virtuous woman).
गृहदेवता f. pl. the deities of a house.
गृहद्वार n. house-door.
गृहप m. guardian of a house.
गृहपति m. master of a house, householder, (f. **गृहपत्नी**) E. of Agni.
गृहपाल m. = **गृहप**.
गृहबलि m. domestic oblation; **°भुज्** m. a sparrow or crow (eater of it).
गृहभर्तृ m. master of a house.
गृहमयूर m. domestic or tame peacock.*
1**गृहमेध** m. domestic sacrifice.
2**गृहमेध** a. performing domestic rites, partaking of or belonging to them; m. householder = **गृहस्थ**.
गृहमेधिन् = prec. adj. & m., f. **°नी** a. housewife.
गृहमेधीय a. pertaining to the domestic sacrifice or the householder; n. domestic sacrifice.
गृहरक्षा f. the guarding of a house.
गृहवास m. = **गृहाश्रम**.
गृहशिखण्डिन् m. = **गृहमयूर**.
गृहशुक m. house-parrot or house-poet.
गृहसंवेशक m. house-builder.
गृहसारस m. domestic crane.
गृहस्थ a. living in the house of (—°); m. householder, a Brahman in the second stage of his religious life.
गृहार्थ m. household affairs or care.
गृहाश्रम m. the order of the householder (cf. **गृहस्थ**).
गृहि m. master of a house.
गृहिन् a. having a house; m. householder, f. **गृहिणी** house-wife.
गृहीत a. grasped, taken, conceived, etc.; often °— having taken or conceived; taken by, provided with.
गृहीतचाप a. armed with (lit. having taken) a bow.*
गृहीतधनु & **°धन्वन्** a. the same.*
गृहीतनामधेय a. named, mentioned.*
गृहीतपश्चात्ताप a. seized by repentance.*
गृहीतपाथेय a. furnished with provisions.*
गृहीताक्षर a. having conceived the words or meaning of (gen.).*
गृहीतार्थ a. having conceived the purpose.*
गृहीतावगुण्ठन a. veiled, covered (carriage).*
गृहीति f. taking, conceiving.
गृही w. **भू** become a house or habitation.
गृह्नु m. beggar.
गृहेश्वर m. master of a house; f. **ई** housewife.
1**गृह्य** a. to be seized or taken, perceptible.
2**गृह्य** = **गृहीत्वा** (v. **ग्रभ्**).
3**गृह्य** a. belonging to a house, domestic. m. the house-fire, pl. the inmates of a house, the family or servants; f. **आ** & n. domestic rite or rule.

गृह्यसूत्र n. manual of domestic rules.
*गेण्डुक m. ball for playing.
गेय a. to be sung or praised; *singing (gen.); n. song.
1गेष्ण m. singer, chanter.
2गेष्ण m. joint, juncture.
गेह n. house, mansion; गेहिनी f. = गृहिणी.
गेहदाह & गेहपति = गृहदाह & गृहपति.
गेहपारावत m. = गृहकपोत.*
गेहीय्, °यति take for a house.
1गेह्य a. being in a house, domestic.
2गेह्य n. household, domestic wealth.
गैरिक n. (आ f.) red chalk.
गो m. bull, ox, ox-hide, leather, sinew; pl. cattle, herds, the stars or rays of light (as the herds of the sky); pieces of flesh, cow-milk (also sgl.). — f. cow, the earth (as the milch cow of kings); speech and Sarasvatī, the goddess of speech.
गोअग्र a. having cows or milk as chief part or object.
गोअर्णस् a. swarming with cows or stars.
1गोकर्ण m. cow-ear.
2गोकर्ण a. cow-eared; m. a kind of antelope, N. of a place of pilgrimage sacred to Çiva, of Çiva himself, & of sev. men.
गोकाम a. desirous of kine.
गोकाम्या f. love of cows.
गोकुल n. herd or station of cattle.
गोक्षीर n. cow-milk.
गोघ्न a. noxious to kine, kine-killing; m. a cow-slayer.
गोचन्दन n. a kind of sandal-wood; f. आ a kind of leech.
गोचर m. reach, scope, sphere, range (lit. field for cattle); adj. being within range or reach of, subject to, accessible, perceptible, attainable by (—° or gen.).
गोजा a. sprung from the cow.
गोजात a. star-born (the gods).
गोण m. ox.
गोण्ड m. N. of a people.
गोतम m. the biggest ox; N. of sev. men, pl. their race.
गोत्र n. cow-stall (m.); race, family; family name, name i.g.; a grandson & cert. further descendants, also a patron suffix (g.).
गोत्रज a. born in the family, noble; m. a relative.
गोत्रनामन् (& °नामधेय*) n. family name.
गोत्रनामाभिजानतस् adv. by race, name, and family.
गोत्रभिद् a. opening the cow-shed or destroying families. m. E. of Indra.
गोत्ररिक्थ n. du. the family name and inheritance.
गोत्राख्या f. family name, patronymic.
गोत्रिन् a. belonging to the same race; m. a relative.
गोत्व n. state or nature of a cow.
गोद a. giving cows; f. आ N. of a river.
गोदा a. = prec. a.
1गोदान n. the gift of cows.
2गोदान n. the part of the head close to the ear & a cert. ceremony performed with it.
गोदावरी f. N. of a river.
गोदुह (nom. °धुक्) m. a cow-milker or herd.
गोदोह m., °न n. the milking of cows.
गोध m. pl. N. of a people. f. गोधा bow-string, sinew, arm-leather (cf. अङ्गुलित्र); a kind of lizard.
गोधन n. possession, herd, or station of cows; m. N. of a man.
गोधूम m. wheat.
गोनन्द or गोनर्द m. pl. N. of a people.
गोनसा or °नासा f. a kind of snake.
गोप m. cow-keeper, cowherd (f. ई), keeper or guardian i.g., E. of Kṛṣṇa.
गोपति m. bull, the sun or moon (lit. lord of the cows or stars); lord or chief i.g.; E. of Kṛṣṇa, Varuṇa, & Çiva.
गोपथ m. way for cows; T. of a Brāhmaṇa.
गोपन n. guarding, protecting (also गोपना f.); hiding, concealment.
गोपनीय a. to be guarded from (abl.).
गोपय्, °यति & °यते, pp. गोपित guard, preserve, hide, keep secret.
गोपा m. cowherd, guardian, protector; f. the wife of a cowherd etc.

गोपाय्, °यति & °यते guard, protect, keep secret. — अभि & परि A. guard, shelter.

गोपाल m. cowherd; prince, king; E. of Kṛṣṇa.

गोपालक m. cowherd (f. °लिका); E. of Kṛṣṇa.

गोपालदारक m. a cowherd's boy, a young cowherd.*

गोपावन्त् a. granting protection.

गोपिष्ठ (superl.) protecting best.

1**गोपीथ** m. a draught of milk.

2**गोपीथ** m. protection, shelter.

गोपुच्छ n. cow's tail; m. a kind of monkey.

गोपुर n. town-gate, gate i.g.

गोपेन्द्र & **गोपेश** m. chief herdsman, E. of Kṛṣṇa.

गोप्तृ m. guardian, protector (f. गोप्त्री, n. गोप्तृ); who hides or conceals.

गोबन्धु a. kin to a cow.

गोबीजकाञ्चन n. pl. cows, grain, and gold.

गोब्राह्मण n. sgl. a cow and (or) a Brahman.

गोभाज् a. earning a cow.

गोभिल m. N. of an author.

गोभुज् & **गोभृत्** m. king.

गोमन्त् a. possessing, containing, consisting of, cows or milk, milky (draught); f. गोमती a place abounding in herds, गोमती N. of sev. rivers; n. गोमत् possession of cattle.

गोमय a. consisting of cattle; n. (often pl.) m. cow-dung.

गोमातृ a. having a cow for mother.

गोमायु a. lowing like a cow; m. a kind of frog, a jackal & N. of a jackal.

गोमिथुन (n. sgl. & m. pl.) a pair of cattle, a bull and a cow.

गोमिन् m. owner of cattle or kine.

गोमुख m. a cert. musical instrument; N. of sev. men.

गोमूत्र n. a cow's urine.

गोमृग m. the Bos Gavaeus.

गोमेध & **गोयज्ञ** m. the sacrifice of a cow.

गोयान n. a carriage drawn by oxen or cows, carriage i.g.

गोयुक्त a. yoked with or drawn by cattle.

गोरक्षक a. guarding cattle; m. cow-herd.

गोरक्षा f., °क्ष्य n. keeping or breeding cattle.

गोरस m. cow-milk, milk i.g.

गोरोचना f. a bright yellow pigment prepared from the bile of a cow.

गोल & °क m. ball, globe; a widow's bastard.

गोलाङ्गूल m. = गोपुच्छ m.

गोवध m. the killing of a cow.

गोवर्धन m. N. of a mountain and an author; E. of Kṛṣṇa.

गोवाल m. a cow's hair.

गोविद् a. getting cows.

गोविनत m. a form of the horse-sacrifice.

गोविन्द m. E. of Kṛṣṇa-Viṣṇu (lit. = गोविद्).

__गोवृन्दारक__ m. an excellent bull.

गोवृष m. bull, E. of Çiva.

गोवृषण m. the scrotum of a bull.

गोव्रज m. cow-pen.

गोशकृत् n. cow-dung.

गोशकृद्रस m. liquid (lit. the juice of) cow-dung.

गोशाला f. cow-stall.

गोशीर्ष m. N. of a serpent-demon (lit. cow-head); n. a cert. weapon, a kind of sandal-wood.

गोशृङ्ग n. a cow's horn.

गोऽश्व n. sgl. oxen and horses; m. N. of a mountain.

गोषणि, **गोषन्**, & **गोषा** a. getting cattle.

गोषाति f. getting cattle, fighting for booty.

गोष्ठ m. cow-pen, stable, station, place; n. a kind of Çrāddha; f. गोष्ठी assembly, meeting, society, party, fellowship, conversation.

गोष्ठीयान n. carriage of an assembly.

गोष्ठ्य a. being in a cow-pen.

गोष्पद n. the mark or impression of a cow's foot, a small puddle; fig. a trifle.

गोसव m. a kind of (orig. cow-) sacrifice.

गोस्तन m. the udder of a cow; *a kind of garland.

गोस्वामिन् m. the owner of a cow.

गोह m. hiding place, lair; (N. of a man*).

गोहत्या f. the killing of a cow.

गोहन् & **गोहन्तृ** killing cattle, m. a cow-killer.

गौड, f. **ई** made of sugar or belonging to the Gauḍas. m. n. N. of a country; m. pl. N. of a people; f. **ई** rum made of sugar.

गौण, f. **ई** secondary, subordinate, also = seq.

गौणिक, f. **ई** relating to or depending on the qualities.

गौतम, f. **ई** descending from Gotama. m. N. of sev. men; f. N. of a river and sev. women.

गौतमारण्य n. N. of a forest.

गौर, f. **ई** white, yellowish, reddish; brilliant, beautiful. m. = **गौरमृग** or = **गौरसर्षप**, N. of a teacher; f. **ई** a female buffalo, a young girl before puberty, E. of the wife of Çiva, N. of sev. women.

गौरमुख m. N. of sev. men.

गौरमृग m. a kind of buffalo (Bos Gaurus).

गौरव a. relating to a Guru or teacher; n. weight, heaviness, (prosodical) length; importance, gravity, authority, respect, reverence.

गौरसर्षप m. yellow mustard or the seed of it (considered as a weight).

गौरीगुरु m. the father of Gaurī, i.e. the Himālaya.

गौरीनाथ & **गौरीपति** m. the husband of Gaurī, i.e. Çiva.

गौरीपूजा f. the adoration of Gaurī, a cert. festival.

गौरीभर्तृ & **गौरीश** m. the lord of Gaurī, i.e. Çiva.

गौरीव्रत n. the vow of Gaurī (a kind of rite).

ग्ना f. a superhuman female, a kind of goddess or female genius; poss. **°वन्त्**.

ग्नास्पति m. the husband of a divine wife.

ग्नास्पत्नी f. a divine wife.

†ग्मन् v. **पृथुग्मन्**.

ग्मा f. the earth (only abl. gen. **ग्मस्**).

ग्रथ्, **ग्रन्थ्**, **ग्रथ्नाति**, pp. **ग्रथित** tie or string together, arrange, compose, write. — **उद्** tie up, fasten, wind; also = C. **उद्ग्रथयति** unbind, loosen. **वि** & **सम्** bind together, connect. — Cf. **संग्रथित**.

ग्रथन n., **आ** f. tying, binding, connecting.

ग्रथिन् a. playing tricks, artful.

ग्रप्सु m. bunch, tuft.

ग्रन्थ m. arranging of words, composition, text, chapter, section.

ग्रन्थकार & **°कृत्** m. the author of a work.

ग्रन्थन n. = **ग्रथन**.

ग्रन्थि m. knot, tie, joint (also of the body); N. of sev. plants.

ग्रन्थिक m. relater, fortune-teller, astrologer.

ग्रन्थिच्छेदक m. purse-cutter, pick-pocket.

ग्रन्थिन् a. versed in books, learned.

ग्रन्थिभेद m. = **ग्रन्थिच्छेदक**.

ग्रन्थिमन्त् a. tied, bound.

ग्रन्थिल a. knotted, knotty.

ग्रप्स s. bunch, tuft.

ग्रभ् or **ग्रह्**, **गृभ्णाति**, **गृभ्णीते**, **गृह्णाति**, **गृह्णीते** (**गृह्णति**, **°ते**), pp. **गृभीत** & **गृहीत** (q.v.) grasp, seize, catch; take (in various mgs, e.g.) gather, pluck, collect, take up or draw (a fluid); take away, rob, occupy, buy, chose, marry, esp. w. **पाणिं** or **पाणौ** take (by) the hand (acc.); accept, receive; assume, use, put on or in; undertake, undergo, begin; gain over, win; get, acquire, keep, hold; take into the mouth, mention, name; take in with the mind, perceive, observe, understand, learn; admit, approve, obey, follow; take for, consider as (2 acc.); ger. **गृह्य** having taken i.e. accompanied by, furnished with, with (acc.); P. **गृह्यते** be meant by (instr.). C. **ग्राहयति** cause to grasp, seize, take etc. (**पाणिं** the hand, see above); cause to choose or marry (2 acc.), cause a person (acc.) to be occupied with (instr.), make learn, teach (2 acc.). D. **जिघृक्षति**, **°ते** be about to seize or take, strive to perceive or understand. — **अनु** follow in taking etc., accept, admit, approve, support, uphold; favour (**आसनम्** the seat = deign to sit down), oblige, make happy, esp. **अनुगृहीतोऽस्मि** I am happy or satisfied = thanks for (instr.). **अप** take away, tear off. **अभि** seize, catch, take hold of, take up, put together, put on, set (a blossom or fruit), accept, receive. **अव** let loose; stop, keep from (abl.); separate, divide (g.); perceive, notice, feel. **आ** grasp, seize, draw tight (the reins); take in, learn.

उद् take up, lift, raise, rear (M. refl.); take out, draw (a sword), preserve, save; cease; admit, grant. उप lift, take up, hold under, seize, take, obtain; admit, accept, approve. नि keep down, depress, draw near or together, close, contract, seize, catch, hold fast, stop, oppress, restrain, subdue, conquer. संनि keep down, suppress, stop, subdue, restrain. परि seize on both sides, embrace, surround, enclose, esp. इति, i.e. repeat a word before and after इति (g.); put on, don; grasp, clutch, hold, overpower, surpass; want, lack; get, obtain, acquire, keep in possession; accept, receive, take (a wife), marry, have regard to, obey, follow. संपरि accept, receive, comprehend. प्र hold out, stretch forth, offer; take, draw near or together, accept, receive (ger. = S.); keep, favour; separate, isolate (g.). संप्र hold out or stretch forth (together), seize, take, receive (well). प्रति take hold of, seize, take = eat, drink; take possession of, occupy; attack, assault; receive, accept (शिरसा on the head as a mark of esteem), take = marry, accept willingly, approve. C. cause to accept, present with (2 acc.). वि hold apart, stretch or spread out, separate, divide, analyze (g.); quarrel, rival, war with (instr. ± सह or सार्धम्), fight against (acc.); seize, clutch by (loc.); accept, receive; perceive, understand. सम् seize or hold (together), gather, collect, assemble; enclose, contain; draw together, contract, restrain; concentrate (the mind); accept, receive, take = marry, take into the mouth, name, pronounce; perceive, understand, learn. अनुसम् salute humbly (by clasping a person's feet. उपसम् the same (± पादौ, also w. acc. & पादयोस्); take, get, receive. प्रतिसम् accept, receive, meet. — Cf. अनुगृहीत, परिगृह्य, परिगृहीत, प्रगृह्य, प्रगृहीत, विगृह्य.

ग्रंभ m. seizing, taking possession.

ग्रंभीतृ m. grasper, one who seizes.

ग्रस्, ग्रंसति, °ते, pp. ग्रसितं & ग्रस्त put in the mouth, swallow, devour, consume, vex, afflict; destroy, annihilate. C. ग्रासयति cause to devour. — आ, उप, परि, प्र, सम् devour.

ग्रसन n. swallowing, devouring.

ग्रंसिष्ठ (superl.) swallowing most.

ग्रसिष्णु a. accustomed to swallow.

ग्रस्तृ m. devourer.

ग्रह् v. ग्रभ्.

ग्रंह a. grasping, seizing, etc. (v. ग्रभ्). — m. one who seizes, esp. the demon Rāhu (who seizes and obscures the moon), a planet or star (as seizing or influencing the destinies of men), demon of illness, crocodile, one of the eight organs, house, vessel for drawing water; anything seized, e.g. booty, prey, ladleful, spoonful, the middle of the bow; seizing, grasp, robbery, theft; tenacity, insisting upon (loc. or —°); taking, receiving; choice, favour; mention, apprehension, conceiving, understanding.

ग्रहण a. seizing, holding (—°). f. ई an imaginary organ in the belly. — n. grasp, seizure (esp. by Rāhu, i.e. eclipse, cf. ग्रहं), taking, holding, marrying, buying, choosing, drawing (water), putting on, donning, undergoing, acquiring, learning, study, perception, apprehension, mentioning, naming, the use of a term & the term itself.

ग्रहणान्त & °णान्तिक a. lasting to the close of study.

ग्रहणीय a. acceptable.

ग्रहयुति f. conjunction of the planets.

ग्रहयुद्ध n. opposition (lit. strife) of the planets.

ग्रहयोग m. = ग्रहयुति.

ग्रहवर्ष m. a planetary year.

ग्रहसमागम m. = ग्रहयुति.

†ग्राहि v. फलग्राहि & फलेग्राहि.

ग्रहिल a. accepting of, inclined to (—°); sensible, irritable, crazy, mad.

ग्रहीतृ m. seizer, taker, buyer, observer, hearer.

ग्रहीतव्य a. to be taken or received.

ग्राभं m. grasper or grasp.
ग्रा॑म m. dwelling-place, village (also n.), community, tribe, race, multitude, troop, collection; pl. inhabitants, people.
ग्रामकुक्कुट m. village or house cock.
ग्रामघात m. plundering of a village.
ग्रामज & °जात a. village-born, grown in cultivated ground.
ग्रामजि॑त् a. conquering troops.
ग्रामणी॑ m. chief of a troop or a community; *barber.
ग्रामदशेश m. the head of ten villages.
ग्रामयाजिक & °याजिन् a. sacrificing for a whole village or community.
ग्रामशकटिक n. village cart.*
ग्रामशताध्यक्ष & °शतेश m. the chief of a hundred villages.
ग्रामाधिप m. chief of a village.
ग्रामान्तर n. another village.
ग्रामान्तीय a. lying near a village.
ग्रामिक m. the chief of a village.
ग्रामि॑न् a. surrounded by a tribe or community; m. villager, peasant.
ग्रामीण a. rustic, vulgar.
ग्रामीयक m. member of a community.
ग्राम्य॑ a. village-, domestic, cultivated; rustic, vulgar. m. villager, peasant; domestic animal. n. = ग्राम्यधर्म m. copulation, lust.
ग्राम्यता f., °त्व n. rusticity, vulgar speech.
ग्रा॑वन् m. stone for pressing out the Soma; stone, rock i.g.
ग्रास a. swallowing (—°); m. mouthful, lump, bit, piece, food; eating, devouring, eclipse (cf. ग्र॑ह).
ग्रासाच्छादन n. sgl. food and clothing.
ग्राह॑, f. ई seizing, catching, taking, accepting (—°). m. beast of prey, crocodile, shark, serpent; seizure, grasp, hold, attack, disease; naming, mentioning.
ग्राहक, f. °हिका taking, receiving, containing, enclosing; perceiving, observing; m. seizer, catcher, receiver, buyer, observer.
ग्राहकत्व n. power of perception.
ग्रा॑हि f. a female spirit of evil; swoon, fainting fit.
ग्राहिन् a. grasping, seizing, holding (—°), catching, gathering, enclosing, containing, gaining, buying, choosing, keeping; attracting, alluring; searching, perceiving.
ग्राह्य a. to be seized, taken, held, gathered, gained, received, perceived, understood, learned, recognized, considered.
ग्रा॑ङ्क m. seizing (acc.).
(ग्रीव m.,) ग्रीवा॑ (& ग्रीवालिका*) f. the neck.
ग्रीष्म॑ m. summer.
ग्रीष्ममयूरी f. a peahen in summer.*
ग्रीष्मसमय m. summer-time, the hot season.
ग्रैव n., ग्रैवेय m. n. the chain on the neck of an elephant.
ग्रैवेयक n. the same, necklace, collar i.g.
ग्रै॑व्य a. relating to the neck.
ग्रैष्म & ग्रैष्मिक a. relating to the summer.
ग्लप्, ग्लपति be sorry about (inst.).
ग्लपन a. tiring; n. fading, withering.
ग्लप्स s. = ग्रप्स.
ग्लह्, ग्लहते play with dice.
ग्ल॑ह m. game at dice, stake in playing; die, dice-box; contest, bet, prize.
ग्ल॑हन n. playing at dice.
ग्ला, ग्ला॑यति (ग्लायते & ग्लाति), pp. ग्लान॑ (q.v.) be loth, displeased, averse to (loc. or instr.); be wearied, exhausted, fade away. C. ग्लाप॑यति & ग्लपयति; pp. ग्लापित wearied, faded, withered. — प्र fade, wither. — Cf. परिग्लान.
ग्लान n., ग्लानि f. exhaustion, depression.
ग्लाविन् a. wearied, inactive.
ग्लास्नु a. exhausted, languid.
ग्लौ s. a kind of ball or round lump of flesh of the sacrificial victim.

घ

1घ, घा (encl.) surely, indeed, even, at least; lays stress upon a prec. particle, pronoun, or preposition; is often followed by ईद् or ईम्.

2घ (—°) striking, killing.

घट्, घटते (°ति) be eager or busy, work at, exert one's self for, strive after (loc., dat., or acc.); be accomplished, come round, succeed, be possible, fit, or suitable; meet, join (instr.). C. घटयति (°ते), pp. घटित bring together, unite, place upon (loc.), bring near, procure, cause, effect, produce, make, form. — उद् open (intr.); C. उद्घाटयति open (trans.), reveal. प्र exert one's self, devote one's self to (loc.); commence, begin. वि go asunder, burst. C. विघटयति tear asunder, destroy, annihilate. सम् come together, meet. C. संघटयति & संघाटयति assemble, collect.

घट m. jar, ewer; f. आ multitude, troop, ई = m.

घटक a. producing, arranging, procuring; m. & f. घटिका = prec. m.

घटकर्पर m. N. of a poet; n. his poem.

घटकार & घटकृत् m. potter.

घटन n. joining, union with (instr. or —°). f. आ the same, arranging or shooting (of an arrow), action, way of acting, effort, endeavour at (loc. or —°); success, accomplishment; getting, procuring, producing; literary work or composition.

घटीयन्त्र n. machine for raising water.

घटोत्कच m. N. of a myth. giant.

घट्ट्, घट्टते (only —°) & C. घट्टयति stroke, touch (also with words = mock), shake, set in motion. — अव C. touch, stroke, rub, also = उद् & उप C. stir about. परि C. rub or touch on all sides. वि C. break asunder, burst open, stir about, shake, open. सम् rub or crush to pieces, bruise. C. cause to rub against (instr.), stir about, touch, collect, meet.

घट्ट m. landing or bathing place.

घट्टजीविन् m. ferry-man (a cert. caste).

घट्टन n. pushing, stirring, touching.

घण्टा f. a bell; घण्टिका f. a small bell.

घण्टाकर्ण m. N. of a Rākṣasa, E. of sev. gods.

घण्टाताड a. ringing a bell.

घण्टापथ m. chief road, high way; T. of a commentary.

घण्टारव & °राव m. the sound of a bell.

घण्टावन्त् a. furnished with a bell or bells.

घण्टिक m. alligator.

घण्टिन् a. = घण्टावन्त्.

घन a. slaying, striking; compact, solid, firm, tight (n. adv.); dark, deep (sound); uninterrupted, whole, entire; full of (—°). m. slaughter, slayer; mace, club, hammer; compact mass, cloud; nothing but (—°).

घनकाल m. the season of the rains (clouds).

घनता f. compactness, thickness (also °त्व n.); state of a cloud.

घनतामस a. deep-dark.

घनतिमिर n. thick darkness, blindness.

घनपद्वी & घनवीथि f. the sky (lit. the path of the clouds).

घनसमय m. = घनकाल.

घनसार a. solid, strong; m. camphor.

घनाघन a. fond of slaughter; compact, thick.

घनात्यय & घनान्त m. autumn (lit. the end of the clouds or rains).

घनी w. कृ harden, thicken; w. भू become hard or thick.

घरट्ट & °क m. grindstone.

घर्घर a. gurgling.

घर्घरिका f. a small bell, used as an ornament.

घर्म m. heat, warmth; any hot (sacrificial) beverage, esp. milk; boiler, cauldron; also = seq.

घर्मकाल m. the hot season.

घर्मच्छेद m. cessation of the heat, the rainy season.

घर्मजल & घर्मतोय n. perspiration.

घर्मदीधिति, घर्मद्युति, °भानु, & °रश्मि m. the sun.

घर्मवन्त् a. glowing.
घर्मवारि n. घर्मजल.
घर्मस्तुभ् a. shouting in the heat.
घर्मांशु m. = घर्मदीधिति.
घर्मान्त m. = घर्मच्छेद.
घार्माम्बु & घर्माम्भस् n. = घर्मजल.
घर्मार्त a. suffering from heat.
घर्मित a. heated, hot.
घर्मिन् a. who prepares the hot sacrificial drink.
घर्मोदक n. = घर्माम्बु.
घर्म्य n. a vessel for preparing the hot sacrificial drink.
घर्ष m. rubbing, friction.
घर्षण n. rubbing, grinding, anointing.
घस्, घस्ति devour, swallow, eat. D. जिघत्सति.
घस m. devourer, N. of a Rakṣas.
घसन n. devouring.
घसि m. food.
घस्मर & घस्वर a. voracious.
घात a. slaying, destroying; m. the same as subst.
घातक, f. ई = prec. a.; m. slayer, murderer.
घातन n. killing, murder; f. ई a kind of club.
घातय्, °यति (°यते) punish, slay, kill, destroy; also C. — व्या impede, disappoint. नि slay, kill. प्रति repel. वि beat, vex, afflict; impede, interrupt.
घातिन् a. = घातक.
घातुक a. killing, harmful, mischievous.
घात्य a. to be killed or destroyed.
घासं & घासि m. food.
घुण & °कीटक m. wood-worm.
घुणाक्षर n. a strange incident (lit. letter produced by the wood-worm.
घुरघुराय्, °यते grunt, growl.
घुष्, घोषति (°ते), pp. घुष्ट sound, cry, call out, proclaim. C. घोषयति cause to sound etc., also = S. — अव proclaim aloud, offer. आ listen to; also = C. cry aloud, proclaim. उद् sound, cry aloud. C. proclaim. वि make noise, sound, proclaim. सम् sound, fill with noise, proclaim, praise, offer. — Cf. उद्घुष्ट & परिसंघुष्ट.
घुष्टान्न n. offered food.
घूक m. owl.
घूत्कार m. screeching (of the owl).
घूर्ण्, घूर्णति, °ते, pp. घूर्णित move to and fro, tremble, shake, whirl. C. घूर्णयति cause to move to and fro etc. — अव, आ, परि, वि = S.
घूर्ण a. moving to and fro, trembling, whirling.
घूर्णन n., आ f. the same as subst.
घूर्णिका f. N. of a woman.
घृ, जिघर्ति, pp. घृत (q.v.) sprinkle, moisten. — व्या C. the same. — Cf. अभिघृत, विघृत.
घृणा m. heat, sunshine, instr. घृणा; f. घृणा compassion, pity, contempt.
घृणालु a. compassionate.
घृणि m. heat, sunshine, ray of light, day; wave, billow.
घृणित्व n. = घृणा.
घृणिन् a. fierce, wild; meek, tender.
घृणीवन्त् a. glowing, shining.
घृत n. clarified butter, ghee; butter, fat i.g. (esp. as emblem of fertility).
घृतकुम्भ & घृतघट m. a jar of ghee.
घृतनिर्णिज् a. clothed in fat.
घृतपशु m. an animal made of ghee.
घृतपृष्ठ a. (having a back or surface) smeared with ghee.
घृतप्रतीक a. (having a face) smeared with ghee.
घृतप्राश m., °न n. eating of ghee.
घृतप्रुष् a. sprinkling ghee.
घृतवन्त् a. abounding in fat or butter; containing the word घृत.
घृतवर्तनि a. whose tracks are in ghee.
घृतश्चुत् a. sprinkling ghee.
घृतस्ना a. dipped in ghee or dropping it.
1घृतस्नु a. the same.
2घृतस्नु a. = घृतपृष्ठ.
घृताक्त a. smeared with ghee.
घृताची (only f.) greazy, fat; as subst. the sacrificial ladle (± जुहू); N. of an Apsaras.
घृतान्न a. feeding on fat.
घृतासुति a. receiving the ghee drink.
घृताहवन & घृताहुत a. receiving the ghee oblation.
घृताहुति f. the ghee oblation.
घृत्य a. consisting of ghee.

घृष्, **घर्षति**, pp. **घृष्ट** rub (M. refl.), polish. crush, pound. C. **घर्षयति** rub, grind. — **अव** rub off. **उद्** the same, rub over, strike against. **नि** rub into, graze, chafe; try, examine. **निस्** rub against (loc.) **सम्** grind to pieces, crush, wound; contend, vie with (**सह**). — Cf. **विघुष्ट**.

घृ॑षु & **घृ॑ष्वि** a. lively, sprightful, gay.

†**घृ॑ष्विराधस्** a. gladly giving.

घे॑ट्ट & **घेम्** v. 1**घ**.

घोट & **०क** m. horse.

घोणा f. nose, snout, beak.

घोर॑ a. awful, terrific, horrible, violent; n. awe, horror, magic, incantation.

घोरता f., **०त्व** n. awfulness, horror.

घोरदर्शन a. of terrible aspect.

घोररूप & **घोर॑वर्पस्** a. of dreadful appearance.

घोराकार & **घोराकृति** a. the same.

घोल m. buttermilk.

घो॑ष m. noise, tumult, cry, sound, rumour, report, proclamation; a station of herdsmen.

घोषण a. sounding; f. **आ** & n. proclamation, judgment.

घोषणस्थान n. place for proclamation.*

घोषवन्त् a. sounding, roaring; sonant (g).

घो॑षि & **घोषि॑न्** a. sounding, noisy.

घोष्टृ m. proclaimer.

घ्न slaying, killing, destroying, removing (—०).

घ्रंस् & **घ्रंस॑** m. the heat of the sun.

घ्रा, **जि॑घ्रति** (**०ते** & **घ्राति**), pp. **घ्रात॑** (—० w. act. & pass. mg) smell, sniff, kiss, perceive. — **अव** smell, kiss. **आ** the same, touch, seize. **समा** & **उप** smell, touch with the mouth, kiss.

घ्राण m. n. smell, sniff, odour; f. **आ** & n. nose, snout.

घ्रातृ॑ m. one who smells.

घ्राति f. smelling, smell.

घ्रेय a. to be smelled; n. odour, smell.

च

च (encl.) and, also; even, just; but, yet; if. It is often joined with **अपि** & **एव**. — **च—च** as well—as, both—and (also **च—तु**), no sooner—than, although—yet; w. neg. neither—nor. **च—न च** (**तु**) although—yet not, **न च—च** although not—nevertheless.

चक् (**चकति**), pp. **चकित** (q.v.) tremble, shake, be alarmed.

चकार m. the word **च**.

चकास्, **चकास्ति** shine, beam.

चकित a. & n. trembling.

चकोर m. a kind of partridge.

चकोरव्रत m. the practice (lit. vow) of the Cakora (said to feed on moon-beams); **०व्रतमालम्ब्** follow the practice of the Cakora (i.e. enjoy the sight of a moon-like face).

चकोरनेत्र & **०राक्ष**, f. **ई** partridge-eyed.

चक्र॑ n. m. wheel (lit. & fig.), discus (esp. of Viṣṇu); orb, circle; troop, multitude, army; circuit, district, province, domain. — m. a kind of duck, also a man's name; f. **चक्री** wheel.

चक्रगोप्तृ m. guardian of the wheel (scil. of the king's chariot), trabant.

चक्रधर a. & m. having a wheel or a discus, a sovereign or Viṣṇu.

चक्रनाभि f. the nave of a wheel.

चक्रभङ्ग m. the breaking of a wheel.

चक्ररक्ष (& **०रक्षिन्***) m. = **चक्रगोप्तृ**.

चक्ररत्न n. an excellent (lit. jewel of a) discus.

चक्रवद्गति a. moving like a wheel, turning round.

चक्रवर्तिता f., **०त्व** n. abstr. to seq.

चक्रवर्तिन् a. rolling on wheels; m. supreme ruler, emperor, chief of (gen. or —०).

चक्रवाक॑ m., **ई** f. the Cakravāka, a kind of goose or duck.

चक्रवात m. whirlwind, hurricane.

चक्रवाल n. orb, circle, troop, multitude.

चक्रवृद्धि f. compound interest or freight-money (lit. wheel-profit).

चक्रव्यूह m. a circular array of troops.
चक्राङ्कित a. marked with a (mystic) circle.
चक्राङ्ग, f. ई a kind of goose or flamingo.
चक्राह्व & चक्राह्वय m. = चक्रवाक.
चंक्रि a. making, active.
चक्रिन् a. having wheels or a discus, driving in a chariot; m. sovereign, king, serpent, E. of Viṣṇu or Çiva.
चक्ष्, चंष्टे, चंक्षते (°ति) see, look at, perceive; consider as (2 acc.); appear, become, visible; show, announce, declare, tell, say. — अनु look after or at; name, term. अभि behold, view, survey; see with favour, address; name, term. अव look down upon (acc.), behold, perceive. आ look at, inspect; proclaim, announce, relate, tell, speak to (acc.); signify, mean (acc.); name, term. प्रत्या refuse, reject; reply to, answer (acc.). व्या recite, explain. परि overlook, neglect, despise, condemn; name, term; speak to (acc.), answer. प्र relate, tell; consider as, take for, call, name. संप्र explain, suppose. प्रति see, perceive, behold, expect; cause to appear, show. वि appear, shine, see, behold, look at, observe; also = C. cause to appear, show, reveal; proclaim, announce, tell. सम् view, behold, survey, examine, observe; enumerate, report; call, name, term. — Cf. अभिचंष्टे, विचंष्टे.
चंक्षण n. appearance, aspect.
चक्षणि m. who illuminates.
चंक्षन् n. eye.
चंक्षस् n. brightness, clearness; seeing or being seen (dat. as infin.).
चंक्षु m. eye.
चक्षुर्विषय & चक्षुष्पथ m. range of sight, visibility.
चक्षुष्प्रीति f. joy of the eye.
चंक्षुष्मन्त् a. having eyes, seeing.
चक्षुष्य a. wholesome or agreeable to the eyes, pleasing, beautiful, dear.
चंक्षुस् a. seeing. m. N. of a Marut & sev. Rishis; n. brightness, light, view, sight, eye.
चक्षूराग m. delight of the eye.
चङ्क्रम m., आ f. walk (abstr. & concr.).
चङ्क्रमण a. walking; n. = prec.
चञ्च a. acquainted with, clever at (—°); abstr. °ता f.
चचरं a. movable.
चञ्च्, चञ्चति leap, jump.
चञ्चरिन् & °रीक m. bee.
चञ्चल a. movable, unsteady, unconstant, fickle; abstr. °त्व n. — m. lover, libertine.
चञ्चललोचन a. having rolling eyes.
चञ्चा f. mat-work.
चञ्चु a. known or renowned by (—°); abstr. °ता f., °त्व n. — m. N. of a man & sev. plants; f. (also चञ्चू) beak, bill.
चञ्चुपुट n., °पुटी f. the hollow of a bird's beak.
चञ्चूपुट n., °पुटी f. the same.
चट्, चटति, pp. चटित happen, take place; arrive, get to or into (loc.). — उद् go away, disappear. C. उच्चाटयति drive away, expel. वि break (intr.).
चटक m., आ f. a sparrow.
चटु s. courtesy, flirtation.
चटुल a. trembling, movable, unsteady, fickle; courteous.
चटूपमा f. a kind of comparison.
चण a. known, famous (—°), abstr. त्व n.; m. = seq.
चणक m. the chick-pea.
चंण्ड, f. आ & ई fierce, violent, wrathful, angry; n. adv. — m. N. of sev. myth. beings, E. of Çiva or Skanda. f. आ & ई E. of Durgā.
चण्डकर & चण्डकिरण m. the sun.
चण्डकौशिक m. N. of a man; n. T. of a drama.
चण्डता f., °त्व n. abstr. to चंण्ड a.
चण्डदीधिति & चण्डरश्मि m. = चण्डकर.
चण्डसिंह m. N. of a king.
चण्डांशु m. = चण्डकर.
चंण्डातक n. a short petticoat.
चण्डाल m. a Caṇḍāla or outcast.
चण्डिका f. E. of Durgā.
चण्डी w. कृ make angry.
चण्डीश & चण्डीश्वर m. E. of Çiva.
चण्डोस्तोत्र n. praise of Durgā (T. of a hymn).

चण्डेश्वर m. = चण्डोश.

चत्, only चंतन्त् & चत्त hide one's self. C. चातयति, °ते scare, drive away. — निस्, प्र, & वि C. M. the same.

चंतसृ or चतसृं v. चत्वार्.

चतिंन् a. hiding one's self.

चतुर् (°—) v. चत्वार्.

1चतुर a. swift, quick, dexterous, clever, skilful in (—°); abstr. °ता f., °त्व n.

2चतुर (—°) v. चत्वार्.

चतुरक, f. °रिका = 1चतुर; m. N. of a jackal; f. N. of a woman.

चतुरर्च, f. ई four-eyed.

चंतुरक्षर a. consisting of four syllables.

चंतुरङ्ग a. consisting of four members or parts; n. (± बल) a complete army (infantry, cavalry, elephants, chariots); f. आ the same, a sort of chess.

चतुरङ्गिन् a. = prec. adj.

चंतुरनीक a. four-faced.

चतुरन्त a. surrounded (by the sea) on all four sides; f. आ the earth.

चतुरर्णव (°—) the four oceans which surround the earth.

चतुरश्र a. four-cornered, regular, harmonious; abstr. °ता f.

चंतुरश्रि a. four-cornered, quadrangular.

चतुरहं m. a period of four days.

चतुरानन a. four-faced, E. of Brahman.

चतुरुत्तरं a. increasing by four.

चंतुर्गुण a. fourfold, quadruple.

चतुर्थ, f. ई the fourth, n. adv. the fourth time; subst. the fourth part. f. ई the fourth day in a lunar fortnight; the fourth case or its endings (g.).

चतुर्थकाल m. the fourth meal-time, a. = seq.

चतुर्थकालिक a. keeping only the fourth meal-time.

1चतुर्थांश m. the fourth part, a quarter.

2चतुर्थांश a. receiving a quarter.

चतुर्दश, f. ई the fourteenth, consisting of fourteen; f. ई the 14th day in a lunar fortnight.

चतुर्दशधा adv. fourteenfold.

चंतुर्दशन् or चतुर्दशंन् a. fourteen.

चतुर्दशम a. the fourteenth.

चतुर्दिक्कम् & चतुर्दिशम् adv. towards the four quarters of the sky, all around.

चतुर्धा adv. in four parts, fourfold.

चतुर्बाहु a. four-armed.

चतुर्भाग m. the fourth part, a quarter.

चतुर्भुज a. = चतुर्बाहु, m. E. of sev. gods.

चतुर्भूमिक a. having four stores.

चतुर्मुख (°—) four faces; a. four-faced, m. E. of sev. gods.

चतुर्मूर्ति a. four-shaped or four-faced, m. E. of sev. gods.

चतुर्युक्त a. drawn by four.

1चतुर्युग n. the four ages of the world.

2चंतुर्युग a. containing the four ages of the world, also = चतुर्युक्त.

चतुर्युज् a. yoked or put to the chariot by four; drawn by four.

चतुर्वक्त्र a. four-faced.

चंतुर्वय a. fourfold.

चतुर्वर्ग m. a collection of four; esp. the four chief objects (virtue, pleasure, wealth, and final beatitude; cf. त्रिवर्ग).

चतुर्विंश, f. ई the twenty-fourth.

चतुर्विंशत् & चंतुर्विंशति f. twenty-four.

चतुर्विंशतितम a. the twenty-fourth.

चंतुर्विध a. fourfold; n. adv.

1चतुर्वेद m. pl. the four Vedas.

2चतुर्वेद a. containing the four Vedas, also = seq.

चतुर्वेदविद् (& चतुर्वेदिन्*) a. knowing the four Vedas.

चतुश्चत्वारिंश, f. ई the forty-fourth.

चंतुश्चत्वारिंशत् f. forty-four.

चंतुःशत n. 104 or 400.

चंतुःशफ a. four-hoofed.

चतुःशाल a. containing four halls; m. such a building.

चतुःशालक m., °शालिका f. = prec. m.

चतुष्क a. consisting of four or increased by four; n. = seq. n., also a kind of hall or square.

चंतुष्टय, f. ई fourfold, consisting of four; n. the number four or a collection of four.

चंतुष्पञ्चाशत् f. fifty-four.

चतुष्पथ m. n. cross-way.

चतुष्पद् & °पाद्, f. °पदी four-legged; m. a quadruped.

चतुष्पद, f. ई a. having four feet, consisting of four words or lines; m. = prec. m.

चतुष्पदवस्तुक a. having as object (referring to) four lines or verses.

चतुष्पदोत्थ a. consisting of four lines or verses.*

चतुष्पाद, f. ई = चतुष्पद्.

चतुस् adv. four times.

चतुस्त्रिंश, f. ई the thirty-fourth.

चतुस्त्रिंशत् f. thirty-four.

1चतुःसमुद्र (°—) the four seas.*

2चतुःसमुद्र, f. ई containing the four seas or surrounded by them.

चतुःसहस्र n. four-thousand.

चतुःसौवर्णिक a. containing four Suvarṇas (in weight).

चतूरात्र s. four days (nights); acc. for f. d.

चत्वर m. n. quadrangular place or yard; quarter of a town.

चत्वार् (चतसृ & चतुर्) a. four; m. pl. the four dice for playing.

चत्वारिंश, f. ई the fortieth.

चत्वारिंशत् & चत्वारिंशति f. forty.

चन् (only aor. चनिष्टम) delight in, enjoy.

चन (also च न) indecl. also not, even (not), (not) even, nor; in l. l. usually with another negation & only after an interrog. which it makes indefin., e.g. न कश्चन not any one = none, न क्व चन not anywhere = nowhere.

चनस् n. delight, satisfaction, only w. धा delight in, be satisfied with (acc. or loc.), enjoy, accept, approve.

चनस्य, °स्यति delight in (acc.).

चनिष्ठ (superl.) most welcome or gracious.

चनोधा a. gracious.

चन्दन m. n. sandal (tree, wood, or unguent).

चन्दनक m. N. of a man.

चन्दनपङ्क m. unguent prepared from sandal.

चन्दनपुर n. N. of a town.

चन्दनमय a. made of sandal.

चन्दनरस m. (& चन्दनवारि n.*) sandal-water.

चन्दनाय, °यते become or be like sandal.

चन्दनोदक n. sandal-water.

चन्द्र a. shining, glittering, brilliant, bright. — m. the moon (often personif.), moon i.e. chief among (—°).

चन्द्रक m. (adj. —° f. चन्द्रिका) moon; f. चन्द्रिका also moonshine; illumination, elucidation (—° in titles of books).

चन्द्रकान्त a. beautiful as the moon; m. the moon-stone (a fabulous gem.).

चन्द्रक्षय m. new-moon (lit. end of the moon).

चन्द्रगुप्त m. N. of sev. kings.

चन्द्रचूड m. E. of Çiva (lit. the moon-crested).

चन्द्रचूडामणि m. T. of a work.

चन्द्रतारक n. sgl. the moon and stars.

चन्द्रत्व n. abstr. to चन्द्र moon.

चन्द्रनिभानना f. having a moonlike face.

चन्द्रपाद m. a moon-beam.

चन्द्रप्रभ m., आ f. moon-like; a man's & woman's name.

चन्द्रबिम्ब & चन्द्रमण्डल n. the orb of the moon.

चन्द्रमस् m. moon or god of the moon.

चन्द्रमास m. a lunar month.

चन्द्रमुकुट, चन्द्रमौलि, & °मौलिन् m. = चन्द्रचूड.

चन्द्ररेखा f. a digit of the moon.

चन्द्रलेखा f. the same, a woman's name.

चन्द्रवंश m. the lunar race (mythol.).

चन्द्रवन्त् a. brilliant as the moon; rich in gold. f. चन्द्रवती a woman's name.

चन्द्रवपुस् a. beautiful as the moon.

चन्द्रवर्ण a. of shining or bright colour.

चन्द्रविशुद्ध a. pure as the moon.*

चन्द्रशाला f. moon chamber (on the top of the house).

चन्द्रशेखर m. = चन्द्रचूड; a man's name.

*चन्द्रसंज्ञ m. camphor.

चन्द्रसरस् n. moon-lake (mythol.).

चन्द्रसिंह m. N. of a king.

चन्द्रांशु m. moon-beam.

चन्द्रातप m. moon-shine.

चन्द्रापीड m. = चन्द्राचूड.

चन्द्रार्ध m. half-moon, crescent.

चन्द्रिन् a. golden.

चन्द्रोदय m. moon-rise.

चपल a. moving to and fro, tremulous, unsteady, agitated, rash, nimble, fickle, inconsiderate, n. adv. — f. आ lightning, a wanton woman, N. of two metres.

चपलगण m. wanton troop, goblins.

चपलता f. (&°त्व n.*) nimbleness, fickleness, wantonness.

चपेट m., आ & ई f. slap with the open hand.

चम्, चामति & चमति sip, drink. — आ sip, rinse the mouth, lick up, absorb, cause to disappear. C. आचमयति & आचामयति cause to sip. — Cf. आचान्त, पर्याचान्त.

चमत् adv., only w. कृ utter or excite surprise; pp. चमत्कृत surprised, astonished, infatuated, proud, arrogant.

चमत्करण n., °कार m., °कृति f. astonishment, amazement, surprise, wonder.

चमन n. sipping.

चमर m., ई f. the Yak (Bos Grunniens); m. n. the chowrie, a long brush made of the tail of the Yak.

चमस m. vessel for drinking, a wooden cup.

चमू f. the bottom of the Soma-press; squadron, army.

चमूगति f. movement of an army, march.

चमूनाथ, चमूप, °पति, & °पाल m. leader of an army.

चम्प m. N. of the founder of चम्पा f. a town.

चम्पक m. N. of a tree, n. its fruit; f. आ a town.

चम्पकवती m. N. of a forest and a town.

चम्पावती f. = चम्पा.

चम्पू f. a kind of composition, prose and verse mixed.

1**चय** m. layer, heap, pile, wall; troop, multitude, collection.

2**चय** a. revenging, punishing (—°).

चयन n. heaping up, gathering; heap, pile.

चर्, चरति (°ते), pp. चरित (q.v.) & चीर्ण move, go, drive (w. instr.), walk, roam, wander through or along (acc.), pervade, explore (only pp. चरित); behave, conduct one's self, act or deal with (instr. or loc.), be engaged or busy with (instr.), have sexual intercourse with (instr.); continue doing or being (pp., adj., ger., or adv.); exercise, perform, produce, cause, effect, do, make, render (2 acc.); consume, eat, feed, pasture. — C. चारयति cause to move, walk, roam, eat, pasture, approach sexually, set in motion, impel; cause to do (2 acc.). D. चिचरिषति or चिचर्षति try to go, be willing to approach sex. (instr.). I. चर्चरीति or चर्चूर्यते (w. act. & pass. mg) move quickly or repeatedly, wander, roam (acc. or loc.). — अच्छ move towards (acc.). अति escape, go past (acc.), transgress, also = seq. व्यति commit offence against (acc.). अधि move on or over. अनु move along or through, follow; move towards, strive after, endeavour to, keep or take to, behave, conduct one's self. C. cause to be pervaded or explored by (instr.). अन्तर् move between or within, be inside (acc., loc., or gen.). अप depart, also = seq. अभि act wrongly towards (acc.). व्यभि the same; M. bewitch, practise sorcery. अव descend. आ come near, approach, enter, visit; use, employ, treat (like—वत्), apply to (acc.); behave, conduct one's self; deal with, have intercourse with (instr. ± सह), undertake, practise, perform, accomplish, effect, do, make. समा proceed, deal or converse with (instr.), perform etc. = prec. उद् rise (l. & f.); emit, esp. the excrement, also = C. उच्चारयति utter, pronounce. अभ्युद् rise over (acc.). प्रोद् cause to sound. व्युद् go forth in different directions; be unfaithful to (acc.), commit adultery with (instr.); perform, accomplish. उप come near, approach, wait on (acc.), attend, treat with (instr.), undertake, begin. निस् & विनिस् go or come forth. परा go away, depart. परि walk about, circumambulate; wait upon, serve. C. be attended by (instr.). प्र come forth, appear, succeed, thrive; go towards, arrive at, reach, visit; proceed, undertake, begin; be active or busy with (loc.); perform, do. संप्र begin to move, go on, take place, happen. वि go asunder, open, spread, be diffused; fall on, attack; walk about, roam, wander, go through, pervade; have intercourse with (instr.); go astray, fail, sin; practise, fulfil, do. C. cause to roam or go astray, corrupt, seduce; move to and fro (in the mind) i.e. deliberate, consider, reflect, ponder, examine, ascertain, state. **प्रवि** advance, proceed, go about, roam. **सम्** come together, meet, approach, arrive, appear, reach to (**आ**); spread through, pervade; stay, remain; exercise, fulfil. C. make to meet, bring into contact, set in motion, cause to go. **अनुसम्** go after or along, spread through, penetrate, also = seq. **अभिसम्** go towards, seek for. — Cf. **आचरित, आचरितव्य, विचारित.**

†**चर** a. moving, movable; as subst. an animal (opp. **स्थावर**); n. going, walking, being, living, doing, performing, having been formerly (—∘); m. spy, secret emissary; f. **चरा.**

चरक m. wanderer, traveller, esp. a religious student or a spy; m. N. of an ancient physician, pl. a branch of the Yajurveda.

चरकाध्वर्यु m. a priest of the Carakas (v. prec.).

चरण m. n. foot, m. pl. the feet of— i.e. the venerable (—∘); line or verse of a stanza; sect or school of the Veda. n. moving, walking, course, way; practice, performance, esp. rel. observance; behaving, conduct, esp. good conduct, morality.

चरणगुरु m. teacher of a Vedic school.

चरणन्यास m. setting down of the feet, footstep, walk, gait.

चरणपतन n., **∘पात** m. foot-fall.

चरणराग m. paint or unguent for the feet.

चरणविक्षेप m. foot-step.

चरणव्यूह m. T. of a treatise.

चरणसंस्कार m. ornament of the feet.

चरण्यु a. moving, movable.

चरथ a. the same; n. going, stirring; way, course (dat. as inf.).

चरध्यै (dat. inf.) to go.

चरम a. the last, final, ultimate, extreme, lowest, least.

चरमवयस् a. of extreme age, aged.

1**चराचर** a. movable, stirring.

2**चराचर** a. movable and immovable, s. animals and plants, the whole world.

चरित n. going, course, way, practice, behaviour, conduct; acts, deeds, adventures.

चरितपूर्व a. done before.

चरितवे (dat. inf.) to go.

चरितव्रत a. having accomplished a vow or an act of devotion.

चरितार्थ a. having attained one's object, successful, satisfied; abstr. **∘ता** f., **∘त्व** n.

चरित्र n. foot, leg (m.); also = **चरित** + custom, law.

चरिष्णु a. moving, wandering, unsteady.

चरु m. pot, kettle; sacrificial food, esp. boiled rice.

चर्कृति f. praise, glory.

चर्कृत्य a. worthy of praise, glorious.

चर्च्, C. **चर्चयति**, pp. **चर्चित** (q.v.) repeat, esp. by inserting **इति.**

चर्चरिका & **चर्चरी** f. a kind of march or song.

चर्चा f. repetition (also **चर्चन**); unguent, ointment; the being penetrated by, thought, care, or talk of (gen. or —∘).

चर्चित a. repeated; smeared, covered with (—∘); wiped off; determined, decided; n. unguent, ointment.

चर्पट a. flat.

चर्म (—∘) = **चर्मन्.**

चर्मकार m. worker in leather, shoemaker.

चर्मकारिन् & **∘कृत्** m. the same.

चर्मकार्य n. working in leather.

चर्मज a. leathern.

चर्मण्य n. leather-work.

चर्मण्वन्त् a. covered with skin; f. **∘ण्वती** N. of a river.

चर्मन् n. skin, leather, hide, shield.

चर्ममय, f. **ई** leathern.

चर्मावकर्तिन् & **∘कर्तृ** m. leather-cutter, shoemaker.

चर्मिन् a. covered with skin; m. shield-bearer.

चर्य a. to be done, practised, kept, etc.; f. **आ** going, wandering, visiting; behaviour, conduct, morality, piety; practice, performance, occupation with (instr. or —∘).

चर्व्, C. **चर्वयति**, pp. **चर्वित** chew, munch, sip, suck.

चर्वण n. chewing, sipping, tasting (also f. **आ**); food, nourishment.

चर्षणि a. agile, swift, active; f. pl. men, people, w. **पञ्च** the five races of men.

चर्षणिप्रा a. filling or nourishing men.

चर्षणीधृत् a. bearing or supporting men.

चर्षणीधृति f. support or protection of men.

चर्षणीसह् a. ruling or overpowering men.

चल्, **चलति** (°ते), pp. **चलित** (q.v.) get into motion, stir, budge; tremble, quiver, totter; set out, start, depart, pass away; walk, march; spread, be diffused; be troubled or disappointed; swerve, deviate, fall off from (abl.). C. **चलयति** or **चालयति** set in motion, shake, push, disturb, agitate; expel or turn off from (abl.). — **आ**, C. **आचालयति** set in motion, stir. **उद्** get off from, leave (abl.); also = **प्रोद्** set out, depart. **समुद्** start up or set out together. **परि** C. move, stir, turn round. **प्र** get in motion, shake, tremble; come forth, rise, start up; swerve or deviate from (abl.); proceed, advance, depart; be perplexed or troubled. C. set in motion, shake, stir. **वि** move to and fro, waver, totter, set out, start, fall off or down, depart, swerve or deviate from (abl.); be perplexed or disappointed. C. **विचालयति** set in motion, excite, turn from (abl.), shake, destroy. **प्रवि** get in motion, shake, tremble, swerve, deviate, leave from (abl.). **सम्** move, shake, tremble, proceed, advance, start or set off from (abl.). C. **संचालयति** set in motion, cause to tremble, remove, push away from (abl.).

†**चल** a. moving, shaking, trembling, stirring, tremulous, inconstant, fickle, variable, perishable; m. agitation, motion, trembling (also °**ता** f., °**त्व** n.); wind.

चलचित्त a. fickle-minded, inconstant; n. fickleness (also °**ता** f.).

चलन a. moving, going on foot, tremulous, fickle, wanton (woman); f. **ई** = seq.; n. stirring, trembling, shaking; motion, activity, function; swerving, leaving off (abl.)

चलनक m. n. a short petticoat.

चलाचल a. moving to and fro, wavering, unsteady, variable.

चलात्मन् a. fickle-minded, frivolous.

चलित n. moving to and fro.

चव्य n., **आ** f. a sort of pepper.

चषक s. vessel, cup, goblet.

चषाल m. n. top of a sacrificial post; p. °**वन्त्**.

चाक्रिक m. carrier, potter, oil-maker.

चाक्षुष, f. **ई** pertaining to the eye or sight, visible; m. patron. of the sixth Manu.

चाक्ष्म a. content, forbearing, gracious.

चाञ्चल्य n. unsteadiness, inconstancy.

चाट m. cheat, deceiver, fortune-teller.

चाटु m. n. courtesy, flattery, politeness.

चाटुकार a. courteous, polite; m. a flatterer.

चाणक्य a. made of chick-peas; m. N. of a celebrated minister and poet.

चाणूर m. N. of a king and a myth. wrestler (slain by Kṛṣṇa).

चाण्डाल m. = **चण्डाल**.

चातक m. the bird Cātaka (supposed to live only upon rain drops).

चातकाय्, pp. °**यित** behave like the Cātaka (v. prec.).

†**चातन** a. dispelling, removing (—°).

चातुर्थक & **चातुर्थिक** a. appearing every fourth day; s. the quartan ague.

चातुर्मास्य n. a cert. sacrifice (lasting four months); period of four months.

चातुर्य n. ability, dexterity, grace.

चातुर्वर्ण्य n. the four castes.

चातुर्विद्य & °**वैद्य** a. versed in the four Vedas; n. the four Vedas.

चातुर्होत्र a. performed by the four chief priests; n. such a sacrifice.

चातुष्प्राश्य a. enough for four to eat.

चात्त्र n. a kind of cylinder, esp. used for kindling fire.

चान्द्र (f. **ई**), °**क**, °**म**, & °**मस** (f. **ई**) lunar.

चान्द्रव्रतिक a. acting like the moon, moon-like.

चान्द्रायण m. observer of the moon's path; n. (± **व्रत**) the moon-penance (r.).

चाप m. n. bow.
चापगुण m. bow-string.
चापयष्टि f. the same; also = **चाप** alone.
चापल & **चापल्य** n. agility, haste, inconstancy, wantonness.
चापवेद m. skill in the managing of the bow.
चापाधिरोपण & **चापारोपण** n. the fastening of the string on the bow or the bending of the bow.
चापिन् a. armed with a bow.
चामर a. coming from the Yak; n. chowrie (= **चमर**).
चामीकर n. gold; °**मय**, f. **ई** golden.
चामुण्ड m. N. of an author; f. **आ** a form of Durgā.
चाय्, **चायति**, °**ते** fear, worship, revere; notice, observe, discern. — **अप** fear, revere. **नि** only ger. **निचाय्य** worship, observe, perceive.
चायु a. showing awe or respect.
चार m. course, way, behaviour, conduct; spy, scout.
चारक a. acting, proceeding, setting in motion (—°). m. spy, scout.
1**चारचक्षुस्** n. a spy as the eye (of a king).
2**चारचक्षुस्** a. spy-eyed, i.e. using spies to see.
चारण a. belonging to the (same) sect or school; m. wandering actor, celestial singer; spy, scout.
चारथ a. wandering.
चारितार्थ्य n. attainment of an object, success.
चारित्र n. conduct, esp. good conduct, virtue, reputation; abl. °**तस्**.
चारित्रावशेष a. having lost all but virtue (lit. having v. as rest).
चारित्र्य n. = **चारित्र**.
चारिन् a. movable, moving, going in, on, or to, living in or upon, acting like, doing, performing (—°); m. foot-soldier, spy.
चारु a. pleasant, lovely, beautiful, dear; n. adv.
चारुगीति f. N. of a metre.
चारुता f., °**त्व** n. pleasantness, charm, beauty.
चारुदत्त m. a man's name.
चारुदर्शन a. good-looking.
चारुनेत्र a. having beautiful eyes.
चारुप्रतीक a. of beautiful appearance.
चारुरूप a. of lovely form; m. a man's name.
चारुलोचन a. = **चारुनेत्र**.
चारुहासिन् a. smiling sweetly.
चारेक्षण a. = 2**चारचक्षुस्**.
***चार्चिक्य** n. smearing of the body, unguent (adj. —° besmeared with*).
चार्मिक a. leathern.
चार्य n. a cert. outcast; state of a spy or scout.
चार्वाक m. N. of a Rākṣasa & a sceptic philosopher; a. pertaining to C., m. pl. his followers.
चाल m. shaking (only —°).
चालन n. shaking, wagging, loosening, pushing away; f. **ई** sieve, strainer.
चाल्य a. to be moved or shaken.
चाष m. the blue jay.
1**चि**, **चिनोति**, **चिनुते** (**चेति**, **चयति**, **चिन्वति**), pp. **चित** (q.v.) heap up, pile up, arrange, construct, build (esp. the sacrific. altar); collect, gather; cover, inlay, set with (instr.); P. **चीयते** increase, thrive, abound. C. **चययति** & **चपयति**, **चाययति** & **चापयति**. — **अधि** heap or build upon (loc.). **अप** gather, collect; P. decrease, wane, get rid of (abl.). **अव** gather, pick off (*2 acc.), take off (a garment). **आ** & **समा** collect, accumulate; load, cover, furnish with (instr.). **उद्** gather, collect, pick off. **समुद्** = prec., also connect, add. **उप** connect, join; heap up, accumulate, augment, strengthen, cover, furnish with (instr.); P. increase, grow, get strong. **समुप** heap up, collect; P. increase, grow. **परि** pile up, accumulate; P. increase, grow. **प्र** gather, collect, accumulate, augment, strengthen; P. increase, become strong. **वि** pick out, select, segregate, sever, disperse, distribute. **संवि** select. **सम्** pile up, arrange, prepare, gather, accumulate. — Cf. 1**अपचित**, **आचित**, **उपचित**, 1**निचित**, 1**परिचित**, **प्रचित**, **समुपचित**, **संचित**.
2**चि**, **चिकेति**, **चिनोति**, **चिनुते** (**चयते**) observe, perceive, notice, seek for, search. — **अनु**

remember. अप respect, honour. नि notice, observe. निस् & विनिस् examine, consider, fix upon. परि search, examine, find out, discover. P. get acquainted. वि discern, distinguish, make clear, illustrate, examine, try, look for, strive after. प्रवि examine, try. सम् deliberate, ponder. — Cf. 2अपचित, अभिनिश्चित, 2निचित, निश्चित, 2परिचित, विनिश्चित.

3चि, चयते detest, hate, punish, revenge, take vengeance on (acc.).

चिकित् a. visible, clear, also = seq.

चिकिति a. knowing, wise.

चिकितु a. visible, manifest, clear; f. understanding, intellect.

चिकित्वंस् & °त्वन् a. attentive, knowing, wise.

चिकित्स् v. 1चित्.

चिकित्सक m. physician.

चिकित्सन n., चिकित्सा f., चिकित्सित n. medical attendance, art of healing.

चिकीर्ष् v. 1कृ.

चिकीर्षा f. wish to do; desire of, endeavour at (gen. or —°).

चिकीर्षित n. purpose, intention.

चिकीर्षु a. wishing to act, desirous of (acc. or —°).

चिकुर m. hair.

†चिकेतस् v. नचिकेतस्.

चिक्कण a. smooth, slippery.

चिच्चिक m. a cert. bird.

चिञ्चा f. the tamarind tree.

1चित्, चेतति, °ते, pp. चित्त (q.v.) perceive, observe, attend to (gen. or acc.), aim at, intend (dat.), strive after, desire (acc.), take care of (acc.); conceive, understand, know; intr. appear, be conspicuous or known. C. चेतयति, °ते & चितयति make attentive, remind, instruct, teach; notice, put to mind, attend to; M. (A.) be conscious or sensible, think, reflect, conceive, understand, remember; appear, be conspicuous, shine. D. चिकित्सति (°ते) intend, aim at, care for; treat medically, heal. I. चेकिते appear, shine. — आ attend to, call to mind, understand, know, find out, invent; intr. appear, shine, excel. प्र become visible, appear, also = C. perceive, understand, announce, proclaim. वि observe, discern conceive, know (also C.); M. be perceptible, appear. D. wish to discern, deliberate, doubt, hesitate. सम् perceive (together), survey, notice; be unanimous, agree. — Cf. चिकित्वंस्, चेकितान, विचित्त.

2चित् f. thought, mind, intelligence.

चित a. covered, strewn with (instr. or —°); f. आ layer, pile of wood, esp. funeral pile; n. building.

चिताग्नि m. the fire of the funeral pile.

चिताधूम m. the smoke of the funeral pile.

1चिति f. = चिता.

2चिति f. = 2चित्.

चित्त a. thought, observed, desired; n. attention, observation, idea (adj. —° thinking of); purpose, intent, wish, desire, intelligence, reason; the mind or heart.

चित्तखेद m. sorrow of the heart.

चित्तचौर m. thief of the heart.

चित्तज & °जन्मन् m. love or the god of love.

चित्तनाथ m. lord of the heart.

चित्तभ्रम m., चित्तभ्रान्ति f. confusion of the mind.

चित्तराग m. affection of the heart.*

चित्तवन्त् a. having reason, sensible.

चित्तविकार m. alteration of the mind.

चित्तविक्षेप m. distraction of the mind.*

चित्तवृत्ति f. condition of the mind, sentiment.

चित्ताकर्षिन् a. attracting the soul.

चित्तानुवर्तिन् a. compliant (to one's mind); abstr. °तित्व n. = seq.

चित्तानुवृत्ति f. compliance, obedience.

1चित्ति f. thinking, reason, intelligence, purpose, design; pl. devotion.

2चित्ति f. crackling.

चित्तिन् a. reasonable.

चित्य a. being arranged, heaped or piled (esp. the fire of the sacrif. pile); f. चित्या arranging, piling, building (of an altar or fun. pile).

चित्र a. conspicuous, visible, bright, clear, loud, variegated, manifold, various, excellent, extraordinary, strange, wonderful. f. आ N. of a lunar mansion. n. anything bright or shining, esp. jewel, ornament, picture; extraordinary appearance, wonder (often as exclamation).

चित्रक m. tiger or panther, a kind of snake, N. of sev. plants, also of sev. men, pl. of a people; n. mark, sign (adj. —° marked by), picture.

चित्रकर् & °कार् m. painter.

1चित्रकर्मन् n. painting or picture.

2चित्रकर्मन् a. having various occupations.

चित्रकूट m. N. of sev. mountains.

चित्रग & चित्रगत a. being in a picture, i.e. painted.

चित्रगृह n. a painted or picture house.

चित्रग्रीव m. Speckled-neck, N. of a pigeon king.

चित्रजवनिका f. a painted courtain.

चित्रन्यस्त a. put in a picture i.e. painted.

चित्रपट & °पट्ट m. painting, picture.

चित्रपरिचय m. knowledge i.e. skill in decorating or painting.*

चित्रफलक (m. n.*) tablet for painting, picture.

चित्रफलकगत a.* = चित्रग.

चित्रभानु a. shining bright; m. fire.

चित्रभित्ति f. a painted wall.

चित्रय्, °यति, pp. चित्रित make variegated, speckle, decorate, paint.

चित्ररथ a. having a bright chariot; m. N. of a Gandharva & sev. men.

चित्रराति & °राधस् a. granting brilliant gifts.

चित्रलिखन n. painting, drawing.

चित्रलिखित a. painted, drawn.

चित्रलेखा f. picture; a woman's name.

चित्रवन्त् a. painted or decorated with pictures.

चित्रवर्ति & °वर्तिका f. a painter's brush.

चित्रवाज a. of extraordinary swiftness.

चित्रशाला (& °शालिका*) f. picture-room.

चित्रशिखण्डिन् m. pl. E. of the seven Rishis (lit. having bright crests), as a constellation the Great Bear.

चित्रश्रवस्तम (superl.) uttering or worthy of, loud praise.

चित्रसेन a. furnished with brilliant weapons; m. N. of a serpent-demon, a Gandharva, & sev. men.

चित्राकृति f. picture.*

चित्राङ्ग m. N. of an antilope (lit. having a spotted body).

चित्राङ्गद a. having brilliant bracelets; m. N. of a Gandharva etc., f. आ of sev. women.

चित्रार्पित a. committed to a picture, painted.

चित्री w. कृ make into a picture.

चित्रीय्, °यते wonder, be surprised.

चित्र्य a. brilliant, sparkling.

चिद् adv. even, indeed, also, just, always, at every time; w. neg. not even. Often only emphasizing the prec. word; in l. l. only after an interrog. & जातु.

चिन्त्, चिन्तयति, °ते, pp. चिन्तित (q.v.) think, reflect, consider, find out, invent; think of, care for (acc., dat., loc., or प्रति); w. neg. not care for, not mind. — अनु meditate, consider, call to mind. समनु & अभि consider, ponder upon (acc.). परि meditate, ponder, think of, find out. प्र reflect, consider; invent. वि discern, observe, meditate, think of (acc.) or to (inf.), consider, regard, imagine, invent. सम् think, meditate, consider.

चिन्तक a. mindful of, intent upon (—°).

चिन्तन n. thinking of, consideration, reflection; care for (gen. or —°).

चिन्तनीय a. to be thought of, attended to, or found out.

चिन्तयान = चिन्तयमान.

चिन्ता f. thought, consideration, reflection, care or sorrow about (gen., loc., or उपरि).

चिन्तापर a. thoughtful, sorrowful.

चिन्तामणि m. the gem of thought (= the philosopher's stone); T. of sev. works.

चिन्तामोह m. confusion of the mind.

चिन्तित n. thought, reflection; anxiety, sorrow; purpose, design.

1चिन्त्य a. = चिन्तनीय, also uncertain, questionable.

2चिन्त्य ger. = चिन्तयित्वा (v. चिन्त्).

चिन्मय a. consisting of intelligence, spiritual.

चिन्मात्र a. consisting only of intelligence, quite spiritual.

चिपिट a. blunted, flat.

चिबुक n. the chin.

चिर a. long (of time), lasting, ancient, old.

n. delay; also adv. a long time, too long, long ago, w. कृ make long, put off, delay. चिर (°—) & any of the obl. cases adv. after a long time, long since, too late, at last, at length, finally.

चिरकार, °**कारि**, & °**कारिन्** a. acting slowly, delaying.

चिरकाल m. a long time.

चिरकृत a. done long ago.

चिरक्रमेण adv. slowly, softly.*

चिरजीविका f. long life.

चिरजीविन् a. living long.

चिरदृष्ट a. seen at length.*

चिरन्तन a. old, ancient; m. pl. the ancients.

चिरमित्र n. an old friend.

चिरय्, °**यति** (°**ते**) act slowly, delay.

चिररात्र s. a long time: °—, acc. & dat. adv.

चिरवास m. long sojourn.

चिरवेला f. a late hour.

चिरस्थित a. having stood for a long time.

चिराय्, °**यति** & °**ते** = **चिरय्**; pp. **चिरायित**.

चिरायुष a. giving long life.

चिरायुस् a. long-lived.

चिरि m. parrot.

चिरोषित a. departed long since.

चिर्भट m., **ई** f. a kind of cucumber.

चिर्भिट n., **आ** f. the same.

चिल्लि m. a cert. bird of prey; f. (also **चिल्ली**) a kind of pot-herb.

चिह्न n. sign, mark; adj. —° = seq. pp.

चिह्नय्, °**यति**, pp. **चिह्नित** mark, stamp, sign.

चीर्त्ति f. gathering, collecting.

चीत्कार m. cry, noise (lit. making cīt).

चीत्कारवन्त् a. accompanied by a cry.

चीत्कृत n., **चीत्कृति** f. = **चीत्कार**.

चीन m. pl. the Chinese.

चीनांशुक n. China cloth, silk.

चीर n. strip of bark or cloth, rag; f. **ई** cricket.

चीरचीवर n. bark-garment.

चीरवसन & **चीरवासस्** a. clothed in bark or rags.

चीरिका f. a written publication.

चीरिन् a. = **चीरवसन**.

चीरीवाक m. cricket.

चीर्णव्रत a. having fulfilled one's vow.

चीवर n. the dress of a mendicant; poss. °**वन्त्**.

चुक्र s. a kind of vinegar or the Indian sorrel.

चुचु & **चुचू** m. f. a kind of pot-herb.

चुट्, **चोटयति** w. **आ** scrape.

चुञ्चु m. a cert. mixed tribe.

चुण्टी f. a well.

चुद्, **चोदति**, °**ते** impel, incite, urge; M. hasten, speed. C. **चोदयति** (°**ते**) = S. + animate, accelerate, press; inspire, excite; turn, cast, direct; start (trans.), further, help on, bring or offer quickly; settle, fix. — **अभि** C. incite, encourage, summon, invite, request, command; ask, inquire for (acc.). **परि** C. set in motion, impel, summon, request. **प्र** push on, impel. C. the same + animate, inspire, inflame, summon, urge, request, command, etc. (v. **अभि**). **सम्** C. set in motion, impel, excite, inflame, summon, request, solicit; speed, procure quickly.

चुप्, **चोपति** stir, move (intr.).

†**चुबुक** n. chin, top of the altar.

चुम्ब्, **चुम्बति**, °**ते** kiss, touch; C. **चुम्बयति**. — **व्यति** touch closely. **परि** = S. **वि** kiss.

चुम्बन n. a kiss.

चुम्बिन् a. touching closely (—°).

चुर्, **चोरयति**, °**ते** steal, rob.

चुलुक m. n. the hollow of the hand, a handful or mouthful, a draught.

चुलुकय्, °**यति** swallow out of the hollowed hand, taste.

चुल्ली f. a chimney or a three-winged hall.

चूचुक a. stammering; n. the nipple of the breast.

चूड m. knob or protuberance (on bricks); the tonsure of a child (r.). f. **चूडा** the tuft or hair on the crown of the head, top i.g.; also = m. (r.).

चूडाकरण & °**कर्मन्** n. = prec. m. (r.).

चूडापीड m. chaplet worn on the crown of the head.

चुडामणि m. diadem (crest-jewel); the gem or best of (—°); abstr. °**ता** f.

चूत m. the mango tree.

चूतमञ्जरी f. = seq., N. of a woman.

चूतलतिका f. a mango blossom.

चूतशर m. the mango arrow (of the god of love.

चूर्, चूरयति steal.

चूरू m. a kind of worm.

चूर्ण a. ground, pulverized; m. n. dust, flour, powder.

चूर्णन n. grinding, pulverizing.

चूर्णय्, °यति, pp. **चूर्णित** grind, pulverize, crumble, crush. — **अव** strew with dust, flour, etc. **प्र, वि** & **सम्** = S.

चूर्णवृद्धि m. N. of a man.*

चूर्णग्रस् & **चूर्णी** w. **कृ** = **चूर्णय्**.

चूर्णीकरण n. = **चूर्णन**.

चूलक (adj. —°) tuft, crest; f. **चूलिका** the comb of a cock, crest, summit i.g.

चूलिन् a. having a crest.

चूल्ह m., **ई** f. fire-place, chimney.

चूष् P. boil, burn, be inflamed; C. **चूषयति** suck up. **सम्** P. = S. P.

चूषण n. sucking (of the leech).

चृत्, चृतति, pp. **चृत्त** (only —°) w. **अति** fasten connect, attach. **अव** let loose. **आ** & **उप** fasten, tie, affix. **नि** insert. **निस्** loosen, untie. **परि** wind round. tie together. **वि** untie, loosen, open, spread out. **सम्** be joined to (instr.).

चेकितान a. knowing, wise; N. of a man.

चेट m., **ई** f. male & female servant.

चेटक m., **चेटिका** f. the same.

चेतन (f. **चेतनी**) perceptible, visible, conspicuous, excellent; perceiving, conscious, intelligent. m. a sentient being, a man; f. **चेतना** consciousness, intelligence; n. appearance, perception, soul, mind.

चेतस् n. appearance, aspect, intelligence, consciousness, mind, heart, desire, fancy.

चेतिष्ठ (superl.) very conspicuous or bright.

चेतु m. attention, carefulness.

चेतृ m. avenger.

चेतोभव & °**भू** m. love or the god of love.

चेतोमुख a. whose mouth is intelligence.

चेत्तृ or **चेत्तृ** m. observer, guardian.

चेद् conj. (= **च** + **इद्**) and; also, even (w. prec. **अपि**); when, if (often prec. by **इति** = if thus, in this case). **अथ चेद्** but if. **न चेद् (चेन्न)** or **नो चेद्** if not, else. Rarely **यदि चेद्** = **चेद्** alone.

चेदि m. pl. N. of a people; sgl. their ancestor.

चेय a. to be heaped up or collected.

चेरु a. active, busy (at the sacrifice).

चेल v. **चैल**.

चेष्ट्, चेष्टति, °**ते**, pp. **चेष्टित** (q.v.) move the limbs, stir, exert one's self, be active or busy, be engaged in (acc.); act or behave towards (loc.); make, do, perform. C. **चेष्टयति**, °**ते** set in motion, impel. — **आ** make, perform. **परि** wallow, roam about. **वि** move the limbs, writhe, struggle, stir, be active or busy, act or behave towards (loc.), effect, produce. **सम्** be restless, exert one's self, act. — Cf. **विचेष्टित**.

चेष्ट n. motion, gesture, effort, activity; conduct, behaviour.

चेष्टन n., **चेष्टा** f. the same; making, doing.

चेष्टावन्त् a. movable.

चेष्टित n. = **चेष्ट**.

चैतन्य n. consciousness, intelligence, mind, soul.

चैतन्यचन्द्रोदय m. the moonrise of intelligence (a play).

चैत्त a. mental, spiritual.

1**चैत्य** m. the individual soul.

2**चैत्य** a. relating to the funeral pile; m. monument, tombstone, temple, also = seq.

चैत्यतरु m. a sacred fig tree.

चैत्यद्रुम & **चैत्यवृक्ष** m. the same.

चैत्र m. N. of a month in spring.

चैत्ररथ a. pertaining to the Gandharva Citraratha; n. (± **वन**) C.'s wood.

चैत्रविभावरी f. a night in spring (cf. **चैत्र**).

चैद्य m. descendant of Cedi or king of the Cedis.

चैल n. cloth, garment.

चैलधाव & **निर्णेजक** m. a washerman.

चैलवत् adv. as (of) a cloth.

चैलाशक m. a cert. goblin.

चोक n. a kind of root.

चोक्ष a. clean (of persons).

चोच n. the bark of a kind of cinnamon.

चोड m. pl. N. of a people.

1**चोद** m. goad, whip.

2**चोद** a. impelling, driving.

चोदक a. impelling, driving.
चोदन a. = prec.; f. आ & n. impulse, summons, precept.
चोदयितृ m., °त्री f. impeller, promoter.
चोदितृ m. the same.
चोर & चोरक m. thief; *चोरिका f. theft.
चोरिकाविवाह m. secret (lit. theft-) marriage.*
चोल m. jacket, bodice; pl. N. of a people.
चोलमण्डल n. the coast of Coromandel.
चोष a. sucking (—°); m. heat, inflammation.
चोषण n. sucking.
चौक्ष & चौक्ष्य a. = चोक्ष.
चौड n. = चूड (r.).
चौर m., ई f. thief, robber.
चौरकिल्बिष n. the guilt of a thief.
चौरशङ्किन् a. fearing thieves or robbers.
चौरिका f. theft.
चौरीसुरतपञ्चाशिका f. T. of a poem.
चौर्य & °क n. theft.
चौल n. = चूड (r.).
†च्यव v. भुवनच्यव.
च्यवन a. shaking or shaken. m. a man's name; n. motion, shock, loss of (—°).
†च्यवस् v. तृषुच्यवस्.
च्यवान a. stirring, active; m. N. of a Rishi.
च्यावन a. causing to fall; n. expulsion, deprivation.
च्यु, च्यवते (°ति), pp. च्युत move, stir, waver, shake; go away, escape, fall, flow, retire from, get rid or be deprived of (abl.), sink (l. & f.), decrease, wane, vanish. C. च्यावयति (च्यवयति) set in motion, shake, agitate (M. intr.); cause to fall or drop, pour out, loosen; remove or expel from (abl.), deprive of (2 acc.). — आ C. cause to flow over, pour out. उद् C. draw out, extract. परि get loose; fall, descend, swerve or part from, get rid of (abl.), sink down, decline. प्र start, proceed; get off, flow out, pour down, descend, part from, get rid or be deprived of (abl.). C. move, shake, drive away, expel, drop down, divert from (abl.), cause to fall, ruin. अनुप्र rush after, follow (acc.). वि go or fall asunder; go away, fall off, part from (abl.) fail, be lost. — Cf. प्रच्योतास्.
1च्युत् a. moving (intr.); shaking, destroying (—°).
2च्युत्, च्योतति drop, sprinkle.
3च्युत् a. dropping, sprinkling (—°).
†च्युति f. departing or dropping from (—°), falling down, descending; falling off, swerving, deviating from (abl.); vanishing, perishing, dying.
च्यौत्न a. impelling, promoting. n. shock, concussion, enterprise, exertion, endeavour.

छ

छगल m., ई f. a goat.
छटा f. mass, lump, multitude.
छत्त्र n. parasol (emblem of royalty).
छत्त्रधार m. bearer of a parasol or umbrella; abstr. °त्व n.
छत्त्रधारण n. the bearing of a parasol.
छत्त्रधारिन् a. bearing a parasol.
छत्त्रवन्त् a. having a parasol.
छत्त्रवृक्ष m. N. of a tree.
छत्त्राक n. mushroom.
छत्त्रिन् m. = छत्त्रधार + prince, king.
छत्त्रोपानह n. a parasol and shoes.
1छद्, only pp. छन्न (q.v.) & C. छादयति (°ते) cover, veil, hide, conceal, keep secret. — अभि C. cover. अव C. cover, overspread, hide, veil, obscure, conceal. आ C. cover, clothe (M. also refl.), hide, obscure. परि C. wrap round, envelop, cover. प्र C. cover (M. refl.), hide, veil in (instr:), conceal, keep secret. प्रति C. overspread, clothe, envelop. सम् the same. — Cf. अवच्छन्न, आच्छन्न, उपच्छन्न, परिच्छन्न, प्रच्छन्न, प्रतिच्छन्न, संछन्न.
2छद् & छन्द्, छन्त्ति, छन्दति, छदयति (°ते) seem, appear, pass for (nom.), please; M. like, be pleased with (acc. or loc.).

C. छन्दयति offer (w. acc. of pers. & instr. of th.); allure, strive to corrupt. — उप C. = S. C. सम् offer (= S. C.).

छद् a. covering (—°); m. cover, veil, wing, leaf.

छदन n. = prec. m.

छदि & छदिन् a. covering (—°).

छदिंस् n. cover, roof, thatch.

छद्मन् n. the same + veil, disguise; plea, pretext, trick, deceit, fraud; °— feigned, only apparently (cf. seq.).

छद्मरूपिन् & छद्मिन् a. having the feigned form of, disguised as (—°).

छन्द् v. 2छद्.

छंन्द or छन्दं a. pleasant, alluring. m. appearance, shape; delight, pleasure; wish, desire. Instr. & abl. at one's own pleasure or will, freely; at the pleasure or will of (gen. or —°).

छन्दक & छन्दन a. charming, winning.

छन्दःशास्त्र n. metrical science, prosody.

छंन्दस् n. delight, pleasure, wish, desire; fancy, ideal; incantation, holy song, sacred text or Veda; metre, also = prec.

छन्दस्कृत a. metrically composed; n. any metrical part of the Vedas.

छन्दस्य a. pertaining to hymns, metrical.

छंन्दस्वन्त् a. desirous.

छन्दःसूत्र n. manual of prosody.

छन्दःस्तुत् & °स्तुंभ् a. praising in hymns.

छंन्दु a. pleasing, charming.

छन्दोगं m. chanter of holy songs.

छन्दोमञ्जरि or °री f. garland of metres, T. of a treatise on prosody.

छन्दोमंय (f. ई*) & छन्दोवन्त्* a. = छन्दस्य.

छन्दोविचिति f. question about metres, T. of a treatise on prosody.

छन्दोवृत्त n. metre.

छंन्द्य a. pleasing.

छन्न a. covered, veiled, concealed, secret; n. cover, secret place, also adv. = °— secretly, low.

छर्दन n., छर्दि f. vomiting.

1छर्दिस् n. refuge, secure place.

2छर्दिस् n. vomiting.

छल n. (m.) fraud, deceit, pretence, delusion, appearance, fiction. °— & instr. with fraud, deceitfully; छलतस् unter the disguise of (— °).

छलन n. deceiving, cheating.

छलय्, °यति, pp. छलित deceive, cheat. — उप = S.

छलिक n. a kind of song or dance.

छवि or (older) छवी f. skin, hide; complexion, colour; beauty, splendour.

छा, छाति, pp. छित (only —°) & छात (q.v.) cut off. — अव flay, skin. आ the same, cut off. प्र bleed, scarify.

1छांग m. ram, goat; f. छांगा & छागी she-goat.

2छाग a. coming from a goat.

छागमांस n. flesh of a goat.

छागल = छाग 1 m. & 2.

छात a. lean, thin, weak.

छात्त्र m. pupil; abstr. °ता f.

छादक a. covering, veiling.

छादन n. cover, screen, clothing.

छादिन् (— °) = छादक.

छाद्मिक a. deceitful, fraudulent.

छान्दस, f. ई Vedic, archaic; metrical.

छान्दोग्य & °ब्राह्मण n. T. of a Brāhmaṇa.

छान्दोग्योपनिषद् f. T. of an Upanishad.

छाय a. shadowing; f. छाया shadow (lit. & fig., also personif. as wife of the Sun); image, reflection; translation (esp. from Prākrit into Sanskrit); lustre, colour, complexion, beauty, charm, grace.

छायातप m. du. shadow and sunlight.

छायातरु & छायाद्रुम m. an umbrageous tree.

छायाद्वितीय a. casting a shadow (lit. having one's shadow as second).

छायानाटक n. a kind of drama.

छायामंय a. shadowy, reflected.

छायावन्त् a. shadowy.

छायासंज्ञा f. Chāyā as Saṁjñā.

छालिक्य n. a kind of song.

छिक्कर m. a cert. animal.

छिक्का f. sneezing.

छिक्कार m. a kind of antelope.

1छिद्, छिनंत्ति, छिन्ते (छिन्दति), pp. छिन्न (q.v.) cut, hew or tear off, chop, rend, split, pierce, separate, divide, interrupt, disturb, destroy. C. छेदयति cause to cut etc., also = S. — अन्तर् cut off, intercept. अव reject; P. be severed from (abl.). व्यव cut off, split, sever from (abl.), interrupt. आ the same; take away, rob, remove, destroy; disregard, neglect. P. उद् cut out or off, destroy, interrupt, impede, disturb: P. cease, fail. समुद् tear out, exterminate. परि cut on both sides, clip round, mow; limit on all sides, fix accurately, define, decide. प्र tear, cut or hew off, split, pierce, snatch away, rob. वि tear or break asunder, separate, divide, disturb, interrupt, destroy. सम् cut or hew off, split, pierce, destroy (a doubt), decide (a question). — Cf. अवच्छिन्न, उच्छिन्न, विच्छिन्न.

2छिद् a. cutting off, breaking, splitting, piercing, destroying, removing (—°); f. as subst.

छिदुर a. easily breaking, decreasing; destroying (—°).

छिद्र a. torn, rent, pierced; n. hole, fissure, opening, interruption, defect, weakness, flaw, fault. Abstr. °ता† f.

छिद्रय्, °यति, pp. छिद्रित making holes, pierce.

छिद्रानुसारिन् a. looking out for the faults of (gen.).

छिद्रिन् a. having holes, hollow.

छिन्न a. cut off or in, carved, incoherent; included by (—°), broken, destroyed, vanished.

छिन्नद्वैध a. whose doubts have been destroyed.

छिन्ननास्य a. having the nose-string cut or broken.

छिन्नपक्ष a. having the wings torn off.

छिन्नमूल a. cut up by the root.

छिन्नसंशय a. whose doubts are dispelled.

छिन्नाभ्र n. a cloud torn asunder.

छुच्छु m. a cert. animal.

छुच्छुन्दर & °रि m. the musk rat.

छुच्छून्दर m., °री f. the same.

छुट्, C. pp. आच्छोटित torn.

छुड्, C. प्रच्छोडयति stretch out.

छुबुक n. chin.

छुर्, छुरयति (छोरयति), pp. छुरित bestrew, beset, inlay. — आ pp. clothed. वि pp. = S. pp.

छुरिका f. knife.

छूरिका f. the same, a cow's mouth.

छृद्, छृणत्ति, pp. छृण्ण pour out or upon, eject, spue, vomit. C. छर्दयति the same, make overflow. — आ pour upon, fill. प्र C. vomit, eject. वि C. cast off, abandon.*

छेक a. clever, shrewd.

छेकोक्ति f. clever speech, insinuation.

छेत्तव्य a. to be cut or split.

छेत्तृ m. cutter, esp. wood-cutter; destroyer.

छेद m. cutter; a cut, section, piece, portion; cutting, dividing, separation, interruption, disturbance; decrease, cessation, loss, want; decision, definition.

छेदक a. cutting off.

छेदन a. the same, hewing, splitting, destroying, removing; n. the act of cutting off etc.

छेदनीय a. = छेत्तव्य.

छेदिन् a. = छेदन a.

छेद्य a. = छेत्तव्य; n. the act of cutting off etc.

छेलक m., छेलिका f. goat.

छोटन n. cutting off.

छोटिका f. snapping of the thumb and forefinger.

ज

ज a. born, produced, caused by, in, or from; made of, living at, belonging to, connected with (—°). f. जा race; —° daughter.

जंहस् n. wing.

1जक्ष्, जक्षिति (जक्षति), pp. जग्ध (q.v.) eat, consume. — प्र & वि = S. pp.

2जक्ष्, only pp. जक्षत् laughing.

जंगत् a. moving, alive. m. pl. men; f. जंगती

a female animal, the earth or world, N. of a metre; n. what moves or is alive, men and (or) animals, the earth, world or universe, du. heaven and the lower world.

जगतीगत a. existing on earth.

जगतीतल n. the surface of the earth.

जगतीपति, °पाल, & °भर्तृ m. king.

जगत्कारण n. the cause of the world.

जगत्त्रय & जगत्त्रितय n. the three worlds, i.e. heaven, earth, and the lower world.

जगत्पति m. the lord of the world, E. of sev. gods.

जगत्प्रकाश a. illuminating the world or known in the world.

जगत्प्रभु m. = जगत्पति.

जगत्स्रष्टृ m. the creator of the world, Brahman.

जगत्स्वामिन् m. = जगत्पति, abstr. °स्वामित्व n.

जगदण्ड n. the egg of the world, the universe.

जगदीश m. = जगत्पति.

जगदीश्वर m. the same; prince, king.

जगद्गुरु m. father of the world, E. of sev. gods.

जगद्दीप m. light of the world, the sun.

जगद्धातृ m. creator of the world, E. of sev. gods.

जगद्योनि f. the womb of the world.

जगन्नाथ m. lord of the world, N. of sev. gods & men.

जगन्निवास m. abode of the world (Viṣṇu-Kṛṣṇa or Çiva).

जगन्मातृ f. mother of the world (Durgā or Lakṣmī).

जंगुरि a. leading (a way).

जग्धं a. eaten, consumed; exhausted by (instr.).

जग्धतृण a. having eaten grass.

जग्धार्ध a. half eaten.

जंग्धि f. eating, food, victuals.

जंग्मि a. going, stirring; hastening towards —°).

जघंन m. n. hinder part, rear of an army (also जघनार्ध m.); the hips or pudenda.

जघनचपला f. libidinous woman (lit. moving the hips); N. of a metre.

जघंनेन (instr. adv.) behind, after (w. gen. or acc.).

जघन्य a. hindmost, last, latest, lowest.

जघन्यज a. last born, youngest.

जघन्यप्रभव a. of low origin.

जंघ्नि a. striking.

जंघ्रि a. sprinkling about.

जङ्ग m. N. of a man.

जङ्गम a. going, moving, living (abstr. °त्व n.); n. what is moving or alive.

जङ्गिड m. N. of a plant.

जंङ्घा f. leg, esp. its under part.

जङ्घानलक m. n. bone of the leg.

जङ्घाबल n. the power of the legs, i.e. running, flight.*

जङ्घाल a. running, swift.

जज m. warrior.

जंज्ञि a. germinating, shooting.

जझ्झ्, only pp. f. pl. **जंझ्झतीस्** splashing waters.

जञ्झ् pp. f. **जंञ्झती** glittering, flashing.

जञ्झणा w. **भंवन्त्** glittering.

जटा f. twisted or matted hair (worn by ascetics and mourners).

जटाकलाप m. tress of hair twisted on the top of the head.

जटाचीरधर a. wearing matted hair and a garment of bark.

जटाजूट m. = जटाकलाप.

जटाधर a. wearing matted hair; m. an ascetic or Çiva.

जटाधारिन् a. = prec. adj.

जटाभार m. = जटाजूट.

जटाभारधर a. wearing a tuft of matted hair.

जटामण्डल n. hair braided in a coil on the top of the head.

जटायु & °युस् m. N. of a fabulous vulture.

जटाल a. wearing a coil of twisted hair.

जटिन् a. the same; m. an ascetic or Çiva.

जटिल a. = prec. a. + confused, full of (—°); m. = prec. m.

1**जठंर** n. belly, stomach, womb; cavity, hole.

2**जठर** a. = जरठ.

जड a. cold, cool; apathetic, stupid, idiotic; m. an idiot. — Abstr. °ता f., °त्व n.

जडप्रकृति a. of a stupid nature.

जडबुद्धि & जडमति a. of a stupid mind.

जडय्, °यति stun, stupify.

जडांशु m. the moon.
जडात्मक & ॰त्मन् a. cool or stupid (by nature).
जडाय्, ॰यते be insensible or dumb.
जडिमन् m. coolness, frigidity, apathy, stupidity.
जडी w. कृ = जडय् ; ॰भू become stupid.
जडीभाव m. = जडिमन्.
जतु n. lac, gum.
जतुगृह & ॰गेह n. the lac-house (in the Mahābhārata).
जतुमुद्रा f. lac-seal.*
जतू f. a bat.
जत्रु m. pl. cert. bones (supposed to be 16); n. the collar bone.
जन्, जायते (॰ति), older जनति, ॰ते, pp. जात (q.v.) be born or produced, grow, be born again, be by birth or nature, be destined for (acc.), become (nom. or *dat.); be, take place, happen, be possible or suitable; generate, beget with (loc.), bring forth, produce, cause, effect. The older pres. stem & C. जनयति, ॰ते have only the trans. mgs. — अधि be born, become, be. अनु be born later or after (acc.); take after, resemble (acc.). अभि be born or destined to (acc.), be born, become (nom.). आ be born. C. beget; cause to be born for (dat.), make prolific. उद् beget, produce; be born, arise. उप be produced in addition, be born (again), appear, arise. C. procreate, cause, effect, attempt. समुप arise, appear, be born (again). C. produce, cause. प्र be born (again), arise, propagate offspring through or in (instr.), bring forth, beget with (loc. or instr.). C. cause to propagate offspring or to be born, beget, generate. प्रति be born again. वि be born, arise, become, be changed into (nom.); propagate offspring, beget, bring forth. सम् be born with (instr.), come forth, appear, take place, become, pass; bring forth. C. beget, bring forth, produce, generate, cause. — Cf. अनुजात, अभिजात, प्रजात.
1जन m. creature, man, person, tribe, race, nation; pl. & sgl. coll. people, folks. Often —॰ w. collect. or indiv. mg, e.g. प्रेष्यजन a servant or the servants. — अयं जनः & एष जनः this person (= I or he, she). f. जना birth, production.
2जन m. N. of a man.
जनक a. generating, producing, causing. m. progenitor, father, N. of sev. kings etc.
जनकतनया, ॰सुता, & जनकात्मजा f. the daughter of Janaka (Sītā).
जनता f. assemblage of men, community, people, subjects, mankind.
जनदेव m. a king (god of men).
जनन, f. ई = जनक a.; m. progenitor, creator, f. ई mother; n. producing, causing; birth, life.
जनपति m. a king (ruler of men).
जनान्तर n. some other or former birth.
जननि f. = जननी, v. जनन.
जनपद m. district, country (lit. tribe-place); (also pl.) people, esp. country people, subjects (opp. prince).
जनप्रवाद m. sgl. & pl. talk of men, rumour.
जनमरक m. epidemic disease, pestilene.
जनमार m., ॰मारी f. the same.
जनमेजय m. N. of sev. men, esp. princes.
जनयितृ m. progenitor, father; f. ॰त्री mother.
जनरव m. = जनप्रवाद.
जनराज् & ॰राजन् m. king (of men).
जनवाद m. = जनप्रवाद.
जनस् n. race; as indecl. (also जनर्) N. of a cert. world.
जनसंमर्द m. throng of people, crowd.
जनस्थान n. N. of a part of the Daṇḍaka forest.
जनाधिप m. ruler of men, king.
जनान्तिकम् adv. to a (single) person, i.e. secretly, under one's breath.
जनापवाद m. pl. evil talk of men.
जनारव m. = जनप्रवाद.
जनार्णव m. crowd (lit. sea) of men, caravan.
जनार्दन m. E. of Viṣṇu-Kṛṣṇa.
जनि & जनी f. woman, wife, pl. metaph. the fingers; जनि also birth, origin, birthplace.
जनिकर्तृ a. originating or generating, producing (f. ॰त्री).

जनितृ or जनितृ m. progenitor, father; f. जनित्री mother.

जनित्र n. birthplace, home, origin; pl. parents, relatives.

1जनित्व a. to be born or produced.

2जनित्व n. the state of a wife.

जनिमन् n. birth, origin; offspring, descendants; creature, being; race, kind.

जनिमन्त् & जनिवन्त् a. having a wife or wives.

जनिष्ठ (superl.) very generative.

जनिष्य a. = 1जनित्व.

जनी v. जनि.

जनुस् n. birth, origin, birthplace; creature, being; creation, production, work; race, kind. Instr. जनुषा by birth or nature, essentially, necessarily.

जनेन्द्र, जनेश, & जनेश्वर m. lord of men, king.

जन्तु m. creature, being, any animal, esp. worms, insects, etc.; man, person (sgl. also coll.); attendant, servant; child, descendant.

जन्त्व a. = 1जनित्व.

जन्मकाल m. time of birth.

जन्मकृत् m. progenitor, father.

जन्मक्षेत्र n. birthplace.

जन्मतस् adv. according to birth or age.

जन्मद a. giving birth to (—°); m. father.

जन्मदिन n. birthday.

जन्मन् n. birth, origin, new birth; existence, life; birthplace, home; progenitor, father (esp. —° begotten by); creature, being; relatives, people i.g.; race, kind; nature, quality.

जन्मप्रतिष्ठा f. mother (lit. support of the race).

जन्मभाज् m. living creature, a being (lit. possessing birth).

जन्मभू & °भूमि f. birthplace, home.

जन्ममृत्यु m. du. birth and death.

जन्मलाभ m. (the gain of) birth.*

जन्मस्थान n. birthplace, home.

जन्मान्तर n. another birth or life. °गत newborn.

जन्मान्तरगत a. born anew.

जन्मास्पद n. birthplace.

जन्मिन् m. creature, man.

1जन्य a. born, produced, rising from (—°); abstr. °ता f., °त्व n. — n. body.

2जन्य a. belonging to the (same) race, national, native; common, vulgar. — m. the bridegroom's friend; f. आ bridesmaid; n. people, tribe, race (also जन्य), pl. inimical tribes; fighting, war.

जन्ययात्रा f. the procession of the bridegroom's friend.

जप्, जपति, °ते, pp. जपित & जप्त whisper, mutter, esp. prayers, invoke in a low voice. — आ mutter into (कर्णे). उप whisper to i.e. bring over secretly. सम् whisper or talk about.

जप a. whispering, muttering; m. muttering prayers, a muttered prayer or spell.

जपन n. = prec. m.

जपमाला f. a rosary.

जपयज्ञ m. a sacrifice consisting of muttered prayers.

जपहोम m. sgl. & pl. the same or (= du.) muttered prayers and ablations.

जपा f. the China rose.

जपापीड m. a garland of Japā flowers.*

जपिन् a. muttering prayers.

जप्य a. the same; n. (m.) whisper or prayer.

जभ् or जम्भ् snap at (अपि), seize with the mouth. C. जम्भयति crush, destroy. I. जञ्जभ्यते open the jaws, snap at; w. अभि the same.

जमदग्नि m. N. of a Rishi.

जम्बाल s. mud, clay.

जम्बीर m. the citron tree; n. a citron.

जम्बु or जम्बू f. the rose-apple tree; n. its fruit.

जम्बुक m. a jackal (used also as an abusive word).

जम्बुद्वीप m. the continent abounding in rose-apple trees, i.e. India, thought as one of the 7 Dvīpas.

जम्बूक m. = जम्बुक.

जम्बूखण्ड m. n., जम्बूद्वीप m. = जम्बुद्वीप.

1जम्भ m. tooth, tusk, the jaws, mouth; swallowing, devouring.

2जम्भ m. crusher, devourer; N. of a cert. demons.

जंभक a. crushing, devouring (—°); m. E. of cert. demons.

जंभन, f. **ई** crushing, destroying.

जम्भलिका f. a kind of song.

जंभ्य m. front- or back-tooth; pl. the jaws.

1**जय** a. conquering, winning (—°); pl. cert. verses or formulas causing victory.

2**जय** m. conquest, victory, gain.

जयकुञ्जर m. a victorious elephant.

जयकृत् a. causing victory.

जयघोष m., **°ण** n., **°णा** f. shout of victory.

जयद a. giving victory.

जयदेव m. N. of sev. poets.

जयद्रथ m. a man's name.

जयध्वज m. flag of victory.

जयन्त m. N. of a son of Indra; E. of sev. gods.

जयपताका f. = **जयध्वज**.

जयपराजय (m. du. & n. sgl.) victory or defeat, gain or loss.

जयप्रेप्सु a. desirous of victory.

जयलक्ष्मी f. the fortune or goddess of victory.

जयवर्मन् m. a man's name.

जयशब्द m. = **जयघोष**.

जयश्री f. = **जयलक्ष्मी**.

जयसेन m , **आ** f. a man's & woman's name.

जयाजय (m. du. & n. sgl.) victory or defeat.

जयादित्य m. a man's name.

जयाशिस् f. prayer for or cheer of victory.

जयितृ, f. **°त्री** victorious.

जयिन् a. conquering, winning, a conqueror (gen. or —°); granting victory.

जयिष्णु & **जयुस्** a. victorious.

जयेन्द्र m. a man's name.

जयेश्वर m. lord of victory, E. of Çiva.

जयैषिन् a. wishing to conquer (—°).

जयोत्तर a. full or certain of victory.

जय्य a. to be won or conquered.

जर्, **जरते** (cf. **चर्**) awake, stir, move, approach (acc.). C. **जरयति**, **°ते** awaken, set in motion.

जर m. wearing out, wasting; f. **जरा** the same; decay, old age.

जरठ a. old, aged; hard, solid, strong.

जरण a. infirm, old; f. **आ** old age.

जरणा f. decrepitude.

जरण्यु a. calling aloud, calling to (dat.).

जरत्कारु m. f. N. of an ancient Rishi & his wife.

जरत्कारुप्रिया f. = prec. f.

जरदष्टि a. long-lived; f. longevity.

जरद्गव m. an old bull; N. of a vulture.

जरद्योषित् f. an old woman.

जरन्त्, f. **जरती** decayed, infirm, dry; old, ancient, former; m. an old man.

जरस् f. decrepitude, old age.

1**जरा** f. v. **जर**.

2**जरा** f. crackling, roaring; calling, greeting.

जराजर्जर a. infirm with age.

जरायु n. the cast-off skin of a serpent; (also f.) the chorion or outer skin of the embryo, after-birth, secundines.

जरायुज a. born from the womb.

जरावन्त् a. old, aged.

जरासंध m. N. of sev. kings.

जरिता f. N. of a myth. bird.

जरितारि m. N. of the son of Jaritā (v. prec.).

जरितृ m. invoker, singer, worshipper.

जरिमन् m. old age, decay, death.

जर्जर & **°रित** a. decayed, worn out, broken, hurt, tattered, perforated; abstr. **°रत्व** n.

जर्जरी कृ wear out, hurt, break, split; **°भू** the same pass.

जर्भरि a. supporting, nourishing.

जर्भुर् v. **भुर्**.

1**जल** n. water (also pl.); abstr. **°ता** f.

2**जल** a. = **जड**.

जलक्रिया f. offering water, funeral ceremony.

जलखग m. aquatic bird.

जलचर m. aquatic animal, fish.

जलचारिन् a. living in or near water; m. = prec.

जलज a. born or produced in water; m. = prec. m.; n. product of the sea, pearl, shell, the lotus.

जलजन्तु m. aquatic animal.

जलजीविन् a. living in, near, or on water; m. fisherman.

जलत्रास m. hydrophobia.

जलद m. a cloud (rain-giver).

जलदागम m. coming of the clouds, the rainy season.

जलद्रव्य n. product of the sea, pearls etc.
जलधर m. cloud (lit. water-bearer).
जलधारा f. flood or gush of water.
जलधि m. ocean, sea.
जलनिधि m. the same.
जलनिधिनाथ m. the Ocean (personif.).
जलपान n. drinking water.*
जलबिन्दु m. drop of water.
जलबुद्बुद m. bubble of water.
जलभाजन n. vessel for water.
जलमय, f. **ई** consisting of water, watery.
जलमुच् a. shedding water; m. a cloud.
जलयन्त्र & **°क** n. water-engine.
जलराक्षसी f. N. of a sea-monster.
जलराशि m. the ocean.
जलरुह (*m.) lotus (growing in water).
जलरुह m. aquatic animal; n. = prec.
जलवन्त् a. abounding in water.
1**जलवास** m. residence in water.
2**जलवास** a. = seq.
जलवासिन् a. living in water.
जलवाह a. bearing water; **°क** m. w.-carrier.
जलविहंगम m. water-fowl.
जलशय्या f. lying in water.
जलसंध m. N. of a son of Dhṛtarāṣṭra.
जलस्थ a. being in water.
जलस्थान n., **°स्थाय** m. pond, lake.
जलस्नान n. bathing, bath.
जलहार m. water-carrier, f. **ई**.
जलहीन a. waterless, dry.
जलागम m. rain (coming of water).
जलाञ्जलि m. two handfuls of water (for the dead), the last farewell.
जलाधार m. pond, lake.
जलायुका f. leech.
जलार्थिन् a. desirous of water, thirsty.
जलार्द्र a. wet with water; f. **आ** a wet cloth.
जलावसेक m. shower of rain.
1**जलाशय** m. pond, lake, sea.
2**जलाशय** a. lying or resting in water.
जलाष a. appeasing, healing.
जलाषभेषज a. having healing medicines.
जलेचर, f. **ई** living in water; m. (adj. —° f. **आ**) aquatic animal.
जलेश m. the sea or its lord i.e. Varuṇa.
जलेशय a. resting or living in water.
जलेश्वर m. Varuṇa (the lord of the waters).
जलोदर n. dropsy (water-belly).
जलोद्धतगति f. N. of a metre.
जलोद्भव a. born in water; m. aquatic animal.
जलौक (m.), **आ** f. leech.
जलौकस् a. living in or near water; m. aquatic animal, f. leech.
जलौकावचारणीय a. relating to the application of leeches.
जलौकोऽवसेक m. bleeding by (the application of) leeches.
जलौकोव्रण s. a wound made by a leech.
जल्प्, **जल्पति** (**°ते**), pp. **जल्पित** (q.v.) murmur, chatter, talk; address, speak to (acc. or instr. ± **सार्धम्**), speak of (acc.). — **अभि** address, answer, talk over, suggest, advise. **उप** & **परि** chatter. **प्र** speak, announce, proclaim. **वि** speak, utter. **सम्** talk, speak. — Cf. **प्रजल्पित**.
जल्प m., **°न** n. chat, talk, conversation.
जल्पक or **जल्पाक** a. talkative.
जल्पि f. murmur, speaking in an undertone.
जल्पित n. chat, talk.
जल्पिन् a. speaking, talking (—°).
जल्प्य n. chat, talk.
जव a. hastening, quick; m. haste, speed.
जवन, f. **ई** impelling; quick, swift; n. = prec. m.
जवनिका f. screen, curtain.
जवस् n. quickness, velocity.
जवा f. = **जपा**.
जविन् a. hastening, running, quick.
जविष्ठ (superl.) quickest, fleetest.
जवीयंस् (compar.) quicker, speedier.
जष m. a cert. aquatic animal.
जस्, **जसते** be exhausted, languish. C. **जासयति** exhaust, weaken. — **उद्** C. destroy (gen. or acc.). **नि** (**जस्यति**) perish, disappear. C. exhaust.
जसु f. exhaustion, weakness.
जसुरि a. exhausted, tired.
†**जस्र** v. **अजस्र**.
जस्वन् a. needy, wretched, poor.
जहका f. hedge-hog.
जहल्लक्षणा f. a rhet. figure in which a word loses its original meaning.

जहितं a. abandoned, forlorn.
जहु m. a young animal.
जह्नु m. N. of an ancient king; pl. his race.
जह्नुकन्या & जह्नुसुता f. the daughter of Jahnu, E. of Gaṅgā.
जा (—°) = ज; m. f. (nom. जास्) offspring.
जागत a. composed in the Jagatī metre, pertaining to it, etc.; n. the Jagatī metre.
जागर & °क m. state of waking.
जागरण a. awake; n. = prec.
जागरित a. having waked; n. = n. prec.
जागरितस्थान a. being in the state of waking.
जागरितान्त m. the state of waking.
जागरिष्णु a. wide or much awake.
जागरूक a. waking, watchful, attentive.
जागृ v. 3गृ.
जागृवंस् a. watchful, eager, indefatigable.
जागृवि a. watchful, attentive, quick, exciting.
जाग्रत् a. waking; s. the state of waking.
जाग्रत्स्वप्न m. du. waking and sleeping.
जाघनी f. tail.
जाङ्गल a. arid, level, fertile (land); living in such a country. m. a kind of partridge; n. deer, game.
जाङ्घिक a. quick-footed; m. runner.
जाठर, f. ई being on or in the belly; m. offspring of the womb, son.
जाड्य n. coldness, frigidity, stiffness, dulness, stupidity, want of intelligence.
जात a. born, begot with (loc.), by (instr. or abl.); born—ago, —old (—°); grown, arisen, appeared, happened, passed, become, turned to (dat.), being, present; often °— (or —°) having born, grown, or existing—, i.e. having got, endowed with, possessed of. — m. son (f. जाता daughter*), living creature; n. being, creature; birth, origin, race, kind, sort; the whole of, all that is (gen. or —°).
जातक a. born, begot (—°); m. a new-born child; n. birth (esp. a former birth of Çākyamuni & its history), nativity, also = seq.
जातकर्मन् n. the ceremony after birth.
जातदन्त a. having teeth (grown).
जातपक्ष a. fledged (having grown wings).
जातपूर्व a. born before.*
जातबल a. having strength (grown or gained).
जातमात्र a. just born.
जातरूप a. beautiful, golden; n. gold.
जातरूपमय, f. ई golden.
जातविद्या f. knowledge of (all) beings.
जातविश्वास a. having got confidence or courage.
जातवेदस् m. E. of Agni (knower or possessor of all beings); in l. l. also = fire.
जातवेश्मन् n. lying-in room.
जातसंकल्प a. who has made up his mind.
जाति (जाती) f. birth, origin, new birth, form of existence, position, rank, caste, family, race, kind, sort, genus, genuine or true state of anything; a kind of jasmine. °—, जात्या, & जातितस् by birth or nature, from the beginning.
जातिजानपद a. relating to castes and districts.
जातितस् adv. according to (one's) caste.
जातिधर्म m. law or duty of caste.
जातिभ्रंश m. loss of caste.
जातिभ्रंशकर a. causing loss of caste.
जातिमन्त् a. of (high) birth or rank.
जातिमात्र n. mere birth or caste; °त्रोपजीविन् a. subsisting only by (the name of) one's caste.
जातिसंपन्न a. born of a noble race.
जातिस्मर a. recollecting a former existence; abstr. °ता f., °त्व n.
जातिस्मरण n. recollection of a former birth.
जातिहीन a. base born (lit. destitute of birth).
जातीकोश m. nutmeg.
*जातीफला f. N. of a plant.
जातु (जातु) adv. at all, ever, once, possibly, perhaps; w. न not at all, never.
जातुष, f. ई made of or covered with lac.
जातूकर्ण m., ई f. a man's & woman's name.
जातेष्टि f. birth-rite.
जात्य a. belonging to the family, caste, or race (of —°); kin, legitimate, genuine, noble.
जात्यन्ध a. born blind.
जात्यन्धबधिर a. born blind and deaf.
जान n. birth, origin.

जानक m. a patron. name; f. ई patron. of Sītā.

जानकीनाथ, °कीवल्लभ, & °कीश m. the lord of Sītā, E. of Rāma.

जानपद a. living in the country; m. countryman (in both mgs), subject.

जानराज्य n. supreme power.

जानि f. wife (only adj. —°).

जानु n. (m.) knee.

जानुक m. N. of a man; n. = prec. (esp. a. —°).

जानुका f. bearing, bringing forth.

जानुदघ्न, f. ई reaching up to the knees.

जान्वस्थि n. shin- (lit. knee-)bone.

जाप m. muttering (esp. prayers).

जापक & जापिन् a. muttering, whispering (—°).

जाप्य a. to be muttered, n. a prayer.

जामदग्न, f. ई belonging to Jamadagni.

जामदग्न्य a. the same.

जामातृ m. son- or brother-in-law.

जामि a. related by blood; kindred, own, native, customary; f. sister (± स्वसृ, metaph. also the fingers), daughter in law, female relative i.g.; n. = seq.

जामित्व n. consanguinity, relationship, friendship.

जाम्बवन्त् m. N. of a monkey prince.

जाम्बिल & जाम्बील n. the knee-pan.

जाम्बुक a. belonging to a jackal.

1जाम्बूनद n. a kind of gold; gold i.g.

2जाम्बूनद, f. ई golden.

जाम्बूनदमय, f. ई the same.

*जायक n. a kind of fragrant wood.

जाया f. wife, consort; abstr. जायात्व n.

जायिन् a. conquering, fighting (—°).

जायु & जायुक a. victorious.

1जार a. becoming old.

2जार m. paramour, lover, friend.

जारज, जारजात, & °जातक a. born of a woman by her paramour.

जारता f. love-affair.

जारवृत्तान्त m. the same.

जारासंधि m. patr. of Sahadeva.

जारिणी f. having a paramour, enamoured.

जारूथ्य a. E. of अश्वमेध.

1जाल n. net, web, springe, snare, coat or helmet of wire, grate, lattice, (lattice-) window, the membrane between the toes of waterbirds (supposed also to exist between the toes and fingers of godlike personages), mane (of a lion); collection, multitude.

2जाल a. watery.

जालक n. net, web, grate, grated window, bundle of beeds or flowers, collection, multitude i.g.; m. a kind of tree; f. जालिका net, veil, armour; multitude.

जालपाद m. a webfooted bird.

जालबन्ध m. net, springe.

जालमार्ग m. the way of the window; instr. through the window.

जालमाला f. net.

जालवन्त् a. having a net, a mail, lattice-windows, etc.

जालाक्ष m. lattice-window.

जालाष n. a cert. soothing medicine.

जालिक m. fowler.

जालोपजीविन् m. fisherman.*

जाल्म, f. ई wretched, low, vulgar; m. wretch.

†जावन् v. पूर्वजावन्.

जावन्त् a. having or granting offspring.

जास्पति m. the father of a family.

जास्पत्य n. the state of a householder.

जाहक m. hedgehog.

जाहुष m. N. of a man.

जाह्नव m. patr. of sev. man; f. ई of Gaṅgā.

जाह्नवीय a. belonging to (the) Gaṅgā.

जि, जयति, °ते, pp. जित conquer, win, subdue, overcome, suppress, expel from (abl.), deprive of (2 acc.); absol. vanquish (in a game or a suit of law), be victorious. जयति, °तु (w. nom.), जितम् (w. instr.) = victorious is or be—, hail to—! C. जापयति cause to conquer or win (2 acc.); salute with reverence*. D. जिगीषति wish to win, seek for prey. — अप keep off, prevent. अभि win, conquer, obtain. अव win, gain, reconquer, vanquish, ward off. आ & उद् conquer, win, subdue. निस् gain, attain, subdue, conquer, overcome, surpass. विनिस् the same. परा (mostly M.) lose, be deprived of (acc.), succumb (abl.*); vanquish, overcome. परि, प्र, प्रति

win, conquer, vanquish. वि (mostly M.) the same; surpass, excel; also = S. absol. D. (mostly M.) wish to win or conquer, attack. सम् win, conquer, obtain (together). — Cf. पराजित.

जिगत्नु a. hastening, quick.

जिगमिषु a. wishing or about to go.

जिगीषा f. wish to conquer or win, ambition.

जिगीषु a. wishing to conquer or obtain.

जिग्यु a. victorious.

जिघत्सा f. wish to eat, hunger.

जिघत्सु a. wishing to devour.

जिघांस्, °सति v. हन्.

जिघांसा f. wish to kill or destroy.

जिघांसिन् a. wishing to kill (—°).

जिघांसु a. wishing to kill or destroy (acc. or —°).

जिघृक्षा f. wish to take or seize.

जिघृक्षु wishing to take, seize, grasp, rob, gather, learn (acc. or —°).

जिङ्गी f. N. of a plant.

जिजीविषा f. wish to live; a. °विषु or जिजीषु.

जिज्ञासन n. wish to know, investigation.

जिज्ञासा f. the same; °सार्थम् for information.

जिज्ञासु a. wishing to know, inquiring.

जित् a. winning, conquering (—°).

जितकाशिन् a. appearing victorious, certain of victory.

जितक्लम a. having overcome or shaken off fatigue.

जितक्रोध a. having conquered anger.

जितात्मन् a. self-subdued.

जिति f. gain, victory, conquest.

जितेन्द्रिय a. having suppressed the organs of sense, abstr. °त्व n.

जित्या f. gain, victory (—°).

जित्वन् *a. victorious; m. N. of a man.

जित्वर a. victorious; vanquishing (—°).

जिन m. a Buddha or Arhant.

जिनेन्द्र m. = जिन.

जिन्व्, जिन्वति (°ते), जिनोति be lively, hasten; put in motion, quicken, impel, refresh, further, favour, bring or help to (dat.); fill, satisfy. — प्र quicken, speed on, favour, help to (dat.). उपप्र urge on, impel.

†जिन्व v. धियंजिन्व & विश्वजिन्व.

जिव्रि a. decayed, old.

जिषे (dat. inf.) to win or conquer.

जिष्णु a. victorious, triumphant, superior, winning, conquering (—°); m. E. of Viṣṇu or Arjuna; N. of sev. men.

जिहासा f. wish to give up.

जिहासु a. wishing to give up.

जिहीर्षा f. wish to seize or take, a. °र्षु.

जिह्म a. not straight or upright, oblique, transverse, crooked; w. इ, गम्, etc. go awry or astray, fail, miss (abl.). — n. & °ता† f. falsehood, dishonesty.

जिह्मग a. going crookedly; m. snake.

जिह्मशी a. lying crookedly or athwart.

जिह्मित a. bent, curved.

जिह्व m. E. of Agni; r. = f. जिह्वा tongue.

जिह्वक (adj. —°, f. इका) -tongued.

जिह्वामूल n. the root of the tongue.

जिह्वामूलीय m. the Visarga before क & ख.

†जीति v. अजीति.

जीन or जील m. a leather bag.

जीमूत m. thunder-cloud; m. N. of sev. plants, E. of the Sun, a man's name.

जीमूतवाह & °वाहन m. a man's name.

जीर a. quick, active, driving, exciting; m. quick movement (esp. of the Soma stones).

जीरदानु a. dropping, sprinkling, causing to flow abundantly.

जीराश्व a. having quick horses.

1जीरि (m. or f.) quick or flowing water.

2जीरि f. old age.

जीर्ण a. decayed, infirm, old, frail, dry; n. digestion; also = seq.

जीर्णता f., °त्व n. decrepitude, old age.

जीर्णदेवायतन n. a temple in ruins.

जीर्णवस्त्र n. a worn or tattered raiment.

जीर्णारण्य n. an old or desert wood.

जीर्णि a. decrepit with age.

जीर्णोद्यान n. an old or desert garden.

जील (or जीन) m. a leather bag.

जीव्, जीवति (°ते), pp. जीवित (q.v.) live, revive (± पुनर्), subsist on (instr.). Imper. जीव (± चिरम्) may you live (long)! C. जीवयति (°ते) make or keep alive, nourish, bring up; wish a pers. to live (by calling जीव). D. जिजीविषति (°ते) or जुज्यूषति

wish to live, seek a livelihood by (instr.). — अति survive. अनु live after i.e. like (acc.); live for, be devoted to (acc.); live on, subsist by (instr.). आ live on, make use of, enjoy (acc.). उद् & प्रत्युद् revive; C. restore to life. उप subsist (± वृत्तिम्); live on, make use of, practise (acc., gen., or instr.); live under, depend on, serve (acc.). प्रत्युप C. restore to life.* वि revive. सम् live (together), subsist on (instr.), revive. C. vivify, keep alive, nourish.

जीव a. living, alive; living on or causing to live, vivifying (—°). m. the principle of life, the living or personal soul; E. of the planet Jupiter; n. life; m. n. living being, creature; f. जीवा pl. water as the living or vivifying element.

जीवक, f. इका a. = prec. adj.; f. जीविका life, livelihood, pl. = prec. f. pl.

जीवगृभ् a. taking alive, catcher.

जीवज a born alive.

जीवजीवक & जीवंजीवक m. a kind of fowl.

जीवदत्त m. N. of a man.

जीवदायक a. life-giving, generating.

जीवन, f. ई causing to live, vivifying; n. life, existence, mode of life; livelihood, subsistence (adj. —° living on); making alive, enlivening; water.

जीवनश् (nom. °नट्) a. where life is lost.

जीवनस्या f. love of life.

जीवनहेतु m. mode of subsistence.

जीवनीय a. vivifying; n. (impers.) vivendum, as subst. water.

जीवन्मुक्त a. liberated in life, abstr. °क्ति f.

जीवन्मृत & °क a. alive and dead, half dead; abstr. °त्व n.

जीवपति, f. °पत्नी a. whose husband or wife is alive.

जीवपितृ & °क a. whose father is alive.

जीवपुत्र a. whose son is alive.

जीवपुरा f. the abode of the living.

जीवप्रज a. whose offspring is alive.

जीवभूत a. being alive, living, vital.

जीवमय a. animated, living.

जीवल a. living or enlivening; N. of a man.

जीवलोक m. the world of the living.

जीववध m. the killing of a living creature.

जीवशंस a. praised by the living.

जीवशेष a. having only life (left).

जीवसर्वस्व n. the whole or substance of a life, the highest treasure.*

जीवसुत a. whose children are alive.

जीवसू f. bringing forth a living child or whose children are alive.

जीवसे (dat. inf.) to live.

जीवातु f. life.

जीवात्मन् m. the living or individual soul.

जीवाशङ्किन् a. thinking (a person to be) alive.

जीवित a. lived, living, alive, restored to life; n. living creature, life, subistence.

जीवितक्षय m. loss of life, death.

जीविततृष्णा f. thirst for life.*

जीवितनाथ m. lord of life, husband.

जीवितप्रदायिन् a. life-giving or l.-preserving.*

जीवितप्रिय a. dear as life.

जीवितमरण n. death in life.*

जीवितव्य n. vivendum (impers.), as subst. life.

जीवितसंशय m. risk of life.

जीवितसम a. dear as (lit. equal to) life.

जीवितसर्वस्व* n. = जीवसर्वस्व.

जीवितात्यय m. danger of life.

जीवितान्त m. end of life, death.

जीवितान्तक a. ending life, E. of Çiva.

जीवितावसान n. end of life, death.*

जीविताशा f. hope or love of life.

जीवितेश m. lord of life (Yama), f. आ mistress, wife.

जीवितेश्वर m. lord of life (Çiva); f. °री = prec. f.

जीवितोद्वहन n. carrying on life.*

जीविन् a. alive, living on or by (loc. or —°); m. living creature.

जीव्य n. vivendum (impers.); life.

जु v. 1जू.

जुगुप्स्, जुगुप्सति v. गुप्.

जुगुप्सा f. horror, disgust, aversion.

जुगुप्सित n. the same, horrible deed.

जुगुर्वणि a. fond of praise.

(जुटक n.*), जुटिका f. tuft, bunch.

जुम्बक m. E. of Varuṇa.

जुर्, जुरति, जूर्यति, pp. जूर्ण (q.v.) grow old, decay, perish, जुरति also trans.

जुवस् n. quickness, speed.

1जुष्, जुषते, °ति, pp. जुष्ट or जुष्ट (q.v.) be pleased or satisfied; be fond of, delight in, enjoy (acc. or gen.); like to, resolve upon (dat. or inf., esp. in ध्यै); prefer or choose (a cert. place), i.e. visit, inhabit. C. जोषयते (°ति) like, love, approve of, choose. — अभि like, visit, frequent. उप cheer, gladden. प्रति cherish, fondle; delight in, be pleased with (acc.). C. fondle, caress. — Cf. प्रजुष्ट, संजुष्ट.

2जुष् a. (mostly —°) delighting in, attached to, visiting, frequenting.

जुष्ट or जुष्ट a. acceptable, welcome, pleasant; wont, visited, frequented; surrounded by, endowed with, possessed of (instr. or —°).

जुष्टि f. favour, love, satisfaction.

जुहू f. tongue, esp. tongue of Agni, flame; a wooden ladle used for pouring butter into the fire.

जुहूषु a. wishing to sacrifice.

जुहोति m. burnt oblations (opp. यजति).

जुहोतियजतिक्रिया f. pl. burnt oblations and other sacrifices.

जुह्वास्य a. tongue- or flame-mouthed (Agni).

1जू, जवते & जुनाति, pp. जूत press on, speed; impel, incite, promote, inspire; expel, drive, away. — प्र press on (tr. & intr.). — Cf. जूजुवंस् & जूजुवान.

2जू a. quick, speedy, pressing, urging; s. horse.

जूजुवंस् & °वान a. speedy, quick.

जूति f. impulse, speed, energy.

जूतिमन्त् a. impetuous, speedy.

जूर्ण a. decayed, old.

1जूर्णि f. blaze, fiery weapon.

2जूर्णि a. singing, praising.

जूर्णिन् a. glowing.

जूर्णी f. a cert. snake.

जूर्य a. old, aged.

जूर्व्, जूर्वति singe, burn. — नि burn down. सम् = S.

1जॄ, जरति, pp. जीर्ण (q.v.) make or grow old; जीर्यति (°ते) grow old, age, decay, wither, waste away; be dissolved or digested. C. जरयति (°ते) make old, wear out, digest. — सम् (जीर्यति) grow old (together). — Cf. जरन्त्.

2जॄ, जरते crackle, roar (fire); sound, call, invoke. — प्रति call to, salute. सम् sound.

जृम्भ्, जृम्भते (°ति), pp. जृम्भित (q.v.) gape, yawn, open (of a flower), blossom; spread, extend; come forth, rise; be or feel at ease. C. जृम्भयति cause to yawn. I. जरीजृम्भते extend far. — उद् & समुद् open wide, come forth, appear, arise. परि spread round. प्र begin to yawn. वि yawn, gape, blossom, expand, break forth, appear; be or feel at ease. सम् expand, break forth, appear. — Cf. विजृम्भित.

जृम्भ m., आ f. gaping, yawning, opening, blowing.

जृम्भण a. causing to yawn; n. = prec.

जृम्भणकर a. = prec. a.

जृम्भित n. = जृम्भ.

जेतव्य & जेत्व a. to be conquered or won.

जेतृ m. conqueror, winner.

जेन्य a. noble, genuine, true.

1जेमन् a. superior.

2जेमन् m. superiority.

जेमन n. eating, food.

जेय a. to be vanquished.

जेष m. gain, acquirement.

जेह्, जेहते open the mouth, gasp, gape. — वि = S.

जैत्र, f. ई victorious, triumphant.

जैत्रयात्रा f. triumphal procession.

जैत्ररथ m. triumphal chariot.

जैत्रिय n. victory, triumph.

जैन, f. ई belonging to the Jinas; m. a Jaina.

जैमिनि m. N. of a saint and philosopher.

जैमिनीय a. relating to Jaimini (v. prec.); m. pl. his followers, n. his work.

जैव, f. ई relating to the individual soul.

जैवातृक a. long-lived.

जैह्म्य n. falsehood, deceit.

जैह्व a. being on or belonging to the tongue.

जैह्व्य n. pleasure of taste (lit. of the tongue).

जोगू a. singing, praising.

*जोङ्ग & °क n. aloe wood.

जोष m. satisfaction, pleasure. जोषम् after one's satisfaction, sufficiently, abundantly (also अनु ° or ° आ); w. अस्, आस्, or स्था be silent, keep quiet.

जोषण n. satisfaction, delight in (—°).

जोष्टृ & जोष्टृ a. loving, fostering.

जोहूत्र a. calling aloud, neighing.

ज्ञ a. knowing, versed in, conversant or familiar with (gen., loc. or —°); intelligent, wise.

ज्ञता f., ज्ञत्व n., ज्ञप्ति f. abstr. to prec.

ज्ञप्तिक (adj. —°) = ज्ञप्ति (v. prec.).

1ज्ञा, जानाति, जानीते (जानति, °ते), pp. ज्ञात know, be or get aware of (acc., r. gen.), recognize, ascertain, investigate, acknowledge, approve, perceive, observe, notice (acc.), remember (gen.); consider or regard as, understand or suppose that— (2 acc.), know how to (infin.); *M. have to do with, deal with (gen.) With न know nothing of (acc.). C. ज्ञापयति, °ते & ज्ञपयति, °ते, pp. ज्ञप्त & ज्ञापित inform, teach; announce, notify; make a person acquainted with (2 acc.); M. beg, request (acc.). D. जिज्ञासते (°ति) wish to know, try, examine; ascertain, suppose. D. C. ज्ञीप्सति wish to make a person acquainted with (2 acc.); pp. ज्ञीप्स्यमान wished or intended to be informed. — अनु permit, grant, approve, forgive, pardon (gen. of pers.); empower, authorize to (dat. or *प्रति w. acc.); dismiss, bid farewell (acc.), be gracious or kind to (acc.). C. ask for permission or leave, take leave of (acc.). अभ्यनु & समनु the same. अभि perceive, notice, understand, know; acknowledge as, think that (2 acc.), concede, grant; agree, approve. प्रत्यभि recognize again, notice, understand, come to one's self, recover one's consciousness. समभि know, recognize. अव despise, surpass. आ attend to, notice, hear, learn, understand. C. command, appoint a pers. (acc.) to (dat. or loc.). समा perceive, notice. C. bid, appoint. उप & समुप think out, invent. निस् & विनिस् discern, find out. परि observe, understand, ascertain, know thoroughly, know as (2 acc.). प्र understand, distinguish, discern, be clever or wise, perceive, become aware of, find out. प्रति acknowledge, recognize, approve, consent, agree, promise (dat., gen., r. loc. of pers., acc. of th.); M. state, affirm, answer; perceive, observe, become aware of. संप्रति consent to, promise. वि perceive, find out, observe, notice, hear from (gen.); consider as, understand or know that (2 acc.); distinguish, discern, know thoroughly, become or be wise; विज्ञायते it is well known or recognized (a rule, dogma, etc.); मा विज्ञायि this (prec. nom.) is not to be understood (g.). C. make known, report, communicate, say that (2 acc.); make one understand, apprise, teach; interrogate, beg, ask for (dat., प्रति, अर्थम्, or निमित्तम्*). अभिवि become aware of, notice. सम् M. be of one mind, agree together, harmonize with (loc., *instr. or *acc.), obey (dat.); direct, appoint (acc.), understand, know. C. cause to agree together, unite; appease, satisfy; make understood, make signs or hints to (अन्योऽन्यम्), order, command. अभिसम् agree in (acc.), acknowledge. — Cf. अनुज्ञात, अभ्यनुज्ञात, परिज्ञात, प्रजानन्त्, प्रज्ञात.

2ज्ञा (—°) knowing, acquainted with.

ज्ञात a. known, understood, learnt, noticed; thought to be (nom.). — आ ज्ञातम् Ah! I know; मया ज्ञातम् I was of opinion.

ज्ञातव्य a. to be learnt or understood.

ज्ञाति m. near relation, kinsman.

ज्ञातित्व n. abstr. to prec.

ज्ञातिप्रभुक a. powerful among the relatives.

ज्ञातिप्राय a. destined chiefly for the paternal relations.

ज्ञातिभाव m. relationship.

ज्ञातिभेद m. dissension among relatives.

ज्ञातिमन्त् a. having near relations.

ज्ञातृ m. knower; acquaintance, witness.

ज्ञात्र n. capacity of understanding, intelligence.

ज्ञान n. knowing, understanding, knowledge.

esp. higher knowledge, science, wisdom; conscience, organ of intelligence or sense. Abstr. °त्व n.

ज्ञानगम्य a. accessible to knowledge.

1ज्ञानचक्षुस् n. the mind's eye.

2ज्ञानचक्षुस् a. using the mind's eye.

ज्ञानतस् adv. from knowledge.

ज्ञानद a. imparting knowledge.

ज्ञानपण्य a. dealing in knowledge or science.

ज्ञानपूर्व a. preceded by (the acquisition of) knowledge.

ज्ञानमय, f. ई consisting of knowledge.

ज्ञानयज्ञ m. the sacrifice of knowledge.

ज्ञानयुत a. endowed with knowledge.

ज्ञानयोग m. the practice of knowledge.

ज्ञानवन्त् a. knowing, intelligent, wise.

ज्ञानशक्तिमन्त् a. having the capacity of knowing.

ज्ञानसङ्ग m. attachment to knowledge.

ज्ञानाग्नि m. the fire of knowledge.

ज्ञानार्थिन् a. wanting to know (—°).

ज्ञानासि m. the sword of knowledge.

ज्ञानिन् a. = ज्ञानवन्त्; m. astrologer, fortuneteller, abstr. °नित्व n.

ज्ञानेच्छाक्रियाशक्तिमन्त् a. endowed with the capacity of knowing, wishing, and acting (ph.).

ज्ञानेन्द्रिय n. organ of perception or sensation.

ज्ञापक (f. °पिका) making understood, teaching, hinting, insinuating. — m. the master of requests (a kind of officer); n. precept, rule, esp. an implicit or indirect rule (g.).

ज्ञापन n. information, insinuation.

ज्ञापनीय & ज्ञाप्य a. to be made known.

ज्ञास् m. a near relative.

ज्ञीप्स्, ज्ञीप्सति v. 1ज्ञा.

ज्ञीप्सा f. wish to know, question.

ज्ञु (only °— & —°) n. knee.

ज्ञुबाध् a. bending the knees.

ज्ञेय a. to be known, understood, learnt, found out; to be regarded as or supposed to be (nom.). Abstr. °ता f., °त्व n.

ज्मन् (loc.) course or way.

ज्मया a. following one's course.

ज्मा f. the earth (only ज्मा instr. & ज्मस् abl. gen.).

ज्मायन्त् a. striving to the earth.

1ज्या, जिनाति, pp. जीत overpower, oppress, deprive of (2 acc.), P. जीयते (जीयते), D. जिज्यासति — अधि & प्र overwhelm.

2ज्या f. force, violence.

3ज्या f. bow-string.

ज्याका f. the same.

ज्याकृष्टि f. the straining of the bow-string.

ज्याघोष m. twang of the bow-string.

ज्यान n. oppression.

ज्यानि f. the same, deprivation, loss.

ज्यापाश m. bow-string.

ज्यायंस् (compar.) superior, greater, stronger, elder; excellent, best.

ज्यायस्वन्त् a. having a senior or superior.

ज्यायिष्ठ (superl.) first, best, excellent.

ज्युत्, ज्योतति (°ते) shine; C ज्योतयति (± अव) illuminate.

ज्युति f. light; °मन्त् shining.

ज्येष्ठ or ज्येष्ठ (superl.) principal, best, eldest, highest, greatest, worst; superior to (abl.). m. chief, senior, eldest brother, N. of a man. f. ज्येष्ठा the eldest wife. n. the chief, best (of things); adv. most, much.

ज्येष्ठतम (superl. to prec.) the first or best of all.

ज्येष्ठतर (compar. to ज्येष्ठ) an elder one; f. आ or °तरिका old woman, duenna.

ज्येष्ठता f., °त्व n. superiority, primogeniture.

ज्येष्ठबन्धु m. head of a family.

ज्येष्ठराज् m. sovereign.

ज्येष्ठवयस् a. older than (—°).

ज्येष्ठवृत्ति a. behaving like an elder brother.

ज्येष्ठसामग a. who sings the Jyeṣṭhasāman (v. seq.).

ज्येष्ठसामन् n. N. of a Sāman; a. = prec. a.

ज्येष्ठांश m. the eldest brother's share.

ज्यैष्ठ m. a cert. month in summer; f. ई the full-moon in this month.

ज्यैष्ठ्य n. preeminence, sovereignty, primogeniture.

ज्योक् adv. long; w. कृ delay, tarry. Superl. ज्योक्तमाम् adv. longest.

ज्योतिर्गण m. the troops of the heavenly bodies.

ज्योतिर्ज्ञ m. star-knower, astrologer.

ज्योतिर्मय a. consisting of light.

1ज्योतिर्विद् m. = ज्योतिर्ज्ञ.
2ज्योतिर्विद् a. creating light.
ज्योतिर्विदाभरण n. T. of an astrological work.
ज्योतिःशास्त्र & ज्योतिष n. astronomy.
ज्योतिष्कृत् a. creating light.
ज्योतिष्मन्त् a. luminous, shining, celestial; m. the sun, a man's name.
ज्योतिःष्टोम m. a cert. Soma ceremony.
ज्योतिस् n. light (l. & f.), brightness, fire, moonshine, light of the eyes; pl. the heavenly bodies; du. sun and moon.
ज्योतीरथ a. whose chariot is light (sev. gods).
ज्योत्स्ना f. moonlight night, moonshine.
ज्योत्स्नाढ्य a. shining brightly (lit. rich in light).
ज्योत्स्निका f. a woman's name.*
ज्यौत्स्न m. the light half of a month.
†ज्रय v. पृथुज्रय.
ज्रयस् n. stretch, expanse.
ज्रि, ज्रयति w. उप stretch out to (acc.).
ज्वर्, ज्वरति be hot or feverish. C. ज्वरयति make feverish. — सम् be grieved or sorry. अनुसम् be sorry for (acc.), also = अभिसम् be grieved or envious.
ज्वर m. fever, pain, grief, sorrow.
ज्वरित & ज्वरिन् a. feverish.
ज्वल्, ज्वलति (°ते), pp. ज्वलित (q.v.) blaze, flame, burn, glow, shine. C. ज्वलयति & ज्वालयति set on fire, illuminate. I. जाज्वलीति & जाज्वल्यते flame violently, be brilliant. — अभि shine, C. = अव C. illuminate. उद् blaze up, flame, shine; C. = S. C. प्र flame up, shine forth; C. set on fire, kindle. अभिप्र & संप्र flame up, catch fire. प्रति blaze, burn. अभिवि flame against or opposite to. सम् blaze, flame; C. kindle, illuminate.
ज्वल m. flame.
ज्वलन a. burning, flaming, combustible; m. fire (also ज्वलन or ज्वलन); n. burning, blazing.
ज्वलनसप्रभ a. fiery, burning.
ज्वलन्त् a. burning, flaming; m. fire.
ज्वलित n. blazing, shining.
†ज्वार v. नवज्वार.
ज्वाल m. light, flame (also ज्वाला f.); torch, hot infusion.
ज्वालन n. kindling.
ज्वालिन् a. flaming.

झ

झंकार m. clattering, murmuring, noise.
झंकारित n. the same (adj. —° sounding with*).
झंकारिन् a. clattering, humming, buzzing, etc.
झंकृति f. = झंकार.
झञ्झा f. roaring (of the wind etc.).
झञ्झानिल, °मरुत्, & °मारुत m. storm, hurricane.
झट् w. उद् v. उज्झटित.
झटिति adv. instantly, on the spot; झटिति—झटिति no sooner—than.*
झण्, झणति tinkle.
झणझण an onom. sound.*
झणझणाय्, °यते jingle, tinkle.
झणत्कार m. tinkling.
झम्प m., आ f. a jump.
झर्, only झरन्त् flowing or falling down.
झरा f. waterfall, cascade.
झरी f. the same, river.
झर्झर m., ई f. a sort of drum.
झर्झरित a. exhausted, withered.
झल्ल m. cudgel-player (a caste).
झल्लक n. a kind of cymbal.
झष m. a large fish, fish i.g.
झषकेतन & झषध्वज m. the god of love; love.
झिङ्गिनी & झिङ्गी f. N. of a plant.
झिल्लिक m. pl. N. of a people; f. आ = seq.
झिल्ली f., झिल्लीक m. a cricket.
झौलिक s. small bag, purse.

ट

टङ्क s. hoe, chisel, stamp.
टङ्कच्छेद m. stamping (lit. cutting or hewing with the chisel).
टङ्कण m. (also **टङ्कन**) borax.
टङ्कय्, °**यति** cover, shut up. — Cf. **उट्टङ्कित** & **विटङ्कित**.
टंकार m. howling, crying, humming, clattering.
टंकारित & **टंकृत** n. the same.
टल्, **टलति** be confused or disturbed.
टसत्, **टसिति** & **टात्** (onomat.) crash!
टांकार m. & **टांकृत** n. clinking, sound.
टाल a. tender (of fruits).
टिट्टिभ m., **ई** f. a kind of bird.
टिण्ठा f. gaming house.
टीक्, **टीकते** trip. C. **टीकयति** explain, make clear.
टीका f. a commentary, esp. on some other commentary.
टीत्कार m. crashing.
टोपर s. small bag, purse.

ठ

ठकार m. the sound or letter **ठ**.
ठक्कुर m. deity, idol, object of reverence, often —° as honorary title after a pr. n.
ठार m. rime, hoar-frost.
ठिण्ठा f. = **टिण्ठा**; also a woman's name.

ड

डम्, **डमति** sound (of a drum).
डम m. N. of a caste.
डमर m. riot, tumult.
डमरिन् m., **डमरु** (*m.) a kind of drum.
डम्ब्, **विडम्बयति**, pp. **विडम्बित** imitate, equal (acc.); mock, cheat, deceive.
डम्बर m. noise, confusion, sound of words, bombast, heap, mass, extent, course.
डवित्थ m. N. of a man.
डाकिनी f. female imp, witch.
डांकृति & **डात्कृति** f. sound, roaring.
डामर a. extraordinary, strange (abstr. °**त्व** n.); m. astonishment, wonder.
डाल s. branch.
डाहल or **डाहाल** m. N. of a people.
डिण्डिम m. a kind of drum (also **आ** & n.); humming, sound.
डित्थ m. N. of a man; abstr. °**ता** f., °**त्व** n.
डिम m. a kind of drama; a cert. caste.
डिम्ब s. affray, riot, tumult, danger, distress; m. egg.
डिम्भ m. a new-born child, fool, ignorant; young animal, sprout of a plant; egg, globe.
डिम्भलीला f. a child's play.*
डिल्लि & **डिल्ली** f. the town of Delhi.
डी, **डयते**, **डीयते**, pp. **डीन** fly, move through the air. — **उद्** fly up, C. **उड्डापयति** scare. **प्रोद्** fly up and away. **प्र** fly up. — Cf. **उड्डीन**.
डीन n. flying, flight (of a bird).
(***डुडुभ**) **डुडुम** & **डुण्डुभ** m. a kind of lizard.
डेरिका f. musk-rat.
डोम्ब m. a cert. low caste; f. **ई** a kind of drama.
डौण्डुभ a. lizard-like (cf. **डुण्डुभ**).
डुल्, C. **डुालयति** w. **आ** mix.

ढ

ढक्क m. a kind of building, N. of a city or district; f. **आ** a large drum.

ढामरा f. goose.

ढाल n. shield.

ढालिन् a. armed with a shield.

ढेङ्क m. a kind of bird.

ढोल m. a kind of large drum.

ढौक्, **ढौकते** approach (acc.). C. **ढौकयति** cause to approach, bring near to (gen.). — **उप** C. present, offer.

ढौकन n. offering, present.

त

त pron. stem of 3ᵈ pers. (cf. **स**; n. **तद्** q.v.) he, she, it; this, that (adj. & subst.), also = the def. article. Repeated, mostly in the plur. = this and that, various, several. **य त** (in the same sentence) whoever, anybody; **य (य)—त त** or **य क** w. **चिद्—त** whoever—he. — It often lays stress on another pronoun of any pers. separately expressed or contained in a verbal form, as **तं त्वा—अहूषत** thee (there) they have invoked, **स नः—भव** be thou to us, **ते वयम्** we here.

†**तंस्**, **तस्** pour out (fig.); C. **तंसयति** shake. — **अभि** shake out of, rob. **परि** C. shake, stir. **वि** the same. — Cf. **अवतंसय्**.

तक्, **तक्ति**, pp. **तक्त** rush, fly. — **निस्** M. rush on, attack (acc.).

तक pron. stem, demin. to **त**.

तकु a. rushing, hastening.

तक्मन् m. a kind or whole class of diseases.

तक्र n. buttermilk (mixed with water).

तक्व a. quick, fleet.

तक्वन् & **तक्ववी** m. a cert. bird of prey.

तक्ष्, **तक्षति**, °**ते**, **तक्ष्णोति**, & **ताष्टि**, pp. **तष्ट** hew, cut, work, fashion, make, invent. — **अनु** procure, get. **अप** split or cut off. **आ** produce, procure. **उद्** fashion out of (abl.). **निस्** shape or form. **प्र** fashion, make. **वि** = **अप**. **सम्** = S. (± together). — Cf. **वितष्ट**.

तक्ष a. cutting off, destroying (—°); m. a carpenter (—°); N. of a serpent-demon etc.

तक्षक m. cutter, carpenter; as pr. n. = prec.

तक्षण n. hewing, cutting, planing.

तक्षन् m. carpenter.

तक्षशिल m. pl the inhabitants of T. (v. seq.).

तक्षशिला f. N. of a town; °**तस्** from T.

तक्ष्य a. to be shaped or formed.

तङ्गण or **तङ्गन** m. pl. N. of a people.

तच्चरित a. of that conduct.

तच्छील a. of that character or nature.

तज्ज a. produced by that.

तज्ज्ञ a. knowing that, familiar with (—°).

तञ्च्, **तनक्ति** contract. — **आ** coagulate.

तट्, **तटति** rumble, groan.

तट m., **ई** f. slope, declivity (lit. & fig.); shore, bank.

तटस्थ a. standing on a slope, bank or shore; also = **मध्यस्थ** q.v.

तटाक n. pond, lake, poss. °**किन्**; f. °**किनी** a large lake.

तटिनी f. river (having banks); °**पति** m. the ocean.

†**तड्**, C. **ताडयति** beat, strike, hurt, hit. — **अभि** & **आ** C. the same. **परि** strike, pelt. **वि** pound, crush; C. pelt, wound, strike against (loc.). **सम्** beat, strike, hit.

तडाग n. pond, lake; °**भेदक** m. the piercer or drainer of a pond.

तळित् & **तळितस्** (= **तडित्** & **तडितस्**) adv. closely, near.

तडित् f. lightning.

तडित्वन्त् a. having or emitting a flash of lightning; m. a cloud.

तडिन्मय a. consisting of lightning.
तडिन्माला f. flash of lightning.
तडिल्लता & **°ल्लेखा** f. the same.
तण्डुल m. grain, esp. of rice (used also as a weight).
तण्डुलकण m. a grain of rice.
तण्डुलकण्डन n. rice-bran.
तण्डुलोदक n. rice-water.*
1**तत** m. father; voc. also = my son.
2**तत** a. stretched out, expanded, wide; overspread or covered with (instr. or —°).
ततस् (adv. abl. of **त**) thence, there, thither; then, therefore. — **ततस्ततस्** & **इतस्ततस्** (from) here and there, (from) everywhere; the former also interr. = **ततः किम्** what then? **ततः परम्** moreover, further, also = **ततः पश्चात्** thereupon, afterwards. **ततः प्रभृति** (or **तत आरभ्य***) thenceforth, since. **ततो ऽन्यतस्** elsewhere. **ततो ऽपरम्** later, afterwards. **यतस्ततस्** from what (person or place) soever, (from) wherever. **यतो यतस्** (from) wheresoever; correl. **ततस्ततस्**.
1**तति** (only as pl.) so many.
2**तति** f. extension, spreading, offering (of a sacrifice); multitude, abundance, high degree.
ततिथ, f. **ई** the so maniest.
ततिधा adv. so manifold.
ततुरि a. overcoming, victorious.
ततोमुख a. directed thither.*
तत्कर्तृ a. doing that.
तत्कर्मकारिन् a. performing the same action.
तत्कारण a. doing or causing that.
तत्कारिन् a. doing the same.
तत्कार्यकारणात् (abl. adv.) for that (precise) reason.
1**तत्काल** m. that time, the time (now or then) being; (°—*) or acc. = at or during that time, just, directly, immediately.
2**तत्काल** a. happening at the same time or immediately.
तत्कालविदिन् a. knowing that time.*
तत्कालीन a. = 2**तत्काल**.
तत्कृत a. caused by that (those); loc. therefore.
तत्क्षण m. the same moment; °—, acc., abl., & loc. at the same moment, just, immediately, forthwith.
तत्तुल्य a. equal or corresponding to, worthy of that (those).
तत्त्व n. the state of being that, i.e. the true state or real nature; truth, reality, first principle (ph.). °—, instr., & adv. in **तस्** in truth, really, exactly.
तत्त्वकथन n. telling the truth.
तत्त्वज्ञ a. knowing the truth or true state of (—°).
तत्त्वज्ञान n. knowledge of the truth, T. of a work.
तत्त्वदर्शिन् & **°दृश्** a. seeing or knowing the truth.
तत्त्वबोध m. = **तत्त्वज्ञान**.
तत्त्वभाव m. true being or nature.
तत्त्वभूत a. being truth, i.e. true.
तत्त्वविद् a. = **तत्त्वज्ञ**.
तत्त्वशुद्धि f. exact knowledge of the truth.
तत्त्वाख्यानोपमा f. & **तत्त्वापह्नवरूपक** n. two kinds of comparison (rh.).
तत्त्वाभियोग m. accusation on ground of facts (j.).
तत्त्वार्थ m. the exact truth; the true meaning of (—°).
तत्पद n. the place of that or the word **तद्**.
1**तत्पर** a. following that or thereupon, inferior; abstr. **°त्व** n.
2**तत्पर** a. (lit. = seq.) quite given to or intent upon (loc. or —°), abstr. **°ता** f.
तत्परायण a. having that as highest object.
तत्पुरुष m. his servant; a class of compounds (g.).
तत्प्रतिपादक a. suggesting or teaching that.
तत्प्रधान a. depending chiefly on that (pers. or thing).
तत्प्रयोजक a. impelling him (her or them).
तत्र (**तत्रा**) adv. = loc. of **त**, there, therein, then. **तत्र तत्र** here and there, everywhere. **यत्र तत्र** (± **अपि**) wherever, at every place or time.
तत्रत्य a. relating to that place, i.e. being there, coming thence, etc.
तत्रभवन्त्, f. **°वती** his or her reverence (there).

तत्रस्थ a. standing or dwelling there.
तत्रान्तरे (loc. adv.) meanwhile (lit. in that interval).
तत्सख m. his (her, their) friend.
तत्संख्याक a. being in that number, counting so much.
तत्सम a. equal, of equal meaning to (—°).
तत्समक्षम् adv. before his (her, their) eyes.
तत्संबन्धिन् a. connected with that (pers. or th.).
तत्सहाय a. joined with that (those).
तत्स्पृष्टिन् a. touching that (—°).
तत्स्वरूप a. having the nature of that.
तथा adv. so, thus; also, likewise (± **च** or **अपि**); as well, as truly (in asseverations, correl. **यथा**); well, surely, certainly. — **तथापि** (± **तु**) even thus, nevertheless, yet (mostly after **यद्यपि** or **कामम्**). **तथा हि** for thus (it is), for instance, namely. **तथैव** (± **च**) just so. **न तथा** = **अन्यथा** (q.v.). **यथा तथा** howsoever, anyhow; w. neg. by no means. **यथा यथा—तथा तथा** in what manner or degree, the more—in that manner etc.
तथागत a. being in that condition, of such a quality or nature; m. a Buddhist.
तथागुण a. having such qualities or virtues.
तथाभाव m. the being so.
तथाभाविन् a. who will be so.
तथाभूत a. being so, of such a kind or nature.
तथारूप & **°रूपिन्** a. of such a form or shape.
तथाविध a. of such a sort or kind.
तथावीर्य a. of such strength or power.
तथाव्रत a. observing such conduct.
तथ्य a. real, true; n. truth, reality; instr. & **°तस्** according to truth.
तद् n. sg. of **तं** (°— used also as stem), as adv. there, then; therefore, accordingly; now, and; often connecting two sentences & correl. to **यद्**, **येन**, **यतस्**, **यदि**, or **चेद्**. — **तदपि** nevertheless, even; **तद्यथा** for instance.
तदनन्तर a. nearest to that, immediately connected with (gen.); n. adv. immediately upon that, thereupon.
तदनु adv. thereupon, then.
तदनुकृति adv. accordingly (to that).
तदनुगुण a. answering or corresponding to (—°).
तदन्त a. ending with that.
तदन्तर्भूत a. being among or within (that).
तदपत्य a. having offspring by that (woman); abstr. **°ता** f.
तदपस् a. doing that work, used to do that.
तदपेक्ष a. having a regard for that.
तदभिमुखम् adv. towards or against that.
1**तदर्थ** m. the meaning of that (those).
2**तदर्थ** a. having that purpose or meaning; n. adv. therefore, on that account.
तदर्थिन् a. wishing for that (those).
तदर्थीय a. having that object.
तदर्धिक a. half of that.
तदवस्थ a. being in that state or condition; being unaltered or safe.
तदा adv. at that time, in that case, then; sometimes redundant, esp. before **अथ** & after **ततस्** & **पुरा**. Often strengthened by **एव** (**तदैव**); correl. to **यदा**, **यत्र**, **यद्**, **यदि**, & **चेद्**. — **तदा प्रभृति** thenceforward. **यदा तदा** at every time, always.
तदात्मन् a. having that nature.
तदात्व n. present state (opp. **आयति**).
तदानीम् adv. at that time, then.
तदाश्रय & **°यिन्** a. relating to that (those).
तदीय a. belonging to or coming from that (those); his, her, their; such.
तदुपकारिन् a. helping to that, conducive.
तदुपहित a. dependent on that.
तदून a. diminished by that.
तदोकस् a. delighting in that.
तद्गत a. directed towards that, pertaining to (—°).
1**तद्गुण** m. the quality or virtue of that (those).
2**तद्गुण** a. poss. to prec.
तद्द्विगुण a. double of that.
तद्धित m. a kind of suffix & a word formed by it (g.).
तद्बुद्धि a. having that mind.
तद्भव a. originating in that, i.e. coming from Sanskrit (g.).
तद्भागिन् a. responsible for that.

तद्युत & तद्युक्त a. joined with that (pers. or thing), together.

तद्रूप a. thus shaped or formed.

तद्वंश्य a. being of that race.

तद्वक्तृ a. teaching that.

तद्वचन a. expressing or meaning that.

तद्वत् adv. so, in that manner (correl. to यद्वत् or यथा); likewise, also.

तद्वत्ता f. abstr. to prec.

तद्वयस् a. being the same age.

तद्वशं a. desirous of that.

तद्विद् a. = तज्ज्ञ.

तद्विध a. of that kind, answering to that; abstr. °त्व n.

तद्विषय a. having that for object, relating to that.

तद्वृत्ति a. living according to that.

1तन्, तनोति, तनुते, pp. तत (q.v.) extend, stretch, spread (intr. & tr.); last. continue; protract, prolong, lengthen; spin out, weave (l. & f.); prepare, arrange, direct, accomplish, perform, compose, make. P. तायते be extended, increase, grow. — अधि string (the bow), cover. अनु extend along (intr.), continue; carry on, maintain. अभि extend or reach over (acc); spread out, unfold, place in front. अव sink down; overspread, cover; loosen, let off (esp. the bow-string). आ spread over, penetrate, cover (esp. with light); expand, diffuse, stretch (a bow); bring forth, produce, effect, show, betray. अन्वा stretch or reach over; spread (tr. & intr.). व्या diffuse, produce, effect. समा the same, stretch (esp. the bow). परि stretch around, surround, envelop. प्र spread, extend (tr. & intr.); cause, produce; show, betray. वि spread over, cover, fill, stretch out (a cord, web, etc.) string (a bow); diffuse, extend; prepare, arrange, sacrifice; produce, effect; make, render (2 acc.). सम् join one's self with, hold together; cover, fill; connect, continue, protract; effect, accomplish; exhibit, evince. अनुसम् add, join, annex; spread, expand; carry on, prosecute. — Cf. आतत, प्रवितत, वितत, संतत.

2तन् (only dat. & instr.) spreading, continuation, propagation, offspring; instr. तना (तना) adv. uninterruptedly, continually.

3†तन्, तन्यति roar.

तन n., आ f. offspring, child.

तनय a. propagating a race or belonging to a family. m. son (du. also son and daughter); f. तनया daughter; n. posterity, offspring, child, descendant.

तनयितु a. roaring, thundering.

तनस् n. posterity, offspring.

तनिमन् m. thinness, weakness; n. the liver.

तनिष्ठ & तनीयंस् superl. & compar. to seq.

तनु (f. तनु, तनू & तन्वी) thin, slender, small, minute, little, spare (abstr. °ता† f, °त्व† n.). f. तनु or तनू body, form, nature (abstr. तनुता f.); person, esp. one's own person or self (often = a refl. pron.; cf. आत्मन्). f. तन्वी a (slender) woman.

तनुगात्र, f. ई slender (-limbed).

तनुच्छद m. feather, pl. plumage; armour, attire (lit. what covers the body).

तनुज m., आ f. son, daughter (born from the body or self).

तनुत्यज् a. giving up one's person.

तनुत्याग m. giving up or risk of one's own life.

तनुत्र & °त्राण n. armour, mail (lit. body-protector).

तनुधी a. of small understanding.

तनुभाव m. thinness, slenderness.

1तनुमध्य n. the middle of the body, waist.

2तनुमध्य a. having a slender waist.

तनुमध्यम a. = prec.

तनुवर्मन् n. armour (of the body).

तनुशरीर a. having a slender body.

तनू w. कृ make thin, attenuate, diminish; w. भू wane, decrease.

तनूकृथं s. preservation of body and life.

तनूजं a. born from or belonging to one's own body or person; m. & f. आ son, daughter.

तनूत्यज् a. = तनुत्यज्.

तनूनपात् m. Agni or the fire (lit. son of one's own self).

तनूपा a. protecting body and life.
तनूपान, f. **ई** the same; n. protection of body and life.
तनूबल n. the strength of the body or self.
तनूरुच् a. brilliant in person.
तनूरुह n. hair of the body, feathers, wings; m. son (lit. what grows out of the body).
तन्ति or **तन्ती** f. cord, rope, line.
तन्तु m. thread, string, cord, wire, warp of a weft; uninterrupted line i.e. continuation of a sacrifice, propagation of a race, etc.; also concr. the propagator of a family (cf. seq.).
तन्तुभूत a. being the propagator of a family.
तन्तुमन्त् a. forming a thread; uninterrupted, lasting.
तन्तुवान n. weaving.
तन्तुवाय m. a weaver.
तन्त्र n. loom, the warp of a weft; anything continuous, regular, lasting, firm, constant, prevalent, or essential; series, troop, army; foundation, basis, regular order, chief part, main point; rule, theory, authority, doctrine, science; book, esp. a kind of mystic works, a magical formula; means, expedient, stratagem; medicine, esp. a specific. f. **तन्त्री** (nom. **°स्**) string, lute.
तन्त्रक *a. recent from the loom, quite new (cloth); adj. — ° doctrine, scientific work.
तन्त्रकार m. writer of a book, author.
तन्त्रय्, **°यति** keep up, perform, conform one's self to, care or provide for (acc.).
तन्त्रवाय m. weaver.
तन्त्रायिन् a. drawing out a thread.
तन्त्रीस्वन n. time of a lute.
†**तन्द्**, **तन्दते** relax, give way.
तन्द्र्, C. **तन्द्रयते** grow weary.
तन्द्र n. series, line.
तन्द्रयु a. lazy, slothful.
तन्द्रा f. weariness, laziness.
तन्द्राय्, **°यते** grow or be weary.
तन्द्री f. = **तन्द्रा**.
तन्निमित्त a. caused by that, abstr. **°त्व** n.
तन्निष्ठ a. intent on that.
तन्मनस् a. having the mind turned upon that.
तन्मय a. consisting or made up of that; abstr. **°ता** f., **°त्व** n.
तन्मांसाद् m. eater of that flesh.
तन्मात्र a. only so much or little. n. a trifle; atom, elementary matter (ph.).
तन्मूल a. caused by (lit. rooted in) that.
तन्यता (instr. f.) thundering, roaring.
तन्यतु m. the same.
तन्यु a. roaring, howling.
तन्वङ्ग, f. **ई** slender (-limbed); f. a maiden or woman.
तप्, **तपति** (**°ते**), pp. **तप्त** (q.v.) be warm or hot, burn (instr.), shine; castigate one's self, do penance, suffer; heat, burn (tr.), distress, pain, torment. P. **तप्यते** (also **तप्यते**, **°ति**) has only the intr. mgs. C. **तापयति**, **°ते** make hot, consume by heat, distress, pain, castigate (one's self). — **अति** make warm or hot, trouble, distress. **अनु** heat, pain; P. suffer pain, repent, long for (acc.). **प्रत्यनु** & **समनु** P. repent. **अभि** make hot, shine upon, pain, ache; P. suffer pain. **आ** glow, shine, heat; P. suffer pain, w. **तपस्** castigate one's self. **अभ्या** heat, pain, torment. **उद्** the same. **उप** make hot, vex, hurt; also = P. suffer, pain, get unwell (A. also impers. w. gen. or acc. of pers.). **निस्** (**निष्**) heat, singe. **परि** burn all round, set on fire, kindle; also = P. feel pain, suffer, do penance (± **तपस्**). C. pain, afflict. **प्र** A. give out heat, burn, shine (l. & f.); shine upon, warm, heat, singe, roast, pain, torment; also = P. feel pain, suffer, castigate one's self. C. heat, warm, illumine, kindle; pain, distress. **प्रति** give out heat towards, make hot or warm. **वि** give out strong heat, burn; pervade, penetrate. **सम्** heat, burn, pain, torment (also C.); suffer pain, repent. P. be distressed, grieve, do penance. **अभिसम्** vex, distress. — Cf. **उत्तप्त**, **उपतप्त**, **प्रतपन्त्**, **प्रतप्त**, **संतप्त**.
तप a. heating, burning, tormenting (—°); m. heat, fire, penance, religious austerity.
तपःक्लम a. exhausted by austerities.
तपःक्षम a. fit to bear austerities.

तपती f. N. of a daughter of the Sun & of a river.

तपन a. warming, burning, shining (of the sun); vexing, tormenting. m. the sun, a cert. hot hell. f. **तपनी** heat, ardour. n. **तपन** the same + pain, penance, religious austerity.

तपनीय m. a sort of rice; n. (purified) gold.

तपनीयाशोक m. a kind of Açoka.*

तपश्चरण n., **°श्चर्या** f. the practice of penance.

तपस् n. warmth, heat, ardour; pain, grief; religious austerity, penance, meditation; (*m.) a cert. month or season.

तपस्य्, **तपस्यति** do penance.

तपस्य a. produced by heat; m. a cert. cool month, a man's name; f. **आ** & n. penance, austerity.

तपस्वन्त् a. glowing; ascetic, devout.

तपस्विकन्या f., **°जन** m. a female devotee.

तपस्विजन m. = seq. m. (also coll.).

तपस्विन् a. distressed, miserable; devout, pious, doing penance; m. & f. **तपस्विनी** an ascetic, a religious man or woman.

तपात्यय & **तपान्त** m. the end of the heat, the rainy season.

तपिष्ठ (superl.) very hot or burning.

तपिष्णु a. burning, glowing, hot.

तपीयंस् (compar.) extremely ascetic; more ascetic than (gen.).

तपु a. burning, hot.

तपुषि a. the same; m. or f. a burning weapon.

तपुष्पा a. drinking hot (drinks).

तपुस् a. = **तपु**.

तपोधन a. rich in penance, ascetic, pious; m. a devout or pious man.

तपोनिधि m. a treasure of penance, i.e. a very pious man.

तपोऽन्त a. ending with austerity.

तपोभृत् a. bearing penance, ascetic; m. = prec.

तपोमध्य a. having austerity in the middle.

तपोमूल a. founded on austerity.

तपोयज्ञ a. having austerity as sacrifice.

तपोयुक्त a. devout, religious (lit. furnished with penance).

तपोयोग m. practice of austerities.

तपोरत & **°रति** a. delighting in penance.

तपोलुब्ध a. eager for penance, devout.

तपोवन n. penance grove, hermitage.

तपोवन्त् a. ascetic, devout, pious.

तपोवृद्ध a. strong by or rich in penance, very devout or religious.

तप्त a. heated, burnt, hot, molten, scorched, distressed, afflicted; (having) undergone (**तपः**); n. adv.; as subst. hot water.

तप्तकृच्छ्र m. n. a kind of penance.

तप्तायस् n. red-hot iron.

तप्ति & **तप्यति** f. heat, warmth.

तप्तृ a. making hot or warm.

तप्यतु a. hot, glowing; f. = **तप्ति**.

तम्, **ताम्यति** (°ते), pp. **तान्त** become dark, dull, or stiff; faint away, be exhausted, languish, perish (also impers. w. acc. of subj.). — **आ**, **उद्**, & **सम्** languish, be perplexed. **प्र** be out of breath, be exhausted, languish. — Cf. **अवतान्त**, **नितान्त**.

तमक m. a kind of asthma.

तमन n. the becoming breathless.

तमस् n. darkness, gloom; mental darkness, illusion; error, ignorance (ph.).

तमस a. dark-coloured; n. darkness.

तमस्वन्त् (f. **°स्वती** & **तमस्वरी**) dark, gloomy.

तमाम् (—° in adv., later also in fin. verbs) in a high degree, very, much.

तमाल m. N. of a tree.

तमिस्र n. darkness (also f. **तमिस्रा**), a dark night; a cert. dark hell, hell i.g.

तमोघ्न a. destroying darkness; m. the sun.

तमोनिष्ठ a. founded on darkness.

तमोनुद् & **°नुद** a. expelling darkness.

तमोभूत a. dark, ignorant, stupid.

तमोमय, f. **ई** consisting of darkness.

तमोरूप & **°रूपिन्** a. the same.

तमोवन्त् a. dark, gloomy.

तमोवृध् a. delighting in darkness.

तमोहन् a. destroying darkness.

तम्र a. obscuring or choking.

तर् m. (only nom. pl. **तारस्**) star.

तर a. crossing, surpassing, overcoming (—°); m. passage, ferry, freight.

तरक्ष or **तरक्षु** m. hyena.

तरंग्, **°गति**, **°ते** wave, heave.

तरंग m. a wave (fig. of a section in a book); jumping motion, leap; waving, moving to and fro.

तरंगय्, °यति, pp. **तरंगित** (q.v.) move to and fro (trans.), toss.

तरंगवात m. air or wind coming from the waves.

तरंगित a. waving, fluctuating, restless, agitated; n. as abstr.

तरंगिन् a. waving, moving to and fro; f. °णी a river; fig. = **तरंग**.

तरण n. crossing, surpassing.

तरणि a. running through or onward, quick, fleet; eager, ardent; helpful, favourable; m. the sun.

तरणित्व n. eagerness, zeal.

तरणीय a. to be crossed or surpassed.

तरतमतस् adv. more or less.

तरद्द्वेषस् a. overwhelming enemies.

तरध्यै dat. inf. to **तॄ**.

तरल a. moving to and fro, trembling, glittering, shining; inconstant, fickle, perishable (abstr. °ता f., °त्व n.); m. wave, billow, the central gem in a necklace, pl. N. of a people; f. **आ** & n. rice-gruel.

तरलय्, °यति, pp. **तरलित** move to and fro, shake (tr. & intr.).

तरलिका f. N. of a woman.*

1**तरस्** n. speed, energy, efficacy, strength; ferry, raft. Instr. speedily, quickly, violently.

2**तरस्** a. rash, energetic.

तरस m n. flesh; a. °**मय** consisting of flesh.

तरस्वन्त् & **तरस्विन्** a. rash, energetic, bold, valiant.

तराम् adv. very, much (—° in adv., later in verbs); w. **न** by no means.

तरि or **तरी** f. boat, ship.

तरिक m. ferry-man; f. **आ** boat.

तरिणी f. boat, ship.

तरिवार sword; °**धारा** f. sword-blade.*

1**तरी** f. v. **तरि**.

2**तरी** f. = **स्तरी**.

तरीयंस् (compar.) running through (acc.).

तरीषणि (inf.) to run through (acc.).

1**तरु** a. rash.

2**तरु** m. tree.

तरुकोटर n. the hollow of a tree.

तरुगहन n. the thicket of a tree.

तरुच्छाया f. the shade of a tree.

तरुण, f. **ई** young, tender, new, fresh; just begun (heat), just risen (sun, moon, etc.). m. young man, N. of sev. plants, also a man's name; f. **तरुणी** young woman, girl; n. cartilage; sprout, stalk.

तरुणय्, °यति refresh, strengthen.

तरुणादित्य m. the young (i.e. just risen) sun.

तरुणिमन् m. youth, juvenility.

तरुतल n. the place under a tree.

1**तरुतृ** a. winning, conquering (acc.).

2**तरुतृ** m. conqueror, impeller (gen.).

तरुत्र a. carrying across; gaining or granting victory.

तरुमण्डप s. arbour, bower.

तरुमूल n. root of a tree, also = **तरुतल**.

तरुराजि f. row of trees, avenue.

तरुष्, **तरुषति**, °ते overcome, vanquish. — **आ** pass over, cross.

तरुष m. conqueror, vanquisher; f. **ई** victorious fight.

तरुषण्ड n. a group of trees.

तरुष्य्, pp. **तरुष्यन्त्** fighting (tr.).

तरुस् n. fight, contest; superiority.

तरूट m. the root of the lotus.

तरूषस् a. victorious, superior.

तर्क्, **तर्कयति** (°ते) suppose, conjecture, guess, reflect, regard as (2 acc.), think of (acc.), think to (inf.). — **परि** ponder, think over, consider as (2 acc.). **वि** suppose, conjecture, reflect on (acc.), ascertain. **सम्** regard as (2 acc.).

तर्क m. supposition, conjecture, opinion; meditation, discussion, philosophical doctrine or system, refutation.

तर्कसंग्रह m. T. of a work (v. prec.).

तर्किन् a. supposing, thinking, reasoning, skilled in speculation or philosophy.

तर्कु s. spindle.

तर्ज्, **तर्जति** (°ते), pp. **तर्जित** (q.v.) threaten, menace, abuse, revile. C. **तर्जयति**, °ते = S. + deride, mock; frighten, terrify. — **अभि** & **वि** C. scold, revile. **परि** C. threaten. **सम्** C. = S.C.

तर्जन n. = seq., also = f. आ censure, blame; f. ई the fore-finger.
तर्जित n. threat, menace.
तर्णक m. calf; any young animal.
तर्दृ m. a sort of insect (lit. borer).
तर्दन & तर्द्मन् n. hole, opening, cleft.
तर्पण, f. ई satiating, refreshing, comforting. n. the action of satiating etc.; satiety, fulness, comfort, pleasure, satisfaction; restorative, nourishment, food.
तर्पणीय a. to be satiated or satisfied.
†तर्मन् v. सुतर्मन्.
तर्य m. N. of a man.
तर्ष m., °ण n. thirst, greediness, desire.
तर्षित a. thirsty, desirous of (—°).
तर्ष्यावन्त् a. thirsty.
तर्हण, f. ई crushing.
तर्हि adv. at that time, in that case, then (often correl. w. यर्हि, यद्, यदा, यत्र, यदि, चेद्); therefore, then, now, well (esp. w. imper. or interr.).
तल m. n. place on or under (gen. or —°), surface, bottom, plain; often corresp. to a more special word, as पाणितल palm of the hand, नभस्तल vault of the sky, often otiose. n. arm-leather (cf. अङ्गुलित्र).
तलघोष m. clapping of the hands.
तललोक m. the nether world.
तलव m. a musician.
तलवकार m. N. of a Vedic school.
तलवकारोपनिषद् f. T. of an Upanishad.
तलातल n. a cert. hell.
तलाशा f. a cert. tree.
तलित a. fried.
तलिन a. thin, slender; small, little.
तलिम n. floor, pavement.
तलोद्य n. a cert. part of the body.
तल्प m. (आ f.) bed, couch, fig. = wedlock.
तल्पग a. going to the bed of (—°); cf. prec.
तल्पज a. born in a marriage bed (but by an appointed substitute of the man).
तल्प्य a. belonging to a bed; born in wedlock.
तवस् a. strong, bold, m. strength, heroism.
तवस्य n. = prec. m.
तवस्वन्त् a. = तवस् adj.
तवागा a. strong, huge (bull).
तविष a. = तवस् a.; f. तविषी & n. = तवस् m.
तविषीमन्त् a. strong, bold, courageous.
तविषीय्, °यति, pp. °यन्त् & °यमाण be strong, violent, or eager; exert one's self.
तविषीयु & तविषीवन्त् a. = तविषीमन्त्.
तविष्य्, °यति = तविषीय्.
तविष्या f. violence, force.
तवीयंस् compar. to तवस् a.
तव्य or तव्य a. strong, powerful.
तव्यंस a. = तवीयंस्.
तष्टि f. carpentry.
तष्टृ m. builder, carpenter.
तसर n. shuttle.
तस्कर m. thief, robber; abstr. °ता† f., °त्व† n.
तस्थु a. stationary, immovable.
तस्मात् (abl. adv.) therefore, then (correl. to यद् or यस्मात्).
ताक्ष्ण, f. ई belonging to a carpenter.
ताजक् & ताजत् adv. suddenly, at once.
ताजक & ताजिक m. a Persian.
ताड a. beating (—°); m. strike, blow.
ताडक m. killer; f. आ N. of a Yakṣiṇī changed into a Rākṣasī and killed by Rāma.
ताडन a. beating, striking, hurting; n. the act of beating, stroke, blow.
ताडनीय a. to be beaten.
ताडाग a. being in or coming from ponds.
ताड्य a. = ताडनीय.
ताण्डव s. a wild dance, esp. of the god Çiva.
ताण्डवित a dancing, hopping (cf. prec.).
ताण्ड्य m. patr. N. of a teacher.
ताण्ड्यब्राह्मण n. T. of a Brāhmaṇa.
तात् (abl. adv.) thus, then.
तात m. father; voc. also i.g. reverend, dear.
तातृपि a. satisfying, delightful.
तात्कालिक, f. ई lasting that (i.e. the same) time or belonging to it; happening at that moment, i.e. immediate, sudden.
तात्त्विक a. essential, real, true.
तात्पर्य n. the being devoted to or aiming at one object; the real meaning, scope, or purport of a speech or work; °तस् with that intention.

तात्य॑ a. paternal.

तात्स्थ्य n. the being there or contained therein.

तादर्थ्य n. the being intended for that.

तादात्म्य n. the identity of nature with (instr., loc., or —°).

तादी॑त्ना adv. at that time, then.

तादृक्ष a. = तादृ॑श्.

तादृग्गुण a. of such qualities.

तादृग्रूप & °वन्त् a. of such a shape or form.

तादृग्विध a. of such a kind or nature.

तादृ॑श् a. (nom. m. f. तादृ॑ङ् & तादृक्) such like, such a one; n. तादृक् adv. in such a manner.

तादृ॑श, f. ई = prec. a.

तादृूप्य n. the being shaped like that.

ताद्विध्य n. the being qualified like that.

तान m. thread, fibre; n. expanse.

तानव n. thinness, meagreness, slenderness.

तानूनप्त्र n. a cert. ceremony relating to Agni Tanūnapāt (r.).

तान्तव, f. ई made of thread; m. son (cf. त॑न्तु); n. a web or woven cloth.

तान्ति f. choking, suffocation.

तान्त्र s. the music of a string instrument.

तान्त्रिक, f. आ & ई familiar with or contained in a cert. doctrine, esp. relating to the Tantras, mystical.

ताप m. heat, ardour, pain, affliction.

तापक a. heating, burning, purifying.

तापन, f. ई heating, burning, distressing, illumining (—°). m. the sun: n. burning, distressing, chastisement, penance; a cert. hell.

तापनीय a. made of (pure) gold; m. pl. a cert. Vedic school.

तापनीयोपनिषद् f. T. of sev. Upanishads (cf. prec.).

तापयिष्णु॑ a. burning, tormenting.

तापश्चित॑ n. a kind of ceremony (r.).

तापस॑ a. performing penance or belonging to it. m. a devotee, ascetic, hermit (f. ई).

तापसवेषभृत् a. wearing a hermit's clothes.

तापस्य n. the state or condition of an ascetic.

तापिच्छ & तापिञ्छ m. N. of a plant.

तापिन् a. vexing (—°); f. °नी T. of sev. Upanishads.

ताप्य m. n. marcasite.

ताम m. longing, desire.

तामरस n. a red-coloured lotus (adj. —° f. आ); f. ई lotus pond.

तामस, f. ई dark, belonging to ignorance (ph.); N. of the fourth Manu.

तामि or तामी f. suppression of the breath.

तामिस्र (पक्ष) m. the dark half of the moon; m. a Rākṣasa or a cert. hell.

ताम्बल m. a kind of hemp; adj. f. ई.

ताम्बूल n. betel (also f. ई), esp. its leaf.

ताम्बूलवीटिका f. betel-globe.

ताम्बूलिक m. a seller of betel.

1ताम्र॑ a. copper-coloured, dark-red (abstr. °ता† f., °त्व† n.); m. a kind of leprosy; n. copper or a copper vessel.

2ताम्र, f. ई made of copper; f. ई a kind of clepsydra.

ताम्रकुट्ट m. coppersmith (f. ई).

ताम्रचूड a. red-crested; m. cock.

ताम्रधूम्र॑ a. dark-red.

ताम्रनख, f. ई having red (i.e. dyed) nails; °नखाङ्गुलि b. red nails & fingers.

ताम्रपट्ट m. a copper-plate.

ताम्रपात्र n. a copper vessel.

ताम्रमय f. ई made of copper.

ताम्रलिप्त m. pl. N. of a people.

ताम्रवर्ण a. copper-coloured, dark-red.

ताम्राक्ष, f. ई red-eyed; m. a crow.

ताम्रिक a. made of copper.

ताय्, तायते (cf. 1तन्) w. वि & सम् expand.

तायन n. succeeding, prospering.

तायु॑ m. thief.

तार॑ a. all-pervading, esp. of a sound, i.e. loud, high, shrill; or of light, i.e. shining, radiant. — m. passing over, crossing (only —°); saver, deliverer (E. of sev. gods), a clear or beautiful pearl, a man's name. f. आ a star or meteor, the pupil of the eye; N. of sev. goddesses & women. n. descent to a river, bank; a loud or shrill sound (also m.); तारम् as adv. aloud; comp. तारतरम्, superl. तारतमम्.

तारक (f. °रिका) carrying over, rescuing; m. N. of a demon, pl. the children of T.;

f. तारका star (also n.), meteor, pupil of the eye, a woman's name; f. तारिका the juice of palms.

तारकाक्ष a. star-eyed.

तारकान्तक m. the killer of Tāraka, i.e. Skanda.

तारकाराज & **तारकेश्वर** m. the moon (lord of the stars).

तारकोपनिषद् f. T. of an Upanishad.

तारण a. & n. carrying over, rescuing; n. also crossing, surpassing, conquering.

तारतम्य n. the being more or less, difference, gradation, proportion.

तारल्य n. fickleness.

तारव, f. ई belonging to a tree.

ताराक्ष a. = तारकाक्ष.

ताराधिप m. the moon (lord of the stars).

तारापति m. the same; the husband of Tārā, E. of sev. gods.

तारामय, f. ई consisting of stars.

तारामृग m. N. of a lunar mansion.

तारामैत्रक n. spontaneous love (lit. the friendship of the stars).

तारायण m. the holy fig tree.

तारिक n. fare or toll for passage.

तारिन् a. carrying over, rescuing; °णी f. E. of Durgā.

तारुण्य n. youth, juvenility.

तार्किक m. thinker, philosopher.

तार्क्ष m. a cert. bird; E. of Garuḍa & Kaçyapa.

तार्क्ष्य m. N. of a mythical being, conceived as a horse, later as a bird, also = prec.

तार्ण a. made of grass.

तार्तीय a. belonging to the third, the third; n. the third part

तार्तीयीक a. the third; abstr. °त्व n.

तार्प्य or **तार्प्र्य** n. a garment made of a cert. vegetable substance.

तार्य a. to be crossed or conquered; n. fare, toll.

तार्ष्टाघ m. a cert. tree; a. (f. ई) belonging to it.

ताल m. the fan-palm (often mentioned as a banner or a measure of height); clapping of the hands, flapping (esp. of the ears of an elephant); beating time, musical time or measure, dance; E. of Çiva, pl. N. of a people. f. ई a cert. tree, palm-wine, clapping of the hands. n. the nut of the fan-palm.

तालक m. a cert. insect; f. तालिका the palm of the hand, clapping of the hands.

तालकेतु m. bearer of the palm banner, E. of sev. heroes.

तालज a. coming from the fan-palm.

तालजङ्घ a. having long (lit. palm-tree) legs; m. N. of sev. demons & heroes, pl. of a warrior tribe.

तालद्रुम m. the fan-palm tree.

तालध्वज m. = तालकेतु.

तालन n. clapping of the hands.

तालपत्त्र n. leaf of the fan-palm.

तालफल n. the nut of the fan-palm.

तालवृन्त (& *क) n. a palm-leaf or fan.

तालव्य a. palatal.

तालशब्द & **तालस्वन** m. (sound of the) clapping of the hands.

तालोयक s. a cymbal.

तालु n. (m.) palate.

तालुक (adj. —°) the same.

***तालूर** m. whirlpool.*

तालूषक s. palate.

तान्प्य a. born of the marriage-bed.

तावक, f. ई thy, thine.

तावकीन a. the same.

तावच्छत, f. ई consisting of as many hundreds.

तावच्छस् adv. so manifoldly.

तावज्ज्योक् adv. so long.

तावत्कालम् adv. the same.

तावत्कृत्वस् adv. so many times.

तावत्तात् adv. just as much or many.

तावत्फल a. yielding so much fruit (fig.).

तावद्गुण a. having so many qualities.

तावन्त् a. so great, so much (many), so long, so far (correl. w. यावन्त् q.v.). n. तावत् adv. so much, so long, so far; for a while, in the mean time (also instr. or loc.); first, at once, just, now (esp. w. imperat. or 1. pers. pres. or fut.); indeed, of course, it is true, one must admit. Often only emphasizing (± एव). — न तावत् not yet, not at all, मा तावत् by no means! तावत्—यावत् (± न) as long or as far—as. यावद्यावत्—तावत्तावत् gradually as—(so). तावत्—च no sooner—than.

तावन्मात्र, f. ई just as much.

तासून m. a sort of hemp, a. (f. ई) hempen.

तास्कर्य n. theft, robbery.

तिक्त a. sharp, pungent, bitter, fragrant.

तिक्ताय्, °यते taste bitter.

तिगित a. sharp, pointed.

तिग्म a. = prec. + poignant, hot; abstr. °ता f.

तिग्मकर m. the sun.

तिग्मजम्भ a. sharp-toothed.

तिग्मतेजन a. sharp-edged or pointed.

तिग्मतेजस् a. the same + violent, fiery; m. the sun.

तिग्मदीधिति & **तिग्मरश्मि** m. the sun.

तिग्मवीर्य a. violent, strong, intense.

तिग्महेति a. having sharp or fiery weapons.

तिग्मांशु m. the sun, fire.

तिग्मायुध a. having sharp weapons.

तिग्मेषु a. having sharp arrows.

तिज्, तेजते, pp. तिक्त (q.v.) be or make sharp. C. तेजयति sharpen, incite. D. तितिक्षते (°ति) wish to be sharp or firm against, i.e. endure, bear (acc.). I. तेतिक्ते = S. tr. & intr. — उद् & सम् C. incite, impel. — Cf. निंतिक्त.

तितउ s. sieve, cribble.

तितिक्षा f. endurance, patience; a. °क्षु.

तितीर्षा f. wish to pass over; a. °र्षु.

तित्तिर m. partridge.

तित्तिरि or **तित्तिरि** m. the same (abstr. °त्व† n.), N. of an ancient teacher & a serpent-demon.

तिथि m. f. a lunar day (also तिथी f.); °विशेष a particular l.d.*

तिनिश m. N. of a tree.

तिन्तिडिका & **तिन्तिडी** f. tamarind.

तिन्दुक m., ई f. N. of a plant.

तिम्, **तिम्यति**, pp. **तिमित** become quiet (or *damp*).

तिमि m. a large fish, fish i.g.

तिमिंगिल m. swallower of the Timi, a large fabulous fish.

तिमिंगिलगिल m. swallower of the Timingila (v. prec.).

तिमिर a. dark, gloomy; n. darkness, dimness of the eyes.

तिमिरय्, °यति darken, obscure.

तिमिरौघ m. deep (lit. flood of) darkness.

तिरय्, °यति veil, cover, hide; restrain, oppress; pervade, fill

तिरश्चीन a. transverse, oblique.

तिरश्चीनवंश m. cross-beam.

तिरस् prep. through, across, beyond, past, without, against (acc.), apart, secretly, or safely from (abl.); adv. crossways, aside, awry; privately, covertly. — Cf. कृ, धा, भू.

तिरस्कर, f. ई surpassing (gen.).

तिरस्करिन् m., °रिणी f. veil, curtain.

तिरस्कार m. abuse, reproach, contempt (adj. °रिन्); armour, mail.

तिरस्कृति (—°) & **तिरस्क्रिया** f. = तिरस्कार abstr.

तिरीट (*n. a kind of head-dress); p. °टिन्.

तिरोअह्न्य a. having lasted beyond a day; left from the day before yesterday.

तिरोजनम् adv. apart from men.

तिरोधा f. concealment, secrecy.

तिरोधान n., °भाव m. disappearance, vanishing.

तिरोभूत a. disappeared, vanished.

तिरोहित a. hidden, concealed, vanished.

तिरोऽह्न्य a. = तिरोअह्न्य.

तिर्यक्ता f., °त्व n. condition of a beast.

तिर्यक्प्रतिमुखागत n. the coming sideways or backwards.

तिर्यगायत a. stretched out obliquely.

तिर्यग्ग a. going obliquely.

तिर्यग्गत a. going horizontally.

तिर्यग्गति f. condition of a beast.

तिर्यग्ज a. born from an animal.

तिर्यग्जन & **तिर्यग्योन** m. a beast (lit. = pr.).

तिर्यग्योनि f. the womb of an animal; condition or race of animals (incl. plants), organic nature.

तिर्यग्वलन n. oblique movement, deflection.

तिर्यञ्च् (nom. m. तिर्यङ्, f. तिरश्ची, n. तिर्यक्) transverse, oblique, horizontal; m. n. an animal (as horizontal, not erect), esp. an amphibious animal, i.g. any creature except man; n. breadth, adv. = तिरश्चा or °श्चि sideways, obliquely, across.

तिल (**तिल**) m. the sesamum plant or seed; mole or spot, small particle of anything.

तिलक m. N. of a tree; freckle, mole, spot under the skin; coloured mark, esp. on the forehead either as an ornament or a sectarian distinction (also n.); the ornament or pride of (—°).

तिलकक्रिया f. painting, ornamenting (v. prec.).

तिलकभूत a. being the ornament of (gen.).*

तिलकय्, °यति, pp. तिलकित mark, ornament, glorify.

तिलतैल n. sesamum-oil.

तिलद्रोण s. a Droṇa of sesamum.

तिलपर्ण & °पर्णिक n. sandal-wood.

तिलपर्णिका & °पर्णी f. the sandal-tree.

तिलपोड m. sesamum-grinder.

तिलप्रद a. giving sesamum.

तिलमय, f. ई made of sesamum.

तिलमिश्र & °मिश्र† a. mixed with sesamum.

तिलशस् adv. in small (lit. sesamum-) pieces.

तिलसंबद्ध a. mixed with sesamum.

तिलसर्षप n. pl. sesamum and mustard-seed.

तिलाम्बु n. water with sesamum.

तिलिङ्ग & °देश m. N. of a country.

तिलोत्तमा f. N. of an Apsaras.

तिलोदक n. = तिलाम्बु.

तिलोदन or **तिलौदन** n. boiled rice with sesamum.

तिल्पिञ्ज & **तिल्वक** m. names of plants.

तिल्विल a. fertile, rich.

तिष्य or **तिष्य** m. N. of a heavenly archer (cf. कृशानु) & of a lunar mansion.

तिसृ f. pl. three.

तीक्ष्ण a. sharp, hot, pungent, acid; harsh, rude, noxious; eager, quick; subtle, keen, intelligent. m. a man's name; f. N. of sev. plants; n. adv., as subst. *iron, poison, slaughter.

तीक्ष्णकर m. = तीक्ष्णांशु.

तीक्ष्णता f., °त्व n. sharpness, pungency.

तीक्ष्णदंष्ट्र a. having sharp teeth.

तीक्ष्णदण्ड a. inflicting severe punishment.*

तीक्ष्णधार a. sharp-edged.

तीक्ष्णभङ्ग a. knocked (sharply) asunder.*

तीक्ष्णविपाक a. burning in digestion.

तीक्ष्णशृङ्ग a. sharp-horned.

तीक्ष्णहृदय a. hard-hearted; abstr. °त्व n.

तीक्ष्णांशु a. having hot rays; m. the sun.

तीक्ष्णाग्र a. sharp-pointed.

तीक्ष्णाम्ल a. bitter-sour.*

तीक्ष्णार्चिस् a. having hot rays.

तीक्ष्णेषु a. having sharp arrows.

तीर n. shore, bank, brim (of a vessel).

तीरज a. growing near a shore; m. such a tree.

तीरय्, °ति get through, bring to an end.

तीररुह a. & m. = तीरज.

तीरिका f. a sort of arrow.

तीर्थ n. (m.) passage, access, approach (esp. to a water or the altar); descent into a water, landing or bathing-place (poss. °वन्त्†), shrine or holy place of pilgrimage, any venerable or worthy thing or person, esp. counsellor, adviser, teacher (also counsel, instruction); certain lines or parts of the hand sacred to sev. gods; the right way, place, or moment.

तीर्थक a. worthy, sacred. m. an ascetic, the chief of a sect; n. a holy bathing-place.

तीर्थकर a. creating a passage, sc. through life (Viṣṇu & Çiva); m. a venerable person, esp. the chief of a sect.

तीर्थमृत्तिका f. earth from a holy bathing-place.*

तीर्थयात्रा f. visit to a sacred shrine or bathing-place, pilgrimage.

तीर्थोदक n. water from a sacred bathing-place.

तीर्थ्य a. belonging to a ford or bathing-place; m. = तीर्थक m.

तीवर m. hunter (a mixed caste).

तीव्र a. strong, violent, intense, fierce; m. & °ता† f. abstr.

1**तु**, **तवीति** be strong. — उद् & सम् (I. तंवीत्वत्) effect, bring about.

2**तु** (**तू**) (indecl.) pray, do (w. imperat.); but, on the contrary (± एवं or वै); often only explet. — किं तु & परं तु yet, however (esp. after a concess. sent.); न तु yet not, rather than (esp. after कामम्, भूयस्, वरम् etc.). तु—तु on the one hand—on the other, indeed—but.

तुक् m. child, boy.

तुग्र m. N. of the father of Bhujyu & an enemy of Indra.

तुग्र्य m. patron. of Bhujyu; pl. the race of Tugra.

तुग्वन् n. ford.

तुङ्ग a. high, lofty, sublime (abstr. °त्व n.); m. height, eminence, mountain.

तुङ्गबल m. a man's name.

तुङ्गिमन् m. height, sublimity.

तुच् s. (only dat. तुचे) offspring.

तुच्छ a. empty, void, vain, s. a paltry thing; abstr. °त्व n.

तुच्छय्, °यति make empty or poor.

तुच्छ्य a. void, empty, vain; n. as abstr.

1तुज्, तुजति, °ते (तुञ्जति & तुञ्जते 3 pl.) push on, impel, stir up; press out, emit, promote, further; M. dash together or wave to and fro, hasten, rush on; P. be vexed or angry. C. तुजयति hasten, run. — Cf. आतुजे, तूतुजान.

2तुज् a. & s. urging, pressing, impelling.

3तुज् s. (only तुजम् & तुजे) = तुच्.

तुजसे dat. inf. to 1तुज्.

1तुजि (only dat. तुजये) propagation.

2तुजि m. N. of a man protected by Indra.

तुज्य a. to be pushed or impelled.

तुञ्ज m. shock, impulse.

तुण्ड n. beak, snout, trunk (of an elephant), mouth, face; point; chief, head; E. of Çiva, N. of a Rakṣas; f. ई a kind of cucumber.

तुण्डिक a. having a trunk.

तुण्डिकेर m. N. of a people.

तुण्डिभ & तुण्डिल a. having a prominent navel.

तुण्डेल m. a cert. evil spirit or goblin.

तुतुर्वणि a. striving to bring near or to obtain.

तुत्थ n. blue vitriol.

तुद्, तुदति (°ते), pp. तुन्न strike, push, prick; pound, crush. C. तोदयति goad, prick. — आ goad, urge on. नि pierce, penetrate. प्र strike at, prick at; C. urge, impel. वि pierce, strike, tear.

तुद a. striking (—°).

तुन्द n. belly, f. ई navel.

तुन्दिल a. having a large belly.

तुन्नवाय m. tailor.

तुबर a. astringent.

तुमुल a. noisy, tumultuous, confused; m. n. noise, tumult, uproar.

तुम्ब m., ई f. a kind of long gourd.

तुम्बुरु m. N. of a Gandharva & sev. men.

तुम्र a. big, strong.

1तुर्, तुरति, °ते, तुरयति, °ते hasten, advance, run; तूर्यति overcome. D. तूतूर्षति press forwards.

2तुर् a. hastening, speeding; conquering.

1तुर a. quick, eager, prompt, willing.

2तुर a. strong, mighty, victorious, wealthy, abundant.

3तुर a. hurt, wounded.

तुरक m. pl. the Turks.

तुरग m. a horse (lit. = seq.); f. ई a mare.

तुरगातु a. going quickly.

तुरंग & तुरंगम m. (ई f.) = तुरग.

तुरंगिन् a. consisting of horses or horsemen.

तुरण a. quick, nimble.

तुरण्य्, °यति be quick, hasten, speed (trans. & intr.).

तुरण्यु a. quick, eager, zealous.

तुरम् adv. quickly.

तुरया a. going quickly.

तुरायण n. a cert. sacrifice.

तुरि f. victorious strength (only dat. तुर्यै), also = seq.

तुरी f. the weaver's brush.

तुरीप n. seminal fluid; adj. spermatic.

तुरीय (तुरीय or तुरीय) a. the fourth, consisting of four; n. one fourth.

तुरीयभाज् a. partaking of a fourth.

तुरुष्क m. pl. N. of a people, the Turks.

तुर्य a. = तुरीय.

तुर्यवह् (nom. °वाट्) a. four years old; m. such an ox, f. तुर्यौही such a cow.

तुर्या f. superior strength.

तुर्व्, तूर्वति overpower.

तुर्व m. = तुर्वश.
तुर्वणि a. conquering (acc.), victorious.
तुर्वणे dat. inf. to तुर्व्.
तुर्वश m. N. of an Aryan hero, mostly connected with Yadu; pl. his race. तुर्वशायदू du. Turvaça and Yadu.
तुर्वसु m. N. of a son of Yayāti.
तुर्वीति m. N. of a man.
तुल्, तोलयति & तुलयति, °ते, pp. तुलित lift up, weigh, examine, compare; equal, match, resemble. — आ lift up. उद् raise, weigh. सम् weigh against each ofter.
तुलन n lifting, weighing. rating.
तुला f. balance, scales; measure, weight; equal weight, resemblance, similarity, likeness with (instr.); the Libra in the zodiac. Acc. w. इ, गम्, आ-या, अधि-रुह्, etc. equal, resemble, be like (instr.); instr. w. धृ weigh, compare with (instr.).
तुलाकोटि m. = तुलायष्टि or an ornament on the feet of a woman.
तुलाधारण n. weighing.
तुलामान n. weights and measures.
तुलायष्टि f. the end of the beam of a balance.
तुलायोग m. pl. the various modes of employing a balance.
तुलावन्त् a. having a pair of scales.
तुलिम a. to be or being weighed.
तुल्य a. equal in (instr. or loc.), to (instr. ± सह, gen., or —°), like, resembling, similar. °— & n. adv. similarly, in like manner as (instr. or —°).
तुल्यजातीय a. of like kind, similar.
तुल्यप्रभाव a. of equal dignity.
तुल्यभाग्य a. of like destiny.
तुल्ययोगोपमा f. a kind of comparison (rh.).
तुल्यवर्चस् a. of equal strength.
तुल्यशीलता f. like disposition.
तुल्यान्तरम् adv. in equal intervals.
तुल्याभिजन a. of like descent, related.
तुल्यारिमित्रता f. the state of having the same enemies and friends, defensive and offensive alliance.
तुल्यार्थ a. equally rich.
तुल्यावस्थ a. being in a similar condition.
†तुवि a. (only °—) much, many, great, strong.
तुविजात a. powerful (lit. strong born).
तुविकूर्मि & †°र्मिन् a. powerful in work.
तुविक्रतु a. having great power.
तुविद्युम्न a. very glorious.
तुविनृम्ण a very valiant or courageous.
†तुविमन्यु a. very zealous or furious.
तुविराधस् a. granting abundantly.
तुविष्टम (superl.) strongest, most powerful.
तुविष्मन्त् a. powerful, mighty.
तुविष्वणस् a. calling loud, roaring.
तुविष्वणि & °ष्वन् a. the same.
†तुविस् v. तुविष्टम & तुविष्मन्त्.
तुवीमघ a. giving abundantly.
तुवीरव a. roaring awfully, thundering.
1तुश्, तोशते drip (intr.). — नि drip down (tr. & intr.); C. grant, distribute.
2तुश्, तोशते be pleased or content, feed on (instr.); appease, satisfy.
तुष्, तुष्यति (°ते), pp. तुष्ट become quiet, be satisfied or pleased with, delight in (gen., dat., instr., loc., or acc. w. प्रति); also = C. तोषयति, °ते (तुषयति) satisfy. — उप C. satisfy. परि be delighted or charmed, be happy. C. satisfy completely, please much. सम् be calm, content, or happy. C. gratify, rejoice, comfort. — Cf. परितुष्ट, संतुष्ट.
तुष m. the husk or chaff of grain.
तुषधान्य n. a leguminous plant.
तुषाग्नि & तुषानल m. fire of chaff.
तुषाम्बु n. sour rice or barley-gruel.
तुषार a. cold; m. frost, rime, dew, ice, snow.
तुषारकण m. a flake of snow.
तुषारकर m. the moon (h. cold rays).
तुषारकिरण & तुषारद्युति m. the same.
तुषारगिरि m. the Himālaya (l. snowy mountain).
तुषारपतन n. snowfall.
तुषाररश्मि & तुषारांशु m. = तुषारकर.
तुषाराद्रि m. = तुषारगिरि.
तुषित m. pl. a cert. class of gods.
तुष्टप्रकृति a. having contented subjects.
तुष्टि f. satisfaction, pleasure.
तुष्टिकर a. causing satisfaction, sufficient.
तुष्टिमन्त् a. satisfied. contented.
तुहिन n. = तुषार m.; °कण m. snowflake.
तुहिनकर & तुहिनकिरण m. the moon.

तुहिनगिरि m. the Himālaya.
तुहिनद्युति & तुहिनमयूख m. the moon.
तुहिनाचल & तुहिनाद्रि m. = तुहिनगिरि.
तूण m., ई f. (adj. —° तूणक) quiver.
तूणव m. a flute.
तूणवध्म m. flute-player.
तूणि m. quiver; poss. तूणिन्.
तूणीर m. = prec. m.
तूत m. mulberry-tree.
तूतुजान or तूतुजान a. eager, quick.
1तूतुजि a. quick, swift, nimble.
2तूतुजि a. furthering, promoting (w. gen.).
तूतुम a. strong, big, copious.
तूपर a. hornless; m. such a goat.
तूय a. strong, vigorous; n. eagerly, quickly.
तूर् f. haste, speed; instr. swiftly.
तूर्ण a. quick, swift; n. adv.
तूर्णाश n. shoot of water.
तूर्णि a. quick, eager.
तूर्त a. quick, swift.
†तूर्ति v. विश्वतूर्ति.
1तूर्य n. a musical instrument.
2तूर्य a. the fourth.
3†तूर्य v. वृचतूर्य.
तूर्यघोष m. sound of musical instruments.
तूर्व् v. तुर्व्.
तूर्वयाण a. overpowering; m. N. of a man.
तूर्वि a. victorious, superior.
तूल n. panicle of a flower or plant, tuft of grass; cotton (also तूलक n. & तूली f.).
तूलिक m. seller of cotton.
तूलिनी f. the silk-cotton tree.
†तूष m. n. border or fringe of a garment.
तूष्णीक a. silent.
तूष्णीम् adv. silently, still; w. भू be silent.
तूष्णीभाव m. silence.
तूस्त n. dust.
तॄ, तरति, °ते, तिरति, °ते, तुरति, °ते, तितर्ति, तरुते, pp. तीर्ण (w. act. & pass. mg) cross over, get through, overcome, subdue, escape; float, swim, rush on; be saved, survive; M. emulate, content, also = C. तारयति, °ते lead or help over (acc.), bring to (acc. or dat.), further, save. D. तितीर्षति, °ते wish to pass over or to arrive at (acc.). I. तर्तरीति, तरीतर्ति, pp. तरीचत् get through, be victorious or fortunate. — अति & व्यति cross, pass, overcome. अभि overtake, get up to (acc.). अव come down, descend (esp. from heaven to earth, ± महीम्), alight; betake one's self from (abl.) to (acc.); take place, happen; overcome, surpass. C. make descend, lead or bring (down) from (abl.) to (acc. or loc.); remove, take off, avert from (abl.); introduce, establish. आ pass, cross, overcome; enlarge, increase. उद् the same + come up from (abl.), esp. out of the water (± जलात्), escape, be saved from (abl.). C. cause to come out, vomit up, take off; lead or fetch over, save from (abl.), deliver, rescue. अभ्युद् cross, pass, get through unto (dat.). समुद् = उद्. नि overthrow, humiliate. निस् come forth from, get out of (abl.); pass, finish, accomplish; overcome, master. C. save, deliver; overcome, vanquish. प्र take to the water, cross over; start on, advance, increase, grow; lead on, further, strengthen, promote, prolong (esp. आयुस् the life); M. live on. C. extend, lengthen; cheat, deceive; lead astray, seduce to (dat. or loc.). विप्र C. cheat, deceive. वि cross through, traverse; further, promote, prolong; remove from (abl.); destroy, frustrate; grant, bestow, give, offer; perform, cause, effect. सम् cross over, pass through (l. & f.), escape, be saved; also = C. bring over, save. — Cf. अवतीर्ण, उत्तीर्ण, निस्तीर्ण, वितीर्ण.
तृच m. n. a stanza of three verses.
तृण n. grass, herb, grass-blade, straw; fig. small or worthless thing, trifle.
तृणवत् or तृणी कृ & तृणं मन् = तृणय्.
तृणकाष्ठ n. grass and wood.
तृणकुटि f. hut of grass or straw.
तृणकुटीर & °क s. the same.
तृणकूट m. n. heap of grass.
तृणच्छेदिन् a. who tears off grass.
तृणजलायुका & °जलूका f. caterpillar.

तृणतन्तु m. grass-blade.
तृणप्राय a. full of grass.
तृणभुज् a. eating grass; m. grass-eater.
तृणमय a. consisting of grass, grassy.
तृणय्, °यति value like grass, i.e. slighten, despise.
तृणराज् m. the vine-palm (lit. king of the grasses).
तृणराज m. the palmyra tree (lit. = prec.).
तृणलव m. grass-blade.
तृणवन्त् a. full of grass.
तृणस्कन्द m. N. of a man.
तृणाग्नि m. a grass or straw-fire.
तृणाङ्कुर m. young (lit. shoot of) grass.
तृणाद a. eating grass, graminivorous.
तृणाश, °न & तृणाशिन् a. the same; m. ruminant.
तृणेन्द्र m. = तृणराज्.
तृणोदक n. sgl. grass and water.
तृणोल्का f. a torch of hay.
1तृतीय a. the third; n. adv. thirdly, for the third time. f. आ the third day in a half month; the endings of the third case & the third case itself (g.).
2तृतीय a. forming the third part; n. one third.
तृतीयदिवस m. the third day; loc. (on) the day after to-morrow.
तृतीयसवन n. the third Soma offering (in the evening).
1तृतीयांश m. a third part.
2तृतीयांश a. receiving a third as share.
तृतीयासमास m. a third (case) compound (g.).
तृतीयिन् a. = 2तृतीयांश.
तृत्सु m. N. of a race or people.
तृद्, तृणत्ति, तृन्त्ते, pp. तृण्ण split, bore, open, let free. — अनु bore after i.e. for (water), make flow. अभि split, open, release; win, acquire. आ split, pierce, separate. वि pierce, cleave, open, break through, excavate. सम् hollow out, connect by a hole, fasten, together.
तृदिल a. having holes, porous.
तृप्, तृप्यति (°ते), तृप्णोति (तृप्नोति), तृम्पति (तर्पति), pp. तृप्त satiate one's self, be satisfied or content with (gen., instr. or —°); enjoy (abl.). C. तर्पयति, °ते satisfy, please, nourish; M. refl. — अभि C. satiate, refresh. आ be satiated or satisfied; C. satiate. परि C. satiate or refresh thoroughly. प्र C. satiate, fill. वि be satiated or pleased. सम् be satiated or satisfied with (gen.). C. satiate, refresh, gladden.
तृपत् adv. one's fill.
तृपल a. restless, eager; n. adv.
तृप्तता f. satiety, satisfaction.
तृप्तांशु a. having abundant juice or strong shoots (Soma).
तृप्ति or तृप्ति f. = तृप्तता; p. °मन्त्†.
तृप्तिकर & °कारक a. giving satisfaction, pleasing.
तृप्र a. restless, anxious; °— & n. adv.
तृभि m. ray.
1तृष्, तृष्यति, pp. तृषित be thirsty, be greedy, desire. C. तर्षयति cause to thirst. — वि thirst, languish. C. cause to languish.
2तृष् f. thirst (lit. & fig.).
तृषा f. the same.
तृषार्त a. tormented by thirst.
तृषु a. greedy, eager, quick; n. adv.
तृषुच्यवस् & °च्युत् a. moving eagerly or quickly.
तृष्ट a. dry, rough, harsh.
तृष्टामा f. N. of a river.
तृष्णज् a. thirsty.
तृष्णा f. thirst; greediness, strong desire for (—°).
तृष्णार्त a. = तृषार्त.
तृष्णासङ्ग m. attachment to desire.
तृष्यावन्त् a. thirsty.
तृह्, तृणेढि, pp. तृढ (तृह्ळ) crush, bruise, dash to pieces. — वि = S.
तेजिष्ठम् (n. superl. adv.) sharpest, hottest.
तेज m. sharpness; N. of a man.
तेजन n. sharpening, kindling; point or shaft of an arrow, reed, bamboo; f. °नी† mat of straw, tuft, bunch, etc.
तेजस् n. sharpness, edge, (pungent) heat, fire, light, radiance, lustre, beauty, vigour, strength, energy, esp. male energy, concr.

semen virile; violence, fierceness; power, authority, dignity.

तेजस्काम a. desiring strength, energy, or dignity.

तेजस्य a. conspicuous, splendid.

तेजस्वन्त् a. burning, shining, splendid, beautiful.

तेजस्विता f., °त्व n. abstr. to seq.

तेजस्विन् a. sharp, burning, shining, radiant, bright; strong, mighty, energetic, violent; dignified, noble, glorious.

तेजिष्ठ (superl.) most sharp, hot, shining, bright, strong, or violent. n. adv.

तेजीयंस् (compar.) sharper, keener; (more) powerful or glorious.

तेजोद्वय n. the two lights (sun and moon).

तेजोमय, f. ई consisting of fire, light, or splendour; shining, bright, clear.

तेजोमूर्ति a. whose form is light.

तेजोराशि m. nothing but (lit. a heap of) splendour.

तेजोरूप a. = तेजोमूर्ति.

तेजोवन्त् a. shining, radiant.

तेजोवृत्त n. noble or dignified behaviour.

तेदनि or °नी f. (clotted) blood.

तेन (instr. adv.) in that direction, there; or in that manner, so (correl. to येन); therefore; then (correl. to येन, यद्, यस्मात्, & यतस्). — तेन हि now then.

तैक्ष्ण्य n. sharpness, pungency, harshness, severity.

तैजस, f. ई luminous, bright, splendid; metallic.

तैत्तिर, f. ई coming from a partridge or from Tittiri.

तैत्तिरीय m. pl. N. of a cert. school of the Yajurveda; °क a. belonging to it.

तैत्तिरीयब्राह्मण n. a Brāhmaṇa of the Taittirīyas (v. prec.).

तैत्तिरीयसंहिता f. the Saṁhitā of the Taittirīyas (i.e. the black Yajurveda).

तैत्तिरीयारण्यक n. an Āraṇyaka of the Taittirīyas.

तैत्तिरीयिन् m. = तैत्तिरीय.

तैत्तिरीयोपनिषद् f. an Upanishad of the Taittirīyas.

तैमिर (+ रोग) m. = तैमिर्य.

तैमिरिक a. whose eyes are dim (cf. seq.).

तैमिर्य n. dimness of the eyes.

तैर्थिक a. sectarian, heretical. m. a worthy person, an authority; n. water from a sacred bathing-place.

तैर्यग्योन a. of animal origin; m. animal.

तैर्यग्योनि & °न्य a. = prec. a.

तैल n. sesamum oil, oil i.g.

तैलकार m. oil-miller.

तैलकुण्ड n. oil-pot.

तैलघृत n. ghee with sesamum-oil.*

तैलपक m. a kind of bird.

तैलपर्णिक m. a kind of sandal-tree.

तैलपात्र n. oil-cup.

तैलप्रदीप m. oil-lamp.

तैलयन्त्र n. oil-mill.

तैलिक m. oil-miller, f. ई.

तैष, f. ई belonging to the lunar mansion Tiṣya; m. N. of a month.

तोक n. offspring, race, child (o. connected w. तनय); p. °वन्त्.

तोकसाति f. winning or breeding of children.

तोकिनी f. having or bringing forth children.

तोक्म m., **तोक्मन्** n. a young green blade, esp. of corn.

तोटक a. quarrelsome; n. violent speech, N. of a metre & a kind of drama.

तोत्त्र n. stick for driving cattle.

तोद m. instigator, exciter; the sun (as pricking or driving horses); also = seq.

तोदन n. stinging, pricking.

तोद्य n. a kind of cymbal.

तोमर m. n. spear, lance; m. pl. N. of a people.

तोय n. water (p. °वन्त्†); acc. w. कृ make a libation of water.

तोयकण m. drop of water.

तोयकर्मन् n. any ceremony with water.

तोयचर a. moving in water; m. aquatic animal.

तोयज a. born in water; n. lotus flower.

तोयद m. cloud (lit. giving water).

तोयदात्यय m. autumn (end of the clouds).

तोयधर a. bearing or containing water.

तोयधार m., आ f. stream of water.

तोयधि m. the sea (receptacle of water).
तोयपात m. rain (fall of water).
तोयमय, f. ई consisting of water.
तोयमुच् m. cloud (pouring out water).
तोयराज् m. the sea (king of the waters).
तोयराशि m. sea or lake (mass of water).
तोयवाह m. cloud (bearing water).
तोयाञ्जलि m. two handfuls of water (r.).
तोयाधार m. water reservoir, pond.
तोयालय m. sea (receptacle of water).
तोयाशय m. pond, river (lit. = prec.).
तोरण n. arch, arched doorway, portal.
तोलन n. lifting up, weighing.
तोल्य a. to be weighed.
तोश & **तोशस्** a. trickling, streaming; granting, abundant.
तोष m. satisfaction, contentment, joy in (loc., gen., or —°).
तोषण a. (f. ई) & n. satisfying, pleasing.
तोषणीय a. to be pleased or pleasant.
तोषयितव्य a. to be satisfied or pleased.
तोषिन् a. satisfied with, delighting in (—°); satisfying, pleasing.
तौग्र्य m. patr. of Bhujyu.
तौर्य n. music; °त्रय & °त्रिक n. the musical triad, i.e. instrumental music, song, and dance.
तौल्य n. weight.
तौषार a. snowy, dewy.
त्मन् m. the vital breath; one's own person or self. Instr. त्मना (f. त्मन्या) & loc. त्मन् yet, really, even, indeed; used as an emphatic particle, esp. after अध, इव, & उत. before च & न.
त्य (pron.-st.) that (person or thing); o. = the defin. article; n. त्यद् (q.v.).
त्यक्तजीवित a. prodigal of life; °योधिन् fighting with peril of life.
त्यक्तव्य a. to be abandoned, removed, given up or sacrificed.
त्यक्ताग्नि a. having forsaken the sacred fire.
त्यक्तुकाम a. desirous to abandon.
त्यक्तृ a. abandoning, prodigal of (gen. or acc.).
त्यक्त्वा ger. having left, i.e. excepting, with exception of (acc.).
1**त्यज्**, त्यजति (°ते), pp. त्यक्त (त्यजित) leave, abandon, let alone, spare, avoid, shun, dismiss, shoot off, cast away, put off, get rid of (also P. त्यज्यते w. instr.); disregard, neglect, renounce, give up; w. तनुम्, जीवितम्, प्राणान् = set aside or risk body or life, also = die. C. त्याजयति cause to leave or abandon, deprive of (2 acc.), expel, turn out (± बहिस्). — अभि quit. समभि give up, renounce, risk (जीवितम्). परि leave, abandon, expel, reject, put off, give up, disregard, neglect, set aside, risk (cf. S.). सम् leave, abandon, reject, shun, avoid, withdraw from (acc.), deliver, give up, etc. (= परि). C. deprive of (2 acc.). – Cf. त्यक्त्वा, नित्यक्त, परित्यक्त, परित्यज्य, संत्यज्य, संत्यक्त.
2**त्यज्** a. leaving, giving up (—°).
त्यजन n. abandoning.
1**त्यजस्** n. abandonment, distress.
2**त्यजस्** m. offspring, descendant.
त्यद् (n. adv. of pron. st. त्य) indeed, you know (always preceded by ह or यस्य).
त्याग m. leaving, abandoning, rejecting, avoiding, giving up; donation, sacrifice (also fig. of one's life); also = seq.
त्यागिता f. liberality. prodigality.
त्यागिन् a. leaving, abandoning, rejecting, dismissing, sacrificing, renouncing, liberal, prodigal; w. आत्मनस् giving up one's life, dying voluntarily.
त्याजक a. leaving, dismissing, rejecting.
त्याजन n. abandoning, renouncing.
त्याज्य a. to be left, abandoned, rejected, removed, avoided, given up or away.
त्रद् m. who opens or lets free.
त्रप्, त्रपते (°ति) become perplexed or ashamed. C. त्रपयति make perplexed or ashamed. — अप & व्यप turn perplexed away.
त्रप (m.), त्रपा f. perplexity, shame.
त्रपु & **त्रपुस्** n. tin.
त्रय, f. ई triple, threefold; n. a triad; f. त्रयी the same (esp. the three Vedas); त्रयी विद्या the threefold knowledge (r.).
त्रयःपञ्चाशत् f. fifty-three.
त्रयधा = त्रेधा.
त्रयाय्य a. to be guarded or protected.
त्रयस्त्रिंश, f. ई the thirty-third.

त्रयस्त्रिंशत् f. thirty-three (r. pl.).
त्रयीधर्म m. the duty taught by the three (Vedas).
त्रयीधामवन्त् a. whose light are the three (Vedas), i.e. the sun.
त्रयीनिष्कर्ष m. the extract or essence of the three (Vedas).
त्रयीमय, f. ई consisting of or based upon the three (Vedas).
त्रयोदश, f. ई the thirteenth.
त्रयोदशधा adv. in (into) 13 parts.
त्रयोदशन् or त्रयोदशन् a. thirteen.
त्रयोविंश, f. ई the twenty-third.
त्रयोविंशति f. twenty-three.
त्रस्, त्रसति (°ते) & त्रस्यति (°ते), pp. त्रस्त tremble, quake, be afraid of (abl., gen., or instr.). C. त्रासयति (°ते) shake, agitate, frighten, scare. — अप start back, flee. उद् C. frighten, rouse up. समुद् C. frighten, terrify. निस् flee. परा C. frighten away. प्र flee in terror. C. affright, scare. वि & सम् tremble, fear; C. terrify, frighten. — Cf. उत्त्रस्त, परित्रस्त, समुत्त्रस्त.
त्रस a. movable, moving; n. what moves or lives, beasts and men.
त्रसदस्यु (& त्रसद्दस्यु) m. N. of a prince.
त्रसर m. a shuttle.
त्रसरेणु m. mote of dust, atom.
त्रस्तनयन a. looking timid (lit. having frightened eyes).
त्रस्नु a. afraid, timorous.
1त्रा, त्रायते, त्राति (°ति), pp. त्रात (q.v.) protect, shelter, rescue from (abl. or gen.). — परि & सम् = S.
2त्रा m. protector.
त्राण n. = seq. + armour, mail.
त्राणन n. protection, guard.
त्रात a. protected; n. protection.
त्रातव्य a. to be protected.
त्रातृ m. protector, guardian.
त्रात्र n. protection.
त्रापुष a. made of tin.
त्रामन् n. protection, guard.
त्रास m. terror, fright.
त्रासन a. (f. ई) & n. terrifying, frightening.
त्रासनीय a. to be dreaded, dreadful.
त्रासिन् a. fearful, timid.
त्रि m. n. pl. three.
त्रिंश, f. ई the thirtieth.
त्रिंशच्छत n. one hundred and thirty.
त्रिंशत् & त्रिंशति f. thirty.
त्रिंशत्तम, f. ई = त्रिंश.
त्रिंशद्वर्ष a. thirty years old.
त्रिक a. trine, forming a triad, consisting of three; ± शत three per cent. — m. a triangular place or yard; n. a triad.
त्रिककुद् a. having three peaks, points, or horns; m. E. of Viṣṇu-Kṛṣṇa, Brahman, etc.
त्रिककुभ् a. = prec. a.; m. thunderbolt, E. of Indra.
त्रिकद्रुक m. pl. three cert. Soma-vessels.
त्रिकर्मकृत् & त्रिकर्मन् a. performing the three (chief) duties (of a Brahman, i.e. sacrifice, study of the Vedas, & liberality).
1त्रिकाल n. the three times (past, present, & future, or morning, moon, & evening).
2त्रिकाल a. belonging to the three times.
त्रिकालज्ञ & °दर्शिन् a. knowing the three times, omniscient.
त्रिकालरूप a. appearing in the form of the three times (the sun).
त्रिकूट a. having three peaks, m. N. of sev. mountains.
त्रिकृत्वस् adv. thrice, three times.
त्रिकोण a. triangular; n. triangle.
त्रिगर्त m. pl. N. of a people.
1त्रिगुण m. pl., n. sgl. the three qualities (ph.).
2त्रिगुण a. consisting of three threads or strings; threefold, triple, n. adv.
त्रिगुणात्मक a. containing the three qualities (ph.).
त्रिच m. n. = तृच.
त्रिचक्र a. three-wheeled; n. such a carriage.
त्रिचक्षुस् a. three-eyed.
त्रिचतुर pl. three or four.
त्रिजगत् n. sgl. & pl., °ती f. the triple world (heaven, earth, & the lower w.).
त्रिजट a. wearing three braids of hair; f. आ N. of a Rākṣasī.
त्रिणाचिकेत a. who has thrice kindled the Nāciketa fire.
त्रित m. N. of a god, pl. a class of gods.

त्रितय n., **त्रिता** f., **त्रित्व** n. a triad.
त्रिदण्ड n. the three staves (of a mendicant Brahman) or the triple subjection (of words, thoughts, & acts); poss. **°ण्डिन्**, as m. a religious mendicant.
त्रिदश a. pl. three times ten i.e. thirty; m. pl. the thirty (round for 33) deities.
त्रिदशता f., **°त्व** n. divinity.
त्रिदशपति m. the chief of the gods (Indra).
त्रिदशश्रेष्ठ m. the best of the gods (Brahman or Agni).
त्रिदशाधिप m. = **त्रिदशपति**.
त्रिदशाधिपति m. E. of Çiva (lit. = prec.).
त्रिदशायुध n. the divine bow, the rainbow.
त्रिदशारि m. an Asura (foe of the gods).
1**त्रिदशालय** m. the residence of the gods, i.e. heaven.
2**त्रिदशालय** m. a dweller in heaven, a god.
त्रिदशेन्द्र & **°शेश** m. = **त्रिदशपति**.
त्रिदशेश्वर m. = prec., also E. of Agni, Varuṇa, & Yama.
त्रिदिव n. the third i.e. highest heaven (in Veda always w. gen. **दिवस्**).
त्रिदिवेश्वर m. lord of the third heaven (Indra).
त्रिदिवौकस् m. an inhabitant of the third heaven, a god.
त्रिधा adv. in three ways, in (into) three parts; at three times.
त्रिधातु a. tripartite, triple; n. = **त्रिजगत्**.
1**त्रिधामन्** a. = prec. adj.; m. E. of Viṣṇu & Brahman.
2**त्रिधामन्** n. = **त्रिदिव**.
त्रिनयन a. three-eyed, m. E. of Rudra-Çiva.
त्रिपक्ष n. three fortnights.
त्रिपञ्चाश, f. **ई** the fifty-third, consisting of 53.
त्रिपथ n. the triple path (the sky, earth, & atmosphere or lower world).
त्रिपद् or **त्रिपद्** (**°पाद्**), f. **त्रिपदी** = seq., also making three steps; s. three quarters, m. E. of Viṣṇu.
त्रिपद (f. **त्रिपदा** or **त्रिपदा**) three-footed or consisting of three Pādas.
त्रिपद्य a. tripartite.
त्रिपाठिन् a. studying the three (Vedas).
त्रिपादक, f. **°दिका** three-footed.
त्रिपिटक n. the three baskets (i.e. collections of Buddhistic writings).
त्रिपिण्डी f. the three sacrificial cakes.
त्रिपिष्टप n. the (third) heaven, Indra's residence (cf. **त्रिदिव**).
त्रिपुट & **°क** m. a kind of pease.
त्रिपुण्ड्र & **°क** n. three lines made across the forehead and other parts of the body with ashes etc., esp. by the followers of Çiva.
त्रिपुर n. the triple city or the three cities (of the Asuras, destroyed by Çiva); also N. of the capital of the Cedis.
त्रिपुरघातिन् m. E. of Çiva (cf. prec.).
त्रिपुरद्रुह् & **°द्विष्** m. the same.
त्रिपुरहन्, **°पुरहर**, **°पुरान्तक** m. = **त्रिपुरघातिन्**.
त्रिपुराराति & **त्रिपुरारि** m. = **त्रिपुरद्रुह्**.
त्रिपृष्ठ a. having three backs or summits.
त्रिप्रकार a. threefold.
त्रिफल a. having three fruits.
त्रिबन्धु a. connected or related in three ways.
त्रिबाहु a. three-armed.
त्रिभाग m. the third part.
त्रिभुज a. threefold.
त्रिभुज a. = **त्रिबाहु**.
त्रिभुवन n. the three worlds (cf. **त्रिपथ**).
त्रिभुवनगुरु & **°पति** m. E. of Çiva & Viṣṇu (cf. prec.).
त्रिभुवनेश्वर m. E. of Indra or Çiva.
त्रिभौम a. three-storied.
त्रिमात्र a. containing three (prosodical) instants.
त्रिमूर्ति a. having three forms; subst. °— the trinity (i.e. Brahman, Viṣṇu, & Çiva).
त्रिमूर्धन् a. three-headed.
त्रियान n. the three vehicles (r.).
त्रियाम a. containing three watches (= 9 hours); f. **आ** night.
त्रियुग n. three periods or ages.
त्रिरश्रि n. three-cornered, triangular.
त्रिरात्र a. lasting three days (lit. nights); m. such a festival; n. such a period i.g., acc. for three days, abl. & instr. after three days.
त्रिरूप a. of three shapes or colours.

त्रिलिङ्ग a. having the three qualities (ph.), or three genders (g.). — n. the country of the Telingas.

त्रिलोक n. (only °— & loc.), **ई** f., & m. pl. the three worlds (cf. **त्रिभुवन**).

त्रिलोकनाथ m. E. of Indra or Çiva (v. prec.).

त्रिलोकीनाथ, **°पति**, & **त्रिलोकेश** m. E. of Viṣṇu or Çiva.

त्रिलोचन a. three-eyed; m. E. of Çiva, a man's name.

त्रिवत्स a. three years old (ox or cow).

त्रिवन्धुर a. three-seated (chariot).

त्रिवरूथ or **त्रिवरूथ** a. granting threefold protection.

त्रिवर्ग m. any group of three, esp. the three aims (virtue, pleasure, & wealth, cf. **चतुर्वर्ग**), the three qualities (cf. **त्रिगुण**), or the three higher castes.

त्रिवर्ण a. three-coloured.

त्रिवर्तु a. threefold.

त्रिवर्ष a. three years old; n. a period of three years.

त्रिवलि (°—) or **°वली** f. the three folds (across the belly, esp. as a mark of female beauty).

त्रिविक्रम n. the three steps; m. E. of Viṣṇu.

त्रिविक्रमसेन m. N. of a king.

त्रिविद्य a. containing the three Vedas.

त्रिविध a. of three kinds, threefold.

त्रिविधा adv. into three parts.

त्रिविष्टप n. = **त्रिपिष्टप**.

त्रिविष्टि adv. three times.

त्रिवृत् a. threefold; m. a kind of recitation, a cord or amulet of three strings.

त्रिवृत्करण n. tripling, combining three things.

त्रिवृत्ता f. abstr. to **त्रिवृत्** a.

1**त्रिवेद** (°—) the three Vedas (also **त्रिवेदी** f.).

2**त्रिवेद** a. knowing or containing the three Vedas (also **°दिन्**).

त्रिशङ्कु m. N. of an ancient sage and king (conceived as a constellation in the southern hemisphere).

त्रिशत a. 103; 300 (f. **ई**) or the 300th

त्रिशततम a. the 103d or 300th.

त्रिशस् adv. by threes.

त्रिशाख a. having three branches.

त्रिशिख a. = seq.; n. trident.

त्रिशिखर a. three-pointed.

त्रिशिरस् a. three-headed or three-pointed; a man's name.

त्रिशीर्ष & **त्रिशीर्षन्** a. three-headed.

त्रिशुच् a. having threefold splendour.

त्रिशूल n. trident (weapon of Çiva); a. bearing the trident.

त्रिशृङ्ग a. having three horns or peaks; m. N. of a mountain.

त्रिशोक a. = **त्रिशुच्**; m. N. of a Rishi.

त्रिःश्वेत a. white on three places.

त्रिषत्य a. triply true.

त्रिषधस्थ a. being in three seats or places.

त्रिषप्त a. pl. three times seven, twenty one; an indef. number i.g.

त्रिषवण n. pl. the (daily) three Soma oblations, a. connected with them.

त्रिषष् a. three times six, eighteen.

त्रिषाहस्र a. consisting of 3000.

त्रिष्टुभ् f. N. of a metre.

त्रिष्ठ a. three-seated (chariot).

त्रिष्ठिन् a. standing on threefold ground.

त्रिस् adv. three times, thrice; **त्र्यह्नस्** thrice a day.

त्रिसंध्य adv. the thee divisions of the day (dawn, noon, & sunset); a. belonging to them.

त्रिसप्त a. pl. = **त्रिषप्त**.

त्रिसवन a. & n. pl. = **त्रिषवण**.

त्रिसाधन a. dependent on three things.

त्रिसुपर्ण m. n. N. of cert. sacred texts; a. knowing these texts.

त्रिस्तन, f. **ई** three-breasted; f. **ई** N. of a Rākṣasī.

त्रिस्रोतस् f. E. of Gaṅgā (lit. having three streams, cf. **त्रिपथ**).

त्रिहायण, f. **ई** three years old.

त्रीरात्रीण a. three days (nights) old.

त्रुट्, **त्रुटति** & **त्रुट्यति** (**त्रुड्यति**), pp. **त्रुटित** burst, break (intr.), fall asunder. C. **त्रोटयति** tear, break, cut, divide.

त्रुटि f. a little bit, atom; a very minute space of time.

त्रेता f. a triad, the three sacred fires, the die

or side of the die marked with three points; the second Yuga or age of the world.
त्रेधा adv. triply, in three parts, ways, or places.
त्रैकालिक, f. **ई** relating to the three times (cf. seq.).
त्रैकाल्य n. past, present, & future.
त्रैकाल्यदर्शिन् a. knowing the three times (v. prec.); m. fortune-teller.
त्रैगुण्य n. triplicity, three qualities; also = 1**त्रिगुण**, a. = **त्रिगुणात्मक**.
त्रैत m. trilling.
त्रैतन m. N. of a cert. divine being.
त्रैदशिक a. relating to the 33 (gods).
त्रैधम् adv. = **त्रेधा**.
त्रैपद n. three quarters.
त्रैपुर a. belonging to the three cities (cf. **त्रिपुर**); m. pl. the inhabitants of them.
त्रैमासिक a. three months old or lasting three months.
त्रैयम्बक a. belonging or consecrated to Tryambaka; m. such a cake.
त्रैरूप्य n. tripleness of form.
त्रैलिङ्ग्य a. tripleness of gender.
त्रैलोक्य n. the three worlds (cf. **त्रिलोक**).
त्रैलोक्यदर्शिन् a. knowing the three worlds; m. a sage.
त्रैलोक्यराज्य n. the sovereignty over the three worlds.
त्रैवणि m. N. of an ancient teacher.
त्रैवर्गिक & **त्रैवर्ग्य** a. belonging to the Trivarga.
त्रैवर्षिक a. three years', triennial.
त्रैवार्षिक a. lasting three years.
त्रैविद्य a. studying the three Vedas or familiar with them; n. the three Vedas or the knowledge of them.
त्रैविध्य a. triple; n. triplicity.
त्रैविष्टप & **°पेय** m. pl. the gods (lit. inhabitants of heaven).
त्रैवेदिक, f. **ई** belonging to the three Vedas.
त्रैष्टुभ, f. **ई** relating to the Triṣṭubh metre.
त्रैस्रोतस a. belonging to (the) Gaṅgā.
त्रैस्वर्य n. the three accents (g.).
त्रैहायण n. a period of three years.
त्रोटक a. tearing, breaking. — m. a cert. poisonous insect; n. angry speech; a kind of drama.
त्र्यंश m. three portions or shares; adj. having three shares.
त्र्यक्ष (f. **ई** & **आ**) three-eyed; m. E. of Çiva; f. **ई** N. of a Rākṣasī.
त्र्यक्षक & **त्र्यक्षन्** m. = prec. m.
त्र्यक्षर a. consisting of three sounds or syllables; n. such a word.
1**त्र्यङ्ग** n. pl. cert. portions of the sacrificial animal.
2**त्र्यङ्ग** n. a threefold (lit. three-membered) army (= **चतुरङ्ग** without elephants).
1**त्र्यङ्गुल** n. abstr. to seq.
2**त्र्यङ्गुल** a. three fingers long or broad.
त्र्यधिष्ठान a. having three stations.
त्र्यनीक a. three-faced.
त्र्यब्द n. a period of three years.
त्र्यम्बक m. E. of Rudra-Çiva, f. **°का**† E. of Pārvatī (lit. the three-eyed).
त्र्यर a. having three wheel-spokes.
त्र्यरुण m. N. of a man.
त्र्यरुष, f. **ई** red in three places.
त्र्यवर a. pl. three at least; n. = seq.
त्र्यवरार्ध्यम् adv. at least three times.
त्र्यवि m. a calf eighteen months old; f. **त्र्यवी**.
त्र्यशीत, f. **ई** the eighty-third.
त्र्यशीति f. eighty-three.
त्र्यश्र a. three-cornered.
त्र्यष्टवर्ष a. twenty-four years old.
1**त्र्यह** m. a period of three days; acc. for three days; abl., loc., & instr. after three days.
2**त्र्यह** a. lasting three days.
***त्र्यहवृत्त** a. happened three days before.
त्र्यहीन a. = 2**त्र्यह**.
त्र्यहैहिक a. having provision for three days.
त्र्यायुष n. the threefold life (childhood, youth, & old age).
त्र्याशिर a. mixed with three products of milk.
त्र्याहिक a. three days', tertian.
त्र्यूधन् a. three-uddered.
त्र्यृच n. a stanza consisting of three verses.
त्र्येणी or **त्र्येनी** f. spotted in three places.

1त्व (nom. त्वम्) pron. stem. of 2nd pers.
2त्व a. thy, thine.
3त्व a. one, several, many. त्व—त्व the one—the other; this—that (one); n. त्वद् partly; त्वद्—त्वद् partly—partly.
त्वक्त्र n. armour (lit. protection for the skin).
त्वच् (only pp. त्वचाणं) = तच्. — Cf. प्रत्वचाणं.
त्वचस् n. energy, vigour.
त्वचीयंस् (compar.) very vigorous.
त्वक्सार a. having the skin or bark as chief part; m. cane.
त्वग्दोष m. disease of the skin; poss. °षिन्.
त्वग्भेद m. breaking of the skin; a scratch.
त्वग्भेदक a. who breaks or cuts the skin.
त्वंकार m. the addressing with Thou.
त्वङ्, त्वङ्गति, pp. त्वङ्गित jump, leap, gallop.
त्वच् f. skin, hide, bark, rind, cover, surface, cloud.
त्वच n. hide, skin (esp. —°); cinnamon.
त्वचन n. skinning, flaying.
त्वचस्थ a. being in the skin.
त्वच्य a. good for the skin.
त्वत्कृत a. made by thee.
त्वत्तस् adv. from thee etc. = abl. of 1त्वं.
त्वंद् = 1त्वं (°—); also = abl. of 1त्वं.
त्वदीय a. thy, thine.
त्वद्रिक् a. towards thee.
त्वद्विध a. like thee, of thy kind.
त्वन्मय a. consisting of thee.
त्वम् (nom. to 1त्वं) thou.
त्वंपद n. the word thou.
त्वर्, त्वरते (°ति), pp. त्वरित, तूर्त, & तूर्ण (q.v.) hurry, hasten to (dat., loc., or inf.). C. त्वरयति (°ते, त्वरयतितराम्) quicken, accelerate; snatch away. — अति hasten very much. परि hasten about. प्र & सम् hasten, speed.
(त्वर m.), आ f haste, speed; त्वरेण & त्वरया quickly.
त्वरणं a. making haste, quick.
त्वरावन्त् a. the same.
त्वरित a. hastening, quick (also त्वरितत्वरित*); °— & n. adv. (also त्वरितं त्वरितम्); n. as subst. haste, hurry.
त्वरितदान n. a quick gift.
त्वष्टि f. carpentry.
त्वष्टृ m. carpenter, workmann, creator; N. of a god.
त्वादत्त & त्वादात a. given by thee.
त्वादूत a. having thee as a messenger.
त्वादृश् & °श, f. °शी like thee, of thy kind.
त्वायन्त् a. longing for thee, seeking thee.
त्वाया (instr. adv.) out of love towards thee, for thy sake.
त्वायु a. longing for thee, loving thee.
त्वावन्त् a. like thee.
त्वाष्ट्र or त्वाष्ट्र a. belonging to Tvaṣṭṛ; m. his son, a patron. name.
1त्विष् (no pres.) pp. त्विषित stir, move (tr. & intr.); glitter, sparkle.
2त्विष् f. stir, agitation, violence; light, splendour, beauty.
त्विषि f. = prec.; poss. °मन्त् or त्विषीमन्त्.
त्वी adv. well; now then.
त्वेष (f. आ & ई) impetuous, vehement; awful, dire; brilliant, shining.
त्वेषथ m. violence, fury.
त्वेषद्युम्न a. of impetuous strength.
त्वेषनृम्ण a. of impetuous courage.
त्वेषप्रतीक a. of brilliant appearance.
त्वेषयाम a. of impetuous course.
त्वेषस् n. vehemence, energy.
त्वेषसंदृश् a. of brilliant aspect.
त्वेष्य a. shaking, agitating, awful.
त्वोत a. helped or protected by thee.
त्वोति a. enjoying thy help or favour.
त्सर्, त्सरति creep, sneak, steal upon. — अभि & उप = S. अव sneak away.
त्सरा f. stealing near.
त्सरु m. a creeping animal; stalk of a leaf; hilt or handle of a sword, poss. °मन्त्†.
त्सारिन् a. creeping, stealing near; crooked, hidden, secret.

थ

थरथराय्, °यते reel, stagger, shake, tremble.
थूर्व्, only pp. थूर्वन्त् E. of Agni.

द

1द (—°) giving, granting, causing.

2द (—°) cutting off, destroying.

दंश्, दंशति (°ते & दंशति), pp. दष्ट, r. दंशित (q.v.) bite. C. दंशयति cause a pers. (acc.) to be bitten by (instr.). — निस्, परि, & वि bite through. सम् bite, seize with the teeth, press together. — Cf. संदष्ट.

दंश m. biting, a bite or the spot bitten; gadfly; armour, mail.

दंशच्छेद m. the cutting out of a bitten spot.

दंशन n. biting; armour, mail.

दंशमशक n. sgl. gadflies and gnats.

दंशित a. bitten, stung; mailed, armed; prepared, ready for (loc.); pressed together, crowded.

दंशुक a. biting (acc.).

दंश्मन् n. a bite or the place bitten.

दंष्टृ m. biter.

दंष्ट्र m., दंष्ट्रा f. large tooth, tusk, fang.

दंष्ट्राकराल a. having terrible tusks.

दंष्ट्रायुध a. having tusks as weapons.

दंष्ट्रिन् a. tusked; m. beast of prey or snake.

दंस् (only दंसयस्) possess wonderful power.

दंसन n. marvellous power or deed.

दंसना f. the same; poss. °वन्त्.

दंसस n. = prec. f.

दंसिष्ठ superl. to seq.

दंसु a. wonderfully strong (°—); n. adv. wonderfully.

दंसुपत्नी f. having a powerful lord or master.

दक्ष्, दक्षति, °ते A. satisfy, please (dat.); M. be able or strong. C. दक्षयति make able or strong.

दक्ष a. able, capable, appropriate, suitable, fit for, clever in (loc. or —°); strong, mighty; intelligent, wise, right (not left). m. ability, power, fitness, cleverness, intelligence, energy, will, disposition, (evil) design; N. of an Āditya, also identif. w. Prajāpati.

दक्षकन्या f. Dakṣa's daughter.

1दक्षक्रतु m. du. will and intellect.

2दक्षक्रतु a. having a strong intellect.

दक्षत् a. gleaming, glittering.

दक्षता f. ability, dexterity, cleverness.

दक्षपितृ a. having Dakṣa as father or gifted with cleverness.

दक्षस् a. able, strong, clever.

दक्षसुत m., आ f. son & daughter of Dakṣa.

दक्षाय्य a. to be obeyed or pleased.

दक्षिण or दक्षिण a. able, capable of, fit for (—°); right (not left), southern; upright, honest; amiable, polite, chivalrous. दक्षिणं w. परि-इ walk round a person with the right side towards him; w. कृ = दक्षिणतः कृ q.v. — m. the right hand or arm, the right hand horse; the right side, the south (m. or n.). f. आ (scil. गो) a good milch-cow; a present given to officiating priests (orig. a cow); fee, donation, gift i.g.; (± दिश्) the south.

दक्षिणतस् adv. from the right or the south; on the right side or south of (gen.). With कृ turn the right to a person (as a mark of esteem).

दक्षिणत्रा adv. on the right side.

दक्षिणत्व n. honesty, amiableness.

दक्षिणपवन m. the south-wird.

दक्षिणपश्चिम a. south-western.

दक्षिणपूर्व a. south-eastern.

दक्षिणा adv. on the right or on the south of (abl.).

दक्षिणात् (abl. adv.) from or on the right or south.

दक्षिणापथ m. the Dekhan (lit. southern path or country).

दक्षिणापर a. south-western.

दक्षिणाप्रत्यञ्च्, f. °तीची south-western.

दक्षिणाप्रवण a. sloping to the south.

दक्षिणाभिमुख a. facing or flowing southwards.

दक्षिणामुख a. turning the face to the right or to the south; n. adv.

दक्षिणायन n. the southern progress (of the sun), the summer.

दक्षिणारण्य n. the southern forest.

दक्षिणावन्त् a. able, fit; rich in offerings or presents, pious.

दक्षिणावर्त m. = दक्षिणापथ.

दक्षिणाशिरस् a. turning the head towards the south.

दक्षिणावृत् a. turned or going round towards the right.

*__दक्षिणाहि__ adv. far on the right or in the south of (abl.).

दक्षिणी w. कृ = दक्षिणां कृ.

दक्षिणीय a. worthy of the sacrificial fee.

दक्षिणेतर a. other than right, left.

दक्षिणेन (instr. adv.) = दक्षिणा, w. acc.

दक्षिणैस् (instr. pl. adv.) on the right side.

दक्षिणोत्तर a. right and left, south and north.

दक्षिण्य = दक्षिणीय.

दक्षु & **दक्षुस्** a. burning.

दग्ध a. burnt, destroyed.

दग्धकिल्बिष a. whose sins are burnt or destroyed.

दग्धृ or **दग्धृ** a. & m. burning, a burner.

दघ्, **दघ्नोति** reach, attain. — **अति** reach beyond, pass.

दघ्न (f. आ & ई) reaching up to, as tall as (—°).

दङ्क्ष्णु a. mordacious.

दच्छद m. lip (covering of the teeth).

दण्ड m. (n.) stick (+ वैतस cane), staff (esp. of the twice-born), pole, cudgel, mace, club; flag-staff handle, on a chariot; (the rod as symbol of) power, force, (concr. forces = army); assault, violence; sovereignty, dominion of (gen. or —°), authority; punishment of all kinds.

दण्डक m. stick, staff (also f. दण्डिका), flag-staff; n. = seq.

दण्डकारण्य n. N. of a forest.

दण्डकाल m. N. of a man.*

दण्डकाष्ठ n. a wooden stick.

दण्डघ्न a. striking with a stick, committing assault.

दण्डचक्र n. body of troops, detachment.

दण्डजित a. subdued by force or punishment.

दण्डदास m. slave from a fine (not paid).

दण्डधर a. bearing the scepter or power; m. king, general, judge.

दण्डधार a. = prec. a. (°क police officer).*

दण्डधारण n. the carrying a staff (r.). the wielding a rod i.e. employing force, chastising, punishment.

दण्डधारिन् a. bearing the rod, punishing.

दण्डन n. beating, punishing.

दण्डनायक m. judge (bearer of the rod).

दण्डनिगड s. chain or fetter (of punishment).*

दण्डनीति f. application of the rod i.e. administration of justice.

दण्डनीय a. to be punished.

दण्डनेतृ m. = दण्डनायक; abstr. °त्व n.

दण्डपाणि a. stick in hand; m. police officer; E. of Yama.

दण्डपात m., °न n. applying the rod, punishment.

दण्डपारुष्य n. assault (with a stick).

दण्डपाल m. judge (keeper of the rod).

दण्डपाश m. du. staff and rope (as attributes of Yama).

दण्डभाज् a. deserving punishment, culpable; being punished by (gen.).

दण्डभृत् a. carrying a staff; m. E. of Yama

दण्डय्, °यति punish, chastise, fine (acc. of pers. & fine).

दण्डयात्रा f. warlike expedition; solemn or festive procession.

दण्डयोग m. infliction of punishment.

दण्डलेश m. a small fine.

दण्डवत् adv like a stick; w. प्र-नम् fall prostrate on the earth.

दण्डवध m. capital punishment, pain of death.

दण्डवन्त् a. having a stick or handle; having a large army.

दण्डवाचिक a. real or verbal (j.).

दण्डविकल्प m. arbitrary punishment.

दण्डविधि m. mode of punishment.

दण्डव्यूह m. arraging an army in long lines (like a staff).

दण्डशूर m. N. of a man.*

दण्डहस्त a. = दण्डपाणि adj.

दण्डाधिप & °पति m. superior judge.

दण्डानीक n. = दण्डचक्र.

दण्डाय्, °यमान resembling the stem of (—°).*

दण्डिक a. chastising, punishing; m. staff-bearer, police officer.

दण्डिन् a. carrying a stick or staff; m. = prec. m., also a Brahman in the fourth stage of his life; E. of Yama, N. of an author etc.

दण्डोद्यम m. raising the stick, threatening; pl. application of force.

दण्डोपानह m. du. a stick and shoes.

दण्ड्य a. to be or being punished (w. acc. of the fine).

दत्त a. given etc.; often °— having given or having been given i.e. having received; m. = seq., a man's name; n. gift, donation, liberality.

दत्तक (पुत्र) m. a son given away (to be adopted by others).

दत्तदृष्टि a. turning the eye upon, looking at (loc.).

दत्तवर a. allowed to choose a boon or granted as a boon.

दत्तशुल्का f. having been bought with money (a bride).

दत्तातङ्क a. making fear, frightening (gen.).

दत्ति f. gift, donation, offering.

दत्तोत्तर a. passing a judgment.

दत्त्रिम a. received by gift (son or slave).

दत्र n. wealth, pl. goods; p. **°वन्त्**.

दत्वन्त् a. having teeth, biting.

दद् or **दद** a. giving (—°).

ददाति m. gift.

ददि a. giving.

ददितृ m. giver or owner.

दद्रु or **दद्रू** f. a kind of leprosy.

दद्रुण a. leprous.

दधन् & **दधन्वन्त्** v. 2**दधि** & **दधिवन्त्**.

1**दधि** a. giving, bestowing.

2**दधि (दधन्)** n. sour milk.

दधिकर्ण m. N. of a serpent-demon & a cat.

दधिक्रा & **°क्रावन्** m. N. of a cert. myth. being.

दधित्थ m. the wood-apple tree.

दधिद्रप्स m. sgl. & pl. whey of sour milk.

दधिभक्त s.=**दध्योदन**.*

दधिभाण्ड n. a vessel with sour milk.

दधिमण्ड m. sour cream.

दधिवन्त् a. having (i.e. prepared with) sour milk.

दधिषु m. suitor, husband.

दधिसंभव a. prepared from sour milk.

दधीय्, **°यति** wish for sour milk.

दधृष् (nom. **°धृक्**) & **दधृष** a. daring, bold, strong, victorious; n. **दधृक्** adv.

दधृष्वणि a. = prec. adj.

दध्यञ्च् (दधीच्) m. N. of a cert. myth. being.

दध्योदन m. boiled rice mixed with sour milk.

1**दन्** only in **पतिर्दन्** & **पती दन्** (voc. du.) = **दंपति** & **दंपती**.

2**दन्**, only **दनस्** & **दन्** straighten.

दनु f. N. of a daughter of Dakṣa, the mother of the Dānavas.

दनुज m. a son of Danu, a Dānava.

दन्त् m. (adj. —° f. **दती**) tooth.

दन्त m. (n.) (adj. —° f. **आ** & **ई**) tooth, fang; an elephant's tusk, ivory.

दन्तक (adj. —°) tooth.

दन्तघाट & **°क** m. an artisan in ivory.

दन्तघात m. a bite (cut with the teeth).

दन्तच्छद m. lip (covering of the teeth).

दन्तजात a. having already teeth (grown).

दन्तधाव m., **°न** n. cleaning the teeth.

दन्तपाञ्चालिका f. a doll of ivory.

दन्तप्रक्षालन n. the same.

दन्तमय a. made of ivory.

दन्तमांस n. the gums.

दन्तमूल n. the root of a tooth.

दन्तमूलीय a. belonging to the root of the teeth, dental (g).

दन्तरचना f. cleaning the teeth.

दन्तवेष्ट m. the gums (also du.).

दन्तशुद्धि f., **°शोधन** n. cleaning of the teeth.

दन्ताग्र n. the point of a tooth.

दन्तादन्ति adv. tooth to tooth (of a hard fight).

दन्तालि & **दन्तावली** f. row of teeth.

दन्तिदन्त m. ivory, **°मय** a. made of ivory.

दन्तिन् a. having teeth or tusks; m. elephant.

दन्तुर a. having long teeth, jagged, notched, uneven; beset with, full of (—°); ugly.

दन्तुरय्, **°यति** beset with, pp. **दन्तुरित** (—°) = prec.

दन्तोलूखलिक & °लिन् a. using the teeth as a mortar, i.e. eating unground corn.
दन्त्य a. belonging to the teeth, dental (g).
दन्दशूक a. mordacious, mischievous; m. a snake.
दभ् or दम्भ्, दभति, दभ्नोति, pp. दब्ध harm, injure, deceive, beguile. P. suffer damage or loss. C. दम्भयति, °ते ward off, strike down. D. दिप्सति wish to hurt or destroy. — आ hurt, injure. उप C. destroy, annihilate.
दभ a. deceiving; dat. दभाय as infin.
दभीति m. deceiver, enemy; N. of a man.
दभ्य a. to be harmed or deceived.
दभ्र a. small, little, scanty; n. as adv. & abstr.
1दम्, दाम्यति, pp. दान्त (q.v.) be or make tame; conquer, master, control. C. दमयति = S. tr.
2दम् s. (only °— & gen. pl. दमाम्) = seq.
1दम m. or n. house, home.
2दम a. taming, subduing; m. self-control, self-command, punishment, fine, mulct, a man's name.
दमक a. (—°) = prec. a.
दमघोष m. N. of a prince.
दमदान n. du. self-control and liberality.
दमन a. (f. ई) & n. taming, controlling, chastising; m. tamer of horses, charioteer, a man's name.
दमनक m. N. of a man & a jackal.
दममय a. consisting of self-control.
दमयन्ती f. N. of the wife of Nala.
दमयितृ m. tamer, subduer, chastiser.
दमाय्, °यति subdue or control (also one's self).
दमितृ m. tamer, subduer.
दमिन् a. tamed; controlling one's self.
दमूनस् a. belonging to the house or family, domestic, homely; m. friend of the house, E. of Agni, Savitṛ, Indra, etc.
दमोपेत a. endowed with self-control.
दंपति m. master of the house, householder; du. husband and wife, male and female.
दम्भ m. deceit, fraud, hypocrisy.
दम्भक a. deceiving, deluding (—°).
†दम्भन a. (—°) & n. harming, deceiving.
दम्भिन् a. deceitful, m. deceiver, hypocrite.
दम्भोलि m. Indra's thunderbolt.
दम्भोलिपाणि m. E. of Indra (cf. prec.).
1दम्य a. to be tamed or subdued; m. (n.) a young bullock that is to be tamed.
2दम्य a. being in a house, homely.
दय्, दयते (°ति), pp. दयित (q.v.) divide, allot (acc. or *gen.); possess, partake; sympathize with, love (acc. or gen.); repent. — अव & निरव satisfy. वि divide, distribute; separate, destroy, be liberal with (instr.), i.e. impart. — Cf. seq.
दयमान a. compassionate, tender, enamoured.
दया f. sympathy, pity for (loc., gen., or —°); poss. °वन्त्.†
दयालु a. pitiful, tender; abstr. °ता† f., °त्व† n.
दयित a. beloved, dear; m. husband, the beloved one, f. आ mistress, wife.
†दर a. cleaving, rending, opening (—°); °— & n. little, a little. m. a hole in the earth, pit, cavern (also f. ई); fear, terror.
दरण n. cleaving, rending, bursting.
दरद् & दरद m. N. of a people.
†दरि a. = दर (—°); m. N. of a serpent-demon.
दरिद्र or दरिद्र a. vagrant, strolling, poor, needy, m. beggar; abstr. °ता† f., °त्व† n.
दरिद्रतातुर a. suffering from poverty.*
दरिद्रा v. 1द्रा.
दरिद्रातुर* a. = दरिद्रतातुर.
दरीमन् s. destruction.
दरीवन्त् a. cavernous.
दर्तृ or दर्तृ a. & m. breaking, a breaker.
दर्तु m. the same.
दर्दुर m. frog, flute; N. of a mountain & sev. men.
दर्दु m. a cert. bird.
दर्प m. extravagance, petulance, temerity, arrogance, pride in (instr. or —°).
दर्पज a. sprung from pride.
दर्पण m. looking-glass, mirror; often —° in titles of books.
दर्भ m. bundle or bunch of grass, esp. of the sacred Kuça grass.
दर्भण n. matting, texture.
दर्भपिञ्जुल, °पिञ्जूल, & °पुञ्जील n. a bunch of grass.

दर्भमय, f. **ई** made of Darbha grass.
दर्भमुष्टि m. f. a handful of Darbha grass.
दर्भस्तम्ब m. a bunch of Darbha grass.
दर्म & **दर्मन्** m. breaker, destroyer.
दर्व m. ladle, spoon.
दर्वि & **दर्वी** f. the same; the hood of a snake.
दर्वीकर m. a kind of snake with an expanded hood.
दर्श or **दर्श** a. looking or aiming at (—°); m. sight, view, m. (n.) the new moon, its day and festival.
दर्शक a. seeing, viewing, looking at, spectator; examining, trying, showing, revealing (gen. or —°); w. **लोहितस्य** who fetches blood.
दर्शत a. visible, conspicuous, beautiful.
दर्शन, f. **ई** (—°) = **दर्शक**; n. seeing, looking, observing; sight, view, vision; appearance, (also in court), occurrence; apparition, dream; visit, meeting with (gen., instr. ± **सह** or —°); trying, examining, understanding; judgment, opinion, knowledge, doctrine; showing, eye.
दर्शनकाङ्क्षिन् a. longing for the sight of (gen.).
दर्शनगोचर & **दर्शनपथ** m. range (lit. path) of sight, horizon.
दर्शनप्रातिभाव्य n. surety for appearance (j.).
दर्शनविषय a. being within sight of (gen.).
दर्शनान्तरगत a. accessible to the eye, visible.
दर्शनीय a. = **दर्शत** + to be shown, to be made to appear (in court).
दर्शनीयाकृति a. of handsome appearance.
दर्शनोत्सुक a. = **दर्शनकाङ्क्षिन्**.*
दर्शपूर्णमास m. du. new and full moon.
दर्शयितव्य a. to be shown.
दर्शयितृ m. shower, guide.
दर्शिन् a. (—°) seeing, beholding, knowing, understanding, finding out, inventing, showing, teaching.
दर्श्य a. to be shown or seen.
दल्, **दलति**, pp. **दलित** (q.v.) burst, split, open (intr.). C. **दालयति** & **दलयति** cause to burst, divide, tear or drive asunder. — **अव** burst or fly open. **उद्** C. split, cleave, tear up. **वि** burst or fly open; tear asunder, split.

दल n. a piece split off, fragment, portion; blade, petal, leaf.
दलन a. (f. **ई**) & n. bursting, splitting, crushing.
दलशस् adv. to pieces.
दव m. fire, heat, also = **दवाग्नि**.
दवथु m. fire, heat; vexation, distress.
दवाग्नि m. conflagration of a forest.
दवानल m. the same.
दविष्ठ (superl.) the farthest; n. **°ष्ठम्** adv.
दवीयंस् (compar.) very remote or distant; n. **दवीयस्** farther away.
दश (—°) = **दशन्**.
दशक a. tenfold; n. a decad.
दशकण्ठ & **°कंधर** m. ten-necked (E. of Rāvaṇa).
दशगुण (n. adv.) & **°गुणित** a. tenfold.
दशग्रामपति m. chief of ten villages.
दशग्रीव m. = **दशकण्ठ**.
दशग्व & **दशग्विन्** a. tenfold (lit. going by tens or in ten ways).
दशत् f. a decad.
दशतय, f. **ई** tenfold.
दशति f. = **दशत्**; also a hundred (= a decad, scil. of decads), **दशतीर्दश** a thousand.
दशदशिन् a. consisting of repeated decads.
दशदिङ्मुख n.* = seq.
दशदिश् f. the ten quarters of the heavens.
दशधा adv. in ten parts, tenfold.
दशन् or **दशन्** a. ten.
दशन m. tooth.
दशनख a. having ten finger-nails.*
दशनच्छद m. the lip (teeth-covering).
दशपल n. sgl. ten Palas.
दशपुर n. N. of sev. towns.
दशबन्ध m. a tenth part.
दशम, f. **ई** the tenth; n. adv. for the tenth time; f. **ई** the tenth day of the half moon, the tenth decad of the life.
दशमास्य a. ten months old.
दशमीस्थ a. between 90 and 100 years old (cf. **दशम**).
दशमुख a. ten-faced (E. of Rāvaṇa).
दशरथ a. having ten chariots; E. of sev. kings.
दशरात्र a. lasting ten days; m. such a festival.

दशरूप n. the ten forms of Viṣṇu, also = seq.

दशरूपक n. the ten forms of the drama, T. of a rhet. work.

दशर्च m. a strophe of ten verses.

दशलक्षणक a. having a tenfold character.

दशवर्ष & °र्षीय a. ten years old.

दशवार्षिक, f. ई the same; lasting ten years or happening after ten years.

दशविध a. of ten kinds, tenfold.

दशशत a. & n. 110; n. also = f. ई 1000.

दशशतकरधारिन् a. having a thousand rays (the moon).

दशशिरस् & दशशीर्ष a. ten-headed; m. E. of Rāvaṇa.

दशसाहस्र a. consisting of 10000, n. 10000.

दशस्य्, °स्यति serve, obey, honour, worship; grant, bestow (dat. of pers. & acc. of th.), help to (dat.). — आ = S. सम् pardon, forgive.

दशस्वर्ण n. ten Suvarṇas.

दशा f. fringe of a garment, wick of a lamp; fig. state or condition of life; situation, circumstances i.g.

दशाक्षर a. containing ten syllables.

दशाङ्गुल a. ten fingers long.

दशानन a. = दशमुख.

दशान्तरुष्य n. a distance of ten stations.

दशार्ण a. ten-syllabled; m. pl. N. of a people.

दशार्ध a. pl. half of ten, five.

दशार्ह m. pl. N. of a people.

दशावर a. containing ten at least.

दशाविपाक m. the fulfilment of fate.

दशास्य a. = दशमुख.

दशाह m. a period or ceremony of ten days.

दशिन् a. consisting of ten parts; m. chief of ten villages.

दशेरक & °रुक m. pl. N. of a people.

दशेश m. chief of ten villages.

दशोत्तर a. the eleventh.

दशोनास m. a kind of snake.

दष्ट a. bitten or stung; n. biting.

दष्टमात्र a. just bitten or stung.

दस्, दस्यति, pp. दस्त suffer want, languish. C. दसयते exhaust, consume. — अप, उप, प्र, & वि be exhausted, be wanting, fail.

दस m. an inimical demon.

दस्म & दस्मन्त् a. miraculous, extraordinary.

दस्मवर्चस् a. of miraculous strength.

दस्म्य a. = दस्म.

दस्यु m. foe, enemy (either a superhuman enemy, an evil demon, or an enemy of the gods, an unbeliever or barbarian, opp. आर्य).

दस्युहत्य n. fight with the Dasyus (v. prec.).

दस्युहन् a. destroying the Dasyus.

दस्र a. = दस्म; m. du. the two Açvins.

दह्, दहति (°ते), pp. दग्ध (q.v.) burn, inflame (l. & f.), consume, destroy. P. दह्यते (°ति) be burnt, burn (intr.), suffer, pine. C. दाहयति (cause to) burn. D. दिधक्षति, °ते be about to burn or destroy. I. दन्दहीति & दन्दग्धि burn completely (tr.); दन्दह्यते the same (tr. & intr.). — अति burn over, dry up. अनु burn over again, burn thoroughly. उप kindle. नि burn down, P. intr. निस् & विनिस् burn out, destroy by fire. परि burn round (tr.); P. burn, glow. प्र burn, consume, destroy. प्रति burn against. वि burn out, damage or consume by fire; P. be burnt or inflamed, glow. सम् A. burn or destroy (together); P. be burnt or tortured. — C. विदग्ध.

दहन a. (f. ई) & n. burning, consuming, destroying; m. (adj. —° f. आ) fire or the god Agni.

दहर a. small, fine.

दभ्र a. the same; n. दभ्रम् adv. little.

1दा, ददाति, दत्ते, ददति, °ते (दाति, दद्मि), pp. दत्त (q.v.) give, grant, bestow, impart (w. acc. or partit. gen. of th., gen. or loc. of pers.), give in marriage (± भार्याम्), give back, restore (± पुनर्); pay (ऋणम्); open *(द्वारम्); deliver up, hand over (± हस्ते); make over, surrender; concede, allow, permit; give away, sell (instr. of price); offer, sacrifice; communicate, teach, pronounce; put in or on, turn to (loc.); w. पावकम् set fire to (loc.); w. अग्नीन् burn (dat.); do, make, cause, perform, bring about. M. receive, carry, bear, keep, guard from (abl.). C. दापयति

cause to give, grant, etc. (1 or 2 acc.), make pay (2 acc.), demand from (abl.); put in or on (loc.).* D. दित्सति, °ते. दिदासति wish or be ready to give. — अनु concede, yield, remit, grant, admit. अभि give. आ M. (A.) accept, receive, conceive (गर्भम्); take, grasp, seize, rob; take or separate from (abl.); take along with one's self, carry off; put on, don; take = eat, gnaw (± दशनैस्); perceive, comprehend, mark; keep, retain (in the memory); undertake, begin. अपा M. take off. अभ्या M. (A.) appropriate, put on, take up (वाक्यम्). उपा M. accept, receive, acquire, appropriate, take, seize, choose, employ, mention; undertake, begin. समुपा M. obtain, get, take, rob, put on, employ. प्रत्या M. receive or take back, recall, repeat. व्या M. (± मुखम्) open the mouth, gape. समा A. give, restore; M. take (together), seize, grasp, gather, collect; comprehend, understand, observe, take to heart; undertake, begin. उद् add, grant, give. परा deliver, surrender, give up; exchange for (dat.), barter. परि surrender, deliver up; intrust, deposit with or in (dat., loc., or gen.); grant, bestow. प्र A. (M.) give up, deliver, present, offer, give in marriage (± भार्याम्); pay, discharge (a debt), restore, sell (w. instr. of price); teach, communicate, impart; grant, permit; put in, set (fire) to (loc.). संप्र give up, deliver, concede, grant, impart, teach, communicate. प्रति restore, return, give. वि distribute. सम् give (together), grant, concede; M. P. meet together. — Cf. आत्त, आदाय, उदात्त, उपात्त, उपादाय, परीत्त, प्रत्त, व्यात्त.

2दा m. giver; often —° giving, granting.

3दा, दाति, द्यति, pp. दिन & दित cut, mow. — अव cut off, divide (esp. the sacrif. cake). निस् distribute, among (2 acc.). समव cut in pieces and collect them. आ, वि, & सम् cut up, bruise, crush. — Cf. अवत्त, समवत्त.

4दा, द्यति, pp. दित (only —°) bind. — आ & नि tie, fetter. वि loosen. सम् bind together, fasten, tie. — Cf. निदित, संदित.

5दा, pp. दात (—°) clean, purify. – Cf. अवदात.

दाक्ष a. southern or belonging to Dakṣa.

दाक्षायण, f. ई descended from or belonging to Dakṣa; m. n. a cert. sacrifice.

दाक्षिण a. belonging to a sacrificial gift.

दाक्षिणात्य a. southerly, belonging to the Dekhan; m. or n. the south, m. pl. the inhabitants of the Dekhan.

दाक्षिण्य = दाक्षिण; n. civility, kindness, gallantry towards (loc., gen., or —°); the south.

दाक्षिण्यवन्त् a. kind, polite, amiable.

दाक्ष्य n. dexterity, shrewdness, skill, industry.

दाडिम m., ई f. the pomegranate tree; n. its fruit.

दाडिमपुष्प n. pomegranate-flower.

दाढिका f. beard, whiskers.

दाण्डिक a. inflicting punishment, punishing.

दातवे & दातवै dat. inf. to 1दा.

दातव्य a. to be given (also in marriage), to be imparted, taught etc.; n. impers.

†दाति f. gift, liberality.

दातिवार a. giving freely, liberal (lit. choosing or liking to give).

दातु n. share, allotted portion.

1दातृ or दातृ a. giving (esp. in marriage), bestowing, granting, conceding, paying; imparting, teaching; causing, producing (gen. or —°); liberal, generous. m. giver, donor; payer, creditor. Abstr. °ता† f., °त्व† n.

2दातृ m. cutter, mower, reaper.

दातृप्रतीच्छक m. du. giver and receiver.

दात्यूह m., ई f. a kind of cock or hen.

दात्यौह m. = prec. m.

1दात्र n. distribution, share, possession.

2दात्र n. sickle, scythe.

दाद m. gift.

दाधृवि a. capable, able to (dat. inf.).

दाधृषि a. courageous, daring.

1दान n. giving, imparting, bestowing of (gen. or —°) on (loc. or —°); giving in marriage, giving up, sacrificing, offering, paying;

teaching, communicating; granting, conceding; gift, present, donation.
2दान m. distribution (concr. distributer, dispenser), liberality, (sacrificial) meal, share, portion, possession.
3दान n. cutting, dividing; pasture.
4दान n. the rut (of an animal) & the rut-fluid (flowing from an elephant's temples in the time of rutting).
दानकाम a. loving to give, liberal.
दानधर्म m. the duty of liberality, charity.
दानपति m. a very liberal man (lit. master of liberality).
दानपर a. liberal, abstr. °ता f.
दानप्रतिभू m. a surety for payment (j.).
दानव m., ई f. son or daughter of Danu, a demon or enemy of the gods.
दानवन्त् a. rich in gifts, liberal.
दानवीर m. = दानपति.
दानशील a. of liberal disposition, munificent.
दानशूर m. = दानपति.
दानस्तुति f. praise of liberality (cert. hymns).
दानिन् a. = दानवन्त्.
1दानु m. f. a class of demons.
2दानु f. n. any dripping fluid, drop, dew; poss. °मन्त्.
दानुचित्र a. shining with dew or moisture.
दानौकस् a. liking offerings (Indra).
1दान्त a. tamed, subdued, patient, passionless; m. a man's name.
2दान्त a. made of ivory.
दापनीय a. to be made to give or pay.
दापयितव्य & दाप्य a. the same.
†दाभ, f. ई harming, injuring (—°).
दाम n., आ f. = 3दामन्.
1दामन् m. giver, a liberal man.
2दामन् n. gift, donation; p. °न्वन्त्.
3दामन् m. or f. allotment, share.
4दामन् n. band, fetter; thread, rope; wreath, garland; p. °न्वन्त्.
दामोदर m. E. of Viṣṇu-Kṛṣṇa; N. of a month & of sev. men.
दामोदरगुप्त & °मिश्र m. names of poets.
दांपत्य n. conjugality.
दाम्भिक a. deceitful; m. cheat, hypocrite.
1दाय a. giving (—°); m. gift.
2दाय m. share, portion, inheritance.
1दायक, f. °यिका giving, granting, imparting, effecting, producing (mostly —°).
2दायक a. heir, kinsman.
दायभाग m. partition of inheritance, N. of a work.
दायहर m. = 2दायक.
दायाद m. the same, also son or brother; f. आ daughter.
दायाद्य n. inheritance.
दायिन् a. giving, granting, conceding, permitting; causing, producing (—°).
1दार m., ई f. rent, cleft.
2दार m. sgl. & pl. (f. आ & n. pl.) wife; दारान् कृ or प्र-कृ take a wife, marry.
1दारक, f. °रिका rending, splitting (—°); f. also = 1दार.
2दारक m. boy, son, a young animal; du. two boys or a boy and a girl. f. दारका (दारकी) girl, daughter.
दारकर्मन् n. taking a wife, marrying.
दारक्रिया f., दारग्रहण n. the same.
दारण, f. ई bursting, tearing, splitting (gen. or —°); n. the act of bursting etc. f. ई E. of Durgā.
दारत्यागिन् a. rejecting one's wife.
दारपरिग्रह m. = दारकर्मन्.
दारव, f. ई & दारवीय a. wooden.
दारसंग्रह m. = दारकर्मन्.
दाराधिगमन n. taking a wife, marriage.
दारि a. bursting, tearing (—°).
दारिन् a. the same (also w. gen.).
1दारु a. breaking.
2दारु n. a piece of wood, wood i.g.; adv. °वत्† like a piece of wood.
दारुक m. a man's name.
दारुज a. wooden.
दारुण or दारुण, f. आ (ई) hard, rough, harsh, cruel, severe; n. & °ता† f. abstr.
दारुणात्मन् a. hard-hearted, cruel.
दारुण्य n. hardness.
दारुपात्र n. a wooden vessel.
दारुमय, f. ई wooden.
दार्ढ्य n. firmness, corroboration, strength, constancy.
दार्दुर, f. ई belonging to a frog.

दार्दुरक, f. °रिका = prec.
दार्भ, f. ई made of Darbha grass.
दार्व, f. ई wooden.
दार्वाघाट m. woodpecker.
दार्श, f. ई relating to the new moon; m. the new moon sacrifice.
दार्शिक, f. ई, & दार्श्य a. = prec. adj.
†दाल v. रज्जुदाल; f. दाला & दालिका colocynth.
दालिम m. = दाडिम m.
दाल्भ्य m. a patron. name.
दाव m conflagration, esp. of a forest; m. n. forest.
दावदहन m. = prec. m.
दावन् a. giving (—°).
दावने (dat. inf.) to give.
दावाग्नि & दावानल m. the fire of a forest conflagration.
1दाश्, दाशति, दाष्टि, & दाश्नोति make offering, sacrifice, grant, bestow, dedicate, serve a god (dat.) with (instr.), be pious or religious. C. दाशयति offer. — Cf. दाश्वंस्.
2दाश् f. worship, m. (nom. दास्) worshipper.
दाश m. fisherman, ferryman, mariner.
दाशतय, f. ई tenfold.
दाशरथ a. belonging to or descending from Daçaratha.
दाशरथि m. descendant of Daçaratha, patron. of Rāma & Lakṣmaṇa, du. R. & L.
दाशराज्ञ n. the fight with the ten kings.
दाशार्ह m. king of the Daçārhas (f. ई), E. of Kṛṣṇa.
दाशिवंस् a. = दाश्वंस्.
दाशुरि a. worshipping the gods, pious.
दाशेरक m. fisherman, pl. N. of a people.
दाश्वंस् a. worshipping the gods, sacrificing; merciful, gracious, granting, bestowing; m. a pious servant of a god.
दास्, दासति w. अभि bear ill-will towards, try to harm, persecute.
1दास m. foe, esp. an evil demon or an infidel (opp. आर्य); servant, slave, f. दासी. दास्याः पुत्रः or पुत्री son or daughter of a slave (abusive words).
2दास, f. ई inimical, demoniacal; m. foe, infidel, demon (f. दासी).
दासजन m. slave, servant (also coll.).
दासजीवन a. living like a slave.
दासता f., °त्व n. slavery, servitude.
दासदासी f. the female slave of a slave.
दासभाव m. condition of a slave, slavery.
दासवत् adv. like a slave.
दासीत्व n. the state of a female slave.
दासीभाव m. the same.
दासेरक m. young camel (f. ई); pl. N. of a people.
दास्य n. slavery, servitude, dependence.
दास्वन्त् a. giving, liberal, munificent.
दाह m. burning (tr. & intr.), combustion, burning-place; heat, glow, fire.
दाहक, f. °हिका burning, setting on fire.
दाहज्वर m. inflammatory fever.
दाहन n. causing to burn or be burnt, combustion.
दाहात्मक a. easily burning, inflammable.
दाहिन् a. burning (tr. & intr.).
दाहुक a. burning; m. conflagration.
दाह्य a. to be or being burnt.
दिक्क (—°) = 2दिश्.
दिक्करिन् m. elephant of a region (myth.).
दिक्कुञ्जर m. the same.
दिक्चक्र & दिक्चक्रवाल n. circuit of the quarters of the compass, horizon.
दिक्छब्द m. a word denoting a direction (g.).
दिक्पति m. the regent or guardian of a quarter of the world (myth.).
दिक्पथ m. = दिक्चक्र.
दिक्पाल & दिगधिप m. = दिक्पति.
दिगन्त m. end of the horizon, remotest distance.
दिगन्तर n. another region, a foreign country.
दिगम्बर a. unclad, naked (lit. sky-clothed), abstr. °त्व n.; m. a naked mendicant.
दिगीश & दिगीश्वर m. = दिक्पति.
दिग्गज m. = दिक्करिन्.
दिग्जय m. the conquest of the world.
दिग्दाह m. uncommon redness (lit. burning) of the horizon.
दिग्देवता f. the deity of a region.

दिग्देश m. remote distance, space (lit. region of the horizon).
दिग्ध a. smeared, anointed, soiled, covered; poisoned (arrow).
दिग्भाग m. direction (of the sky).
दिग्वसन & **दिग्वासस्** a. & m. = **दिगम्बर**.
दिग्विजय m. = **दिग्जय**.
दिग्विभाग m. = **दिग्भाग**.
दिङ्नाग m. = **दिक्करिन्**.
दिङ्नाथ m. = **दिक्पति**.
दिङ्मण्डल n. = **दिक्चक्र**.
दिङ्मात्र n. a mere direction.
दिङ्मुख n. quarter of the heavens (lit. face of the sky).
1**दिति** f. distribution, liberality.
2**दिति** f. N. of a goddess (cf. **अदिति**).
दितिज m. a son of Diti, a Daitya.
दित्यवह् (nom. **°वाट्**), f. **दित्यौही** a bull or cow two years old.
दित्सा f. the wish to give; a. **दित्सु** & **दिदित्सु**.
दिदृक्षा f. the wish to see; a. **दिदृक्षु**.
दिदृक्षेण्य & **दिदृक्षेय** a. worth seeing, conspicuous.
दिद्यु m. dart, arrow.
दिद्युत् a. shining, blazing; f. = prec. + thunderbolt, flame, N. of an Apsaras.
दिधक्षा f. the wish to burn; a. **°क्षु**.
दिधिषु a. wishing to gain; m. suitor, husband, f. (also **°षू**) a woman married twice.
दिधिषूपति m. the husband of a woman married a second time.
1**दिन** v. 3**दा**.
2**दिन** n. day.
दिनकर & **दिनकर्तृ** m. the sun (day-maker).
दिनकर्तव्य & **दिनकार्य** n. daily work (esp. religious observance).
दिनक्षय m. evening (end of day).
दिननक्तम् adv. day and night.
दिननाथ m. the sun (lord of the day).
दिननिश् f. du. day and night.
दिनपति & **दिनभर्तृ** m. = **दिननाथ**.
दिनमणि m. the sun (jewel of the day).
दिनमुख n. break (lit. mouth) of day.
दिनाधिनाथ & **दिनाधीश** m. = **दिननाथ**.
दिनान्त m. evening (end of day).
दिनार्ध s. noon (half of the day).
दिनावसान n. = **दिनान्त**.
दिनेश & **दिनेश्वर** m. = **दिननाथ**.
दिनोदय m. daybreak, morning.
दिप्सु a. wishing to harm.
दिलीप m. N. of sev. kings.
दिलीपसूनु m. the son of Dilīpa (Raghu).
1**दिव्**, **दीव्यति**, **°ते**, pp. **द्यूत** (q.v.) shine, play (orig. throw, sc. rays of light or the dice); play at dice (**अक्षैस्** or ***अक्षान्**), gamble with (instr.) for (acc., instr., dat., or *gen.), sport, joke; trifle with, mock, rally (acc.). C. **देवयति** cause to play. — **अति** play higher; put to stake. **प्रति** play against (acc.); *put to stake (gen. or acc.). **वि** play for (acc.), joke, sport.
2**दिव्**, **देवति**, **°ते**, pp. **द्यून** (q.v.) lament, be distressed. — **परि** (A. & M.) the same; C. **परिदेवयति**, **°ते** lament, deplore. — Cf. **आद्यून**, **परिदेवित**, **परिद्यून**.
3**दिव्**, **द्यु** (nom. sgl. **द्यौस्**) m. sky, heaven (also f.), the god of heaven; day (also n.); light, fire-flame (only instr. pl. **द्युभिस्**). — **द्यावा** m. du. heaven and earth or day and night. **अनु द्यून्** & **द्यवि द्यवि** day by day. **अभि द्यून्** in the course of the days, in a long time. **उप द्युभिस्** by day & = prec.
दिव n. heaven, day; **दिवे दिवे** day by day.
दिवंगम a. going or leading to heaven.
दिवस m. heaven or day.
दिवसकर, **°कृत्**, & **°क्षय** = **दिनकर** etc.
दिवसचर a. going about by day (animal).
दिवसनाथ m. = **दिननाथ**.
रिवसमुख n. = **दिनमुख**.
दिवसी w. **कृ** make a day (of a night).
दिवसेश्वर m. = **दिनेश्वर**.
दिवस्पति m. lord of heaven, E. of Indra & Viṣṇu.
दिवस्पृथिवी du. heaven and earth (only **°व्यास्**).
दिवा (instr. adv.) by day.
दिवाकर m. the sun (day-maker).
दिवाकीर्ति m. a Caṇḍāla.
दिवाकीर्त्य a. to be recited at day-time; n. cert. recitations or songs.
दिवाचर & **°चारिन्** a. = **दिवसचर**.

दिवातन f. **ई** & **दिवातर** a. daily, diurnal.
दिवानक्तम् & **दिवानिशम्** adv. day and night.
दिवान्ध a. blind by day; m. owl.
दिवारात्रम् adv. day and night.
दिवासंकेत m. a rendezvous by day.*
दिविक्षय & **दिविक्षित्** a. dwelling in heaven.
दिविचर & **°चारिन्**† a. moving in the sky.
दिविज & **दिविजा** a. born in the sky.
दिवित् a. going to heaven.
दिवित्मन्त् a. the same, celestial.
दिविषद् a. dwelling in heaven; m. a god.
दिविष्टि f. devotion, prayer, sacrifice.
दिविष्ठ a. dwelling in heaven, celestial.
दिविस्पृश् & **°स्पृशन्त्** a. touching the sky, going to heaven.
दिवोजा a. born in heaven.
दिवोदास m. N. of a man (slave of heaven).
दिवौकस् m. an inhabitant of heaven, a god.
दिव्य a. heavenly (opp. earthly), divine (opp. human), wonderful, splendid. n. anything heavenly or divine, esp. celestial good, the celestial regions (pl.), ordeal, oath.
1**दिव्यचक्षुस्** n. a heavenly eye.
2**दिव्यचक्षुस्** a. having a divine (prophetic) eye.
दिव्यज्ञान a. having divine or supernatural knowledge.
दिव्यता f., **°त्व** n. divine nature.
दिव्यदर्शन a. of a divine aspect.
दिव्यदर्शिन् a. = 2**दिव्यचक्षुस्**.
दिव्यदृश् a. the same; m. astrologer.
दिव्यनारी f. divine female, Apsaras.
दिव्यरूप & **°पिन्** a. of a celestial form.
दिव्यवर्मभृत् a. wearing a celestial armour.
दिव्यविज्ञानवन्त् a. = **दिव्यज्ञान**.
दिव्यसंकाश a. heaven-like, divine.
दिव्यस्त्री f. = **दिव्यनारी**.
दिव्याकृति a. of heavenly appearance, very beautiful.
दिव्यास्त्र n. a cert. magical weapon.
दिव्यौषध n. a cert. magical drink.
1**दिश्**, **दिदेष्टि**, **दिशति**, **°ते**, pp. **दिष्ट** (q.v.) point out, show, produce (a witness); assign, grant, bestow; order, command, bid (inf.). C. **देशयति**, **°ते** show, assign, direct, bid. I. **देदिष्टे** exhibit, show, bid, order or direct urgently; **देदिश्यते** show or prove one's self. — **अति** assign, transfer, extend to (gen.). **अनु** point at (acc.), direct, bid, assign. **समनु** assign. **अप** the same; indicate, state, denounce; feign, pretend. **व्यप** designate, name; feign, pretend. **आ** aim at, menace, challenge (acc.), assign, announce, teach, designate, term; foretell, prophesy of a pers. (acc., P. w. nom.); direct, order, appoint to (loc., dat., inf., or **अर्थम्**). C. indicate, show. **उपा** assign, give in marriage to (gen.); announce, tell. **प्रत्या** direct, order, recommend; invite, summon; reject, despise; vanquish, surpass. **व्या** assign or distribute (separately); explain, indicate, teach; direct, order, appoint to (loc., dat., or **प्रति**); foretell, prophesy of a pers. (acc., P. w. nom.). **समा** assign, impart, communicate (dat. or gen.); teach, designate, name (2 acc.); direct, appoint to (dat., inf., or **अर्थम्**), also = C. order, command (absol.). **उद्** stretch out towards (acc.); indicate, explain, teach, designate as, mean by (2 acc.), predict or prophesy of (acc); point out i.e propose or offer as (2 acc.). **समुद्** mention, enumerate; designate, name (2 acc.). **उप** point to (acc.), show; indicate, explain, mention, speak of (acc.); advise, recommend; inform, instruct, teach (2 acc.); command, rule over (acc.). **प्रत्युप** teach in return (2 acc.). **समुप** point to (acc.), teach, show (2 acc.). **निस्** point to (acc.), assign, destine, designate, name, regard as, take for (2 acc.); mention, proclaim, predict; advise, suggest (2 acc.). **अभिनिस्** name, designate (2 acc.); settle, determine. **विनिस्** assign, destine for (loc.); indicate, proclaim; designate, name (2 acc); resolve, determine; appoint to, charge with (loc.). **परि** indicate, state. **प्र** the same + announce, proclaim, direct, order; assign, grant, impart. **संप्र** indicate, designate, state. **सम्** assign, destine for; direct, instruct, order; appoint to, charge with (2 acc.). **प्रतिसम्** give a pers. (acc.) a commission (in return) to (gen.); direct,

command. — Cf. उद्दिश्य, निरादिष्ट, समुद्दिश्य.

2दिश् f. point, esp. cardinal point, quarter of the sky (4—10), region, place, (foreign) country, space (opp. काल); direction, precept, rule; manner, way. — दिशि दिशि in all directions, everywhere; दिशो ऽन्तात् from the end of the world; pl. all quarters, the whole world; दिशो ऽवलोक्य staring into the air.

दिशा f. direction, region.

दिश्य a. relating to the quarters of the sky or to the horizon, coming from afar, foreign, outlandish.

दिष्ट a. pointed out, appointed, bidden, assigned, settled, decided. n. appointed place; order, decree; destiny.

दिष्टान्त m. the appointed end, death.

दिष्टि f. direction, order, command; juncture, good luck, only instr. दिष्ट्या (± वृध् M.*) how fortunate! thank heaven!

दिह्, देग्धि, pp. दिग्ध (q.v.) anoint, smear. — अभि wreath, also = S. अव, परि, प्र = S. सम् the same; M. P. be doubtful or dubious; P. also be confounded with (instr.). C. confound, perplex, M. be uncertain. — Cf. आदिग्ध, उपदिग्ध, निर्दिग्ध, संदिग्ध.

1दी, दीयति, °ते fly. — निस् fly away. परि fly about.

2दी v. दीदि.

दीक्ष्, दीक्षते, pp. दीक्षित (q.v.) be consecrated. C. दीक्षयति, °ते consecrate. D. दिदीक्षिषते wish to be consecrated. — अभि = S.

दीक्षण n. consecrating (one's self); f. आ religious preparation for (—°).

दीक्षणीय a. relating to consecration, f. आ the ceremony of consecration.

दीक्षा f. preparation or consecration for a religious ceremony, initiation; dedication, devotion to (—°); personif. as the wife of Soma.

दीक्षापति m. lord of consecration (Soma).

दीक्षापाल m. guardian of consecration (Agni or Viṣṇu).

दीक्षित, f. °ता consecrated for (dat., loc., instr., or —°), prepared, ready for (dat., instr., loc., or —°); abstr. °त्व† n. — Often °— or —° in names, esp. of Brahmans.

†दीति v. सुदीति.

†दीदि, 3 pl. दीद्यति intr. shine, gleam, be bright or visible, please; tr. bestow by shining (dat. or loc. of pers., acc. of th.). — अभि bestow by shining. आ shine upon. नि = S. tr. प्र shine forth. सम् shine together, also = S. tr. — Cf. दीद्यत्, दीद्यान, दीदिवंस्.

†दीदिति v. सुदीदिति.

दीद्यत् & दीद्यान a. shining, radiant.

दीदिवंस् (दीदुष्) & दीदिवि a. the same.

दीधि, दीध्ये, अदीधेत्, pp. धीत (q.v.) appear, seem (A.); perceive, look at (acc.); think, consider (± मनसा), desire. — अनु observe, think over. अभि think of, consider. आ attend to, care for (gen.), make up one's mind. उद् look up to (acc.). प्रति hope, expect. वि hesitate, be irresolute. — Cf. दीध्यत् & दीध्यान.

1दीधिति f. religious reflection, devotion.

2दीधिति f. brightness, splendour.

दीध्यत् & दीध्यान a. thinking, reflecting, thoughtful, attentive.

दीन a. scarce, scanty, weak, feeble (abstr. °ता f.); depressed, sad, wretched, n. as abstr. & adv. (also दीनकम्).

दीनचित्त & °चेतन a. distressed in mind.

दीनमनस् & °मानस a. the same.

दीनरूप a. of sad appearance, mournful, dejected.

दीनसत्त्व a. low-spirited.

दीप्, दीप्यते or दीप्यते (दीप्यति), pp. दीप्त (q.v.) blaze, flame, shine, be brilliant (l. & f.). C. दीपयति, °ते kindle, inflame, illuminate; excite, raise. I. देदीप्यते blaze brightly, be radiant. — आ C. inflame, kindle. उद् flame up, burn; C. = S. C. उप C. kindle, set fire to (acc.). प्र flame forth, burn. C. kindle, inflame, rouse. वि blaze, flame; C. kindle, illuminate. सम् flame; C. inflame, excite. — Cf. अतिदीप्त, आदीप्त, प्रदीप्त, संदीप्त.

दीप m. light, lamp.
दीपक a. kindling, inflaming, illuminating; m. & f. दीपिका = prec.
दीपद a. who gives a lamp.
दीपन, f. ई kinding, inflaming (lit. & fig.); n. the act of kindling etc.
दीपमाला & °मालिका f. a row of lamps, illumination.
दीपालोक m. lamp-light, a burning lamp.
दीपावलि f. = दीपमाला.
दीपिन्, f. ई kindling, inflaming (—°).
दीप्त a. blazing, flaming, glowing, hot, bright, radiant.
दीप्तकिरण a. having hot rays.
दीप्तवीर्य a. of fiery strength.
दीप्ताक्ष, f. ई having flaming eyes.
दीप्ति f. flame, brilliancy, brightness (p. °मन्त्†); lustre, beauty.
दीप्तौजस् a. of burning energy, hot-blooded.
दीप्र a. flaming, shining.
दीर्घ a. long (sp. & t.); n. adv.; abstr. °ता† f., °त्व† n.
दीर्घकर्ण m. Long-ear, N. of a cat.
दीर्घकालम् (acc. adv.) a long time.
दीर्घजिह्व a. long-tongued; m. N. of a Dānava, f. आ & ई N. of a Rākṣasī & some other female demon.
दीर्घजीविन् a. long-lived.
दीर्घतमस् m. N. of a Rishi.
दीर्घतीक्ष्णमुख, f. ई having a long and sharp mouth.
दीर्घदर्शिता f., °त्व n. abstr. to seq.
दीर्घदर्शिन् a. far-sighted, provident.
दीर्घनिःश्वास m. a long sigh.*
दीर्घप्रयज्यु a. offering or receiving constant prayers and sacrifices (of gods & men).
दीर्घबाहु a. long-armed; a man's name.
दीर्घमुख. f. ई long-mouthed or long-beaked.
दीर्घयशस् a. far renowned.
दीर्घराव m. Long-yell, N. of a jackal.
दीर्घरोष a. persevering in anger, slow to forgive; abstr. °ता f.
दीर्घलोचन a. long-eyed.
दीर्घश्रवस् a. far renowned.
दीर्घश्रुत a. hearing afar or = prec.
दीर्घसत्त्र n. a long-continued Soma sacrifice; p. °त्त्रिन्.
दीर्घसंध्य a. prolonging the twilight devotions; abstr. °त्व n.
दीर्घसूत्र a. dilatory, slow (lit. spinning a long thread); abstr. °ता f.
दीर्घसूत्रिन् a. = prec. a.; abstr. °सूत्रिता f.
दीर्घाक्ष, f. ई long-eyed.
दीर्घाधी a. looking or thinking far.
दीर्घापाङ्ग a. having long outer corners of the eyes; m. N. of an antelope.*
दीर्घायु a. long-lived; abstr. °त्व.
दीर्घायुष्ट्व & °युष्य n. abstr. to seq.
दीर्घायुस् a. long-lived or who may live long.
दीर्घिका f. a (long) lake or pond.
दीर्घी कृ lengthen (°भू pass.); lead far away.
दीर्घोच्छ्वासम् adv. with a long sigh.
दीव् f. (only dat. & loc.) game at dice.
1दु, दुनोति (दुन्वते), pp. दून q.v. (& दुत) burn, grieve (tr. & intr.); P. दूयते (°ति) only intr. C. दावयति = S. tr. — अभि burn (tr.). आ M. grieve, be afflicted. परि burn violently (intr.), be distressed. प्र burn (intr.), vex, afflict. वि burn, destroy; M. be distressed.
2दु = 1दिव्; only दविषाणि.
दुःख a. uneasy, unpleasant; n. uneasiness, pain, sorrow (comp. °तर† n.), as adv. = instr., abl., & °— with difficulty, scarcely, hardly, unwillingly.
दुःखकर (& °कारिन्*) a. causing pain (gen.).
दुःखग्रह a. hard to conceive.
दुःखजीविन् a. living in distress.
दुःखता f. discomfort, pain, sorrow.
दुःखदुःखेन (instr. adv.) with great pain or difficulty.*
दुःखप्राय a. consisting of pain, miserable, wretched.
दुःखभागिन् & °भाज् a. having pain as one's portion, unhappy.
दुःखमरण a. having a painful death.
दुःखय्, °यति to pain or distress.
दुःखयोग m. infliction of pain.
दुःखयोनि m. a source of misery.
दुःखशील a. having a difficult temper, full of pretensions, irritable.

दुःखहन् a. destroying pain.
दुःखाकुल a. troubled with pain, aggrieved.
दुःखाभिज्ञ a. knowing woe.
दुःखाय्, °यते feel pain, be distressed.
दुःखार्त a. afflicted by pain.
दुःखालय m. a home of woes.
दुःखित a. pained, afflicted, miserable.
दुःखिता f., °त्व n. abstr. to seq.
दुःखिन् a.=दुःखित.
दुःखीय्, °यति=दुःखाय्.
दुःखोत्तर a. followed by pain.
दुःखोपचर्य a. difficult to be treated or satisfied.
दुःप्रसह v. दुष्प्रसह.
दुकूल m. a cert. plant; n. a kind of fine cloth or garment.
दुग्ध a. milked, sucked out, extracted; n. milk, the water in the cloud.
दुग्धदोह a. milked out.
दुग्धसिन्धु m. the sea of milk.
दुग्धस्रोतस् n. a stream of milk.
दुघ a. milking, yielding (—°); f. दुघा milch-cow.
दुच्छुना f. misfortune, harm.
दुच्छुनाय्, °यते seek to harm.
दुध्, only दोधत् impetuous, wild, fierce, & दुधित confused (darkness).
दुधि & दुध्र a.=दोधत् (v. prec.).
दुध्रकृत् a. stirring.
दुन्दुभ m. a cert. aquatic animal.
दुन्दुभि m. f. drum (f. also ई); m. also E. of Kṛṣṇa & N. of sev. men, f. ई N. of a Rākṣasī.
दुन्दुभ्याघात m. beater of a drum, drummer.
1दुर् f. door (only दुरस् & दुरस्).
2दुर् (°—)=दुस्.
दुर् m. opener, giver of (gen.).
दुरक्ष a. weak-eyed.
दुरतिक्रम a. difficult to be overcome or escaped.
दुरत्यय a.=prec. & seq.
दुरधिग & °म difficult to be attained.
दुरन्त a. taking a bad end or taking no end, endless; abstr. °ता f.
दुरभिसङ्ग m. a bad inclination.*
दुरवगाह a. difficult to be fathomed or found out.*
दुरवबोध a. difficult to be understood.
दुरवाप a. difficult to be attained.
दुरस्य्, °स्यति wish to harm; a. °स्यु.
दुराकृति a. disfigured, ugly.
दुरागम m. bad gain or corrupt tradition.
दुराचर, f. ई difficult to be handed or treated.
1दुराचार m. bad conduct, wickedness.
2दुराचार a. ill-behaved, depraved, wicked.
दुरात्मन् a. of bad nature, evil, wicked.
दुरात्मवन्त् a. the same.
दुराधर a. difficult to be restrained, obtained, or kept.
दुराधर्ष a. difficult to be attacked, untractable, dangerous.
दुराधी a. evil-minded.
दुराप & दुरापन a. difficult to be reached or attained.
दुराराध्य a. difficult to be won or conciliated.
दुरारुह & दुरारोह a. difficult to be ascended.
दुरालक्ष्य a. difficult to be perceived.
दुरालभ a. difficult to be laid hold of.
दुरालम्ब a. difficult to be kept or maintained.
दूरालम्भ a.=दुरालभ.
दुरालोक a. difficult to be perceived, indistinct.
दुरावह a. difficult to be led towards (—°).
दुरावार a. difficult to be kept back.
दुराशय a. having wicked thoughts.
दुराशा f. bad hope, despair at (loc.).
दुराशिर् a. badly mixed.
दुराशिस् a. having evil wishes or intentions.
दुरासद a. difficult to be approached or met, unaccessible, impracticable, unheard of.
दुरासह a. difficult to be accomplished.
दुरित (दुरित) n. difficulty, danger, distress, damage, discomfort, evil, sin; adj. difficult, evil, bad, sinful, wicked.
दुरिति f. difficulty, distress, trouble.
दुरिष्टि f. failure in a sacrifice.
दुरीह a. badly meant.
दुरुक्त a. ill or badly spoken; n. such a word.
दुरुक्ति f.=prec. n.
दुरुत्तर a. difficult to be overcome.
दुरुत्सह & दुरुद्वह a. difficult to be borne.
दुरुद्गीथ s. a wrong Udgītha.

दुरुपचार a. difficult to be approached or treated.

दुरुपसद् a. unaccessible.

दुरुपसर्पिन् a. approaching carelessly.

दुरूह a. difficult to be perceived or understood; abstr. °त्व n.

दुरेव a. evil-minded, wicked; m. evil-doer.

दुरेवम् adv. uneasily.

दुरोण n. dwelling, home.

दुरोणसद् a. sitting in the house.

दुरोदर m. player at dice or a die; n. game at dice.

दुर्ग a. hard to go through or to, difficult of access or attainment, impassable, unaccessible. m. N. of an Asura & sev. men; n. rough ground, difficult place; mountain, hill, crag, stronghold, castle; difficulty, danger, distress; f. आ N. of a goddess, the daughter of Himavant and wife of Çiva.

दुर्गत a. faring ill, miserable, poor; n. = seq.

दुर्गति f. ill condition, misery, poverty.

दुर्गन्ध a. ill-smelling; m. = seq.

दुर्गन्धता f. bad smell, stink.

दुर्गन्धि a. = दुर्गन्ध adj.

दुर्गपति & °पाल m. governor of a fortress.

दुर्गम a. = दुर्ग a., s. difficult situation.

दुर्गमनीय & दुर्गम्य a. hard to go or enter.

दुर्गसिंह & दुर्गसेन m. names of authors.

दुर्गह n. dangerous place or way, danger.

दुर्गाचार्य m. N. of a scholiast.

दुर्गाढ a. difficult to be fathomed.

दुर्गादत्त & दुर्गादास m. names of men.

दुर्गाध a. = दुर्गाढ.

दुर्गापूजा f. the festival in honour of the goddess Durgā.

दुर्गाह्य a. difficult to be fathomed; abstr. त्व n.

दुर्गृभि a. difficult to be seized or held fast.

1दुर्ग्रह a. the same + difficult to be overcome, gained, understood.

2दुर्ग्रह m. stubbornness, a foolish whim; an evil demon (causing diseases).

दुर्ग्राह्य a. = 1prec.; abstr. °त्व n.

दुर्जन m. a bad man, villain.

दुर्जनी w. कृ make a villain of (acc.), i.e. offend, compromise, mortify.*

दुर्जय a. difficult to be subdued or overcome, invincible; m. N. of a Dānava, a Rakṣas, & sev. men.

दुर्जल n. bad water.

दुर्जात a. wretched, miserable, bad (lit. ill-born or natured); n. misery.

1दुर्जाति a. = prec. a.

2दुर्जाति f. misfortune.

दुर्जातीय a. = 1दुर्जाति.

दुर्जीव n. a hard life, also impers. it is hard to live.

दुर्जेय a. difficult to be vanquished.

दुर्ज्ञान a. difficult to be known; abst. °त्व n.

दुर्ज्ञेय a. = prec. adj.

दुर्णश a. difficult to be attained.

दुर्णामन् m. a kind of demon (lit. of bad name).

दुर्दम & दुर्दम्य a. difficult to be subdued.

दुर्दर्श & °न a. difficult or unpleasant to behold.

दुर्दशा f. bad situation, misfortune.

दुर्दान्त a. badly tamed or hard to tame; m. N. of a lion.

दुर्दिन n. a bad day, rough weather.

दुर्दिवस m. the same.

दुर्दुहा f. difficult to be milked (a cow).

दुर्दृश् a. seeing badly.

दुर्दृश a. = दुर्दर्श.

दुर्देश m. a bad or unwholesome place.

दुर्दैव n. bad luck, misfortune.

दुर्द्यूत n. bad or unfair game.

दुर्धर a. hard to be borne, held, restrained, administered (punishment), kept in mind or recollected; m. a man's name.

दुर्धरीतु & दुर्धर्तु a. difficult to be restrained, irresistible.

दुर्धर्ष a. difficult to be assaulted or approached, invincible, dangerous, terrible; abstr. °ता f., °त्व n.

दुर्धा f. derangement, bad order.

दुर्धार्य a. difficult to be borne or kept.

दुर्धित a. badly arranged, not in order.

दुर्धी a. weak- or evil-minded; stupid or wicked.

दुर्धुर a. badly yoked.

दुर्नय m. evil or imprudent conduct.
दुर्निग्रह a. difficult to be kept down or restrained.
दुर्निमित्त a. an ill omen.
दुर्निरीक्ष, °क्षण, & °क्ष्य difficult to be looked at.
दुर्निवार & °वार्य a. difficult to be checked, hard to get rid of.
दुर्नीत a. badly managed; n. a bad situation or conduct.
दुर्न्यस्त a. badly arranged.
दुर्बल a. weak, feeble, thin, unwell; poor, scanty. Abstr. °ता f.
दुर्बलेन्द्रिय a. having weak organs.
1दुर्बुद्धि f. folly or wickedness.
2दुर्बुद्धि a. foolish, wicked.
दुर्बोध & °ध्य a. hard to understand.
दुर्ब्राह्मण m. a bad Brahman.
दुर्भग a. uncomfortable, unpleasant, unhappy; abstr. °त्व† n.
दुर्भर a. hard to bear or suffer, to please or satisfy.
दुर्भर्तृ m. a bad husband.
दुर्भाग्य a. unfortunate.
दुर्भार्या f. a bad wife.
दुर्भाष a. speaking ill or badly; m. ill speech.
दुर्भाषित, f. आ w. वाच् = prec. m.
दुर्भाषिन् a. = दुर्भाष a.
दुर्भिक्ष n. (m.) famine, want; abstr. °त्व n.
दुर्भिद् a. difficult to be cleft or broken.
दुर्भूत n. ill luck, evil.
दुर्भृति f. scanty or difficult maintenance.
दुर्भेद् & दुर्भेद्य a. = दुर्भिद्.
दुर्भ्रातृ m. a bad brother.
1दुर्मति f. ill-will or false opinion.
2दुर्मति a. foolish or wicked.
1दुर्मद m. false, pride, infatuation.
2दुर्मद a. drunken, fierce, extravagant; very fond of, all eager for (—°).
1दुर्मनस् a. bad disposition, perversity of mind.
2दुर्मनस् a. discouraged, sad.
दुर्मनस्क a. = prec., abstr. °ता f.
दुर्मनाय्, °यते become or be sad or sorrowful. — अति be quite melancholy.
दुर्मनुष्य m. a wicked man, villain.
दुर्मन्तु a. difficult to be understood.
दुर्मन्त्र m. bad advice.
दुर्मन्त्रित a. badly advised; n. = prec.
दुर्मन्त्रिन् m. evil adviser or bad minister; a. as poss.
दुर्मन्मन् a. evil-minded.
दुर्मर a. dying with difficulty; n. impers.
दुर्मरण & °रत्व n. a hard death.
दुर्मर्ष a. not to be forgotten, imperishable; also = seq.
दुर्मर्षण a. unbearable, unsufferable.
दुर्मित्र a. unfriendly, inimical (also °मित्रिय); m. a man's name.
दुर्मुख, f. ई having an ugly face or a foul mouth; m. a man's name.
दुर्मेध, °धस्, & °धाविन् a. dull-witted, silly, stupid.
दुर्मैत्र a. inimical.
दुर्मोचहस्तग्राह a. holding fast (lit. the grasp of whose hand is difficult to unloose).*
दुर्य a. belonging to the door or house; m & f. आ pl. residence, home.
दुर्यशस् n. disgrace, ignominy.
दुर्युग n. a bad age (of the world).
दुर्युज् a. difficult to be yoked.
दुर्योग m. bad contrivance, offence.
दुर्योण n. residence, home.
दुर्योनि a. of low origin, base-born.
दुर्योधन a. difficult to be conquered, invincible (abstr. °ता f.); m. N. of the eldest son of Dhṛtarāṣṭra.
दुर्लक्ष्य a. difficult to be observed, hardly visible.
दुर्लङ्घन a. difficult to be overcome or escaped.
दुर्लङ्घ्य a. the same; abstr. °ता f.
दुर्लभ a. difficult to be obtained or seen; rare, precious, dear; difficult i.g. (w. infin.).
दुर्लभदर्शन a. out of sight, invisible (lit. whose sight is difficult to be obtained).
दुर्ललित a. fondled too much, ill-bred; n. ill behaviour, a roguish trick.
दुर्वच a. hard to be spoken (of); abstr. °त्व n.
दुर्वचन n. = seq.*
1दुर्वचस् n. evil speech, abuse.
2दुर्वचस् a. speaking harshly.
1दुर्वर्ण m. bad colour, impurity.

2दुर्वर्ण a. bad-coloured, low-born.
दुर्वर्तु a. difficult to be restrained, irresistible.
दुर्वस n. (it is) bad dwelling.
दुर्वसति f. bad residence.
दुर्वह a. difficult to be borne or managed.
1दुर्वाच् f. evil speech.
2दुर्वाच् a. speaking ill.
दुर्वाच्य a. hard to be uttered, harsh (words); n. harsh language or bad news.
दुर्वाद m. hard speech, censure, abuse.
दुर्वान्त a. (leech) that has not well vomited.
दुर्वार & °ण a. difficult to be checked or stopped, irresistible.
दुर्वार्त्ता f. bad news.
दुर्वार्य a. = दुर्वार; abstr. °ता f.
दुर्वाल a. bald-headed or red-haired.
दुर्वासस् a. badly clad, naked; m. N. of a Rishi.
दुर्विगाह & °ह्य a. = दुर्गाढ.
1दुर्विज्ञान n. difficulty understanding with.
2दुर्विज्ञान a. difficult to be understood.
दुर्विज्ञेय a. the same.
दुर्विदग्ध a. badly taught, i.e. ignorant, stupid or cunning, crafty, subtle.
दुर्विद्य a. uninformed, uneducated.
दुर्विद्वंस् a. evil-minded.
दुर्विधि m. a bad fortune.
दुर्विनय m. ill behaviour.
दुर्विनीत a. ill-behaved.
1दुर्विपाक m. evil consequences.
2दुर्विपाक a. having evil consequences.
दुर्विभाव, °भावन, & °भाव्य a. difficult to be conceived or understood.
दुर्विलसित n. ill behaviour, bad manners.
दुर्विवाह m. bad marriage, mesalliance.
दुर्विषह & °ह्य a. unbearable, irresistible.
1दुर्वृत्त a. ill-behaved, wicked.
2दुर्वृत्त n. ill behaviour, misconduct, villany.
दुर्वृत्ति f. misery, distress, also = prec.
दुर्व्यसन n. bad inclination, vice.
दुर्हणा f. damage, misfortune, p. °वन्त्.
दुर्हणाय्, pp. °यन्त् = seq.
दुर्हणायु a. meditating evil.
†दुर्हणु a. having ugly jaws.
दुर्हार्द् a. bad-hearted.
दुर्हित a. ill-conditioned, miserable.
दुर्हृणाय्, pp. °यन्त् = seq.
दुर्हृणायु a. raging, furious.
दुर्हृद् a. bad-hearted; m. enemy.
दुल्, दोलयति, pp. °लित raise, swing.
1दुवस् n. honour, worship.
2दुवस् a. stirring, restless.
दुवस्य्, °स्यति honour, worship; present (acc. of pers. & instr. of th. or dat. of pers. & acc. of th.).
दुवस्यु & दुवस्वन्त् a. reverent, respectful.
दुवोया f. (instr.) honour, worship.
दुवोयु a. = दुवस्यु; n. adv.
दुश्चर a. difficult to be gone, entered, or overcome; inaccessible, impracticable. Abstr. °त्व n.
1दुश्चरित n. misbehaviour, wickedness, folly.
2दुश्चरित a. misbehaving, wicked.
दुश्चर्मन् a. having a cutaneous disease.
दुश्चारित्र & °रिन् a. = 2दुश्चरित.
दुश्चित् a. thinking evil.
दुश्चित्त a. afflicted, sad.
दुश्चेतस् a. = दुश्चित्.
दुश्चेष्टा f., °ष्टित n. ill conduct or practice.
दुश्च्यवन a. difficult to be shaken.
दुःशंस a. speaking or thinking evil.
दुःशल m., °आ f. N. of a son & a daughter of Dhṛtarāṣṭra.
दुःशासन m. N. of a son of Dhṛtarāṣṭra.
दुःशासुस् a. evil-minded, malevolent.
दुःशिक्षित a. badly taught, uneducated.
दुःशिष्य m. a bad pupil.
दुःशील a. having a bad character or disposition; abstr. °ता f.
दुःशेव a. malevolent, envious.
1दुष् (°—) = दुस्.
2दुष्, दुष्यति (°ते), pp. दुष्ट (q.v.) be or become bad, corrupted, defiled, impure; sin, be guilty. C. दुषयति q.v. — प्र get worse, be spoiled or contaminated, do amiss, sin against (प्रति). वि act improperly, commit a sin. सम् be polluted. — Cf. प्रदुष्ट, विप्रदुष्ट, संदुष्ट.
दुष्कर a. difficult, arduous, uncommon, extraordinary; difficult to or to be (infin.); n. hardly, scarcely (w. यद् or यदि).

दुष्कर्मन् n. misdeed, sin; a. & m. who does evil, villain.
1दुष्कुल n. a low race.
2दुष्कुल a. of low race, base-born; abstr. °ता f.
दुष्कृत् = दुष्कर्मन् a. & m.
1दुष्कृत a. ill done.
2दुष्कृत n. evil deed, crime, sin.
दुष्कृतकर्मन् & °कारिन् a. doing evil deeds; reprobate, criminal.
दुष्कृति & °तिन् a. doing evil; m. evil-doer.
दुष्ट a. spoiled, corrupt, injured, damaged, vicious, bad, guilty. m. villain, wicked man; n. guilt, sin. Abstr. °ता f., °त्व n.
दुष्टचरित्र a. ill-behaved; m. evil-doer.
दुष्टचारिन् a. & m. the same.
दुष्टचेतस् a. evil-minded.
†दुष्टतनु a. having an ugly body.
दुष्टबटुक m. bad fellow.*
दुष्टभाव a. evil-natured, wicked; abstr. °ता f.
दुष्टर a. unconquerable, irresistible, unbearable, unsufferable.
दुष्टरीतु a. the same.
दुष्टवाच् a. speaking evil; m. a defamer.
दुष्टशोणित n. corrupt blood.
दुष्टात्मन् & दुष्टान्तरात्मन् a. evil-naturcel.
दुष्टि f. corruption, depravity.
दुष्टुति v. दुःष्टुति.
दुष्परिहन्तु a. difficult to be destroyed.
दुष्पार a. difficult to be crossed, overcome, or accomplished.
दुष्पूर a. difficult to be filled or satisfied.
दुष्प्रणीत a. ill-managed, failed; n. bad conduct.
दुष्प्रधर्ष a. unassailable, untouchable.
दुष्प्रयुक्त a. badly employed.
दुष्प्रसह a. difficult to be borne or overcome, irresistible.
दुष्प्रसाद् & °न a. difficult to be propitiated.
दुष्प्राप & °ण a. hard to attain.
दुष्प्रेक्ष, °क्षणीय, & °क्ष्य a. difficult or unpleasant to be looked at.
दुष्मन्त, दुष्यन्त, or दुःषन्त m. N. of a king, the husband of Çakuntalā.
दुःष्टुति or दुःष्टुति f. bad i.e. faulty hymn or praise.
दुःष्वप्न्य n. evil dream, restless sleep.

दुस् (°—) = Gr. δυς.
दुस्तर a. difficult to be crossed or overcome.
दुस्तरण, f. ई the same.
दुस्त्यज a. difficult to be relinquished or quitted; abstr. °ता f.
दुस्थ & दुस्थित v. दुःस्थ & दुःस्थित.
दुःसह a. difficult to be borne, irresistible; (abstr. °त्व n.*).
दुःसाध्य a. difficult to be accomplished or managed.
दुःस्थ & दुस्थित a. ill-faring, miserable, unhappy, poor, ill.
दुःस्थिति f. abstr. to prec.
दुःस्पर्श & दुःस्पृश a. difficult or unpleasant to be touched.
दुःस्वप्न m. an evil dream.
1दुह्, दोग्धि, दुग्धे (दुहति, °ते, दोहति, °ते, दुह्यति, °ते), pp. दुग्ध (q.v.) milk, i.g. extract, derive, draw the good out of (2 acc.); yield, grant, bestow (mostly M.). C. दोहयति, °ते cause to milk, also = S. milk, extract. D. दुदुक्षति & दुधुक्षति wish to milk. — निस् A. M. milk out, extract. विप्र A. suck out. वि M. milk out, empty. सम् A. M. milk or suck (together); M. yield or grant together.
2दुह् & दुह a. (—°) milking; milching or yielding.
दुहितामातृ f. du. daughter and mother.
दुहितृ f. daughter; abstr. °तृत्व n.
दू f. = 1दुवस्.
दूडभ a. difficult to be deceived, infallible.
दूडाश a. not worshipping, irreligious.
दूढी a. evil-minded.
दूणश a. unattainable.
1दूणाश a. the same.
2दूणाश a. imperishable, everlasting.
दूत m. messenger, ambassador, envoy, go-between; f. ई (also दूति) esp. confidante, procuress.
दूतक, f. दूतिका the same.
दूतकर्मन् & दूतत्व n. office or state of a messenger.
दूत्य n., दूत्या f. the same; message, news.
दून a. burnt, pained, vexed.
दूर a. far, distant from (abl. or gen.); n

distance (in sp. & t.); as adv. far, high above, in a high degree, very much, (also दूर °—); w. कृ surpass. दूरेण far, from afar, comp. दूरतरेण; by far. दूरात् (from) afar, far from (abl.). दूरे far, a long way off, comp. दूरतरे at some distance from (abl.).

दूरंआधी a. whose longing is in the distance.

दूरकम् & °के (acc. & loc. adv.) far.

दूरक्ष्य a. difficult to be preserved or kept.

दूरग a. going far, remote.

दूरगत a. gone far away.

दूरंगम a. going far away.

दूरतस् adv. from afar, far away, far, not at hand; w. भू keep in distance.

दूरत्व n. remoteness, distance.

दूरदर्शन & °दर्शिन् far-seeing (lit. & fig.).

दूरपथ m. long way, distance.

दूरपातिन् a. flying or sending far.

दूरभाव m. remoteness, distance.

दूरय्, °यति remove, deprive.

दूरवर्तिन् a. being far.

दूरविलम्बिन् a. hanging far down.

दूरसंस्थ a. being in the distance.

दूरसूर्य a. having the sun far i.e. high, shone upon from above.

दूरस्थ & दूरस्थित a. = दूरसंस्थ.

दूराकृष्ट a. far stretched or extended.

दूरारूढ a. risen high (lit. far).*

दूरारोहिन् a. the same.*

दूरालोक m. sight from afar, remote distance.

दूरी w. कृ leave behind, remove, reject; w. भू go back, retire, be far.

दूरेअन्त a. ending in the distance, boundless.

दूरेचर a. staying (lit. moving) far.

दूरेदृश् a. visible from afar.

दूरेभा a. shining far and wide.

दूरेवध a. far-striking or hitting.

दूरोत्सारित a. driven far away.*

दूरोह a. ascending with difficulty.

दूरोहण a. difficult to be ascended; n. N. of a cert. rite.

दूर्व m. N. of a king; f. दूर्वा a kind of grass.

दूर्वाचत्वर s. grass plot.*

दूर्श n. a kind of woven cloth or garment.

दूष a. defiling, polluting (—°).

दूषक, f. इका (gen. or —°) = prec. + corrupting, disgracing, offending; f. दूषिका also = दूषी q.v.

दूषण, f. ई = prec.; m. N. of a Rakṣas; n. the act of defiling or corrupting, seduction, defamation, objection, refutation; want, fault, guilt, sin, offence.

दूषय्, दूषयति (°ते), pp. दूषित spoil, corrupt, defile, pollute, harm, injure, blame, revile. — प्र spoil, attack, defame. वि the same, w. उपहासैस् mock, laugh at (acc.). सम् spoil, dishonour. — Cf. प्रतिदूषित.

दूषि a. defiling, destroying (—°).

दूषिन् a. polluting, disgracing (—°).

दूषी & दूषीका f. the rheum of the eyes.

1दूष्य a. liable to be corrupted or defiled.

2दूष्य n. a kind of cloth, tent, garment.

दूष्यगन्धिन् a. smelling of rags (cf. prec.).*

1दृ, दृणाति (दर्षि), pp. दीर्ण burst, break asunder, split open (tr. & intr.); P. दीर्यते (°ति) the same (intr.). C. दरयति & दारयति (°ते) = S. tr. + drive asunder, disperse, scatter. I. (st. दर्दृ & दादृ) = S. tr. — अव S. & C. split, break, burst asunder (tr.); P. the same (intr.). आ split, go asunder; also = I. rend, break, open, make accessible. निस् S. & C. rend, split, cleave. परि M. rend on all sides, P. peel or drop off on all sides (skin). प्र break, tear; P. split. open, burst asunder (intr.). वि split, tear, rend asunder, open; P. burst, go asunder; C. rend or saw in pieces, break through, open, drive asunder, chase away; I. split, open (tr.). — Cf. अवदीर्ण, परिदीर्ण, विदीर्ण.

2दृ, द्रियते, w. आ, आद्रियते (°ति), pp. आदृत (q.v.) regard, respect, mind (w. acc. or inf.); also w. pass. mg. — अत्या have much regard or consideration. प्रत्या be regardful towards (acc.).

दृंहण n. making firm, fortifying.

दृंहित a. made firm, fortified; n. = prec.

दृंहितृ m. strengthener, fortifier.

दृक्पथ m. range of sight.

दृक्पात m. (the letting fall) a glance.

दृगन्त m. the outer corner of the eyes.

दृग्गोचर m. range of sight.

दृग्रुध् a. obstructing the sight.

दृढ (**दृळ्ह**) a. firm, strong, solid, durable, steady, sure, certain; n. adv., as subst. anything firm or solid, esp. stronghold, fortress.

दृढकारिन् a. persevering (lit. acting firmly).

दृढता f., **°त्व** n. firmness, steadiness, perseverance in (loc.).

दृढधन्वन् & **°धन्विन्** a. having a strong bow.

दृढनिश्चय a. of firm determination, resolute.

दृढमति a. firm-minded, strong-willed.

दृढमुष्टि f. strong or close fist; also as a. poss.

दृढय्, **°यति** make firm, fasten, confirm, strengthen.

दृढव्रत a. strict, faithful (lit. whose vows are firm); firmly insisting on (loc.) or devoted to (—°).

दृढायु & **°युस्** m. a man's name.

दृढायुध a. having strong weapons; E. of Çiva.

दृढी w. **कृ** = **दृढय्**, w. **भू** become or be firm.

दृढीकरण n., **°कार** m. making firm, confirmation.

दृति m. (f.) bag of leather, bellows (also **दृती** f.).

दृध्र a. holding tightly, fastening.

दृप्, **दृप्यति** (**दर्पति**), pp. **दृप्त** rave, be foolish, insolent, or proud. C. **दर्पयति**, pp. **दर्पित** make mad, foolish, etc.

दृब्धि f. stringing together.

दृभ्, **दृभति** bunch, make into tufts, string together, connect. — **सम्** connect, compose, write. — Cf. **संदृब्ध**.

दृभीक m. N. of a demon.

दृवन् a. tearing asunder, rending.

1**दृश्** (cf. **पश्**), pp. **दृष्ट** (q.v.) see, behold, know by (instr.); see with the mind, notice, observe, try, examine; find out, invent (esp. a sacred song). P. M. **दृश्यते** (**°ति**) be seen or visible, appear or be regarded as, pass for (nom.); be found, occur. C. **दर्शयति** cause a pers. (acc., gen., dat., or *instr.) to see (acc.), show, w. **आत्मानम्** one's self, i.e. appear, pretend to be; produce, point out, make known as or prove to be (2 acc.); – pp. **दर्शितम्** (impers.) appearance has been made by (instr.).* D. **दिदृक्षते** (**°ति**) desire or like to see. — **अनु** look at (acc.), behold, see (**मनसा** with the mind); P. M. be seen, appear; C. cause to see, teach, show (2 acc.). **अभि** behold, see; P. be seen, appear; C. cause to see, show, betray. **आ** M. appear; C. show. **उद्** C. pp. **उद्दर्शितम्** = **दर्शितम्** (v. S.). **उप** look on, notice, observe; P. M. be visible, appear; C. cause to see, show, explain; exhibit, pretend, feign. **नि** C. cause to see, show, point out, explain, teach, proclaim. **परि** see = visit; behold, notice, know, understand, find out; P. be visible, appear; C. show, explain. **प्र** P. M. be visible, appear; C. make visible, show, point out, make known or clear, explain, teach. **संप्र** behold; P. be seen, appear; C. cause to see, show, **आत्मानम्** pretend to be (adv. in **वत्**), point out etc. = prec. **प्रति** behold, notice; P. M. be seen or visible, appear as (nom.); C. cause to see, show. **वि** P. M. be clearly visible, come forth, appear; C. = prec. **सम्** A. M. behold, observe; P. M. be seen or appear (together), resemble; C. cause to see, make manifest, show; w. **आत्मानम्** etc. = **संप्र** C. — Cf. **अभ्युद्दृष्ट**, **उद्दृष्ट**, **संदृष्ट**.

2**दृश्** f. (nom. **दृक्**) seeing, looking; f. the action of seeing, —° look, appearance; n. eye.

दृशति f. looking, sight.

दृशि f. seeing, power of sight, eye, poss. **°मन्त्**.

दृशीक a. worth seeing, conspicuous; n. sight.

दृशीका f. sight, appearance.

दृशेक a. looking at (—°); m. spectator.

दृशेन्य a. = **दृशीक**.

दृश्य a. to be seen, visible to (instr. or —°); worth seeing, beautiful; abstr. **°ता**† f., **°त्व**† n.

दृषत्कण m. small stone, pebble.

दृषद् f. rock, large stone, esp. the nether mill-stone.

दृषदुपल n. sgl. du. & °ला f. du. the nether and the upper mill-stone.

दृषदोलूखल n. sgl. mill-stone and mortar.

दृषद्वन्त् m. N. of a man; f. °द्वती N. of a river & sev. women.

दृष्ट a. seen, visible, apparent, known, foreseen, destined; decided, acknowledged, valid; n. perception, observation, sight, view, glance.

दृष्टदोष a. having found out faults or being found out as a fault.

दृष्टपूर्व a. seen before.

दृष्टमात्र a. only seen.*

दृष्टवीर्य & **दृष्टसार** a. of proved strength.

दृष्टश्रुत a. seen and (or) heard.

दृष्टान्त a. serving for an example or standard; m. example, standard, precedent.

दृष्टार्थ a. whose aim is apparent, also = prec. a.

दृष्टि f. seeing, looking at (gen.); viewing, beholding (lit. & fig.); sense or power of sight; look, glance; eye.

दृष्टिक्षम a. worth seeing (lit. bearing the sight).

दृष्टिक्षेप m. glance, look (lit. the throwing about of the eyes).

दृष्टिगोचर m. = दृग्गोचर.

दृष्टिपथ m. = दृक्पथ.

दृष्टिपात m. = दृक्पात.

दृष्टिपूत a. purified by the sight.

दृष्टिप्रसाद m. the favour of a look; °दं कृ grant an audience.

दृष्टिमन्त् a. having sight or insight.

दृष्टिराग m. expression of the eyes.*

दृष्टिविक्षेप m. = दृष्टिक्षेप.

दृष्टिसंभेद m. mutual glance (lit. mixing or meeting of glances).*

दृह् (**दृंह्**), दृंहति, pp. दृढ or दृळ्ह (q.v.) make or be firm; M. दृंहते or दृह्यति, °ते only intr. C. दृंहयति, pp. दृंहित (q.v.) make firm, fortify, fix; m. hold fast, be firm.

देय a. to be given, granted, married, restored, committed; n. impers., as subst. gift, offering, present, pay.

देव, f. **ई** divine, heavenly. — m. celestial being, god (esp. Indra), idol; priest, Brahman; king, prince. f. **ई** goddess (esp. Durgā), queen, princess.

देवक (adj. —°) god; N. of a Gandharva & of sev. men. f. **देविका** a goddess of low rank; **देवकी** N. of Kṛṣṇa's mother.

देवकन्यका & °**कन्या** f. celestial maiden, nymph.

देवकर्मन् n. any action pertaining to the gods; pious work, offering.

देवकल्प a. god-like.

देवकार्य n. = देवकर्मन्, also divine command.

देवकिल्बिष n. sin against the gods.

देवकीनन्दन, **देवकीपुत्र** & °**सूनु** m. E. of Kṛṣṇa.

देवकुल n. temple.

देवकृत a. made or done by the gods.

देवकृत्य n. = देवकर्मन्.

देवखात a. hollow by nature (lit. dug by the gods).

देवगण m. a troop or class of gods.

देवगर्भ m. divine child.

देवगवी f. pl. the cows of the gods.

देवगिरि m. N. of a mountain.

देवगुप्त a. guarded by a god or gods.

देवगुरु m. god and teacher (°—); father or teacher of the gods, E. of Kaçyapa & Bṛhaspati.

देवगुह्य n. a secret of the gods.

देवगृह m. n. temple, chapel; palace.

देवच्छन्द m. a necklace of 81 strings.

देवज a. god-born.

देवजन m. pl. (sgl.) host of gods or demons.

देवजननी f. the mother of the gods.*

देवजा a. born or produced by gods.

1**देवजात** a. the same.

2**देवजात** n. a race or class of gods.

देवजुष्ट a. liked by the gods.

देवजूत a. sped by the gods.

1**देवता** f. godhead, divinity (abstr. & concr.); a god or idol.

2**देवता** (instr. adv.) like a god or among the gods.

देवतागार & **देवतागृह** n. a temple (lit. house of the gods).

देवतात् & **देवताति** f. divine service or a troop of gods.

देवतामन्दिर n. = देवतागार.*

देवतामय, f. **ई** containing (all) the gods.

देवतार्चन n. worship of the gods.

देवताशेष* v. देवशेष.

देवतासहायिन् a. alone (lit. having only the gods as companions).

देवतुमुल n. thunder (noise of the gods).

देवत्त a. given by the gods.

देवत्य or **देवत्य** a. having — as deity, consecrated to (—°).

देवत्रा adv. among or to the gods.

देवत्व n. divinity (only abstr.).

देवदत्त a. given by a god or by the gods; m. Arjuna's conch-shell, one of the vital airs, a man's name.

देवदर्शन & **°र्शिन्** a. seeing the gods.

देवदारु m. a species of pine.

देवदूत m. a messenger of the gods.

देवदेव m. the god of the gods, the highest god (Brahman, Çiva-Rudra, Viṣṇu-Kṛṣṇa, or Gaṇeça).

देवदेवेश m. E. of Çiva or Viṣṇu (cf. prec.).

देवदैवत्य a. sacred to the gods (lit. having the gods as deity).

देवद्र्यञ्च्, f. **°द्रीची** turned towards the gods.

देवन n. shining, beaming; playing, game at dice.

देवनदी f. celestial river, E. of sev. sacred rivers.

देवनाथ m. lord of the gods, Çiva.

देवनामन् n. divine name.

देवनिकाय m. host of gods.

देवनिद् m. a god-hater.

देवनिर्मित a. created by the gods.

देवपति m. lord of the gods (Indra.).

देवपत्नी f. having a god as husband.

देवपशु m. cattle sacred to the gods.

देवपात्र n. cup of the gods.

देवपान a. serving the gods for drinking.

1**देवपुत्र** m. the son of a god.

2**देवपुत्र** a. having gods as children.

देवपुर् f., **°पुर** n., **°पुरा** f. castle or city of the gods.

देवपूजा f. worship of the gods.

देवपूर्व+°गिरि m. = **देवगिरि**.

देवपूर्वकम् adv. beginning with the gods.

देवप्रिय a. dear to the gods (Çiva).

देवभक्ति f. devotion (to the gods), piety.

देवभिषज् m. the physician of the gods.

देवभोग m. pleasure of the gods, heavenly joy.

देवमणि m. divine amulet, esp. the jewel on Kṛṣṇa's breast.

देवमनुष्य or **°ष्य** m. pl. gods & men.

देवमय a. containing the gods.

देवमातृ f. the mother of the gods.

देवमुनि m. a divine Muni.

देवय्, pp. **°यन्त्** serving the gods, religious.

देवयज् a. worshipping the gods, making oblations to them.

देवयजन, f. **ई** = prec. or serving for an oblation; n. place of offering.

देवयज्ञ m. sacrifice to the gods, esp. a burnt sacrifice.

देवयज्य n., **°यज्या** f. worship of the gods, a sacrifice.

देवया a. going to or desirous of the gods; religious, pious.

देवयाजिन् a. = **देवयज्**.

देवयात्रा f. idol procession, pilgrimage i.g.; **°गत** being on a pilgrimage.

देवयान, f. **ई** going or leading to the gods; f. **ई** N. of a daughter of Uçanas; n. path of the gods.

देवयु & **°यू** (f. **ऊ**) loving the gods; religious, pious.

देवयुक्त a. yoked by the gods.

देवयुग n. the age of the gods, i.e. the first age of the world.

देवयोषा f. the wife of a god.

देवर m. husband's brother.

देवरत a. delighting in the gods, pious.

देवरथ m. the car of a god.

देवराज् m. king of the gods, E. of Indra.

देवराज m. a divine ruler, also = prec.

देवराज्य n. dominion over the gods.

देवरात m. God-given, a man's name.

देवरूपिन् a. having a divine form, godlike.

देवर्षि m. a celestial saint.

देवल m. a man's name or = seq.

देवलक m. attendant upon an idol (who carries it about and shows it).

देवलिङ्ग n. the characteristic of a god.

देवलोक m. the world of the gods.

देववध m. a celestial weapon.

देववधू f. = **देवयोषा**.

देववन्त् a. surrounded or accompanied by gods.

देववन्द् a. praising the gods.
देववाहन a. carrying the gods.
देवविद् a. knowing the gods.
देवविश् & °विशा f. race or host of the gods.
देववी a. gratifying or comforting the gods; superl. °तम.
देववीति f. a feast or meal for the gods.
1देवव्रत n. religious observance, also = prec.
2देवव्रत a. devoted to the gods, pious, religious; E. of Bhīṣma & Skanda.
1देवशत्रु m. an enemy of the gods, an Asura or Rakṣas.
2देवशत्रु a. having the gods as enemies.
देवशर्मन् m. a man's name.
देवशिष्ट a. directed by the gods.
देवशुनी f. the divine female dog, i.e. Saramā.
देवशेष n. the remnants of (a sacrifice offered to) the gods.
देवश्रुत् a. audible to or heard by the gods.
†देवसख m. friend of the gods.
देवसद् a. dwelling among the gods.
देवसद्मन् n. seat of the gods.
देवसृष्ट a. sent forth or created by the gods.
देवसेन m. a man's name; f. °ना the army or host of the gods (often person.).
देवस्तुत् a. praising the gods.
देवस्व n. the property of the gods.
देवहविस् & देवहव्य n. oblation to the gods.
देवहित a. arranged or settled by the gods.
देवहिति f. divine arrangement.
देवहू a. invoking the gods.
देवहूति f. & देवहूय n. invocation of the gods.
देवहेति f. a divine weapon.
देवागार m. n. a temple.
देवाङ्गना f. a divine female.
देवाञ्च् (f. देवाची) turned towards the gods.
देवात्मन् m. the divine soul.
देवाधिप m. lord of the gods (Indra).
देवानीक n. army of the gods.
देवान्न n. food of (i.e. offered to) the gods.
देवाय्, देवायन्त् = देवय्.
देवायु, °यू a = देवयु, °यू.
देवारि m. enemy of the gods, an Asura.
देवार्चन n. worship of a god.
देवावन्त् a. = देववन्त्.
देवावी a. = देववी.

देवावृध् a. gladdening the gods.
देवाश्व m. the horse of a god.
देवासुर m. pl. the gods and the Asuras.
देवितृ m. dice-player.
देविन् a. playing at dice.
देवीगृह & °भवन n. the temple of the goddess (Durgā).
देवी w. भू be a god i e. represent an idol.
देवृ m. husband's brother.
देवेद्ध a. kindled by the gods.
देवेन्द्र m. lord of the gods (Indra).
देवेश m. the same (also Brahman, Viṣṇu & Çiva), prince, king; f. ई E. of Durgā & Devakī.
देवेश्वर m. lord of the gods (Çiva).
देवेषित a. impelled or sent by the gods.
देवेषु m. a divine arrow.
देव्य n. divine dignity or power.
देव्युपनिषद् f. T. of an Upanishad.
देश m. place, spot, region, country; देशे in the right place (o. w. काले q.v.). — f. देशी language of the country, vulgar speech, provincialism.
देशक a. & m. pointing out, showing, directing, teaching, teacher.
देशकाल m. du. place and time, sgl. pl. & t. for (gen.); °ज्ञ or °विद् a. knowing pl. & t.
देशदृष्ट a. customary (lit. seen) in a country, local.
देशधर्म m. local law or custom.
देशना f. direction, instruction.
देशभाषा f. the dialect of a country.
देशभाषान्तर n. a foreign language (lit. another dialect than that of the country).*
देशाटन n. travelling (in a country).
देशातिथि m. foreigner (guest in a country).
देशान्तर n. another country, abroad.
देशान्तरगमन n. a travelling abroad.*
देशान्तरस्थ a. being abroad.
देशिक a. & m. showing the way, guide, teacher.
देशिन् a. pointing out, showing; f. °नी the index or forefinger.
देशीकोश m. vocabulary of provincialisms.
देशीनाममाला f. garland of provincial words (T. of a glossary).

देशीय a. belonging to the country, provincial; native of, contiguous to, resembling (—°).
देश्य a. to be pointed out, exemplary, standard; being on the spot, present, m. eye-witness; also = prec.
देष्टृ m. (देंष्ट्री) f. pointer, guide, instructor.
देष्ट्र n. direction, assignation, promise.
देष्ठ (superl.) giving most.
देष्णं n. gift, donation.
देह m. n. body, person, abstr. °त्व n.; f. देही mound, wall.
देहकर, °कर्तृ & °कृत् m. father (lit. former of the body).
देहज m. son or the god of love (lit. born of the body).
देहत्याग m. death (lit. relinquishing the body).
देहदाह m. heat of the body, fever.
देहधारण n. life (lit. supporting of the body).
देहभृत् a. carrying or having a body; m. living creature, esp. man, E. of Çiva.
देहयात्रा f. support of the body, prolonging life.
देहरक्षा f. chastity (lit. care of the body).
देहली f. threshold.
देहवन्त् a. having a body; m. living creature, man.
देहवृत्ति f. support of the body.
देहिन् a. = देहवन्त्; m. man or soul.
देहोत्कम्प m. trembling of the body.
दैक्ष a. relating to initiation.
दैतेय m. descendant of Diti, an Asura, f. ई; a. belonging or pertaining to a Daiteya
दैत्य m. & a. = prec.
दैत्यदानवमर्दन m. the crusher of the Daityas and Dānavas (Indra).
दैत्यनिबर्हण, °निषूदन, °हन्तृ, & दैत्यान्तक m. killer of the Daityas (Viṣṇu).
दैत्यारि m. enemy of the Daityas, a god.
दैत्येन्द्र m. the king of the Daityas.
दैन्य n. dejection, wretchedness, misery; acc. w. कृ or विधा be querulous or humble.
दैर्घ्य n. length.
दैव or दैवं, f. ई belonging to or coming from the gods; divine, celestial, royal; fatal (v. seq.). — m. (± विवाह) a certain form of marriage, f. ई a woman married by it; n. deity, religious work (sc. कर्मन् or कार्य), divine appointment i.e. fate, destiny.
दैवगति f. a fatal chance.
दैवज्ञ a. knowing fate; m. astrologer.
दैवत, f. ई belonging to a deity, divine; n. deity, a god or an idol; adj. —° = देवत्य.
दैवतस् adv. by fate or chance.
दैवत्य (adj. —°) = देवत्य.
दैवदुर्विपाक m. a bad fatality (lit. the hard ripening of destiny).
दैवनिर्मित a. formed by destiny or nature.
दैवपरायण a. putting fate above all, m. fatalist.
दैवमानुषक a. belonging to gods and men.
दैवयानेय m. metron. from देवयानी.
दैवयोग m. fatality, chance, °तस् by chance.
दैववश m. = prec. (also abl.).
दैवविद् a. & m. = दैवज्ञ.
दैवहतक a. struck by destiny, cursed, damned; n. the cursed destiny.*
दैवाद्यन्त a. beginning and ending with the gods.
दैविक a. relating to the gods, divine.
दैवोढा f. a woman married according to the Daiva rite; °ज a. born of such a woman.
दैव्य (f. आ & दैवी) the same; n. divine power, fate, destiny.
दैशिक a. belonging to a place, local, provincial; also = देशिक
दैहिक, f. ई bodily, corporeal.
दोग्धृ m. milker; f. दोग्ध्री having or yielding milk (cow or wet-nurse), also = seq.
दोग्ध्र n. milk-pail.
दोघ a. & m. milking.
दोधक n. N. of a metre.
दोर्दण्ड m. an arm (resembling a stick).
दोल m. swinging, rocking; f. आ (r. m.) swing, litter, hammock.
दोलाघर & °क s. a house with a swing.*
दोलाय्, °यते swing, waver; be restless or unsteady.
दोलारूढ a. restless, unsteady (lit. mounted on a swing); doubtful, uncertain.
दोलोत्सव m. a swinging-feast.
दोःशालिन् a. having strong arms.

1(दोष m.), mostly दोषा f. evening, dark; दोषाम् & °षा (instr.) in the evening, at dusk.

2दोष m. (n.) fault, defect, want; sin, transgression; harm, evil consequence; disadvantage, damage, bad condition.

दोषगुण n. sgl. faults and virtues.

दोषज्ञ a. knowing faults, wise i.g.

दोषणु a. being in the arm.

दोषन् n. fore-arm, arm i.g.

दोषमय a. consisting of faults.

दोषल a. faulty, corrupt, bad.

दोषवत् adv. like a fault or sin.

दोषवन्त् a.=दोषल+guilty, sinful, noxious, dangerous.

दोषस् n. evening, dusk.

दोषाकर m. the moon (night-maker).

दोषाक्षर s. a word of blame or reproach.

दोषातन a. nocturnal, nightly.

दोषानुदर्शिन् a. perceiving faults.

दोषाय्, °यते appear as a fault.

†दोषावस्तृ m. illuminer of the darkness.

दोस् n. (m.) fore-arm, arm i.g.

दोह a. yielding, granting (—°); m. milking, making profit out of (—°); milk, milk-pail.

दोहद m. the longing of pregnant women, i.g. ardent wish or desire of (loc. or —°); pregnancy, fig. of plants before blossoming.

दोहदिन् a. desirous of, eager for (loc. or —°).

दोहन a. giving milk (—°); n. milking or milk, also=f. दोहनी milk-pail.

दोहल m.=दोहद.

दोहस् n. milking; dat. दोहसे as infin.

दोह्य a. to be milked.

दौत्य & °क n. message, mission.

दौरात्म्य n. wickedness, malice.

दौरित n. mischief, harm.

दौर्ग a. relating to Durgā.

दौर्गत्य n. misery, distress, poverty.

दौर्गह m. patron. of Purukutsa, horse.

दौर्जन्य n. wickedness, meanness.

दौर्बल्य n. weakness.

दौर्भाग्य n. ill luck, esp. unrequited love.

दौर्मनस्य n. melancholy, sadness.

दौर्व्रत्य n. disobedience, ill conduct.

दौर्हृद m. villain, enemy; n. evil disposition, enmity.

दौवारिक m., ई f. door-keeper, porter.

दौश्चर्म्य n. a disease of the skin.

दौःशील्य n. evil disposition, wickedness.

दौष्कुल or °लेय a. of low family.

1दौष्कुल्य a. the same.

2दौष्कुल्य n. a low family or race.

दौष्कृत्य & दौष्ट्य n. badness, wickedness.

दौष्मन्त & दौष्मन्ति v. seq.

दौष्यन्त & °न्ति a. belonging to or descended from Duṣyanta.

दौःषन्ति v. दौष्यन्ति.

दौःष्वप्न्य n. (state of) having evil dreams.

दौहित्र m., ई f. a daughter's son or daughter.

दौहृद n. (a. —° f. आ) the longing of a pregnant woman.

द्यावा v. 3दिव्.

द्यावाक्षम् f. du. (nom. °क्षामा) heaven and earth.

द्यावापृथिवी f. du. (nom. °वी & °व्यौ) the same.

द्यावाभूमि f. du. (nom. °मी) the same.

द्यु v. 3दिव्.

द्युक्ष a. heavenly, light, brilliant.

द्युगत् adv. through or across the sky.

द्युचर a. moving in the sky, an inhabitant of heaven.

1द्युत्, द्योतते (°ति), pp. द्युत्त shine, beam, twinkle, glitter. C. द्योतयति, pp. द्योतित make brilliant, illuminate, make clear or manifest. I. दविद्युतति (3 pl.) shine bright.— अभि C. illuminate, irradiate. उद् shine forth; C. illuminate; I. shine intensely. प्र begin to shine; C. irradiate. वि beam, glitter, shine forth (impers. विद्योतते it lightens), also = C. illumine, irradiate. सम् shine together, emulate in shining.

2द्युत् f. splendour, lustre.

3द्युत्, pp. द्युत्त broken; C. द्योतयति break asunder.

द्युतय्, °यति w. वि twinkle, glitter.

द्युति f. splendour, beauty, majesty; poss. °मन्त्.

द्युनिश् (n. sgl. & f. du.) day and night.

द्युनिश (n. sgl. & du.) the same.

द्युपति m. a god (lord of heaven).
द्युपथ m. the air (heavenly path).
द्युभक्त a. given by heaven.
द्युमणि m. the sun (sky-jewel).
द्युमत्सेन m. N. of a king.
द्युमन्त् a. heavenly, bright; clear, loud (n. adv.), splendid, excellent; powerful, vigorous, energetic.
द्युम्न n. splendour, glory; vigour, power; inspiration, enthusiasm; wealth, opulence.
द्युम्नवन्त् & द्युम्निन् poss. to prec.
द्युयोषित् & द्युवधू f. divine female, Apsaras.
द्युषद् m. a god (inhabitant of heaven).
द्युसरित् f. the heavenly river (Ganges).
द्युस्त्री f. = द्युयोषित्.
द्यु a. gambling; f. play at dice.
द्यूत n. gambling, play (at dice); war, fight & its prize.
द्यूतकर, °कार, & °कृत् m. a gambler.
द्यूतजित a. won at dice.
द्यूतदास, f. ई a slave won at dice.
द्यूतधर्म m. rule of playing (at dice).
द्यूतपलायित a. run away from gambling.*
द्यूतलेखक s. gambling-bill.*
द्यूतवृत्ति m. a gambler by profession.
द्यूतशाला, & °सदन n. gaming-house.
द्यूतसमाज m. assembly of gamblers.
द्यून a. distressed, sorrowful.
द्योत m. light, lustre.
द्योतक a. shining, illuminating, explaining, meaning.
द्योतन or द्योतन a. & n. shining, illuminating, enlightening, showing.
द्योतनि f. brightness, splendour.
द्योतिन् a. = द्योतक.
द्योत्य a. to be (being) expressed or explained.
द्यौर्लोक m. the heavenly world.
द्रङ्ग m., आ f. town, city.
द्रढय्, °यति make firm, strengthen, corroborate.
द्रढिमन् m. firmness, resolution, corroboration.
द्रढिष्ठ & *द्रढीयंस superl. & compar. to दृढ.
द्रधस् n. garment.
द्रप्स m. drop, spark; the moon (as the spark on the sky), a flag.
द्रप्सवन्त् a. dropping, besprinkled.
द्रप्सिन् a. falling in drops or carrying a banner.
द्रम्, I. दन्द्रम्यते run about, roam.
द्रमिल m. N. of a people.
द्रव a. running, swift, flowing, liquid, overflowing or full of (—°); m. course, flight; liquid substance, juice, essence.
द्रवण n. running, flowing, melting.
द्रवत् adv. speedily, quickly.
द्रवता f., °त्व n. fluidity.
द्रवमय a. liquid.
†द्रवय्, °यते run, flow.
द्रवर a. running quickly.
द्रवि m. a smelter.
द्रविड m. N. of a country, pl. of a people (considered also as a caste); f. ई w. स्त्री a Dravidian woman.
द्रविण n. movable property, wealth, money; substantiality, essence, power, strength; poss. °वन्त्†.
द्रविणस् n. wealth, property (v. prec.); concr. giver of wealth.
द्रविणस्यु a. desiring or procuring wealth.
द्रविणाधिपति m. lord of wealth (Kubera).
द्रविणेश्वर m. owner of wealth, also = prec.
द्रविणोद, °दस्, & °दा a. giving wealth.
द्रविणोविद् a. procuring wealth.
द्रवितृ m. runner.
द्रवित्नु a. running, quick.
द्रवी w. भू become fluid, melt.
1द्रव्य n. property, wealth; substance, thing, object, esp. worthy object or fit person.
2द्रव्य a. belonging to a tree.
द्रव्यगर्वित a. proud of money.*
द्रव्यजात n. a cert. substance; various objects.
द्रव्यदातृ m. giver of money.
द्रव्यमय a. material, substantial.
द्रव्ययज्ञ m. sacrifice of wealth.
द्रव्यवन्त् a. having property, wealthy, opulent; inherent in the substance (ph.).
द्रव्यवृद्धि f. increase of wealth.
द्रव्यशुद्धि f. cleansing of (soiled) objects.
द्रव्यहस्त a. carrying any object (with the hands).
द्रव्यार्जन n. acquisition of wealth.

द्रव्याश्रित a. inherent in the substance (ph.).
द्रष्टृ m. one who sees (also as 2d sgl. fut.), examines. tries, or decides; m. judge.
द्रष्टुकाम a. wishing to see.*
द्रष्टव्य a. to be seen, visible; to be considered as (nom.); to be understood, investigated, examined, tried (j.).
द्रह्यत् adv. firmly, strongly.
1द्रा, द्राति run, hasten; C. द्रापयति; I. दरिद्राति run about, be in need. — अप run away. अभि overtake. वि run asunder or away. disappear.
2†द्रा, द्राति, द्रायते sleep. — अव fall asleep. नि go to sleep, sleep. — Cf. निद्राण & निद्रित.
द्राक् adv. speedily, quickly, soon.
द्राक्षा f. vine, grape.
द्राघय्, °यति lengthen, extend; tarry, delay.
द्राघिमन् m. length.
द्राघिष्ठ & द्राघीयंस् superl. & compar. to दीर्घ.
द्राघ्मन् m. = द्राघिमन्; instr. द्राघ्मा adv.
1द्रापि m. mantle, garment.
2†द्रापि a. causing to run.
द्रावण a. & n. causing to run, putting to flight.
द्रावयत्सख a. speeding the friend (horse).
द्रावयित्नु a. melting.
द्राविड, f. ई belonging to the Draviḍas; m. sgl. & pl., f. ई = द्रविड, ई.
1द्रु, द्रवति (°ते), pp. द्रुत (q.v.) run, hasten, flee; become fluid, melt (l. & f.). C. द्रावयति (°ते). — अति run past (acc.). अधि run towards, mount, leap upon, cover. अनु run after, follow, pursue; run through i.e. recite quickly. अप run away. अभि run near. hasten towards, attack, assail; visit, befall. आ run near, approach. समा run (together) towards or against (acc.). उद् run up or out. उप & समुप rush at (acc.); attack, visit, befall. निस् run out or away. परि run about. प्र hasten, on, rush at (acc.); run away, flee, escape. विप्र run asunder, also = संप्र run away, flee. वि run asunder or away, flee. C. drive away. chase, put to flight. सम् run together. — Cf. विद्रुत.
2द्रु m. n. wood or any wooden implement, as a cup or an oar, a wooden handle, etc.
द्रुग्ध m. injurer, foe; n. impers. (it has been) plotted or sinned, as subst. offence, injury.
द्रुघण m. a wooden mace.
द्रुघ्नी f. a felling (lit. wood-) axe.
द्रुत a. run, fled; speedy, quick (n. adv., compar. °तरम्†); fluid, melted (l. & f.), wet with (—°).
द्रुतत्व n. the being melted or touched.
द्रुतपद n. N. of a metre, as adv. speedily, quickly.
द्रुतविलम्बित n. N. of a metre.
द्रुति f. = द्रुतत्व.
द्रुपद n. a wooden pillar or post; m. N. of a king.
द्रुम m. tree; °मय a. wooden.
द्रुमवन्त् a. poss. to prec. m.
द्रुमाग्र m. n. the top of a tree.
*द्रुमामय m. lac, resin (lit. tree-disease).
द्रुमाय्, °यते pass for a tree.
द्रुवय m. a wooden vessel, esp. the cylinder of a drum.
1द्रुह्, द्रुह्यति (°ते), pp. द्रुग्ध (q.v.) be hostile, hurt, offend, strive to harm (dat., gen., loc., or acc.); *emulate, vie. — अभि hurt, injure, plot against (acc., dat., or loc.); commit (acc.); pp. w. act. & pass. mg.
2द्रुह् (nom. ध्रुक्) a. hurting, injuring, offending against (gen., mostly —°); m. f. = द्रुग्ध m.; f. = द्रुग्ध n.
द्रुहिण m. E. of Brahman, Viṣṇu, or Çiva.
द्रुह्व m. f. injury, hurting.
द्रुह्यु m. N. of an ancient king, pl. of a people.
द्रुह्वन् a. hurting, damaging.
द्रू, द्रूणाति hurl.
द्रेका f. N. of a plant.
द्रोग्धृ a. & m. malevolent, injurer.
द्रोघ a. deceitful, malicious.
द्रोण n. trough, bucket, cup, a cert. measure; m. N. of an ancient hero, the teacher of the Kurus and Pāṇḍavas, & of sev. other men; also = द्रोणमेघ; f. द्रोणा a woman's name; f. द्रोणी = n. + channel, valley.
द्रोणकलश m. a large Soma-vessel.

द्रोणमेघ m. a cloud pouring forth water as from a trough; द्रोणवृष्टि the rain from such a cloud.

द्रोण्य a. belonging to the trough.

द्रोह m. injury, wrong, offence, treachery.

द्रोहभाव m. inimical disposition.

द्रोहिन् a. hurting, injuring, deceiving, betraying (gen. or —°).

द्रौणि m. Açvatthāman, the son of Droṇa.

द्रौपदी f. patron. of Kṛṣṇā, the daughter of Drupada and wife of the five Pāṇḍu princes.

द्रौपदेय m. a son of Draupadī.

द्व f. du. two, both (± अपि); द्वयोस् (g.) occurring in both genders (sc. m. & f.), and also in both numbers (sgl. & pl.).

द्वक a. du. two and two together.

द्वंद्व n. pair, couple, esp. a pair of opposites (as male & female, heat & cold, etc.); duality, contrast; duel, strife, fight; m. n. a copulative compound (g.). – Acc. & instr. by pairs.

द्वंद्वभाव m. discord.

द्वंद्वशस् adv. two by two, by couples.

द्वंद्विन् a. forming a couple.

द्वंद्वी w. भू pair off; become embroiled; be uncertain or irresolute about (loc.).

द्वय, f. ई twofold, double; n. a pair or couple (also f. ई), double nature, falsehood; the masc. & fem. gender (g.).

द्वयाविन् & द्वयु a. false, dishonest (lit. double-natured or tongued).

द्वर, द्वरि, & द्वरिन् a. obstructing.

द्वा (°—) = द्वि.

द्वात्रिंश, f. ई the thirty-second.

द्वात्रिंशत् f. thirty two.

द्वात्रिंशल्लक्षणक & °लक्षणोपेत a. having the 32 (auspicious) marks or spots on the body.

द्वादश, f. ई the twelfth, consisting of twelve; n. the number twelve or an aggregate of 12.

द्वादशक a. & n. = prec.

द्वादशधा adv. in (into) twelve parts.

द्वादशन् or द्वादशन् a. pl. twelve.

1द्वादशरात्र n. a period of 12 days (nights).

2द्वादशरात्र a. lasting 12 days.

द्वादशवार्षिक, f. ई twelve years old.

द्वादशविध a. twelvefold.

द्वादशशत n. one hundred and twelve.

द्वादशसाहस्र, f. ई consisting of twelve thousand (years).

द्वादशाब्द a. lasting twelve years.

द्वादशार a. having twelve spokes.

1द्वादशाह m. a period of 12 days.

2द्वादशाह a. lasting 12 days.

द्वापञ्चाश, f. ई the fifty-second.

द्वापञ्चाशत् f. fifty-two.

द्वापर or °पर m. the Two-side of the die; N. of the third age of the world.

द्वार् f. gate, door, opening; entrance or issue; way, means; द्वारा (—°) by means of.

द्वार n. (m.) = prec., also —° occasioned by; द्वारेण (—°) = द्वारा (cf. prec.); f. द्वारी door.*

द्वारक n. door, gate; f. द्वारका (°रिका) N. of Kṛṣṇa's capital.

द्वारप m. door-keeper, servant.

द्वारपक्ष & °क m. fold of a door.

द्वारपति & द्वारपाल m. door-keeper, warder.

द्वारपिधान m. or n. bolt of a door; shutting (of a door), conclusion, close.

द्वारफलक n. = द्वारपक्ष.

द्वारबाहु m. door-post.

द्वारमुख n. opening (lit. door-mouth).*

(द्वाररक्षक*) & द्वाररक्षिन् m. door-keeper.

द्वारवती f. N. of Kṛṣṇa's capital.

द्वारशोभा f. a splendid portal.*

द्वारस्थ a. standing at the door; m. door-keeper, porter.

द्वारिक & द्वारिन् m. = prec. m.

द्वारी w. कृ use as a means (lit. as a door).

द्वार्बाहु m. door-post.

द्वार्य a. belonging to or being at a door; f. आ = prec. n.

द्वाविंश, f. ई the twenty-second.

द्वाविंशति f. twenty-two.

द्वाविंशतिधा adv. in 22 parts or ways.

द्वाषष्ट a. the sixty-second.

द्वासप्तति f. seventy-two.

द्वास्थ v. seq.

द्वाःस्थ a. standing at the door; m. door-keeper.

द्वि (°—) two.

1द्विक a. consisting of two, two.
2द्विक m. a crow (cf. काक).
द्विकर्मक a. having two objects or accusatives (g.).
द्विगु m. a cert. class of compounds (g.).
द्विंगुण or द्विगुणं a. double, twofold, twice as much as (abl. or —°); द्विगुण & द्विगुणतर (°—) adv., also n. °तरम्. Abstr. °ता† f., °त्व† n.
द्विगुणय्, °यति double, multiply by two; pp. द्विगुणित doubled, folded, double.
द्विगुणी कृ = prec. act., °भू = prec. pass.
द्विजं adj. twice-born (lit. & fig.). — m. a man of the first three castes, esp. a Brahman; bird; tooth.
द्विजधर्मिन् a. having the duties of the twice-born.
द्विजंन्मन् a. having a double birth, birth-place, or nature; m. = prec.
द्विजर्षभ m. chief (lit. bull) of the twice-born, a Brahman.
द्विजर्षि m. = ब्रह्मर्षि.
द्विजलिङ्गिन् a. wearing the external marks of a Brahman.
द्विजवत्सल a. fond of Brahmans.
द्विजवर, °श्रेष्ठ, & °सत्तम m. a Brahman (best of the twice-born).
द्विजा a. twice or doubly born.
द्विजाग्र्य m. a Brahman (chief of the twice-born).
द्विजाग्र्यार्चा f. the veneration of Brahmans.
द्विजाति a. twice-born; m. a member of the three upper castes, esp. a Brahman.
द्विजादि m. Brahman and so on, i.e. caste.
द्विजानि a. having two wives.
द्विंजिह्व a. two-tongued, double-tongued (lit. & fig.); m. a snake.
द्विजेन्द्र, द्विजेश्वर, & द्विजोत्तम m. a Brahman (chief of the twice-born).
द्विट्सेविन् a. serving the enemy; m. a traitor.
द्वितं m. N. of a Vedic god & of a Rishi.
द्वितय a. consisting of two, twofold, double, pl. both; n. a pair.
द्वितां adv. just so, so also, likewise.
द्वितींय a. second, n. adv. secondly, for the second time. — m. companion, fellow, follower, friend or enemy, adj. —° followed by, endowed with, possessed of. f. आ female companion (*the second day of a half-month*); the second case (accusative) and its endings, also a word standing in the accusativ (g.).
द्वितीयभाग & द्वितीयांश m. a half.
द्वितीयाचन्द्र m. the moon of the second day of a half-moon; the young moon.*
द्वित्र (& द्वित्रि) pl. two or three.
द्वित्रिचतुरभाग pl. a half, a third, or a fourth.
द्वित्व n. doubleness, duality; dual or reduplication (g.).
*द्विद्रोण n. two Droṇas; instr. by such a measure.
द्विध a. twofold, divided or split in two.
द्विधा adv. in two parts, in twain; w. कृ double.
द्विधाभूताकृति a. of twofold shape.
द्विधास्थित a. existing double.
द्विप m. elephant (lit. drinking twice).
द्विंपद् or द्विपंद् (°पाद्) a. having two feet (m. man, n. mankind) or consisting of two verses (f. द्विपाद् or द्विपंदी), m. & f. °दी such a metre.
द्विंपद = prec. a., also consisting of two words; m. the two-footed i.e. man.
द्विपदिका f. a kind of metre or tune.
द्विपदीखण्ड m. or n. a piece in Dvipadikā (v. prec.).
द्विंपाद्, f. ई two-footed.
द्विपारि m. lion (lit. the elephant's enemy).
द्विपेन्द्र & द्विपेश्वर m. a large elephant (lit. prince of the elephants).
द्विबाहु a. two-armed; m. a man.
द्विभाग m. a half.
द्विभुज a. = द्विबाहु.
द्विमात्र a. twice as large.
द्विमासादि a. more than two months (pregnant).
द्विमुख, f. ई having two mouths or faces.
द्विंमूर्धन् a. two-headed.
द्विरद a. two-toothed; m. elephant.
द्विरात्र a. lasting two days; m. such a ceremony.
द्विरुक्त a. twice said, repeated, doubled, reduplicated; n. = seq.

द्विरुक्ति f. repetition.
द्विरुच्चारित n. the repeated execution (of a musical piece).
द्विरूप a. bicolour, biform, twofold.
द्विरेफ m. a kind of bee.
द्विर्वचन n. repetition, reduplication.
द्विलक्ष n. a distance of 200,000 (Yojanas).
द्विलक्षण a. twofold, of two kinds.
द्विलय s. double time (tempo) or measure.
द्विवक्त्र a. = द्विमुख.
द्विवचन n. the dual & its endings (g.).
द्विवर्ण a. two-coloured.
द्विवर्ष & °क (f. °र्षिका) two years old.
द्विवार्षिक a. the same.
द्विविध a. twofold, °धा adv.
द्विशत, f. ई consisting of or amounting to two hundred, the two hundredth. f. ई two hundred; n. the same, hundred and two.
द्विशफ a. cloven- (lit. double-)footed.
द्विंशवस् a. doubly strong.
द्विशस् adv. two by two, in couples.
द्विशिरस् a. two-headed.
द्विशृङ्ग a. having two horns or points.
1द्विष्, द्वेष्टि, द्विष्टे (द्विषति & °ते), pp. द्विष्ट (q.v.) hate, be hostile or a rival (w. acc., r. dat. or gen.). — प्र dislike, hate, show enmity against (acc.). वि A. M. the same; M. also hate each other mutually, be hostile towards one another. — Cf. द्विषन्त्, विद्विषन्त्, विद्विषाण, विद्विष्ट.
2द्विष् (nom. द्विट्) f. hatred, concr. hater, enemy (also m.); adj. —° = seq.
द्विष a. hating, disliking (—°).
द्विषदन्न n. food from an enemy.
द्विषदायुस् m. an enemy (life-hater).
द्विषन्त् (f. द्विषन्ती) hating, hostile, averse; m. enemy.
द्विष्ट a. hated, odious; averse, hostile.
द्विस् adv. twice (*अह्नस्, अह्ना, or अह्नि twice a day).
द्विसहस्र n. two thousand.
द्विःसम a. twice as large.
द्विहायन, f. ई two years old.
द्वीप m. n. island, peninsula, sandbank; esp. one of the (4, 7, 13, or 18) islands or continents of which the earth is supposed to consist.
द्वीपिचर्मन् n. an elephant's skin.
द्वीपिन् m. panther, leopard, or elephant; f. °नी† stream, river, sea.
द्वीप्य a. living on an island.
द्वेधा adv. in two, asunder.
द्वेष m. aversion, hate, dislike.
द्वेषण a. hating, inimical; n. = prec.
द्वेषणीय a. = द्वेष्य.
द्वेषस् n. = द्वेष; hater, enemy.
द्वेषस्थ a. feeling a dislike.
द्वेषिन् & द्वेष्टृ a. disliking, hating, inimical; m. hater, enemy.
द्वेष्य a. to be hated, m. enemy.
द्वेष्यता f., °त्व n. abstr. to prec.
द्वैगुण्य n. the double, double the amount, value, measure, etc.
द्वैजात a. belonging to or consisting of the twice-born.
द्वैत n. duality, dualism.
द्वैतभान n. appearance of dualism.
द्वैतवाद m. the doctrine of dualism.
द्वैतिन् m. a dualist (ph.).
द्वैध a. twofold, double; n. adv., as subst. duality, difference, division (esp. of the forces), contest, strife.
द्वैधीभाव m. duality, double state or nature; duplicity, fraud, uncertainty, doubt.
द्वैधी w. भू go asunder into two parts, become separated or disunited.
1द्वैप a. being in or coming from an island.
2द्वैप a. coming from a tiger or panther.
द्वैपायन m. the island-born, E. of Vyāsa.
द्वैप्य a. living in or coming from an island.
द्वैमातुर a. having two mothers (a natural m. and a stepmother).
द्वैमास्य a. lasting two months.
द्वैरथ n. (± युद्ध) a duel with chariots, duel or fight i.g.; m. adversary.
द्वैराज्य a. dominion divided between two princes.
द्वैविध्य n. duality, twofold nature or manner.
द्व्यंश m. two shares (also f. ई); a. having two shares.
द्व्यक्ष, f. ई two-eyed.

1द्व्यक्षर n. two syllables.

2द्व्यक्षर or द्व्यक्षर a. consisting of two syllables; n. such a word.

द्व्यणुक n. aggregate of two atoms.

द्व्यधिक a. consisting of two more.

द्व्यभियोग m. a twofold accusation.

द्व्यर्थ a. having two meanings; ambiguous.

द्व्यर्ध a. one and a half.

द्व्यह a. lasting two days. — m. a period or ceremony of two days; acc. two days long, abl. & loc. after two days.

द्व्यहवृत्त a. happened two days before.

द्व्यास्य a. having two mouths.

द्व्युरण a. having two lambs.

द्व्येकान्तर a. separated by one or two.

ध

ध a. putting, placing (—°), f. धा as subst.

धक्षत् & धक्षु a. = दक्षत् & दक्षु.

धट m. pair of scales, balance; f. ई a rag of cloth.

धत्तूर m. thorn-apple; n. its fruit, gold.

धन् (दधन्ति) set in motion. C. धनयति, °ते = S., M. also = be quick, run. — प्र spring forth, flow.

धन n. prize (of contest or game), booty, wealth, property, money; adj. —° possessed of, rich in. – हितं धनम् the proposed prize or the opened match. धनं w. भृ M. carry off the prize or booty; धनं जि win the prize or match.

धनकोश m. treasure of money.

धनक्षय m. loss of money.

धनजित् a. winning treasures or booty.

धनंजय a. the same, victorious i.g.; m. fire, a cert. wind in the human body, E. of Arjuna, N. of a serpent-demon & sev. men.

धनंजयविजय m. T. of a drama.

धनद a. giving money or wealth, munificent, liberal; m. E. of Kubera, N. of a serpent-demon & sev. men.

धनदण्ड m. fine, amercement.

धनदत्त m. a man's name.

धनदा a. bestowing the prize, the booty, or treasures.

धनदेश्वर m. the wealth-giving god (Kubera).

धननाश m. loss of wealth.

धनपति m. lord of wealth (a rich man or Kubera).

धनपाल m. guardian of treasure.

धनमद m. pride of wealth; p. °वन्त्.

धनमित्र m. a man's name.

धनयौवनशालिन् a. gifted with wealth and youth.

धनरक्ष a. guarding one's money; °क m. E. of Kubera.

धनर्च & धनर्चि a. shining with booty.

धनलोभ m. greediness for money.

धनवन्त् a. wealthy; m. a rich man, the sea.

धनवर्जित a. destitute of wealth, poor.

धनवृद्ध a. rich in money.

धनवृद्धि m. N. of a merchant.

धनव्यय m. spending of money, liberality, munificence.

धनसंचय m., °न n. accumulation of riches.

धनसनि & धनसा a. winning or granting treasures.

धनसाति f. abstr. to prec.

धनस्पृत् a. carrying the prize or booty.

धनस्वामिन् m. owner of money, capitalist.

धनहार्य a. to be won by money.

धनहीन a. = धनवर्जित; abstr. °ता f.

धनागम m. income or property of money.

धनाढ्य a. opulent, rich; abstr. °ता f.

धनादान n. acceptance of money.

धनाधिप & °पति m. lord of wealth (Kubera).

धनाध्यक्ष m. treasurer, E. of Kubera.

†धनायु a. earning money.

धनार्थिन् a. greedy for money.

धनिक a. rich; m. a rich man, creditor, a man's name; *f. आ a (good or young) woman.*

धनिन् = धनिक a. & m.

1धंनिष्ठ (superl.) very quick.
2धनिष्ठ (superl.) very rich; f. आ sgl. & pl. E. of lunar mansion.
1धनु m. bow.
2धंनु & धनू f. sandbank, sandy shore, island (fig. of a cloud).
धंनुतृ a. running, swift.
धनुरार्त्नी f. bow-end.
धनुर्ग्रह, °ग्रीह, & °ग्रीहिन् m. bowman, archer.
धनुर्ज्या f. bow-string.
धनुर्दुर्ग n. = धन्वदुर्ग q.v.
धनुर्धर & °धारिन् a. bearing a bow; m. archer.
धनुर्भृत् a. & m. = prec.
धनुर्यष्टि & धनुर्लता f. the bow (conc. as f.).
धनुर्विद्या f., °वेद m. science of archery.
धनुःशत n. a hundred bows' length.
धनुष्क (—°) = धनुस्.
धनुष्काण्ड n. sgl. bow and arrow.
धनुष्कार & °ष्कृत् m. bow-maker.
धनुष्कोटि or °टी f. bow-end.
धनुष्पाणि a. bow in hand; m. archer.
धनुष्मन्त् a. having a bow; m. = prec. m.
धंनुस् n. bow or a bow's length (a cert. measure).
धनेश m. lord of treasure, rich man or = seq.
धनेश्वर m. E. of Kubera, a man's name.
धनैश्वर्य n. the dominion of wealth.
धनैषिन् a. craving money; m. creditor.
धनापचय m. expense of money.
धनोष्मन् m. the (burning) wish for treasures.
धंन्य a. having or bringing wealth, wealthy, opulent; rich in, full of (—°); auspicious, fortunate.
धन्यता f. fortune, bliss.
धन्व्, धंन्वति (°ते) run, speed (intr. & tr.); swing or bend (the bow). — अच्छ, अनु, & अभि run towards or near. प्र run (asunder), dissolve, perish. सम् M. run near or together with (instr.).
धन्व (adj. —°) bow; m. N. of a man.
धन्वच्युत् a. shaking the ground.
धन्वदुर्ग n. a fortress protected by a desert.
1धंन्वन् n. bow (later mostly —°).
2धंन्वन् n. m. dry land, desert, shore.
धन्वन्तरि m. N. of a cert. mythol. being, E. of the Sun, in l. l. the physician of the gods.
धन्वन्य a. being on dry land.
धन्वायन, f. ई carrying a bow.
धन्वायिंन् & धन्वाविन् a. the same.
धन्वार्ति f. bow-end.
धन्वासंह a. strong with the bow.
धन्विन् a. armed with a bow; m. an archer, E. of Çiva, a man's name.
धम (ध्मा), धंमति (°ते), pp. धमित & ध्मात blow, exhale; kindle (fire by blowing), melt (ore). — अनु blow upon. अप blow off. अभि blow at, terrify by blowing. आ inflate, blow, sound, proclaim aloud; P. be inflated or puffed up. उपा & समुपा blow, sound. उद् exhale, breathe out, proclaim. उप blow at (acc.). निस् & परा blow away. प्र blow forth, blow away i.e. terrify by blowing, blow at (acc.); M. proclaim aloud. C. blow into (a conch-shell), sound. वि blow i.e. drive asunder, scatter, disperse, destroy. सम् blow or melt together; proclaim aloud.
धम a. blowing, melting (—°).
धमधमाय्, °यते quake, tremble.*
धमन a. blowing away, scaring (—°); n. the melting (of ore).
धमंनि f. piping; reed, pipe; tube or canal of the human body, vessel, vein, nerve, etc.
धम्मिल्ल m. the braided hair of a woman tied round the head.
धय a. sucking, drinking (gen. or —°).
धर a. bearing, supporting, wearing, carrying, keeping, preserving, knowing, owning, possessing (—°); m. a man's name; f. आ the earth.
धंरण, f. ई bearing, holding; m. N. of a serpent-demon, m. n. a cert. weight; f. धरणी the earth; n. holding, support, bringing, procuring.
धरणि f. the earth (also personif.).
धरणिधर a. holding or supporting the earth; m. a mountain, E. of Viṣṇu-Kṛṣṇa.
धरणिपति & °भृत् m. prince, king.
धरणीधर a. & m. = धरणिधर.

धरणीधृत्, **°ध्र**, & **°भृत्** m. a mountain.
धरणीरुह m. tree (grown from the earth).
धराधर a. & m. = **धरणिधर**.
धराधिप, **धरापति**, & **°भुज्** m. prince, king.
धराभृत् m. a mountain (earth-holder).
धराशय a. sleeping on the (bare) earth.
धरित्री f. female bearer, the earth.
धरिमन् m. balance, weight; **धरिममेय** a. sold (measured) by the weight.
धरीमन् m., only loc. **°मणि** according to custom or nature.
1**धरुण**, f. **ई** bearing, supporting, holding, capacious. m. bearer, supporter; n. support, basis, foundation; receptacle (also f.).
2**धरुण** m. a sucking calf.
धर्णस a. = seq. a.
धर्णसि a. strong, firm, powerful; n. bearing, keeping.
धर्णि m. keeper.
धर्तृ m. bearer, supporter, preserver.
धर्त्र n. hold, support.
धर्म m. statute, established order, custom, practice; law, right, justice (o. personif.); good works, merit, virtue; nature, character, quality, mark, attribute; E. of Yama & Prajāpati. — Instr. **धर्मेण** according to law or virtue; **धर्मे स्थितः** abiding by the law, virtuous. — Abstr. **°ता**† f., **°त्व**† n.
धर्मकञ्चुक m. the breastplate of righteousness.*
धर्मकामार्थ m. pl. virtue, pleasure, and wealth; **°संबन्ध** m. matrimony (lit. union of virtue, pleasure, & wealth).
धर्मकाम्या f. (only instr.) love or sense of duty.
धर्मकार्य & **°कृत्य** n. an act of duty.
धर्मकोश m. the treasury of law or duties.
धर्मक्रिया f. = **धर्मकार्य**.
धर्मक्षेत्र n. = **कुरुक्षेत्र** q.v.
धर्मघ्न a. immoral, unlawful (lit. destroying law).
धर्मचक्षुस् a. having an eye or a sense for what is right.
धर्मचरण n., **°चर्या** f. observance of the law, doing one's duty, virtuousness.
धर्मचारिन् a. virtuous (cf. prec.); f. **°णी** a (virtuous) wife.
धर्मज a. begot or produced by a sense of duty; m. patron. of Yudhiṣṭhira.
धर्मजीवन a. living by (the fulfilment of) pious works.
धर्मज्ञ a. knowing the law or one's duty; abstr. **°ता** f. = seq.
धर्मज्ञान n. knowledge of the law or one's duty.
धर्मतत्त्वतस् adv. according to the true nature of law.
धर्मतस् adv. according to law or rule, rightly, justly, from a virtuous motive. Also = abl. of **धर्म**.
धर्मदत्त m. a man's name.
धर्मदार m. pl. a lawful wife.
धर्मदृष्टि a. = **धर्मचक्षुस्**.
धर्मदेव m. the god of justice.
धर्मधृत् a. observing the law.
धर्मध्वज a. whose banner is virtue, also = seq.; m. a man's name.
धर्मध्वजिन् a. hypocritical.
1**धर्मन्** m. bearer, supporter.
2**धर्मन्** n. support, foundation; law, order, custom, manner, modality; arrangement, direction; right conduct, duty; nature, quality, characteristic (esp. — °). — **धर्मणा** & **धर्मभिस्** according to rule or nature; **धर्मणस्परि** in (natural) order or succession.
धर्मनिष्ठ a. grounded on or devoted to virtue.
धर्मपति m. the lord of order and law.
धर्मपत्नी f. a lawful wife.
धर्मपर & **°परायण** a. holding law or virtue above all, righteous, virtuous.
धर्मपाठक m. reciter or teacher of the law.
धर्मपुत्र m. lawful son i.e. a son begot from a sense of duty, also a pupil; *E. of Yudhiṣṭhira.*
धर्मप्रतिरूपक m. counterfeit of virtue.
धर्मप्रधान a. devoted to duty (lit. having d. as chief object).
धर्मप्रवक्तृ m. interpreter of the law.
धर्मप्लव m. boat of virtue (fig. of a son).
धर्मबुद्धि a. having a virtuous mind, virtuous.

धर्मभगिनी f. a female having the right of a sister; a sister in the faith.
धर्मभागिन् a. possessed of virtue, virtuous.
धर्मभिक्षुक m. a mendicant from a sense of virtue.
धर्मभृत् a. maintaining the law, just.
धर्ममय a. consisting of law or virtue.
धर्ममार्ग m. the path of law or virtue.
धर्मयुक्त a. virtuous, pious, just.
धर्मरत & **°रति** a. delighting in virtue, virtuous.
धर्मराज्, **°राज**, & **°राजन्** m. king of justice, E. of Yama & Yudhiṣṭhira.
धर्मरुचि a. delighting in or devoted to virtue.
धर्मलोप m. neglect of duty.
धर्मवन्त् a. righteous, just.
धर्मविद् a. = **धर्मज्ञ**.
धर्मविधि m. theory of law.
धर्मवृद्ध a. rich in virtue, m. a man's name.
धर्मशासन & **°शास्त्र** n. a law-book.
धर्मशील a. of a virtuous disposition or character, religious, pious.
धर्मशुद्धि f. a correct knowledge of law.
धर्मसंयुक्त a. legal, lawful.
धर्मसंहिता f. a code or collection of laws.
धर्मसंचय m. store of good works.*
धर्मसंज्ञा f. sense of duty.
धर्मसमय m. a lawful obligation.
धर्मसु a. promoting order or justice.
धर्मसूत्र n. a manual on law and custom.
धर्मसेवन n. performance of duties.
धर्मस्थ m. a judge (lit. abiding in the law).
धर्मस्वरूपिन् a. having justice as one's own nature or character; w. **भगवन्त्** m. Yama.
धर्महन्तृ, f. **°हन्त्री** transgressing (lit. killing) law or justice.
धर्महानि f. neglect of duty.
धर्माक्षर n. pl. formula or confession of faith.*
धर्माचार्य m. teacher of law.
धर्मातिक्रम m. transgression of law or duty.
धर्मात्मता f. abstr. to seq.
धर्मात्मन् n. of a virtuous disposition, pious-minded, just, virtuous.
धर्माधर्म m. du. right and wrong; **°ज्ञ** a. knowing r. & w.
धर्माधिकरण n. administration of the laws; m. judge, magistrate.
धर्माधिकरणस्थान n. court of justice (v. prec.).
धर्माधिकार m. = **धर्माधिकरण** m.
धर्माधिकारणिक, **°कारिन्**, & **°कृत** m. judge.
धर्माधिष्ठान n. court of justice.
धर्माध्यक्ष m. overseer of justice, superior judge.
धर्मानुकाङ्क्षिन् a. striving after justice, having a sense for what is right.
धर्मानुष्ठान n. performance of duty.
धर्माभिषेकक्रिया f. the performance of a religious ablution.
धर्मारण्य n. a sacred grove; N. of a wood & a town.
धर्मार्थ m. du. virtue and wealth; **°थम्** adv. for a pious purpose.
धर्माविरुद्धम् adv. according (lit. not opposed) to law or duty.
धर्मावेक्षिता f. respect for the law, sense of duty.*
धर्माशोक m. the Açoka of justice (E. of king A.).
धर्माश्रित a. just, virtuous.
धर्मासन n. throne of justice, seat of the judge.
धर्मिता f., **°त्व** n. abstr. to seq.
धर्मिन् a. knowing or observing the law, virtuous, just; having the right, duty, manners or characteristics of (—°).
धर्मिष्ठ (superl.) perfectly virtuous, just, or lawful; abstr. **°ता** f.
धर्मेन्द्र, **धर्मेश**, & **°श्वर** m. king of justice, E. of Yama.
धर्मेप्सु a. wishing to gain merit.
धर्मोपघातक a. unlawful (lit. killing the law).
धर्मोपदेश m., **°देशना** f. instruction in law.
धर्मोपमा f. a kind of comparison (rh.).
धर्म्य a. lawful, legal, customary, just, righteous; endowed with qualities (ph.), suitable or corresponding to (gen.).
धर्म्यामृत n. the nectar of right or faith.
धर्षक a. attacking, assailing (—°).
धर्षण n., **आ** f. attack, assault, offence, violation.
धर्षिन् a. = **धर्षक**.
†धव्, **धवते** run, flow. — **अव** flow down, descend.

1धवं m. N. of a plant.
2धव m. man, husband, master, lord.
धवल (f. आ & ई) white; abstr. °ता f., °त्व n.
धवलगिरि m. N. of a mountain.
धवलय्, °यति make white, illumine.
धवलाय्, °यति become or shine white.
धवलिमन् m. whiteness, white colour.
धवितव्य or °तंव्य a. to be fanned.
धवित्र n. fan, brush.
धंवीयंस् (compar.) running, hastening.
1धा, दंधाति, धत्ते; दंधति, °ते (धाति, धायते), pp. हितं (q.v.) & धित (only —°) put, set, lay; put upon, bring to, direct towards (loc. or dat.), fix (esp. the mind) upon, think of (loc. or dat.); resolve, determine to (dat., loc., acc. w. प्रति, or infin.); establish, constitute, appoint (2 acc.); create, produce, cause, do, make; hold, keep, wear, bear, maintain; M. take to one's self, receive, obtain, get, win, conceive (गंर्भम्); w. श्रोकम् & चंनस् enjoy, delight in (loc. or dat.); assume, incur, show, betray (M. & A.). C. धापयति (only —°). D. दिंधिषति, °ते wish to give; M. wish to win or get, w. अवद्यम् bid defiance (gen.); धिंत्सति wish to put or place upon (loc.). — अधि A. set upon (esp. the fire); bestow on (dat. or loc.), grant, impart; M. acquire, get, exhibit. अनु put on additionally; induce to (dat.). व्यनु unfold, exhibit. अन्तर् A. M. put into (loc.) or between, separate, exclude; hide, conceal, cover; A. receive or contain within; keep from (abl.), withhold; P. be covered or hidden, disappear. अप A. take or drive away. अपि or पि put in (loc.); offer or present to (dat.), bestow on (loc.); cover, shut up, hide, conceal; P. be hidden, become invisible, disappear in (loc.). अभि put on or to, surround or cover with (instr.), give up to (dat.), deliver; practice, apply, commit; name, designate; tell (2 acc.); P. be called. प्रत्यभि draw back, reabsorb; answer, consent. अव put down or in, immerse (in water), shut up or enclose in (loc.); be immersed in (loc.), be attentive. C. cause to be laid in. व्यव put asunder, place between, separate, interrupt; P. be separated or interrupted. आ put on (esp. wood on the fire), lay, set, place in or on, direct towards, fix upon (loc. or dat.), lay down, deposit; impart, grant, bestow, offer (dat., loc., or gen. of pers.), bring to (dat.), employ at (loc.); produce, cause, effect; M. seize, take, receive, conceive (गंर्भम्), appropriate to one's self. अत्या place above, extol. अध्या place upon. अन्वा put on (esp. wood), i.e. set up or kindle (the fire). अभ्या the same. उपा put on, place upon (loc.); M. seize, take. निरा take out or away. पर्या lay about, surround. व्या P. be divided, be separated from (abl.); be uncomfortable or ill. समा put on (wood), set up or kindle (fire); lay, set, place on or in (loc.), turn or fix (the eyes or mind) upon (loc.), collect or concentrate the mind (± आत्मानम्); impose, adjust, apply; unite, keep together, reconcile, restore, settle, arrange, cause, produce. M. put on (a garment), conceive (of women), accept, appropriate to one's self, manifest, betray, devote one's self entirely to (acc.); establish, state, concede, agree. उपसमा = अन्वा + put a thing in its place. प्रतिसमा adjust (the arrow), put in order, restore. उद् shut up, erect; cast away, expose. उप put on or in, w. अधस्तात् under; put on the fire, put (the horse) to the yoke, put to mind (हृदि); lie down upon (acc.), (g.) precede immediately (only P.); commit to (dat.), impart, teach; add, join; use, employ. तिरस् set aside, remove, drive back, overwhelm; hide, conceal. M. be hidden from (abl.), vanish, disappear. नि lay down, take off, put, set, place in or on (loc. ± अन्तंर् or अन्तर् —°), put before one (dat.), turn (the eyes) to (loc.), set the mind i.e. resolve upon (dat.); deposit, keep, guard; appoint, commit, entrust; keep down, suppress, remove, finish. With क्रियाम् take pains with (loc.); w. भूमौ or अवटे

bury; w. मौलौ esteem highly; w. मनसि or हृदये reflect, ponder; w. मनो मनसि consent (lit. put mind to mind). C. cause to deposit or to put in (loc.). अधिनि lay upon, bestow, impart. अपनि put aside, remove, drive away. अभिनि lay on, impose; approach, touch. उपनि place near, put before (dat.); lay down, bury (a treasure); deposit, commit, entrust (loc.); bring about, effect. प्रणि lay down, prostrate (the body); put on or in (loc.); touch, approach with (instr.), turn or fix (eyes or mind) on (loc.); be intent upon or attentive to (acc.); stretch forth, send out (esp. spies, ± चरान्), explore, search; find out to be (2 acc.). प्रतिनि put instead, substitute; order, command. विनि lay apart, distribute, take off or down; put in, fix on, appoint to (loc.). संनि lay down (together) in or at (loc.); place near or aside; keep, preserve, heap up, collect; M. appoint, assign; w. दृष्टिम् fix on (loc.), w. हृदयम् concentrate, collect; M. P. be near or present. C. bring near, fetch. निस् find out. परि A. M. lay or set around, put on, don (± वासस् etc.); surround, clothe, dress; A. conclude the recitation (r.). C. cause to put on (2 acc.), surround or clothe with (instr.). विपरि change, esp. clothes (± वासस्). पुरस् M. (A.) put before, place in front or at the head, prefer, choose, be intent on or eager for (acc.); appoint (esp. to priestly functions); commit, entrust to (dat. or gen.). प्र present, offer; set forward, send out (spies). प्रति put instead, replace; adjust (the arrow), take aim; put to the lips, set the foot upon (loc.), stride out; present, offer, restore; M. commence, begin. वि distribute, divide; impart, procure, grant; appoint, arrange, settle; destine, design; exhibit, show, betray; find out, produce, found, form, cause, effect, make (in various mgs & w. various nouns = 1कृ q.v.); make, render (2 acc.); lay, place, put, fix in or on (loc.); set forward or send out (spies). D. (धित्सति, °ते) wish to impart, fix, settle, find out, procure, make or render (2 acc.); intend or purpose i.g. अनुवि M. appoint or regulate (in due order); cause or effect (after another), bring about, perform; P. be regulated according to, i.e. obey, follow (acc. or gen.). प्रतिवि arrange, prepare, make ready; counteract, take measures against (loc.). संवि M. dispose, arrange; settle, direct, order, appoint; hold up, carry on, manage, employ, use; make or render (2 acc.). सम् put together, connect, compose, unite; close, collect (lit. & fig.); repair, restore; lay down, put in or on (loc., esp. शरम् ± धनुषि, also absol. = aim, shoot); impart, grant, bestow (together) on (loc.); M. bring together, unite; make peace or agree with (instr., r. acc.); stand out against (acc.), rival, vie. P. be united with = get possessed of (instr.); be held or contained in (loc.). अनुसम् add, connect; follow (lit.* & fig.), observe, explore, ascertain. अभिसम् snap at (loc.), unite or join, esp. the arrow with the bow (instr.); bring about, beget; aim at (dat. or loc.), purpose, intend (acc. or dat.); call to mind, ponder; consent, agree about (acc.); win over, take in, cheat, deceive. उपसम् add, increase; join or connect with (instr.); aim at, keep in view; cheat, deceive. प्रतिसम् put together (again), readjust; M. put on (esp. the arrow on the bow), restore, return. — Cf. अत्याहित, अन्तर्हित, अपिहित, अभिहित, अवहित, आहित, उद्धित, उपसंहित, उपहित, उपाधाय, उपाहित, तिरोहित, निहित, परिहित, पुरोहित, प्रणिहित, विनिहित, विहित, व्यवहित, व्याहित, संहित, संनिहित, समाहित.

2धा a. & f. putting, placing, etc. (— °).

3धा, धयति, pp. धीत suck, drink, imbibe. C. धापयते suckle, nourish. — उप C. M. = S. C. निस् suck out.

धाटी f. assault, attack.

1†धातु m. layer, part of a whole, ingredient,

esp. element or elementary matter (ph.), mineral, metal, ore; a verbal root (as the primary elements of the earth and the language).

2धातु a. fit to be sucked or sipped; f. a milch cow.

धातुक्रिया f. metallurgy.

धातुपाठ m. list of verbal roots.

धातुमत्ता f. abstr. to seq.

धातुमन्त् a. rich in minerals or metals.

धातुमय, f. ई metallic, also = prec.

धातुवाद m. metallurgy, mineralogy.

धातुवादिन् m. metallurgist, assayer.

धातुवृत्ति f., °समास m. titles of works.

धातृ m. bearer, supporter, preserver, author, creator; in l. l. N. of sev. gods etc., E. of Brahman, also = Fate, Destiny (person.). — f. धात्री nurse, mother, the earth.

धात्र a. relating to Dhātṛ.

धात्रेयिका & धात्रेयी f. foster-sister.

धात्वाकर m. a mine.

धान a. holding, containing; n. & f. ई receptacle, seat.

धानक m. a cert. coin; n. coriander.

धाना f. pl. grains of corn; poss. °वन्त्.

धानुष्क a. having a bow; m. archer.

धान्य a. consisting or made of grain or corn; n. sgl. & pl. corn i.g., p. °वन्त्†.

धान्यक (adj. —°) = prec. n.; n. coriander.

धान्यकूट s. granary.

धान्यखल m. corn-floor.

धान्यचौर m. a stealer of grain.

धान्यद m. a giver of grain.

धान्यधन n. corn and wealth.

धान्यपञ्चक n. the five sorts of corn.

धान्यमय a. consisting of grain.

धान्यमिश्र a. mixing or adulterating corn.

धान्यवत् adv. like corn.

*धान्यांश m. a grain of corn.

धान्याद a. eating corn.

धान्यार्घ m. price of corn.

धान्व m. N. of an Asura prince.

धान्वन a. situated in a desert.

धाम m. a kind of superhuman beings.

धामन् n. seat, home, residence, realm (of the gods); wont or favourite place, thing, or person; inmates, family, troop, host (also pl.); law, rule; custom, rite, manner; strength, power, majesty, splendour (also pl.); N. of a Rishi.

धामवन्त् a. powerful, strong.

धाय m. layer.

धायस् a. nourishing, refreshing; n. (only dat. as inf.) sucking, drinking; feeding, supporting; refreshment, enjoyment, satisfaction.

1धायु a. liberal, generous.

2धायु a. thirsty.

धाय्या f. additional verse (r.).

1धार, f. ई holding, bearing; (debtor*).

2†धार m. n. (only °— & —°), धारा f. stream, jet, gush, flood.

धारक a. bearing, holding.

धारका f. vulva.

धारण, f. ई holding, bearing, maintaining (gen. or —°). — f. आ wearing, keeping, retaining, maintenance, assistance; remembrance, memory; abstraction of mind, fixed attention (ph.); precept, rule (j.). n. धारण holding, supporting, wearing, keeping (esp. in the memory); bearing, suffering; abstraction or concentration (of the mind).

धारणक a. holding, bearing, consisting of (—°); m. debtor.

धारपूत a. clear as water.

धारयत्कवि a. supporting sages.

धारयत्क्षिति a. supporting creatures.

धारयितव्य a. to be borne or held.

धारयितृ m. bearer, holder.

धारयु a. flowing, dropping.

1धारा v. 2धार.

2धारा f. edge, blade (p. °वन्त्); margin, circumference (esp. of a wheel); continuous line or series.

धाराङ्कुर m. hail (sprout of water).

धाराधर m. cloud (water-bearer).

धाराधिरूढ a. having reached the highest point (lit. the edge).

धारानिपात & धारापात (pl.) m. shower (lit. downfall) of rain.

धारायन्त्र n. water-machine, fountain.
धारावर् a. sending showers of rain.
धारावर्ष m. n. torrent of rain.
धाराश्रु n. a flood of tears.
धारासंपात & **धारासार** m. downfall or shower of rain.
धारि a. holding, bearing (—°).
1**धारिन्** a. holding, bearing, wearing, possessing, keeping (also in one's memory), retaining, supporting, observing. f. °**णी** the earth, a woman's name.
2**धारिन्** a. streaming.
धारु a. sucking.
धार्तराष्ट्र, f. **ई** belonging to or descending from Dhṛtarāṣṭra.
धार्म, f. **ई** relating to justice or Dharma.
धार्मिक, f. **ई** righteous, lawful, just, virtuous, pious (abstr. °**ता** f., °**त्व** n.); m. a juggler.*
1**धार्य** a. to be held, borne, worn, kept, turned, fixed, retained, upheld, supported, observed; n. clothing.
2**धार्य** n. water.
धार्ष्ट्य n. boldness, audacity.
1**धाव्**, **धावति** (°**ते**) run, stream, pour, ride, swim, glide; hasten, rush, run after or against (acc.). C. **धावयति** cause to run, impel; ride or drive (w. instr. of the vehicle); jump, dance. — **अति** run over or past (acc.). **अनु** run after, through, towards, against (acc.); succour, assist (acc.). **अप** run away, depart (from a previous statement), prevaricate (j.). **अपि** run into (acc.). **अभि** run towards or against, attack or succour (acc.). **अव** run or drop down from (abl.). **आ** run or flow towards (loc.), come near, return; run against (acc.). **उप** run near, approach, hasten towards, resort to (acc.); M. run, glide. **निस्** stream or spring forth, run out, escape from (abl.). **परि** run or flow about or through (**मृगयाम्** go hunting), run near or after (acc.). **प्र** run forth or away, hasten, rush on, resort to (acc.), penetrate. **प्रति** run back; rush against, assail (acc.). **वि** run away or through, be scattered or lost in (loc.). **अनुवि** run after in different directions. **सम्** run together, rush against, assail (acc.).
2**धाव्**, **धावति**, °**ते**, pp. **धौत** (q.v.) rinse, wash, cleanse, purify; M. also refl. C. **धावयति** wash. — **आ** knead, press out, cleanse (esp. the Soma-stems). **नि** M. rub or anoint one's self; rub one's self against i.e. cling to (loc.). **प्र** rub off, C. wash. **वि** wash or cleanse off. **सम्** M. run or wash one's self. — Cf. **निर्धौत**, **विधौत**.
धाव a. & s. washing, cleansing.
1**धावक** a. running.
2**धावक** a. washing; m. washer.
3**धावक** m. N. of a poet.
1**धावन** n. running, galloping; onset, assault.
2†**धावन** (adj. —° & n.) rubbing.
धावल्य n. the white colour.
धावितृ m. runner, courser.
धाविन् a. running or washing (—°).
1**धासि** f. seat, home.
2**धासि** m. milk-beverage; drink or nourishment i.g.
धास्यु a. desirous of drinking or of eating.
1**धि**, **धिनोति** nourish, refresh, gladden.
2†**धि** m. receptacle (only —°).
धिक् (excl. of sorrow & displeasure) alas! shame! fie! (w. nom., voc., gen., or acc.). **धिग्धिक्**, **अहो धिक्**, **हा धिक्** (± **कष्टम्**), **हा हा धिक्**, & **हहा धिक्** the same; also **धिगस्तु** (w. gen. or acc.). With **कृ** reproach, mock, despise.
धिक्कार m., **धिक्कृत** n. reproach, censure.
धिग्दण्ड m. reprimand, reproof.
धिग्वण m. a cert. mixed caste.
धितावन् a. rich in gifts, bounteous.
†**धिति** v. **नेमधिति**.
धिप्सु a. wishing to deceive.
धियंजिन्व a. exciting or cherishing devotion.
धियंधा & **धियायु** a. devout, pious.
धियावसु a. rich in devotion.
धिषंण a. intelligent, wise; m. E. of Bṛhaspati. — f. **आ** a cert. Soma-vessel, also fig. = the Soma-juice & its effects; intelligence, wisdom, knowledge, a woman's name; du. the two worlds (lit. bowls), i.e. heaven and earth; pl. heaven, earth, and air.

धिषण्य्, only धिषण्यन्त् attentive, devout.
धिषा (instr. adv.) readily.
1धिष्ण्य a. spiritual, transcendental, holy, devout, pious. — m. (f. आ & n.) a heap of earth, forming a sort of inferior or side-altar; n. meteor (also f.); place, abode, region, star, asterism.
2धिष्ण्य a. placed upon the earth-altar (v. prec.); m. (± अग्नि) such a fire.
धिष्ठित v. अधिष्ठित.
1धी v. दीधी & ध्या.
2धी f. thought, idea, notion, intention, opinion, intelligence, wisdom, art; devotion, prayer, (often personif.).
धीत a. thought of, reflected on; n. thought, idea.
*धीता f. daughter.
धीति f. thought, idea, reflection, perception, devotion, prayer (o. personif.); intelligence, skill (pl.), intention, design.
धीमन्त् a. intelligent, skilful, wise.
1धीर (f. धीरी & धीरा) intelligent, skilful, clever, wise; abstr. °ता† f., °त्व n.†
2धीर a. firm, steady, grave, deep (sound); insisting on (—°), constant, persevering, resolute, courageous; °— & n. adv.; abstr. °ता f., °त्व n.
3*धीर n. saffron.
धीरचेतस् a. strong-minded, resolute.
धीरण a. devout, pious.
धीरप्रशान्त a. grave and calm.
धीरभाव m. firmness, constancy.
धीरसत्त्व a. strong-minded, courageous.
1धीर्य a. = 1धीर.
2धीर्य n. intelligence, wisdom.
धीवन् a. clever.
धीवन्त् a. intelligent; devout, pious.
धीवर (f. ई) & °क m. a fisher.
धु v. धू.
धुक्ष्, धुक्षते, only w. सम् S. & C. संधुक्षयति kindle.
धुङ्क्षा f. a cert. bird.
†धुनय्, °यति rush; w. आ rush on.
धुनि, धुनिमन्त्, & धुनेति a. boisterous, tempestuous, wild; m. N. of a demon.
धुनिव्रत a. wont to rave or roar.
धुन्धु m. N. of an Asura; °मार m. the slayer of D., i.e. Kuvalayāçva.
धुर् f. (m.) yoke or pole (of a carriage, esp. its fore-part); fig. load, burden; top, highest place, place of honour.
धुर m., f. आ load, burden; peg on the axle-tree (only m.); pole (only f.).
धुरंधर a. bearing the yoke or burden (l. & f.), patient; m. foreman, leader.
धुरा (instr. adv.) violently.
धुर्य a. fit to be yoked or harnessed, draught-; being at the top of (—°); eminent, highest, best. — m. beast for draught; chief, foreman; n. fore-part of the pole.
धुर्यासन n. seat of honour.
धुर्व् v. धूर्व्.
धुस्तूर m. thorn-apple.
धू, धूनोति, धूनुते, धुनोति, धुनुते (धूवति, धुवति, धुनाति, धुनोते), pp. धूत & धुत shake, toss, agitate; shake off a thing from (2 acc.), cast away, remove; fan, kindle (fire); intr. struggle, resist. I. दोधवीति & दोधूयते shake violently, flourish, swing, fan; intr. move to and fro, totter, rush on. — अप shake off. अभि shake, fan. अव shake or throw down, shake off from (abl.) upon (loc.), reject; move to and fro, toss. व्यव shake off, reject, renounce. आ & व्या shake, toss, stir. उद् rouse up, stir, lift, swing, fan, kindle, move, excite; throw off, reject. समुद् shake up, raise, stir, toss. निस् shake out or off, drive away, remove, expel; swing, brandish. विनिस् shake off, drive asunder, reject; move to and fro, toss. प्र move onward (tr.), blow away or out. I. shake or blow out (the beard). वि shake, toss, swing (M. also refl.), fan, kindle, drive asunder or away, remove, destroy; M. shake off (1 or 2 acc.), give up, renounce. सम् shake towards i.e. bestow on (dat.); M. raff up together. — Cf. अवधूत, आधूत, उद्धूत, निर्धूत.
धूक m. N. of a plant.
धूता f. daughter.*

धूति m. shaker, agitator; f. = seq.
धूनन n. shaking, stirring.
धूनय्, °यति, °ते shake, move, toss. — अव & वि = S.
धूप (m. sgl. & pl.) incense, perfume; smoke, vapour.
धूपक m. perfume or perfumer.
धूपन n. incensing, fumigation.
धूपय्, धूपयति, pp. धूपित besmoke, fumigate, perfume, incense. — अव, आ, उप, प्र = S.
धूपाय्, °यति smoke, fume, fumigate.
धूपि (m. pl.) cert. winds bringing rain.
धूपिन् a. perfuming.
धूम (m. sgl. & pl.) smoke, vapour, incense.
धूमक (adj. —°) & धूमिका f. the same.
धूमकेतन m. fire (lit. = seq. a.).
धूमकेतु a. whose sign is smoke, marked by smoke; m. fire or a comet, E. of Agni or the sun, N. of a Yakṣa.
धूमग्रह m. E. of Rāhu.
धूमध्वज m. fire (whose flag is smoke).
धूमपथ m. sacrifice (lit. path of smoke).
धूमपात m. sgl. & pl. rising smoke.
धूममय, f. ई consisting of smoke or vapour.
धूमय्, only P. धूम्यते be obscured by smoke or vapour, be eclipsed or darkenend.
धूमवन्त् a. smoking, steaming; abstr. °वत्त्व n.
धूमवर्त्मन् n. = धूमपथ.
धूमशिखा f. a column of smoke.
धूमाक्ष, f. ई dim-eyed.
धूमानुबन्ध m. a compact cloud of smoke.
धूमाय्, °यति, °ते smoke, steam.
धूमिन् a. smoking, steaming.
धूमोद्गम m. the rising of smoke.
धूमोद्गार m. = prec.
धूम्या f. thick smoke, a cloud of smoke.
धूम्र a. smoke-coloured, grey, dark-red; dim, obscured (lit. & fig.).
धूम्रय्, °यति colour grey.
धूम्रवर्ण a. grey-coloured.
धूम्राक्ष a. grey-eyed.
धूम्रिमन् m. dark colour, obscurity.
धूर्गत a. standing at the head, being the first or best of (—°).
धूर्जटि & °टिन् m. E. of Rudra-Çiva.
धूर्त a. shrewd, sly, cunning; m. rogue, cheat; abstr. °ता f., °त्व n.
धूर्तक a. & m. = prec.
धूर्तचरित n. pl. roguish tricks.
धूर्तनर्तक & धूर्तसमागम n. T. of comedies.
धूर्ति f. injury, harm.
धूर्व्, धूर्वति injure, damage.
धूर्वन् n. bending, damaging.
धूर्वोढ़ m. cattle for draught.
धूर्षद् m. leader (of a carriage).
†धूर्षह् (°र्षाह्) a. bearing the yoke.
धूलन n. covering with dust.
धूलय्, pp. धूलित covered with dust. — Cf. उद्धूलय्.
धूलि or धूली f. dust, powder, farina.
धूलीमय, f. ई covered with dust.
धूसर a. dust-coloured, grey.
धूसरित a. made grey, greyish.
धूसरिमन् m. grey colour.
धृ (धरति, °ते), pp. धृत (q.v.); C. धारयति, °ते = S. hold, bear, carry on, keep down, suppress, keep back i.e. own to (dat. or gen.); withstand, resist; uphold, maintain, preserve, support, wear, use, possess; turn the mind or set the heart on (loc. or dat.), be determined to (infin.). With गर्भम् become or be pregnant; w. दण्डम् or दमम् inflict punishment on (loc.); w. व्रतम् observe a vow; w. मूर्ध्ना (°र्ध्नि) or शिरसा (°सि) honour highly; w. तुलया weigh, measure; ± मनसा bear in mind, remember; ± आत्मानम्, प्राणान्, शरीरम्, etc. live on, survive. P. ध्रियते (°ति) be held, borne, etc., mostly = A. intr. I. दर्धर्ति & दाधर्ति hold fast; establish, fix. — अधि bring upon, carry over to, communicate (loc.). अभि maintain, uphold, withstand. अव settle, establish, state, assume as certain, consider as (2 acc. or acc. & nom. w. इति); learn, hear, understand, perceive, observe, ponder. आ uphold, preserve, keep (esp. in the memory), put on or to (loc.). P. आध्रियते be (contained) in (loc.). उद् draw out, elevate, raise, further. समुद् maintain, support. उप bear,

support, take for, consider as (2 acc.); learn, hear, perceive, observe, think over. नि lay down in, bring to (loc.); appoint, render (2 acc.). निस् take out, set off, ascertain, decide. प्र keep in mind, think over, ponder; w. मनस् set the mind on (dat.), determine; w. दण्डम् = S. संप्र commit, entrust to (dat.); w. बुद्धिम् & loc. = prec. w. मनस् & dat., ± मनसा = S.; make up the mind, resolve, settle. वि hold, bear; keep asunder, separate, distribute, arrange; keep from (abl.), withhold, suppress; support, preserve, guard; w. मनस् set the mind upon (loc.). सम् keep together, bear, support, maintain; keep in mind, remember; keep back, withhold, resist; hold, wear, possess; w. मनस् = prec. — Cf. विधृत.

धृक् (only nom. sgl.) & धृत् a. holding, bearing, supporting, having, possessing (—°).

धृत a. held, borne, worn, kept, detained, turned or fixed upon, ready for (loc. or dat.), upheld, maintained, observed; existing, alive; o. °— holding, bearing, etc.

धृतदण्ड a. punishing or being punished (lit. by or over whom the stick is carried).

धृतद्वैधीभाव a. bearing doubt or suspense.

धृतधनुस् m. carrying a bow; m. bowman, archer.

धृतनिश्चय a. firmly resolute upon (dat.).

धृतपूर्व a. worn before.

धृतप्रज a. having descendants.

धृतराष्ट्र m. N. of an ancient king, the elder brother of Pāṇḍu (pl. his sons).

धृतव्रत a. of fixed law or order, resolute, firm, devoted, faithful; N. of a serpent-demon etc.

धृतशरीर a. bearing up one's body, living on, existing.

धृतसंकल्प a. firmly resolute upon (loc.).

धृतात्मन् a. firm-minded, constant.

धृति f. holding fast, firmness, solidity, constancy, resolution; satisfaction, contentment. — धृतिं कृ hold fast or be satisfied; °बन्ध् set the mind on (loc.).

धृतिगृहीत a. armed with constancy or resolution.

धृतिपुष्प n. the flower of content or happiness; °ष्पं बन्ध् be satisfied or blessed.

धृतिमन्त् a. steadfast, constant, firm; satisfied, content.

धृतिमुष् a. robbing fortitude, agitating.

धृष्, धृष्णोति, धर्षति, pp. धृषित & धृष्ट q.v. be bold, dare or venture to (inf.), defy (acc.). C. धर्षयति, pp. धर्षित attack, injure, violate; M. overwhelm. — अप overwhelm, conquer. अभि S. & C. the same. आ venture against, attack. C. injure, offend. प्र venture against, assail, injure, harass. C. the same + violate (a woman), destroy, lay waste. संप्र C. assail, defy. प्रति hold out against, withstand. वि C. venture against, injure, harass, also = seq. सम् C. violate (a woman), destroy. — Cf. आधृषि & धृषन्त्.

धृषज a. a hero.

धृषद्विन् a. bold, corageous.

धृषन्त् a. bold, daring, courageous (also धृषाण & धृषमाण); n. धृषत् & instr. धृषता adv.

धृषित a. bold, courageous, brave.

धृष्ट a. bold, audacious; abstr. °ता† f., °त्व† n.

धृष्टकेतु m. a man's name.

धृष्टद्युम्न m. N. of a prince.

धृष्टि a. bold, daring; m. a pair of tongs (also du.); a man's name; f. boldness, courage.

धृष्णु a. bold, courageous, valiant, strong, firm, n. adv. — Abstr. °त्व† n.

धृष्णुया (instr. adv.) = prec. n. adv.

धृष्णुषेण a. carrying a strong weapon or leading a valiant army.

धृष्ण्वोजस् a. having powerful strength.

धृष्य a. assailable.

धेना f. milch cow or milk.

धेनु a. milching; f. = prec., fig. the earth.

धेनुका f. milch cow, female animal i.g.

धेनुमन्त् a. containing milk, nourishing.

धेन्वनडुह m. milch cow and bull.

धेष्ठ (superl.) giving most.

1धैर्य n. wisdom, prudence.

2धैर्य n. firmness, constancy, courage, calmness, gravity (also °ता f.), p. °वन्त्.
धैवर a. relating to a fisherman.
धोरणि or °णी f. an uninterrupted series.
धौत a. washed, clean, polished, bright; n. & f. ई washing.
*धौतकौशेय n. bleached silk.
धौति f. spring, brook.
धौम्य & धौम्र m. patron. names.
धौरेय a. standing at the head of; m.=seq.
धौरेयक m. beast of burden, horse.
धौर्जट, f. ई relating to Çiva.
धौर्त्य n. deceit, fraud; (°ज्ञ deceitful*).
ध्मा, ध्मात v. धम्.
ध्मातव्य a. to be blown or kindled.
1ध्मातृ m. blower, smelter.
2ध्मातृ n. melting (only ध्मातरि).
ध्मान n. blowing, puffing, swelling.
1ध्या, ध्यायति (°ते, ध्याति), pp. ध्यात think of (acc.), reflect, meditate, ponder (± मनसा or °सि etc.). D. दिध्यासते. — अनु=S. + regret, remember. समनु muse, ponder. अप think ill of (acc.), bewitch by evil thoughts. अभि set the mind on (acc. or loc.); intend, wish, desire; take for (2 acc.); absol. meditate, ponder. अव despise, curse. नि perceive, notice; also=D. निदिध्यासते be thoughtful or attentive. निस् ponder on, think over, consider (regard, contemplate, observe closely or intently*). प्र meditate upon, reflect, consider, find out. सम् reflect, ponder.
2ध्या f. thinking, meditation.
ध्यातव्य a. to be thought of.
ध्यातृ m. thinker, abstr. °त्व n.
ध्यान n. thought, reflection, (religious) meditation; p. °वन्त् & ध्यानिन्.
ध्यानतत्पर & ध्यानपर a. lost in thought.
ध्यानपटह s. the drum of meditation (fig.).*
ध्यानयोग m. the practice of meditation.
ध्यानस्थित a. sunk in meditation.
ध्यानिक a. based upon meditation.
ध्याम n. a kind of fragrant grass.
ध्यायिन् a. lost in meditation, quite intent on or devoted to (—°).
ध्येय a.=ध्यातव्य.

ध्रज्, ध्रजति sweep, glide (of the wind, birds, etc.).
ध्रजस् n. gliding or sweeping course.
ध्रजीमन्त् a. gliding, sweeping.
1ध्राज्, ध्राजति=ध्रज्.
2ध्राज् f. pl. the action or power of gliding.
ध्राज m. who glides.
ध्राजि (ध्राजि) f.=ध्रजस्.
ध्रुति f. seduction.
ध्रुव a. steady, firm, constant, certain, safe; n. adv. — m. the polar star, a man's name; f. आ the largest of the three sacrificial ladles.
ध्रुवक्षित्, ध्रुवक्षिति, & ध्रुवक्षेम a. firmly fixed solid.
ध्रुवच्युत् a. moving what is firm.
ध्रुवसद् a. resting on firm ground.
ध्रुवसिद्धि m. N. of a physician.
ध्रुवसे (dat. inf.) to stop or rest.
ध्रुवि a. resting firmly.
ध्रौव a. being in the ladle called Dhruvā.
ध्रौव्य n. fixedness, constancy.
ध्वंस्, ध्वंसति, °ते, pp. ध्वस्त (q.v.) sink down, fall to dust, perish (also P. ध्वस्यते); be gone (only imper.). C. ध्वंसयति, pp. ध्वंसित strew, fell, destroy, violate (a woman). ध्वसयति spatter, sparkle. — अप be gone (only imper.). अव M. be scattered or dispersed. नि C. (ध्वसयति) scatter, destroy. विनि be gone (only imper.). प्र M. flow away, subside (water); fall to dust, perish. वि M. (A.) be scattered, crumble down. C. (°ध्वंसयति) crush, waste, destroy. — Cf. अपध्वस्त, आध्वस्त, उपध्वस्त, परिध्वस्त, विध्वस्त.
ध्वंस m. decay, ruin, fall.
ध्वंसक a. destroying, ruining (—°).
ध्वंसकारिन् a. the same.
ध्वंसन a. & n. the same.
ध्वंसिन् a. decaying, perishing; destroying, ruining.
ध्वज m. (n.) banner, standard, flag, sign of any trade, mark, emblem, symbol, characteristic; the ornament of (—°).
ध्वजपट m. banner (-cloth), standard.
ध्वजयष्टि f. flag-staff.

ध्वजवन्त् a. adorned with flags, having a mark or sign; m. standard-bearer or vendor of spirituous liquors.

ध्वजाहृत a. robbed at the standard, i.e. won on the battlefield.

ध्वजिन् a. & m. = ध्वजवन्त्.

1**ध्वन्**, pp. ध्वान्त (q.v.); C. veil, cover.

2†**ध्वन्**, ध्वनति, pp. ध्वनित (q.v.) sound; C. ध्वनयति or ध्वानयति cause to sound. — अभि & प्र = S. — Cf. अपध्वान्त.

ध्वन m. a cert. wind.

ध्वनन n. sounding; hinting at, allusion (rh.).

ध्वनि m. sound, noise, roar, thunder; hint, figure of speech.

ध्वनित a. sounded; n. sgl. & pl. sound, noise, thunder.

ध्वरस् f. a kind of female demons.

ध्वरा f. bending, causing to fall.

ध्वस् v. ध्वंस्.

ध्वसन् m. N. of a king.

ध्वसनि m. sprinkler (cloud).

ध्वसन्ति m. N. of a man.

ध्वसिर a. scattered, covered.

ध्वस्त a. fallen, decayed, perished, destroyed, vanished; bestrewn, covered with (instr. or —°).

ध्वस्ति f. cessation, destruction.

ध्वस्मन् m. pollution, obscuration.

ध्वस्मन्वन्त् a. polluted, obscured.

ध्वस्र a. decayed, withered, faded; falling off, withdrawing from (gen.).

ध्वाङ्क्ष m. a crow.

ध्वान m. hum, murmur, sound, noise.

1**ध्वान्त** a. dark; n. darkness.

2**ध्वान्त** m. a cert. wind.

ध्वृ, ध्वरति bend, cause to fall, ruin.

न

1**न** pron. stem. of 1st pers. du. & pl.

2**न** (indecl.) not (also °— = 2अ), nor, neither (± उ, उत, अपि, चापि, वा, अथ वा); no (absol.); lest (w. opt.); like, as (only in a. l.). In the negat. mgs often followed by एव & खलु. Two negations in the same sentence generally form an emphatic affirmation. — Cf. खलु, चेद्, तु, नहि, नो.

नंश् v. 1 & 2नश्.

नंश m. getting, acquisition.

नंशुक a. perishing.

नक् (nom.) night.

नकार m. the sound n or the negation न.

नकिंचन a. having nothing, quite poor.

नकिंचिद् n. nothing.

नकिस् (ind.) none, nobody, also = seq.

नकीम् (ind.) not, not at all, never.

नकुल m. the ichneumon (f. ई); E. of Çiva, N. of a Pāṇḍava etc.

नक्त n. night, acc. by night.

*__नक्तक__ m. rag, wiper.

नक्तंचर a. walking about at night (also °चारिन्); m. a night-animal or nocturnal demon (f. ई).

नक्तन् (only instr. pl. नक्तभिस्) night.

नक्तंदिन n. sgl. night and day; acc. adv. by night and day.

नक्तया (instr. sgl.) by night.

नक्ति f. night.

नक्तोषस् f. du. night and dawn.

नक्र m. crocodile or alligator.

नक्ष्, नक्षति, °ते get at, obtain. — अभि = S. अव overtake. परि get round. प्र come near.

नक्षत्र n. a star or constellation (sgl. also coll.); esp. a lunar mansion (27, later 28; o. personif. as the daughters of Dakṣa and wives of the moon).

नक्षत्रदर्श m. star-gazer.

नक्षत्रनाथ m. the moon.

नक्षत्रमाला f. garland i.e. group of stars or of the lunar mansions; a necklace containing 27 pearls.

†**नक्षत्रराज** m. the king of the stars, the moon.

नक्षत्रलोक m. pl. the worlds of the stars.

नक्षत्रविद्या f. knowledge of the stars, astronomy.

नक्षत्रिय a. belonging or relating to the stars.

नक्षत्रेश m. = नक्षत्रराज.
नक्षद्दाभ a. slaying the approaching.
†नक्ष्य a. to be approached.
नख m. n. (adj. —° f. ई) nail (of finger or toe), claw.
नखखादिन् a. biting the nails.
नखच्छेदन n. nail-cutting.
नखपद n. nail-mark, scratch.
नखर a. shaped like a claw; n. such a knife or dagger, also = नख.
नखविष्किर m. scratcher (kind of bird).
नखाग्र n. nail-point.
नखाघात m. hurt or injury by the nails.
नखाङ्क m. = नखपद.
नखानखि adv. nail against nail (of a hard fight).
नखायुध a. having nails or claws as weapons; m. a claw-footed animal, abstr. °त्व n.
नखिन् a. having nails or claws; m. = prec. m.
नग m. mountain; tree, plant i.g.
नगनदी f. N. of a river.
नगनिम्नगा f. mountain-river.
नगर n. (m.), ई f. town, city.
नगरगामिन् a. going or leading to the town.
नगरजन m. pl. towns-folk.
नगरदैवत n. the deity of a town, adv. °वत्.
नगरद्वार n. city-gate.
नगररक्षा f. government of a town.
नगररक्षिन् m. civic guard, watchman of a town.
नगरवृद्ध m. eldest of a town, alderman.
नगरस्थ a. dwelling in a town.
नगराधिप & °पति m. lord of a town.
नगराध्यक्ष & नगरिन् m. the same.
नगरीय a. belonging to a city.
नगरीरक्षिन् m. = नगररक्षिन्.
नगरोपान्त n. neighbourhood of a town.
नगरौकस् m. townsman, citizen.
नगर्यन्न n. food given by the lord of a town.
नगवन्त् a. rich in trees.
नगाग्र n. mountain-top.
नगापगा f. mountain-river.
नगेन्द्र, नगेश, & नगेश्वर m. king of mountains, the Himālaya, Kailāsa, etc.
नगोदर n. mountain-rift.
नग्न a. naked, bare; m. a naked mendicant, f. आ a naked i.e. wanton woman, also = seq. f.
नग्नक (f. नग्निका) a. naked, wanton; m. = prec. m., f. a girl before puberty (allowed to go naked).
नग्नता f., नग्नत्व n. nakedness, nudity.
नग्नहु m. yeast, ferment.
नग्नी w. कृ make a person naked i.e. a mendicant.
नचिकेत & नचिकेतस् m. N. of a man.
नचिर a. not long (time); n. not long, for a short time (also °कालम्). Instr., abl., & dat. shortly, soon.
नट्, नटति dance, play. C. नाटयति perform, represent (d.). —*उद् play a trick (w. gen.).
नट & °क m., नटी f. a dancer or mime (also as a caste).
नटता f. the state of a dancer or actor.
नटन n. dance, pantomime.
नटनीय n. impers. it must be danced.
नड or नळ m. a species of reed.
नडक n. the hollow of a bone.
नडमय, f. ई consisting of reeds.
नड्वल n., °ला f. reed-bed.
नत a. bent, curved, rounded; bowing before (gen. or acc.); sunk, depressed; cerebralized (g.).
नतभ्रू f. having arched brows or bending the brows, frowning.
नतराम् (compar.) not at all, by no means.
नताङ्गी f. a beautiful (lit. round-limbed) woman.
नति f. bending, stooping, humility; the change of a dental letter into a cerebral (g.).
नद्, नदति (°ते) sound, roar, cry, hum (± स्वनम्, शब्दम्, etc.). C. नदयति or नादयति, °ते, pp. नादित (q.v.) make resound. I. नानदति (3. pl.) sound violently, howl, neigh. — अनु & अभि sound towards (acc.); C. (also व्यनु) make resound, fill with noise. उद् & समुद् sound, howl, roar, cry. उप C. make resound. नि sound, cry out, shriek; C. = prec. C. प्र (प्रणदति) begin to cry or roar. प्रति sound back, answer with a cry or howl. वि sound, cry, roar (± रवम्, स्वनम्, etc.), also = C. make resound, fill

with noise. सम् sound, roar, cry out. C. = prec. C., abs. cry aloud.

नदं m. roarer, bellower, neigher, esp. bull, stallion, etc; also reed, rush, sedge; river, stream. f. नदी flowing water, river; a kind of fem. themes in ई or ऊ (g.).

नदथु m. sounding, roaring.

नदनदीपति m. the lord of the rivers (conc. as males & females), i.e. the ocean.

नदनदीभर्तृ m. the same.

नदनिमंन् a. sounding, humming.

नदनुं m. noise, sound.

नदनुमंन्त् a. sounding, thundering.

नदभर्तृ m. the ocean (lord of the streams).

नदराज m. the same.

नदिं m. crier, caller.

नदी v. नदं.

नदीज a. river-born, m. E. of Bhīṣma; living near a river (horses).

नदीतट m., °तीर n. the bank of a river.

नदीन m. the ocean (also personif.).

नदीनद m. pl. & n. sgl. the rivers (conceived as males & females).

नदीनाथ & नदीपति m. = नदराज.

नदीपूर m. the flood of a river.

नदीमुख n. the mouth of a river.

नदीश m. = नदराज.

नदीष्ण a. familiar with rivers; i.g. clever, skilful, versed in (loc.).

नदीसंतार m. the crossing of a river.

नदृश्य a. invisible.

नद्धं a. tied, bound on, attached to, covered or inlaid with (—°); n. band, knot.

नद्धि f. tying, binding.

ननां f. mother (fam. expression).

नंनान्दृ f. the husband's sister.

ननुं adv. not, by no means, never; also interr. = nonne, or affirm. (± च) = certainly, I suppose, I dare say etc.); w. an imperat. = pray, do, just.

नन्तृ a. (g.) bending, changing (a nasal into a cerebral).

नंन्त्व a. to be bent.

नन्द्, नंन्दति (°ते) rejoice, be satisfied with (instr., r. abl.). C. नन्दयति gladden. — अभि please; be pleased with, delight in (acc.), greet, take leave of (acc.), accept, approve; w. न reject, decline. प्रत्यभि greet (in return). समभि congratulate. आ rejoice; C. gladden, make happy, bless. प्रति greet joyfully or in return, bid farewell (acc.), speak kindly or humbly to (acc.); accept, approve; w. न decline, refuse. C. gladden, make happy.

नंन्द m. joy, happiness, a son (as the chief object of joy); E. of Kṛṣṇa, N. of a cowherd (K.'s foster-father) etc.; f. आ a woman's name, नन्दी a cert. tree, a kind of musical instrument, E. of Durgā.

नन्दक a. delighting in (—°); m. N. of Kṛṣṇa's sword, a serpent-demon, etc.

नन्दन a. gladdening, making happy; m. son, descendant of (—°), N. of sev. myth. beings & of a minister; f. आ daughter; n. gladdening, joy, bliss, N. of Indra's grove.

नन्दनन्दन, नन्दसूनु, & नन्दात्मज m. Nanda's son, i.e. Kṛṣṇa.

नन्दनवन n. the grove Nandana.

नन्दि m. the Joyful, E. of Viṣṇu, Çiva & one of his attendants; f. joy, happiness, a woman's name.

नन्दिकर a. causing joy to (gen.); m. son of (—°).

नन्दिग्राम m. N. of a village.

नन्दिघोष m. sound of joy.

नन्दिदेव m. a man's name.

नन्दिन् a. delighting in or gladdening, m. son of (—°); E. of Çiva, a man's name. f. °नी daughter, E. of Durgā etc., N. of a myth. cow.

नन्दिवर्धन a. increasing the happines of (gen.); m. E. of Çiva, a man's name.

नन्दीमुख, नन्दीश, & नन्दीश्वर m. E. of Çiva.

नंपात् v. नंप्तृ.

नपुंस m. eunuch (lit. not a man).

नंपुंसक m. n. neither male nor female, i.e. a eunuch or hermaphrodite; n. a word in the neuter gender, the neuter gender.

(नप्तिं) & नप्ती f. daughter or grand-daughter.

नंप्तृ m. descendant, son, (esp. & in l. l. only) grandson; f. नप्त्री grand-daughter.

नभ्, नंभते burst (tr. & intr.). C. tear open, rend asunder. — उद् C. = S. C. प्र burst, split (intr.).

नभ m. a man's name.

नभनु m., °नू f. spring, river.

नभन्य a. breaking forth, penetrating (lit. & fig.).

नभश्चर a. moving in the sky; m. a god or Vidyādhara (f. ई).

नभःश्रित् a. reaching to the sky.

नंभस् n. mist, vapour, clouds, atmosphere, sky; a cert. month in the rainy season (*m.); du. heaven and earth.

नभसं m. a man's name.

नभस्तल n. the celestial vault, cope of heaven.

नभस्तस् adv. down from heaven.

नभस्मय a. misty, vaporous.

नभस्य a. the same; m. a cert. month in the rainy season.

नंभस्वन्त् a. misty, cloudy; m. wind.

नभःसद् m. inhabitant of heaven, a god.

नभःसिन्धु f. the celestial river (Gaṅgā).

नभःस्थल n., °स्थली f. canopy or vault of heaven.

नभःस्पृश् & °स्पृश a. touching the sky.

नभीत a. not afraid, adv. °वत्.

नभोजा a. born in the clouds or mist.

नभोज a. driving the clouds.

नभोमण्डल n. the vault of heaven.

नभोयोनि a. sky-born, E. of Çiva.

नंभोरूप a. dark (lit. cloud-) coloured.

नभोविद् a. knowing the sky or dwelling therein.

नभोवीथी f. the path of the sun.

1नभ्य a. misty, cloudy.

2नंभ्य n. nave of a wheel, centre i.g.

नभ्यस्थं a. being in the nave of a wheel or in the centre.

नम्, नंमति, °ते, pp. नतं (q.v.) bend, bow (mostly intr.), yield or submit to (dat. or gen., r. acc.); aim at (gen.) with (instr.). C. नमयति or (mostly —°) नामयति (नाम्यति) cause to bend, curve; w. चापम् or धनुस् bend a bow; cerebralize (g.). I. नन्नमीति bend (intr.), bow very low. — अति hold aside. अनु incline to (dat.). अभि bow or incline to (dat.). अव bend down (intr.), bow; C. the same (trans.), w. धनुर्ज्याम् bend the bow. आ (intr.) bend, stoop, bow before (acc.); tr. bend down, overthrow, subdue. C. = prec. tr., w. धनुस् bend a bow. उद् rise, ascend (lit. & fig.), also = C. raise, lift, erect. समुद् rise; C. = prec. C. उप come or repair to, befall, occur, come into the mind (w. acc., later also w. dat. or gen. of pers.), approach or wait upon (acc.) with (instr.). C. bring near, offer or present to (gen.). नि bend (tr. & intr.), bow to (acc.), humble one's self, submit. परि (intr.) bend aside, stoop; change, develop, ripen, fade, be accomplished. C. ripen, bring to an end, pass (time). प्र bend or bow before (dat., gen., loc., or acc.). C. bow (tr.); make a person (acc.) bend before (dat.). अभिप्र bend or bow before (dat. or acc.), प्रति incline towards (acc.). वि bow, bend (intr.); C. the same trans. सम् bow, bend, humble one's self, submit to (dat., gen., or acc.); M. yield or conform one's self to, obey (dat.); make straight or right, arrange, prepare (A. M.). C. bend down, make sink, change, arrange, prepare, accomplish. — Cf. अंपनत, अभ्युन्नत (add.), अवनत, आनत, उन्नतं, उंपनत, निर्णत, परिणत, प्रणत, प्रोन्नत, विनत, संनत समभ्युन्नत, समुन्नत.

नंम m. abode, pasture-ground.

नंमउक्ति f. (expression of) homage.

नमन a. (—°) & n. bending.

†नमयिष्णु a. = prec. a.

नंमस् n. bow, obeisance, adoration, homage w. कृ pay homage, revere, worship (dat. loc., or acc.).

नमसानं a. doing homage, worshipping.

नमस्कारं m. exclamation of नंमस्, worship, adoration.

नमस्कार्य a. to be adored or worshipped.

नमस्कृति & नमस्क्रिया f. = नमस्कार.

नमस्य्, नमस्यंति (°ते) do homage, worship, bless (acc.). — सम् = S.

नमस्य a. to be worshipped, venerable; respectful, humble.

नमस्या f. worship, homage.
नमस्यु a. bowing, worshipping.
नमस्वन्त् a. the same; inspiring veneration.
नमस्विन् a = नमस्यु.
नमुचि m. N. of a demon.
नमुचिहन् m. the slayer of Namuci (Indra).
नमोवृध् a. honoured by adoration.
नमोवृध a. increasing or furthering adoration.
नम्र a. bowing, bent, curved, humble; abstr. °ता† f., °त्व† n., the latter also = suppleness, nimbleness.
नम्रवक्त्र a. bending down the face.
नम्री w. कृ bend down, humiliate.
नय m. leading (of an army), conduct, behaviour, way of life, policy, worldly or political wisdom.
नयकोविद & **नयज्ञ** a. skilled in policy, prudent, wise.
नयन m. a man's name; n. leading, conduct, the eye as the leader (adj. —° f. आ, r. ई).
नयनगोचर a. being within seeing distance.
नयनजल n. tears (lit. eye-water).
नयनपथ m., °पदवी f. path or range of sight.
नयनप्रीति f. delight of the eyes.
नयनमधु n. the same (lit. honey of the eyes).*
नयनवन्त् a. having eyes to see.
नयनविषय m. range of sight, horizon.
नयनसलिल n. = नयनजल.
नयनाञ्चल n. corner of the eyes.
नयनाञ्जन n. ointment for the eyes.
नयनाम्बु & **नयनोदक** n. = नयनजल.
नयनोदबिन्दु m. a tear-drop.
नयवन्त् a. prudent, wise, virtuous.
नयविद् a. = नयकोविद.
नयशालिन् a. = नयवन्त्.
नयशास्त्र n. the doctrine of policy.
नयहीन a. opp. to नयवन्त्.
नयितव्य a. to be led or brought.
नयिष्ठ (superl.) leading best.
नयुत m. pl. a myriad.
नर m. man, husband, hero; the primal man or spirit (always connected with नारायण); person or personal ending (g.).
नरक or **नरक** m. (n.) the lower world, hell (also personif.); m. N. of a demon killed by Kṛṣṇa.
नरकजित् & °रिपु m. E. of Kṛṣṇa (cf. prec.).
नरकस्थ a. being in hell.
नरजाङ्गल n. man's flesh.
नरता f., °त्व n. humanity, human condition.
नरदन्त m. a human tooth.
नरदेव, °नाथ, & °पति m. king, prince.
नरपशु m. man-beast.
नरपाल m. king, prince.
नरपुंगव m. the best (lit. bull) of men or heroes.
नरबलि m. human sacrifice.
नरमांस n. man's flesh.
नरमेध m. = नरबलि.
नरराज m. king (of men); abstr. °राज्य n.
नररूप a. formed like a man.
नरलोक m. the world of men, earth.
नरवाहन a. carried or drawn by men; m. E. of Kubera, a man's name.
नरवाहिन् a. = prec. a., w. यान n. palankin.
नरवीर m. a (man-)hero.
नरव्याघ्र & °शार्दूल m. man-tiger, an eminent man or hero.
नरसिंह m. man-lion (a great hero or Viṣṇu); a man's name.
नरहरि m. E. of Viṣṇu or a man's name.
नराधम a. lowest of men, a wretch.
नराधिप & °पति m. king, prince.
नराश m. man-eater, a Rakṣas.
नराशंस m. E. of Agni or Pūṣan.
नराशन m. = नराश.
नरिष्टा or °ष्ठा f. chattering, sport.
नरिष्यन्त् & °ष्यन्त m. N. of a son of Manu Vaivasvata.
नरेन्द्र m. king, prince; abstr. °ता f., °त्व n.
नरेन्द्रमार्ग m. the king's road, high way.
नरेश & **नरेश्वर** m. = नरेन्द्र.
नरेष्ठा a. standing or serving as standing-place for men.
नरोत्तम a. the best of men.
नर्तक a. causing to dance; m. & f. ई dancer.
नर्तन m. dancer; (f. आ &) n. dance.
नर्तयितृ a. = नर्तक; m. a dancing master.
नर्तित a. danced or made to dance; n. dancing.
नर्तितव्य n. the necessity to dance.*
†**नर्तिन्** v. वंशनर्तिन्.

नर्द्, नर्दति (॰ते), pp. नर्दित bellow, roar, scream, sound. — अभि roar to (acc.). प्रति roar or scream against (acc.); roar after (food etc.). वि roar out, cry, thunder. सम् roar.
नर्दन n. roaring, crying.
नर्दित n. the same, a cert. throw with the dice.
नर्म m. sport.
नर्मद a. causing sport, sporting; f. आ N. of a river.
नर्मन् n. sport, jest; नर्मार्थम् for sport.
नर्मयुक्त a. jocular (lit. connected with a joke).
नर्मसचिव & ॰सुहृद् m. = कार्यान्तरसचिव q.v.
नर्मोक्ति f. a facetious word.
नर्य a. manly, human, strong, capable, good or agreeable to men. — m. man, person; n. manly deed or gift for men.
नर्यापस् a. doing manly deeds.
नल m. a kind of reed-grass; N. of sev. kings & myhol. beings; f. ई a kind of fragrant substance.
नलक m. n. = नडक; f. नलिका = prec. f., quiver.
नलकूबर m. N. of a son of Kubera.
नलगिरि m. N. of Pradyota's elephant.
नलद n. nard; f. नलदी N. of an Apsaras.
नलिन n. lotus flower; f. ई lotus plant, group, or pond.
नलिनदल, ॰निदल, & ॰नीदल n. lotus leaf.
नलिनीपत्त्र n. the same.
नलोदय m. Nala's rise, T. of a poem.
नलोपाख्यान n. the Nala-episode.
नल्व m. a cert. measure of distance.
1नव a. new, fresh, young; ॰— adv. newly, lately, just.
2नव m. sneezing.
1नवक a. = 1नव.
2नवक a. consisting of nine; n. the number nine.
नवकृत्वस् adv. nine times.
नवगत् a. bearing the first time.
नवग्व a. ninefold, consisting of nine; m. a mythol. family (cf. दशग्व).
नवज, नवजा, & नवजात a. recently born or risen, young, fresh.
नवज्वार m. new pains.
नवत a. the ninetieth.
नवता f. novelty, freshness.
नवति f. ninety.
नवतितम a. the ninetieth.
1नवत्व n. = नवता.
2नवत्व n. the number nine.
नवदश a. the 19th or consisting of 19.
नवदशन् or नवदशन् a. nineteen.
1नवद्वार n. pl. the nine gates (of the body).
2नवद्वार a. having nine gates; n. the body.
नवधा adv. in nine parts or ways.
नवन् or नवन् a. nine.
नवन n. praise.
नवनी f., नवनीत n fresh butter.
नवपद्, f, ई nine-footed.
नवम, f. ई the ninth.
नवमल्लिका or ॰मालिका f. Arabian jasmine.
नवमेघकाल m. spring (time of the new clouds).
1नवयौवन n. the first youth.
2नवयौवन a. being in the first youth.
नवरात्र m. a period or festival of nine days.
नवर्च a. consisting of nine verses.
नववधू f. bride, newly-married woman.
नववार्षिक a. nine years old.
नवविध a. ninefold.
नवसस्य n. the first fruits of the harvest; ॰स्येष्टि f. a sacrifice of them.
नवसू f. (a cow) that has recently calved.
नवाक्षर a. consisting of nine syllables.
नवान्न n. the first fruits; नवान्नेष्टि f. sacrifice of the first fruits.
नविद्य a. ignorant.
नविन् a. consisting of nine.
नविष्टि f. eulogium, panegyric.
नविष्ठ (superl.) the newest, youngest; n. adv.
नवी w. कृ renew, revive; ॰भू pass.
नवीन a. fresh, young.
नवीय a. = 1नव्य.
नवीयंस् (compar.) fresh, young, near; नवीयस् & ॰सा newly, just.
(नवेद &) नवेदस् a. knowing (w. gen.).
नवोढा f. newly-married.
1नव्य a. = 1नव.

2नव्य or नव्यं a. to be sung or praised.
नव्यंस् (f. नव्यसी) = नवीयंस्; also n. as adv.
1नश्, नश्यति (°ते) & नशति (°ते), pp. नष्ट (q.v.) be lost or missing, vanish, disappear, wane, perish, fly, escape, be gone. C. नाशयति (°ते), pp. नाशित make disappear, expel, destroy, violate, deflower; lose, also from memory, i.e. forget. — अप be gone. अव wane, disappear. निस् C. expel, drive away. प्र (णश्यति) be lost, disappear, run away. विप्र be lost, vanish, have no effect or result. संप्र disappear, cease. वि be lost, vanish, perish, have no effect or success; be deprived of (abl.). C. make disappear, destroy, annihilate, kill. अनुवि disappear or perish after (acc.). — Cf. प्रनष्ट, विनष्ट, विप्रनष्ट.
2नश् (नंश्), नशति, °ते attain, get, meet with (loc.); reach, befall. D. इनक्षति q.v. – अच्छ come near. अभि, उद्, परि, प्र, वि, & सम् reach, attain.
नशन n. disappearance, loss.
नश्वर, f. ई perishable.
नष्ट a. lost, disappeared, invisible, fled, escaped (n. impers.), perished, damaged, destroyed; deprived of, -less (abl. or °—); having lost a cause in court (j.).
नष्टचेतन a. senseless.
नष्टचेष्ट a. motionless.
नष्टरूप a. invisible, unknown.
नष्टसंज्ञ a. unconscious.
नष्टसलिल a. waterless.
नष्टात्मन् a. = नष्टचेतन.
नष्टार्थ a. impoverished.
नष्टाशङ्क a. fearless, n. adv.
नष्टासु a. lifeless, inaminate.
नष्टि f. loss, ruin.
1नस्, नंसते meet, encounter; copulate (man and wife). — सम् meet, join with (instr.).
2नंस् f. nose (only नसा, नसि, नसोस्, नस्तस्, & adj. —°).
3नस् (encl.) us, to us, or of us (acc., dat., & gen. pl. of 1st pers. pron.).
नस (adj. —°) = 2नंस्.
नस्तक m. the septum of the nose.
नस्तस् (abl. adv.) from the nose or into the nose.
नस्ता f. a hole bored in the septum of the nose.
नंस्य a. being in the nose; f. आ the string through the nose of an animal (cf. prec.); n. a sternutatory.
नस्यकर्मन् n. the application of a sternutatory.
नस्योत a. bound with a nose-string (cf. नस्या); m. such a bull.
नस्वन्त् a. having a nose, nosed.
नह्, नंह्यति (नहति), pp. नद्ध (q.v.) tie, bind on; M. put on, esp. armour, arm one's self. C. नाहयति cause to tie together. — अप unbind, loosen. अपि or पि tie on, fasten, bind under, cover, obstruct. अव bind on, put over, cover. आ bind on; M. be stopped up. उद् push off, remove; break forth, rise from (abl.). उप tie up, bind together. परि tie round, gird, encircle. सम् tie together, bind over, fasten; gird, clothe, arm (M. refl.); A. M. put on, make ready or prepare to (inf.). — Cf. अपिनद्ध, आनद्ध, उन्नद्ध, निनद्ध, परिणद्ध, विनद्ध, संनद्ध.
नंहन n. binding, tying round; bond, fetter, bolt.
नहिं (न हिं) adv. indeed not, by no means, not at all.
नंहुष m. race, lineage; m. N. of an ancient king etc., E. of Kṛṣṇa-Viṣṇu.
नहुष्य a. belonging to or descendent of Nahuṣa, human i.g.
नंहुस् m. race, lineage, tribe; neighbour, comrade, friend.
नं adv. not (= 2नं).
नाक m. celestial vault, heaven, sky (± दिवस्); adj. painless, sorrowless.
नाकचर a. moving in the sky.
नाकनारी f. divine woman, Apsaras.
नाकपति m. a god (lord of the sky).
नाकपाल m. = prec.
नाकपृष्ठ n. cope of heaven.
नाकसद् m. a god (dwelling in heaven).
नाकस्त्री f. = नाकनारी.
नाकिन् m. a god.
नाक्षत्र & नाक्षत्रिक (f. ई) belonging to the stars, sidereal.

1नाग m. serpent or serpent-demon; a cert. wind in the body, elephant, a man's name. f. नागी a serpent-maid or fem. elephant.
2नाग a. relating to serpents or elephants.
नागकन्यका f. a serpent-maid.
नागकुमार m. a serpent-prince.
नागदन्त m. an elephant's tooth or tusk, ivory; a peg to hang things on.
नागदेव & °नाथ m. serpent-king, a man's name.
नागनायक & °पति m. leader or king of the serpents.
नागपुर n. = हास्तिनपुर.
नागमातृ f. the mother of the serpent-demons.
नागमुद्रा f. seal showing a serpent.*
नागर a. born or bred in town, civic, urbane; clever, cunning (abstr. °ता f.). – m. citizen; n. dry ginger.
नागरक (f. °रिका) coming from or living in town; m. citizen, chief of a town or police; f. °रिका a woman's name; n. = prec. n.
नागराज् m. serpent-king.
नागराज m. the same, also king of the elephants, i.e. a large elephant.
नागराजन् m. = नागराज्.
नागरिक a. urbane, polite; m. citizen.
नागरिकवृत्ति f. town manners, politeness.
नागलोक m. the world of the serpents.
नागवधू & °वशा f. female elephant.
नागवन्त् a. consisting of elephants.
नागसाह्वय a. named after elephants; w. नगर n. = हास्तिनपुर.
नागह्रद m. serpent-lake.
नागानन्द n. the Joy of the Serpents, T. of a play.
नागाह्वय a. & n. = नागसाह्वय.
नागिन् a. surrounded by serpents.
नागेन्द्र m. = नागराज.
नागोजि & °भट्ट m. N. of a grammarian.
नाचिकेत a. pertaining to Naciketa; m. (± अग्नि) a cert. sacred fire.
नाट m. pl. N. of a people; f. ई its language.
नाटक m. actor, dancer, mime; n. & f. नाटिका plays of a cert. kind.
नाटकीय a. dramatic; f. आ actress.
नाटयितव्य a. to be played or represented.
नाटित & °क n. mimic representation, gesture.
नाट्य n. dancing, mimic representation.
नाट्यवेद m. art of dancing or dramatic representation.
नाट्यवेदी f. scene.
नाट्यशाला f. dancing-room.
नाट्यशास्त्र n. = नाट्यवेद.
नाट्याचार्य m. dancing master or teacher of dramatic art.
नाडि f. vein, artery, any tubular organ of the body.
नाडिक (a. —°) the same; f. आ a tubular stalk of a plant or organ of the body, a cert. measure of time.
नाडी f. tube, pipe, flute; cranny, fissure; vein, pulse, etc. (v. नाडि); wheel-box.
नाडीका f. the wind-pipe or throat.
नाणक n. a coin.
नातिचिर a. not very long (time); °रे & °रात् soon.
नातिदीर्घ a. = prec. a., n. adv.
नातिदूर a. not too far; abl., & loc. adv., as prep. w. abl. or gen.
नातिदूरग a. not too distant.
नातिदूरवर्तिन् & °रस्थित a. being not too far.
नातिनीच a. not too low.
नातिपरिस्फुट a. not fully manifest.
नातिप्रमनस् a. not very cheerful.
नातिभिन्न a. not too different from (abl.).
नातिमात्रम् adv. not too much.
नातिमानिन् a not too self-conceited; abstr. °नित्व n.
नातिरूप a. not very beautiful.
नातिश्लिष्ट a. not quite tight or fast.
नातिस्वस्थ a. not quite well.
नात्युच्छ्रित a. not too high.
नाथ्, नाथते (°ति), pp. नाथित (q.v.) seek aid; beg or ask for (gen. or *dat. of th. or 2 acc.). C. नाथयति cause to ask. — अनु & *उप A. ask.
नाथ n. refuge, aid; m. protector, lord, husband; o. adj. dependent on, occupied by, endowed with (—°).
नाथवत्ता f. abstr. to seq.
नाथवन्त्, f. °वती having a protector (husband).

नाथितं a. wanting help, being in need, oppressed; n. entreaty, request.

नाथिन् a. having a patron or protector.

नादं m. loud sound, cry, roaring, thunder, sound or noise i.g.

नादि a. sounding, noisy.

नादित n. sound, roar, noise.

नादिन् a. sounding, roaring, thundering, resonant (often —°).

नादेयं & नाद्यं a. belonging to or coming from a river, fluvial.

नाध् = नाथ्, only नाधमान seeking aid, supplex, & नाधितं = नाथितं a.

नाधस् n. refuge, aid.

नाधीत a. who has learned nothing.

नाना adv. differently, variously, distinctly, separately, o. adj., esp. °—; *as prep. without (instr., abl., or acc.).

नानाकार a. multiform, manifold.

नानात्व n. variety, diversity, difference.

नानादिग्देश m. sgl. the different quarters of the sky, all countries of the world.

नानादेश m. different countries; °देशीय & °देश्य a. coming from everywhere.

नानाधी a. having different knowledge.

नानानम् adv. differently.

नानारस a. variously flavoured or disposed.

1नानारूप n. pl. various forms or shapes.

2नानारूप a. variously formed, different, manifold.

नानार्थ a. having a different aim or purpose; having different meanings, s. such a word.

नानाविध a. manifold, different.

नानास्त्री f. pl. women of various castes.

नान्दनं n. pleasure-ground, paradise.

नान्दी f. joy, satisfaction; the introductory prayer (d.).

नान्दीमुख, f. ई showing a merry face, m. pl. a class of Manes; f. ई N. of a metre.

नान्यगामिन् a. running to nothing else.

नान्यचेतस् a. thinking of nothing else.

नापितं m. barber; f. °ती.

नापितगृह n. a barber's shop.

नाभ् f. opening or spring.

नाभ (adj. —°) = नाभि q.v.

नाभस, f. ई celestial, heavenly.

नाभाग m. a man's name.

नाभागारिष्ट & नाभानेदिष्ठ m. sons of Manu Vaivasvata.

नाभि f. (m.) the navel or any navel-like cavity, the nave of a wheel (also नाभी f.) centre, middle, rallying point, community of race or family, home, concr. relative, friend; (*f.) musk, musk animal.

नाभिक (adj. —°) navel or nave, f. आ a navel-like cavity.

1नाभिजात a. sprung from a navel.

2नाभिजात a. not of noble birth.

नाभिदघ्न a. reaching up to the navel.

नाभिभू m. navel-born, E. of Brahman.

नाभिमान m. non-arrogance, meekness.

नाभिलक्षित a. unobserved.

नाभिवर्धन n. cutting of the navel (-string).

नाभी v. नाभि.

नाभ्य a. = 1नाभिजात.

नाम (adj. —° & adv.) v. नामन्.

नामक (adj. —°, f. नामिका) = नामन्.

नामकरण m. nominal suffix; n. = seq.

नामकर्मन् n. name-giving (r.).

नामकीर्तन n. mentioning the name of (gen.).

नामग्रह m., °ग्रहण n., °ग्राह m. mentioning of the name.

नामतस् adv. by name, namely; w. कृ call, name (2 acc.); w. प्रछ् inquire after the name of (acc.). नाम नामतस् by name; cf. नामन्.

नामथा adv. by name.

नामधं & °धा m. name-giver.

नामधारक a. bearing (only) the name of, i.e. being only by name (nom.).

नामधारिन् a. bearing the name of, i.e. being called (—°).

नामधेय n. appellation, name; also = नामकर्मन्.

नामन् n. (adj. —° f. नाम्नी, r. नामन्) name, appellation, esp. personal name (opp. गोत्र); characteristic form, nature, species; noun (g.). नाम्ना or नाम (also both together or w. नामतस्) by name, called. — नाम ग्रभ् (ग्रह्) call or address by name, mention (gen.); नाम भृ bear a name, be called, नाम कृ, दा, or धा give a name, call; नाम्ना कृ or विधा call, term (2 acc.). Acc. नाम also adv. namely, indeed, of course; perhaps, probably, indeed, then (esp. after an interr. pron.). अपि नाम I wonder if, perhaps, मा नाम would that not —, if only not (opt.).

नामन a. bending.

नाममात्र n. only the name, a. having only the name.

नाममाला f. vocabulary (garland of nouns).

नाममुद्रा f. seal-ring (with a name).

नामरूप n. name and form.

नामवन्त् a. having a name.

नामशेष a. having (only) the name left, i.e. dead.

नामाक्षर n. pl. inscription (lit. the letters) of a name.

नामाङ्क & नामाङ्कित a. marked with a name.

1नामिन् a. = नामवन्त्.

2नामिन् a. bending; changing into a cerebral (g.).

नाम्ब m. a species of grain; a. consisting of it.

नाम्य a. to be bent.

नाय m. leader, guide; (wise) conduct, policy.

नायक m. (adj. —° आ) leader, guide (abstr. °त्व n.); chief, general (± सैन्यस्य); lord, husband; lover, hero, f. नायिका (d.).

नार adj. belonging to a man, human; m. man, pl. water; f. नारी woman, wife.

1नारक, f. ई hellish, infernal; m. inhabitant or lord of the infernal regions.

2नारक m. hell or the infernal regions.

नारङ्ग m., ई f. the orange tree.

1नारद or नारद m. N. of sev. myth. persons, esp. of an ancient Rishi often associated with Parvata, of a Gandharva, etc.

2नारद, f. ई pertaining to Nārada.

नारदीय a. = prec.

नाराच m. a kind of arrow.

1नारायण m. the son of (the primeval) man (cf. नर), often identified with Viṣṇu or Kṛṣṇa; a man's name.

2नारायण a. relating to Nārāyaṇa.

नाराशंस, f. ई relating to the praise of a man or men, belonging or sacred to Agni Narāçaṅça; m. a sort of Soma vessels.

नारि f. = नारी.

नारिकेर m. the cocoa-nut tree or cocoa-nut.

नारिकेल m. the same.

नारी v. नार.

नारीष्ठ a. fond of women.

नार्य m. N. of a man.

नाल a. consisting or made of reeds; n. a hollow stalk, esp. of the lotus, pipe, tube, handle.

नालिकेर (f. ई) & °केल m. = नारिकेर.

नालीक m. a kind of arrow.

1नाव m. shout of joy.

2नाव (—°) & नावा f. = नौ.

नावनीत, f. ई coming from or being like butter; soft, meek.

नावाज & नाविक m. mariner, pilot.

नावोपजीवन & °जीविन् m. the same.

नाव्य a. navigable; n. & f. आ river.

नाश m. loss, ruin, destruction, death.

नाशक (f. नाशिका) = seq. a.

नाशन, f. ई destroying, removing (gen. or —°); n. as subst.

नाशिन् a. = seq.; —° = prec. a.

नाशुक a. disappearing, perishing.

नाश्य a. to be removed or destroyed.

नाष्टिक m. the owner of anything lost.

नाष्ट्रा f. danger, destruction, evil spirit.

नासत्य m. E. of the Açvins.

नासा f. (du. & sgl.) nose.

नासाग्र n. the tip of the nose; °रन्ध्र s. nostril.

नासान्तिक a. reaching to the nose.

नासापुट m. wing of the nose, nostril.

नासामूल n. root (upper part) of the nose.

नासिका f. nostril; nose (mostly du.).

नासिकाग्र n. the tip of the nose.

नासिकापुट m. = नासापुट.

नासिकामूल n. = नासामूल.

नासिकारज्जु f. nose-string* (cf. नस्या).

नासिक्य a. being in or uttered through the nose, nasal; m. nasal sound (g.), pl. N. of a people.

नास्तिक a. & m. atheist(ical), sceptic(al).

नास्तिकवृत्ति a. leading the life of or deriving one's livelihood from, an atheist.

नास्तिकता f., **नास्तिक्य** n. abstr. to **नास्तिक**; **°क्य** w. **कर्मणाम्** denial of the future results of works.

नास्तिता f., **°त्व** n. non-existence (ph.).

नास्य n. nose-cord (cf. **नस्य**).

1**नाहुष** f. **ई** belonging to the same race, kin.

2**नाहुष** m. descendant of Nahuṣa, patr. of Yayāti, N. of a serpent-demon.

नि (°—) in, within, down, back.

निंस् (**निंस्ते**) kiss.

निंसिन् a. kissing (—°).

निः before **क** v. **निष्क**.

निःक्षत्र & **°क्षत्रिय** a. without the warrior caste.

निः before **प** & **फ** v. **निष्प** & **निष्फ**.

निकक्ष m. armpit.

निकट a. near; s. nearness, proximity; **°टम्**, **°टे** & **°टात्** adv.

निकर m. heap, pile, mass, abundance, multitude (often —°).

निकर्ष m. decrease, reduction.

निकष m. rubbing in, anointing; a roller or harrow; the touchstone, n. the streak of gold or test made on it.

निकषण n. rubbing off; m. or n. touchstone.

निकषा adv. close by (w. acc.).

1**निकाम** m. desire, wish, pleasure, satisfaction; °—, acc., & abl. in **°तस्** adv.

2**निकाम** a. desirous, eager, greedy.

निकामन् a. the same.

निकाय m. group, class, troop, assemblage, multitude.

निकार m. humiliation, insult.

निकारिन् m. oppressor.

निकाश m. horizon, proximity; adj. —° appearance, likeness, abstr. **°त्व** n.

निकाष m. scratching, rubbing, grinding.

निकिल्बिष n. expiation.

निकुञ्ज m. thicket, bower, vault.

निकुम्भ m. N. of a plant & sev. men.

निकुरम्ब, **°रुम्ब**, & **°रुम्बक** m. n. multitude.

निकृत a. bent down, humiliated, injured; mean, vile.

निकृति f. baseness, meanness, deceit, fraud (also personif.).

निकृतिन् & **निकृत्वन्** a. base, false, deceitful.

निकृन्तन a. cutting down or off, destroying; n. as abstr.; m. a cert. hell.

निकृष्ट a. brought down, debased, mean, low; (brought) near; n. vicinity.

निकेत m. (n.) habitation, abode, house; order of the relig. life of a Brahman; mark, sign.

निकेतन n. habitation, abode, temple.

निकोच m., **°न** n. contraction.

निक्त a. washed, rinsed, cleansed, purified, besprinkled.

निक्रमण n. stamping (with the foot), footstep.

निक्ष्, **निक्षति** pierce. — **वि**= S.

निक्षेप m. putting down, placing, throwing, casting (also **°ण** n.); deposit, pledge, trust (j.).

निक्षेप्तृ m. depositor (j.).

निक्षेप्य a. to be put down or thrust into (loc.).

निखिल a. entire, whole; instr. adv.

निखिलार्थ a. complete.

निगड n. chain (for the feet), fetter; as adj. (= poss. **°वन्त्** *) chained, fettered.

निगडन n. binding, fettering.

निगडपूरित a. chained, fettered.*

निगडय्, **°यति** bind, fetter.

निगद m. recitation, prayer or sacrif. formula; mention, speech.

निगन्तव्य a. to be studied.

निगम m. insertion (r.); source, root, etymon (g.); sacred text or precept; lesson, rule i.g.

निगमन n. insertion, quotation; conclusion (ph.).

निगरण n. swallowing, devouring.

निगिरण n. = **निगरण**.

निगुत् m. enemy.

निगूढ a. hidden, concealed, secret, n. adv.; **°चारिन्** walking in secret.

निगूहन n. covering, hiding.

निगृहीति f. subduing, restraint.

निग्रभीतृ m. who holds or binds fast.

निग्रह m. seizing, holding, restraining, subduing; chastisement, punishment, censure, blame.

निग्रहण a. & n. suppressing, chastising.

निग्रहीतृ m. = **निग्रभीतृ**.

निग्रहीतव्य a. to be chastised.

निग्राभ m. pressing down; N. of a verse (r.).

नियाह्य a. to be (or being) kept down or punished.

निघण्टु m. vocabulary, pl. T. of the Vedic glossary explained by Yāska.

निघर्ष m., °**ण** n. rubbing.

निघात m. stroke, blow.

निघातिन् a. striking, destroying (—°).

निघ्न a. dependent, subject to (—°); abstr. °**ता** f.

निचक्रया (instr. adv.) with down-rolling chariots.

निचमन n. sipping.

निचय m. heaping or piling up, heap, multitude, accumulation, provisions.

1**निचित** a. heaped or piled up, covered or endowed with, full of (instr. or —°).

2**निचित** a. seen, visible.

निचिर a. attentive, watchful.

निचुल m. N. of a tree & a poet.

निचुलक m. cover, wrapper, case.

निचृत् f. a defective metre.

निचेतृ or **निचेतृ** m. observer.

निचेय a. to be heaped or piled up.

निचेरु a. gliding, sneaking.

निचोल m. = **निचुलक**.

निज्, pp. **निक्त** (q.v.), I. **नेनेक्ति**, **नेनिक्ते** wash, cleanse, purify; M. refl. — **अव** = S.; C. **अवनेजयति** cause to wash off. **अभ्यव** A.M. wash, cleanse; C. = prec. C. **निस्** A. wash off, cleanse; M. wash, dress, or adorn one's self. **प्र** wash off, cleanse. **वि** wipe off. — Cf. **निर्णिक्त**.

निज a. inborn, indigenous, native, own; w. **रिपु** m. a foe in one's own camp. In l. l. = a poss. pron. of all persons.

निजघ्नि a. striking down.

निजुर् f. burning, consuming.

निटल, **निटाल**, & **निटिल** n. forehead.

निर्णिक् adv. secretly.

निण्य a. inner, private, secret, n. a secret or = prec.

नितम्ब m. the buttocks, esp. of a woman (mostly du.); ridge or side (of a mountain); the sloping bank (of a river).

नितम्बवती f. a buxom woman (cf. prec.).

नितम्बस्थल n., °**ली** f. the region of the buttocks.

नितम्बिनी f. = **नितम्बवती**.

नितराम् adv. downwards, in a low tone; completely, extremely, especially, by all means.

नितल n. a cert. hell.

नितान्त a. extraordinary, excessive, much; °— & n. adv.

नितिक्त a. impelled, urged on.

नितोद m. piercing, hole.

नितोदिन् a. piercing, boring.

नितोशन a. sprinkling, distributing; m. distributer (gen.).

नित्य a. inner, interior, indigenous, own; constant, continual, eternal (**नित्य** °— & n. adv.); abiding or persevering in, devoted to (—°); regular, essential, necessary, obligatory. Abstr. °**ता**† f., °**त्व**† n.

नित्यकर्मन् n. a constant act or duty.

नित्यकालम् (acc. adv.) always, constantly.

नित्यकृत्य n., °**क्रिया** f. = **नित्यकर्मन्**.

नित्यक्त a. driven away, vanished.

नित्यजात a. being constantly born.

नित्यतृप्त a. always contented.

नित्यदा adv. always, constantly.

नित्ययुक्त a. always devoted, always intent upon (loc.).

नित्यशस् adv. always, constantly.

नित्यसंन्यासिन् m. always an ascetic.

नित्यसेवक a. always serving (others).

नित्यस्नायिन् a. always bathing.

नित्याभियुक्त a. constantly devoted.

नित्योदक & °**किन्** a. always provided with water.

नित्योदित a. risen spontaneously (of a knowledge).

1**निद्** or **निन्द्**, **निन्दति** (°**ते**), pp. **निन्दित** (q.v.) revile, abuse, blame, despise; ridicule, mock, surpass. D. **निनित्सति** be willing to revile. — **प्रति** & **वि** revile, censure, reproach.

2**निद्** f. mocking, contempt; mocker, blamer, reviler; adj. mocking, reviling (—°).

निदर्शक a. seeing, perceiving (—°); also = seq. a.

निदर्शन, f. **ई** pointing at, proclaiming, teaching (—°). f. **आ** a cert. comparison (rh.);

n. pointing or looking at, evidence, example, symptom, omen, °नार्थम् for instance.
निदर्शिन् a. seeing, knowing (—°).
निंदा f. blame, contempt.
निदाघं m. heat, the hot season, summer.
निदातृं m. who ties on or restrains.
निदांन n. band, rope, halter; first cause, original form, essence (ph.), cause, reason i.g. — Instr. निदानेन originally, essentially, really.
निदानसूत्र n. T. of a metrical work.
निंदिग्ध a. clinging to (loc.).
निंदित a. tied on; kept, hidden.
निदिध्यासन n. meditation.
निदिध्यासितव्य a. to be meditated upon.
निदिध्यासु a. wishing to meditate on (acc.).
निदेश m. direction, command.
निदेशकारिन् & °कृत् a. executing orders, obedient.
निदेशवर्तिन् a. the same; m. servant.
निद्रा f. sleep, °कर† a. causing sleep.
निद्रागम m. sleepiness (the coming of sleep).
निद्राचौर m. stealer of sleep.*
निद्राण a. sleeping, asleep.
निद्रालस a. drowsy (lit. lazy from sleep).
निद्रालस्य n. drowsiness (cf. prec.).
निद्रालु a. sleepy.
निद्रित a. asleep.
निधंन n. going or lying down, i.e. settlement, abode, receptacle; or conclusion, end, death.
(*निधन a. destitute of wealth, poor, miserable); abstr. °ता f.
निधां f. net, snare.
निंधातोस् abl. inf. to नि + धा.
निधांन n. laying down, depositing, keeping, preserving; receptacle, vessel (r. also m., adj. —° f. ई); (hidden) treasure.
निधिं m. setting down or serving up (of food etc.); receptacle, vessel, (hidden) treasure.
निधिप m. guardian of treasure.
निधिंपति m. the same; a very rich man, E. of Kubera.
निधिपा & °पाल m. = निधिप.
निधीश m. E. of Kubera.
निधुवन n. coition.
निधेय a. to be put down or on.
निध्यर्थिन् a. wishing for treasures.
निंध्रुवि a. constant, faithful.
निनद m. n. sound, noise, cry, hum.
निंनद्ध a. tied fast to (loc.).
निनयन n. pouring out, offering.
निनाद m., °दित n. the same.
निनादिन् a. sounding or crying, causing to sound (—°).
निनित्सुं a. wishing to blame.
निनीषु a. wishing to lead or spend (time).
निन्दक a. s. reviling, reviler (mostly —°).
निन्दन n. reviling, blaming, reproaching.
निन्दा f. the same + shame, disgrace.
निन्दार्ह a. worthy of censure.
निन्दित a. reviled, blamed, rejected, prohibited, forbidden.
निन्दितृं m. scoffer, blamer.
निन्दिन् a. blaming, reproaching (—°).
निन्दोपमा f. a kind of comparison (rh.).
निंन्द्य a. blamable, abstr. °ता† f.
1निप m. chief, master.
2निप m. water-jar.
निपतन n. falling or flying (down); fall, ruin, loss.
निंपात m. fall, ruin, loss, death; falling down from (abl.) into or upon (—°), flying down, descending; falling against, assault, onset; accidental occurrence or mention, exception, irregularity, particle (g.).
निपातन n. letting fall, throwing down, killing, destroying; occasional mention or use of a word (g.); falling or flying down, descent.
निपातनीय a. to be caused to fall.
निपातिन् a. falling or flying down; descending upon (—°); felling, destroying (—°).
निपादं m. low ground, valley.
निपान n. drinking; watering place, pond.
निपुण a. clever, skilful; versed in, familiar with (loc., *gen., *instr., infin., or —°); exact, complete, perfect. °— & n. adv.; abstr. °ता f., °त्व n.

निपुणिका f. N. of a woman.
निपूत a. filtered, strained.
निबद्ध a. tied or fastened to (loc.), dependent on (instr.); joined together, built; composed or consisting of, accompanied by, endowed or adorned with (—°); enclosed, contained in, turned towards, being in or on (loc. or —°); used, employed (word or sound).
निबन्द्धृ m. composer, author.
निबन्ध m. tying on, fastening; band, fetter; foundation, literary composition.
निबन्धन, f. **ई** tying, fastening; n. ligation, construction, literary composition; bond, fetter (also f. **ई**); cause, means, condition; adj. caused by, dependent on, related to (—°).
निबन्धिन् a. binding, fettering; connected with, causing (—°).
निबर्हण a. & n. destroying, removing.
निबिड a. low; thick, dense, close, tight; full of (instr. or —°).
निबिडय्, °**यति**. pp. **निबिडित** embrace closely, make tight.
निभ a. like, equal to (—°).
निभृत a. loaden or filled with (instr. or —°); firm, steady, unmoved, constant, faithful; devoted to, intent upon (—°); settled, certain; hidden, secret. n. secret, mystery, silence, also adv.
निमग्न a. plunged, immersed in, sunk down or fallen into (loc. or —°), set (sun), entered, penetrated; deepened, depressed.
निमग्ननाभि & °**मग्नमध्या** f. slender (lit. having a depressed navel or waist).
निमज्जन n. diving, bathing.
निमज्जनस्थान n. bathing-place.
निमन्त्रक m. inviter.
निमन्त्रण n. invitation.
निमय m. barter, change.
निमि m. N. of sev. kings.
निमित a. measured out; caused by (instr.).
निमित्त n. mark, aim, sign, token; presage, omen; reason, cause, esp. the efficient cause; in the obl. cases = because or on account of; adj. caused, produced, occasioned by (—°).
निमित्तक a. caused by, dependent on (—°).
निमित्तकारण n. causa efficiens.
निमित्ततस् adv. by or from a special cause or reason
निमित्तत्व n. the being a cause, causality.
निमित्तनैमित्तिक n. du. cause and effect.
निमित्तमात्र n. only the cause or instrument.
निमित्तहेतु m. = **निमित्तकारण**.
निमिश्ल a. attached or devoted to (—°).
निमिष् f. winking, shutting the eyes.
†**निमिष** n. the same; an instant.
निमीलन n. shutting (esp. of the eyes).
निमीलित a. having shut the eyes; closed, shut; disappeared, vanished.
निमृग्र a. clinging or yielding to (loc. & **आ**).
निमृद् m. crusher.
निमेष m. = **निमिष**.
निमेषण n. the shutting of the eyes, a. (f. **ई**) causing it.
निम्न n. depth, lowland; a. deep, depressed, sunk, instr. pl. downwards.
निम्नगा f. a river (going downwards).
निम्नोन्नत a. depressed and elevated i.e. voluptuously shaped (woman).
निम्ब m. N. of a tree, °**तैल** n. the oil coming from it.
निम्रुक्ति f. sunset, evening.
निम्रुच् f. the same; a. withered, faded.
निम्लोचन n., **निम्लोच** m. = prec. f.
नियत a. tied or fastened to (loc.); kept back, checked, restrained, suppressed, settled, fixed; regular, exact, constant; confined or reduced to (—°); limited, concentrated or quite intent upon (loc.).
नियतकाल a. limited in time, temporary.
नियतव्रत a. firm in one's vow or faith, faithful, pious.
नियतात्मन् a. self-controlled.
नियताहार a. restricting one's food.
नियति f. the fixed order of things; necessity, destiny (also pers.).
नियतेन्द्रिय a. having one's organs or passions restrained.
नियन्तव्य a. to be restrained or tamed.

नियन्तृ m. restrainer, tamer, charioteer.
नियन्त्रण n. restraining, confining (also आ f.).
नियम m. = prec. + limitation, restriction to (loc. or प्रति); definition, statement; fixed rule or law, strict necessity; promise, vow; voluntary restraint, minor duty (r.); common-place (rh.). Instr. & abl. necessarily, absolutely, by all means.
नियमन a. restraining, subduing; n. also limiting, defining.
नियमार्थम् adv. for the sake of restriction.
नियमोपमा f. a kind of comparison (rh.).
नियम्य a. to be restrained, subdued, limited, or defined.
नियान n. coming down, arrival; way, path.
नियामक, f. °मिका restraining, subduing, confining, deciding; m. leader, ruler.
नियुक्त a. tied on, fettered or fastened to (loc.); commissioned, ordered, appointed to (loc., dat., अर्थम्, or infin.), turned or directed to (loc.); prescribed, enjoined. – m. functionary, official; n. necessarily, by all means.
नियुक्ति f. injunction, appointment.
नियुत् f. team of horses, esp. the steeds of Vāyu; series, row (of objects); gift, donation.
नियुत a. tied on, fastened; n. a million.
नियुत्वन्त् a. having a team of horses (E. of sev. Gods); forming a line or series, i.e. uninterrupted, continual, everlasting.
नियुद्ध n. fight, esp. fistic combat.
नियोक्तृ m. who ties or fastens; employer, ruler, lord, master.
नियोक्तव्य a. to be turned to (loc.); to be appointed to or commissioned with (loc.); to be called to account.
नियोग m. attaching, fastening (only °—); use, employment; injunction, commission, appointment, command, order; necessity, destiny.
नियोगकृत् a. executing a commission.
नियोगार्थ m. the object or purpose of an appointment.
नियोजन n. tying, attaching; bond, fetter; commission, appointment to (loc.); f. °नी† a halter.
नियोज्य a. to be fastened; endowed with (instr.); enjoined, authorized, or appointed. m. servant, dependant.
निरंशक a. getting no share.
निरंशु a. rayless.
निरग्नि a. having no fire or hearth.
निरघ a. sinless, blameless.
निरत a. satisfied with, delighting in, devoted to, intent upon (loc., instr., or —°).
निरङ्कुश a. unchecked (lit. unhooked), independent, free, extravagant, n. adv.; abstr. °त्व n.
निरञ्जन a. without unguent or paint, deceitless, honest.
निरतिशय a. unsurpassed, highest.
निरत्यय a. dangerless, secure, infallible.
1**निरनुक्रोश** m. mercilessness, cruelty; °तस् adv.
2**निरनुक्रोश** a. merciless, cruel towards (loc.); abstr. °ता f.
निरनुरोध a. regardless, unkind, indifferent to (loc.).
निरन्तर a. having no interval, continuous, uninterrupted, constant, dense, compact; abounding in, full of (instr. or —°); not different, equal, identical. n. adv. tight, fast; constantly, regularly; immediately, forthwith.
निरन्तरपयोधरा f. having thick clouds (breasts).
निरन्तरोत्कण्ठा f. continual longing.*
निरन्तरोद्भिन्न a. densely blossomed.*
निरन्वय a. childless, unrelated; n. adv. behind one's back, not openly (opp. अन्वयवत् q.v.).
निरप a. waterless.
निरपत्य a. childless, abstr. °त्व n.
निरपत्रप a. shameless.
निरपराध a. faultless, innocent (also °वन्त्); abstr. °ता f.
निरपाय a. imperishable (also °यिन्); infallible, secure
निरपेक्ष a. regardless, careless, indifferent to or about (loc. or —°). — Abstr. °क्षा & °क्षता f., °क्षत्व n.

निरपेक्षित a. regardless or disregarded.
निरपेक्षिन् a. careless, indifferent.
निरभिलाष a. not wishing for, indifferent about (—°).
निरभ्र a. cloudless, loc. in a cloudless sky.
निरमित्र a. free from enemies.
निरम्बर a. unclothed, naked.
निरम्बु a. having or drinking no water.
निरय m. hell (also personif.).
निरयण n. egression, issue.
निरर्गल a. unchecked, free; n. adv.
1निरर्थ m. disadvantage; nonsense (pl.).
2निरर्थ a. = seq. + destitute of wealth, poor.
निरर्थक a. purposeless, useless, unmeaning, nonsensical.
निरवकाश a. offering or finding no space.
निरवग्रह a. unchecked, free; n. adv.
निरवद्य a. blameless; abstr. °त्व n.
निरवधि a. unlimited, incessant.
निरवयव a. not consisting of parts, indivisible.
निरवरोध a. unrestrained.
निरवलम्ब & °न a. having or offering no support.
निरवशेष a. complete, whole, entire; °षेण & °षतस् adv.
निरष्ट a. emasculated.
निरसन a. (f. ई) & n. expelling, rejecting.
निरस्त्र a. weaponless.
निरहंकार & °कृति a. free from selfishness.
निरहंक्रिया f. abstr. to prec.
निराकरण n. rejecting, removing, forgetting.
निराकरिष्णु a. rejecting; forgetful.
निराकाङ्क्ष & °ङ्क्षिन् a. expecting or wanting nothing.
निराकार a. shapeless, formless; insignificant, unassuming, modest.
निराकुल a. not over-filled; unconfused, clear, calm, steady; n. adv. & as abstr.
1निराकृति a. shapeless, formless.
2निराकृति f. disturbance, interruption.
निराक्रिया f. = निराकरण.
निराग a. passionless, calm.
निरागस् a. sinless, innocent.
निरागार a. houseless, shelterless.
निरातङ्क a. not uneasy, comfortable.
निरातप a. not exposed to the heat of the sun.
निरातपत्र a. having no parasol.
निरादिष्ट a. paid off (pers. & th.); °धन a. having been paid off with money.
निरानन्द a. joyless, sorrowful.
निरानन्दकर, f. ई causing woe or sorrow.
निरापद् f. prosperity; adj. prosperous.
निराबाध a. undisturbed, harmless (n. adv.).
1निरामय m. health, happiness.
2निरामय a. healthy, well, wholesome, perfect.
निरामिन् a. staying in (loc.).
निरामिष a. having no meat or prey, free from sensual desires.
निरामिषाशिन् a. eating no flesh.
निरालम्ब & °न a. = निरवलम्ब.
निरालोक a. not looking about, blind (lit. & fig.); dark.
निराश a. hopeless, despairing of (loc., dat., abl., acc. w. प्रति, or —°); abstr. °त्व n.
निराशङ्क a. fearless, n. adv.
निराशा f. hopelessness.
निराशिन् a. hopeless.
निराशिस् a. without a hope or blessing.
निराश्रय a. without (i.e. not having or offering) shelter, refuge, or support.
निरास m. ejection, removal.
निरास्वाद & °स्वाद्य a. tasteless, yielding no enjoyment.
निराहार a. & m. not eating, fasting; abstr. °ता f.
निरिङ्ग a. immovable, not flickering.
निरिच्छ a. desireless.
निरिन्द्रिय a. having no organs (of sense), impotent, barren, weak, frail.
निरीक्षक a. looking at, observing (—°).
निरीक्षण a. = prec.; n. look, sight.
निरीक्षा f. consideration.
निरीक्षितव्य & निरीक्ष्य a. to be looked at or considered.
निरीह a. inactive, indolent; abstr. °ता f.
निरुक्त a. uttered, pronounced, declared as (2 nom.), explained, distinctly said or enjoined; n. explanation, etymological interpretation, T. of a work.
निरुक्ति f. = prec. n.

निरुज a. free from sickness, healthy, wholesome.

निरुत्कण्ठ a. free from desire or longing.*

निरुत्तर a. having no superior, having or making no reply.

निरुत्सव a. having no festivals.

निरुत्सवारम्भ a. showing no preparations for a festival.*

1**निरुत्साह** m. want of energy, indolence.

2**निरुत्साह** a. devoid of energy or courage, indolent; abstr. **°ता** f.

निरुत्सुक a. unconcerned, calm; having no desire for (**प्रति**)

1**निरुत्सेक** m. modesty, humbleness.

2**निरुत्सेक** a. pretenceless, modest.

निरुदक a. waterless.

निरुदर a. having no belly or trunk.

निरुद्ध a. held back, obstructed; expelled, rejected; stuffed or filled with (instr. or —°).

निरुद्गति a. not jerking (waggon).

निरुद्यम a. inactive, indolent.

निरुद्योग a. effortless, lazy.

निरुद्विग्न & **निरुद्वेग** a. undisturbed.

निरुपद्रव a. inflicting or suffering no harm; harmless, undisturbed.

निरुपधि a. deceitless, honest.

निरुपपद a. having no epithet.

निरुपप्लव a. = **निरुपद्रव**.

निरुपम a. having no like, matchless.

निरुपाय a. unsuccessful, idle.

निरूढ a. grown, risen.

निरूपण a. (—°) & n. determining, defining.

निरूपयितव्य & **°रूप्य** a. to be determined or defined.

निर्ऋति f. decay, destruction (o. personif. as the goddess of death); depth, abyss.

निर्ऋथ m. destruction or destroyer.

निरोध m. shutting in, confinement, restraint, coercion, oppression.

निरोधन a. confining, obstructing (—°); n. = prec.

निरौषध a. incurable, irremediable (lit. where there is no healing plant).

निर्गन्ध a. scentless, abstr. **°ता** f.

निर्गम m. going out (also **°न** n.), ceasing, vanishing, issue, end.

निर्गर्ह a. blameless

निर्गलित a. flowed out, poured forth.

निर्गुण a. having no thread or string; devoid of attributes, qualities, or virtues, abstr. **°ता** f., **°त्व** n.

निर्गृह, f. **ई** houseless.

निर्ग्रन्थ a. freed from all ties; m. a Jaina beggar.

निर्ग्रह m. finding out, recognizing.

निर्घण्टु & **°क** m. vocabulary.

निर्घर्षण n. rubbing.

निर्घात m. removal, destruction; hurricane, whirlwind.

निर्घृण a. unmerciful, cruel, hard-hearted, n. adv.; abstr. **°ता** f., **°त्व** n.

1**निर्घोष** m. sound, noise.

2**निर्घोष** a. soundless, noiseless.

निर्जन a. unpeopled, lonely, s. solitude, desert; abstr. **°ता** f., **°त्व** n.

निर्जय m. conquest, victory.

निर्जर a. not growing old; young, fresh.

निर्जरायु a. having cast its skin (serpent).

निर्जल a. waterless, s. such a land.

निर्जिति f. = **निर्जय**.

निर्जिह्व a. tongueless.

निर्जीव a. lifeless, dead, **°करण** n. killing, slaughter.

निर्जीवित a. = prec. a.

निर्जेतृ m. conqueror.

निर्ज्ञाति a. having no relatives.

निर्ज्ञान a. ignorant, stupid.

निर्झर m. (n.) **°ण** n. waterfall, cataract.

निर्झरिणी f. torrent, river.

निर्णय m. taking away, removal; composing, settling; decision, determination; sentence, verdict (j.).

निर्णयोपमा f. a kind of comparison (rh.).

निर्णत a. bent outwards, projecting, high.

निर्णानक a. moneyless, poor.*

निर्णाम m. bent, curve.

निर्णिक्त a. washed off, cleansed, polished, purified, expiated.

निर्णिक्ति f. expiation.

निर्णिज् f. shining dress or ornament.
निर्णीत a. found out, ascertained, settled, fixed.
निर्णेक m. ablution, expiation.
निर्णेजक m. washerman.
निर्णेजन n. = **निर्णेक**.
निर्णेतृ m. who pronounces a sentence, judge, umpire.
निर्णोद m. expulsion.
निर्दय a. pitiless or unpitied, cruel, passionate, n. adv.; abstr. °**त्व** n.
निर्दर or **निर्दरि** s. cave, cavern.
निर्दलन n. splitting, breaking.
निर्दश a. more than ten days old.
निर्दहन a. (f. **ई**), & n. burning.
निर्दातृ m. weeder.
निर्दाहं a. & m. = **निर्दहन**.
निर्दुःख a. feeling or causing no pain, abstr. °**त्व** n.
निर्दैव a. forsaken by the gods.
निर्देश m. pointing out, direction, order, command to (—°), description, designation.
निर्देश्य a. to be determined, described, announced, or foretold.
निर्दोष a. faultless, guiltless, innocent, abstr. °**ता** f.
निर्द्रव्य a. immaterial; wealthless, poor.
निर्द्वंद्व a. free from or indifferent about the opposites (as heat and cold etc.); not standing in mutual relation; uncontested, undisputed.
निर्धन a. having no property, indigent, poor.
निर्धर्म a. unjust, lawless, impious.
निर्धार m. taking out, separating.
निर्धारण n. the same, determining, settling.
निर्धुत v. seq.
निर्धूत a. shaken out or off, driven away, rejected (also **निधुत**); raised, brandished, swung; troubled, vexed; bereft of (—°).
निर्धूम a. smokeless; abstr. °**त्व** n.
निर्धौत a. washed off, cleansed.
निर्नमस्कार a. doing or deserving no homage, despised by all.
निर्नर a. devoid of men, deserted.
निर्नाथ a. protectorless, abstr. °**ता** f.
निर्नायक a. guideless, abstr. °**त्व** n.
निर्नाशन a. & n. removing, expelling.
निर्नाशिन् a. (—°) = prec. a.
निर्नास a. noseless or snubnosed.*
निर्निद्र a. sleepless, abstr. °**ता** f.
निर्निमित्त a. causeless, groundless, °— & n. adv.
निर्निमेष a. not winking (eye).
निर्बन्ध m. insisting upon (loc. or —°), pertinacity, perseverance.
निर्बन्धिन् a. insisting upon (loc. or —°).
निर्बल a. strengthless, weak.
निर्बाध a. unchecked, undisturbed.
निर्बीज a. seedless, empty; abstr. °**त्व** n.
निर्बुद्धि a. senseless, stupid, ignorant.
1**निर्भय** n. safety, security.
2**निर्भय** a. fearless, dangerless, secure.
निर्भर a. excessive, violent, full of (—°); °— & n. adv.
निर्भर्त्सन n. threat, reproach.
निर्भात a. shining forth, radiant, bright; appeared, arisen.
निर्भासन n. illuminating (lit. & fig.).
निर्भिन्न a. cleft or burst asunder; budded, blossomed; separated, disunited.
निर्भी & °**क** a. fearless, not afraid of (—°).
निर्भीत a. the same.
निर्भूति f. ceasing to be.
1**निर्भेद** m. bursting, splitting asunder (tr. & intr.); blurting or blabbing out.
2**निर्भेद** a. uninterrupted.
निर्भेदिन् a. splitting, piercing.
निर्भोग a. not devoted to enjoyment.
निर्भ्रान्ति f. stepping out, roaming.*
***निर्मक्षिक** (a. free from flies); °**कं कृ** purify the air, chase away the bystanders.*
निर्मत्सर a. free from envy or egoism.
निर्मथन n. stirring, churning, rubbing (esp. kindle fire by rubbing).
निर्मद a. not in rut (elephant); not proud, humble, modest.
निर्मनस्क a. mindless, senseless, abstr. °**ता** f.
निर्मन्त्र a. not accompanied by sacred verses (a marriage).
निर्मन्थन n. = **निर्मथन**.
निर्मम a. unselfish, disinterested, careless about (loc,); abstr. °**ता** f., °**त्व** n.

निर्मर्याद a. unlimited, countless; extravagant, criminal, impious. n. confusion, chaos, also as adv.

निर्मल a. stainless, clean, pure; abstr. °ता f., °त्व n.

निर्मा f. measure, value, equivalent.

निर्मांस a. fleshless, meagre.

निर्माण n. measuring, measure; making, production, creation, work.

निर्मातृ m. maker, builder, creator, author.

निर्मान a. free from pride or egoism.

निर्मानुष a. unpeopled, desolate.

निर्माय a. strengthless or deceitless.

निर्मार्जन n. sweeping away, cleaning.

निर्माल्य a. cast out or left (from a garland), useless; n. the leavings of a sacrifice, esp. flowers.

निर्मित a. produced, made, built, formed, created by (instr. or —°), out of (abl., instr. or —°); effected, caused, settled, determined.

निर्मिति f. formation, production, creation.

निर्मुक्त a. unbound, loosened; delivered, escaped; saved from, rid of (instr., or abl.); given up, lost, disappeared (°—); having cast the skin (serpent).

निर्मुक्ति f. liberation, deliverance from (abl. or —°).

निर्मूल a. rootless, unfounded, abstr. °ता f.

निर्मोक m. a hide or skin (taken or cast off).

निर्मोच m., निर्मोचन n. = निर्मुक्ति.

निर्यन्त्रण a. unrestrained, n. adv.

निर्याण n. going out or off, departure, disappearance, death.

निर्यातन n. giving back, returning, requital.

निर्यात्य a. to be restored or delivered.

निर्यापण n. expelling, banishing from (abl.).

निर्यास m. exudation of trees, juice, resin, milk, etc.

निर्यूह n. prominence, projection, pinnacle, turret.

निर्योगक्षेम a. neither acquiring nor enjoying.

निर्लक्षण a. unmarked, undistinguished, unimportant.

निर्लक्ष्य a. unobservable.

निर्लज्ज a. shameless; abstr. °ता f.

निर्लुण्ठन n. robbing, plundering.

निर्लेप a. unsmeared, stainless, pure.

निर्लोभ a. free from avarice.

निर्वंश a. having no family, single.

1निर्वचन n. speaking out, utterance, saying, proverb, explanation, etymology.

2निर्वचन a. not speaking, silent; unobjectionable, blameless.

निर्वत्सल a. untender towards (loc.).

निर्वपण a. & n. pouring out, offering, bestowing.

निर्वर्तन n. accomplishment, completion.

निर्वर्तनीय, °र्तयितव्य, (°र्तितव्य*, &) °त्य a. to be accomplished.

निर्वर्तिन् a. accomplishing, performing (—°).

निर्वल्कल a. barkless.*

निर्वश a. having no free will, dependent; abstr. °ता f.

निर्वसु a. wealthless, poor; abstr. °त्व n.

निर्वहण n. issue, end, close.

निर्वाक्य & निर्वाच् a. speechless, silent.

निर्वाच्य a. to be explained or defined.

1निर्वाण n. blowing out, extinction, disappearance; liberation i.e. annihilation or eternal bliss (r.); joy, satisfaction i.g.

2निर्वाण a. extinguished, set (sun), liberated, blessed.

निर्वाणयितृ (°तृक) a. extinguishing, cooling.*

निर्वात a. windless, sheltered; s. such a place.

निर्वाद m. censure, blame.

निर्वाप m. scattering, strewing, pouring out, offering.

निर्वापक a. extinguishing; soothing, refreshing.

1निर्वापण n. = निर्वाप.

2निर्वापण a. & n. extinguishing, cooling.

निर्वापयितृ (°तृक*) = निर्वाणयितृ.

निर्वास m. departure, banishment from (abl.); travelling, living abroad.

निर्वासन n. expulsion, banishment.

निर्वासनीय & निर्वास्य a. to be expelled or banished.

निर्वाह m. accomplishment, performance; competency, subsistence.

निर्वाहक (f. °हिका) & °हिन् a. accomplishing, performing, effecting.

निर्वाह्य a. to be accomplished or performed.
निर्विकल्प & °**क** a. having or offering no alternative, free from difference or doubt; n. °**ल्पम्** without hesitation or reflection.
निर्विकार a. unchanged, immutable, firm; abstr. °**ता** f.
निर्विघ्न a. undisturbed, n. & instr. adv.
निर्विचार a. inconsiderate, n. adv.
निर्विचेष्ट a. motionless.
निर्विण्ण a. despondent, depressed; disgusted with, weary of (abl., gen., loc., or —°); **अ-निर्विण्णचेतस्** a. having an undesponding heart, constant.
निर्विद्य a. unlearned.
निर्विनोद a. having no pastime.
निर्विन्ध्या f. N. of a river.
निर्विमर्श a. inconsiderate.
निर्विशङ्क & °**ङ्कित** fearless, confident, n. adv.
निर्विशेष a. making or showing no difference, not differing from (—°); equal, similar; n. as adv. or as abstr. = °**ता** f., °**त्व** n.
निर्विष a. poisonless (serpent).
निर्विषय a. having no residence, support, or sphere; banished, driven from (—°).
निर्विष्ट a. entered, sticking in (loc. or —°); restored, paid; enjoyed, earned, won.
निर्वीर a. destitute of men or heroes, abstr. **निर्वीरता** f.
निर्वीर्य a. unmanly, powerless, impotent, exhausted; abstr. °**ता**† f.
निर्वृक्ष a. treeless.
निर्वृत a. extinct, allayed; satisfied, happy.
निर्वृति f. extinction, tranquillity, happiness, bliss; poss. °**मन्त्**.
निर्वृत्त a. come forth, arisen; accomplished, finished, ready.
निर्वृत्ति f. completion, fulfilment; want of manners, ill behaviour.
निर्वेद m. despondency, despair, indifference; disgust for, aversion to (loc., gen., or —°); poss. °**वन्त्**.
निर्वेददुःसहम् adv. in a manner unbearable to (or on account of) despair.*
निर्वेपन a. not trembling or flickering.
निर्वेश m. requital, payment, expiation.
निर्वेश्य & **निर्वेष्टव्य** a. to be paid or requited.
निर्वैर a. peaceable, free from enmity towards (loc.); n. adv. & = abstr. °**ता** f.
निर्वोढृ a. going to carry away.
निर्व्यपेक्ष a. regardless, indifferent to (loc. or —°)
निर्व्याकुल a. undisturbed, calm; abstr. °**ता** f.
निर्व्याज a. deceitless, honest, sincere, pure, genuine; n. adv., abstr. °**ता** f.
निर्व्याधि a. free from sickness, healthy.
निर्व्यापार a. free from occupation, not busy.
निर्व्यूढ a. finished, successful; n. completion.
निर्व्यूढि f. issue, end; top, summit.
निर्व्यूह m. prominence, turret, battlement.
निर्व्रण a. free from wounds, unhurt, undamaged.
निर्व्रत a. neglecting religious observances.
निर्व्रस्क a. uprooted.
निर्व्रीड a. shameless.
निर्हरण n. taking out or off, removing, carrying away.
निर्हस्त a. handless.
निर्हार m., **निर्हृति** f. = **निर्हरण**.
निर्हेति a. weaponless, unarmed.
निर्हेतु a. causeless; abstr. °**ता** f., °**त्व** n.
निर्ह्राद m. sound, noise; a. °**दिन्**.
निर्ह्लाद a. joyless, uncomfortable.*
निलय m. settling down, rest, repose; hiding-place, dwelling, abode, receptacle; a. —° living or staying in.
निलयन n. settling down upon (loc.); refuge, dwelling-place, camp.
निवचन n. speaking out, utterance, address; saying, proverb.
निवत् f. depth, valley; instr. = seq.
निवता adv. downhill, adown.
निवपन n. pouring out, scattering; an oblation to the Manes.
निवर m. covering, protection or protector.
†**निवर्त** a. causing to return.
निवर्तन a. the same; n. return, cessation, desisting from (abl.); causing to return, bringing back from (abl.).
निवर्तनीय a. to be brought or kept back.
निवर्तयितव्य, **निवर्तितव्य**, & **निवर्त्य** a. = prec.
निवर्तिन् a. returning, abstaining from (abl.).

निवसन n. putting on; cloth, garment.
निवस्तव्य n. (it is) to be lived or spent.
निवह a. bringing, causing; m. sgl. & pl. troop, multitude, heap, mass.
1**निवात** a. windless; n. such a spot.
2**निवात** a. unimpeded, secure; n. security.
निवातस्थ a. standing in a windless place.
निवाप m. seed or a sown field; also = seq.
निवापाञ्जलि m. an oblation to the Manes.
निवापोदक n. a libation to the Manes.
निवारण a. & n. keeping back, warding off (acc. or —°).
निवारणीय & **निवार्य** a. to be kept off.
1**निवास** m. clothing; a. clothed in (—°).
2**निवास** m. stopping, dwelling; resting-place, abode, home.
निवासरचना f. architecture, edifice.
निवासन n. dwelling, abode.
निवासवृक्ष m. a tree (serving) as resting-place (for a bird).
1**निवासिन्** a. clothed in (—°).
2**निवासिन्** a. dwelling, staying or being in (loc. or —°); m. inhabitant.
निविड v. **निबिड**.
निविद् f. instruction, precept, doctrine; a kind of short address or invocation of the gods (r.).
निविष्ट a. entered, settled down, gone to rest; lying, resting, dwelling, staying, sitting, sticking in, on, or at; turned to, intent upon (loc. or —°); established, founded; occupied, cultivated.
निवोत a. = seq.; also n. as subst.
निवीतिन् a. wearing the sacred thread round the neck.
निवृत a. surrounded, enclosed, stopped; n. covering, mantle.
निवृत्त a. returned, gone, departed, fled; having escaped, desisted or abstained from (abl. or —°); deprived of (abl.); ceased, vanished, disappeared, no more to be supplied (g.); independent of wordly motives (an action).
निवृत्ति f. return; cessation, vanishing, disappearance, desisting or escaping from (abl. or —°); abstaining, esp. from action, inactivity.
निवेदक (f. °**दिका***) telling, relating (—°).
निवेदन a. & n. relating, announcing.
निवेदयितुकाम a. wishing to relate.*
निवेदिन् a. knowing, aware of; telling, relating; offering, presenting (—°).
निवेद्य a. to be related or communicated.
निवेश m. entering, stopping; putting down, pressing against; settling down, halting- or dwelling-place, settlement, habitation, home; founding a household, matrimony.
निवेशन, f. **ई** entering, penetrating (—°); laying down, lodging. – n. entrance, putting down, laying on, employing, introducing, fixing, impressing; settling down etc. = prec.
निवेशिन् a. being in, lying near, resting on (—°).
निवेश्य a. to be founded (town) or married (man).
निवेष्ट m., °**न** n. covering, clothing.
निवेष्टव्य n. (it is) to be married (of a man).
निवेष्टुकाम a. wishing to marry.
1**निवेष्य** m. whirlpool or whirlwind.
2**निवेष्य** a. belonging to a whirlpool, whirling.
निश् f. night.
निश (—°) n. & **निशा** f. the same.
निशाकर m. the moon (night-maker).
निशागम m. evening, coming of night.
निशाचर a. night-walking; m. a Rakṣas (f. **ई**).
निशात्यय m. close of night, day-break.
निशाधीश m. the moon (lord of night).
निशानाथ m. the same.
निशानिशम् adv. day by day (lit. night by n.).
1**निशान्त** a. tested, approved, usual, customary.
2**निशान्त** n. dwelling-place, house.
3**निशान्त** s. close of night, day-break.
निशापति m. = **निशाधीश**.
निशाम m., °**न** n. observing, perceiving.
निशामुख n. the face or the coming of the night.
निशित a. sharpened, whetted; eager for (loc.).
निशिता f. night.
निशिताङ्कुश s. a sharp or pointed hook.

निःशिति f. stimulation, invitation, entertainment, treat.
निशीथ m. (n.) midnight, night i.g.
निशीथदीप m. night lamp.
निशुम्भ m. killing, slaughter, N. of a Dānava.
निश्चय m. ascertainment, conviction, persuasion, decision, resolution, fixed opinion or purpose.
निश्चल a. immovable, invariable.
निश्चित a. having settled a thing, resolved upon, sure of (dat., loc., अर्थम् or —°); settled, fixed upon, certain, n. adv.
निश्चिन्त a. thoughtless, careless, unconcerned.
निश्चेतन a. unconscious, unreasonable; abstr. °त्व n.
निश्चेतस् a. = prec. a.
निश्चेष्ट a. motionless; n. adv.
निश्छन्दस् a. not studying the Veda.
निश्छिद्र a. having no rent, openings, or weak points; whole, complete, uninterrupted.
निःश्वसित n. breathing out.
निश्वास m. breathing in or out, sigh.
निःशङ्क a. fearless, not afraid of (—°), confident; °— & n. adv.
निःशङ्का f. fearlessness; instr. = prec. adv.
निःशङ्कित a. = निःशङ्क.
निःशत्रु a. free from enemies.
निःशब्द a. noiseless, silent; s. silence.
निःशरण a. defenceless.
निःशलाक a. free from (high) grass (a forest).
निःशल्य a. freed from the point of an arrow; n. adv. without pain or reluctance, willingly.
निःशस्त्र a. weaponless, unarmed.
निःशुक्र a. having no splendour.
निःशेष a. having no remainder, whole, entire; acc. w. कृ = निःशेषय् (q.v.). °—, instr. & adv. in तस् entirely, completely. — Cf. अशेष.
निःशेषता f. abstr. to seq.
निःशेषय्, **यति** destroy totally.
निःश्रीक a. ugly, unhappy, inglorious.
निःश्रेयस, f. **ई** best, most excellent (lit. having no better or superior); n. bliss, deliverance, final beatitude, happiness, welfare.
निःश्रेयसकर a. creating supreme bliss.
निःश्वसित a. breathing out, sighing.
निःश्वास m. breathing out, breath i.g.
निषङ्ग m. quiver or sword (lit. what is attached); poss. °ङ्गिन्.
निषक्त a. hanging on, clinging to, sitting in, turned towards (—°).
निषण्ण a. seated; sitting, lying, or resting on (loc. or —°).
निषत्त or **निषत्त** a. seated.
निषत्ति f. sitting, seat.
निषत्नु a. sitting fast.
निषद् a. sitting inactive; n. the state of sitting, esp. near the altar.
निषदन n. sitting down; seat, abode.
निषद्वर a. sitting (inactive or near the altar).
निषध m. N. of a mountain & sev. men; pl. N. of a people.
निषाद m. Non-Aryan, barbarian.
निषादिन् a. sitting, lying on or in (loc. or —°); m. elephant-driver.
निषिद्ध a. kept off, prohibited, forbidden (pers. & th.).
निषिद्धि f. keeping off.
निषूदक or **°दन** m. killer, destroyer.
निषेक m. sprinkling, infusion; impregnation (r.); water used for washing.
निषेचन n. pouring out, sprinkling.
निषेद्धव्य a. to be kept off or back.
निषेद्धृ m. who keeps off.
निषेध m. keeping off, probition (also °न n.); denial, negation, contradiction.
निषेधिन् a. repelling, beating (—°).
निषेध्य a. = निषेद्धव्य.
निषेव a. practising, frequenting, enjoying; devoted to, intent upon (—°); m., f. आ, & °न n. as abstr.
निषेवित a. inhabited, frequented, tenanted, occupied, approached, enjoyed.
निषेवितव्य a. = निषेव्य.
निषेविन् a. practising, observing, enjoying (—°).
निषेव्य a. to be practised, observed, or enjoyed.
निष्क m. (n.) a golden ornament for breast or neck (p. निष्किन्); a. cert. coin.

निष्कण्टक a. free from thorns or enemies.
निष्कम्प a. not trembling, unshaken, immovable; abstr. °ता f., °त्व n.
निष्कर a. free from duties or taxes.
निष्करुण a. pitiless, cruel (abstr. °ता f.*).
निष्कर्मन् a. inactive.
निष्कर्ष m. drawing out, extracting, taking off (also °ण n.); extract or essence of anything, main point, chief matter.
निष्कल a. without parts, undivided; maimed, impotent, barren.
निष्कलङ्क a. stainless, sinless, pure.
निष्कल्मष a. = prec. a.
निष्काम a. desireless, disinterested.
निष्कारण a. having no reason, cause, motive, or purpose; °—, n., & abl. adv.
निष्कासन n. expulsion, driving away.
निष्कासनीय a. to be driven away.
निष्किंचन a. having nothing, poor.
निष्कुट m. n. grove, pleasure-ground.
निष्कुतूहल a. free from curiosity.
निष्कुल a. having no family, single.
निष्कूज a. soundless, mute.
निष्कृत n. expiation; fixed place, rendezvous.
निष्कृति f. restoration, healing; also = prec.
निष्कृप a. pitiless, cruel.
निष्कोश a. unsheathed.
निष्क्रम m., °ण n. going out (esp. for the first time with a child).
निष्क्रय m. redemption, ransom, acquittance; reward, wages.
निष्क्रयण a. & n. redeeming, ransoming.
निष्क्रान्त a. gone out; exit, exeunt (d.).
निष्क्रिय a. inactive (abstr. °ता f.); not performing or not performed with, ceremonious rites.
निष्क्रियात्मन् a. inactive, lazy; abstr. °त्मता f.
निष्क्रीति f. redemption.
निष्क्रोध a. not angry with (gen.).
निष्टाप m. warmth.
निष्टुर a. throwing down, felling.
निष्ट्य a. external, foreign.
निष्ठ a. staying, lying, being, resting, footing, dependent, or intent upon; relating, attached, or devoted to (—°), abstr. °ता f. — f. आ stand-point, basis, foundation; devotion to, familiarity with (loc.); height, summit, close, end (adj. —° ending with); decision, sentence, verdict (j.); the endings त & तवन्त् and the participles formed with them (g.).
निष्ठा or **निःष्ठा** a. excelling, leading.
निष्ठावन्त् a. perfect, consummate.
निष्ठाशून्य a. wanting firmness, unsteady.
1**निष्ठित** a. standing on, being in (loc.).
2**निष्ठित** (**निःष्ठित**) a. grown forth, risen, accomplished, ready.
निष्ठीवन n., °विका f., °वित n. spitting out, spittle.
निष्ठुर a. rough, hard, cruel, merciless; abstr. °ता f., °त्व n.
निष्ठ्यूत a. bespat; n. spittle.
निष्ण a. clever, skilful, versed in (—°).
निष्णात a. the same (also w. loc.); agreed upon, settled.
निष्पतन n. rushing forth.
निष्पत्ति f. coming out or forth, completion, result.
निष्पंद f. excrement.
निष्पद a. footless.
1**निष्पन्द** m. motion.
2**निष्पन्द** a. motionless; °न्दी w. कृ make m.
निष्पन्न a. come forth, arisen, descended or derived from (abl.); brought about, effected, ripened; succeeded, prospered, thriven.
निष्परामर्श a. incapable of thinking.
निष्पर्यन्त a. unlimited.
निष्पादक a. accomplishing; abstr. °त्व n.
निष्पादनीय & **निष्पाद्य** a. to be accomplished.
निष्पाप a. sinless.
निष्पार a. boundless, unlimited.
निष्पीडन n. pressure.
निष्पुत्र a. sonless.
निष्पुरुष a. destitute of men (males), unpeopled.
निष्पेष m., °ण n clashing against, bounce, shock.
निष्प्रज्ञ a. ignorant, stupid.
निष्प्रताप a. void of dignity.
निष्प्रत्याश a. hopeless; °शी w. भू lose all hope of (प्रति).
निष्प्रत्यूह a. unimpeded, unlimited.

निष्प्रभ a. deprived of light, splendourless, dark, obscure; abstr. °**ता** f., °**त्व** n.

निष्प्रयोजन a. having no motive, purpose, or object; useless, harmless, inoffensive, n. adv.; abstr. °**ता** f., °**त्व** n.

निष्प्रवाणि a. fresh from the loom, quite new (cloth).

निष्प्राण a. breathless, exhausted; abstr. °**ता** f.

निष्प्रीति a. joyless, not rejoicing in (—°).

निष्फल a. bearing no fruit, fruitless, useless, unsuccessful; abstr. °**त्व** n.

निष्फली w. **कृ** leave unrewarded.

निष्फार m. yawning, gaping.

निष्फेन a. foamless.

निष्यन्द & °**न्दिन्** v. **निस्यन्द** & °**न्दिन्**.

निष्षह (°**षाह**) a. overpowering, powerful.

निष्षिध् f. preparation, dish, food; grant, gift, oblation.

निःषेचन n. pouring out, sprinkling with (—°).

निःष्पन्द = **निष्पन्द**; abstr. °**ता** f.

निस् prep. out of, away from (abl.), mostly °— as prep. or neg. pref. (cf. 2**अ**) in subst. & adj.

निसर्ग m. evacuation, discharging (esp. of the body); giving forth, ceding, granting, bestowing; dismission, creation; natural state or character, nature; °—, instr., & abl. by nature, originally.

निसर्गज a. innate, natural, originally given by (—°).

निसर्गनिपुण a. clever by nature.

निसर्गशालीन a. modest by nature.

निसर्गसौहृद n. natural friendship.

निसृष्ट a. hurled on or against (loc. or —°); turned, directed; let loose, dismissed, sent forth; kindled (fire); committed, entrusted, granted, bestowed; made, accomplished.

निस्तमस्क a. free from darkness, light.

निस्तरण n. passing over; escape, rescue.

निस्तार m. = prec. + payment, acquittance.

निस्तारण n. passing over, overcoming.

निस्तीर्ण a. crossed, passed, overcome; saved or escaped from (—°).

निस्तेजस् a. deprived of splendour or energy.

निस्त्रिंश a. cruel, merciless (lit. more than thirty), abstr. °**त्व** n. – m. a sword, p. °**शिन्**.

निस्त्रिंशकर्कश a. cruel and hard.

निस्त्रैगुण्य a. exempt from the three qualities (ph.).

निस्यन्द or **निष्यन्द** a. & m. flowing or trickling down; m. also discharge of any fluid, gush, stream.

निस्यन्दिन् or **निष्यन्दिन्** a. = prec. adj., also trans. (—°).

निस्रव or **निस्राव** m. flowing down, stream, torrent.

निस्वन or **निःस्वन** m. sound, noise, voice.

निस्वनित or **निःस्वनित** n. the same.

निस्वर a. noiseless, mute.

निःसंशय a. doubtless, infallible, certain (pers. & th.); n. adv.

निःसङ्ग a. unattached, unobstructed, indifferent to (loc.); disinterested, unselfish; m. & °**ता** f., °**त्व** n. as abstr.

निःसंचार a. & m. not roaming.

निःसंज्ञ a. senseless, unconscious.

निःसत्त्व a. unreal, abstr. °**त्व** n.; wanting courage or strength, weak, cowardly, abstr. °**ता** f.

निःसत्य a. untrue, false; abstr. °**ता** f.

निःसंदिग्ध a. doubtless, certain (things); n. adv.

निःसपत्न a. having no rival or equal; abstr. °**ता** f.

निःसरण n. going out, issue; means, expedient.

निःसलिल a. waterless.

निःसह a. unable to bear or resist (—°); defenceless, weak, impotent, abstr. °**ता** f.

निःसाध्वस a. fearless, confident, bold, n. adv.; abstr. °**त्व** n.

1**निःसार** m. going forth.

2**निःसार** a. sapless, pithless, worthless, vain; abstr. °**त्व** n.

निःसारण n. going or driving out.

निःसार्य a. to be driven out or excluded from (abl.).

निःसीमन् a. boundless, immeasurable.

निःसुवर्णक a. having no gold.*

निःसूनु a. sonless.

निःस्नेह a. having no grease or oil; loveless, unfeeling; unloved, hated.

निःस्पृह a. desireless, not wishing or caring for (loc. or —°); turning away from (abl).

निःस्फुर a. not throbbing (heart).*

निःस्व a. having no property, indigent, poor.

निःस्वन a. soundless. v. also **निस्वन**.

निःस्वाध्यायवषट्कार a. neither studying nor sacrificing.

निःस्वामिका f. having no lord or husband.

निहन्तव्य a. to be killed or destroyed.

निहन्तृ m. killer, destroyer.

निहाका f. whirlwind.

निहित a. laid (down), situated, deposited, hidden, kept, turned, placed, fixed, given, delivered.

निह्नव m. denial, concealment, contradiction, excuse, expiation.

निह्नुत a. denied, disowned, concealed, secreted, hidden, covered, falsely represented.

निह्नुति f. denial.

1**नी**, **नयति**, **°ते**, pp. **नीत** lead, guide, conduct, direct (l. & f.); carry away, remove; draw near, attract; bring to or into (acc., esp. of an abstr., **प्रति**, dat., or loc.); M. (A.) lead home, i.e. marry (a wife); pass or spend (time); make out, ascertain, settle. — With **अग्रम्** take the lead, head (gen.); w. **दण्डम्** bear the rod, i.e. inflict punishment; w. an adv. in **सात्** reduce to or change into, e.g. **भस्मसात्**; w. **शूद्रताम्** make a person (acc.) a Çūdra; **समताम्** make equal; w. **दुःखम्** make unhappy, pain; w. **परितोषम्** gratify; w. **क्षयम्** destroy (cf. **इ** & **गम्**). C. **नाययति** cause a pers. or th. to be led or carried away by (instr.) to (acc.). D. **निनीषति**, **°ते** be willing to lead etc., to carry off, to bring into (acc.); to find out or ascertain. I. **नेनीयते** lead away as a captive, have power of (acc.). — **अच्छ** lead near or towards (acc.). **अति** lead over or beyond (acc.); I. bring forward. **अनु** bring near or towards (acc.); try to win, conciliate; ask, request. **प्रत्यनु** conciliate, deprecate, ask pardon for (acc.). **अप** lead or take away, put off, remove. **व्यप** the same. **अभि** lead near or towards (acc.); fetch, procure; represent, act, perform (d.). **अव** lead down, push or put into (acc. or loc.); pour down, off, or over. **अभ्यव** lead down or pour into (acc.). **व्यव** pour out singly. **समव** lead or pour together, mix, unite. **आ** lead or bring near, fetch, cause; lead or bring towards or into (acc., w. **वशम्** subject, subdue), lead or bring back (± **पुनर्**); pour in, mix; offer, sacrifice. **उदा** lead up or out (esp. out of the water). **उपा** lead or bring near, draw towards (acc.); get or cause to (gen. of pers. & acc. of th.); lead away, carry off. **पर्या** lead round or near. **प्रत्या** lead or bring back, recover; pour to, fill up by pouring in. **समा** conduct together, gather, collect; lay together (the hands); conduct towards, unite with (instr. ± **सह**); pour together, mix; lead or bring near; carry away, lead home; offer, sacrifice. **उद्** lead upwards, bring up, erect; lead out, deliver, rescue; draw out (water), fill up by drawing; lead off (**वधाय** to death); find out, investigate, infer. **समुद्** lift up, raise (lit. & fig.), investigate, ascertain; pay off (a debt). **उप** lead near, bring to, present, offer, communicate; carry off, lead away, take to one's self, receive (esp. as a pupil); bring or put into a state or condition, **आत्मानम्** betake or expose one's self to (acc. or loc.*); bring about, cause, produce. C. cause a person (acc.) to be received as a pupil. **समुप** draw near, admit, lead to (acc.), present, offer; lead away, take to one's self; bring about, cause. **नि** lead to (dat. or loc.), cause to (dat. inf.); bend, incline; pour out or in; offer, sacrifice; perform, accomplish. **निस्** lead or take away; find out, settle, decide. **परा** lead away or back. **परि** lead or carry round, esp. lead a bride round the fire, i.e. marry; lead away, carry off, lead near, bring to (acc.); find out, explore. C. परिणययति & परिणाययति marry a man (acc.) with a woman (acc.). प्र bring forwards, lead further, promote; convey (r.); conduct or take to (M. to one's self), present, offer; bring or reduce to (a state); employ, inflict (punishment); state, decide, teach, compose, promulgate; perform, accomplish; show, betray (esp. one's feelings), love, desire. संप्र bring together, collect, raise (taxes); employ, inflict (punishment); compose, promulgate. प्रति lead back or towards, put together, mix. वि lead or drive away, remove; spend, pass (time); mix, stir up (Soma etc.); part (the hair); spread, extend; train, discipline, teach, instruct; cause or induce to (dat. inf.); perform, accomplish. सम् lead together, gather, collect, unite; mix together, stir up (r.); bring near, fetch, get, procure; present with (instr.); give back, restore, return. — Cf. अपनीत, अभिनीत, अभिविनीत, निर्णीत, परिणीत, प्रणीत, विनीत.

2नी (—°) leading, bringing, etc.

नीकाश m. appearance, look, only adj. —° resembling, like.

नीच a. low, deep (lit. & fig.), inferior, mean, base; abstr. °ता f., °त्व n.

नीचा (instr. adv.) below, down.

नीचात् (abl. adv.) from below.

नीचीन a. turned downwards, °बार t. d. with the opening.

नीचैस् (instr. adv.) low, below, down, downwards; humbly, modestly; in a low or deep tone (comp. °स्तराम्†).

नीड or नीळ m. n. resting-place, esp. a bird's nest; the interior or seat of a carriage.

नीति f. conduct, esp. right or wise conduct; also = नीतिविद्या q.v.

नीतिकुशल & °ज्ञ a. skilful in politics or human affairs.

नीतिमन्त् a. of right or discreet conduct.

नीतिविद्या f., °शास्त्र n. moral or political science.

नीथ m. a man's name (lit. leader); n. नीथ musical mode or song; f. नीथा way, trick, artifice.

नीध्र n. (the edge of a) roof.

नीप a. situated low, deep. — m. N. of a tree, n. its blossom & fruit; m. pl. N. of a princely race.

नीप्य a. = prec. adj.

नीर n. water (also pl.).

1नीरज m. n. lotus (water-born).

2नीरज a. = seq.

नीरजस् & °जस्क a. free from dust or passion.

1नीरद m. cloud (water-giver).

2नीरद a. toothless.

नीरधि & °निधि m. sea, ocean (lit. receptacle of waters).

नीरन्ध्र a. having no holes or openings, uninterrupted, close, thick; abstr. °ता f.

नीरव a. soundless.

नीरस a. sapless, dried up, withered, tasteless, insipid, dull; abstr. °ता f.

नीराग a. colourless, passionless; abstr. °ता f.

नीराजन n., °ना f. a kind of lustration (r.).

नीरुज्, नीरुज, & नीरोग a. free from sickness, healthy, well.

नीरोह m. shooting forth.

नील a. dark-coloured, esp. dark-blue or black. — m. sapphire; N. of a serpent-demon, sev. men, etc.; f. नीला a woman's name, नीली indigo (plant or dye); n. dark colour or substance, indigo.

नीलकण्ठ a. blue-necked; m. peacock, E. of Çiva, a man's name.

नीलगिरि m. N. of a mountain.

नीलग्रीव a. blue-necked, E. of Çiva.

नीलपक्ष्मन् a. having dark eyelashes.

नीलपट m. dark garment.

नीलपृष्ठ a. black-backed, E. of Agni.

नीलमणि m., नीलरत्न n. sapphire (blue gem.).

नीललोहित a. blue-red, E. of Çiva.

नीलवन्त् a. blackish, dark.

नीलवर्ण a. blue-coloured.

नीलवसन & °वस्त्र n. blue cloth or garment.

नीलसंधानभाण्ड n. vat for (preparing) indigo.

नीलसरोरुह n. blue lotus.

नीलाञ्जन n. (black) antimony.

नीलाब्ज & नीलाम्भोज n. blue lotus.

नीलिमन् m. blackness, dark colour.
नीलीभाण्ड n. indigo vat.
नीलीवर्ण a. having the colour of indigo.
नीलोत्पल n. blue lotus.
नीव m. a kind of tree.
नीवार m. wild rice.
नीवारकण m. rice-grain.
नीवि or नीवी f. a cloth or girdle worn round a woman's waist.
नीशार m. a blanket or shawl.
नीषह् (°षाह्) a. overpowering.
नीहार m. (n.) fog, mist (also pl.).
1नु, नू (indecl.) now, still, then, indeed (esp. in questions ± खलु); -ever or -soever (w. a rel., which it makes indefin.); w. neg. certainly not, never. — नू चिद् just now, for ever; never, never more; नु—नु (—नु) either—or (—or), also in questions without an interr. pron.
2नु, नौति, नुवति, नवते, °ति, pp. नुत roar, sound, exult, praise. I. नोनवीति, नवीनोत् howl, thunder. — अच्छ call or shout to (acc.). अनु I. cheer after (acc.). अभि hail, shout to (acc.). आ M. sound, scream; I. sound through (acc.). प्र roar, sound, howl, hum, utter (esp. the syllable Om). अभिप्र shout to, hail (acc.). सम् sound or roar together.
3नु, नवते (नौति) move (trans & intr.); C. नावयति move from a place, remove. — अप A. lay by. अभि & अव M. turn to (acc.).
नुति f. praise.
नुत्ति f. driving away, removal.
1नुद्, नुदति, °ते, pp. नुत्त & नुन्न push, thrust; impel, incite; expel, drive away, remove, reject. C. नोदयति impel. I. नोनुद्यते drive away repeatedly, chase. — अप, व्यप, अपा, & व्यपा push or drive away, chase, remove. निस् push out, expel, remove, reject. परा push away, chase, remove. प्र push or drive away, chase; impel, incite. प्रति push back, repel, avert. वि drive asunder or away; strike, wound. C. drive away, pass or spend (time); divert, amuse; delight in, enjoy (instr.). सम् press or bring together. C. bring near, fetch; impel, incite. उपसम् = prec. S.
2नुद् (—°) chasing, removing.
नुद a. = prec. + hurting, injuring.
नू v. 1नु.
नूतन a. new, recent, fresh, young.
नूत्न a. = prec. + future.
नूनम् adv. now, just; immediately, in future; then, therefore; certainly, indeed.
नूपुर m. n. an ornament for the toes or ancles of women; p. °रिन् & °रवन्त्.
नृ m. man, hero (used also of gods); a masculine word (g.); pl. men, people.
नृकलेवर s. human body, corpse.
नृकेसरिन् m. man-lion, i.e. Viṣṇu.
नृग m. a man's name.
नृचक्षस् a. beholding men.
नृजित् a. conquering men.
नृज्याय m. the conquering of men.
1नृत्, नृत्यति (°ते), pp. नृत्त dance; play, act, represent (d.). C. नर्तयति (°ते) cause to dance or to move to and fro. I. नरिनर्त्ति, नरीनर्त्ति, नरीनृत्यति, °ते (cause to) dance about or to and fro. — अनु dance after or before (acc.). आ dance or hasten near. C. cause to dance or move gently. उप dance before (acc.). परि dance about (acc.). प्र dance (forwards), begin to dance. सम् dance together.
2नृत् f. gesture, gesticulation.
नृतम a. manliest, strongest.
नृता f. the masculine sex.
नृति f. dancing, acting.
नृतु a. gesticulating, lively.
नृतू s. dancer.
नृत्त n. dance.
नृत्य n. dance, pantomime.
नृत्यगीत n. du. dance and song.
नृदुर्ग n. a fortress (protected) by men.
नृदेव (f. ई) & नृप m. king (god or lord of men).
नृपकार्य n. the king's affair or commission.
नृपजन m. sgl. the kings (coll.).
नृपति m. = नृप.
नृपतिकन्यका f. royal maid, princess.

नृपत्नी f. the king's wife, queen.
नृपत्व n. royalty, dominion.
नृपशु m. a brute of a man or a man serving as a sacrificial victim.
नृपसुत m. a king's son, prince.
नृपाङ्गण or °न n. a royal court.
नृपाण a. giving drink to men.
नृपातृ m. protector of men.
नृपात्मज m. = नृपसुत; f. आ princess.
नृपाय्य a. protecting men; n. large building, hall.
नृपाल m. king (protector of men).
नृपासन n. royal seat, throne.
नृपीति f. guard of men.
नृबाहु m. a man's arm.
नृभर्तृ m. king (lord of men).
नृमणस् a. kind towards men.
†नृमणस्य्, °स्यते denom. to prec.
नृमांस n. man's flesh.
नृमादन a. gladdening men.
नृमेध m. man-sacrifice, N. of a man.
नृम्णं n. manliness, courage, strength.
नृयज्ञ m. sacrifice to men, i.e. hospitality.
नृलोक m. the world of men, the earth.
नृवत् adv. like a man, strongly, bravely.
नृवन्त् a. manly, having or belonging to men.
नृवराह m. the man-boar (Viṣṇu).
नृवाहण & नृवाहस् a. carrying men.
नृवीर m. (man-)hero.
नृशंस a. cursing or wronging men, malicious, base (also °वन्त्); abstr. °ता f.
नृशंसहृदय a. cruel-hearted, mischievous.
नृशंस्य a. = नृशंस; n. as abstr.
नृशृङ्ग n. a man's horn, non-entity.
नृषच् (°षाच्) a. friendly to men, kind.
नृषद् a. dwelling in or among men.
नृषदन n. assemblage or residence of men.
नृषद्मन् & नृषद्वन् a. = नृषद्.
नृषह (°षाह्) a. conquering men.
नृषह्य n. abstr. to prec.
नृषा a. winning or procuring men.
नृषाति n. abstr. to prec.
नृषाह्य a. = नृषह; n. = नृषह्य.
नृषूत a. impelled by men.

नृसिंह m. man-lion, a great hero or Viṣṇu; a man's name.
नृहन् a. man-killing.
नृहरि m. = नृसिंह.
नेक्षण n. a sharp stick or fork.
नेजक m. a washerman.
नेजन n. washing, cleansing.
नेतव्य a. to be carried or brought.
1नेतृ a. leading or (as 3^d fut.) he will lead also = seq.
2नेतृ m. leader, guide, conductor, bringer, inflicter (दण्डस्य); f. नेत्री.
नेतृत्व n. abstr. to prec.
नेत्र m. leader, guide (only adj. —°); a man's name; n. नेत्रं guidance, conduct, the eye.
नेत्रगोचर a. within range of sight, visible.
नेत्रचपल a. restless with the eyes.
नेत्रज a. coming from the eyes.
नेत्रजल & °वारि n. tears (lit. eye-water).
नेत्राञ्जन n. ointment for the eyes, collyrium.
नेत्रोत्सव m. delight of the eyes, beautiful sight.
1नेद्, नेदति w. अति overflow.
2नेद् indecl. not, by no means; that not, lest (w. conj., opt., or imper.).
नेदिष्ठ (superl.) the nearest, very near; n. adv. very nearly, next.
नेदिष्ठतम (superl.) the nearest of all; °तमाम् adv.
नेदीयंस् (compar.) nearer, quite near; n. adv.
नेपथ्य n. ornament, decoration, attire, dress, adj. —° dressed in, adorned with; also = seq., loc. behind the scene.
नेपथ्यगृह n. tiring-room, postscenium.
नेपथ्यसवन n. a cert. ceremony.
नेपाल m. N. of a country & (pl.) a people.
नेम adj. the one, some; नेम—नेम the one—the other; half (°—).
नेमंधिति f. (only loc. °ता) discord, conflict, seclusion.
नेमि f. the circumference of a wheel; rim, edge i.g.
नेमिशब्द m. noise of carriage-wheels.*
नेय a. to be carried, brought, passed (time); to be guessed (rh.).

नेयार्थ & °**क** a. the meaning of which is only to be guessed, not evident (rh.).
नेष्ट a. not wished for, unpleasant.
नेष्टृ m. one of the chief priests at a Soma sacrifice.
नेष्ट्र n. the Soma vessel or office of the Neṣṭṛ (cf. prec.).
नैक a. not one, i.e. many, several.
नैकट्य n. proximity, neighbourhood.
नैकधा adv. manifoldly, in various ways or parts.
नैकरूप a. multiform, various.
नैकवर्ण a. many-coloured.
नैकविकल्प & °**विध** a. manifold, different.
नैकशस् adv. repeatedly, often.
नैकृतिक a. dishonest, mean, wicked.
नैगम, f. **ई** relating to Vedic quotations or the Veda itself, Vedic. m. an interpreter of the Veda; means, expedient; citizen, trader.
नैघण्टुक a. mentioned by the way; n. = **निघण्टु**.
नैत्यक a. constant, perpetual, regular.
नैत्यिक a. the same.
नैदाघ, f. **ई** belonging to the hot season, summer-like; m. summer time.
नैदाघिक & **नैदाघीय** a. = prec. adj.
नैद्र a. relating to sleep.
नैधन a. having an end, perishable, relating to death, death's; n. decay, death.
नैपुण & °**ण्य** n. cleverness, skill.
नैबिड्य n. closeness, uninterruptedness.
नैमित्तिक, f. **ई** having a cause, as s. effect (cf. **निमित्त°**); having some particular cause, occasional, accidental. — m. fortune-teller, soothsayer.
नैमिष n. N. of a sacred forest, m. pl. its inhabitants.
नैमिषारण्य n. = prec. n.
नैमिषीय a. relating to the Naimiṣa forest; m. pl. = **नैमिष** m. pl.
नैयग्रोध a. belonging to or made of the Indian fig-tree.
नैयमिक a. fixed, regular.
नैयायिक a. belonging to the Nyāya system; m. an adherent of it.
नैरन्तर्य n. uninterruptedness, close succession, immediate consequence.
नैरपेक्ष्य n. disregard, indifference.
नैरर्थ्य n. meaninglessness.
नैराश्य n. hopelessness, despair.
नैरुक्त a. based on etymology, explained etymogically; m. etymologist.
नैरुज्य n. health.
नैर्ऋत, f. **ई** belonging or consecrated to Nirṛti (also **नैर्ऋत्य**); m. a child of N., demon, Rakṣas; n. E. of a lunar mansion.
नैर्गन्ध्य n. inodorousness.
नैर्गुण्य n. want of qualities or virtues.
नैर्घृण्य n. pitilessness, cruelty.
नैर्धन्य n. want of property, poverty.
नैर्मल्य n. stainlessness (lit. & fig.).
नैर्लज्ज्य n. shamelessness, impudence.
नैवार a. consisting or made of wild rice.
नैवेद्य n. offering of eatables to a deity.
नैवेशिक n. furniture of a house.
नैश, f. **ई** nocturnal, nightly.
नैशिक, f. **ई** the same.
नैश्चिन्त्य n. absence of care or anxiety.
नैःश्रेयस, (f. **ई**) & °**सिक** a. giving supreme bliss.
नैषध m. a prince of the Niṣadhas, esp. Nala; pl. the Niṣadhas. n. T. of a poem about Nala.
नैषधीय & °**चरित** n. = prec. n.
नैषाद, f. **ई** belonging to the Niṣāda; m. a Niṣāda.
नैष्कर्म्य n. exemption from acts, inactivity.
नैष्किंचन्य n. want of anything, poverty.
नैष्कृतिक v. **नैकृतिक**.
नैष्ठिक, f. **ई** forming the end, last, definitive; highest, perfect, complete.
नैष्ठुर्य n. severity, harshness.
नैष्फल्य n. fruitlessness, uselessness.
नैसर्ग & °**र्गिक** a. natural, original.
नैःस्नेह्य n. absence of love, unkindness.
नैःस्व्य n. want of property, poverty.
नो (**न** + **उ**) adv. neither, nor; not.
नोत् adv. almost, nearly.
नोद m. = seq. n.
नोदन a. & n. pushing, impelling, driving away.

नोदिन् a. (—°)=prec. adj.
नोधस् m. N. of a Rishi.
नोधा (=नवधा) adv. ninefold.
नोनुव a. sounding.
नोपलक्षित a. not perceptible.
नोपस्थातृ & °स्थायिन् a. not appearing (in court).
1नौ acc., dat., & gen. du. of pron. of 1st pers.
2नौ f. ship, boat, vessel.
नौक (adj. —°)=prec.; f. आ small boat or ship.
नौकर्णधार m. helmsman, pilot.
नौकर्मन् n. the occupation of a boatsman; °मजीविन् a. living as a b.
नौचर a. going in a ship; m. sailor.
नौजीविक m. sailor, boatsman.
नौबन्धन n. N. of the highest peak of the Himālaya.
नौयान n. going in a ship, navigation; vessel.
नौयायिन् a. going in a boat; m. a passenger.
नौव्यसन n. shipwreck.
न्यक्कार m., न्यक्कृति f. bringing down, humiliation, contempt.
न्यग्भाव m degradation, debasement.
न्यग्भावन n.=न्यक्कार.
न्यग्रोध m. the Indian fig-tree (lit. growing downwards).
न्यङ्क m. du. cert. parts of a carriage.
न्यङ्कु m. a kind of deer.
न्यङ्ग m. something clinging or adhering; mark, sign; offensiveness, invective.
न्यच्छ n. mole or spot on the body.
न्यञ्च् (नीच्, f. नीची) directed downwards, going down, deep (l. & f.); n. न्यक् adv. downwards, down, w. कृ bring down, humiliate, contemn, w. भू humble one's self.
न्यञ्चन n. hollow, recess, hiding-place; f. ई the lap.
न्यन्ते (loc.), न्यन्तेन (instr.) adv. near, close to (—°).
न्ययन n. entrance or receptacle.
न्यर्ण a. waterless.
न्यर्थ n. destruction, ruin.
न्यसन n. casting down; putting, placing, mentioning.
न्यस्त a. thrown down, put aside, stretched or laid out, mystically touched, leaned upon, put on or donned, applied to (—°).
न्यस्तदण्ड & °शस्त्र a. harmless, peaceful (lit. having laid down the stick or the weapons).
न्यस्तव्य & न्यस्य a. to be put (down).
न्यह्न (only loc.) the closing day.
न्याचम् ger. lowering, bending down.
न्याय m. norm, standard (lit. that to which a thing goes back); rule, axiom, method; manner, way, esp. the right way, fitness, propriety; law-suit, judicial sentence, judgment; logical argument, syllogism, N. of a phil. system. — Instr. & abl. in the right way, regularly, duly (also °—); in the way or after the manner of (—°).
न्यायवन्त् & न्यायवर्तिन् a. acting rightly, behaving properly.
न्यायवादिन् a. speaking properly.
न्यायविद्या f. logic.
न्यायवृत्त a.=न्यायवन्त्.
न्यायशास्त्र n. manual of logic.
न्याय्य a. regular, customary, usual; proper, fit to (infin. w. pass. sense); n. adv.
न्यास m. putting in, placing, settling; putting down, writing, painting; depositing, deposit, pledge (j.); giving up, abandoning, renunciation.
न्यासधारिन् m. the holder of a deposit, depositary (j.).
न्यासी w. कृ deposit a thing with a person.
न्युब्ज a. turned downwards, lying on the face.
न्यूङ्ख m. the insertion of the sound O into the recitation.
न्यून a. wanting, incomplete, defective, inferior, smaller, less by (instr. or —°), less than (abl.); low, vile.
न्यूनय्, °यति lessen, diminish.
न्यूनाधिक a. too little or too much; n. as subst. (also °क्य n.).
न्यूनी w. कृ lessen, diminish.
न्योकस् a. delighting in, used to (—°); homely, comfortable.
नृधीश m. lord of men, king.
न्वै (=नु वै) adv. really, indeed.

प

1प (—°) drinking.
2प (—°) protecting, keeping.
पक्तव्य a. to be cooked or baked.
पक्ति or पंक्ति f. cooking, food, digestion, ripening (fig. = bearing consequences), development.
पक्तिदृष्टि f. du. digestive organs and sight.
पक्तृ m. who cooks or bakes.
पकथ m. N. of a man, pl. of a people.
पक्व a. cooked, prepared (on fire), ripened, matured, developed (abstr. °ता† f.); n. = seq.
पक्वान्न n. cooked food.
पक्वेष्टक a. made of burnt bricks; f. आ a burnt brick.
पक्ष m. wing, feather, flank or side, half, esp. of the month, a fortnight; party, faction, troop, class; one of two cases, alternative (पक्षे on the other hand, —° with regard to); supposition, statement, thesis, the subject of a syllogism; action, law-suit. Abstr. °ता† f., °त्व† n.
पक्षक (adj. —°) wing.
पक्षग्रहण n. abstr. to seq.
पक्षग्राह & °ग्राहिन् a. choosing a party.
पक्षद्वार (& °क*) n. a side- or inner door.
पक्षधर a. maintaining the party of (gen.), adhering to (loc.); m. bird.
पक्षपात m. moult or flight (lit. the falling or flying of the wings), partisanship (lit. the falling to one side) predilection for (loc., gen., प्रति, or —°).
पक्षपातिन् a. flying, partial to (loc. *or —°); abstr. °तिता f.
पक्षपुच्छ n. pl. wings and tail.
पक्षवन्त् a. winged or belonging to a party.
पक्षविकल a. with lamed wings.
पंक्षस् n. wing, side.
पक्षान्त m. the end of the wings of an army or the last day of a fortnight.
पक्षाभास m. feigned or ungrounded lawsuit; abstr. °त्व n.
पक्षिन् a. winged (lit. & fig.); taking the side of, partial to (—°). m. bird; f. °णी a female bird, ± रात्रि a night with the preceding and following day.
पक्षिमृगता f. the condition of a bird or of a beast.
पक्षिराज् & °राज m. the king of the birds (E. of Garuḍa or Jaṭāyu).
पक्षिशावक m. young bird, birdling.
पक्षिस्वामिन् & पक्षीन्द्र m. = पक्षिराज्.
पक्षोत्तर s. cover formed by the wings.
पंक्ष्मन् n. eyelash.
पक्ष्मल a. having (strong or long) eyelashes, hairy, shaggy i.g.; °नेत्र having eyes with long eyelashes.
पक्ष्य a. being in the wings; changing by halves or half-months; belonging to the party of (—°).
पंङ्क s. mud, dirt.
पङ्कच्छिद् m. N. of a plant, whose fruit is used to clear water (lit. destroying mud).
पङ्कज n. a kind of lotus (lit. mud-born).
पङ्कजजन्मन् m. E. of Brahman (lotus-born).
पङ्कवन्त्, पङ्किन्, & पङ्किल a. muddy.
पङ्केरुह & °रुह n. = पङ्कज.
पङ्क्ति & पङ्क्ती f. a set or row of five; group, troop, assembly, party; a kind of metre.
पङ्क्तिक्रम m. successive order.
पङ्क्तिपावन a. purifying or adorning a society.
पङ्गु (f. पङ्ग्वी) lame (also °क); abstr. °ता f., °त्व n.
पच्, पंचति, °ते cook, bake, boil, roast, burn (bricks), digest; mature, ripen, develop (trans., पंच्यते intr.); P. पच्यंते be cooked etc., also intr. = पंच्यते. C. पाचयति, °ते cook or cause to cook (tr.), bring to maturity or perfection. — परि P. be cooked or roasted, grow mature (lit. & fig.), bear results. वि cook thoroughly; P. be cooked or digested, ripen i.e. have results (of an action).

पच a. cooking, boiling, roasting (—°).
पचत॑ a. cooked; n. cooked food.
प॑चन a. cooking, roasting (—°); n. the act of or an instrument for cooking. also = **पचना** f. ripening, maturing.
पचेलिम a. cooking or ripening quickly.
पच्छस् adv. by Pādas or hemistichs.
पच्छौच n. cleansing the feet.
पज्र॑ a. solid, stout, sturdy; m. N. of a race of Rishis.
पज्रिय॑ a. belonging to the Pajras, E. of Kakṣīvant.
पञ्चक a. consisting of five, five days old, etc.; w. **शत** n. five per cent. — m. a man's name; f. **पञ्चिका** a book of 5 chapters; n. aggregate of five.
पञ्चकृत्वस् adv. five times.
पञ्चकृष्णलक a. equal to five Kṛṣṇalas.
पञ्चकोण m. a pentagon.
पञ्चगव्य n. the five (products) of the cow, i.e. milk, sour milk, butter, urine, & dung.
प॑ञ्चचत्वारिंशत् f. forty-five.
पञ्चजन॑ m. the five (classes of) beings, i.e. gods, men, Gandharvas, Apsaras, serpents, & Manes.
पञ्चतन्त्र & **°क** n. T. of a collection of fables (lit. having five divisions or books).
1**पञ्चतपस्** n. the five fires (i.e. four fires and the sun).
2**पञ्चतपस्** a. exposed to the five fires.
पञ्चतय, f. **ई** fivefold.
पञ्चता f. fivefoldness, also = **पञ्चत्व**.
पञ्चत्रिंश॑ a. the thirty-fifth.
प॑ञ्चत्रिंशत् & **पञ्चत्रिंशति** f. thirty-five.
पञ्चत्व n. the five elements or the dissolution of the body into them, i.e. death.
पञ्चथ a. the fifth.
पञ्चदण्डच्छत्त्रप्रबन्ध m. T. of a tale.
पञ्चदश॑, f. **ई** the fifteenth, increased by or consisting of 15; f. **ई॑** the 15th day.
पञ्चदशकृत्वस् adv. fifteen times.
पञ्चदशधा adv. in or into 15 parts.
प॑ञ्चदशन् a. fifteen.
पञ्चदशर्च॑ a. consisting of 15 verses.
पञ्चदशवार्षिक a. fifteen years old.
पञ्चदशाह m. a period of 15 days, a. **°हिक**.
पञ्चदशिन् a. consisting of 15 parts.
पञ्चधा॑ adv. in five parts or ways.
पञ्चधातु n. sgl. the five elements.
प॑ञ्चन् or **पञ्च॑न्** a. five.
पञ्चनख a. having five nails or claws; m. a five-toed animal.
पञ्चनद n. the (country of the) five rivers, the Pañjāb; m. pl. the inhabitants of it.
प॑ञ्चनामन् (f. **°नाम्नी**) having five names.
प॑ञ्चपञ्चाशत् f. fifty-five.
पञ्चपट्टिक m. N. of a man.
प॑ञ्चपद a. containing five verses.
प॑ञ्चपाद a. five-footed.
पञ्चबाण m. the god of love (lit. the five-arrowed).
पञ्चभूत n. pl. the five elements.
पञ्चम॑, f. **ई॑** fifth or forming the fifth part, w. **अंश** m. a fifth. — f. **ई** the fifth day of the half month, the fifth case & his endings (g.); n. a fifth, adv. for the fifth time, fifthly.
पञ्चमाषिक a. amounting to five Māṣas.
पञ्चमास्य a. containing five months.
पञ्चमुख a. having five faces or points.
1**पञ्चरात्र** m. five days (nights).
2**पञ्चरात्र॑** a. lasting five days.
पञ्चर्च॑ a. containing five verses.
पञ्चवक्त्र a. five-faced; m. E. of Çiva.
पञ्चवर्ग॑ m. a group of five.
पञ्चवर्ण a. five-coloured, many-coloured.
पञ्चवर्ष, **°क**, **°वर्षीय**, & **°वार्षिक** a. five years old.
पञ्चविंश॑, f. **ई** the twenty-fifth or consisting of twenty-five.
पञ्चविंशत् & **प॑ञ्चविंशति** f. twenty-five.
पञ्चविंशब्राह्मण n. T. of a Brāhmaṇa.
प॑ञ्चविध or **पञ्च॑विध** a. of five kinds.
पञ्चशत a. five hundred (pl.), amounting to 500 (fine) or fined 500; the 500th, **°ते काले** in the 500th year. — n. 105 or 500, f. **ई** 500, a period of 500 years.
पञ्चशर m. = **पञ्चबाण**.
पञ्चशस् adv. five by five.
पञ्चशाख a. five-fingered; m. the hand.
पञ्चशीर्ष a. five-headed.
पञ्चष pl. five or six.

पञ्चसहस्री f. sgl. five thousand.
पञ्चसांवत्सरिक & **पञ्चहायन** a. five years old.
पञ्चांश m. the fifth part.
पंञ्चाक्षर a. five-syllabled.
1**पञ्चाग्नि** (°—) the five sacred fires.
2**पञ्चाग्नि** a. maintaining the five sacred fires or exposing one's self to them.
पञ्चाङ्ग (°—) five limbs, members, or parts; a. having five limbs, members, or parts.
पञ्चात्मक a. consisting of the five elements, abstr. °त्व n.
पञ्चाब्दाख्य a. so called for ten years.
पञ्चाभ्यधिक a. best of five.*
पञ्चामृत n. sgl. & pl. the five kinds of divine food or the five elements.
पंञ्चार a. having five spokes.
पञ्चाल m. pl. N. of a warrior-tribe.
पञ्चावयव a. five-membered.
पञ्चाशक a. pl. fifty; f. °शिका T. of sev. works.
पञ्चाशत् f. fifty.
पञ्चाशद्भाग m. the fiftieth part.
पञ्चास्य a. five-faced or five-pointed.
पञ्चिन् a. fivefold.
पञ्ची w. **कृ** render fivefold; abstr. °करण n.
पञ्चेन्द्रिय a. having five organs.
पञ्चेषु m. = **पञ्चबाण**.
पञ्जर n. cage, skeleton.
पञ्जरकपिञ्जल, °**कपोत**, & °**शुक** m. a partridge, a dove, and a parrot kept in a cage.*
पञ्जिका f. a kind of commentary.
पञ्जो f. almanac, calendar.
पट्, **पटति** split, burst, open (intr.). C. **पाटयति** cause to split etc., break asunder, rend, tear, cut off, hurt, injure. — **अव** C. split, tear asunder, open. **उद्** & **समुद्** C. the same + expel, remove, dethrone. **वि** split, tear, rend, divide, root out, remove, drive away.
पट m. (woven) cloth, blanket, garment; picture, image of (—°); f. **ई** piece of cloth, screen, curtain (d.).
पटगत a. painted on cloth.
पटच्चर m. thief, robber.
1**पटर** m. or n. ray (of sunlight).
2**पटर** m. E. of Varuṇa.
पटल n., **ई** f. cover, veil, screen, roof, basket, chest, heap, mass, multitude; n. & m. division, section, chapter of a book.
1**पटवास** m. cloth, tent.
2**पटवास** (& *°**क**) m. perfumed powder.
पटवेश्मन् n. tent (house of cloth).
पटह m. (f. **ई** & n.) kettle-drum, abstr. °**ता** f.
पटहघोषक m. crier who beats a drum.
पटहघोषणा f. proclamation by sound of a drum.
पटाञ्चल & **पटान्त** m. the edge of a garment.
पटि & **पटिका** f. a kind of woven cloth.
पटिष्ठ (superl.) most clever with (—°).
पटीक्षेप m. tossing up the curtain.
पटीयंस् (compar.) very clever in (—°) or fit for (loc. or —°).
पटीर m. the sandal tree.
पटु a. sharp, pointed, pungent, acute, fierce; piercing (ray of light), clear, shrill (sound); violent, strong, intense; clever, skilful in, fit for (loc. or —°); n. adv. — m. N. of a man, pl. of a people.
पटुता f., °**त्व** n. sharpness, cleverness.
पटुमति a. sagacious.
पटोत्तरीय n. upper garment (of cloth).
पटोल m. a kind of cucumber.
पटौर m. a cert. member of the body.
पट्ट m. plate, tablet; cloth, bandage, ligature, frontlet, turban (cf. **पट**).
पट्टक m., **पट्टिका** f. plate, tablet, cloth, bandage; n. also patent, document.
पट्टदोल n. or °**ला** f. a swing made of cloth.*
पट्टन n. town, city.
पट्टांशुक n. a kind of garment.*
पट्टिश m. a kind of spear, p. °**शिन्**.
पठ्, **पठति** (°**ते**) read aloud, recite, rehearse; teach, mention; repeat to one's self, study, learn from (abl.). C. **पाठयति** teach to talk or read, teach i.g. (2 acc.); read, peruse. I. **पापठीति** & **पापठ्यते** recite often, read or study diligently. — **अनु** speak after, repeat. **परि** enumerate, name, mention. **प्र** recite aloud; C. teach, explain. **वि** & **सम्** read, peruse.
पठक m. reader, reciter.

पठन n. reciting, studying.
पठनीय & पठितव्य a. to be studied or read.
पठितसिद्ध a. effective while being (only) uttered.
पड्बीश, पड्वीश, & पड्विंश n. fetter (esp. for a horse); fettering or halting-place.
पण्, पणते (°ति), pp. पणित (q.v.) bargain, barter, buy; bet, wage, stake, risk, play for (gen.); win a thing (instr.) from (acc.) at play. — वि sell; bet, stake (gen.).
पण m. bargain, stipulation, contract; play, game, bet, wager; the thing staked, deposited, or agreed upon; a cert. coin.
पणन n. purchasing, bartering.
पणबन्ध m., °न n. making a treaty, stipulation.
पणयितृ m. seller.
पणव m. a kind of drum.
पणस्त्री f. venal woman, harlot.
1पणाय्, infin. °यितुम् sell.
2पणाय्, °यति, °ते worship, revere.
पतायितृ m. seller.
पणाय्य a. to be praised, venerable.
पणि m. bargainer, niggard, a stingy sacrificer or a malicious demon.
पणित a. & m. having betted, a better; n. bet, wager, stake.
पणितृ m. trader, seller.
पणी w. कृ lay at stake, risk.
पण्ड, पण्डक, & पण्डग m. eunuch, weakling.
पण्डित a. learned, educated, wise, clever in, familiar with (—°); m. scholar, teacher. — Abstr. °त्व† n.
पण्डितगर्व m. pride in wisdom.*
पण्डितमानिक & °मानिन् a. thinking one's self learned or clever, self-conceited.
पण्डितंमन्य & °मन्यमान a. the same.
पण्ड्र & °क m. = पण्ड etc.
1पण्य a. to be sold, vendible; n. article of trade, ware (poss. °वन्त्†); traffic, business; warehouse, shop.
2पण्य a. to be praised.
पण्यजन m. trader.
पण्यभूत a. forming an article of trade.
पण्ययोषित् f. = पणस्त्री.
पण्यस्त्री & पण्याङ्गना f. = पणस्त्री.

पत्, पतति (°ते), pp. पतित (q.v.) fly, soar, rush; come down, descend, fall or sink (lit. & fig. ± अधस्), lose caste, rank, or position; fall or light upon (loc.); incur or get into (loc.); come to pass, happen. C. पातयति, °ते (& पतयति q.v.) cause to fly or fall, pour out or shed (water, tears, etc.); hurl, cast, throw; put, turn, direct to, impose or inflict upon (loc.); throw down, fell, ruin, cut off or asunder, divide (द्विधा); M. rush on, hasten. D. पिपतिषति & पित्सति being about to fly or to fall in. — अच्छ fly towards (acc.). अति fly or fall beyond or past. अनु fly to, through, or after; go after, follow, pursue. अन्तर् fly into (loc.). अभि fly or hasten near, go towards or against; fall down or upon, come into (acc.). C. throw on (dat. or loc.); throw down, kill. समभि rush upon (acc.). अव fly, jump, fall down or upon (acc.). आ fly or hasten near, fall into or upon (acc. or loc.); happen, occur, fall to one's (gen.) share. C. throw or cut down, let fall, shed (tears). अभ्या hasten near, rush upon (acc.). समा fly or hasten near, rush upon (acc.); come to, obtain; have sexual intercourse with (सह). उद् fly or spring up, come forth, rise, start, set out, escape. C. cause to fly up, lift, raise. अभ्युद् fly or jump up. C. cause to fly up to (acc.). समुद् fly or spring up (together) etc. = उद् S. उप fly near, hasten towards (acc. or loc.). नि fly down, alight, descend, fall or rush upon (acc. or loc.), get or fall into (loc.), tumble down, throw one's self down (पादयोस्); happen, occur (w. gen. = come into the mind*), fall to the share of (loc.), fall into ruin, be lost or in vain. C. cause to fall, let fall, drop, throw down; put in, turn upon (loc.); fell, destroy, kill; put down, establish (g.). प्रणि throw one's self down, bow to (acc., dat., or loc.). C. cause to fall down or bow. विनि fly, fall, rush, descend upon or into (loc.); attack, assail. C. throw down, cut off or split (the head), inflict (punishment); destroy, ruin, kill. संनि fly, fall, or descend upon (loc.); assemble, meet, encounter; come together with (instr. ± सह). C. throw down, shoot off; collect, unite, bring together. निस् & विनिस् fly or rush out, come forth, depart, retreat, escape. परा fly away or past, fall out or down, depart, escape, retreat, stay away, fail; fly along, hasten; come near, arrive. परि fly or run about, round, or to and fro; leap down from (abl.), rush or fall upon (loc.). C. cause to fall down, shoot off, throw into. प्र fly forth or along, hasten to (loc.); fall down, rush upon, come into (loc.). C. cause to flee, pursue. वि fly along or through; split, burst asunder (intr.). C. cause to fly away, shoot off; rend asunder, throw down, destroy, kill. सम् fly or rush together; meet, encounter (of friends & foes); hasten on or towards (acc.), come to, arrive at (acc. or loc.); fall down upon, get into (loc.), happen, pass, occur. C. hurl upon, throw down into (loc.).

पतग m. a winged animal, bird.

पतगपति & °**राज** m. the king of the birds, E. of Garuḍa.

पतगेश्वर m. = prec., also E. of Jaṭāyu.

पतंग a. flying; m. bird, insect, esp. grasshopper, butterfly, or moth (also **पतंग**).

पतंगर a. bird-like.

पतंगराज m. = **पतगराज**.

1**पतंगवृत्ति** f. rashness, temerity, lit. the way of a moth (attracted by a light).

2**पतंगवृत्ति** a. very thoughtless or rash (cf. prec.).

पतञ्चल m. N. of a man.

पतञ्जलि m. N. of a philosopher, grammarian, etc.

पतत्र n. wing, pinion, feather.

पतत्रिन् a. winged, feathered, flying; m. bird, horse, arrow.

पतत्रिराज् & **पतत्रिराज** m. = **पतगराज**.

पतद्ग्रह & **पतद्ग्राह** m. spitting-pot or alms-box (receiver of what falls).

पतन m. N. of a Rakṣas; n. flying, descending, rushing; getting into (loc.), ruin, fall (lit. & fig.).

पतनीय a. causing fall or the loss of caste; n. such a crime.

पतन्त a flying. m. a bird.

पतय्, **पतयति** fly, hasten, M. drive away or fell. — **अच्छ** & **आ** A. fly to (acc.). **वि** A. open, go or fly asunder.

पतयालु, °**यिष्णु**, & °**यिष्णुक** a. flying.

पतर & **पतरु** a. flying, fugitive.

पताका f. flag, banner; the flag or symbol of (—°).

पताकांशुक n. flag or banner (-cloth).

पताकादण्ड m. flag-staff.

पताकिन् a. having or bearing a flag; m. flag-bearer, flag, chariot, f. °**नी** army.

पति m. master, owner, ruler, lord, husband.

पतिंवरा f. choosing her husband.

पतिक (adj. —°) = **पति**.

पतिघातिनी & °**घ्नी** f. husband-slaying.

पतिजुष्ट a. loved by her husband.

पतित a. fallen, sunk, degraded, an outcast; often —° fallen from, at, or upon, got into. n. flying, flight.

पतितसावित्रीक a. having lost the Sāvitrī (r.).

पतितान्न n. food from an outcast.

पतितोत्थित a. fallen and risen (l. & f.).

पतित्व & °**त्वन** n. matrimony, wedlock.

पतिदेवता & °**देवा** f. a wife regarding her husband as a divinity.

पतिप्राणा f. a wife whose life is her husband.

पतिमती f. having a husband, married.

पतिलोक m. the husband's world (in a future life).

पतिवती & **पतिवत्नी** f. = **पतिमती**.

पतिव्रत n. devotion to a husband.

पतिव्रता f. a wife devoted or obedient to her husband.

पतिष्ठ (superl.) flying most or best.

पतिसेवा f. devotion to the husband.

पतीय्, °**यति** wish for a husband.

पतीयस् (compar.) w. **पत्** fly better or well.

पत्ततस् adv. = **पत्तस्**.

पत्तन n. town, city; m. pl. N. of a people.

पत्तवे dat. inf. to 1**पद्**.

पत्तस् adv. from or at the feet.

पत्ति m. foot-soldier, pedestrian; f. the smallest division of an army.

पत्तिक a. walking on foot.

पत्त्र n. wing, feather (also on the arrow), any vehicle as chariot, cart, horse etc.; the leaf of a tree or a leaf for writing on, paper, a letter or any written document; a thin plate of metal, blade.

पत्त्रक, f. पत्त्रिका wing or leaf (adj. —°).

पत्त्रच्छेदभक्ति f. interval between the veins of a leaf.*

पत्त्रच्छेद्य n. a piece of leaf.

*पत्त्रपाश्या f. a kind of ornament on the forehead.

पत्त्रभङ्ग m. figures or lines painted on the face or body.

पत्त्रय्, °यति, pp. पत्त्रित (q.v.) to feather.

पत्त्ररथ m. a bird (having wings as a vehicle).

पत्त्रल a. leafy.

पत्त्रलेखा f. = पत्त्रभङ्ग.

पत्त्रविशेषक m. the same.

पत्त्रशाक n. vegetables consisting of leaves, greens.

*पत्त्राङ्ग n. red sandal.

*पत्त्राङ्गुलि or °ली f. = पत्त्रभङ्ग.

पत्त्रारूढ a. written down (on a leaf).

पत्त्रावलि or °ली f. = पत्त्रभङ्ग.

पत्त्रित a. feathered (arrow).

पत्त्रिन् a. winged, feathered; m. bird, arrow.

पत्त्रोर्ण n. woven silk or a garment made of it; m. pl. N. of a people.

पत्नी f. mistress, lady, wife; abstr. °त्व† n.

पत्नीक (adj. —°) = prec.

पत्नीय्, °यति regard or treat as a wife.

पत्नीवन्त् a. having a wife or wives.

पत्मन् n. flight, path, way.

पत्य्, पत्यते be master, get possessed of, own (acc. or. instr.); partake of (loc.), be fit for, serve as (dat.).

पत्वन्, f. पत्वरी flying; n. flight.

पत्सुतःशी a. lying at the feet.

पत्सुतस् adv. at the feet.

पथ्, पथि, पन्थन् (nom. पन्थास्) path, road, course, way, manner; a cert. hell. — पन्थानं दा give the way to, go out of the way of (gen.). पथि in the way, on the journey; पथानेन in this way or manner.

पथ m. path, course, way (mostly a. —°).

पथि v. पथ्.

पथिक m. traveller, wanderer.

पथिकसार्थ m. company of travellers, caravan.

पथिकृत् a. preparing a path.

पथिपा, पथिरक्षस्, & °रक्षि a. protecting ways.

पथिष्ठा a. standing in or on a way.

पथिस्थ a. the same + being on the way, going.

पथेष्ठा a. = पथिष्ठा.

पथोपदेशक m. guide, leader (of the way).

पथ्य a. customary, normal, regular, suitable, fit, proper. n. fortune, good lock; hail to (gen. or dat.)! — f. पथ्या path, way; w. रेवती & स्वस्ति the rich path (personif. as the goddess of fortune).

1पद्, पद्यते (°ति), pp. पन्न (q.v.) fall, drop, fall out, sink down, perish; (mostly —°) go, step, tread; go to (acc.). C. पादयति, °ते bring to fall. — अति go beyond (acc.); transgress, neglect (also C.). अनु go after, follow, betake one's self to or into; get at, befall. अप escape. अपि enter. अभि approach, appear, betake one's self to or into, meet with (acc., r. loc.); catch, seize, overpower, master, undertake, accept. अव fall down or out; lose, be deprived or fall short of (abl.). आ come near, approach, enter; get into, meet with (acc.), esp. get in trouble, meet with an accident; happen, occur, be; एवमापद्यते so is it. C. cause to go or enter, bring to or into (acc.), esp. bring to fall, ruin, destroy; bring near, procure, occasion; get, obtain. अभ्या get into (acc.). प्रत्या come back, return. व्या perish, be lost; C. destroy, kill. समा attack, assail; get into (acc.); occur, appear. उद् come forth or out of (abl.), be born, happen, occur, appear, arise, begin. C. A. (M.) procreate, beget with (loc.), cause, effect, produce, bring forth; grow (plants or animals), spill (blood), kindle (fire). व्युद् originate (scil. from a root), have an etymology (g.). C. produce, cause; derive, trace back to a root (g.). समुद् come forth, be born of (loc.), happen, occur, present one's self. C. bring forth, effect, cause, produce. उप fall upon, attack; come near, approach (esp. for aid or insruction); get to or into (acc. or loc.), fall to the lot of (gen.); happen, occur, take place, appear as (nom.), turn to (dat.); be fit or right. C. bring about, cause, effect, arrange, prepare; make or appoint (2 acc.); present or furnish with (2 acc. or acc. of pers. & instr. of th.); give (also in marriage), offer, procure, bestow on (acc. of th. & dat., r. loc. of pers.); find out, ascertain, prove. अभ्युप approach, ask for help (acc.); endow or furnish with (instr.). नि lie down, rest; lie with (acc.); C. lay down, fell, destroy. अनुनि & उपनि (acc.) lie with. निस् come forth, spring up, arise, ripen, be accomplished. C.A.(M.) bring about, make ripe, prepare, accomplish, settle, decide. अभिनिस् come to, enter (acc.), come forth, appear. प्र come or resort to (acc.), visit, enter, get, obtain, meet with (acc.), undertake, begin; happen, take place, become, be; assent, agree. अनुप्र enter after (acc.), follow, obey. अभिप्र approach, enter, undertake, begin; get at, resort to (acc.). संप्र enter (together), repair or resort to (acc.); be accomplished or brought about. प्रति step to, enter upon, resort to, get at or into, meet with (acc.), undertake, begin; happen, take place; perform, accomplish, make = reddere (2 acc.), do anything to, behave towards (loc., gen., or acc.); find out, learn, understand, think, judge (w. अन्यथा falsely); accede, yield, consent, confess, promise, answer (± उत्तरम्). C. lead or bring to (acc.); get, procure; give (also in marriage) to, present, bestow on (2 acc. or acc. of th. & loc., dat., or gen. of pers.); cause, effect, produce; make clear, explain, teach, show. विप्रति go hither and thither, be perplexed or uncertain, waver. संप्रति go to, get at (acc.); obtain, recover; consent, agree, acknowledge; take for (2 acc.). वि fall asunder, go amiss, fail, perish, die. C. destroy, kill. सम् fall to, devolve upon (loc. or gen.); turn out well, succeed, prosper; come together, meet with, get at (acc. or instr.); arise, be born, become (nom. or dat. = turn out to be, be changed into). C. A. (M.) procure, furnish, present, provide (acc. of th. & dat. or gen. of pers. or acc. of pers. & instr. of th.); bring about, accomplish, make ready, prepare, transform, make into (2 acc.), get, obtain; agree, consent. अभिसम् be changed into, become like (acc.); get at, obtain (acc. or loc.). C. make into or like (acc.). उपसम् come to, arrive at (acc.). C. bring near, procure. — Cf. अवपन्न, आपन्न, उत्पन्न, उपपन्न, उपसंपन्न, निष्पन्न, प्रतिपन्न, प्रत्युत्पन्न, प्रत्युपपन्न, प्रपन्न, विपन्न, विप्रतिपन्न, व्युत्पन्न, समुत्पन्न, संपन्न.

2पद् (पाद्) m. (adj. —° f. पद् or पदी) foot, step, quarter.

पद n. (m.) step, pace, stride; footstep, vestige, mark; footing, stand-point, place, spot, position, station; office, (high) rank, dignity; object, cause, often adj. subject or obnoxious to (—°); foot (also as a measure of length), quarter of a stanza, line; word or a kind of base of a noun (g.); also = पदपाठ q.v. — पदेन on foot; पदे पदे at every step, everywhere; पदं दा (or पदात्पदं गम्*) make a step, stride; पदं कृ put the foot on or in, enter, occupy (loc.); C. bring together a person (acc.) with (loc. or acc. w. प्रति).

पदगति f. manner of going, gait.

पदज्ञ a. knowing (places), wise.

पदनी a. following the steps of (gen.).

पदनीय a. to be investigated; abstr. °त्व† n.

पदन्यास m. putting down the feet, tread, footmark.

पदपङ्क्ति f. = seq.; N. of a metre.

पदपद्धति f. a row of footsteps.

पदपाठ m. the word-recitation (of the Veda, cf. क्रम° & संहितापाठ).

पदपूरण a. & n. filling out a verse.
पदबन्ध m. poem (lit. = seq.).
पदरचना f. arrangement of words, literary composition.
पदवी m. (nom. **°वीस्**) leader, guide, usher; f. (nom. **°वी**) path, way, track; reach, range (of eyes, ears, etc.); position, rank. — **पदं पदव्यां** (w. gen. or —°) **धा** or **निधा** tread in the footstep of a person, i.e. rival with him.
पदवीय n. footstep, vestige.
पदशब्द m. the sound of footsteps.*
पदशस् adv. step by step or word by word.
पदश्रेणि f. = **पदपङ्क्ति**.
पदस्थ a. going (lit. standing) on foot; having a rank or position.
पदाक्रान्त a. following at one's heels.*
पदाङ्क m. footmark.
पदाति a. going on foot; m. pedestrian, foot-soldier.
पदादि m. the beginning of a verse or word.
पदानुग a. = **पदाक्रान्त** + suitable, agreeable to (—°); m. attendant, companion.
पदानुसार m. following at one's heels; **°रेण उपलभ्** overtake.*
पदान्त m. the end of a verse or word.
1**पदान्तर** n. a step's interval.
2**पदान्तर** n. another word.
पदार्थ m. the meaning of a word or the thing corresponding to it; thing, object, matter; man, person; category or predicament (ph.).
पद्धति f. footstep, track, way, path; leader, guide, guide-book.
पद्म m. n. lotus, esp. the flower (which closes at evening), fig. an army arrayed in the form of a lotus or a cert. posture of the body in religious meditation; one of the treasures of Kubera, a cert. high number (1000 billions).
पद्मक m. n. = prec., m. N. of a tree & a man.
1**पद्मगर्भ** m. the interior or calyx of a lotus.
2**पद्मगर्भ** a. containing lotuses or sprung from a lotus; m. N. of a lake, E. of Brahman, Viṣṇu, & Çiva.
पद्मगृहा f. E. of Lakṣmī (lit. the lotus-housed).
पद्मज m. E. of Brahman (cf. 2**पद्मगर्भ**).
पद्मता f. abstr. to **पद्म**.
पद्मदलेक्षण a. lotus (leaf-)-eyed.
पद्मनाभ m. E. of Viṣṇu (the lotus-naveled).
पद्मपाणि m. E. of Brahman (the lotus-handed).
पद्मपुर n. N. of a town.
पद्मपुराण n. T. of a Purāṇa.
पद्मभव & **पद्मभू** m. = **पद्मज**.
पद्ममय, f. **ई** made or consisting of lotus.
पद्मयोनि m. = **पद्मज**.
पद्मरति f. a woman's name.
पद्मराग m. a ruby (lotus-coloured).
पद्मवन्त् a. full of lotus-flowers; f. **°वती** N. of a woman and a town.
पद्मवर्चस् & **°वर्ण** a. lotus-coloured.
पद्मव्याकोश a. lotus-blossom or flower.
पद्मशस् adv. by thousands of billions.
पद्मषण्ड n. a group of lotuses.
पद्मसंभव m. = **पद्मज**.
पद्मसरस् n. lotus-lake.
पद्माकर m. lotus group or pond.
पद्माक्ष, f. **ई** lotus-eyed; m. E. of Viṣṇu.
पद्मादित्व n. the being a lotus-flower etc.
पद्मालय m. E. of Brahman (the lotus-housed).
पद्मावती f. = **पद्मवती**.
1**पद्मासन** n. lotus-seat.
2**पद्मासन** m. E. of Brahman (the lotus-seated).
पद्मिन् a. spotted (elephant); f. **°नी** the lotus plant or a lotus pond.
पद्मिनीखण्ड n. a multitude of lotuses.
पद्मिनीपत्त्र n. a lotus-leaf.
पद्मोद्भव m. = **पद्मज**.
पद्य a. relating to the foot or consisting of parts of verses; f. **आ** pl. footsteps, horses' hoofs; n. verse, poetry (opp. **गद्य**).
पद्यमय a. consisting of verses.
पद्र m. a village.
पद्वन्त् a. having feet, running; n. such an animal.
पन्, **पनते**, pp. **पनित** be wonderful; admire, praise, commend. C. **पनयति**, **°ते** = S. tr.; M. also rejoice at, be glad of (acc. or gen.). — **आ** admire, praise. **वि** P. pride one's self.
पनयाय्य a. admirable. wonderful.
पनस m. the bread-fruit tree, N. of a monkey.
पनस्य्, **°स्यते** show one's self admirable or glorious.

पनस्यु a. glorious or boastful.
पनाय्य a. = **पनयाय्य**.
पनितृ a. praising, welcoming.
पनिष्ठ (superl.) very admirable or glorious.
पनीयंस् (compar.) more or very glorious.
पनु or **पनू** f. admiration, praise.
पन्थन् v. **पथ्**.
पन्न s. creeping on the ground.
पन्नग m., **ई** f. serpent or s.-demon (cf. prec.).
पन्नगनाशन m. E. of Garuḍa (serpent killer).
पन्नगभोजन m. E. of Garuḍa (serpent-eater).
पन्नगराज m. the serpent-king.
पन्नगारि m. E. of Garuḍa (enemy of serpents).
पन्नगेन्द्र & **°गेश्वर** m. = **पन्नगराज**.
पन्य a. wonderful, glorious.
पन्यंस् a. = **पनीयंस्**.
पपि a. drinking (acc.).
पपुरि a. liberal, abundant.
पपृक्षेण्य a. desirable.
1**पप्रि** a. liberal, granting (gen. or acc.).
2**पप्रि** a. leading over, saving.
पम्पा f. N. of a river and a lake.
पयःपूर m. flood or jet of water.
पयस् n. juice, fluid, esp. water or milk; semen virile, strength, vital power; pl. drops, floods, streams.
पयस्पा a. drinking milk.
पयस्य a. made of milk; f. **°स्या** curds.
पयस्वन्त् a. juicy, succulent, liquid, milky; exuberant, strong.
पयस्विन् a. succulent, milky; f. **ई** a milch-cow.
पयोग्रह m. oblation of milk.
पयोद a. giving milk or water; m. cloud.
पयोदुह a. giving milk or semen.
पयोधर m. a cloud or a woman's breast (water- or milk-holder).
पयोधा a. sucking milk.
पयोधारा f. stream of water; **°गृह** n. bathing-room.
पयोधि & **पयोनिधि** m. the ocean (receptacle of waters).
पयोभृत् m. a cloud (water-holder).
पयोमय a. consisting of water.
पयोमुख a. showing milk on the surface.
पयोमुच् a. yielding milk (water); m. cloud.
पयोराशि m. the sea (mass of water).
पयोवाह m. a cloud (water-bearer).
पयोवृध् a. succulent, overflowing, exuberant.
पयोव्रत a. living on mere milk (r.).
पयोष्णी f. N. of a river.
पर a. far, distant, different; either in space, i.e. remote, opposite, foreign, hostile — or in time, i.e. past, previous, former, ancient, old; subsequent, future, later, last, extreme; —or in number, order, & degree, i.e. exceeding, more than; following, standing after, worse, worst; surpassing, superior, better, best (in the compar. mgs mostly w. abl. or —°). — m. another, stranger, foe, the supreme Spirit, the Absolute, a man's name. n. remotest distance, highest point or degree, final beatitude; chief matter or occupation, esp. adj. —° quite consisting of, filled with, devoted to, intent upon; as adv. & prep. beyond, after (abl.); hereafter, next, moreover, further (± **अतस्**, **इतस्**, or **ततस्**), excessively, beyond measure; at the best, at the utmost; at least, at any rate; but, however (± **तु** or **किं तु**). — Abstr. **परता** f., **°त्वं** n.
परकथा f. pl. talk about others.
परकार्य n. another's business.
परकीय a. belonging to another, strange, inimical; abstr. **°त्व** n.
परकृत्य n. = **परकार्य**.
परक्षेत्र n. another's field or wife.
परच्छिद्र n. another's fault or flaw.
परजन m. strangers.
परतस् adv. farther, thereafter, then, as prep. after, beyond, above (abl.); often = abl. of **पर**.
परत्र adv. elsewhere, in another world, hereafter (w. **भीरु** anxious about the other world); farther on, below.
परदार m. sgl. & pl. another's wife; adultery.
परदारिन् a. committing adultery.
परदारोपसेवन n., **°सेवा** f. intercourse with another's wife.
परदेश m. foreign or hostile country.
परदोषज्ञ a. knowing another's faults.
परद्रव्य n. another's property or goods.

परधन n. another's wealth.
परंतप a. vexing foes.
परपक्ष m. the party of the foe.
परपरिग्रह m. another's property or wife.
परपाक m. food or meal of a stranger.
परपिण्डपुष्टक m. who feeds on another's food, parasite.*
परपुरंजय a. conquering the foe's city or cities.
परपुरुष m. the husband of another woman.
परपुष्ट m., **आ** f. the Kokila or Indian cuckoo (lit. nourished by a stranger, sc. the crow).
परपूरुष m. = **परपुरुष**.
परपूर्वा f. a woman who has had a former husband, **°पति** m. the husband of such a woman.
परप्रेष्यत्व n. service (of another), slavery.
परभाग m. supremacy, excellency, might; abl. **°तस्**.
परभृत m. = **परपुष्ट**.
परभृतिका f. female Kokila, a woman's name.*
परम a. farthest, last, extreme, best or worst, highest, chiefest; surpassing, better or worse than (abl.). °— as adj. supreme, chief, adv. highly, exceedingly; —° = **पर**; n. **परमम्** yes, very well, with pleasure.
परमक (f. **°मिका**) a. utmost, best or worst.
परमत n. the opinion of others.
परमता f. the highest point, position, or rank.
परमदारुण a. most dreadful.
परमधर्मात्मन् a. very dutiful or virtuous.
परमपुंस् m. the supreme spirit (Viṣṇu).
परमप्रीत a. very glad.
परमर्षि m. an excellent Rishi.
परमसमुद्य a. quite perfect or satisfactory.
परमाक्षर n. the highest syllable (i.e. Om) or Brahman.
परमाणु m. infinitely small part or atom.
परमात्मन् m. the supreme spirit, the soul of the universe; abstr. **°त्मत्व**.
परमानन्द m. the highest bliss.
परमार्तवत् adv. very mournfully.
परमार्थ m. the highest or whole truth, reality (abstr. **°ता** f.). °—, instr., abl., & adv. in **तस्** really, truly (**°तः संकल्प्य** taking for real*).
परमेश m. the supreme lord, i.e. Viṣṇu.
परमेश्वर m. a rich or noble lord, a prince or king (abstr. **°ता** f., **°त्व** n.); also = prec. & E. of sev. gods, f. **ई** E. of Durgā.
परमेष्ठिन् a. standing in the highest place, chief, supreme; E. of sev. gods (esp. Prajāpati), heroes, or sages.
परमेष्वास m. an excellent archer; abstr. **°ता** f.
परंपर a. following one another, successive, repeated; f. **आ** uninterrupted series, thick mass, instr. in the course of, along (—°).
परलोक m. the other or future world.
परलोकहस्त a. sure of (lit. holding in the hand) the future world.*
परवत्ता f. abstr. to seq.
परवन्त् a. subject to another, powerless, helpless, beside one's self; dependent on, devoted to (loc., gen., or —°).
परवश a. subject to another's wish, dependent on another; mastered or ruled by (—°).
परवारण m. chaser of foes.*
परवीरहन् a. killing hostile heroes.
परशु m. hatchet, axe.
परशुमन्त् a. poss. to prec.
परशुराम m. E. of Rāma (R. with the axe).
परश्वध m. hatchet, axe; p. **°धिन्**.
परश्वस् adv. the day after to-morrow.
परःशत a. pl. more than a hundred.
परस् adv. beyond, on the other or opposite side, (as prep. w. acc., instr., or abl.); further, later, afterwards, in future; without, except (instr. or abl.); above, more than (acc., instr., or °— in numerals).
परस्तरम् or **°तराम्** adv. farther away.
परस्तात् adv. & prep. (w. gen.) beyond, on the other side, below or above, in future, later, after; afterwards, towards or away; from above, before, or behind.
परस्थान n. foreign place.
परस्पा protecting; n. = seq.
परस्पात्व n. protection.
परस्पर (only the obl. cases of m. sgl., n. & °— adv.) each other, one another, mutual(ly)
परस्परतस् adv. = abl. to prec.
परस्परादिन् a. eating each other.
परस्पा m. protector.

परस्मैपद n. the form for another, i.e. the active or transitive form of the verb.

परस्व n. another's property.

परस्वन्त् m. the wild ass.

परस्वादायिन् a. seizing another's property.

परःसहस्र or **परःसहस्र** a. more than a thousand.

परा adv. (only °— in subst. & verbs) away, off, forth.

पराक s. distance (only loc. & abl.); m. a kind of penance.

पराकात्तात् adv. from afar.

पराक्रम m. sgl. & pl. bold advance, courage, strength.

पराग m. sgl. & pl. the pollen of a flower (poss. °गिन्), dust i.g.

परागम m. the arrival or attack of an enemy.

पराग्वदन & °शालिन् a. = पराङ्मुख.

पराङ्ग n. the hinder part of the body.

पराङ्मनस् a. having the mind directed backwards.

पराङ्मुख, f. ई a. having the face turned backwards, averted, turned away; flying from, avoiding, shunning, not caring for (abl., loc., gen., प्रति w. acc., or —°); contrary, unfavourable. — n. adv., abstr. °ता f., °त्व n.

पराङ्मुखी w. कृ put to flight; w. भू take to flight, turn the back upon (gen.), be contrary or unfavourable.

पराचीन a. turned away, averted, opposite; not caring for, indifferent about (abl.); n. adv. beyond, away, after (as prep. w. abl.).

पराचैस् adv. away, aside, off.

पराजय m. conquest, victory (gen. or —°); defeat, deprivation, loss (abl. or —°).

पराजित a. conquered, overthrown; having lost (a lawsuit).

†**पराजिष्णु** a. succumbent or victorious.

पराञ्च् (f. पराची, n. पराक् & पराङ्) directed away, averted, opposite to, turning from (abl.), behind or after one another, following upon (abl.); departed, lost; turned outwards (the organs of sense); n. adv.

परातरम् adv. further away.

परात्मन् m. the supreme spirit.

परादद् a. giving up, delivering (acc.).

परादान n. the action of giving up.

पराधीन a. subject to another, dependent or intent upon, occupied with (—°); abstr. °ता f.

परानीक n. hostile troop.*

परानुदे (dat. inf.) to push away.

परान्त m. the final end, death.

परापर n. the far and near, more and less, better and worse, earlier and later, cause and effect; abstr. °ता f., °त्व n.

पराभव m. going away, parting, vanishing, disappearance, also = seq.

पराभाव m. defeat, humiliation.

पराभूति f. = prec.

परामर्श m. seizure, touch; attack, injury loc., gen., or —°); relation, insinuation, recollection, reflection, consideration, thought.

परायण n. going away, departure, last way or exit; final end or aim, last resort or refuge; essence, sum, chief matter; N. of a work. —° having a thing as highest object or occupation, i.e. quite filled with, devoted to, or intent upon (cf. पर). — Adj. violent, strong, being the last refuge or essential matter of, conducive to, dependent on (gen.).

परायत्त a. dependent on, subject to (—°).

1**परार्थ** m. highest (or another's) advantage, interest, business, or matter. °—, acc. & loc. adv. for another's sake, for others.

2**परार्थ** a. having another object, dependent on another person or thing.

परार्थवादिन् a. speaking for another, representative (j.).

परार्ध m. the other or more remote side or half; the highest number (also n.).

परार्ध्य a. being on the other or more remote side or half; finest, best, most excellent; more excellent than (abl.).

परावत् f. distance.

परावर n. = परापर; also adj. more distant

and nearer, higher and lower, all-including; m. pl. ancestors and descendants.

परावृज् m. outcast.

पराशर m. destroyer, a man's name.

1**पराश्रय** m. dependence on others.

2**पराश्रय** a. dependent on others.

परासु a. dying or dead (lit. whose breath is going or gone out).

परासेध m. arrest, prison.

परास्य or **परास्य** a. to be cast away.

पराह्ण m. the afternoon.

परि adv. round, about (often °—, also to denote abundance or high degree); prep. round, about, against, opposite to, beyond, above, more than (acc.); from, out of, after, in consequence or on account of, according to (abl.); *around i.e. outside or with exception of (abl., also **परि परि**).

परिकर m. attendance, assistance, followers, servants, troop, multitude (also pl.); a girdle.

परिकर्मन् n. the being about or intent upon something, preparation for (—°), attendance, worship, veneration, care, esp. of the body, as anointing, perfuming, toilet i.g.

परिकर्मिन् m. assistant, servant.

परिकर्ष m., °**ण** n. dragging about.

परिकल्पना f. bringing about, contrivance.

परिकीर्तन n. proclaiming aloud, boasting.

परिकोप m. violent anger.

परिक्रम m., °**ण** n. walking about, roaming.

परिक्रय m. purchase, hire, wages.

परिक्रयण n. hiring, engaging.

परिक्रामितक (only instr.) walking about (d.).

परिक्लिन्न a. thoroughly wet.

परिक्लिष्ट a. much vexed or troubled, suffering, uneasy, weak; n. adv. unwillingly.

परिक्लेश m. vexation, hardship, fatigue.

परिक्लेष्टृ m. tormentor, torturer.

परिक्षत a. hurt, wounded.

परिक्षति f. hurting, wounding.

परिक्षय m. disappearing, decay, end.

परिक्षाम a. quite emaciated or exhausted.

परिक्षित् a. spreading or dwelling around; m. N. of an ancient king.

परिक्षीण a. exhausted, vanished, perished, brought down, poor, weak in (instr.).

परिक्षेप m. tossing about, moving to and fro; surrounding, enclosing.

परिखचित a. inlaid, set or strewed with (—°).

परिखा f. a ditch or trench round a town.

परिखिन्न a. wearied, annoyed.

परिखेद m. weariness, exhaustion.

परिगणन n., °**ना** f. accurate enumeration or statement.

***परिगणितिन्** a. thoroughly versed in (loc.).

परिगत a. gone round or through, diffused, spread; deceased, dead; surrounded by, endowed or affected with, possessed of (instr. or —°); known, learnt of (abl.).

परिगतार्थ a. acquainted with or initiated into a matter.

परिगम m. surrounding, extending; meeting, getting acquainted with, partaking of (—°)

परिगलित a. dropped down, sunk into (—°).

परिगाढम् adv. intensely, strongly.

परिगृह्य ger. along, with (lit. taking); without (lit. wanting).

परिगृहीत a. seized, received, connected with, possessed of (instr. or —°).

परिगृहीति f. taking together, comprehending.

परिग्रह m. surrounding, enclosing (lit. & fig.); putting on, assuming; taking or holding together, seizing, grasping; taking, receiving, getting, obtaining; acquisition, possession (adj. —° possessed of); undertaking, incurring, occupation or business with (loc. or —°); taking to, i.e. favouring, revering; honour, grace; taking to wife, marrying; wife (also coll.), household, family, attendants etc.

परिग्रहण n. putting on, wrapping round.

परिग्रहीतृ m. helper, assister, ruler, husband.

परिग्राह m. enclosure (of the Vedi).

परिग्लान a. wearied, exhausted; *averse to (dat.).

परिघ m. iron bar for locking a gate, du. gate; iron club, fig. obstacle, hindrance, esp. a current of clouds before the sun.

परिघस्तम्भ m. door-post.*

परिघर्म्य m. an implement for preparing the hot sacrificial beverage.

परिचर्चा f. rejection, disapproval.

परिचर्च्य a. to be rejected or disapproved.

1**परिचय** m. heaping up, accumulation.

2**परिचय** m. knowledge, acquaintance, familiarity or intercourse with (gen., loc., instr. ± **समम्**, or —°).

1**परिचयवन्त्** a. heaped up, accumulated; full, complete.

2**परिचयवन्त्** a. acquainted, familiar.

परिचर a. roaming about, moving, flowing. — m. companion, assistant; attendance, homage.

परिचरण m. servant, assistant; n. going about, attendance, service, devotion.

परिचर्य a. to be served or waited upon; f. **आ** = seq.

परिचार m. attendance, devotion.

परिचारक, f. **°रिका** male or female attendant.

परिचारिन् a. going about, movable, attending to, serving; m. servant.

1**परिचित** a. heaped up, increased, acquired, got; filled with i.e. containing (instr.).

2**परिचित** a. known, accustomed, familiar.

परिचिति f. acquaintance, familiarity.

परिच्छद m. cover, garment, dress, surroundings, domestic implements, baggage, retinue, train, attendants; adj. —° possessed of, covered or adorned with.

परिच्छन्न a. covered, filled, concealed, disguised.

परिच्छेद m. cutting, severing, separation, section, chapter of a book; discrimination, definition, decision, judgment.

परिजन m. servant, mostly coll. retinue, suite.

परिज्ञात a. known, learnt; known as (—°).

परिज्ञान n. perception, knowledge.

परिज्ञेय a. to be known or learnt.

परिज्मन् a. moving or being around; as loc. adv. round about, everywhere.

परिज्रि a. running or spreading round.

परिणत a. bent outwards or aside, altered, changed into (instr. or —°), developed, ripe, mature, abundant, advanced (age), full (moon), setting (sun), digested (food), faded, passed.

परिणति f. change, transformation, development, ripening, maturity, accomplishment; consequence, result, issue, end.

परिणद्ध a. bound or wrapt round; girt or encirled by (—°); broad, large.

परिणमयितृ a. ripening (gen.).

परिणय m., **°न** n. leading round (the sacred fire), marriage.

परिणाम m. change, alteration, transformation, development, evolution into (instr.), transformation of food i.e. digestion; fading, decay; course (of time), advancement (of age), old age; consequence, result, end. °— & loc. finally, at last.

परिणाममुख a. verging to the issue.*

परिणामिन् a. altering, subject to change.

परिणायक m. leader, husband (cf. **परिणीत**).

परिणाह m. compass, circumference, extent, width.

परिणाहवन्त् & **°हिन्** a. poss. to prec.

परिणीत n. marriage; f. **°ता** a married wife (lit. leading and led round, scil. the sacrificial fire).

परिणीतपूर्वा f. married before.

परिणेतृ m. husband (cf. **परिणीत**).

परितक्म्य a. causing anxiety, insecure, dangerous; f. **आ** danger, fear.

परितस् adv. round about, on all sides, everywhere; prep. round (acc., r. gen.).

परिताप m. glow, heat, pain, grief, sorrow, repentance.

परितापिन् a. burning, heat; causing pain or sorrow.

परितुष्ट a. much pleased by (instr.), very glad.

परितुष्टि f. high satisfaction, delight.

परितोष m. the same; poss. **°वन्त्** or **°षिन्**.

परितोषक a. satisfying.

परितोषण a. & n. the same.

परित्यक्त a. left by, deprived of, wanting (instr. or —°).

परित्यज्य (ger.) letting aside, i.e. at a distance from or with exception of (acc.).

परित्यक्तृ m. forsaker, deserter.

परित्याग m. leaving, quitting, abandonment, giving up, rejection, renunciation.

परित्यागिन् a. leaving, abandoning, forsaking, renouncing.

परित्याज्य a. to be left, abandoned, given up, renounced, omitted.

परित्रस्त a. frightened, afraid.

परित्राण n. protection, rescue from (abl.), refuge.

परित्रातव्य a. to be protected or defended.

परित्रातृ m. protector, defender.

परिदा f., **॰दान** n. giving one's self up, surrender, devotion.

परिद्यूर्ण a. dropsical.

परिदेव m. lamentation, wailing.

परिदेवित a. mournful, sad; n. lament.

परिदेविन् a. lamenting, wailing.

परिद्यून a. distressed, miserable.

परिधान or **॰धान** n. laying round, putting on, wrapping; garment, vesture.

परिधि m. enclosure, fence, wall; cover, garment; circumference, compass, horizon; fire-frame (r.).

परिधूसर a. quite gray or dusty.

परिध्वंस m. mischief, disaster, ruin, trouble; loss of caste (also f. **आ**), an outcast.

परिध्वंसिन् a. falling off or destroying.

परिध्वस्त a. covered with (—°); destroyed, annihilated.

परिनिन्दा f. strong censure.

परिनिर्मित a. measured, marked out, fixed, settled.

परिनिष्ठा f. extreme limit, highest point; completion, perfection.

परिनिष्ठित a. being in (loc.); thoroughly versed in or familiar with (loc.).

परिपक्व a. completely burnt (brick); quite ripe or mature.

परिपतन n. flying round.

परिपन्थिन् a. besetting the path; m. waylayer, opponent, enemy.

परिपाक m. being completely cooked or digested; ripening, maturity, perfection.

परिपाटि or **॰टी** f. succession, order.

परिपाठ m. complete enumeration.

परिपाण m. n. protection, refuge.

परिपाण्डु & **॰र** a. very pale or white.

परिपान n. drink, beverage.

परिपार्श्व a. being at one's side; **॰चर** & **॰वर्तिन्** a. going or standing near.

परिपालक a. guarding, protecting.

परिपालन n. protection, guard, nurture, maintenance, care (also f. **आ**).

परिपालनीय & **॰ल्य** a. to be protected or maintained.

परिपीडन n., **॰पीडा** f. squeezing, vexing, injuring.

परिपुष्ट a. nourished, fostered, cherished, increased, blessed or abundantly furnished with (instr. or —°).

परिपूत a. cleaned, husked; purified by (—°).

परिपूरक a. filling or causing fulness.

परिपूर्ण a. filled or covered with (—°), full, entire, complete, accomplished, attained.

***परिपूर्णता** f., **॰त्व** n. fulness.

परिपूर्णेन्दु m. the full moon.

परिपूर्ति f. getting full, completion.

परिपेलव a. very fine or delicate.

परिप्रश्न m. question, inquiry.

परिप्री a. dear, valued.

परिप्रुष् a. sprinkling, splashing.

परिप्रेप्सु a. wishing to obtain, desirous of (acc. or —°).

परिप्लव a. swimming, moving to and fro. m. ship, boat; wavering, unsteadiness, unquietness.

परिबाध् f. obstructor, hinderer.

परिबाधा f. trouble, pains.

परिबृंहण n. increase, addition; supplement.

परिबृढ v. **परिवृढ**.

परिभग्न a. broken, interrupted, troubled, prevented.

परिभव m. ill treatment, injury, humiliation, offence, transgression; disrespect, contempt for (loc., gen., or —°).

परिभवन n. humiliation, contempt.

परिभवनीय a. to be offended or humiliated.

परिभविन् a. injuring, humiliating, mocking.

परिभाव & **॰विन्** = **परिभव** & **॰विन्**.

परिभावुक a. contemning, humbling (acc.).

परिभाषण n. talk, conversation; blame, censure.

परिभाषा f. the same; a kind of rule (g.).

परिभाषेन्दुशेखर m. T. of a work.
परिभू a. being around, encompassing, pervading, ruling, superior.
परिभूति f. superior strength; humiliation, injury.
परिभोक्तृ m. enjoyer, parasite.
परिभोग m. enjoyment, esp. sexual intercourse; means of enjoyment, subsistence.
परिभोगिन् a. enjoying.*
परिभ्रंश m. escape.
परिभ्रंशन n. falling from, losing (abl.).
परिभ्रम m. going to and fro, roaming; digression.
परिभ्रमण n. moving round, circumference.
परिभ्रष्ट a. fallen down, dropped off, fallen from (abl.) upon or into (loc. or —°); sunk, ruined, vanished, gone, escaped from (abl.); abstaining from (—°), deprived or void of (abl. or —°).
परिभ्रामण n. turning round (trans.).
परिमण्डल n. circle, circumference; a. circular, round.
परिमन्थर a. very slow or tardy.
परिमन्द a. very tired or languid; abstr. °ता f.
परिमन्यु a. wrathful, angry.
परिमर m. dying around; w. ब्रह्मणः a cert. magical rite.
परिमर्द m. crushing, grinding.
परिमर्दन n. rubbing.
परिमर्श m. consideration, reflection.
परिमल m. fragrance, perfume.
परिमलय्, °यति (pp. °मलित*) to perfume.
परिमा f. measure in circumference.
परिमाण n. measuring, measure, compass, size, number, value; a. amounting to (—°).*
परिमाथिन् a. torturing, vexing.
परिमार्ग m., °ण n. searching, seeking for.
परिमार्जन n. wiping off, cleaning.
परिमित a. meted out, measured; limited, little, few.
परिमिति f. measure, quantity.
परिमिलन n. touch, contact.
परिमूढ a. confounded, perplexed.
1परिमृष्ट a. polished, clean; wiped off, purged away, destroyed.
2परिमृष्ट a. caught, found out.*
परिमेय a. measurable, calculable, finite, small in number.
परिमोक्ष m., °ण n. liberation, deliverance.
परिमोष m. theft.
परिमोषक a. stealing.
परिमोषण n. taking away.
परिमोषिन् a. stealing; m. thief.
परिमोहन n. bewilderment, fascination.
परिमोहिन् a. bewildered, perplexed.
परिम्लान a. faded, withered, diminished, impaired, vanished, gone.
परियज्ञ m. a secondary rite.
परिरक्षक m. guardian, keeper.
परिरक्षण, f. ई guarding, protecting, keeping; n. = seq.
परिरक्षा f. protection, saving.
परिरक्षितृ m. = परिरक्षक.
परिरम्भ m., °ण n. an embrace.
परिरम्भिन् a. embracing.
परिरोध m. obstructing, keeping back.
परिलग्न a. stuck, held fast.*
परिलघु a. very light or small, minute, paltry; abstr. °ता f.
परिलङ्घन n. jumping to and fro.
परिलम्ब m., °न n. lingering, tarrying.
परिलेख m., °न n. outline, delineation.
परिवत्सर m. a full year; adj. °रीण.
परिवर्ग m. shunning or removing.
परिवर्ग्य a. to be avoided.
परिवर्जक a. shunning, avoiding.
परिवर्जन n. avoiding, giving up, resigning, escaping.
परिवर्जनीय a. to be avoided.
परिवर्त m. turning round, moving to and fro, roaming, revolving, revolution (of a planet), lapse (of time); change, barter; abode, spot, place.
परिवर्तक a. causing to turn round or back; m. change, barter.
परिवर्तन, f. ई = prec. a.; n. turning round, revolving; revolution, lapse or end (of time), change, barter.
परिवर्तिन् a. moving round, revolving, circling, ever recurring; changing, passing into (—°); abiding in, about, or with (loc. or —°).

परिवर्धन n. increasing, augmenting.
परिवह m. N. of a wind.
परिवाद m. abuse, reproach, censure.
परिवादकर m. censurer, slanderer.
परिवादिन् a. speaking ill of, blaming.
परिवार m. cover, covering, surroundings, train, retinue (adj. —° followed by).
परिवारण n. = prec. + warding off.
1परिवास m. abode, stay, residence.
2परिवास m. fragrance, odour.
परिवासन n. shred, chip.
परिवाह m. overflow; a. °हिन्.
परिविंशत् f. full twenty.
परिवित्त or परिवित्त m. an elder brother who marries after the younger.
परिवित्ति m. the same; abstr. °ता f., °त्व n.
परिविन्न m. the same.
परिविश्रान्त a. thoroughly rested.
परिविष्टि f. service, attendance.
परिवी a. wound round.
परिवीत a. surrounded, enveloped, covered, veiled.
परिवृक्त a. rejected, despised; f. परिवृक्ता or परिवृक्ती a disliked or despised wife.
परिवृज् f. avoiding, removing.
परिवृढ m. lord, chief (lit. the surrounded one).
परिवृत a. covered, veiled, or hung with, surrounded or accompanied by (instr. or —°); n. a covered place of sacrifice.
परिवृत्त a. rolling (n. as subst.), turned or spread round, lasting, finished, ended, gone; °भाग्य unfortunate (lit. whose fortune has gone).
परिवृत्ति f. rolling, turning round, turn, return, change, barter.
परिवृद्धि f. increase, growth.
परिवेत्तृ m. a younger brother that marries before the elder.
परिवेद m. complete knowledge.
1परिवेदन n. the same.
2परिवेदन n. the marrying of a younger brother before the elder.
परिवेष m. arrangement, preparation or distribution of food, waiting at meals; circumference, circle, esp. a halo round the sun or moon.
परिवेषक m. attendant, distributer of food.
परिवेषण n. = परिवेष.
परिवेष्टन n. cover, veil; ligature, bandage (also °ना f.).
परिवेष्टृ m., °ष्ट्री f. attendant, waiter.
परिव्यय m. seasoning, condiments; (expense, cost*).
परिव्ययण n. winding round, covering.
परिव्याण n. the same.
परिव्रज्या f. strolling, wandering (esp. of a religious mendicant).
परिव्राज् m. (nom. °व्राट्) vagrant, religious mendicant.
परिव्राजक m. the same.
परिशङ्कनीय a. to be distrusted or feared; n. impers.
परिशङ्कित a. afraid, suspicious; suspected, distrusted.
परिशङ्किन् a. fearing, anxious.
परिशप्त n. cursing, a curse.
परिशिष्ट a. left, remaining; n. supplement, appendix.
परिशीलन n. frequent contact or occupation with (—°).
परिशुद्ध a. clean, pure; diminished by (—°).
परिशुद्धि f. purification, justification.
परिशुष्क a. quite dry or parched.
परिशेष a. left, remaining; m. n. remnant, rest, supplement.
परिशोधन n. purification, paying off.
परिशोष m. getting dry, dryness.
परिशोषण a. & n. drying up, parching.
परिशोषिन् a. drying up (tr. & intr.).
परिश्रम m. fatigue, pain, exertion, labour.
परिश्रय m. enclosure, fence.
परिश्रान्त a. much tired, worn out.
परिश्रित् f. encloser (r.).
परिश्रुत a. heard, learnt from (gen., instr., or —°, also n. impers.); known as, passing for, called (nom.); celebrated, famous.
परिषत्त्व n. abstr. to seq. f.
परिषद् a. sitting around, besetting; f. assembly, congregation.
परिषूति f. enclosing, oppressing.
परिषेक m. sprinkling over, moistening, bathing.

परिषेचन n. sprinkling, watering.
परिषोडश a. pl. full sixteen.
परिष्कार m. arranging, adorning, ornament.
परिष्कृत a. prepared, arranged, adorned, accompanied by (—°).
परिष्टि f. surrounding, impeding, oppression, distress.
परिष्टुति f. praise.
परिष्टुभ् a. shouting or exulting around.
परिष्ठा a. obstructing, impeding; f. impediment, barrier.
परिष्ठित a. obstructed, hindered.
परिष्यन्द m. stream, river; sandbank, island.
परिष्वङ्ग m. embrace, contact.
परिष्वजन n. the same.
परिष्वज्य a. to be embraced.
परिष्वञ्जन n. = परिष्वजन.
1परिसंवत्सर m. a full year.
2परिसंवत्सर a. a full year old.
परिसंख्या f., °न n. enumeration, sum, total.
परिसंघुष्ट a. resonant all around.
परिसमाप्त a. finished, perfect.
परिसमाप्ति f. completion, end.
परिसर a. adjacent, contiguous, lying near or upon (—°); m. standing-place, position, environs, proximity.
परिसरण n. running about, moving to and fro.
परिसर्पण n. = prec., creeping upon (—°).
परिसर्पिन् a. going about, roaming.
परिसहस्र a. pl. full thousand.
परिसाधन n. bringing about, accomplishing, arranging, settling.
परिस्कन्न a. scattered (semen).
परिस्तर m., °स्तरण n. strewing, covering, cover.
परिस्तोम m. cover, cushion.
परिस्थित a. remaining in (loc.).
परिस्पन्द m., °स्पन्दित n. stirring, motion.
परिस्पर्धिन् a. vying with (—°).
परिस्पृध् f. rival.
परिस्फुट a. very clear or distinct, n. adv.
परिस्यन्द m. = परिष्यन्द.
परिस्रज् f. wreath, garland; p. °जिन्.
परिस्रव m. overflowing, gliding down; stream, gush.

परिस्राव m. fluxion.
परिस्रुत् a. streaming round or over, foaming, fermenting; f. a kind of liquor.
परिहर m. reserve, concealment.
परिहरण n. moving, placing, or carrying round, avoiding.
परिहरणीय & °हर्तव्य a. to be avoided.
परिहाणि or °हानि f. decrease.
परिहार m. leading round, avoiding, escaping, forsaking, leaving out, passing over, reserve, concealment; exemption, immunity, privilege (j.).
परिहारिन् a. avoiding (—°).
परिहार्य a. to be avoided or left alone; to be exempted or presented with an immunity.
परिहास m. jest, joke, sport.
परिहासनिमित्तम् adv. for sport.*
परिहासशील a. fond of jesting; abstr. °ता f.*
परिहित a. placed round, seated or standing round; put on, donned; covered, clothed, surrounded.
परिहीण a. left out, ceased, disappeared; wanting, being without (abl., instr., or —°).
परिहृति f. shunning, avoiding.
परिहृष्ट & °हृषित a. greatly delighted.
परिह्रुत् a. causing to fall.
परिह्रुति or परिह्रूति f. going or leading astray, damage, injury.
परीक्षक m. examiner, investigator.
परीक्षण n., °णा f. examination, investigation.
परीक्षा f. the same.
परीक्षिन् a. proving, testing; m. examiner.
परीणस् n. plenty, abundance; instr. richly, abundantly.
परीणसं n. = prec.
परीणह् f. (nom. °णत्) enclosure; trunk or chest on a carriage.
परीणाम & °णाह m. = परिणाम & °णाह.
परीत a. standing round; filled with, seized, surrounded by (instr. or —°); abstr. °ता f.
परीताप & °तोष m. = परिताप & °तोष.
परीत्त a. given up, delivered.
परीत्ति f. delivering.

परीपाक m. = परिपाक.
परीप्सा f. desire of obtaining or saving, a. °प्सु.
परीमन् s. bounty, abundance.
परीमाण n. = परिमाण.
परीरम्भ m. = परिरम्भ.
परीवर्त m. exchange, barter.
परीवाद, °वार, & °वाह m. = परिवाद, °वार, & °वाह.
परीवृत a. = परिवृत.
परीवेत्तृ m. = परिवेत्तृ.
परीशास m. excision; du. a kind of tongs (r.).
परीषेक m. = परिषेक.
परीष्टि f. investigation, research.
परीसर m. circumference, surroundings.
परीहार m. avoiding, reserve.
परीहास m. = परिहास.
†परु m. limb, member.
परुच्छेप m. N. of a Rishi.
*परुत् adv. last year.
परुत्क a. knotted or limbed.
परुशस & परुःपरुस् adv. limb by limb, member by member.
परुष (f. old परुष्णी) knotty (reed), bristly, shaggy (hair); spotted, many-coloured, dirty; piercing, keen, rough, harsh. — m. reed, arrow; f. परुष्णी cloud, N. of a river; n. sgl. & pl. harsh language.
परुषाक्षर a. containing or using harsh words (language or person).
परुषोक्ति f. harsh language.
परुस् n. knot, joint (of a plant or the body), member, portion, section.
परे (loc. adv.) later, in future.
परेण (instr. adv.) beyond, past (acc.), farther; later. after (abl. or gen.).
परेत a. gone, dead; m. pl. the Manes.
परेति f. departure.
परेद्यवि (loc. adv.) next day, to-morrow.
परेश m. supreme lord, E. of Brahman or Viṣṇu.
परोऽक्ष a. beyond the eye, out of sight, invisible, imperceptible, unintelligible, obscure. Loc. behind one's back, in one's absence; °— & instr. secretly, mysteriously; acc. & abl. in the absence or without the knowledge of (instr. or gen.).
परोऽक्षता f., °त्व n. the being out of sight, invisibility, imperceptibility.
परोऽक्षानुराग m. love without seeing (the beloved object).*
परोपकार m. abstr. to seq.
परोपकारिन् a. assisting or helping others.
परोपकृति f. = परोपकार.
परोविंश a. pl. more than twenty.
परोऽशीत a. pl. more than eighty.
†पर्क v. मधुपर्क.
पर्कटी f. a kind of fig-tree.
पर्जन्य m. rain-cloud or rain, personif. as the rain-god.
पर्जन्यजिन्वित a. animated by the rain(-god).
पर्जन्यवृद्ध a. nourished by the rain(-god).
पर्ण n. wing, plume, feather (also of an arrow), leaf; m. = पलाश m.
पर्णधि m. the part of an arrow to which the feathers are fastened.
पर्णमय, f. ई made of Palāça-wood.
पर्णवन्त् a. leafy.
पर्णशय्या f. couch of leaves.
पर्णाद m. a man's name.
पर्णाशन n. abstr. to seq.
पर्णाशिन् a. eating leaves.
पर्णिन् a. winged, plumed, leafy.
पर्ण्य a. relating to leaves.
पर्तृ s. protector or protection (only instr. pl.).
पर्द्, पर्दते fart.
पर्पट m., ई f. names of plants.
पर्यक् adv. round about.
पर्यग्नि m. the circumambient fire (r.); as adv. w. कृ carry the fire round (cf. seq.).
पर्यग्निकरण n. carrying the fire round (the sacrificial animal).
पर्यङ्क m. couch, bed; the sitting with bent legs upon the hams.
पर्यटन n. wandering about, roaming through (gen. or —°).
पर्यन्त m. circumference, limit, edge, end; adj. —° surrounded by, reaching to. पर्यन्तम् to the end of, as far as, until (—°).
पर्यन्तस्थ a. limitative, adjoining.
पर्यय m. revolution, lapse (of time); change, mutation, inversion.

पर्ययन n. going round, circumambulation.
पर्यवसान n., **°साय** m. close, end.
पर्यवसित a. living farther off, having removed to (acc.); thoroughly finished or closed, settled, definitive.
पर्यश्रु a. tearful, weeping.
पर्यश्रुनयन a. having tears in the eyes.
पर्यसन n. throwing about, moving to and fro.
पर्यस्त a. inverted, overturned, upset, fallen on (loc.), spread about (—°).
पर्यस्तमयम् adv. about sunset.
पर्याकुल a. filled, full of (—°); troubled, confused, excited. Abstr. **°त्व** n.
पर्याकुलय्, **°यति** trouble, confound.
पर्याकुली कृ = prec., **°भू** P.
पर्याचान्त (अन्न) n. food left by a person who has rinsed his mouth prematurely.
पर्याप्त a. got, obtained, finished, complete, large, copious, sufficient to, enough for (gen. or dat.); n. adv., w. **एतावता** this is enough for (gen.).
पर्याप्तभोग a. having sufficient enjoyment.
पर्याप्ति f. conclusion, end; satisfaction, sufficiency; capability of (—°).
पर्याय m. turning round, revolving; course, lapse (of time); turn, succession; formula, stanza; convertible term, synonym. °— & instr. successively, in turn.
पर्यालोच m., **°न** n. circumspection, deliberation.
पर्यालोचना f. = prec. + plan, intention.
पर्यावर्त m., **°न** n. return.
पर्यास m. turning round, revolution; edging, bordering, close, end, concluding strophe in a recitation.
पर्युक्षण n. sprinkling; f. **ई** a vessel for sprinkling.
पर्युत्सुक a. very restless, sorrowful, eager, desirous of or longing for (dat.); abstr. **°त्व** n.; **°की भू** become or be very sad.
पर्युपस्थित a. standing round (acc.); approached, imminent, impending.
पर्युपासन n. sitting around, surrounding, veneration, friendliness, courtesy.
पर्युषित a. having passed a night, stale, night-flat, not fresh, insipid.
पर्येतृ m. conqueror, lord.
पर्येषण n. searching, inquiring.
पर्येष्टव्य a. to be sought or striven after.
पर्येष्टि f. searching for (—°).
पर्व (adj. —°) = **पर्वन्**.
पर्वकाल m. = seq. f.
पर्वण m. N. of a demon; f. **ई** the period of a change of the moon.
पर्वत a. knotty, rugged (of a mountain). — m. mountain (also fig. of a cloud), height, hill, rock, stone, N. of sev. men, esp. of a Rishi (cf. **नारद**); f. **पर्वती** rock, stone.
पर्वतच्युत् a. shaking mountains.
पर्वतपति m. lord of the mountains.
पर्वतमस्तक s. top (lit. head) of a mountain.
पर्वतराज् & **°राज** m. = prec., E. of the Himavant.
पर्वतशिखर m. n. mountain-top.
पर्वताग्र n. the same.
पर्वतात्मजा f. E. of Durgā (mountain-daughter).
पर्वतायन m. = **पार्वतायन**.
पर्वति f. rock, stone.
पर्वतीय a. mountainous, mountain-.
पर्वतेश्वर m. = **पर्वतपति**; N. of a man.
पर्वतेष्ठा a. dwelling on mountains.
पर्वतोपत्यका f. land at the foot of a mountain.
पर्वत्य or **°त्य** a. = **पर्वतीय**.
पर्वन् n. knot, joint (esp. of a plant or of the body), limb, member (lit. & fig.), break, division, portion, section (esp. of a book); period, fixed time (esp. the 2 or 4 changes of the moon and the Cāturmāsya festival).
पर्वशस् adv. limb by limb, piece by piece.
पर्वसंधि m. change of the moon, esp. the time of new- and full-moon.
पर्शान m. chasm, precipice.
1**पर्शु** f. rib; curved knife, sickle.
2**पर्शु** m. = **परशु**.
पर्ष m. bundle, sheaf.
1**पर्षणि** a. carrying over (ship).
2**पर्षणि** loc. inf. to 2**पृ**.
पर्षद् f. = **परिषद्**.
पर्षिष्ठ (superl.) carrying over or rescuing best.
पल n. a cert. weight (also m.) or measure; flesh, meat.

पलच, f. ई white.
पलल n. ground sesamum seeds, pap; mud, mire.
पललौदन n. a pap made of ground sesamum seeds.
पलाण्डु m. (n.) onion.
पलाय्, °यति & पलायते flee. — प्र run away, escape. वि flee asunder.
पलायन n. flight, escape.
पलायिन् a. flying, fugitive.
पलाल n., ई f. stalk, straw.
पलालभार & °क m. a load of straw.
पलालोच्चय m. a heap of straw.
पलाव s. fishing-hook; m. pl. chaff, husks.
पलाश n. (adj. —° f. ई) leaf, petal; m. a kind of tree (= पर्ण m.), n. its blossom.
1पलाशिन् a. leafy; m. tree.
2पलाशिन् a. eating flesh, carnivorous.
पलिक्नी v. seq.
पलित, f. पलिक्नी grey, hoary; n. grey hair.
पल्पूलन n. lye.
पल्पूलय्, °लयति, pp. पल्पूलित wash in lye, wash or cleanse i.g.; tan.
पल्य n. sack for corn.
पल्यङ्क m. couch, bed.
पल्ल m. a large granary; f. ई = पल्लिका.
पल्लव m. n. sprout, shoot, twig (lit. & fig.); edge of a garment.
पल्लवका f. a woman's name.*
पल्लवय्, °यति sprout, shoot, spread; pp. पल्लवित also full of (—°).
पल्लविन् a. having young shoots.
पल्लि f. a small village, esp. a settlement of wild tribes.
पल्वल n. small tank, pond, pool.
पव m. N. of a man; f. पवा purification.
पवन m. wind (often personif.), N. of a man; n. instrument for purifying, sieve, strainer, etc.
पवनज & °तनय m. son of the wind, E. of Hanumant.
पवनाशन & °शिन् m. snake (l. wind-eater).
पवनोत्कम्पिन् a. trembling in the wind.*
पवमान a. being purified or strained; m. wind, N. of cert. Stotras.
पवयितृ m. purifier.
पवस्त n. du. heaven and earth.
पवि m. tire of a wheel, metallic point of a spear or arrow.
पवितृ m. purifier.
पवित्र n. instrument for cleansing, esp. filter, strainer, etc.; i.g. anything cleansing or purifying (l. & f.); a. purifying, pure, holy, sinless. m. a cert. sacrifice.
पवित्रकीर्ति a. of stainless renown.
पवित्रपूत a. clarified by a strainer.
पवित्रय्, °यति, pp. पवित्रित cleanse, purify.
पवित्री w. कृ = prec.
पवीतृ m. = पवितृ.
पव्या f. purification.
1पश्, only pres. पश्यति, °ते (cf. स्पश् & दृश्) see, behold, perceive, look, look on, try, examine, ponder; regard or consider as, take for (2 acc. or acc. & adv. in वत्), see with the spiritual eye (of seers and poets), find out, invent. — अति look beyond. अनु look at, behold, discover, regard or consider as etc. = S. अव look at, observe. उद् look up, foresee, expect, behold, perceive. परि look over, survey, descry. discover, learn, understand, know as (2 acc.). प्र look forward, foresee, view, behold, know, recognize, take for (2 acc.). प्रति look at, behold, experience, learn. वि see in different places or in detail, discern, distinguish; perceive, observe, know, understand. अभिवि behold, perceive. सम् see (together or at the same time), look over, survey, observe, consider, try, examine, perceive, behold, know, understand; M. look at each other, be together.
2पश् (only instr. पड्भिस्) look, eye.
3पश् (only instr. पड्भिस्) bond, rope.
पशव्य a. belonging to or fit for cattle; n. a herd or drove of cattle.
पशु or पशु m. cattle (singly or coll.), animal, esp. domestic a. or sacrificial victim (sometimes including man, sometimes said contemptuously of a man. — Abstr. °ता† f., °त्व† n.
पशुकर्मन् n., °क्रिया f. the act of animal sacrifice.

पशुघात m. slaughter of cattle.*
पशुघ्न a. killing cattle.
पशुतृप् a. taking away (lit. feeding on) cattle.
पशुप a. guarding cattle; m. herdsman.
पशुपति m. lord of the animals, E. of sev. gods.
पशुपा m. keeper of cattle, herdsman.
पशुपाल m. the same.
पशुपाश m. the cord for (binding) the victim.
पशुबन्ध m. an animal sacrifice.
पशुमन्त् a. connected with, relating to, or rich in cattle. m. a herdsman; n. possession of cattle.
पशुमार (only instr. & acc. adv.) as if killing cattle.
पशुमारण & °कर्मन् n. slaughtering cattle.*
पशुयज्ञ m. an animal sacrifice.
पशुयाजिन् a. offering an animal sacrifice.
पशुरक्षि & °रक्षिन् m. herdsman, herd.
पशुवत् adv. like an animal or as in an animal (sacrifice).
पशुविद् a. procuring cattle.
पशुव्रत a. acting like an animal.
पशुशिरस् & °शीर्ष n. the head of an animal.
*पशुशृङ्ग n. the horn of an animal.
पशुषा & °षा a. bestowing cattle.
पशुसनि a. the same.
पशुसंभव a. coming from cattle.
पशुसोम m. pl. the animal and Soma sacrifices.
पशुहव्य n. animal sacrifice.
पशूखा f. a vessel to cook the sacrificial animal in.
पश्चा (instr. adv.) behind, afterwards, later, westward.
पश्चात् (abl. adv.) from behind, from the back, behind, after, later, west (as a prepos. w. gen. & abl.). — With कृ leave behind, surpass, excel, w. गम् go back; ततः पश्चात् after that, thereupon.
पश्चातात् (abl. adv.) from behind.
पश्चात्काल m. later time.
पश्चात्ताप m. sorrow, repentance (l. after-pain).
पश्चात्तापिन् a. feeling regret or repentance.
पश्चाद्वात m. wind from behind, west wind.
पश्चार्ध m. the hinder or western part.
पश्चार्ध्य a. being on the west side.

पश्चिम a. hinder, hindmost, westerly, latter, last; f. आ + संध्या the evening twilight, + क्रिया the last rite i.e. burning the dead, ± दिश् the west.
पश्चिमदक्षिण a. south-westerly.
पश्चिमोत्तर a. north-westerly.
पश्य a. looking, knowing, intelligent.
†पश्यत a. visible, conspicuous.
पश्वङ्ग n. anything belonging to the sacrificial animal.
पश्वनृत n. untruth concerning cattle.
पश्विज्या f. animal sacrifice.
पश्विष् a. wishing for cattle.
पंसस् n. the membrum virile.
पस्त्य n. habitation, stall, stable; f. आ pl. house, dwelling, family, sgl. the goddess of a house.
पस्त्यसद् m. house-mate.
पस्त्यावन्त् a. being kept in a stable, having or offering a fixed abode; m. householder, a wealthy man.
पह्लव m. pl. the Parthians or the Persians.
1पा, पिबति, °ते (पाति), pp. पीत (with pass., r. with act. mg), drink, imbibe, swallow, draw in, enjoy. C. पाययति, pp. पायित give to drink (2 acc.). D. पिपासति (पिपीषति) wish to drink, be thirsty. I. पेपीयते drink greedily or repeatedly (also w. pass. mg). — आ drink up, drink out of (abl.) or at (acc.); imbibe, absorb, draw in, enjoy. नि drink in, imbibe, absorb. परि drink before and after (acc.), drink or draw up. प्र begin to drink, drink in, sip. वि drink up, drink largely, drink out of (abl.). सम् A. & M. drink in together. — Cf. पिपासन्त् & पिपासित.
2पा a. drinking (—°).
3पा, पाति (pp. पात) protect, watch, shelter from or defend against (abl.); rule, govern; keep, observe. — अभि guard, observe. नि protect, shelter from (abl.), watch, observe, keep. निस् protect from (abl.). परि protect on all sides, observe, keep, maintain. प्र protect or shelter from (abl.).
4पा a. protecting, guarding, keeping (—°).
पांसन, f. ई defiling, disgracing (—°).

पांसव a. formed of dust.

पांसव्य a. to seq.

पांसु m. pl. (sgl.) dust, sand.

पांसुक m. pl. = prec.

पांसुक्रीडन n. playing with sand.

पांसुर a. dusty.

पांसुल a. the same + impure, defiled; defiling, disgracing.

पांसुवर्ष m. n. falling (lit. rain) of dust.

पांसुसंचय m. a heap of sand.

पांसुसमूहन a. raising dust (wind).

पांसुस्नान n. rolling (lit. bathing) in dust.

पांसूप्त a. covered with dust.

1पाक a. very young, simple, ignorant, stupid, artless, honest. — m. the young of animals, N. of a Daitya.

2पाक m. (adj. —° f. ई) cooking, baking (tr. & intr.), burning (bricks), cooking in the stomach, i.e. digestion; ripening, maturity, development (esp. of consequences), perfection.

पाकत्रा adv. simply, artlessly.

पाकपात्र n. cooking-utensil.

पाकबलि m. = पाकयज्ञ.

पाकभाण्ड n. = पाकपात्र.

पाकयज्ञ m. a simple or domestic sacrifice.

पाकयज्ञिक & °यज्ञिय a. relating to the P. (v. prec.).

पाकल a. quite black.

पाकवत् adv. = पाकत्रा.

पाकशंस a. speaking honestly.

पाकशासन m. the punisher of Pāka or the instructor of the ignorant (E. of Indra).

पाकारु m. a cert. disease.

पाकिम a. obtained by cooking or burning (pot etc.), red-hot.

पाक्य a. cookable or obtained by cooking.

पाक्या f. (instr.) in simplicity or honesty.

पाक्षपातिक a. favouring a party, partial.

पाक्षिक a. = prec. or subject to an alternative.

पाखण्ड = पाषण्ड.

पाङ्क्त a. fivefold.

पाङ्क्तता f., °त्व n. abstr. to prec.

पाङ्क्तेय & पाङ्क्त्य a. worthy (of a society), decent.

पाङ्क्त m. a kind of mouse.

पाचक, f. °चिका cooking, ripening (tr.).

पाचन, f. ई the same; n. as subst.

पाजक m. cooking-basket.

पाजस् n. glimmer, sheen, brightness, cheerfulness, vigour; du. heaven and earth (as the two sheens or shining surfaces).

पाजस्य n. the region of the belly or flanks (of an animal).

पाजस्वन्त् a. shining or vigorous.

पाञ्चजन्य a. relating to or containing the five tribes.

पाञ्चभौतिक a. consisting of the five elements.

पाञ्चयज्ञिक a. relating to the five sacrifices.

पाञ्चरात्रिक a. lasting five days (nights).

पाञ्चवार्षिक. f. ई five years old.

पाञ्चाल, f. ई belonging to the Pañcālas. m. a prince of the P., pl. the people of the P.; f. ई a princess of the P., esp. Draupadī.

पाञ्चालक, f. °लिका = prec. adj.

पाञ्चाल्य a. the same; m. a prince of the Pañcālas.

पाट m. intersection; f. पाटा N. of a cert. plant.

पाटक m. who splits or tears asunder.

पाटच्चर m. thief, robber.

पाटन n. splitting, tearing asunder.

पाटल a. pale-red; m. pale-red colour, redness; N. of a tree, n. its blossom, f. आ = both.

पाटलावती f. N. of a river.

पाटलि f. N. of a tree.

पाटलिपुत्र n. N. of a city, pl. its inhabitants.

पाटव n. sharpness, acuteness, dexterity.

पाटिन् a. splitting (—°); m. a cert. fish.

पाटीर m. the sandal-tree.

पाटूर m. the part near the ribs (of an animal).

पाठ m. recitation, perusal, study, text.

पाठक m. reciter, reader, student, scholar, teacher.

पाठदोष m. error of the text, false reading.

पाठन n. teaching, instruction.

पाठवन्त् a. well-read, learned.

पाठिन् a. well-read in (—°); m. student, scholar.

पाठीन m. a kind of fish.

पाठ्य a. to be recited.

पाण m. a stake at play.

पाणि m. hand, hoof; adj. —° carrying in the hand. पाणिं ग्रह् or दा take or give the hand i.e. marry (the former of the man, the latter of the woman).
पाणिग्रह m., °ग्रहण n. marriage (cf. prec.).
पाणिग्रहणिक & °ग्रहणीय a. nuptial.
पाणिग्रहीतृ, °ग्राह, & °ग्राहक m. bridegroom, husband (lit. hand-taker).
पाणितल n. the palm of the hand.
पाणिधर्म m. form of marriage.
पाणिन् (—°) = पाणि.
पाणिनि m. N. of a celebrated grammarian.
पाणिनीय a. relating to or coming from Pāṇini; m. a disciple or follower of P., n. his grammar.
पाणिपद्म s. a lotus (like) hand.
पाणिपाद् n. sgl. & m. pl. hands and feet.
पाणिपीडन n. marriage (lit. pressing the hand).
पाणिबन्ध m. marriage (union of the hands).
पाणिमन्त् a. having hands.
पाणिमित a. to be measured or spanned with the hands, very thin or slender.
पाणिस्थ a. being in the hand.
†पाण्डर a. whitish yellow.
पाण्डरवासस् a. wearing a yellow garment.
पाण्डव m. a son or descendant of Pāṇḍu; a., f. ई belonging to the Pāṇḍavas.
पाण्डवीय a. = prec. a.
पाण्डवेय m. & a. = पाण्डव.
पाण्डित्य n. learning, erudition, knowledge; cleverness, dexterity.
पाण्डिमन् m. = seq. abstr.
पाण्डु a. whitish yellow, white, pale (abstr. °ता† f., °त्व† n.), N. of an ancient king.
पाण्डुनन्दन m. a son of Pāṇḍu.
पाण्डुपत्त्र n. a yellow leaf.
पाण्डुभूम m. a whitish soil.
पाण्डुर a. whitish, pale.
पाण्डुरता f., °रिमन् m. abstr. to prec.
पाण्डुरोग m. the yellow disease, jaundice.
पाण्डुलेख s. first outline or sketch (lit. pale writing).
पाण्डुसोपाक or सोपाक m. a cert. mixed caste.
पाण्ड्य m. pl. N. of a people.
पाण्ड्व n. an uncoloured woolen garment.
पाण्य a. relating to the hand.
पाण्यास्य a. whose mouth is his hand.
पात m. flying, flight; fall, downfall; attack, inroad; case, possibility; happening, event.
पातक a. causing to fall (—°); m. crime, sin.
पातकिन् a. criminal, wicked; m. sinner.
पातञ्जल m. composed by Patañjali; m. a follower of P., n. his system (ph.), the Mahābhāṣya (g.).
पातन n. causing to fall, felling (also adj.), throwing, removing, destroying; w. दण्डस्य chastising, punishing.
पातनीय a. to be caused to fall or thrown.
पातयितृ m. who causes to fall or throws.
पातवे & पातवै dat. inf. to 1पा.
1पातव्य a. to be drunk.
2पातव्य a. to be protected.
पाताल n. lower world, abode of serpents or demons, also a cert. hell.
पातिन् a. flying, falling, sinking; felling, throwing down (—°).
पातुक a. falling, losing caste or going to hell.
1पातृ or पातृ m. drinker.
2पातृ m. protector, defender.
1पात्य a. = पातनीय.
2पात्य n. dominion, sway.
पात्र n. instrument of drinking, cup, bowl, vessel, dish, utensil or receptacle i.g., fig. a (worthy) recipient, a person worthy of or fit for (gen., loc. or —°), a master in (gen.); an actor or a part in a play; a cert. measure of capacity. — m. a king's counsellor or minister; f. पात्री (पात्री) vessel, pot, dish.
पात्रता f., °त्व n. capacity, fitness, worthiness (lit. the being a receptacle).
पात्रिन् a. provided with a drinking vessel or a dish.
पात्री w. कृ make a receptacle or worthy object, honour, dignify; w. भू P.
पाथस् n. spot, place (also °थिस् n.); water.
पाथेय n. provender for a journey; p. °वन्त्.
पाथोज n. lotus-flower, °जिनी f. the lotus plant.
पाथोद & °धर m. cloud (water-giver or -bearer).

पाथोधि m. the see (receptacle of water).
पाथोनाथ m. the ocean (lord of the waters).
पाथोनिधि m. = पयोधि.
पाद m. foot, leg (lit. & fig.), foot as a measure; column, pillar; ray, beam (as the foot of a heavenly body); fourth part, quarter of anything, esp. of a four-versed stanza, also part or verse i.g., section, chapter. Often pl. the feet of (—°) i.e. the venerable —.
पादक s. little foot; a. —° foot i.g. (f. °दिका).
*पादकटक m. n. foot-ring, anklet.
पादगृह्य (ger.) seizing one's feet.
पादग्रहण n. clasping a person's feet (as a reverential salutation).
पादचार & °चारिन् a. going on foot.
पादजल n. water for washing the feet.
पादतल n. the sole of the foot.
पादतस् adv. from or at the feet; step by step, by degrees.
पादत्र & °त्राण n. a shoe (foot-protecting).
पादधावन n. washing the feet.
पादनख m. a toe-nail.
पादन्यास m. placing the feet or throwing the rays, step, footprint.
पादप m. plant, tree (drinking with the foot or root).
पादपतन n. falling at another's feet, prostration.
पादपद्धति f. line of footsteps, track.
पादपद्म m. a lotus (like) foot.
पादपीठ n. foot-stool.
पादपूरण a. & n. filling out a verse.
पादप्रक्षालन n. washing the feet.
पादप्रहार m. a kick (foot-blow).
पादबन्ध m. fetter for the feet.
पादभट m. foot-soldier.
पादभाग m. fourth parth, quarter.
पादमुद्रा f. foot-print, trace; °पङ्क्ति f. a row of foot-prints.
पादमूल n. root or sole of the foot; the foot of a mountain; also = पाद (—°). पादमूले निपत् fall at one's feet.
पादरजस् n. the dust of the feet.
पादलग्न a. sticking in the foot or lying at one's feet.
पादवन्त् a. having feet.
पादवन्दन n. respectful salutation (lit. saluting the feet).
पादशस् adv. foot by foot or by a fourth.
पादशौच n. cleaning the feet.
पादाग्र n. point of the foot, toe.
पादाघात m. a kick (blow with the feet).
*पादाङ्गद n. foot-ring, anklet.
पादाङ्गुलि or °ली f. toe (foot-finger).
पादाङ्गुष्ठ m. the great toe (foot-thumb).
पादात m. foot-soldier, foot-man.
पादान्त m. the extremity of the foot or the end of a verse.
पादान्तर n. interval or distance of a foot.
पादाभिवन्दन & °वादन n. = पादवन्दन.
पादार्ध n. half a quarter or half a stanza.
पादार्पण n. setting down the feet, stepping upon.
पादावनेजन, f. ई used for washing the feet.
पादावसेचन n. water for washing the feet or in which the feet have been washed.
पादाहति f. = पादाघात.
पादिन् a. = पादवन्त्; also being entitled to one fourth.
पादु m. foot, step; place.
(पादुक &) °का f. shoe, slipper.
पादू f. the same.
पादून a. = पादोन.
पादोदक n. water for washing the feet.
पादोन a. less by one fourth.
पाद्य a. relating to the feet; n. water for washing the feet.
1पान n. drinking, beverage.
2पान v. 3पा.
3†पान v. तनूपान.
पानक m. n. drink, beverage, potion.
पानप a. drinking spirituous liquors.
पानपात्र & °भाण्ड n. drinking-vessel.
पानभोजन n. drinking and eating.*
पानमत्त a. mad from drinking, intoxicated.
पानमद m. intoxication.
पानीय a. drinkable; n. drink, beverage, esp. water.
पानीयवर्ष s. (water-)rain.
पान्त m. drink, beverage.
पान्थ m. wanderer, traveller; abstr. °त्व n.

पापं (पाप), f. ई (later आ) bad, wicked, evil, inauspicious; n. पापम् & f. instr. पापया (± अमुया q.v.) badly, wrongly. m. bad fellow, wretch, profligate; n. evil, sin, harm, trouble. शान्तं पापम् may the sin be destroyed = heaven forbid.

पापक, f. °पिका (& °पकी) bad, evil; n. evil, wrong, sin; m. wicked person, villain.

1पापकर्मन् n. evil deed, crime.

2पापकर्मन् a. doing evil; m. evil-doer, sinner, villain.

पापकल्प m. villain.

पापकारिन् & °कृत् (superl. °कृत्तम) = prec.

पापकृत n., °कृत्या f. evil deed, sin.

पापचेतस् a. evil-minded, wicked.

पापत्वं n. bad condition, misery.

पापनिश्चय a. malevolent.

पापबन्ध m. an uninterrupted series of evil deeds.

1पापबुद्धि f. bad intention, malevolence.

2पापबुद्धि a. evil-minded.

पापभाज् a. partaking of a wrong, guilty.

पापमति a. = 2पापबुद्धि.

पापयोनि f. bad or low birth-place.

पापरहित a. free from guilt, innocent.

पापरोग m. a bad disease; p. °गिन्.

पापलोक m. the evil world, place of the wicked.

पापशील a. of bad character, wicked; abstr. °त्व n.

पापसम n. a bad year.

पापहन् a. destroying sin or the sinful.

पापात्मन् a. evil-minded; m. a bad person, sinner, wretch.

पापानुबन्ध m. evil consequences.

पापारम्भक a. doing evil, wicked.

पापाह s. an inauspicious day.

पापिन् a. doing evil; m. evil-doer.

पापिष्ठ (superl. to पापं) worst, lowest, most wicked; comp. °तर† worst off, superl. °तम† worse than (abl.). — m. a bad man, villain.

पापीयंस् (compar. to पापं) worse off, more wretched or miserable; also = prec. adj. & m.

पाप्मन् m. evil, harm, trouble, crime, sin.

पामन् m. skin disease, scab.

पामन a. scabbed.

पाय्, पायते cacare.

पायक, f. °यिका drinking (gen. or. —°).

पायन n. giving to drink.

पायम् (ger., doubled) drinking or sucking continually.

पायस a. prepared with milk; m. n. such a food, esp. rice boiled in milk.

पायसपिण्डारक m. rice-eater.*

पायसापूप m. a cake of milk, rice, etc.

पायिन् a. drinking, sucking (—°).

1पायु m. guard, protector.

2पायु (पायु) m. the anus.

†पाय्य a. to be caused to drink; n. drink, beverage.

1पार a. carrying over. m. crossing (only —°), a man's name; n. (m.) the further shore or bank, i.g. limit, end, aim. पारं गम् cross over, go through, carry out. f. पारा N. of a river, पारी milk-pail.

2पार m. = पाल keeper, protector.

पारक्य a. belonging to others, strange, alien, hostile, inimical; m. enemy.

पारग a. crossing over, going through (lit. & fig.); thoroughly familiar or conversant with (gen., loc., or —°).

†पारण a. carrying over, rescuing. – n. fulfilling, accomplishing; ending, esp. a fast, i.e. breakfast; reading through, perusal, study (also f. आ).

पारणीय a. to be gone through or brought to an end.

पारत m. quicksilver, pl. N. of a people.

पारतन्त्र्य n. dependence (on others).

पारतस् adv. on the other side, beyond (gen.).

पारद m. = पारत.

पारदारिक a. having intercourse with another's wife; m. an adulterer.

पारदार्य n. intercourse with another's wife, adultery.

पारदेश्य a. coming from a foreign country, foreign.

पारभृतीय a. of a Kokila or sacrificial (flesh).*

पारमार्थिक, f. ई real, essential, true.

पारमेश्वर, f. ई belonging to the supreme lord.

पारमेष्ठ्य a. = prec.; n. highest rank, supremacy.
पारंपर्य n. uninterrupted series, continuous succession or tradition; intercession, intermediation.
पारंपर्यक्रमागत a. handed down by tradition.
पारंपर्यागत a. the same.
पारयितृ a. going or about to lead over.
पारयिष्णु a. bringing through, overcoming, victorious.
पारलौकिक a. belonging to the other world.
पारवश्य n. dependence, the being subject or obnoxious to (—°).
पारशव, f. **ई** made of iron; m. a cert. mixed caste.
पारस, f. **ई** Persian, f. **ई** (± **भाषा**) the Persian language.
पारसिक or **°सीक** m. pl. the Persians.
पारस्कर m. N. of an ancient teacher; a. composed by P.
पारायण n. going through, perusal, study.
पारार्थ्य n. altruism, unselfishness.
पारावत a. remote, coming from afar; m. turtle dove, pl. N. of a people.
पारावार s. the nearer and further shore; m. the sea.
पाराशर & **पाराशर्य** (f. **°शरी**) patron. from **पराशर**.
पाराशर्यायण m. patron. from **पाराशर्य**.
पारिक्षित् & **°क्षित** m. descendant of Parikṣit, patron. of Janamejaya.
पारिजात & **°क** m. the coral tree, N. of one of the five trees of paradise, a man's name.
पारिणाय्य n. furniture, marriage-portion.
***पारितथ्या** f. a kind of pearl-string.
पारितोषिक n. gratuity, present, reward (abstr. **°त्व** n.*).
पारिपन्थिक m. waylayer, robber, thief.
पारिपार्श्वक or **°र्श्विक** a. standing at the side, attending. m. servant, attendant; assistant of the manager of the play; f. **°र्श्विका** female attendant (d.).
पारिप्लव a. swimming or moving to and fro, unsteady, fickle. abstr. **°ता** f., **°त्व** n.; m. ship, vessel.
पारिभद्र & **°क** m. N. of a tree.
पारिषद a. fit for an assembly, decent. m. assessor at a council, pl. the attendants of a god.
पारिहार्य m. a kind of bracelet.
पारीन्द्र m. lion.
पारुषेय a. spotted, freckled.
पारुष्ण m. a kind of bird.
पारुष्य n. harshness, esp. harsh speech, insult.
पारेश्मशानम् adv. on the other side of the burial-place.
पारोऽक्ष्य a. out of sight or mind, indiscernible, invisible; n. mystery.
पार्जन्य a. belonging to Parjanya.
पार्ण a. made of Parṇa-wood.
1**पार्थ** m. patr. from Pṛthi; n. cert. sacred texts.
2**पार्थ** m. descendant of Pṛthā, E. of the Panduids.
पार्थव, f. **ई** belonging to Pṛthu; n. extent, width.
1**पार्थिव**, f. **ई** earthly, terrestrial; m. inhabitant of the earth, lord of the earth, prince, king, warrior. Abstr. **°ता**† f., **°त्व**† n.
2**पार्थिव**, f. **ई** royal, princely.
पार्य a. opposite, upper, last, final, decisive, effective, helpful. n. end, decision.
पार्वत, f. **ई** belonging to or coming from a mountain, mountainous; f. **ई** a mountain stream or the daughter of the mountain (Himavant), i.e. Durgā.
पार्वतायन m. a patron. name.
पार्वतीपरिणय m. T. of a play.
पार्वतीय a. living in the mountains; m. mountaineer.
पार्वायनान्तीय a. relating to the changes of the moon and the solstices.
पार्श्व n. (m.) the region of the ribs, pl. the ribs; flank, side, immediate neighbourhood. Acc. near to, towards, loc. close to, near; abl. away from, on the part or by means of.
पार्श्वग a. going at the side, accompanying (also **°गत**); m. pl. attendants, retinue.
पार्श्वतस् adv. sideways, aside (gen. or —°).
पार्श्वपरिवर्तित a. directed sideways.*

पार्श्वपरिवर्तिन् a. being at the side, near.
पार्श्ववर्तिन् & °विवर्तिन् a. the same.
पार्श्वस्थ a. standing near.
पार्श्वानुचर m. attendant.
पार्षत a. belonging to the spotted antelope, made of its skin; m. & f. ई patron. names of Drupada & his race.
पार्षद्र pl. = seq. m. pl.
पार्षद m. attendant, esp. of a god, partaker of an assembly, spectator; n. text-book of a gramm. school.
पार्ष्टेय a. being within the ribs.
पार्ष्णि f. the heel, fig. = back; acc. w. ग्रह् attack from behind.
पार्ष्णिग्रह a. attacking or threatening from behind; °ग्रहण n. abstr.
पार्ष्णिग्राह a. = prec. a.; m. an enemy in the rear.
1पाल m. guard, protector, herdsman (f. ई), king; a man's name.
2पाल m. n. alms-pot.
पालक m. guard, protector (f. °लिका), prince, ruler; a man's name.
पालन a. (f. ई) & n. keeping, guarding, protecting, observing.
पालनकर्मन् n. protectorship, superintendence.*
पालनीय a. to be kept or protected.
पालय्, पालयति (पालयते), pp. पालित protect, keep, watch, rule, observe, maintain. — अनु, अभि, परि, प्र the same. प्रति the same + wait for, expect. सम् protect, guard, keep.
पालयितृ m. protector, guardian, keeper (gen., acc., or —°).
पालागल m. runner, messenger.
पालाश, f. ई made of Palāça wood; m. = पलाश.
पालि or °ली f. the tip of the ear; edge, margin, side i.g.; row, range, line; raised bank, dike; pot, boiler; an oblong pond (only पाली).
पालित्य n. greyness (of age).
पालिन् a. guarding, protecting; m. ruler, king.
पाली v. पाल & पालि.
पाल्य a. to be protected, guarded, kept, maintained, observed.
पाल्वल, f. ई coming from a pond.
पाव m. a cert. wind-instrument.
पावक a. pure, clear, bright, shining; m. fire or the god of fire.
पावकार्चिस् f. flash of fire.
पावकि m. son of Fire, E. of sev. gods.
†पावन् a. drinking or protecting.
पावन, f. ई purifying or purified, pure, holy; n. the act or a means of purifying.
पावमान a. relating to the Soma-juice while being purified; f. ई N. of cert. Vedic hymns.
पावर s. a cert. die (= द्वापर).
पावा f. N. of a city.
पावित्र्य n. purity.
पाश m. bond, snare, trap (lit. & fig.).
पाशकण्ठ a. having a sling on the neck.
पाशकपीठ m. board for playing at dice.*
पाशय्, °यति, pp. पाशित bind, fetter.
पाशव a. coming from or belonging to cattle.
पाशहस्त m. E. of Yama (lit. snare in hand).
पाशिन् a. having a snare or sling; m. fowler, E. of Varuṇa.
पाशुक, f. ई belonging to cattle, esp. to the sacrificial animal.
पाश्चात्त्य or °त्य a. hinder, western, last.
पाषण्ड, f. ई heretical; m. heretic, m. n. = seq.
पाषण्डता f. heresy.
पाषण्डस्थ a. being in heresy, heretical.
पाषण्डिन् m. heretic.
पाषाण m. stone; °मय, f. ई made of stone.
पाष्य n. pl. stones; du. the two stones for pressing Soma.
पास्त्य a. belonging to a house, as s. domestic affairs.
पि v. 2पी.
पिंश् & पिंष् v. पिश् & पिष्.
पिक m., ई f. the Indian cuckoo.
पिङ्ग a. reddish brown, tawny; m. a man's name.
पिङ्गल a. = prec. a.; m. a man's name, esp. N. of an author on Chandas or metrics, E. of sev. gods & demons; f. पिङ्गला a kind of leech, a woman's name.

पिङ्गलक, f. °लिका = prec. adj.; f. a kind of owl, a woman's name.
पिङ्गलाक्ष, f. ई tawny-eyed.
पिङ्गलिमन् m. a reddish-brown colour.
पिङ्गलोचन a. = पिङ्गलाक्ष.
पिङ्गाक्ष, f. ई = prec.; m. ape, E. of Agni, N. of a Rakṣas, a Daitya, etc.
पिचु m. cotton.
पिचुल m. N. of a tree.
पिच्छ n. feather of a tail (esp. of the peacock); pl. the feathers of an arrow. f. आ the scum of boiled rice etc.; lump, mass, heap, multitude.
पिच्छक m. sgl. = prec. n. sgl.; f. पिच्छिका the tail of a peacock tied in a bunch.
पिच्छल & **पिच्छिल** a. slimy, slippery.
पिच्छोरा & °ला f. fife, flute.
पिञ्जर a. reddish yellow, gold-coloured, hoary.
पिंजरय्, °यति*, pp. पिञ्जरित to colour reddish yellow.
पिञ्जरी w. कृ = prec.
पिञ्जला f. N. of a river. °ली f. bundle of stalks or grass (r.).
पिञ्जूल, °ञ्जूल n., °ली f. = prec. °ली f.
पिटक m. n., आ f. basket, box; boil, blister.
पिठर n., ई f. pot, pan.
पिठरक m. the same.
पिंठीनस् m. N. of a man.
***पिडक** m., आ f. a small boil or pimple.
पिंण्ड m. n. (पिण्डी f.) a round mass, lump, globe, ball, knob, clod; esp. a cake of meal offered to the Manes, also i.g. a mouthful or lump of bread, victuals, subsistence.
पिण्डक m. lump, knob, meal-cake (v. prec.); f. पिण्डिका a round swelling or protuberance, esp. a fleshy one, du. the calves of the leg.
पिण्डखर्जूर m. a species of date tree.
पिण्डद a. giving the (funeral) cake; m. patron, master.
पिण्डदान n. offering of the funeral cake.
पिण्डनिर्वपन n. the same.
पिण्डपात m. a meal received as an alms; °वेला f. the time for it.*
पिण्डपितृयज्ञ m. a cert. sacrifice to the Manes consisting of meal-cakes.
पिण्डभाज् a. partaking of the funeral cake; m. pl. the Manes.
पिण्डमय a. made of a lump (of clay).*
पिण्डय्, °यति, pp. पिण्डत roll or press together, heap up, collect.
पिण्डाग्र n. a small portion of a (funeral) cake.
पिण्डान्वाहार्यक a. offered after the funeral cakes (श्राद्ध).
पिण्डार & °क m. N. of a serpent-demon.
पिण्डालक्तक s. thick lac.*
पिण्डितार्थ a. having many reasons or advantages.*
पिण्डी w. कृ make into a lump, press together; pp. °कृत thickened, strengthened, thick, strong.
पिण्डोपनिषद् f. T. of an Upanishad.
पिण्याक s. oil-cake.
पितापुत्रं m. du. father and son.
पितामहं m. father's father, grandfather, E. of Brahman, pl. the Manes; f. °मही paternal grandmother.
पितुं m. (n.) drink; nourishment, food.
पितुकृत् a. providing food.
पितुभाज् a. enjoying food.
पितुभृत् a. bringing food.
पितुमन्त् a. rich in food, nourishing.
पितुषणि a. getting food.
पितृं m. father, E. of sev. gods; du. the parents; pl. the father and his brothers, also the forefathers & their spirits, the Manes.
पितृक (adj. —°) = prec.
पितृकर्मन् n. sacrifice to the Manes.
पितृकानन n. cemetery (grove of the fathers).
पितृकार्य & °कृत्य n., °क्रिया f. = पितृकर्मन्.
पितृघातक, °घातिन्, & °घ्न m. parricide.
पितृंतम m. the best of the fathers.
पितृतर्पण n. offering to the Manes (lit. refreshing or feeding the M.).
पितृतस् adv. on the father's side.
पितृत्व n. abstr. to पितृ.
पितृदाय m. patrimony.

1पितृदेव m. pl. the Manes and the gods or the divine Manes.
2पितृदेव a. having the father as a god.
पितृदेवत a. having the Manes for deities.
पितृदेवता f. pl. the Manes and the gods.
पितृदेवत्य a. = पितृदेवत.
पितृदैवत, f. ई relating to the worship of the Manes.
पितृपीत a. drunk by the fathers.
पितृपूजन n. worship of the Manes.
पितृपैतामह, f. ई derived from father and grandfather.
पितृबन्धु m. kinsman by the father's side; n. as abstr.
पितृभक्ति f. devotion to a father.
पितृमंन्त् or पितृमन्त् a. having a father or belonging to the Manes.
पितृमात्रर्थ a. begging for father and mother.
पितृमेध & °यज्ञ m. sacrifice to the Manes.
पितृयाण or °यान a. trodden by the Manes; m. the path trodden by or leading to the Manes.
पितृराज & °राजन् m. king of the Manes, E. of Yama.
पितृलोक m. the father's house; the world or abode of the Manes.
पितृवंश m. the father's family, °वंश्य belonging to it.
पितृवंत् adv. like a father or the Manes.
पितृवध m. parricide.
पितृवन n. = पितृकानन; °सुमनस् n. flower from a cemetery, pl. funeral wreath.
पितृवित्त a. acquired by the fathers.
पितृवेश्मन् n. the father's house.
पितृव्य m. father's brother, paternal uncle.
पितृव्यपुत्र m. cousin (cf. prec.).
पितृव्रत a. worshipping the Manes.
पितृषंद् a. sitting or dwelling with the father i.e. unmarried; living with the Manes.
पितृष्वसृ f. the father's sister.
पितृष्वस्रीय m. a father's sister's son.
पितृसद्मन् n. cemetery (seat of the father's).
†पितृहन् m. parricide.
पितृह्वय n. invocation of the Manes.
पित्तं n. the bile.
पित्तज्वर m. bilious fever.
पित्तल a. bilious.
पित्राद्यन्त a. beginning and ending with the Manes.
पित्र्यं a. paternal, ancestral, belonging or sacred to the Manes.
†पित्व v. अभिपित्वं.
पिद्व m. a cert. animal.
पिधातव्य a. to be covered, shut, or stopped.
पिधान n. covering, shutting up; cover, lid.
पिधायक a. covering, veiling (—°); abstr. °ता f.
पिधित्सु a. wishing to conceal.
पिनद्ध v. अंपिनद्ध.
पिनाक n. staff, stick; the club and the bow of Rudra-Çiva.
पिनाकिन् m. E. of Rudra-Çiva (v. prec.).
पिन्व्, पिंन्वति, °ते cause to swell or stream; fill, moisten; pour forth, discharge; intr. swell, overflow. C. पिन्वयति = S. tr. — प्र = S.
पिन्व a. causing to swell or flow (—°).
पिंन्वन n. a cert. vessel (r.).
पिपतिषु a. about to fall.
पिपासन्त् & °सवन्त् a. thirsty.
पिपासा f. desire to drink, thirst.
पिपासार्त a. tormented by thirst.
पिपासित & °सु a. thirsty.
पिंपिष्वन्त् a. swelling, overfull, abundant.
पिपील m. ant.
पिपीलक m., पिपीलिका f. the same.
पिपीलिक m. the same.
†पिपीषु a. wishing to drink, thirsty.
पिपृच्छिषु a. wishing to ask.
पिप्पका f. a cert. bird.
पिप्पल m. the holy fig-tree; f. आ N. of a river, ई berry; n. पिंप्पल berry, esp. of the holy fig-tree.
पिप्पलाद m. N. of an ancient teacher, pl. his school.
पिप्रीषा f. desire of pleasing.
पिप्रीषु a. wishing to please.
पिंप्रु m. N. of a demon.
पिप्लु m. freckle, mark, mole.
पिब a. drinking (—°).
पिंबध्यै dat. inf. to 1पा.

पिब्द्, only pp. पिब्दमान being firm or compact.

पिब्दन a. firm, compact, solid.

1पिश्, पिंशति, °ते, pp. पिशित & पिष्ट (q.v.) cut up, carve (esp. meat), arrange, prepare, adorn, shape, form; M. also refl. adorn one's self, be brilliant or beautiful. — अभि & आ adorn, embellish. — Cf. पेपिश्त्, पेपिशान.

2पिश् f. ornament, decoration.

पिश m. a kind of deer.

पिशङ्ग, f. ई reddish brown.

पिशङ्गाश्व a. having reddish horses.

पिशाच m. a cert. class of demons or devils.

पिशाचक, f. ई the same.

पिशाचाङ्गना f. female demon, witch.

पिशाचि m. N. of a demon.

पिशित n. flesh (cut up or prepared).

पिशिताश, °शन, & °शिन् a. eating flesh; m. a Rakṣas or Piçāca, demon, fiend.

पिशील n. a (wooden) vessel or dish.

पिशुन a. backbiting, slanderous, treacherous; betraying or showing (—°). m. betrayer, traitor, slanderer, a man's name; n. = seq.

पिशुनता f. slander, calumny.

पिशुनय्, °यति, pp. पिशुनित betray, manifest.

पिष्, पिनष्टि (पिंषति), pp. पिष्ट (q.v.) grind, pound, crush, destroy. C. पेषयति = S. — निस् & विनिस् pound, crush, rub (the hands). प्र crush or grind down. प्रति rub or beat against (together), pound, crush. वि beat asunder, pelt with (instr.). सम् pound, squeeze, crush or grind down. — Cf. उत्पिष्ट, प्रपिष्ट.

1पिष्ट a. adorned, decorated.

2पिष्ट s. bread, cake; f. ई & n. flour, meal.

पिष्टक m. = prec. s.; n. = prec. f. & n.

पिष्टप v. विष्टप.

पिष्टपशु m. an animal made of meal.

पिष्टमय, f. ई made of meal.

(*पिष्टात &) °क s. perfumed powder.

पिष्टान्न n. farinaceous food.

पिष्टि f. powder.

पिष्टोदक n. water mixed with flour.

पिस्, पिस्यति stretch.

पिस्पृक्षु a. wishing to touch.

पिहित v. अपिहित.

पिहिति f. covering, stopping.

1पी (पि), पयते (पीपेति), pp. पीन & पीपिवंस् (q.v.) swell, be exuberant, overflow; cause to swell or overflow, fill, bless. — अभि swell, be exuberant. आ & प्र swell or cause to swell. — Cf. 2आपीत & आपीन.

2पी, पीयति v. पीय्.

पीठ n. seat, stool, bench, pedestal.

पीठक s., पीठिका f. = prec.

पीठमर्द m., °मर्दिका f. the hero's or heroine's companion (d.).

पीठसर्प & °सर्पिन् a. moving with the help of a board, i.e. lame; m. cripple.

पीड्, पीडयति (°ते), pp. पीडित (q.v.) press, squeeze, oppress, suppress, vex, harass, pain, beleaguer (a city), eclipse (sun or moon). — अभि press against, tread upon, press, squeeze, vex, pain, beleaguer. अव press down, vex, harass. आ press out, vex, plague. उद् press upwards or out of. उप press, suppress, vex, pain. नि press against or together, plague, annoy. निस् press out or together. परि press together, compress, plague or torment greatly. प्र press, squeeze, pain. सम् press together, pain, torment.

पीडन a. & n. vexing, paining.

पीडा f. pain, ache, harm, wrong.

पीडाकर & पीडाकृत् a. causing woe or harm.

पीडित n. harm, mischief.

1पीत v. 2पा.

2पीत a. yellow; abstr. ता f.

पीतक, f. °तिका = prec.

पीतन m. N. of a tree; *n. saffron.

पीतवन्त् a. having drunk.

पीतवासस् a. dressed in yellow; m. E. of Viṣṇu.

पीतसोमपूर्व a. having formerly drunk the Soma-juice.

पीताम्बर a. & m. = पीतवासस्.

पीति f. drinking; drink, beverage.

पीतिमन् m. a yellow colour.

पीतोदक a. having drunk water.

†पीथ m. drink or protection.

पीथिन् a. drinking (—°).
पीन a. fat, brawny, thick solid, firm. Abstr. °ता† f., °त्व† n.
पीनस m. rheum, catarrh; p. °सित & °सिन्.
पीपिवंस्, f. पिप्युषी exuberant, luxurious; abounding in, flowing with (gen. or acc.).
पीय्, पीयति abuse, blame.
पीयक m. abuser, scoffer.
पीयतु & पीयु a. scornful, scoffing.
पीयूष m. n. biestings, cream, juice, Soma, nectar.
पीयूषगरल n. sgl. nectar and poison.
पीला f. N. of an Apsaras.
पीलु m. N. of a tree (n. its fruit); elephant, atom.
पीलुमती (द्यौस्) f. the central sky.
पीव & पीवंस् (only nom. पीवान्) a. fat.
पीवन्, f. पीवरी swelling, fat, stout, plump, thick; m. a man's name; f. a woman's name.
पीवर a. fat; swelling with, rich in (—°); abstr. °त्व n.
पीवस् n. fat.
पीवस a. fat, swelling, abundant.
पीवस्वन्त् a. rich in fat.
पीविष्ठ (superl.) very fat.
पुंलिङ्ग n. the masculine gender, a. masculine (g.).
पुंवत् adv. like a man or like the masculine (g.).
पुंश्चली f. harlot (lit. running after men).
पुंश्चलीपुत्र* & पुंश्चलीय m. whore-son.
पुंश्चलू f. a harlot; m. fornicator.
पुंस् v. पुमंस्.
पुंसवन a. bringing forth a male; n. (± व्रत) a cert. ceremony to get a son.
पुंसवन्त् a. having a son.
पुंसुवन n. begetting a male child.
पुंस्क (adj. —°) = पुमंस्.
*पुंस्कटी f. a man's hip.
पुंस्कोकिल m. the male Kokila.
पुंस्त्री du. a male and a female (child).
पुंस्त्व n. the being male, the masculine gender (g.); manhood, semen virile.
पुक्कश or °स m. a cert. mixed caste.
पुङ्ख m. the lowest (feathered) part of an arrow, poss. पुङ्खित.
पुङ्खितशर a. having feathered arrows.
पुंगव m. bull; hero among, chief of (—°).
पुच्छ m. n. tail; poss. °वन्त् †.
पुच्छधि m. the root of the tail.
पुच्छाग्र n. the tip of the tail.
पुञ्ज m. heap, lump, mass, multitude of (—°).
पुञ्जय्, °यति, pp. पञ्जित heap up, press together.
पुञ्जशस् adv. in heaps.
पुञ्जिष्ठ m. a fisherman or a birdcatcher.
पुञ्जी w. कृ = पुञ्जय्, w. भू pass. & refl.
पुट्, पुटति to fold or cover.
पुट m. n., ई f. fold, cavity; cover, envelope.
पुटक m. fold, pocket, cavity; chink.
पुटकिनी f. plant or group of lotus-flowers.
पुण्डरिस्रजा f. garland of lotus-flowers.
पुण्डरीक n. a lotus-flower, esp. a white one (poss. °वन्त्); m. a man's name, f. आ a woman's name.
पुण्डरीकनयन a. lotus-eyed, E. of Viṣṇu or Kṛṣṇa.
पुण्डरीकमुख a. lotus-faced; f. °खी a kind of leech.
(पुण्डरीकलोचन*) & °काक्ष a. = पुण्डरीकनयन.
पुण्ड्र m. N. of an ancient hero; pl. N. of a people.
पुण्य a. prosperous, auspicious, favourable, fair, beautiful, right, just, pure, good, holy. n. good, right, good work (also collect), virtue, merit; also = seq.
पुण्यक n. a cert. religious ceremony.
पुण्यकर्तृ, °कर्मन्, & °कृत् a. right-doing, virtuous, honest.
पुण्यकृत्या & °क्रिया f. a right or good action.
पुण्यगन्ध a. sweet-scented, fragrant.
पुण्यगन्धि & पुण्यगन्धिन् a. = prec.
पुण्यजन m. pl. a kind of genii (lit. good people.)
पुण्यता f., °त्व n. holiness, purity, virtue.
1पुण्यतीर्थ n. a holy bathing-place.
2पुण्यतीर्थ a. rich in holy bathing-places.
पुण्यपापेक्षितृ a. seeing good and bad deeds.
पुण्यफल n. the fruit of good works.
पुण्यलोक a. belonging to or partaking of the good world.

पुण्यवन्त् a. virtuous, fortunate.
पुण्यशील a. of virtuous or honest character.
पुण्यश्लोक a. of good fame; m. E. of Nala, f. आ E. of Sītā & Draupadī.
पुण्यात्मन् a. holy-minded, virtuous, honest.
पुण्याहं n. a god or happy day, also = seq.
पुण्याहवाचन n. wishing a person a happy day.
पुत् v. पुट्.
पुत्तल & °क m. (°लिका f.) puppet, statue.
पुत्तिका f. the same; termite or a small species of bee.
पुत्रं m. son, child, the young of an animal; f. ई daughter.
पुत्रक m. little son, boy, N. of a man; f. पुत्रिका daughter, esp. adopted daughter (j.), puppet, dole.
पुत्रंकाम a. wishing for sons or children.
पुत्रकाम्या f. wish for a son or children.
पुत्रकार्य n. a son's duty.
पुत्रकृतक a. adopted as a son.
पुत्रकृत्य n. = पुत्रकार्य.
पुत्रकृथ s. procreation of children.
पुत्रता f., °त्व n. sonship.
पुत्रदार n. sgl. son and wife.
पुत्रपिण्डपालन s. a cert. religious ceremony.*
पुत्रपितृ m. du. son and father.
पुत्रपौत्र n. sgl. (also °क) & m. pl. sons and grandsons; p. °त्रिन्.
पुत्रमय a. consisting of a son.
पुत्रवत् adv. like a son (sons).
पुत्रंवन्त् a. having a son, sons, or children.
पुत्रस्नेह m. a son's love.
पुत्राचार्य a. having a son for one's teacher.
पुत्रार्थिन्, f. °र्थिणी wishing for children.
पुत्रिण्याप्त a. begot with a female that has already a son.
पुत्रिंन्, f. °णी = पुत्रंवन्त्.
पुत्रिय्, °यति wish for a son or children.
पुत्रिय a. relating to a son.
पुत्री v. पुत्र.
पुत्री w. कृ adopt as a son, abstr. °करण n.
पुत्रीय्, °यति = पुत्रिय्.
पुत्रीय & पुत्र्य a. = पुत्रिय.
पुथ्, C. पोथयति (°ते) crush, destroy. — अव, नि, वि = S.

पुद् s. hell or a kind of hell.
पुद्गल a. beautiful; m. body, matter, soul, individual, man, E. of Çiva.
पुनःकरण n. doing again, transforming.
पुनःकर्मन् n., °क्रिया f. repetition.
पुनःपाक m. repeated cooking or baking.
पुंनर् adv. back, home, again, once more ± भूयस्); again and again, repeatedly (mostly पुंनः पुनः); further, moreover, besides or in turn, on the other hand, however, but. Lays stress on a prec. वा, अथ वा, & अपि वा; पुनः — पुनः now—now. — Cf. किम्.
पुनरागम m., °न n. return.
पुनरागामिन् a. returning.
पुनराधान n. setting up again (the sacred fires).
पुनरानयन n. leading back.
पुनरावर्तिन् a. returning or leading back (to mundane existence).
पुनरावृत्ति f. return (esp. to mundane existence); repetition.
पुनरुक्त a. said again, repeated; superfluous, useless; n. adv. or = seq.
पुनरुक्तता f., °त्व n. repetition, tautology.
पुनरुक्तवादिन् a. repeating the same thing, talking idly.*
पुनरुक्ति f. repetition, tautology.
पुनरुपलब्धि f. obtaining again, recovery.
पुनर्गर्भवती f. again pregnant.
पुनर्जन्मन् n. re-birth.
पुनर्जात a. born again.
पुंनर्णव a. new again, renewed.
पुनर्दर्शन n. seeing again.
पुनर्दारक्रिया f. taking a second wife.
पुंनर्नव a. = पुनर्णव.
पुनर्भव a. born again; m. new birth.
1पुनर्भू a. = prec. a.; f. a female marrying again (with her own consent).
2पुनर्भू a. be born or marrying again (cf. prec.).
पुनर्भोग m. enjoying again.
पुनर्लाभ m. obtaining again, recovery.
पुनर्लेखन n. writing down again.
पुनर्वचन n. saying again, repeating.
पुंनर्वसु a. restoring goods; m. (sgl. & du.) N. of a lunar mansion.

पुनर्वाद m. saying again, tautology.
पुनर्हन् a. destroying again.
पुनर्हविस् n. repeated oblation.
पुनश्चर्वण n. chewing again (the cud).
पुनश्चिति f. piling up again.
पुनःसंभव m. re-birth.
पुंनपुंसक n. masculine and neuter (g.).
पुंनाग m. N. of a tree.
1पुंनामन् a. having a masculine name.
2पुन्नामन् a. having the name पुद् (q.v.).
पुमंस् (पुंस्) m. a man or male, a word in the masculine gender (g.); man = human being; servant, attendant; the soul, spirit.
पुंभाव m. masculine sex, manliness.
1पुर् f. fullness, abundance (only पूर्भिस्).
2पुर् (nom. पूर्) f. stronghold, castle, (fortified) town; the body.
पुर n., ई f. the same.
पुरउष्णिह् f. N. of a metre.
पुरएतृ m. who goes before, leader.
पुरजन m. townsfolk.
पुरजित् m. the conqueror of castles, E. of Çiva.
पुरंजय m. N. of sev. heroes (lit. = prec.).
पुरतस् adv. & prep. in front, before (sp. & t.), in presence of (gen. or —°).
पुरद्वार n. a city-gate.
पुरंदर m. E. of sev. gods (lit. destroyer of castles).
पुरंधि a. prolific (lit. bearing a body), bounteous, liberal; f. liberality, also = seq.
पुरंध्रि or °ध्री f. wife, woman.
पुरभिद्, °मथन, & °मथितृ m. of Çiva (lit. = पुरंदर).
पुरय m. N. of a man.
पुररक्ष & °रक्षिन् m. watchman of a town.
पुरराष्ट्र (°—) town and country.
पुरवासिन् m. city-dweller, townsman.
पुरश्चरण a. making preparations for (—°), abstr. °ता f.; n. a preparatory rite.
पुरस् adv. in front, forward, before (also prep. w. gen., abl., acc., or —°); eastward, at first. With गम् go first, take the lead. — Cf. 1कृ & धा.
पुरस्कार m. preference, veneration, honour.
पुरस्कृत a. placed before, appointed, chosen, preferred, honoured; accompanied by, possessed of, connected or occupied with; n. adv. in company with (—°).
पुरस्कृत्य ger. having placed before or appointed, having paid respect to; as adv. or prep. with regard to, on account of, about (acc.).
पुरस्तात् adv. in front, before, eastward or from the east, at first, previously (also as prep. w. gen., abl., acc., or —°).
पुरस्तान्मुख a. having the face turned towards, looking into a person's face.*
पुरःसद् a. sitting in front or towards the east.
पुरःसर, f. ई going before, preceding. m. forerunner, attendant, servant; adj. preceded or accompanied by, connected with, n. adv. with, after (—°).
पुरःस्थ a. evident, clear (lit. standing before, scil. one's eyes).
पुरा adv. formerly, once upon a time, of yore; up to the present time, hitherto (w. pres. ± स्म); at first, firstly; soon, shortly (w. pres.); w. a neg. never. — As a conj. ere, before (w. pres. ± न, मा, or यदि); as a prep. before, from, except, without (abl.).
पुराकल्प m. the past or a tale of the past.
पुराकृत a. done before; n. former deed.
पुराजा a. existing from of old.
पुराण, f. ई former, ancient, old; n. things of the past, ancient history or legend, T. of a class of sacred works.
पुराणवत् adv. as of old.
पुराणविद् a. knowing past things.
पुराणविद्या f., °वेद m. abstr. to prec.
पुराणसंहिता f. collection of the Purāṇas.
पुरातन, f. ई existing from of old, former, ancient, loc. in the times of old; m. pl. the ancients.
पुराधिप & पुराध्यक्ष m. governor of a city, prefect of police.
पुरारि m. E. of Çiva or Viṣṇu (lit. foe of the castles).
पुराविद् a. knowing past things.

पुरावृत्त a. happened long since, past, ancient; n. past event, old story.

पुरिशय a. resting in the body.

पुरीतत् m. n. the pericardium, intestine i.g.

पुरीष n. crumbling or loose earth, rubbish, excrement, ordure; poss. °वन्त्.

पुरीषिन् & °ष्य a. dwelling in or on the earth; earthy, muddy.

पुरु, f. पूर्वी much, many (in l. l. only °—); m. N. of an ancient king; n. पुरु or पुरू much, often, greatly; superl. पुरुतम or पुरूतम very much or many, very frequent, often repeated, n. adv.

पुरुकुत्स m. a man's name.

पुरुकुत्सानी f. the wife of Purukutsa.

पुरुकृत् & °कृत्वन् a. doing much, active, busy, efficacious.

पुरुक्षु a. rich in food, i.g. abundant in, liberal with (gen.).

पुरुजित् m. a man's name.

पुरुत्रा adv. in many places or ways, variously, often.

पुरुदंस & °दंसस् a. rich in wonders or deeds.

†**पुरुदत्र** a. rich in gifts.

पुरुद्रप्स a. rich in drops, dropping.

पुरुध & °धा adv. in many ways, variously, frequently.

पुरुप्रिय a. beloved of many.

पुरुप्रैष or °प्रैष a. inciting many.

†**पुरुभुज्** a. possessing much.

पुरुमित्र m. a man's name (friend of many).

पुरुरूप a. multiform, many-coloured.

पुरुवीर a. rich in men (children or followers).

पुरुशाक a. helpful, powerful.

पुरुश्चन्द्र a. shining much or bright.

पुरुष (पूरुष) m. man, human being, male, person, individual of a cert. generation; man = hero; man = servant, attendant; official, agent; the primal man or spirit; the life-giving principle in man and other beings; the supreme spirit or soul of the universe. — f. पुरुषी a woman.

पुरुषकार m. manly deed, human effort; manhood, virility.

पुरुषकेसरिन् m. man-lion (E. of Viṣṇu).

पुरुषज्ञान n. knowledge of men.

पुरुषता f. manhood, manliness; as instr. adv. = seq.

पुरुषत्रा adv. among men or in the manner of men.

पुरुषत्व n. manhood, virility.

पुरुषपशु m. a man as a sacrificial victim or a beast of a man.

पुरुषमानिन् a. thinking one's self a man or hero; abstr. °नित्व n.

पुरुषमृग m. the male of the antelope.

पुरुषमेध m. the sacrifice of a man.

पुरुषर्षभ m. man-bull, i.e. excellent man.

पुरुषवर m. the best of men, E. of Viṣṇu.

पुरुषविध a. man-like; abstr. °ता† f.

पुरुषव्याघ्र m. man-tiger, excellent man.

पुरुषसिंह m. man-lion, hero.

पुरुषाकार a. of human form.

पुरुषाद् a. eating or consuming men.

पुरुषाद, f. ई = prec.; m. a Rakṣas.

पुरुषादक a. & m. the same.

पुरुषानृत n. falsehood regarding a human being.

पुरुषार्थ m. any object or aim of men; °प्रयोजन n. means for obtaining it.

पुरुषी v. पुरुष.

पुरुषोत्तम m. the best of men or of servants; the supreme spirit (Viṣṇu or Kṛṣṇa).

पुरुष्टुत a. praised by men.

पुरुष्य a. human.

पुरुहूत a. invoked by many; m. E. of Indra.

पुरू v. पुरु.

पुरूची f. many, abundant; long.

पुरूतम v. पुरु.

पुरूरवस् a. crying loudly; m. N. of a myth. king and hero.

पुरूवसु a. rich in goods.

पुरोग a. going before, first, excellent, best; m. forerunner, leader, chief (f. आ), adj. led or accompanied by, furnished with (—°).

पुरोगम a. & s. = prec.

पुरोगव m. forerunner (lit. fore-bull); leader (f. ई).

पुरोगा m. = prec.

पुरोडाश् (°ळाश्; nom. °ळास्) m. sacrificial cake, oblation i.g.

पुरोडाश m. = prec.; offering of (gen.).
पुरोधस् m. appointed priest, house-priest of a king.
पुरोधा f. the office of a house-priest.
पुरोऽनुवाक्यवन्त् a. poss. to seq.
पुरोऽनुवाक्या f. invitatory verse (r.).
पुरोभाग m. forepart; obtrusiveness, impudence, malevolence, envy.
पुरोभागिन् a. obtrusive, troublesome (abstr. °गिता f.*).
पुरोभू a. being in front, excelling (acc.).
पुरोमुख a. turned forward or eastward (with the mouth or face).
पुरोमूल n. the root of a tree that is turned eastward.
पुरोयुध् & °योधं a fighting in front.
पुरोरथ a. whose chariot is foremost; i.g. excelling, superior.
पुरोरुच् a. shining in front or before; f. N. of cert. sacred formulas.
पुरोवर्तिन् a. being in front or before.
पुरोवात m. wind from before, east wind.
पुरोहन् a. destroying castles.
पुरोहित a. set before, commissioned, appointed; m. an appointed priest, esp. house-priest of a prince.
पुरोहिति f. the office of the house-priest.
पुर्य a. being in a strong place.
पुलक m. N. of a plant; n. pl. the erection of the hairs of the body (as a sign of rapture or desire).
पुलकय्, °यति, pp. पुलकित having the hairs erect (cf. prec.).
पुलस्त्य & पुलह m. names of ancient Rishis.
पुलाक m. empty or bad grain.
पुलिन n. sandbank, small island.
पुलिन्द m. pl. N. of a people.
†पुलु (°—) = पुरु.
पलुकाम a. desiring much, covetous.
पुलोमन् m. N. of a demon.
पुलोमा f. N. of a female demon.
पुलोमारि m. foe of Puloman, i.e. Indra.
पुल्कस m., ई f. N. of a cert. mixed caste.
पुल्वघ a. doing much evil.
पुष्, पुष्यति (°ते, पुष्णाति, & पोषति), pp. पुष्ट (q.v.) intr. thrive, bloom, grow, prosper; tr. cause to thrive etc.; cherish, foster, develop, unfold, display, possess, enjoy. C. पोषयति cherish, foster, rear, bring up, cause to be nourished by (instr.). — उद् (उत्पुष्णाति) nourish, make fat. उप = S.* — Cf. परिपुष्ट, विपुष्ट.
पुष्कर n. a blue lotus-flower (fig. of the heart); head of the ladle (r.); the skin of a drum; the tip of an elephant's trunk; water, air, the sky; N. of sev. places of pilgrimage. — m. a species of crane, E. of Kṛṣṇa, Çiva, etc.; a man's name.
पुष्कराक्ष a. lotus- or blue-eyed.
पुष्करारण्य n. N. of a forest.
पुष्करावर्तक m. pl. a cert. class of clouds.
पुष्करिन् a. rich in lotuses; m. elephant, f. °रिणी lotus-pond.
पुष्कल a. abundant, numerous, rich, splendid, resounding, loud; m. a kind of drum, a man's name; n. the head of a ladle.
पुष्कलक m. the musk-deer.
पुष्ट a. having thrived; nourished, fat, strong; abundant, rich in, furnished with; n. wealth, prosperity.
पुष्टाङ्ग a. fat-limbed.
पुष्टि or पुष्टि f. thriving, prosperity, comfort, wealth, opulence; breeding, rearing (of cattle), nourishment (o. personified).
पुष्टिमन्त् a. thriving, abundant.
पुष्टिवर्धन a. augmenting prosperity.
पुष्प n. bloom, flower (adj. —° f. आ or ई); m. topaz, a man's name.
पुष्पक m. a kind of snake, N. of a mountain; n. (m.) N. of Kubera's chariot.
पुष्पकरण्ड n. flower-basket, also = seq.
पुष्पकरण्डकोद्यान n. N. of a grove.
पुष्पकाल m. spring (time of flowers).
पुष्पकेतु m. E. of the god of love (lit. having flowers as attribute).
1पुष्पचाप m. a bow of flowers.
2पुष्पचाप m. E. of the god of love (lit. having a bow of flowers).
पुष्पदन्त m. flower-tooth, E. of Çiva or of an attendant of Çiva.
पुष्पध m. the son of an outcast Brahman.
पुष्पधनुस् & °धन्वन् m. = 2पुष्पचाप.

पुष्पपेशल a. as delicate as a flower.
पुष्पफल n. blossom and fruit.
पुष्पबाण m. E. of the god of love (the flower-arrowed).
पुष्पभद्र m. a man's name.*
पुष्पभाजन n. a flower-basket.
पुष्पमय, f. ई consisting of flowers.
पुष्पमाला f. garland of flowers.
पुष्पमित्र m. N. of sev. kings.
पुष्पमेघ m. a cloud raining flowers.
पुष्पराग m. topaz.
पुष्पलावी f. flower-gatherer or seller, flower-girl.
पुष्पवन्त् a. rich in blossoms or flowers.
पुष्पवर्ष n., °वृष्टि f. rain of flowers.
पुष्पशय्या f. a couch of flowers.
पुष्पशेखर m. garland of flowers.
पुष्पसायक m. = पुष्पबाण.
पुष्पसार m. the juice of flowers.
पुष्पसूत्र n. T. of a Sūtra work.
पुष्पागम m. spring (the coming of flowers).
पुष्पायुध m. = पुष्पबाण.
पुष्पाराम m. flower-garden.
पुष्पावन्त् = पुष्पवन्त्; f. °वती† N. of a town.
पुष्पित a. blooming, flowery.
पुष्पिताग्र a. flower-pointed; f. आ N. of a metre.
पुष्पिन् a. = पुष्पित.
पुष्पेषु m. = पुष्पबाण.
पुष्पोत्कटा f. N. of a Rākṣasī.
पुष्प्य्, पुष्प्यति to blossom.
1पुष्य n. nourishment; the blossom i.e. the best part of anything.
2पुष्य m. N. of a lunar mansion; f. पुष्या a cert. plant.
पुष्यसे dat. inf. to पुष्.
पुस्त m., आ f. manuscript, book.
पुस्तक m., पुस्तिका f. the same.
1पू, पुनाति, पुनीते, पवते (°ति), pp. पूत (q.v.) cleanse, purify, make clear or bright, sift, discern; contrive, invent, compose; M. also clear itself, flow clear; grow or be pure (lit. & fig.). C. पवयति or पावयति purify. — अति purify, strain over or through (acc.); M. pass through (the body). अभि M. clear itself, flow clear towards or for (acc.). आ M. flow clear towards (acc.) or in (loc.), bestow by flowing (also A.). उद् cleanse, purify. निस् winnow. परा clear off. परि strain, filter, purify; M. flow off clear. वि cleanse thoroughly. सम् cleanse, purify; C. the same. — Cf. निपूत, परिपूत.
2पू purifying (—°).
3पू drinking (—°).
पूग m. association, corporation, multitude; betel-palm, n. its nut.
पूगयज्ञ m. a sacrifice for a corporation.
पूज्, पूजयति, °ते, pp. पूजित (q.v.) reverence, worship, honour, present with (instr.); respect, regard. — अभि receive or greet reverentially, honour or present with (instr.), praise, celebrate. परि esteem highly. प्र honour, praise, esteem, present with (instr.). प्रति honour (in turn), salute respectfully, esteem, present with (instr.), praise, extol. सम् do honour to, salute respectfully, praise, celebrate, esteem, present with (instr.). — Cf. अभिपूजित.
पूजक, °जिका f. worshipper (gen. or —°).
पूजन n. worship, veneration.
पूजनीय a. to be honoured, honourable.
पूजयितव्य a. = पूजनीय.
पूजयितृ m. worshipper, adorer.
पूजा f. honour, worship, respect.
पूजागृह n. house of worship, temple.
पूजार्ह a. worthy of reverence, venerable.
पूजासत्कार m. revering by worship, adoration.*
पूजासंभार m. the apparatus of worship.
पूजित a. honoured, respected, acknowledged recommended, initiated; frequented or inhabited by; furnished with (—°).
पूजोपकरण n. the apparatus of worship.*
पूज्य a. to be honoured, honourable.
पूज्यता f., °त्व n. honourableness.
पूतदक्ष & °दक्षस् a. pure-minded.
पूतन m. a kind of demon; f. आ, abstr. °त्व n.
पूतपाप a. purified from sin.
पूतमूर्ति a. (whose body has been) purified.
पूति a. putrid, stinking.
पूतिक a. = prec.; m. a cert. herb.

पूतिगन्ध m. fetid odour, stench.
पूतिगन्धि a. fetid, stinking.
पूतित्व n. putrid state, stench.
पूतिभाव m. the same.
पूतिमृत्तिक m. N. of a cert. hell.
पूतिवक्त्र a. having a stinking breath, abstr. °ता f.
पूतीक m. a kind of herb (cf. पूतिक).
पूत्रिम a. purified, clean.
पूप m. cake.
पूपशाला f. cake-room, a baker's shop.
पूय्, पूयति become foul or putrid, stink.
पूय m. n. pus.
पूयभुज् a. eating pus.
पूयशोणित n. purulent blood.
पूर a. filling, completing, satisfying (—°); m. completion, fulfilment, satisfaction; flood, gush, stream; a cake.
पूरक a. = prec. (—° or *gen.); m. stream, gush, f. पूरिका a sort of cake.
पूरण a. (f. ई) & n. (पूरण) making full, completing, accomplishing, satisfying; m. & f. ई an ordinal number in the masc. & fem. gender (g.).
पूरणीय a. to be completed, supplied, or satisfied.
पूरय्, °यति v. 1पृ.
पूरयितृ (°तृक*) a. filling up; m. fulfiller, satisfier.
पूरु m. man, people (coll.); N. of a tribe & an ancient prince.
पूरुष v. पुरुष.
पूरुषाद् a. eating men.
पूर्ण a. filled, full; full of, rich in (instr., gen., or —°), complete, abundant; fulfilled, accomplished, satisfied.
पूर्णक m. a cert. tree; f. पूर्णिका a cert. bird.
पूर्णकुम्भ m. a full cup or jar; m. n. a breach or gap of a cert. shape.
पूर्णचन्द्र m. the full moon.
पूर्णता f., °त्व n. fulness.
पूर्णपात्र m. n., °पात्री f. a full vessel or cup; °पात्रवृत्त्या plentifully, abundantly.
पूर्णमास् m. the full moon.
पूर्णमास m. the same, full-moon sacrifice; f. ई the day or night of full moon.
पूर्णविंशतिवर्ष a. full twenty years old.
पूर्णश्री a. completely fortunate.
पूर्णामृतांशुवदना f. having a face like the full moon.
पूर्णार्थ a. having one's wishes fulfilled, successful.
पूर्णिमा f. the day or night of full moon.
पूर्णेच्छ a. whose wish has been fulfilled.
पूर्णेन्दु m. the full moon.
पूर्त a. filled, full of (gen.); bestowed, fulfilled; n. = seq.
पूर्ति f. fulfilment, reward; merit, esp. charity.
पूर्तिन् poss. to पूर्त.
पूर्त्वन् a. having filled one's self (with food).
पूर्पति m. the lord of a castle or city.
पूर्भिद् a. breaking castles; abstr. °भिद्य n.
पूर्व a. being before (sp. & t.), fore, first, eastern, to the east of (abl.); prior, preceding, ancient, previous to, earlier than (abl. or —°, often °— or —° w. pp. in the sense of an adv., e.g. पूर्वोक्त or उक्तपूर्व spoken before or already); accompanied by, following; with, under, according to (—°); w. वयस् n. youth; w. आयुस् n. old age. — m. elder brother, pl. the ancestors or ancients. f. पूर्वा (± दिश्) the east. n. forepart, as adv. in front, before (as prep. w. abl.), first, previously, already, long since; —° accompanied by etc. (cf. adj. —°). पूर्व-उत्तर former–latter, n. adv. first–last; अद्य पूर्वम् until now, hitherto.
पूर्वक, f. पूर्विका ealier, former, previous; —° adj. & n. adv. accompanied by etc. = prec.; m. ancestor, forefather.
पूर्वकर्मन् n. a former or the first action.
पूर्वकाय m. the fore or upper part of the body.
पूर्वकाल & °लिक a. of former times.
पूर्वकृत a. done before, n. a former act.
पूर्वग & °गत a. going & gone before.
पूर्वगत्वन् a. going to meet.
पूर्वचित्ति f. foreboding, presentiment, only dat. forthwith, immediately.
पूर्वचोदित a. mentioned or stated before.
पूर्वज a. born or produced before, former, previous, ancient, very old, the elder or

eldest; m. forefather, ancestor; eldest (elder) brother.
पूर्वजन m. pl. men of former times, the ancients.
1पूर्वजन्मन् n. a former birth of life.
2पूर्वजन्मन् m. the elder brother.
पूर्वजा & °जावन् a. born before, former, ancient.
पूर्वतस् adv. in front, eastward, first.
पूर्वतस्कर m. a former thief.
पूर्वत्र adv. before, above; also = loc. to पूर्व.
पूर्वत्व n. precedence, priority, former state.
पूर्वथा adv. formerly, from old or as of old, at first, before.
पूर्वदक्षिण a. south-eastern.
पूर्वदत्त a. given before.
पूर्वदिश् f. the eastern region.
पूर्वदृष्ट a. seen before, looked upon by the ancients as (nom.).
पूर्वदेव m., °देवता f. a primal god or deity.
पूर्वदेश m. the eastern region or country.
पूर्वनिपात m. the irregular precedence of an element of a compound (g.).
पूर्वनिविष्ट a. dug before (tank).
पूर्वपक्ष m. the fore part or side; the first half of a month or year; action or law-suit; the first objection (ph.).
पूर्वपथ m. the former path.
पूर्वपद n. first member of a compound (g.).
पूर्वपा a. drinking before or first.
पूर्वपाद m. forefoot.
पूर्वपाय्य n. the first drink.
पूर्वपितामह m. forefather, ancestor.
पूर्वपीति f. = पूर्वपाय्य.
पूर्वपुरुष m. forefather, ancestor; the primeval spririt i.e. Brahman.
पूर्वपूर्व a. each previous or former one; m. pl. the forefathers.
पूर्वपूर्वोक्त a. the one always mentioned before.
पूर्वपेय n. = पूर्वपाय्य.
पूर्वबन्धु m. first i.e. best friend.
पूर्वभाग m. the fore or upper part.
पूर्वभाज् a. receiving the first share, preferred.
पूर्वभुक्ति f. old or long possession.
पूर्वभूभृत् a. the eastern mountain or a former king.
पूर्वमारिन् a. dying before.
पूर्वमीमांसा f. the former Mīmāṅsā (ph.).
पूर्वरात्र m. the first part of the night.
1पूर्वरूप n. indication, forerunner, prognostic of (प्रति); a cert. figure of speech.
2पूर्वरूप a. having the previous form, being as before.
पूर्ववत् adv. as before, as aforesaid.
पूर्ववन्त् a. having or relating to something precedent; f. °वती having been married before.
पूर्ववह् (°वाह्) a. drawing in front or for the first time.
पूर्ववाद m. action at law.
पूर्वविद् a. knowing (the things of) the past.
पूर्वविधि m. a preceding rule.
पूर्वविहित a. deposited or buried before (treasure).*
पूर्ववृत्त a. past before; n. a former event.
पूर्ववैरिन् m. first i.e. worst foe.
पूर्वशिष्य m., आ f. former pupil.
पूर्वसद् a. sitting in front.
पूर्वसभिक m. chief of a gaming house.
पूर्वसमुद्र & °सागर m. the eastern sea.
पूर्वसाहस n. the first or heaviest fine (j.).
पूर्वसू f. first bringing forth.
पूर्वहूति f. first invocation, morning prayer.
पूर्वाचल m. the eastern mountain.
पूर्वाचार्य m. an ancient teacher.
पूर्वाद्य a. beginning with the east.
पूर्वाद्रि m. = पूर्वाचल.
पूर्वाधिक a. more important or greater than before.
पूर्वापर a. fore and hind, eastern and western, first and last, prior and subsequent.
पूर्वार्ध m. (n.) the front or upper part; the east side; the first half.
पूर्वार्धकाय m. the front or upper part of the body.
पूर्वावधीरित a. despised before.
पूर्वावेदक m. plaintiff.
पूर्वाह्ण m. forenoon (lit. earlier day); loc. early in the morning.
पूर्वाह्णिक, f. ई relating to the forenoon.
पूर्वी v. पुरु.

पूर्वेण adv. in front; before, to the east of (acc. or gen.).

पूर्वेद्युस् adv. on the day before, yesterday.

पूर्वोक्त a. said or mentioned before.

पूर्वोपकारिन् a. who has rendered a person a service before.

पूर्वोपनिहित a. deposited before.

पूर्व्य (पूर्विय) a. previous, former, ancient, old; first, best, next, nearest; n. adv. formerly, long, since, hitherto.

पूल & °क m. bunch, bundle.

पूल्य n. an empty grain of corn.

पूषण्वन्त् a. protected by Pūṣan (cf. seq.).

पूषन् m. N. of a Vedic divinity, often identif. with the Sun.

1पृ, पिपर्ति, पृणाति, पृणति, pp. पूर्त & पूर्ण (q.v.) fill, make full; sate, nourish, refresh; give abundantly, lavish (dat. of pers. & acc. of th.), present with (acc. of pers. & instr. of th.), fulfil, accomplish. M. & P. पूर्यते (पूर्यते & पूर्यति) fill or sate one's self, become full of (instr.). C. पूरयति, °ते make full, complete, fulfil, accomplish; fill, cover, present with (instr.). — अभि make full; M.P. become full, be filled with (gen.); C. fill, complete, load, cover, present abundantly with (instr.), increase, augment, fulfil, accomplish. आ fill, sate; make full, complete, fulfil, accomplish; M.P. be or become full, increase, be rich in (instr.); C. fill wholly, cover with (instr.). नि put down, pour out (r.). परि M.P. be filled, become full or complete by (instr.); C. fill, make full, accomplish. प्र fill, make up, complete, accomplish; M.P. refl.; C. = S. प्रति bestow in return; C. fill, satiate, satisfy, accomplish. सम् M.P. be or become filled; C. fill, make full, fulfil, accomplish. — Cf. अभिपूर्ण, आपूर्ण, परिपूर्ण, पृणन्त्, प्रतिपूर्ण, संपूर्ण.

2पृ, पिपर्ति pass (trans.), bring across or to (acc.), rescue, save from (abl.); protect, further, promote. C. पारयति (°ते) the same + come through, overcome; resist, keep one's ground; be capable of or able to (infin.). — अति lead over, bring across (acc.); pass (trans.), go through (acc.). C. lead over, pass (trans.); M. rescue, deliver from (abl.). निस् draw or help out of (abl.), escape; C. = S. सम् C. bring over; finish, perform.

3पृ, पृणोति, pp. पृत (only —°), w. आ be busy or active; w. व्या (प्रियते or पृणुते) be busy or occupied with (अर्थम्). C. व्यापारयति set to work, employ in or at (loc., instr., or अर्थम्). — Cf. आपृत (add.), व्यापृत.

पृक्त a. mixed, mingled; united with, full of (instr. or —°).

पृक्ष् f. refreshment, food, satiation.

पृक्ष a. spotted, dappled; m. such a horse.

1पृच्, पृणक्ति, पृङ्क्ते etc., pp. पृक्त (q.v.) mix, mingle, unite or combine with (instr., r. loc.); fill, satiate; bestow richly, lavish upon (loc.); augment, increase. — आ mix or unite with (instr.); fill, satiate (M. refl.); pervade, penetrate. उप add to (loc.), increase, augment; approach, esp. for sexual intercourse. वि bring asunder, separate from (instr.); scatter, disperse, fill, satiate. सम् A.M. mix, mingle, join, touch; fill, endow, present with (instr.). — Cf. अनुपृक्त, संपृक्त.

2पृच् f. refreshment.

पृच्छक (f. पृच्छिका*) asking, inquiring after (gen. or —°).

पृच्छा f. asking, question, inquiry.

पृच्छ्य a. to be asked or inquired after.

पृणन्त् a. giving richly, liberal.

पृत् f. fight, battle (only loc. pl.).

पृतन n. hostile army; f. आ the same or = prec.

पृतनाज् a. rushing in battle.

पृतनाजित् a. victorious in battle.

पृतनाज्य n. contest, fight.

पृतनाय्, to fight, only pp. °यन्त्.

पृतनायु a. hostile, inimical.

पृतनाषह् (°षाह्) a. conquering hostile armies.

पृतनाषाह्य or °साह्य n. abstr. to prec.

पृतन्य्, °न्यति attack, fight (tr.).
पृतन्यु a. attacking; m. enemy.
पृत्सुति m. f. hostile attack.
पृत्सुषुतुर् a. victorious (in battle).
पृथ m. the palm of the hand.
पृथक् adv. separately, severally, respectively, singly, here and there (often doubled); prep. apart from, except, besides (abl., *instr., or *gen.). — With कृ separate, sunder, keep off, avert from (abl.); w. भू become separate, sever (intr.).
पृथक्करण n., पृथक्क्रिया f. separation, disunion.
पृथक्ता f., °त्व n. separateness, singleness, individuality.
पृथक्पिण्ड a. distantly related (opp. सपिण्ड).
पृथक्सुख a. pl. having different (not the same) enjoyments.
पृथक्स्थिति f. separation, singleness.
पृथगर्थ a. pl. having different (not the same) advantages.
पृथगुपादान n. particular mention.
पृथग्गण m. pl. several classes.
पृथग्जन m. a man of the lower classes; sgl. & pl. low people.
पृथग्भाव m. separateness, difference, individuality.
पृथग्वर्ष n. pl. always one year.
पृथग्विध a. of different kinds, various.
पृथाजन्मन् & पृथात्मज m. son of Pṛthā, E. of Yudhiṣṭhira.
पृथाभू & पृथासूनु m. the same.
पृथि m. N. of a man.
पृथिवी f. the earth (lit. the wide one, often personif.); land, country, realm.
पृथिवीकम्प m. earthquake.
पृथिवीक्षित् a. inhabiting or ruling the earth; m. prince, king.
पृथिवीतल n. the surface of the earth.
पृथिवीद्यावा (nom. du.) earth and heaven.
पृथिवीनाथ, °पति, °पाल, & भुज् m. prince, king (lord of the earth).
पृथिवीभृत् m. mountain (earth-bearer).
पृथु (f. पृथ्वी & पृथु) wide, broad, large, extensive, ample, abundant; n. adv. — m. a man's name; f. पृथ्वी the earth, land, realm.
पृथुक m. n. half-ripe rice; m. boy, young animal.
पृथुज्रय (f. ई) & °ज्रयस् a. far-spreading.
पृथुतरी w. कृ open wider (the eyes.)
पृथुता f., °त्व n. breadth, width.
पृथुधार a. broad-edged.
पृथुनितम्ब a. broad-hipped.
पृथुपर्शु a. having large sickles.
पृथुपाजस् a. far-shining, resplendent.
पृथुपाणि a. broad-handed.
पृथुबुध्न or पृथुबुध्न a. broad-based.
†पृथुयामन् a. broad-pathed.
पृथुल a. broad, wide, large.
पृथुलवक्षस् a. broad-breasted.
पृथुलेक्षण & पृथुलोचन a. large-eyed.
पृथुशिरस् a. broad-headed.
पृथुश्रवस् a. far-famed.
पृदाकु m., पृदाकू f. adder, snake.
पृशन n. clinging to, tenderness.
पृशनायु & °नी f. clinging to, attached, tender.
पृश्नि a. speckled, dapple; pl. manifold, various. — m. N. of a prince, pl. N. of a race of Rishis; f. a dappled cow, milk, the earth, a cloud, the starry sky, N. of the mother of the Maruts.
पृश्निमातृ a. having Pṛçni for a mother (cf. prec.).
पृषत m. the spotted antelope; drop of water; spot, mark.
पृषत्क m. arrow.
पृषदश्व a. having spotted horses or having antelopes for horses.
पृषद्वत् a. spotted, many-coloured.
पृषन्त्, f. पृषती spotted, dappled. — m. the spotted antelope; f. a spotted cow, mare, or female antelope; n. drop of water.
पृषित n. rain.
पृष्ट a. asked, questioned, n. that which is asked or inquired after.
पृष्टि or पृष्टी f. rib, पृष्टितस् on the ribs.
पृष्ट्या f. side-horse.
पृष्ठ n. back (esp. of an animal); hinder part, rear; upper side, surface, top (of a hill or palace); loc. behind the back, behind or from behind.

पृष्ठग a. being on the back, mounted on (gen. or —°).

पृष्ठतस् adv. from the back, from behind; at the back of, behind (gen. or —°); with the back i.e. with averted face; behind the back i.e. secretly, privately. — With **कृ** take on the back; place behind the back i.e. neglect, forsake, abandon.

पृष्ठभाग m. hinder part, back.

पृष्ठमांस n. back-flesh; **°सं खाद्** bite the back-flesh i.e. backbite, speak ill.

पृष्ठयज्वन् a. worshipping on hills.

पृष्ठवास्तु n. the upper story or top of a house.

पृष्ठानुग & **°गामिन्** a. going behind, following.

पृष्ठानुपृष्ठिका f. following, persecuting.*

पृष्ठ्य a. carrying on the back; m. (± **अश्व**) pack- or riding-horse.

पृष्व a. consisting of dew or rime.

पेट m. or n., **आ** & **ई** f. basket, bag.

पेटक m. n., **°टिका** f. the same; n. troop, multitude.

पेट्टालक s. basket, bag.

पेडा f. the same.

पेत्व m. ram, sheep.

पेदु m. N. of a man.

पेपिशत् & **पेपिशान** a. adorned, embellished, brilliant, many-coloured.

पेय a. to be drunk, drinkable; n. drink, beverage.

पेयूष = **पीयूष**.

पेरा f. a cert. musical instrument.

1**पेरु** a. penetrating, leading through, rescuing.

2**पेरु** a. swelling or causing to swell.

3**पेरु** a. drinking or thirsty.

पेलव a. tender, delicate.

पेश m. ornament, decoration; adorner, shaper, fabricator; f. **पेशी** a lump of flesh.

पेशन, f. **ई** well formed, decorated.

पेशल a. = prec. + handsome, beautiful, charming, pleasant, n. as abstr.; clever, dexterous, abstr. **°त्व**† n.

पेशस् n. shape, form; ornament, decoration, embroidery, p. **पेशस्वन्त्**.

पेशितृ m. who cuts, carver.

पेष, f. **ई** (—°) & m. grinding.

पेषण n. = prec. m.; f. **ई** grind-stone.

पेषी w. **कृ** pound, grind, crush.

पेष्टृ m. grinder.

पेष्ट्र n. bone.

पेष्य a. to be ground into (—°).

पेसुक a. spreading, extensive.

पैङ्गल, **°लायन**, & **°लायनि** m. patron. from **पिङ्गल**.

पैङ्गल्य n. brown colour.

पैङ्गि m. patron. of Yāska.

पैङ्गिन् m. a follower of Paiṅgya (cf. seq.).

पैङ्ग्य & **पैज** m. N. of ancient teachers.

पैजवन m. patron. of Sudās.

पैठर adj. cooked in a pot.

पैतामह, f. **ई** coming from a grandfather or from Brahman. m. Brahman's son; n. E. of a lunar mansion.

पैतृक, f. **ई** paternal, parental, relating to the Manes.

पैतृयज्ञिक & **°यज्ञीय** a. relating to a sacrifice to the Manes.

पैतृष्वसेय, f. **ई** descended from a father's sister; m. her son.

पैत्र (f. **ई**) & **पैत्र्य** a. relating to the Manes.

पैद्व a. belonging to Pedu; m. his horse.

पैनाक a. relating to Pinākin i.e. Çiva.

पैप्पल a. made of the wood of the holy fig-tree.

पैप्पलाद a. derived from Pippalāda; m. pl. his followers.

पैलव a. made of Pīlu wood.

पैशल्य n. versatility, affability.

पैशाच, f. **ई** belonging to the Piçācas; f. **ई** their language.

पैशुन & **°न्य** n. backbiting, slander.

पैष्ट (f. **ई**) & **पैष्टिक** a. made of meal or flour.

पोटक m. servant.

पोटल & **पोटलक** m., **°लिका** f. bundle.

पोटी f. the rectum.

पोत m. a young animal or plant, a young or fresh (—°); m. n. ship, vessel, abstr. **°त्व** n.

पोतक m. = prec. (—°); f. **°तिका** cloth, garment.

पोतप्लव m. seaman, mariner.

पोतभङ्ग m. shipwreck.
पोतवणिज् m. a seafaring merchant.
पोतृ or पोतृ m. purifier (a kind of priest).
पोत्र n. the Soma-vessel or the office of the Potṛ (cf. prec.); the snout of a hog.
पोत्रिन् m. a wild boar (cf. prec.).
पोत्रीय a. belonging to the Potṛ.
पोथ m. blow, strike with (—°).
पोया f. a cert. wind-instrument.
पोलिका f. a kind of cake.
पोष m. thriving, growth, welfare; nourishing, fostering.
पोषक, f. °षिका nourishing, breeding, keeping.
पोषण a. = prec.; n. as abstr.
पोषणकर a. effecting nourishment.
पोषणीय a. to be nourished.
पोषयितृ & °यिष्णु a. nourishing, causing to grow or thrive.
पोषितृ m. nourisher, breeder.
पोषिन् a. nourishing, bringing up (—°).
पोषुक a. growing, thriving.
पोष्टृ m. = पोषितृ.
पोष्य a. to be (being) nourished or well fed; thriving or causing to thrive.
पोष्यावन्त् a. causing prosperity.
पौंश्चलीय a. relating to harlots.
पौंश्चलेय m. whoreson.
पौंश्चल्य n. running after men, harlotry.
पौंस्न a. human, manly; n. manhood, virility.
पौंस्य n. = prec. n.; also manly deed, pl. hosts of men.
पौच्छ a. being on the tail.
पौञ्जिष्ठ or °ष्ठ m. a fisherman.
पौण्डरीक a. made of lotus-flowers.
पौण्ड्र m. N. of Bhīṣma's conch-shell, pl. N. of a people.
पौण्ड्रक m. pl. a cert. mixed caste or = prec. pl.
पौण्य a. honest, virtuous.
पौतन s. N. of a region.
पौतिनासिक्य n. stench of the nose.
पौत्र, f. ई coming from or belonging to a son or to children; m. a grandson (°वत्† adv.); f. पौत्री granddaughter.
पौत्रक m. grandson, poss. पौत्रिन्.
पौनःपुन्य n. frequent repetition.
पौनरुक्त्य n. repetition, tautology.
पौनर्भव a. relating to a woman remarried with her own consent; m. her son, w. भर्तृ her (second) husband.
1पौर m. filler, increaser.
2पौर m. townsman, citizen.
पौरकार्य n. the citizens' affairs.
पौरजन m. townsfolk, the citizens.
पौरंदर a. belonging to the destroyer of the castles (Indra).
पौरव, f. ई descended from or belonging to Pūru; m. a descendant of P., pl. his race, N. of a people.
पौरस्त्य a. foremost, eastern.
पौरस्त्यपवन m. east wind.
पौराण, f. ई belonging to or derived from the olden times; primeval, ancient.
पौराणिक, f. ई = prec., also knowing the past.
पौरिक m. townsman, citizen.
पौरुष, f. ई human, manly, belonging or consecrated to Puruṣa. — m. a man's load; f. ई a woman; n. manhood, virility, manly deed, a man's length.
पौरुषेय, f. ई a relating to man, human. — m. hireling, day-labourer; n. human deed or work.
पौरुहूत a. relating to Puruhūta-Indra.
पौरूरवस a. belonging to Purūravas.
पौरोगव m. inspector of a royal household, esp. of the kitchen.
पौरोभाग्य n. envy, malevolence.
पौरोहित्य n. the office of a house-priest.
पौर्णमास, f. ई relating to the full moon; m. n. festival of the full moon; n. day of full moon; f. ई day or night of full moon.
पौर्णमास्य n. full-moon sacrifice.
पौर्त w. कर्मन् n. a meritorious work.
पौर्तिक a. relating to a meritorious work.
पौर्वदेहिक or °दैहिक a. relating to a former life or existence.
पौर्वापर्य n. priority and posteriority; succession, continuity.
पौर्वाह्णिक, f. ई belonging to the morning, matutinal, as s. mat. ceremony.
पौर्विक, f. ई former, ancient, old.
पौलस्त्य m. patron. of Kubera.

पौलोम a. relating to Puloman or Pulomā. m. N. of a Rishi, pl. a cert. class of demons; f. **ई** patron. of Indra's wife.

पौष m. N. of a cert. month.

पौष्टिक, f. **ई** conducive to welfare.

पौष्ण, f. **ई** consecrated to Pūṣan (the Sun); n. E. of a lunar mansion.

पौष्प, f. **ई** coming from or made of flowers.

पौष्य m. N. of an ancient king.

प्या, प्यायते swell, overflow. — **आ** swell, become full of or rich in (instr.); make full, enlarge, strengthen. C. **आप्याययति, °ते** cause to swell, make full, esp. pour water upon the Soma; nourish, refresh; excite, rouse. **समा** swell, grow, increase; C. nourish, strengthen, vivify. **प्र** swell, C. make swell.

†**प्युक्षण** s. covering for a bow.

1**प्र** adv. forward, onward, forth, away, fore (mostly °— in subst. & verbs); very, much, greatly (°— in adjectives).

2**प्र** filling, sating, nourishing (—°); n. fulfilment.

प्रउग n. the forepart of the shafts of a chariot.

प्रकट a. manifest, apparent; °— & n. adv.

प्रकटन n. manifesting, showing.

प्रकटय्, °यति, pp. **प्रकटित** manifest, reveal, bring to light.

प्रकटशीर्ष a. with uplifted head.*

प्रकटी कृ = **प्रकटय्, °भू** w. pass. mg.

प्रकटीकरण n. manifesting, revealing.

प्रकम्प a. & m. trembling, shaking.

प्रकम्पन m. wind; n. = prec. m.

प्रकम्पिन् a. trembling, moving to and fro.

प्रकर m. heap, multitude.

प्रकरण n. bringing forth, creation; treatment, discussion or object of it; section, chapter, book; a kind of drama.

प्रकर्ष m. excellence, superiority, high degree; °—, abl., & instr. eminently, perfectly, very much.

प्रकर्षण m. vexer, tormentor; n. drawing away or along.

प्रकल्पना f. fixing, settlement.

प्रकाण्ड m. the stem or trunk of a tree; best or chief of (—°).

प्रकाम m. desire, delight, pleasure. **प्रकाम** (°—), **°मम्**, & **°मतस्** willingly, at will, very much, indeed.

प्रकामोद्य n. loquacity (talking to heart's content).

प्रकार m. manner, way, sort, kind; °— adj. -like, -fold, abstr. **°त्व** n.

प्रकाश a. shining forth, clear, open, manifest; famed, celebrated, renowned, glorious; °— & n. openly, clearly, publicly, aloud. — m. clearness, light, elucidation, explanation esp. in titles of books), shine, appearance (adj. °— resembling, like); publicity, fame, renown; loc. adv. openly, publicly, before the world. — Abstr. **°ता**† f., **°त्व**† n.

प्रकाशक, f. **°शिका** = prec. + seq. adj.; abstr. **°त्व** n.

प्रकाशन a. & n. illuminating, disclosing, explaining, expressing.

प्रकाशनारी f. public woman, prostitute.

प्रकाशय्, °यति v. **काश्**.

प्रकाशवन्त् a. bright, brilliant.

प्रकाशिता f., **°त्व** n. clearness, brilliancy.

प्रकाशिन् a. clear, bright; manifesting, disclosing.

प्रकाशी w. **कृ** illuminate, disclose, make known.

प्रकाशेतर a. invisible (lit. the opposite of visible).

प्रकाश्य a. to be illuminated or manifested; abstr. **°ता** f.

प्रकिरण n. scattering, throwing about.

प्रकीर्ण & **°क** a. scattered, dispersed, mixed, miscellaneous; n. miscellanea.

प्रकीर्तन n. announcing, proclaiming; f. **आ** mentioning, naming.

प्रकीर्ति f. commendation, praise.

प्रकुपित a. agitated, moved, angry (**प्रति** or loc.).

प्रकृत a. made, done; commenced, mentioned, in question.

प्रकृति f. the original or natural form or cause of anything; nature or the material world (ph.); the (5—8) constituent elements of the state, e.g. the king, the ministers, subjects etc.; i.g. nature, character, disposition, temper.

प्रकृतिज a. springing from nature, innate.
प्रकृतिपुरुष m. minister of state.
प्रकृतिमन्त् a. natural, normal, ordinary.
प्रकृतिष्ठ or °स्थ a. being in the natural state or condition, healthy, normal, genuine.
प्रकृतिस्थदर्शन a. normal-sighted.*
प्रकृष्ट a. long, protracted; extraordinary, excellent; violent, strong.
प्रक्लृप्त a. prepared, arranged, settled; n. adv. readily, easily.
प्रकेत m. appearance; observation, intelligence; observer, knower.
प्रकोप m. violent anger, rage, wrath.
प्रकोपण or °पन, f. ई a. (—°) & n. irritating, exciting, provoking.
प्रकोष्ठ m. fore-arm; a room near the gate (or a court*) of a royal palace.
प्रक्रम m. step, stride (also as a measure of distance); commencement, beginning, proportion, measure.
प्रक्रमण n. stepping forward, advancing towards (—°); going out.
प्रक्रान्त n. setting out, departure.
प्रक्रिया f. bringing forth, producing; proceeding, way, manner; ceremony; privilege, superiority, high rank and its insignia; chapter, section.
प्रक्री a. to be bought.
प्रक्रीड m. play, sport; play-ground.
प्रक्रीडिन् a. playing, sporting.
प्रक्रोश m. shriek, scream.
प्रक्लेद m. wetness, humidity.
प्रक्षय m. destruction, ruin, fall.
प्रक्षालक a. washing, m. washer.
प्रक्षालन a. performing ablutions (r.); n. washing, purifying, water for washing.
प्रक्षीण a. destroyed, diminished, exhausted.
प्रक्षीणपाप a. whose sins have been destroyed.
प्रक्षेप m. & °ण n. throwing, strewing, pouring upon or into.
प्रक्ष्वेडा f., °डित n. humming, grumbling.
प्रखल m. a great villain.
प्रख्य a. visible, clear, distinct; f. आ look, appearance, adj. —° resembling, -like, shining, brilliant.
प्रख्यात a. acknowledged, known, famous.
प्रगर्धिन् a. impetuous, eager.
प्रगल्भ्, °ल्भते be bold etc. (cf. seq.).
प्रगल्भ a. bold, resolute, confident; abstr. °ता f.
प्रगाढ a. steeped, soaked, impregnated; mixed with, rich in (—°), excessive, abundant, advanced (time); n. adv. much, vehemently, intensely.
1†प्रगाण n. access, approach.
2प्रगाण n. singing, song.
प्रगाथ m. N. of a cert. mixed metre.
प्रगीत a. sung, filled with song; having begun to sing, singing.
प्रगुण a. all right, excellent.
प्रगुणय्, °यति, pp. प्रगुणित set right, make straight.
प्रगुणी w. कृ make straight or smooth, strengthen, foster, nourish.
1प्रगृह्य a. to be taken (separately), not subject to the rules of Saṁdhi (g.).
2प्रगृह्य (abs.) having taken, along with (acc.).
प्रगे adv. early in the morning or to-morrow morning.
प्रगेतन a. matutinal, to-morrow's, future.
प्रग्रह m. holding or stretching forth (also adj. —°); taking, seizing; friendly reception, kindness, favour; taking to, being fond of or eager for, obstinacy, pertinacity; rein, bridle, rope; leader, chief, comrade, satellite.
प्रग्रहण m. guide, leader (only adj. —° led by). n. taking, seizing; rein, bridle; offering, presenting.
प्रग्रहवन्त् a. having seized, holding (—°); receiving kindly, obliging.
प्रघस m. Voracious, N. of a Rakṣas & a monkey.
प्रघासिन् & °स्नु a. voracious.
प्रघोष m. sound, noise, roar.
प्रचण्ड a. very violent or wrathful, abstr. °ता f.
प्रचण्डातप m. excessive heat.
प्रचण्डपाण्डव n. T. of a drama.
प्रचंता adv. secretly, mysteriously.
प्रचय m. plucking, gathering; heap, quantity, multitude.
प्रचयस्वर m. a kind of accent (g.).

प्रचरण n. going forth, proceeding; f. **ई** a cert. wooden ladle used at a sacrifice.
प्रचर्या f. proceeding, action.
प्रचल a. being in motion, trembling.
प्रचलन n. trembling, shaking, tottering.
प्रचार m. going forth, coming off, appearing; occurrence, existence; proceeding, behaviour, conduct; use, employment; play- or pasture-ground.
प्रचित a. gathered, heaped up, covered or filled with (instr. or —°).
प्रचुर a. much, many, abundant; rich in, filled with (—°). Abstr. **°ता** f., **°त्व** n.
प्रचेतस् a. attentive, knowing, wise; m. E. of Varuṇa.
प्रचेतुन a. affording a wide prospect.
प्रचोद m., **°न** n. impelling, inciting.
प्रच्छद् f. cover, covering.
प्रच्छद & *°पट* m. coverlet, sheet.
प्रच्छन्न a. covered, veiled, hidden, secret; n. adv.
प्रच्छन्नपाप a. having secret sins.
प्रच्छादक a. (—°) = seq. a.
प्रच्छादन a. (—°) & n. covering veiling.
प्रच्छाय s. a shadowy place, shade.
प्रच्छिद् a. cutting off or to pieces.
प्रच्छेद m. slip, strip.
प्रच्यव m. falling off, fall.
प्रच्यवन n., **प्रच्युति** f. = prec.; being deprived of (abl.).
प्रच्योतोस् (gen. inf.) to break down.
प्रछ्, **पृच्छति** (°ते), pp. **पृष्ट** (q.v.) ask, question, inquire, w. acc. of pers. or (&) th.; seek, request, entreat; P. **पृच्छ्यते** be asked after (acc., r. dat., loc., **अर्थे**, **अधिकृत्य**, or **हेतोस्**). With **न** not care for (acc.). — **अनु** ask, ask some one after (2 acc.). **आ** M. (A.) bid farewell to (acc.), invoke (a god), ask, inquire. **उपा** & **समा** bid farewell. **परि** ask, question, interrogate a person (acc.) about (acc. ± **प्रति**, r. loc. or gen.). **प्रति** ask, interrogate a person about (2 acc.). **वि** ask, inquire, ascertain. **सम्** M. consult, converse or talk with (abl.), absol. with each other; ask, question, inquire (2 acc.).
प्रज a. bringing forth (—°); f. **आ** procreation, offspring, descendants, children, family; creature, esp. man, folk, subjects.
प्रजन m. generation (also n.), generator.
प्रजनन a. begetting, generating; n. procreation, production, procreative power, semen.
प्रजननवन्त् a. generative.
प्रजनयितृ m. generator.
प्रजनिष्णु a. procreative.
प्रजनु m. f. the vulva.
प्रजय m. victory, conquest.
प्रजल्प m., **°ल्पन** n. talk, conversation.
प्रजल्पित n. talk, spoken words.
प्रजव m. haste, rapidity.
प्रजवन & **प्रजविन्** a. rapid, swift.
प्रजस् f. (—°) = **प्रजा**.
प्रजाकाम a. desirous of offspring.
प्रजागर a. waking, watchful; m. waking or watching, a guardian.
प्रजात a. born; f. **आ** having born.
प्रजाति f. generation, propagation, offspring.
प्रजादान n. the breeding of children.
प्रजाधर्म m. rule for the breeding of children.
प्रजानन्त्, f. **°नती** knowing, wise.
प्रजापति m. lord of creatures or of procreation, the Creator, E. of sev. gods & Rishis, also N. of a separate god & sev. men.
प्रजापाल m. protector of creatures i.e. Kṛṣṇa, or protector of subjects i.e. king, sovereign.
प्रजापालन n. the protection of subjects.
प्रजायिनी f. bearing, bringing forth, a mother.
प्रजावन्त् a. having or granting offspring, prolific; f. **°वती** pregnant, mother of (—°), the wife of the (elder) brother.
प्रजाहित a. good for (all) creatures.
प्रजीवन n. livelihood, subsistence.
प्रजुष्ट a. delighted with (loc.).
प्रजेश & **°श्वर** m. lord of creatures, creator; or lord of subjects, king.
प्रज्ञ a. intelligent, wise, knowing (—°); f. **प्रज्ञा** intelligence, wisdom, discernment, judgment, reason.
प्रज्ञता f. intelligence, wisdom.
प्रज्ञप्ति f. communication, information.

1प्रज्ञाचक्षुस् n. the mind's eye.
2प्रज्ञाचक्षुस् a. seeing with the mind's eye.
प्रज्ञात a. well-known, renowned; common, usual.
प्रज्ञातृ a. knowing; m. guide.
प्रज्ञान, f. ई knowable, distinguishable. — n. knowledge, discrimination; mark, sign; organ of perception.
प्रज्ञानघन m. nothing but intelligence.
प्रज्ञावाद m. word of wisdom.
प्रज्वलन n. blazing up, flaming.
प्रज्वलित n. the same.
प्रज्वालन n. kindling.
प्रज्वाला f. flame.
प्रणत a. bent, stooped; bowing to (gen. or acc.); subject, humble.
प्रणति f. bending, bowing, salutation.
प्रणपात् & प्रणप्तृ m. great-grandson.
प्रणमन n. = प्रणति.
प्रणय m. leader, guide; leading, conduct; manifestation, betrayal, esp. of one's feelings, confidence, familiarity, love, desire.
प्रणयन n. bringing near, fetching, means for fetching, vessel; manifestation, betrayal; use, employment of (—°).
प्रणयभङ्ग m. breach of confidence.
प्रणयवन्त् a. acting confidently or without restraint; attached or used to, familiar with (loc. or —°).
प्रणयस्पृश् a. showing confidence.
प्रणयिजन m. a lover.
प्रणयिता f love, desire, longing for (loc., gen., or —°).
प्रणयिन् a. loved, dear; affectionate, tender, loving, kind; pleased with, fond of, connected with (instr. or —°). — m. favourite, friend, lover, husband; f. ई mistress, wife.
प्रणव or प्रणव m. the sacred syllable Om (—° also प्रणवक).
प्रणाद m. sound, shout, roar.
प्रणाम m. bow, reverent salutation.
प्रणाली & °लिका f. channel, water-course, stream.
प्रणाश m. disappearance, loss, death.
प्रणाशन, f. ई = seq. a.; n. as abstr.
प्रणाशिन् a. destroying, removing (—°).
प्रणिधान n. laying on, applying, employment, endeavour, effect; consideration, attention or submission to (—°); meditation, devotion.
प्रणिधि m. watching, spying, sending out (spies); spy, emissary.
प्रणिपतन n. falling at a person's feet.
प्रणिपात m. the same, reverence, humility.
प्रणिहित a. laid down, put on (—°); set forward, stretched out; turned upon (—°), committed, entrusted; concentrated or intent on one thing.
प्रणी m. guide, f. guidance.
प्रणीत a. brought, presented (of a son); f. आ holy water.
प्रणीति f. guidance, conduct; leading away.
प्रणेजन, f. ई wiping away (—°); n. washing away, bathing, water for washing.
प्रणेतृ m. leader, guide; maker, creator; author, teacher.
प्रणेय a. to be (being) guided or led, obedient; to be applied, effected, fixed, settled.
प्रतट s. a high bank or shore.
प्रतनु a. very thin, slender, delicate, or small.
प्रतपन्त् a. shining, majestic, powerful.
प्रतप्त a. heated, hot (l. & f.), pained, vexed by (—°).
प्रतमम् adv. chiefly, particularly.
प्रतरण, f. ई carrying on, furthering, increasing; n. crossing over, navigation.
प्रतरम् or प्रतराम् adv. further, longer, in future.
प्रतर्क m. conclusion, supposition.
प्रतर्दन a. piercing through; m. destoyer, E. of Viṣṇu.
प्रतवस् a. active, powerful.
प्रतान m. shoot, tendril, a plant with tendrils; ramification (lit. & fig.).
पताप m. heat, glow, splendour, brilliancy, highness, majesty, power.
प्रतापन a. burning, paining. m. a cert. hell; n. burning, heating.
प्रतापमुकुट m. N. of a prince.
प्रतापरुद्रीय m. T. of a work.
प्रतापवन्त् a. majestic, glorious, powerful.

प्रतापिन् a. = **प्रतापन** a. + **प्रतापवन्त्**.
प्रताम्र a. deep-red.
प्रतार m. crossing over; taking in, deceiving.
प्रतारक a. deceiving; m. deceiver.
प्रतारण n. = **प्रतार**.
प्रति adv. towards, against, again, back, in return (°— in verbs & substantives, in adv. comp. also at the time of, about, with regard or according to, before, on, at, mostly with the idea of constant repetition); as a prep. (w. preceding, rarely following acc.) towards, against, before, over against, opposite, near, on, by, at, in; at the time of, about (also abl. or gen.); with regard to, in favour of (also gen.); according to, on account or in consequence of; *w. abl. instead of or in return for; on a par with or as a match for (also adv. in **तस्**). — **आत्मानं प्रति** to one's self, aside (d.); **मां प्रति** according to me, in my opinion.
प्रतिकर, f. **ई** counteracting; m. requital, compensation.
प्रतिकर्कश a. as hard as (—°).
प्रतिकर्मन् n. counterworking, cure, remedy; dress, decoration.
प्रतिकामम् adv. at will.
प्रतिकार m. requital, retaliation, counteraction, remedy.
प्रतिकूल a. adverse (lit. against the shore), contrary, opposite, unfavourable, inauspicious, rebellious, inimical; abstr. **°ता** f. — n. inverted order, also as adv. **°कूलम्** inversely, contrarily.
प्रतिकूलकारिन् a. offering opposition.
प्रतिकृति f. resistance, defence; (reflected) image, picture.
प्रतिक्रम m. inverted order.
प्रतिक्रमण n. stepping towards.
प्रतिक्रिया f. requital, retaliation, defence; remedy of, return for (—°).
प्रतिक्षणम् adv. at every moment, constantly.
प्रतिगमन n. going back, return.
प्रतिगर m. response (r.).
प्रतिगु adv. against a cow.
प्रतिगृहम् adv. in every house.
प्रतिग्रह m. receiving, accepting from (gen. ± **सकाशात्**, abl., or —°), acceptance (esp. of gifts, as a prerogative of Brahmans); gift, donation; kind reception, favour, grace; taking to wife, marriage; seizer, receiver.
प्रतिग्रहण n. receiving, accepting.
प्रतिग्रहीतव्य a. to be received or accepted.
प्रतिग्रहीतृ m. who receives or marries.
***प्रतिग्राह** m. spittoon (as a receptacle).
प्रतिग्राहिन् a. receiving, accepting.
प्रतिघात m., **°न** n. warding off, resistance, hindrance.
प्रतिघातक (f. **°तिका**) & **°तिन्** a. warding off, disturbing.
प्रतिचक्षण n. look at, view; appearance.
†**प्रतिचक्षिन्** a. looking at, viewing.
प्रतिचक्ष्य a. visible.
प्रतिच्छन्द & **°क** m. reflected image.
प्रतिच्छन्न a. covered, clothed, veiled, concealed, unknown.
प्रतिच्छाया f. reflected image, shadow.
प्रतिजन m. adversary.
प्रतिजन्मन् n. re-birth.
प्रतिजन्य a. adverse, hostile.
प्रतिज्ञा f. = seq. + plaint, indictment (j.).
प्रतिज्ञान n. agreement, promise, statement, assertion.
प्रतिज्ञापरिपालन n. the keeping of a vow or promise.
प्रतिज्ञापूर्वकम् adv. by beginning with the indictment (j.).
प्रतिदर्श m., **°न** n. look, view, appearance.
प्रतिदान n. restoring, gift in return.
प्रतिदिनम् & **°दिवसम्** adv. day by day, daily.
प्रतिदिशम् adv. in every direction, everywhere.
प्रतिदीवन् m. adversary at play.
प्रतिदूषित a. stained, polluted.
प्रतिदोषम् adv. about evening.
प्रतिद्वंद्व m. opponent, adversary.
प्रतिद्वंद्विन् m. = prec., adj. —° outvying.
प्रतिधा f. putting to (the lips), draught.
प्रतिधान n. putting on (—°).
प्रतिधि m. the cross-bar on the pole of a carriage.
प्रतिनन्दन n. greeting, salutation.

प्रतिनयन (°—) towards the eyes.
प्रतिनव a. new, fresh.
प्रतिनायक m. the hero's adversary (d.).
प्रतिनिधि m. substitution, substitute; image of, resembling (—°).
प्रतिनिर्यातन n. giving back, restoring.
प्रतिनिवृत्ति f. return, coming back.
प्रतिपक्ष m. opposite side or party, rivality; also = seq. + equal to, a match in (—°).
प्रतिपक्षिन् m. adversary, rival.
प्रतिपच्चन्द्र m. the young moon* (cf. **प्रतिपद्**).
प्रतिपत्ति f. acquiring, getting, perceiving, understanding, wisdom, intelligence, supposition, assertion, statement; agreement, admission; giving, bestowing on (loc. or —°); honouring, respecting; causing, effecting; undertaking, beginning, proceeding at or with (gen. or loc.); means against (gen.) to (loc.).
प्रतिपद् f. access, entrance, beginning, commencement, first day of a half-month; introductory verse or stanza (r.).
प्रतिपद (°—) & **°दम्** adv. at every step or word.
प्रतिपन्न a. approached, arrived, (having) got to or met with; begun, acted, done; undertaken, performed; learnt, understood, promised, consented to.
प्रतिपाण m. counter-stake or game.
प्रतिपात्रम् adv. in every character (d.).
प्रतिपादक, f. **°दिका** giving, bestowing; treating, discussing, explaining, teaching.
प्रतिपादन n. bringing, imparting, bestowing on (loc. or —°); restoring, appointing to (loc.); causing, effecting, producing; treating, discussing, explaining, teaching; undertaking, beginning.
प्रतिपादनीय a. to be given (esp. in marriage*); to be discussed or expounded.
प्रतिपादयितृ m. giver, expounder, teacher.
प्रतिपाद्य a. to be produced, treated, discussed, or taught.
प्रतिपान n. drinking or water for drinking.
प्रतिपालन n. keeping, protecting, maintaining, observing, (expecting*).
प्रतिपालिन् a. keeping, guarding.
प्रतिपाल्य a. to be kept or guarded; to be waited on or for.
1**प्रतिपुरुष** m. substitute, companion; a puppet employed by a thief.*
2**प्रतिपुरुष** (°—) & **°षम्** adv. man by man.
प्रतिपूजक a. honouring, revering.
प्रतिपूजन n., **°पूजा** f. abstr. to prec.
प्रतिपूज्य a. to be honoured or revered.
प्रतिपूरण n. filling or being filled with (instr.).
प्रतिपूर्ण a. full, filled with (instr. or —°); satisfied, pleased.
प्रतिप्रति m., n., **°तिनी** f. counterpart; match for, equal to (acc.).
प्रतिप्रश्न m. counter-question.
प्रतिप्रस्थातृ m. a cert. priest, **°स्थान** n. his office.
प्रतिप्रिय n. kindness or service in return.
प्रतिबद्ध a. tied to, plaited, twisted, connected with, dependent on (—°).
प्रतिबन्ध m. binding to, connection, conjunction; obstruction, hindrance, resistance.
प्रतिबन्धक, f. **°न्धिका** obstructing, impeding (—°).
प्रतिबन्धवन्त् a. encountering obstacles, difficult.
प्रतिबन्धिन् a. = prec. or = **प्रतिबन्धक**.
1**प्रतिबल** n. hostile army.
2**प्रतिबल** a of equal strength, a match for (gen. or —°); able to (infin.).
प्रतिबाधक a. repelling, rejecting (—°).
प्रतिबाधन n. abstr. to prec.
प्रतिबिम्ब n. (m.) reflected disk of sun or moon; image, shadow i.g.
प्रतिबिम्बित a. reflected, mirrored back.
प्रतिबुद्ध a. awakened, awake (lit. & fig.); illuminated, enlightened, perceived, known.
प्रतिबुद्धि f. awaking (fig.).
प्रतिबोध m. awaking, a. **°धिन्**; knowledge, p. **°वन्त्**.
प्रतिबोधक a. awakening; m. instructor, teacher.
प्रतिबोधन a. awakening, refreshing (—°); f. **आ** awaking, recovering consciousness, n. awaking, awakening, teaching, enlightening.
प्रतिबोधनीय a. to be awakened.

प्रतिभट a. vying with, a match for (gen. or —°).
प्रतिभय a. formidable, terrible; n. adv., as subst. dread, peril.
प्रतिभा f. image, light, splendour, look, appearance, understanding, intelligence, presence of mind, fancy, idea, conception.
प्रतिभाग m. distribution, portion, share.
प्रतिभान n. intelligence, understanding.
प्रतिभानवन्त् & **°भावन्त्** a. intelligent, wise.
प्रतिभास m. appearance, semblance, occurring to the mind, idea
प्रतिभू m. substitute, surety or bail for (gen., dat., *loc., or —°).
प्रतिभेद m. splitting, piercing; betrayal.
प्रतिभोग m. enjoyment.
प्रतिमल्ल m. antagonist, rival.
प्रतिमा m. framer, creator; f. measure, image, likeness, picture, idol, symbol, emblem; adj. —° resembling, equal to.
प्रतिमान n. measure, weight, counterpart, match, model, pattern, likeness, similarity.
प्रतिमार्ग m. way back.
प्रतिमित् f. support, stay.
प्रतिमित a. reflected, mirrored back.
1**प्रतिमुख** n. epitasis (d.).
2**प्रतिमुख**, f. **ई** standing opposite, facing, °— & n. adv.; imminent, present.
प्रतिमुहूर्त (°—) & **°र्तम्** adv. at every moment, constantly.
प्रतिमोचन n. loosening, getting rid of (—°).
प्रतियत्न m. care for anything, effort, endeavour; arrangement, preparation.
प्रतियातन n. requital, retaliation; f. **आ** counterpart, image.
प्रतियुद्ध n. fighting against or in return.
प्रतियोग m. opposition, resistance.
प्रतियोगिक a. correlative (ph.).
प्रतियोगिन् a. = prec.; m. = seq.
प्रतियोद्धृ & **°योध** m. adversary, rival, match.
प्रतियोधन n. = **प्रतियुद्ध**.
प्रतिर or **प्रतिर** a. carrying over, furthering, promoting.
प्रतिरथ m. = **प्रतियोद्धृ**.
प्रतिरव m. crying out to; crying back, echo.
प्रतिराज & **°राजन्** m. anti-king, hostile king.
प्रतिरात्रम् & **°रात्रि** adv. each night, nightly.
1**प्रतिरूप** n. counterpart, image, model.
2**प्रतिरूप** a. similar, corresponding, suitable.
प्रतिरूपक n. & a. = prec. 1 & 2.
प्रतिरोद्धृ m. opposer, adversary.
प्रतिरोध m. obstruction, hindrance.
प्रतिरोधक a. obstructive, hindering.
प्रतिरोधन n. obstructing, hindering.
प्रतिरोधिन् a. = **प्रतिरोधक**.
प्रतिलभ्य a. to be received or obtained.
प्रतिलम्भ m. = seq. + conceiving, understanding.
प्रतिलाभ m. receiving, finding, obtaining.
प्रतिलोम a. against the hair or grain, reverse, inverted, contrary; °—, n., & **°तस्†** adv.
प्रतिवचन n. final clause (g.); also = seq.
प्रतिवचस् n. answer, reply.
प्रतिवत्सर m. year, **°रम्** adv. annually.
प्रतिवर्ष (°—) & **°र्षम्** adv. = prec. adv.
प्रतिवस्तु n. counterpart, equivalent.
प्रतिवस्तूपमा f. a kind of comparison.
प्रतिवाक्य n., **°वाच्** f., **°वाचिक** n. answer.
प्रतिवात m. contrary wind; n. against the w.
प्रतिवाद m. rejection, refusal.
†**प्रतिवादिन्** a. contradicting, disobedient; m. adversary, opponent; defendant (j.).
प्रतिवारण a. & n. warding off.
प्रतिवासरम् adv. daily.
प्रतिविधान n. arrangement against, prevention of (gen. or —°); care about (—°).
प्रतिविधि m. remedy or measure against (—°).
प्रतिविधेय a. to be counteracted or done in return; n. impers.
प्रतिवीर m. opponent, match.
प्रतिवेश a. neighbouring, auxiliary; m. neighbour.
प्रतिवेशिन् a. neighbouring; m. neighbour, f. **°नी**.
प्रतिवेश्मन् n. a neighbour's house.
प्रतिशत्रु m. adversary, enemy.
प्रतिशब्द & **°क** m. resonance, echo.
प्रतिशाप m. curse in return.
प्रतिश्रय m. refuge, help, assistance; shelter, abode, dwelling.
प्रतिश्रव a. answering; m. promise, agreement.
प्रतिश्रवण n. = prec. m.

प्रतिश्रुत् & °श्रुति f. = prec.; echo, resonance.

प्रतिषिद्ध a. warded off, prohibited, forbidden, refused, contradicted; suppressed, omitted.

प्रतिषिद्धवाम a. refractory when driven back.*

प्रतिषेक m. besprinkling.

प्रतिषेद्धृ m. hinderer, prohibiter.

प्रतिषेध m. warding off, driving away, expulsion; prohibition, denial, refusal; negation or a negative particle (g.).

प्रतिषेधक, f. °धिका prohibiting, refusing; negative (g.).

प्रतिषेधन a. warding off; n. expulsion, refusal, refutation.

प्रतिषेधात्मक a. of a negative character (g.).

प्रतिष्ठ a. steady, resisting; f. आ stead, standing-place, support, receptacle, basis, foundation, abode, home; state of rest, quiet, comfort; position, high rank, celebrity, preeminence, accession of a prince.

प्रतिष्ठान n. stead, basis, pedestal, foundation (lit. & fig.); N. of a town.

प्रतिष्ठि f. resistance.

प्रतिष्ठित a. standing; being or abiding in, founded or resting on (loc. or —°); established, settled, firm.

प्रतिसंहार m. taking back, withdrawing.

प्रतिसंदेश m. answer to a message.

प्रतिसंधान n., °संधि m. reunion, connection, juncture.

प्रतिसर m. a bracelet or ribbon used as an amulet.

*प्रतिसीरा f. curtain, screen.

प्रतिस्पर्धिन् a. vying with (gen.), equal to (—°).

प्रतिहरण n. throwing back, rejecting.

प्रतिहर्तृ m. averter, destroyer; a kind of priest.

प्रतिहस्त & °क m. substitute, proxy.

प्रतिहार m. striking against, pushing back; door, gate (which keeps off), porter (f. ई).

प्रतिहारभूमि f. door-place, threshold.

प्रतीक n. exterior, surface; face, mouth (poss. °वन्त्); look, appearance, image, symbol, copy; (also m.) first verse or word.

प्रतीकार m. = प्रतिकार.

प्रतीकाश m. reflected image; look, appearance, adj. —° similar to, -like.

प्रतीक्ष a. waiting for, having regard for (—°); f. आ expectation, attention to, regard for (—°).

प्रतीक्षण n. consideration, regard; observance, fulfilment.

प्रतीक्षणीय a. to be waited for.

प्रतीक्षिन् a. looking or waiting for (—°).

प्रतीक्ष्य a. to be waited for or expected; to be observed or fulfilled; to be considered or regarded.

प्रतीघात a. warding off, repelling; m. = प्रतिघात.

प्रतीची v. प्रत्यञ्च्.

प्रतीचीन a. turned towards or against (also प्रतीचीन), turned away or back, being behind or west, imminent, future, later than (abl.); n. adv. behind.

प्रतीचीनग्रीव a. having the neck turned to the west.

प्रतीच्य a. westerly.

प्रतीत a. convinced, resolute, relying on (—°); satisfied, glad, pleased; known, famous for (instr.).

प्रतीतात्मन् a. confident, resolute (in mind).

प्रतीति f. coming near, approaching; conclusiveness, intelligibility; insight, knowledge, conviction, persuasion, confidence, faith, belief.

प्रतीप a. contrary (lit. against the stream), inverted, cross, refractory, hostile, troublesome, unpleasant; m. adversary, antagonist. — n. adv. contrarily, against, back, in inverted order; w. गम् oppose, resist.

प्रतीपविपाकिन् a. resulting in the contrary.

प्रतीमान n. counter measure.

प्रतीष्टम् adv. according to one's wish.*

प्रतीहार m., ई f. door-keeper, porter.

प्रतुद & प्रतुद m. pecker (a kind of bird).

प्रतुष्टि f. satisfaction.

प्रतूर्ति a. rapid, violent; f. haste, hurry.

प्रतोद m. goad.

प्रतोली f. broad way, high street.

प्रतोलीद्वार n. gate of a street.*

प्रत्ति f. giving away, delivery.

प्रत्न a. former, old, ancient; traditional, customary.

प्रत्नथा & **प्रत्नवत्** adv. as formerly, as usual.

प्रत्यक् v. **प्रत्यञ्च्**.

प्रत्यक्ष a. before the eyes, plainly visible, clear, distinct, actual, immediate. — n. superintendence, care of (gen.); ocular evidence. immediate apprehension or intelligence; as adv. before one's face, publicly, distinctly, immediately, personally (also abl., instr., & °—).

प्रत्यक्षचारिन् a. moving before one's (gen.) eyes.

प्रत्यक्षता f., **°त्व** n. ocular evidence, visibility, explicitness, distinctness.

प्रत्यक्षदर्शन n. the seeing with one's own eyes, esp. the power of seeing a god bodily.

प्रत्यक्षदर्शिन् a. seeing or having seen (gen.) with one's own eyes.

प्रत्यक्षदृष्ट a. seen with one's own eyes.

प्रत्यक्षभूत a. become visible, manifested.

प्रत्यक्षी w. **कृ** take a view of, look at, see (w. acc.); w. **भू** catch the eye, be visible or manifest.

प्रत्यक्षीकरण n. abstr. to prec. w. **कृ**.

प्रत्यगात्मन् m. the inner soul (ph.).

प्रत्यगानन्द a. appearing as inward joy (ph.).

प्रत्यग्दक्षिणतस् & **°दक्षिणा** adv. southwesterly.

प्रत्यग्र a. fresh, new, young, recent; °— & n. adv.

1**प्रत्यङ्ग** n. a minor or secondary member of the body.

2**प्रत्यङ्ग** (°—) & **°ङ्गम्** adv. limb by limb, member by member.

प्रत्यङ्गदक्षिणा f. fee for each part (of a sacrifice).

प्रत्यङ्मुख a. turned to the west.

प्रत्यञ्च्, f. **प्रतीची** or **प्रतीची** turned towards, facing, being in front of or opposite to (acc.); turned backwards, averted; westerly, west of (abl.); turned inwards, inner, interior; equal to, a match for (acc.); n. **प्रत्यक्** adv. backwards, back, away; behind, west of (abl.), inwardly. — m. the inner soul; f. **प्रतीची** (± **दिश्**) the east.

प्रत्यनन्तर a. being nearest or next; n. adv.

प्रत्यनीक a. hostile, opposite; m. enemy, rival; n. enmity, hostile army.

प्रत्यभिघारण n. besprinkling afresh (r.).

प्रत्यभिज्ञा f., **°न** n. recognition.

प्रत्यभियोग m. counter plaint (j.).

प्रत्यभिवाद m., **°न** n. regreet, return of salutation.

प्रत्यय m. belief, conviction, confidence, trust in (loc., gen., or —°), evidence, certainty, knowledge, notion, idea; suffix (g.).

प्रत्ययकर, **°कारक**, & **°कारण*** a. producing confidence.

प्रत्ययप्रतिवचन n. a certain answer.

प्रत्ययित a. tested, tried, unsuspected; confidential, intimate.

प्रत्ययिन् a. trustworthy, sure, certain.

प्रत्यर्थिता f. abstr. to seq.

प्रत्यर्थिन् a. hostile, inimical; emulating with (—°). m. opponent, adversary, rival; defendant (j.).

प्रत्यर्पण n. giving back, restoring.

प्रत्यर्पणीय a. to be given back or restored.

प्रत्यवमर्श m., **°न** n. inner contemplation or meditation.

प्रत्यवर a. lower, meaner, viler.

प्रत्यवरूढि f. descending towards.

प्रत्यवरोधन n. obstruction, disturbance.

प्रत्यवरोह m., **°रोहण** n. = **प्रत्यवरूढि**.

प्रत्यवरोहिन् a. descending, moving downwards.

प्रत्यवसान n. consuming, eating.

प्रत्यवहार m. drawing back or in; reabsorption, dissolution.

प्रत्यवाय m. decrease, diminution; inversion, inverted order; annoyance, uneasiness; offence, sin.

प्रत्यवेक्षण, **°क्षणा*** & **°क्षा** f. regard, attention, care.

प्रत्यवेक्ष्य a. to be considered.

प्रत्यह a. daily; n. adv.

प्रत्याख्यान n. refusal, rejection, refutation.

प्रत्याख्येय a. to be refused or rejected.

प्रत्यागति f. coming back, return.

प्रत्यागम m., **°न** n. the same.

प्रत्यादान n. recovery; repetition.
प्रत्यादेश m. direction, order, command; repudiation, putting to shame or confusion, warning, caution.
प्रत्यादेशिन् a. rejecting, contemning (—°).*
प्रत्यानयन n. leading or bringing back.
1**प्रत्यायन** n. setting (of the sun).
2**प्रत्यायन** a. convincing, trustworthy; f. **आ** convincing, appeasing, comforting; n. showing, explaining, proving.
प्रत्याययितव्य a. to be explained or proved.
प्रत्यावृत्ति f. return.
प्रत्याशा f. confidence, trust, hope; abstr. **°शात्व** n.
प्रत्याश्वास m. breathing up again, recovery.
प्रत्याश्वासन n. bringing to life again, recomforting.
प्रत्यासत्ति f., **°सन्नता** n. proximity, nearness.
प्रत्याहरण n. drawing or keeping back; detention from (abl.).
प्रत्याहार m. = prec., dissolution, destruction; comprehension or comprehensive word (g.).
प्रत्युक्त n., **°क्ति** f. answer, reply.
प्रत्युज्जीवन n. coming back or restoring to life.
प्रत्युत्तर n. rejoinder, reply.
प्रत्युत्थान n. rising up to meet (as friend or foe), esp. respectful reception.
प्रत्युत्पन्न a. present; **°मति** a. having presence of mind; m. Ready-wit, N. of a fish.
प्रत्युदाहरण n. counter example.
प्रत्युद्गति f. going to meet (respectfully or hospitably).
प्रत्युद्गम m., **°न** n. = prec.
प्रत्युपकार m. return of a service or kindness; adj. **°रिन्**.
प्रत्युपपन्न a. present; **°मति** a. having presence of mind; abstr. **°त्व** n.
प्रत्युपस्थित a. approached, present, standing opposite, assembled, happened, imminent, standing or being in (loc.).
प्रत्युपहार m. giving back, restitution.
प्रत्यूष s. dawn, day-break (**महति प्रत्यूषे** early in the morning*).
प्रत्यूषस् n. dawn, day-break.
प्रत्यूह m. obstacle, impediment.
प्रत्यृचम् adv. at each verse or stanza.
प्रत्यृतु adv. in each season.
प्रत्येक a. each one, each single; °— & n. = seq.
प्रत्येकशस् adv. one by one, singly.
प्रत्वक्षस् & **प्रत्वक्षाणं** a. powerful, mighty.
प्रथ्, **प्रथते**, pp. **प्रथित** (q.v.) spread, extend (intr., r. **प्रथति** trans.); become larger or wider, increase, grow; appear, arise; become famous or celebrated. C. **प्रथयति** trans. (M. intr. or refl.) spread, broaden, extend, augment; proclaim, celebrate, disclose, show, manifest. — **अनु** M. (intr.) spread along (acc.). **अभि** M. (intr.) stretch before or against; C. (tr.) spread about (acc.), divulge. **आ** C. (trans.) spread, expand. **प्रति** M. (intr.) spread round or over. **वि** A. spread, expand; M. (intr.) stretch, increase, be large or wide. C. spread, extend, disclose, unfold, manifest.
प्रथ m. N. of a man, f. **आ** = seq. + fame, renown.
प्रथन n. spreading, displaying.
प्रथम a. first, primal, foremost, earliest, principal, best, chief. °— & n. first, before (n. as prep. w. gen.), for the first time, just, now, immediately; often also adj. pro adv. — m. the first (third) person; f. **आ** the first or nominative case and its endings.
प्रथमकल्प m. first or primary rule.
प्रथमकल्पित a. first in rank or importance.
प्रथमज & **°जा** a. firstborn, primary, original.
प्रथमजात a. firstborn.
प्रथमतस् adv. first, at first; forthwith, immediately; before, rather than (gen. or —°).
प्रथमभक्ति f. the former devotion.*
प्रथमवयस् n. earliest age, youth.
प्रथमश्री a. having just become rich or fortunate.
प्रथमसाहस m. the first (lowest) fine (j.).
प्रथस् n., **प्रथिमन्** m. width, extension.
प्रथित a. spread, divulged. **°यशस्** a. farfamed.
प्रथिष्ठ & **प्रथीयंस्** superl. & comp. to **पृथु**.
प्रद a. giving, uttering, causing (mostly —°).
प्रदक्षिण a. standing on or moving to the right, turning the right towards a person,

i.e. respectful, reverential; °— & n. °णम् adv., the latter also = towards the south. Acc. w. कृ or °णी कृ turn the right side towards a person or an object. m., n., & f. आ as abstr., also circumambulation from left to right.

प्रदक्षिणार्चिस् a. flaming towards the right.

प्रदाक्षिणात् adv. = प्रदक्षिण adv.

प्रदक्षिणी w. कृ v. प्रदक्षिण.

प्रदर m. splitting, rending; crack, crevice.

प्रदर्श m. look (—°); direction.

प्रदर्शक a. showing, announcing, teaching; m. teacher.

प्रदर्शन n. look, aspect (often a. —°); showing, pointing out; instruction, lesson.

प्रदर्शिन् a. looking, seeing; showing, indicating (—°).

प्रदातृ m. giver, bestower, granter, esp. who gives a daughter in marriage.

प्रदान n. giving, esp. in marriage, presenting, offering, yielding, granting, applying; gift, donation, oblation; communicating, teaching, proclaiming; putting on, applying; effecting, producing.

प्रदाय n. gift, present.

प्रदायक & °यिन् a. giving, presenting.

प्रदाह m. burning, heating; destruction.

1**प्रदिव्** f. (nom. प्रद्यौस्) the third or fifth of the heavens.

2**प्रदिव्** a. ancient, old; abl. long since, from of old, also = loc. always, ever.

प्रदिश् f. pointing to or out; direction, order, command; quarter, region of the sky, intermediate region (e.g. north-east etc.).

प्रदीप m. lamp, light (fig. = ornament); explanation, commentary.

प्रदीपक m., °पिका f. a small lamp, light, or commentary.

प्रदीपन a & n. inflaming, kindling.

प्रदीपाय्, °यते represent a lamp.

प्रदीप्त a. flaming, glowing, hot, shining.

प्रदीप्तशिरस् a. having a hot head.

प्रदुष्ट a. corrupt, bad, wicked, libidinous; m. villain, ruffian.

प्रदेय a. to be given, esp. in marriage, marriageable; to be presented, offered, communicated, taught; m. gift, present.

प्रदेश m. pointing out, direction, destination; place, spot, region; appealing to a precedent; instance, example.

1**प्रदोष** m. disorder (of body or state); mutiny, insurrection.

2**प्रदोष** a. bad, evil.

3**प्रदोष** m. evening, nightfall; °षम् adv. at dusk.

प्रदोषागम m. the coming on of evening.

प्रदोषानिल m. the evening wind.

प्रद्युम्न m. E. of the god of love (lit. the powerful), N. of sev. men, a mountain, & a river.

प्रद्योत m. flashing up, light, splendour; N. of a Yakṣa & sev. kings.

प्रद्वेष m., °षा n. dislike, hatred.

प्रधन n. the prize of the contest; contest, fight.

प्रधर्षक a. attacking, molesting (—°).

प्रधर्षण a. = prec. (—°); f. आ & n. as abstr.

प्रधान n. the main thing or person, chief, head; original matter or supreme spirit (ph.); often —° having—as chief thing or person i.e. devoted to, excelling or delighting in, full of. Adj. & °— chief, main, principal, best.

प्रधानतस् adv. according to rank or eminence.

प्रधानता f., °त्व n. preeminence, superiority.

प्रधानपुरुष m. chief person, man of rank or authority; supreme spirit (E. of Çiva).

प्रधानप्रकृति s. chief minister.

प्रधानभूत a. being the chief person.

प्रधानवासस् n. rich garment.

प्रधानसभिक m. = पूर्वसभिक.

प्रधि m. the circumference or rim of a wheel; pl. the fellies.

प्रधुर n. the point of carriage-pole.

प्रधृष्टि f. overwhelming.

प्रध्यान n. reflection, thought.

प्रध्वंस m. destruction, ruin.

प्रध्वंसन a. destroying, ruining.

प्रध्वंसिन् a. perishable, also = prec. (—°).

प्रनष्ट a. lost, disappeared, missing; gone, past, fled, escaped.

प्रनष्टस्वामिक a. whose owner has disappeared.
प्रनष्टाधिगत a. lost and found.
प्रपञ्च m. expansion, development, prolixity, amplification; the visible world or universe (ph.).
प्रपञ्चन n. circumstantial explanation.
प्रपञ्चय्, °यति develop, amplify, explain copiously.
प्रपतन n. flying forwards or falling down.
प्रपथ m. journey, way, road.
प्रपथिन् a. wandering, travelling.
1**प्रपद्** f. way; entrance (cert. sacred texts).
2**प्रपद्** f. the forepart of the foot.
प्रपद n. = prec.; point of the foot, tip of the toes.
प्रपन्न a. approached, arrived, come (esp. as a suppliant); happened, appeared; having resorted to, h. entered, incurred, got, obtained (acc.); acknowledged, agreed to; furnished with (instr.).
प्रपलायन n. running away, flight.
प्रपा f. watering-place, well, cistern.
प्रपाठ & °क m. lesson, chapter.
†**प्रपाण** n. watering-place or a drink.
प्रपात m. a mode of flying; rushing forth, starting off; fall, falling out, falling from (abl. or —°), on or into (loc. or —°).
प्रपातन n. causing to fall, throwing down.
प्रपान n. drinking, sipping.
प्रपापालिका f. female well-keeper.
प्रपालक m. guardian, protector.
प्रपालन n. guard, protection.
प्रपितामह or **प्रपितामह** m. great-grandfather (also E. of Brahman & Kṛṣṇa), pl. great-grandfathers, ancestors i.g.; f. °मही great-grandmother.
प्रपित्व n. going away, flight, retreat; evening.
प्रपिष्ट a. rubbed or ground down.
प्रपौत्र m., ई f. great-grandson or -daughter.
प्रप्रोथ m. snorting.
प्रप्लुत a. dipped in water.
प्रफर्वी f. a wanton girl.
प्रफुल्ल a. blossomed, blooming, expanded, opened.
प्रबद्ध a. attached to, dependent on (—°); suppressed, checked, stopped.
प्रबन्द्धृ m. author.
प्रबन्ध m. connection, bond, tie (also °न n.); continuation, uninterrupted series; literary composition.
प्रबल a. strong, mighty, intense, violent, important, great (also °वन्त्; abstr. °ता f., °त्व n.); n. °लम् greatly, much; m. a man's name.
प्रबुद्ध a. awakened, expanded, blossomed, appeared; enlivened, brightened; clear-sighted, clever, wise.
प्रबुध् a. awake, attentive; f. awaking.
प्रबोध m. awaking (also of flowers); appearing, rising; watching, perceiving, understanding, intellect, knowledge; awakening, reviving (esp. a lost fragrance).
प्रबोधक a. awakening.
प्रबोधचन्द्र m. the moon of knowledge; °चन्द्रोदय m. the rise of the moon of knowledge, T. of a drama.
प्रबोधन a. awakening, rousing; n. awaking, understanding, or awakening, enlightening; *the reviving of a fragrance.
प्रभङ्ग m. breaker, crusher; breaking, crushing, destruction.
प्रभङ्गिन् a. breaking, crushing, destroying.
प्रभञ्जन a. = prec.; wind, storm.
प्रभर्तृ m. bringer.
प्रभर्मन् n. bringing, placing before.
प्रभव a. excelling; m. origin, source, home, a. —° sprung or descended from, being in or on.
प्रभवितृ a. powerful; m. lord, ruler.
प्रभविष्णु a. the same; abstr. °ता f.
प्रभा f. splendour, light, beauty (often —°), pl. rays; a woman's name.
प्रभाकर m. the sun (light-maker); a man's name.
प्रभात a. shone forth, begun to be light; n. day-break.
प्रभातकरणीय a. morning-work.*
प्रभातकल्प a. nearly begun to be light (night).
प्रभामण्डल & °क n. circle or garland of light.

प्रभामय, f. **ई** consisting of light.

प्रभाव m. might, majesty, superhuman strength, power over (loc.); splendour, brilliancy. — Instr. & abl. by means or in consequence of.

प्रभावन्त् a. shining, radiant; f. **॰वती** N. of a metre & of sev. women.

प्रभाववन्त् & **प्रभाविन्** a. potent, mighty.

प्रभाषित a. said, told, explained; n. word, speech.

प्रभास m. N. of sev. gods & men, also of a celebrated place of pilgrimage.

प्रभासन n. irradiating, illuminating.

प्रभासुर, ॰स्वन्त्, & ॰स्वर a. shining bright, splendid.

प्रभीत a. afraid, timid.

पभु (or **॰भू**, f. **प्रभ्वी**) excelling, surpassing, mighty, abundant; being a master of (gen.) or a match for (*dat.); capable of or able to (infin., loc., or —॰). — m. lord, ruler, prince, E. of Brahman etc.

प्रभुता f., **॰त्व** n. lordship, supremacy, power, possession; preponderance, preference, instr. chiefly.

प्रभूत a. come forth, become (—॰); much, abundant, numerous, great, important (॰— adv.); rich in, blessed with (—॰), able to (infin.).

प्रभूतता f., **॰त्व** n. might, multitude.

प्रभूति f. origin, source; sufficiency, power, might.

प्रभृति f. bringing forth, offering, presenting, beginning; often adj. (—॰) or adv. (after an abl. or —॰) beginning with, since, from, — and so on.

प्रभृथ m. offering, donation.

प्रभेद m. splitting, division, separation, difference, species, kind.

प्रभेदक, f. **॰दिका** cleaving, piercing (—॰).

प्रभेदन a. = prec.

***प्रभ्रष्टक** n. a wreath of flowers hanging down from the crown of the head.

प्रभ्रष्ट a. fallen down; run away, escaped from (abl.).

प्रमणस् v. **प्रमनस्**.

प्रमति f. care, providence, protection, concr. protector.

प्रमत्त a. intoxicated, excited; rutting, lascivious; negligent, careless about (abl., loc., or —॰).

प्रमथ m. tormentor (a kind of goblin); N. of a man, f. **आ** of a woman.

प्रमथन (f. **ई**) & **॰थिन्** tormenting, destroying.

प्रमद् or **प्रमद्** f. joy.

1**प्रमद** m. joy, pleasure, delight.

2**प्रमद** a. gay, merry, wanton, petulant; f. **आ** a wanton young woman, woman i.g.

प्रमदन n. amorous desire.

प्रमदवन n. pleasure-grove of the wives of a prince, harem's garden.

प्रमदाजन m. a woman or women (coll.).

प्रमदावन n. = **प्रमदवन**.

प्रमदावनपालिका f. woman guarding a harem's garden.*

प्रमद्वर a. foolish; m. fool, f. **आ** woman's name.

प्रमनस् a. loving, tender; cheerful, merry, gay.

प्रमन्थ m. rubbing-stick (to produce fire).

प्रमन्यु a. wrathful or sorrowful.

प्रमय m. perishing, death.

प्रमयु a. perishable.

प्रमर m., **प्रमरण** n. death.

प्रमर्दन a. & n. crushing, destroying; m. E. of Viṣṇu, a man's name.

प्रमर्दितृ m. crusher, destroyer.

प्रमर्दिन् (—॰) = **प्रमर्दनन** a.

प्रमहस् a. of great might.

प्रमा f. basis, foundation, ground-measure, right notion or conception.

प्रमाण n. measure, scale, standard; extent, size, weight, distance, duration, prosodical length; norm, rule of action, authority; proof, argument (ph.).

प्रमाणय्, **॰यति** adapt; take as authority or argument, prove, demonstrate.

प्रमाणसूत्र n. measuring cord.

प्रमाणाधिक a. beyond measure, excessive.

प्रमाणी w. **कृ** = **प्रमाणय्**.

प्रमातृ m. a person fit to perceive or judge; an authority, a proof (ph.).

प्रमाथ m. tearing, rape (of a woman), overwhelming, destruction.

प्रमाथिन् a. tearing, stirring, harassing; N. of a Rākṣasa & a monkey.

प्रमाद m. drunkenness, intoxication, negligence, carelessness.

प्रमादिन् a. neglectful, careless.

प्रमापण, f. **ई** murdering; n. slaughter.

प्रमायु & **प्रमायुक** a. = **प्रमयु**.

प्रमार m. dying, death.

प्रमार्जक a. wiping off, destroying.

प्रमार्जन n. abstr. to prec.

प्रमित a. meted out, measured, limited, little, few; (—°) measuring, of such and such extent or size; n. a hall.

प्रमिताक्षरा f. N. of a metre.

प्रमिति f. correct notion, true knowledge or inference.

प्रमीत a. deceased, dead; **°पतिका** f. whose husband is dead, a widow.

प्रमीति f. ruin, destruction, death.

प्रमुक्ति f. liberation.

प्रमुख (f. **ई***) turning the face towards, facing (acc.); foremost, first, principal, best; often —° having as first or chief, headed by, — and so on. °— before one's face, publicly; loc. & **°तस्** as prep. w. gen. or —°.

प्रमुग्ध a. fainted, unconscious; very charming.

प्रमुद् f. joy, pleasure, esp. sensual pl.

प्रमुदित a. glad, merry, gay; n. joy, delight.

प्रमूढ a. bewildered, unconscious, foolish, stupid, dull.

प्रमृड a. gracious, kind.

प्रमृण a. destroying.

प्रमृत a. dead; n. death.

प्रमृश a. touching.

प्रमृष्ट a. polished, clean, bright; smeared with (instr.); wiped off, removed, destroyed.

प्रमृष्टि f. smearing with (instr.).

प्रमेय a. measurable, provable, discernible; n. object of certain knowledge, the thing to be proved.

प्रमोक m. liberation, deliverance.

प्रमोच m. letting fall, losing, also = prec.

प्रमोचन a. (f. **ई**) & n. letting free, liberating from (—°).

प्रमोद m. joy, delight, a man's name.

प्रमोदन a. gladdening, delighting; n. joy, mirth.

प्रमोदनृत्य n. dance of joy, merry dance.

प्रमोदिन् a. gladdening.

प्रमोष m. robbing, taking away.

प्रमोह m. bewilderment, perplexity.

प्रमोहन (f. **ई**) & **°हिन्** a. bewildering, perplexing.

प्रयज् f. offering, oblation.

प्रयज्यु a. rushing on, impetuous.

प्रयत a. stretched or held out, far-reaching; placed upon (loc.); offered, given, returned; restrained, composed, well-prepared, purified, pure (r.).

प्रयतता f. purity, holiness.

प्रयतात्मन् a. pure in heart.

प्रयति f. offering, oblation, gift; endeavour, intention.

प्रयत्न m. effort, endeavour, pains at (loc. or —°), activity; °—, instr., & abl. with pains, carefully; hardly, scarcely.

प्रयत्नवन्त् a. assiduous, careful.

प्रयन्तृ m. giver, bringer; leader, driver.

प्रयमण n. purification (r.).

प्रयस् n. pleasure, enjoyment; object of enjoyment, e.g. food & drink, dainties, etc.

प्रयस्त a. boiling over; hot, eager.

प्रयस्वन्त् a. having or offering enjoyment.

प्रया f. onset.

प्रयाग m. N. of a region (lit. the place of sacrifice), pl. its inhabitants.

प्रयाचन n. imploring.

प्रयाज m. fore-offering (r.).

प्रयाण n. setting out, starting, going forth; journey, march; onset, beginning.

प्रयामन् n. setting out or moving on.

प्रयास m., **°सित** n. effort, exertion.

प्रयुक्त a. yoked, used, employed, acted, proceeded (n. impers.), lent; usual, answering to the purpose.

प्रयुक्ति f. impulse.

प्रयुज् f. team of horses; impulse, activity, acquisition.

प्रयुत n. a million.

प्रयुद्ध n. fight, combat.

प्रयुध् a. attacking.

प्रयोक्तव्य a. = **प्रयोज्य**.

प्रयोक्तृ m. hurler, archer; employer, executor; agent (g.); performer (d.); lender on interest; speaker, reciter, author, poet.

प्रयोग m. hurling, throwing, position or addition (of a word); employment, use, practice; usual form (g.); means (only instr. plur. by means of); commencement, beginning, enterprise, execution; device, plan, contrivance; offering, bestowing; lending at interest or the invested capital; recitation, delivery, performance, representation.

प्रयोगनिपुण a. clever in practice.*

प्रयोगिन् a. being employed, usual.

प्रयोजक, f. °जिका causing, effecting, essential; m. author (abstr. °ता f., त्व n.), composer, lender, creditor.

प्रयोजन n. cause, reason, motive, aim, purpose, use of (instr.). — किं (or भवतु*) प्रयोजनं what is the use of, enough of (instr.); केन प्रयोजनेन, *कस्मै-°नाय, (also *abl., *gen. & *loc.) the same.

प्रयोज्य a. to be shot off, to be used, employed, recited, performed.

प्रयोतृ m. remover.

प्ररक्षण n. protecting

प्ररुज m. N. of a Rākṣasa.

प्ररूढ a. grown up, grown with (—°); strong, old; born or sprung from (—°).

प्ररूढि f. growth, increase.

प्ररेक m., **प्ररेचन** n. abundance, superfluity.

प्ररोचन (f. ई) & n. inciting, seducing.

प्ररोधन n. ascending.

प्ररोह m., °ण n. growing or shooting forth (lit. & fig.); sprout, shoot, twig.

प्ररोहिन् a. shooting up from (—°).

प्रलपन n. prattling, talking.

प्रलपित n. talk, chaff; lament, wail.

प्रलम्ब a. hanging down, pendulous; m. N. of a Daitya etc.

प्रलम्बकेश a. whose hair hangs down.

प्रलम्बिन् a. = प्रलम्ब a.

प्रलम्भ m. gain, acquisition, also = seq.

प्रलम्भन n. taking in, deceiving.

प्रलय m. dissolution, destruction, esp. of the universe; °घन m. & °दहन m. the cloud and the fire causing the end of the world.

प्रलयन n. layer, bed.

प्रलव m. part cut off, chip, fragment.

प्रलवन n. cutting off, mowing.

प्रलाप m. talk, prattle, chattering, unintelligible or delirious speech; lament (also n.).

प्रलापवन्त् & °पिन् poss. to prec.

प्रलीन a. vanished, gone, dead; dissolved i.e. tired, wearied.

प्रलोभ m. seduction.

प्रलोभक m. seducer (N. of a jackal).

प्रलोभन a. (f. ई) & n. seducing, alluring.

प्रलोभ्य a. to be desired, attractive.

प्रव a. hovering, soaring.

प्रवक्तव्य a. to be announced or taught.

प्रवक्तृ m. speaker, announcer, expounder, teacher.

प्रवचन m. = प्रवक्तृ; n. speaking, announcing, recitation, exposition, sacred writings, esp. the Brāhmaṇas.

प्रवचनपटु a. skilled in speaking, eloquent.

प्रवचनीय a. to be recited.

प्रवण s. slope, steep descent, precipice, gulf, depth; a. declined, bent, sloping towards (—°); prone, inclined or attached to (loc., dat., gen., infin., or —°).

प्रवत् f. slope of a mountain, sloping path, easy or rapid course; instr. sgl. & pl. downwards or rapidly.

प्रवत्वन्त् a. poss. to prec.

प्रवद a. sounding forth (drum); m. proclaimer, herald.

प्रवदन n. announcement.

प्रवत्त् a. directed forwards or towards.

1**प्रवपण** n. shaving (of the beard).

2**प्रवपण** n. sowing.

प्रवयस् a. advanced in age; robust, vigorous; aged, old.

1**प्रवर** m. cover, upper garment.

2**प्रवर** m. call, either a summons of a Brahman to priestly functions or an invocation of Agni; a line of ancestors (so named in such an invocation) or a member of it.

3**प्रवर** a. chief, principal, best of (gen. or —°),

the eldest son; higher, better, greater than (abl.); distinguished by (—°).

प्रवरजन m. a person of quality.

प्रवर्ग m. a cert. sacrificial vessel.

प्रवर्ग्य m. a cert. ceremony introductory to the Soma sacrifice.

प्रवर्तक a. proceeding (—°); setting in motion or activity, causing, effecting, promoting, furthering; m. promoter, prompter, instigator.

प्रवर्तन n. moving forwards or onwards, coming forth from (abl.), arising, appearing, happening; acting, dealing with (instr. or loc.); causing, producing, fetching, applying, introducing.

प्रवर्तनीय a. to be applied or begun.

प्रवर्तितव्य n. impers. (it is) to be proceeded.

प्रवर्तिन् a. coming or streaming forth, moving on, flowing, active, busy; causing, effecting, applying, introducing.

प्रवर्धक, f. **°र्धिका** augmenting, increasing (—°).

प्रवर्धन a. the same.

प्रवर्ष m., **°ण** n. rain.

प्रवसथ n. setting out, leaving (pl. w. abl.).

प्रवसन n. setting out, departing, dying.

प्रवह a. carrying (—°); m. a cert. wind.

प्रवहण n. letting go, marrying (a girl); any vehicle, carriage, ship (also f. **ई**, adj. —° f. **आ**).

प्रवहणबलीवर्द m. draught-ox.*

प्रवहणभङ्ग m. shipwreck.

प्रवहणवाहक m. coachman, driver.*

प्रवहणिक m. the same.*

प्रवाचन n. proclamation, praise.

प्रवाच्य a. to be proclaimed, praiseworthy.

प्रवात (a. windy*); n. a draught of air or an airy place.

प्रवातशयन n. an airy couch.

प्रवातेज or **°जा** a. grown in an airy place.

प्रवाद m. speaking out, expressing, naming, mentioning, saying, talk, rumour; pl. ill report, slander, calumny.

प्रवादिन् a. speaking out, telling.

प्रवापिन् a. sowing upon (—°).

प्रवार m. cover, cloth.

प्रवारण n. satisfying, gratifying.

प्रवार्य a. to be satisfied.

प्रवाल m. n. shoot, sprout, coral.

प्रवास m. the being abroad or on a journey; acc. w. **गम्** go abroad.

प्रवासन n. sending abroad, banishment.

प्रवासिन् a. being abroad or on a journey.

प्रवास्य a. to be sent abroad or banished.

प्रवाह m. stream, current, course, continuance, series.

प्रवाहण a. & n. carrying off, driving forth.

प्रवाहिन् a. carrying, drawing, flowing; m. beast for draught.

प्रविक्त a. shaken, trembling.

प्रविख्यात a. universally known, renowned as (nom.).

प्रवितत a. extended, wide; performed, accomplished; numerous, various.

प्रविद् f. knowledge, wisdom.

प्रविद्ध a. hurled, cast away, scattered, dispersed, spilt; omitted given up.

प्रविद्वंस् a. knowing, wise.

प्रविभक्त a. distributed, divided, separate.

प्रविभाग m. division, part, portion.

प्रविरल a. rare, isolated, very few.

प्रविविक्त a. separated, detached, single or simple, solitary.

प्रविविक्तभुज् a. enjoying the simple (ph.).

प्रविष्ट a. entered (act. & pass.), come into or being in, turned towards, intent upon (acc., loc., or —°).

प्रविष्टक n. (only instr.) entrance (d.).

प्रवीण a. clever, versed in, familiar with (loc or —°); abstr. **°ता** f.

प्रवीर m. great hero, chief among (gen. or —°).

प्रवृत्त a. having turned forward, advanced, set out, come forth, arisen, appeared, happened; being, existing; (having) begun, going to, intending (infin., dat., loc., or —°); occupied with, devoted to, engaged in (loc. or —°); acting, proceeding; interested, done on purpose (**कर्मन्**).

प्रवृत्तपारण n. N. of a cert. ceremony (r.).*

प्रवृत्ति f. coming forth, rising, appearance, origin; progress, advance, activity, endeavour, application or devotion to, occupation or dealing with (loc. or —°); acting, proceeding; use, employment; continuance, validity of a rule (g.); fate, destiny; news, tidings.

प्रवृत्तिवचन a. expressing activity.

प्रवृद्ध a. grown up, adult, developed, mature; strong, great, large, high, mighty, old.

प्रवृद्धि f. growth, increase, prosperity, welfare.

प्रवेदन n. making known, announcing.

प्रवेदिन् a. knowing well (—°).

प्रवेप m., °**न** n. trembling, shaking.

प्रवेपिन् a. trembling.

प्रवेश m. entering, ingress, penetration; entrance (d.).

प्रवेशक (adj. —°) = prec.; a kind of interlude (d.).

प्रवेशन n. entering, going into (loc., gen., or —°), sexual intercourse.

प्रवेशिन् a. entering (—°).

प्रवेश्य a. to be entered or introduced.

प्रवेष्टव्य a. = prec.; n. impers.

प्रवेष्टृ m. who enters into (—°).

प्रवोढृ (°**व्ळ्हृ**) m. who carries off (gen. or —°).

प्रव्रजित a. gone abroad; m. religious mendicant, ascetic.

प्रव्रज्या f. going abroad, emigration (also °**ज्य** n.); retirement into solitude, the order of a religious mendicant or ascetic.

प्रव्रस्क m. a cut.

प्रव्राज् m. religious mendicant.

प्रव्राज m. the bed of a river.

प्रव्राजक m. religious mendicant; f. °**जिका** female ascetic.

प्रव्राजन n. expulsion, banishment.

प्रव्राजिन् a. running after (—°); m. = **प्रव्राजक** m.

प्रशंसन n., °**सा** f. commendation, praise, eulogy.

प्रशंसिन् a. commending, praising (—°).

प्रशंसोपमा f. a kind of comparison (rh.).

प्रशंस्य a. to be praised, better than (abl.).

प्रशम m. calmness, tranquillity (esp. of the mind), ceasing, disappearance, extinction (of fire).

प्रशमन a. & n. tranquillizing, suppressing, healing, securing

†**प्रशर्ध** a. valiant, bold.

प्रशस् f. axe, hatchet, knife.

प्रशस्त a. praised, extolled, commended or commendable, good, better, best, auspicious, lucky; abstr. °**त्व**† n.

प्रशस्तवचन n. pl. commendatory words, praises.

प्रशस्ति f. praise, eulogy, panegyric; direction, guidance.

प्रशस्तिकृत् a. giving praise, praising.

प्रशस्य a. praiseworthy, commendable, excellent; abstr. °**ता**† f.

प्रशाखा f. branch, limb (of the body).

प्रशाखिका f. a small branch or bough.

प्रशान्त a. tranquillized, quiet, calm, indifferent; extinguished, removed, ceased, disappeared, gone, died.

प्रशान्तता f. tranquillity of mind.

प्रशान्ति f. becoming tranquil or calm, quiet, rest, ceasing, vanishing, extinction, destruction, also = prec.

प्रशासन n. direction, guidance, government, dominion.

प्रशासितृ m. governor, ruler.

प्रशास्तृ m. director (a class of priests).

प्रशिथिल a. very loose.

प्रशिष्टि & **प्रशिस्** f. direction, command.

1**प्रश्न** m. question, demand, inquiry, controversy; task, lesson.

2**प्रश्न** m. basket-work, a plaited basket.

प्रश्नकथा f. a tale ending with a question.

प्रश्नपूर्वक a. beginning with a question.

प्रश्नय्, °**यति** inquire after (2 acc.).

प्रश्नाख्यान n. du. question and answer.

प्रश्निन् m. inquirer.

प्रश्नोत्तर n. question and answer.

प्रश्नोत्तरमाला f. garland of questions and answers, T. of a work.

प्रश्रय m., °**ण** n. respectful demeanour, civility, modesty.

प्रश्रयवन्त् & °**यिन्** poss. to prec. m.

प्रश्रित a. modest, humble, n. adv.; secret, mysterious.

प्रश्लिष्ट a. twisted (a kind of Saṁdhi).

प्रश्लेष m. twisting together, close contact, euphonic coalition of vowels.

प्रष्टव्य a. to be asked or inquired into.

प्रष्टि m. side-horse; bystander, companion.
प्रष्टृ m. inquirer.
प्रष्ठ a. standing in front, preceding, best of (—°); m. foreman, leader.
प्रसक्त a. attached or devoted to, turned upon, connected or endowed with (loc. or —°); absol. clinging to objects, worldly, enamoured; following, resulting; lasting, constant. °— & n. adv.
प्रसक्ति f. adherence, attachment, devotion, inclination; bearing upon, applicability.
प्रसङ्ग m. = prec. + union, connection, business with (adj. —° connected with); occurrence of a possibility, case, event, occasion, opportunity. Instr., abl., & loc. occasionally, incidentally; on the occasion, on account, or in the course of (—°).
प्रसङ्गवन्त् a. occasional, incidental.
प्रसङ्गिन् a. attached or devoted to, dependent on (—°); belonging to something else, secondary, unessential, also = prec.
प्रसत्त a. satisfied, pleased with (—°).
प्रसत्ति f. grace, favour.
प्रसन्न a. clear, bright, pure; distinct, plain, just; propitiated, pleased, delighted, content; gracious or kind to (loc., gen., or acc. w. प्रति). — Abstr. °ता f., °त्व n.
प्रसन्नजल a. containing clear water.
प्रसन्नतर्क a. thinking just.
प्रसन्नप्राय a. almost plain or just.
प्रसन्नमुख a. having a tranquil face.
प्रसन्नरस a. clear-juiced.
प्रसन्नसलिल a. = प्रसन्नजल.
प्रसन्नात्मन् a. of gracious or tranquil mind.
प्रसभ (°—) & प्रसभम् adv. forcibly, violently.
प्रसभदमन n. violent subduing.
प्रसर m. coming forth, rising, appearing, spreading, free course, bold behaviour; flood, stream, multitude.
प्रसरण n. running away, escape.
प्रसर्ग or प्रसंर्ग m. rushing forth, discharge, emission.
प्रसलवि adv. to the right.
1प्रसव m. pressing out the Soma.
2प्रसव m. urging, setting or getting in motion, impulse, animation; furtherance, assistance; activity, pursuit; impeller, vivifier.
3प्रसव m. procreation, generation, conception, bringing forth, childbirth; birthplace; offspring, blossom, flower.
प्रसवन n. bringing forth; fecundity.
प्रसववेदना f. the pangs of childbirth, throes.
1प्रसवितृ m. impeller, promoter.
2प्रसवितृ m. procreator, father.
प्रसविन् a. bringing forth, producing.
प्रसवोतृ m. = 1प्रसवितृ.
प्रसव्य a. directed to the left; n. adv.
प्रसंह् (°साह्) a. overpowering.
प्रसह a. & m. bearing. resisting (—°).
1प्रसह्य ger. forcibly, by force.
2प्रसह्य a. to be resisted or overpowered.
प्रसह्वन् a. overpowering.
प्रसाद् m. clearness, brightness, serenity, calmness, tranquillity, kindness, grace, favour, aid, assistance, gratuity, present.
प्रसादक a. clearing, soothing, propitiating, gladdening, comforting.
प्रसादन a. (f. ई) & n. the same.
प्रसादयितव्य a. to be propitiated.
प्रसादवित्त a. rich in favour; m. favourite.
प्रसादसुमुख a. inclined to do grace.
प्रसादिन् a. clear, bright; brightening (—°).
प्रसादी w. कृ favour or present a person (gen.) with (acc.).
प्रसाद्य a. = प्रसादयितव्य.
प्रसाधक, f. °धिका dressing, adorning; man- or maid-servant.
प्रसाधन a. accomplishing; n. bringing about, arranging, ornament, dress, °कला†* f. the art of dressing or decorating. — f. ई comb.
प्रसार m. stretching, spreading, rising.
प्रसारण n. stretching, spreading, exhibiting, showing, increasing, augmenting.
प्रसारिन् a. coming forth, flowing from (—°); stretching, extending to (—°).
1प्रसित a. devoted to, intent upon, anxious about (loc. or *instr.).
2प्रसित a. flying along.
प्रसिति f. track, path, course, stretch, reach, dominion, continuation, duration.

प्रसिद्ध a. accomplished, brought in order, arranged, settled; famous, celebrated; abstr. °ता† f., °त्व† n.

प्रसिद्धि f. success, accomplishment, perfection; celebrity, notoriety.

प्रसुत् a. flowing forth (from the press); f. continued pressing of Soma.

प्रसुत a. (having) pressed out continually; n. = prec. f.

प्रसुति f. = prec. n.

प्रसुप् a. sleeping, asleep.

प्रसुप्त a. fallen asleep, sleeping, senseless, at rest.

प्रसू n. bearing, bringing forth (—°), fruitful. f. mother; shoot, young grass or herb.

प्रसूत a. born, brought forth (f. आ also act.), produced, sprung from (abl., gen., or —°), in (loc.); sent forth, impelled, bidden, allowed.

प्रसूति f. bringing forth, bearing, birth, production, coming forth, growth; f. father or mother, child, offspring, grown fruit; urging, impelling, bidding, permission.

प्रसूतिका f. having brought forth recently.

प्रसूतिविकल a. having no progeny.

प्रसून n. bud, blossom, fruit.

प्रसूनमाला f. garland of flowers.

प्रसूमन्त् & **प्रसूवन्** (f. **प्रसूवरी**) furnished with flowers.

प्रसृत a. streamed or broken forth, spread, extensive, mighty, strong, widely spread, common, usual; run away, fled. — m. the stretched out and hollowed hand (also as a measure.

प्रसृति f. streaming, flowing, also = prec. m.

प्रसेक m. flowing forth, discharge; the bowl of a spoon or ladle.

प्रसेन & °**जित्** m. names of sev. princes.

प्रस्तब्ध a. stiff, rigid.

प्रस्तर m. stramentum, layer, straw; bunch of grass (r.); surface, plain; stone, rock.

प्रस्तव m. praise, eulogy.

प्रस्तार m. spreading, extension, high degree; straw, cushion, bed, layer, plain, surface.

प्रस्तारपङ्क्ति f. N. of a metre.

प्रस्तारिन् a. spreading, stretching over (—°).

प्रस्ताव m. mentioning, subject or opportunity of conversation, opportunity i.g., occasion of (—°); introduction (r.); prologue (d.). — Instr. occasionally, by the bye.

प्रस्तावना f. announcing, proclaiming; introduction, prologue (cf. prec.).

प्रस्तीर्ण a. spread, extended, flat.

प्रस्तुत a. praised, mentioned, in question, commenced, begun; n. beginning, purpose.

प्रस्तुति f. praise.

प्रस्तोतृ m. a class of priests.

प्रस्थ m. n. table-land on a mountain, surface, plain; a cert. weight & measure.

प्रस्थान n. going forth, setting out, departure.

†**प्रस्थावन्** a. hastening on, rapid.

प्रस्थित a. standing ready (to sacrifice), rising; prominent, appointed (to an office); started, set out, having left for (acc. ± **प्रति**, dat., or loc.).

प्रस्थिति f. = **प्रस्थान**.

प्रस्नव m. what flows forth, esp. milk or urine, pl. tears.

प्रस्निग्ध a. very slippery, soft, or delicate.

प्रस्फुट a. manifest, clear.

प्रस्यन्द m., °**न** n. flowing forth.

प्रस्यन्दिन् adj. to prec.

प्रस्रव m. the flowing forth, esp. of the milk from the udder, also the milk itself; gush, flood, stream.

प्रस्रवण n. flowing fort. efflux; spring (also m.).

प्रस्वादस् a. pleasant, charming.

प्रस्वेद m. sweat, perspiration.

प्रहति f. stroke, throw.

प्रहर m. a watch i.e. a period of about 3 hours (lit. a stroke, scil. on a gong).

प्रहरण n. striking, beating, fighting, war, battle, weapon.

प्रहर्तव्य a. to be struck or assailed; n. impers.

प्रहर्तृ m. sender, striker, assailant, champion.

प्रहर्ष m. great joy, delight, rapture.

प्रहर्षण a. making stiff (the hairs of the body) i.e. exciting, gladdening; n. erection (of the hairs); delighting or delight.

प्रहर्षिन् a. gladdening (cf. prec.).

प्रहसन n. laughing, mocking; n. a kind of comedy or farce.

1**प्रहस्त** m. the outstretched hand.

2**प्रहस्त** a. long-handed; m. N. of a Rakṣas etc.

प्रहा f. start, advantage.

प्रहाण n., **°णि** f. ceasing, vanishing.

प्रहार m. stroke, blow, shot.

प्रहारिन् a. striking, fighting; m. warrior, hero.

प्रहास m. laughter, sarcasm; p. **°सिन्**.

प्रहि m. a well.

प्रहीण a. left alone, deprived of, wanting (—°); vanished, gone.

प्रहुत m. a kind of sacrifice.

प्रहुति f. oblation, sacrifice.

प्रहृष्ट a. rigid, erect; delighted, joyful, glad.

प्रहृष्टमनस् a. rejoiced in mind.

प्रहेति m. weapon, spear.

प्रहेतृ m. impeller.

प्रहोष m., **°षिन्** a. offering.

प्रह्राद m. N. of the chief of the Asuras.

प्रह्लाद m. refreshment, comfort, joy, happiness; N. of a Daitya, also = prec., pl. N. of a people.

प्रह्लादन a. (f. **ई**) & n. refreshing, gladdening.

प्रह्लादिन् a. = prec. adj.

प्रह्व a. bent forwards, stooping; humble.

1**प्रा**, pp. **प्रात** = 1**पृ**; 2**प्रा** = 2**प्र** (—°).

प्रांशु a. tall, high.

प्राक् v. **प्राञ्च्**.

प्राकार m. encircling wall, rampart.

प्राकारखण्ड m. a piece or the ruins of a wall.*

प्राकारस्थ a. standing on a wall.

प्राकृत, f. **आ** & **ई** natural, normal, usual, common, vulgar, vernacular; n. the vulgar language, the Prākrit.

प्राकृतभाषिन् a. speaking the vulgar language.

प्राक्छाय n. the falling of a shadow towards the east.

प्राक्तन, f. **ई** former, previous, ancient.

प्राक्तस् & **प्राक्तात्** adv. from the front or from the east.

प्राक्कूल a. having the points turned towards the east (blades of grass).

प्राक्प्रस्तुत a. mentioned before.

प्राक्शस् adv. eastward.

प्रागग्र a. having the point directed to the front or to the east.

प्रागनुराग m. the former affection.

प्रागल्भी f., **°ल्भ्य** n. confidence, boldness.

प्रागवस्था f. the former condition.

प्रागुत्तर a. north-eastern; **°रेण** & **°रतस्** north-east of (abl. or gen.). f. **आ** the north-east.

प्रागुदञ्च् a. north-eastern; f. **°दीची** = prec. f.

प्रागूढा f. having been married before.

प्राग्गमनवन्त् a. moving forwards.

प्राग्ग्रीव a. having the neck turned eastward.

प्राग्जन्मन् n. a former birth.

प्राग्जात n., **°जाति** f. the same.

प्राग्दक्षिण a. south-eastern; **°णा** adv.

प्राग्भार m. slope, inclination (lit. & fig.), mass, heap.

प्राग्र n. the extreme point; **°सर** a. first of all, best of (gen.).

प्राग्वत् adv. as before.

प्राघुण, **°घुणक**, & **°घुणिक** m. guest.

प्राघूर्ण & **°क** m. the same.

प्राघूर्णिक m. = prec.; n. hospitable reception.

प्राङ् v. **प्राञ्च्**.

प्राङ्गण or **°न** n. fore-court, court-yard.

प्राङ्मुख, f. **ई** facing the east; inclined towards (—°); abstr. **°त्व** n.

प्राचण्ड्य n. violence, passion.

प्राचीन a. turned forward or eastward; former, prior, ancient, old; n. adv. forwards, in front or to the east of, before (abl.).

प्राचीनावीत n. & **°तिन्** a. wearing the sacred cord over the right shoulder.

प्राचुर्य n. multitude, plenty.

प्राचेतस m. patron. from **प्रचेतस्**.

प्राचैस् (instr. adv.) forwards.

प्राच्य or **प्राच्य** a. being in front, eastern, former, ancient; m. pl. the ancients or the inhabitants of the east.

प्राछ् m. (nom. **प्राट्**) inquirer.

प्राजक m. driver.

प्राजापत्य a. coming from or belonging to Prajāpati; m. (± **विवाह**) a cert. form of marriage; n. procreative power.

प्राजिक m. falcon.

प्राज्ञ a. intellectual; intelligent, wise, clever (abstr. °त्व† n.). m. a wise man.

प्राज्ञमानिन् & प्राज्ञंमानिन् a. thinking one's self wise.

प्राज्य a. abundant, much, great, important.

प्राज्यकाम a. having plenty of enjoyments.

प्राज्यवृष्टि a. giving plenty of rain.

प्राञ्च्, f. प्राची turned forwards, being in front, facing; turned eastwards, easterly; previous, former; m. pl. the eastern (people or grammarians). Acc. w. कृ bring, offer, promote, further; w. कल्पय् turn one's front towards. n. प्राक् (प्राङ्) in front, before (w. abl. of pl. & t.); eastward, in the east of (abl.); formerly, previously, first, at first, from now. Instr. प्राचा forwards; abl. प्राचंस् from the front. f. प्राची (± दिश्) the east.

प्राञ्जल a. straight, plain; abstr. °ता f.

प्राञ्जलि (f. °लि or °ली) making hollow hands (cf. अञ्जलि).

प्राड्विवाक m. judge.

प्राण m. breath, esp. vital breath, vitality; wind, esp. one of the winds in the human body; pl. life, the vital organs or organs of sensation.

प्राणकर्मन् n. a vital function.

प्राणकृच्छ्र n. danger of life.

प्राणत्याग m. abandonment of life.

प्राणत्राण n. saving a life.

प्राणथ m. breathing.

प्राणद & °दातृ a. giving or saving life.

प्राणधारण n. support or prolongation of life.

प्राणन a. & n. vivifying; n. also breathing.

प्राणनाथ m. lord of life, i.e. husband, lover.

प्राणनान्त m. death (end of life).

प्राणनाश m. death (loss of life).

प्राणनिग्रह m. checking the breath.

प्राणपरित्याग m. = प्राणत्याग.

प्राणप्रद a. saving or having saved a person's life.

प्राणप्रिय a. dear as life; m. husband, lover.

प्राणभृत् a. supporting life, alive; m. living creature, man.

प्राणमन्त् a. vigorous, strong.

प्राणमय a. consisting of breath, breathing.

प्राणयात्रा f. support of life, subsistence.

प्राणयात्रिकमात्र a. having only what is necessary for the support of life.

प्राणयुत a. endowed with life, living.

प्राणलाभ m. saving of life.

प्राणलिप्सु a. wishing to save a life.

प्राणलाभ m. preservation of life.

प्राणवन्त् a. having breath, living, vigorous, strong.

प्राणवृत्ति f. vital function, activity.

प्राणव्यय m. loss of life.

प्राणसम a. dear as (lit. equal to) life.

प्राणसार a. full of life, vigorous.

प्राणहर, °हारक, & °हारिन् a. robbing life, destructive.

प्राणहीन a. robbed of life, lifeless.

प्राणात्यय m. danger of life.

प्राणाधिक & °प्रिय a. dearer than life.

प्राणानुग a. following the life of, i.e. following in death (—°).

1प्राणान्त m. end of life, death.

2प्राणान्त a. causing the end of life; w. दण्ड m. punishment of death.

प्राणान्तिक a. = prec. a. + lifelong; n. peril of life.

प्राणापानं m. du. inspiration and expiration.

प्राणाबाध m. injury or danger of life.

प्राणायाम m. restraining of breath.

प्राणार्थिन् a. greedy for life.

प्राणावरोध m. = प्राणायाम.

प्राणित्व n. abstr. to seq.

प्राणिन् a. having breath or life; m. living creature, man or animal.

प्राणिवध m. killing a living creature.

प्राणेश m. lord of life, i.e. husband, lover; f. आ wife, mistress.

प्राणेश्वर m., ई f. the same.

प्रातःकार्य & °कृत्य n. morning ceremony.

प्रातर् adv. early, in the morning, to-morrow.

प्रातरभिवाद m. morning salutation.

प्रातरशन n. morning-meal, breakfast.

प्रातरह्न m. early morning.

प्रातराश m. morning-meal, breakfast; °शित a. who has breakfasted.

प्रातराहुति f. morning oblation.

प्रातर्यज्ञ m. early sacrifice.

प्रातर्युक्त a. yoked early in the morning.
प्रातश्चन्द्र m. the moon in the morning, °द्युति a. having the colour of it i.e. pale.
प्रातस्तन a. matutinal; n. morning.
प्रातस्त्य a. = prec. a.
प्रातःसंध्या f. morning twilight, dawn.
प्रातःसव m., °सवन n. the morning libation of Soma.
प्रातिकूलिक a. opposed to, adverse, inimical, abstr. °ता f. & °कूल्य n.
प्रातिपदिक a. explicit; n. the crude form or base of a noun, abstr. °त्व n.
प्रातिभाव्य n. surety (j.).
प्रातिलोम्य n. inverted order; instr. adv.
प्रातिवेशिक & °श्मिक m. neighbour.
प्रातिवेश्य a. neighbouring; m. a neighbour living opposite, neighbour i.g.
प्रातिशाख्य n. a cert. class of works.
प्रातिश्रुत्क a. being in the echo.
प्रात्ययिक a. perceptible by the senses.
प्राथमकल्पिक a. being the first in rank or importance.
प्राथमिक a. primary, first.
प्राथम्य n. priority.
प्रादक्षिण्य n. circumambulation from the left to the right.
प्रादुर्भाव m. the becoming visible, rising, appearance.
प्रादुष्करण n. the making visible, production.
प्रादुस् adv. forth to view, into sight. With अस् & भू become visible, appear, rise; w. कृ make visible, reveal, show.
प्रादोष & °षिक a. vespertine.
प्राधानिक a. predominant, chief.
प्राधान्य n. predominance, prevalence; °—, instr., abl., & °तस् adv. chiefly, principally.
प्राधीत a. learned in the Veda.
प्राध्व m. start; °ध्वे कृ place at the head of (gen.).
प्राध्वम् adv. far away (w. कृ lay aside); kindly, humbly.
प्राध्वन m. the bed of a river.
प्रान्त m. n. edge, margin, border, point, end.
प्रान्तर n. a long and solitary path.
प्रान्तवृति s. horizon.
प्रापक a. leading towards (—°), getting, procuring.
प्रापण, f. ई leading towards (—°); n. reaching, attaining, coming, entering, getting at (loc.), gain, acquisition.
प्रापणीय a. to be attained or brought to (acc.); abstr. °त्व n.
प्रापिन् a. reaching, getting at.
प्राप्त a. (having) reached or obtained; come, arrived at (—°); existing, being, often °— whose— is come, who has got –, provided with; following from a rule, valid, correct (g.).
1प्राप्तकाल m. the arrived time, i.e. the right or favourable moment.
2प्राप्तकाल a. whose time is come, seasonable, suitable, fit, proper, f. आ marriageable.
प्राप्तजीवन a. having recovered life, saved from death.
प्राप्तप्रभाव a. mighty (lit. having attained might).
प्राप्तयौवन a. having attained adolescence, f. आ marriageable.
प्राप्तरूप a. fit, proper; learned, wise.
प्राप्तविकल्पत्व n. alternativeness (g.).
प्राप्तव्य a. to be met with or attained.
प्राप्तापराध a. having committed a fault.
1प्राप्तार्थ m. the attained object.
2प्राप्तार्थ a. having made money.
प्राप्तावसर a. seasonable, suitable, proper.
प्राप्ति f. reaching, attaining (conc. also as a superhuman faculty), arriving at, coming, entering, pervading; finding, meeting with; acquisition, rescue from (abl.), gain, profit, fortune; resulting from a rule, validity, correctness (g.).
*प्राप्तोदक a. having got water.
प्राप्य a. = प्राप्तव्य + fit, proper.
प्राबल्य n. might, force.
प्राभवत्य n. superiority, power.
प्राभाकर m. a follower of Prabhākara; n. his work (ph.).
प्राभृत & °क n. present, offering.
प्रामाण्य n. the being an authority or a proof, °तस् adv.
प्राय m. going forth, esp. to fight, onset; de-

parture, esp. from life, seeking death by fasting (acc. w. आस्, उपास्, आस्था, कृ etc. devote one's self to death); what is prominent, most or principal part. Adj. —° mostly consisting of, abounding in; resembling, like; nearly, as it were.

प्रायण a. going; n. entrance, beginning, course of or departure from life; acc. w. कृ = prec. w. आस् etc.

प्रायत्य n. purity (r.).

प्रायशस् adv. mostly, generally, likely.

प्रायश्चित्त n., °त्ति f. expiation, atonement, amends.

प्रायश्चित्तीय्, °यते be obliged to do penance.

प्रायश्चित्तीयता f. abstr. to prec.

प्रायस् adv. = प्रायशस्.

प्रायुस् n. a very long life.

प्रायेण (instr. adv.) = प्रायशस्.

प्रायोपगमन & **प्रायोपवेशन** n. seeking death by abstaining from food.

प्रारब्ध a. (having) begun or undertaken.

प्रारम्भ m. beginning, undertaking.

प्रारोह m. shoot, sprout.

प्रार्थ a. ready to set out.

प्रार्थक a. wooing; m. a suitor.

प्रार्थन n., °ना f. desire, wish; requesting, begging; petition or suit for (loc. or —°).

प्रार्थनीय a. to be asked or desired.

प्रार्थयितृ m. wooer, suitor.

प्रार्थयितव्य a = प्रार्थनीय.

प्रार्थित a. wished, desired, wanted, asked, requested; n. wish, desire.

प्रार्थिन् a. wishing, desiring, longing for; attacking (—°).

प्रार्थ्य a. = प्रार्थनीय.

प्रार्पण m. impeller.

प्रालम्ब a. hanging down; s. a kind of pearl ornament.

***प्रालम्बिका** f. a golden necklace.

प्रालेय s. hail, snow, rime, dew.

प्रालेयाद्रि m. the Himālaya (snow-mountain).

प्रावरण n. covering, cover, cloak, mantle.

प्रावर्ग a. distinguished, eminent.

प्रावार & °क m. upper garment, mantle.

प्रावितृ m. protector, guardian.

प्रावित्र n. protection, guard.

प्रावी a. heedful, zealous.

प्रावीण्य n. cleverness, skill in (loc. or —°).

प्रावृट्काल m. the rainy season.

प्रावृण्मेघ m. rain-cloud.

प्रावृत a. covered or filled with (instr.); put on (clothes); n. = प्रावरण.

प्रावृष् f. the rainy season, the rains.

प्रावृष m. = prec.; adj. belonging to the rainy season, rainy.

प्रावृषिक, °षीण, & °षेण्य a. = prec. adj.

प्रावेप m. swinging, hanging down.

प्रावेशिक, f. ई relating to the entrance (d.).

प्राश् f. assertion in a dispute.

प्राश m. eating, food.

प्राशन n. eating, feeding.

प्राशस्त्य n. excellence, perfection, high quality.

प्राशा f. ardent desire.

प्राशित a. eaten or drunk; m. a kind of sacrifice.

प्राशितव्य or °तव्य a. to be eaten, eatable.

प्राशितृ m. eater.

प्राशित्र n. the Brahman's portion of food at a sacrifice; प्राशित्रहरण n. the vessel for holding it.

प्राशु a. very quick, swift.

प्राश्निक a. containing many questions; m. inquirer, umpire.

प्रास m. cast, throw; spear.

प्रासङ्गिक, f. ई relating to attachment or connection; occasional, accidental.

प्रासह् a. powerful, victorious; f. force, victory.

प्रासह m. power, force.

प्रासाद m. lofty seat or platform for spectators, tower, upper story, palace, temple.

प्रासादगर्भ m. inner apartment; sleeping-room in a palace.

प्रासादपृष्ठ & °दाग्र n. terrace on the top of a palace.

प्रास्ताविक, f. ई introductory (d.).

प्राहुण m., ई f. guest.

प्राहुणक or °णिक m., °णिका f. the same.

प्राह्ण m. morning, forenoon.

प्रिय a. dear, valued, pleasing to, beloved of, one's own (gen., loc., dat., or —°); loving,

fond of, devoted to (loc., °—, or —°). — m. friend, lover, husband (also प्रियतम), son-in-law; f. आ mistress, wife, (also प्रियतमा). n. love, kindness, favour, as adv. agreeably, pleasantly, instr. willingly.
प्रियंवद a. speaking, kindly; f. आ a woman's name.
प्रियकाम a. well-wishing, kind.
प्रियकाम्या f. benevolence, kindness.
प्रियकार, °कारक, & °कारिन् a. doing a kindness, obliging.
प्रियकृत् & प्रियंकर (f. ई & आ) the same.
†प्रियक्षत्र a. ruling kindly.
प्रियंगु m. f. a medicinal plant and perfume.
प्रियचिकीर्षा f. desire to do a kindness or to please; adj. °चिकीर्षु.
प्रियजन m. the beloved person.
†प्रियजात a. born beloved or desired.
प्रियता f., °त्व† n. dearness, affection, love.
प्रियदर्श & °न a. pleasant to look at.
प्रियदर्शिका f. N. of a play & its heroine.
प्रियनिवेदन n. glad tidings.
प्रियनिवेदयितृ (°तृक) m. messenger of glad tidings.*
प्रियनिवेदिका* f., °दितृ *m. = prec.
प्रियबन्धु m. a dear friend.
प्रियभाषण n. friendly speech; a. °षिन्.
प्रियरूप a. pleasantly formed.
प्रियवचन n. & a. = प्रियभाषण & °षिन्.
प्रियवचस् n. & a. = prec.
प्रियवसन्तक m. the pleasant spring or (and) dear Vasantaka.
1प्रियवाच् f. kind or pleasant speech.
2प्रियवाच् a. speeking kindly or tenderly.
प्रियवाद m. = prec. 1, °वादिन् a. = prec. 2.
प्रियसंवास m. society of friends.
प्रियसख m., ई f. a dear friend.
प्रियहित a. pleasant and good.
प्रियातिथि a. kind to guests, hospitable.
प्रियाप्रिय n. sgl., du., & pl. pleasant and unpleasant things, comfort and discomfort.
प्रियाल m. N. of a tree.
प्रियालापिन् a. talking kindly.
प्रियोक्ति f. friendly speech.
1प्री, प्रीणाति, प्रीणीते, प्रीयते (°ति), pp. प्रीत (q.v.) A. please gladden, rejoice, propitiate; also = M. be glad or cheerful, delight in, be content or pleased with, be fond of (gen., instr., loc., or abl.). C. प्रीणयति = S.A.; D. पिप्रीषति wish to please or propitiate. — आ A. please, satisfy, gladden, propitiate. M. be glad, rejoice. सम् (प्रीयते) be glad or cheerful, delight in (loc. or abl.). — Cf. आप्रीत, परिप्रीत, संप्रीत.
2प्री (—°) friendly to, delighting in.
प्रीणन a. & n. pleasing, gratifying.
प्रीणय्, °यति v. 1प्री.
प्रीत a. pleased, satisfied with (instr., loc., or —°), glad, cheerful; loved, dear.
प्रीतात्मन् a. pleased in mind.
प्रीति f. pleasure, satisfaction, or delight in (loc. or —°); friendship, love (also personif. as the wife of the god of love).
प्रीतिकर a. causing pleasure.
प्रीतिकर्मन् n. labour of love.
प्रीतिच्छेद m. disturbance of joy.*
प्रीतिदान n., °दाय m. gift of love.
प्रीतिपूर्वकम् adv. out of love.
प्रीतिप्रमुख a. kind from the beginning.
प्रीतिमन्त् a. pleased, content; feeling love or friendship for (loc., gen., or acc.); fond, kind (words); having Prīti (cf. s. v.).
प्रीतिवचस् n. kind talk, friendly words.
प्रु, प्रवते flow, spring up. — अति jump away. अप jump down. अभि jump near. उद् jump up or forth. नि sputter about. — Cf. विप्रुत.
प्रुथ्, प्रोथति snort. — प्र = S.
प्रुष्, प्रुष्णाति, प्रुष्णुते (प्रुष्यति), pp. प्रुषित sprinkle, wet, moisten. — अभि M. sprinkle anything on one's self. परि sprinkle about. वि drip off or down.
प्रुषितप्सु a. speckled, dapple.
प्रुष्वा or प्रुष्वा f. hoar-frost, ice.
प्रेक्षक, f. प्रेक्षिका looking at, viewing; considering, judging.
प्रेक्षण n. look, view, sight, spectacle.
प्रेक्षणक a. looking at; m. spectator, beholder; n. spectacle, show.
प्रेक्षणालम्भ s. looking at and touching (women).
प्रेक्षणीय a. to be seen or viewed, visible, worth seeing, sightly, beautiful; abstr. °ता f.

प्रेक्षा f. look, view, sight, show, spectacle; consideration, reflection.
प्रेक्षागार m. n., °**गृह** n. play-house.
प्रेक्षावन्त् a. considerate, wise.
प्रेक्षासमाज n. sgl. public spectacles or assemblies.
प्रेक्षित n. look, view, glance.
प्रेक्षितृ m. spectator, beholder.
प्रेक्षितव्य a. to be seen.*
प्रेक्षिन् a. looking at, watching (—°).
प्रेक्ष्य a. = **प्रेक्षितव्य** + worth seeing.
प्रेङ्ख a. rocking, swinging; m. n. & f. **आ** a swing.
प्रेङ्खण n. swinging.
प्रेङ्खोल a. swinging, moving to and fro; m. a swing.
प्रेङ्खोलन n. swinging; a swing.
प्रेङ्खोलित a. swung, moved to and fro.
प्रेणा instr. = **प्रेम्णा**, v. **प्रेमन्**.
प्रेत a. deceased, dead, adv. °**वत्**†; m. a ghost.
प्रेतकर्मन् n. funeral rite.
प्रेतकाय m. dead body, corpse; abl. °**तस्**.
प्रेतकार्य & °**कृत्य** n. = **प्रेतकर्मन्**.
प्रेतगत a. gone to the dead, dead.
प्रेतधूम m. the smoke of a burned corpse.
प्रेतगति f. the way of the dead; °**तिं गत** died, dead.
प्रेतनाथ & °**पति** m. lord of the dead (Yama).
प्रेतनिर्यातक m. a carrier of dead bodies.
प्रेतपुरी f. the city of the dead.
प्रेतभाव m. the being dead.
प्रेतराज m. = **प्रेतनाथ**.
प्रेतशुद्धि f. the purification after a death.
प्रेतहार m. carrier of dead bodies.
प्रेताधिप & °**पति** m. the same.
प्रेतान्न n. the food destined for the dead.
प्रेति f. going away, flight.
प्रेतेश & °**श्वर** m. = **प्रेतनाथ**.
प्रेत्य ger. after death, in the other world.
प्रेत्यभाव m. the state after death.
प्रेत्वन्, f. **प्रेत्वरी** rushing on, straying about.
प्रेदण्ड & °**क** m. ruffian, villain.*
प्रेप्सा f. wish to attain, adj. **प्रेप्सु**.
प्रेम (adj. —°) = seq.
प्रेमन् m. n. love, affection, kindness.
प्रेमबन्ध m., °**न** n. the ties of love.
प्रेमाबन्ध m. = prec.
प्रेमार्द्र a. overflowing with love.
प्रेयंस् (compar.) dearer, more valued or wished for; m. & f. **प्रेयसी** the beloved one; n. joy, happiness.
प्रेरक a. & m. impelling, impeller.
प्रेरण n., **आ** f. impulse, activity.
प्रेरणीय a. to be urged on or incited.
प्रेरितृ m. inciter, impeller.
प्रेष् f. pressing, urging on.
प्रेष m. impulse, zeal.
प्रेषण n. sending forth, commissioning, order, command; °**कृत्** a. executing an order.
प्रेष्ठ (superl.) most dear or beloved, very pleasant. m. lover, husband, f. **आ** mistress, wife.
प्रेष्य a. to be sent. m. & f. **आ** man- & maid-servant; n. service, order, command.
प्रेष्यजन m. servant (also collect.).
प्रेष्यता f., °**त्व** n. servitude, service.
प्रेष्यभाव m. the same.
प्रैषं m. request, direction, command.
प्रैष्यं m., **आ** f., man- or maid-servant; n. **प्रैष्य** servitude.
प्रैष्यजन & °**भाव** m. = **प्रेष्यजन** & °**भाव**.
प्रोक्त a. spoken to, addressed; said, uttered, announced, declared, stated, mentioned, called.
प्रोक्ष m. sprinkling (r.).
प्रोक्षण n. the same; f. °**णी** water for sprinkling, holy water.
प्रोक्षितव्य a. to be sprinkled.
प्रोच्चैस् (instr. adv.) very loudly or intensely.
प्रोञ्छ् v. **उञ्छ्**.
प्रोञ्छन n. wiping out (lit. & fig.).
प्रोत a. tied, strung; pierced, put on (a spit); set, inlaid.
प्रोति m. N. of a man.
प्रोत्कट a. very great or high, chief.
प्रोत्तुङ्ग a. very high or lofty.
प्रोत्थित a. broken forth, appeared (leaf); sprung from (—°).
प्रोत्फुल्ल a. widely expanded, full-blown.
प्रोत्साह m. great effort, zeal, ardour.
प्रोत्साहन n. instigation, stimulation.

प्रोथ s. the nostrils of a horse or the snout of a hog.

प्रोथथ m. snorting, panting.

प्रोदक a. dripping, wet.

प्रोद्यत a. lifted up, raised (voice); going or about to (infin.).

प्रोन्नत a. raised up, prominent, very high, superior in (—°).

प्रोष m. burning.

प्रोषित a. away from home, abroad, absent; vanished, gone, dead.

प्रोष्ठ m. bench, stool; pl. N. of a people.

प्रोष्ण a. burning hot.

प्रोष्णु a. wandering, roaming.

प्रौढ a. grown up, full-grown, mature, developed; adult, buxom (woman), confident, bold; great, mighty, strong; full of, rich in (—°).

प्रौढत्व n. confidence, audacity.

प्रौढपाद् a. holding the feet in a cert. position (r.).

प्रौढाचार a. of confident or audacious behaviour.

प्रौढि f. growth, maturity, also = **प्रौढत्व**.

प्रौष्ठपद m. a cert. month, f. **ई** the full-moon's day in it.

प्लक्ष m. the holy fig-tree.

प्लति m. N. of a man.

प्लव a. swimming, floating, verging towards (—°), perishable. — m. boat, raft (also n.), a kind of duck, swimming, bathing, flood; jump, leap.

प्लवग m. frog or ape (lit. going by leaps).

प्लवंग m. ape; **°म** m. frog or ape (cf. prec.).

प्लवन a. sloping towards (—°); n. swimming, bathing in (—°), flying, jumping over (—°).

प्लवितृ m. leaper.

प्लाक्ष a. coming from the holy fig-tree.

प्लाव m. flowing over; jump.

प्लावन n. bathing, ablution.

प्लाविन् a. flowing from; spreading, promulgating (—°).

प्लाशि m. sgl. & pl. a cert. part of the intestines.

प्लाशुक a. growing swiftly again.

प्लिहन् & **प्लीहन्** m., **प्लीहा** f. the spleen.

प्लु, **प्लवते** (**°ति**), pp. **प्लुत** (q.v.) float, swim, bathe, sail; vibrate, hover, soar, fly; blow (wind), pass away (time); spring, jump, dance. C. **प्लावयति, °ते** make float or swim, inundate, overflow, cover with (instr.), bathe, cleanse, wash away, remove. I. **पोप्लूयते** swim about. — **अभि** sail or move towards (acc.), spring or hasten near, attack, visit. **समभि** inundate, submerge, attack, visit. **अव** immerse; jump down or off. **आ** bathe, plunge, or wash (tr. & intr.); overflow, inundate, cover; jump near, over, up, or off. C. = S. tr.; M. also bathe (intr.). **उपन्या** swim near or towards (acc.). **समा** bathe (intr.); overflow, cover thoroughly. **उद्** spring up, emerge, rise. **उप** swim on the surface, float upon, hover towards, overflow, cover, veil, eclipse, attack, assail. **परि** swim about, bathe; flood, inundate; soar about, fly through; spring about, move restlessly, waver, go astray. **प्र** go to sea (acc.); C. cause to float away, wash or flood with water. **वि** go asunder, be dispersed, fall into disorder, go astray, be ruined, perish. C. make swim; flood, inundate; spread abroad, divulge; ruin, destroy. **सम्** flow together, gather, contract (intr.); fluctuate, waver (mind). C. gather, contract (trans.), flood, inundate. — Cf. **अभिपरिप्लुत** (add.), **अभिप्लुत**, **आप्लुत**, **उपप्लुत**, **प्रप्लुत**, **विप्लुत**, **संप्लुत**.

प्लुत a. floated, bathed, inundated, overflowed, covered or filled with (instr. or —°); protracted (g.); flown, jumped, n. leap, jump.

प्लुति f. overflowing, flood; leap, jump; prolation (g.).

प्लुष्, **प्लोषति**, pp. **प्लुष्ट** burn, singe.

प्लुषि m. a kind of insect.

प्लेङ्ख m. swing.

प्लोत s. cloth, rag.

प्लोष m. burning, conflagration.

प्लोषण & **प्लोषिन्** a. burning, singeing (—°).

†प्सर (—°) shyness, shame.
1†प्सरस् (—°) the same.
2प्सरस् n. food, feast, enjoyment.
प्सा, प्साति, pp. प्सात chew, devour.
1प्सु (—°) food.
2प्सु (—°) form, aspect.
प्सुरस् n. food, fruit.

फ

फक्क्, फक्कति swell.
फञ्जी f. N. of a plant.
फट् interj. & mystic syllable.
फटा f. the hood of a serpent.
†फण्, फणति spring. C. फाणयति cause to spring or run.
फण m. scum, froth; the hood of a serpent (also f. आ).
फणधर & फणभृत् m. hooded serpent, snake i.g.
फणवन्त् a. hooded; m.=prec.
फणाभृत् & फणावन्त् a. & m. the same.
फणि m. serpent.
फणिन् m. = prec., E. of Rāhu & Patañjali.
फणिपति m. serpent-king, E. of Çeṣa.
फणीन्द्र, फणीश, & फणीश्वर m. = prec.
1फल्, फलति, pp. फुल्ल (q.v.) burst, split (intr.). — उद् burst out, rush forth. C. उत्फालयति tear open, open wide (eyes). प्रति rebound, be reflected. वि & सम् burst or split asunder. — Cf. उत्फुल्ल, प्रफुल्ल, प्रोत्फुल्ल, समुत्फुल्ल, संफुल्ल.
2फल्, फलति, °ते, pp. फलित (q.v.) fruit, bear fruit, have results or consequences, be fulfilled. — प्रति & वि bear fruit, ripen, be accomplished.
3फल् interj. = फट्.
फल n. (adj. —° f. आ & ई) fruit, esp. of a tree, kernel, testicle; fruit i.e. result, profit, gain, reward or punishment, compensation, interest on capital; tablet, board, blade, point of an arrow. f. आ & ई names of plants.
फलक (adj. —° f. °लिका) result, advantage, gain; abstr. °त्व n. — फलक n. tablet, board etc. = फल + a wooden bench, the palm of the hands, shield.
फलकोश m. sgl. & du. the scrotum.
फलग्रह a. & m. deriving fruit or profit.
फलग्रहि & °ग्रहिष्णु a. fruit-bearing, fruitful.
फलतस् adv. concerning the fruit or reward.
फलता f., °त्व n. the state of fruit.
फलद a. yielding fruit or profit.
फलदर्भोदक n. fruit, Darbha grass, and water.
फलनिर्वृत्ति f. fulfilment of consequences, final retribution.
फलपाक m. the ripening of fruit or the fulness of consequences.
फलपाकान्त a. perishing after the ripening of its fruit (plant).
फलपातन n. causing a fruit to fall.
फलप्रद a. bringing gain or a reward.
फलप्राप्ति f. obtaining a result, success.
फलबन्धिन् a. forming fruit.
फलभाग m. share in any product, advantage, or reward; poss. °गिन्.
फलभूमि f. the land of retribution.
फलभृत् a. fruit-bearing, fruitful.
फलमिश्र a. accompanied by fruits.*
फलयोग m. remuneration, reward.
फलवन्त् a. fruitful, yielding results or advantages; abstr. °वत्ता† f., °वत्त्व† n.
फलसाधन n. obtaining a result.
फलसिद्धि f. success, prosperity.
फलहक m. board, plank.
फलहेतु a. having results for a motive.
फलाकाङ्क्षिन् a. desirous of results or consequences.
फलागम m. autumn (arrival of fruits).
फलाढ्य a. rich in fruit (tree).
फलार्थिन् a. wishing for fruits or a reward.
फलाशिन् & फलाहार a. living on fruits.
फलिग m. receptacle for water; barrel, cask, etc., fig. a cloud.
फलित a. fruitful, having yielded fruits or consequences, resulted, fulfilled; n. also impers.

फलिंन् a. fruitful, having gain or advantage. m. fruit-tree, f. फलिनी a. cert. plant.

फलिन a. bearing fruit.

फली w. कृ winnow, thrash.

फलीकरण n. abstr. to prec.; m. pl. the refuse from the cleaned grain.

फलेग्रहि a. bearing fruit, fruitful.

फलोदय m. the appearance of consequences; reward or punishment for (loc. or —°).

फलोद्गम m. pl. the appearance of fruit.

फल्गु (f. फल्गु, °ल्गू, & °ल्ग्वी) reddish; small, minute, weak (abstr. °ता† f.); f. du. N. of a lunar mansion.

फल्गुन a. reddish, red. m. E. of Arjuna; f. ई sgl. & du. N. of a double lunar mansion.

फल्ग्व a. small, weak.

फाल m. (*n.) ploughshare or a kind of shovel; bundle, bunch, nosegay.

फालकृष्ट a. tilled with the plough, s. ploughed land; growing on tilled ground, m. such fruit.

फाल्गुन, f. ई belonging to the lunar mansion Phalgunī; m. N. of a month, E. of Arjuna, f. ई the day of full moon in the month Ph., also = फल्गुनी.

फिट्सूत्र n. T. of a grammatical work.

फुट s. the hood of a snake.

फुत् (interj.) w. कृ blow, scream, shriek.

फुत्कार m. abstr. to prec.

फुत्कृत n., फुत्कृति f. the same.

फुराफुराय्, °यते tremble, flicker.*

फुल्ल्, फुल्लति bloom, expand.

फुल्ल a. burst or torn open, loose, expanded, blooming.

फुल्लनलिनी f. a lotus plant in full bloom.*

फुल्लोत्पल n. N. of a lake (lit. having blooming lotuses).

फूत्कृ, फूत्कार m., फूत्कृति f. = फुत्कृ etc.

फेञ्चक m. a cert. bird.

फेट्कार m. howling.

फेत्कार m., फेत्कृत n. the same.

फेत्कारिन् a. howling.

फेन m. (n.) foam; फेनी a kind of food.

फेनप a. drinking foam.

फेनवन्त् a. frothy, foaming.

फेनिल a. = prec., m. N. of a tree.

फेन्य a. being in foam.

फेरव & फेरु m. a jackal.

ब

बंह्, pp. बाढ (q.v.), C. बंहयते make firm, strengthen, increase. — सम् C. = S.C. — Cf. अवबाढ, निबाळ्ह (add.).

बंहिष्ठ (superl.) & बंहीयंस् (compar.) very firm, strong, thick, or fat.

बक m. a kind of heron; hypocrite, flatterer, a man's name.

बकवृत्ति a. acting like a heron i.e. hypocritical.

बकव्रत n. the conduct of a heron i.e. hypocrisy; °व्रतचर, °व्रतिक, °व्रतिन् a. = prec. adj.

बंकुर s. war-trumpet.

बकुल m. a kind of tree; n. its flower.

बकुलदामन् n. a garland of Bakula flowers.

बकुलमाला & बकुलावलि f. the same.

बकुलावलिका f. a woman's name.

बकोट m. a kind of heron.

बंट् adv. indeed.

बटु m. lad, fellow, boy, esp. a young Brahman.

बडा or बळा adv. = बंट्.

बडिश m. n. hook, esp. fish-hook.

बण्ड a. maimed, crippled.

1बत interj. of astonishment or regret (also बतारे, अहो बत, & अयि बत).

2बतं m. weakling.

बदर s., ई f. the jujube tree, n. बंदर its fruit, f. also = seq.

बदरिका f. N. of one of the sources of the Gaṅgā & a neighbouring hermitage of Nara & Nārāyaṇa.

बंह्नक m. a prisoner.

बद्धकदम्बक a. forming groups.
बद्धचित्त a. fixing the mind upon (loc.).
बद्धदृष्टि a. fixing the gaze upon (loc.).
बद्धनेत्र a. fixing the eyes upon (loc.).
बद्धपरिकर a. having tucked up one's garments.*
बद्धपल्लव a. having formed shoots, abstr. °ता f.*
बद्धमण्डल a. forming circles.
बद्धमूल a. having struck root, deeply rooted; abstr. °ता f.
बद्धलक्ष a. turning the eyes (lit. taking aim).
बद्धवत् adv. as if bound.
बद्धाञ्जलि a. putting the hollowed hands together (cf. अञ्जलि).
बद्धाश a. placing one's hope upon (—°).
बद्बधानं v. बाध्.
बद्व n. (m.) troop, number, multitude.
बधिर a. deaf, abstr. °ता† f.
बधिरय्, °यति, pp. बधिरित make deaf, deafen.
बन्दिग्रह m. capture, captivation.
बन्दिता f. abstr. to seq. 1.
1**बन्दिन्** m. praiser of a prince, bard.
2**बन्दिन्** m. captive, prisoner, slave.
बन्दी f. = prec., also a female captive or robbery.
बन्दीकृत a. taken prisoner, seized, overcome; m. a prisoner.
बन्ध्, बध्नाति, बध्नीते (बन्धति), pp. बद्ध (q.v.) bind, tie, attach, fix, fasten, put on (mostly M.); bind (a victim for the gods), i.e. sacrifice; bind together, join, construct, compose; effect, produce, perform, make, get, show, manifest, betray; obstruct, stop, close, dam up (± सेतुना); catch, take or keep prisoner; direct, turn (the eyes or mind) upon (loc. or infin.). C. बन्धयति cause to be bound, caught, constructed, dammed up, etc. — अनु tie to, attach (l. & f.), join, connect; stick to, adhere, follow, (*equal, resemble); adduce, cause, effect; show, betray; hold together, last; insist upon, be urgent with (acc.). P. be tied to etc., be added as indicatory letter (g.). अव tie to, attach. आ bind or tie on, join, unite, bring together; begin, enter into (conversation). उद् tie up, hang. उप bind, fetter. नि bind on, fasten, tie to (loc.); fetter, chain (l. & f.); join, unite; build, construct; close up, stop, restrict; fix, put or turn upon (loc.); compose, write down; betray, manifest. परि bind or put on, tie round (M.), surround, obstruct, stop. प्र tie, fasten, fetter. प्रति tie to, fasten; enchase, set in (loc.); join, connect; fix, direct; shut out, keep off, exclude; stop, interrupt. सम् bind together, connect, attach; P. be bound together, be connected with i.e. belong to (instr.). अभिसम् connect with, mean by. P. be connected with, belong to, be to be supplied. — Cf. अनुबद्ध (add.), अवबद्ध, आबद्ध, उद्बद्ध, उपनिबद्ध, निबद्ध, निर्बद्ध (add.), प्रतिबद्ध, प्रबद्ध, संबद्ध.
बन्ध m. binding, tying to (esp. the sacrificial post), fettering, capturing; custody, prison; band, string, sinew (of the body); chain, tether, bondage (opp. मुक्ति); joining together, connection, position (esp. of hands, feet, etc.); union, intercourse with (—°); forming, constructing; embankment, covering with a bridge; fixing or turning upon (loc.); manifestation, exhibition, show, display (—°).
बन्धक m. binder, catcher; rope, halter. — f. ई an unchaste woman.
बन्धन, f. ई binding, fettering, holding fast; n. the act of binding etc., capture, custody, prison; band, string, sinew, muscle; stem, stalk; chain, fetter, bondage (opp. मुक्ति); constructing, building, covering with a bridge, embanking; dam, mole; union, connection, fixing or turning upon (loc.) etc. = बन्ध.
बन्धनकोश s. stalk-cavity.
बन्धनस्थ a. being in prison, prisoner.
बन्धनागार m. prison-house.
बन्धनीय a. to be (being) tied or caught.
बन्धपाश m. bond, fetter.
बन्धिन् a. binding, catching; causing, effecting; showing, betraying (—°).

बन्धु m. connection, association, relation (adj. f. ऊ only nominally connected with, only by name —°); concr. relative, kinsman, friend, brother, husband; f. ऊ wife (only adj. —°).
बन्धुकृत्य n. the duty of a kinsman or friend.
बन्धुजन m. kinsman or kinsfolk; friend(s).
बन्धुता f., बन्धुत्व n. connection, relation, affinity (the former also concrete).
बन्धुदायाद m. kinsman and heir.
बन्धुबान्धव s. kith and kin.
बन्धुप्रिय a. dear to friends or relations.
बन्धुमन्त् a. having relations or surrounded by relations.
बन्धुर a. bent, inclined (lit. & f.), favourable; delightful, charming.
बन्धुल m. a bastard.
बन्धुवत् adv. like a relative.
बन्धूक m. N. of a plant.
1बन्ध्य a. to be bound, fettered, stopped, caught, joined together.
2बन्ध्य v. वन्ध्य.
बन्ध्वेष m. inquiring after kindred.
बबर m. N. of a man.
बभस m. eater, devourer.
बभ्रि a. bearing or borne.
बभ्रु (f. बभ्रु or बभ्रू) reddish brown, tawny; m. a large kind of ichneumon, E. of sev. gods & men.
1बभ्रुक a. = prec. a.
2बभ्रुक m. a kind of ichneumon.
बभ्रुलोमन्, f. °म्नी brown-haired.
बभ्रुवाह & °वाहन m. N. of a prince.
बम्भरालि f. fly.
बम्भारव m. lowing (of cows).
बरासी f. a kind of garment.
बर्कर m. kid.
बर्कु m. N. of a man.
बर्जह m. udder.
बर्जह्य n. nipple.
बर्बर a. stammering or curled. — m. pl. the barbarians or Non-Aryans, sgl. a man of the lowest origin, adj. mean, vile.
बर्स m. tip, point, thin end.
बर्स्व m. the socket of a tooth.
बर्ह m. tail-feather, tail of a bird, esp. a peacock's tail.
†बर्हण a. & n. pulling out, uprooting.
बर्हणा (instr. adv.) firmly, strongly; really, indeed.
बर्हणावन्त् a. solid, strong, earnest; n. adv.
बर्हभार m. a peacock's tail.
बर्हापीड m. a garland made of the feathers of a peacock.
बर्हि n. = बर्हिस्.
बर्हिण or बर्हिन् m. a peacock (cf. बर्ह).
बर्हिषद् a. sitting on the sacrificial grass; m. a class of Manes.
बर्हिष्ठ (superl.) the largest or strongest; n.adv.
बर्हिष्मन्त् a. poss. to बर्हिस्; m. worshipper, sacrificer.
बर्हिष्य a. belonging to the sacrificial grass.
बर्हिःष्ठ or °ष्ठा a. standing on the sacrificial grass.
बर्हिस् n. (m.) the sacrificial grass or bed (often personif.).
1बल n. (sgl. & pl.) might, power, strength, force; forces i.e. troops, army. बलेन, बलात्, & बलतस् by force, forcibly; by the power or by means of, through, by.
2बल m. a crow; N. of a demon (cf. वल), a brother of Kṛṣṇa, etc.; f. आ a woman's name; n. बल = वल cave, cavern.
बलकृत a. done by force.
बलकृति f. a mighty deed.
बलक्ष, f. बलक्षी white.
बलक्षगु m. the moon (lit. having white rays).
बलचक्र n. dominion, sovereignty, army.
बलज m., आ f. heap of corn.
बलद m. ox.
बलदा & °दावन् a. giving strength.
बलदेय n. abstr. to prec.
बलदेव m. N. of the elder brother of Kṛṣṇa.
बलपति m. lord of strength or chief of an army.
बलपुर n. the castle of Bala.
बलप्रद a. giving strength.
बलभ m. a kind of insect.
बलभद्र m. = बलदेव.
बलभिद् m. the destroyer of Bala (Indra).
बलभृत् a. strong (bearing strength).

बलमद् m. pride in strength or power.
बलमुख्य m. chief of an army.
बलयुक्त & °युत a. endowed with force, strong.
बलराम m. = बलदेव.
बलवत्ता f., °त्त्व n. abstr. to seq.
बलवन्त् a. powerful, mighty, strong, prevalent, superior to (abl.); n. °वत् adv. greatly, much, well.
बलवृत्रघ्न, °निषूदन, & °हन् m. the slayer of Bala and Vṛtra, i.e. Indra.
बलसमूह m. armed force, host.
बलसेना f. army, troops.
बलस्थ a. strong, vigorous; m. warrior.
बलहीन a. wanting strength, weak, feeble.
बलाक m., बलाका f. a kind of crane; poss. °किन्†.
बलात्कार m. (acting with) force or violence; °— & instr. by force, violently.
बलात्कृत a. treated violently, overpowered.
बलाधिक a. superior in strength.
बलाध्यक्ष m. commander of an army or minister of war.
1बलाबल n. strength or weakness, (relative) strength or importance.
2बलाबल a. now strong, now weak.
बलार्थिन् a. desirous of power.
बलास m. a cert. disease; p. बलासिन्.
बलाहक m. cloud; N. of a serpent-demon etc.
बलि m. tax, impost, tribute, gift, present, pious offering (opp. the real sacrifice; poss. बलिमन्त्); handle of a fly-flapper; N. of a Daitya.
बलिकर्मन् n. the presenting of a pious oblation (v. prec.).
बलिन् a. mighty, strong.
बलिपुष्ट m. crow (fed by offerings).
बलिभुज् & °भोजन m. the same.
बलिभृत् a. paying tribute.
बलिवर्द m. ox.
बलिविधान n = बलिकर्मन्.
बलिष्ठ (superl.) mightiest, strongest, stronger than (abl.).
*बलिसुत s. arrow.
बलिहरण n., °हार m. = बलिकर्मन्.
बलिहृत् a. paying tribute.
बलीयंस् (compar.) mightier, stronger; very strong or important, n. adv.
बलीवर्द m. = बलिवर्द.
बल्कस n. dregs, sediment.
बल्बज m. a kind of grass.
बल्बला w. कृ stammer, stutter.
बल्बूथ m. N. of a man.
बल्बूल m. N. of a serpent-demon.
बल्य a. strengthening.
बल्लव m. cowherd (f. ई); abstr. °ता f., °त्व n.
बल्हिक m. N. of a man, pl. of a people.
बस्त m. a goat.
बस्ताजिन n. a goat's skin.
बस्ति v. वस्ति.
बस्नि adv. quickly.
बहल a. thick, dense, wide, large, intense; filled with, consisting mostly in (—°).
बहिर्गेहम् adv. outside the house.
बहिर्ग्रामप्रतिश्रय a. living outside the village.
बहिर्द्वार n. outer door or the place outside a door.
बहिर्धा adv. & prep. (w. abl.) outside, without, out of.
बहिर्यान a. going or driving out.
1बहिर्वेदि f. the place outside the Vedi.
2बहिर्वेदि adv. outside the Vedi.
बहिष्टात् adv. outside, without.
बहिष्पवमान m. n. a cert. sacred song; f. ई pl. its single verses.
बहिष्प्रज्ञ a. whose perception is directed outward.
बहिस् adv. & prep. (w. abl. or —°) outward, abroad, outside, out. — With कृ (pp. बहिष्कृत) drive away, turn out of (abl.), exclude from (abl. or loc.); cast off, give up, renounce; w. भू come forth or out of (abl.).
बहु, f. बह्वी much, many, numerous, frequent, abundant, rich in (instr.), large, great, mighty. — n. subst. w. gen.; as adv. much, frequently, often, greatly; almost, nearly, as it were (only °—); w. मन् cf. s. v.
बहुकृत्वस् adv. many times, often.
बहुगु, f. ऊ rich in cows.
बहुगुण a. many-threaded, manifold, various, having many (good) qualities or virtues.

बहुजल्प a. talkative; m. °जल्पितृ as subst.
बहुतनय a. having many sons.
बहुतय a. pl. manifold.
बहुतराम् adv. highly, greatly, much.
बहुता f. multiplicity, multitude.
बहुतिथ a. manifold, many, much, °थे ऽहनि for many days; n. adv. highly, greatly.
बहुतृष्ण a. very thirsty.
बहुत्रा adv. among or to many.
बहुत्रिवर्ष a. nearly three years old.
बहुत्व n. multiplicity, multitude, majority; the plural number (g.).
1**बहुदान** n. a rich gift.
2**बहुदान** a. giving richly, liberal.
बहुदायिन् a. = prec. 2.
बहुदेय n. munificence, liberality.
1**बहुदोष** m. great evil or harm.
2**बहुदोष** a. full of faults, very bad.
बहुधन a. having much wealth, very rich; abstr. °त्व n.
बहुधा adv. in many ways, forms, parts, or places, much, variously, repeatedly; w. कृ multiply, divulge.
बहुपत्नीक a. having many wives; abstr. °ता f. polygamy.
बहुपद् a. many-footed.
बहुपर्ण a. many-leaved.
बहुपशु a. rich in cattle.
बहुपाक्य a. who has much cooked (for the poor).
बहुपाठिन् a. studying much.
बहुपाद् a. many-footed or composed of many verses.
बहुपाय्य n. a large hall (lit. protecting many).
बहुपुष्ट a. being in high prosperity.
बहुप्रकार a. manifold; n. adv.
बहुप्रज & °प्रजस् a. rich in offspring.
बहुप्रतिज्ञ a. containing many counts (plaint).
बहुप्रत्यवाय a. connected with many difficulties.
बहुप्रिय a. dear to many.
बहुभाषिन् a. talkative; n. °भाष्य abstr.
बहुभुज् & °भोजक a. eating much, voracious.
बहुभोजिन् a. = prec.; abstr. °जिता f.
बहुमत्स्य n. a place abounding in fish.
बहुमध्यग a. belonging to many.
बहुमन्तव्य a. to be esteemed highly.
बहुमान m. high esteem or consideration, high opinion of (loc. or gen.).
बहुमानिन् a. highly esteemed.
बहुमान्य a. = **बहुमन्तव्य**.
बहुमुख a. many-mouthed, speaking variously.
1**बहुमूल्य** n. a large sum of money.
2**बहुमूल्य** a. costly, precious.
बहुरजस् a. very dusty or having much pollen.
बहुरस a. very juicy or succulent.
बहुरूप a. many-coloured, multiform, manifold.
बहुल a. thick, dense, wide, large, numerous, many, much, abounding in (--°); n. adv. often. Abstr. °ता† f., °त्व† n.
बहुलायास a. giving much effort.
बहुलित a. increased, augmented.
बहुली w. कृ v. **बहुलीकृत**; w. भू increase, spread (intr.), get public.
बहुलीकृत a. made (to appear) thick or dense*; increased, spread, public.
बहुलौषधिक a. rich in herbs.
बहुवचन n. the plural number and its endings (g.).
बहुवल्लभ a. having many favourites or wives.*
बहुवासर m. pl. many days.
बहुविघ्न a. connected with many difficulties, abstr. °ता f.
बहुविद् a. rich in knowledge.
बहुविद्य a. = prec.; abstr. °ता f.
बहुविध a. manifold, various; n. adv.
बहुविधाकार a. of many kinds.
बहुवीर्य a. very strong or powerful.
बहुवृत्तान्त a. rich in adventures (house).*
बहुव्रीहि m. possessive compound, lit. (having) much rice; adv. °वत् (g.).
बहुशस् adv. manifoldly, repeatedly.
बहुशाख a. having many branches or ramifications (also °खिन्); abstr. °त्व† n.
बहुश्रुत a. very learned, well taught.
बहुसंस्थित a. frequented by many.
बहुसार a. pithy, solid.
बहुसाहस्र a. containing many thousands, f. ई sgl. many thousands.
बह्वृदक a. having much water; m. a kind of religious mendicant.

बह्वुदर a. big-bellied or many-bellied.
बहूपमा f. a kind of comparison (rh.).
बह्वन्न a. rich in food.
बह्वपत्य a. having or promising a numerous progeny.
बह्वपाय a. connected with many dangers.
बह्वश्व a. rich in horses; m. N. of a man.
बह्वादिन् a. eating much, voracious.
बह्वाशिन् a. = prec., abstr. °शित्व n.
बह्वृच् a. having many verses, E. of the Rig-veda.
बह्वृच a. = prec. a.; m. a student, adherent, or priest of the Rigveda.
बह्वेनस् a. very sinful.
बाकुर a. + दृति m. a kind of bag-pipe.
बाढ (**बाळ्ह**) a., only loc. **बाळ्हे** adv. strongly, aloud; n. **बाढम्** adv. indeed, certainly, yes, very well.
1**बाण** or **बाण** m. reed-shaft, arrow, N. of an Asura etc.; **बाणवत्** adv. like an arrow.
2**बाण** v. **वाण**.
बाणधि m. quiver (receptacle of arrows).
बाणपथ m. reach of a shot (lit. arrow-path).
बाणपात m. shot (lit. arrow-fall), also = prec.
बाणपात(पथ)वर्तिन् a. being within the reach of a bow-shot.
बाणवन्त् m. arrow or quiver.
बाणशब्द m. the sound of an arrow.
बाणासन n. bow (arrow-thrower).
बाणिन् a. having an arrow.
बादर a. coming from the jujube tree, n. its berry; pl. N. of a people.
बादरायण m. N. of sev. men, esp. of an ancient sage; a. composed by B.
बाध्, **बाधते** (°ति), pp. **बाधित** oppress, torment, beset, hurt, injure, remove, annul. C. **बाधयति** oppress, vex, pain, fight. D. **बीभत्सते** feel aversion or loathing (abl.). I. **बाबधे** or **बद्बधे** press heavily, confine, hem in. — **अति** afflict or distress hard (acc. or gen.). **अप** drive away, remove (also C.). D. have a loathing for (abl.). **अभि** press hard, pain, vex, obstruct. **अव** keep off. **आ** press against, torment, distress. **उद्** break forth. **नि** press down, hem in, beset. **निस्** keep off. **परि** keep off, exclude or prevent from (abl. or gen.), protect from (abl.); vex, harass, pain. **प्र** press forwards, urge on, further; drive back, repel, torment, afflict, molest, injure, abolish, undo. **प्रति** drive back, ward off, hem in, disturb, afflict. **वि** press or drive asunder, repel, afflict, pain, hurt, injure. **सम्** press together, oppress, afflict, torment.
बाध m. oppressor, tormentor; (also f. **आ**) oppression, annoyance (also **बाध**), opposition, resistance, pain, distress, injury, damage, expulsion, removal, annulment, contradiction, absurdity.
बाधक, f. °**धिका** molesting, afflicting, paining, injuring, removing.
बाधन a. oppressing, molesting, opposing; n. the action of oppressing etc., expulsion, removal, annulment; f. **आ** discomfort, uneasiness.
बाधितत्व n. the being suspended or set aside.
बाधितव्य a. to be oppressed, molested, pained, suspended, annulled, or set aside.
बाधितृ m. oppressor, harasser.
बाधिर्य n. deafness.
बाध्य a. = **बाधितव्य**, abstr. °**त्व** n.
बाध्व m. N. of a Rishi.
बान्धव m., **ई** f. relation, kinsman or kinswoman (esp. on the mother's side), friend.
बान्धवधुरा f. friendly turn, kindness (lit. the burden of friendship).
बान्धव्य n. relationship.
बाभ्रव m. patr. from **बभ्रु**.
बाभ्रव्य m. = prec., N. of sev. men.
†**बार** (—°) opening, aperture.
बार्ह a. made of the tail-feathers of a peacock.
बार्हत, f. **ई** relating to the metre Bṛhatī.
बार्हतक m. N. of a man.
बार्हस्पत, f. **ई** relating to Bṛhaspati.
बार्हस्पत्य a. = prec.
बाल् (interj.) crack!
1**बाल** a. young, not full-grown, newly risen (sun), waxing (moon); childish, ignorant. m. child, boy, fool, N. of a Rakṣas etc.; f. **आ** girl, young woman, a cow of one year.

2बाल v. वाल.
बालक, f. लिका = 1बाल.
बालकमलिनी f. a young lotus plant.*
बालकेलि or °केली f. a child's play.
बालक्रीडन n., °क्रीडा f. the same.
बालक्रीडनक m. a child's toy or plaything, a ball etc.
बालघ्न m. a child-slayer.
बालचन्द्र m. the young or waxing moon.
बालता f., °त्व n. childhood.
बालदेव m. N. of a man.
बालधन n. the property of infants.
बालपुत्रक m. a little son.
बालबन्धन m. N. of a demon (lit. child-binder).
बालभारत n. T. of an epic poem & a play.
बालभाव m. childhood or childishness.
बालमति a. having a childish mind.
बालमित्र n. an early friend.*
बालरामायण n. T. of a drama.
बालरोग m. disease of children.
बाललीला f. a child's play.
बालवैधव्य n. widowhood in early age.
बालसखि & °सुहृद् m. friend from childhood.
बालहन्, f. °घ्नी murdering children, infanticide.
बालातप m. early heat, i.e. the heat of the morning sun.
बालादित्य a. the newly risen sun, N. of two kings.
बालाध्यापक m. a teacher of boys.
बालापत्य n. young offspring (of men and animals).
बालार्क m. the young (newly risen) sun.
बालिश a. young, childish, ignorant, simple.
बालिशता f., °त्व n., & बालिश्य n. abstr. to prec.
बालेय a. fit for an oblation or descended from Bali. — m. ass; patron. from Bali.
बाल्बज, f. ई made of Balbaja-grass.
बाल्य or बाल्य n. childhood, infancy; childishness, simplicity, stupidity.
बाल्हि or बाल्हि m. N. of a country.
बाल्हिक or बाल्हिक m. pl. N. of a people.
बाल्हीक or बाल्हीक m. pl. = prec.; a (f. ई) belonging to or coming from the B.; n. saffron.
बाष्प m. (sgl.) tears, vapour.
बाष्पकण्ठ, f. ई choking with tears (lit. having tears in the throat).
बाष्पमोक्ष m. the shedding of tears.
बाष्पसलिल & बाष्पाम्बु n. flood of tears.
बाष्पाय्, °यते to shed tears.
बाष्पासार & बाष्पोत्पीड m. flood of tears.
बास्त a. belonging to or coming from a goat.
बास्तिक n. a multitude of goats.
बाहव m. arm.
बाहीक a. being outside, exterior; m. pl. N. of a people.
बाहु m. arm, esp. fore-arm, (of beasts) fore-leg, esp. its upper part; a cert. measure of length; N. of a Daitya & sev. princes.
बाहुक (adj. —°) arm; N. of a serpent-demon etc.
बाहुगुण्य n. possession of many advantages, superiority.
बाहुजूत a. swift with the arms.
बाहुता adv. in the arms.
बाहुदण्ड m. a long arm (lit. arm-stick).
बाहुदा f. N. of a woman & sev. rivers.
बाहुपाश m. the encircling arms (lit. arm-fetter).
बाहुबन्ध a. fettered on the arms.
बाहुबन्धन n. = बाहुपाश.
1बाहुबल n. strength of the arm.
2बाहुबल a. = seq.; m. N. of a king.
बाहुबलिन् a. strong in the arm.
बाहुमन्त् a. having (strong) arms.
1बाहुमात्र n. a distance of an arm's length.
2बाहुमात्र, f. ई as long as an arm.
बाहुमूल n. the root of the arm, armpit.
बाहुयुद्ध n. arm-fight, wrestling.
बाहुयोध & °योधिन् m. pugilist, wrestler.
बाहुलता f. a little or slender arm (lit. arm-creeper).
बाहुल्य n. abundance, multitude, commonness, ordinary state of things; abl. adv. usually, likely, probably.
1बाहुवीर्य n. strength of the arm.
2बाहुवीर्य a. strong in the arm.
बाहुशालिन् a. = prec.; warlike, valiant.
बाहुश्रुत्य n. much learning, scholarship.
बाहूत्क्षेपम् adv. with uplifted arms or hands.

बाहूबाहवि adv. arm against arm i.e. in close combat.

बाह्य a. external, being outside or without, opposite or contrary to, extra-, anti- (abl. or —°), strange, foreign; m. a foreigner or an outcast. °—, acc. instr., & loc. outside, without, abl. from without. — Abstr. **°ता**† f., **°त्व**† n.

बाह्यकरण n. external organ of sense.

बाह्यतस् adv. & prep. (w. abl.) outside, without.

बाह्यस्पर्श m. contact with external objects.

बाह्यान्तर् adv. from without and within.

बाह्येन्द्रिय n. = **बाह्यकरण**.

बाह्लि etc. v. **बाह्लिह** etc.

बाह्वङ्क m. bending the arm, encircling.

बाह्वृच्य n. the Rigveda (cf. **बह्वृच**).

बाह्वोजस् a. strong in the arm.

बिडाल m., **आ** f. cat.

बिडालक m., **°लिका** f. the same.

बिडालाक्ष, f. **ई** cat-eyed.

बिदल v. **विदल**.

बिन्दु m. drop, globule, point, dot; the sign of the Anusvāra (g.).

बिन्दुक m. drop.

बिन्दुमन्त् a. formed into drops or globules.

बिन्दुसार & **बिन्दुसेन** m. names of kings.

बिन्दूय्, pp. **°यमान** dripping, wet with (—°).*

बिम्ब m. n. disk (of sun or moon), globe, hemisphere; orb, circle i.g.; mirror, image, picture, shadow. — m. lizard, chameleon; f. **ई** a kind of gourd, n. its red fruit.

बिम्बाधर m. the red (lit. Bimba-like, v. prec.) lip.

बिम्बित a. mirrored back.

बिम्बिसार m. N. of a king.

बिल n. cleft, hollow, cavern, den.

बिलवास & **°वासिन्** a. living in holes; m. such an animal.

बिलशय, **°शायिन्**, & **बिलेशय** a. & m. = prec.

बिलिश a. fishing hook or bait.

बिलौकस् a. & m. = **बिलवास**.

बिल्म n. slip, chip; a broken helmet.

बिल्मिन् a. having a helmet.

बिल्व m. N. of a tree; n. its fruit, also a cert. weight.

1**बिल्वमात्र** n. the weight of a Bilva fruit.

2**बिल्वमात्र** a. having the weight or the size of a Bilva-fruit.

बिल्हण m. N. of a poet.

†**बिष्कला** f. parturient.

†**बिस** n. the film or fibre of a lotus plant.

बिसतन्तु m. the same.

बिसप्रसून n. a lotus flower.

बिसवती f. a place rich in lotus flowers.

बिसिनी f. the lotus-plant.

बीज n. seed (of plants and animals), seed-corn, grain, germ, element, origin, beginning, adj. caused by (—°).

बीजक m. a citron; n. seed.

बीजकाण्डप्ररोहिन् & **°ण्डरुह** a. springing up from seed or from slips (plants).

बीजकोश s. seed-vessel, esp. of a lotus-flower.

बीजपूर & **°क** m. the citron-tree; n. a citron.

बीजप्रद a. giving the seed (father).

बीजवन्त् a. provided with seed or grain.

बीजवाप m. the sowing (seed).

बीजाङ्कुर m. seed-shoot; du. seed and shoot; adv. **°वत्**.

बीजाढ्य m. = **बीजपूर**.

बीजाश्व m. stallion (lit. seed-horse).

बीजिन् a. = **बीजवन्त्**; m. the (real, not nominal) begetter or father.

बीजोत्कृष्ट m. the extractor of seed- (i.e. of good) corn (scil. in selling, while the rest is bad).

बीभत्स्, **°त्सते** v. **बाध्**.

बीभत्स a. loathsome, disgusting, hideous (abstr. **°ता** f.); f. **आ** (& n.*) disgust, horror.

बीभत्सु a. loathing, detesting, disgusted, revolted; m. E. of Arjuna.

बुक m. N. of a plant.

बुक्का f. heart.

बुडिल m. N. of a man.

बुद्ध a. awakened (lit. & fig.), completely conscious, enlightened; m. the Enlightened One, the Buddha, E. of Gautama of the Çākya tribe.

बुद्धत्व n. abstr. to prec.
बुद्धधर्म m. the law of Buddha.
बुद्धमार्ग m. the path or doctrine of Buddha.
बुद्धरक्षित m., आ f. a man's & woman's name.
बुद्धागम m. the doctrine of Buddha
बुद्धान्त m. waking state or condition.
बुद्धि f. insight, intellect, reason, mind, judgment; perception, comprehension, knowledge; opinion, persuasion, supposition, notion, idea, conjecture, the taking for (—°); design, intention, purpose; instr. for the sake, on account, or because of (—°).
बुद्धिकृत a. acted wisely.
बुद्धिग्राह्य a. attainable by intellect.
बुद्धिजीविन् a. subsisting by intelligence, rational.
बुद्धिपूर्व & °क (n. adv.) premeditated.
बुद्धिभेद m. disturbance of the mind.
बुद्धिमन्त् a. intelligent, wise, abstr. °मत्त्व n.
बुद्धिमोह m. confusion of the mind.
बुद्धियुक्त a. endowed with understanding, intelligent.
बुद्धिवर्जित a. opp. to prec.
बुद्धिविवर्धन a. increasing the understanding.
बुद्धिवृद्धि f. growth of the understanding.
बुद्धिशरीर & बुद्धिसागर m. names of men.
बुद्धिशालिन् a. = बुद्धियुक्त.
बुद्धिशुद्ध a. pure in heart or intention.
बुद्धिशुद्धि f. purification of the heart.
बुद्धिहीन a. = बुद्धिवर्जित; abstr. °त्व n.
बुद्धीन्द्रिय n. a perceptive organ of sense.
बुद्धोपासक m., °सिका f. a worshipper of Buddha.
बुद्ध्यधिक a. superior in wisdom.
बुद्बुद m. a bubble in water.
बुध्, बोधति (°ते), बुध्यते (°ति), pp. बुद्ध (q.v.) wake, awake (intr., r. trans.); watch, notice, heed (acc. or gen.); perceive, learn, know, understand, regard or know as, take for (2 acc.), present with (acc. of pers. & instr. of th.). C. बोधयति awaken, revive, restore to consciousness, cause to notice, attend, or understand; remind of, teach (2 acc.). D. बुभुत्सते wish to know or learn. I. बोबुधीति have knowledge of (acc.). — अनु awake. watch, notice, perceive, think of, consider. C. remind of, teach, inform. अव awake; perceive, learn, understand. C. awaken, remind, inform, explain. समव perceive, learn. आ attend to (acc.). उद् M. awake. नि (बोधति) attend to, learn or hear from (gen., r. सकाशात्), understand, know. प्र (बुध्यते) wake up, be awake, watch; expand, blossom; (बोधति) know, understand. C. awaken, cause to expand or blossom, make sensible of, admonish, persuade; teach, instruct (2 acc.). प्रति awake, expand, blossom, notice, perceive. C. awaken, admonish, remind, inform, teach. वि awake; perceive, learn. C. awaken, make conscious, bring to reason. सम् awake, watch, perceive, notice. C. awaken (lit. & fig.), make attentive to or aware of, exhort, admonish, teach (2 acc.). — Cf. उद्बुद्ध, प्रतिबुद्ध, प्रबुद्ध, विबुद्ध, संबुद्ध.
बुध a. intelligent, clever; m. a wise or learned man, a knower; a god; a man's name.
बुध्न (or बुंध्न) m. n. bottom, ground, depth, lowest part, foot of a tree, root.
बुध्न्य a. being on the ground or in the depth; w. अहि m. the serpent of the deep.
बुन्द m. arrow.
बुभुक्षा f. desire of eating, hunger.
बुभुक्षित & बुभुक्षु a. hungry.
बुभुत्सा f. desire of knowing, curiosity.
बुभुत्सु a. wishing to know (— °), curious.
बुभूर्षा f. desire of supporting (gen.).
बुभूर्षु a. wishing to support (acc.).
बुभूषा f. desire of being or living.
बुभूषु a. wishing for welfare or power.
बुरुड m. basket-maker.
बुल्ल m. N. of a man.
बुल्व a. oblique, transverse.
बुस n. vapour, mist, rubbish, chaff and other refuse of grain.
बृंहण a. & n. making fat, strengthening, nourishing.
1बृंहित a. strengthened, increased by or furnished with.
2बृंहित n. roaring.
†बृगल n. morsel, piece, fragment.

बृबंदुकथ a. E. of Indra.
बृबु m. N. of a man.
बृसी f. bunch of grass, a kind of seat or cushion.
1बृह् (वृह्), बृहंति (वृहंति), pp. बृढ (वृढ) pluck, tear out. — आ tear off, root out. उद् & समुद् draw forth. नि throw down; C. the same, destroy, annihilate. प्र tear out or off, snatch away; tear asunder, destroy; M. = उपप्र M. draw towards one's self, attract. वि rend asunder, break up, split, destroy, remove. सम् rend asunder, draw out (together).
2बृह्, बृहति (only बृहन्त् q.v.) & बंृहति, °ते; C. बृंहयति, °ते, pp. बृंहित (q.v.) make great or big, strengthen, augment, further. – अभि C. strengthen, increase, augment. उप the same; I. (बर्बृहि) press or embrace close. समुप C. strengthen, supply, complete. परि A. M. enclose, encircle, make tight or firm, strengthen, fortify. C. strengthen, augment. सम् join firmly together. C. संवर्हयति join together, attach (dat.); संबृंहयति strengthen, encourage. — Cf. उपबृंहित, परिबृढ, परिवृढ.
3बृह् (वृह्) बृंहति (वृंहति), pp. बृंहित (q.v.) roar.
4†बृह् v. बृहस्पति.
बृहच्छोक a. having great sorrow.
बृहच्छ्रवस् a. loud-sounding or = seq.
बृहच्छ्लोक a. far-famed.
बृहज्जातक n. T. of a work.
बृहज्ज्योतिस् a. shining bright.
बृहत m. N. of a man.
*बृहतिका f. cover, mantle.
बृहत्कथा f. the large narrative, T. of a work.
बृहत्कीर्ति a. far-famed.
बृहत्केतु a. of great brightness.
बृहत्तृण n. coarse grass.
बृहत्त्व n. greatness, size, extent.
बृहत्पलाश a. large-leaved.
बृहत्पाद a. large-footed.
बृहत्संहिता f. T. of a work.
बृहत्सुम्न a. very gracious or benevolent.
बृहत्सेन m. N. of sev. kings, f. आ a woman's name.
बृहदश्मन् a. containing big rocks (mountain).
बृहदश्व m. a man's name.
बृहदारण्यक n. T. of an Upanishad.
बृहदुक्थ a. having loud praise, far-famed; m. a man's name.
बृहदुक्ष् or बृहदुक्ष a. sprinkling abundantly, raining.
बृहदुक्षन् a. having great bulls.
†बृहद्गिरि a. calling loudly.
बृहद्ग्रावन् a. resembling a large stone.
1बृहद्दिव a. belonging to the lofty sky, heavenly. m. N. of an ancient Rishi; n. pl. the lofty sky.
2बृहद्दिवं a. = prec. a.; f. आ N. of a goddess.
बृहद्देवता f. T. of a work.
बृहद्द्युति a. shining bright.
बृहद्द्युम्न m. N. of a prince.
बृहद्भानु a. shining bright; m. a man's name.
बृहद्भास् a. = prec. a.
1बृहद्रथ m. a great hero.
2बृहद्रथ m. a man's name.
बृहद्रयि a. having much wealth.
बृहद्रवस् a. loud-sounding.
बृहद्रि a. = बृहद्रयि.
बृहद्वयस् a. very vigorous or powerful.
बृहद्वसु m. a man's name.
बृहद्वादिन् a. boastful, vain-glorious.
बृहद्व्रत n. the great vow (scil. of chastity); a. observing it.
बृहन्त्, f. बृहती high, tall, great, much, abundant, important, mighty, grown-up, old, clear, loud; n. height, as adv. highly, widely, thickly, firmly, aloud, much, greatly. m. a man's name; f. ई N. of a metre.
बृहन्त a. great.
बृहन्नड & बृहन्नल m. a kind of reed-grass, a feigned name of Arjuna.
†बृहन्मति a. high-minded.
बृहन्मध्य a. great in the middle.
बृहस्पति m. N. of a god (the lord of prayer, later of wisdom and eloquence), the planet Jupiter; a man's name.
बेकनाट m. usurer.
बेकुरा f. voice, sound. बेटी f. whore.
बैजवाप & °पायन m. patron. names.

बैजिक a. relating to seed or the semen virile, sexual.

बैडाल a. peculiar to cats, feline.

बैडालव्रतिक a. acting like a cat, hypocritical, false.

बैन्द m. N. of a despised tribe.

बैल a. living in holes, m. such an animal.

बैल्व a. coming from the Bilva tree or made of its wood.

बोद्धव्य a. to be observed, perceived, understood, recognized; to be taught or admonished; n. impers. (it is) to be waked.

बोद्धृ m. perceiver, knower; abstr. °त्व n.

बोध a. perceiving, understanding; m. waking, becoming or being awake (lit. & fig.); expanding, budding; perception, knowledge, intelligence, wisdom.

बोधक, f. °धिका awakening, teaching, explaining, conducive to the knowledge of (—°); m. instructor, teacher.

बोधन, f. ई causing to expand or blossom, exciting, rousing, explaining, teaching; n. awaking, state of waking, perception, knowledge; awakening, rousing, instructing, teaching.

बोधनीय a. to be reminded, to be made known or explained.

बोधमय a. consisting of knowledge.

बोधयितृ m. waker, awakener, teacher.

बोधयितव्य a. to be made acquainted with (acc.).

बोधयिष्णु a. wishing to awaken.

बोधि m. f. perfect wisdom; m. the tree of wisdom or knowledge (r.).

बोधितव्य a. to be taught or imparted.

†बोधिन् a. awakening, instructing, causing to perceive or know; knowing, familiar with, thinking of (—°).

बोधिसत्त्व m. a Buddha immediately before the attainment of perfect knowledge.

बोध्य a. to be known or understood, to be taught or explained.

बौद्ध a. borne in mind (not spoken out), relating to the intellect or to Buddha; m. a Buddhist.

बौद्धदर्शन & °मत n. the doctrine of the Buddhists.

बौधायन m. patron. of an ancient teacher, m. pl. his school; a. belonging to or composed by B.

ब्रध्न a. reddish-yellow; m. the sun.

†ब्रह्म m. priest (only —°).

1ब्रह्मकल्प a. like (a) Brahman.

2ब्रह्मकल्प m. the age of Brahman (a cert. period of remote antiquity).

ब्रह्मकार a. offering prayers, devout.

ब्रह्मकिल्बिष n. crime against Brahmans.

ब्रह्मकूर्च n. a kind of penance.

ब्रह्मकृत् a. = ब्रह्मकार.

ब्रह्मकृति f. devotion, prayer.

ब्रह्मक्षत्र n. sgl. & du. Brahmans and warriors.

ब्रह्मक्षत्रसव m. pl. sacrifices offered by Brahmans and warriors.

ब्रह्मगीतिका f. the song of Brahman (cert. verses).

ब्रह्मगुप्त m. a man's name.

ब्रह्मघातक m. a Brahman-killer.

ब्रह्मघातिन् m. = prec , f. °नी a woman on the second day of her menses.

ब्रह्मघ्न m. = prec. m.

ब्रह्मचर्य n. sacred study, the life and condition of a Brahman student, esp. abstinence, chastity; poss. °वन्त् †.

ब्रह्मचर्याश्रम m. the state of a Brahman student (as the first of the four periods of a Brahman's life).

ब्रह्मचारिन् a. poss. to ब्रह्मचर्य; m. a Brahman student.

1ब्रह्मजन्मन् n. rebirth effected by sacred knowledge.

2ब्रह्मजन्मन् a. sprung from Brahman.

ब्रह्मजाया f. a Brahman's wife.

ब्रह्मजुष्ट a. delighted by prayer or devotion.

ब्रह्मजूत a. incited by prayer or devotion.

ब्रह्मज्ञ a. knowing the sacred writings.

ब्रह्मज्ञान n. knowledge of sacred things or writings.

ब्रह्मज्य a. oppressing Brahmans.

ब्रह्मज्येय n. abstr. to prec.

ब्रह्मणस्पति m. = बृहस्पति.

ब्रह्मणस्पत्नी f. the wife of the Brahman priest.

ब्रह्मण्य्, only **ब्रह्मण्यन्त्** praying, devout.
ब्रह्मण्य a. devoted to sacred knowledge or friendly to Brahmans; religious, pious i.g.
ब्रह्मण्यता f. devotion towards Brahmans.
ब्रह्मण्वत् adv. like a Brahman.
ब्रह्मण्वन्त् or **ब्रह्मण्वन्त्** a. devout, pious.
ब्रह्मता f. abstr. to **ब्रह्मन्** n. (i.e. the impersonal divinity).
ब्रह्मत्व n. abstr. to 1**ब्रह्मन्** & 2**ब्रह्मन्**.
ब्रह्मद् a. imparting sacred knowledge.
ब्रह्मदण्ड m. Brahman's staff (a myth. weapon) or a B.'s punishment i.e. his curse.
ब्रह्मदत्त a. given by Brahman; a man's name.
ब्रह्मदातृ a. = **ब्रह्मद्**.
ब्रह्मदान n. the gift of the Veda.
1**ब्रह्मदाय** a. imparting or teaching the Veda.
2**ब्रह्मदाय** m. the Veda as an heritage, **°हर** a. receiving it from (gen.).
ब्रह्मदेय a., f. **आ** married after the Brahma rite, w. **विधि** m. this rite itself; n. instruction in the sacred writings.
ब्रह्मद्विष् a. hating devotion or the Brahmans.
ब्रह्मद्वेष m. hatred of devotion, impiety.
1**ब्रह्मन्** n. devotion (lit. swelling, sc. of the soul), worship, piety, holy life, chastity; hymn of praise, prayer; sacred text, magic formula, incantation, the syllable Om, the Veda, i.g. divine science, theology or theosophy; the priestly or sacerdotal class; the supreme Being regarded as impersonal, the Absolute.
2**ब्रह्मन्** m. one who prays, any devout person or a priest; a knower of sacred knowledge, a Brahman of caste or the priest so called; the supreme Being, personif. as the highest god or creator of the world.
ब्रह्मनिर्वाण n. extinction in Brahman.
ब्रह्मनिष्ठ a. quite absorbed in (the contemplation of) the Absolute.
ब्रह्मपथ m. the way to Brahman (m. or n.).
ब्रह्मपुत्र m. a son of a Brahman or of the god Brahman.
ब्रह्मपुर n., **ई** f. Brahman's city (in heaven), also N. of sev. cities on the earth.
ब्रह्मपुराण n. T. of a Purāṇa.
ब्रह्मप्राप्त a. having attained Brahman.
ब्रह्मप्रिय & **°प्री** a. loving devotion or the Veda.
ब्रह्मभवन n. the abode of Brahman.
ब्रह्मभाग m. the share of a Brahman or chief priest.
ब्रह्मभाव m. the entrance into Brahman (n.).
ब्रह्मभुवन n. the world of Brahman.
ब्रह्मभूत a. entered into Brahman; n. the absorption into Brahman.
ब्रह्मभूय n. = prec. n., Brahmanship.
ब्रह्मभूयंस a. & n. = **ब्रह्मभूत**.
ब्रह्ममय, f. **ई** consisting of Brahman (n.).
ब्रह्ममीमांसा f. the investigation into Brahman, i.e. the Vedānta.
ब्रह्मयज्ञ & **°याग** m. the offering of prayer, the study or recital of the Veda.
ब्रह्मयुज् a. yoked by prayer.
ब्रह्मयोग m. the application of prayer or devotion.
1**ब्रह्मयोनि** f. home in Brahman, **°स्थ** a. = seq.
2**ब्रह्मयोनि** a. dwelling in Brahman as in one's home.
ब्रह्मरक्षस् n., **°राक्षस** m. a kind of evil demon.
ब्रह्मराजन्यौ m. du. a Brahman and a prince.
ब्रह्मरात m. a man's name (lit. given by Brahman).
ब्रह्मराशि m. the whole mass of sacred texts or knowledge.
ब्रह्मर्षि m. a priestly sage; abstr. **°ता** f., **°त्व** n.
ब्रह्मर्षिदेश m. the country of the priestly sages.
ब्रह्मलोक m. the world of Brahman.
ब्रह्मवध m., **°वध्या** f. the murder of a Brahman.
ब्रह्मवध्याकृत n. the (committed) murder of a Brahman.
ब्रह्मवनि a. devoted to Brahmans.
ब्रह्मवन्त् a. possessed of sacred learning.
ब्रह्मवर्चस n. preeminence in sacred learning or holiness, poss. **°सिन्** or **°स्विन्**; **°स्य** a. conducive to it.
ब्रह्मवर्चसकाम a. desirous of holiness (cf. prec.).
ब्रह्मवाच् f. the sacred text.
ब्रह्मवाद m. speaking of sacred matters, **°दिन्** m. theologian, sage.
ब्रह्मवित्त्व n. abstr. to seq.

ब्रह्मविद् a. having sacred knowledge; m. theologian, philosopher, sage.

ब्रह्मविद्या f. abstr. to prec.

ब्रह्मविद्वंस् a. knowing Brahman.

ब्रह्मविद्विष् a. = **ब्रह्मद्विष्**.

ब्रह्मवृद्ध a. grown by devotion.

ब्रह्मवेद m. the Veda of the Brahmans or the Veda of sacred spells, the Atharvaveda.

ब्रह्मवेदिन् a. = **ब्रह्मविद्**.

ब्रह्मवैवर्त & **°क** n. T. of a Purāṇa.

ब्रह्मव्रत n. a cert. religious observance; the vow of chastity, **°धर** a. performing it.

ब्रह्मशाला f. Brahman's hall.

ब्रह्मशिरस् & **°शीर्षन्** n. Brahman's head, N. of a mythical weapon.

ब्रह्मसंशित a. sharpened by devotion or prayers.

ब्रह्मसंसद् f. Brahman's hall or an assembly of Brahmans.

ब्रह्मसंस्थ a. wholly devoted to sacred knowledge.

ब्रह्मसत्त्र n. the sacrifice of devotion or prayer, adj. **°त्त्रिन्**.

ब्रह्मसदन & **°सदस्** n. Brahman's seat or hall.

ब्रह्मसरस् n. Brahman's lake, N. of a holy bathing-place.

ब्रह्मसव m. gush of prayer, N. of a cert. libation.

ब्रह्मसार्ष्टिता f. equality or union with Brahman.

ब्रह्मसिद्धान्त m. T. of sev. works.

ब्रह्मसुवर्चला f. a cert. plant, also an infusion or a decoction of it.

ब्रह्मसूत्र n. the Brahmanical thread worn over the shoulder; a theological or philosophical Sūtra work, esp. that of Bādarāyaṇa on the Vedānta philosophy.

ब्रह्मस्तेन m. a stealer of holy things, esp. who gets possessed of the Veda by illicit means.

ब्रह्मस्तेय n. abstr. to prec.

ब्रह्मस्थल n. N. of a town.

ब्रह्मस्व n. the property of Brahmans.

ब्रह्महत्या f. killing of a Brahman.

ब्रह्महन् m. the murderer of a Brahman.

ब्रह्माञ्जलि m. joining the hands for the sake of (or while studying) the Veda; **°कृत** a. performing it.

ब्रह्माणी f. Brahman's wife, E. of Durgā.

ब्रह्माण्ड n. Brahman's egg, i.e. the Universe.

1**ब्रह्माद्य** a. to be eaten by Brahmans.

2**ब्रह्माद्य** a. beginning with Brahman.

ब्रह्माधिगमिक a. relating to the sacred study.

ब्रह्माभ्यास m. the study of the Veda.

ब्रह्मारण्य n. N. of a forest.

ब्रह्मारम्भ m. beginning of the sacred study.

ब्रह्मार्घ a. worthy of Brahman or of sacred knowledge.

ब्रह्मावर्त m. the holy land (between Sarasvatī and Dṛṣadvatī).

ब्रह्मास्त्र n. Brahman's weapon (myth.).

ब्रह्माहुति f. sacrifice of prayer or devotion.

ब्रह्मिष्ठ (superl.), **ब्रह्मीयंस्** (compar.) a most holy or a holier Brahman.

ब्रह्मेद्ध a. kindled with prayers.

ब्रह्मोज्झ a. having neglected or forgotten the Veda, abstr. **°ता** f.

ब्रह्मोद्य a. forming the conversation among Brahmans, w. **कथा** f. discussions about or riddles from the Veda; n. rivalry in sacred knowledge.

ब्रह्मोपनिषद् f. T. of an Upanishad.

ब्रह्मौदन n. boiled rice for Brahmans.

ब्राह्म, f. **ई** pertaining to (the) Brahman i.e. divine, holy, spiritual; or pert. to Brahmans i.e. belonging or favourable to, consisting of the sacerdotal class, Brahmanical. — f. **ई** E. of Durgā or Sarasvatī; a woman married according to the Brahman rite.

1**ब्राह्मण** m. a priest or theologian, a Brahman; f. **ई** a woman of the priestly caste.

2**ब्राह्मण**, f. **ई** Brahmanical; n. the Brahman or Absolute, sacred or divine power, a cert. class of Vedic writings.

ब्राह्मणक m. a bad Brahman, a Brahman only by name.

1**ब्राह्मणकल्प** m. pl. Brāhmaṇas and Kalpas (two kinds of Vedic works).

2**ब्राह्मणकल्प** a. like a Brahman.

ब्राह्मणकाम्या f. love of Brahmans.

ब्राह्मणकुमार m. a Brahman boy.

ब्राह्मणकुल n. a Brahman's house.

ब्राह्मणघ्न m. the killer of a Brahman.

ब्राह्मणचाण्डाल m. a degraded or outcast (lit. a Caṇḍāla of a) Brahman.

ब्राह्मणजातं n. the Brahmanical race or caste.

ब्राह्मणडिम्भ m. infant or weakling of a Brahman.

ब्राह्मणता f., °त्व n. the state or dignity of a Brahman.

ब्राह्मणधन n. the fee given to Brahmans.

ब्राह्मणपुत्रक m. a Brahman boy or lad.

ब्राह्मणप्रिय m. a friend of Brahmans.

ब्राह्मणब्रुव m. calling one's self a Brahman, i.e. a B. only in name, a bad B.

ब्राह्मणभोजन n. feeding Brahmans.

ब्राह्मणवचन n. the statement of a Brāhmaṇa.

ब्राह्मणवध m. killing a Brahman.

ब्राह्मणवर्चसं n. the dignity of a Brahman.

ब्राह्मणवाक्य n. = ब्राह्मणवचन.

ब्राह्मणविधि m. precept of a Brāhmaṇa.

ब्राह्मणविलाप m. the Brahman's Lament, T. of an episode of the Mahābhārata.

ब्राह्मणविहित a. enjoined in a Brāhmaṇa.

ब्राह्मणसात् w. कृ present to Brahmans, w. अस् belong to B.

ब्राह्मणस्पत्यं a. relating to Brahmaṇaspati.

ब्राह्मणस्व n. the property of Brahmans.

ब्राह्मणाच्छंसिन् m. a cert. priest; °स्य a. belonging to him, n. his office.

ब्राह्मणायनं m. a (mere) descendant of a Brahman.

1ब्राह्मणी v. 1ब्राह्मणं.

2ब्राह्मणी w. भू become a Brahman.

ब्राह्मणोक्त a. enjoined in a Brāhmaṇa.

ब्राह्मण्य a. fit for Brahmans; n. state or dignity of a Brahman, an assembly of Brahmans.

ब्राह्मि a. Brahmanical, holy, divine.

ब्राह्मीपुत्र m. the son of a woman married according to the Brahman rite.

ब्राह्मोढा f. a woman married according to the Brahman rite.

ब्राह्म्य a. pertaining to Brahman or the Brahmans.

ब्रुव a. calling one's self—, only in name a (—°).

ब्रू, ब्रवीति, ब्रूते say, tell (acc. of th. & gen., dat., loc. of pers.; or 2 acc.), speak to (acc., r. gen.); name, call (2 acc.), speak of (acc. ± प्रति or अधिकृत्य); answer (± पुनर्); announce, foretell; M. (A.) call one's self or profess one's self to be (nom., r. + इति). — अच्छा M. call near. अति abuse, revile. अधि encourage, console, comfort (dat.), speak in favour of or intercede for (dat.). अनु pronounce, recite; teach, rehearse to (dat.), address reverentially (dat.), invite a person (dat.) to (gen.); say, speak; take for, recognize; M. repeat, learn by heart. अप speak off, i.e. conjure, charm with words; console a person (abl.) for the loss of (acc.). आ M. converse. उद् renounce, give up (acc. or gen.). उप M. (A.) speak to (acc.), beg for (dat., r. acc.), invoke, persuade. निस् pronounce (clearly and singly), explain. प्र tell forth, proclaim, announce, teach, praise, relate, betray, call, describe as (2 acc.). प्रति speak back, answer; M. return (an attack etc.). वि speak out, utter, state, explain, answer a question; declare falsely; contradict, disagree; M. dispute, contend. सम् A. M. talk together, converse; M. consent, agree, say anything to (2 acc.).

ब्लेष्क m. snare, noose.

भ

भ n. star, asterism, lunar mansion.

भंसस् n. a cert. part of the abdomen.

भक्तं a. distributed, divided; attached or devoted to, faithful, m. a worshipper or adorer (loc., gen., acc., or —°); n. food, nourishment, meal.

भक्तद् & °दायक a. giving food to (gen.).

भक्तदास m. a slave who serves for food.

भक्तद्वेष m. aversion from food, want of appetite.

भक्तरुचि f. desire of food, appetite, hunger.

भक्तशरण n. receptacle for food, store-room or kitchen.

भक्ति f. distribution, partition, division, portion, share; division by lines, variegation, decoration, line, streak; devotion, attachment, love or piety for (loc., gen., or —°).

भक्तिच्छेद m. pl. division by lines or streaks, variegation.

भक्तिनम्र a. bent down in devotion.

भक्तिभाज् a. full of faith or devotion.

भक्तिमन्त् a. = prec. (w. loc. or —°).

भक्तियोग m. faithful devotion.

भक्तिवंस् & °वंन् a. partaking of (gen.).

भक्तिवाद m. assurance of devotion.

भक्तिहीन a. wanting piety or devotion.

भक्ष्, भक्षति, °ते, older भक्षयति, °ते, pp. भक्षित (q.v.) partake of, enjoy, eat, drink, devour, consume, waste, destroy. C. भक्षयति *cause a pers. (instr. or acc.) to eat (acc.); cf. also S. D. बिभक्षिषति & बिभक्षयिषति wish to eat or devour. — परि enjoy or drink (esp. what belongs to another), eat, feed on. सम् enjoy or devour (together).

भक्ष m. enjoyment, eating or drinking, food or drink; adj. feeding or living on (—°).

भक्षक a. eating, feeding on (gen. or —°); m. enjoyer, eater, devourer.

भंक्षण a. enjoying (—°); n. enjoyment, eating or drinking; being eaten by (inst.); drinking vessel.

भक्षणीय a. to be (being) devoured.

भक्षयितव्य a. to be enjoyed or eaten.

भक्षित a. eaten; munched (g.); the being devoured by (instr.).

भक्षितव्य a. = भक्षयितव्य.

भक्षितृ m. enjoyer, eater.

भक्षिन् a. enjoying, eating (mostly —°).

भक्षिवंन् a. enjoying.

भक्ष्य a. to be (being) enjoyed or eaten, enjoyable, eatable; n. food.

भक्ष्यभोज्य (°—) all kind of enjoyments.

भक्ष्याभक्ष्य n. allowed and forbidden food.

भंग m. distributer, dispenser, gracious lord, protector, N. of an Āditya & E. of sev. gods; portion, lot, fortune; abundance, happiness; dignity, majesty; loveliness, beauty; affection, love; the vulva.

भंगत्ति f. a gift of fortune.

भगदत्त m. N. of a king.

भगदेवत a. having Bhaga for a deity.

भगदैवत a. = prec.; n. E. of a lunar mansion.

भगवद्गीत a. sung or declared by Bhagavant i.e. Kṛṣṇa; f. आ pl. (± उपनिषद्) T. of a philosophical poem.

भंगवन्त् a. fortunate, prosperous, happy, glorious, illustrious, excellent, holy, divine (of gods & men, esp. in the voc. sgl. m. भगवन्, भगवस्, & भगोस्, f. भगवति, pl. m. भभवन्तस्, or in the nom. w. 3ᵈ pers. as reverential address). m. E. of Viṣṇu-Kṛṣṇa, Çiva, etc., f. भगवती a holy woman (abstr. °त्व n.*); E. of Lakṣmī & Durgā.

भगिंन् a. fortunate, happy, splendid; f. भगिनी sister.

भगिनीपति m. a sister's husband.

भगीरथ m. N. of an ancient king.

भगेश m. the lord of fortune.

भगोस् v. भंगवन्त्.

भग्न a. broken, bent, curved; scattered, defeated, disappointed, marred, destroyed, annihilated, lost; abstr. °ता f.

भग्नमनस् a. broken-hearted, discouraged.

भग्नयुग n. (loc.) when the yoke is broken.

भग्नव्रत a. who has broken a vow.

भग्नाश a. whose hopes are broken, disappointed.

भग्नास्थि a. whose bones are broken.*

भङ्क्तृ m. breaker, destroyer.

भङ्गं a. breaking. — m. the act of breaking, bending, or curving; breach, fracture, division, separation, downfall, ruin, destruction, interruption, disturbance, frustration, disappointment, defeat; bend, fold, wave; hemp (also f. भङ्गा).

भङ्गकारिन् a. causing a breach, breaking (—°).

भङ्गि or भङ्गी f. breaking, bending; curve, step (of a stair-case), crooked path, indirect manner of speech, circumlocution; way, manner i.g.; mere appearance or semblance.

भङ्गिन् a. breaking down, fragile, perishable (—°); defeated in a law-suit.

भङ्गिमन्त् a. curled (hair).

भङ्गु m. N. of a demon.

भङ्गुर a. fragile, transitory, changing, fickle; crisp, curled, wrinkled. Abstr. °ता f.

भङ्गुरय्, °यति break, destroy; crisp, curl (trans.).

भङ्गुरावन्त् a. insidious, malignant.

भज्, भंजति, °ते, pp. भक्त (q.v.) deal out, apportion, dispense, distribute (w. gen. or dat. of pers.), share, divide (M. among each other); M. grant, bestow, endow, furnish with (instr.); M. (A.) receive as a portion, partake of, enjoy, prefer, choose, take or go to, pursue, practise, belong or be attached to, revere, honour, worship, love, court. C. भाजयति deal out, distribute, divide; make a pers. (acc.) share in (gen.). — अप give a pers. (gen. or dat.) a share of (gen.); content, satisfy; divide, distribute. आ A. (M.) deal out, give a pers. (acc.) a share in (loc.). अन्वा M. make a person share in (loc.) after or along with others. निस् exclude from (abl.), content or satisfy with (instr.); C. disinherit. परि divide. प्रति fall again to the share of (acc.). वि part asunder, divide, distribute (2 acc., acc. of th. & dat. or loc. of pers., or acc. of pers. & instr. of th.); M. also share among each other or with (instr.). प्रवि divide, distribute. संवि sever, sunder; divide with (instr. ± सह, dat., or gen.); give a share, present with (instr.). सम् distribute, divide, share, present with a gift, endow. — Cf. अन्वाभक्त (add.), आभक्त, प्रविभक्त, विभक्त, संभक्त.

भजक m. distributer.

भजन n. adoration, worship; °ता f. the same.

भजनीय a. to be loved or adored.

भजितव्य & भजेन्य a. the same.

भञ्ज्, भनक्ति, pp. भग्न (q.v.) break, bend, curve; scatter, disperse; defeat, conquer; frustrate, disappoint, destroy, annihilate; P. भज्यते with intr. mg. (C. भञ्जयति w. शूले pierce with a pale*). — अभि break, destroy. अव break down (tr.). निस् break asunder, split. प्र break, destroy; rout, defeat (an army). वि break to pieces; scatter, distribute; frustrate, disappoint. सम् break, crush. — Cf. परिभग्न, संभग्न.

भञ्जक m. breaker; f. भञ्जिका breaking (—°).

भञ्जन a. & m. breaking, breaker, destroyer (—°); n. the act of breaking, destroying, interrupting, disturbing.

भञ्जिन् a. breaking, dispelling (—°).

भट्, भाटयति hire.

भट m. hireling, soldier, servant.

भट्ट m. lord, E. of learned men (°— & —° in names).

भट्टनारायण m. N. of a poet.

भट्टाचार्य m. illustrious teacher (E. of Kumārilabhaṭṭa).

भट्टार & °क m. lord (applied to gods & learned men).

भट्टारकवार m. the lord's day, Sunday.

भट्टि m. N. of a poet.

भट्टोजि & °दीक्षित m. N. of a grammarian.

भड m. N. of a cert. mixed caste.

भण्, भणति, pp. भणित (q.v.) speak, say, relate; call, name (2 acc.). C. *भाणयति (भणापयति*) cause to speak. — प्रति answer, reply.

भण m. telling (—°).

भणन a. telling, announcing.

भणनीय a. to be told.

भणित n., भणिति f. speech, talk, description.

भण्ड m. jester, buffoon, a cert. mixed caste.

भण्डि m. N. of a man.

भद्र a. bright, pleasing, good, happy; voc. भद्र, भद्रे, & भद्रास् good sir, good lady, & good people! भद्रम् & भद्रया adv. luckily, fortunately. n. luck, prosperity, good fortune, भद्रं ते or वः happiness to thee or you (often only explet.).

भद्रक, f. भद्रिका good; m. pl. N. of a people.

भद्रकारक & °कृत् a. causing prosperity.

भद्रकाली f. N. of a goddess (in l. l. Durgā).

भद्रतस् adv. fortunately.
भद्रता f. goodness, honesty.
भद्रत्व n. prosperity, good fortune.
भद्रपाप n. sgl. good and evil; m. pl. the good and evil.
भद्रपीठ n. splendid seat, throne; m. a cert. winged insect, used by thieves.
भद्रभुज a. whose arms cause prosperity.
भद्रमुख a. whose face causes prosperity (in voc. as reverential address).
भद्रमुस्त m., **आ** f. a kind of fragrant grass.
भद्रवन्त् a. causing happiness or prosperity, auspicious, f. **°वती** wanton girl.
*भद्रश्री f. sandal.
भद्रसेन m. a man's name.
भद्रावह a. bringing happiness.
भद्राश्व m. a man's name.
भद्रासन n. splendid seat, throne.
भद्राह n. a lucky day, favourable time.
भद्रेश m. E. of Çiva.
भन्, **भनति** speak, tell.
भन्द्, **भन्दते** be bright, shine; resound, praise.
भन्ददिष्टि a. hastening along with shouts.
भन्दन a. shouting, cheering; f. **आ** as abstr.
भन्दिष्ठ (superl.) shouting or praising most loudly.
भय n. fear, dread, anxiety, terror, danger, distress (w. abl. or —°).
भयकर a. causing fear.
भयकर्तृ, **°कृत्**, **भयंकर** (f. **ई**), & **°कर्तृ** a. = prec.
भयद, **°दायिन्**, & **°प्रद** a. inspiring fear.
भयस्थ s. dangerous situation.
भयानक a. dreadful, terrible.
भयापह a. warding off fear or peril.
भयाभय n. du. danger and security.
भयार्त a. tormented by fear.
भयालु (°क) a. timid.
भयावह a. causing fear or danger.
भयैडक m. wild ram.
भय्य n. impers. (it is) to be feared.
भर m. bearing, carrying (also a. mostly —°); obtaining, getting, carrying away, theft, fight, battle, burden, load, a cert. weight or measure; mass, quantity, abundance (instr. & abl. adv.); song, hymn.
भरण n. bearing, wearing, bringing, procuring, maintaining, nourishing; wages, hire.
भरणीय a. to be maintained or nourished.
भरत m. E. of Agni (lit. to be maintained or kept alive); N. of sev. princes & other men, esp. of a patriarchal hero & the mythical author of dramatic art, also = seq.; pl. the race of the Bharatas.
भरतपुत्र m. actor, mime.
भरतर्षभ m. the best (lit. bull) among the Bharatas, E. of sev. men.
भरतवाक्य n. epilogue, lit. speech of Bharata (d.).
भरतशार्दूल, **°श्रेष्ठ** & **°सत्तम** a. tiger or best of the Bharatas.
भरद्वाज m. field-lark, N. of a Rishi.
भरध्यै dat. inf. to **भृ**.
भरस् n. bearing, supporting.
भरहूति f. battle-cry, shouting in battle.
भराक्रान्त a. heavy (lit oppressed by a load).*
†**भरि** v. **उदरंभरि** & **सहोभरि**
भरित a. filled, full of (gen. or —°).
भरित्र n. arm or hand.
भरिष a. rapacious, greedy.
भरीमन् m. support, maintenance, nourishment.
भरु m. E. of Viṣṇu & Çiva.
भरूज m. roasted barley.
भर्ग m. = seq., a man's name, pl. N. of a people.
भर्गस् n. radiant light, glory.
भर्गस्वन्त् a. majestic.
भर्जन a. frying, roasting; n. frying or frying-pan.
†**भर्णस्** v. **सहस्रभर्णस्**.
भर्तव्य a. to be borne, maintained, nourished, or fed.
1**भर्तृ** (**भर्तृ**) m. bearer, supporter, maintainer, lord, chief; f. **भर्त्री** female supporter, mother.
2**भर्तृ** m. husband; abstr. **°त्व**† n.
भर्तृक (adj. —°) = 2**भर्तृ**.
भर्तृघ्नी f. husband-slaying.
भर्तृचिन्ता f. thinking of the husband.

भर्तृदारक m., °रिका f. a king's son or daughter; prince, princess.
भर्तृप्रिय & °भक्त a. devoted to a lord or husband.
भर्तृमती f. having a husband, married.
भर्तृमेण्ठ m. N. of an author, abstr. °ता f.
भर्तृरूप a. formed like a (the) husband.
भर्तृलोक m. the husband's world.
भर्तृवत्सला f. affectionate to the husband.
भर्तृव्रत n. devotion to the husband.
भर्तृव्रता f. devoted to the husband.
भर्तृहरि m. N. of an author.
भर्त्स्, भर्त्सति & भर्त्सयति, °ते, pp. भर्त्सित (q.v.) threaten, revile, mock, deride. अभि, अव, निस्, परि, सम् = S.
भर्त्सन n., °ना f. threatening, scolding.
भर्त्सित n. threat, menace.
भर्मन् n. support, nourishment.
भर्व्, भर्वति munch, devour.
भल्, निभालयति, °ते look at, behold, perceive; (निस् the same*).
भल adv. certainly, indeed.
भल्ल m. a kind of arrow (also f. ई); bear.
भल्लूक m. bear, °युवन् m. a young bear.
भव m. coming into existence, birth, birthplace, origin (often a. —° born of, sprung from, being in); becoming (—°); being, existence, world; means of existence, wealth, prosperity; N. of a god.
भवच्छिद् a. destroying mundane existence.
भवच्छेद m. abstr. to prec.
भवजल n. the ocean of existence.
भवत्पूर्व a. beginning with ,your honour', n. adv.
भवदीय a. your, your honour's.
भवदुत्तरम् adv. with ,your honour' at the end.
भवद्वसु a. rich in goods.
भवद्विध a. one like you or your honour.
भवन n. coming into existence, place of existence, dwelling, abode, house, palace, temple.
भवनद्वार n. the door of a palace.
भवनीय a. being about to take place.
भवनोद्यान n. garden of a house or palace.*
1भवन्त् (nom. भवन्) a. being, present; f. °न्ती the present time or tense.
2भवन्त् (nom. m. भवान्, f. भवती) pers. pron. of 2nd pers., with 3d pers. of the verb, used in respectful address (pl. also for sgl. & msc. for n.) = your honour, your worship, you.
भवन्मध्य a. having ,your honour' in the middle; n. adv.
भवभावन m. creator of the world.
भवभूति f. welfare, m. N. of a poet.
भवव्यय m. du. production and dissolution.
भवसागर m. the ocean of existence.
(*भवादृच्), भवादृश्, & °दृश (f. ई) your like.
भवानी f. N. of a goddess, the wife of Bhava, in l. l. = पार्वती.
भवानीपति & °वल्लभ m. E. of Çiva (cf. prec.).
भवान्तर n. another existence, a former or future life.
भवाब्धि m. = भवसागर.
भवारुद्र m. du. Bhava and Rudra.
भवार्णव m. = भवसागर.
भवाशर्व m. Bhava and Çarva.
भविक a. benevolent, pious.
भवितव्य a. = seq., n. impers. w. instr. of subj. & pred.; abstr. °ता† f. necessity, fate, destiny.
भवितृ, f. °त्री what is to be, future.
भवितास् gen. abl. infin. to 1भू.
भविन् m. living being, esp. man.
†भविष्ठ v. प्रभविष्ठ.
भविष्णु a. being, becoming (only —°); thriving, prospering.
भविष्य a. future, imminent; n. the future.
भविष्यत्काल a. relating to the future (g.).
भविष्यत्ता f., °त्त्व n. futurity.
भविष्यत्पुराण n. T. of a Purāṇa.
भविष्यद्वाचिन् a. expressing the future (g.).
भविष्यन्त् a. future; n. the future (time or tense).
भवीत्व a. future.
भवीयंस् (compar.) more abundant.
भवोदधि m. = भवसागर.
भव्य a. being, present, future; proper, fit, right, good, excellent, fine, beautiful, auspicious,

fortunate, gracious, favourable, religious, pious. n. existence, presence, future; good luck, fortune.

भष्, भषति, °ते bark.

भष a. barking

भषक m. barker, dog.

1भस्, बभस्ति, बप्सति, pp. भसित (q.v.) chew, devour, consume.

2भस् (only loc. भसि) ashes.

भसद् f. the hinder parts, pudendum muliebre.

भसद्य a. being on the hinder parts (v. prec.).

भसित a. consumed to ashes.

भस्त्रा f. bag, sack, bellows.

भस्त्रिका f. little bag, pouch, purse.

भस्मकृत a. made into ashes.

भस्मता f. abstr. to seq. n.

भस्मन् a. chewing, devouring. n. (also pl.) ashes, abl. भस्मतस्.

भस्मभूत a. reduced to ashes.

भस्मराशी w. कृ change into a heap of ashes.

भस्मरेणु m. dust of ashes.

भस्मशायिन् a. lying on ashes.

भस्मसात् w. कृ & नी reduce to ashes; w. गम् & भू become ashes.

1भस्मान्त n. neigbourhood of (loc. near) ashes.

2भस्मान्त a. ending in ashes, being finally burnt.

भस्मान्ति adv. = prec. 1 loc.

भस्माप् f. pl. water with ashes.

भस्मावशेष a. reduced to ashes (lit. of what only ashes remain).

भस्मित a. made into ashes, consumed, destroyed.

भस्मी w. कृ & भू = भस्मसात् w. the same.

भस्मीकरण n. burning to ashes.

भस्मीभाव m. being or becoming ashes.

भस्मीभूत a. reduced to or being mere ashes.

1भा, भाति, pp. भात be bright, shine, be splendid or beautiful, please (acc. w. प्रति or प्रतिभाति w. acc.); show one's self, appear; look or be like (nom. ± इव or adv. in वत्), pass for (nom.). — अति shine bright or brighter than (acc.). अनु shine after (acc.). अभि shine forth, appear. अव shine down or upon. आ shine upon, illumine; shine forth, appear, look or be like (इव, यथा or adv. in वत्). उद् shine out, become manifest. निस् & विनिस् shine forth. प्र shine forth, begin to be bright (as the night), appear or be like (nom. ± इव). प्रति shine upon, illumine; become manifest, offer or present one's self, come into the mind, occur to (acc. or gen.); appear to (gen. or acc. ± प्रति), look or be like, resemble (= S.); seem fit, please. संप्रति appear, come into the mind, occur. वि shine forth, shine far and wide, begin to be bright (night), be brilliant, make a show, catch the eye, appear, arise, look or be like (= S.); shine upon, illumine. सम् shine out, become manifest, arise, appear as (nom. ± इव or यथा). — Cf. आभात, निर्भात, प्रभात, विभात.

2भा f. light, brightness, splendour, adj. —° resembling, like.

भाःकूट m. a kind of fish.

भाक्त a. subordinate, secondary; m. N. of cert. sects.

1भाग m. part, portion, share, property; lot, esp. happy lot, good fortune; place, spot, region, side.

2भाग a. relating to Bhaga.

भागदुघ m. distributer, dispenser.

भागधेय n. portion, share, property; lot, esp. happy lot, luck, fortune; a. (f. ई) due as a share.

भागभाज् a. having a share of anything, m. a partner.

भागलक्षणा f. insinuation of a part (rh.).

भागवत, f. ई relating to Bhagavant (Viṣṇu), m. a follower of Bh.; n. = seq.

भागवतपुराण n. T. of a Purāṇa.

भागशस् adv. in parts, part by part; in turns, by and by.

भागहर a. receiving a share; m. heir.

भागहारिन् & भागापहारिन् a. & m. = prec.

भागानुभागेन (instr. adv.) in greater and smaller portions.

भागार्थिन् a. claiming a share.

भागिन् a. sharing in, partaking of, responsible for, entitled to (loc., gen., or —°); m. partaker, owner.

भागिनेय & °क m. a sister's son.

भागीरथ, f. ई relating to Bhagīratha; f. ई E. of Gaṅgā.

भागुरि m. a man's name.

1भाग्य a. relating to Bhaga; n. E. of lunar mansion.

2भाग्य a. lucky, fortunate; n. lot, fortune, welfare, reward, fate, destiny.

भाग्यक्रम m. course of fortune.

भाग्यरहित a. deserted by fortune, unhappy, miserable.

भाग्यवत्ता f. abstr. to seq.

भाग्यवन्त् a. having good luck, happy, fortunate.

भाग्यवश m. the power of destiny.

भाग्योदय m. pl. luck, welfare.

भाङ्ग a. hempen.

भाङ्गासुरि m. patron. of Ṛtuparṇa.

भाज् a. partaking of, entitled to, connected with, belonging to, sharing, enjoying, practising, occupying, inhabiting, revering (–°, r. gen.).

भाजन n. vessel, dish, receptacle i.e. fit place or person for (gen. or —°, cf. पात्र), substitute; adj. —° sharing, partaking of, relating or belonging to, serving or equivalent for.

भाजयु a. liberal, bounteous.

भाजिन् a. partaking of, connected with (—°).

भाज्य a. to be distributed or divided.

भाट & °क n. wages, hire, rent.

भाटि f. the same.

भाट्ट m. a follower of (Kumārila) Bhaṭṭa; n K's work.

भाण् an onomat. word.

भाण m. a kind of drama.

भाणक m. proclaimer; f. भाणिका a kind of drama.

भाण्ड n. vessel, pot, dish, chest, trunk; implement or utensil, esp. musical instrument; horse-trappings, harness, ornament i.g.; wares, merchandise.

भाण्डवादन n. playing on a musical instrument.

भाण्डवाद्य n. a musical instrument.

भाण्डागार n. store-, treasure-, or warehouse; °रिक m. the overseer of such a house, treasurer.

भाण्डार m., °गृह n. = भाण्डागार.

भाण्डावकाशद a. giving room (to a thief) for (concealing his) implements.

भाति f. light, splendour; perception, knowledge.

भात्वक्षस् a. luminous (lit. light-strong).

भाद्र & °पद m. N. of a month.

भान n. = भाति.

भानव & °वीय a. relating to the sun.

भानु m. light, beam, the sun; N. of an Āditya, pl. the Ādityas.

भानुमन्त् a. beaming, luminous, splendid; m. the sun, a man's name, f. °मती a woman's name.

भानुमित्र & भानुरथ m. names of kings.

भाम् v. भामित.

भाम m. light, beam, splendour; heat, passion, fury, rage, wrath.

भामित a. wrathful, angry.

भामह m. N. of an author.

भामिन् a. shining, beaming, beautiful, fair; f. भामिनी a beautiful or an angry woman.

भामिनीविलास m. T. of a poem.

भार m. burden, load, quantity, mass, multitude.

भारत, f. ई descended from Bharata or relating to the Bharatas, also E. of Agni (cf. भरत). — m. descendant of Bharata, pl. the race of Bh. = भरतास्. f. ई N. of a deity, in l. l. the goddess of speech = Sarasvatī; speech, word, eloquence. n. the country of Bharata i.e. India, or the story of the Bharatas, often = महाभारत (q.v.).

भारतीय n. T. of a work.

भारद्वाज, f. ई belonging to or descended from Bharadvāja; m. pl. N. of a people or = seq.

भारद्वाजिन् & °जीय m. pl. N. of a Vedic school.

भारभारिन् & °भृत् a. bearing loads.

भारवन्त् a. heavy; abstr. °वत्त्व n.

भारवाह a. bearing burdens, m. carrier.

भारवाहन & °वाहिन् a. & m. = prec.

भारवि m. N. of a poet.

भारसह a. burden-bearing, very strong or powerful.

भारसाधन & **°साधिन्** a. effecting much, most powerful (weapons).

भाराक्रान्त a. heavily laden (cf. **भराक्रान्त**).

भारिक m. carrier.

भारिन् a. bearing, m. = prec.

भारूप a. shining, bright.

भार्ग m. N. of a man, pl. of a people.

भार्गव, f. **ई** relating to or coming from Bhṛgu, m. descendant of Bh.; also = seq.

भार्गवग्रह m. the planet Venus.*

भार्गायण m. patron. from **भर्ग**.

भार्मन् s. support; board, table.

भार्य a. to be supported or maintained. m. servant, soldier; f. **भार्या** wife.

भार्यात्व n. abstr. to prec. f.

भार्याद्रोहिन् a. injuring one's own wife.

भार्यावन्त् a. having a wife.

भाल n. forehead.

भाव m. becoming, being (often —°); passing or change into (loc. or —°); occurrence, appearance, existence, duration; state, condition; conduct, behaviour; nature, character, temper, disposition; sentiment, feeling (rh.); supposition, conjecture, meaning, sense; the abstract idea of a verb (g.); affection, inclination; heart, soul, mind; a being, thing, creature; a clever man, in respectful address = honourable sir (d.).

भावक a. causing, effecting, furthering, promoting (—° or gen.); fancying, imagining (gen. or —°).

भावकर्तृक a. whose agent is an abstract noun (g.).

भावन, f. **ई** = **भावक**. — f. **आ** & n. effecting, bringing about; imagination, conception, conjecture, supposition, thought, idea; ascertainment, evidence (only f.).

भावनीय a. to be effected or accomplished; to be fancied or imagined (n. impers.).

भावबन्धन a. binding hearts.

भावमधुर a. sweet or pleasant by (following) nature (picture).*

भावमिश्र m. honourable sir (d.).*

भावयितव्य a. to be cherished or promoted.

भावयितृ m. cherisher, promoter.

भावयु a. cherishing, promoting.

भावरूप a. real, actual; n. thing (ph.).

भाववचन a. expressing the abstract idea of a verb (g.).

भाववन्त् a. being in a state or condition.

भावशुद्धि f. purity of mind.

भावशून्य a. void of affection.

भवसंशुद्धि f. = **भावशुद्धि**.

भावसमाहित a. concentrated in mind.

भावस्खलित n. offence committed only in thought.

भावस्थ a. being in love.

भावाकूत n. the first emotions of the heart.

भाविक, f. **ई** real, actual; sentimental, expressive; n. lively expression.

भावित a. brought into being, produced; enlivened, refreshed, comforted, exalted; got, obtained; thought of, known; stated, convicted; full of, occupied with (instr. or —°), turned upon (loc.); perfumed.

भावित्व n. abstr. to seq.

भाविन् a. becoming, being (often —°); what ought or is about to be, impending, future. f. **°नी** a beautiful woman.

भावुक a. becoming (w. nom. or —° after an adv. in **अम्**); a sister's husband (d.).

भावोदय m. the rising of passion or emotion.

भाव्य a. what ought to be, future (n. impers.); to be caused or effected; to be (being) conceived or imagined, to be convinced, to be demonstrated.

भाव्यता f., **°त्व** n. abstr. to prec.

भाष्, **भाषते** (**°ति**), pp. **भाषित** (q.v.) speak, talk, say, tell (acc. of pers. & th.); name, call (2 acc.). C. **भाषयति**, **°ते** cause to speak; tell, say. — **अनु** call after or to (acc.), speak to or about (acc.); pronounce, confess. **अप** abuse, revile. **अभि** speak, say, tell (acc. of th. or – & – pers.), proclaim, confess. **आ** speak to, address (acc.), converse with (**सह**); say, tell (1 or 2 acc.); name, call; exclaim, promise. **व्या** & **समा** address, speak to, communicate. **परि** speak to, admonish, remind, pronounce, explain, teach. प्र speak out, name, proclaim, communicate, expound, explain, converse with (acc.). प्रति speak back, answer (acc. of pers. or th.); relate, communicate. वि revile, abuse; P. admit an alternative, be optional (g.). सम् talk to, converse with (instr. ± सह), address, salute, persuade. C. = S. — Cf. विभाषित.

भाषक a. speaking, talking about (—°).

भाषण n. speaking, talking.

भाषा f. speech, language, esp. vernacular l., dialect; description, definition; accusation, plaint.

भाषाज्ञ a. knowing languages.

भाषिक a. dialectical; f. आ language.

भाषित a. spoken, told, uttered; n. speech, language, talk, conversation.

भाषितव्य a. to be spoken to.

भाषितृ a. speaking (acc. or —°).

भाषिन् a. speaking, talking (mostly —°); loquacious.

भाष्य n. speech, talk; any work in the vulgar speech, esp. explanatory work, commentary, also = महाभाष्य q.v.

भाष्यकार & °कृत् m. the writer of a commentary, E. of Patañjali.

1भास् n. (older than) f. light, brightness.

2भास्, भासति, °ते, pp. भासित (q.v.) shine, be bright, appear as or like (nom. or instr.), become clear or obvious, be imagined or conceived. C. भासयति, °ते make shine, illuminate, cause to appear as (instr.), show, manifest. — अव M. shine, light, become manifest, appear as (instr. or adv. in वत्). C. shine upon, illumine. आ M. appear as (इव). उद् shine forth, make a show, catch the eye. C. illumine (M.), illustrate, embellish. समुद् shine with (instr.). निस् C. illumine. परि M. appear, look like (इव). C. beautify, adorn. प्र shine, be bright, appear like (इव). C. illumine, illustrate. प्रति M. shine forth, become manifest, appear like (nom.) or as (instr. of an abstr.), be brilliant, make a show. C. show, manifest. वि shine, be bright.

भास m. light, brightness; a cert. bird of prey (f. भासी their mother), a man's name.

भासक a. causing to shine or appear, making evident or known; m. N. of a poet.

भासता f. the state of the bird Bhāsa.

भासद् m. buttock.

भासन n. shining, glittering, excelling.

1भासस् n. light, lustre.

2भासस् n. food.

भासित a. shining, brilliant.

भासिन् (—°) & भासुर a. = prec.

भासुरदेह a. of radiant aspect (body).

भास्कर a the same; m. the sun, a man's name, n. a kind of breach (made by a thief).

भास्करनन्दिन् m. son of the god of the sun.

भास्मन a. ashy.

भास्य a. to be (being) brought to light or made visible; abstr. °त्व n.

भास्वन्त् a. shining, brilliant; m. the sun.

भास्वर a. = prec. a.

भिक्ष्, भिक्षते (°ति) wish for (acc. or gen.); request, beg (1 or 2 acc.), esp. go begging for food. C. भिक्षयति cause to beg.

भिक्षण n. begging, asking for alms.

भिक्षा f. begging or begged food, alms; acc. w. या, चर्, or अट् go begging for food.

भिक्षाचरण & °चर्य n., °चर्या f. going about begging.

भिक्षाटन n. the same; °नं कृ beg for alms.

भिक्षान्न n. begged food.

भिक्षापात्र & °भाण्ड n. vessel for begged food.

भिक्षार्थिन् a. asking for alms; m. beggar.

भिक्षावन्त् a. begging.

भिक्षावृत्ति a. living on alms.

भिक्षाशित्व n. abstr. to seq.

भिक्षाशिन् a. eating begged food.

1भिक्षाहार m. begged food, alms.

2भिक्षाहार a. eating begged food.

भिक्षितव्य a. to be begged or asked for.

भिक्षिन् a. begging.

भिक्षु m. beggar, religious mendicant, esp. a Brahman in the last stage of his life, also a Buddhist mendicant.

भिक्षुक m. = prec., f. ई a female mendicant.

भिक्षुचर्या f. begging, a beggar's life.

भित्त n. fragment, broken piece; partition, wall.

भित्ति f. breaking, splitting, dividing; a mat (made of split reeds); partition, wall.

भित्तिवेदिकाबन्ध m. a kind of altar.*

1**भिद्**, **भिनत्ति** (**भिन्त्ते**), pp. **भिन्न** (q.v.) split, cleave, cut asunder, break in twain, destroy, annihilate; pierce, open, expand; loose, extricate; interrupt, disturb, trouble; disclose, betray; divide, separate, part; change, alter; distinguish, discriminate. P. **भिद्यते** (°ति) be split etc., mostly intr. burst, open, expand, blossom, get loose or free; separate or keep aloof from (instr.); change, alter, differ from (abl.). C. **भेदयति**, °ते split, break, destroy, divide, disunite, seduce. D. **बिभित्सति** wish to break or destroy. — **अव** cleave asunder, pierce. **उद्** break through (disclose, betray*); P. burst open, become manifest **निस्** split or tear asunder, pierce, hurt, wound, loose, unveil, discover; P. split, burst, open (intr.). **परि** P. be split, broken, changed, disfigured. **प्र** split forth, tear asunder, open, pierce, divide. **प्रति** pierce, penetrate; disclose, betray; reproach, censure. **वि** split or break asunder, pierce, destroy, divide, disunite, change, alter. C. alienate, estrange from (abl.). **सम्** cleave, split, break, pierce, hurt, wound, interrupt, give up; combine, mingle, join, associate with (acc.). **अनुसम्** & **उपसम्** bring together, mingle, mix. – Cf. **उद्भिन्न**, **निर्भिन्न**, **प्रोद्भिन्न** (add.), **विभिन्न**, **संभिन्न**.

2**भिद्** a. breaking, dividing, piercing, destroying (—°); f. the act of splitting or dividing; difference, species, kind; partition, wall.

भिदा f. breaking, splitting, piercing; division, separation, difference; species, kind.

भिदुर a. easily split or broken, fragile, brittle; breaking, destroying; coming into contact, mingling or joining with (—°).

†**भिद्य** m. a rushing river; n. breaking, splitting (—°).

भिन्दिपाल & °**क** m. a kind of spear.

भिन्दु m. splitter, breaker, destroyer; drop (cf. **बिन्दु**).

भिन्न a. split, cleft, broken, destroyed, annihilated; loosened, opened, burst, blossomed; divided, disunited, seduced; changed, altered, distinct, different from (abl.); mingled, mixed with (instr. or —°), cleaving or sticking to (loc. or —°). — n. piece, fragment.

भिन्नगति a. of a broken or unsteady gait.

भिन्नत्व n. the being different from (—°).

भिन्नदेश a. belonging to different places, abstr. °**त्व** n.

भिन्नभाजन or °**भाण्ड** n. a broken dish or vessel.

भिन्नरुचि a. having a different taste.

भिन्नवृत्त & °**वृत्ति** a. leading an evil life, abstr. °**वृत्तिता** f.

भिन्नस्वर a. speaking with a broken voice.

भिन्नाञ्जन n. collyrium mixed with oil.

भिन्नार्थ a. having a clear meaning, intelligible; abstr. °**त्व** n.

भियस् m. fear (only acc., instr., & dat. as infin.).

भियसान a. timid.

भिल्ल m. pl. N. of a people; m. sgl. a king of the Bh., f. **ई** a Bh. woman.

भिषक्तर & °**तम** compar. & superl. to seq. 2 adj.

1**भिषज्**, **भिषक्ति** heal.

2**भिषज्** a. healing; m. physician or medicine.

भिषज्य्, °**ज्यति** heal, cure.

भिषज्य a. sanative, healthy; f. **आ** cure, remedy.

†**भिषण्ज्य्**, °**ज्यति** heal, cure.

1**भी**, **भयते**, **बिभेति** (**बिभ्यति**), pp. **भीत** (q.v.) fear, be afraid of (abl. or gen., r. instr. or acc.); fear for, be anxious about (abl.). C. **भीषयते** (°ति) & **भाययति** frighten, terrify. — **नि** C. put in fright. **वि** take fright. — Cf. **प्रभीत**, **विभीत**, **संभीत**.

2**भी** f. fear, horror at (abl., loc., acc w. **प्रति**, or —°).

भीत a. frightened, terrified, afraid of (abl., gen., or —°); anxious about (—°); n. or °**वत्**† adv., n. also as abstr.

भीतभीत a. much frightened, afraid of (abl.).

भीति f. fear, danger of (abl. or —°); **भीतितस्** from fear of (—°).

भीतिमन्त् a. timid, shy.

भीम॑ a. fearful, terrible, abstr. **°ता†** f.; E. of Rudra-Çiva, N. of sev. men, esp. of a Vidarbha king.

भीमकर्मन् a. doing terrible deeds.

भीमदर्शन a. of terrible aspect.

1**भीमनाद** m. a terrible sound.

2**भीमनाद** a. sounding terribly.

भीमन्त् a. fearful, afraid.

भीमपराक्रम a. possessing terrible power or courage.

भीमबल a. possessing fearful strength.

भीमयु॑ & **भीमल॑** a. dreadful, terrible.

भीम॑संदृश् a. of terrible aspect.

भीम॑सेन m. N. of one of the sons of Pāṇḍu etc.

भीमाङ्गद m. N. of a man.*

भीमौजस् a. having terrible strength.

भीर a. inspiring fear, frightening.

भीरु॑ (f. **भीरु** & **°रू**, voc. **भीरु**) timid, cowardly, shy, afraid of (abl. or —°, **परत्र** of the other world). — Abstr. **°ता†** f., **°त्व†** n.

भीरुक & **भीलुक** a. timid, cowardly, afraid of (—°).

भीषण, f. **आ** & **ई** terrifying, frightening (gen. or —°), awful, horrible.

भीषय् v. 1**भी**.

1**भीषा** f. frightening, intimidation.

2**भीषा॑** (instr. adv.) from fear.

भीषिका f. N. of a goddess.

भीष्म॑ a. dreadful, horrible; N. of an ancestor of the Bharatas, the son of Gaṅgā.

भु (—°) = 2**भू**.

भुं॑क् (interj.) crack!

भुक्त a. enjoyed, eaten; feeding on (—°); n. eating, food.

भुक्तपीत a. having eaten and drunk.

***भुक्तपूर्वन्** a. having enjoyed (acc.) before.

भुक्तमात्रे (loc. adv.) immediately after eating.

भुक्तवन्त् a. heaving eaten; **°वज्जने** (loc. adv.) when people have eaten.

भुक्तशेष n. the remnants of a meal.

भुक्ति f. eating, enjoyment, food; fruition, possession.

भुग्न a. bent, curved, distorted; broken, discouraged.

1**भुज्**, **भुज॑ति**, pp. **भुग्न** (q.v.) bend, turn, make crooked. — **अव** & **आ** bend in. **नि** bend down. **निस्** & **विनिस्** bend aside, turn away. **परि** encompass, embrace. **प्र** bend, fold. — Cf. **आभुग्न**, **व्याभुग्न**.

2**भुज्**, **भुन॑क्ति**, **भुङ्क्ते॑** (**भुञ्जति**, **°ते**), pp. **भुक्त** (q.v.) enjoy (in older lang. w. instr., later mostly w. acc.), esp. food (i.e. eat, feed on, ± acc.), but also the earth, a country or town (i.e. rule), a woman (i.e. love carnally), etc.; experience, endure, atone for (acc.) at the hands of (gen.); be of use to, serve (acc.). C. **भोजयति** (**°ते**) cause to enjoy or eat, feed (acc. of pers. & acc. or instr. of th.). D. **बुभुक्षते** (**°ति**) wish to eat, be hungry. I. **बोभुजीति** enjoy. — **अनु** reap the fruit of (acc.), partake of, enjoy. **अभि** be of service to (acc.). **उप** enjoy (also carnally), eat, consume, use, possess, partake of, live on, reap the fruit of (acc.); be of use or service to (acc.). **परि** eat before another or leave another without food (acc.); eat, devour, use, employ. **सम्** eat together, keep a common meal, enjoy (also carnally). C. cause to eat, feed with (instr.).

3**भु॑ज्** f. enjoyment, profit, advantage, service, use, possession, wealth (dat. **भुजे॑** also as infin.); adj. —° enjoying, eating, ruling, loving etc. (v. prec.)

भुज m. arm, branch, trunk of an elephant; f. **आ** the coil of a snake, arm.

भुजग m., **ई** f. snake (lit. going crookedly), serpent-demon or s.-maid; abstr. **°त्व** n.

भुजगपति & **°राज** m. the king of snakes.

भुजगात्मजा f. serpent-daughter.

भुजगेन्द्र & **°गेश्वर** m. the same.

भुजंग m. = **भुजग**, lecher, parasite.

भुजंगप्रयात n. N. of a metre.

भुजंगम m. = **भुजग**.

भुजंगशत्रु m. E. of Garuḍa (enemy of snakes).

भुजंगेन्द्र & **°गेश** m. the king of snakes.

भुजच्छाया f. protection (shadow of the arms).

भुजदण्ड m. a long arm (lit. arm-staff).
भुजबन्धन n. an embrace.
भुजमध्य n. breast (middle of the arms).
भुजमूल n. shoulder (root of the arms).
भुजयष्टि f. = भुजदण्ड.
भुजलता f. a slender arm (lit. arm-creeper).
भुजस्तम्भ m. a strong arm (lit arm-post).*
भुजान्तर n. the breast or chest (interval between the arms).
भुजान्तराल n. the same.
1भुजि f. enclosure.
2भुजि f. protection or protector.
भुजिष्य a. yielding food or profit, useful; m. & f. आ servant.
भुज्मन् a. fruitful.
भुज्यु a. flexible, pliant; N. of a man.
भुर्, भुरति, °ते quiver, jerk, struggle, stir, flash. I. जर्भुरीति = S. — परि I. = S. I. सम् I. rush along.
भुरण a. stirring, active.
भुरण्य्, °ण्यति quiver, stir (tr. & intr.).
भुरण्यु a. stirring, restless, eager, active.
भुरिज् f. a pair of shears or scissors; a kind of two-armed chopping bench used by a wheelwright, N. of a metre.
भुर्वणि a. restless, impatient.
भुर्वन् s. restless motion (of water).
भुवन n. being, existence, thing; world (2, 3, 7, or 14), earth; place of existence, abode, dwelling.
भुवनच्यव a. shaking the world.
भुवनतल n. the surface of the earth.
भुवनत्रय n. the three worlds (heaven, atmosphere & earth).
भुवनद्वय n. the two worlds (heaven and earth).
भुवनपति m. the lord of the world.
भुवनभर्तृ m. = prec.
भुवनभावन m. creator of the world.
भुवनेश m. the lord of the world.
भुवनेश्वर m. = prec., also king, prince, E. of Çiva.
भुवनेष्ठा a. being in the world or in the existing creatures.
भुवस् (indecl.) air or atmosphere.
भुविष्ठ a. standing on the ground or dwelling on the earth.
भुशुण्डि or भुशुण्डी f. a. cert. weapon.
1भू, भवति (°ते), pp. भूत (q.v.) become, be (nom. or adv. in ई or ऊ), rise, appear, happen, occur; exist, live (w. न cease to be, perish, die), stay, abide; be possible or suitable; befall, fall to the lot of, belong to (gen., r. dat. or loc.); serve for, tend or conduce to (dat. of th.), devote one's self to, be occupied with (loc.); get something i.e. thrive, prosper, be lucky (± इदम्); turn out well, succeed. भवेत् may be, granted; भवतु good, possible, enough of this. C. भावयति, °ते, pp. भावित (q.v.) bring into existence or being, produce, effect, cause; cherish, further, refresh, comfort; practise, exercise; get possessed of, obtain; show, manifest, call to mind, imagine, consider, know, take for (2 acc.); convince, convict, state, establish; mingle, mix, saturate, steep. D. बुभूषति (°ते) wish to become or be, to rise or thrive, endeavour at (acc.); like, prefer, honour, esteem. I. बोभवीति be repeatedly, use to be. — अति be or become in a high degree; excel, overcome (acc.). अनु be after, come up with, attain, equal; embrace, comprehend, include; help, serve, further; enjoy, feel, experience, suffer; perceive, hear, learn. समनु enjoy, experience. अन्तर् be within, penetrate. अप be absent or wanting. अभि be against, surpass, overcome, oppress, harass, humiliate; turn to, approach or present with (instr.). आ be present or at hand; exist, live on; come forth, spring from (abl.). अन्वा follow, imitate. अभ्या occur, happen. उद् come forth, arise, grow, increase, be sufficient or equal. C. bring forth, produce, develop, display. समुद् spring forth, arise, increase. उप approach, assist. तिरस् be absent or lost, disappear, vanish. C. cause to disappear, dispel. निस् be off, move on. परा perish, be lost, succumb, yield; overcome, conquer, harm, hurt, injure.

C. overthrow, destroy. परि surround, encompass, comprehend, include; attend, manage, take care of (acc.); surpass, overcome, vanquish; hurt, injure, despise, disgrace; mock, scoff. प्र come forth, spring up, arise, appear, happen, occur, spread, expand, increase, grow; be numerous or strong, prevail, rule over, dispose of (gen., loc., or dat.); be equal to or a match for (dat.), be able to or capable of (infin.); be of use, profit, avail (dat.). C. augment, increase, strengthen, nourish, further. प्रति equal (acc.). C. observe, learn, know. वि expand, develop, arise, appear; suffice for, be equal to, attain, pervade, fill (dat. or acc.), be able to (infin.). C. cause to expand or develop, open, show, manifest; separate, divide; discern, discover, perceive, know, recognize or acknowledge as, take for (2 acc.), deliberate, ponder, fancy, imagine, suppose, establish, prove, convict, convince. P. be considered as, pass for, appear, seem (nom.). सम् come or be together, assemble, meet, be united with (instr. ± सह or loc.), have sexual intercourse with (instr. ± सह or सार्धम् & acc.); be held or contained in (loc.); originate, be produced or engendered, be born, spring from (abl.), happen, occur, exist, become, be, fall to a person's (loc. or gen.) share or lot, be possible, be able to or capable of (infin.). C. bring together, produce, accomplish, make that– (pp.); go to meet, betake one's self to, salute, honour, gratify or present with (instr.); combine, think, judge (अन्यथा falsely); imagine, suppose, give a person (loc.) credit for (acc.), consider as, take for (2 acc.) P. be possible. अभिसम् attain, get possessed of, participate in (acc.). — Cf. अन्तर्भूत, उद्भूत, प्रभूत, समुद्भूत, संभूत, संभव.

2भू a. becoming, being, sprung from (—°); f. becoming, existing, the universe (pl. the worlds), the earth, land, country, place, ground.

भूकम्प m. earthquake.

भूगत a. being or living on the earth.

भूगोल & °क m. the terrestrial globe.

भूचर a. going or living on the earth; m. inhabitant of the earth.

भूत a. become, either been, past, gone, former; or being (often — °), present, real. — m. N. of a Yakṣa etc. n. being, creature, the world; ghost, goblin, demon (m.); the past, fact, reality, welfare, prosperity; element (ph.). — Abstr. °ता† f., °त्व† n.

भूतकर्तृ m. the creator of (all) beings.

भूतकाल m. the past time.

भूतकृत् m. = भूतकर्तृ.

भूतगण m. host of beings or demons.

भूतग्राम m. the same.

भूतजननी f. the mother of beings (E. of sev. goddesses).

भूतधरा f. the earth (supporting beings).

भूतधारिणी f. = prec.

भूतपति m. lord of (evil) beings (E. of sev. gods).

भूतपूर्व & °क a. having been before.

भूतभर्तृ a. supporting all beings, m. = भूतपति.

भूतभव्य n. past and future.

भूतभव्येश m. the lord of past & future.

भूतभावन a. creating all beings.

भूतभाविन् a. = prec. or past and present.

भूतभाषा f. the language of demons or Piçācas; °मय, f. ई written in this language.

भूतभृत् a. supporting all beings.

भूतमय, f. ई containing all beings or consisting of the five elements.

भूतमहेश्वर m. the great lord of all beings or demons (E. of Viṣṇu or Çiva).

भूतमातृ f. = भूतजननी.

भूतमात्रा f. pl. the subtile elements (ph.).

भूतयज्ञ m. oblation to all created beings.

भूतयोनि f. the origin of all beings.

भूतल n. the surface of the earth.

भूतवत् adv. as if past.

भूतविद् a. knowing (evil) beings.

भूतविद्या f. the knowledge of (evil) beings.

भूतसंसार m. the world of beings.

भूतसंप्लव m. end (lit. submersion) of all being or of the world.

भूतसर्ग m. creation of beings or elements.
भूतसाक्षिन् m. witness of all beings, the All-seer.
भूतस्थ a. being in beings.
1भूतात्मन् m. the soul of beings, the individual soul.
2भूतात्मन् m. the body (lit. whose soul are the elements).
भूतादि m. the first of all beings, E. of Viṣṇu.
भूताधिपति m. lord of all beings.
भूतानद्यतन v. अनद्यतन.
भूतार्थ m. matter of fact, reality, truth.
भूतावास m. the abode of the elements, the body; also E. of Viṣṇu & Çiva.
भूति or भूति f. being, esp. well-being, welfare, wealth, fortune; ornament, decoration.
भूतिकर्मन् n. any auspicious rite.
भूतिकाम a. desirous of welfare.
भूतिकृत् a. causing welfare (Çiva).
भूतिकृत्य n. = भूतिकर्मन्.
भूतिद a. causing welfare, E. of Çiva.
भूतिमन्त् a. having welfare, prosperous.
भूतेज्य a. worshipping evil beings.
भूतेश & °श्वर m. lord of (evil) beings, E. of sev. gods.
भूदेव m. a Brahman (god on earth).
भूधर a. bearing or supporting the earth; m. mountain.
भूधरारण्य n. mountain-forest.
भूना v. 2भूमन्.
भूप m. earth-protector, king.
भूपति m. lord of beings (Rudra) or of the earth (a king).
भूपतित a. fallen on the earth.
भूपाल & भूभर्तृ m. = भूप.
भूभार m. the bearing or the burden of the earth.
भूभुज् m. earth-possessor i.e. king.
भूभृत् m. earth-holder i.e. mountain, king, or Viṣṇu.
भूम (—°) = भूमि.
भूमण्डल n. the terrestrial globe.
1भूमन् n. earth, country, world, a being; pl. all existing things.
2भूमन् m. plenty, abundance, multitude, wealth; adj. full of (—°). Instr. भूम्ना & भूना abundantly, mostly, generally.
भूमहेन्द्र m. great lord of the earth, i.e. king.
भूमि (भूमी) f. the earth, ground, soil, land, country, place, site, abode; floor or story of a house; step, degree (fig.); position, part or character (d.); a person or thing worthy of (—°).
भूमिकम्प m., °कम्पन n. earthquake.
भूमिका f. the earth, ground, place for (—°); floor or story of a house, step, degree (fig.), part, character, costume (d.).
भूमिकाभाग m. floor, threshold.*
भूमिगत a. = भूपतित.
भूमिगर्त m. a pit in the ground.
भूमिगृह n. an under-ground chamber.
भूमिचल m., °चलन n. earthquake.
भूमिज & °जात a. sprung from the earth.
भूमितल n. the surface of the earth.
भूमित्व n. abstr. to भूमि.
भूमिद a. giving land.
भूमिदान n. donation of land.
भूमिदुन्दुभि m. earth-drum (a pit in the ground covered with a skin)
भूमिदेव m. = भूदेव.
भूमिधर m. earth-holder, mountain or king.
भूमिप, °पति, & °पाल m. king (cf. भूप etc.).
भूमिपरिमाण n. square-measure.
भूमिप्र a. filling the earth (fame).
भूमिप्रचल m. earthquake.
भूमिबुध्न a. having the earth as bottom.
भूमिभाग a. portion of land, place, spot.
भूमिभुज् & °भृत् m. king (cf. भूभुज् & °भृत्).
भूमिलोक m. the terrestrial world.
भूमिवज्रमणि m. pl. land, diamonds, and (other) jewels.
भूमिशय a. lying or living on (in) the earth; m. such an animal.
भूमिष्ठ a. standing or lying on the earth; being in one's own country.
भूमिसुत m. the planet Mars (the son of the earth).
भूमिस्पृश् a. touching the earth.
भूमी v. भूमि.
भूमीरुह & °रुह m. tree, plant (earth-growing).

भूम्य a. terrestrial.

भूम्यनृत a. untruth concerning land.

भूयंस् (compar.) more, greater, larger, mightier, more numerous, abundant, or important; also w. the mgs of the positive or superl. (very) great, etc.; full of, abounding in (instr. or —°). **भूयस्** n. adv. more, most, very much, further, moreover, again (often doubled, also **भूयोऽपि**, **भूयश्चापि**, & **पुनर्भूयस्**); instr. **भूयसा** exceedingly, in a high degree, mostly, generally.

भूयस्त्व n. the being more or greater, multitude, abundance.

भूयिष्ठ (superl.) most, greatest, chiefest; very abundant, numerous, or important; mostly consisting of, chiefly filled with or accompanied by (—°); nearly, almost (—° after a pp., e. g. **गतभूयिष्ठ** nearly gone). n. adv. mostly, chiefly, very much (also instr).

भूर् (indecl.) earth.

भूरि a. abundant, much, frequent, numerous, strong, mighty; n. adv.

†**भूरिगु** a. rich in herds.

भूरिता f. numerousness, multitude.

भूरितेजस् a. rich in splendour, glorious.

भूरितोक a. having many children.

भूरिद a. much-giving, munificent.

भूरिदक्षिण a. rich in sacrificial fees, liberal, bounteous i. g.

भूरिदात्र a. rich in gifts.

भूरिदावन्, f. °**दावरी** liberal, munificent.

भूरिधन a. having much wealth.

भूरिधामन् a. having much power.

भूरिधायस् a. nourishing or sating many.

भूरिपाश a. having many fetters (Mitra-Varuṇa).

भूरिपोषिन् a. nourishing many.

भूरिभार a. bearing a heavy load.

भूरिरेतस् a. rich in seed, prolific.

भूरिवर्चस् a. very splendid or glorious.

भूरिवर्पस् a. many-shaped.

भूरिवसु m. N. of a minister.

भूरिवार a. rich in treasures or gifts.

भूरिशस् adv. manifoldly, variously.

भूरिविलम्बिन् a. hanging deeply down.

भूरिशृङ्ग a. many- or strong-horned.

भूरिश्रवस् m. N. of a prince.

भूरिस्थात्र a. having many stations, being in many places.

भूरुह & °**रुह** m. = **भूमिरुह्**, °**रुह**.

भूर्ज m. a kind of birch; n. its bark (used for writing on).

भूर्जकण्टक m. a cert. mixed caste.

भूर्जद्रुम m. birch-tree.

भूर्णि a. excited, irritated, shy, wild, fierce, active, busy.

भूर्यक्ष a. many-eyed.

भूर्योजस् a. having great power.

भूर्लोक & **भूलोक** m. the terrestrial world.

भूशय a. = **भूमिशय**.

भूष्, **भूषति** be busy for, endeavour at, attend upon (dat.). C. **भूषयति** (°**ते**), pp. **भूषित** adorn, embellish (M. refl.). — **आ** observe, maintain; conform one's self to (loc.). **उप** consider, regard, follow (acc.). **परि** serve, attend upon (acc.); honour, obey, follow. C. adorn. **प्रति** make ready, prepare; wait on, serve, honour, obey. **वि** C. adorn.

भूषण, f. **ई** adorning, embellishing (—°). n. (m.) ornament, decoration; adj., f. **आ** adorned with (—°).

भूषयितव्य a. to be adorned.

भूषा f. ornament, decoration.

भूषाय्, °**यते** serve as ornament.

भूषिन् a. adorned with (—°).

भूष्णु a. growing, wishing to thrive.

भूष्य a. = **भूषयितव्य**.

भूसुर m. = **भूदेव**.

भूस्तृण m. a kind of fragrant grass.

भूस्थ a. standing or living on the earth.

भृ, **बिभर्ति** (**बिभर्ति**), **भरति**, °**ते** (**भर्ति**), pp. **भृत** bear (in all mgs), hold, carry, wear, keep (also in memory), contain, possess, have, maintain, support, nourish; hire, pay; convey, transport (M. move on rapidly), take away (M. for one's self, obtain, win); procure, offer, present, bestow; experience, undergo (w. **आज्ञाम्** obey); raise (the voice or a sound, M. refl.); fill, load. D. बुभूर्षति wish to keep or maintain. I. भंरिभ्रत्, बरीभर्ति bear hither and thither or repeatedly. — अप carry off, take away. अव bear down, ward off; thrust or push in, introduce; imprint, impress; sever, cut off. आ bring near, procure, cause, produce; fill. पर्या bring near from (abl.). समा bring together or near. उद् take out, select; deliver from (abl.); lift up, hold high. उप bring near, procure, get. निस् take out of (abl.). परि A. M. bring; M. spread (tr. & intr. w. acc.). प्र bring forward or near, place before, make ready; offer, present; stretch out, hurl, cast; bring in, introduce; M. flash, vibrate, rush on, fly along. अभिप्र hurl, shoot; M. = प्रति present, offer. वि take asunder, spread out, diffuse; M. place here and there, distribute. सम् bring together, collect, concentrate, compose, make ready, arrange, prepare, pay back, restore; nourish, foster. — Cf. आभृत, निभृत, संभृत.

भृकुटि or °टी f. contraction of the eyebrows, a frown.

भृगु m. pl. N. of a mythical race of beings, m. sgl. N. of an ancient Rishi regarded as their ancestor.

भृगुतुङ्ग m. N. of a sacred mountain.

भृगुनन्दन m. Bhṛgu's son, patron. of Çaunaka, Ruru, & Paraçurāma.

भृगुपति m. E. of Paraçurāma (cf. prec.).

भृगूद्वह m. = भृगुनन्दन.

भृङ्ग m. a large black bee (f. आ & ई).

भृङ्गसार्थ m. a flight of bees.

भृङ्गाय्, °यते be like a bee.

भृङ्गार m. n. water-pot, pitcher.

भृङ्गालि f. = भृङ्गसार्थ.

भृज्ज्, भृज्जति, pp. भृष्ट roast, parch (esp. grain). C. भर्जयति = S. — अव, परि, सम् the same.

भृज्जन n. roasting-pan.

भृत् a. bearing, maintaining, possessing, having, bringing, procuring (—°).

भृत a. borne, held, kept, supported, nourished, hired, paid; acquired, won, loaden or filled with (—°); m. hireling, mercenary.

भृतक a. hired, paid; m. a hired servant.

भृतकाध्यापक m. a hired teacher.

भृतकाध्यापित a. taught by a hired teacher.

भृति or भृति f. bearing, carrying, maintaining, nourishing; wages or service for wages.

भृत्य m. dependant, servant, minister of a king; abstr. °ता f., °त्व n.

भृत्यभाव m. the state of a servant, servitude.

भृत्यवात्सल्य n. love to servants.

भृत्याय्, °यते behave like a servant towards (loc.).

भृथ s. oblation.

भृम m. error, mistake.

भृमल a. stunned, torpid.

1भृमि a. quick, agile; m. whirlwind.

2भृमि f. quickness, agility.

भृश a. powerful, strong, intense, exceeding, mostly °— or n. adv.; abstr. °ता f.

भृशदण्ड a. inflicting severe punishment on (loc.).

भृष्टि f. point, top or peak (of a mountain), corner, edge.

भृष्टिमन्त् a. pronged, toothed.

भेक m., ई f. frog.

भेकीपति m. a male frog.

भेड m., ई f. a man's & woman's name.

भेतव्य a. to be feared; n. impers.

भेत्तृ m. breaker, piercer, disturber, traitor, conqueror.

भेद m. breaking, splitting, breach, division, separation, seduction, winning over (of another's ally), interruption, disturbance, hurt, injury; bursting, expanding, blossoming; alteration, change, difference; fissure, cleft, pudendum muliebre; part, portion; species, variety.

भेदक a. breaking, piercing, digging through, destroying, seducing; distinguishing, defining.

भेदकर, f. ई breaking, piercing; separating, disuniting.

भेदकारिन् a. disuniting; different, n. adv.

भेदन a. breaking, tearing, piercing, perforating; n. the action of breaking etc., disclosing, betraying, disuniting; bursting, opening, breach, rupture, disunion, discord.

भेदनीय a. to be cleft or cut through.

भेदिन् a. breaking, splitting, piercing, opening, causing to flow, separating, dividing, disuniting.

भेद्य a. to be cleft or pierced; to be betrayed, seduced, refuted; distinguished, defined.

भेय a. to be feared, n. impers.

(**भेरि** or) **भेरी** f. kettle-drum.

भेरुण्ड a. terrible, awful. m. a kind of bird or beast of prey; f. **आ** N. of a goddess.

भेषज, f. **ई** healthy, sanative; n. a remedy or cure for (—°).

भेषजकृत a. healed, cured.

भेषजता f. healing power.

भेषज्य a. curative, sanitary.

भैक्ष a. living by alms; n. asking alms, mendicancy, begged food, alms. **भैक्षं चर्** & **भैक्षाय गम्** go about begging, beg.

भैक्षचरण & °**चर्य** n., °**चर्या** f. going about begging.

भैक्षभुज् a. eating begged food.

भैक्षवृत्ति a. subsisting on alms, f. as abstr.

भैक्षान्न n. begged food.

भैक्षाशिन् & **भैक्षाहार** a. eating begged food.

भैक्षाश्य n. the living on alms.

भैक्षोपजीविन् a. subsisting on alms.

भैम a. descended from Bhīma; f. **ई** the daughter of Bh., i.e. Damayantī.

भैरव, f. **आ** & **ई** formidable, awful, horrible, n. adv. — m. a form of Çiva, a man's name; f. **ई** a form of Durgā.

भैषज्य n. curativeness, a cert. sanative ceremony, remedy against (—°).

भोक्तव्य a. to be enjoyed or eaten (n. impers.), to be fed; to be used or employed.

भोक्तुकाम a. wishing to eat, hungry.

भोक्तृ m., °**क्त्री** f. enjoyer, possessor; abstr. °**क्तृत्व** n.

1**भोग** m. winding, curve, coil.

2**भोग** m. enjoyment, fruition, use, application, possession, dominion, government; feeling, perception, gain, advantage, pleasure, joy.

भोगतृष्णा f. longing after enjoyments, egoism.*

भोगपति m. lord of possession i.e. governor, viceroy etc.

1**भोगवन्त्** a. having windings or rings, ringed; m. serpent or serpent-demon, f. °**वती**.

2**भोगवन्त्** a. having enjoyments, happy, prosperous; f. °**वती** E. of the city of Ujjayinī.

भोगाय्, °**यते** ringle, coil.

भोगायतन n. place of enjoyment.

1**भोगिन्** a. & m. = 1**भोगवन्त्**.

2**भोगिन्** a. enjoying, eating (—°); or = 2**भोगवन्त्** a.

भोगीन्द्र & **भोगीश** m. the serpent-king.

भोग्य a. to be (being) enjoyed, used or experienced; useful, profitable. Abstr. °**ता**† f., °**त्व**† n.

भोज a. bountiful, liberal; or = 2**भोगवन्त्** a.; m. N. of sev. kings, pl. N. of a people.

भोजक a. eating (—°) or *about to eat.

भोजदेव m. N. of a king.

भोजन a. feeding, nourishing. m. enjoying, eating. feeding, nourishing, meal, food, wealth, possession, pleasure, joy; adj. —° feeding on or serving as food for.

भोजनकाल m., °**वेला** f. meal-time.

भोजनार्थिन् a. desirous of food, hungry.

भोजनीय a. to be (being) eaten or fed; n. food.

भोजयितव्य a. to be fed or nourished.

भोजिन् a. enjoying, eating (—°).

भोज्य a. to be enjoyed or eaten, fed or nourished; to be used, employed, perceived. n. eating, food, enjoyment, advantage; abstr. °**ता**† f., °**त्व**† n.

भोज्यान्न a. whose food one may eat.

भोट m. Tibet; **भोटीय** a. Tibetan.

भोभवत्पूर्वकम् adv. (to address) with **भोस्** and **भवन्त्**.

भोभाव m. the nature of **भो** (cf. seq.).

भोस्, **भोः**, **भो** (= **भवस्**, voc. of 2**भवन्त्**) interj. of address, sorrow, or interrogation, often repeated or connected with other interjections.

भौजंग, f. **ई** relating to a snake, snaky.

भौजिष्य n. slavery, servitude.

भौत a. relating to beings or ghosts; demoniacal, crazy, mad; m. idiot.

1भौतिक a. = prec. adj.

2भौतिक m. E. of Çiva; a class of monks.

भौम, f. ई relating to the earth, earthly, terrestrial; or consisting of earth, earthy. — n. dust; grain, corn; ground, floor, story (only adj. —°).

भौमक m. animal living in the earth.

भौमिक & भौम्य a. being on the earth.

भौरिक m. treasurer.

भौर्ज a. birchen.

भौवन a. belonging to the world.

भ्यस्, भ्यसते fear, tremble at (abl.).

भ्रंश्, भ्रंशते, भ्रश्यते (°ति), pp. भ्रष्ट (q.v.) fall, drop, bounce against (loc.) or from (abl.); sink, decline, decay, disappear, be gone or lost; be deprived of, lose (abl.). C. भ्रंशयति cause to fall, throw down, drop (trans.); precipitate, overthrow, cause to be lost, deprive of (abl.). — प्र fall down, disappear, vanish, be deprived of. C. bring to fall, deprive of (abl.). वि fail, have no success in (loc.); turn away from, abandon (abl.). C. cut or break off, fell, ruin, destroy; deprive of (abl.). सम् fall down. — Cf. अपभ्रष्ट, परिभ्रष्ट, प्रभ्रष्ट, विभ्रष्ट.

भ्रंश m. fall, ruin, disappearance, loss; aberration or deviation from (—°).

भ्रंशन a. causing to fall, throwing down; n. being deprived or depriving of (abl.).

भ्रंशिन् a. falling, dropping down from (abl.), sinking, declining, perishing; causing to fall, destroying.

भ्रज् f. stiffness.

भ्रम्, भ्रमति (°ते), भ्राम्यति, pp. भ्रान्त (q.v.) roam, wander, stroll; go through, perambulate (acc.); fly about, flutter; move round, rotate; stagger about, waver, go astray, be perplexed or mistaken. C. भ्रमयति & भ्रामयति (°ते) cause to roam etc., whirl round, swing, roll; cause to err, perplex, embarrass, confuse; pp. भ्रमित fasely taken for or confounded with (—°)*. I. बभ्रमीति & बम्भ्रम्यते wander about or through, the latter also w. pass. mg. — उद् start up, rise. C. whirl around, swing, rouse, agitate, trouble, disturb. परि wander about, roam, turn round. C. move to and fro, shake, stir. प्र roam, wander through, permeate. वि wander about or through, move to and fro (tr. & intr.), stagger, tumble, waver, be perplexed or agitated. सम् wander, rove, be perplexed or bewildered. — Cf. उद्भ्रान्त, विभ्रान्त, संभ्रान्त.

भ्रम m. roaming, wandering, moving to and fro; wandering through (—°); whirling flame, whirlpool, eddy, a potter's wheel; giddiness, wandering of mind, confusion, mistake, error.

भ्रमण n. roaming, wandering through (—°); tottering, wavering, unsteadiness; turning round, revolution (of a star), giddiness, dizziness.

भ्रमणीय a. to be roamed through.

भ्रमर m., ई f. bee (adj. —° f. आ).

भ्रमि f. turning round, revolution; whirlpool, eddy; a potter's wheel.

भ्रष्ट a. fallen, dropped down from (abl. or —°) into (loc.); sunk, ruined, lost, gone; separated from, deprived of (abl. or —°).

भ्राष्ट्र n. roasting pan.

भस्ता f. bag (cf. भस्त्रा).

1भ्राज्, भ्राजते, °ति shine, flash, beam. — C. भ्राजयति make shine, irradiate. परि shine all around. प्र, वि, सम् = S.

2भ्राज् (nom. भ्राट्) f. sheen, glitter.

भ्राज a. shining, glittering.

भ्राजज्जन्मन् a. having a brilliant home or origin (Maruts).

भ्राजदृष्टि a. having bright weapons (Maruts).

भ्राजस् n. sheen, lustre, splendour.

भ्राजस्वन्त् a. shining, glittering.

भ्राजस्विन् a. the same.

भ्राजि f. = भ्राजस्.

भ्राजिन् a. shining, sparkling.

भ्राजिष्ठ (superl.) shining brightest.

भ्राजिष्णु a. shining, radiant; abstr. °ता f.

भ्राजिष्मन्त् a. = prec. adj.

भ्रातृ m. brother (in confidential address also = friend, dear!).

भ्रातृक (m. brother*), mostly adj. —°.

भ्रातृजाया f. a brother's wife, sister-in-law.
भ्रातृत्व n. brotherhood.
भ्रातृदत्त a. given by a brother.
भ्रातृभार्या f. = **भ्रातृजाया**.
भ्रातृमन्त् a. having a brother or brothers.
भ्रातृव्य m. a father's brother's son; nephew, cousin; rival, adversary, enemy.
भ्रातृव्यवन्त् a. having rivals.
भ्रात्र & **भ्रात्र्य** n. brotherhood.
भ्रान्त a. roaming, roamed (also pass., n. impers.); turning round, rolling, perplexed, confused, mistaken; n. roaming, wandering (also in mind), mistake, error.
भ्रान्ति f. roaming, wandering; moving round (—°), revolution; tottering, wavering, confusion, perplexity, uncertainty, doubt, error.
भ्रान्तिमन्त् a. roaming, turning round; erring, mistaken.
भ्राम m. roaming about, unsteadiness, fickleness.
भ्रामक, f. **°मिका** deceitful, false.
भ्रामण n. swinging or turning round.
भ्रामरिन् a. epileptic.
भ्रामिन् a. confused, perplexed.
भ्राश्य a. to be broken or cut off.
भ्राष्ट्रक s. roasting pan.
भ्री, भ्रीणाति hurt.
भ्रुकुटि & **°टी** f. = **भ्रुकुटि**.
भ्रुकुटिबन्ध m., **°रचना** f. knitting the brows, frowning.
भ्रुकुटीमुख n. a frowning face (cf. prec.), adj. having a frowning face.
भ्रुव adj. (—°) = seq.).
भ्रू f. brow (adj. —° **भ्रु, भ्रू,** & **भ्रूक**, cf. also prec.).
भ्रूकुटीमुख n. = **भ्रुकुटीमुख**.
भ्रूक्षेप m., **°क्षेपण** n. contraction of the eyebrows.
भ्रूण n. embryo, unborn child; m. a Brahman of high rank.
भ्रूणघ्न & **°भिद्** m. the killer of an embryo.
भ्रूणवध m., **°हति,** & **°हत्या** f. the killing of an embryo.
भ्रूणहन् & **°हन्तृ** m. = **भ्रूणघ्न**.
भ्रूभङ्ग & **भ्रूभेद** m. contraction of the eyebrows.
भ्रूलता f. an arched eyebrow (lit. brow-creeper).
भ्रूविकार & **°विक्षेप** m. = **भ्रूभङ्ग**.
भ्रूविलास m. amorous play of the brows.
†**भ्रेष्, भ्रेषति, °ते** totter, go astray.
भ्रेष m. tottering, going astray, trespass; loss.

म

म pron. stem of 1st pers.
मंह्, मंहते, मंहयति grant, bestow, w. **वि** distribute.
मंहना f. gift, donation, as instr. adv. readily, willingly, quickly.
मंहयु a. liberal, generous.
मंहिष्ठ (superl.) most liberal or generous.
मंहीयंस् (compar.) more liberal or generous.
मकमकाय्, °यते croak (of a frog).
मकर m., **ई** f. a kind of sea monster (the emblem of the god of love); array of troops in the form of a M.
मकरकेतन, °केतु, & **°ध्वज** m. the god of love (cf. prec.).
मकरन्द m. the juice of flowers, a man's name; n. = seq.
मकरन्दोद्यान n. N. of a pleasure grove near Ujjayinī.
मकरालय & **मकरावास** m. E. of the sea (lit. multitude or abode of monsters).
मकार m. the sound **म**.
मक्ष् & **मक्षा** f. a fly.
(**मक्षिक** m.), **मक्षिका** f. = prec. or bee.
(**मक्षु**) or **मक्षू** adv. quickly, instantly, directly; superl. **मक्षूतम** as adj.
मक्षूयु a. quick, swift.
मख a. gay, jocund; m. occasion of joy, festivity, sacrifice; N. of a demon.
मखद्विष् m. a demon or Rakṣas (lit. enemy of sacrifices).
मखमथन n. the disturbance of (Dakṣa's) sacrifice.

मखस्य्, °स्यति, °ते be cheerful or merry.
मखस्यु a. cheerful, merry.
मखहन् m. the slayer of Makha (E. of sev. gods).
मखांशभाज् m. a god (lit. partaker of sacrifices).
मग m. a magian; pl. N. of a people.
मगध m. pl. N. of a country and people.
मगधदेश m. the country of the Magadhas.
†मगन्द m. usurer.
†मगुन्दी f. N. of the mother of cert. female demons.
मग्न a. sunk, dived, immersed or penetrated into (loc. or —°); went down, set (moon), fallen, ruined, decayed.
मघ n. gift, donation, reward; f. आ sgl. & pl. N. of a lunar mansion.
मघत्ति f. the giving and receiving of presents.
मघदेय n. the giving of presents.
मघव m. E. of Indra.
मघवत्त्व n. liberality, munificence.
मघवन् & मघवन्त् (f. मघोनी) a. rich in gifts, liberal, generous; m. the institutor or patron of a sacrifice, E. of Indra.
मङ्कणक m. N. of a Rishi & a Yakṣa.
मङ्कि m. N. of a man.
मङ्कु a. tottering, reeling.
मङ्क्तव्य n. impers. to be dived.
मङ्क्षु adv. instantly, directly.
मङ्ख m. a man's name.
मङ्ग m. pl. N. of a people.
†मङ्गल n. welfare, luck, prosperity; anything lucky, auspicious, or of good omen (also as adj. = मङ्गल्य), ancient or traditional usage; m. the planet Mars, a man's name.
मङ्गलकरण (& कर्मन्*) n. prayer for success (lit. luck-causing act).
मङ्गलकलश s. auspicious pot or vase.*
मङ्गलगृह (& क*) n. auspicious chamber or house.
मङ्गलतूर्य n. festive instrument.
मङ्गलसमालम्भन n. auspicious unguent.*
मङ्गलवचस् n., °शब्द m. benedictory speech, congratulation.
मङ्गलाचार m. auspicious custom or ceremony.
मङ्गलादेशवृत्त m. fortune-teller.
मङ्गलार्थम् adv. for the sake of good fortune.
मङ्गलीय a. auspicious.
मङ्गलोद्गीत n. festive song.*
मङ्गल्य a. lucky, auspicious, festive, solemn, holy. m. & f. आ names of sev. plants; n. anything auspicious or of good omen, esp. a prayer.
मङ्गिनी f. boat, ship.
मङ्गीर & मङ्गु m. names of men.
मच्चित्त a. having the mind (fixed) on me, thinking of me.
मज्ज्, मज्जति (°ते), pp. मग्न (q.v.) sink (in water), dive, bathe, be submerged or drowned, be ruined, perish. C. मज्जयति (°ते) = S. trans. or act. — उद् emerge or plunge. C. cause to emerge or come up. उप sink, dive. नि sink down, plunge or penetrate into (loc.); disappear, perish; cause to sink or fall. C. cause to dive, drown. संनि sink down, fall. निस् sink; overflow. प्र & वि plunge, rush into (acc. or loc.). — Cf. आमग्न, उन्मग्न, निमग्न, संमग्न.
मज्जन् m. marrow; poss. मज्जन्वन्त्.
मज्जन n. sinking, diving, bathing, overflowing.
मज्जयितृ a. causing to sink.
मज्जस् n., मज्जा f. marrow.
मज्मन् s. greatness, might; instr. adv. together, generally, at all.
मञ्च m. stage, platform.
मञ्चक m. n. = prec., f. मञ्चिका chair.
मञ्जर n. cluster of blossoms, panicle.
मञ्जरि & °री f. = prec., blossom or bud i.g., °री often in titles of books (—°).
मञ्जिष्ठा f. the Indian madder (bright red).
मञ्जीर s. foot-ornament, anklet.
मञ्जु a. pleasant, sweet; n. adv.
मञ्जुभाषिन् & °वादिन् a. speaking sweetly.
मञ्जुल a. = मञ्जु; m. a kind of hen.
मञ्जुस्वन a. sweet-voiced.
मञ्जूषा (& मञ्जूषिका*) f. box, basket.
मटक s. dead body, corpse.
मटची m. hail.
मठ m., ई f. hut, also = seq.
मठायतन n. monastery, convent, college.
मठिका f. hut, cottage, cell.

मण s. a cert. measure of grain.
मणि m. pearl, jewel, gem, ornament i.g., fig. a jewel of (—°); magnet, water-jar.
मणिक m. a large water-jar.
मणिकर्णिका f. an ornament for the ears made of pearls; N. of a sacred pool & a woman.
मणिकार m. jeweller (f. ई).
मणित n. sound or murmur (during the sexual intercourse).
मणिधनु m. & °धनुस् n. rainbow.
मणिनाग m. N. of a serpent-demon.
मणिपुष्पक m. the conch-shell of Sahadeva.
मणिपूर (or °पुर) n. N. of a town.
मणिबन्ध m. the fastening or putting on of jewels, the wrist (as the place for it).
मणिबन्धन n. = prec., also string or ornament of pearls.
मणिभद्र m. N. of a king of the Yakṣas.
मणिमन्त् a. adorned with jewels; m. N. of a Yakṣa, a Rakṣas, etc.
मणिमय, f. ई consisting of jewels.
मणिमाला & मणियष्टि f. string of pearls.
मणिरत्न n. jewel, precious stone.
मणिरत्नमय, f. ई = मणिमय.
मणिरत्नवन्त् a. containing jewels.
मणिल a. dewlapt.
मणिसूत्र n. string of pearls.
मणिस्तम्भ m. a crystal post or pillar.
मणिस्रज् n. wreath of jewels.
मणिहर्म्य n. N. of a palace (lit. Crystal P.).
मणीन्द्र m. diamond (jewel-chief).
मण्ड्, मण्डयति, pp. मण्डित deck, adorn, embellish, glorify. — परि & प्रति = S.
†मण्ड m. n. broth, scum.
मण्डक (adj. —°) f. इका = prec.
मण्डन n. adorning (also adj.), ornament.
मण्डप s. open hall, pavilion, temple.
मण्डपिका f. small pavilion or shed.
मण्डल a. round, circular. — n. disk, circle, ring; district, territory, country (also f. ई); assemblage, collection, totality, multitude, group, company, band (also m. & f. ई); circular array of an army (also m.); the circle of a king's neighbours, a cert. division of the Rigveda.
मण्डलक n. disk, circle, ring; f. °लिका troop, multitude.
मण्डलन्यास m. drawing a circle.
मण्डलित a. ringled.
मण्डलिन् a. forming a circle or ring; possessing or ruling a country.
मण्डली w. कृ & भू make & become round.
मण्डलेश & °श्वर m. the ruler of a country.
मण्डितृ m. adorner, ornament.
मण्डु m. N. of a Rishi.
मण्डूक m. frog (adj. —° f. आ), N. of a Rishi; f. मण्डूकी female frog.
मण्डूकप्लुति f. frog-leap (g.).
मण्डूकिका f. female frog.
मण्डूर s. rust of iron.
मत a. thought, believed, supposed; considered as, taken for (nom. & adv.); esteemed, honoured, approved or liked by (gen.); intended, designed; known, understood.
मतङ्ग & °ज m. elephant.
†मतवचस् a. mindful of thoughts or prayers.
मतवन्त् a. having a purpose or object.
मतस्न n. du. a cert. internal organ of the body.
मताक्ष a. well skilled in dice.
मति or मति f. devotion, prayer, worship, hymn or song of praise; thought, purpose, mind, intention to (loc., dat., or infin.); thought, meditation, opinion, belief; understanding, intelligence. मत्या on purpose or at discretion.
मतिपूर्व a. premeditated; °र्वम् & °र्वे = seq.
मतिपूर्वकम् adv. intentionally, on purpose.
मतिभेद m. change of opinion.
मतिभ्रम m. confusion or error of mind.
मतिमन्त् a. intelligent, wise, clever.
मतिविद् a. knowing (one's) mind or heart.
मतिविभ्रम m. = मतिभ्रम.
मतिशालिन् a. endowed with intelligence, wise, clever.
मतिहीन a. opp. of prec.
मतुथ m. a wise man.
मत्क a. my, mine.
मत्कुण m. bug.
मत्कृत a. done by me.

मत्त a. intoxicated, drunk (lit. & fig.), excited, in rut.

मत्तकाशिनी f. a wanton or charming woman (lit. one appearing intoxicated).

मत्तमयूर m. an excited peacock; n. N. of a metre.

मत्तवारण m. an elephant in rut; n. top, turret.

मत्तस् adv. (= abl. of **म**) from me.

मत्तहस्तिन् m.*= **मत्तवारण** m.

मत्पर, **°परम**, & **°परायण** a. devoted to me.

मत्य n. harrow, roller; club.

मत्संस्था f. union with me.

मत्समत्व n. likeness with me.

मत्सर a. exhilarating, intoxicating, gay, merry; selfish, envious, jealous. m. the exhilarater (Soma); envy, jealousy of, eagerness for (loc. or —°), indignation.

मत्सरवन्त् a. exhilarating, intoxicating.

मत्सरिन् a. = prec. + envious, jealous of, eager for (loc. or —°).

मत्स्थ a. living in me.

मत्स्य m., **आ** f. fish.

मत्स्यघात m. killing fish.

मत्स्यण्डिका f. sugar-juice.

मत्स्यपुराण n. T. of a Purāṇa.

मत्स्यबन्ध m. fisherman.

***मत्स्यबन्धन** n. fishing hook (or fish-catching*).

मत्स्यमांस n. the flesh of fish (or fish and flesh*).

मत्स्याद् or **°द** a. eating fish.

1**मथ्**, **मन्थ्**, **मथ्नाति**, **मथ्नीते**, **मंथति** (**°ते**), **मंन्थति**, **°ते**, pp. **मथित** stir, whirl (w. **अग्निम्** excite fire by attrition), churn, produce by churning; shake, agitate, confuse, crush, grind, oppress, afflict, destroy, annihilate. C. **मन्थयति** cause (milk) to be churned. — **अभि** twirl, turn round, w. **अग्निम्** produce fire by attrition. **आ** churn (the sea), shake, agitate. **उद्** shake up, excite, disturb, mix, mingle; strike, hurt, cut off, tear or root out, destroy, kill. **उप** stir up, mix, mingle. **निस्** elicit by attrition out of (2 acc.), shake or tear out of (abl.), wipe off; stir about, agitate, excite, hurt, harass, crush, pound, break in pieces, destroy. **प्र** stir about, churn (the sea), tear away, cut out or off, harass, annoy, hurt, injure, lay waste, devastate, destroy. C. **प्रमाथयति** handle roughly, harass, kill. **वि** M. tear away, rend asunder, crush down; A. rout, disperse, perplex, bewilder. **सम्** pound, crush. — Cf. **उन्मथ्य**.

2**मथ्** a. killing (—°); m. churning stick.

मथन, f. **ई** (**आ**) afflicting, injuring, destroying; n. the act of afflicting etc., whirling, churning.

मथाय्, **°यति** produce fire by attrition.

मथितृ m. crusher, slayer (—°).

मथुर m. N. of a man, f. **आ** N. of sev. cities.

†**मथ्य** a. to be rubbed, to be churned out of (—°).

मथ्र a. whirling round.

1**मद्** or **मन्द्**, **मंदति**, **°ते**, **मंन्दति**, **°ते**, **ममंत्ति**, **मांद्यति**, pp. **मत्त** (q.v.) bubble, undulate, boil, be agitated or (pleasantly) excited; rejoice at, revel in (instr., gen., or loc., r. acc.), be mad or drunk with (instr.); gladden, delight, exhilarate, intoxicate. C. **मदयति**, **°ते**, **मादयति**, **°ते**, & **मन्दयति**, **°ते** A. (M.) = S. tr.; M. the same refl. — **अनु** shout or hail to, acclaim (acc.). **अभि** be glad or gladden. **उद्** be excited or out of one's senses; gladden, exhilarate. C. excite, confuse, madden. **उप** rouse, encourage. **प्र** rejoice, exult, be careless about (abl.) not attend to, take it easy. **अभिप्र** gladden, exhilarate; perplex, confound. **वि** be perplexed or confused; confound, embarrass, disturb. **सम्** rejoice together at (instr.). — Cf. **अभिमत्त**, **आमत्त** (add.), **उन्मत्त**, **प्रमत्त**, **विमत्त**, **संमत्त**.

2**मद्** (°—) = **म**; also = abl. of the same.

मंद m. excitement, inspiration, enthusiasm, intoxication, ardent passion, lust, rut, the rut-juice of an elephant; arrogance, conceit, pride in (gen. or —°); any intoxicating drink, as spirituous liquor, Soma, etc.

मदकल a. sounding or singing softly (in love or rut).

मदखेल a. playful, wanton.
1मदच्युत् a. exciting intoxication or excited by intoxication, gladdening, exhilarating, cheerful, merry.
2मदच्युत् a. dropping rut-juice.
मदच्युत a. staggering with intoxication.
मदन m. love or the god of love.
मदनमह & मदनोत्सव m. (great) festival held in honour of the god of love.
(मदनलेख m.*) & आ f. love-letter.
मदनसंदेश m. message of love.*
मदनसारिका f. a kind of bird.
मदनातुर a. love-sick.
मदनावस्थ a. enamoured; f. आ amorousness.
मदनिका f. a woman's name.
मदनोद्यान n. N. of a garden.
मदन्ती f. pl. boiling water.
मदपटु a. in rut, furious (elephant).
†मदपति m. lord of the inebriating drink (Soma).
मदप्रसेक m. the aphrodisiacal fluid.
मदयन्तिका & °यन्ती f. names of women.
मदयितृ m. intoxicater, delighter.
मदर्थम् adv. for my sake.
मदर्पण n. an offering to me.
मदलेखा f. a line of rut-juice (on an elephant's temples.
मदान्ध a. blind through drunkenness, love, or arrogance.
मदामद a. constantly excited.
मदाम्बु & मदाम्भस् n. the rut-juice of an elephant.
मदालस a. lazy from intoxication.
मदावन्त् a. intoxicated, drunk.
मदावस्था f. rut (of an elephant).
मदाश्रय a. resorted to me.
मदि & °का f. a kind of harrow or roller.
मदिन् a. gladdening, charming, intoxicating.
मदिर a. = मदिन्; f. मदिरा any inebriating drink.
मदिरदृश् & °नयन a. having beautiful (lit. intoxicating) eyes.
मदिराक्ष (f. ई) & मदिरेक्षण a. the same.
मदिष्ठ superl. to मदिन्.
मदीय a. my, mine.
मदुघ m. a kind of honey-plant or liquorice.
मदोत्कट a. excited by drink, rage, or rut.
मदोदग्र a. much excited or furious.
मदोद्धत a. puffed up with pride, haughty.
मदोन्मत्त a. intoxicated by rut or arrogance.
मद्गत a. being in me.
मद्गु m. a kind of aquatic bird or animal, N. of a mixed caste.
मद्गुर m. a kind of fish; a diver or pearl fisher (a cert. caste).
मद्भक्त a. devoted to me.
मद्भाव m. my essence.
मद्य a. exhilarating, intoxicating, charming, pleasant. n. intoxicating drink, spirituous liquor.
मद्यप m. drinking spirituous liquors, m. a drunkard.
मद्यपान n. the drinking of spirituous liquors; any spirituous drink.
मद्यभाण्ड n. vessel for spirituous liquor.
मद्यान्नविक्रय m. the sale of spirituous liquors and victuals.
मद्याजिन् a. worshipping me.
मद्र m. pl. N. of a people, sgl. the country or a prince of the M.; *n. joy or hail to (gen. or dat.)!
मद्रिक् adv. towards me.
मद्र्यञ्च् a. turned towards me; n. मद्र्यक् adv. = prec.
मद्वत् adv. like I or me.
मद्वन् a. addicted to merriness or intoxication; also = seq.
मद्वन्त् a. gladdening or intoxicating.
मद्विध a. one like me.
मधु (f. मधु, मधू, & मध्वी) sweet, pleasant, agreeable. m. N. of the first month of the year, the spring, N. of two Asuras & sev. princes; n. sweet food or drink, esp. milk, honey, Soma, mead, wine, etc.
मधुकर m., ई f. honey-maker, bee.
मधुकरिका a. woman's name.
मधुकशा f. honey-whip (myth.).
मधुकार, f. ई = मधुकर.
मधुकृत् a. making sweetness; m. bee.
मधुग्रह m. libation of honey.
मधुच्छन्द & °न्दस् m. names of men.

मधुच्युत् & °च्युत a. dropping honey or sweetness.
मधुजात a. sprung from honey.
मधुजिह्व a. honey-tongued.
मधुत्व n. sweetness.
मधुद्विष् m. foe of Madhu (Kṛṣṇa).
मधुधा a. giving sewetness.
मधुनाडी f. honey-cell.
मधुन्तम (superl.) very sweet.
मधुप a. sipping honey or sweetness; m. bee.
मधुपटल m. bee-hive.
मधुपर्क m. a mixture or offering of honey (r.).
मधुपर्णी, °पर्णी, & पर्णिका f. names of plants.
मधुपवन m. vernal wind.
मधुपा a. = मधुप.
मधुपान n. sipping honey; a cert. sweet beverage.
मधुपिङ्ग a. yellow as honey; °ङ्गाक्ष a. having such eyes.
मधुपेय a. sweet to drink; n. the drinking of sweetness.
मधुप्सरस् a. greedy for sweetness.
मधुमत्त a. excited by wine or by the spring.
मधुमद m. the intoxication of wine.
मधुमन्त् a. sweet, honied, pleasant, agreeable; f. °मती† N. of a metre, a river, a town, & sev. women.
मधुमय, f. ई made of honey, sweet as h.
मधुमांस n. honey and (or) meat.
मधुमाधवी f. a kind of spring flower or a cert. intoxicating drink.
मधुमाधव m. du. & n. sgl. the two spring months, the spring.
मधुमास m. spring month, spring time.
मधुमिश्र a. mixed with honey or sweet milk.
मधुर a. sweet, pleasant, charming, melodious, n. adv.; abstr. °ता f., °त्व n.
मधुरप्रलापिन् a. singing sweetly.*
मधुरभाषिन् a. speaking sweetly or kindly.
मधुरमय, f. ई full of sweetness.
मधुररविन् a. sounding sweetly.
मधुरस m. honey-juice, sweetness.
मधुरस्वर a. sweet-voiced, sounding sweetly; n. adv.
1मधुराक्षर n. pl. sweet or kind words.
2मधुराक्षर a. sounding sweetly.
मधुरास्वाद a. tasting sweet.
मधुरिमन् m. sweetness, suavity.
मधुरोपन्यास m. friendly address or speech.*
मधुल a. sweet.
मधुलिह् a. honey-sucking; m. bee.
मधुवचस् a. speaking kindly.
मधुवत् adv. like honey.
मधुवन n. the Honey-Wood (myth.).
मधुवर्ण a. honey-coloured or of sweet aspect.
मधुवाहन & °वाहिन्† a. bearing sweetness.
मधुव्रत a. intent upon sweetness; m. bee.
मधुश्चुत् & मधुश्च्युत a. dropping sweetness, flowing with honey.
मधुश्री f. the beauty of spring (personif.).
मधुषुत् a. producing sweetness.
मधुष्ठाल n. honey-pot.
मधुस् n. sweetness.
मधुसर्पिस् n. du. honey and clarified butter.
मधुसूदन m. the Madhu-slayer (Kṛṣṇa).
मधुस्तोक m. drop of honey.
मधुस्रव a. dropping honey.
मधुहन् & °हन्तृ m. the Madhu-slayer (Kṛṣṇa).
मधूक m. bee, N. of a tree.
मधूच्छिष्ट n. bees-wax, wax.
मधूत्सव m. the spring festival.
मधूद्यान n. a spring garden.
†मधूयु a. greedy for sweetness.
मधूलक n. honey or sweetness i.g.; f. °लिका† a kind of bee & = seq.
मधूली f. a cert. corn-fruit.
मध्य a. middle, central, moderate, indifferent, neutral; n. (also मध्ये) adv. in the midst of, inside, in or into, between, among (gen. or —°, मध्ये also °— in adv.), as subst. the middle, centre, interior, esp. the middle of the body, the waist (also m.).
मध्यग & °गत a. being (going) in the middle of, contained in, staying among (gen. or —°).
मध्यचारिन् a. going amidst (gen.).
मध्यतस् adv. from or in the middle, (from) among, out of (gen. or —°).
मध्यता f. mediocrity.
मध्यदेश m. middle region or part, esp. middle

of the body, the waist; the midland country (between Himālaya & Vindhya), pl. its inhabitants.

मध्यंदिन m. midday or midday offering.

मध्यभाग m. the middle part, esp. of the body, the waist.

मध्यम a. = **मध्य**; m. n. = prec.

मध्यमक n. = **मध्य** n., °**कं प्रविश्** enter.

मध्यमजात a. middle-born (son).

मध्यमपुरुष m. the 2nd (middle) person (g.).

मध्यमरात्र m. midnight.

मध्यमलोक m. the middle world, the earth.

मध्यमवयस n. the middle age.

मध्यमश्री m. intercessor (lying between).

मध्यमस्था a. being in the middle of (gen.); abstr. °**स्थेय** n.

मध्यमस्वर m. the middle sound (dominant).

मध्यमेषा f. a cert. part of a waggon.

मध्यमेष्ठ or °**ष्ठा** a. = **मध्यमस्था**.

मध्यरात्र m., °**रात्रि** f. midnight.

मध्यवयस् a. middle-aged.

मध्यवर्तिन् a. being in, among, or between.

मध्यस्थ a. being in the middle, being within, among, or between (gen. or —°); moderate, indifferent, neutral, impartial.

मध्यस्थता f. indifference, impartiality.

मध्यस्थान n. the middle space i.e. the air.

मध्यस्थित a. being between (gen.); indifferent, impartial, abstr. °**ता** f.

मध्या (instr. adv.) in the midst (gen.), meanwhile.

मध्यावर्ष n. the middle of the rainy season.

मध्याह्न m. midday.

मध्येनदि adv. in or into the river.

मध्येपद्मम् adv. in a lotus-flower.

मध्येपृष्ठम् adv. on the back.

मध्येरणम् adv. in the battle.

मध्येसमुद्रम् adv. in the middle of the sea.

मध्व m. N. of a man.

मध्वक m. bee.

मध्वद् & **मध्वाशिन्** a. eating sweets.

मध्वापात m. honey at the beginning.

मध्वासव m. decoction of honey.

मन्, **मन्यते**, °**ति**. **मनुते**, pp. **मत** (q.v.) think, believe, imagine; consider as or take for (2 acc., acc. & dat., or acc. & adv. in **वत्**), also refl. consider one's self as, pass for, appear as (nom. ± **इव**); think fit or right, approve of (acc.); think of, meditate on (as in prayer), intend or wish for, remember, mention, declare (acc., r. gen.); find out, invent; perceive, observe, know, understand, comprehend (gen. or acc.). With **बहु** esteem, honour, w. **लघु** disesteem, despise, w. **साधु** (± **इति**) approve, commend, w. **तृणाय** (cf. above) value at a straw, esteem lightly, w. **न** think nothing of, disregard; **मन्ये** methinks (often inserted parenthetically). C. **मानयति** (°**ते**), pp. **मानित** honour, esteem. D. **मीमांसते** (°**ति**) consider, examine, call in question. — **अति** value lightly, slighten; be proud or conceited. **अनु** assent, approve, like; acknowledge as (2 acc.); grant, impart; allow, permit; indulge, forgive; w. **न** have no patience with, dislike. C. ask (acc.) for permission, take leave of (acc.), beg for (acc.); honour, regard, consider. **अव** disregard, despise. **अभि** put one's mind upon, wish for (acc.), love, like; have (evil) intentions against (acc.), threaten, menace, hurt, injure, kill; think, suppose, take for or consider as (2 acc., P. 2 nom.). **अव** despise, treat contemptuously, disregard. **अभ्यव** the same. **परि** overlook, neglect, forget. **प्रति** answer, return, oppose (2 acc.). C. honour, applaud, regard, consider, deign to accept. **वि** distinguish. C. disgrace, disregard, slighten. **सम्** think, suppose, take for (2 acc.); intend, purpose; esteem, honour. C. honour, revere. — Cf. **अनुमत**, **अभिमत**, **विमत**, **संमत**.

मनं m. du. a cert. ornament.

मनःपूत a. pure of mind.

मनन a. thoughtful, careful; n. thought, reflection, consideration.

मनना (instr. adv.) thoughtfully, carefully.

(**मनःशिल** m. n.) & °**शिला** f. red arsenic.

मनःषष्ठ a. being six with the Manas (cf. seq.).

मनस् n. mind, soul, heart; the internal organ of perception and cognition (ph.); intellect, reason, thought; excogitation, invention; wish, inclination, desire, endeavour; sentiment, disposition; adj. —° wishing or intending to (esp. w. an infin. in तु). — Instr. मनसा in the mind, in thought; with the heart, willingly. मनः कृ take to (gen.); determine, resolve; also = ° धा, विधा, बन्ध्, etc. direct the mind towards, think of (loc., dat., acc. w. प्रति, or infin.); मनसि कृ or निधा take to heart, consider, imagine.

मनस m. N. of man, f. आ N. of a goddess, n. (—°) = prec.

मनसिज m. love or the god of love (lit. the heart-born).

मनसिजतरु m. love conceived as a tree.

मनसिजरुज् f. love-sickness.

मनस्क n. (mostly a. —°) = मनस्.

मनस्कृत m. idea (of the mind).

मनस्ताप m. heart-ache.

मनस्तेजस् a. endowed with acuteness (of mind).

मनस्मय a. spiritual (opp. material).

मनस्य्, °स्यति, °ते have in mind, intend.

मनस्यु a. wishing, desiring.

मनस्वन्त् a. full of sense or spirit.

मनस्विन् a. intelligent, wise, clever, abstr. °स्विता† f.

मनःसंताप m. grief, sorrow of heart.

1मना f. zeal, ardour, jealousy, anger.

2मना f. a cert. vessel or weight of gold.

मनाक् adv. a little, slightly, somewhat; only, merely. With न almost, nearly; न मनाक् (± अपि) not at all, by no means.

मनाय्, °यति be zealous or devout, mind, remember.

मनायी f. Manu's wife.

मनायु a. zealous, devout.

†मनावसु a. rich in devotion, faithful.

मनावी f. = मनायी.

मनीषा f. thought, reflection, understanding, wisdom; notion, idea; prayer, hymn; wish, desire.

मनीषिका f. intelligence, wisdom.

मनीषित a. desired; n. wish, desire.

मनीषिता f. intelligence, wisdom.

मनीषिन् a. thoughtful, wise, devout.

मनु m. man, coll. mankind (also मनु in मनावधि); N. of a class of divine beings (in later times thought to be 7), esp. of the father of mankind & suppositious author of a law-book.

मनुज m. man (lit. sprung from Manu or men).

मनुजनाथ & °पति m. lord of men, king.

मनुजात a. sprung from Manu or men; m. man.

मनुजाधिप & °पति m. = मनुजनाथ.

मनुजेन्द्र & °जेश्वर m. the same.

मनुर्हित a. friendly to or good for men.

मनुष m. man.

मनुष्य a. human or humane; m. man, husband.

मनुष्यकृत a. committed by men (sin).

मनुष्यजा a. born of men.

मनुष्यजात n., °जाति f. mankind.

मनुष्यत् adv. = मनुष्वत्.

मनुष्यता f. the condition of man, manhood, humanity.

मनुष्यत्रा adv. among men.

मनुष्यत्व n. = मनुष्यता.

मनुष्यदेव m. human god, i. e. a Brahman or a king.

मनुष्यमारण n. manslaughter.

मनुष्ययज्ञ m. sacrifice to men, i.e. charity, hospitality, etc.

मनुष्यराज & °राजन् m. a human king.

मनुष्यरूप n. human shape.

मनुष्यलोक m. the world of men.

मनुष्यविश् f., °विश n., °विशा f. the race of men, mankind.

मनुष्वत् adv. like (with) man or Manu.

मनुस् m. man, mankind.

मनोगत a. resting in the heart, innermost; n. thought, opinion, wish, desire.

मनोग्रहण n. captivation of the mind.

मनोग्राहिन् a. captivating the mind, ravishing.

मनोज & °जन्मन् m. = मनसिज.

1मनोजव m. the swiftness of thought.

2मनोजव a. swift as thought.

मनोजवस् (superl. °विष्ठ) & मनोजविन् a. = prec.

मनोजात a. born in the mind.

मनोजु a. = 2**मनोजव**.

मनोज्ञ a. agreeable (to the mind), pleasant, charming; abst.°**ता** f.

मनोतृ or **मनोतृ** m. inventor, disposer.

मनोदण्ड m. control over the thoughts.

मनोदुष्ट a. defiled with (evil) thoughts.

मनोभव a. born in the mind or heart; m. love, °**द्रुम** m. the love-tree (poet.).

मनोऽभिप्राय m. heart's desire.

मनोऽभिराम a. delighting the heart.

मनोभू m. = **मनोभव** m.

मनोमय, f. **ई** spiritual, mental.

मनोमृग m. the heart conceived as a deer.

मनोयुज् a. heart-yoked (harnessed by mere wish, or suited to the mind i. e. judicious, wise).

मनोरथ m. wish, desire, fancy (lit. heart's joy).

मनोरथान्तर m. inhabitant of the heart, the beloved of (gen.).*

मनोरम a. charming (the mind), lovely, beautiful.

मनोराग m. affection of the heart.

मनोरुज् f. affliction of the heart.

मनोलौल्य n. fancy (of the mind), caprice.

मनोवाक्कर्मन् n. pl. thoughts, words, or acts.

मनोवृत्ति f. operation or state of the mind.

मनोहन् a. heart-killing.

मनोहर (f. **आ** & **ई**) captivating, charming, delightful (lit. heart-taking); abstr. °**त्व** n.

मनोहराकार a. having a fine figure.

मनोहारिन् a = **मनोहर**.

मन्तव्य or **मन्तव्य** a. to be thought or supposed (n. impers.), to be taken for (nom.).

मन्तु m. adviser, manager, ruler (also f.); advice, counsel, direction, plan, intention.

मन्तुमन्त् a. (only voc. **मन्तुमस्**) good counsellor, ruler.

मन्तृ m. thinker, assenter.

मन्त्र m. (n.) speech, esp. sacred speech or text, prayer, hymn, etc.; charm, spell; deliberation, counsel, advice; plan, intention, secret.

मन्त्रकाल m. time of deliberation.

मन्त्रकृत् m. composer or reciter of a sacred text; counsellor, emissary.

मन्त्रज्ञ a. kowing sacred texts or experienced in counsel.

मन्त्रण n., °**णा** f. consultation, deliberation.

मन्त्रतत्त्वविद् a. experienced in (the nature of) counsel.

मन्त्रतस् adv. with respect or according to the sacred texts.

मन्त्रद a. teaching the sacred texts or giving advice.

1**मन्त्रदर्शिन्** a. knowing the sacred texts.

2**मन्त्रदृश्** a. = prec.; m. poet of hymns or counsellor.

मन्त्रपद n. magical word, spell.

मन्त्रपुस्तिका f. magical book.

मन्त्रप्रभाव m. the power of magic.*

मन्त्रबल n. the same.

मन्त्रभेद m. a kind of magical incantation; breach or betrayal of counsel.

मन्त्रमूल a. rooted in counsel or deliberation.

मन्त्रय्, **मन्त्रयति** & **मन्त्रयते**, pp. **मन्त्रित** (q.v.) speak, utter; deliberate with (instr. ±**सह**) about (dat.); talk over, consider; determine to (infin.); counsel, advice (acc. of pers. or thing); consecrate with sacred or magical texts, (cause a person to speak.*). — **अनु** follow with sacred texts (— **इति**); consecrate, dismiss, exhort, take leave of (acc.). **अभि** address, speak to (2 acc.), woo (a girl), conjure, charm, salute, bid farewell to (acc.). **आ** speak to, address, ask, invite, summon, greet (in coming or going). **उपा** address, invite or appoint to (loc. or dat.), take leave of (acc.). **उप** call near, invite to (dat.), persuade, conciliate. **नि** call or summon to (loc.); also = **उपनि** invite, esp. by means of i.e. by offering (instr.) **परि** consecrate (cf. S.). **प्रति** call to (acc.), consecrate. **सम्** consult together, deliberate with (inst. ± **सह** or **समम्**) consider, salute. — Cf. **आमन्त्रित** (also add.).

मन्त्रवन्त् a. accompanied by or familiar with sacred texts, n. adv.

मन्त्रवर्ण m. the syllables or contents of a sacred text.

मन्त्रवाद m. the purport or contents of a sacred text; w. **श्लोक** m. a sacred stanza.

मन्त्रवादिन् m. reciter of magical formulas, conjurer.

मन्त्रविद् a. knowing sacred texts or magical incantations.

मन्त्रविद्या f. magic art.

मन्त्रशक्ति f. the power or a means of incantation.

मन्त्रसंस्कार m. a rite performed with sacred texts, **°कृत्** a. performing such a rite.

मन्त्रसंहिता f. collection of Vedic hymns.

मन्त्रसिद्ध a. thoroughly versed in the art of magic.

मन्त्राधिराज m. the king of spells (a Vetāla).

मन्त्राराधन n. winning by spells, conjuring.

मन्त्रित a. deliberated, talked over (n. impers.); advised, counselled, consecrated with sacred texts or magical formulas; n. deliberation, plan.

मन्त्रिता f., **°त्व** n. the office of a king's minister or councillor.

मन्त्रिदुहितृ f. a minister's daughter.*

मन्त्रिन् a. wise, clever. m. enchanter, conjurer; a king's minister or councillor.

मन्त्रिपुत्र, °सुत, & °सूनु m. a minister's son.

मन्थ् v. 1**मथ्**.

मन्थ m. stirring, churning, killing, slaying; a mixed beverage; spoon for stirring, churning-stick; a kind of antelope.

मन्थन a. & n. kindling fire by friction; n. also stirring, shaking i.g.

मन्थर a. slow, lazy, tardy; dull, stupid; f. **आ** N. of a woman. °— & n. adv.; abstr. **°ता** f.

मन्थरक m. N. of sev. men & a tortoise.

मन्थरित a. tired, languid.

मन्था f. churning or churning-stick.

मन्थान m. shaker (E. of. Çiva); churning-stick or a cert. instrument for kindling fire.

मन्थितव्य a. to be rubbed or kindled by friction.

मन्थितृ m. stirrer, shaker.

मन्थिन् a. stirring, shaking; m. Soma juice mixed with meal.

मन्थिप a. drinking mixed Soma (cf. prec.).

मन्थ्य a. to be kindled by friction (fire).

मन्द a. slow, lazy, tardy in (loc. or —°); dull, inert, weak (lit. & fig.), stupid. °— & n. (also doubled) slowly, tardily, gradually, softly. Abstr. **°ता** f., **°त्व** n.

मन्दग & **°गति** a. moving slowly.

मन्दचेतस् a. of slow or weak understanding, stupid, dull.

मन्दच्छाय a. of little brilliance or beauty.

मन्दधी a. = **मन्दचेतस्**.

मन्दन a. merry, gay.

मन्दपाल m. N. of a Rishi.

मन्दप्रज्ञ a. = **मन्दचेतस्**.

मन्दफल a bearing little fruit or having few results.

मन्दबुद्धि a. = **मन्दचेतस्**.

मन्दभागिन् a. having little luck, unfortunate.

मन्दभाग्य a. = prec.; n. & **°ता** f. misfortune.

मन्दभाज् a. = prec. a.

मन्दमति = **मन्दचेतस्**; m. N. of a man & a lion.

मन्दमन्दम् adv. very slowly, by small degrees.

मन्दमेधस् a. = **मन्दचेतस्**.

मन्दय्, °यति weaken, diminish.

मन्दयत्सख a. rejoicing friends.

मन्दयु a. cheerful, gay.

मन्दर m. N. of a sacred mountain, a tree in paradise, & sev. men.

मन्दविचेष्टित a. moving slowly.

मन्दवीर्य a. of little strength, weak.

मन्दसान a. enjoying one's self, delighted, pleased, glad, intoxicated.

मन्दाकिनी f. N. of sev. rivers & a mountain.

मन्दाक्रान्त a. slowly approaching; f. **आ** N. of a metre.

मन्दात्मन् a. = **मन्दचेतस्**.

मन्दादर a. having little regard for, careless about (loc.).

मन्दाय्, °यते tarry, linger, be weak or faint.

मन्दार m. coral tree (also a tree of paradise, cf. **मन्दर**).

मन्दारक m. = prec.; f. **°रिका** a woman's name.

मन्दारवती f. a woman's name.
मन्दि & मन्दिन् a. delightful, charming; cheerful, gay, inspirited.
मन्दिर n. dwelling, house, castle, palace, temple.
मन्दिष्ठ (superl.) most delightful.
मन्दी कृ weaken, diminish, slacken; w. भू P.
मन्दु a. exhilarated, inspirited.
मन्दुरा f. horse-stable; °पाल m. groom.
मन्दोत्साह a. having little energy or zeal; not very enthusiastic.
मन्दोदरी f. N. of a wife of Rāvaṇa.
मन्दौत्सुक्य a. having little desire to (प्रति).
मन्द्र a. pleasant, charming, sweet, esp. well sounding, pleasant to the ear, deep, hollow (voice or sounds i.g.); n. adv.
मन्द्रजिह्व a. pleasant-voiced.
मन्द्रयु a. sounding merrily or sweetly.
मन्धातृ m. thinker, devout or pious man.
मन्निमित्तम् adv. for my sake.
मन्मथ m. love or the god of love (lit. the shaker or agitator).
मन्मथलेख m. love-letter.
मन्मथानल m. the fire of love.
मन्मन् n. thought, devotion, prayer, praise, hymn.
मन्मय a. sprung from (lit. consisting of) me.
मन्य a. thinking one's self—, appearing as, passing for (—°).
मन्या f. du. & pl. the muscles of the neck, neck i.g.
मन्यु m. mood i.e. temper of mind, esp. high spirit, ardour, zeal; passion, wrath, anger at (loc. or acc., w. प्रति), fury, rage (often personif.); distress, grief, sorrow; abl. मन्युतस् adv.
मन्युमन्त् a. spirited, zealous, wrathful, angry.
मन्युमी a. destroying (hostile) fury or in fury.
मन्युमोक्ष m. abandoning anger, reconciliation.
मन्वन्तर n. (m.) the age of a Manu (now the seventh & seven others are to follow).
मन्विद्ध a. kindled by men.
ममक a. my, mine.
ममत् (repeated & w. चन or चिद्) now—then—at another time.
ममता f., ममत्व n. selfishness, egoism.
ममाय्, °यते to envy (acc.).
ममृवंस्, f. मम्रुषी moribund.
मम्म & °क m. a man's name.
मम्मट m. N. of a writer.
1मय, f. ई made or consisting of (only —°); m. the Former, N. of an Asura.
2मय m. horse, f. मयी mare.
मयन्त or मयन्द n. N. of a metre.
मयस् n. refreshment, cheer, delight.
मयस्कर a. causing delight.
मयु m. a Kimpuruṣa or some other man-like animal.
मयूख m. peg; ray of light; p. °वन्त् † & °खिन् †.
मयूर m., ई f. peacock or hen; abstr. °ता† f., °त्व† n.
मयूरपक्षिन् a. adorned with peacock's feathers (arrow).
मयोभव a. refreshing, gladdening; m. = मयस्.
मयोभु, °भू (f. °भू), or °भुव a. = prec. a.
मय्य m. N. of a Brahman.
मर m. dying, death.
मरक m. epidemic, plague.
मरकत n. emerald.
मरकतमय (f. ई) made of emerald.
मरण n. = मर; °णं कृ to die.
मरणदशा f. the hour of death.
मरणभीरुक a. fearing death.*
मरणान्त & °न्तिक a. ending in death.
मराय a. mortal.
मराल m. a kind of swimming bird; *an elephant.*
मरिच m. the pepper shrub; n. grain of pepper.
मरीच m. & n. = prec.; m. also = मरीचि m.
मरीचचूर्ण s. ground pepper.*
मरीचि f. mote in the air, beam of light (also मरीची); m. N. of a Prajāpati, the father of Kaçyapa.
मरीचिका f. mirage.
मरीचिन् m. the sun (lit. = seq. a.)
मरीचिमन्त् a. having rays; m. the sun.
मरीचिमालिन् a. wreathed with rays; m. = prec. m.
मरीमृश a. touching, groping.
मरु m. waste, desert (often pl.); mountain.

मरुत् m. wind, god of the wind (only pl.), breath, air.
मरुत्त m. N. of sev. princes.
मरुत्तम (superl.) quite like the Maruts.
मरुत्पति m. lord of the Maruts (Indra).
मरुत्वन्त् a. having the Maruts (Indra).
मरुत्सख a. having the wind for a friend (clouds or fire).
मरुत्सखि a. having the Maruts for friends.
मरुत्सहाय a. = मरुत्सख (fire).
1मरुद्गण m. the host of the Maruts.
2मरुद्गण a. belonging to the host of the Maruts.
मरुद्वृध a. rejoicing in the Maruts.
मरुधन्वन् m. desert land, wilderness.
मरुस्थल n., °ली f. the same.
1मर्क m. eclipse (of the sun).
2मर्क m. N. of the Purohita of the Asuras etc.
मर्कट m., ई f. ape, monkey.
मर्डितृ m. pitier.
मर्त m. a mortal, man.
मर्तव्य n. impers. it must be died.
मर्त्य a. mortal, m. man.
मर्त्यता f., °त्व n. mortality, human condition.
मर्त्यत्रा adv. among men.
मर्त्यभुवन n., °लोक m. the world of mortals, the earth.
मर्त्येषित a. sent by mortals.
मर्द a. (—°) = seq. a.; m. violent pressure, hard rubbing.
मर्दन, f. ई crushing, grinding, rubbing, pressing, afflicting, destroying (gen or —°); n. the action of crushing etc., also anointing with (°—).
मर्दनीय a. to be crushed or trodden down.
मर्दल m. a kind of drum.
मर्दितव्य a. = मर्दनीय.
मर्दिन् a. (—°) = मर्दन a.
मर्मग, °च्छिद्, & °च्छेदिन् a. going to (cutting through) the vitals, very painful.
मर्मच्छेद m. abstr. to मर्मच्छिद् (v. prec.).
मर्मज्ञ a. knowing the weak spots; i.g. knowing, clever, deeply versed in or familiar with (—°).
मर्मन् n. open part of the body, vulnerable or weak spot.
मर्मभेदिन् a. = मर्मच्छिद्, m. arrow.
मर्ममय a. consisting of or relating to the mortal parts of man.
मर्मर a. & m. rustling, murmuring.
मर्मविद् & °वेदिन् a. = मर्मज्ञ.
मर्मस्पृश् & मर्महन् (f. °घ्नी) touching or striking the vitals, very painful or injurious (lit. & fig.).
मर्य m. man, esp. young man, lover, suitor; pl. men, servants, attendants.
मर्यक m. little man.
मर्यतस् adv. from or amongst young men.
मर्यादा f. limit, boundary, frontier; coast, shore; the legal or moral bounds, order, law, rule, agreement, contract.
मर्यादाभेदक m. destroyer of landmarks.
मर्यादिन् a. observing the boundaries; m. borderer, neighbour.
मर्श m. a cert. sternutatory.
मर्शन n. touching, inquiring, examining.
*मर्ष m. patient endurance.
मर्षण a. bearing, forgiving (—°); n. = prec.
मर्षणीय a. to be borne or forgiven.
मर्षिन् a. patient, forbearing.
मल n. m. dirt, impurity (lit. & fig.); a dirty garment (only n.).
मलग m. fuller, washerman.
मलपङ्क s. dirt, mire; poss. °ङ्किन्.
मलय m. N. of a mountain (also °गिरि m.); pl. N. of a people.
मलयज a. grown on the Malaya mountains; m. n. sandal tree or wood.
मलयद्रुम m. the sandal tree.
मलयपर्वत & °भूभृत् m. the Malaya mountains.
मलयाचल & मलयाद्रि m. the same.
मलयानिल m. a wind from the Malaya mountains.
मलवन्त् a. dirty.
मलावह a. causing impurity.
मलिन a. dirty, impure (lit. & fig.); dark-coloured, gray, black. m. a religious mendicant; n. meanness, fault, sin.
मलिनय्, °यति, pp. मलिनित soil, defile.
मलिनिमन् m. darkness, meanness, wickedness.
मलिनी w. कृ = मलिनय्, P. °भू.
मलिनीकरण n. soiling, contamination.

मलिनीकरणीय a. fit to cause pollution.

मलिम्लु or मलिम्लुं m. robber.

मलिम्लुसेना f. band of robbers.

मलिम्लुच् & °म्लुचं m. robber, thief.

मलीमस a. = मलिन a.

मल्ल m. wrestler by profession, athlete; pl. N. of a caste & a people.

मल्लघटी f. a kind of pantomime.

मल्लयुद्ध n. fistic combat.

मल्लिका f. a kind of jasmine.

मल्लिकाक्ष m. a kind of swan (lit. jasmine-eyed).

*मल्लिगन्धि n. a kind of Agallochum.

मल्लिनाथ m. N. of an author.

मल्ली f. = मल्लिका.

मल्वं a. inconsiderate, foolish, silly.

मल्हं a. dewlapt.

मशंक m. biting insect, gnat, fly.

मषि or मषी f. powder, esp. bone-black, ink.

मसार m. sapphire or emerald.

मसि or मसी f. = मषि & मषी.

मसीगुडिका f. globule or blot of ink.*

मसूर m. lentil.

मसूस्य n. a kind of grain.

मसृण a. soft, smooth, tender.

मसृणय्, °यति, pp. मसृणित soften, smoothen.

*मस्कर m. bamboo.

मस्करिन् m. religious mendicant (p. to prec.).

मस्तक m. n. head, skull, top, point.

मस्तकोत्तंस m. head-wreath, diadem.

मस्तिष्क m. n. the brain.

मंस्तु n. sour cream.

मस्तुलुङ्ग m. n. the brain.

1मह्, महते, महयति, °ते, pp. महित (q.v.) A. (M.) gladden, delight, exalt, refresh, excite, impel; esteem highly, honour; M. be glad, rejoice at (instr. or acc.); grant, bestow. — सम् stir up, excite; honour, celebrate.

2मंह (f. मंह & मही) great, mighty, powerful, strong, abundant; old, aged. f. मही the earth (as the great one), ground, soil, land, country, kingdom; space; host; cow; du. heaven and earth; pl. rivers, waters.

1मह m. feast, festival.

2मह a. great, rich, abundant, abstr. °ता† f.; n. pl. great deeds.

महत्तम (superl.) very great or high; m. an eminent man.

महत्तर (compar.) greater, mightier, stronger than (abl.); very great etc. m. chief, principal, courtier, chamberlain (also °क* m.).

महत्ता f., °त्व n. greatness, power, high rank, importance, authority.

महद्भय n. great danger or distress.

महन् n. greatness, abundance, might (only instr. sgl. & pl.).

महन n. praise.

महनीय a. to be praised or celebrated.

महन्त् (महान्त्, f. महती; °— mostly महा q.v.) great (in all mgs, i.e.) big, large, tall; extensive, long, protracted, far advanced; much, many, abundant, numerous; intensive, thick, dense; mighty, important, high, noble, distinguished, eminent. — m. a great or noble man, (± आत्मन्) the intellect; n. anything great or important; greatness, might.

महये (dat. inf.) for joy.

महय्य a. to be honoured or delighted.

महर् & महर्लोक m. N. of a cert. world.

महर्त्विज् or महत्विज् m. great or chief priest.

महर्द्धि & °क a. very rich or mighty.

महर्द्धिन् a. the same.

महर्षभ m. great bull.

महर्षि m. great Rishi.

महल्ल (& °क) m. eunuch in a harem.

1मंहस् n. greatness, might, lustre, splendour, abundance, plenty, feast, festival, joy, pleasure; instr. pl. मंहोभिस् with might, greatly.

2महस् adv. joyfully, willingly, quickly.

मंहस्वन्त् a. great, mighty, splendid, glorious, delightful.

महस्विन् a. splendid, brilliant.

महा (only °— & acc. sgl. महाम्) = महन्त्.

महाकथा f. great tale.

महाकपाट m. large door.

महाकल्प m. great cycle of time.

महाकवि m. great poet.

महाकाय a. of great stature, gigantic.
महाकाल m. a form and a temple of Çiva; f. ई a form of Durgā.
महाकाव्य n. great or classical poem.
1महाकुल n. noble family.
2महाकुल a. of noble family or race.
महाकुलीन a. = prec. 2, abstr. °ता f.
महाक्रतु m. great sacrifice.
महाक्रोध a. very angry, wrathful.
महागण m. great multitude or crowd.
1महागद m. great sickness.
2महागद m. great antidote.
3महागद a. armed with a large club.
महागल a. long- or thick-necked.
महागिरि m. great mountain.
1महागुण m. chief or cardinal virtue.
2महागुण a. possessing great qualities or merits, distinguished; abstr. °त्व n.
महागुरु m. a very venerable person.
महागृह m. great or noble house.
महाग्राम m. great multitude or village.
महाग्रीव a. long-necked (Çiva).
महाघोर a. most horrible.
महाघोष a. loud-sounding, noisy.
महाचपला f. N. of a metre.
महाचल m. great mountain.
महाज m. a large he-goat.
महाजन m. a great or eminent man (also coll.); a great number of men, people (also pl.).
महाजव a. very swift, rapid.
महाजानु m. N. of a Brahman (large-kneed).
महाज्वर m. great fever or affliction.
महाज्वाल a. of great splendour.
महाढ्य a. very rich or wealthy.
महातपस् a. much afflicted or doing severe penance; m. N. of a sage.
महातपस्विन् a. = prec. a.; m. a great ascetic.
महातल n. N. of a cert. hell.
महातिघोर a. = महाघोर.
महातेजस् a. possessing great fire or lustre; glorious, mighty.
1महात्मन् m. the supreme spirit, the intellect (ph.).
2महात्मन् a. large-minded, magnanimous, generous, noble, eminent.
महात्यय m. great sorrow, a. causing gr. s.
महात्याग m. great liberality; a. = seq.
महात्यागिन् a. very liberal or generous.
महादुःख n. great sorrow.
महादेव m. the great god, esp. Rudra-Çiva or Viṣṇu; f. ई the great goddess i.e. Pārvatī or Lakṣmī, the first wife of a king.
महादेवकृत्या f. a sin committed against Çiva.
महादोष m. great fault or wrong.*
महाद्युति a. of great splendour or glory.
1महाधन n. great contest or booty; great wealth.
2महाधन a. having or costing much money; rich, wealthy, costly, precious.
महानग्न m. lover or athlete; f. आ & ई whore (lit. quite naked).
महानद m. a great river or stream; f. ई the same, E. of Gaṅgā.
महानरक m. a cert. hell.
महानस n. freight-waggon, kitchen.
महानाग m. great serpent or elephant.
महानाटक n. a great drama.
1महानाद m. lound sound.
2महानाद a. loud-sounding.
महानाम्नी f. pl. E. of cert. Vedic verses.
महानिश् & °निशा f. dead of night, midnight.
महानील a. dark blue, black; m. sapphire.
महानुभाव a. high-potent or magnanimous; abstr. °ता f., °त्व n.
महान्त a. great; m. N. of a king.
महापक्ष a. having many relatives or adherents.
महापङ्क m. n. deep mire.
महापङ्क्ति f. N. of a metre.
महापण्डित a. greatly learned.
महापथ m. chief road or the long journey i.e. death.
महापराध m. great crime.
महापरिभव m. great outrage or indignity.*
महापशु m. large cattle.
महापात m. long flight; a. far-flying.
महापातक n. great crime; poss. °किन्.
महापाप n. great evil or sin.
महापाप्मन् a. very wicked.
महापार्श्व a. broad-sided (leech); m. N. of a Dānava & a Rākṣasa.

महापुण्य a. very auspicious or fortunate; very good, pure, or holy.
महापुर n., °री f. great stronghold or city.
महापुरुष m. a great man or the great spirit.
महापृष्ठ a. broad-backed.
महाप्रकरण n. a great drama of a cert. kind.
महाप्रजापति m. the great lord of creatures (Viṣṇu).
महाप्रपञ्च m. the great universe.
महाप्रभ a. very resplendent; f. °प्रभा great brightness.
महाप्रभाव a. of great power or might.
महाप्रभु m. great lord or king.
महाप्रमाण a. of great extent or size.
महाप्रस्थान n. the great journey, i.e. death; °प्रस्थानिक or °प्रास्थानिक a. relating to it.
महाप्रश्न m. great or puzzling question.
महाप्राज्ञ a. very wise.
1**महाप्राण** m. strong breath or great strength.
2**महाप्राण** a. poss. to prec.
1**महाफल** n. great fruit or reward, large testicle.
2**महाफल** a. bringing great reward.
महाबल a. very strong or mighty.
महाबाहु a. long-armed (E. of gods & heroes).
महाबिल n. deep cave or hole.
महाबुद्धि a. of great understanding, very wise or clever.
महाबृहती f. N. of a metre.
महाब्राह्मण m. a great Brahman.
महाभय n. great danger or dread; a. very dangerous or dreadful.
महाभाग & °गिन् a. having a great portion or a good lot; fortunate, prosperous, distinguished, eminent.
महाभागधेय a. of high rank or power.*
महाभाग्य n. high power or importance.
महाभारत s. (± आहव or युद्ध) the great war of the Bharatas; n. (± आख्यान) the great narrative of the war of the Bh.
महाभाष्य n. the great comment (of Patañjali on the grammatical Sūtras of Pāṇini).
महाभिजन m. high or noble descent.
महाभियोग m. great accusation (j.).
महाभीशु a. very resplendent.
महाभीषणक a. very dreadful.
महाभुज a. = महाबाहु.
महाभूत a. (being) great; m. great creature or being; n. grosser element (ph.).
महाभूमि f. great realm or dominion.
1**महाभोग** a. of great extent.
2**महाभोग** a. having great windings or coils (also °वन्त् or °भोगिन्); m. a serpent.
3**महाभोग** m. great enjoyment; a. causing it.
महाभोज m. great prince, N. of a king.
महाभ्र n. great or dense cloud.
महामख m. great or chief sacrifice.
महामणि m. great or precious jewel.
महामति a. = महाबुद्धि.
महामत्स्य m. a large fish.
महामनस् a. high-minded, proud or generous.
महामनुष्य m. great person, gentleman.
महामन्त्रिन् m. chief councillor, prime minister.
महामह a. very mighty.
महामहार्घ a. most precious or dear.*
महामांस n. precious meat, esp. human flesh, °विक्रय m. sale of h. f.
महामात्य m. = महामन्त्रिन्.
महामात्र a. great (in measure), best, first of (-°). — m. great man, high official, minister; elephant-driver or keeper.
महामाय a. very deceitful or illusory; m. E. of sev. gods, f. आ & ई E. of Durgā.
महामाया f. the Great Illusion (ph.).
1**महामुख** n. large mouth.
2**महामुख**, f. ई large-mouthed.
महामुनि m. great sage.
महामूर्धन् a. large-headed.
महामृग m. large deer, elephant.
महामृध n. great battle.
महामेघ m. great or dense cloud.
महामेरु m. the great mountain Meru.
महायज्ञ m. great or chief sacrifice.
महायशस् a. very glorious.
महायुग n. a great Yuga (= 4 ages of the world).
महायुद्ध n. great battle.
महायोगिन् m. great Yogin, E. of Viṣṇu & Çiva.
महायोगेश्वर m. great lord of devotion (Viṣṇu).

महाय्य a. to be gladdened or honoured.
1महारजन n. safflower.
2महारजन a. dyed with safflower.
महारण m. great battle.
महारण्य n. large wood.
महारत्न n. precious jewel or pearl.
1महारथ m. great chariot or great hero.
2महारथ a. having a great chariot.
महारथ्या f. great or high street.
महारव m. loud sound or cry; a. loud-sounding, crying, roaring.
महाराज m. great king, sovereign.
महाराज्ञी f. great queen, E. of Durgā.
महारात्र n., °त्रि f. dead or close of night.
महाराव m. great howl or cry.
महाराष्ट्र m. pl. the Mahrattas; f. ई the language of the M.
महारौरव m. a cert. hell.
महार्घ a. precious, costly, dear; abstr. °ता f.
महार्णव m. (great) ocean.
महार्थ m. great thing, important matter; adj. great, important, wealthy.
महार्ह a. = महार्घ.
महावद m. proclaimer of great things, i.e. teacher of sacred knowledge.
महावध a. wielding a mighty weapon.
महावन n. large forest.
महावसु a. having much wealth.
महावाक्य n. great speech, i.e. either literary work or chief sentence.
महावात m., °वात्या f. tempest, storm-blast.
माहाविक्रम a. having great might or courage; m. N. of lion.
महाविपुला f. N. of a metre.
महावीचि m. a cert. hell.
महावीर m. great hero, E. of Viṣṇu.
महावीरचरित n. T. of a play.
महावीर्य a. of great strength or energy.
महावृक्ष m. large tree.
महावृष m. great bull; pl. N. of a people.
महावेग a. very impetuous or rapid; stormy (sea).
महाव्याहृति f. great word (r.).
1महाव्रत n. great vow.
2महाव्रत a. having undertaken a great vow.
महाशङ्ख m. a great conch-shell.
महाशन a. eating much, voracious.
महाशनिध्वज m. flag with a great thunderbolt.
1महाशब्द m. loud sound.
2महाशब्द a. loud-sounding.
1महाशय m. the sea (lit. great receptacle).
2महाशय a. high-minded, magnanimous.
महाशर m. great arrow.
महाशरीर a. big-bodied.
महाशल्क m. a kind of sea-crab.
1महाशाल m. the owner of a great house.
2महाशाल m. a great Çāla-tree.
महाशिरस् a. large-headed.
महाशिव m. great Çiva.
महाशैल m. great rock or mountain.
महाश्मन् m. precious stone.
महाश्मशान n. a large burial-place.
महासती f. a virtuous woman or wife.
महासतोबृहती f. N. of a metre.
महासत्त्र n. great Soma sacrifice.
1महासत्त्व m. great creature or being.
2महासत्त्व a. great-minded, noble, virtuous, courageous; abstr. °ता f.
महासन n. great or splendid seat, throne.
महासाधु a. very good, excellent; f. °साध्वी = महासती.
महासार a. solid, pithy, strong, precious.
महासिंह m. great lion.
महासेन a. having a great army; E. of Skanda, N. of sev. kings.
महासेना f. great army.
महास्त्र n. great weapon or bow.
महास्य a. large-mouthed.
महास्वन m. loud sound or cry; adj. loud-sounding.
महास्वर a. = prec. a.
महाहनु a. large-jawed.
महाहव m. great fight or war.
1महाहविस् n. chief oblation or clarified butter; E. of Çiva.
2महाहविस् m. N. of a Hotṛ.
महाहस्त & °हस्तिन् a. large-handed.
महाहि m. great serpent.
महाह्न m. great (cf. broad) day, afternoon.
महाह्रद m. large tank or pool.
मंहि adj. (only °— & nom. acc. sgl.) great; adv. greatly, much.

मंहिकेरु a. praising highly.
महित a. honoured, celebrated, highly esteemed by (gen. or —°).
महिता f., °त्वं & °त्वनं n. greatness, might.
महिंन् & महिंन a. great, mighty.
माहना instr. = महिम्ना (cf. seq.).
महिमंन् m. greatness, might, majesty; instr. also as adv. greatly, mightily.
महिमन्त् a. much, abundant.
†महिरत्न a. having great treasures.
महिला f. woman, wife.
मंहिव्रत a. having great power or dominion.
महिषं, f. मंहिषी mighty, strong. — m. the sun (w. सुपर्ण), buffalo (± मृगं), high priest, a man's name; f. मंहिषी buffalo-cow, woman of high rank, esp. the (first) wife of a king.
महिष्ठ (superl.) greatest.
मही v. 2मंह्.
महीकम्प m. earth-quake.
महीक्षित् m. earth-ruler, king.
महीचर & °चारिन् a. moving on the earth.
महीज a. earth-born; m. plant, tree.
महीतल n. surface of the earth.
महीदुर्ग n. earth-fortress.
महीधर a. earth-bearing; m. mountain or Viṣṇu.
महीध्र m. = prec. m.
महीनाथ & महीन्द्र m. earth-lord, king.
महीन्द्रेन्द्र m. king of kings.
महीप, °पति, & °पाल m. earth-protector or ruler, king.
महीपृष्ठ n. surface (lit. back) of the earth.
महीभर्तृ m. king (lit. = seq.).
महीभुज् m. king (earth-possessor).
महीभृत् m. king or mountain (earth-bearer).
महीमय, f. ई earthen.
महीय्, °यंते be great, happy, or blessed; be exalted or honoured by (gen.).
मंहीयंस् (compar.) greater or very great.
महीयां f. joy, bliss, °यै dat. as inf.
महीयु a. joyful, merry.
महीरुह् m. (nom. °रुट्) tree (earth-grower).
महीरुह m. = prec.
महोलुका f. cow.
महीश्वर m. earth-lord, king.

महें (dat. inf.) for joy.
†महेनदि (voc.) large river.
महेन्द्रं m. the great Indra (abstr. °त्व † n.) or a great king, N. of sev. kings.
महेन्द्रचाप m. Indra's bow i.e. the rainbow.
महेन्द्रमन्दिर n. Indra's palace.
†महेमते (voc.) high minded.
महेश m. the great lord or god, E. of Çiva; a man's name.
महेश्वर m. = prec., also E. of sev. other gods, esp. of the 4 world-protectors; f. ई E. of Durgā.
महेषु m. great arrow.
महेषुधि f. great quiver.
महेष्वास m. great bowman or archer.
महोक्षं m. large bull, abstr. °ता † f.
महोत्सव m. great festival.
महोत्साह a. having great energy or perseverance.
महोदधि m. sea, ocean.
1महोदय m. great happiness, bliss.
2महोदय a. very fortunate or lucky.
1महोदर n. large belly, dropsy.
2महोदर a. big-bellied; N. of a serpent-demon etc.
महोपाध्याय m. great teacher.
महोरग m. great serpent.
महोरस्क a. broad-breasted.
महोल्का a. great firebrand or meteor.
महोष्ठ a. large-lipped (Çiva).
महौजस् a. having great strength or might.
महौषध n. a very efficacious remedy.
महौषधि or °धी f. a very efficacious medicinal plant.
मह्मन् m. greatness.
1मां (adv. & conj.) not, that not, lest, would that not, w. imperat. or an augmentless form of a past tense (± स्म); rarely with an optative; or with aor. or fut.; often without verb. — मैवम् or मा तावत् may it not be so; मैं (= मां उ) and not, neither (prohib.).
2मा, मिंमीते (मभाति & माति), pp. मितं (q.v.) measure, mete, compare with (instr.); measure across i.e. pass through, traverse; measure out = apportion, give, grant; help

a pers. (acc.) to (dat.); prepare, arrange, form, make, create, develop, display (also refl.) show, manifest; conclude, infer; intr. (pres. माति) correspond in measure, find room in (loc.); w. न be beside one's self with (instr.). C. मापयति, °ते cause to be measured or built, build, erect. — अनु be inferior in measure, be not equal to (dat.) in (acc.); form after i.e. recreate in thought, conclude or infer from (abl.). उप apportion, grant; compare with (instr.). निस् measure out; fashion or make out of (abl. or instr.), construct, build, form, make, create, compose, produce, show, betray. अभिनिस् produce, create, make, compose. विनिस् the same; fashion out of (abl. or instr.). परि measure around; limit, measure through, complete. प्र measure, tax, estimate; frame, create, make, arrange; conceive, understand. वि measure out, pass through, count over, arrange, settle. सम् measure, make equal to or compare with (instr.), apportion, distribute, grant, bestow. — Cf. अनुमित, उपमित (add.), निर्मित, परिमित, प्रतिमित, प्रमित, संमित.

3मा f. measure.

4मा, मिमाति bellow, roar, low; w. अनु & आ bellow etc. towards (acc.).

5मा, मयते w. नि exchange, barter for (instr.).

मांस् (only °—) = seq.

मांस n. sgl. & pl. meat, flesh, abstr. °त्व† n.

मांसखण्ड n. a bit of flesh.

मांसगृध्नि a. gready for flesh.

मांसपेशी f. = मांसखण्ड.

मांसभूत a. being flesh.

मांसभेत्तृ m. who cuts a flesh-wound.

मांसमय, f. ई consisting of flesh.

मांसरुचि a. liking meat.

मांसल a. fleshy, muscular, strong.

मांसलुब्ध a. desirous of meat.

मांसविक्रय m. sale of meat.

मांसविक्रयिन् & °विक्रेतृ m. meat-seller.

मांसशोणितलेपन a. having flesh and blood for mortar (the body).

मांसाद्, °द, & °दिन् a. flesh-eating, carnivorous.

मांसाशन n. flesh-meat.

मांसाशिन् a. = मांसाद्; abstr. °शित्व n.

मांसीय्, °यति long for flesh.

माकन्द m. the mango tree.

माकर, f. ई relating to the sea monster Makara.

माकरन्द a. coming from the juice of flowers.

माकिस् adv. = ne or ne quis.

माकी f. du. heaven and earth.

माकीन a. my, mine.

माकीम् adv. ne.

माकुलि m. a kind of snake.

माक्षिक a. coming from a bee, n. honey.

माक्षीक m., आ f. spider; n. = prec. n.

मागध, f. ई relating to, coming from, or born among the Magadhas. — m. a prince of the Magadhas, pl. N. of a people (= मगध) & a caste; f. आ a princess of the M., f. ई the same or the language of the Magadhas.

माघ, f. ई relating to the constellation Maghā; m. N. of a cert. month, of a poet (cf. seq.), etc.

माघकाव्य n. Māgha's poem i.e. the Çiçupālavadha.

माघशुक्ल s. the bright half of the month Māgha.

मांघोन n. liberality.

माङ्गलिक a. bringing or wishing for happiness; n. any auspicious thing, e.g. amulet etc.

माङ्गल्य a. & n. = prec., n. also benediction, auspicious ceremony or festival.

माचिरम् adv. shortly, quick, mostly w. imper., lit. (be) not long!

माञ्जिष्ठ, °क, & °ष्ठिक a. red as madder.

माठर n. a man's name.

माठव्य m. N. of a Brahman.

माणव m. boy, lad, youngster, esp. a young Brahman.

माणवक m. = prec.; f. °विका lass, wench.

माणिक m. jeweller.

माणिक्य n. ruby; m. N. of a man.

माण्डलिक m. governor of a province.

मातङ्ग m. elephant, greatest or best of (—°); a man's name.

मातरिश्वन् m. N. of a divine being closely connected with Agni, or of A. himself.

मातलि m. N. of Indra's charioteer.

मातलिसारथि m. E. of Indra (cf. prec.).

मातली m. N. of a divine being closely connected with Yama.

मातादुहितृ f. du. mother and daughter.

मातापितृ m. du. father and mother.

मातामह m., ई f. maternal grandfather and grandmother; du. maternal grandparents.

मातुल & °क m. maternal uncle (applied also to others in confidential address).

मातुलङ्ग, °लिङ्ग, or °लुङ्ग m. citron tree; n. a citron.

मातुलानी f. the wife of a maternal uncle.

मातुलिङ्ग & °लुङ्ग v. मातुलङ्ग.

मातुलेय m., ई f. son or daughter of a maternal uncle, cousin.

1मातृ f. mother (applied also to the earth, the cow, the sticks of attrition, in respectful address to near relatives or elderly women i.g.); E. of Lakṣmī & Durgā; du. father and mother, heaven and earth; du. & pl. the sticks of attrition; pl. the (7, 8, 9, or 16) divine mothers, or the (8) female Manes.

2मातृ m. measurer (acc.), knower.

मातृक a. the mother's, maternal. m. maternal uncle; f. आ mother or grandmother.

मातृगुप्त m. N. of a king.

मातृतमा (superl.) f. very motherly.

मातृतस् adv. from the mother, on the mother's side.

मातृभक्ति f. devotion to a mother.

मातृमन्त् a. having a mother.

मातृवत् adv. as one's mother.

मातृवत्सल (a. mother-loving*;) m. E. of Skanda.

मातृष्वसृ f. a mother's sister.

मातृष्वसेय m., ई f. a mother's sister's son & daughter.

†मातृहन् m. matricide.

मात्रा f. measure, limit (in sp. & time), quantity, size, duration (also मात्र n.); unity of measure, foot; prosodial instant, moment i.g.; particle, atom; element, matter (ph.); wealth, money, utensils; n. —° in subst. all—whatever, or only, mere—; in adj. (f. आ & ई) so and so long, high, large, etc.; having or being only, consisting only of—; after a pp. just, scarcely.

मात्रक, f. °त्रिका (—°) = prec. (—°).

मात्रता f., °त्व n. abstr. to मात्र n.

मात्राछन्दस् n. a metre measured by prosodial instants.

मात्रावन्त् a. having a certain measure.

मात्रावृत्त n. = मात्राछन्दस्.

मात्राशिन् a. eating moderately.

मात्रासङ्ग m. devotion to one's utensils.

मात्रीय्, °यति take for or treat as (one's own) mother.

मात्सर्य n. envy, jealousy, discontent.

मात्स्य a. fishy or fish-like.

माथ m. destruction, annihilation.

माथक m. destroyer.

माथव m. patron. = माधव.

माथुर, f. ई coming from or belonging to Mathurā; m. an inhabitant of M., a man's name.

मादक, मादन, & मादनीय a. inebriating.

मादयितृ & मादयिष्णु a. the same.

मादृश् & मादृश (f. ई) one like me.

माद्रवती f. = माद्री.

माद्रवतीपुत्र or °सूनु m. son of M. (Nakula or Sahadeva).

माद्री f. princess of the Madras, E. of the second wife of Pāṇḍu.

माद्री f. a princess of the Madras, E. of the wives of Pāṇḍu, Kṛṣṇa, etc.

माधव, f. ई vernal; m. the second month of the spring, spring i.g.; descendant of Madhu, E. of Viṣṇu-Kṛṣṇa, Paraçurāma, etc., a man's name; f. माधवी the Mādhavī-(i.e. spring-) flower, a woman's name.

माधविका f. = prec. f.

माधवसेन m. N. of a king.

माधवाचार्य m. the teacher Mādhava, N. of a celebrated scholar.

माधवीय a. relating to Mādhava or to Mādhavācārya.

माधवीमण्डप s. Mādhavī-bower.*

माधवीलता f. Mādhavī-creeper (**°गृह** n. = prec.*).

माधुपर्किक, f. **ई** relating to the ceremony Madhuparka.

माधुरी f. & **°धुर्य** n. sweetness, charm, grace.

माधूक a. sweet-voiced.

माध्य a. middle, central.

माध्यंदिन a. meridional, midday-; m. pl. N. of a Vedic school.

माध्यम & **°क** (f. **°मिका**) central.

माध्यमिक a. = prec.; m. pl. N. of a mid-land people.

माध्यस्थ a. showing indifference; n. = seq.

माध्यस्थ्य n. indifference, neutrality.

माध्याह्निक, f. **ई** belonging to midday, noon-.

माध्विक m. who collects honey.

माध्वी a. f. sweet, du. E. of the Açvins.

माध्वीक n. a kind of liquor.

1**मान** m. opinion, conception; intention, will; pride, arrogance; respect, honour; anger, caprice, pouting, sulkiness anger (esp. in women).

2**मान** m. building, edifice, castle, house; n. the act of or an instrument for measuring, measure, extent, dimension, size, weight, esp. a cert. measure of weight, duration; picture, likeness, similarity; proof, evidence.

3**मान** m. thinker or maker, poet; N. of an ancient Rishi, pl. his race.

मानग्रहण n. (taking to) pouting.*

मानद a. giving or showing honour (to others); m. honour-giver (address of a woman to her husband or lover).

मानन n., **°ना** f. veneration, reverence.

माननीय a. to be revered or honoured.

मानभाज् a. receiving respect from (—°).

मानभृत् a. bearing pride, proud.

मानयितृ m. honourer, who respects.

मानयितव्य a. = **माननीय**.

मानयोग m. pl. the different modes of measuring or weighing.

मानव, f. **ई** descended from or relating to Manu, human. — m. human being, man; pl. the tribes of men (5 or 7), mankind, people, the subjects (of a king); N. of a Vedic school. f. **ई** daughter of Manu or man, a woman. n. a man's length (as a measure), the law-book of Manu.

मानवकल्पसूत्र n. T. of a work.

मानवगृह्यसूत्र n. the same.

मानवदेव m. king (man-god).

मानवधर्मशास्त्र n. Manu's law-book.

मानवन्त् a. enjoying honour, high-spirited, disdainful; f. **°वती** = **मानिनी** (v. **मानिन्**).

मानवपति m. man-lord, king.

मानवर्जित a. wanting or breaking honour.

मानवर्धन a. increasing honour.

मानवेन्द्र m. man-lord, king.

1**मानस**, f. **ई** (**आ**) sprung from the mind, the mind's, mental, spiritual; n. (adj —° f. **आ**) mind, spirit, heart, soul, N. of a sacred lake and place of pilgrimage.

2**मानस** a. dwelling on the lake Mānasa.

मानसक (adj. —° f. **°सिका**) = 1**मानस** n.*

मानससंताप m. mental anguish, grief.

मानाधिक a. exceeding the measure.

मानापमान n. du. honour and dishonour.

मानार्ह a. worthy of honour.

मानिता f., **°त्व** n. abstr. to seq.

मानिन् a. thinking, being of opinion; considering, regarding as, honouring, also considering etc. (one's self) as, passing for (—°); high-minded, haughty, arrogant, proud of (**तस्**) to (**प्रति**); highly honoured or esteemed; f. **°नी** an angry or pouting woman.

मानुष & **मानुष**, f. **ई** human or humane. m. (adj. —° f. **आ**) human being, man, pl. the (5) tribes of men; f. **मानुषी** a woman; n. = seq.

मानुषता f., **°त्व** n. condition of man, manhood, humanity.

मानुषदैविक a. human and divine.

मानुषराक्षस, f. **ई** a fiend in human form.

मानुष्य n. = **मानुष** n.

मानुष्यक a. human; n. = prec.

मान्त्रिक m. reciter of a text or spell, enchanter, sorcerer.

मान्थर्य n. slowness, weakness.
मान्थाल m. a kind of animal.
मान्थालव & मन्थीलव m. = prec.
मान्द a. gladdening (E. of the water).
मान्दार्य m. N. of a man.
मान्द्य n. slowness, weakness, torpor.
मान्धातृ m. N. of an ancient king.
मान्धाल m. = मान्थाल.
मान्मथ, f. ई relating to love or the god of love.
1मान्य a. to be respected, venerable; abstr. °त्व n.
2मान्य m. a patron. name.
मान्यस्थान n. ground for respect.
मापना f. meting out, measuring.
माम m. only voc. in confidential address = uncle.
मामक (f. मामिका & °मकी) my, mine.
मामकीन a. = prec.
मामतेय m. metron. of Dīrghatamas.
मायवन्त् a. = मायावन्त्.
माया f. art, supernatural or wonderful power, wile, trick, deceit, sorcery, illusion, phantom, unreality (ph.); °— being only in appearance, a feigned or phantom — (cf. seq.).
मायाकपोत m. a phantom-pigeon, °वपुस् a. having the form of it.
मायादेवी f. N. of Çākyamuni's mother.
मायाधर a. skilled in magic.
मायापटु a. the same.
मायामय, f. ई illusory, unreal.
मायामृग m. a phantom antelope.
मायायन्त्र n. magical work, enchantment.
मायायोग m. the employment of illusion or magical art.
मायावचन n. a deceptive speech.
मायावन्त् a. possessing magical power or skilled in magical art; deceptive, illusory.
मायावाद m. the doctrine of illusion (ph.).
मायाविद् a. knowing magical arts.
मायाविन् a. = मायावन्त्; m. magician, juggler.
मायिक a. deceptive, illusory.
मायिन् a. possessing magical powers, artful, wise, cunning, deceitful; m. magician, juggler; n. magic, magical art.

1मायु, charm, spell (only —°).
2मायु m. bleating, roaring, a cert. animal.
मायुक a. lowing, roaring.
मायूर, f. ई a peacock's.
मायोभव m., °भव्य n. gladness, happiness.
मार a. killing, destroying (—°). m. death, pestilence, slaughter, murder, hindrance, obstruction, the god of love, the Destroyer or Devil (with Buddhists). f. ई killing, pestilence.
मारक, f. °रिका killing, murdering (—°); m. pestilence (also r. °रिका), the god of death.
मारकत. f. ई smaragdine.
मारण n. killing, slaughter, murder (w. प्राप् suffer death); N. of a cert. magical ceremony & a mythical weapon.
मारमोहित a. infatuated by the god of love.
माररिपु m. the foe of the god of love, i.e. Çiva.*
मारव, f. ई forming or belonging to a desert.
मारात्मक a. murderous.
मारारि m. = माररिपु.
मारिन् a. dying or killing (—°).
मारिष m. honourable man (often in voc. as a respectful address).
मारीच a. relating to Marīci; m. = seq.
मारीचि & °च्य m. patron. from मरीचि.
मारीय a. belonging to the god of love.
मारुक a. perishing.
मारुत or मारुत, f. ई relating to the Maruts or the wind. — m. wind, air, the god of wind (adj. —° f. आ), E. of Viṣṇu & Rudra; f. आ N. of a woman, f. ई (sc. दिश्) the north-west.
मारुतसूनु m. the son of the god of wind, E. of Hanumant.
मारुतात्मज & मारुति m. the same.
मारुतान्दोलित a. swung or tossed by the wind.*
मारुतोद्वेल्लित a. the same.*
मार्कट f. ई apish, monkey-like.
मार्कण्डेय m. patron. of an ancient sage, pl. his race.
मार्कण्डेयपुराण n. T. of a Purāṇa.
मार्ग्, मार्गति, °ते (मार्गयति), pp. मार्गित track,

hunt, (cf. seq.), seek for, strive after, ask, request (2 acc.) परि = S.

मार्ग a. relating to game or deer. — n. (± मांस) game, venison. m. track, way, path, road, passage; mode, manner, esp. right manner, proper course; custom, use; title or head (j.), stile, diction. मार्गेण & मार्गेस् through, along (—°).

मार्गण a. asking, requiring (—°). — m. beggar, suppliant; arrow (abstr. °ता f.), n. searching, inquiring.

मार्गदर्शक m. guide (way-shower).

मार्गव m. N. of a mixed caste.

मार्गशीर्ष m. N. of a month.

मार्गस्थ a. being on the (right) way (l. & f.).

मार्गागत & मार्गायात a. coming from a journey, m. a traveller.

मार्गावलोकिन् a. waiting, impatient (lit. looking out at a persons's way).

मार्गितव्य a. to be searched for or striven after.

मार्जन, f. ई wiping away, cleansing, washing; washerman & woman. f. आ wiping out, washing; skin or sound of a drum; f. ई cleansing, purifying, brush, broom; n. wiping out, sweeping, cleansing, effacing.

मार्जार (f. ई) & °क m. cat, esp. wild cat.

मार्जारलिङ्गिन् a. having the nature of a cat.

मार्जालीय a. fond of washing (E. of Çiva); m. (scil. धिष्ण्य) a heap of earth to the right of the Vedi (r.)

मार्जाल्य a. = prec. a.

मार्जित a. cleaned, polished, smeared with (instr.); wiped off, removed, destroyed.

मार्डीक n. mercy, grace.

मार्तण्ड m. the sun or the god of the s. (cf. seq.).

मार्ताण्ड m. bird, esp. the bird in the sky i.e. the sun.

मार्त्तिक, f. ई made of clay, earthen.

मार्त्स्न a. ground fine or small.

मार्दव n. softness, meekness, kindness.

मार्ष्टि f. *washing, cleaning.

माल m. N. of a country, pl. of a people; f. आ wreath, garland, chaplet, necklace, row, line, collection, esp. of words, dictionary; n. field, garland (only °—).

मालक m. arbour, bower; f. °लिका garland, necklace; row, line, multitude; n. garland, ring.

मालति f. a kind of jasmine.

मालती f. = prec., a woman's name.

मालतीमाधव n. Mālatī and Mādhava, T. of a play.

मालय a. coming from the Malaya mountain.

1मालव m. N. of a country (Malwa), pl. its inhabitants.

2मालव, f. ई relating to the Mālavas, a prince or princess of the M.

मालवविषय m. the country of Malwa.

मालविका f. N. of a woman.

मालविकाग्निमित्र n. Mālavikā and Agnimitra, T. of a play.

मालाकार m., ई f. wreath-maker, florist.

मालावन्त् a. wreathed, crowned.

मालिक m. wreath-maker.

मालिन् a. = मालावन्त् (mostly —°). m. garland-maker, gardener; f. °नी a gardener's wife, N. of a river & a metre, a woman's name.

मालिन्य n. foulness, defilement, impurity.

मालूर m. a cert. fruit tree.

मालोपमा f. a kind of comparison (rh.).

माल्य n. wreath, crown; poss. °वन्त्, m. also N. of a Rākṣasa, a mountain, etc.

मौल्व्य n. thoughtlessness, foolishness.

मावन्त् a. one like me.

माविलम्बम् adv. without delay (cf. माचिरम्).

माष m. bean; a small weight of gold (also माषक m. n.).

माषतिलौ m. du. sesamum and beans.

1मांस n. flesh, meat.

2मांस् m. moon, month.

मास m. (adj. —° f. ई) moon (only —°), month.

मासधा adv. by the month, monthly.

मासर n. a cert. dish or drink.

मासशस् adv. month by month.

माससंचयिक a. gathering (provisions) for a month.

मासानुमासिक a. performed every month.

मासिक, f. ई pertaining to a month, happening every month, lasting a month, monthly.

मासिकान्न n. food given at a monthly Çrāddha.
मासीन a. monthly.
मासुर, f. **ई** lentil-shaped.
मास्य a. a month old.
माहात्मिक a. magnanimous, glorious.
माहात्म्य n. magnanimity, highness, majesty.
माहारजन, f. **ई** dyed with saffron.
माहाराज्य n. sovereignty.
माहाराष्ट्र, f. **ई** belonging to the Mahrattas; f. **ई** the M. language.
माहित्र n. N. of a cert. hymn.
माहिन a. joyous, glad.
माहिष, f. **ई** relating to or coming from a buffalo.
माहिषिक m. a keeper or breeder of buffaloes.
माहिषेय m. a son of the first wife of a king.
माहिष्य m. a cert. mixed caste.
माहेन्द्र, f. **ई** great Indra's, eastern; w. **धनुस्** n. rainbow.
माहेय a. earthen, f. **ई** cow.
माहेश्वर a. relating to great Çiva; m. a Çivaite.
1**मि**, **मिनोति**, **मिनुते**, pp. **मित** (q.v.) fix, establish, build, erect, measure, observe, perceive. — **उद्** set up, erect. **नि** dig in, fix, build, construct. **प्र** erect, build; perceive, understand. **वि** fix, set up, build. **सम्** fix or set up together. — Cf. **विमित**.
2**मि** v. **मी**.
1**मिक्ष्**, **मिमिक्षति** mix, stir up; prepare. C. **मेक्षयति** stir up, mix with (instr.).
2**मिक्ष्** v. **म्यक्ष्**.
मिघ् v. 1**मिह्**.
मित् f. post, pillar.
1**मित** a. measured, defined, limited; scanty, succinct, small, concise; examined, known.
2**मित** a. fixed, firm, solid.
मितज्ञु a. having firm or fixed (i.e. bent) knees.
मितद्रु a. running quickly (lit. having a firm course).
मितभाषितृ & **॰भाषिन्** a. speaking little.
मितभुक्त, **॰भुज्**, & **॰भोजन** a. eating little.
मिताक्षर a. composed in measured (i.e. metrical) language, concise, short, comprehensive; f. **आ** T. of sev. commentaries.
मिताशन a. eating little or sparingly.
मिताहार a. the same; m. as subst.
1**मिति** f. measure, weight, value.
2**मिति** f. erecting, establishing.
मित्र m. friend, comrade (mostly n., esp. in l.l.), N. of an Āditya etc.; n. friendship.
मित्रकर्मन् & **॰कार्य** n. friendly office.
मित्रकृति f., **॰कृत्य** n. the same.
मित्रगुप्त a. protected by Mitra; m. N. of a man.
मित्रता f., **॰त्व** n. friendship, intimacy.
मित्रद्रुह् (nom. **॰ध्रुक्**) treacherous or faithless to friends.
मित्रद्रोह m. abstr. to prec.
मित्रधा adv. in a friendly manner.
मित्रधित n. friendly compact.
मित्रधिति f., **मित्रधेय** n. = prec.
मित्रनन्दन a. gladdening one's friends.
†**मित्रपति** m. lord of friends or of friendship.
मित्रभाव m. friendly relation, friendship.
मित्रभेद m. separation of friends.
मित्रमहस् a. rich in friends.
मित्रलाभ m. acquisition of friends.
मित्रवत् adv. as a friend.
मित्रवत्सल a. affectionate to friends.
मित्रवन्त् a. having friends.
मित्रसंप्राप्ति f. acquisition of friends.
मित्रसह m. N. of a king & a Brahman (lit. = seq.).
मित्रसाह a. indulgent towards friends.
मित्रस्नेह m. love to friends, friendship.
†**मित्रातिथि** m. N. of a man.
मित्रामित्र n. sgl. friend and foe.
मित्रायु a. seeking friendship.
मित्रावरुण m. du. Mitra and Varuṇa.
मित्रावसु m. N. of a prince.
मित्रिन् a. befriended, allied.
मित्रिय a. friendly, coming from or relating to a friend.
मित्रीय्, **॰यति** treat or gain as friend.
मित्र्य a. = **मित्रिय**.
मिथ्, **मेथति**, **॰ते** (& **मिथति**) meet together, either associate, pair; or (more commonly) altercate, wrangle, reproach (acc.); M. contest with each other.
मिथत्या (instr. adv.) alternately or emulously.

मिथंस् adv. together, mutually, alternately, secretely, privately.
मिथ:प्रस्थान n. mutual or common departure.
मिथ:समय or °समवाय m. mutual agreement.
मिथ(:)स्पृध्य ger. rivalling with each other.
मिथिल m. pl. N. of a people.
मिथु or मिथू adv. alternately; wrongly, falsely.
मिथुनं a. paired, forming a pair; n. pair (male and female), twin couple, couple or pair i.g. (in Veda mostly m. du.); cohabitation, copulation, union, junction i.g. Abstr. मिथुनत्वं n., मिथुनभाव m.
मिथुनी w. कृ & भू or अस् pair (tr. & intr.).
मिथुया (instr. adv.) wrongly, falsely.
मिथुस् adv. mutually or = prec.
मिथ्या adv. wrongly, falsely, in vain. With ब्रू, वच्, etc. speak falsely, tell a lie; w. कृ make false, cheat; contradict, deny, w. कृ & न keep (a given word).
मिथ्याकृत a. done wrongly.
मिथ्याकोप m. feigned anger.
मिथ्याक्रय m. false price.
मिथ्याग्रह m. useless obstinacy.
1मिथ्याचार m. improper conduct.
2मिथ्याचार a. acting falsely, hypocritical.
मिथ्याज्ञान n. misapprehension, error.
मिथ्याभियोगिन् a. bringing forth a false accusation (j.).
मिथ्याभिशंसिन् a. = prec.; °शस्त a. accused falsely.
मिथ्याभिशस्ति & °भिशाप m. false accusation.
मिथ्यायोग m. wrong use or employment.
मिथ्यावचन & °वाक्य n. falsehood, lie.
मिथ्यावाद m. = prec., adj. = seq.
मिथ्यावादिन् a. speaking untruly, lying.
मिथ्याव्यापार m. wrong occupation.
मिथ्यासाक्षिन् m. false witness.
मिथ्योपचार m. feigned service or kindness.
मिद्, मेद्यति (मेदते) be fat. C. मेदयति make fat.
मिन्दा f. a bodily defect.
मिमङ्क्षु a. desirous of bathing or diving.
मिमर्दयिषु & मिमर्दिषु a. wishing to crush.
मिमिक्ष & °क्षु a. mixed, mingled.
मियेध m. sacrificial meal.
मियेध्य a. partaking of a sacrificial meal.
मिल्, मिलति, pp. मिलित (q.v.) meet, assemble, join (instr. ± सह, gen., or loc.), mix, combine; occur, happen. C. मेलयति bring together with (gen.), assemble (tr.). — सम् come together, be present, get into possession of (gen.).
मिलन n. meeting, contact.
मिलित a. met, joined, happened, occurred.
मिलिन्द m. bee.
मिश्र a. mixed, mingled; manifold, various; joined, connected, or furnished with, accompanied by (instr. ± समम्, gen., or —°); abstr. °ता† f. —° (pl.) —and his followers, —and others; °— & —° (sgl.) as title of honour in proper names, esp. those of scholars (cf. भट्ट); n. adv. among (—°).
मिश्रक a. mingled, miscellaneous; mixing, adulterating.
मिश्रकेशी f. N. of an Apsaras.
मिश्रण n. mixing, uniting.
1मिश्रधान्य n. mixed grain.
2मिश्रधान्य a. mixed of various kinds of grain.
मिश्रय्, °यति, pp. मिश्रित mix, mingle with (instr. or loc.). — वि & सम् = S.
मिश्री w. कृ = prec., w. भू mix, associate with (instr.), also of sex. intercourse.
†मिश्र (—°) = मिश्र.
मिष्, मिषति (°ते) open the eyes, look, behold (only the pres. pp. मिषन्त्, esp. in constructions as मिषतो बन्धुवर्गस्य before the eyes of the friends). — उद् = S. + blossom, expand. नि close the eyes, wink, fall asleep. — Cf. उन्मिषित.
मिष n. deceit, fraud, illusion; instr., abl., & adv. in तस् under the appearance or pretext of (—°).
मिष्ट a. savoury, dainty, sweet; n. = seq.
मिष्टान्न n. sweetmeat, dainty dish.
मिसि f. N. of sev. plants.
1मिह्, मेहति (°ते), pp. मीढ (q.v.) make water; wet, sprinkle. C. मेहयति cause to make water. — अभि urine upon (acc.). अव make water upon or towards (acc.). नि = S. परि wet by urining upon. प्र = S. प्रति

make water in the direction of (acc.). — Cf. मीढ्वंस्.

2मिंह् f. mist, fog.

मिहिका f. snow.

मिहिर् m. the sun.

मी, मिनाति (मिनोति) damage, lessen, diminish; fail, transgress; frustrate, annul; M. P. मीयते, मीयते perish, be lost. C. मापयति only with प्र (q.v.) — आ disturb, remove, annul, change, alter (M. intr., refl., or recipr.). उद् M. disappear. प्र frustrate, annul, destroy, annihilate; change, alter; transgress, neglect, miss, forget; outstrip, surpass. P. M. perish, die. C. destroy, kill; cause to be killed by (instr.). — Cf. प्रमीत.

मीडम् adv. softly, gently.

मीढ (मीळ्ह) n. prize, reward; content, struggle.

मीढुष्मन्त् (मीळ्हुष्मन्त्) a. = seq.

मीढ्वंस् (मीळ्हुष्) a. bestowing richly, bountiful, liberal, gracious; superl. मीळ्हुष्टम.

मीन m. fish, poss. °वन्त्.

मीनकेतु & मीनध्वज m. the god of love (lit. the fish-bannered).

मीमांसक m. examiner (—°); follower of the Mīmāṅsā system (cf seq.).

मीमांसा f. reflection, consideration, examination, N. of a philos. system.

मील्, मीलति, pp. मीलित (q.v.) close the eyes, wink (also = मिल्). C. मीलयति close, shut. — आ & व्या C. close (the eyes). उद् open, expand, (trans. & intr.); come forth, appear. C. open, expand, manifest. प्रोद् & समुद् = उद् (also C.). नि shut the eyes, wink; close, contract (intr.); disappear, vanish. C. shut or cause to shut. सम् close the eyes; close up, contract (intr.). C. close, shut. — Cf. उन्मीलित, निमीलित, संमीलित.

मीलन n. closing the eyes, winking.

मीलित a. having closed the eyes, sleepy or asleep; closed, shut; vanished, disappeared, gone; also = मिलित.

मीव्, मीवति, pp. मूत (q.v.) & मीवित push, move. — आ push aside, wrench open (door). प्र push towards. प्रति push back, shut to.

मुकुट m. diadem, crown; p. °टिन्.

मुकुन्द m. E. of Viṣṇu.

मुकुर m. mirror, also = seq.

मुकुल n. bud (also fig. of a tooth).

मुकुलय्, °यति, pp. मुकुलित (q.v.) close.

मुकुलाय्, °यते bud, blossom (cf. seq.).

मुकुलायित a. blossomed.*

मुकुलित a. budded or closed (like buds).

मुकुलितनयन a. with closed eyes.

मुकुलिन् a. having buds.

मुक्त a. released, freed from, rid of (abl. or instr.); loosened, relaxed, fallen off or down; set free, dismissed; relinquished, given up; put off, laid aside, cast away; discharged, shed; thrown, hurled; liberated, emancipated (from sin or worldly existence) — f. मुक्ता pearl.

मुक्तकेश, f. आ & ई having flowing or dishevelled hair.

मुक्तचेतस् a. whose mind is liberated.

मुक्तता f., °त्व n. emancipation, liberation.

मुक्तबुद्धि a. = मुक्तचेतस्.

मुक्तसङ्ग a. free from (worldly) attachment.

मुक्तशिख a. = मुक्तकेश.

मुक्तागुण m. string of pearls.

मुक्ताजाल n. ornament of pearls; °मय, f. ई made or consisting of pearls.

मुक्तात्मन् a. = मुक्तचेतस्.

मुक्ताफल n. pearl (-fruit); abstr. °ता f.

मुक्तामणि m. pearl (-jewel); °सर m. string of pearls.

मुक्तामय, f. ई made or consisting of pearls.

मुक्तारत्न n. pearl (-gem).

मुक्तारुच् a. shining like pearls; f. as abstr.

मुक्तावलि or °ली f. string of pearls.

मुक्ताशुक्ति f. pearl-oyster.

मुक्तासन a. having left a seat, risen.

मुक्ताहार m. string of pearls.

मुक्ति f. liberation, release from (—°); final emancipation or beatitude; putting off, giving up, relinquishing (—°); casting, throwing, hurling.

मुक्तिवन्त् a. freed from (abl.).
मुक्ते prep. except (instr.).
मुचोजा f. snare, net.
मुख n. mouth, face, beak, snout, (adj. —° having — in the mouth etc. or having a -like mouth); direction, quarter (adj. —° turned towards, facing, n. adv.); opening, aperture, entrance into (gen. or —°); fore-part, top, point, edge, surface; head, chief, best; commencement, introduction (adj. —° ± आदि beginning with); cause, occasion, means of, instr. मुखेन by means of (gen. or —°).
मुखगत a. being in the mouth or in the face.
मुखचन्द्र & °मस् m. a moon-like face.
मुखचपल a. talkative, garrulous (lit. whose mouth is ever moving, abstr. °त्व n. — f. आ N. of a metre.
मुखज a. sprung from or being in the mouth; m. a Brahman.
मुखतस् adv. from, at, or by the mouth; at the head or in front.
मुखदघ्न a. reaching to the mouth.
मुखदोष m. loquacity (mouth-sin).
मुखपङ्कज n. a lotus-like face.
मुखपट m. veil, screen (for the face).
मुखप्रसाधन n. the adorning (washing, painting etc.) of the face.
मुखभेद m. distortion of the face.
मुखमधु a. having honey in the mouth, sweet-speaking.*
मुखमारुत m. breath (mouth-wind).
मुखर a. talkative, loquacious, garrulous, noisy; eloquent on, resonant with (—°); abstr. °ता f. — m. chief, ringleader; f. ई bit of a bridle.
मुखरय्, यति, pp. मुखरित make resound or speak.
मुखराग & °वर्ण m. colour of the face.
मुखरी कृ = मुखरय्.
मुखवन्त् a. mouthed.
मुखविपुला f. N. of a metre.
मुखव्यादान n. opening the mouth; gaping.
मुखशशिन् m. a moon-like face.
मुखश्री f. beauty of a face.
मुखाङ्ग n. part of the face.
मुखादित्व n. the being face etc.
मुखाब्ज & मुखाम्बुज n. = मुखपङ्कज.
मुखासव m. nectar of the lips.
मुखास्वाद m. kissing the mouth.
मुखीय a. being at the entrance or at the head of (—°).
मुखेन्दु m., °बिम्ब n. a moon- (disk-) like face.
मुख्य a. being in (on) the mouth or face, coming from the mouth; being at the head or at the beginning, best, principal, original, primary, first among (—°). m. chief, leader.
मुख्यता f., °त्व n. first place, highest rank, preeminence among (gen. or —°).
मुख्यशस् adv. principally, first.
मुख्यसदृश a. similar to the principal (person or thing).
मुख्यार्थ m. the primary meaning (of a word); adj. employed in or having the primary meaning.
मुग्ध a. stupefied, perplexed; gone astray, lost; foolish, silly; careless, innocent, charming, lovely.
मुग्धता f., °त्व n. simplicity, grace, charm.
मुग्धदूर्वा f. young Dūrvā-grass.*
मुग्धदृश् f. fair-eyed.
मुग्धधी & °बुद्धि a. of simple mind.
मुग्धबोध n. T. of a grammar (lit. instruction of the ignorant).
मुग्धभाव & °स्वभाव m. simplicity, inexperience.
मुग्धाक्षी f. a fair-eyed woman.
मुग्धात्मन् a. = मुग्धधी.
मुग्धेक्षणा f. = मुग्धाक्षी.
मुग्धेन्दु m. the young moon.
मुञ्ज & मुञ्जट m. names of men.
1मुच्, मुञ्चति, °ते & मुचति, °ते, pp. मुक्त, ger. मुक्त्वा (q.v.) release, deliver from (abl. or तस्) unloose, open; let go, set free; relinquish, abandon, forsake, quit, put off, lay aside, give up, grant, bestow; discharge, shed; emit, utter; send forth, shoot, throw, hurl against (loc., dat,, gen.,

or acc. w. प्रति). P.M. मुच्यते (मुच्यति, मुच्यति) be released from, get rid of, escape (abl. & instr., r. gen.), be deprived of, want (instr.); be liberated from sin or mundane existence. C. मोचयति, °ते release, deliver or redeem from (abl., r. instr.), set free, let loose; unbind, open etc., cause to give up or discharge (2 acc.). D. मुमुक्षति, °ते A. be about to give up or send forth, M. (also मोक्षते) wish to be liberated from (abl.), esp. desire final liberation. — अति P. avoid, escape (acc.). अभि let loose, emit, stream forth; throw, hurl, shoot off. अव loose, release, unyoke, unharness; take off, doff. आ put on (a garment); let loose, emit, hurl, throw, cast. उद् free or save from (abl.); unfasten, loosen, open; take off, doff; leave, relinquish; give back, restore; send forth, emit, throw, hurl. C. deliver from (abl.), loosen, untie (the hair), take off. उप put on, don. निस् loosen, untie, free from (abl.). P. cast the skin (of a snake), be stripped or deprived of (instr.). विनिस् abandon, give up; P. be delivered from (instr.). परि free from (abl.), loose, unbind, take off, abandon, give up, send forth, emit. P. get rid of (abl., gen., or instr.), be liberated from worldly ties. प्र let go, release from (abl.), loosen, untie, shake off, scare away, abandon, give up, emit, discharge, shed; hurl, shoot off. P. get rid of (abl. or instr.); become loose, fall off (fruit); leave off, cease. विप्र free, deliver, loosen, unfasten, take off. P. be liberated from (abl.), escape. प्रति fasten on (loc.), put on, dress a person (dat., loc., or gen.); with (acc.). M. dress one's self, assume (a form etc.); set free, release, dismiss, give up, abandon, return, restore (a debt). P. get rid of (abl.). C. rescue, save. वि loosen, unharness, take off (clothes); abandon, quit, give up, avoid, loose, w. न not rest or leave off; forgive, pardon; emit, pour forth, utter; hurl, cast, shoot off, take, assume (a shape). M. (also A.) unharness, put up, stop; (also P.) get loose, fall off; P. be freed or escape from, be deprived of, lose (abl., adv. in तस्, or instr.). C. unloose, unharness, liberate from (abl.), ward off. प्रवि dismiss, let loose, give up. सम् pour forth, shed (tears). C. liberate. — Cf. अतिमुक्त, आमुक्त, उन्मुक्त, निर्मुक्त, विनिर्मुक्त, विप्रमुक्त, विमुक्त.

2मुच् a. freeing from, sending forth, emitting, throwing, hurling (—°).

मुंज m. a sort of rush or grass.

मुञ्जनेजन a. cleaned from grass or rushes.

मुञ्जमय, f. ई made of Muñja grass.

मुट्, मोटते w. उद् break or pluck off. C. मोटयति (± प्रति) strangle, smother, kill.

मुट s. basket or bunch.

मुण्ड a. shaved, bald; hornless (cow or goat), lopped (tree); pointless, blunt. m. baldhead, N. of a Daitya etc., pl. N. of a people; n. head.

मुण्डक m. trunk or stem of a tree.

मुण्डकोपनिषद् f. T. of an Upanishad.

मुण्डधारिन् a. wearing (a garland of) heads or sculls.*

मुण्डन n. shaving the head, tonsure.

मुण्डय्, °यति, pp. मुण्डित shave (the head).

मुण्डितशिरस् a. shaven-headed.

मुण्डिन् a. = prec., also hornless.

मुण्डिभ m. N. of a man.

मुतव s. a kind of grass.

मुतिब m. pl. N. of a people.

1मुद्, मोदते (°ति), pp. मुदित (q.v.) be glad or merry, rejoice at, have pleasure in (loc. or instr.). C. मोदयति (°ते) gladden. — अनु rejoice after, with, or at (acc. of pers. & th.); agree to, approve of, applaud, permit. C. gladden; approve of etc. = S. प्र become or be joyful, exult. C. gladden. प्रति meet or welcome with joy, rejoice at (acc., r. gen.). C. delight, exhilarate. — Cf. प्रमुदित.

2मुद् f. joy, delight.

मुदा f. = prec., poss. °वन्त्.

मुदित a. joyful, glad, merry; delighted with (instr. or —°).

मुदिर m. cloud.

मुद्ग m. a sort of bean.

मुद्गर m. hammer, mallet.
मुद्गल m. N. of a Rishi etc., pl. N. of a people.
मुद्गवर्ण a. bean-coloured.
मुद्र a. joyous, glad.
मुद्रण n. sealing up, closing.
मुद्रय्, °यति, pp. मुद्रित seal, stamp, shut, print. — उद् unseal, open. वि seal up, shut.
मुद्रा f. seal, seal-ring, ring i.g., stamp, print, mark, impression; shutting, closing, lock, mystery.
मुद्राङ्क & °ङ्कित a. stamped, sealed, marked with (—°).
मुद्राराक्षस n. Rākṣasa (a minister) and the seal-ring, T. of a drama.
मुद्रिका f. seal-ring, signet.
मुद्रिताक्ष, f. ई having closed eyes.
मुधा adv. in vain, for nothing.
मुनि m impulse or a man driven by (inward) impulse; an inspired saint or seer; ascetic, devotee, hermit, monk, esp. one who has taken the vow of silence; pl. the seven stars of the Great Bear (cf. ऋषि).
मुनितनया f. the daughter of a Muni.
मुनिदौहित्र m. the grandson of a Muni.
मुनिपत्नी f. the wife of a Muni.
मुनिपुत्र m. the son of a Muni.
मुनिवन n. a hermit's grove.
मुनिवर m. the best of the Munis, E. of Vasiṣṭha.
मुनिवेष m. a hermit's garment; also = seq.
मुनिवेषधर a. wearing a hermit's garment.
मुनिव्रत a. keeping a Muni's vow (i.e. the vow of silence).
मुनिसुत m. = मुनिपुत्र.
मुनीन्द्र, मुनीश, & °श्वर m. the chief of Munis, i.e. a great sage or ascetic.
मुन्यन्न n. pl. the food of ascetics.
मुमुक्षा f. desire of liberation.
मुमुक्षु a. desirous of freeing (acc. or —°) or of being freed, esp. from mundane existence.
मुमुक्षुता f., °त्व n. desire of liberation or final emancipation.
मुमूर्षा f. desire of death.
मुमूर्षु a. wishing to die, moribund.
मुमोचयिषु & °चयिषु a. wishing to liberate.
मुर m. N. of a demon slain by Kṛṣṇa.
मुरज m. a kind of drum or tambourine.
मुरजित् m. the conqueror of Mura (Kṛṣṇa).
मुरद्विष् or °रिपु m. the foe of Mura (Kṛṣṇa).
मुरल m. a cert. fish; pl. N. of a people.
मुरारि m. = मुरद्विष्, also N. of a poet.
मुर्मुर m. burning chaff or a burning coal about to be extinguished.
1मुष्, मुष्णाति (मोषति, मुषति), pp. मुषित (q.v.) rob, steal, plunder, rob or bereave of (2 acc.); carry off, ravish (lit. & fig.); surpass, excel. — अभि rob of (2 acc.). अव, आ, & निस् take away, carry off. परि rob of (2 acc.). प्र rob, take away, withdraw. वि & सम् rob, carry off.
2मुष् robbing, taking away, destroying, surpassing (—°).
मुषाय्, °यति rob, snatch away. — आ = S. प्र plunder.
मुषित a. robbed, stolen (also मुष्ट) plundered or stripped of (acc.), ravished, enraptured; destroyed, disappointed, surpassed, exceeded; stripped off, naked; taken in, deceived, cheated, mocked.
मुषितक n. stolen property.
मुषीवन् m. robber, thief.
मुष्क m. testicle, du. the vulva.
मुष्कदेश m. the region of the scrotum.
मुष्कभार a. having testicles.
मुष्कर & मुष्कवन्त् a. = prec.
मुष्टि f. fist, handful; handle, esp of a sword.
मुष्टिप्रहार m. blow with the fist.
मुष्टियुद्ध n., °हत्या f. a fight with fists, hand to hand engagement.
मुष्टिहन् m. fighting hand to hand.
मुष्टी कृ clench the fist.
मुसल m. n. pestle, mace, club, bell-clapper.
मुसलिन् a. armed with a club.
मुस्त m. n., आ f. a kind of grass.
मुस्तक m. n., आ f. the same.
मुह्, मुह्यति (°ते), pp. मुग्ध & मूढ (q.v.) be confused or faint; err, lose one's senses; fail, not turn out well. C. मोहयति, °ते

confuse, bewilder, disarrange, cause to err or fail. I. मोमुह्यते be in great confusion. — अति = S. I. अनु become perplexed after (acc.). व्या M. become perplexed; C. perplex, bewilder, confuse. परि err, go astray (fig.). C. make confused, throw into disorder. प्र become perplexed or embarrassed, lose consciousness, faint. वि & सम् the same; C. stupefy, deprive of consciousness, cause to err or fail. — Cf. अतिमुग्ध, अतिमूढ, उन्मुग्ध (add.), परिमूढ, प्रमुग्ध, प्रमूढ, विमुग्ध, विमूढ, व्यामूढ, संमुग्ध, संमूढ.

मुंहु or मुहुं adv. suddenly, at once.

मुहुक n. moment; instr. pl. = prec.

मुंहुर् = मुहु (± आ); for a moment, awhile; every moment, repeatedly (also doubled); on the other hand, however. मुहुर्—मुहुर् at one moment—at another, now—now.

मुहूर्त m. n. moment, instant; hour (= $^1/_{30}$ day); instr. & abl. in a moment, after a little while, immediately, directly.

मुहूर्तक s. moment or hour (cf. prec.).

मूक (मूक) a. dumb, silent; abstr. °ता† f., °त्व† n.

मूंजवन्त् m. N. of a mountain, pl. of a people.

मूढ a. erred, gone astray, confused, uncertain, silly, stupid; n. & °ता† f., °त्व† n. as abstr.

मूढचेतन & °चेतस् a. perplexed in mind.

मूढदृष्टि a. stupid, silly (lit. having an uncertain look).

मूढधी, °बुद्धि, & °मति = मूढचेतन.

1†मूत v. काममूत.

2मूंत m. n. a woven basket.

मूतक n. a little basket.

मूंत्र n. urine.

मूत्रपुरीष n. du. urine and excrement.

मूत्रय्, °यति, °ते, pp. मूत्रित discharge urine, make water upon (acc.). — अव = S. tr.

मूत्रोच्चार (°—) = मूत्रपुरीष; °समुत्सर्ग m. discharge of urine and excrement.

मूत्र्य a. relating to urine.

1मूंर a. stupid, dull.

2मूंर a. rushing, impetuous.

3मूंर n. = मूंल.

मूरु N. of a country.

मूर्ख a. stupid, dull, silly; inexperienced in (loc.); m. fool, blockhead.

मूर्खता f., °त्व n. abstr. to prec.

मूर्छ्, मूर्छति, pp. मूर्त & मूर्छित (q.v.) become rigid, coagulate, thicken, increase, grow, sound loudly; become torpid or senseless, faint away, swoon. C. मूर्छयति (°ते) cause to thicken; form, shape, strengthen, augment, excite, rouse. — सम् thicken, coagulate, become firm or solid, sound loudly. C. stupefy, stun. — Cf. विमूर्छित, संमूर्छित.

मूर्छन a. stunning; strengthening (—°). n. increase, growth; f. आ fainting, swooning; swelling or rising of sounds, intonation, note, tone or semitone (in the scale), melody.

मूर्छा f. thickening, coagulation; swoon, faint, stupefaction, astonishment; melody.

मूर्छित a. rigid, stiff, thick, strong, intensive, full of, mixed with (—°); roused, excited; stupefied, senseless; n. a kind of song.

मूर्त a. thickened, coagulated, solid, substantial, corporeal; stupefied, insensible.

मूर्ति f. (firm) body, embodiment, form, shape, image, person, adj. —° formed of; pl. the solid parts of the body.

मूर्तितस् (abl. adv.) out of the body.

मूर्तिमन्त् a. embodied, material, incarnate, personified; adj. —° formed of.

मूर्ध (—°) = मूर्धन्.

मूर्धग a. being on the head.

मूर्धज m. pl. hair or mane (l. head-born).

मूर्धतस् adv. from or on the head.

मूर्धन् m. forehead, scull, head, highest part, top, point, summit, chief, leader. मूर्ध्ना & मूर्ध्नि कृ put on the head i.e. esteem highly, w. धृ the same, w. वृत् stand above all.

मूर्धन्य a. being on the head, uppermost, highest, first; cerebral (g.).

मूर्वा f. a kind of hemp, °मय a. made of it.

मूंल n. (adj. —° f. आ & ई) root (lit. & fig.), foot, basis, foundation, ground, bottom, immediate neighbourhoud; origin, source commencement, cause; the chief person or thing, e.g. text (opp. commentary), capital (opp. interest), also capital = chief city, holder (opp. owner); N. of a lunar mansion (also m.). — मूलं कृ or बन्ध् take root; मूल (—°) sprung from, rooted in, resting on; (°—) original, chief, first, also =(± आ) मूलात् or मूलतस्, & मूलादारभ्य from the bottom or the beginning.

मूलक, f. °लिका = prec. (—°); n. an esculent root, radish.

मूलकर्मन् n. magic with roots.

मूलखानक m. root-digger.

मूलता f., °त्व n. the being a root or origin.

मूलदेव m. a man's name.

मूलपुरुष m. the representative of the (original) race.

मूलप्रकृति f. the primary matter (ph.).

मूलप्रणिहित a. having been watched by spies.

मूलफल n. sgl. roots and fruits; the interests of capital.

मूलफलाशन a. eating roots and fruits.

मूलभृत्य m. an old or hereditary servant.

मूलव्यसनवृत्तिमन्त् a. living by an hereditary vice.

मूलसाधन n. chief instrument or expedient.

मूलस्वामिन् m. du. holder and owner.

मूलहर a. taking away the roots, uprooting, destroying; abstr. °त्व n.

मूलायतन n. original seat or residence.

मूलाशिन् a. living on roots.

मूलिक a. radical, original.

मूलिन् a. having a root.

मूल्य a. being at the root. — n. original value, price, wages, pay, earnings, gain, capital.

मूष् s. mouse.

मूष m. the same.

मूषक m. thief, robber; mouse, rat.

मूषिक m. mouse, rat; f. मूषिका the same, a kind of leech.

मूषिकशावक m. young mouse, mousey.

मूषिकोत्कर m. mole-hill or mouse-hole.

1मृ, मरति, मरते, also P. म्रियते (°ति), pp. मृत (q.v.) die, depart from life. C. मारयति (°ते) kill, slay, put to death. D. मुमूर्षति wish or be about to die. I. मरीमर्ति suffer the pangs of death. — अनु die after (acc.), follow in death. अभि affect or soil by dying. परि die around (acc.). — Cf. प्रमृत & ममृवंस्.

2मृ, मृणाति, pp. मूर्ण crush, destroy. — उप P. (मृर्यते) be destroyed. नि, प्र, & वि = S.

मृकण्ड & °ण्डु m. N. of an ancient sage.

मृच्, मृचति, म्रचति stroke, rub, smear. C. म्रचयति, pp. म्रचित = seq. — अभि S. & C. smear, anoint. नि rub on, touch (loc.)

मृच m. curry-comb.

मृचिणी f. torrent.

मृग m. wild animal, beast of the forest, esp. deer, gazelle (seen also as spot in the moon), musk deer; a cert. high-flying bird; f. मृगी hind, doe.

मृगग्रहण n. capture of a deer.

मृगजीवन m. hunter (lit. who lives by hunting).

मृगयु a. hunting wild beasts.

मृगतृष्णा & °तृष्णिका f. mirage (l. deer-thirst).

मृगदृश् f. deer-eyed.

मृगद्विज m. pl. beasts and birds.

मृगनाभि m. musk or musk-deer (lit. deer's navel).

मृगपक्षिन् m. pl. = मृगद्विज.

मृगपति m. lord of the beasts (lion, tiger, or roebuck).

मृगमद m. musk (l. deer's moisture).

मृगय्, मृगयते (°ति) chase, hunt, pursue, seek for, strive after (acc.), request or beg anything (acc.) from (abl., adv. in तस्, or gen. ± सकाशात्). — परि seek. वि search, investigate, examine.

मृगयस् m. wild beast, deer.

मृगया f hunting, chase.

मृगयारण्य & मृगयावन n. hunting park.

मृगयाशील a. addicted to hunting.*

मृगयु m. hunter.

मृगराज् & °राज m. lord of the beasts (lion or tiger).

मृगराजधारिन् m. E. of Çiva.

मृगरोचना f. a yellow pigment prepared from the bile of a deer (cf. गोरोचना).*

*मृगरोमज a. woollen (lit. produced from animal's hair).

मृगलक्ष्मन् & **°लाञ्छन** m. the moon, lit. having a deer (scil. as its spot).
मृगलिप्सु a. wishing to catch or kill a deer.
***मृगलोचना** f. deer-eyed.
मृगवधू f. female deer, doe.*
मृगवन n. deer-park.
मृगव्य n. hunting, chase.
मृगव्याध m. hunter (deer-slayer).
मृगशाव m. young deer, fawn.
मृगशावाक्षी f. fawn-eyed.
मृगशिरस् & **मृगशीर्ष** n. N. of a lunar mansion.
मृगहन् m. hunter (lit. = seq.).
मृगहन्तृ m. deer-slayer.
मृगाक्षी f. deer-eyed.
मृगाङ्क m. = **मृगलक्ष्मन्**.
मृगाङ्गना f. = **मृगवधू**.
मृगाधिप m. king of beasts, lion.
मृगाराति & **मृगारि** m. foe of deer, lion.
मृगोदृश् & **मृगेक्षणा** f. deer-eyed.
मृगेन्द्र m. = **मृगाधिप**.
मृगेभ n. sgl. deer and (or) elephant.
मृगेश्वर m. = **मृगाधिप**.
मृग्य्, **मृग्यति** hunt, search.
मृग्य a. to be sought for or inquired after.
1**मृच्**, pp. **मृक्त**; C. **मर्चयति** injure, hurt.
2**मृच्** f. injury, threat.
मृचय a. perishable, transitory.
मृच्छकटिका f. a toy-cart made of clay; T. of a drama.
मृज्, **मार्ष्टि**, **मृष्टे** (**मृजति**, **°ते**, **मार्जति**, **°ते**), **मर्जयति**, **°ते** & **मार्जयति**, **°ते**, pp. **मृष्ट** (q.v.), **मृजित**, & **मार्जित** (q.v.) wipe, clean, polish, rub, stroke, adorn (M. also refl.); wipe off, remove, destroy, get rid of (acc.); (also M.) wipe off (a guilt, i.e. throw it) upon (loc.); M. take away, carry off, win. I. **मर्मृज्यते**, **मरीमृज्यते**, etc. wipe or clean repeatedly, M. one's self. — **अनु** wipe down, smooth, purify. **अप** wipe off, remove, throw upon (loc.). **अव** stroke downwards, wipe away. **आ** wipe off, clean, purify. **उद्** stroke upwards; wipe off, clean, adorn; M. refl., also carry off, win. **उप** stroke, wipe, polish. **नि** rub in or upon (loc.), rub or wipe off (M. refl.), lead to, bestow on (loc.); M. take for one's self, carry off. **निस्** wipe off, destroy. **परि** wipe all round, rub, stroke, polish, clean, purify; wipe away, remove, destroy, get rid of (acc.). **प्र** wipe, polish, clean, stroke; wipe off, remove, destroy, frustrate. **वि** wipe off, rub dry, clean, purify, embellish, adorn (**तन्वम्** refl.), stroke, smear, anoint. **सम्** rub off, sweep clean, strain, filter, purify, stroke; wipe off, remove, destroy. — Cf. **उन्मृष्ट**, 1**परिमृष्ट**, **प्रमृष्ट**, **संमृष्ट**.
मृज a. wiping off, removing, destroying (—°); f. **आ** purification, ablution, purity, cleanliness; poss. **°वन्त्**.
मृज्य a. to be wiped off or destroyed.
मृड्, **मृडति** (**मृळति**), **°ते** & **मृडयति** (**मृळयति**), **°ते** be gracious, forgive (dat. of pers. & acc. of th.); treat graciously, make happy. **अभि** forgive.
मृड a. merciful, gracious; m. E. of Agni & Çiva.
मृडन n. showing grace, favouring.
मृळयाकु a. merciful, gracious.
मृडानी f. Mṛḍa's wife, i.e. Pārvatī.
मृडितृ m. = **मर्डितृ**.
मृडीक (**मृळीक**) n. grace, mercy.
मृण्, **मृणति** crush, pound, thrash. — **नि**, **प्र**, **वि**, **सम्** = S.
मृणाल n., **ई** f. lotus-root or fibre; poss. **°वन्त्**.
मृणालक, f. **°लिका** (adj. —°) = prec.
मृणालवलय n. bracelet of lotus-fibres.
मृणालसूत्र n. necklace of lotus-fibres.
मृणालिनी f. lotus plant or group.
मृत a. dead, deceased, vanished, gone, useless; m. dead body, corpse, n. death.
मृतक m. dead man, corpse; n. death.
मृतकल्प a. like dead, almost dead.
मृतचेल n. garment of a dead person.
मृतजात a. dead-born.
मृतजीवन, f. **ई** reviving the dead.
मृतदेह m. dead body, corpse.
मृतधार & **°क** a. carrying a corpse.
मृतपुरुषदेह m. a human corpse.

मृतपुरुषशरीर n. = prec.
मृतवत् adv. as if dead.
मृतवस्त्रभृत् a. wearing the clothes of the dead.
मृतसंजीवन a. reviving the dead.
मृताङ्ग n. dead body, corpse.
मृताह m., °हन् & °हस् n. the day of one's death.
मृति f. death; °मन् m. mortality.
(मृत्तिक s. &) मृत्तिका f. clay, loam.
मृत्तोय n. pl. earth and water.
मृत्पात्र n. an earthen vessel.
मृत्पिण्ड m. a lump of clay.
मृत्पिण्डबुद्धि a. stupid, foolish (lit. having the wisdom of a lump of clay).*
मृत्प्रक्षेप m. scattering earth over anything.
मृत्यु m. death or the god of death; pl. the various kinds of death.
मृत्युकाल m. the time of death.
मृत्युदूत m. messenger of death.
मृत्युद्वार n. the door of death.
मृत्युपाश m. death's noose or sling.
मृत्युबन्धु or मृत्युबन्धु m. death-fellow (man).
मृत्युभय n. danger or fear of death.
मृत्युमन्त् a. subject to death.
मृत्स्न s. dust, powder.
1मृद्, मृद्नाति, मर्दति, °ते (म्रदति, °ते) pp. मृदित, rub, squeeze, crush, smash; wipe off, destroy. C. मर्दयति, °ते press or rub hard, pound, crush, grind down, destroy, harass, afflict, also cause to be rubbed etc. — अभि crush, smash, destroy, lay waste. अव the same. उद् rub in, mix with (instr.). नि smash, destroy, rub or strip off. परि trample down, squash, wear away, wipe off. प्र crush down, bruise, pound, destroy, ravage. वि & सम् the same.
2मृद् f. clay, loam, mound of earth or lump of clay.
मृदङ्ग m. a kind of drum.
मृदा f. clay, loam.
मृदु (f. मृदु & मृद्वी) soft, tender, delicate, mild, gentle, weak, moderate; m. n. softness, gentleness.
मृदुक a. soft, gentle, n. adv.
मृदुक्रूर n. du. softness or harshness.
मृदुगिर् a. sweet-voiced.
मृदुतीक्ष्ण a. gentle and harsh.
मृदुपूर्व a. soft, gentle (at first); n. adv.
मृदुभाव m. softness, meekness.
मृदुभाषिन् a. speeking mildly.
मृदुल a. soft, tender, mild.
मृदुवाच् a. = मृदुभाषिन्.
मृदुसूर्य a. having a mild sun (day).
मृदुस्पर्श a. soft to the touch.
मृदुहृदय a. soft-hearted, kind.
मृदू भू become soft, soften.
मृद्ध a. forsaken, helpless.
मृद्भाण्ड n. an earthen vessel.
मृद्वङ्ग, f. ई tender-limbed.
मृद्वीका f. a vine or bunch of grapes.
1मृध्, मर्धति, pp. मृद्ध (q.v.) neglect, forsake, contemn, despise. — परि slacken, relent, cease.
2मृध् f. combat, fight; foe, enemy.
मृध m. battle, fight.
मृधस् n. contempt, disdain, only w. कृ contemn, despise.
मृध्र n. disdain, insult; insulter.
मृध्रवाच् a. speaking injuriously, insulting.
मृन्मय, f. ई made of earth, w. गृह the grave; s. an earthenware vessel.
मृन्मयूर m. a peacock made of clay.
मृल्लोष्ट n. lump of clay.
मृश्, मृशति, °ते, pp. मृष्ट & मृशित touch, stroke, grasp, take hold of (lit. & fig.); think of, consider. — अनु grasp, seize, take into consideration. अभि touch, feel, bring into contact with (instr.). अव touch, grope, consider. आ touch, feel, enjoy, consider, examine. परा touch, seize, grasp, violate (a woman); point to, mean, P. be meant. परि touch, grope, seize, examine, try, consider. प्र touch, feel. वि touch, feel, stroke, try, examine, find out. C. consider, reflect upon. सम् take hold of, seize, touch. — Cf. आमृष्ट, 2परिमृष्ट.
मृष्, मृष्यते (°ति) not heed, forget, suffer, bear, put up with (acc.). C. मर्षयति, °ते make forget (acc.); suffer, endure, bear, forgive, pardon; w. न not let alone,

molest, disturb. — अपि forget, neglect. आ (also C.) bear patiently. उप C. the same. प्र forget, neglect (acc. or dat.).
मृषा adv. in vain, uselessly, wrongly, falsely. With मन् or ज्ञा not believe, w. कृ feign.
मृषाज्ञान n. false knowledge, ignorance, folly.
मृषाभाषिन् a. speaking falsely, lying.
मृषावचन n., °वाच् f. untrue or satirical speech, irony.
मृषावाद m. = prec.; a. = मृषाभाषिन्.
मृषावादिन् a. = prec. adj.
मृषोद्य n. = मृषावचन.
मृष्ट a. cleansed, washed, polished, clean, pure; smeared with (instr.); savoury, dainty (food); pleasant, charming.
मृष्टि f. cleaning, dressing (of food).
†मेक v. सुमेक.
मेकल m. pl. N. of a people.
मेक्षण n. wooden stick or spoon.
(मेखल s. &) मेखला f. girdle (lit. & fig.); also = seq.
मेखलापद n. the place of the girdle, the hips.
मेखलावन्त् a. having a girdle, girt.
मेखलिन् a. = prec.; m. a Brahmanical student.
मेघ m. cloud, abstr. °त्व† n.
मेघकाल m. the time of clouds, the rainy season.
मेघदूत m. the Cloud-Messenger, T. of a poem.
1मेघनाद m. thunder (lit. cloud-noise).
2मेघनाद a. sounding like thunder, roaring.
मेघनादिन् & °निर्घोष a. = prec. 2.
मेघमाला f. wreath of clouds, lit. = seq.
मेघराजी f. line of clouds.
मेघरेखा & °लेखा f. the same.
मेघवात a. wind with clouds or rain.*
मेघोदक n. rain (lit. cloud-water).
मेघोदय m. rising or gathering of clouds.
मेचक a. dark blue, black; m. an eye in a peacock's tail.
मेडि or मेळि m. crackling, rustling.
मेढी f. = मेथि, मेथी.
मेढ्र n. (m.) the membrum virile.
मेण्ठ m. elephant-keeper, N. of a poet.
मेतृ m. who erects or builds.
मेथन n. abusive speech.
मेथि m., मेथी f. pillar, post (esp. to bind cattle to), prop for supporting the shafts of a carriage.
मेद m. = मेदस्; a cert. mixed caste.
मेदन n. fattening.
मेदस् n. (m.) fat, corpulence.
मेदस्वन्त् & मेदस्विन् a. fat, corpulent.
मेदिन् m. partner, companion; f. मेदिनी the earth, land, soil, spot, place.
मेदिनीपति m. earth-lord, king.
मेदिनीश m. the same.
मेदुर a. fat, thick, dense; as thick as, full of (—°).
मेद्य a. fat, thick.
मेध m. juice of meat, broth; sap or essence, esp. of the sacrificial animal; the victim or sacrifice itself.
मेधपति or मेधपति m. lord of sacrifice.
1मेधस् n. sacrifice.
2मेधस् a. intelligent, wise; —° intelligence, wisdom.
मेधसाति f. gain of a prize or reward.
मेधा f. prize, reward; mental vigour or power, intelligence, wisdom.
मेधाजनन a. producing wisdom; n. N. of a cert. rite.
मेधातिथि m. N. of sev. sages.
मेधाविन् a. intelligent, wise, judicious.
मेधि & मेधी = मेथि & मेथी.
†मेधिन् v. गृहमेधिन्.
मेधिर a. = मेधाविन्.
मेध्य a. full of sap or pith, vigorous, mighty; fit for a sacrifice, pure, undefiling.
मेध्यता f., °त्व n. abstr. to prec.
मेध्यातिथि m. N. of a Rishi.
मेनका f. N. of an Apsaras etc.
मेना f. wife, female.
मेनि f. weapon, thrust, punishment, vengeance, anger, wrath.
मेय a. to be (being) measured; discernible, provable, demonstrable.
मेरु m. N. of a mountain.
मेरुकूट & °पृष्ठ n. the summit of Meru.
मेरुसर्षप m. du. mount Meru and a mustard-seed.
मेल m., आ f. meeting, assembly.

मेलक m. = prec., °कं कृ assemble.
मेलन n. meeting, assembling, union.
मेषं m. ram, sheep, in Veda also a fleece or anything woollen; f. ईं ewe.
मेषिका f. = prec. f.
1**मेषवृषण** m. du. the testicles of a ram.
2**मेषवृषण** a. having the testicles of a ram.
मेष्क m. a cert. rapacious animal.
मेह m. urine; acc. w. कृ make water.
मेंहन n. the membrum virile, also = prec.
मेहंना (instr. adv.) in streams, abundantly.
मेहंनावन्त् a. bestowing abundantly.
मेहिन् a. making water (—°).
मैंघ, f. ई coming from clouds, cloudy.
मैत्रं, f. ईं belonging to or coming from a friend, friendly, kind, benevolent, affectionate; also relating to Mitra. — m. N. of a cert. mixed caste & of a cert. alliance (scil. संधि), a man's name; f. मैत्री friendship, benevolence, likeness with (—°); n. friendship, N. of a lunar mansion, the evacuation of excrement (presided over by Mitra).
मैत्रक n. friendship.
मैत्राक्षज्योतिक m. a kind of phantom or demon.
मैत्रायण m. pl. N. of a Vedic school.
मैत्रायणीसंहिता f. T. of a Saṃhitā.
मैत्रावरुणं, f. ईं relating to Mitra and Varuṇa.
मैत्रिन् m. friend.
मैत्रीभाव m. friendship.
मैत्रेय a. benevolent, kind; m. & f. ई patron. of sev. men & women, m. also = seq.
मैत्रेयक m. N. of a cert. mixed caste.
मैत्र्य n. friendship.
मैथिल, f. ई relating to Mithilā. m. sgl. & pl. the king & the people of M., f. ई the princess of M., i.e. Sītā.
मथुनं, f. ई paired, coupled; relating to copulation; n. copulation, marriage.
मैथुनिन् a. having sexual intercourse.
मैथुन्य a. relating to copulation.
मैनाकं m. N. of a mountain & a Daitya.
मैनालं & **मैनिक** m. fisherman.
मैन्द m. N. of a monkey.
मैरव, f. ई relating to (mount) Meru.
मैरेय m. n. a kind of intoxicating drink.
मैं v. 1मा.
मोक n. a skin flayed or cast off; f. मोंकी night.
मोक्तव्य a. to be freed, relinquished, given up, hurled upon (loc.).
मोक्तृ m. releaser, deliverer, restorer.
मोक्ष्, मोंक्षते v. 1मुच्.
मोक्ष m. deliverance, release from (abl., gen., or —°), esp. final emancipation, death; loosening, unbinding, solution (of a question), shedding (of tears or blood), uttering (of a curse), throwing, shooting off; scattering, strewing; giving up, abandoning.
मोक्षक a. loosening, untying, setting free.
मोक्षण a. freeing, delivering; n. deliverance, acquittance, loosening, untying, letting go or flow, giving up.
मोक्षणीय a. to be let go or given up.
मोक्षपरायण a. having final emancipation as chief object.
मोक्षभाव m. deliverance, emancipation.
मोक्षय्, °यति (°ते) set free, deliver, draw out of, release from (abl.), emancipate; let flow, shed, cast, hurl. — वि & सम् liberate, set free.
मोक्षयितव्य a. to be liberated.
मोक्षयितृ m. deliverer, liberator.
मोक्षशास्त्र n. the doctrine of emancipation.
मोक्षसाधन n. means of emancipation.
मोक्षिन् a. striving after or partaking of emancipation.
मोक्षेच्छा f. desire of emancipation.
मोक्ष्य a. to be liberated or saved.
मोंघ (**मोघं**) a. vain, useless, causeless, good for nothing; °— & n. adv.
मोघकर्मन् a. of vain acts.
मोघज्ञान a. of vain knowlege.
मोघता f. vainlessness, uselessness.
मोघाश a. of vain hopes.
मोघी w. कृ frustrate, disappoint; w. भू P.
मोच m., आ f. names of plants.
मोचक a. liberating, freeing from (—°).
मोचन, f. ई delivering from, hurling (—°); n. release, deliverance from (abl. or —°), loosening, unyoking, discharging, emitting.

मोचनीय & **मोचयितव्य** a. to be liberated or set free.

मोच्य a. the same, to be given back or restored.

मोटक m. n. globule, pill.

मोटन a. (—°) & n. crushing, breaking, strangling.

मोद m. delight, gladness; fragrance.

मोदक a. delighting (—°); m. n. small round comfit, smeetmeat.

मोदन a. & n. gladdening, delighting.

मोदनीय a. to be rejoiced at, delightful.

मोदिन् a. rejoicing, pleased, happy; gladdening (—°).

मोमुघ a. crazy, mad.

मोरट m. a kind of plant.

मोष m. robber, thief; robbery, theft; robbed or stolen property.

मोषण a. (—°) & n. robbing, stealing.

मोष्य a. to be stolen.

मोह m. unconsciousness, bewilderment, perplexity, swoon; error, infatuation, darkness or delusion of mind (ph.), ignorance, folly.

मोहन, f. **ई** stupefying, perplexing, deceiving (—°); n. the act of stupefying etc., error, delusion, fascination, seduction, sexual intercourse.

मोहनीय a. producing or relating to illusion.

मोहमय, f. **ई** consisting of error or delusion.

मोहमुद्गर m. T. of sev. works (lit. the hammer of ignorance).

मोहयितृ m. perplexer, infatuator.

मोहवन्त् a. perplexed, infatuated.

मोहिन् a. perplexing, bewildering.

मोहुक a. falling into confusion.

मोहोपमा f. a kind of comparison (rh.)

मौक्तिक a. desirous of emancipation; n. (m.) a pearl.

मौक्तिकावलि or **°ली** f. string of pearls, necklace.

मौक्तिकाहार m. the same.*

मौक्य n. dumbness.

मौख a. relating to the mouth.

मौखर्य n. talkativeness.

मौग्ध्य n. simplicity, inexperience, innocence.

मौघ्य n. uselessness.

मौच n. banana (the fruit).

मौजवत a. coming from the mountain Mūjavant.

मौञ्ज, f. **ई** made of Muñja-grass, f. **ई** (sc. **मेखला**) such a girdle.

मौञ्जिन् a. wearing a girdle of Muñja-grass.

मौञ्जीनिबन्धन & **मौञ्जीबन्धन** n. the tying of the girdle (v. prec.).

मौढ्य n. simplicity, stupidity.

मौण्ड्य n. shaving of the head, tonsure.

मौद्गल्य m. patron. from Mudgala; a cert. mixed caste.

मौन n. the condition of a Muni or holy sage; silence.

मौनवृत्ति a. = seq. 2.

1**मौनव्रत** n. the vow of silence.

2**मौनव्रत** a. observing the vow of silence.

मौनिन् a. keeping silence; abstr. **°नित्व** n.

मौर्ख्य n. stupidity, folly.

मौर्य m. pl. N. of a dynasty.

मौर्व, f. **ई** Mūrvā (a kind of hemp); f. **ई** (scil. **मेखला**) such a girdle.

मौर्वीज्या f. a bowstring made of Mūrvā fibres.

मौल a. coming from roots, radical, original, native, traditional, hereditary.

मौलि m. head, top, point; crest, diadem (also f.). — **मौली निधा** put on the head i.e. receive with submission.

मौलिन् a. diademed, crested; being at the head of, excelling (—°).

मौलिमाला & **°मालिका** f. a crown worn on the head.

मौल्य a. being at the root.

मौसल a. shaped like a club or fought with clubs (battle).

मौहूर्त m. an astrologer (knower of hours).

मौहूर्तिक a. lasting an instant, momentary; m. astrologer.

म्ना, **मनति**, w. **आ** mention, repeat, regard as, take for (acc.). **समा** the same. – Cf. **आम्नात** (add.), **समाम्नात**.

म्यक्ष्, **म्यक्षति** be fixed in, rest on (loc.); be present. — **अप** keep off. **आ** be present in or on (loc.). **नि** hold; M. be present in (loc.). **परा** be beside. **सम्** keep together.

म्रच् v. मृच्.
†म्रच a. rubbing, destroying.
म्रचण n. rubbing, anointing; ointment, oil.
म्रद् v. मृद्.
म्रदिमन् m. softness, meekness.
म्रदीयंस् (compar.) softer, milder.
म्रित्, म्रित्यति (± वि) dissolve, decay.
म्रुच्, म्रोचति, w. नि set (of the sun), w. अभिनि set upon (acc.). – Cf. अभिनिम्रुक्त (add.).
म्रेड्, आम्रेडयति, pp. आम्रेडित (q.v.) repeat.
म्ला, म्लायति, °ते (म्लाति), pp. म्लात & म्लान (q.v.) relax, languish, wither, fade, decay. C. म्लापयति cause to wither or langish, weaken. — परि, प्र, वि = S. — Cf. आम्लान & परिम्लान.
म्लात a. made soft by tanning.
म्लान a. withered, faded, languid, weak, vanished, gone; n. & °ता f. = seq.
म्लानि f. withering, decay, languor, dejection.
म्लायिन् a. withering, fading away.
म्लित् = म्रित्.
म्लुच्, म्लोचति, pp. म्लुक्त go to rest. — अनु rise. उप retire to, hide behind (acc.). नि go down, set. अभिनि set upon (acc.). — Cf. अपम्लुक्त (add.).
म्लुप् = म्लुच्.
म्लेच्छ्, म्लेच्छति speak barbarously or unintelligibly.
म्लेच्छ m. barbarian or barbarism.
म्लेच्छता f. abstr. to prec.
म्लेच्छदेश m. the country of the barbarians.
म्लेच्छन n. barbarian or unintelligible speech.
म्लेच्छवाच् a. speaking a barbarous or foreign language.

य

यं pron. rel. (n. यद् q.v.) who, which; if anybody (mostly w. opt.). Repeated or connected with त (q.v.) or कश्च, कश्चन, कश्चिद्, कोऽपि whoever, whichever, whatever, any. यो ऽहम्, यस्त्वम् I who, thou who etc.
यक = यं who, which.
यकन् & यकृत् n. the liver.
यकार m. the sound य.
यकृद्वर्ण a. liver-coloured.
यक्ष्, यक्षति, °ते w. प्र press on, strive after (acc.), overtake.
यक्ष n. a supernatural being or apparition, ghost, spirit; m. a class of genii, attendants on Kubera (f. ई); abstr. °ता† f., °त्व† n.
यक्षकर्दम & °धूप m. kinds of ointment or perfume.
यक्षदृश्य a. having the look of a supernatural apparition.
यक्षपति, °राज्, & °राज m. king of the Yakṣas, E. of Kubera.
यक्षाधिप & °पति m. the same.
यक्षिन् a. pressing on, avenging; or agile, lively; f. °णी† a female Yakṣa.
यक्षु m. N. of a people.
यक्षेन्द्र & यक्षेश्वर m. = यक्षपति.
यक्ष्म & यक्ष्मन् m. disease, esp. consumption.
यक्ष्मिन् a. consumptive.
यक्ष्य a. lively, agile.
यच्छ्रद्ध a. of what (rel.) faith.
1यज्, यजति, °ते, pp. इष्ट (q.v.) worship, esp. with sacrifices or oblations, consecrate, hallow, offer, sacrifice (A. mostly on account of another, M. on one's own account or by the help of another). C. याजयति °ते sacrifice (as priest) for (acc.) with (instr.), cause a person (acc.) to sacrifice with (acc. or instr.) by means of a priest (instr.). D. यियक्षति, °ते wish to sacrifice. — अनु worship afterwards with (instr.). अप drive away, M. purchase by a sacrifice. अपि sacrifice (acc. of the god or the oblation). अव avert, drive away, or satisfy by a sacrifice. आ consecrate, hallow, worship, win by a sacrifice (for men from the gods, M. also for one's self). परि get or procure by a sacrifice; worship or sacrifice before or after another.

प्र worship, sacrifice; offer the Prayāja. सम् worship or sacrifice (together); do homage to, revere. C. cause to sacrifice together, act as sacrificing priest for (acc.). — Cf. इष्ट, यजमान.

2यज् worshipping, sacrificing (—°).

यजत & यजत्र a. venerable, holy.

यजति m. any oblation not burnt (opp. जुहोति).

यजथाय & यजध्यै dat. inf. to 1यज्.

यजन n. sacrificing or a place of sacrifice.

यजनीय (± अहन्) n. the day of sacrifice or consecration.

यजमान m. a person who institutes or performs a sacrifice and pays the expenses of it; also sacrificer, Brahman i.g.

यजमानशिष्य m. the pupil of a Brahman.

यजस् n. worship.

यजा f. N. of a tutelary goddess.

यजि a. worshipping, sacrificing (—°); m. sacrifice.

यजिन् m. worshipper, sacrificer.

यजिष्ठ (superl.) sacrificing best or most.

यजिष्णु a. worshipping or adoring (the gods).

यजीयस् (compar.) sacrificing better or best.

यजुर्विद् a. knowing sacrificial formulas.

यजुर्वेद m. the Veda of the Yajus or sacrificial texts.

यजुष्टस् adv. on the side or with regard to the Yajus.

यजुष्मन्त् a. accompanied with a sacrificial formula.

यजुष्य a. relating to worship.

यजुस् n. sacred awe, worship, sacrifice; sacrificial text, also = यजुर्वेद (sgl. & pl.).

यज्ञ m. worship, devotion, homage, praise, prayer; sacrifice, oblation.

1यज्ञकर्मन् n. sacrificial act.

2यज्ञकर्मन् a. performing a sacrifice.

यज्ञकाम a. eager for worship or sacrifice.

यज्ञकृत् a. performing or causing a sacrifice.

यज्ञक्रतु m. sacrificial rite or ceremony.

यज्ञक्रिया f. sacrificial act.

यज्ञच्छाग m. a goat for sacrifice.

यज्ञतुरंग m. a horse for sacrifice.

यज्ञदत्त m. a man's name.

यज्ञदीक्षा f. initiation into sacrifices.

यज्ञधीर a. experienced in worship.

यज्ञनी a. directing the sacrifice.

यज्ञपति m. lord (either performer or receiver) of the sacrifice, E. of sev. gods.

यज्ञपशु m. animal for sacrifice, victim.

यज्ञपात्र n. sacrificial utensil.

यज्ञप्रिय & °प्री a. liking sacrifices.

1यज्ञभाग m. share of a sacrifice.

2यज्ञभाग a. having a share in a sacrifice.

यज्ञभागेश्वर m. E. of Indra (lit. lord of prec. 1).

यज्ञभूमि f. place for sacrifice.

यज्ञभृत् m. arranger of a sacrifice, E. of Viṣṇu.

यज्ञमन्मन् a. intent on sacrifices.

यज्ञमुख n. mouth or opening of a sacrifice.

यज्ञमुष् m. N. of a demon (lit. stealer of sacrifices).

यज्ञवनस् a. loving sacrifice.

यज्ञवन्त् a. worshipping, adoring.

†यज्ञवर्धन a. promoting sacrifice.

*यज्ञवल्क m. N. of a man.

यज्ञवाट m., °वास्तु n. place for sacrifice.

यज्ञवाह a. conducting the sacrifice, conveying it to the gods.

यज्ञवाहन a. the same, E. of Viṣṇu & Çiva.

यज्ञवाहस् a. offering or receiving sacrifice.

यज्ञविद् a. skilled in sacrifice.

यज्ञविद्या f. skill in sacrifice.

यज्ञवृद्ध a. exalted or delighted with sacrifices.

यज्ञवृध् a. delighting in sacrifices.

यज्ञशरण n. sacrificial shed.

यज्ञशाला f. sacrificial hall.

यज्ञशास्त्र n. the science of sacrifice.

यज्ञशिष्ट n. the remnants of a sacrifice; °ष्टाशन n. the eating of them.

यज्ञशील a. zealous about offering sacrifices.

यज्ञशेष m. = यज्ञशिष्ट.

यज्ञश्री a. promoting sacrifice.

यज्ञश्रेष्ठ m. the best of sacrifices.

यज्ञसंस्था f. the ground-form of a sacrifice.

यज्ञसदन n. sacrificial hall.

यज्ञसदस् n. an assembly at a sacrifice.

यज्ञसाध् & °साधन a. performing sacrifice or worship.

यज्ञसूत्र n. the sacrificial cord.

यज्ञसेन m. N. of sev. men, E. of Viṣṇu etc.

यज्ञहन् a. disturbing sacrifice.

यज्ञहुत् & †°होतृ m. offerer at a sacrifice.
यज्ञाङ्ग n. limb i.e. part, means, or implement of a sacrifice; m. E. of Viṣṇu-Kṛṣṇa.
यज्ञायतन n. place for sacrifice.
यज्ञायुध n. sacrificial instrument; poss. °धिन्.
यज्ञार्थम् adv. for a sacrifice.
यज्ञिन् a. rich in sacrifices (Viṣṇu).
यज्ञिय a. relating to, skilful in, or worthy of sacrifice; sacrificial, pious, holy, divine. m. offerer or a god.
यज्ञीय a. sacrificial.
यज्ञेश & °श्वर m. lord of the sacrifice (Viṣṇu).
यज्ञोपवीत n. the investiture with the sacrificial cord or the s. cord itself.
यज्ञोपवीतिन् a. invested with the sacrificial cord.
यंज्यु a. performing or receiving worship.
यंज्वन् m., **यंज्वरी** f. worshipper, sacrificer, pious man or woman; adj. sacrificial.
यत्, **यंतति**, °ते, pp. **यत्त** (q.v.) & **यतित** A. join, connect, unite; A. (M.) associate one's self with, rival with (instr.); M. join one's self with, meet (as friends or foes); M. (A.) try to join, strive after, endeavour at, be devoted to or intent upon (loc., dat., acc. ± **प्रति**, or infin.); absol. exert one's self, take pains, be cautious or careful. C. **यातंयति**, °ते A. put in order, arrange, join, connect (M. refl.), remind (gen.) of (acc.); requite with reward or punishment (also M.). — **अधि** M. fasten, stick or put on. **आ** arrive, enter, stay or abide in (loc.), strive after (dat.). **अन्वा** C. A. connect, unite, cause to join or partake of (loc. or acc.). **उप** M. befall. **नि** M. get at (loc.). **निस्** C. carry off, lead away; fetch out of, get, procure, give back, restore, requite. **प्रतिनिस्** C. give back, restore. **परि** surround. **प्र** make effort, take pains, strive after, endeavour at (loc., dat., acc., or infin.). **प्रति** thwart, oppose; retaliate, requite. **वि** C. arrange; do penance; vex, harass. **सम्** A. join, connect; M. intr. join with (instr.), assemble, meet together, encounter. — Cf. **अन्वायत्त** (sic!), **आयत्त**, **समायत्त**, **संयत्त**.

यत a. held, restrained, checked, controlled.
यतचित्तात्मन् a. restraining one's mind and self.
यतचेतस् a. restrained in mind.
यतनीय n. impers. = **यतितव्य**.
यतम a. who or which (rel.) of many.
यतमथा adv. in which (rel.) of many ways.
यतर a. who or which (rel.) of two.
यतरथा adv. in which (rel.) of two ways.
यतव्रत a. observing vows; devout, firm, constant.
यंतस् adv. (= abl. of **य**) from whom, what or which, (from) where (repeated from whom etc. soever); wherefore, why, because, as; since (+ **प्रभृति**); as soon as; that, so that, in order that. — Cf. **ततस्**.
यतंस्रुच् a. lifting up or stretching out the sacrificial ladle.
यतात्मन् & °त्मवन्त् a. self-restrained.
1**यंति** pl. as many (correl. of **तति**).
2**यंति** m. controller, esp. of self i.e. ascetic, devotee; N. of a myth. race of ascetics etc.
3**यंति** f. restraint, control; pause, caesura.
यतिचान्द्रायण n. a kind of penance.
यतितव्य n. impers. to be striven after (loc.).
यतित्व n. the state of an ascetic.
यतिथ, f. **ई** the as (rel.) maniest.
यतिधा adv. in as (rel.) many parts or ways.
यतिन् m. ascetic.
यतिपात्र n. an ascetic's vessel.
यतिवेष a. wearing an ascetic's garments.
यंत्काम a. which desiring.
यत्काम्या (instr. adv.) in which design.
यात्कारणम् adv. for which motive or reason; because, since.
यत्कृते adv. wherefore, why.
यत्न m. endeavour, effort, labour, pains about (loc. or —°). °—, instr., abl. & adv. in **तस्** with effort, diligently, carefully; **यत्नं कृ** take pains, strive after, endeavour at (loc. or infin.).
यत्नवन्त् a. making effort, energetic, zealous about (loc.).
यत्प्रभाव a. of what power.
यंत्र (**यंत्रा**) adv. (= loc. of **य**) where, when,

while, as, if. — यत्र कुत्र (± अपि) wherever, everywhere. यत्र क्व च (± न) the same, at any time. यत्र क्वापि anywhere, here and there.

यत्रत्य a. where being or dwelling.

यत्रसायंगृह a. resting where evening (comes).

यत्रेच्छक (°—) where one likes, at pleasure.

यत्रोद्भूत a. where arisen.

यत्संख्याख a. being in what number, counting how many.

यथा adv. as, in which way (correl. तथा, एव or एवम्), as truly as (corr. तथा), as for example (also तद्यथा). As conj. that (also before a direct quotation with इति), so that, in order that; as, since; as if. Often °— in adject. & adv., where sometimes not to be translated. - Cf. कथम्, तथा, & तद्.

यथाकथित a. (as) already mentioned.

यथाकर्तव्य a. to be done under certain circumstances; n. the proper course of action.

यथाकर्म adv. according to (the respective) actions.

यथाकामम् (or °कामम्) adv. according to wish, agreeably, at one's ease.

यथाकार्य a. = यथाकर्तव्य adj.

यथाकालम् adv. according to time, in due time.

यथाकृत a. well done, agreed; n. °कृतम् adv. as has been done, as usually, as agreed.

यथाक्रमम् adv. according to order, in regular series.

यथाखेलम् adv. with playful or gentle motion.

यथागत a. (n. & instr. adv.) on which (way) one came before.

यथागमनम् adv. as it has been got or found (of a ring, lit. according to its arrival).*

यथाङ्गम् adv. limb after limb.

यथाचित्तम् adv. according to a person's thought or will.*

यथाचिन्तितानुभाविन् a. judging by one's own frame of mind.

यथाज्ञानम् adv. according to (the best of one's) knowledge.

यथाज्येष्ठम् adv. according to age or rank.

यथातत्त्व (°—) & n. adv. according to truth.

यथातथम् adv. as it really is, exactly, accurately, duly.

यथातथ्यम् adv. in accordance with the truth.

यथादर्शितम् adv. as shown.

यथादिक् & °दिशम् adv. according to the various quarters of the sky.

यथादृष्टम् adv. as seen.

यथादैवतम् adv. deity after deity.

1यथादेशम् adv. according to places.

2यथादेशम् adv. according to direction.

यथाधर्मम् adv. according to duty or right.

यथाधीत a. as has been read, corresponding to the text.

यथानिर्दिष्ट a. as before mentioned.

यथान्यायम् adv. according to rule, justly.

यथापण्यम् adv. according to the wares.

यथापूर्व a. (being) as before; n. °पूर्वम् adv. one after another, as before.

यथाप्रतिज्ञम् adv. according to promise or agreement.

यथाप्रदेशम् adv. according to direction or place.

यथाप्रधानम् adv. according to precedence or superiority.

यथाप्रस्तुतम् adv. as intended or begun.

यथाप्राणम् & °णेन adv. according to one's might.

यथाप्राप्त a. suitable to circumstances, in conformity with a particular state or rule, proper; n. adv. regularly, correctly (g.).

यथाबलम् adv. according to power or to (the condition of) the army.

यथाबीजम् a. according to the seed.

यथाभागम् adv. according to shares or portions; in the respective or proper places.

यथाभिप्रेत a. as wished or desired; n. adv. according to wish, at pleasure.

यथाभिमत a. & adv. = prec. (also °—).

यथाभिरुचित a. as wished for, agreeable.

यथाभिलषित & यथाभीष्ट a. the same.

यथाभ्यर्थित a. as requested or asked for.

यथामति adv. according to one's opinion or judgment.

यथामुख्य a. according to the chief or first, according to rank and dignity; n. adv.

यथाम्नातम् & °म्नायम् adv. according to text or tradition.

यथायतनम् adv. according to place, in the right place.
यथायथम् adv. as is fit, in regular order.
यथायोगम् adv. according to circumstances.
यथायोग्यम् adv. as is fit or proper.
यथारूप a. of which kind or sort; n. **°पम्** adv. in a suitable way, properly, duly.
यथार्थ a. accordant with the thing or fact, true, exact, proper, fit; °— & **°र्थम्** adv., n. also as subst. the pure truth.
यथार्थनामक a. having a true name.
यथार्थनामन् n. a true name; a. = prec.
यथार्थित a. = **यथाभ्यर्थित**.
यथार्ह a. according to worth or merit, fit, right; °— & n. adv.
यथार्हणम् & **°र्हतस्** n. = prec. adv.
यथालब्ध a. as obtained or met with, previously found.
यथालाभ (°—) & **°भम्** adv. just as it happens to occur; justly, accidentally.
यथालिखितानुभाविन् a. perceiving that a thing is (only) painted.*
यथालोकम् adv. according to room or place; in the proper place.
यथावकाशम् adv. = prec.
यथावत् adv. according to propriety, as is fit or right, properly, duly.
यथावयस् & **°वयसम्** adv. according to age.
यथावशम् adv. according to pleasure.
यथावसरम् adv. on every occasion.
यथावस्तु a. according to the state of the matter, exact.
यथाविद्यम् adv. according to knowledge.
यथाविध a. of which kind or sort.
यथाविधानम् & **°धानेन** adv. according to precept or rule.
यथाविधि adv. = prec.; i.g. properly, duly.
यथाविषयम् adv. according to the object or matter.
यथावीर्य a. of what strength; n. adv. according to strength or courage.
यथावृत्त a. as happened or as (how) behaving; n. the actual occurrence of a thing or adv. as it really happened.
यथावृद्धम् adv. according to age.
यथावेदित a. as stated or deposed (j.).
यथाव्यवसितम् adv. as determined.*
यथाशक्ति or **°शक्त्या** adv. according to power or ability.
यथाशास्त्र (°—) & **°स्त्रम्** adv. according to precept or rule.
यथाश्रद्धम् adv. according to inclination.
यथाश्रुत a. as heard or handed down by tradition; n. adv.
यथाश्रुति a. according to the sacred precepts.
यथासंवृत्तम् adv. as has happened.*
यथासंकल्पित a. corresponding to wishes or expectations.
यथासंख्यम् adv. number for number, in due correspondence.
यथासङ्गम् adv. according to need, as required.
यथासन्न a. at every approach, n. adv.
यथासमयम् adv. according to time or circumstances.
यथासमर्थितम् adv. as settled.
यथासमीहित a. as desired; n. adv.
यथासर्वम् adv. as everything is, in all particulars.
यथासुखम् adv. at ease or pleasure.
यथासुखमुख a. turning the face as one pleases.
1**यथास्थान** n. the right or proper place.
2**यथास्थान** a., **°नम्** adv. (being) in the proper place or in regular order.
यथास्व a. each his own; n. each in his own way.
यथाहार a. eating as opportunity offers.
यथेच्छ a. according to wish or desire; °—, n., & **°च्छया** adv.
यथेप्सया (instr. adv.) = prec. adv.
यथेप्सित & **यथेष्ट** a. & n. adv. = **यथेच्छ**.
यथेष्टसंचारिन् a. going according to will or inclination.
यथेष्टाचरण n. arbitrary proceeding.
यथोक्त a. as aforesaid or mentioned above; n. adv.
यथोक्तकारिन् a. acting as told or directed.
यथोचित a. fit, proper, suitable, becoming; n. adv.
यथोत्तर a. following in regular succession; n. adv.
यथोत्साहम् adv. according to power, with all one's might.

यथोदित a. as said or spoken, previously told; n. adv.

यथोद्दिष्ट a. as indicated or mentioned, n. adv.

यथोपपत्ति adv. according to occasion, as may happen.

यथोप्त a. as sown, answering to the seed.

यद् n. sg. of **य** (used also as stem °—); as conj. that (after such verbs as say, think, etc.), in order that, as for the fact that; when, if; wherefore, why; as, because, since. Often correl. to **तद्** q.v. — **अथ यद्** & **यद्यपि** although, however; **यद्वा** or else; however, nevertheless; **यत्सत्यम्** certainly, indeed.

यदर्थ a. having which object or intention.

यदर्थम् & °**र्थे** a. for which purpose, wherefore.

यदा conj. when, if; often strengthened by **एव** (**यदैव**). In the correl. clause esp. **अथ, तद्, तदा, तेन,** etc. — **यदा कदा च, यदा यदा** or **यदा** w. doubled verb = whenever; **यदा कदा चिद्** at every time, always.

1**यदि** (**यदी**) conj. if, when (also **यदि चिद्, यदि चेद्, यदीद्, यद्यु,** in the correl. clause often followed by **अथ, तद्, तदा, ततस्, तर्हि, तेन,** etc.); that, but (after a neg.); if not, perhaps that; how if? — **तद्यपि** or **अपि यदि**—(**तथापि** or **तदपि**) = although, however — (still, nevertheless). **यदि (वा)**—**यदि (वा)** whether—or; **यदि—न वा** whether—or not.

यदीय a. whose, belonging to whom, which, or what.

यदु m. N. of an ancient hero & his race; cf. **तुर्वश**.

यदृच्छ a. accidental; f. **आ** accident, change, °—, instr., & °**तस्** accidentally, unexpectedly, spontaneously.

यदृच्छालाभ m. earning of what comes spontaneously; °**तुष्ट** a. satisfied with it.

यद्गोत्र a. belonging to what family.

यद्देवत a. having which godhead or divinity.

यद्धेतोस् (abl. adv.) from which reason or motive.

यद्भविष्य m. Fatalist, N. of a fish (lit. what will be, scil. will be).

यद्र्यञ्च् & **यद्र्यञ्च्** a. moving or turned in which direction.

यद्वत् adv. as, in what manner, as surely as (correl. to **तद्वत्** or **एवम्**).

यद्वा v. **यद्**.

यद्विध a. of what sort.

यद्वृत्त n. occurrence, event, adventure.

यन्तृ m. holder, manager, driver, ruler.

यन्तव्य a. to be held in or restrained.

यन्त्र n. hold i.e. means for holding, prop, support, fence, barrier; trace (of a carriage); i.g. any instrument or machine.

यन्त्रण n., **आ** f. restriction, limitation, control.

यन्त्रदृढ a. locked up (door).

यन्त्रधारागृह n. a room with a shower-bath, a bathing-room; abstr. °**त्व** n.

यन्त्रय्, °**यति**, pp. **यन्त्रित** restrain, curb, bind, fetter. — **उप, नि, सम्** = S.

यन्त्रारूढ a. mounted on a machine.

यन्त्रिन् a. having a harness (horse); m. tormentor, harasser.

यन्निमित्त a. caused by what; n. adv. wherefore, for which reason.

यभ्, **यभति**, °**ते** futuere.

यम्, **यच्छति**, °**ते**. (**यमति**, °**ते**), pp. **यत** (q.v.) hold, hold up, lift, raise, erect, sustain, support; hold back, restrain, check, stop; hold out, offer, grant, furnish, give (dat. or loc. of pers. & acc. of th., or acc. of pers. & instr. of th.); stretch, extend, show; M. rest on (loc.), stretch or extend with (instr.); hold out, persevere, be obedient or faithful to (dat.). C. **यमयति** (°**ते**) hold back, restrain, control, bring in order. — **अधि** erect, raise towards (loc.), extend over (dat.). **अनु** direct, turn, arrange, M. conform one's self to, follow (acc.). **अन्तर्** restrain, check (inwardly). **आ** hold out, stretch, extend, lengthen, bend (a bow), put on or draw back (an arrow), throw (a lance), abs. take aim; stop, check, restrain, draw near, bring. **अभ्या** draw, extend, protract; aim at (acc.). **निरा** stretch out. **व्या** tear asunder, stretch out, extend; M. (A.) struggle or contend about (loc.). C. (**व्यायाम्य**) take excercise. **समा**

draw together, contract, pull, stretch. उद् lift up, raise (lit. & fig.); hold forth, offer, present; shake up, stir, agitate; check, restrain, stop; A. M. strive, prepare for, endeavour at (dat. or अर्थम्). प्रोद् raise, uplift. समुद् the same, check, curb, restrain. उप take hold of, seize; offer, present; take to wife, marry. नि hold, restrain, stop (M. intr.); fasten, lie to, bind up (the hair); take, assume; offer, present; govern, control, limit; fix, establish. C. restrain, curb; fasten, tie to (loc.), suppress, limit. विनि & संनि hold, restrain, suppress. प्र stretch, hold out, offer, give; produce, cause; pronounce, utter; restore, pay back, return. प्रतिप्र offer in turn, give back, restore. संप्र offer or present (together), grant, bestow, give in marriage; return, restore. वि hold asunder, stretch out, extend. सम् hold together, draw tight (reins), restrain, curb, check, control, govern, bind together or up, attach, fasten, fetter; suppress, omit, annul, destroy. C. bind, fetter, bind up, arrange (hair); check, curb, subdue. — Cf. अभ्युद्यत (add.), आयत, उद्यत, नियत, प्रयत, प्रोद्यत, वियत, व्यायत, संयत.

1यम m. holder, i.e. bridle or driver; restraint, self-control, any paramount moral duty or observance (ph.).

2यम, (f. आ & ई) paired, twin; m. a twin (du. twins), N. of a god, either the Twin (with his sister यमी f.) or the Restrainer, the god of death. n. pair, twin letter (g.)

यमक a. double, twofold; n. a kind of paronomasia (rh.).

यमकिंकर m. Yama's servant.

यमक्षय m. Yama's realm.

यमगाथा f. a verse or hymn relating to Yama.

यमज, °जात, °जातक a. twin-born; m. du. twins.

यमदण्ड m. Yama's rod.

यमदूत m. Yama's messenger.

यमधानी f. Yama's abode.

यमन a. (f. ई) & n. restraining.

यमनेत्र a. having Yama as a guide.

यमपुरुष m. = यमकिंकर.

1यमराजन् m. king Yama.

2यमराजन् a. having Yama as king; m. a subject of Yama.

यमराज्य & °राष्ट्र n. Yama's dominion.

यमल a. twin, paired, doubled; m. a twin.

यमलोक m. Yama's world.

यमवन्त् a. having self-possession, who governs or controls himself.

यमविषय m. Yama's realm.

यमश्रेष्ठ a. pl. having Yama as chief.

यमश्व m. Yama's dog.

यमसदन n. Yama's seat or abode.

यमसादन n. the same.

यमसू f. bringing forth twins.

यमिन् a. = यमवन्त्.

यमिनी f. bringing forth twins.

यमिष्ठ a. restraining best.

यमुना f. N. of river (identif. w. यमी).

यमेष्ट n. a sacrifice offered to Yama.

ययाति m. N. of an ancient patriarch.

ययि or ययी a. running, hastening; m. cloud.

यय a. = prec. a.; m. horse.

यर्हि conj. when, if (correl. तर्हि); as, because.

1यव m. any grain or corn, esp. barley or a barley-corn.

2यव m. pl. the bright halves of the months.

3यव a. warding off, keeping away.

यवक्षेत्र n. field of barley.

यवखल m. thrashing-floor.

यवगोधूमवन्त् a. producing barley and wheat.

यवन् m. = 2यव.

1†यवन a. keeping off (—°).

2यवन m. a Greek or Muhammedan (f. ई), i.g. a foreigner.

यवनिका f. curtain (cf. जवनिका).

यवपिष्ट n. barley-meal.

यवमध्य a. thick in the middle (lit. having the middle of a barley-corn).

यवमध्यम n. a kind of penance (r.).

यवमन्त् a. containing or mixed with barley. m. corn-grower; n. abundance of corn.

यवमय a. consisting or made of barley.

यवयावन् a. warding off.

यवयु a. wishing for grain.

यवस m. n. grass, pasture, food.
यवसाद् a. feeding on grass.
यवागू f. rice-gruel.
यवाचित a. laden with barley.
यवाद् a. eating barley.
यवाशिर् a. mixed with barley.
यवासक m. the manna-plant.
यवाहार a. living on barley.
यविष्ठ (superl.) youngest, E. of Agni as the fire just kindled or set on the altar.
यविष्ठ्य a. the same.
यवीयंस् (compar.) younger; lesser, worse; the least or worst. m. & f. **°यसी** a younger brother & sister.
यवीयुध् a. fond of war, warlike.
1**यव्य** m. a stock of barley or corn i.g.
2**यव्य** m. a month.
यव्या f. stream, river; only instr. sgl. & pl. in streams i.e. abundantly.
1**यशस्** n. glory, fame, honour, beauty.
2**यशस्** a. glorious, honoured, splendid.
यशस्कर, f. **ई** causing renown, glorious.
यशस्काम a. eager for renown, ambitious.
यशस्कृत् & **यशस्य** a. = **यशस्कर**.
यशस्यु a. seeking favour.
यशस्वन्त् a. glourious, splendid, excellent.
यशस्विन् a. the same.
यशोघ्न a. destroying renown, disgracing.
1**यशोदा** a. causing renown or splendour.
2**यशोदा** f. N. of Nanda's wife, Kṛṣṇa's foster-mother.
यशोधन a. rich in glory or renown.
यशोधा a. conferring splendour or fame.
यशोभगिन् a. rich in glory.
यशोभृत् a. bearing fame, renowned.
यशोवर्मन् m. N. of sev. men.
यशोहन्, f. **°घ्नी** destroying glory or beauty.
यशोहर a. robbing fame, disgracing.
यष्टवे dat. inf. to 1**यज्**.
यष्टव्य a. to be sacrificed or worshipped; n. impers.
यष्टि f. staff, stick, stalk (often to compare an arm or a slender body with); string of pearls, necklace.
यष्टृ or **यष्टृ** m. worshipper, sacrificer.
यष्ट्युत्थान n. the rising by the help of a stick.

यस्, **यस्यति**, **ययस्ति**, pp. **यस्त** be hot or eager, exert one's self. — **आ** = S., C. **आयासयति** strain, stretch, tire, vex, harass (w. **आत्मानम्** refl.*). **प्र** commence to boil up or be agitated, be hot or eager. — Cf. **आयस्त** (add.), **प्रयस्त**.
यस्मात् (abl. to **य**) because, since, that.
यह्व a. young, lively; m. child.
यह्व, f. **ई** youngest, newest, always young or fresh (of Agni = **यविष्ठ**, of the waters etc.). f. **ई** pl. flowing water.
यह्वन्त्, f. **यह्वती** = prec.
1**या**, **याति** (**°ते**), pp. **यात** (—° mostly w. act. mg) go, travel, march, set out, depart, fly, escape, pass, vanish, perish; go off, speed, succeed; proceed, act, behave; go to (acc., loc., or dat.), reach, attain to a condition (acc. of an abstr., cf. **गम्**), go to a woman, have sexual intercourse with (acc.), approach with a request, ask for (2 acc.); make out, learn, understand. With **आख्याम्** be called (nom. + **इति**), w. **खण्डशस्** or **दलशस्** fall to pieces, w. **शतधा** fall into a hundred pieces; **क्व तद्यातम्** how is it with it? **यातु** let it go, no matter. C. **यापयति** make or bid go (to *acc.), dismiss, send out, drive away, pass, spend. D. **यियासति** wish or be about to go etc. — **अच्छ** approach, arrive. **अति** pass by, overtake, omit. **अनु** go to (acc.), go after, follow (esp. in death), obey, imitate, equal, reach, attain. **अप** go away, depart, retreat, flee, cease, desist. **प्रत्यप** retreat, fly back. **व्यप** go away, set out, flee. **अभि** approach, go to or against; take to, partake of (acc.). **अव** come down, descend from (**आ** w. abl.); go away, depart; avert, remove. **आ** approach, arrive, come from (abl.) to or into (acc., r. loc.), get at, enter into, partake of (acc.); appear to (gen.), befall (acc.). **अत्या** pass by (acc.). **अभ्या** come near or to (acc.). **उपा**, **अभ्युपा**, **समुपा** the same. **प्रत्या** return, come back to (acc.), go to meet or against (acc.). **समा** come near (together), arrive; assemble, meet, come out of or from (abl.) to (acc. or loc.);

pass away; get into a state or condition (acc.). उद् rise, go forth or out, depart from (abl.). प्रत्युद् rise and go to meet or against (acc.). उप come near, arrive, visit, approach (acc., also loc. of place); enter (acc.), meet, encounter, undergo (acc.); occur to, fall to one's share (acc.). अभ्युप come to, get at, go against (acc.). प्रत्युप return, come back to or into (acc. ± प्रति or loc.). समुप come near (together), go or resort to (acc.). नि come down to or upon (acc.), run over (with a carriage), get into (acc.). निस् go or come out of (abl.) to or into (acc.); pass away, vanish. C. cause to go away, expel from (abl.). अभिनिस् & विनिस् go out, depart from (abl.). परि go round, circumambulate, surround, keep, guard; go through, pervade; pass by, avoid; flow off (Soma). प्र go forth, set out, go towards (acc. ± अच्छ or प्रति, & loc.) or against (acc.); walk, run, ride, drive, flow, etc.; vanish, pass away, die; get into, partake of (acc.); proceed, act, behave. अनुप्र set out after (acc.), follow. अभिप्र approach (acc.), set out, leave for (acc.), attack, assail. प्रतिप्र come near or back. संप्र set out (together), walk or flow towards (acc. ± प्रति). प्रति come near or back to (acc. ± प्रति); go against (acc.); comply with, gratify (acc.). वि pass or cut through, go or turn away. सम् go or come together, meet, encounter (as friends or foes), approach, arrive, get into a state or condition. अनुसम् go to and fro, go to, visit. अभिसम् go to or against (acc.). प्रतिसम् go against, attack.

2या going (—°).

याग m. sacrifice.

याच्, याचति, °ते, pp. याचित ask, beg, request (acc. or abl., r. gen. of pers.; acc. ± प्रति of th., also अर्थम् or अर्थे & dat. of an abstr.); woo, ask a girl (acc.) from (abl., r. acc.); offer a thing (acc.) to (dat.). C. याचयति cause to ask or sue; ask a thing (acc.) for (अर्थे). — अनु ask, entreat. अभि ask, request (2 acc.); ask (a girl) in marriage from (acc.). आ & उप ask, implore. निस् beg off from (2 acc. or acc. of th. & instr. of pers.). प्र ask, beg (2 acc.). संप्र & सम् the same.

याचक m., ई f. petitioner, beggar.

याचन n. asking (also in marriage), begging for (—°).

याचनक m. beggar, mendicant.

याचनीय a. to be asked or requested (n. imp.).

याचितव्य a. to be asked (also for a girl).

याचितृ m. petitioner, beggar, suitor.

याचिन् a. asking, begging for (—°).

याचिष्णु a. asking, soliciting, suppliant; abstr. °ता f.

याच्ञा f. asking, begging for (—°); petition, request.

याच्ञ्यं s., आ f. = prec.

याच्य a. to be asked or solicited; to be wooed, abstr. °ता f.

याज m. sacrificer.

याज m. = prec. (—°) or sacrifice.

याजक m. sacrificing priest.

याजन n. performance of a sacrifice for (gen. or —°).

याजिन् a. & m. sacrificing, sacrificer.

याज्ञ a. relating to sacrifice.

याज्ञवल्क्य m. patron. of a teacher.

याज्ञसेन m., ई f. patron. of Çikhaṇḍin & Draupadī.

याज्ञिक, f. ई relating to sacrifice; m. sacrificer, liturgist.

याज्ञिक्य n. the rules of the liturgists.

याज्ञिय a. & m. = याज्ञिक.

याज्य a. for whom or what is sacrificed; m. sacrificer or tutor of a sacrifice, abstr. °ता f., °त्व n. — f. याज्या the consecrating text, poss. याज्यवन्त्.

1यात् (abl. adv.) in as much as, as long as, since.

2†यात् v. ऋणयात्.

यात a. gone, passed, etc.; n. gait, march, motion; (*the place where a person has gone); the past time.

यातन n. requital; f. आ the same, punishment, fine, pains, esp. of hell.

यातनार्थीय a. subject to torments.

यातयंज्जन a. arranging men.
यातयाम & °**मन्** a. exhausted, used, spoiled; useless, stale, flat (lit. having walked one's way); abstr. °**त्व** n.
1**यातृ** a. going, driving, riding etc., ceasing, perishing; m. the driver of a carriage.
2**यातृ** m. avenger.
3**यातृ** f. a husband's brother's wife.
यातवे dat. inf. to 1**या**.
1**यातव्य** a. used against witchcraft.
2**यातव्य** a. to be gone or set out (n. impers.); to be gone against, to be attacked or assailed.
यातव्यपक्ष m. the inimical party (lit. the side to be gone against).
यातु m. sorcery, witchcraft; also = seq.
यातुधान m., **ई** f. a kind of demons or evil spirits.
यातुमन्त् or °**मावन्त्** a. practising sorcery.
यातुविद् a. skilled in sorcery.
यातुहन् a. destroying witchcraft.
यात्रा f. going, setting off, journey, travel, march, expedition; festive train, procession, feast, festival; livelihood, subsistence; custom, usage; a kind of dramatic entertainment.
यात्रिक a. belonging to a march or an expedition, requisite for the support of life; n. march, campaign.
यात्रिन् a. being on a march or in procession.
यात्रोत्सव m. festive procession.
यात्सत्र n. N. of a cert. ceremony.
याथाकामी f., °**काम्य** n. acting according to will or desire, arbitrariness.
याथातथ्य n. the proper state or condition, reality, truth; °**तथ्यम्**, °**तथ्येन**, & °**तथ्यतस्** in truth or as is proper.
याद्, only **याद्मान** closely connected with (instr.).
यादव, f. **ई** relating to Yadu; m. & f. his descendant, m. pl. his race.
यादवशार्दूल & **यादवेन्द्र** m. E. of Kṛṣṇa.
यादस् n. sea monster.
यादुर a. embracing voluptuously.
यादृग्गुण a. of what qualities.
यादृच्छिक a. spontaneous, accidental.
यादृश् & °**दृश**, f. **ई** which like, qualis.
याद्राध्यम् adv. as well or as quickly as possible.
याद्व a. belonging to the race of Yadu.
यान a. leading (of a way) to (gen. or adv. in **त्रा**). n. going, riding, marching; way, course; ship, vehicle i.g., waggon, chariot.
यानक n. carriage, vehicle.
यानकर m. wheelwright.
यानग a. riding in a carriage.
यानपात्र n. ship, boat (lit. going-vessel).
यानभङ्ग m. shipwreck.
यानस्वामिन् m. the owner of a carriage.
यानासन n. du. marching and sitting.
यानास्तरण s. waggon-cushion.*
यापक a. bringing, procuring.
यापन a., n. & f. **आ** causing to go, bringing to an end (time), prolonging or supporting (life); as subst. also procrastination, delay.
याप्य a. to be expelled or rejected (abstr. °**त्व** n.); low, vile, trifling, unimportant.
याभ m. sexual intercourse, p. °**वन्त्**.
1**याम** m. close, end.
2**याम**, f. **ई** belonging to or coming from Yama.
3**याम** m. course, going, way, progress; carriage, chariot; watch of the night (3 hours).
यामश्रुत a. renowned for speed.
यामन् n. going, motion, course, fight; march, expedition, approaching with prayers, invocation.
यामहू a. to be called or being ready to help.
यामहूति f. invocation for help.
यामि or **यामी** f. = **जामि** f.
यामिक a. keeping watch; m. watchman, night-watcher.
यामिनी f. night; a woman's name.
याम्य a. relating to Yama, southern; m. a servant of Yama, f. (± **दिश्**) the south.
याम्योत्तर a. southern and northern.
याયजूक a. sacrificing eagerly.
यायावर a. wandering about, having no fixed abode; m. a vagrant mendicant, pl. N. of a race of Brahmans.
यायिन् a. going, running, flying, travelling.

1यांव m. pl. = 2यंव.
2याव a. consisting or made of barley.
3याव m. lac-dye.
1यावक m. n. a kind of food prepared from barley.
2यावक m. = 3याव.
यावच्छस् adv. as manifoldly as.
यावच्छेषम् adv. as much (many) as is left.
यावच्छ्रेष्ठ a. the best possible.
यावज्जीवम् & °वेन† adv. throughout life.
यांवत् v. यांवन्त्.
यावतिथ a. the as manieth.
यावत्कालम् adv. as long as anything lasts, a while.
यावत्कृत्वस् adv. as often as, whenever.
यावत्स्वम् adv. as many (much) as one has.
यावदध्ययनम् adv. during the lesson.
यावदन्तम् & °न्ताय adv. to the end.
यावदर्थ a. as much as necessary, corresponding to want; n. adv.
यावदहं n. the corresponding (as manieth) day.
यावदायुषम् & °युस् adv. through life.
यावदुक्त a. as much as stated; n. adv.
यावद्धा adv. as often or as many times as.
यावद्बलम् adv. with all one's strength.
यांवन् m. aggressor, pursuer.
1यावन a. born among the Yavanas; m. *incense.
2यावन n. removing, keeping off.
यांवन्त् a. as great, as far or long, as much or many (correl. तांवन्त् q.v.). n. यांवत् as adv. or conj. as far or as long as, while (also instr. & loc., correl. तांवत्, °ता & °ति); meantime, at once, just, now (w. 1. pers. pres., 3. pers. imper.); as prep. during (acc.), till or as far as (acc. or abl.). यावन्न as long as not, before, until; if not, unless. — Cf. अद्य, इति, तावन्त्.
यावन्मात्रं a. of which measure or size, far extending; n. adv. as long as, a little, in some degree.
यावयंद्द्वेषस् a. driving away foes.
यांसु n. embrace, coition.
†यास् v. अयांस्.
यास m. N. of a plant.
यास्क m. N. of a teacher.
यियक्षु a. going to sacrifice.
यियासा f. desire of going.
यियासु a. being about to go.
1यु, यौति, युते, युवंति, °ते, pp. युतं (q.v.) fasten, hold fast, bind, harness, join, unite, draw towards one's self, attract get possession of. D. युयूषति wish to attract or hold fast. — आ draw onwards or towards, seize, occupy, get, procure, mix, mingle. पर्या & समा mix, stir up. नि tie on, fasten; procure, bestow; take to one's self, appropriate. प्र stir up, mix; disturb, destroy. सम् take to one's self, consume; put together, join, connect; share with, bestow on (instr.). — Cf. अभियुत, आयुत, नियुत, संयुत, समायुत.
2युं companion, comrade.
3यु, युयोति, युच्छति, °ते, pp. युत tr. repel, keep or ward off, separate, protect from (abl.); intr. keep apart, be or remain separate. C. यवंयति or यावंयति = S. tr. I. pp. यायुवत् yield, give way. — अप remove, avert from (abl. or dat.). निस् keep off, repel. प्र remove; keep away (intr.), be indolent or heedless. वि part (tr. & intr.); separate or be separated from, deprive or be deprived of (instr.); scatter, disperse, open. — Cf. वियुत.
4युं driving, going, moving.
युक्तं a. yoked, harnessed, set to work, appointed, instituted, occupied with, (loc. or —°); active, zealous, attentive, concentrated, absorbed in thought; skilful, clever in (loc.), joined or furnished with; accompanied by (instr. or —°) relating to, dependent on (—°); fit, proper, right to (w. यद् or infin.).
युक्तग्रावन् a. having set in motion (lit. harnessed) the Soma-stones.
युक्तचेष्ट a. acting or behaving properly.
युक्तमद a. intoxicated.
युक्तरूप a. suitable, fit, proper (loc. or gen.); n. adv.
युक्तरूपक n. a fit comparison (rh.).

युक्तात्मन् a. with concentrated mind.
युक्तार्थ a. sensible, rational.
युक्ति f. junction, connection (also of words, i.e.) sentence, preparation, application, use, employment, practice, means, expedient, trick, contrivance, stratagem, cause, motive, argument, correctness, fitness, propriety. — **युक्तिं कृ** find a means or try an art. **युक्त्या** & **युक्तितस्** properly, fitly, duly; by means or by virtue of (—°).
युक्तिमन्त् a. joined or connected with (—°); fit, able, competent.
युग n. (m.) yoke, team; couple, pair, race or generation of men, age of the world (4) a cert. measure of length.
युगक्षय m. the end of (an age of) the world.
युगधार m. the peg by which the yoke is fixed on the pole.
युगंधर n. pole of a carriage.
युगपद् adv. simultaneously, at once.
1**युगमात्र** n. the length of a yoke.
2**युगमात्र**, f. **ई** as long as a yoke.
युगल m. n. pair, couple.
युगलक n. = prec., esp. a couple of Çlokas.
युगशम्य n. yoke and peg.
युगशरम् adv. along with (instr.).
युगादि m. the beginning of (an age of) the world.
युगान्त m. the end of a yoke or of an age.
युगान्तर n. the other (half of the) sky.
युग्म & **°क** a. paired, even; n. pair, double Çloka.
युग्मन् & **युग्मन्त्** a. = prec. adj.
युग्य n. carriage or beast for draught.
युग्यवाह m. coachman, driver.
युग्यस्थ a. sitting in a carriage.
युङ्गिन् m. a cert. mixed caste.
युच्छ्, **युच्छति** v. 3**यु**.
1**युज्**, **युनक्ति**, **युङ्क्ते**, **युजते** & **युञ्जति**, **°ते** pp. **युक्त** (q.v.) yoke, harness (of waggon and steed); make ready, fit out, prepare, arrange, set to work (P. refl.); apply, use, fasten or fix on, put or place (**धुरि** at the head lit. at the thill), turn or direct (esp. the mind) upon (loc.); (± **योगम्**) be intent on, meditate (also M.); appoint, institute; bid, order, enjoin; unite, connect, join with (instr.); P. M. cling to, adhere, marry; A. present or furnish with (acc. of pers. & instr. of th., or loc. gen. of pers. & acc. of th.); M. become possessed of (acc.); P. the same (instr. ± **सह**) or fall to one's (gen.) share or lot, be fit or suitable for (loc., gen. or instr.), be proper or right. C. **योजयति °ते** yoke, harness, fit out, array; use, employ, undertake, begin; appoint to or charge with (loc.), fasten, fix (esp. the mind) or place on (loc.); unite, connect, furnish, endow with (instr.). D. **युयुक्षति** wish to lay on or to appoint. — **अनु** strive to overtake, pursue; ask, question (acc. of pers. or & th.). **अभि** A. appoint to, charge with (loc.); A. (M.) prepare or get ready for (acc. or infin.); M. (A.) yoke, harness, put to; attack, march against; P. be sued for or be accused of (acc.). C. furnish with, make a pers. (acc.) share in (instr.). **प्रत्यभि** attack or accuse in return. **आ** harness, put to (loc.); M. fasten, put on, place in (loc.). C. fix upon (loc.), put together. **समा** arrange, prepare; join, bring together with (instr.). **उद्** make one's self ready, set to work; set off, be gone. C. urge on, impel, also = **समुद्** C. incite or animate to (dat.). **उप** M. (A.) yoke, harness, put to (loc.); use, employ, appropriate, enjoy; consume, eat. P. be applied, be useful, necessary, requisite, or qualified for (loc., dat. of th., gen. of pers.). **नि** M. (A.) fasten or put to (loc., **धुरि** = S.); join, put together; bind or attach to, fix or turn upon (loc. or dat.); put (a task) upon, commission, elect (2 acc.), appoint to, charge with (acc. of pers. & loc. or dat. of th.; or loc. of pers. & acc. of th.); use, employ. C. harness, put to (loc.); tie on, fasten, set (jewels); direct, impel, exhort or constrain to (dat., acc. w. **प्रति**, loc., or **अर्थम्**), appoint to (loc.), choose for, elect (2 acc.); commit or entrust to (loc.); set, lay, fix; place in or upon, take into

or to (loc.); employ, set to work; furnish with, cause to partake of (instr.). विनि M. (A.) loosen, untie, unharness, shoot of—at (loc.), appoint to, destine for (loc., dat. or अर्थम्); place, fix (the mind) upon; use, employ; eat, consume. C. appoint to, charge with (loc., अर्थाय or अर्थम्); commit to (loc.), present, offer to (dat.), use, employ. संनि place in or on (loc.); commission, appoint, employ. C. the same, charge with (= विनि C.); urge on, impel; destine, assign. प्र M. (A.) harness, put to (loc.), prepare (instr.) for (dat.), join with (instr.), set in motion, hurl, cast shut off—at (loc. or dat.), turn or fix upon (loc.), utter, pronounce, show, manifest; animate, impel, bid, direct to (dat. or loc.), elect, choose for (2 acc.), bring to or into (acc.), place at or upon (loc.), add; use, employ; effect, produce; arrange, execute, perform (d.). P. be fit or suitable. C. hurl, cast; bring forth, utter, show, betray; fix, concentrate (the mind); direct, instruct, appoint to (loc.), commit to (dat.), begin, undertake; represent, perform; use, employ; exact (interest). अनुप्र M. add after (abl.); pursue, overtake; follow. विप्र sever from (instr.); C. deprive or rid of (instr.). संप्र yoke, harness, set in motion, let loose; execute, perform (music). P. be joined or added; partake or be guilty of (instr.). C. fit out, make ready; join or connect with (instr.); bring forth, use, employ. वि detach or sever from (instr.); A.M. liberate from or deprive of (instr., r. abl.); M.P. relax, yield, give way. C. separate, rid or deprive of (abl. or instr.). सम् A. put together, join, unite, bind, fetter; endow or furnish with (instr.), fix (the mind) upon (loc.). C. yoke, harness; fit out, equip (an army), lay on, shoot off (an arrow), turn or fix (the mind) on (loc.), appoint (to a commission), intrust or commit to (gen.); perform, accomplish; add to (loc.), put together, join, etc. = S. — Cf. अभियुक्त, आयुक्त, उद्युक्त, उपयुक्त, नियुक्त, निर्युक्त (add.), प्रयुक्त, विप्रयुक्त, वियुक्त, विसंयुक्त, संयुक्त, संप्रयुक्त, समायुक्त.

2युज् a. yoked together, harnessed with, drawn by (—°), endowed or furnished with (instr. or —°); pair, even. m. comrade, companion.

युजे dat. inf. to 1युज्.

युज्य a. united, allied, related, homogeneous, suitable, fit, proper. m. companion, ally; n. union, alliance.

युञ्ज् (nom. युङ्) a. yoked together; m. yokefellow, comrade.

युत a. fastened to (—°); added, united or connected with, consisting of, increased by, possessed of (instr. or —°).

युति f. union with, possession of (instr. or —°).

युत्कार a. making war.

युद्ध a. fought; n. fight, battle.

युद्धभू & °भूमि f. field of battle.

युद्धविशारद a. skilful in war.

युद्धशालिन् a. warlike, valiant.

युद्धाचार्य m. military instructor.

1युध्, युध्यते, °ति, योधति, pp. युद्ध (q.v.) fight, combat, contend with (instr. ± सह or समम्) for or about (loc.); fight (tr. w. acc.), vanquish. C. योधयति, °ते cause to fight, fight (tr.), defend. D. युयुत्सति, °ते wish to fight with (instr. or acc.). — अभि fight (acc. or instr.), vanquish, win by fighting. आ fight (tr.). उद् rise against (dat.) नि fight with (सह or साकम्). प्र (begin to) fight, attack (acc.). C. cause to open the fight. संप्र (begin to) fight. प्रति fight against, vanquish, be a match for (acc.). C. the same. सम् fight together, fight with (acc. or instr. ± सार्धम्). — Cf. प्रयुद्ध, प्रतियुद्ध.

2युध् m. warrior; f. fight, battle.

युधामन्यु m. N. of a warrior.

युधिष्ठिर m. N. of the eldest son of Pāṇḍu etc. (lit. firm in battle).

युध्म m. warrior, champion.

युध्वन् a. warlike.

युप्, only pf. **युयोप** & pp. **युपित** obstruct, thwart, hurt. C. **योपयति** efface, destroy. I. **योयुप्यते** make smooth or straight (hair). **सम्** C. efface, smooth.

युयुत्सा f. desire for war, pugnacity.

युयुत्सु a. eager for battle, wishing to fight with (instr. ± **सार्धम्**); N. of a prince.

युयुधान m. a man's name.

युव pron. st. (du.) of 2[d] pers. (°— often **युवा**).

युवति & °**ती** a. & f. young, young woman.

युवन् (**यून्**) a. & m. young, young man, youth (E. of sev. gods); a younger descendant (g).

युवन्त् a. = prec. adj.

युवन्यु a. juvenile.

युवयु a. longing for both of you.

युवराज m. young king i.e. heir-apparent, crown prince.

युवराजत्व & °**राज्य** n. the rank of an heir-apparent.

युवश a. young; m. a youth.

युवाकु a. belonging or devoted to both of you.

युष्म pron. st. (pl.) of 2[d] pers. (°— **युष्मा** & **युष्मद्**).

युष्मदीय a. your, yours.

युष्मद्विध a. one like you.

युष्माक a. your, yours.

युष्मादत्त a. given by you.

युष्मादृश् & °**दृश** a. one like you.

युष्मानीत a. led by you.

युष्मावन्त् a. belonging to you.

युष्मेषित a. sent by you.

युष्मोत a. befriended by you.

यूक m., **आ** f. house.

यूथ n. m. herd, troop, multitude.

यूथनाथ m. protector or leader of a herd or troop.

यूथप, °**पति**, & °**पाल** m. the same.

यूथशस् adv. in troops or herds.

यूथिका f. a kind of jasmine.

यूथ्य a. belonging to a herd or troop; f. **आ** herd, flock, troop.

यून n. band, cord, string.

यूप m. post, esp. the stake to which the sacrificial victim is fastened, poss. °**वन्त्**†.

यूपाहुति f. offering at the erection of the sacrificial post.

यूयुवि a. removing.

यूष m. n. broth, soup.

यूषन् (only weak cases) & **यूस्** (only nom.) = prec.

येन (instr. adv. & conj.) whither, where, in what manner, wherefore, why, that (quod or ut).

येष्, **येषति** boil up, bubble. — **निस्** boil or sweat forth.

येष्ठ (superl.) going most quickly.

योक्तव्य a. to be set to work, to be applied or appointed, to be collected or concentrated, to be endowed or furnished with (instr.); n. impers. preparations are to be made for (loc.).

योक्तृ m. harnesser, driver.

योक्त्र n. band, cord, halter.

योक्त्ररश्मि m. du. halter and bridle.

योग m. yoking, harnessing, drive, yoke, team; fitting out (an army), fixing (an arrow); setting to work, use, application; means, expedient, trick, stratagem, art, fraud, deceit, magic, charm; enterprise, work; union, combination, relation, contact with (instr. ± **सह** or —°); conjunction (of stars); pursuit, acquisition, property; succession, order, fitness, propriety; effort, endeavour, zeal, attention; collection or concentration of the mind, meditation, contemplation, N. of a phil. system; etymology & etym. meaning of a word, grammatical construction, rule or aphorism (g.). — Instr. & abl. in the right way, as is proper, according to, by means or in consequence of (—°).

योगक्षेम m. (n.) sgl., m. pl. (du.) security or secure possession of property; fortune (esp. if destined for pious uses), prosperity, welfare; °**मं वह्** get a pers. (dat.) a livelihood.*

योगक्षेमकर a. causing welfare.

योगधर्मिन् a. devoted to meditation.

योगधारणा f. perseverance in devotion.

योगनिद्रा f. contemplative sleep, i.e. a state

between sleeping and waking, slumber, esp. that of Viṣṇu at the end of an age of the world.

योगभ्रष्ट a. fallen from devotion.

योगमाया f. magic, charm, spell.

योगयज्ञ m. the sacrifice of devotion.

योगयात्रा f. the way of meditation, T. of a work.

योगयुक्त a. sunk in meditation.

योगरोचना f. a cert. magical ointment.

योगवन्त् a. joined, united; adhering to the Yoga system.

योगविद् a. knowing the (right) means or the Yoga system.

योगविभाग m. division of a rule (g.).

योगशास्त्र n. the Yoga doctrine.

योगस्थ a. persevering in devotion.

योगाचार्य m. a teacher of the art of magic or of the Yoga system.

योगात्मन् a. whose essence or nature is devotion or the Yoga system.

योगायोग m. du. propriety or impropriety.

योगिता f., **०त्व** n. abstr. to seq. adj. (—°); n. also abstr. to seq. m.

योगिन् a. united or connected with, relating to (—°); m. a Yogin, a follower of the Yoga system (f. **०नी**), a devotee or ascetic i.g.; f. **०नी** also a kind of witch or female demon.

योगीश्वर m. a master of sorcery or the chief among devotees, E. of Yājñavalkya.

योगेश्वर m. = prec.

योग्य a. fit for the yoke, i.g. fit, suitable, useful, conducive to, qualified for, capable of (gen., loc., dat., infin., or —°). m. beast for draught; f. **योग्या** setting to work, preparation, contrivance, practice.

योग्यता f., **०त्व** n. abstr. to prec. adj.

योजक m. harnesser, employer (—°).

योजन n. harnessing, yoke, team, drive, course, way, stage (a cert. measure of distance); direction, instruction, collection or concentration of the mind; arrangement, preparation, conjunction, combination (also f. **आ**).

योजनीय a. to be employed, to be joined with (instr.).

योजयितव्य a. to be used or selected, to be furnished with (instr.).

योज्य a. turned to (loc.), to be appointed or compelled to (loc. or —°); to be used or employed, to be added to (loc.) or furnished with (instr.).

योत्र n. rope, cord.

योद्धव्य a. to be fought, n. impers.

योद्धुकाम a. wishing to fight.

योद्धृ m. fighter, warrior.

योध m. = prec.

योधधर्म m. the law for warriors.

योधन n. combat, fight.

योधनीय a. to be fought.

योधमुख्य m. chief in war, leader.

योधवीर m. hero (in war).

योधिन् a. fighting.

योधीयंस् a. more warlike.

योध्य a. to be fought.

योनि m. f., **योनी** lap, womb, vulva; place of origin or abiding, home, lair, nest, etc.; family, race, caste; source, spring; seat, place i.g.; adj. born among, sprung from (—°); **योनितस्** by birth or blood.

योनिसंकर m. mixture of caste (lit. origin), intermarriage.

योन्य a. forming a womb or a receptacle.

योषणा (योषणा) f. girl, woman, wife.

योषन्, योषा, & योषित् f. the same.

योस् (only w. **शंम्**) welfare, happiness.

यौगंधरायण m. patron. of a minister.

यौगपद् & **०पद्य** n. simultaneousness; instr. **०पद्येन** adv.

यौगिक, f. **ई** agreeing with the etymology or derived from it.

यौतक a. belonging privately to a person; n. gift, donation, private property, esp. a woman's dowry.

यौध a. warlike.

यौधेय m. N. of a prince.

यौन n. relating to marriage or connected by it; n. matrimonial connection.

यौवन n. youth.

यौवनवन्त् a. youthful, young.
यौवनश्री f. the beauty or bloom of youth.
यौवनसुख n. the joys of love (lit. of youth).*
यौवनस्थ a. being in (the bloom of) youth.
यौवनारम्भ m. first (lit. beginning of) youth, juvenility.*
यौवनीय a. young, juvenile.
यौवराज्य n. the rank of an heir-apparent, °स्थ a. having this rank.
यौषिण्य n. womanhood.
यौष्माक & °कीन a. your, yours.

र

र (—°) possessing, having.
रंसु a. delightful.
रंसुजिह्व a. sweet-tongued (Agni).
रंह्, रंहते, °ति, pp. रंहित M. run, hasten, A. make run or hasten. C. रंहयति, °ते = S. — Cf. रारहाणं.
रंहस् n. speed, swiftness.
रंहि f. running, a running stream; speed, haste, flight.
रकार m. the sound र.
रक्त a. dyed, coloured, red, charming, beautiful, excited, agitated, impassioned, fond of (loc., gen., or —°), delighted with (instr.), loving, enamoured. f. आ lac; n. blood, *saffron.
रक्तक a. red, bloody.
रक्तकण्ठ, f. ई sweet-voiced; m. the Indian cuckoo.
रक्तकण्ठिन् a. = prec. a.
रक्तकदम्ब m. a red Kadamba (flower).
रक्तचन्दन n. red sandal.
रक्तच्छद a. red-leaved; abstr. °त्व n.
रक्तता f., °त्व n. redness.
रक्तदन्त् a. having red (i.e. dirty) teeth.
रक्तनेत्र a. red-eyed; abstr. °ता f., °त्व n.
रक्तपाद m. red-foot (a bird).
1**रक्तपुष्प** n. a red flower.
2**रक्तपुष्प** a. red-flowered.
रक्तभाव a. enamoured.
रक्तमुख a. red-mouthed.
रक्तमूलक m. a kind of mustard.
रक्तमोक्ष m., °ण n. blood-letting, bleeding.
1**रक्तवर्ण** m. red colour.
2**रक्तवर्ण** a. red-coloured.
रक्तवासस् & °वासिन् a. clad in red.
*__रक्तसंकोच__ n. safflower.
रक्ताक्ष, f. ई red-eyed.
रक्ताभ a. having a red appearance.
1**रक्ताम्बर** n. a red garment.
2**रक्ताम्बर** a. wearing a red garment.
रक्ताशोक m. red-flowering Açoka.
रक्तिमन् m. redness.
रक्तिमन्त् a. charming, lovely.
रक्ष्, रक्षति, °ते, pp. रक्षित protect, guard, keep, save from (abl.), take care of (acc.); beware of, prevent (acc.). C. रक्षयति protect from (abl.), save. D. रिरक्षति wish to protect from (abl.). — अनु guard or protect (by following). अभि & समभि keep, protect. आ protect, guard from (abl.). परि keep, guard, watch, protect, save from (abl.), take care of, maintain, observe. प्र preserve, rescue or deliver from (abl.). प्रति keep, observe. वि the same. सम् guard, watch, keep, maintain, take care of, defend, save.
रक्ष, f. ई protecting, guarding, keeping, watching; m. protector, keeper. f. आ guard, watch, protection, preservation; any preservative, esp. a sort of bracelet or amulet.
रक्षक m., रक्षिका f. guardian, protector.
रक्षण m. = prec. m.; f. आ & n. रक्षण protecting, guarding, saving, preserving.
रक्षणीय a. to be guarded or protected, shunned or avoided.
रक्षपाल m. protector, guard.
रक्षपालक m., °लिका f. = prec.
1†**रक्षस्** a. protecting, cf. पथिरक्षस्.
2**रक्षस्** n. harm, injury, damage; harmer, N. of a kind of evil beings or demons (also रक्षस).

†रक्षस v. असुररक्षस.
रक्षस्त्वं n. demoniacal nature, malice.
रक्षस्य a. anti-demoniacal.
रक्षस्विन् a. demoniacal, malignant.
रक्षाकरण्डक n. a basket as amulet.*
रक्षागण्डक m. a kind of talisman.*
रक्षाधिकृत a. appointed to protect; m. = seq.
रक्षाधिपति & रक्षापति m. superintendent of police.
रक्षाप्रतिसर m. an amulet (for protection).
रक्षामङ्गल n. ceremony (performed) for protection.
रक्षामणि m. a jewel as talisman.
रक्षावन्त् a. enjoying protection, guarded by (instr.).
†रक्षि v. पथिरक्षि.
रक्षितव्य a. to be guarded or protected from (abl.).
रक्षितृ m. keeper, guardian, protector.
रक्षिन् a. protecting, guarding; bewaring of (—°); m. = prec.
रक्षोघ्न a. driving back or killing Rākṣasas.
रक्षोजन m. pl. the band of Rākṣasas.
रक्षोदेवता f. pl. the deities of the Rākṣasas.
रक्षोदेवत्य & °दैवत a. having the Rākṣasas as deities.
रक्षोयुज् m. comrade of the Rākṣasas.
रक्षोहत्य n. the killing of Rākṣasas.
रक्षोहन्, f. °घ्नी = रक्षोघ्न.
रक्षण m. protection, guard.
रक्ष्य = रक्षणीय.
रंघीयंस् (compar.) lighter (in weight).
रघुं, f. रघ्वी running, swift, fleet, light; m. runner, courser; N. of an ancient king, pl. his race.
रघुनन्दन m. Raghu's son i.e. Rāma.
रघुनाथ, °नायक, & °पति the chief of the Raghus, i.e. Rāma.
रघुपत्वन् a. flying quickly.
†रघुमन्यु a. quick-tempered.
रघुयन्त् a. moving quickly.
रघुया (instr. adv.) quickly, lightly.
रघुयामन् a. moving lightly.
रघुवंश m. the race of Raghu, T. of a poem.
रघुवर & °वीर m. the best or the hero of the Raghus, i.e. Rāma.
रघुवर्तनि a. rolling or moving quickly.
रघुष्यद् a. rapid, swift.
रङ्क m. starveling, beggar.
रङ्कु m. a kind of deer or antelope.
रङ्ग्, रङ्गति move hither and thither, rock.
रंङ्ग m. colour, hue; theatre, play-house, stage, arena.
रङ्गद्वार n. prologue (d.).
रङ्गनाथ m. a man's name.
रङ्गभूमि f. place for acting, stage, arena.
रङ्गमङ्गल n. a cert. theatrical ceremony.
रङ्गमण्डप s. play-house, theatre.
रङ्गवाट s. place for contest or plays; stage, theatre.
रङ्गाङ्गण n. place for a public show.
रङ्गावतरण n. entering on the stage, the profession of an actor.
रङ्गावतारक & °तारिन् a. who enters the stage, m. an actor.
रङ्गिन् a. attached or devoted to, also = prec. a.
रङ्घ्, रङ्घते hasten, run.
रङ्घस् n. haste, speed.
रच्, रचयति, pp. रचित (q.v.) produce, form, make (also w. 2 acc.); contrive, arrange, prepare; cause, effect; compose, write; place or fix on or in (loc.). — आ arrange, prepare; write, compose; put on, furnish with (instr.). उप produce, make, form, cause, effect. वि produce, fabricate, construct, cause, effect, arrange, prepare; compose, write; invent, find out; put, place, fix on or in (loc.); furnish with (instr.).
रचन n. arranging, managing, preparing, writing, composing; f. आ arrangement, disposition, preparation, contrivance, bringing about, putting in or on, finding out, invention, fiction; style, literary composition.
रचयितृ m. composer, author.
रचित a. produced, arranged, prepared, made of (instr. or —°), composed or written, placed or fixed on, turned towards (loc.), provided or occupied with (instr. or —°).
रचितार्थ a. who has attained his object.
रज् or रञ्ज्, रज्यति, °त, pp. रक्त (q.v.) be coloured or red, be exited or agitated, be

affected with a strong feeling, esp. be delighted with, fond of, be in love with or have pleasure in (loc.). C. रञ्जयति (रजयति), pp. रञ्जित colour, redden; brighten, illumine; rejoice, delight, please, satisfy. — अनु be coloured or reddened after, take the tinge of, be delighted with, feel affection towards (acc. or loc.). C. colour after or according to (instr.); brighten, exalt, gratify, win, conciliate. अप lose colour; C. estrange, alienate (acc.). अभि be charmed or delighted with (instr.). उप eclipse, cast a shade upon (loc.). वि lose colour, become cold or indifferent towards (abl. or loc.). सम् be coloured or reddened. C. colour, redden, rejoice, gratify. — Cf. अनुरक्त, अपरक्त, उपरक्त, विरक्त, संरक्त.

रज m. dust, the pollen of flowers, a man's name.

रजःकण m. a grain of dust, pl. dust.

रजक m. (रजिका & रजकी f.) washerman (woman), who is also a dyer (a mixed caste).

रजत॑ a. whitish, silver-coloured, silvery; n. silver.

रजतपात्र॑ & °भाजन n. silver vessel.

रजतमय, f. ई made of silver, silver.

रजतान्वित a. adorned with silver.

र॑जन, f. ई colouring; m. ray, beam, N. of a man, f. ई night.

रजनि f. = रजनी (v. prec.).

रजनिकर m. the moon (night-maker).

रजनिचर m. a Rākṣasa (night-rover).

रजनिराक्षसी f. night regarded as a Rākṣasī.

रजनीचर m. night-walker, the moon or a Rākṣasa.

रजनीपति m. the moon (lord of night).

रजनीमुख n. evening, (beginning of night).

रजनीरमण & रजनीश m. the moon (husband or lord of night).

रजयित्री॑ f. a female dyer.

रजःशय॑ a. of silver.

र॑जस् n. atmosphere, air, esp. the lower region of clouds and vapours (opp. दिव् or रोचन); the sky (conc. also as twofold, रजसी) mist, gloom (i.g.); dust, pollen of flowers, any small particle of matter; foulness, impurity, esp. the menstrual secretion, darkness or soul-darkening passion (ph.).

रजस॑ a. obscure, dark.

रजस्क (adj. —°) = र॑जस्.

रजस्यु॑ a. vaporous, dusty.

रजस्वल a. dusty or full of passion; f. आ menstruating, a woman during the menses.

1रजि॑ m. N. of a demon or king.

2र॑जि f. direction.

र॑जिष्ठ (superl.) straightest or most honest.

रजोमेघ m. a cloud of dust.

रज्जव्य॑ n. materials for a rope.

र॑ज्जु (र॑ज्जू) f. cord, rope.

रज्जुक (adj. —°) = prec.

र॑ज्जुदाल m. a kind of tree or = seq.

रज्जुदालक m. the wild fowl.

रज्जुपीठिका f. a kind of rope-ladder.

रज्जुपेडा f. a rope-basket.

रज्जुबन्ध m. fettering with ropes.

रज्जुमय a. consisting of ropes.

रज्जुलम्ब m. a hanging rope.

रज्जुवाल v. रज्जुदाल.

रज्जुसर्ज॑ m. rope-maker.

रञ्जक, f. रञ्जिका colouring, dyeing; gladdening, charming, pleasing.

रञ्जन a. (f. ई) & n. = prec.; n. also colour.

रञ्जनीय a. to be rejoiced (at).

रट्, रटति, pp. रटित (q.v.) howl, yell, cry, roar. I. रारटीति scream aloud, croak. — आ = S.

रटन n. cry, applause.

रटरटाय्, °यते croak.

रटित a. shouted at; n. cry, yell, sound.

रण॑ m. joy, delight; (also n.) battle, fight about (—°).

रणकर्मन् n. battle, fight.

रणकृ॑त् a. causing joy or making war.

रणक्षिति f., °क्षेत्र n. field of battle.

रणत्कार m. rattling, humming.

रणदुन्दुभि m. battle-drum.

रणप्रिय a. fond of war, warlike.

रणभू & °भूमि f. field of battle.

रणमुख n., °मूर्धन् m., °शिरस् & °शीर्ष n. the front of battle or the van of an army.
रणरणक m. longing for, ardent desire; love or the god of love.
रणरसिक a. fond of war, pugnacious.
रणलक्ष्मी f. the fortune or the goddess of war.
रणशिक्षा f. the art or science of war.
रणशूर m. hero in war, warrior.
रणशौण्ड a. experienced in war.
रणस्थान n. battle-place.
रणाङ्गण, रणाङ्गन, & रणाजिर n. the same.
रणातोद्य n. war-drum.
रणावनि f. field of battle.
रणित a. & n. tinkling, rattling, humming.
रंणितृ m. who rejoices in (loc.).
रण्डा f. a slut or widow.
रंण्य a. delightful, pleasant; n. pleasure, delight, war, battle.
रण्व्, रण्वति, pp. रण्वितं (q.v.) delight.
रण्वं a. delightful, lovely, also = seq.
रण्वसंदृश् a. of lovely appearance.
रण्वितं a. merry, gay.
रतं a. content, happy, glad, merry; pleased with, devoted to, fond of (loc., instr., or —°); dallying or having sexual intercourse with (—°).
रंति f. rest, repose, quiet, comfort, pleasure in (loc. or —°); the pleasure of love, sexual intercourse (person. as the wife of the god of love).
रतिकर, f. ई causing joy or being in love, enamoured.
रतिक्रिया f. sexual intercourse.
रतिज्ञ a. skilled in love.
रतिपति m. Rati's husband (cf. seq.).
रतिप्रीति f. du. Rati and Prīti (the wives of the god of love).
रतिबन्धु m. husband, lover.
रतिमन्त् a. cheerful, gay; accompanied by Rati.
रतिरमण m. Rati's lover i.e. the god of love.
1रतिरस m. sexual enjoyment.
2रतिरस a. sweet as love.
रतिसंयोग m. sexual intercourse.
रतिसर्वस्व n. the fulness of delight.
रतिसहचर & रतीश m. the god of love (Rati's husband).
रतोत्सव m. the feast of love.
रंत्न a. gift, present, riches, treasure, esp. precious stone, jewel, pearl; often —° the jewel called—, a jewel of i.e. the best of; °— set or adorned with jewels.
रत्नकुम्भ m. a jar set with jewels.*
रत्नगर्भ a. filled with jewels; f. आ the earth.
रत्नच्छाया f. splendour of jewels.
रत्नतल्प m. a couch set with jewels.
रत्नदीप m. jewel-lamp (i.e. a lamp with jewels serving as light).
रत्नधं & °धा a. bestowing riches or blessings; superl. °धातम.
रत्नधेय n. abstr. to prec.
रत्ननिधि m. receptacle of pearls or jewels, E. of the sea, mount Meru, & Viṣṇu.
रत्नपर्वत m. jewel mountain, E. of Meru.
रत्नपुर n. N. of a city.
रत्नप्रदीप m. = रत्नदीप.
रत्नप्रासाद m. a palace adorned with jewels.
रत्नभाज् a. distributing or possessing treasures.
रत्नभाजन & °भाण्ड n. jewel-box.*
रत्नभूत a. jewel-like (lit. being a j.).
रत्नमय, f. ई made of jewels or pearls.
रत्नमाला f. a pearl necklace (poss. °लिन्); T. of sev. works (also —°).
रत्नरत्न n. the jewel of jewels.
रत्नराशि m. heap or collection of jewels.
रंत्नवन्त् a. abounding in gifts or jewels.
रत्नवर्धन & °वर्मन् m. names of men.
रत्नषष्ठी f. a cert. observance.*
रत्नसू a. producing jewels (the earth).
रत्नहविस् n. N. of a cert. oblation.
रत्नाकर m. jewel-mine, the sea.
रत्नाङ्कुर s. small (lit. sprout of) a pearl.
रत्नाङ्गुरीयक & °लीयक n. a ring set with jewels.
रत्नावली f. pearl necklace, a woman's name; T. of a play.
रत्निन् a. abounding in gifts or jewels.
1रंथ m. waggon, esp. war-chariot, also any

vehicle of the gods; charioteer, warrior, champion, hero.

2रथ m. pleasure, joy.

रथकार & रथकृत् m. wheelwright.

रथकेतु m. the banner of a chariot.

रथघोष m. the sound of a chariot.

रथचक्र & रथचरण n. chariot-wheel (foot).

रथचर्या f. (often pl.) going by carriage.

रथजङ्घा f. the hinder part of a carriage.

1रथजित् a. winning chariots.

2रथजित् a. winning affection, charming.

रथज्ञान n. knowledge of chariots, skill in driving; poss. °निन्.

रथतुर a. speeding or overtaking a chariot.

रथधुर् f. the pole of a carriage.

रथनाभि f. nave of a chariot-wheel.

रथनेमि f. the rim of a chariot-wheel.

रथपथ m. carriage-road.

रथप्रा a. filling or furthering chariots.

रथभङ्ग m. the breaking of a carriage.

रथमार्ग m. = रथपथ.

रथमुख n. the front or forepart of a chariot.

रथयान n. the going in a chariot.

रथयावन् a. going in a chariot.

रथयु a. wishing for chariots.

रथयुज् a. yoking the chariot or yoked to it; m. charioteer.

रथयुद्ध n. a chariot fight.

रथयोग m. the team of a chariot.

रथयोध m. who fights from a chariot, a charioteer.

रथरश्मि m. waggon-string, trace.

रथर्य्, रथर्यति go in a chariot.

रथवन्त् a. abounding in chariots; n. possession of chariots.

रथवर्त्मन् n. carriage-road.

रथवाह, f. ई drawing a chariot; m. chariot-horse or = seq.

रथवाहक m. charioteer.

रथवाहन n. a movable frame to place carriages upon.

रथविज्ञान n., °विद्या f. skill in (managing) chariots.

रथविमोचन n. unyoking of a chariot; °नीय a. relating to it.

रथवीथी f. = रथपथ.

रथवेग m. the speed of a chariot.

रथशिक्षा f. = रथविज्ञान.

रथशिरस् & °शीर्ष n. = रथमुख.

रथसङ्ग m. throng of chariots.

रथस्थ a. standing on a chariot.

रथस्पति m. the deity of comfort or chariots.

रथाक्ष m. a carriage axle.

रथाङ्ग n. any part of a carriage, esp. a wheel, also a potter's wheel & the discus of Viṣṇu-Kṛṣṇa. m. a kind of goose or duck.

रथाङ्गनामन्, °संज्ञ, & °साह्व m. = prec. m.

रथाङ्गपाणि & रथाङ्गिन् m. E. of Viṣṇu.

रथानीक n. an array of war-chariots.

रथारथि adv. chariot against chariot.

रथारोह m. charioteer or the mounting a chariot.

रथाश्व m. carriage-horse, n. carriage & horse.

रथाहस् n., रथाह्न m., & रथाह्न्य n. a day's journey by carriage.

रथिक m. owner or driver of a carriage.

रथिन् a. having or going in a carriage, carriage- or cart-; m. charioteer or = prec.

रथिर a. = prec. a. or quick, swift.

रथी a. & m. = रथिन्; as m. also guide, ruler, lord i.g.

रथीय्, only रथीयन्त् moving in a chariot.

रथेश m. owner of a chariot or a warrior fighting from a chariot.

रथेशुभ् a. hastening along in a chariot.

रथेषा f. the pole of a carriage.

रथेषु m. a kind of arrow.

रथेष्ठ or °ष्ठा a. & m. standing on a chariot, charioteer.

†रथोढ a. carried on a chariot.

रथोद्धत a. proud of a chariot; f. आ N. of a metre.

रथोपस्थ m. the seat (lap) of a chariot.

रथ्य or रथ्य a. belonging or accustomed to a carriage, chariot-; m. a carriage-horse. f. रथ्या road, high-road. n. chariot-trappings or a wheel; a race or contest with chariots.

रथ्यामुख n. mouth or entrance of a road.*

रथ्योपसर्पण n. walking on a road.

रद्, रदति, °ते, pp. रदित scratch, gnaw, rend, dig open (a way), guide, lead into a course (a river), convey or bring to (dat.). — प्र scratch, dig. वि separate, open.

रद् a. scratching, gnawing at (—°); m. tooth.

रदच्छद m. lip (lit. tooth-covering).

रदन m. tooth, tusk.

रदनच्छद m. = रदच्छद.

रदनिका f. a woman's name.

†रदावसु a. dispensing wealth.

रध्, रन्ध्, रध्यति, pp. रद्ध be or make subject to (dat.); harass, pain. C. रन्धयति (°ते) = S. trans. I. (रारन्धि) subdue. — नि give into the power of (dat.).

रध्र a. wretched, poor; a miser.

रध्रचोद & °चोदन a. impelling the miser.

रध्रतुर a. the same.

1रन्, रणति, °ते, & रण्यति be pleased, rejoice, take pleasure in (loc., r. acc.). C. रणयति, °ते delight a pers. with (instr.) or in (loc.), or = S. (w. loc.).

2रन्, रणति, pp. रणित (q.v.) ring, sound, tinkle. C. रणयति make ring etc.

रन्ति f. delight in (loc.).

रन्तिदेव m. N. of an ancient king.

रन्तृ a. liking to stay with (loc.).

रन्त्य a. delightful, pleasant.

रन्धन a. & n. destroying; n. also cooking, preparation of food.

†रन्धनाय्, °यति make subject, deliver into the power of (dat.).

रन्धि f. subjugation; the being cooked.

रन्ध्र n. (m.) opening, cleft, hole, pit; defect, flaw, weak part.

रन्ध्रानुसारिन् a. searching out the weak parts.

रन्ध्रोपनिपातिन् a. rushing in through holes.

रप्, रपति chatter, whisper; I. रारपीति = S.

रपस् n. defect, fault, hurt, injury.

†रप्श्, रप्शते (S. only in seq.) be full. — प्र reach beyond (abl.). वि be overfull, have plenty of (gen. or instr.).

रप्शदूध्न् a. having a full udder.

रफ्, only pp. रफित brought down, wretched.

रब्धा f. food.

रभ् or रम्भ्, रभते, °ति (रम्भति, °ते), pp. रब्ध (—° w. act. & pass. mg) take hold, seize, embrace. C. रम्भयति & D. रिप्सते (only —°). — अनु grasp, seize. आ take hold upon, touch, seize, lean or stay upon (acc.), reach to, attain; undertake, begin to (acc. or infin.). अन्वा take hold of from behind, hold on to (acc.). समन्वा take hold of each other or together. अभ्या grasp, touch, get at, undertake, begin. प्रा & समा the same. परि & संपरि embrace (together). सम् take hold of (each other), seize upon, partake of, enjoy (instr.); M. P. be excited or agitated. अभिसम् grasp, hold fast. — Cf. आरब्ध (sic!), आरभ्य, प्रारब्ध, संरब्ध.

रभ m. N. of a monkey.

रभस् n. impetuosity, fierceness, violence; instr. adv. violently, furiously, rapidly.

रभस a. impetuous, fierce, violent, strong. m. = prec. + energy, zeal, ardent desire of (—°); °—, instr., & abl. = prec. adv.

रभस्वन्त् a. impetuous, violent.

रभि f. a cert. part of a chariot.

रभिष्ठ (superl.) very impetuous or fierce.

रभीयंस् & रभ्यस् (compar.) the same.

रभोदा a. giving impetuous strength.

रम्, रमते, °ति, रम्णाति, pp. रत (q.v.) tr. stop, fix, settle; gladden, delight, enjoy (esp. carnally); intr. stop, rest, stay gladly with (loc. or dat.); delight in, be pleased with or to (loc., instr., or infin.); be happy or content; dally or have sexual intercourse with (instr. ± समम्, सह, साकम्, or सार्धम्). C. रमयति or रामयति = S. trans. — अनु A. stop (intr.), stay; M. find pleasure or delight. अभि M. stop, stay; delight in, be satisfied or pleased with (loc. or instr. ± सह). उपाव M. feel comfortable. आ A. stop, cease; take delight in (loc.), enjoy carnally (instr. ± समम्). उपा A. (M.) rest, repose, desist from (abl.). व्युपा & समा the same. उप A. stop (tr.); A. M. stop (intr.), rest, stay repose; cease from, renounce, resign (abl.). व्युप A. M. come to rest, cease, desist from (abl.). नि M. go to rest, cease, end. C. निरामयति stop, check, restrain. परि A. take pleasure in, rejoice at (abl.). वि A. (M.)

stop, cease, pause, rest; desist from (abl.), renounce, resign (abl. or absol.). C. विरमयति or विरामयति bring to rest or to an end. — Cf. अनुरत, उपरत (add.), निरत (to be placed after निरञ्जन). विरत.

रम a. gladdening, delighting (—°); f. आ fortune, riches, splendour, E. of Lakṣmī.

रट or °क m. pl. N. of a people.

रमण, f. ई = रम adj. — m. lover, husband; f. ई mistress, wife, N. of a serpent-maid; n. joy, pleasure, esp. sensual pleasure, sexual intercourse.

रमणीय a. enjoyable, delightful, charming; f. आ N. of a singer.*

रमणीयजन्मन् a. whose birth is pleasant, born under an auspicious star.

रमणीयडामरत्व n. delight and wonder.

रमणीयता f., °त्व n. loveliness, beauty.

1रमति f. a pleasant abode.

2रमति a. liking to abide, not straying.

रमानाथ & °पति m. lord of Ramā i.e. Viṣṇu.

रमेश & °श्वर m. the same.

रम्ब्, रम्बते hang down.

1रम्भ् v. रभ्.

2रम्भ्, रम्भति, °ते roar, bellow.

रम्भ m. prop, support, staff, N. of an Asura etc.; f. आ the plantain, N. of an Apsaras etc.

रम्भिन् a. carrying a stick; m. old man or door-keeper.

रम्भोरु, f. °रू or °रु having beautiful (plantain-like) thighs.

रम्य a. enjoyable, charming, beautiful.

रम्यता f., °त्व n. charm, beauty.

रम्यदारुण a. beautiful and terrible.

रम्यान्तर a. offering pleasant intervals.

रय m. current, stream, course, quick motion, haste; instr. & abl. quickly, rapidly.

रयि m. (f.) wealth, treasure.

रयिद or °दा a. bestowing riches.

रयिन्तम (superl.) very wealthy.

रयिपति m. lord of wealth or treasures.

रयिमन्त् & °वन्त् a. wealthy, rich, opulent.

रयिविद् a. obtaining or possessing wealth.

रयिवृध् a. rejoicing in wealth.

रयिषच् (°षाच्) a. partaking of wealth.

रयिषह् (°षाह्) a. ruling over wealth.

रयिष्ठ a. wealthy (lit. standing in wealth); m. a rich man.

रयिष्ठान & °स्थान a. & m. = prec. (lit. a receptacle of wealth).

रयीयन्त् a. wishing for wealth.

रराट n. forehead (cf. ललाट).

रला f. a cert. bird.

रल्लक m. a kind of deer.

रव m. roar, howl, thunder, yell, cry; sound or noise i.g.

रवण a. roaring, howling, singing.

रवत & रवथ m. = रव.

रवि m. the sun.

रविकिरण m. sun-beam.

रवितनय m. the son of the sun; E. of the planet Saturn & of Yama.

रवितृ m. crier, screamer.

रविबिम्ब & °मण्डल n. the sun's orb or disk.

रविसुत m. the son of the sun; E. of the planet Saturn & of the monkey Sugrīva.

रशना f. cord, strap, rein; girdle, esp. of a woman, adj. —° girt or surrounded by.

रशनाकलाप m. a woman's girdle twisted of several strings.

रश्मन् m. rein (only instr. रश्मा & —°).

रश्मि m. (f.) line, cord, trace, rein, whip, measuring rope; ray or beam of light.

रश्मिजाल n. a net or garland of rays.

रश्मिपुञ्ज m. heap or multitude of rays.

रश्मिमन्त् a. having rays, radiant; m. the sun.

रश्मिमय a. consisting of rays.

रश्मिमालिन् a. garlanded with rays.

रश्मिवन्त् a. & m. = रश्मिमन्त्.

1रस्, रसति, °ते, pp. रसित (q.v.) roar, howl, cry, sound. — अभि neigh to (acc.). आ & वि roar, scream. — Cf. अनुरसित, आरसित.

2रस्, रसति, रस्यति, रसयति, °ते taste, relish, feel, perceive.

रस m. the sap or juice of plants and fruits, fluid, liquid i.g., poet. = water; the best or finest or strongest part of anything, its essence or bloom; taste or the organ of taste, relish or inclination for, desire of (loc. ± उपरि or —°), any object of taste or enjoyment; pleasure, charm, beauty; feeling, sentiment, affection; style, character (esp. of a work of art). — f. रसा moisture, humidity, N. of a river & a mythol. stream; the lower world, hell.

रसगुण a. possessing the quality of taste.

रसज a. produced from liquids.

रसज्ञ a. knowing tastes (lit. & fig.), i.g. judicious, wise, familiar with (loc. or —°), abstr. °ता f. — n. & f. आ tongue.

1रसन n. roaring, screaming, sounding i.g.

2रसन m. phlegm; f. आ tongue; n. tasting, feeling.

रसनीय a. what is tasted.

रसप्रबन्ध m. poetical composition, esp. a drama.

रयमय, f. ई consisting of juice or fluids.

रसयति s. tasting.

रसयितव्य a. to be tasted, tasty.

रसयितृ m. taster.

रसवत्ता f. abstr. to seq.

रसवन्त् a. juicy, savoury; pithy, strong; graceful, elegant.

रसवर्जम् adv. except taste.

रसविक्रयिन् m. liquor-seller.

रसविद् a. knowing tastes or having good taste (lit. & fig.).

रसातल n. the lower world, hell.

रसात्मक a. whose essence is juice or taste; juicy, tasteful, elegant.

रसाधिक a. full of taste or enjoyments.

रसान्तर n. another taste, sentiment or character; difference of tastes.

रसान्तरविद् a. knowing the different tastes.

रसायन n. medicine for prolonging life, an elixir.

रसाय्य a. juicy, tasty.

रसाल m. the mango tree.

रसाशिर् a. mixed with juice (milk).

रसास्वाद m. the perception of enjoyment.

रसिक a. having (good) taste; having a liking for, be fond of or familiar with (loc. or —°); tasteful, elegant. Abstr. °ता f., °त्व n.

रसिकजन m. elegant people.

रसित a. & n. roaring, crying, tinkling, sounding i.g.

1रसितृ m. roarer.

2रसितृ m. taster.

रसिन् a. juicy, pithy, strong, tasteful, elegant.

रसोन m. a kind of garlic.

रस्य a. palatable, tasty, savoury.

रह्, रहति, pp. रहित (q.v.) leave, desert, abandon. C. रहयति = S. or cause to leave etc. — वि C. abandon, desert. — Cf. विरहित.

रह (°—) = रहस्.

रहण n. abandonment, separation.

रहस् n. solitude, lonely place, as adv. secretely.

रहसू f. bringing forth (a child) in secret.

रहस्य a. secret, private; n. a secret, mystical doctrine, mystery, also adv. = रहस्.

रहस्यधारिन् a. keeping a secret.

रहस्यभेद m., °भेदन n. disclosure of a secret.

रहस्यसंरक्षण f. the keeping of a secret.

रहस्याख्यायिन् a. telling a secret or making secret reports.

रहःस्थ a. being in private, alone.

रहित a. left, deserted, alone; destitute of, wanting (instr., °— or —°).

रहूगण m. pl. N. of a race of Rishis.

रहोगत a. being in a lonely place, private, secret.

1रा, राति, राते, pp. रात (q.v.) give, grant, bestow. — सम् = S.

2रा (—°) giving, bestowing.

3रा, रायति bark, bark at. — अभि bark at.

4रा v. रै.

राका f. the goddess or the day of full moon; N. of a Rākṣasī & a river.

राकाचन्द्र m. full moon (cf. prec.).

राकानिशा f. the night of full moon.

राकापति & °रमण m. the full moon (husband of Rākā).

राकाशशाङ्क & °शशिन् m. = राकाचन्द्र.

राक्षस, f. ई belonging to the Rakṣas, demoniacal, m. an evil demon, a Rakṣas.

राक्षसता f., °त्व n., °भाव m. the state or condition of a Rakṣas.

राक्षसेन्द्र m. the king of the Rakṣas, Rāvana.

*राचा f. lac (cf. लाचा).

राग m. colouring, colour, esp. redness; charm, loveliness; affection, feeling, passion; joy, pleasure, delight in, longing after, love of (loc. or —°); musical mode (6).

रागद्वेष m. du. love and hatred.

रागबन्ध m. manifestation of love or affection.

रागमय a. red or enamoured.

रागलेखा f. line of paint; N. of a woman.

रागवन्त् a. = रागमय.

रागात्मक a. consisting in passion.

रागिता f. longing after, desire for (loc. or —°).

रागिन् a. coloured, red; impassioned, loving, affectionate; attached to, fond of, delighting in (loc. or —°). f. °णी a modification of the Rāga (cf. s. v.).

राघव m. descendant of Raghu, E. of sev. princes, esp. of Rāma.

राघवपाण्डवीय n. T. of poem.

राङ्कव a. belonging to the antelope called Raṅku, made of deer's hair, woollen; m. a woollen cover.

राङ्ग m. actor.

1राज्, राजति, °ते, राष्टि reign, rule, direct, be master of (gen.); shine, glitter, be illustrious or eminent, distinguish one's self, appear as (इव). C. राजयति, °ते rule, govern. — अनु imitate. निस् C. cause to shine or glitter. परि shine all around. वि = S. + excel, surpass (abl.). अतिवि shine very bright. अनुवि follow (acc.). सम् reign, rule (gen.). — Cf. इरज्य्.

2राज् (nom. राट्) m. sovereign, king.

राज m. (only —°) prince, king, first or best of.

राजक m. little king, also = राजन् (—°); n. a multitude of kings.

राजकन्यका & °कन्या f. a king's daughter.

राजकर्तृ m. king-maker (who sets a king on the throne).

राजकर्मन् n. = राजकृत्य, also royal service.

राजकार्य n. = prec.

राजकिल्बिषिन् a. sinning as a king.

राजकीय a. royal, princely.

राजकुमार m., °रिका f. a king's son & daughter.

राजकुल n. a king's or a royal family; the court of a king.

राजकृत् m. = राजकर्तृ.

राजकृत्य n. a king's duty or business.

राजक्रिया f. = prec.

राजगवी f. a kind of buffalo.

राजगामिन् a. going to the king.

राजगुरु m. councillor or minister of a king.

राजगुह्य n. royal mystery.

राजगृह n. a king's house, palace; n. (& f. ई) N. of a town.

राजघातक m. king-killer, regicide.

राजजम्बू f. a species of date tree.

राजत n. silver, also adj. (f. ई).

राजतनय, f. आ a king's son & daughter.

राजतरंगिणी f. T. of sev. works.

राजतस् adv. from the king.

राजता f., °त्व n. kingship, royalty.

राजदण्ड m. royal authority or a punishment inflicted by a king.

राजदन्त m. principal tooth, front-tooth.

राजदर्शन m. a royal audience (lit. the act of seeing a king).

राजदार m. pl. a king's wife (wives).

राजदारिका f. a king's daughter, princess.*

राजदुहितृ f. = prec.

राजद्वार् f., °द्वार n. the king's gate, gate of a palace.

राजधर्म m. a king's duty; Pl. the laws relating to kings.

राजधर्मभृत् & °विद् a. maintaining & knowing the duties of a king.

राजधानी f. a king's residence; abl. °तस्.

1राजन् m. king, ruler (often of gods, esp. of Soma). a man of the military caste; f. राज्ञी queen.

2राजन् s. direction, guidance.

राजनय m., °नीति f. policy or politics (lit. royal conduct.

राजन्य a. royal, princely; m. a man of the military caste; abstr. °त्व† n.

राजन्यक n. an assemblage of warriors.

राजन्यकुमार m. a king's son, prince.

राजन्यबन्धु m. friend of a prince, also = राजन्य m.

राजन्वन्त् a. having a (good) king.

राजपट्ट m. a kind of precious stone.
राजपति m. a lord of kings.
राजपत्नी f. a king's wife.
राजपथ m. principal (lit. king's) street.
राजपरिवर्त m. change of government (l. king) *
1राजपुत्र m. a king's son, prince (f. °पुत्री); a Rājpoot.
2राजपुत्र a. having princes as sons.
राजपुत्रक m., °त्रिका f. a king's son or daughter, prince, princess.
राजपुमंस् m. a royal servant.
राजपुर n., °री f. N. of a city.
राजपुरुष & °पूरुष m. = राजपुमंस्.
राजप्रकृति f. minister of a king.
राजप्रदेय a. to be given to a king.
राजप्रिया f. a king's favourite wife.
राजप्रेष्य m. royal servant; n. royal service.
राजबान्धव m., ई f. a royal relation.
राजभट m. a king's soldier.
राजभवन n. a king's palace.
राजभाव m. royalty.
राजभृत्य m. a king's servant.
राजभ्रातृ m. a king's brother.
राजमन्दिर n. = राजभवन.
राजमातृ f. a king's mother.
राजमानत्व n. the being radiant, brilliancy.
राजमानुष m. a royal officer.
राजमार्ग m. = राजपथ.
राजमुख n. a king's face.
राजयक्ष्म & °यक्ष्मन् m. a kind of disease.
राजयज्ञ m. a king's sacrifice.
राजयोषित् f. a king's wife.
राजराज् m. a king of kings.
राजराज m. = prec. (abstr. °ता f., °त्व n.); E. of Kubera.
राजराज्य n. reign over all kings.
राजर्षि m. a royal sage.
राजलक्षण n. royal sign or token.
राजलक्ष्मी f. royal fortune or splendour (often personif.).
राजलोक m. a company of kings.
राजवंश m. a family of kings.
राजवंश्य a. belonging to a royal family.
राजवत् adv. like a king.
राजवध m. a king's weapon.
राजवन्त् a. having a king.
राजवल्लभ m. a king's favourite.
राजविद्या f. royal science, state policy.
राजवीथी f. = राजपथ.
राजवेश्मन् n. a king's abode, palace.
राजवेष m. a royal garment.
राजशासन n. royal edict or order.
राजशास्त्र n. royal science, state policy.
राजशेखर m. N. of a poet.
राजश्री f. = राजलक्ष्मी.
राजस, f. ई relating to passion (ph.); abstr. °त्व n.
राजसंसद् f. a king's court of justice.
राजसत्त्र n. a king's sacrifice.
राजसद्मन् n. a royal dwelling.
राजसभा f. royal hall or assembly.
राजसर्षप m. black mustard or the seed of it (used as a weight).
राजसिंह m. king-lion, an illustrious king.
राजसुत m., आ f. a king's son or daughter.
राजसूनु m. = prec. m.
राजसूय m. n. a great sacrifice at a king's consecration.
राजसेवक & °सेविन् m. a king's servant.
राजसेवा f. king's service.
राजस्यालक m. the brother of a king's concubine.*
राजस्व n. the property of a king.
राजहंस, f. ई a sort of goose or swan.
राजहर्म्य n. a king's palace.
राजहार m. bringer of Soma.
राजादन m. a kind of tree.
राजाधिराज m. king of kings, supreme king.
राजाधिष्ठान n. royal capital.
राजाधीन m. subject or servant of a king.
राजानुज m. the younger brother of a king.*
राजानुजीविन् m. a king's servant.
राजान्न n. food from a king.
राजाभिषेक m. consecration of a king.
राजार्थ royal property, treasury, abstr. °ता f.
राजार्ह a. worthy of a king, royal, princely; n. Agallochum.
राजाश्व m. a strong (lit. royal) stallion.
राजासन n. royal seat, throne.
राजासन्दी f. a stool to place the Soma upon (r.).

राजि or राजी f. streak, line, row.
राजिन् a. shining.
राजिमन्त् a. striped.
राजिल m. a kind of snake.
राजी & °मन्त् v. राजि & °मन्त्.
राजीकृत a. striped, forming stripes.
राजीव a. striped; m. a cert. fish; n. a blue lotus-flower.
राजीवनेत्र & °लोचन a. lotus-eyed.
राजेन्द्र m. lord of kings.
राजोपकरण n. the ensigns of royalty.
राजोपचार m. homage or service rendered to a king.
राजोपसेवा f. royal service.
राजोपसेविन् m. a king's servant.
राज्ञी v. 1राजन्.
राज्य a. fit to reign, royal; n. (also राज्य or राज्य्र) kingship, sovereignty, reign, kingdom, country.
राज्यच्युति f. loss of a realm, dethronement.
राज्यभङ्ग m. decay of a realm.
राज्यभाज् a. enjoying sovereignty.
राज्यलक्ष्मी & °श्री f. splendour of a reign.
राज्यसुख n. the sweetness of sovereignty.
राज्यस्थ & °स्थायिन् a. being in a kingly office, reigning.
राज्यस्थिति f. abstr. to prec.
राज्याभिषेक & राज्योपकरण = राजा° & राजो°.
रात a. given (often °— or —°).
रातहविस् & °हव्य a. willing to present offerings.
राति a. ready (to give); f. grace, favour.
रातिन् a. rich in gifts.
रातिषाच् a. granting favours, liberal, bounteous.
रात्र n. night, mostly —° as m. or n.
रात्रक, f. °त्रिका nocturnal, nightly.
रात्रि v. रात्री.
रात्रिक a. nocturnal, nightly; —° after a num. lasting or sufficient for so and so many nights or days.
रात्रिचर्या f. night-roving; a nightly act or observance.
रात्रिजागर m. night-watching.
रात्रिंदिव n. day and night, °दिवम् also as adv. = instr. °दिवा by d. & n.
रात्रिमय a. nocturnal.
रात्रिरक्षक m. night-guard, watchman.
रात्रिविहारिन् a. roaming at night.*
रात्रिशेष m. the remainder or last part of a night.
रात्रिसत्त्र n. a night ceremony.
रात्री (later रात्रि) f. night.
रात्र्यहन् n. du. night and day.
रात्र्यागम m. approach of night, evening.
रात्र्युपाय m. the same.
1राथ्य n. possession of chariots.
2राथ्य a. fit for a chariot.
राद्ध a. accomplished (n. impers. w. instr. of pers. & th.), ready, perfect, successful, happy.
राद्धि f. success, good fortune.
राध्, राध्नोति, राध्यते, °ति, pp. राद्ध (q.v.) succeed, prosper (of pers. & th.); be happy, have luck with (instr.); partake of, get at or to (dat. or loc.); *prophesy to (राध्यति w. dat.); accomplish, bring about; win over, gratify, conciliate. C. राधयति bring about, satisfy. — अप miss (the mark), fail; be at fault, offend, sin against (loc. of th. or gen. of pers.). अभि C. satisfy, content. अव fail, make a fault. आ C. make happy, satisfy, conciliate, try to win, honour, serve (acc.); gain, partake of (acc.). उपा serve (acc.). समा C. = आ C. प्रति counteract, oppose (acc.). वि be deprived of (instr.); hurt, injure, offend. सम् C. agree about or upon (loc.); satisfy, content. — Cf. अपराद्ध, अभिराद्ध, इरध्.
†राध s. = seq.; m. a man's name; f. आ a cert. attitude in shooting, N. of Kṛṣṇa's foster-mother, of Kṛṣṇa's consort, etc.
राधस् n. favour, gracious gift, blessing, liberality, munificence.
†राधस्पति m. lord of gifts.
राधाकान्त m. the beloved of Rādhā i.e. Kṛṣṇa.
राधेय m. metron. of Karṇa and Bhīṣma.
राधोदेय n. bestowing wealth or showing favour.
राध्य a. dark-coloured, black (m. ± शकुनि a crow); charming, lovely, beautiful. —

m. a kind of deer, N. of three celebrated heroes etc. f. रामा a dark or beautiful woman, mistress, wife, (young) woman i.g.; N. of an Apsaras etc.; f. रामी darkness, night; n. dusk.

रामकृष्ण m. a man's name.

रामगिरि m. N. of a mountain.

रामचन्द्र m. Rāma-moon, E. of Rāma & N. of sev. men.

रामठ m. pl. N. of a people.

रामणीयक n. loveliness, beauty.

रामतापनी f., °तापनीय n. T. of an Upanishad.

रामतीर्थ n. N. of a place of pilgrimage.

रामदेव & °नाथ m. E. of Rāma, N. of sev. men.

रामह्रद m. Rāma's lake (a sacred bathing-place.

रामायण, f. ई relating to Rāma; n. N. of an epic poem.

रामेश्वर m. a man's name.

राम्या or राम्या f. night.

रायस्काम a. desirous of wealth.

†रायस्पोष m. increase of wealth, a. = seq.

रायस्पोषदा, °दावन्, & °वनि a. giving increase of wealth.

राव m. roaring, crying, sound, noise.

रावण m. N. of a Rākṣasa (lit. causing to cry or lament).

रावणि m. descendant of Rāvaṇa.

1रावन् a. giving, bestowing.

2रावन् a. sounding, calling (only —°).

रावित n. sound.

राविन् a. roaring, sounding, crying like (–°).

राशि m. heap, mass, multitude.

राशिशस् adv. by heaps.

राशिस्थ a. standing in a heap, heaped up.

राशीकृ A., °भू P. heap or pile up.

राष्ट्र n. kingdom, sovereignty, country, region, people, subjects.

राष्ट्रक (adj. —°) = prec.

राष्ट्रकर्षण n. harassing of a country.

राष्ट्रगोप, राष्ट्रपति, & राष्ट्रपाल m. king (lit. protector of a kingdom).

राष्ट्रभङ्ग m. decay of a kingdom.

राष्ट्रभृत् m. dependent prince, tributary; f. pl. cert. sacrifices or sacrif. formulas.

राष्ट्रभृति f., °भृत्य n. maintenance of dominion.

राष्ट्रभेदिन् m. rebel (divider of a country).

राष्ट्रवर्धन a. increasing dominion.

राष्ट्रि f. female ruler.

राष्ट्रिक m. inhabitant (subject or ruler).

राष्ट्रिन् a. holding a kingdom.

राष्ट्रिय m. successor of a king, pretender; also = seq.

राष्ट्रियस्याल m. a king's brother-in-law (d.).

राष्ट्री f. female ruler or manager.

राष्ट्रीय m. = राष्ट्रिय.

रास्, रासति, °ते roar, howl. I. रारास्यते cry aloud, lament.

रास m. a kind of rustic dance (performed by Kṛṣṇa); play, sport i.g.

रासभ m., °भी f. ass.

रास्ना f. girdle; poss. रास्नावं.

रास्पिनं & रास्पिरं a. noisy.

राहवीय a. belonging to Rāhu.

राहित्य n. the being without (—°).

राहु m. the Seizer, E. of a demon supposed to swallow the sun and moon and thus cause eclipses.

राहुग्रह m. the demon Rāhu.

राहुग्रसन & °ग्रहण n. seizure & swallowing by Rāhu, i.e. eclipse of sun or moon.

राहूगण m. patron. from रहूगण.

रि or री, रिणाति, रिणीते, रीयते, pp. रीण A. let loose, sever from (abl.); cause to run or stream, emit, grant, bestow; M. flow, run, dissolve. — अनु M. flow after (acc.). आ A. cause to run; M. run. नि loosen, unveil, tear asunder, destroy. निस् sever from (abl.). वि hew asunder, cleave. सम् put together, restore.

रिक्त a. empty, void; wanting, -less (—°), poor, indigent, worthless, vain.

रिक्तक a. empty, void, unladen.

रिक्तपाणि & °हस्त a. empty-handed.

रिक्थ n. inheritance, property.

रिक्थग्राह, °भागिन्, °भाज्, & °हर a. receiving etc. an inheritance; m. heir.

रिक्थाद a. taking an inheritance; m. heir.

रिक्थिन् a. poss. to रिक्थ; m. heir or bequeather.

रिख्, रिखति = लिख्.

रिङ्ख्, **रिङ्खति**, or **रिङ्ग्**, **रिङ्गति** creep, crawl, move slowly.

रिङ्खण or **रिङ्गण** n. creeping, crawling.

रिङ्गि f. going, motion.

रिङ्गिन् a. creeping, crawling.

रिच्, **रिणक्ति**, pp. **रिक्त** (q.v.) leave, clear (a room), let go, let free; deliver up, part with, sell; leave behind, supplant. P.M. **रिच्यते**, **रिच्यते** be emptied, be deprived of or freed from (instr.), be destroyed, perish. C. **रेचयति** make empty, give up, abandon; emit breath (± **मारुतम्**). **अति** M.P. leave behind, reach beyond, surpass, predominate over (acc. or abl.). C. cause to preponderate, overdo. **अभ्यति** M.P. be left in favour or for the sake of (acc.). **व्यति** P. reach beyond, surpass, excel, differ from (acc. or abl.). **आ** cede, yield (dat. of pers. & acc. of th.). **उद्** & **प्र** M.P. reach beyond, exceed, preponderate over (abl.). **वि** M.P. the same, be emptied or purged. C. empty, purge. — Cf. **अतिरिक्त**, **उद्रिक्त**, **विरिक्त**, **व्यतिरिक्त**.

रित् a. flowing, moving.

1**रिप्**, only pp. **रिप्त** smear, stick, cleave to; cheat, impose upon (only **रिरिपुस्**).

2**रिप्** f. cheat (abstr. & concr.).

रिपु a. deceitful, treacherous; m. impostor, cheat, adversary, enemy, abstr. **°ता†** f.

रिपुंजय a. conquering foes; m. N. of sev. princes.

रिप्र n. dirt, impurity.

रिप्रवाह a. removing impurity.

रिफ्, **रिफति**, **रेफति**, pp. **रिफित** snarl. — **अव** the same. **आ** snore.

रिभ्, **रेभति** crackle, creak, murmur, chatter, talk, sing, shout, praise.

रिरंसा f. desire of (sexual) enjoyment; **°सु** a. lustful, lascivious.

(**रिरक्षा** &) **रिरक्षिषा** f. desire to watch or guard.

रिरक्षिषु (& **रिरक्षु**) a. to prec.

रिरिक्षु a. wishing to hurt.

रिश्, **रिशति**, pp. **रिष्ट** (q.v.) tear, pull, bite off, crop.

रिशा f. a cert. animal (tearer).

रिशादस् a. E. of the Maruts etc.

रिश्य m. = **ऋश्य**.

1**रिष्**, **रिष्यति**, **°ते**, **रेषति**, pp. **रिष्ट** (cf. **रिश्**) be hurt, receive harm, suffer wrong, fail, perish; harm, injure. C. **रेषयति** = S. tr., M. = S. refl. or intr. D. **रिरिक्षति** wish to harm.

2**रिष्** f. injury or injurer.

रिषण्य्, **°ण्यति** fail, wrong.

रिषण्यु a. injurious, malevolent.

रिष्ट a. torn, rent asunder, broken, hurt, destroyed, missed, failed; n. = seq.

रिष्टि f. bad luck, failure, misfortune.

रिह्, **रेढि**, pp. **रीढ** lick, caress, kiss. I. **रेरिह्यते**, pp. **रेरिहत्** & **रेरिहाण** lick repeatedly, kiss. — **आ** lick, gnaw at (acc.). **परि** & **प्रति** the same. **सम्** lick together.

री v. **रि**.

रीति f. going, motion, course, stream; line, row; way, manner; style, diction.

रीत्यप् a. streaming forth water.

1**रु**, **रौति**, **रुवति**, **रवति**, **°ते**, pp. **रुत** (q.v.) roar, howl, shriek, croak, sound, thunder. C. **रावयति** cause to roar or cry, fill with cries. I. **रोरवीति**, **रोरूयते**, **°ति** roar or cry out loudly. — **अभि** & **आ** roar etc. (at or against). **प्र** roar or cry aloud. **वि** roar, yelp, shout, creak, rattle, tinkle; cry or call at. C. cry aloud, make resound. — Cf. **अभिरुत**, **विरुत**.

2**रु**, only **राविषम्** & **रुत** (q.v.) crush.

रुंष्, pp. **रुंषित** covered with dust, smeared, soiled.

रुक्म m. (n.) ornament of gold; n. gold.

रुक्मन्त् a. shining (Agni).

रुक्मपाश m. a string on which golden ornaments are worn.

रुक्मपुङ्ख a. having a golden butt-end (arrow).

रुक्मपृष्ठ a. overlaid with gold, gilded.

रुक्ममय a. made of gold, golden.

1**रुक्मरथ** m. a golden chariot.

2**रुक्मरथ** a. having a golden chariot, E. of Droṇa.

रुक्मवक्षस् a. golden-breasted (Maruts).

रुक्मस्तेय n. stealing gold.

रुक्माभ a. bright like gold.
रुक्मिणीश m. E. of Kṛṣṇa (cf. seq.).
रुक्मिन् a. having golden ornaments. — m. N. of an ancient hero, f. रुक्मिणी his sister, Kṛṣṇa's wife.
रुक्ष a. shining, bright.
रुगन्वित & रुगार्त a. visited by pains, ill.
रुग्ण a. broken, crushed; n. cleft, fissure.
1रुच्, रोचते (°ति), pp. रुचित (q.v.) shine, be bright, make a show, appear beautiful or good, please (dat. or gen.); delight in (acc.), long for (dat.). C. रोचयति, °ते A. cause to shine, illuminate, make bright or pleasant; cause a person (acc.) to like or long for (dat.); A.M. take delight in, approve, like (acc. or infin.); choose (2 acc.); intend, purpose; be agreeable, please (also P.). — अति shine over or outshine (acc.). अभि shine, be brilliant or splendid, please (dat.). C.A. content or satisfy with (instr.), entertain, amuse; A.M. take delight in, have a taste for, like (acc. or infin.). उद् M. shine forth. उप M. approach with brightness. प्र shine forth, be brilliant or clear, please. C.A. make shine, illumine, make agreeable or pleasant, commend, approve, like. प्रति M. please (acc.). वि M. shine forth, glitter, be bright or radiant, become visible, appear like (nom.), excel, outshine (acc.), appear good, please (gen.). C.A. make shine, illumine; take delight in (acc.). सम् M. shine (together or in emulation). C.A. take delight in, approve of, resolve upon (acc.); choose for (2 acc.). — Cf. अभिरुचित.
2रुच् f. light, lustre, brightness, splendour, beauty, colour; appearance (—°); delight in, taste or longing for.
रुच a. bright, f. रुचा pleasure, liking.
रुचक n. tooth; a cert. golden ornament, necklace; a kind of building.
†रुचय्, °यते shine.
रुचि or रुची f. light, splendour, beauty, colour; wish, desire, pleasure in, taste for (loc., acc. w. प्रति, infin., or —°), appetite; adj. —° delighting in, eager or longing for. Abstr. °ता† f., °त्व† n.
रुचिकर a. causing desire.
रुचित a. shining, bright, splendid, beautiful, delicate, dainty.
रुचिर a. bright, splendid, beautiful, pleasant, agreeable to (gen. or —°).
रुचिष्य a. pleasing, agreeable, desired.
रुच्य a. splendid, beautiful.
1रुज्, रुजति, pp. रुग्ण (q.v.) break, crush down, destroy; pain, afflict. C. रोजयति give one a blow upon (loc.). — अव break off. आ break open or asunder, tear out, lacerate, dislimb. प्र break to pieces. वि & सम् break, crush, rend.
2रुज् a. breaking, crushing; f. grief, sorrow, pain, illness.
रुज a. = prec. adj.; f. रुजा breaking, pain.
रुजस्कर & रुजाकर (f. ई) causing pain.
रुजाय्, pp. रुजायमान causing pain, aching.*
रुण्ड a. mutilated; m. (also °क) cripple, a mere trunk.
1रुत a. sounding with (—°); n. roaring, shouting, neighing, singing (of birds), etc.
2रुत a. broken down, ill.
रुतज्ञ a. knowing the language (of beasts and birds); m. an augur.
रुतवेत्तृ m. & रुताभिज्ञ a. = prec. m. & a.
रुद्, रोदिति, रुदति, °ते, रोदति, °ते, pp. रुदित (q.v.) cry, weep, lament. C. रोदयति cause to weep or lament. I. रोरुद्यते weep very much. — अनु weep after or for (acc.). प्र burst into tears, begin to weep or lament; cry aloud; weep with (acc.). वि weep or cry aloud, sob.
रुदित a. weeping, wet with tears; n. weeping, howling, crying.
रुद्र a. E. of sev. gods (as the red or howling); m. N. of the god of tempests (later identif. w. Çiva), ruler of the Maruts, pl. his sons, the Rudras or Maruts.
रुद्रगर्भ m. Rudra's offspring, i.e. Agni.
रुद्रजप m. a cert. prayer addressed to Rudra.
रुद्रजापक & °जापिन् a. reciting the Rudrajapa.
रुद्रदेव m. a man's name.

रुद्रयज्ञ m. a sacrifice offered to Rudra.
रुद्रवन्त् a. accompanied by Rudra or the Rudras.
रुद्रवर्तनि a. E. of the Açvins.
रुद्रशर्मन् & **°सोम** m. names of Brahmans.
रुद्राणी f. Rudra's wife.
रुद्रिय a. belonging to Rudra or the Rudras; m. sgl. & pl. the host of the Maruts; n. Rudra's power.
1**रुध्**, **रोधति** grow, sprout. — **वि** = S.
2**रुध्**, **रुणद्धि**, **रुन्द्धे** (**रुन्धति**, **°ते**, **रोधति**), pp. **रुद्ध** obstruct, hold back, keep off, hinder, suppress, shut up, close, stop or fill up, besiege, invest, cover, veil. C. **रोधयति**, **°ते** hold back, stop, cause to be confined or besieged by (2 acc. or acc. & instr.). — **अनु** obstruct (a way), hem in, surround; fetter, master, govern; follow immediately (acc.); mostly P. **रुध्यते** (**°ति**) cleave or cling to, be devoted to, intent upon, engaged in (acc.); conform one's self to, have a regard for (acc.). **अप** keep or ward off, remove, expel or exclude from (abl.). **अव** hold back, keep away from (2 acc.), hold fast, confine in, shut up (loc., r. acc.); obstruct, hinder; surround, besiege; cover, veil; remove, expel from (abl.); cling or be devoted to (acc.). M. hold, contain; get, attain. **समव** shut up, confine; get, attain; P. be contained in (loc.). **आ** shut up, confine, invest, surround, besiege; ward off, expel, drive away. **उप** the same, drive in (cattle); keep back, retain; molest, pain, harass, trouble, disturb, prevent; menace, compromise; cover, veil. **नि** hold back or fast, stop, overtake, check, restrain, obstruct, hinder, shut up, confine. **संनि** hold back or fast, shut up, confine, check, restrain, suppress; stuff, fill. **परि** shut up, confine, keep back. **प्र** hold back, obstruct, hinder. **प्रति** hold back, resist, disturb, trouble, shut up, confine; veil, cover. **वि** hinder, obstruct, restrain, suppress, surround, besiege, confine, shut up; M. be opposed by (instr.); P. **विरुध्यते** (**°ति**) be opposed or contrary to (instr.); disagree, contend or fight with (instr. ± **सह**, gen., loc., or **प्रति**). C. render hostile, disunite, exasperate. **सम्** drive in (cattle), confine, keep prisoner, invest, besiege, hold back, stop, detain, hold fast, fetter, withold, refuse; veil, cover. — Cf. **अवरुद्ध** (add.), **उपरुद्ध**, **निरुद्ध**, **विरुद्ध**, **संरुद्ध**.
3**रुध्** (—°) stopping, hindering.
रुधिर a. red, bloody; m. the planet Mars; n. (**रुधिर**) blood, saffron.
रुधिरपात m. flow of blood.
रुधिरलेप m. stain of blood.
रुधिरवर्ष n. blood-rain.
रुधिराशन a. drinking blood (Rākṣasa or arrow).
1**रुप्**, **रुप्यति** have racking pain in the belly.
2**रुप्** f. the earth.
रुम m. N. of a man.
रुमण्वन्त् m. N. of sev. men.
रुरु m. a kind of deer.
रुरुक m. N. of a prince.
रुरुक्षणि a. able to destroy.
रुरुत्सु a. wishing to hold back.
रुरुदिषा f. abstr. to seq.
रुरुदिषु a. about to weep or cry.
†**रुवण्य्**, **°यति** scream, yell.
रुवण्यु a. sounding, loud.
रुवथ m. lowing, bellowing.
रुशत्पशु a. having white cattle.
†**रुशदूर्मि** a. having bright waves.
रुशद्गु a. having white cows.
रुशद्वत्स a. having a white calf.
रुशन्त्, f. **रुशती** light, bright, white.
1**रुष्**, **रोषति**, **रुष्यति**, **°ते**, **रुषति**, **°ते**, pp. **रुषित** & **रुष्ट** (q.v.) be vexed, be cross or angry. C. **रोषयति**, **°ते** vex, annoy, irritate. — Cf. **अभिरुषित**, **आरोषित**, **विरुष्ट**, **संरुषित**.
2**रुष्** f. (nom. **रुट्**) anger, wrath, rage.
रुषा f. (only —°) = prec.
रुषित & **रुष्ट** a. enraged, irritated, wrathful, angry with (gen., loc., or acc. w. **प्रति**).
1**रुह्**, **रोहति**, **°ते** (& **रुहति**, **°ते**), pp. **रूढ** (q.v.) rise, mount up, climb, spring up, grow, develop, thrive; grow together, i.e. cicatrize,

heal. C. रोहयति & रोपयति, °ते raise up, erect, place on, fix, fasten, commit, intrust; grow (trans., i.e.) plant, sow; heal, cure (cf. S.). — अति rise beyond (acc.), grow higher. अधि ascend, mount (acc., r. loc.), w. तुलाम् be a match for (instr.); rise into, get at, obtain (परां कोटिम् the highest degree). C. raise above, place or fix upon (loc. or acc.); put in, appoint to (loc.), intrust, commit to (loc.), bend (a bow). अनु ascend, M. grow up or together. अपि & समपि grow together. अभि & समभि mount, ascend, rise to (together). अव descend from (abl.) upon (acc.), tread on (loc.), enter. C. descend (tr.) or take down from (abl.); set, plant (trees); deprive of (abl.), decrease, diminish, destroy. आ mount, ascend climb; rise to (acc. or loc.), bestride, enter (also = inire, कक्षाम् = तुलाम्, cf. sub अधि), spring forth, develop, increase; get to, arrive at, reach, attain. C. cause to mount, ascend, or enter (acc., w. तुलाम् = संशयतुलाम् expose to danger, compromise, w. पत्त्रम् commit to paper, write down); set, plant; string (a bow); raise, promote; place in or upon, appoint to (loc. or acc.); cause, produce, show, betray. अत्या exceed all limits. अध्या mount, ascend, enter; rise into the air. C. cause to ascend (2 acc.), promote or appoint to (loc.); falsely suppose or transfer to (loc.), exaggerate. अन्वा rise after (acc.), mount, ascend, enter, bestride. अभ्या mount, ascend, rise to or above. उपा mount, ascend, approach, get at (acc.). समा ascend or rise to or upon (acc. or loc.), approach (as friend or foe), enter upon, engage in (acc., w. तुलाम् cf. sub अधि). C. cause to mount or ascend (2 acc. or acc. & loc.), load or place upon; raise, erect, promote, exalt; put in (loc. or acc.), deposit (the sacred fire), string (a bow), intrust, commit, transfer, attribute to (loc.); show, manifest. उप grow together; C. cause to grow together, heal. प्र grow forth, sprout; grow together, cicatrize or heal; increase, thrive. C. plant, fix on or in (loc.). प्रति grow or sprout again; C. plant again, restore. वि grow out, germinate. C. cause to grow, plant, cause to cicatrize, heal; expel, remove from (abl.). सम् grow, esp. grow together, cicatrize, heal; grow forth, germinate, appear. C. cause to grow etc., plant, sow = propagate (आत्मानम् refl.). — Cf. अत्यारूढ (add.), अधिरूढ, अभ्यारूढ, अवरूढ, आरूढ, उपरूढ, निरूढ, प्ररूढ, विरूढ, संरूढ, समारूढ.

2रुह् f. growing, sprouting, also a. = seq.

रुह a. growing on, springing from (—°).

रूक्ष a. rough, dry, arid, unpleasant, harsh, abstr. °ता† f., °त्व† n., °भाव† m.

रूक्षण a. & n. attenuating, emaciating.

रूक्षय्, °यति make thin, emaciate, ± वि smear.

रूक्षवाच् f. harsh language.

रूक्षस्वन a. harsh-sounding, n. adv.

रूक्षी w. कृ smear, soil.

रूढ a. risen, mounted, grown; grown together i.e. healed, cicatrized; sprung up, produced from (—°); spread, public, notorious, traditional, special, conventional (cf. seq.).

रूढि f. mounting, ascent, growth, extent, publicity, notoriety; custom, traditional use, esp. of a word; special or conventional (opp. etymological) meaning.

रूप n. (adj. —° f. आ, r. ई) outward appearance, colour, form, shape (often —° adj. -coloured or -shaped, -like, consisting of or in—), the right form i.e. beauty; nature, character, mark, peculiarity; circumstances; drama, play (cf. दशरूप). — Abstr. °ता† f., °त्व† n.

रूपक a. figurative; m. a cert. coin; f. रूपका bitch-fox or female jackal, रूपिका N. of a plant; n. form, appearance, shape, image, kind, species; a cert. figure of speech (rh.), a drama.

रूपकरूपक n. a kind of Rūpaka (rh.).

रूपकार m. maker of images, sculptor.

रूपकृत् a. forming, shaping; m. = prec.

1रूपगुण a. possessing the quality of colour.

2रूपगुण m. beauty of form or appearance.
रूपगुणोपेत a. beautiful.
रूपण n. metaphorical description; investigation, examination.
रूपतस् adv. according to form, from without.
रूपधर & °धारिन् a. having the colour, shape, or form of (—°).
रूपधृत् & °भृत् a. = prec.
रूपनाशिन् a. destroying form or beauty, disfiguring.
रूपय्, °यति, pp. रूपित form, model, figure; represent, perform (d.). — नि = S. (d.); behold, perceive, find out, try, examine, ascertain, fix, settle, determine, choose for (2 acc.); appoint to (loc., dat., or infin.).
रूपयौवनवन्त् a. possessing beauty and youth.
रूपवन्त् a. having form or colour, embodied, bodily; having the form of, shaped like, appearing as (—°); beautiful.
रूपविपर्यय m. change of bodily form.
रूपशस् adv. according to peculiar formation.
रूपशालिन् a. handsome, beautiful.
रूपसंपद् f. perfection of form, beauty.
रूपसंपन्न a. endowed with beauty.
रूपाजीव a. prostitute (lit. living by one's form or beauty); m. whore.
रूपिदारक m. a fine boy.*
रूपिन् a. = रूपवन्त्.
रूप्य a. to be (being) metaphorically indicated; n. silver.
रूप्यद a. giving silver.
रूप्यरज्जु f. a rope of silver.
रूर a. hot, burning.
रूष्, pp. रूषित covered or smeared with, cleaving to (—°).
रूषण n. covering, smearing, soiling.
रे interj. of address.
रेक्कु a. empty, void.
रेक्णस् n. (inherited) property, wealth.
रेक्णस्वन्त् a. poss. to prec.
रेखा f. streak, line (r. रेख m.); also = seq.
रेखान्यास m. drawing lines, a sketch.
रेच & °क m., °न n. emission of breath.
रेज्, रेजति, °ते A. shake (trans.); M. shake (intr.), tremble. C. रेजयति = S. tr. — प्र M. tremble; C. shake (tr.). सम् M. tremble.
रेणु m. dust, pollen of a flower.
रेणुगुण्ठित a. covered with dust.
रेत (°—) = रेतस्.
रेतज a. born from (one's own) seed (son).
रेतस् n. flow, flood, gush, flow of semen, the seminal fluid itself, seed; offspring, progeny.
रेतस्य a. conveying seed.
रेतस्वन्त् & रेतस्विन् a. rich in seed, prolific.
रेतःसिच्य n., °सेक m. discharge of semen.
रेतःस्कन्दन & °स्खलन n. the same.
रेतिन् a. rich in seed, impregnating.
रेतोधस् a. impregnating; m. (± पितृ) father.
1रेतोधा a. impregnating, fertilizing.
2रेतोधा f., °धेय n. impregnation.
रेपस् n. spot, stain.
रेफ m. the snarling sound, i.e. र्.
रेभ a. crackling, tinkling, splashing, sounding loudly; m. reciter, chatterer, N. of a man.
रेभिन् a. making resound (—°).
रेभिल & °क m. N. of a man.
रेरिह a. licking constantly.
रेव m. N. of a man; f. आ N. of a river (= नर्मदा).
रेवन्त् a. wealthy, rich, opulent, abundant, splendid; n. रेवत् adv. — f. रेवती pl. the rich ones (fig. = the cows or the waters); N. of a lunar mansion (also sgl.); sgl. N. of a female demon, the wife of Balarāma, etc.
रेशी f. pl. E. of the water.
†रेष m. hurt, injury.
रेषण a. hurting; n. damage, failure.
रेषिन् a. hurting, injuring (—°).
रेष्मन् m. whirlwind, storm-cloud.
रै m. (f.) possession, wealth, riches.
रैक्क m. N. of a man.
रैतस a. seminal.
रैतिक & रैत्य a. brazen.
रैभ्य or रैभ्य m. patr. of sev. men, also a class of gods.
रैवत, f. ई descended from a wealthy family, rich, opulent; N. of a Manu.
रैवतक m. N. of a mountain, pl. its inhabitants.

रैवत्य n. wealth, riches.
1रोक m. brightness, light.
2रोक m., रोकस् n. phenomenon of light.
रोग m. infirmity, disease; sore place.
रोगघ्न a. removing sickness.
रोगनाशन, °हन् (f. घ्नी), & °हर a. = prec.
रोगार्त a. visited by sickness, ill.
रोगार्दित & रोगाविष्ट a. the same.
रोगिन् a. sick, ill.
रोच a. shining.
रोचक a. causing appetite.
रोचकिन् a. having appetite (cf. अ°); delighting in (loc.).
रोचन, f. ई & आ shining, bright, beautiful; f. आ the bright sky, firmament, a cert. yellow pigment (cf. गोरोचना); n. light, sheen, the ethereal space or (3) spaces (cf. रजस्).
रोचनावन्त् a. shining, light.
रोचस् n. brightness, light, sheen.
रोचिष्णु a. shining, brilliant.
रोचिष्मन्त् a. the same.
रोचिस् n. light, splendour, beauty.
रोचुक a. pleasant.
रोद m. wail, lament.
रोदन n. weeping.
रोदस् n. (only °— & gen. du.) = seq. 1.
1रोदसी f. du. heaven and earth.
2रोदसी f. Rudra's wife.
रोदितव्य n. impers. (it is) to be wept.
रोद्धव्य a. to be closed or shut.
रोद्धृ m. oppressor, besieger.
रोध m. obstruction, restraint, prevention, suppression; confinement in (loc.); siege, blockade; dam, bank, shore.
रोधक a. investing, besieging (—°).
रोधन n. confining, investing, shutting up; restraining, suppressing.
रोधस् n. dam, wall, mound, high bank, bluff.
रोधस्वन्त् a. having high banks (river).
रोधिन् a. keeping back, obstructing, hindering, preventing, disturbing (—°).
रोध्र m. N. of a plant.
रोप m. planting (of trees).
रोपक m. planter; f. °पिका seed.
रोपण a. (f. ई) & n. putting or placing on, erecting, planting; causing to grow together, healing, curing.
रोपणीय a. to be erected or planted.
रोपयितृ m. erecter, planter.
रोपि f. pain in the bowels, colic.
रोपिन् a. planting, growing (—°).
रोप्य a. to be planted or healed.
रोम (—°) = रोमन्.
रोमक m. pl. the Romans.
रोमण्वन्त् a. covered with hair, hairy.
रोमन् n. hair (on the body of men or beasts), the feathers of a bird or the scales of a fish.
रोमन्थ m. ruminating, chewing the cud.
रोमराजि or °राजी f. row or line of hair (esp. above the navel of women).
रोमवन्त् a. = रोमण्वन्त्.
रोमश a. covered with thick hair, very hairy.
रोमहर्ष m. the erection of the hair on the body, a thrill or shudder; °हर्षण a. causing it.
रोमाञ्च m. = prec. m.; poss. °ञ्चित or °ञ्चिन्.
रोमाली & रोमावली f. = रोमराजि.
रोमोद्गति f., °द्गम m. = रोमहर्ष.
रोमोद्भेद m. the same.
रोर m. a cert. part of the body.
रोलम्ब m. bee.
रोष m. anger, wrath, fury against (—°).
रोषण a. angry, wrathful, passionate, enraged at or against (gen. or —°).
रोषाग्नि m. the fire of wrath.*
रोषिन् & रोष्टृ a. wrathful, furious.
रोह a. rising, mounted on (—°); m. rising, growiug, increasing, height.
रोहक a. riding, m. a rider.
रोहण m. N. of a mountain; n. mounting, ascending; entering in, riding, sitting, or standing on (—°); putting on, fastening; growing together, healing.
रोहस् n. elevation, height.
रोहसेन m. N. of a boy.
रोहि m. a kind of deer.
रोहिण m. a kind of tree.
रोहिणी v. रोहित.
रोहित् a. red (—°); f. a red mare or a doe.

रोहित, f. **रोहिणी** red, reddish. — m. a red horse, a kind of deer or fish, a cert. form of rainbow, a man's name. f. **रोहिणी** a red cow or mare; (also **रोहिणी**) a cert. lunar mansion (personif. as a daughter of Dakṣa and the favourite wife of the Moon), N. of sev. myth. women.

रोहिताक्ष a. red-eyed; m. N. of a man.

रोहिताश्व m. N. of a man (lit. = seq.).

रोहिदश्व a. having red horses.

रोहिन् a. rising, growing.

रोही f. a doe.

रौक्म, f. **ई** golden, adorned with gold.

रौक्ष्य n. roughness, harshness.

रौद्र or **रौद्र**, f. **आ** & **ई** relating to Rudra or the Rudras; Rudra-like i.e. fierce, violent, formidable, inauspicious, n. adv. — m. a descendant or worshipper of Rudra, pl. a class of evil demons, N. of a people. n. fierceness, formidableness, horror (also **°ता†** f.), N. of a lunar mansion.

रौधिर a. consisting of blood, bloody.

रौप्य & **°मय** (f. **ई**) made of silver, silver or silvery.

रौप्यमाषक m. a Māṣaka (coin or weight) of silver.

रौम्य m. pl. a class of evil demons.

रौरव, f. **ई** coming from the Ruru (a kind of deer); m. a cert. hell.

रौहिण a. relating to Rohiṇī (cf. **रोहित**); m. N. of a demon etc.

रौहिणायन m. a patron. name.

रौहिणेय m. metron. of Bālarāma.

रौही f. a doe (cf. **रोही**).

ल

ल m. the common name for all tenses & moods or verbal terminations.

लकार m. the sound **ल**.

लकुच m. a kind of tree, n. its fruit.

लकुट m. a club, poss. **°टिन्**.

लक्ष्, **लक्षते**, **°ति** mark, notice; cf. **लक्षय्**.

लक्ष n. mark, sign, aim, prize; a lac i.e. one hundred thousand (also m.).

लक्षक a. marking or indicating indirectly (rh.), n. = prec. n. (m.).

लक्षण a. = prec. a.; f. **आ** aim, goal, indirect indication (rh.). — n. mark, sign, token, characteristic, attribute, lucky or favourable mark, the genitals; accurate description, definition, designation, appellation, name, kind, species; aim, intention, direction; cause, occasion; adj. —° appearing as, relating to.

लक्षणवन्त् a. showing lucky marks, marked with (—°).

लक्षणान्वित a. endowed with auspicious marks.

लक्षणसंनिपात & **°संनिवेश** m. the impressing of a mark, branding.

लक्षणीय a. visible or imaginable.

लक्षण्य a. serving as a mark or having good marks.

लक्षय्, **°यति** (**°ते**), pp. **लक्षित** (q.v.) mark, note, distinguish, define, signify, express, esp. indirectly (rh.), aim at, intend, mean, consider as, take for (acc. & acc ± **इव**), know by (instr.), observe, examine; notice, perceive, behold. P. **लक्ष्यते** be marked, meant, or intended; be called or termed (2 nom.); be perceived or observed, appear, seem (nom. ± **इव**). — **अभि** mark, note, aim at, notice, perceive, behold; P. appear. **आ**, **उपा**, & **समा** see, P. videri. **उप** mark, distinguish, define, express indirectly or figuratively (rh.), notice, observe, consider as, take for (2 acc.); see, behold, hear, learn. P. be seen etc., appear to be (nom.). **समुप** notice, perceive, observe. **वि** mark, notice, perceive. **सम्** mark, see, hear, learn; P. videri. — Cf. **विलक्षित**.

लक्षवेधिन् a. piercing or hitting the aim.*

लक्षान्तर n. a distance of a hundred thousand (Yojanas).

लक्षित a. marked with or knowable by (instr.

or —°), aimed at, meant; expressed, esp. indirectly, abstr. °त्व n. (rh.); noticed, observed, seen, heard, learnt, understood.

लक्षितव्य a. to be defined.

लक्षिन् a. showing lucky marks.

लक्षी कृ make a mark of, aim or point at; °भू become the mark or aim of (—°).

लक्ष्मण a. having marks or signs. — m. the Indian crane, N. of Rāma's brother etc.; f. आ N. of sev. plants, a woman's name; n. mark, sign.

लक्ष्मण्य a. serving as a mark, visible far and wide; m. N. of a man.

लक्ष्मन् n. mark, sign, token; any special mark or characteristic (good or bad).

लक्ष्मी f. (nom. लक्ष्मीस् & लक्ष्मी) mark, sign; (±पापी) bad sign or omen, (±पुण्या) good sign, good luck (also pl.); prosperity, wealth, splendour, esp. royal splendour or dignity (often personif.); beauty, grace, loveliness, N. of the goddess of fortune and beauty (often identif. w. श्री q.v.).

लक्ष्मि (°—) = prec.

लक्ष्मीक (adj. —°) the same.

लक्ष्मीवन्त् a. fortunate or beautiful.

लक्ष्य a. to be defined, to be expressed indirectly or implicitly (rh.); to be taken for or regarded as (nom.); to be aimed at, intended, noticed, observed; visible, perceivable, knowable by (instr. or —°). — n. mark, aim, object, prize, a lac (100,000); appearance, pretence.

लक्ष्यता f., °त्व n. abstr. to prec.

लक्ष्यार्थ m. the meaning expressed indirectly or implicitly.

लक्ष्यालक्ष्य a. visible and invisible, i.e. hardly visible.

लक्ष्यी कृ = लक्षी कृ.

लग्, **लगति**, pp. लग्न (q.v.) attach or fasten one's self to (loc.), cling to, adhere, approach, near, follow immediately, happen, occur, pass away. — अव abide, stay, tarry. आ cling to, adhere. वि cling or stick to (loc.). — Cf. अनुलग्न, अवलग्न, आलग्न, परिलग्न*, प्रतिलग्न* (add.), विलग्न, संलग्न.

लगनीय n. impers. (it is) to be clung to (loc.).

लगुड m. club, cudgel, poss. °डिन्.

लगुडप्रहार m. a blow with a cudgel.

लगुडहस्त a. cudgel in hand.

लग्न (loc. or —°) a. attached, stuck, held fast; following, immediately; clinging to, fastened on, intent on or about to (infin.); m. (n.) auspicious time or moment for (—°).

लग्नकाल m., °दिन n., °दिवस m. auspicious time or day.

लग्नवेला f., °समय m. = prec.

लघय्, °यति make light, lessen, diminish.

लघिमन् m. lightness (conceived also as a supernatural faculty), levity, fickleness, frivolity.

लघिष्ठ & **लघीयस्** superl. & compar. to seq.

लघु (f. लघ्वी & लघु) swift, quick, light, easy, soft, gentle (sound), pleasant; insignificant, small, low, mean; short (prosod.), young or younger. — n. adv., w. मन् slight, despise (w. कृ mock, scoff*).

लघुकौमुदी f. T. of a grammatical work (lit. the easy explanation).

लघुक्रम a. having a light step, hastening; n. adv.

लघुगति a. moving quickly.

लघुचित्त a. light-minded, fickle; abstr. °ता f.

लघुचेतस् a. little-minded, illiberal.

लघुच्छेद्य or **लघूच्छेद्य** a. easy to be extirpated or destroyed.

लघुता f., °त्व n. quickness, lightness, freshness, agility; smallness, insignificance, shortness (pros.); fickleness, frivolity; humbleness, meanness, contemptibleness.

लघुपतनक m. N. of a crow (lit. quickly flying).

लघुपातिन् m. the same.

लघुभाव m. lightness.

लघुभ्रातृ m. a younger brother.

लघुवासस् a. lightly or cleanly dressed.

1**लघुविक्रम** m. a quick step.

2**लघुविक्रम** a. stepping quickly, light-footed.

लघुसत्त्व a. of a weak character, abstr. °ता f.

लघुहस्त a. light-handed, clever; p. °वन्त्.

लघुहस्तता f., °त्व n. abstr. to prec.

लघुहृदय a. light-hearted, fickle.

लघू कृ lighten, lessen, diminish, humble, despise.

लघूय्, °**यति** slight, despise.

लघ्वाशिन् & **लघ्वाहार** a. eating little or moderately.

लङ् s. the imperfect & its endings (g.).

लङ्का f. N. of the chief town in Ceylon & the island itself.

लङ्ग a. lame.

लङ्घ्, **लङ्घति**, °**ते** leap; mostly C. **लङ्घयति** (°**ते**), pp. **लङ्घित** spring over, go beyond (acc.); travel over (**अध्वानम्**); mount, ascend, enter; get off, escape; overstep, transgress; violate, offend; excel, surpass, outstrip. — **अति** C. transgress. **अभि** C. leap or step over, transgress, offend. **उद्** C. the same + pass by, escape; pass or travel over (way). **वि** C. leap over, pass by; transgress, violate; neglect, omit; surpass, excel; wrong, offend.

लङ्घक m. offender.

लङ्घन n. leaping, springing over (gen. or —°), mounting, rising to (—°), assault, capture, conquest; transgression, offence, repudiation.

लङ्घनीय a. to be passed or travelled over; passable, attainable, transgressible; to be violated or wronged.

लङ्घ्य a. the same.

लज्ज्, **लज्जते** (°**ति**), pp. **लज्जित** (q.v.) be abashed or embarrassed, be ashamed of (instr. or gen.) or to (infin.). C. **लज्जयति** make ashamed, confound. — **वि** & **सम्** = S. — Cf. **विलज्जित**.

लज्जा f. shame, bashfulness.

लज्जाकर, f. **ई** causing shame, shameful.

लज्जापयितृ (°**तृक**) a. = prec.*

लज्जाय्, pp. °**यित** = **लज्जित** a. & n.

***लज्जालु** & °**क** a. bashful, modest.

लज्जावन्त् a. full of shame, bashful, modest; abstr. °**वत्त्व** n.

लज्जावह a. causing shame, shameful.

लज्जित a. abashed, embarrassed, ashamed of (instr. or —°); n. shame, bashfulness.

लञ्चा f. donation.

लट् s. the present & its endings (g.).

लटभ, **लटह** (**लडह***) a. nice, pretty; f. **आ** a nice girl.

लड्डु & °**क** s. a kind of cake.

लण्ड n. excrement.

लता f. creeper, creeping plant or tendril, twig (often —° in comparisons); lash of a whip, string of pearls, a (slender) woman.

लतागृह n. a summerhouse formed of creepers.

लतापाश m. a sling or noose made of a creeper.

लतामण्डप m. = **लतागृह**.

लतालय m. dwelling (of an owl) made of creepers.

लतावलय n. = **लतागृह**, poss. °**वन्त्**.

लतावितान s. an awning or canopy formed of creepers.

लतिका f. a small creeper or winding plant.

लप्, **लपति** (°**ते**), pp. **लपित** (q.v.) chatter, prate, talk, lament. C. **लापयति** cause to talk. I. **लालपीति** chatter senselessly, prattle, **लालप्यते** (°**ति**) wail, lament. — **अप** deny, refuse, conceal. **अभि** talk, speak of; name, call. **आ** address, speak to (acc.), converse with (**समम्** or **सह**), say, tell (2 acc.). C. cause to speak, engage in conversation, question. **उद्** C. = prec. C. or caress. **समुद्** raise the voice; (wail, lament*). **प्र** prattle, chatter, talk, lament. C. compel to speak. **वि** wail, moan, chatter, talk confusedly or at random. **सम्** converse, C. address. — Cf. **आलपित**, **प्रलपित**, **विलपित**.

लपन n. mouth.

लपित n. chaff, humming.

लप्सुदिन् a. bearded (goat).

लब m. a cert. bird.

लब्ध a. caught, seized, taken; got, obtained (esp. °— having caught etc.).

लब्धनामन् a. having gained a name, celebrated or famous for (—°).

लब्धप्रत्यय a. having acquired confidence, abstr. °**ता** f.*

लब्धप्रसर a. having got free course, let loose, unimpeded, bold.

लब्धलक्ष a. experienced, versed in (loc.), lit. having hit the mark or won the prize.

लब्धवर्ण a. learned, skilful, clever (lit. having learned the letters or got distinction).

लब्धव्य a. to be attained or received.

लब्धान्तर a. having got an opportunity, abstr. °त्व n.

लब्धावकाश & **लब्धावसर** a. the same.

लब्धास्पद a. having got a situation.

लब्धि f. acquisition, perception.

लब्धृ m. receiver, gainer, recipient.

लभ्, **लभते** (°ति & **लम्भते**), pp. **लब्ध** (q.v.) catch, seize; meet with, find; obtain, get, receive; be capable of or able to, succeed in (dat. or infin.); possess, have, enjoy; perceive, know, learn, understand. P. be caught etc., be allowed or permitted; result, follow. C. **लम्भयति** cause to take or receive (2 acc. or acc. of pers. & instr. of th.); get, obtain, find out, learn. D. **लिप्सते** (°ति) wish to catch or obtain. — **अनु** catch or seize from behind. **अभि** seize, touch, get, attain. D. wish to catch or seize. **आ** catch, seize, touch, take hold of (esp. the sacrificial animal to kill it); undertake, begin; gain, acquire, get, attain. C. cause to seize, touch, or begin. D. wish to touch or kill. **अन्वा** seize or touch (from behind); hold or stick to (acc.). **उपा** touch, also = C. reproach, blame. **समा** take hold of, seize, touch, get, obtain, rub over, anoint. **उप** catch, meet with, find, obtain (P. fall to one's share), recover; conceive (**गर्भम्**); perceive, learn, ascertain, understand, know as (2 acc.). C. let have or know. **प्रत्युप** receive back, recover. **समुप** get, obtain; learn, understand. **प्र** seize; take hold of, get, obtain, also = C. take in, dupe, fool, mock. **विप्र** = prec. C. **प्रति** receive back, recover, get, obtain; get it i.e. be punished; perceive, learn, understand, know as (2 acc.); wait for, expect. **वि** take asunder or away; get, procure; cede, surrender, yield. C. let a pers. have a th. (2 acc.). **सम्** wrestle or struggle with (instr.), take hold of one another; obtain, receive.

लभ v. **दुर्लभ** & **सुलभ**.

लभन n. obtaining, meeting with.

लभ्य a. to be found or met with, attainable, intelligible, suitable, fit, proper.

लम् only **ललाम**, enjoy (sexually).

लम्पट a. covetous, greedy for (loc. or —°).

लम्पा f. N. of a city & a kingdom.

लम्ब्, **लम्बते** (°ति), pp. **लम्बित** (q.v.) hang down, sink; hang upon, cling to (loc., w. **रश्मिषु** let free); stay behind, tarry, lag, linger. C. **लम्बयति** hang up, suspend; w. **करम्** put the hand to (dat.). — **अव** hang down, descend, sink, sit down; hang, lean, rest, depend or rely upon, belong to (acc., r. loc. or instr.); take hold of, seize, uphold, maintain; take to, affect, pursue (acc.); linger, tarry. C. hang or let down, suspend on (loc.); seize, take hold of, support, uphold; load upon, impose. **आ** hang down; hang or lean, depend or rest upon, hold or stick to (acc., r. loc.); seize, take; support, maintain; take to, affect, pursue assume, show, exhibit. **व्या** hang down (from all sides), descend. **समा** cling to, lean or rely upon (acc.); take hold of, seize, assume; apply or devote one's self to (acc.). C. suspend on (loc.). **उद्** C. hang, suspend. **परि** lag, loiter. **प्र** hang down. **प्रति** C. hang, tie up. **वि** hang (on both sides) on (acc. or loc.); sink, descend; lag, loiter. C. suspend on (loc.); detain, delay, lag or loiter. **प्रवि** C. hang, suspend. — Cf. **अवलम्बित**, **आलम्बित**, **उल्लम्बित** (add.), **प्रलम्बित** (add.), **विलम्बित**, **विलम्ब्य**, **समुल्लम्बित**.

लम्ब a. hanging down (intr.), hanging on or down to (—°).

लम्बकर्ण, f. **ई** having pendulous ears, long-eared; m. a he-goat, N. of an ass & a hare.

लम्बन a. hanging down (tr. & intr.).

लम्बित a. hanging down, pendent, hanging on (instr. or —°), sunk, fallen off; slow, moderate (time of music).

लम्बिन् a. = लम्ब.

लम्बोदर, f. ई having a large belly; m. E. of Gaṇeça.

लम्भ m., °न n. obtaining, finding, recovering.

लम्भनीय a. to be obtained.

लम्भयितव्य a. to be set to work or applied.*

लम्भुक a. going to get or obtain (acc.).

लय m. dulling or hebetating the mind. m. clinging or adhering to (—°), cowering, hiding, vanishing or entering into (loc. or —°); absorption, extinction, death; rest, repose; time or pause in music.

लयन n. rest or resting-place.

लयमध्य (to be performed) in a mean or moderate time (piece of music).

लयशुद्ध a. (to be performed) in pure or just time (as prec.).

लयस्थान n. place of dissolution.

लल्, ललति (°ते), pp. ललित (q.v.) sport, dally, play, coruscate. C. लालयति cause to sport etc., caress, fondle, cherish, love. (आ play. sport*). उप & सम् C. = S. C.

ललन a. sporting, coruscating (light); f. आ a (wanton) woman, mistress, wife.

ललनिका f. little or poor woman.

*ललन्तिका f. a pendulous necklace.

ललाट n. forehead, loc. in front.

ललाटक n. = prec.; f. °टिका (*ornament of) or mark on the forehead.

ललाटंतप a. burning the forehead (sun).

ललाटपट्ट & पट्टक m., पट्टिका f. (the plate or tablet of) the forehead.

ललाटफलक n. the same.

ललाटलिखित a. written (by Fate) on the forehead; लेखा f. such lines or features.

ललाटाक्ष a. having an eye on the forehead (Çiva); f. ई N. of a Rākṣasī.

ललाटिक a. being in front.

ललाम, f. °मी having a blaze or star (cattle); s. ornament, decoration; f. ई N. of a female demon.

*ललामक n. garland worn on the forehead.

ललामन् n. ornament, decoration.

ललित a. sporting, playing, coruscating; lovely, charming, favourite, liked; simple, artless, naive.

ललितललित a. exceedingly beautiful.

ललितलोचन a. fair-eyed; f. N. of a woman.

ललितविस्तर m. T. of a Buddhistic work.

ललित्थ m. pl. N. of a people.

लल्ल m., आ f. a man's & woman's name.

लव m. cutting, plucking, gathering etc.; what is cut, as wool, hair, etc.; fragment, piece, particle, bit, drop.

लवङ्ग m. the clove tree; n. cloves.

लवङ्गिका f. a woman's name.

लवण n. salt, esp. sea-salt, a. salt; f. आ or ई N. of sev. rivers.

लवणजल a. having salt water; m. = seq.

लवणजलधि & °जलनिधि m. the sea.

लवणता f., °त्व n. saltness.

लवणतोय & लवणवारि a. & m. = लवणजल.

लवणाब्धि m. the sea.

लवणाम्बुराशि & लवणाम्भस् m. = prec.

लवणार्णव & लवणालय m. the same.

लवणित a. salted, seasoned with salt.

लवणिमन् m. loveliness, beauty.

लवणोद & °धि m. the (salt) sea.

लवणोदक a. having salt water.

लवन n. cutting or implement for cutting.

लवलि or °ली f. N. of a plant.

लवशस् adv. in small pieces, w. कृ & छिद् C. make or cut in small pieces.

लवितव्य & लव्य a. to be cut.

लशुन n. (m.) leek, garlic.

लष्, लषति (°ते & लष्यति), pp. लषित desire, long for, strive after (acc.). – अभि, समभि, आ, & परि = S.

लस्, लसति, pp. लसित gleam, glance; sound forth; appear, rise (only लसन्त् & लसमान), sport, play. C. लासयति (cause or teach to) dance. – उद् = S. C. cause to gleam etc.; cause, produce i.g. प्रत्युद् shine, appear. प्रोद् shine or sound forth, move hither and thither. समुद् shine or sound forth, appear. वि shine, glitter, appear, arise, sound forth, sport, play, move hither and thither, coruscate. – Cf. उल्लसित, विलसित.

लसूजनी f. a coarse needle.

लहर m. pl. N. of a people.

लहरि or °री f. wave, billow.

ला, लाति grasp, seize, take; ger. **लात्वा** having taken, i.e. with.

लाक्षण a. knowing characteristic signs or marks.

लाक्षणिक, f. **ई** = prec. or indirect, metaphorical; m. prophet, fortune-teller.

लाक्षण्य a. = **लाक्षण**.

†**लाक्षा** f. N. of a plant, lac.

लाघव n. quickness, agility, dexterity in (loc.), lightness, relief; fickleness, inconsiderateness, smallness, shortness, insignificance, meanness, humbleness, contempt.

लाङ्गल n. plough.

लाङ्गलध्वज & **लाङ्गलिन्** m. E. of Balarāma, lit. having a plough (for an ensign).

लाङ्गुल or **लाङ्गूल** n. tail.

लाज m., **आ** f. pl. parched or roasted grain.

लाञ्छ्, C. **लाञ्छयति**, pp. **लाञ्छित** mark, distinguish.

लाञ्छन n. mark, sign, vestige.

लाट m. pl. N. of a people.

लातव्य m. patron. of sev. men.

लापिन् a. speaking, telling (—°); lamenting.

लापु s. a cert. insrument.

लाब & **°क** m. a kind of quail.

लाभ m. finding, meeting with, getting, acquisition (gen. or —°); gain, advantage, capture, conquest; perception, knowledge.

लाभलिप्सा f. greediness of gain.

लाभवन्त् a. having a gain; —° = **लाभिन्**.

लाभालाभ m. du. & n. sgl. gain and loss.

लाभिन् a. finding, obtaining (—°).

लाल m. a man's name (cf. **लल्ल**).

लालक, f. **°लिका** caressing, fondling.

लालन n. abstr. to prec.

लालनीय a. to be caressed or fondled.

लालस a. ardently desirous of, eagerly longing for, thoroughly devoted to (gen. or —°); m., f. **आ** & **°ता** as abstr.

लालसक, f. **°सिका** = prec. adj.*

लाला f. spittle.

लालाट a. being on the forehead (also **°टिक**); f. **°टी** forehead.

लालापान n. the sucking spittle.

लालाय्, **°यते** emit spittle, slaver.

लालित्य n. loveliness, grace, beauty.

लालिन् a. fondling, cherishing.

लाव, f. **ई** cutting, severing, killing.

1**लावक** m. cutter, mower, reaper.

2**लावक** v. **लाबक**.

लावण a. saline, salt, salted.

लावणक s. N. of a place.

लावणिक a. dealing in salt; lovely, charming.

लावण्य n. saltness; charm, beauty.

लावण्यमय, f. **ई** full of loveliness or beauty.

लावण्यवन्त् a. the same.

लावाणक m. = **लावणक**.

लास m. jumping, sporting, dancing.

लासक a. moving hither and thither; m. & f. **°सिका** dancer.

लास्य n. dance; m. dancer.

(**लिक्ष** s. &) **लिक्षा** f. nit (louse-egg).

लिख्, **लिखति** (**°ते**), pp. **लिखित** (q.v.) scratch, furrow, slit, peck at (acc.); draw a line, write, write down, delineate, sketch, paint. C. **लेखयति** cause to scratch etc.; also = S. write, paint. — **अभि** = S., (± **हृदयेन**) ponder upon*; C. cause to write or paint. **आ** scratch, touch, cut in, write, delineate, paint; ponder upon (acc.*). **समा** the same. **उद्** furrow, scratch, scrape, cut in, inscribe, write down; cut out, chisel, form; smooth, polish. **प्रोद्** scratch, furrow. **समुद्** the same, touch (the sky); write down, register, record. **परि** draw a furrow or a line around, enclose in a circle. **प्र** scratch, furrow; sketch, delineate, write; A.M. scrape together; M. comb one's self. **प्रति** write in return, answer. **वि** scratch, tear open, scrape, rub against, touch (the sky); scratch or cut in, write, delineate, paint. **सम्** scratch, engrave, inscribe, touch (a musical instrument) i.e. play.

लिखन s. cratching, writing.

लिखित a. scratched, written, drawn, sketched, painted; **लिखित इव** as if painted i.e. quite immovable. — m. N. of a Rishi; n. scripture, written document.

लिखितत्व n. the being written down.

लिखितृ m. painter.

लिख्य m., **आ** f. = **लिक्ष**, **आ**.

लिङ् s. the potential or precative & their endings (g.).

लिङ्ग् v. आलिङ्ग्.

लिङ्ग n. mark, sign, emblem, badge, characteristic, attribute, sectarian mark; proof, means of proof, evidence (j.); organ of generation, esp. the male organ of Çiva (r.); idol i.g; gender (g.), the subtile frame or body (ph.).

लिङ्गदेह m. n. = prec. (ph.).

लिङ्गधर a. wearing marks; w. only the marks of, a false (—°).

लिङ्गधारण n. the wearing of (one's own) marks.

लिङ्गपुराण n. T. of a Purāṇa.

लिङ्गवन्त् a. having marks or characteristics.

लिङ्गशरीर n. = लिङ्ग (ph.)

लिङ्गस्थ m. a religious student (cf. लिङ्गिन्).

लिङ्गानुशासन n. the doctrine of grammatical gender.

लिङ्गिन् a. = लिङ्गधर; m. a religious student or ascetic (who has a right to wear signs or badges).

लिङ्गिवेष m. a student's dress.

लिच्छिवि m. N. of a princely race.

लिट् s. the perfect & its endings (g.).

लिन्दु a. slimy, slippery.

लिप्, लिम्पति, °ते, pp. लिप्त (q.v.) smear, stain, soil (lit. & fig.), besmear with (instr.) or smear a th. (acc.) over or on a th., stick on to (loc.); P. लिप्यते cleave or stick to (intr.). C. लेपयति & लिम्पयति = S. tr. — अनु smear, anoint with (instr.); M. refl. अव the same; P. be haughty or arrogant. आ smear, anoint with (instr.); C. the same. उप the same. नि smear; cause to disappear; M. disappear, become invisible. प्र, वि, सम् smear, anoint; C. the same. — Cf. अवलिप्त.

लिपि f. smearing, rubbing over, writing.

लिपिकर m. painter (f. ई*), writer.

लिपिन्यास m. writing down.

लिप्त a. smeared, stained, soiled, defiled; cleaving or sticking to (loc.); f. आ minute ($^1/_{60}$ degree).

लिप्ति f. ointment, dough.

लिप्सा f. desire to gain or have, longing for (loc. or —°).

लिप्सु a. wishing to get, longing for (acc. or —°).

लिबुजा f. creeping plant, creeper.

लिम्पि f. writing, scripture.

लिश्, लिशते (only —°) = रिश्.

1लिह्, लेढि, लीढे, लिहति, pp. लीढ lick, lick up, lick at (loc.), lick away i.e. destroy. C. लेहयति cause to lick. I. लेलिह्यते etc. (pp. लेलिहान) lick frequently, play with the tongue. — अव, आ, उद् lick, touch (with mouth or beak). उप M. enjoy by licking. निस् lick off, sip. परि lick at (acc); I. lick frequently. वि the same. सम् & परिसम् lick at, enjoy. — Cf. आलीढ, उल्लीढ.

2लिह् (—°) licking.

लिह a. = prec. (—°).

1ली, लीयते, °ति (लयते only w. नि), pp. लीन (q.v.) cling, adhere, stick, light or sit upon (of birds & insects); stoop, cower; slip into, disappear. C. लापयति & लाययति v. sub वि. — अभि cling to (acc.). अव settle down, cower, hide. व्यव stoop, cower. आ cling or adhere to (loc.), sit down upon or in, stoop, cower, hide. नि cleave or stick to (acc.), lie or settle down upon (loc.); °लयते (also अपनि) hide, disappear from (abl.). संनि settle down, alight; hide or disappear in (loc.). प्र hide one's self; dissolve, be absorbed in (loc.); disappear, perish, die. संप्र vanish, be dissolved or absorbed in (loc.). प्रति disappear. वि cling or stick to, cower upon (loc.); settle down, alight; conceal one's self, disappear, be dissolved, melt. C. (°लापयति & °लाययति) cause to disappear, dissolve, melt (tr.). प्रवि perish, disappear. सम् cling or stick close to (acc.), find room in (loc.); hide, be concealed; stoop, cower, contract. — Cf. अभिलीन, अवलीन (add.), आलीन, निलीन (add.), प्रलीन, विलीन, संलीन.

2ली, only I. लेलायति, °ते be unsteady, waver, tremble.

लीका f. pl. a class of evil demons.

लीन a. clinging or sticking to (n. also as abstr. w. loc.), lying or sitting on, quite devoted to or intent upon; (n. also impers.) hidden, absorbed, or disappeared into (loc. or —°). Abstr. °ता f., °त्व n.

लीला f. play, sport, amusement, pastime; wantonness, grace, beauty, charm; mere play or sport, i.e. either ease or facility in doing anything; or appearance, semblance, pretence. °— & instr. for sport, without effort; feignedly.

लीलाकमल n. a lotus (held in the hand) to play with.

लीलागार n. pleasure-house.

लीलागृह & °गेह n. the same.

लीलानृत्य n. a sham dance, the image of a dance.

लीलापद्म & लीलाब्ज n. = लीलाकमल.

लीलाभरण n. a sham ornament.

लीलाय्, °यति & °ते play, sport, amuse one's self; pp. लीलायित playing, sporting, n. also impers. & as abstr.

लीलारविन्द n. = लीलाकमल.

लीलावन्त् a. graceful, charming; f. °वती a charming or wanton woman, a woman's name, E. of Durgā, T. of sev. works.

लीलावापी f. pleasure-tank.

लीलोद्यान n. pleasure-garden.

लुक् s. disappearance, elision (g.).

लुङ् s. the aorist & its endings (g.).

लुञ्च्, लुञ्चति, pp. लुञ्चित pluck, tear; peel, husk. — अव & वि tear off or out. — Cf. उल्लुञ्चित.

लुञ्चक & लुञ्चन a. tearing out.

1लुठ्, लुठति, °ते, pp. लुठित roll, move to and fro (intr.), stir up, agitate. C. लोठयति = S. D. लुलुठिषते be about to roll. I. लोलुठीति wallow (of a drunkard). — उद्, परि, प्र, & वि = S. intr.

2लुठ्, लुण्ठ्, लुण्ठति = prec. S. tr.; C. लुण्ठयति & लोठयति, pp. लुण्ठित rob, steal, plunder. — निस् & वि = S. C.

लुड्, C. लोडयति stir up, agitate. — अव rummage, investigate. आ stir up, agitate, trouble, disturb, rummage, work one's way through (acc.). समा mix together, mingle with (instr.), stir up etc. = prec. निस् investigate thoroughly. विप्र, प्रति, वि, & सम् stir up, trouble, disturb, confuse.

लुण्ठ् v. 2लुठ्.

लुण्ठ s. a kind of grass.

लुण्ठक m. plunderer.

लुण्ठन n. plundering of (—°).

लुण्ठि f. plundering, pillaging.

लुण्डिका f. ball, round mass.

लुण्डी कृ make into a ball, roll together.

1लुप्, लुम्पति (°ते), pp. लुप्त (q.v.) break, harm, injure, attack, rub, plunder, consume, throw away, suppress, destroy, cause to disappear. P. लुप्यते (लुप्यते, °ति) be broken or harmed etc.; be suppressed or elided, disappear (g.). C. लोपयति, °ते omit, neglect, infringe, violate; divert from (abl.). I. लोलुप्यते etc. confuse, disturb. — अप pluck off, sever; P. fall off. अव strip off, snatch away; seize, attack; suppress, destroy. आ pull out, sever; P. be troubled or disturbed. व्या break, destroy. उद् & समुद् take out, pick up. परि take away, remove, destroy. प्र pluck out, rob, deprive of (तस्). विप्र take away, rob; trouble, disturb. वि tear or break in pieces, pull out or up, take away, rob, plunder, destroy, ruin; P. M. decay, perish, disappear, be gone or missing. सम् pluck, pull, snatch away; C. ruin, destroy.

2लुप् s. elision, suppression.

लुप्त a. broken, harmed, robbed, plundered, deprived of (—°); mutilated, incomplete (opp. पूर्ण); suppressed, elided (g.).

लुप्तदण्डक m. peeled staff, i.e. arch-rogue.*

लुप्तोपमा f. elliptical comparison (rh.).

लुब्ध a. confused, perplexed, troubled; covetous, avaricious; desirous of, longing for (loc. or —°); m. = seq.

लुब्धक m. hunter.

लुब्धता f., °त्व n. greediness, covetousness, eager desire for (—°).

लुभ्, लुभ्यति, pp. लुब्ध (q.v.) go astray, be lustful or covetous, desire eagerly, long for (loc. or dat.); attract, allure. C. लोभयति confuse, disturb, trouble, derange; allure. I. लोलुभ्यते be very greedy of (loc.). — अनु C. long for (acc.). अभि C. entice, allure. आ get into confusion. उप C. allure, seduce. परि S. & C. the same. प्र M. go astray, be lustful, lust after (सह); also = C. allure, entice, seduce. विप्र, संप्र, & प्रति C. = prec. C. वि fall into disorder or confusion; C. lead astray, perplex, confuse, seduce, divert, amuse. सम् be confounded; C. confound, disarrange, tempt, allure, seduce. — Cf. परिलुब्ध (add.).

लुम्बी f. fruit.

लुल्, लोलति, pp. लुलित (q.v.) move hither and thither, roll, wallow; disappear. C. लोलयति set in motion, agitate, confound. — Cf. अभिलुलित, आलुलित, विलुलित, संलुलित.

लुलाप & **लुलाय** m. buffalo.

लुलित a. moving hither and thither, fluttering, waving, tremulous; touched, shaken, agitated, disturbed, damaged; n. motion.

लुश & **लुशाकपि** m. names of men.

लू, लुनोति & लुनाति, लुनोते, pp. लून (q.v.) cut, sever, mow, pluck, hew down, tear asunder, pierce, destroy. — अव cut off. आ tear or pluck off. न्या, व्या, निस्, परि, प्र, विप्र, वि cut or hew off.

लूक्ष a. rough, harsh.

लूता f. spider.

लून a. cut, severed, plucked, reaped, gnawed off, hewn asunder, destroyed; n. tail.

लृट् s. the future in स्य & its endings (g.).

लेख m. streak, line, writing, letter; pl. a class of gods (sgl. a god i.g.). — f. लेखा scratch, streak, line, furrow, row, edge, margin, a faint sickle (of the moon); drawing, likeness, impression.

लेखक m. writer, scribe; writing down, scripture, reckoning, calculation; f. लेखिका a small stripe.

लेखन, f. ई scratching, scraping, attenuating; f. ई writing reed, pen, pencil; n. scratching, writing down, copying.

लेखनसाधन* n. pl. = लेखसाधन.

लेखनीय a. to be painted or written down.

लेखपत्त्र n., °पत्त्रिका f. letter.

लेखसाधन n. pl. materials for writing.*

लेखहार & °क m. letter-carrier.

लेखाविधि m. the action of painting (pl.).

लेखिन् a. scratching, scraping, touching (—°).

लेख्य a. to be scratched, written down, or painted. n. writing, copying, drawing, painting; picture, written document.

लेख्यगत a. being on a picture i.e. painted.

लेट् s. the conjunctive & its endings (g.).

लेट m. a cert. mixed caste.

लेण्ड n. excrement.

लेप m. = seq. + dirt, impurity (l. & f.); the wipings (r.).

लेपन n. smearing, daubing, ointment, plaster, mortar.

लेपभागिन् a. partaking of the wipings (r.).

लेपिन् a. smearing or covering, smeared or covered with (—°).

लेप्य a. to be smeared or soiled.

लेलया (instr. adv.) flickeringly, unsteadily.

लेलिह & **लेलिहान** m. serpent (licker).

लेश m. particle, atom, drop, bit of (gen. or —°); a cert. figure of speech (rh.) °—, instr., & adv. in तस् slightly, very little.

लेश्य & **लेश्या** f. light.

लेष्टु m. clod of earth.

लेष्टुका f. the same.*

लेह m. licker, sipper.

लेहन n. licking, sipping.

लेह्य a. to be (being) licked or sipped.

लोक्, लोकते, mostly लोकयति (°ते) look, look at, view, contemplate; perceive, know. — अभि view, contemplate. अव & समव look, look at, contemplate, see, mark, perceive. आ & समा look at, behold, consider, regard, examine, investigate, perceive, learn, know as (2 acc.). परि look around. (प्र consider*). वि look at, regard, try, examine, study; perceive, see, discover, look over or beyond (acc.). प्रवि look at, observe, behold, see, consider.

1**लोक** m. open splace, free room, place, region, world or one of the (imaginary 2, 3, or 7) worlds, esp. the earth; people, men or mankind (sgl. or pl.); company, community, troop or band of (—°); worldy life, ordinary practice or common usage (opp. to higher things, esp. knowledge).

लोककण्टक m. a thorn to mankind, a wicked man or criminal.

लोककर्तृ m. the creator of the world.

लोककान्त a. liked by the world, popular.

लोककाम a. longing for a cert. world.

लोककार m. = लोककर्तृ.

लोककृत् a. granting space, liberating; also = prec.

लोकक्षित् a. dwelling in heaven.

लोकचर & °चारिन् a. wandering through the world.

लोकचरित & °चारित्र n. the ways or proceedings of the world.

लोकजित् a. winning space or heaven.

लोकज्ञ a. knowing the world, abstr. °ता f.

लोकतन्त्र n. the course of the world.

लोकतस् adv. from the world, from what people say.

लोकत्रय n., °त्रयी f. the three worlds (heaven, earth, and the air or the lower regions).

लोकदम्भक a. deceiving the world.

लोकद्वय n. the two worlds (heaven and earth).

लोकद्वार n. the gate of heaven.

लोकधातृ m. the creator of the world (Çiva).

लोकनाथ m. lord of the worlds (Brahman, Viṣṇu, or Çiva); also ruler of men, king.

लोकप m. = लोकपाल.

लोकपति m. = लोकनाथ.

लोकपाल m. world-protector (4 or 8); prince, king.

लोकप्रवाद m. world-saying, common saying, proverb.

लोकभावन m. the creator of the world (Brahman).

लोकमय, f. ई spacious or containing the world.

लोकमार्ग m. the way or custom of the world.

लोकंपृण a. world-filling; f. आ E. of the bricks used for building the sacrificial altar (set up with the formula लोकं पृण etc.).

लोकयात्रा f. business and traffic of men; support of life, daily bread.

लोकरञ्जन n. pleasing the world, popularity.

लोकवचन n., °वाद m. the talk of the world.

लोकवन्त् a. containing the world.

लोकविज्ञात a. known by the world or universally.

1लोकविद् a. having or granting room.

2लोकविद् a. knowing the world.

लोकविद्विष्ट a. hated by men.

लोकविश्रुत a. universally celebrated.

लोकवृत्त n., °वृत्तान्त m. course or proceedings of the world, universal custom.

लोकव्यवहार m. the same.

लोकश्रेष्ठ a. best in the world.

लोकसंग्रह m. the welfare of the world.

लोकसाक्षिक a. witnessed by the world or by men; n. adv.

लोकहित n. the welfare of the world.

लोकाचार m. usage or practice of the world, general custom.

लोकात्मन् m. the soul of the world.

लोकादि m. the beginning i.e. the author of the world.

लोकाधिप & °पति m. ruler of the world, a god.

लोकानुग्रह m. the welfare of the world.

लोकान्तर n. another world, the Beyond.

लोकान्तरस्थ a. deceased, dead.

लोकापवाद m. the reproach of the world, general evil report.

लोकालोक (n. sgl. & m. du.) world and no world, N. of a myth. mountain.

लोकिन् a. possessing the (best) world; pl. the inhabitants of the universe.

लोकेश & °श्वर m. lord or ruler of the world.

लोकैषणा f. yearning after heaven.

लोकोक्ति f. talk of the world, common saying.

लोकोत्तर a. surpassing the world or what is common; unusual, extraordinary.

लोक्य a. granting free space or sphere of action; world-wide, usual, customary right;. real, actual. — n. free space or sphere.

लोग m. clod of earth.

लोच्, (only —°) लोचते & C. लोचयति, °ते

w. आ consider, reflect; C. the same, r. cause to appear or be seen; pp. आलोचित (n. also impers.). अन्वा, पर्या, समा, & निस् C. call to mind, imagine, consider, reflect, deliberate.

लोचन a. enlightening, n. eye.

लोचनगोचर a. within the range of the eye.

लोचनत्रयपथ m. the range of the three eyes (of Çiva).

लोचनपथ m. path of the eyes, sphere of vision.

लोचनाञ्चल m. corner of the eye.

लोचनानन्द m. delight of the eyes.*

लोट् s. the imperative & its endings (g.).

लोठन n. shaking (of the head).

लोडन n. vexing, annoying.

लोध m. a kind of animal.

लोध्र m. a kind of tree.

लोप m. cutting off, severing, taking away, troubling, disturbing; want, loss; elision (g.). f. लोपा a cert. bird.

लोपक a. troubling, disturbing, destroying (—°).

लोपन n. omitting, violating.

लोपाश m. jackal or fox.

लोपिन् a. wronging, injuring (—°); liable to elision (g.).

लोप्तृ m. violator, injurer.

लोप्त्र n. stolen property, plunder, booty.

लोप्य a. to be rejected or elided.

लोभ m. greed, avarice, impatience, strong desire of (gen., loc., —°).

लोभन n. alluring, enticing.

लोभनीय a. to be desired or longed for; seductive, attractive.

लोभविरह m. freedom from greed or avarice

लोभिन् a. greedy, covetous; longing for or alluring (—°).

लोम & °क (—°) = लोमन्.

लोमकीट m. louse (hair-insect).

लोमकूप m. pore of the skin (hair-hole).

लोमगर्त m. the same.

लोमन् n. hair on the body of men & animals.

लोमपाद m. N. of a king.

लोमवन्त् a. having hair, hairy.

लोमश a. the same.

लोमहर्ष m. erection of the hair, thrill or shudder.

लोमहर्षण a. exciting (cf. prec.); m. E. of Sūta.

लोल a. moving hither and thither, restless, unsteady; greedy, eager or longing for (loc., infin., or —°); abstr. °ता f., °त्व n.

लोलुप a. ardently longing for or desirous of (loc. or —°); आ & °ता f., °त्व n. abstr.

लोलुभ a. greedy after, longing for (—°).

लोलेक्षण a. having a rolling eye.

लोष्ट m. n. clod of earth.

लोष्टक m. the same, masonry.

लोष्टगुटिका f. lump of clay.

लोष्टमय a. made of clay, earthen.

लोष्टमर्दिन् a. who crushes clods.

लोष्ट्र & **लोष्ठ** = लोष्ट.

लोह a. reddish, of copper or iron. m. n. reddish metal, copper, also iron & metal i.g.; n. an iron vessel.

लोहचारक m. a cert. hell.

लोहज a. made of copper or iron.

लोहदण्ड s. an iron bar.

लोहधातु m. iron.

लोहमय, f. ई the same.

लोहवन्त् a. reddish.

लोहशङ्कु m. a cert. hell.

लोहायस a. of reddish metal, coppery; n. coppery metal, any m. alloyed with copper.

लोहाष्ठीला f. a metal ball.

लोहित (f. °ता & लोहिनी) reddish, red, coppery, metallic. — m. a cert. precious stone, (*a kind of fish*), N. of a serpent-demon etc.; n. copper, metal i.g., blood, *saffron.

लोहितकृष्ण a. reddish black.

लोहितग्रीव a. red-necked (Agni).

लोहितवन्त् a. containing blood.

लोहितवासस् a. having a red (bloody) garment.

लोहिताक्ष, f. ई red-eyed.

लोहिताङ्ग m. the planet Mars (lit. the red-limbed).

लोहिताय, °यति & °ते become or be red.

लोहितायस a. made of red metal; n. copper.

लोहितोर्ण, f. ई having red wool.

लौहिनी v. **लोहित**.

लौकिक, f. **ई** worldly, popular, ordinary, common, vulgar. m. pl. ordinary people or men of the world; n. the ways of the world, common usage, abstr. **॰त्व** n.

लौक्य a. belonging to or extended through the world; common, vulgar.

लौल्य n. restlessness, unsteadiness, fickleness; greediness, eagerness or passion for (—॰).

लौह, f. **ई** coppery, metallic, red; n. metal, esp. iron.

लौहायस a. of reddish metal, coppery; n. metallic ware.

लौहित्य m. a kind of rice, N. of a river etc.; n. redness.

व

व indecl. = **इव**.

वंश m. cane, esp. of the bamboo; rafter, lath; reed-pipe, flute (also f. **ई**); the spine; lineage, family, race.

वंशक m. a kind of sugar-cane; f. ***वंशिका** a kind of flute, also = n. Agallochum.

वंशकर & **॰कृत्** m. the founder or propagator of a family.

वंशकृत्य n. playing on the flute.

वंशगोप्तृ m. guardian or maintainer of a race.

वंशज a. made of bamboos or sprung from the race of (—॰).

वंशधर m. maintainer of a family; descendant.

वंशनर्तिन् m. juggler, buffoon (lit. family-dancer).

वंशब्राह्मण n. T. of a work.

वंशभृत् m. supporter of a family.

वंशमय, f. **ई** made of bamboo.

वंशवर्धन a. increasing or propagating a race (also **॰वर्धिन्**); m. son.

वंशस्थ n. N. of a metre.

वंशीय a. belonging to the family of (—॰).

वंश्य a. belonging to the main beam or to the family (—॰ = prec.); m. cross-beam, member of a family, ancestor or descendant.

वंसग m. bull.

वंकल m. the inner bark of a tree.

वकार m. the sound **व**.

वकुल etc. v. **बकुल**.

वक्तव्य or **वक्तव्य** a. to be said or uttered, to be spoken to, of, or against; blamable, reprehensible, accountable, responsible; n. impers., as subst. reproach, censure. Abstr. **॰ता**† f., **॰त्व**† n.

वक्ति f. speech.

वक्तुकाम a. wishing to speak or say.

वक्तृ a. speaking telling; m. speaker, proclaimer of (gen., acc., or —॰); orator, teacher.

वक्त्र n. mouth, face, snout, beak.

वक्त्रद्वार n. mouth (-door).

वक्त्राम्बुज n. a lotus-like face.

वक्त्रेन्दु m. a moon-like face.

वक्त्व a. to be uttered or spoken.

वक्मय a. to be proclaimed or praised.

वक्र a. crooked, tortuous, false, dishonest, ambiguous, malignant, inimical.

वक्रनास a. having a crooked nose or beak.

वक्रपाद a. having crooked legs.

वक्रभणित n. ambiguous speech, falsehood.*

वक्रभाव m. crookedness, falsehood.

वक्रित a. crooked, bent.

वक्रिमन् m. crookedness, ambiguity.

वक्रेतर a. straight, not curled (hair).

वक्रोक्ति f. ambiguous or indirect speech, pun (rh.).

वक्रोलक m. N. of a village; n. N. of a town.

वंक्ष a. turning, rolling, moving to and fro.

वंक्षन्, f. **वंक्षरी** the same.

वक्ष् (cf. 2**उक्ष्**), C. **वक्षयति** cause to grow or increase, strengthen. — **अति** excel, be superior to (acc.).

वंक्षण (f. **ई**) & n. strengthening, refreshing.

वक्षणा f. pl. belly, womb (fig. of clouds, mountains, & rivers).

वक्षणि a. strengthening.

वक्षथ m. gathering strength.

वक्षस् n. breast, chest.

वक्षःस्थल n., °**स्थली** f. (the region of the) breast.

वक्षी f. flame.

वक्षोज & **वक्षोरुह** m. du. the female breast (lit. the two chest-born).

वग्नु m. sound, cry, call.

वग्वन a. talkative chattering.

वग्वनु m. = **वग्नु**.

वंघा f. a kind of noxious animal.

वङ्क m. tramper; f. **आ** pommel (of a saddle).

वङ्कु a. going crookedly or hurriedly.

वङ्क्य a. flexible, pliant.

वंङ्क्रि f. a rib.

वङ्क्षण m. groin, flank, side.

वङ्ग m. tree; the country of Bengal, pl. its inhabitants.

वंङ्गृद m. N. of an evil demon.

वङ्घ m. a kind of tree.

वच्, **विवक्ति**, **वक्ति**, pp. **उक्त** (q.v.) say, speak, tell (2 acc. or dat. gen. of pers. & acc. of th.); name, call (2 acc., M. refl. 2 nom.); reproach, censure, blame (acc.); w. **पुनर्** repeat or reply. P. **उच्यते** be called, pass for (nom.). C. **वाचयति**, °**ते** cause to say, speak etc. (2 acc.); read, recite; agree, promise. D. **विवक्षति** (°**ते**), pp. **विवक्षित** wish to say, speak, etc.; P. be meant or in question. — **अच्छ** call near, salute, invite. **अधि** speak in favour of, intercede for (dat.). **अनु** recite (prayers etc.) for (gen. or dat.), teach, communicate; M. say after (the teacher) i.e. learn, study. C. cause to recite; read. **अभ्यनु** say with regard to something; describe in words. **अभि** = prec., also i.g. say, tell (2 acc.). **आ** address, invoke. **उप** exhort, impel. **निस्** speak out, explain, derive (g.); speak off i.e. drive away with words. **प्र** tell forth, proclaim, praise, mention, teach, communicate to (dat. or gen.); declare to be, name (2 acc.); betray, denounce, deliver, surrender. **परिप्र** scold, reproach. **प्रतिप्र** indicate, denounce. **संप्र** declare (together), announce, indicate. **प्रति** announce, commend (M.); answer, return (2 acc.); refute. **वि** announce, proclaim, explain, decide; M. contend for, quarrel about (loc.). **सम्** proclaim, communicate; say (together) to (acc. ± **प्रति**); M. converse, talk together. – Cf. **अनुक्त**, **अनूचान**, **निरुक्त**, **प्रत्युक्त** (sic!), **प्रोक्त**.

वचन a. speaking, eloquent; saying, meaning (—°), abstr. °**ता**† f., °**त्व**† n.; being said by (instr. or —°), abstr. °**त्व**† n. — n. speaking, pronouncing, sound, voice, utterance, word, speech; affirmation, declaration, mention, statement; command, injunction; counsel, advice, precept, rule; number (g.). — **वचनं कृ** or **वचने स्था** follow the advice of (gen.); **वचनात्** (°**नेन**) in the name of (gen. or —°); **इति वचनात्** as has been said.

वचनकर a. doing what one is told, obedient.

वचनकारक, °**कारिन्**, & °**कृत्** a. the same.

वचनावक्षेप m. mocking or abusive speech.*

वचनावन्त् a. eloquent.

वचनीय a. to be spoken, mentioned, called, or reproved; n. reproach, censure. Abstr. °**ता** f.

वचनोपन्यास m. hinting or insinuating speech.*

वचस् n. speech, word, song; counsel, advice.

वचस a. staggering, reeling (carriage).

†**वचस्य**, °**स्यते** be audible, talk.

वचस्य a. worthy of mention or praise.

वचस्या f. readiness of speech, eloquence.

1**वचस्यु** a. eloquent.

2**वचस्यु** a. = **वचस**.

वचस्विन् a. eloquent.

वचोयुज् a. harnessed at a word.

वचोविद् a. skilful in speech.

वज्र m. n. thunderbolt (flash of lightning), esp. conceived as the weapon of Indra; diamond (mostly n.); m. a form of military array (± **व्यूह**), N. of sev. men, also = **वज्रलेप**. n. a thunder-like i.e. very hard word.

वज्रकील m. thunderbolt; den. **°कीलाय्**.
वज्रदक्षिण a. holding a thunderbolt in the right hand (Indra).
वज्रधर a. wielding the thunderbolt (E. of Indra).
वज्रपतन n.* = **वज्रपात**.
वज्रपाणि a. having the thunderbolt in the hand (the same).
वज्रपात m. the fall of a thunderbolt or a stroke of lightning.
वज्रबाहु a. = **वज्रपाणि**; m. N. of a monkey.
वज्रभृत् a. = **वज्रधर**.
वज्रमय a. made of or hard as diamond, adamantine.
वज्रमुकुट m. N. of a prince.
वज्रमुष्टि a. holding a thunderbolt in the fist, E. of Indra, N. of a Rākṣasa & sev. warriors.
वज्रलेप m. a kind of very hard mortar.
वज्रवह (**°वाह**) a. wielding the thunderbolt.
वज्रवेग m. N. of a Rākṣasa.
वज्रसार a. hard as diamond; s. diamond.
वज्रसारी कृ a. make hard as diamond.
वज्रहस्त a. = **वज्रपाणि**.
वज्राय्, **°यते** become a thunderbolt or diamond; pp. **°यमान** hard, adamantine.
वज्रिन् a. armed with the thunderbolt, E. of Indra.
†**वज्रिवस्** (voc.) = prec.
वञ्च्, **वञ्चति** totter, go crookedly, sneak; P. **वच्यते** move to and fro (lit. & fig.), rock, roll, hurry along. C. **वञ्चयति**, **°ते**, pp. **वञ्चित** (q.v.) mislead, deceive, cheat of (instr. or abl.), escape. — **अच्छ** roll or move towards (acc.). **अभि** C. deceive, cheat. **आ** P. roll or spring forth. **उप** C. & **निस्** M. deceive, cheat. **परि** sneak about; C. cheat. **प्र** C. escape. **सम्** totter.
वञ्चक m. deceiver, jackal (**°वचन*** = **वञ्चनवचन**).
वञ्चन n., **आ** f. deceit, fraud; p. **°नवन्त्**.
वञ्चनवचन n. deceitful speech.*
वञ्चनीय a. to be deceived.
वञ्चयितव्य a. = **वञ्चनीय**.
वञ्चयितृ m. deceiver.
वञ्चित a. deceived, tricked, cheated of (instr., abl. or —°); deluded, imposed upon, surprised; escaped (acc.); f. **आ** a kind of riddle.
वञ्जुल m. N. of sev. plants.
वट m. the Indian fig-tree; also **°वृक्ष** m.
वटक m., **वटका** & **वटिका** f. globule, ball, a kind of cake.
वटारका f. cord, rope; a. **°मय**.
वठर a. stupid, foolish; m. fool.
वडब m. male horse resembling a mare.
वडबा f. mare.
वडबाग्नि m. the hellish fire (supposed to be at the South-pole).
वडबानल m. the same.
वडभि or **°भी** f. = **वलभी**.
वडिश v. **बडिश**.
वणिक्कर्मन् n. trade (a merchant's business).
वणिक्पथ m. = prec. (a merchant's way).
वणिक्पीडा f. a merchant's torment.
वणिक्पुत्र m. a merchant's son.
वणिक्सार्थ m. company of traders, caravan.
वणिक्सुत m., **आ** f. a merchant's son & daughter.
वणिक्सूनु m. = prec. m.
वणिग्जन m. trader or (coll.) traders.
वणिज् m. merchant, trader; trade, merchandise.
वणिज्या f. trade, traffic.
वण्ट a. having no tail.
वण्ठ m. lad, servant.
वत्, **वतति**, only w. **अपि** apprehend, understand; C. **वातयति** reveal, inspire (devotion).
वतंस m. garland, ring (cf. **अवतंस**).
वत्स m. **आ** f. calf, young animal i.g., child (esp. voc. in friendly address); year (only —°); N. of sev. men & a country, pl. its inhabitants.
वत्सक, f. **वत्सिका** little calf (voc. = prec.).*
वत्सतन्ती & **°तन्त्री** f. a long rope to which a calf is tied.
वत्सतर m., **ई** f. weaned calf, bullock or heifer (lit. more than a calf).*
वत्सदन्त m. a kind of arrow (lit. calf-tooth).
वत्सनपात् m. N. of a man.
वत्सप m. keeper of calves; N. of a demon.
वत्सपति m. king of the Vatsas (Udayana).

वत्सभूमि f. the country of the Vatsas.

वत्सर m. year (also personif.).

वत्सराज m. = **वत्सपति**.

वत्सल, f. **आ** loving her calf, as subst. such a cow; adj. affectionate, tender, kind i.g., fond of, wholly given up or devoted to (loc., gen., **प्रति**, or —°). Abstr. **°ता** f., **°त्व** n.

वत्सलय्, **°यति** make affectionate or tender.

वत्सवन्त् a. having a calf.

वत्सिन् a. = prec. (f. **वत्सिनी**).

वत्सेश्वर m. = **वत्सपति**.

वद्, **वदति**, **°ते**, pp. **उदित** (q.v.) A. speak, raise the voice (± **वाचम्**), sing, sound (**उच्चैस्** or **बृहत्** loud); speak or say to, relate, communicate, proclaim, announce (acc. ± **अभि**, gen. or loc. of pers. & acc. of th.), tell, teach, (2 acc.); counsel, advice, foretell, predict; designate as, name, call (2 acc.). M. speak or say to (acc.); talk over, discuss; dispute or quarrel about, lay a claim to (loc.). C. **वादयति**, **°ते** cause to speak or sound, esp. a musical instrument, play on (acc. or loc.), absol. make music; speak, recite. D. **विवदिषति** wish to speak or say. I. **वावदीति** or **वावदति** speak or sound loudly. — **अच्छ** A. salute, invite. **अति** A. speak louder or better, oversound, overspeak, defeat in disputing. **अनु** repeat (words), imitate. **अव** revile, abuse, disapprove of; C. the same. **अभि** speak to, salute; say with regard to, mean by a word etc., express, utter, declare to be, call (2 acc.). C. address, salute; *M. greet a pers. (acc.) by means of another (acc. or instr.); make resound i.e. play on (acc.). **प्रत्यभि** A. greet in return (also C. M.). **अव** depreciate by words. **व्यव** resume speaking. **आ** speak to, address, announce, proclaim. **उद्** raise the voice, speak out. C. call or sound. **प्रत्युद्** C. make resound. **निस्** & **परा** speak off, remove. **परि** express one's self about (acc.), esp. censure, blame. **प्र** speak forth, say, proclaim, anounce; raise the voice, utter sounds (of birds & beasts); suppose, state; declare to be, call (2 acc.). C. make sound, play on a musical instrument. **प्रति** speak to (acc.), answer, return, repeat. **वि** M. (A.) contradict, dispute or quarrel with (instr., r. acc.) about (loc.); C. commence an action or law-suit. **सम्** A. M. say together; converse with (instr.) about (loc.); accord, agree; (be all right*); declare to be, call (2 acc.). C. make speak or sound, cause to converse, cause a conversation about (loc.); consent, agree; describe accurately. **विसम्** break an agreement; C. not stick to, neglect, miss.

वद a. & m. speaking, speaker (—°).

वदन n. speaking, sounding; mouth, face, front, point.

वदनपङ्कज n. a lotus-like face.

वदनपवन m. breath (mouth-wind).

वदनमारुत m. the same.

वदनोदर n. the jaws (lit. the hollow of the mouth).

वदर, **°री** v. **बदर**, **°री**.

वदान्य a. bountiful, liberal.

वदितव्य a. to be spoken or said; n. imp.

वदितृ a. & m. speaking, a speaker.

वदिष्ठ (superl.) speaking best.

वद्मन् a. speaking.

वध् (**वधति**), P. **वध्यते** (**°जि**) strike, slay, kill, destroy. C. **वधयति** = S. — **अप** cut off, cleave; drive away. **अभि** & **समभि** smite upon (acc.). **आ** crush down, dash to pieces. **उद्** tear out or in pieces. **उप** strike on (acc.), slay, kill. **नि** fix or fasten in (loc.); knock down, kill. **निस्** frustrate, annihilate. **परा** cleave, tear asunder. **प्र** beat. **वि** destroy.

वध m. slayer, murderer, destroyer; deadly weapon, esp. Indra's thunderbolt; capital or corporal punishment; place of execution; stroke, blow, hurt, injury, destruction, death.

वधक m. murderer, executioner.

वधकाम्या f. desire to kill or slay.

वधजीविन् m. a living by the death (of animals); m. butcher, hunter, etc.

1वधत्र n. deadly weapon, dart.
2वधत्रं a. protecting from injury.
वधदण्ड m. corporal punishment.
वधना f. deadly weapon.
वधनिग्रह m. pain of death.
वधबन्ध m. du. slaying and fettering.
वधभूमि f. place of execution.
वधर्, वधस् n. dart, weapon (esp. Indra's).
वधर्य्, only वधर्यन्ती f. hurling darts (lightning).
वधस्नं (only instr. pl.) deadly weapons.
†वधस्नु a. wielding deadly weapons.
वधु f. woman, wife.
वधू f. bride or newly married woman, wife or woman i.g., also female of any animal; daughter-in-law, i.g. the wife of a younger relation.
वधूजन m. (coll.) women, womankind.
वधूटिका & वधूटी f. a young woman.
वधूदर्श a. looking at a bride.
वधूपथ m. the path of a bride.
वधूमन्त् a. furnished or harnessed with female animals.
वधूयु a. uxurious, lustful.
वधूसंयान n. a woman's carriage.
वधैषिन् a. wishing to slay or kill.
वधोपाय m. pl. means or kinds of corporal punishment.
वध्य a. to be slain, killed, or destroyed, deserving death or corporal punishment. — m. villain, scape-grace; f. वध्या killing, murder, execution.
वध्यडिण्डिम s. a drum beaten at the time of execution, funeral drum.*
वध्यता f., °त्व n. abstr. to वध्य adj.
वध्यपटह m.* = वध्यडिण्डिम.
वध्यपर्याय m. one's turn to excecute a criminal.*
वध्यपुरुष m. executioner.*
वध्यभू & °भूमि f. place of execution.
वध्यमाला f. funeral wreath (of a criminal).*
वध्यस्थान n. = वध्यभू.
वध्र m., ई f. a leather strap or thong.
वध्रि a. emasculated, unmanly.
वध्रिमती f. having an impotent husband.

1वन् (वा), वनोति, वनुते, वनति (वनति), °ते, pp. वात (—°) & वनित (cf. वनिता) like, love; wish, desire, aim at; get, obtain, acquire, win, conquer, dispose of, possess, enjoy. C. वानयति & D. विवासति, °ते (only —°). — अभि wish for, long or strive after. आ the same, D. wish to win or attract, entice, allure. अभ्या D. approach (as an enemy). उप D. seek to win. प्र win, conquer. सम् C. make well-disposed.
2वन् (only gen. & loc. pl.) wood, wooden vessel.
1वन n. tree, wood, forest, wooden vessel or barrel for the Soma-juice, fig. = cloud. f. वना the wood of attrition (person.), वनी wood, thicket.
2वन n. desire, longing.
वनकपि m wild ape.
वनकरिन् & °गज m. wild elephant.
वनगमन n. the going into a forest.
वनगहन n. thicket of a wood.
वनगुल्म m. forest shrub or bush.
वनगोचर, f. ई living in a wood, m. forester.
वनग्रहण n abstr. to seq. a.; °कोलाहल s. hunting cry.*
वनग्राहिन् a. taking the forest; m. hunter.
वनचर, f. ई wandering in a forest; m. inhabitant of a forest (man or animal).
वनचरवृत्ति a. living like a forester.*
वनचर्य n., °चर्या f. abstr. to वनचर.
वनचारिन् a. & m. = वनचर.
वनज & °जात a. born or produced in a forest, sylvan, wild.
वनज्योत्स्ना f. Light of the Grove (poet. N. of a plant).*
वनदाह m. forest conflagration.
वनदेवता f. forest goddess, dryad.
वनद्विप m. = वनकरिन्.
वनधारा f. avenue of trees.
वनना f. desire.
वननीय a. to be desired.
वनप m. wood protector or keeper.
वनपाल & °क m. the same.
वनभू & °भूमि f. wood region.
वनमाला f. garland of wood flowers; poss. °लिन्, m. E. of Kṛṣṇa.

वनमृग m. a forest deer.

वनराजि or °**जी** f. a row of trees or long track of a forest.

वनर्गु a. wandering in a forest or a wilderness; m. a savage.

वनलता f. a wild (lit. wood-)creeper.

1**वनवास** m. forest-life.

2**वनवास** a. & m. = seq.

वनवासिन् a. living in a wood; m. forester, hermit, ascetic.

वनश्वन् m. jackal (forest-dog).

वनस् n. desire or charm, loveliness.

वनस्थ a. & m. = **वनवासिन्**.

वनस्थली f. region or neighbourhood of a forest.

वनस्पति m. tree (lit. lord of the wood), esp. a large tree with fruit, but without flowers; stem, trunk, beam, timber, the sacrificial post; the Soma plant (as the lord of plants); E. of Viṣṇu.

1**वनान्त** m. (region of a) forest.

2**वनान्त** a. bounded by a forest.

वनान्तर n. the interior of a forest; loc., acc., & abl. in, into, & out of a forest.

वनायु m. N. of a prince (also °**युस्**); pl. N. of a people.

वनालय m. a forest as habitation, °**जीविन्** a. living in forests.

वनाश्रय a. living in a forest; m. inhabitant of a forest.

वनि f. request, desire, wish.

वनिका f. little wood, grove (only — °).

वनिता f. mistress, wife; girl or woman i.g.

वनितृ m. owner or possessor of (acc.).

1**वनिन्** a. requesting or bestowing.

2**वनिन्** m. tree, the Soma-plant.

वनिन n. tree or wood.

वनिष्ठ (superl.) & **वनीयंस्** (compar.) obtaining or bestowing most (more).

वनिष्ठु m. the rectum or a part of the intestines near the omentum.

वनीयक m. beggar, suppliant.

वनीवन् a. requesting.

वनीवाहन n. carrying to and fro.

वनु m. plotter or adherent (cf. **वनुस्**).

वनुष्, **वनुष्यति**, °**ते** aim at, strive after, plot against, attack.

वनुस् a. eager, zealous; either devoted, loving, or plotting, hostile. m. an enemy.

वनेचर, f. **ई** wandering or dwelling in a forest; m. inhabitant of a forest (either man or animal).

वनेजा m. tree (wood-born).

वनैकदेश m. a (one) spot in a wood.

वनोद्देश m. neighbourhood of a wood or = pr.

वनोद्भव m. produced in a forest, grown wild.

वनोपप्लव m. a forest conflagration.

वनोपेत a. resorted to a forest.

वनौकस् a. living in a forest; m. = **वनेचर** m.

वनौषधि f. a wild herb.

वन्तृ m. owner or possessor of (gen.).

वन्द्, **वन्दते** (°**ति**) praise, honour, salute reverentially. C. **वन्दयति** the same. — **अभि** = S., **परि** praise, extol. **प्र** praise aloud or begin to praise. **प्रति** & **सम्** honour, salute reverentially.

†**वन्द्** v. **देववन्द्**.

वन्दध्यै dat. infin. to **वन्द्**.

1**वन्दन** m. N. of a man; n. praise, worship, reverential greeting.

2**वन्दन** n. a parasitical plant or a kind of disease.

वन्दनीय a. to be praised or greeted with homage.

वन्दारु a. praising, respectful, reverential; n. praise.

वन्दितव्य a. = **वन्दनीय**.

वन्दितृ or **वन्दितृ** m. praiser.

वन्दिन् v. **बन्दिन्**.

वन्द्य a. = **वन्दनीय**.

वन्धुर n. the seat or frame-work of a carriage.

वन्ध्य a. barren, sterile (of women, female animals, & plants); fruitless, useless, in vain; wanting, destitute of (—°). Abstr. °**ता** f., °**त्व** n.

वन्य adj. living or growing in woods, sylvan, wild, wooden; m. wild animal, (also n.) wild plant.

वन्यनाग m. wild elephant.

वन्यवृत्ति & **वन्याशन** a. living on wild food.

वन्येतर a. different from wild, tame or civilized.

वन्येभ m. wild elephant.

1**वप्, वपति, °ते**, pp. **उप्त** shear, shave (hair or beard, M. refl.), trim (nails); shear fig. = crop off, graze. C. **वापयति, °ते** cause to shear or to be shorn (M. refl.). — **परि** shear around. **प्र** shear off.

2**वप्, वपति, °ते**, pp. **उप्त** (q.v.) strew, scatter, esp. seed, sow; throw or cast (dice etc.). C. **वापयति** sow, plant. — **अनु** bestrew; scatter, disperse. **अप** disperse, destroy. **अपि** & **अभि** bestrew, cover. **आ** strew or throw upon, mix, mingle, pour out. C. mix, add, arrange, comb (the hair). **उद्** draw out, dig up, raise; cast away. **उप** heap up, bestrew, inter, cover. **नि** heap up, raise, sow upon (loc.); throw down, cast (dice). **निस्** throw or draw out, deal out (from a larger mass), distribute; present an oblation to a god, offer. C. scatter, sow, deal out. **परा** throw aside, remove. **परि** bestrew with (instr.). **प्र** scatter, pour out, throw upon or in (loc.), bestrew. **प्रति** infix, insert; stick or set with (instr.); join, add. **सम्** pour in, mingle.

वप m. sower.

2**वपन** n. shearing, shaving.

1**वपन** n. sowing.

वपनीय a. to be sown; n. impers.

1**वपा** f. caul, omentum; poss. **°वन्त्**.

2†**वपा** v. **वल्मीकवपा**.

वपुष a. = **वपुस्** a., n. wonder.

वपुष्टम superl. to **वपुस्** adj.

वपुष्टर or **वपुष्टर** compar. to the same.

वपुष्मन्त् a. beautiful; embodied, corporeal.

वपुष्य्, °ष्यति wonder, admire.

वपुष्य a. = **वपुस्** adj.

वपुष्या f. (instr.) wonderment.

वपुस् a. wondrous, esp. wondrous beautiful; n. wonder, wonderful or beautiful appearance; form, shape, body.

वपोदर a. having a fat belly.

वप्तव्य a. to be sown, n. impers.

1**वप्तर्** or **वप्तृ** m. shearer, shaver.

2**वप्तृ** m. sower.

वप्र m. n. mound of earth, hillock, rampart; f. **आ** a bed (for plants).

वप्रक्रिया & **°क्रीडा** f. (the elephant's) building of or playing with earth-mounds.

वप्सस् n. beautiful form or appearance.

वम्, वमिति & **वमति**, pp. **वान्त** (q.v.) vomit, spit out, give forth (**वचस्** repent). C. **वामयति** & **वमयति** cause to vomit. — **अभि** spit at. **उद्** & **निस्** spit out, eject.

वमथु m. vomiting.

वमन n. vomiting, ejecting, giving forth.

वमि or **वमी** f. vomiting, sickness, nausea.

वम्र m., **ई** f. ant.

वम्रक m. a small ant.

1**वयस्** n. fowl (coll.), bird, esp. small bird.

2**वयस्** n. food, meal, strength, health, youth; age i.g.

3**वयस्** n. weft.

1**वयस** m. bird.

2**वयस** n. (—°) = 2**वयस्**.

वयसान्वित a. aged.

वयस्क (adj. —°) = 2**वयस्**.

वयस्कृत् a. giving strength or life.

वयस्य a. being the same age; m. contemporary, friend (also **°क**, abstr. **°कत्व** n., **°स्यभाव** m.), f. **°स्या** female friend, a woman's confidante.

वयस्वन्त् a. strong, vigorous.

वयःसम a. equal in age.

वयःस्थ a. grown up, mature, aged, old

1**वया** f. bough, branch; race, family.

2**वया** f. strengthening, refreshment.

वयित्री & **वयी** f. female weaver.

वयुन a. moving, waving. n. what moves or lives; course, path, way, (pl. ways and means); usage, custom, rule, order.

वयुनाविद् a. knowing ways and means.

वयोऽतिग a. advanced in age, old.

वयोधस् a. = seq. adj.

वयोधा a. giving or possessing strength or health, strong, vigorous; f. strengthening, refreshing; **°धै** as infin.

वयोऽधिक a. superior in years or age, old; m. old man.

वयोधेय a. giving strength, strengthening.

वयोबाल a. young of years.

वयोरूपसमन्वित a. endowed with youth and beauty.
वयोऽवस्था f. age, stage of life.
वयोविध a. bird-like.
वयोवृद्ध a. old of years.
वयोवृध् a. increasing strength.
वय्य m. comrade, companion, a man's name.
1वर m. surrounding, stopping (dat. as infin.); circle, extent, space.
2वर a. choosing (=°); m. suitor, lover, bridegroom or the b.'s friend, husband, son-in-law.
3वर a. choice, select; most excellent, fairest, best of (gen., loc., abl., or —°); fairer or better than (abl. or gen.). n. rather or more than (abl. ± आ); वरं — न (च, तु, पुनर्) (it is) better—than; वरं कुर्यात् he had better or he might rather do. m. (n.) choice, wish, request, boon, gift, reward, privilege, dowry, alms. — वरं वृ, याच्, काङ्क्ष्, etc. choose a gift or utter a wish, ° दा or प्रयम् grant a gift, ° लभ् have a wish fullfilled. वरं वरम्, प्रति वरम्, & वरमा according to wish, at pleasure. वराय to satisfaction, at heart's content.
1वरक m. who asks a girl in marriage.
2वरक s. choice, wish.
वरगात्र, f. ई fair-limbed, well-shaped.*
वरट m. a kind of grain; f. *आ *& ई a kind of wasp.
1वरण m. a kind of tree; f. आ N. of a river.
2वरण n. choosing, wishing, suing; m. pl. cert. verses recited at the choice of a priest.
*वरण्ड m. the string of a fish hook.
वरण्डलम्बुक m. the same.*
वरतनु, f. ऊ having a beautiful body; f. ऊ a beautiful woman.
वरत्रा f. strap, thong, strip of leather.
वरद a. granting or fulfilling wishes; m. benefactor; f. आ N. of a river.
वरदान n. the grant of a boon or wish.
वरपुरुष m. the best of men.*
वरप्रद a. = वरद adj.; °प्रदान n. = वरदान.
वरप्रार्थना f. desire for a suitor.
वरयितव्य a. to be chosen.
वरयोषित् f. a most excellent woman.
वररुचि m. N. of a poet and scholar.
वरवर्णिन् a. of a fair complexion; °नी f. a fair-faced woman.
वरवस्त्र n. a beautiful garment.
वरवृत a. accepted as a boon.
वरस् n. width, breadth, room, space.
वरसद् a. sitting in a circle.
वरस्त्री f. = वरयोषित्.
वरस्या f. wish, desire.
वराक, f. ई wretched, miserable.
वराङ्ग n. the best member of the body, i.e. the head.
वराङ्गना f. = वरयोषित्.
वराट m. a cowry (used as a coin).
वराटक m., °टिका f. = prec., cord, rope.
वरानना f. fair-faced.
वरारोह, f. आ having fair hips or buttocks.
वरार्थिन् a. asking for a boon or blessing.
वरार्ह a. exceedingly worthy or precious.
वरासन n. splendid seat, throne.
वराह m. boar, hog; a cert. array of troops, E. of Viṣṇu.
वराहमिहिर m. N. of an astronomer.
वराहु m. = वराह; pl. a class of winds.
1वरिमन् m., वरिमन् n. circumference, compass, width, extent.
2वरिमन् m. the chief or best.
वरिवस् n. room, space, freedom, ease, comfort; w. कृ, धा, or विद् give room or free course to (dat.).
वरिवस्कृत् a. granting room, freeing.
वरिवस्य्, °स्यति = वरिवस् w. कृ etc., also comfort, serve, cherish.
वरिवोद a. granting room or freedom.
वरिवोधा (superl. °तम) & वरिवोविद् (compar. °वित्तर) the same.
1वरिष्ठ (superl.) widest, broadest, largest.
2वरिष्ठ (superl.) most excellent, best, chief among (gen. or —°); better than (abl.); the worst of (gen.).
वरीतृ m. suitor (of a woman).
वरीमन् n. & वरीमन् m. = 1 & 2वरिमन्.
1वरीयंस् (compar.) wider, broader, very wide or broad; n. adv. farther off, as subst. a wider room or freer course; free space, freedom.

2वरीयंस् (compar.) more excellent, better; most excellent, best of (gen.).
वरीवृत a. rolling, winding.
वरुण m. the All-encompasser, N. of a god.
वरुणगृहीत a. seized by Varuṇa, dropsical.
वरुणदेव n. E. of a lunar mansion.
वरुणपाश m. Varuṇa's snare or noose.
वरुणप्रघास m. N. of a cert. sacrifice.
वरुणमेनि f. Varuṇa's wrath.
वरुणराजन् a. having Varuṇa as king.
वरुणलोक m. Varuṇa's world or his domain, the water.
वरुणसव m. a cert. oblation.
वरुणानी f. Varuṇa's wife.
वरुणालय m. Varuṇa's abode, the sea.
वरुण्य a. coming from or belonging to Varuṇa; w. आपस् standing water.
वरुतृ m. coverer, protector, defender; f. वरुत्री female defender, guardian goddess.
वरूथ n. cover, protection, shelter; s. chariot-fender, army, troop, multitude.
वरूथिन् a. wearing armour, having a fender (chariot), affording shelter or protection, sitting in a chariot; surrounded by a multitude of (—°). m. war-chariot, f. °नी† army.
वरूथ्य a. affording shelter or protection.
वरेण्य a. desirable, excellent, dear, best of (gen.).
वरेण्यक्रतु a. benevolent or intelligent.
वरेय्, °यति woo, ask in marriage.
वरेयु m. wooer, suitor.
वरेश & °श्वर a. granting boons or fulfilling wishes.
1वरोरु m. a beautiful thigh.
2वरोरु (f. °रु or °रू) a. having beautiful thighs, f. a well-formed woman.
वर्ग a. & m. removing, remover; m. group, section, division, party, class, esp. of words or sounds (g.).
वर्गशस् adv. by groups.
वर्गस्थ & वर्गिन् a. belonging to a side or party.
वर्ग्य a. = prec.; m. colleague.
वर्चस् n. light, brightness, lustre, colour, the illuminating power of fire or the sun, power or strength i.g., vitality, energy, activity; excrement, ordure.
वर्चस n. light, brightness, colour (—°).
वर्चस्य a. giving vigour or energy.
वर्चस्वन्त् & वर्चस्विन् a. vigorous, energetic.
वर्चिन् m. N. of a demon.
वर्ज a. wanting, excluding (—°).
वर्जन n. avoiding, shunning, excluding.
वर्जनीय a. to be avoided or shunned.
वर्जम् adv. excepting, except (—°).
वर्जयितव्य a. to be avoided.
वर्जयितृ m. who avoids or shuns.
वर्जित a. avoided, shunned; destitute of, free from, -less, —excluded (—°).
वर्ज्य a. to be avoided; —° = वर्ज.
वर्ण m. cover, lid; outside, external appearance, colour, dye, paint, complexion; sort, kind, character, sort of men i.e. caste; letter, sound, vowel, syllable, word; praise, glory.
वर्णक, f. वर्णिका painting, representing; s. specimen, pattern; f. वर्णिका paint, ointment (also m.), mask, dress of an actor.
वर्णकचित्रित a. painted with colours.*
वर्णक्रम m. succession of colours or order of castes.
वर्णचित्रित a. = वर्णकचित्रित.*
वर्णज्यायंस् & °ज्येष्ठ (compar. & superl.) higher or highest in caste.
वर्णता f., °त्व n. abstr. to वर्ण caste.
वर्णदूषक a. sullying the caste.
वर्णधर्म m. sgl. & pl. the laws or duties of castes.
वर्णन n., °ना f. description.
वर्णनीय a. to be painted or described.
वर्णपरिचय m. skill at song or music.*
वर्णमात्र n. the mere (only the) colour.
वर्णय्, °यति (°ते), pp. वर्णित paint, colour, dye, picture, describe, relate, tell; observe. — अनु describe, picture, relate, explain, tell, praise. समनु, अभि, व्या, उप the same. निस् observe, look close at, contemplate; picture, represent. विनिस् observe closely. सम् communicate, relate.
वर्णयितव्य a. to be painted or described.
वर्णयितृ m. who paints or describes.

वर्णवर्ति & **°वर्तिका** f. pencil or painting-brush.

वर्णवृत्त n. a metre measured by the number of syllables.

वर्णसंसर्ग & **°संकर** m. the mixture of castes (by intermarriage).

वर्णापेत a. destitute of caste, degraded.

वर्णावर a. lower in caste.*

वर्णाश्रम m. pl. caste and order (cf. **आश्रम**).

वर्णिन् a. having a cert. colour, coloured, having the appearance or belonging to the caste of (—°); m. a person belonging to one of the four castes, esp. a religious student.

वर्ण्य a. to be painted or described.

वर्तक m., **वर्तिका** f. a quail.

वर्तन a. causing to move or live (Viṣṇu). n. turning, rolling, moving on, wandering, roaming; staying, abiding in (loc.); living on (instr.), support of life, earnings, wages; intercourse or commerce with (**सह**), proceeding with (—°).

वर्तनार्थिन् a. seeking an occupation.

वर्तनि f. the felloe or the track of a wheel; way, road, course.

वर्तमान a. going on, present; n. = **°काल** m. the present time.

वर्तवे dat. inf. to 1**वृ**.

वर्ति or **वर्ती** f. a pad or kind of bandage on a wound; wick of a lamp; paint, ointment, esp. eye-salve.

1**वर्तिका** f. v. **वर्तक**.

2**वर्तिका** f. stalk, wick, paint-brush.

वर्तितव्य a. to be stayed in, attended to, or dealt with; n. impers. (it is) to be stayed in or among (loc.), attended to (loc.) or dealt with (loc., gen. or instr. w. **सह**).

वर्तिन् a. staying, remaining, lying, situated in (—°), engaged in or occupied with (—°), proceeding with, behaving (well) towards (—°).

वर्तिस् n. place to turn to, quarters, abode.

वर्तीर m. a kind of quail or partridge.

वर्तुल a. round; n. a circle.

वर्तृ m. restrainer.

वर्त्मन् n. wheel-track, path, course, way; instr. by way of, through (—°).

वर्त्र, f. **ई** warding off, holding back; n. dam, weir.

1**वर्ध** a. (—°) & n. increasing, furthering.

2**वर्ध** s. separation.*

वर्धक a. cutting, shearing; m. = seq.

वर्धकि & **°किन्** m. carpenter.

1**वर्धन**, f. increasing, growing, thriving; strengthening, furthering, promoting, animating, exhilarating, delighting (mostly —°). — m. increaser, a man's name. n. increase, growth, prosperity; rearing, educating, strengthening, enlargement, refreshment.

2**वर्धन** n. the cutting (cf. **नाभि°**).

वर्धनीय a. to be increased or strengthened.

वर्धापन n. the cutting of the navel-string.

वर्धित s. a kind of dish.

वर्धितव्य n. impers. to be grown.

वर्धितृ m. increaser.

वर्धिनी f. increasing, strengthening (—°).

वर्धिष्णु a. increasing, growing.

वर्ध्र m. & n. leather strap, thong, girth.

वर्पस् n. assumed appearance, image, form; art, stratagem.

वर्म (adj. —°) = **वर्मन्**.

वर्मण्वन्त् a. clad in armour, mailed.

वर्मन् n. armour, coat of mail (lit. cover); shelter, protection.

वर्मि m. a kind of fish.

वर्मित & **वर्मिन्** a. = **वर्मण्वन्त्**.

वर्य a. to be chosen (esp. in marriage), excellent, best of (gen. or —°).

वर्वर a. = **बर्बर** curled, curly.

वर्ष a. raining (—°); n. m. rain (n. pl. the rains as a season), a year, a part of the world; m. N. of a grammarian; f. **आ** rain, pl. (sgl.) the rains.

वर्षण, f. **ई** (mostly —°) & n. raining.

वर्षधर m. eunuch (lit. restrainer of rain, i.e. of semen).

वर्षनिर्णिज् a. clothed with rain.

वर्षन्त् a. raining, m. rain.

वर्षपात m. pl. showers of rain.

वर्षपूग m. n. sgl. & pl. plenty of rain or a series of years.
वर्षवर m. = **वर्षधर**.
वर्षवृद्ध a. grown by rain.
वर्षशतवृत्त a. passed a hundred years ago.
वर्षशतिन् a. a hundred years old.
वर्षसहस्रवृत्त a. passed a thousand years ago.
वर्षाकाल m. the rainy season.
वर्षारात्र m., **°रात्रि** f. = prec. (lit. r. night).
वर्षार्ध s. a half-year.
वर्षाशरद् f. du. the rainy season and autumn.
वर्षासमय m. = **वर्षाकाल**.
वर्षाह्वू f. frog (lit. caller in rain).
वर्षिक a. —years old (—°).
वर्षिता f. abstr. to **वर्षिन्**.
वर्षितृ m. rainer.
वर्षिन् a. raining, sprinkling (—°); or = **वर्षिक**.
वर्षिमन् m. width.
वर्षिष्ठ (superl.) highest, largest, greatest, strongest; n. adv.
वर्षीय a. of —years (—°).
वर्षीयस् (compar.) superior, higher, longer, larger than (abl.); great, important, thriving; better than (abl.); aged, old.
वर्षुक a. rainy, watery.
वर्षोदक n. rain-water.
वर्षोपल m. hail (lit. rain-stone).
वर्षौघ m. mass or shower of rain.
वर्ष्टृ m. rainer.
1**वर्ष्मन्** m. height, top, crown of the head.
2**वर्ष्मन्** n. height, elevation, surface, point; size, extent; body.
वर्ष्य or **वर्ष्य** a. rainy; f. **वर्ष्या** pl. rain water.
वल्, **वलति**, **°ते**, pp. **वलित** (q.v.) turn (intr.), return; break forth, appear. C. **वलयति** or **वालयति** cause to turn or roll. — **वि** turn away. — Cf. **संवलित**.
वल m. cave, cavern; N. of a demon (cf. 2**बल**).
वलक s. cover; n. procession.
वलन n. turning, moving round, undulation, agitation, coming forth, appearance.
वलन्तिका f. a kind of dance.
वलभिद् v. **बलभिद्**.
वलभी (**°भि**) f. roof or turret of a house.
वलय m. n. bracelet (worn by men & women), circle, enclosure, boundary, circumference; adj. —° encircled or surrounded by.
वलयित a. = prec. adj.; forming a circle, circular, round.
वलयिन् a. having a bracelet; encircled by (—°).
वलवृत्रघ्न etc. v. **बलवृत्रघ्न** etc.
वलाहक v. **बलाहक**.
वलि or **वली** f. fold of skin, wrinkle.
वलित a. turned, bent, n. impers.; accompanied by, joined with (—°).
वलिन, **वलिभ**, & **वलिमन्त्** a. wrinkled.
वलीपलित n. wrinkles and grey hair.
वलीमन्त् a. curled.
वलीमुख & **°वदन** m. ape (lit. having a wrinkled face).
वल्क m. n. the bark of a tree.
वल्कल m. n. = prec.; a garment made of bark (worn by hermits).
वल्कलवन्त् a. dressed in bark.
वल्कलाजिनवासस् a. clothed in garments of bark and hides of animals.
वल्कलाम्बरधारण n. the wearing of bark-clothes.
वल्कलिन् a. having bark or dressed in bark.
वल्कवासस् n. a garment made of bark.
वल्ग्, **वल्गति**, **°ते**, pp. **वल्गित** (q.v.) spring, jump (esp. with joy). — **अभि** spring near or towards, boil up (water). (**अव** leap, bound*.) **आ** move quickly, jump, spring. **व्या** gallop, leap, move hither and thither. **प्र** & **वि** leap, spring. **सम्** begin to undulate or boil up.
वल्गक m. jumper, dancer.*
वल्गन n. springing, galloping.
वल्गा f. bridle, rein.
वल्गित a. & n. springing, jumping, moving to and fro.
वल्गितभ्रू a. moving the eyebrows playfully.
वल्गु a. handsome, lovely; beautiful. n. adv.
वल्गुली f. a kind of night-bird.
वल्गूय्, **°यति** treat kindly.
वल्भ्, **वल्भते** eat, taste.
वल्मीक m. ant-hill.
वल्मीकराशि m., **°वपा** f., **°शिखर** n. the same.

वल्मीकाग्र n. N. of a peak of Rāmagiri.
वल्ल m. a kind of wheat or a cert. weight.
वल्लकी (°कि) f. a kind of lute.
वल्लभ a. dearest to (gen., loc., or —°), dearer than (abl.), favourite, also as subst., f. **आ**; abstr. **°ता** f. (**°त्व*** n.).
वल्लभजन m. favourite.
वल्लरि or **°री** f. a creeping or twining plant.
वल्लि or **वल्ली** f. the same.
वल्लूर n. dried flesh.
वल्श m. sprout, twig.
वल्ह्, **वल्हति**, **°ते** challenge.
वव्रं a. hiding (intr.); cavern, deep.
वव्रि m. cover, garment or body.
वश्, **वष्टि**, **विवष्टि**, **ववष्टि**, **वशति** be eager, will, desire, long for, order, command; aver, declare to be (2 acc.). C. **वशयति** subdue. — **अभि** rule over, command; strive after, M. long for (acc.). — Cf. **उशन्त्**, **उशमान** (add.), **वावशानं**.
1**वंश** a. willing, submissive, dependent; m. will, command, control, authority, power, influence; adj. —° being in the power of or subject to. **वशेन**, **°शात्**, **°शतस्** by command, by force, by means of, according to (gen. or —°). — Acc. w. **इ**, **गम्** etc. come into the power of (gen. or —°), w. **नी**, **आनी** etc. bring into subjection, overpower, subdue (also loc. w. **कृ**, **स्थापय्** etc.); loc. w. **भू**, **स्था** etc. be subdued or subject.
2**वंश** n. liquid grease.
वशंवद a. acknowledging a person's will or power, obedient or devoted to (—°).
वशग a. being in the power of, subject or obedient to, dependent on (gen. or —°); abstr. **°त्व** n.
वशगत a. = prec. adj.
वशगमन n. subjection, submission.
वशता f., **°त्व** n. subjection, dependence.
वशनी a. subject to (gen.).
वशवर्तिन् a. = **वशग**.
वशा f. cow, esp. a barren cow (also woman); a female elephant, w. **अवि** f. a ewe.
वशानुग a. following one's own or another's (gen.) will; subject or obedient to (gen. or —°).
वशान्न a. devouring cows.
वशित्व n. self-control or power over (loc.).
वशिन् a. having will or power, either self-control or command over others, ruling, powerful; m. ruler, lord of (gen.), f. **वशिनी**.
वशी कृ A. (M.) make submissive, enthrall, subjugate; **°भू** P.
वशीकरण n. abstr. to prec.
वशीकार m., **°कृति** & **°क्रिया** f. the same.
वश्य a. submissive, obedient, yielding to (gen. or —°); n. might, power. Abstr. **°ता** f., **°त्व** n.
वश्यात्मन् a. whose soul is restrained or controlled.
वषट् an exclamation used on making an oblation; w. **कृ** utter this exclamation.
वषट्कर्तृ a. & m. exclaiming Vaṣaṭ.
वषट्कार m. = prec m.
वषट्कारिन् a. = **वषट्कर्तृ**.
वषट्कृत a. offered with the exclamation Vaṣaṭ.
वषट्कृति f. = **वषट्कार**.
वष्टि a. desirous or desirable.
1**वस्** (encl. pron. of 2nd pers.) you.
2**वस्**, **उच्छति**, pp. **उष्ट** (—°) shine, light up, dawn; bring or drive away (**दूरे**) by shining. C. **वासयति** cause to shine. — **अप** = S. + **दूरे**, extinguish. **वि** shine abroad, light up. C. cause to dawn or grow bright. — Cf. **व्युष्ट**, **व्युषित**.
3**वस्**, **वस्ते** put on, don, enter, assume (an appearance). C. clothe, dress in, cover with (instr.), M. refl. — **अधि** put on. **अनु** clothe, cover (M. refl.), surround, protect. **अभि** cover one's self with (acc.). C. clothe or cover with (instr.). **नि** put on (over another garment). **परि**, **प्र**, **प्रति** don. **वि** change clothes, also = C. put on, don. **सम्** dress one's self in (instr.).
4**वस्**, **वसति**, **°ते**, pp. **उषित** q.v. (& **उष्ट**) stay in a place, esp. over night (± **रात्रिम्**), dwell, live, rest on (eye) or in (loc.); w. **दूरतस्** keep away; w. **सुखम्** be at ease

or comfortable. C. वासयति, °ते cause to stay (over night), lodge; confine in (loc.), stop, detain, keep, support. — अधि settle upon, occupy, inhabit. अनु remove to a place after another person (acc.); dwell, inhabit; pass, spend (time). आ settle or enter upon (acc.), dwell or live in (loc.); cohabit with (acc.); w. गुरोस्तल्पम् commit adultery with the teacher's wife. C. harbour, lodge; take up one's abode in (acc.); stop, stay, esp. over night. अध्या choose as abode, inhabit (acc.), dwell or live in (loc.) enter upon, attend to (acc.). समा stop, stay (esp. over night); settle in, inhabit (acc.). C. make a halt, settle down. उद् C. remove from its place (esp. the fire from the altar ± अग्निम्), sever, cut off (a head), root out (trees), ravage, lay waste. उप abide, stay, wait, esp. with eating i.e. fast; enter upon, attend to (acc.). C. cause to stay (over night) or fast. नि dwell (of men & beasts), live in (loc.), inhabit, occupy, keep; incur, undergo; have sexual intercourse with (acc.). C. cause to stay, receive in one's house, lodge; make inhabitable, populate; inhabit. संनि live with (instr.) in (loc.). निस् finish (w. वासम्); C. expel from home, banish, send away, dismiss. परि stay (over night), live with (instr.); C. keep over night. प्र set out, go abroad (for a night); depart, disappear, be gone; stay or dwell in (loc.); also = C. banish, exile. विप्र go or be abroad. C. banish, remove. प्रति (stay over night*); have one's dwelling. वि change one's abode, go away from (abl.); pass, spend (time) C. drive away (from home or land), banish, exile, dismiss. सम् dwell together, live with (instr. ± सह or acc.), cohabit with (acc.); stay or live in (loc.); pass, spend (acc. of time). C. cause to live together, bring together with (instr. ± सह), give shelter, harbour. — Cf. अध्युषित, अभ्युषित, उपोषित, पर्युषित, प्रोषित, विप्रोषित, व्युषित.

वसति f. staying (over night), dwelling, living, abode, home, house, settlement, nest.

1वसन n. garment, cloth, clothing; du. under and upper garment, adj. —° clothed in.

2वसन n. staying, dwelling, abode.

वसनपर्याय m. change of clothes.*

वसनवन्त् a. clothed.

वसन्त m. spring (the friend of the god of love)

वसन्तक m. = prec., a man's name.

वसन्तकाल m. spring time.

वसन्ततिलक n. N. of a metre.

वसन्तपुष्प n. a spring flower.

वसन्तबन्धु m. the friend of the spring (cf. वसन्त).

वसन्तमहोत्सव m. the great spring festival (in honour of the god of love).

वसन्तश्री f. the beauty of spring.

वसन्तसख & °सहाय m. = वसन्तबन्धु.

वसन्तसमय m. spring time.

वसन्तसेन m., आ f. a man's & woman's name.

वसन्ता or वसन्ता adv. in spring.

वसन्तोत्सव m. spring festival.

वसवान m. (± वस्वस) owner of wealth.

वसव्य a. wealthy; n. wealth (also वसव्य).

वसा or वसा f. fat, grease, brain.

†वसापावन् a. drinking grease.

वसामय, f. ई consisting of fat.

वसाय्, °यते dress one's self in (instr.).

वसाहोम m. oblation of fat.

वसिष्ठ (superl.) most excellent, best, richest; m. N. of an ancient Rishi, deified as a star in the Great Bear.

वसीयंस् (compar.) better than (abl.), more wealthy or glorious.

वसु, f. वस्वी (& वसु) a. good, wholesome; m. E. of the gods or a class of (8) gods, N. of sev. men; n. good, property, wealth, riches.

वसुजित् a. winning good.

वसुता & वसुताति f. wealth or liberality.

वसुत्ति f. enrichment.

वसुत्व & वसुत्वन n. wealth, riches.

वसुद a. bestowing wealth, liberal.

वसुदत्त m., आ f. a man's & woman's name

वसुदा, °दान, & °दावन् a. = वसुद.
वसुदेय n. bestowing of wealth, liberality.
वसुदेव m. N. of Kṛṣṇa's father etc.
वसुधा a. yielding good, liberal. f. the earth, land.
वसुधातल n. the surface of the earth.
वसुधाधर a. supporting the earth; m. king or mountain.
वसुधाधिप & °पति m. lord of the earth, king.
वसुधान, f. ई containing wealth.
वसुधापति m. lord of the earth, king.
वसुधार a. holding treasures.
वसुधारिणी f. the earth (lit. = prec.).
वसुधिति a. possessing or bestowing wealth; f. = seq.
वसुधेय n. bestowal of wealth.
वसुंधर a. containing wealth. f. आ the earth, land.
वसुनीति & †वसुनीथ a. bringing wealth.
वसुपति m. (± वसूनाम्) lord of wealth or of the gods (E. of Agni, Indra, etc.).
वसुभूति m. a man's name.
वसुमत्ता f. wealth, riches.
वसुमन्त् a. containing treasures, wealthy; accompanied by the Vasus. m. a man's name; f. वसुमती the earth, a woman's name.
वसुमय, f. ई a consisting in wealth.
वसुमित्र m. a man's name.
वसुर a. valuable, rich.
वसुरण्व a. delighting in wealth.
वसुरेतस् m. fire or the god of fire (lit. seed of wealth or of the Vasus).
वसुलक्ष्मी f. N. of a woman.*
वसुवनि a. craving or bestowing wealth.
वसुवन्त् a. joined with the Vasus.
वसुविद् a. bestowing good.
वसुशक्ति m. a man's name.
वसुश्रवस् a. having good fame or famed for wealth.
वसुषेण m. E. of Kṛṣṇa and Karṇa.
वसूय्, °र्यति crave good.
वसूया (instr. adv.) from desire for good.
वसूयु a. craving good.
वस्त v. बस्त.
वस्तवे dat. infin. to 2वस्.

वस्तव्य a. to be spent (time); n. impers. (it is) to be stayed, dwelt, or lived.
वस्ति m. f. bladder; *fringe.
1वस्तु f. brightening, dawning; gen. वस्तोस् in the morning, प्रति वस्तोस् towards morning.
2वस्तु n. seat, place; thing, object, reality; matter, circumstance; substance, contents or subject (of a poem etc.).
वस्तुक a. having as subject (—°).
वस्तुतस् adv. in reality.
वस्तुरचना f. arrangement of a matter, treatment of a subject.
वस्तूपमा f. a kind of comparison.
†वस्तृ a. lighting up, m. illuminer.
वस्त्र n. cloth, garment; clothes, dress.
वस्त्रपूत a. purified by a cloth.
वस्त्रवन्त् a. well clothed.
वस्त्रवृत्त n. the real fact.
*वस्त्रयोनि f. material of cloth.
*वस्त्रवेश्मन् n. tent.
वस्त्राञ्चल m. the hem of a garment.
वस्त्रान्त m. the end of a garment.
वस्त्रान्तर n. upper garment, cover.
वस्त्रापहारक m. a stealer of clothes.
वस्त्राय्, °यते be like a garment.
वस्न n. price, value.
वस्न्य a. valuable, purchasable.
1वस्मन् n. cover.
2वस्मन् n. nest.
वस्यइष्टि f. striving after the highest good.
वस्यंस् (compar.) better, more excellent, wealthier than (abl.); n. the better or best, welfare, happiness.
1वह्, वहति, °ते, pp. ऊढ (q.v.) conduct, carry (esp. the oblation), draw (waggon), guide (the horses); bring near, procure, cause, effect; offer, present (a sacrifice); carry off, rob; take to wife, marry; bear, support, feel, suffer; indulge, pardon; wear, have; undergo, incur; pass, spend; intr. travel, go (in or by any vehicle), drive, ride, run, swim, flow, blow (wind), pass away (time); P. उह्यते be conducted etc., be borne along, move, go in or by (instr.). C. वाहयति, °ते

cause to conduct, draw, or carry; guide, drive (cf. S.), ride on (acc.); step upon or travel over (a way); set to work, use, apply; take in, deceive. I. वनीवाह्यते carry hither and thither. — अति carry over or across, pass by; spend (time). C. transport, transpose, let pass i.e. spend (time), escape (a foe etc.). अनु carry along. अप carry or drive away (also C.); take off, remove, give up. अभि convey near or towards, bring. आ the same, also bear (fig.), lead home i.e. take to wife; carry or drive away; intr. flow. C. call near, invite (esp. gods to a sacrifice). अन्वा & अभ्या bring hither or to. उदा & समुदा lead away, esp. lead out a bride from her father's house, i.e. marry. समा bring hither or to (together), assemble; M. meet. उद् & समुद् lead up or away; raise, elevate; draw out, extract; marry (cf. उदा); lead or bring to, offer, present; bear, carry (lit. & fig.); have, possess, enjoy; endure, suffer; manifest, betray. उद् C. (cause to) marry. उप lead or bring near, get, procure, cause, effect; betray into (acc.). समुप carry along, let flow; P. approach, begin, rise. नि lead down or towards (dat. or loc.); bear, support. निस् lead out, extract, save from (abl.); carry off, remove; bring about, effect; succeed (of pers.&th.). C. pass, spend (time); bring about, perform, accomplish. परा lead or take to (dat.). परि lead about, esp. the bride or the wedding procession, i.e. wed; intr. flow about. प्र trans. carry onward or along, lead or bring to (acc.); intr. be borne along, flow, blow. C. set in motion, send away, dismiss. प्रति conduct towards or near. वि lead away, marry (cf. उदा), form a matrimonial alliance with (instr.); M. get married, celebrate a wedding. C. give in marriage or marry. सम् carry (together), conduct, lead, draw, drag, bear along; P. ride on (instr.). C. bring together, assemble, collect; drive (carriage etc.), guide, conduct, lead, take to wife; carry the hand along the body, stroke. — Cf. अपोढ, उदूढ, उपोढ, आेढ, 2व्यूढ.

2वह् (वाह्, उह् & ऊह्) carrying, drawing, bearing, holding (—°).

वंह a. = prec., also intr. flowing towards or through (—°). m. n. the shoulder of the yoked animal or the part of the yoke lying on it.

वहंत् f. vehicle or river.

वहतु m. wedding procession, wedding.

वहन a. (—°) & n. conducting, carrying, bearing; n. also flowing, ship.

वहनभङ्ग m. shipwreck.

वहनीय a. to be carried, drawn, or borne.

वंहन्ती f. pl. flowing water.

वहलं a. used to the yoke (cow).

वहित्र n. ship; °भङ्ग m. shipwreck.

वहिंन् a. = वहलं.

वंहिष्ठ (superl.) & वंहीयंस् (compar.) conducting best (better); most (more) practicable (way).

वंह्नि m. beast for draught, team; conveyer, esp. who brings an oblation to the gods (Agni); the rider or charioteer (sev. gods), the flowing one (Soma); in l. l. mostly fire or the god of fire.

वह्निगृह n. house or place of the sacred fire.

वंह्नितम (superl.) carrying best (the oblation).

वह्निपतन n. entering the fire, self-immolation.

वह्निमन्त् a. containing fire.

वह्निमय a. consisting of fire, fiery.

वह्निशाला f. = वह्निगृह.

वह्निशिखा f. fire-flame.

वह्निसंस्कार m. the burning of a dead body.

वह्निसात्कृ burn, cremate.

वह्निस्फुलिङ्ग m. fire-spark.

वह्यं a. fit to draw or carry; n. portable bed, litter.

वह्यक m. beast for draught.

1वा (indecl.) or (following its word), either—or not, i.e. optionally (g.), as, like (= इव), indeed, even (= एव), but, but if, suppose that (fut.), possibly (after an interr.), often only explet. — वा—वा either—or; वा—न वा either—or not, perhaps—perhaps not, whether—or not; वा न—वा either not—or; यदि वा—वा (न) whether—or (not). न (± वा)—वा neither—nor. — Cf. अथ, उत, किम्, यदि.

2वा, वयति, °ते, pp. उत or ऊत weave, interweave, plait, fig. = compose (hymns etc.). - आ weave or lay in, interweave; also = समा M. string upon (loc.). उद् bind up, suspend. परि interweave; tie round, fetter, ensnare. प्र weave or tie to (loc.). वि plait, twist, weave. सम् weave together, interweave, inlay or adorn with (instr.). — Cf. ओत, प्रोत, व्युत, व्यूत, समुत.

3वा, वाति, वायति, °ते, pp. वात & वान (—°) blow, blow near or towards (tr. & intr.), spread (intr. of odours), smell. — अनु blow towards or after (acc.), inflame, rouse. अभि & आ blow towards or hither. अव blow down. उप cease to blow, be extinguished. निस् blow, also = prec. C. निर्वापयति extinguish, allay, refresh, delight. परा blow away. प्र blow, be exhaled or spread (odour). वि blow asunder or through. सम् blow. — Cf. निर्वाण, प्रवात.

4वा v. 1वन्.

5वा before उ = वै.

वाक m. saying, formula, recitation (r.).

वाकोवाक्य n. dialogue, conversation; E. of cert. parts of the Vedic tradition.

वाक्क्षत n. offence by words.

वाक्चक्षुस् n. speech and look.

वाक्चपल a. restless with words, talking idly.

वाक्पटु a. eloquent, abstr. °ता f.

वाक्पति m. lord of speech.

वाक्पथ m. time or opportunity of speaking.

वाक्पारुष्य n. roughness of speech, verbal injury.

वाक्य n. speech, words; statement, deposition (j.); sentence, periphasis (g.).

वाक्यपदीय n. T. of a work.

वाक्यार्थ m. the meaning or contents of a sentence.

वाक्यार्थोपमा f. a kind of comparison (rh.).

वाक्संयम & °संवर m. restraint or control of speech.

वागपहारक m. stealer of (another's) words or of the Word, i.e. the Veda.

वागीश a. & m. = seq. (often —° in names of learned men).

वागीश्वर m. a master of language.

वागुरा f. snare, net, trap.

वागुरावृत्ति a. who lives by snaring animals.

वागुरिक m. deer-catcher, hunter.

वागृषभ m. master (lit. bull) of language; abstr. °त्व n.

वाग्गुद m. a kind of bird or bat.

वाग्दण्ड m. speech-assault, either reproof, reprimand, or = seq. n., also control over one's speech; du. word and stick.

वाग्दण्डज a. sprung from speech-assault, w. पारुष्य n. verbal injury.

वाग्दुष्ट a. speaking ill or abusively; m. defamer.

वाग्देवता & वाग्देवी f. the goddess of speech (Sarasvatī).

वाग्दैवत्य a. sacred to Sarasvatī (v. prec.).

वाग्बन्धन n. stopping of speech, silence.

वाग्भट m. N. of sev. scholars.

वाग्मिता f., °त्व n. eloquence.

वाग्मिन् a. eloquent.

वाग्यत a. reserved in speech, taciturn.

वाग्वन्त् a. connected with language.

वाग्विद् a. skilled in language.

वाग्विदग्ध a. clever in speech; abstr. °ता f.

वाग्विन् a. eloquent.

वाग्विसर्ग m. ,°सर्जन n. breaking silence; speaking.

वाग्वीर m. master of language.

वाग्वीर्य a. strong-voiced.

वाग्व्यवहार m. discussion, quarrel.

वाग्व्यापार m. speaking, talking (lit. use of speech).

वाघत् m. the institutor of a sacrifice.

वाङ्मधु n. sweet words (speech-honey).

वाङ्मधुर a. sweet in speech.

वाङ्मनस् n. du., °मनस n. sgl. speech and mind.

वाङ्मय, f. ई a. consisting of speech or words, relating to speech; n. speech, eloquence, rhetoric.

वाङ्मात्र n. the mere word.

वाच् f. speech, voice, sound, word, language, discourse; also speech personif. or the goddess of speech, Sarasvatī.

वाचंयम a. = वाग्यत, abstr. °त्व n.

वाचक, f. °चिका a. speaking, saying, expressing (gen. or —°); m. speaker, reciter. Abstr. °ता f., °त्व n.

वाचकपद a. containing words that have a sense or express something.

वाचन n. reciting or causing to recite, reading, expressing; f. आ lesson, chapter.

वाचस्पति m. lord of speech, master of language, E. of sev. gods, esp. of Bṛhaspati, also a man's name.

वाचा f. speech, word; the goddess of speech.

वाचामात्र & °क n. = वाङ्मात्र.*

वाचाट a. talkative, vain-glorious.

वाचारम्भण n. a mere phrase (lit. a hold or support of language).

वाचाल a. = वाचाट; also noisy, resounding with (—°). Abstr. °ता f., °त्व n.

वाचालय्, °यति cause to talk or fill with noise.

वाचिक a. consisting of words, verbal, oral.

वाचिन् a. asserting, expressing (—°).

वाच्य to be spoken or said (n. impers.); being said or meant; to be spoken to or about; to be spoken against, blamable, censurable; n. blame, censure, fault. Abstr. °ता f., °त्व n.

वाच्यार्थ m. the meaning immediately expressed.

वाज m. swiftness, strength, courage; race, struggle, contest & its prize, booty, gain, reward, treasure, good; offering-meat; runner, horse; N. of one of the Ṛbhus, pl. the Ṛbhus together.

वाजजित् a. winning the contest or booty.

वाजदा & °दावन् a. granting good or strength.

वाजपति m. lord of strength (f. °पत्नी).

वाजपेय m. n. a cert. sacrifice.

वाजपेशस् a. embellished with gifts or strength.

वाजंभर a. carrying the prize.

वाजय्, वाजयति & वाजयति, °ते run for the prize, race, hasten; combat, contest; spur on, incite.

वाजयु a. running (for the prize), zealous, eager, strong, bestowing booty or treasure.

वाजरत्न a. rich in goods or treasures.

वाजवन्त् a. consisting of or connected with booty, treasure etc., strong, vigorous; accompanied by the Vājas (i.e. Ṛbhus).

वाजश्रव m. N. of a man.

वाजश्रवस् m. N. of a teacher.

वाजश्रवस m. patron. from prec.

वाजश्रुत a. famed for swiftness.

वाजसनि a. gaining or granting good, booty, strength, etc.; victorious.

वाजसनेय m. patron. of Yājñavalkya; pl. N. of a Vedic school.

वाजसनेयिन् m. pl. the school of Vājasaneya.

वाजसनेयिब्राह्मण n., °संहिता f. Brāhmana & Saṅhitā of the Vājasaneyas.

वाजसा a. = वाजसनि.

वाजसात n., °साति f. gain of the prize or of goods, battle, victory.

वाजसृत् a. running for the prize.

वाजिन् a. swift, courageous, strong, brave, manly. m. hero, warrior; horse, stallion. Pl. the horses of the gods, also the sect of Vājasaneya.

वाजिन n. race, running, contest, manly strength.

वाजिनीवन्त् a. swift or having swift horses, courageous, strong.

वाजिनीवसु a. having swift horses or giving strength.

वाजिनेय m. son of a hero or warrior.

वाजिमेध m. horse-sacrifice.

वाजिरूपधर e. having the shape of a horse.

वाजिवेग a. swift as an horse.

वाञ्छ्, वाञ्छति, pp. वाञ्छित (q.v.) desire, wish. — अभि, समभि, सम्, & अभिसम् = S.

वाञ्छा f. wish, desire for (loc., gen., acc. with प्रति, or —°).

वाञ्छित a. wished for, desired; n. wish, desire.

वाट् an exclamation used on making on oblation.

1**वाट** a. made of the Indian fig-tree.

2**वाट** m. enclosed place, garden (also ई f.); district, way.

वाटक m., **°टिका** f. enclosure, garden.
वाटधान m. pl. N. of a tribe.
1**वाट्य** a. = 1**वाट**.
2**वाट्य** m. parched barley.
वाडब adj. coming from a mare; m. = **वडवाग्नि**, also a Brahman.
वाडबाग्नि m. = **वडबाग्नि**.
वाडव = **वाडब**.
1**वाण** m. instrumental music; a harp with a hundred strings.
2**वाण** v. 1**बाण**.
वाणशब्द m. the sound of a lute or of arrows.
वाणिज m. merchant, trader.
वाणिजिक a. living by trade.
वाणिज्य n. (**°ज्या** f.) a merchant's business, trade.
1**वाणी** f. reed; du. the two spring-bars on a carriage.
2**वाणी** f. music (pl. choir of singers or musicians), sound, voice; speech, words, eloquence or the goddess Sarasvatī.
वाणीची f. a cert. musical instrument.
वात m. wind, air; the god of the wind.
वातजूत a. swift as the wind.
वातत्विष् a. impetuous like the wind.
वातभक्ष a. living upon wind.
वातरंहस् a. swift as the wind.
वातल a. windy, airy.
वातवर्ष m. sgl. & pl. rain and wind.
वातव्य a. to be weft.
वातव्याधि m. wind-disease.
वातस्वन & **°स्वनस्** a. roaring like the wind.
वातात्मज m. E. of Hanumant (son of the Wind).
वातापि a. swelling by wind, fermenting, or having the wind as ally (Soma); m. N. of an Asura.
1**वातायन** m. a patron. name.
2**वातायन** a. moving in the wind or in the air; n. air-hole, round window, i.g. a place to take the air, pavilion, turret etc.
वाताली f. whirlwind.
वातावन्त् a. windy, airy.
वातावली f. = **वाताली**.*
वाताश & **°शिन्** m. serpent (wind-eater).
वाताश्व m. a wind-swift horse, runner.
वाताहति f. a violent gust (lit. stroke) of wind.
वातिक m. wind-maker, i.e. braggart, boaster.
वातुल a. windy; also = seq.
वातूल a. crazy, mad, insane.
वातोपसृष्ट a. affected with a wind-disease.
वातोर्मी f. N. of a metre (wind-wave).
वात्या f. storm, whirlwind.
वात्सल्य n. affection, tenderness towards (loc., gen., or —°).
वात्स्य a. relating to Vatsa; m. as patron.
वात्स्यायन m. patr. from prec. m., N. of an author.
वाद a. speaking of or playing on (—°). m. speech, discourse, mention, assertion, proposition, statement, dispute, controversy; sound, music.
वादन m. & n. player & playing on a musical instrument.
वादयुद्ध n. speech-fight i.e. controversy.
वादिक a. speaking, asserting (—°).
वादित & **°तव्य** n. instrumental music.
वादित्र n. musical instrument or = prec.
वादिन् a. speaking, discoursing, asserting, expressing (—°, r. acc.). m. speaker, explainer, teacher, disputant; plaintiff, accuser, du. plaintiff and defendant.
वाद्य a. to be spoken or to be played (blown) on; n. speech or musical instrument.
वाधूय a. bridal; n. bridal garment.
वाध्रीणस v. **वार्ध्रीणस**.
वान n. weaving, sowing.
1**वानप्रस्थ** m. a Brahman of the third order, hermit, anchorite.
2**वानप्रस्थ** a. relating to a hermit; m. the third stage of a Brahman's life (also **°प्रस्थ्य** n.).
1**वानर** m. (adj. —° f. **आ**) monkey, ape, f. **ई**.
2**वानर**, f. **ई** belonging to a monkey, monkey-like, apish.
वानस्पत्य a. relating to trees or woods, wooden; m. tree, bush, plant i.g.; n. fruit of a tree.
वानायु m. pl. N. of a people.
वानीर m. a kind of reed or cane.
वानेय a. living or growing in a wood.

वान्त a. having vomited; n. = seq.
वान्तान्न n. vomited food.
वान्ताशिन् a. eating vomited food.
वान्ति f. vomiting.
वान्या f. a cow whose calf is dead.
1वाप m. shearing, shaving.
2वाप m. sower, scatterer; scattering, seed.
1वापन n. causing to shear or shearing.
2वापन n. sowing.
वापिका & वापी f. an oblong pond.
वापीजल n. water from a pond.
वापीविस्तीर्ण n. a breach or gap formed like an oblong pond.
वापुष a. wonderful.
1वाप्य a. to be scattered.
2वाप्य a. coming from ponds.
†वाभि v. ऊर्णवाभि.
वाम् (encl.) acc. dat. gen. du. of 2nd pers. pron.
1वाम, f. ई & आ dear, pleasant, lovely, beautiful; fond of, eager or greedy for (—°). m. E. of Çiva, a man's name. f. वामा a (beautiful) woman; f. वामी a female or she-(ass, camel etc.); n. anything dear or precious, wealth, goods, etc.
2वाम a. left (not right), adverse, contrary, refractory, stubborn, prude, coy, cruel, wicked, bad; n. adversity, mischief. Abstr. °ता† f., °त्व† n.
वामक, f. °मिका left (not right), adverse, cruel, hard. m. a cert. mixed caste; n. a kind of gesture.
वामतस् adv. from the left side.
वामदृश् & °दृष्टि f. a fair-eyed woman.
वामदेव m. N. of a Rishi.
1वामन a. dwarfish, short, small, abstr. °ता† f., °त्व† n. — m. dwarf, E. of Viṣṇu etc., N. of sev. men.
2वामन a. relating to a dwarf or Viṣṇu.
वामनयना f. = वामदृश्.
वामभाज् a. enjoying lovely things.
वामलोचन n. a beautiful eye.
वामलोचना f. a fair-eyed woman.
वामशील a. of a stubborn or wicked character.
वामाक्षी f. = वामदृश्.
वामारम्भ a. stubborn, refractory.
वामिन् a. vomiting, ejecting.
वामेतर a. different from left, right.
वामोरू f. a woman with beautiful thighs.
वाम्य n. perversity.
वायक m. weaver, sewer.
वायव, f. ई relating to the wind or to Vāyu, north-western; f. ई (± दिश्) the north-west.
वायव्य a. = prec. a.; n. E. of a lunar mansion.
1वायस m. bird, crow; f. ई crow-hen.
2वायस, f. ई relating to crows.
वायसी w. कृ change into a crow, भू P.
1वायु m. wind, air, esp. vital air (5); the god of wind, pl. the Maruts.
2वायु a. tired, languid.
3वायु a. desirous or desirable.
वायुगीत a. sung by the wind, i.e. universally known.
वायुपुत्र m. Vāyu's son i.e. Hanumant.
वायुपुराण n. T. of a Purāṇa.
वायुभक्ष, °भक्षक, & °भक्ष्य a. living on air.
वायुभूत a. being (like) wind.
वायुमन्त् a. joined or connected with wind.
वायुमय a. having the nature of wind.
वायुर a. windy.
वायुवत् adv. like the wind.
वायुवेग m. the swiftness of wind.
वायुवेगक & °वेगिन् a. swift as wind.
वायुसम a. wind-like.
वायुसूनु m. = वायुपुत्र.
वाय्य m. a patron. name.
वाय्वश्व a. having the winds for horses.
वार् n. water.
1वार m. tail-hair, esp. of a horse; m. n. sgl. & pl. a hair-sieve.
2वार v. दुर्वार.
3वार m. good, treasure; appointed time or place, one's turn, alternation, succession, change, time (w. numerals, वारं वारम् many a time, often); day (of a week). — f. वारा courtezan.
वारकन्यका f. = prec. f.
वारङ्ग m. handle.
वारण, f. ई warding off, resisting (n. a subst.); strong, wild, fierce, dangerous. m. elephant.
वारणशाला f. stable for elephants.

वारणसाह्वय n. (± पुर) the town synonymous with elephants, i.e. Hāstinapura.
वारणावत n. N. of a city.
1वारणीय a. to be kept off.
2वारणीय a. relating to elephants.
वारनारी f. courtezan (cf. 3वार).
वारबाण s. coat of mail.
वारमुख्य m. dancer, singer; f. आ = prec.
वारयितव्य a. to be kept from (abl.).
वारयुवति & °योषित् f. = वारनारी.
वारवधू & °वनिता f. the same.
वारवन्त् a. long-tailed (horse).
वारविलासिनी & वाराङ्गना f. = वारनारी.
वाराणसी f. N. of a city (Benares).
वाराह, f. ई relating to a boar (Viṣṇu), boarish, made of hog's leather, etc.
1वारि n. water.
2वारि & °री f. place where elephants are caught or tied on.
वारिगर्भोदर a. pregnant with rain (cloud).
वारिचर a. living in or near water; m. fish, pl. N. of a people.
वारिचारिन् a. living in water.
वारिज (water-born); m. conch-shell, n. a lotus.
वारितरंग m. (water-)wave.
वारितस् adv. (& adj.) by water (& checked).
वारिति s. water-plant.
वारिद a. giving water or rain; m. cloud.
वारिधर a. carrying water; m. = prec. m.
वारिधानी f. water-tub.
वारिधारा f. sgl. & pl. stream of water.
वारिधि & °निधि m. sea (receptacle of water).
वारिपथ m. water-path, voyage.
वारिपथोपजीविन् a. living by voyages, seafaring.
वारिबिन्दु m. drop of water.
वारिमन्त् a. abounding in water.
वारिमय, f. ई consisting of water.
वारिमुच् a. discharging water; m. cloud.
वारियन्त्र n. water-wheel.
वारिराज m. E. of Varuṇa (water-king).
वारिराशि m. heap of water, the sea.
वारिवह a. carrying or pouring forth water.
वारिवाह a. = prec.; m. cloud or the rain-god.
वारिवाहक & °हिन् a. = prec. a.
वारिविहार m. water-sport (i.e. leaping in the water and splashing others).
वारिसंभव a. born or produced in water.
वारिस्थ a. reflected (standing) in water (sun).
वारीय्, °यते be like water.
वारुक a. choosing (acc.).
वारुण, f. ई relating to Varuṇa or the water, Varuṇa's, western, water-. m. aquatic animal, fish; f. ई the west (± दिश्), Varuṇa's wife or daughter, a kind of spirit or liquor; n. E. of a lunar mansion.
वारुणि m. a patron. name.
वारेवृत a. chosen, elect.
वार्कार्य f. producing water.
वार्क्ष, f. ई relating to trees, wooden.
वार्त्त a. common, regular; f. आ livelihood, subsistence (— ° living on or by); business, trade, profession (esp. that of a Vaiçya); intelligence, news, tale, story, mention of (gen., loc., acc. ± उद्दिश्य, or — °).
वार्त्ताकर्मन् n. & वार्त्तारम्भ m. business, trade, profession.
वार्त्ताहर m. messenger (carrier of tidings).
वार्त्ताहर्तृ & °हार m. the same.
वार्त्ताहारिन् a. bringing a message from (— °).*
वार्त्तिक m. husbandman, trader, spy, messenger; explanatory or complementary rule (g.).
वार्त्रघ्न, f. ई relating to the Vṛtra-slayer, w. हविस् n. offering of victory; m. E. of Arjuna (Indra's son).
वार्त्रहत्य a. & n. (belonging to) the slaying of Vṛtra.
वार्द m. = वारिद m.
वार्द्धक m. old man; n. old age.
वार्द्धकभाव m. & वार्द्धक्य n. = prec. n.
वार्द्धुष, °षि, °षिक, & °षिन् m. usurer.
वार्द्धुषी f., °ष्य n. usury.
वार्धनी f. water-jar.
वार्धि & वार्मुच् m. = वारिधि & °मुच् m.
वार्ध्राणस or वार्ध्रीणस m. an old white he-goat or a kind of crane.
1वार्य a. to be checked or restrained; m. wall.

2वार्य a. to be chosen, precious, dear. m. treasure, jewel.
वार्यनिलाशन a. living on water and air.
वार्योकस् s. leech (whose home is the water).
वार्वाह m. rain-cloud.
वार्ष, f. ई belonging to the rainy season.
वार्षपर्वण a. coming from Vṛṣaparvan, f. ई patron. of Çarmiṣṭhā.
वार्षिक, f. ई = वार्ष or = seq. a.
वार्षिक्य a. annual; n. the rainy season.
वार्ष्ण or वार्ष्ण & वार्ष्णि m. patron. names.
वार्ष्णेय m. patron. of sev. men, also of Kṛṣṇa; N. of Nala's charioteer.
वाल m. tail-hair, horse-hair, tail, bristle; hair-sieve.
वालखिल्य a. (w. मन्त्रास् or ऋचस्) cert. hymns of the Rigveda; m..pl. a class of dwarfish Rishis.
वालधान n. & वालधि m. a hairy tail.
*वालपाश्या f. a string of pearls to bind up the hair.
वालमय a. made of hair, hairy.
वालवासस् a. wearing a hairy garment.
वालव्यजन n. a fly-flap made of tail-hair.
वालिन् (having hair or a tail); N. of of a Daitya & a monkey.
वालुक a. made of sand; f. आ sgl. & pl. sand.
वालुकामय, f. ई = prec. adj.
वालुकाम्बुधि m. sea of sand i.e. desert.
वालुकार्णव m. the same.
वाल्क a. made of bark, n. such a garment.
वाल्गुद m. a kind of bat.
वाल्मीक a. composed by Vālmīki (v. seq.).
वाल्मीकि m. N. of an ancient Rishi, the author of the Rāmāyaṇa, etc.
वाल्लभ्य n. favouriteship, tenderness.
वाव (indecl.) surely, just; lays stress on the preceding word.
वावचन n. the statement of something as optional or arbitrary (g.).
वावदूक a. talkative, loquacious, abstr. °त्व n.
वावशान a. eager, willing, ready.
वावहि a. conducting well.
वावात a. dear, favourite; f. आ a king's favourite wife of a cert. rank.
वावातृ m. follower, adherent.

वाश्, वाशति, °ते, वाश्यते, °ति, pp. वाशित (q.v.) bleat, low, roar, cry (of birds). C. वाशयति, °ते cause to bleat etc.; M. sound loudly. I. वावश्यते howl, croak, sound loudly. अनु & प्रत्यनु low after or in return. अभि bleat or bellow at (acc.). प्रति the same. सम् (also I.) bleak etc. (together).
वाश or वाश a. roaring.
वाशक & वाशन a. croaking.
वाशित n. howling, croaking.
वाशिता f. a cow desiring the bull (also of other animals & female, woman i.g.).
वाशिन् a. howling, croaking.
वाशी f. a pointed knife; p. °मन्त्.
वाश्र a. bleating, bellowing, roaring, sounding; f. आ a (lowing) cow.
1वास m. garment, clothes.
2वास m. staying (esp. over night), abiding in (loc. or —°), abiding-place, house, home, state, condition; adj. —° living or dwelling in.
3वास m. odour, perfume.
वासःखण्ड n. piece of cloth, rag.
वासक (—°) = 1 2 3वास; n. = seq.
वासगृह & °गेह n. sleeping-room.
वासतेय a. deserving or giving shelter.
1वासन n. garment, dress; box.
2वासन n. causing to abide, lodging; f. आ thought or desire of (loc.); impression of (—°), notion, idea.
वासनामय a. consisting in ideas or in impressions from (—°); abstr. °त्व n.
वासनीय a. intelligible only by deep reflection.
वासन्त, f. ई vernal; f. N. of sev. plants.
वासन्तिक, f. ई = prec. a.; m. a cert. festival in spring.
वासपादप m. a tree (serving) as resting place (for birds).*
वासभवन n. sleeping-room.
वासभूमि f. dwelling-place.
वासय्, °यति (°ते), pp. वासित (q.v.) infuse, perfume, make fragrant. — अधि & अनु = S.
वासयष्टि f. pole for a bird to perch on.
वासयितव्य a. to be harboured or lodged.
*वासयोग m. a kind of perfume.

वासर॑, f. **ई** matutinal, early; m. day (opp. night) or day of the week.

1**वासव॑**, f. **ई** relating to or descended from the Vasus; m. E. of Indra.

2**वासव**, f. **ई** belonging to Indra; f. **ई** (± **दिश्**) his region, the east.

वासवज m. Indra's son i.e. Arjuna.

वासवदत्ता f. a woman's name, T. of a novel.

वासवदिश् & **वासवाशा** f. the east (cf. 2**वासव**).

वासवि m. = **वासवज**.

वासवेश्मन् n. sleeping-room.

1**वा॑सस्** n. garment, dress; du. under and upper garment.

2**वासस्** n. night-quarters.

वा॑सात्य a. dawny, dim.

वासार्थम् adv. to dwell or stay over night.

वासित a. perfumed, fragrant.

1**वासिन्** a. clothed in (—°).

2**वासिन्** staying or dwelling in (mostly —°).

वासिष्ठ, f. **ई** belonging to or descended from Vasiṣṭha; w. **शत** n. the hundred sons of V.

वासुकि m. N. of a genius & a serpent-king.

1**वासुदेव॑** m. patr. of Viṣṇu-Kṛṣṇa.

2**वासुदेव** a. relating to Kṛṣṇa (cf. prec.).

वासू f. girl, maiden.

वासोद & **°दा** a. giving clothes.

वास्तव, f. **ई** real, true.

वास्तव्य a. remaining on the spot, left (as worthless); belonging to an abode; m. inhabitant, E. of Rudra (lord of the remainders of a sacrifice).

वा॑स्तु n. (m.) dwelling, home.

वास्तुकर्मन् n. building a house.

वास्तुज्ञान n. art of building, architecture.

वास्तुदेव m., **°देवता** f. house-god.

वास्तुबन्धन n. = **वास्तुकर्मन्**.

वास्तुमध्य s. the centre of a house.

वास्तुविद्या f. = **वास्तुज्ञान**.

वास्तुविधान n., **°विधि** m. = **वास्तुकर्मन्**.

वा॑स्तोष्पति m. the genius of the dwelling.

वास्त्व a. left; n. remainders.

1**वाह्** v. 2**वह्**.

2**वाह्**, **वाहते** press, urge.

वाह॑ a. carrying, drawing, flowing (—°); m. beast for draught, horse, bull etc., waggon or any vehicle; adj. —° riding or going in. n. drawing, driving, riding, carrying, bearing, flowing.

वाहक, f. **°हिका** carrying, bringing.

वाहतक v. **बार्हतक**.

वा॑हन a. carrying, bringing. n. (m.) beast of burden or beast for riding; vehicle i.g., waggon ship, oar, sail (adj. —° riding or going in); n. drawing, carrying, driving, riding, guiding (a horse).

वाहनायुध n. sgl. & pl. vehicle and weapons.

वा॑हस् n. offering, presenting, waiting on.

वाहस॑ m. Boa-constrictor.

वाहितृ m. guide.

वाहिन् a. moving on (carriage); drawing, carrying, bringing, having, flowing or running towards (—°). m. waggon, chariot; f. **वाहिनी** army or a cert. division of an army, river.

वाहिनीपति & **°नीश** m. chief of an army.

वा॑हिष्ठ (superl.) carrying, bringing, or flowing most.

वाहीक v. **बाहीक**.

वाह्य a. what is carried, drawn, ridden, borne on (—°). n. beast for draught or riding, vehicle i.g.

वाह्लि & **°क** v. **बाह्लि** & **°क**.

1**वि॑** m. bird.

2**वि॑** adv. apart, asunder, away, out (mostly °— in verbs & nouns, to express division or distance).

विंश॑ a. the twentieth or twentifold; w. **शत॑** n. one hundred and twenty. m. (± **अंश** or **भाग**) a twentieth part.

विंशक a. accompanied or increased by twenty; w. **शत** n. twenty per cent.

विंशत् (°—) = seq.

विंशति॑ f. twenty.

विंशतिक a. twenty years old or consisting of twenty parts.

विंशतितम & **विंशतिम** a. the twentieth.

विंशतिशत n. one hundred and twenty.

विंशांश m. the twentieth part.

विंशिन् a. consisting of twenty.

विक m. N. of a man.

विकङ्कत m. N. of a plant.

विकच a. hairless, bald-headed; opened, blos-

somed (flower); shining, radiant, resplendent with (—°).
विकचय्, °यति open, pp. **विकचित** blossomed.
1**विकट** a. exceeding the usual measure, huge, monstrous, hideous, wicked, bad; n. adv. m. N. of sev. men & a gander.
2**विकट** a. having no mat or bed.
विकटाक्ष a. having hideous eyes.
विकटानन a. having a hideous mouth.
विकत्थन m. braggart; n. = seq.
विकत्था f., **विकत्थित** n. bragging, boasting.
विकम्पिन् a. trembling.
विकर a. robbed of the hands (as a punishment).
विकरण a. & n. changing, modifying; m. the inserted conjugational suffix (g.).
विकर्ण a. having the ears far asunder, having no ears i.e. deaf. m. a kind of arrow, a man's name.
विकर्तन a. & n. cutting asunder, dividing; m. the sun.
विकर्तृ m. changer, transformer.
विकर्मक्रिया f. commission of bad acts.
1**विकर्मन्** n. bad or prohibited action.
2**विकर्मन्** a. doing no work or = seq.
विकर्मस्थ & °**कर्मिन्** a. doing prohibited acts.
विकर्ष m. drawing towards one's self or drawing asunder, distance.
विकर्षण a. & n. drawing asunder, bending (a bow).
विकल a. defective, imperfect, crippled, mutilated, weak; destitute of, -less (instr. or —°); depressed, sad, unwell. Abstr. °**ता** f., °**त्व** n.
विकलय्, °**यति** afflict, annoy.
विकली कृ the same.
विकलेन्द्रिय a. deficient in organs of sense.
विकल्प m. alternative, choice between two or more; difference, variety; supposition, (false) conception; uncertainty, doubt.
विकल्पक m. distributer, arranger, former.
विकल्पन m. = prec.; f. **आ** & n. giving an option or alternative; fancy, imagination, (false) conception.
विकल्पवन्त् a. having a doubt, uncertain.
विकल्पिन् a. like, to be confounded with (—°).
विकल्मष a. sinless.
विकवच a. having no coat of mail.
विकस्ति f. bursting.
विकस्वर a. open (lit. & fig.), blossomed.
विकार m. change, alteration, perturbation, disorder (of body or mind), modification, preparation, production, passion of any kind, love, hatred.
विकारण a. causeless.
विकारिन् a. producing or undergoing a change etc.; changing into (—°).
विकार्य a. mutable.
विकाल m. evening.
1**विकाश** m. bright sheen.
2**विकाश** v. **विकास**.
विकाशयितृ v. **विकासयितृ**.
1**विकाशिन्** a. shining; illumining (—°).
2**विकाशिन्** v. **विकसिन्**.
विकास m. opening, blossoming, expansion, diffusion; opening of the heart, i.e. cheerfulness, merriment.
विकासक a. opening, developing (—°).
विकासन a. & n. causing to blossom or expand.
विकासयितृ (°**तृक**)* a. = prec. adj.
विकासिन् a. opened, blossoming, expanding, spreading, extensive, great.
विकिर m. a scattered portion of rice etc. (r.); a kind of bird.
विकिरण n. scattering.
विकीर्ण a. scattered, dispersed; spread, covered with, full of (—°).
विकुक्षि a. big-bellied.
विकुञ्चित a. bent, curled, contracted.
विकुण्ठ a. sharp, piercing, irresistible; m. E. of Viṣṇu & N. of Viṣṇu's heaven.
विकुण्ठित a. blunted, dulled.
विकूज m. humming, tinkling, etc.
विकूजन & °**जित** n. the same.
विकूबर a. robbed of the pole (carriage).
विकृत a. altered, changed, deformed, diseased, imperfect, unfinished, unnatural, artificial; inlaid or adorned with (—°). n. change, alteration, monstrous birth.
विकृताकृति a. deformed.
विकृति f. alteration, change, disorder (poss.

°मन्त् †); formation, development; N. of a species of metre.

विकृष्ट a. wide, long.

विकेतु a. robbed of the flag.

विकेशं, f. ई shag-haired; f. ई E. of cert. evil demons.

विकोश a. unsheathed (sword).

विकौतुक a. showing no curiosity or interest.

विक्रमं m. step, stride, going, gait; bold advance, valour, might.

विक्रमकेसरिन् m. N. of a prince.

विक्रमणं n. stepping, striding, bold advance, valour.

विक्रमपुर n. N. of a city.

विक्रमबाहु & °सेन m. names of kings.

विक्रमसिंह m. N. of sev. princes.

विक्रमाङ्क & °देव m. = विक्रमादित्य.

विक्रमाङ्कदेवचरित n. T. of a poem.

विक्रमादित्य m. N. of sev. kings, esp. of the supposed founder of the Samvat era (56 B.C.)

विक्रमिन् a. stepping, bestriding; advancing, courageous, bold.

विक्रमोर्वशी f. T. of a drama.

विक्रय m., °ण n. sale.

विक्रयक & °यिक m. seller, vender.

विक्रयिन् a. selling; m. = prec.

विक्रय्य a. to be sold.

विक्रान्त a. bold, valiant; n. = विक्रमं.

विक्रान्तस्तुतम् adv. with a bold and bounding gait.

विक्रान्ति f. the power of bestriding the whole world; also = prec.

विक्रामं m. a step's width.

विक्रायक m. seller.

विक्रिया f. = विकार + misfortune, mischief, damage.

विक्रियोपमा f. a kind of comparison.

विक्रीड m. play ground, toy; f. आ = seq.

विक्रीडित n. play, sport.

विक्रुष्ट n. = विक्रोश.

विक्रेतृ m. seller, vender.

विक्रेतव्य & °क्रेय a. to be sold.

विक्रोध a. free from anger.

विक्रोश m. cry of alarm or for help.

विक्रोशन m. N. of a myth. being.

विक्रोष्टृ m. who cries for help.

विक्लव a. depressed, timid, shy, afraid, perplexed, troubled, out of order; uncertain about, incapable of (—°). n., °ता f., & °त्व n. as abstr.

विक्लान्त a. wearied, dispirited.

विक्लिन्न a. thoroughly wet; softened, compassionate.

विक्लिष्ट a. hurt, violated.

विक्लेद m. becoming wet, wetness, dissolution.

विक्षत a. grievously hurt or wounded; n. wounding, wound.

विक्षरं a. pouring out

विक्षिप्त a. thrown asunder, scattered, dispersed; absent in mind, inattentive.

विक्षेप m. throwing, scattering, tossing, sending, dispatching; turning off, diversion, distraction; projection (ph.).

विक्षेपशक्ति f. the projective power (ph.); p. °मन्त्.

विक्षोभ्धोस् (gen. inf.) to crush.

विक्षोभ m. violent motion, agitation, confusion; adj. °भिन्.

विखनस् m. E. of Brahman, N. of a Muni.

विखादं m. devouring or devourer.

विखेद a. free from depression, fresh.

विख्यात a. universally known; renowned or known as, called (nom. w. इति).

विख्याति f. notoriety, fame.

विख्यापन n. announcement.

विगत a. gone away, disappeared, ceased, dead, remote; often °— having no—, free from, -less.

विगतज्वर a. free from fever or distress.

विगतसंकल्प a. devoid of purpose or resolution, undetermined.

1विगदं m. cry, confused noise.

2विगद a. free from illness, well.

विगन्ध & °न्धि a. smelling badly, stinking.

विगम m. departure, disappearance, absence, cessation.

विगर्हण n., °णा f. blaming, censure, reproach.

विगर्हित a. blamed, censured, prohibited, forbidden by (instr. gen. or —°); wicked, bad.

विगर्हिन् a. blaming (—°).

विगर्ह्य a. blamable.
विगाढ a. plunged into (act. & pass.), begun, set in, advanced.
विगाथा f. N. of a metre.
विंगामन् n. step, stride.
विगाहं a. plunging into, piercing.
विगीत a. discordant, contradictory.
विगीति f. N. of a metre.
विगुण a. having no string; void of qualities or virtues; defective, incomplete, destitute of (—°); worthless, ineffective, contrary.
विगुल्फ a. abundant.
विगूढ a. hidden, concealed.
विगृह्य (ger.) aggressive(ly).
विंग्र or **विग्रं** a. mighty, strong.
विग्रह m. separation, division; isolation, analysis (g); discord, contest, quarrel, war with (instr. ± **सह, साकम्**, or **सार्धम्**, loc., gen. w. **उपरि**, or —°).
विग्रंहण n. diffusing, distributing, seizing, grasping.
विग्रहवन्त् a. having a form or body, embodied, incarnate.
विग्रहिन् a. making war; m. minister of war.
विघटन n. separating, dispersing, destroying.
विघट्टन a. opening; n. & **आ** f. opening, striking, rubbing, friction.
1**विघनं** a. hurting, damaging; m. stamper, pounder, club, poss. **°निंन्**.
2**विघन** a. cloudless.
विघर्षण n. rubbing, friction.
विघसं m. n. food, esp. the remains of an oblation of food.
विघसाशिन् a. eating the remains of the sacrificial food.
विघात m. stroke, blow; warding off, beating back; obstacle, hindrance, disturbance; destruction, ruin.
विघातक a. impeding, disturbing.
विघातन a. warding off, a. & n. = prec.
विघातिन् a. beating, fighting, hurting, removing, disturbing.
विघूर्णन n., **°ना** f. tottering, reeling.
विंघृत a. sprinkled.
विघृष्ट a. rubbed, sore.
विघ्न m. breaker, destroyer (—°); m. (n.) obstacle, hindrance.
विघ्नकर a. causing obstacles, impeding.
विघ्नकर्तृ, °कारिन्, & **°कृत्** a. the same.
विघ्नजित् m. E. of Ganeça (lit. overcoming obstacles).
विघ्नपति m. = prec. (lit. lord of obstacles).
विघ्नय्, °यति, pp. **विघ्नित** binder, disturb. — **सम्** = S.
विघ्नराज् & **°राज** m. = **विघ्नपति**.
विघ्नवन्त् a. connected with obstacles.
विघ्नेश & **°श्वर** m. = **विघ्नपति**.
विच्, विनंक्ति (विवेक्ति), pp. **विक्त** separate, esp. grain from chaff by winnowing, i.g. sift, sever from (abl.), try, examine. — **अप** sever, separate (= S.). **वि** separate by tossing or blowing, i.g. sift; sever from (abl.); examine, try, distinguish, decide (a question). C. **विवेचयति** = **प्रवि** separate, try, examine. — Cf. **प्रविविक्त, विविक्त**.
विचकिल m. a kind of jasmine.
विचक्र a. having no wheels.
विचक्षणं a. conspicuous, visible, clear, distinct; discerning, intelligent, knowing, wise, skilful or clever in (loc. or —°), abstr. **°त्व†** n.
विचक्षुस् a. eyeless, blind.
विचंक्षे dat. inf. to **चक्ष्**.
विचय m. sifting, searching, investigating.
विचयन n. the same.
विचरणीय n. impers. to be proceeded.
विचरित a. roving about, wandering.
विचर्चिका & **°चर्ची** f. a kind of cutaneous disease.
विंचर्षणि a. stirring, agile, swift, active.
विचार m. proceeding, mode of procedure (= a single case), also = seq.
विचारण n., **°णा** f. change of place; reflection, deliberation, examination, hesitation, doubt.
विचारणीय a. requiring much consideration.
विचारवन्त् a. acting with deliberation.
विचारित a. deliberated, dubious or settled; n. deliberation, hesitation.

विचारिन् a. spreading, wide; roaming, wandering; going through, judging, considering (—°).
विचार्य a. = विचारणीय.
विचिकित्सन n., °त्सा f. uncertainty, doubt.
विचिकित्स्य a. dubitable.
विचित् a. sifting, discerning.
विचिति f. = विचय.
1**विचित्त** a. senseless, perplexed
2**विचित्त** a. perceived, manifest.
विचित्य a. to be sifted.
विचित्र a. variegated, many-coloured; various, manifold, different; extraordinary, strange, wonderful beautiful, surprising, amusing. Abstr. °ता f.
विचित्रवीर्य m. N. of an ancient king.
विचित्रित a. variegated, many-coloured; embellished or adorned with (instr. or —°).
विचिन्तन n. thinking, thought.
विचिन्तनीय a. to be thought of or considered.
विचिन्ता f. thought, care.
विचिन्त्य a. = विचिन्तनीय.
विचृत् f. loosening, untying; du. E. of two stars.
विचेतन a unconscious, senseless, inanimate, dead, stupid, foolish.
विचेतृ m. sifter.
विचेतस् a. catching the eye, conspicuous; wise, clever; unconscious, senseless; stupid, foolish.
विचेय a. to be sifted, searched, examined; n. as abstr.
विचेष्ट a. motionless, not stirring.
विचेष्टन n. stirring, agility, exertion.
विचेष्टा f. the same; conduct, behaviour.
विचेष्टित n. = prec.
विच्छाय a. splendourless, colourless, dim.
विच्छित्ति f. interruption, disturbance, hindrance, frustration.
विच्छिन्न a. torn asunder, severed, interrupted, destroyed, perished.
विच्छेद m. piercing, tearing or breaking asunder, severing from (gen. or —°); interruption, hindrance, prevention, destruction; division, difference.
विच्छेदकारिन् a. causing an interruption.
विच्छेदन a. dividing, interrupting; n. cutting off, removing, dividing, distinguishing.
विच्छेदिन् a. destroying.
विच्युति f. falling off (lit. & fig.); separating from (abl.).
1**विज्**, **विजते** (°ति & वेजते), pp. विग्न (विक्त) dart up or back (intr.), tremble, flee from (abl.). C. वेजयति dart (tr.), frighten, agitate; strengthen, increase. I. वेविज्यते start up at (dat.), flee from (abl.). — उद् start up, take a fright, be afraid of (abl., gen., or instr.); get tired of or disgusted with, desist from (abl.). C. terrify, frighten, vex, annoy, harass. समुद् start for fear, take fright. प्र rush away. वि C. frighten. सम् start up, run away, fall asunder. — Cf. आविग्न, उद्विग्न, प्रविक्त, विविग्न, संविग्न, समाविग्न, समुद्विग्न.
2**विज्** s. stake at game.
विजन a destitute of people or inhabitants, desert, solitary. n. solitary place, loneliness; °नं & °नी कृ remove all witnesses.
विजन्मन् m. a cert. mixed caste.
विजय m. victory, conquest, booty, a cert. array of troops. m. & f. आ a man's & woman's name.
विजयदण्ड m. a cert. detachment of troops.*
विजयदत्त m. N. of sev. men & of the hare in the moon.
विजयप्रत्यर्थिन्, f. °णी desirous of victory.
विजयवन्त् a. victorious.
विजयवर्मन् m. N. of sev. men.
विजयिन् a. victorious; m. victor, conqueror.
विजर a. not aging.
विजल्प m. (talk*); unjust reproach.
विजात & °तीय a. of a different kind, dissimilar.
विजामि a. related (by blood).
†**विजावती** f. who has born.
विजावन् a. corporal, one's own (son).
विजिगीषा f. desire to overcome or to conquer; adj. °षिन् or °षु.
विजित a. conquered, subst. c. land; n. conqust, victory.
विजिति f. contest, victory.
विजितिन् a. victorious.

विजितेन्द्रिय a. having the organs subdued.
विजिह्म a. bent, curved.
विजिह्व a. tongueless.
विजु m. a cert. part of the body of a bird.
विजृम्भ m. stretching.
विजृम्भण n. gaping, blossoming, spreading, expanding.
विजृम्भित a. gaped, opened, blown; n. impers., also = prec.
विजृम्भिन् a. coming forth.
विजेतव्य to be subdued.
विजेतृ m. victor, conqueror.
विज्ज m. a man's name.
विज्जल a. slimy, smeary.
विज्ञ a. knowing, wise, learned.
विज्ञप्ति f. request, petition; report.
विज्ञातव्य a. to be known.
विज्ञाति f. knowledge.
विज्ञातृ m. who knows or understands.
विज्ञान n. knowing, knowledge, intelligence, wisdom, learning, science, art, the capacity or organ of knowledge; the meaning by, knowing as, supposing (—°).
विज्ञानमय a. consisting of knowledge.
विज्ञानवन्त् & °**निन्** a. knowing, wise, learned.
विज्ञापन n., °**ना** f. = **विज्ञप्ति**.
विज्ञापनीय & °**ज्ञाप्य** a. to be made known or to be apprised.
विज्ञेय a. to be known or understood, to be taken for (nom.).
विज्य a. having no string (bow).
विज्वर a. free from fever or pain, well, at ease.
विट m. boon-companion; bon-vivant (d.).
विटङ्क crown, top, summit; a. nice, pretty.
विटङ्कित a. stamped, marked, adorned with (instr. or —°).
विटप m. branch, twig, bush.
विटपिन् a. having branches; m. tree.
विट्पण्य n. the wares of a Vaiçya.
विट्पति m. chief of people (= king) or of the Vaiçyas; a daughter's husband.
विड s. a kind of salt.
विडम्ब a. imitating (—°); m. mockery, derision.
विडम्बक a. = prec. a.
विडम्बन a. the same; n. & f. **आ** imitating, aping; abuse, mockery, derision, profanation.
विडम्बिन् a. imitating, aping, mocking, profaning (—°).
विडोजस् & **विडौजस्** m. E. of Indra.
विड्ज a. growing on dung.
विड्भुज् a. feeding on ordure.
विड्वराह m. house-pig.
विण्मूत्र n. sg. du. faeces and urine.
वितत a. spread out, extended, covered with (instr. or —°); extensive, broad, wide, n. adv.; abstr. °**त्व**† n. extent.
वितति f. stretching out, extension, length, abundance, multitude.
वितथ a. not so, false, in vain; abstr. °**ता** f.
वितथाभिनिवेश m. inclination towards what is false, poss. °**वन्त्**.
वितनु a. very thin or small; bodiless, unsubstantial; m. the god of love.
वितमस् & °**मस्क** a. free from darkness, light.
वितर a. leading on (a path).
वितरण n. leading on; transfer, bestowal, donation.
वितरम् & °**राम्** adv. further, more.
वितर्क m. conjecture, supposition, deliberation, doubt.
वितर्क्य a. to be considered.
वितर्दि & °**का** f. a kind of terrace.
वितल n. a cert. hell.
वितष्ट a. carved out, fashioned.
वितस्ता f. N. of a river (Hydaspes).
वितस्ति f. span (as a measure of length).
वितान m. n. spreading out, extension; awning, canopy; abundance, multitude; sacrificial act; m. the distribution of the sacred fires & these themselves.
वितानक n. awning, canopy, abundance.
वितानवन्त् a. furnished with a canopy.
वितानाय्, pass. °**य्यते** represent an awning.
वितामस a. = **वितमस्**.
वितार a. starless.
वितिमिर a. = **वितामस**.
वितीर्ण a. got over, passed; granted, bestowed; finished, accomplished.
वितुष a. husked.
वितृण a. grassless.

वितृष् & °ष a. free from thirst.
वितृष्ण a. free from thirst or desire; abstr. °ता f.
वितृष्णा f. = prec. f.
वितोय a. waterless.
1वित्त a. known, celebrated.
2वित्त a. got, acquired; seized or visited by (—°); f. आ taken, married; n. anything found or got; wealth, money, property.
वित्तकाम a. desirous of wealth; °काम्या f. abstr.
वित्तनाथ m. lord of wealth (Kubera).
वित्तप, °पति & °पाल m. the same.
वित्तपपुरी f. N. of a town.
वित्तमय, f. ई consisting in wealth.
वित्तवन्त् a. wealthy, rich.
वित्तवर्धन & °विवर्धिन् a. increasing wealth.
वित्तहीन a. destitute of wealth, poor.
वित्तागम m., वित्ताप्ति f. acquisition of property or money.
वित्ताप्पति m. du. the lords of wealth and water (Kubera and Varuṇa).
1वित्ति f. consciousness, intellect.
2वित्ति (वित्ति) f. finding or anything found; gain, acquisition.
वित्तेश & °श्वर m. = वित्तनाथ.
वित्रास a. frightening (—°); m. fright.
वित्रासन a. (f. ई) & n. frightening.
विथुर a. tottering, reeling, trembling; frail, uncertain.
विथुर्य्, °र्यति totter, reel.
1विद्, वेत्ति (वेद्), pp. विदित or वित्त (q.v.) know, understand, learn, perceive, experience, feel; think or be mindful of (acc. or gen.), know how to (infin.); believe, suppose, know or recognize as, declare to be, take for, call, name (2 acc. or acc. & nom. w. इति). C. वेदयते, °ति make known, announce, report; inform of, teach (2 acc.); take for, learn or know—to be (2 acc.); perceive, notice, experience, feel. D. विविदिषति wish to know, inquire after (acc.). — अनु know thoroughly (lit. along). आ know well or exactly. C. address, invite, announce, proclaim, prescribe, inform; offer, present. नि C. cause to know, announce, report, communicate to (dat., gen., or loc.); name, call (2 acc.), offer, present, surrender (आत्मानम् refl.). विनि & संनि C. make known, announce, report, offer, present, surrender. परि know very well. प्र know. C. make known, announce, relate. प्रति understand, know. C. make known, announce, tell; acquaint with (2 acc.); offer, entrust, commit. वि discern, know. सम् know or understand (together); consent, agree. C. cause to know, inform, instruct; make known, communicate.

2विद् (mostly —°) knowing.

3विद्, विन्दति, °ते (वित्ते), pp. वित्त & विन्न (q.v.) find, meet with, get, obtain; visit, befall; have, possess; find out for, procure (dat.); look for, turn to (acc.); M. (A.) take to wife (± भार्याम्), find a husband, marry; bring forth (± सुतम्). P.M. be found, be there (impers.), exist. विद्यते (°ति) there is (esp. w. न), यथा विदे as it is, i.e. as usual or as well as possible. D. विवित्सति wish to find. I. वेविदत्, वेविदान be present. — अधि supersede, supplant. अनु find (after), get, obtain, take hold of; M. भार्याम् take to wife. P. be found, exist. अभि find, find out, know. आ get hold of, get at, acquire, incur, undergo. P. be, exist. निस् divide from (abl.); M. get rid of (gen.), take off (acc.); P. become depressed or dispirited, get weary of or disgusted with (abl., instr., r. acc.). परि P. be married with the younger brother before the elder has married. सम् M. find, get hold of, acquire, win. P. be found, be there (esp. w. न), exist, belong to (gen.). — Cf. अधिविन्न, अनुवित्त, निर्विण्ण, परिवित्त, परिविन्न, 1विदान, संविदान.

4विद् (—°) finding, winning, procuring.
विद (—°) = 2विद्.
विदग्ध a. burnt, inflamed; burnt i.e. taught by experience, knowing, witty, cunning, clever.

विदग्धचूडामणि m. N. of a parrot (the crest-jewel of the wise).
विदग्धता f. cleverness, skill in (loc.).
†विदच v. सुविदच.
विदथ n. direction, order; arrangement, disposition; meeting, assembly, council, congregation, esp. for a festival; array, squadron (esp. of the Maruts); fight, battle.
विदथ्य a. fit for a congregation or a council, festive, solemn.
विदद्वसु a. winning good.
विदरण n. bursting, splitting.
†विदर्भ m. pl. N. of a people, sgl. the country or a king of the V.
विदर्भनगरी f. city of Vidarbha, i.e Kuṇḍina.
विदर्भपति or °राजन् m. king of Vidarbha.
विदर्भीकौण्डिन्य m. N. of a teacher.
विदल a. split, burst, blossomed; n. chip, splint, esp. a split bamboo cane or a split pea.
विदलन n. bursting, splitting (trans.).
1विदान or विदान a. existing, being, real; usual, common.
2विदान n. dividing.
विदार m. rending, tearing, or cutting asunder.
विदारक a. tearing asunder, lacerating (—°).
विदारण a. (f. ई) & n. tearing or breaking asunder, splitting, piercing, crushing, wounding.
विदारिन् a. = prec. a.
विदाहिन् a. heating, burning.
विदित a. known, learnt, understood, known as (nom.), famous, celebrated; n. impers. or adv. with the knowledge of (—°).
विदितधर्मन् a. knowing what is right.
विदितभक्ति a. knowing i.e. practising devotion.
विदितात्मन् a. knowing the soul or the self.
विदिश् f. intermediate region (north-east etc.).
विदिशा f. = prec., N. of a city & a river.
विदीर्ण a. burst, torn asunder, opened.
विदुर a. wise, intelligent, clever in (—°); m. N. of an ancient hero.
विदुस् a. attentive, mindful.
विदूर a. distant, remote. n. विदूरम् far off, विदूरात् or °रतस् from afar, also = °रे far away.
विदूरता f.*, °त्व n. great distance.
विदूषक a. defiling; m. jester, buffoon, the confidential friend of the hero (d.)
विदृति f. the suture on the head.
विदेघ m. N. of a man.
विदेय a. to be given or granted.
1विदेव a. godless, impious.
2विदेव m. dicing.
विदेवन n. the same.
विदेश m. a foreign country, abroad.
1विदेह m. pl. N. of a people; m. the country or a king of the V.
2विदेह a. bodiless, dead, abstr. °त्व n.
विद्ध a. pierced, hit, wounded, hurt; affected or afflicted with (instr. or —°).
विद्मन् n. attention, knowledge; dat. as infin.
1†विद्य n. finding, getting.
2विद्य (adj. —°) = seq.; abstr. °ता f.
विद्या f. knowledge, learning, a discipline or science, esp. sacred knowledge (threefold) or magic, spell.
विद्यागुरु m. the teacher of a science.
विद्याग्रहण n. acquirement of knowledge.
विद्याधन n. the treasure of knowledge.
विद्याधर m. a class of genii (lit. keeper of knowledge); °चक्रवर्तिन् m. king of the Vidyādharas.
विद्याधरमहाचक्रवर्तिन् m. supreme king of the Vidyādharas, abstr. °र्तिता f.
विद्याधरेन्द्र m. king of the Vidyādharas, abstr. °ता f., °त्व n.
विद्याधार m. receptacle of knowledge, a great scholar.
विद्याधिगम m. the study of science.*
विद्यानुपालिन् a. keeping the hereditary science.
विद्याबल n. the power of magic.
विद्याभीप्सिन् a. desirous of knowledge.
विद्यामद m. pride in one's learning.
विद्यामय a. consisting in knowledge.
विद्यार्थ & °र्थिन् a. seeking for knowledge, desirous of learning.
विद्यावन्त् & °विद् a. having or knowing knowledge, learned.

विद्यावयोवृद्ध a. advanced in learning and age.
विद्याहीन a. wanting knowledge, uninstructed.
विद्युत् a. gleaming, glittering; f. lightning or a shining weapon.
विद्युत्य a. relating to lightning.
विद्युत्वन्त् a. containing lightning; m. cloud, N. of a mountain.
विद्युद्दामन् n. flash of lightning.
विद्युद्धस्त a. holding a glittering weapon in the hand.
विद्युन्मन् a. glittering, flashing.
विद्युन्महस् a. having a glittering sheen or whose delight is lightning.
विद्युन्माला f. garland of lightning, N. of a metre.
विद्युन्मालिन् a. poss. to prec.; m. N. of an Asura & Rākṣasa.
विद्युल्लता & **विद्युल्लेखा** f. flash of lightning (lit. a creeper & a line of lightning).
विद्योत a. & m. flashing, glittering.
विद्योतक a. illuminating.
विद्योतन a. = prec.; n. lightning.
विद्योतिन् a. illuminating (—°).
विद्रव m. running asunder, flight, panic.
विद्रावण a. & n. driving asunder, putting to flight; n. also flight.
विद्राविन् a. running away, flying.
विद्रुत a. run asunder, fled (n. impers.); scattered, destroyed; agitated, alarmed.
1**विद्रुम** n. coral.
2**विद्रुम** a. treeless.
विद्वंस् (**विदुंस्**) a. knowing, wise, learned, cunning; versed in, familiar with (acc., loc., or —°). Compar. **विदुंष्टर**, superl. **विद्वत्तम**.
विद्वज्जन m. a wise man.
विद्वत्ता f., **°त्त्व** n. knowledge, learning.
विद्वल a. knowing, cunning.
विद्विष् m. enemy, foe.
विद्विषन्त् & **°षाण** a. hostile, averse; m. = prec.
विद्विष्ट a. odious (abstr. **°ता** f.); hostile, opposite or contrary to (loc. or —°).
विद्विष्टि f. hatred, enmity.
विद्वेष m. = prec., aversion to (loc.), the being hated by (—°).
विद्वेषक a. hating, disliking (—°).
विद्वेषण a. causing hatred; n. the same as subst., also = **विद्वेष**.
विद्वेषिता f. hatred, enmity.
विद्वेषिन् a. hating, rivalling, inimical; m. hater, foe.
विद्वेष्य a. odious, hateful to (—°).
1**विध्**, **विधति** (**°ते**) serve a god (dat.); worship, honour with (instr.); offer, consecrate (acc.); be gracious or friendly (of a god). — **उप** worship, do homage.
2**विध्**, **विन्धते** lack, be destitute of (instr.); be bereft or alone.
3**विध्**, **विध्यति** v. **व्यध्**.
विधन a. having no riches, poor.
विधर्तृ m. distributer, arranger, maintainer, supporter; loc. as inf. to distribute or to hold.
1**विधर्म** m. distribution, disposition.
2**विधर्म** m. injustice, wrong.
3**विधर्म** a. illegal, unjust, wrong.
1**विधर्मन्** m. holder, supporter, arranger; enclosure, receptacle, limits; arrangement, disposition, direction.
2**विधर्मन्**, **°र्मिक**, & **°र्मिन्** a. = 3**विधर्म**.
विधवता f. widowhood.
विधवा f. widow (± **योषित्** **स्त्री**, etc.).
विधा f. part, proportion, measure, sort, kind; adj. —° often -fold, -like.
विधातव्य a. to be arranged, settled, caused, brought about, shown, manifested, aspired to, striven after, used, employed; n. impers.
विधातृ m. disposer, distributer, arranger, creator, N. of a god, often identif. with Brahman or a son of Brahman; also Fate personified, E. of Viṣṇu, Çiva etc.; f. **विधात्री** disposing, arranging, creating.
विधान n. disposing, arranging (also adj., f. **ई**); performing, accomplishing, creating, creation (also concr.); ordering, ordinance, rule, prescription, method; fate, destiny.
विधानोक्त a. prescribed by rule.
विधायक & **°यिन्** a. & m. regulating, ordering; builder, founder, author.

विधारण n. bearing, holding, stopping, restraining, suppressing.
विधारिन् a. ckecking, restraining (—°).
विधावन n. running to and fro.
विधि m. disposition, arrangement, ordinance, prescription, rule, method, way, procedure, means of (dat., loc., or —°); act, the action of (—°), performance, business, work; solemn act, ceremony; creation, fate, destiny; the Creator or Brahman.
विधिज्ञ a. knowing the law.
विधिदृष्ट a. prescribed by rule, regular.
विधिपूर्वकम् & °**पूर्वम्** adv. = **विधिवत्**.
विधिमन्त्रपुरस्कृतम् adv. according to rule and the sacred texts.
विधियज्ञ m. a regular sacrifice.
विधियोग m. observance of a rule; disposition of Fate.
विधिवत् adv. according to rule, in the right manner.
विधिवश m. the power of destiny.
विधिविपर्यय m. change of fortune, adversity.
विधिहीन a. destitute of rule, irregular.
1**विधुं** m. throb (of the heart).
2**विधुं** a. lonely; m. the moon.
विधुक्षय m. the wane of the moon.
विधुति f. shaking, tossing, chasing.
विधुंतुद m. E. of Rāhu (harasser of the moon).
विधुर m. robbed of the pole (carriage); i.g. bereft, alone; separated from, destitute of, lacking (—°); defective, incomplete; depressed, wretched, miserable; adverse, contrary, unfavourable; n. adv., as subst. adversity, misfortune.
विधुरता f., °**त्व** n. deficiency, want, misery.
विधुरदर्शन n. sight of adversity.
विधुरय्, °**यति** deject, depress.
विधूति f. = **विधुति**.
विधूनन a. causing to move hither and thither; n. shaking, agitating; waving, undulating; rejecting, removing.
विधूम a. smokeless.
विधूम्र a. quite grey.
विंधृत a. kept asunder, separated, distributed; shunned, avoided; kept back, detained, preserved; held, borne, worn, possessed, taken (resolution).
विंधृति f. division, partition (also concr.).
विधेय a. to be granted, procured, used, employed; to be (being) ordered or enjoined; to be established or stated; to be performed or done, shown or manifested; subject or obedient to, dependent on (gen. or —°). n. what is to be done, incumbency, duty.
विधेयता f., °**त्व** n. abstr. to prec.
विधेयात्मन् a. having the soul (self) well restrained.
विधेयी कृ make dependent, subdue, °**भू** P.
विधौत a. cleansed by washing.
विध्यात्मक a. having a positive form.
विध्वंस m. fall, ruin, destruction, harm, injury, violation (of a woman).
विध्वंसन a. & n. ruining, spoiling, destroying, violating.
विध्वंसिन् a. = prec. adj. + being ruined, perishing.
विध्वस्त a. raised (dust); decayed, perished, destroyed, lost.
विनत a. bent, curved, stooped; deepened, depressed; bowing to (gen.), humble; cerebralized (g.). m. a kind of ant, a man's name; f. **विंनता** N. of a daughter of Dakṣa.
विनति f. bowing down, bending to (loc.).
विनद m. cry, sound, noise; adj. °**दिन्**.
विंनद्ध a. untied, loosened.
विनम्र a. bent down, humble, modest.
विनयं a. removing. m. removal, withdrawal; training, breeding, discipline, good manners, modesty, courtesy.
विनयदत्त m. a man's name.*
विनयन a. removing, driving away; n. breeding, training, instructing in (loc.).
विनयिन् a. well-behaved, modest.
विनर्दिन् a. roaring.
विनशन n. disappearing, (± **सरस्वती**° or **सरस्वत्यास्**) the place where the river Sarasvatī is lost in the sand.
विनश्वर, f. **ई** perishable, abstr. °**ता** f., °**त्व** n.

विनष्ट a. lost, ruined; disappeared, perished; spoilt, corrupted, wretched.
वि॑नष्टि f. loss.
विनस a. robbed of the nose.
वि॑ना prep. without, except, beside (acc., instr., or abl.). **विनाकृत** separated from, bereft of (instr., abl, or —°); **°भूत** the same (instr.); **°कृत्य** without.
वि॑नाट m. bag.
विनाथ a. having no protector.
विनायक m. guide, conduct; E. of Ganeça, pl. a class of demons.
विनाश m. perdition, destruction, ruin, disappearance, loss.
विनाशक a. causing to disappear, destroying.
विनाशन a. (f. **ई**) & n. = prec.
विनाशिन् a. perishing or destroying.
विनाश्य a. to be destroyed; abstr. **°त्व** n.
विनिग्रह m. keeping separate, division; keeping down, check, control, restraint.
विनिद्र a. sleepless, awake, open, blossomed.
विनिन्द a. surpassing; f. **आ** abuse, blame.
विनिन्दक a. blaming, mocking, surpassing.
विनिपात m. ruin, destruction, death.
विनिमय m. change, permutation, reciprocity.
विनिमीलन n. closing (of a flower).
विनिमेष m. closing (of the eyes).
विनियोग m. distribution; commission, charge; use, employment; relation, correlation.
विनिर्गम m. going out, departure.
विनिर्जय m. conquest.
विनिर्णय m. decision, settled rule concerning (gen. or —°).
विनिर्माण n. meting out; making, building, construction.
विनिर्मुक्त a. hurled, thrown; escaped, freed from or rid of (abl., instr., or —°).
विनिर्याण n. going away, setting out.
विनिर्वृत्त a. proceeded or risen from (—°) finished, complete.
विनिवर्तन n. coming back, return; coming to an end, cessation.
विनिवारण n. keeping back or off.
विनिविष्ट a. dwelling, living, being in (loc. or —°), placed in or on (loc.).
विनिवृत्त a. returned, averted from or deprived of (abl. or —°); ceased, vanished, gone.
विनिवृत्ति f. cessation, discontinuation.
विनिवेश m. setting down, laying on; entrance, impression, vestige.
विनिश्चय m. settled opinion or firm resolution concerning (gen. or —°).
विनिश्चल a. motionless, steady like (—°).
विनिश्चित a. determined to (—°); ascertained, settled, certain, sure, n. adv.
विनिहित a. placed or fixed upon (loc. or —°); appointed, commissioned; disagreeing, not consenting.
विनीत a. broken in, trained, disciplined, educated, taught, versed in (loc. or —°); well-behaved, dignified; modest, humble. Abstr. **°ता** f., **°त्व** n.
विनीतात्मन् a. of modest mind.
विनीति f. good manners, modesty.
विनुत्ति f. expulsion.
विनुद् f. shock.
विनेतृ m. trainer, instructor, teacher.
1**विनेत्र** m. = prec.
2**विनेत्र** a. eyeless, blind.
विनेय a to be removed, taught, or punished.
विनोद m. expulsion, removal, diversion, entertainment, amusement.
विनोदन n. diversion, amusement.
विनोदिन् a. driving away, diverting, amusing.
विन्द a. finding, winning (—°).
1**विन्दु** a. knowing, familiar with (—°).
2**विन्दु** a. finding, winning, procuring.
3**विन्दु** v. **बिन्दु**.
विन्ध्य m. N. of the mountain-range separating Hindustan from Deccan.
विन्ध्यगिरि & **°पर्वत** m. the same.
विन्ध्यवन n. a forest in the Vindhya.
विन्ध्यवासिन् a. dwelling in the Vindhya.
विन्ध्याटवी f. = **विन्ध्यवन**.
विन्न a. found, f. **आ** married.
विन्यास m. putting down or on, placing, distributing, arrangement, order, disposition.
1**विप्**, **वे॑पते** (**°ति**) tremble, quake, vibrate; C. **वेपयति** shake, agitate. — **उद्** tremble, take fright. C. frighten. **परि** tremble. **प्र**

the same. C. shake, agitate. वि tremble, throb. सम् tremble, quake.

2विप् a. agitated, inspired. f. switch, rod, staff (of an arrow).

विपक्व a. cooked, done; ripened, matured.

1विपक्ष m. the day of transition from one half-month to another; adversary, rival; counter assertion or example.

2विपक्ष a. robbed of the wings.

विपक्षभाव m. state of a rival, enmity.

विपक्षस् a. going on both sides (of the chariot).

विपक्षीय a. inimical.

विपञ्ची f. the Indian lute.

विपण m. sale, traffic; bet, wager; trading-place, shop, market.

विपणन n. selling, trade.

विपणि f. sale, trade; shop, market.

विपणिगत a. being on the market, marketable.*

विपत्ति f. failure, adversity, calamity, destruction, ruin, death.

1विपथ s. wrong way, bad road.

2विपथ m. n. a waggon fit for bad roads.

विपथि a. being beside the road.

विपद् f. failure, misfortune, death.

विपन्न a. turned out bad, gone wrong, failed; wretched, ruined, lost, dead; abstr. °ता f.

विपन्या & विपन्यया (instr. adv.) wonderingly or wonderfully.

विपन्यु a. wondering or wonderful.

विपरिणाम m. change, transformation; adj. °मिन्.

विपरीत a. inverted, opposite, different, wrong, bad.

विपर्यय a. inverted, perverse; m. revolution (of the sun), expiration (of a time); failure (of conception); overthrow, inversion; opposition, the contrary of (gen. or —°); change, barter, alteration, esp. to the bad, reverse of fortune, calamity, ill luck, adversity; error, mistake.

विपर्यस्त a. inverted, changed; standing round.

विपर्यास m. upsetting (of a carriage), transposition, expiration (of a time); inversion etc. = विपर्यय.

विपर्यासोपमा f. a kind of comparison (rh.).

विपश्चित् a. agitated, inspired; wise, learned, clever in, familiar with (—°).

†विपस् n. agitation, inspiration.

विपाक a. ripe. m. ripening, maturity, consequence of actions; issue, result i.g.; digestion.

विपाकिन् a. ripening, bearing fruit or having consequences.

विपाट m. a kind of arrow (cf. विपाठ).

विपाटल a. deep-red.

विपाठ m. a kind of arrow (cf. विपाट).

विपाण्डु a. whitish, pale, abstr. °ता f.

विपाण्डुर a. = prec. adj.

विपान n. drinking off.

विपाप & विपाप्मन् a. faultless, sinless.

विपाल a. having no herd or keeper.

विपाश् f. N. of a river.

विपाश a. having no sling or fetters; f. आ = prec.

विपाशन n. untying.

विपाशिन् a. having no stiing.

विपिन n. wood.

विपुल a. large, wide, broad, thick, long, strong, intensive, important, numerous, much, many, loud. f. आ N. of a metre.

विपुलता f., °त्व n. largeness, extent, width.

विपुष्ट a. ill fed, famished.

विपुष्प a. flowerless.

विपृच्छम् acc. infin. to प्रछ्.

विप्र a. stirred inwardly, inspired, wise, learned, clever; m. seer, poet, singer, priest, a Brahman.

विप्रकर्ष m. drawing away, carrying off; distance, remoteness; contrast, difference.

विप्रकार m. doing harm, injuring.

विप्रकीर्ण a. scattered, diffused, loose (hair); expanded, wide.

विप्रकृति f. change, variation.

विप्रकृष्ट a. remote, far (w. *gen. or *abl.); abstr. °त्व n.

विप्रकृष्टान्तर a. separated by a longer distance.

विप्रजित्ति m. N. of a teacher.

विप्रता f. state or rank of a Brahman.

विप्रतापस m. a Brahmanical ascetic.

विप्रतिपत्ति f. false perception, delusion of the senses, error, mistake, discrepancy, conflict.

विप्रतिपन्न a. perplexed, confounded, bewildered; wrong, false.

विप्रतिषिद्ध a. forbidden, contrary; n. adv.

विप्रतिषेध m. checking, restraining; contrariety, discrepancy; negation.

विप्रतीप a. (turned backwards*); refractory, inimical.

विप्रत्यय m. distrust.

विप्रत्व n. = **विप्रता**.

विप्रदुष्ट a. corrupt, bad, libidinous.

विप्रनष्ट a. lost, vanished.

विप्रपुत्र m. a Brahman's son.

विप्रमुक्त a. hurled, shot off; driven away, absent; liberated from (instr. or —°).

विप्रयोग m. separation from (instr. ± **सह**, gen., or —°); absence, want, loss.

विप्रर्षभ m. chief (lit. bull) among Brahmans.

विप्रर्षि m. a priestly sage.

विप्रलम्भ m. deception, illusion or disillusion.

विप्रलम्भक a. deceiving; m. deceiver.

विप्रलम्भयितृ(क)* & **विप्रलम्भिन्** the same.

विप्रलुम्पक a. rapacious.

विप्रवत् adv. like a Brahman.

विप्रवास m. going or staying abroad; being outside (abl. or —°).

विप्रवासन n. banishment.

†**विप्रवाहस्** a. receiving the homage or oblation of singers.

1**विप्रवीर** m. a heroic Brahman.

2**विंप्रवीर** a. inspiring men or having inspired men.

विप्रश्न m. questioning Fate.

विप्रश्निक m. who questions Fate, astrologer.

विप्रस्व n. the property of a Brahman.

विप्रहीण or °**हीन** a. excluded from (abl.); disappeared, gone; destitute of (instr.).

विप्रापवाद m. abuse of a Brahman.

विंप्रिय a. disunited; not dear, unpleasant to (gen. or —°); n. something unpleasant.

विंप्रुत a. submerged, washed away.

विप्रुष् f. (nom. °**प्रुट्**) drop, spot, dot.

विप्रेन्द्र m. an excellent Brahman.

विप्रेमन् m. estrangement, alienation.

विप्रोषित a. abroad, absent, removed to (acc.); banished.

विप्लव m. ruin, fall, destruction, loss, calamity, distress; tumult, rebellion, violation (of a woman).

विप्लुत a. confounded, disturbed, disquieted, agitated, depraved, wicked, ruined, lost.

विप्लुष् f. a drop.

विफल a. fruitless, useless, unsuccessful, idle, vain; having no testicles.

विफलता f. uselessness.

विफलत्व n. fruitlessness (lit. & fig.).

विफली कृ render useless, frustrate, disappoint (°**भू** P.); emasculate.

विबल a. having no strength; weak.

विबाधं m. remover or removal.

विबाधंवन्त् a. driving away (Agni).

विबालीं f. N. of a river.

विबुद्ध a. awakened, expanded, blossomed; clever, skilful, versed in (loc.).

विबुद्धि a. unwise, unseasonable.

विबुध a. very wise; m. a wise man or a god.

विबुधराज m. king of the gods, Indra.

विबुधस्त्री f. divine female, Apsaras.

विबुधाधिप & °**पति** m. the same.

विबुधानुचर m. attendant of a god.

विबुधेश्वर m. lord of the gods.

विबोध m. awaking, perceiving, knowing.

विबोधन m. awaker, rouser; n. awaking or awakening.

विभक्त a. divided, separated by (instr. & —°) or from (instr.), isolated, lonely; distinct, different, manifold; regular, symmetrical. n. separation, isolation, loneliness.

विभक्तृ or **विंभक्तृ** m. distributer, arranger.

विंभक्ति f. division, distinction, modification; inflection, case, case-affix or personal ending (g.).

विभङ्ग m. bending, contracting (of the eyebrows); incision, furrow; interruption, disturbance, frustration.

विभजनीय & **विभज्य** a. to be divided.

विभञ्जनु a. breaking (intr.).

विभय a. dangerless, secure; n. as adv.

विभव a. rich. m. omnipresence, ubiquity,

evolution, development, growth; power, might, majesty, rank, high position; property, wealth, money.

विभवतस् adv. according to rank or fortune.

विभववन्त् & **°विन्** a. wealthy, opulent.

विभा a. shining; f. lustre, splendour, beauty.

विभाग m. distribution, apportionment, division, partition, esp. of an inheritance; share, portion, part; separation, distinction, difference.

विभागशस् adv. in parts, separately.

विभाज्य a. to be divided or distributed.

विभात a. shone forth, bright, luminous; n. daybreak.

†**विभानु** a. shining, resplendent.

विभाव & **विभावन्** a. the same.

विभावन a. & n. developing, manifesting; n. also perceiving, ascertaining; f. **आ** a cert. rhetor. figure.

विभावनीय a. to be perceived or understood.

†**विभावरी** adj. f. to **विभावन्**; f. the starlight night, night i.g.

विभावरीमुख n. evening (beginning of night).*

विभावसु a. resplendent. m. fire or the god of fire; the sun.

विभाविन् a. powerful; showing, manifesting, displaying.

विभाव्य a. to be perceived, perceivable, intelligible; to be heeded or attended to (n. impers.).

विभाषा f. alternative, option (g.).

विभाषित a. optional (g.).

विभास् f. splendour.

विभिन्दु a. splitting; m. N. of a man.

विभिन्न a. pierced, cleft, opened, blossomed, expanded, split asunder, destroyed; altered, disfigured, estranged, disunited, opposite, different.

विभी a. fearless; m. N. of a man.

1**विभीत** a. fearless.

2**विभीत** m. = seq.

विभीतक & **विभीदक** m. N. of a tree; n. its nut (used for dicing).

विभीषण a. terrifying, horrible. m. N. of a Rākṣasa etc.; n. frightening, terror.

विभीषणनामक, f. **°मिका** a. having a terrible name.

विभीषिका f. frightening, terror.

विभु & **विभू**, f. **विभू** & **विभ्वी** far-reaching, pervading, omnipresent; abundant, intense, powerful, mighty, able to (infin.). m. lord, ruler, chief of (—°), E. of Brahman, Viṣṇu, & Çiva; N. of a god etc.

विभुत्व n. omnipresence, might, power.

विभूति a. pervading, abundant, powerful, mighty, disposing of (gen.); f. development, growth, abundance, might, power, glory, majesty, splendour, success, welfare, fortune, prosperity, wealth, riches.

विभूतिमन्त् a. powerful, mighty.

विभूमन् m. growth, might.

विभूवस् a. mighty.

विभूषण a. adorning; n. ornament, splendour, beauty.

विभूषणवन्त् a. adorning.

विभूषा f. ornament.

विभेत्तृ m. breaker, piercer, destroyer.

विभेद m. breaking, splitting, piercing; bending, contracting (of the eyebrows), change, alteration; interruption, disturbance; falling asunder, decay; discord, difference.

विभेदन a. & n. splitting, piercing, separating.

विभेदिन् a. splitting, tearing, destroying.

विभ्रंश m. decay, disappearance, ruin, loss.

विभ्रंशिन् a. decaying, falling down or off.

विभ्रम m. unsteady motion, flurry, going to and fro, esp. of the eyes; coquetry, grace, beauty; confusion, agitation, error, mistake; erroneous application of (gen.); mistaking for, phantom or mere semblance of (—°).

विभ्रष्ट a. fallen, ruined; separated from, deprived of, thwarted in (—°); idle, vain; vanished, gone.

विभ्राज् a. shining.

विभ्रातृव्य n. rivalry, enmity.

विभ्रान्त a. moving to and fro, rolling (eyes); flurried, confused, bewildered.

विभ्रान्ति f. agitation, confusion, error, mistake.

विभ्वतष्ट a. fashioned by Vibhvan or by a skilful artificer; well made, perfect.
1**विभ्वन्** a. far-reaching, pervading.
2**विभ्वन्** a. capable, skilful, clever; m. N. of a Ribhu.
विमत a. disagreed, disunited.
1**विमति** f. disagreement, dislike, aversion.
2**विमति** a. stupid, foolish.
विमत्त a. discountenanced; ruttish.
विमत्सर a. free from envy or selfishness.
विमद a. free from intoxication, rut, or arrogance; m. **विमद** N. of a Rishi.
विमध्य s. middle, centre.
विमनस् a. very wise; out of one's senses or disheartened.
विमनस्क a. depressed, disheartened.
1**विमन्यु** m. longing for, desire.
2**विमन्यु** a. free from anger or wrath.
विमन्युक a. not angry or appeasing anger.
विमर्द m. crushing, pounding, stamping (with the feet); hostile encounter, fight, war, tumult; destruction, disturbance.
विमर्दक & **°कारिन्** a. crushing, destroying.
विमर्दन a. & n. = prec.; n. also war, fight.
विमर्दिन् (—°) = prec. adj.
विमर्श m., **°न** n. consideration, examination, dubitation.
विमर्शच्छेदिन् a. destroying doubt, unequivocal.
विमर्शिन् a. considering, examining (—°).
विमर्ष, **°र्षन** etc. = **विमर्श** etc.
विमर्ष्टव्य a. to be tried or inquired into.*
विमल a. stainless, clean, pure, bright; abstr. **°ता** f., **°त्व** n.
विमलमति a. pure-minded, honest.
विमलय्, **°यति** make pure or clear.
विमलात्मन् a. bright (-natured, the moon).
विमलानन a. bright-faced.
विमलिमन् m. purity, brightness.
विमलीकरण n. purification.
विमहन्त् a. very great.
विमहस् a. merry, gay.
विमांस n. bad meat.
विमातृ f. step-mother.
विमाथ m. shaking, pounding.
विमाथिन् a. crushing.

1**विमान**, f. **ई** measuring, traversing, pervading, esp. the sky. — m. n. sky-chariot (of gods etc.), waggon i.g.; palace, tower; n. extension, measure.
2**विमान** m. despising, contempt.
3**विमान** a. dishonoured.
विमानन n., **°ना** f. = 2**विमान**.
विमानयितव्य & **विमान्य** a. to be despised or dishonoured.
1**विमार्ग** m. wiping off.
2**विमार्ग** m. wrong road; a. being on it.
विमार्जन n. = 1**विमार्ग**.
विमित a. fixed, built; n. building, hall.
विमिश्र a. mixed, mingled, dissimilar; mixed, joined or furnished with (instr. —°).
विमुक्त a. unyoked, unharnessed, unbound, loosened, dishevelled (hair); deprived of (instr.), escaped or freed from (abl., instr., °— or —°); free from sin; clear (ship); emancipated (r.); given up, abandoned, relinquished by (°— or —°); hurled, cast, thrown, sent forth by (—°).
विमुक्तकण्ठम् adv. loudly, aloud (lit. with loosened throat).
विमुक्तमौनम् adv. breaking the silence.
विमुक्ति f. loosening, emitting, giving up (breath); release, liberation from (abl. or —°), final emancipation.
विमुख a. turning the face away or back, averted; turning off or abstaining from (loc., abl., gen. w. **उपरि**, or —°); opposed, unfavourable; abstr. **°ता** f.
विमुखय्, **°यति** turn off, avert.
विमुखी कृ the same, drive or bend back, put to flight; **°भू** P.
विमुखीभाव m. aversion.
विमुग्ध a. confused, perplexed; stupid, foolish, abstr. **°ता** f.
विमुच् f. stopping, halting (lit. unharnessing) or liberating; **विमुचो नपात्** the son of (happy) arrival or liberation, safe-guard or liberator (Pūṣan).
विमूढ a. = **विमुग्ध** + incertain of (—°).
विमूढभाव m. confusion, perplexity.
विमूर्छित a. thickened, coagulated; full of, resonant with (—°).

विमूल a. rooted out, eradicated.
विमृग्वरी f. cleanly.
विमृत्यु a. not subject to death, immortal.
विमृध् m. despiser, averter, enemy.
विमृध a. warding off the despiser.
विमृश m. consideration, dubitation.
1**विमृश्य** ger. after mature consideration.
2**विमृश्य** a. to be considered or examined.
विमेघ a. cloudless.
विमोक m. unharnessing, loosening, release etc. = **विमुक्ति**.
विमोक्तृ m., **°क्त्री** f. releaser.
विमोक्तव्य a. to be let loose, given up, hurled or thrown upon (loc. or dat.).
विमोक्ष m. getting loose, opening (intr.); loosening, setting free, sending forth, shooting off, giving, bestowing; release etc. = **विमुक्ति**.
विमोक्षण a. freeing from (—°); n. loosening, unbinding, emitting, giving up; liberating from (abl. or —°).
विमोक्षिन् a. partaking of liberation.
विमोचक a. liberating from (—°).
विमोचन, f. **ई** unharnessing, loosening, freeing from (—°); n. giving up, abandoning, unharnessing, halting, stopping, liberating from (abl.).
विमोच्य a. to be liberated.
विमोह m. confusion of the mind.
विमोहन a. perplexing, bewildering; n. = prec.
विमोहिन् a. = prec. a.
वियत a. stretched, expanded.
वियन्त् a. going asunder, dissolving, perishing; n. **वियत्** the air or sky (as the space between the two separated, i.e. heaven and earth).
वियुक्त a. divided, du. disunited (man and wife); separated from, rid of, -less (instr. or —°).
वियुत a. separated from, deprived of (instr. or —°); f. **आ** du. heaven and earth.
वियोग m. separation, division, loss of (instr. ±**सह**, abl., or —°); absence, want; getting rid of, abstaining from, giving up (**°यं गम्** be lost*).
वियोगवन्त् a. separated (from the beloved object).
वियोगिता f. separation, parting.
वियोगिन् a. separated (esp. of lovers) from (instr. or —°).
वियोजन n. liberation or separation from (—°).
वियोजनीय & **°ज्य** a. to be separated from (abl.).
1**वियोनि** or **°नी** f. womb of animals, also = **°ज** animal.
2**वियोनि** a. contrary to one's nature.
विरक्त a. discoloured, passionless, indifferent to or averse from (abl., loc., acc. w. **प्रति**, or —°).
विरक्ति f. indifference (cf. prec.); p. **°मन्त्**.
विरचना f. arrangement, putting on.
विरज a. dustless, passionless, pure.
विरजस् & **°जस्क** a. = prec.
विरत a. having desisted or ceased from (abl.), n. impers.; having given up or resigned (abl. or —°).
विरति f. resting, ceasing, abstaining from (abl., loc., or —°); conclusion, end. °— finally, at last.
विरप्श, f. **ई** swelling, full; m. abundance.
विरप्शिन् a. = prec. a.
विरम m., **°ण** n. ceasing, desisting, abstaining from (—°).
विरल a. having interstices or intervals, separated (in space or time), distant, thin, rare; abstr. **°ता** f.
विरलाय्, **°यते** be thin or rare.
विरव m. roaring, thundering.
विरश्मि a. rayless.
विरस a. juiceless, flavourless, insipid, disgusting, repugnant; n. adv.
विरह m. abandonment, separation from (instr. or —°); absence, want.
विरहित a. abandoned, forsaken, lonely, separated from, -less (instr. or —°).
विरहिन् a. separated, absent, -less (—°).
1**विराग** m. change or loss of colour, absence of passion; aversion or indifference to (loc., abl., or —°).
2**विराग** a. many-coloured or = seq.
विरागवन्त् & **°गिन्** a. passionless, indifferent.

विराज् a. shining, radiant, ruling; m. f. ruler, sovereign; f. high rank, distinction, (also m.) N. of a myth. being, the first progeny of Brahman, (ph.) the Intellect ruling over the collective aggregate of bodies, (only f.) N. of sev. metres.

विराज & °जिन् a. shining, resplendent.

विराज्ञी f. queen.

विराज्य n. reign, government.

विराट m. N. of an ancient king.

विरात्र s. the end of night.

विराद्ध m. offender, injurer.

विराध m. N. of a Rākṣasa.

विराधन n. failure.

विराम m. cessation, rest, end, pause, caesura, stop and its sign (g.).

विराव m. cry, sound, noise, hum.

विरावण a. causing to cry or howl.

विराविन् a. crying, bellowing, roaring; resounding with (instr.).

विरिक्त a. having purged.

विरिञ्च or °ञ्चि m. E. of Brahman.

विरुक्मन्त् a. shining; m. a bright ornament or weapon.

1विरुज a. causing pain.

2विरुज a. painless, sound, healthy.

विरुत a. & n. tinkling, sounding, singing (of birds), humming.

विरुति f. = prec. n.

विरुद्ध a. stopped, hindered; opposed, contrary, repugnant, hostile to (instr., gen., or —°); unwished for, hateful, odious, prohibited, dangerous.

विरुष्ट a. very angry.

विरूक्ष a. rough, harsh.

विरूढ a. grown forth, germinated, formed, risen; mounted or ridden by (instr.).

विरूप a. many-coloured, multiform, manifold, various, different from (—°); also = seq. Abstr. °ता† f.

विरूपक a. deformed, ugly.

विरूपय्, °यति deform, disfigure.

विरूपाक्ष, f. ई having deformed eyes; m. N. of a cert. divine being, E. of Çiva etc.

विरोक m. ray of light.

विरोकिन् a. shining.

विरोग m. health, a. healthy.

विरोचन a. illuminating; m. the sun.

विरोचिष्णु a. shining, bright.

विरोद्धव्य a. to be opposed or fought with; n. impers. (it is) to be fought.

विरोध m. obstruction, hindrance, disturbance; opposition, contradiction; adversity, injury, detriment, calamity; hostility, contest between (instr. ± सह or —°).

विरोधक a. opposed to, incongruous with (gen. or —°); also = seq.

विरोधकृत् a. causing hostility or sedition.

विरोधन a. opposed to, fighting with (—°); n. opposing, quarrelling, harming, injuring.

विरोधिता f., °त्व n. abstr. to seq.

विरोधिन् a. obstructing, hindering, (*rivalling, a match); disturbing, injuring, harming, repelling, hostile, inimical; m. adversary, foe.

विरोधोक्ति f. contradiction.

विरोधोपमा f. a kind of comparison (rh.).

विरोपण & °रोहण a. causing to grow together, heating.

विरोह m., °हण n. sprouting, growing; adj. °हिन्.

विलक्ष a. having no aim or missing the aim, ashamed, embarrassed; abstr. °त्व n.

विलक्षण a. of different character or nature; unequal to, different from (abl. or —°); various, manifold.

विलक्षित a. marked, knowable by (instr. or —°); puzzled, vexed.

विलग्न a. hanging, sitting or resting on, sticking or cleaving to, turned or fixed upon (loc. or —°); hanging down, pendulous; gone, past; thin, slender.

विलङ्घन n. springing over, striking against, harming, injuring.

विलङ्घिन् a. overstepping, transgressing (fig.); striking against, touching.

विलङ्घ्य a. to be overstepped or passed over (river); to be borne, tolerable.

विलज्ज a. shameless.

विलज्जित a. ashamed, abashed.

विलपन & °पित n. wailing, lamenting.

विलम्ब a hanging down; n. lagging, loitering.

विलम्बन n., **॰ना** f. retarding, delay.
विलम्बिन् a. hanging down, hanging or leaning on (loc. or —॰), hung with (—॰); lagging, loitering.
विलम्बित a. hanging down; laggering, loitering, retarded, slow; n. impers., as adv., or as subst. delay.
विलम्ब्य ger. lagging, loitering, slowly, so late.
विलय m. dissolution, destruction, disappearance.
विलयन a. dissolving, n. = prec.
विलसन a. coruscating etc. = seq.
विलसित a. shining, radiant, appeared, risen, moving to and fro, coruscating (lightning), sporting, dallying.
विलाप m. lament.
1**विलापन** a. & n. causing to lament.
2†**विलापन**, f. **ई** dissolving, melting, removing, destroying.
विलापिन् a. wailing, lamenting.
विलास m. appearance (rising or semblance); joy, merriment, petulance; joke, sport, play, esp. amorous pastime, dalliance, coquetry; grace, beauty.
विलासक, f. **॰सिका** moving hither and thither, dancing.
विलासगृह n. pleasure house.
विलासचाप or **॰धन्वन्** m. E. of the god of love.
विलासबाण m. the same.
विलासभवन n. = **विासगृह**.
विलासवती f. a coquettish woman.
विलासिकत्व n. abstr. to seq. adj.
विलासिन् a. flashing, beaming, moving to and fro, wanton, sportive, dallying with (—॰). m. husband, lover; f. **॰नी** a (wanton) woman; mistress, wife.
विलीन a. attached to, fixed upon, immersed in, sitting upon (loc. or —॰); covered, hidden; disappeared, vanished, gone; melted or dissolved into (—॰).
विलुण्ठन n. plundering, robbing, stealing.
विलुम्पक m. robber, destroyer.
विलुलित a. moved hither and thither, fallen down or asunder, disordered, confused.
विलेप m., **॰न** n. ointment, rubbing in.
विलेपिन् a. smearing, anointing.
विलोकन & **॰कित** n. look, glance; consideration.
विलोकिन् a. seeing, beholding, perceiving, observing.
विलोचन a. making see or seeing; n. eye.
विलोठिन् a. moving hither and thither.
विलोडन n. stirring up, churning.
विलोप m. loss, disturbance, destruction, injury, theft.
विलोपक a. destroying, plundering.
विलोपन n. destroying, omitting, stealing.
विलोपिन् a. destroying, omitting (—॰).
विलोप्तृ m. thief, robber.
विलोप्य a. to be destroyed.
विलोभन n. attraction, seduction.
विलोम & **विंलोमन्** a. against the hair or grain, contrary, refractory.
विलोल a. moving hither and thither, restless, unsteady.
विल्व v. **बिल्व**.
विवक्तन्त् a. eloquent.
विवंक्षण a. swelling (Soma).
विवक्षा f. desire of saying, teaching, expressing; meaning, sense (loc. or —॰), mere desire of saying etc., i.e. hesitation, doubt.
विवक्षित a. meant, intended, borne in mind (± **हृदि**), abstr. **॰त्व** n.
विवक्षु a. calling aloud; wishing to say or tell.
विवंचन a. decision, authority.
विवत्स a. having no calf; bereft of the young or children i.g.
विवत्सु a. = **विवदिषु**.
विवदन n. quarrel, contest.
विवदिषु a. wishing to speak.
विवध or **वीवध** m. carrying-yoke; burden, load, provisions, stock of grain, etc.
विवयन n. matting-work.
विवर m. n. opening, hole, fissure, interval, distance, flaw, fault.
विवरण n. opening, uncovering, explaining.
विवर्चस् a. splendourless.
विवर्जन n. abandoning, giving up; desisting from (abl.).
विवर्जनीय a. to be abandoned or given up.

विवर्जित a. abandoned by, destitute of, free from, -less (instr. or —°); left out—, not including (—°).
विवर्ण a. colourless or discoloured, pale; abstr. °ता f., °भाव m.
विवर्णवदन a. pale-faced.
विवर्त m. the turning or revolving one, i.e. the sky; whirl-pool, eddy; change, altered condition; the mere semblance of (—°).
विवर्तन a. turning, revolving, changing; n. the action of turning etc., moving hither and thither, wandering, roaming, turning away or back; turning point, change.
विवर्तिन् a. turning (intr.), moving in a circle, turning away or towards (—°), changing.
विवर्धन, f. ई (आ) increasing, strengthening, furthering (—°); n. growth, increase, welfare.
विवर्धिन् = prec. adj. (only f. & —°).
विवव्रि a. uncovered, bare.
विवश a. having no will, irresolute or indolent, acting involuntarily or against one's own will; abstr. °ता f.
विवसन & °वस्त्र a. unclothed, naked.
विवस्वत्सुत m. patron. of Manu.
विवस्वन् a. (only instr. pl.) = seq. adj.
विवस्वन्त् or **विवस्वन्त्** a. lighting up, matutinal; m. N. of a god, later E. of the sun or the god of the sun.
विवाक m. decider.
विवाच् a. calling to (i.e. challenging) each other; f. challenge, contest.
विवाचन m., ई f. arbiter, umpire; n. decision, authority.
विवाद m. (n.) quarrel, contest, dispute.
विवादपद n. the object of a contest.
विवादार्थिन् m. prosecutor, plaintiff.
विवादिन् a. disputing, litigating.
विवास् v. 4वा.
1**विवास** m. the lighting up, daybreak.
2**विवास** m. leaving home, exile.
विवासन n. expulsion, banishment.
विवासस् a. unclothed, naked.
विवास्य a. to be banished.
विवाह m. leading (the bride) home; wedding, marriage.
विवाहनेपथ्य n. wedding ornament.*
विवाहपटह s. wedding drum.
विवाहवेष m. wedding garment.
विवाह्य a. to be married (girl); fit for a matrimonial alliance; related by marriage. m. son-in-law.
विविक्त a. separated, detached, isolated, single, lonely, free from (instr. or —°); clean, pure, dainty, clear, distinct; n., °ता f. & °त्व n. separation, loneliness, etc.
विविक्तसेविन् a. seeking solitude.
विविक्तासन a. sitting in a lonely place.
विविक्ति f. separation, division, (right) distinction.
विविक्षु a. wishing or being about to enter.
विविग्न a. much frightened.
विविध a. of different kinds, various, manifold; n. adv.
विविधागम m. relating to various traditions.
विविधायुध a. having different weapons.
विवृत a. uncovered, bare, open, displayed, manifested, published, explained; n. adv.
विवृतपौरुष a. showing heroism.
विवृतभाव a. open-hearted, candid.
विवृति f. explanation, exposition.
विवृत्त a. turned round or back, whirled, bent.
विवृत्ताक्ष a. rolling the eyes.
विवृत्ताङ्ग a. distorting the limbs (in agony).
विवृत्ति f. expansion; hiatus (g.).
विवृद्ध a. grown, increased, enlarged, important, great, numerous, abundant.
विवृद्धि f. growth, increase, lengthening (of a vowel); thriving, welfare.
विवृद्धिद a. giving welfare.
विवेक m. separation, discrimination, discernment, examination, consideration, judgment insight, penetration; poss. °वन्त् & °किन्.
विवेकज्ञ a. having (lit. knowing) the right insight into (—°).
विवेकविश्रान्त a. void of judgment, unwise, foolish.
विवेकिता f., °त्व n. right discrimination or judgment.
विवेक्तृ a. who discriminates or judges right.
विवेचक a. discriminating (right).

विवेचन a. (f. **ई**) & n. discriminating, examining, or judging (right); for n. also f. **आ**.

विवोढृ m. husband.

विंव्रत a. refractory, stubborn.

1**विश्**, **विशति**, **॰ते**, pp. **विष्ट** (q.v.) enter, go in or into, sit or settle down on (acc. or loc.); go home or to rest, set (of the sun); get into a condition, undertake, begin (acc.); deal with (instr.), fall to the lot of, occur or happen to (acc.). C. **वेशयति** cause to enter (acc.) or sit down upon (loc.). D. **विविक्षति** wish to enter (acc.). – **अनु** follow, enter (acc.); follow a person (acc.) into (acc.). **आ** enter, pervade, settle down on or among (acc., r. loc.); inire (acc.); approach, get at, take possession of (acc.); get into a state or condition (acc.). C. cause to enter, put into (loc., r. acc.), turn or set upon, entrust or commit to (loc.). **अन्वा** enter, take possession of (acc.); follow, conform one's self to (acc.). **अभ्या** enter, penetrate (acc. or loc.). **उपा** the same, get into; visit, befall (acc.). **प्रा** come to (acc.); C. lead in, introduce. **समा** enter, penetrate, pervade (acc.), sit or settle down on (loc. or acc.); visit, befall (acc.); get into a condition (acc.); devote one's self to (acc.). C. lead or put into (acc.), turn upon (loc.), commit, entrust (loc.). **उप** approach (acc.); stop, sit or settle down, set (sun); cohabit (instr.); attend or apply one's self to (acc.). C. cause to sit down on, put in (loc.). **उपोप** sit down beside each other or at a person's (acc.) side. **पर्युप** sit around. **समुप** sit down or be seated (together). **नि** M. (A.) enter, penetrate, pervade (acc. or loc.); bite (of a leech); sit or settle down on (loc.), resort, turn, or attend to (acc. or loc.); establish one's self i.e. marry (man); stop, make a halt, come to rest, cease. C. cause to enter, cause to sit or settle down on (loc.); bring to rest; cause (a man) to marry, draw up or encamp (an army); lead, bring, put, transfer into (loc.); build, found, populate, make inhabitable (town etc.), throw or hurl upon, fix in, put on, turn or direct to (loc.), don (clothes); appoint to (loc.), confer upon (loc.). With **चित्रे** paint, w. **पत्रे** write down, w. **चित्ते** or **हृदये** call to mind. **अभिनि** M. (A.) enter or penetrate into, insist or be bent upon (acc.); belong to (loc.). C. lead into, turn or direct to, place or fix upon (loc.). **उपनि** C. encamp (an army), found (a city). **परिणि** settle down around. **विनि** put, place, fix, turn (loc.), appoint to, set about (loc.). **संनि** C. lead into (a house), lodge, set or lay down, draw up (an army); place, put, fix in or on, hurl upon (loc.); build, found; appoint to (loc.), load or confer upon (loc.). **निस्** enter (acc. or loc., ± **गृहेषु** become a householder, marry); pay back, restore; enjoy, delight in (acc.). **प्र** enter, get into (acc. or loc.); pierce, penetrate; reach, attain (acc.), enjoy carnally (acc.); attend to, be bent upon (acc., r. loc.); enter, make one's appearance (d.). C. cause to enter, lead in, introduce (loc. or acc.); lead home, marry; lay down, place, put etc. in (loc. or acc.); appoint, install; initiate into (acc.); write down. **अनुप्र** enter (after another), get into or among (acc., r. loc.), resort to (acc.). **संप्र** enter, go in, inire, take to, deal with (acc.). C. cause to enter, bring or lead into (acc.). **सम्** come near, approach; join (acc. or instr.); enter, go into (acc., r. loc.), settle down, go to rest; lie or sleep with (instr. ± **सह**, dat., or acc.), lie on or in (loc.). C. cause to lie down, set, place, put etc. on or in, bring into or to (loc.). **अनुसम्** go to rest after (acc.). **अभिसम्** assemble around (acc.). — Cf. **अनुप्रविष्ट**, **अभिनिविष्ट**, **अभिविष्ट**, **आविष्ट**, **उपविष्ट**, **निविष्ट**, **निंविष्ट**, **प्रविष्ट**, **विनिविष्ट**, **संनिविष्ट**, **समाविष्ट**.

2**विंश्** (nom. **विट्**) f. settlement, dwelling-place, house; sgl. & pl. community, tribe, people, esp. the third caste (= **वैश्य**), sgl.

a member of it. विश्पति m. E. of Indra & Agni; विशां पति m. prince, king.

विशङ्क a. fearless, not afraid of (—°), secure; n. adv.

विशङ्कट a. extensive, enormous, huge, awful, terrible.

1विशङ्का f. hesitation, suspicion, doubt, fear, apprehension.

2विशङ्का f. fearlessness, security, ease.

विशङ्कित a fearful, suspicious, uneasy about, anxious over (acc. w. प्रति or —°).

विशङ्किन् a. suspecting, expecting, apprehending.

विशङ्क्य a. to be suspected or apprehended.

विशद a. clear, pure, distinct, intelligible; tender, soft; dexterous, fit for (—°). Abstr. °ता f.

विशदय्, °यति cleanse, purify, make clear or explain.

विशदी w. कृ the same.

विशन n. entering, penetrating (—°).

विशय m. middle, centre; uncertainty, doubt, p. °वन्त् & °यिन्.

विशर a. tearing asunder; m. a cert. disease.

विशरारु a. falling asunder, decaying, frail, abstr. °ता f.

विशरीक m. N. of a cert. disease.

विशल्य a. having no point (arrow); having no (arrow-)point or wound, i.e. free from pain, N. of a man.

विशल्यकरण. f. ई healing arrow-wounds, f. a cert. medicinal herb.

विशसन, f. ई killing, murderous; m. sword; n. killing (an animal), cutting up, slaughter, fight.

विशसितृ & विशस्तृ m. who kills or cuts up (an animal).

विशस्त्र a. weaponless.

विशाख a. branchless or having spreading branches, forked; f. आ sgl. du. pl. N. of a lunar mansion, f. ई a forked pole (also °खिका f.); n. fork, ramification.

विशाखदत्त m. N. of a poet.

विशातन a. (f. ई) & n. hewing down, destroying.

विशारद a. experienced, knowing, wise; clever at, familiar with (loc. or —°).

विशाल a. extensive, wide, large; intensive, great, important. f. आ E. of the city of Ujjayinī.

विशालता f. extent, width.

विशालनेत्र a. large-eyed.

विशाललोचन a. = prec.

विशालाक्ष, f. ई the same.

विशिक्षु a. communicative, liberal.

विशिख & विशिख a. having no tuft of hair, bald; unfeathered or unpointed, blunt (arrow); m. a (blunt) arrow.

विशिरस् a. headless (also °स्क), pointless, topless.

विशिशासिषु a. ready to kill.

विशिष्ट a. separate, distinct, marked by (instr. or —°); peculiar, special; distinguished, eminent, excellent at (instr. or —°), best of (gen.); different from i.e. better or worse than (abl. or —°). Abstr. °ता f., °त्व n.

विशिष्टवर्ण a. & m. (of) a particular colour.

विशिंस् f. explanation.

विशीर्ण a. broken, torn, scattered, decayed, wasted, destroyed; abstr. °ता f.

विशीर्षन्, f. °र्ष्णी headless.

विशील a. bad-natured, immoral.

विशुद्ध a. completely purified or cleansed, pure, clear, bright; settled, absolved, finished. Abstr. °ता f., °त्व n.

विशुद्धभाव & °द्धात्मन् a. pure-hearted.

विशुद्धि f. purification, purity; p. °मन्त्.

विशुष्क a. quite dry, withered.

विशून्य a. quite void or empty.

विशूल a. having no spear or pike.

विशृङ्खल a. unfettered, unrestrained; immoderate, excessive, n. adv.

विशृङ्ग a. hornless, topless.

विशेष m. (n.) distinction, difference, special property, peculiarity; kind, species, individual; eminence, superiority; something extraordinary of, chief, first rate (°— or —°). — Instr., abl., & °— in a high degree, especially, particularly.

विशेषक a. distinguishing, qualifying; m. n. mark on the forehead.

विशेषकरण n. doing better, surpassing.

विशेषज्ञ a. knowing difference or different things; critical, wise, clever.
विशेषण a. & n. distinguishing, specializing; n. also doing better, surpassing; kind, species; the specializing word i.e. attribute, adjective, adverb, or predicate.
विशेषतस् adv. according to the difference of (—°); especially, in particular.
विशेषमण्डन n. a quite peculiar ornament.
विशेषय् v. 2शिष्.
विशेषवन्त् a. doing or having something peculiar or better.
विशेषविद् a. = विशेषज्ञ.
विशेषिन् a. different from or superior to (—°), individual.
विशेष्य a. what is distinguished or specialized; n. substantive, subject.
विशोक a. freed or freeing from grief.
विशोधन a. (f. ई) & n. purifying.
विशोष m. dryness.
विशोषण a. & n. drying up (tr. & intr.).
विशोषिन् a. = prec. a.
विश्पति m. chief of a settlement or a community; du. master and mistress of the house.
विश्पत्नी f. house-wife.
विश्पला f. N. of a woman.
विश्य a. forming or belonging to a community; m. a man of the third caste.
विश्रब्ध a. confident, fearless, secure; °— & n. adv.
विश्रब्धकार्य a. having a confidential or a candid business.*
विश्रब्धप्रलापिन् a. talking without restraint.*
विश्रब्धसुप्त a. sleeping peacefully.
विश्रम m., °ण n. rest, repose, relaxation.
विश्रम्भ m. trust, confidence in (loc., gen., or —°); unrestrained behaviour, ease.
विश्रम्भकथा f., °कथित n. confidential talk.
विश्रम्भगर्भकथा f. the same.*
विश्रम्भण n., °म्भता f. trust, confidence.
विश्रम्भालाप m. familiar conversation.
विश्रम्भिन् a. inspiring or enjoying confidence, confidential.
1**विश्रवस्** n. great renown, glory.
2**विश्रवस्** a. famous, glorious, N. of a Rishi.
विश्रान्त a. rested, refreshed, ceased; desisting from, i.e. destitute of, -less (—°).
विश्रान्ति f. rest, repose, cessation, end.
विश्राम m. rest, repose, deep breath; cessation, tranquillity; also = seq.
विश्रामभू f. place of rest.
विश्रामस्थान n. the same; object of recreation.
विश्रुत a. heard, learnt, understood, known as (nom.); famous, renowned.
विश्रुति f. celebrity, fame.
विश्लथ a. relaxed, languid.
विश्लिष्ट a. loosened, disjoined, seaparated.
विश्लेष m. disunion, disjunction, separation.
विश्लेषण a. dissolving, disuniting; n. = prec.
विश्लेषिन् a. getting loose, falling asunder; separated (from the beloved person).
विश्व a. all, every (n. every one); entire, whole, universal, pervading all (Viṣṇu, the intellect, etc.); pl. विश्वे (± देवास्) all the gods or the All-gods (as a class). m. the intellect (ph.); n. the All or Universe.
विश्वकर्मन् a. all-doing, all-creating; m. N. of a world-creating genius (similar to & often identified with Prajāpati), in l. l. the architect or artist of the gods.
विश्वकृत् a. & m. = prec.
विश्वकृष्टि a. dwelling among or known to all people, common or friendly to all.
विश्वगूर्त & †**विश्वगूर्ति** a. welcome to all.
विश्वचक्षण & °**चक्षस्** a. all-seeing.
विश्वचक्षुस् a. = prec.; n. aii-eye.
विश्वचर्षणि & **विश्वजन्य** a. = विश्वकृष्टि.
विश्वजित् a. all-conquering; m. N. of a cert. sacrifice.
†**विश्वजिन्व** a. all-refreshing.
विश्वज् a. all-impelling.
विश्वतस् adv. from or on all sides, all around.
विश्वतुर् & °**तूर्ति** a. all-surpassing.
विश्वतोमुख a. (having the face) turned everywhere, facing all sides.
विश्वत्र adv. everywhere, evermore.
विश्वथा adv. by all means, at all times.
विश्वदर्शत a. visible to all, all-conspicuous.
विश्वदानीम् a. always, evermore.
विश्वदाव & °**व्य** a. all-burning.
†**विश्वदावन्** a. all-giving.

विश्वदृश् a. all-seeing.
विश्वदृष्ट a. all-conspicuous.
विश्वदेव a. all-divine; m. pl. the All-gods (cf. विश्व).
विश्वदेव्य a. belonging or dear to all gods.
विश्वदोहस् a. milking or yielding all things.
विश्वध or °धा adv. by all means, always.
विश्वधामन् n. the universal home.
विश्वधायस् a. all-nourishing.
विश्वधृक् or °धृत् a. all-supporting.
विश्वधेन a. sating all with drink.
विश्वनाथ m. lord of the universe; E. of Çiva, a man's name.
विश्वनामन्, f. °म्नी having all names.
विश्वपिंश् & विश्वपेशस् a. having all sorts of ornaments or beauties.
विश्वप्सु a. appearing in all forms.
विश्वप्स्न्य a. the same.
विश्वभरस् a. all-supporting.
विश्वभानु a. all-illumining.
विश्वभुज् a. all-enjoying, all-consuming.
विश्वभृत् a. = विश्वभरस्.
विश्वभेषज, f. ई all-healing.
विश्वभोजस् a. all-giving or all-feeding.
विश्वमनस् a. mindful of all.
विश्वमिन्व a. impelling or moving all.
विश्वमूर्ति a. existing in all forms or whose form is the universe.
†विश्वमेजय a. all-exciting.
विश्वंभर a. supporting the universe, all-sustaining; m. fire, E. of Viṣṇu, f. आ the earth.
विश्वंभरकुलाय m. receptacle for fire.
विश्वयोनि m. or f. source or creator of the universe.
विश्वरूप (f. आ & विश्वरूपी) a. many-coloured, multiform, manifold, various. m. E. of Viṣṇu, N. of a son of Tvaṣṭṛ, of an Asura, & of sev. men.
विश्ववार & °वार्य a. containing or granting all goods or treasures.
1विश्वविद् a. all-knowing, omniscient.
2विश्वविद् a. all-possessing.
विश्ववेदस् a. = 1 2विश्वविद्.
विश्वव्यचस् a. all-containing, all-embracing.
विश्वशंभू a. causing welfare or happiness to all.
विश्वश्चुच् & विश्वश्चन्द्र a. all-sparkling.
विश्वश्री a. blessing all.
विश्वसख m. all-friend.
विश्वसत्तम m. the best of all (Kṛṣṇa).
विश्वसनीय a. to be trusted (n. impers.); abstr. °ता f.
विश्वसू f. bringing forth all.
विश्वसृज् m. (nom. °सृक्) all-creator.
विश्वसौभग a. bestowing all blessings.
विश्वस्त a. confident, fearless, trusting in (gen.); n. adv.
विश्वह (°हा) adv. always, at all times.
विश्वा adv. always, evermore.
विश्वाङ्ग a. having all limbs, complete.
विश्वाची f. common, universal.
विश्वात्मन् m. the soul of the universe, E. of Viṣṇu.
विश्वाद् a. all-consuming.
विश्वाधिप m. the lord of the universe.
विश्वानर a. = विश्वकृष्टि.
विश्वामित्र m. N. of a celebrated Rishi, pl. his race.
विश्वायु a. = विश्वकृष्टि.
विश्वावसु a. blessing all (Viṣṇu); m. N. of a Gandharva, a son of Purūravas, etc.
विश्वास m. confidence, trust in (loc., gen., instr. ± सह, or —°); private communication, secret.
विश्वासकार्य n. confidential matter.
विश्वासघात m. breach of faith.
विश्वासन n. producing confidence.
विश्वासपात्र n., °भूमि f. a trustworthy person (lit. vessel & place for confidence).
विश्वासभङ्ग m. breach of faith.*
विश्वासस्थान n. surety.
विश्वासह् (°साह्) a. all-conquering.
विश्वासिक a. trustworthy.
विश्वासिन् a. the same; also trustful.
विश्वास्य a. = विश्वसनीय.
विश्वाहा adv. = विश्वहा.
विश्वेश m. lord of the universe, E. of sev. gods.
विश्वेश्वर m. = prec. (f. ई); a man's name.
विश्वौजस् a. possessing all strength.
विश्वत्रा adv. everywhere.

1विष्, विवेष्टि & वेषति, I. वेवेष्टि, pp. विष्ट stir, bustle, work, be active, not rest (waters); serve, attend; accomplish, finish (food i.e. eat up), overcome, conquer. C. वेषयति clothe, dress. — उप serve, attend. परि the same, dress (food); P. have a halo (sun or moon).

2विष् (nom. विट्) f. excrement, faeces.

1विष m. servant, attendant.

2विष n. venom, poison; adj. f. आ poisonous.

विषकन्या & ॰कन्यका f. venom-girl (said to cause the death of her lovers).

विषकुम्भ m. a jar of poison.

विषकृत a. poisoned.

विषकृमि m. dung-beetle.

विषक्त a. hung, hanging or sticking in, turned upon (loc. or —॰); dependent on (—॰).

विषघात m. destroyer of poison, physician.

विषघ्न a. destroying poison.

विषज a. produced by poison.

विषङ्ग m. sticking, clinging; adj. ॰ङ्गिन्.

विषजिह्व a. venom-tongued.

विषण्ण a. dejected, sad, out of spirits.

विषण्णरूप a. of a sorrowful aspect.

विषण्णवदन a. looking sad or dejected.

विषतरु m. poison-tree.

विषता f., ॰त्व n. the being poison.

विषदायक & ॰यिन् a. giving poison, poisoning.

विषदिग्ध a. smeared with poison, poisoned.

विषदूषण, f. ई destroying poison.

विषद्रुम m. = विषतरु.

विषधर m. a venomous serpent (venom-holder).

विषम a. uneven, unequal, odd (number); different, changing; difficult, hard, adverse, cross, inimical; bad, mean, dishonest, false, wrong. n. unevenness, bad road, pit, precipice; difficulty, pain, distress, adversity; unequality, incongruency, incompatibility.

विषमत्व n. unequality, adversity.

विषमय, f. ई consisting of poison, poisonous.

विषमवृत्त n. an unequal metre (having different verses).

विषमशील a. cross-tempered.

विषमस्थ & ॰स्थित a. being in danger or difficulties.

विषमायुध & विषमेषु m. E. of the god of love, lit. the odd (i.e. five-)arrowed.

विषमी कृ make uneven or adverse, P. ॰भू.

विषमेषु m. = विषमायुध.

विषय m. reach, sphere, domain, province, country; the right place for (gen.); object, esp. of sense, pl. (sgl.) the pleasures of sense or the external world. छन्दसि विषये in the sphere of i.e. only in the Veda (g.). Adj. —॰ falling into the sphere of, belonging or relating to. — Abstr. ॰ता f., ॰त्व n.

विषयपराङ्मुख a. averse from the external world.*

विषयवन्त् a. having an object, objective.

विषयवासिन् a. living in a country; m. inhabitant of a country, countryman.

विषयसङ्ग m. addiction to sensual objects, ॰ज adj. sprung.

विषयात्मक a. given to sensual pleasures.

विषयान्त m. the boundary of a country.

विषयिन् a. sensual; m. sensualist, materialist.

विषयी कृ spread, diffuse; subdue, make a thing an object, P. ॰भू.

विषयीकरण n. abstr. to prec.

विषयोपसेवा f. indulgence in sensual pleasures.

विषरस m. a poisoned drink.

विषवन्त् a. poisoned, envenomed.

विषविटपिन् m. poison-tree.

विषविद्या f. toxicology.

विषवृक्ष m. = विषविटपिन्.

विषवेग m. the effect of poison.

विषवैद्य m. conjurer of poison.

विषहन् a. destroying poison.

विषहर, f. ई removing poison.

विषह्य a. practicable (± कर्तुम्), conquerable.

विषाक्त a. = विषदिग्ध.

विषाग्नि m. burning (l. fire of) poison.

विषाण n. (old also आ f.) horn (adj. —॰ f. आ & ई), tusk (of an elephant or Ganeça), claw (of a crab), nipple; point i.g.

विषाणवन्त् a. having horns or tusks; m. boar.

विषाणिन् a. = prec. adj.; m. elephant.

विषाद् a. eating poison.
विषाद् m. slackness, dejection, depression, aversion, disgust.
विषादन a. & n. causing despondency or depression.
विषादवन्त् a. = seq.
1**विषादिन्** a. dejected, sad.
2**विषादिन्** a. eating poison.
विषानल m. = **विषाग्नि**.
विषान्न n. poisoned food.
विषापह a. destroying poison.
विषाय्, °**यते** (°**ति**) become poison.
विषासहि a. conquering (gen.), powerful.
विषास्वाद् m. tasting poison.
विषित a. loosened, opened, unharnessed (lit. & fig.), let free.
विषितस्तुक a. dishevelled.
विषिन् a. poisoned.
विषु adv. on both sides (—°).
विषुण a. various, changing (moon); averse, hostile.
विषुणक् adv. asunder.
विषुप्त a. fallen asleep.
विषुरूप a. many-coloured, various.
विषुवत्संक्रान्ति f. equinox passage or the time of it (cf. seq.).
विषुवन्त् or **विषूवन्त्** a. belonging to both sides, i.e. middle, central. m. middle day (r.); n. equinox.
विषूचिका f. a kind of disease.
विषूची v. **विष्वञ्च्**.
विषूचीन a. going asunder, diverging, spreading.
विषूवृत् a. balancing (lit. & fig.).
विषोल्बण a. full of poison.
विष्कन्ध n. a cert. disease.
विष्कम्भ m. support; width, diameter; also = seq. m.
विष्कम्भक a. supporting; m. a kind of interlude or introductory scene (d.).
विष्किर m. scratcher, a kind of bird.
विष्ट् v. **आविष्टित**.
विष्ट a. entered etc., contained in (acc. or loc.); filled or joined with (instr.).
विष्टप् f., **विष्टप** n. (m.) highest part, surface, firmament, heaven.
विष्टब्ध a. fixed, firm (also **विष्टभित**); supported, stayed, stopped, hindered; stiff, rigid, motionless.
विष्टम्भ m. support, prop, obstruction, hindrance, resistance.
विष्टम्भन, f. **ई** supporting; n. obstruction, suppression.
विष्टम्भिन् a. supporting (fig.), obstructing.
विष्टर m. a bunch of reed-grass etc. to sit upon.
विष्टार m. straw (of the Barhis).
विष्टारपङ्क्ति f. N. of a metre.
विष्टारिन् a. spread (r.).
विष्टि f. bustle, stirring, activity, service; one's turn, times (—°).
विष्टिर् f. width, extent.
विष्टुत a. praised variously or abundantly.
विष्टुति f. mode of recitation.
1**विष्ठा** f. place, province, domain, division, party; kind, form.
2**विष्ठा** f. = 2**विष्**.
विष्ठित a. standing asunder, scattered, diffused, spread; fixed, standing or being in (loc. or —°).
विष्णु m. N. of a god; abstr. °**त्व**† n.
विष्णुक्रम m. pl. Viṣṇu's paces (r.).
विष्णुगुप्त m. E. of Cāṇakya.
विष्णुचक्र n. the discus of Viṣṇu.
विष्णुदत्त a. given by Viṣṇu, m. a man's name.
विष्णुपत्नी f. Viṣṇu's wife (Aditi).
विष्णुपद n. Viṣṇu's domain (the sky).
विष्णुपुराण n. T. of a Purāṇa.
विष्णुमय, f. **ई** coming from or belonging to Viṣṇu.
विष्णुमित्र m. a man's name.
विष्णुमुख a. headed by Viṣṇu.
विष्णुरूप a. bearing the shape of Viṣṇu.
विष्णुवन्त् a. accompanied by Viṣṇu.
विष्णुशर्मन् m. N. of an author.
विष्पर्धस् a. emulating.
विष्पश् m. (nom. **विष्पट्**) overseer.
विष्फुलिङ्ग m. spark.
विष्यस a. overflowing.
विष्यन्द m. drop; adj. °**न्दिन्**.
विष्यन्दन n. dropping, overflowing.

विष्वक्तन a. spread everywhere; numerous, abundant.

विष्वक्सेन m. E. of Viṣṇu-Kṛṣṇa.

विष्वग्गमनवन्त् a. going everywhere.

विष्वग्वृत्ति a. = **विष्वक्तन**.

विष्वञ्च्, f. **विषूची** turned to or being on both (all) sides; going asunder, splitting, spreading everywhere; diverging, averse or separated from (abl. or instr.). n. **विष्वक्** adv. sideways, all around, everywhere.

विष्वद्र्यञ्च् a. turned everywhere; n. **द्र्यक्** sideways, away.

विसंवाद m. contradiction, disagreement.

विसंवादिन् adj. to prec.

विसंष्ठुल or **°स्थुल** a. loose, tottering, unsteady.

विसंज्ञ & **°ज्ञित** a. unconscious.

विसंदृश, f. **आ** & **ई** unequal, inferior.

विसंधि a. having no joints (body); unallied.

विसंनाह a. without a coat of mail.

विसर m. plenty, abundance.

विसर्ग m. cessation, end; loosening, letting go; dismission, evacuation (of the body); gift, donation; hurling, throwing, casting, shooting off; production, creation (abstr. & concr.); a kind of aspiration & its sign (g.).

विसर्जन n. cessation, end; making cease, remove; letting go, dismission etc. = prec. as far as creation.

विसर्जनीय m. = **विसर्ग** (g.).

विसर्प m. spreading about, a kind of inflammation (also **°पिका** f.)

विसर्पण a. & n. spreading, increasing; n. also moving off, budging.

विसर्पिन् a. springing forth, coming out of (—°); moving to and fro, spreading, expanding.

विसर्मन् m. running asunder.

विसल्प m. a cert. disease.

विसार m. extending, diffusing, dissolving.

विसारथि a. having no charioteer.

विसारिन् a. coming forth, spreading, expanding.

विसूरण n. grief, sorrow.*

विसृत् f. flowing asunder.

विसृत a. expanded, stretched, slackened (bowstring), gone asunder; come forth or sprung from (—°); prominent (eyes).

विसृत्वर a. spreading.

विसृपस् abl. inf. to **विसृप्**.

विसृष्टि f. letting go, emanation, creation, esp. in detail.

विसोढ v. **सह्**.

विस्त m. a cert. weight.

विस्तर a. extensive. m. extent, width; spreading, expanding; abundance, multitude, completeness, prolixity, specification. Instr., abl., **°तस्**, & **°शस्** adv. diffusely, fully, in detail.

विस्तार m. spreading, expansion, diffusion, specification.

विस्तारिन् a. extending, large, broad.

विस्तीर्ण & **विस्तृत** a. strewed, scattered, covered; spread, expanded, developed, broad, wide, ample, numerous, far-sounding.

विस्पर्धा f. emulation.

विस्पर्धिन् a. vying with (—°).

विस्पष्ट a. visible, clear, distinct, intelligible; n. adv.

विस्पष्टार्थ a. having a clear sense.

विस्फार m. gaping, bursting, opening; the twang of a bow-string.

विस्फारित a. opened wide, torn asunder.

विस्फूर्ज m., **°र्जित** n. roaring, thundering.

विस्फोट m. crackling; boil, pustule.

विस्मय m., **°न** n. wonder, surprise.

विस्मयनीय a. wondrous, strange.

विस्मयान्वित (& **°याचिप्त***) a. astonished.

विस्मयिन् a. the same.

विस्मरण n. forgetting, oblivion.

विस्मापक & **°न** (f. **ई**) astonishing.

विस्मित a. astonished, surprised.

विस्मृत a. having forgotten (acc. or —°); being forgotten by (instr. or gen.).

विस्मृति f. forgetfulness, oblivion.

विस्मेर a. astonished, abstr. **°ता** f.

विस्यन्द etc. v. **विष्यन्द्**.

विस्र a. stinking of raw flesh.

विस्रगन्ध m. the stench of raw flesh.

विस्रगन्धिन्* a. = **विस्र**.

विस्रव m. flowing forth, flood.
विस्रंसस् abl. infin. to विस्रंस्.
वि॑स्रस्त a. fallen down or asunder, loosened, detached, slackened, languished.
विस्रुति f. = विस्रव.
विस्वर a. soundless or inharmonious.
विह (°—) air, the sky.
विहग m. bird (sky-goer).
विहगपति & विहंगेन्द्र m. the king of the birds, E. of Garuḍa.
विहंग m. = विहग.
विहंगम a. moving in the sky; m. a bird or the sun.
विहंगवाटी f. aviary, bird-cage.*
वि॑हत a. torn open, struck, hurt, visited, afflicted; hindered, disturbed, warded off.
विहति f. stroke, blow; defence, repulse.
विहन्तृ m. slayer, killer, destroyer.
विहर m. transposition, change.
विहरण n. = prec.; leading or walking about.
विहर्तृ m. robber; roamer, sporter.
विहव॑ m. invocation.
विह॑व्य or विहव्य॑ a. to be invoked or desired.
विहस्त a. handless, robbed of the tusk (elephant); unhandy, awkward; perplexed, helpless; quite intent upon or engaged in (— °).
विहाय ger. leaving behind or out; excluding, notwithstanding (acc.).
1वि॑हायस् a. powerful, vigorous.
2विहायस् n. the open air, space, sky, atmosphere; instr. through the air.
विहार m. (n.) distribution, arrangement, esp. of the sacred fires, & these themselves; expansion, esp. of the organs of speech; relaxation, recreation, amusement, sport, pastime, delight in (—°, also adj.); walking for pleasure, roaming about; place of recreation, pleasure-garden, grove; a Buddhist or Jaina temple or convent (also °रिका f.).
विहारक, f. °रिका finding or giving delight.
विहारदासी f. female servant of a temple or convent.
विहारदेश m., °भूमि f. pleasure-ground.
विहारवन n. pleasure-grove.
विहारवन्त् a. finding delight in (—°).
विहारवारि n. water to sport in.
विहारशयन n. pleasure-couch.
विहारशैल n. pleasure-mountain.
विहारस्थली f., °स्थान n. = विहारदेश.
विहारावसथ m. pleasure-house.
विहारिन् a. wandering about or = विहारक.
विहास m. laughter.
विहिंसक a. harming (gen. or —°).
विहिंसता f., °सन n., °सा f. abstr. to prec.
विहित a. distributed, appointed, settled, arranged, made, done, put, placed; endowed or furnished with (instr.).
विहिति f. proceeding, bringing about.
विहीन a. abandoned, deserted, deprived or destitute of (instr., abl., or —°); wanting, missing; low, mean.
विहृत n. walk, excursion.
विहृति f. extent, increase, sport, pleasure.
वि॑हृदय n. discouragement, despondency.
विहेठक a. harming, hurting.
विह्रुत् f. a snake or worm.
वि॑ह्रुत a. bent, broken.
विह्वल a. discountenanced, perplexed, confused, exhausted; n. adv.
1वी, वे॑ति, pp. वीत॑ (q.v.) seek, pursue, strive after, fall upon, attack, win, take hold of, enjoy; undertake, begin, urge, impel, further, promote; procure, get for, help to (2 acc.). — अति overtake, be superior to (acc). अप turn away (intr.). अभि drive on. अव seek after (acc.). आ approach, drive on or near, undertake, begin, seize, take hold of. उप strive after (acc.). नि (I. वेवेति) penetrate, rush into or among (loc.). प्र drive on, set in motion; impel, inspire; strive on or after, enter into (acc.); fall upon, attack; inire, impregnate. प्रति receive. — Cf. अभि॑वीत.
2वी॑ (nom. वी॑स्) v. देववी॑ & पदवी॑.
3†वी, I. वेवीयते flutter, flicker.
वीक्षण n. looking, viewing, considering; sight, eye.
वीक्षा f. looking at, examining; insight, knowledge.
वी॑क्षित n. look, sight.

वीचितव्य n. impers. to be looked or seen.
वीचितृ m. beholder.
1**वीचि** f. deception, seduction.
2**वीचि** or **वीची** f. wave.
वीज्, **वीजति**, **°ते** fan, blow on; C. **वीजयति** kindle (fire). — **अनु**, **अभि**, **आ**, **उद्**, **उप**, **परि**, **सम्** = S.
वीजन n. fanning or fan.
वीटा f. a small round pebble.
वीटिका f. button of a garment; ball, esp. a preparation of the Areca nut enveloped in a leaf of the betel plant.
वीड्, **वीडयति** (**वीळयति**) make (M. **°ते** be) strong or firm; pp. **वीळित** = seq. a.
वीडु or **वीळु**, f. **वीड्वी** strong, firm; n. stronghold.
वीड्वङ्ग a. strong-limbed.
वीणा f. lute.
वीणागाथिन् m. player on the lute.
वीणावाद m. player or playing on the lute.
वीणिन् a. having a lute or playing on it.
1**वीत** a. straight, even; wished for, desired, n. wish, desire.
2**वीत** a. gone, ceased (—°).
3**वीत** a. hidden, concealed; covered in, girt with (instr.).
वीतचिन्त a. free from care about (loc.).
वीतदर्प a. whose pride is gone, humbled.
वीतभय, **°भी**, & **°भीति** a. fearless.
वीतमन्यु a. free from anger or sorrow.
वीतराग a. dispassionate.
वीतव्रीड a. shameless, impudent.
वीतशोक a. sorrowless, abstr. **°ता** f.
वीतहव्य a. presenting desired oblations.
1**वीति** f. enjoyment, delight, profit, advantage, favourite food or drink.
2**वीति** f. separation.
वीतिहोत्र a. inviting to feasts or meals; m. fire or the god of fire.
वीथि or **वीथी** f. row, line, road, street, way, terrace, gallery, a kind of drama.
(**वीथिक** s.) & **°का** f. the same.
वीध्र (only loc. adv.) clear sky.
वीप्सा f. repetition, succession (g.).
वीर m. man, esp. hero, chief (also E. of sev. gods, esp. of Indra); husband, male child, son, coll. male offspring; also the male of an animal. Pl. men, people, retainers, followers.
वीरक m. little man.
वीरघ्नी v. **वीरहन्**.
वीरचर्या f. manly doing, seeking adventures etc.
वीरण n. a kind of fragrant grass.
वीरणस्तम्ब & **°क** m. bunch of grass.
वीरतम & **°तर** m. greatest & greater hero.
वीरता f., **वीरत्व** n. manliness, heroism.
वीरदेव m. a man's name.
वीरपत्नी f. the wife of a hero.
वीरपुर n. N. of a city.
वीरप्रसविनी & **°प्रसू** f. the mother of a hero.
वीरबाहु a. strong-armed; m. E. of Viṣṇu, N. of sev. princes etc.
वीरभट m. a brave warrior.
वीरमातृ f. the mother of a man (hero).
वीरमानिन् a. thinking one's self a man or hero.
वीरंमन्य a. the same.
वीरय्, **वीरयते** be like a man or hero.
वीरया (instr. adv.) courageously.
वीरयु a. courageous, bold.
वीरवन्त् a. rich in men (retainers or sons), manly, heroic; n. plenty of men.
वीरवर m. excellent hero, a man's name.
वीरवह (**°वाह**) a. carrying men.
वीरशय m. the couch of a (wounded or dead) hero.
वीरशयन n., **°शय्या** f. the same.
वीरसू a. bringing forth heroes; f. the mother of a son.
वीरसेन m. N. of a Dānava & sev. princes.
वीरहत्या f. the killing of a man(-child).
वीरहन्, f. **°घ्नी** & **°हणी** slaying men.
वीरासन n. hero-sitting (a cert. posture).
वीरिण m. n. = **वीरण**.
वीरिणी f. mother of sons, E. of Asiknī, a wife of Dakṣa.
वीरुध् f. (m.) herb, plant, esp. a spreading creeper.
वीरुध n., **वीरुधि** s. the same.
वीरेण्य a. manly, heroic.

वीरेन्द्र m. chief of heroes.
वीत्सा f. desire of frustrating.
वीर्य n. manliness, courage, strength, heroic deed, semen virile.
वीर्यकृत् a. doing manly deeds.
वीर्यवत्ता f., °त्त्व n. strength, might.
वीर्यवन्त् a. strong, effective, powerful, mighty, rich in semen.
1वीर्यशुल्क n. valour as purchase-price (for a wife).
2वीर्यशुल्क a. purchased by valour (wife).
वीर्यावन्त् a. = वीर्यवन्त्.
†वूर्य n. choice, election.
1वृ, वृणोति, वृणुते, वरति, °ते (cf. also ऊर्णु), pp. वृत (q.v.) cover, veil, hide; enclose, encompass, surround, guard; shut (a door); hold back or captive, ward off, hinder, restrain. C. वारयति, °ते keep back, hold prisoner, hide, conceal, hinder, stop, ward off, exclude, forbid, withhold. — अनु cover, veil, enclose, surround; C.M. hinder, stop. अप (अपा) uncover, open; C. hide. अपि veil. अभि cover, C. keep back, ward off. आ cover, veil, hide, surround, confine, bar, obstruct, occupy, fill. C. cover, hide, fill up, ward off. अपा uncover, lay open, show, manifest. प्रा cover, veil; put on, don; fill. समा cover, veil, enclose, surround, fill, stop, hinder. नि ward off; C. keep back, withhold, forbid, remove, banish. विनि C. keep back, hinder, stop, suppress, forbid, remove, dethrone. निस् be satisfied or pleased. परि cover, veil, surround; shut up, obstruct, hinder. C. encompass, surround, attend. संपरि C. surround, hem in. प्र ward off, C. the same. प्रति C. keep or send back, ward off, prohibit, contradict. वि A.M. uncover, open, unsheathe (a sword), illumine, display, manifest, explain. सम् A.M. cover over, hide, conceal, shut (a door); put together, bring in order; M. intr. gather, assemble, increase. अभिसम् cover, veil, surround, fill. — Cf. अपवारित, अपवार्य, अपावृत (sic!), अपीवृत (add.), 1अभिवृत, आवृत, निवृत, निर्वृत, परिवृत, परीवृत (sic!), पर्यावृत (add.), प्रावृत, विवृत, व्राण, संवृत.
2वृ, वृणीते, वृणाति, वृणोति, वृणुते, pp. वृत choose, esp. in marriage, woo, ask for; prefer, desire, wish, like. C. वरयति, °ते choose, ask, beg (2 acc.); esp. choose in marriage (± पतिम् or पत्नीम्). — अप M. content or satisfy with (instr.). अभि choose; prefer to (abl.). आ choose, desire; A. grant. निस् choose, pick out. परि M. choose, select. प्र M.(A.) choose, adopt. — Cf. 2अभिवृत.
वृक a. tearing, harming (cf. अवृक). m. (the tearer, either) wolf or plough, N. of an Asura etc.; f. वृकी a she-wolf.
वृकताति f. attempt at murder or robbery.
वृकति m. murderer, robber.
*वृकधूप m. incense or turpentine.
वृकल m. a bark garment; f. आ a cert. part of the bowels.
वृकलोमन् n. a wolf's hair.
वृकायु a. rapacious, sanguinary.
वृकोदर m. E. of Bhīmasena (wolf-bellied).
वृक्क m. du. the kidneys.
वृक्ण a. cut, torn, broken; n. a cut.
वृक्त a. turned, twisted, plucked (cf. seq.).
वृक्तबर्हिस् a. who has plucked or spread the sacrificial grass, i.e. sacrificing, pious.
वृक्य m. du. = वृक्क.
वृक्ष m. tree, plant, esp. a tree with (visible) flowers or fruits.
वृक्षक m. a small tree.
वृक्षच्छाया f. the shade of a tree.
वृक्षदेवता f. the deity of a tree, dryad.
वृक्षनिर्यास m. the exudation of trees, gum, resin.
वृक्षमय, f. ई made of wood, wooden.
वृक्षमूल n. the root of a tree.
वृक्षारोपक m. a planter of trees.
वृक्षारोहण n. the climbing of trees.
वृक्षवाटिका f. a grove of trees.
वृक्षशाखा f. a branch of a tree.
वृक्षाग्र n. the top of a tree.
वृक्षादन m. a carpenter's chisel (lit. tree-eater); f. ई N. of a plant.

वृक्षाश्रय a. living on trees.
वृक्षौकस् m. ape (lit. tree-dweller).
वृक्ष्य n. fruit of a tree.
वृज्, वृणक्ति, वृङ्क्ते, pp. वृक्त turn, twist off, pluck out (the sacrificial grass), turn or set aside, remove; M. avert, keep away, withhold. C. वर्जयति (°ते), pp. वर्जित (q.v.) abandon, shun, avoid, exempt, spare; renounce, resign; leave out, exclude. P. be deprived of or excluded from. — अप avert, remove, scare away; turn or tear off; finish, conclude. C. abandon, avoid, renounce, yield, grant, present, offer (a funeral meal); keep (a promise), conclude, finish. अपि procure to, turn upon (loc.). अव turn off, sever; C. remove, destroy. आ procure, afford, furnish; take to one's self, appropriate; withhold from (abl.); be favourable to (acc.). C. bend, incline, make favourable, win over. व्या separate, divide. समा take to one's self, appropriate; C. bend, incline. उद् remove, destroy. नि bend down, cause to fall, cast away. परा turn away (trans. & intr.), flee; tear off, remove, reject, abandon. परि turn round, give way, avoid, spare, exempt from (instr.); reject, turn out. C. keep off, remove, shun, avoid, abandon. प्र strew (the sacrificial bed); set in or at the fire, heat or glow. सम् take to one's self, appropriate. — Cf. आवर्जित, परिवृक्त, विवर्जित.
वृजन (वृंजन) n. enclosure, either sacrificial ground or enclosed settlement, dwelling or the dwellers; also = f. वृजिन crooked way, trick, cheat, art, stratagem.
वृजिन a. crooked, false, artful, mischievous; n. & f. आ falsehood, fraud, sin.
1वृत्, वर्तते, °ति, ववर्त्त (वर्त्ति), pp. वृत्त (q.v.) turn, revolve, roll, run off, pass away (time); go on, take place, happen, occur; abide, live, exist, be (also as simple copula), become; find one's self, feel (w. adv.); (± वृत्तिम्) deal with, act, proceed (adv. or instr.); behave towards (loc.), have intercourse with (सह, loc. with a woman); be concerned or occupied with (loc. or dat.); live or subsist on or by (instr.); conduce or tend to (dat.); be valid or supplying from a previous rule (g.). With मूर्ध्नि stand at the head, be chief in importance; w. हृदि or मनसि be turned or thought over in the mind; किं वर्तते how is it with (gen.); आत्मनि न वर्तते he is beside himself (with joy etc.). C. वर्तयति. °ते cause to turn or roll, whirl about, brandish, turn i.e. fabricate by turning; spend, pass (time); lead a life, exist (± जीवितम्); live on or by (instr.); maintain, observe; perform, accomplish, make, do, utter; show, manifest; explain, tell, relate. I. वर्वर्त्ति, वरीवर्त्ति, वरीवृत्यते turn, roll, be present, exist. — अच्छ C. bring near. अति intr. pass away (time), cease or desist from (abl.); trans. pass by, cross over, go beyond; overcome, resist, escape, transgress, neglect, omit, forget. व्यति intr. = prec., tr. (w. acc.) cross over, pass, overcome, escape. समति intr. run away, tr. (w. acc.) pass by, escape. अधि roll over (loc.); move or turn towards (adv. in तस्). अनु intr. pass or rise after, last, continue, also = S. (g.); tr. (w. acc.) roll after, follow, pursue, adhere, cling to, equal in (instr.), consent, agree, obey, oblige, be devoted to or intent upon, conform one's self to or depend upon, fall into or partake of. C. cause to roll on, cause to follow or pursue, join to (loc.); recite, answer. समनु go after, follow, conform one's self to (acc.). अन्तर् C. mix with (loc.). अप turn off or aside, go away, withdraw. व्यप the same, desist from (abl.). अभि move or turn towards (acc. or adv. in तस्), rise, appear, take place; approach, advance (as friend or foe), meet, encounter, attack, conquer. समभि approach, go against (acc.); come near or back; rise, appear. आ A. (M.) turn or roll hither, sc. रथम् = come to; turn around, pass by (acc.); M. roll near or back (intr.),

revolve; go down, set; (± पुनर्) return, also = be born anew; be repeated or renewed. C. turn or come to (± रथम्); bring near, attract; turn round, invert, disturb, destroy; bring back, repeat, recite. I. move quickly, stir. अन्वा M. roll after or along, follow; I. the same. अपा turn away from (abl.). अभ्या turn towards, resort to (acc.). C. approach (sc. रथम्), repeat. उपा turn towards, resort to (acc.), arrive at (acc. or loc.); turn from (abl.), return, come back. C. turn hither (tr.), bring near or back; obtain, win. अभ्युपा turn towards, get to, partake of (acc.). पर्या turn round or away, turn into (instr.). C. put instead of something else. अनुपर्या go after or along, follow. अभिपर्या turn towards or around. प्रत्या turn towards (acc.); return, come back. व्या turn away or back (intr.); separate from or part with, get rid of (instr. or abl.); open, burst, split into (adv. in धा); cease, come to an end. C. sever or free from (instr. or abl.); remove, destroy, annul. समा turn back, return, go home (esp. of a pupil after his apprenticeship); approach, come hither; turn towards (acc.); come off, take place, pass away. C. drive home (cows), dismiss (a pupil). अभिसमा & उपसमा return. उद् spring off, go out, disappear from (abl.), burst asunder, boil up, swell. C. burst asunder (tr.), destroy, ruin. उप tread upon, approach, appear, befall. नि turn round (tr. & intr.); return (also into life i.e. be born again); turn away, flee, abstain or desist from, get rid of (abl.); end with or at (abl.); not belong to, be withheld from (abl.), stop, pause, cease, disappear. C. turn downwards, bring or lead back, keep off, avert from (abl.), give up, let go, withhold, suppress, annul; refuse, deny; grant, procure, perform, accomplish. अभिनि return; C. repeat. उपनि return, be repeated. प्रतिनि turn back from (abl.), escape. C. lead back, turn off, avert. विनि turn back, desist from, renounce (abl.); cease, disappear, vanish, be extinguished (fire). C. lead or draw back, avert, annul, frustrate. संनि turn back, return from (abl.); stop, pause; abstain or desist from (abl.), pass away. C. send or lead back, divert from (abl.); stop (tr.), suppress. निस् roll out, come forth, develop, grow, become (nom.), be performed or finished, return. C. bring forth, create, effect, perform, accomplish. अभिनिस् come forth, develop; C. bring about, accomplish. परा turn the back upon (abl.), turn round (उदक् towards the north), return; abstain or desist from (abl.). परि turn round, move in a circle, roll (w. हृदये run in the mind); roam, walk about (acc.); return, go back to (acc.), be reborn in (loc.), change, alter (± अन्यथा); abide, dwell; act, proceed, behave. C. turn round (tr.), move about, upset, alter, change, renew; turn topsy turvy i.e. confuse, destroy. विपरि turn round, roll (w. हृदये = prec.), roam about, change, alter. संपरि the same + come back, return; get rid of (abl.). प्र turn forward, set out, move on; come forth, rise, appear, originate from (abl.), come off, take place, happen, occur; undertake, begin, set about, prepare for (infin., dat., loc., or अर्थम्); act, proceed, deal with (loc.); work, be valid, cause, effect; rest or be turned upon (loc.); last, continue; become, be present, exist; have the sense or meaning of (loc.). C. set in motion, hurl, cast, or send away; introduce, establish, appoint; produce, accomplish; form, make; show, exhibit; undertake, begin; use, employ. अतिप्र come forth abundantly. अभिप्र move or roll towards, fall into (acc.); set out, get in motion. संप्र come forth, rise, begin, undertake, prepare for (dat. or loc.); deal with, behave towards (loc.). C. set in motion, set abroad, divulge, introduce; undertake, begin. वि roll, run, turn, wallow, struggle; sink (sun); turn or run away, part with (instr.);

come forth, rise from (abl.), expand, develop. C. turn, roll, contract (the brows); form, shape, make of (instr.); remove, keep off or asunder. **सम्** turn towards, approach, meet, encounter (as friends or foes), assemble, unite; take shape, come into being, originate or rise from (abl.), happen, take place, begin, be, become, be present, exist. C. turn to (acc.); roll, clinch (the fist); envelop, cover; hurl, cast; break, destroy; perform, accomplish. **अभिसम्** turn to (acc.), prepare for, begin (infin.). — Cf. **अतिप्रवृत्त, अतिवृत्त, अनुवृत्त, अपवृत्त, अपावृत्त, अभिप्रवृत्त** (add.); **अभ्यावृत्त, अभ्युपावृत्त, आवृत्त, उद्वृत्त, उपावृत्त** (sic!), **निर्वृत्त, निवृत्त, परिवृत्त, प्रवृत्त, विनिर्वृत्त, विनिवृत्त, विवृत्त, व्यावृत्त, संवृत्त, संनिवृत्त, समावृत्त.**

2**वृत्** (—°) enclosing, surrounding; f. attendance, band, troop, army.

3**वृत्** (—°) turning, moving, existing, being; after numerals -fold.

वृत a. covered, veiled, hidden, enclosed or surrounded by, endowed with, full of (instr. or —°).

वृता f. progress, motion.

1**वृति** f. enclosure, hedge, fence.

2**वृति** f. choice, selection, request.

वृत्त a. turned, round; happened, passed; finished, accomplished; ceased, gone, died; being, present (°—); become; having behaved towards (loc.). — n. occurrence, appearance, event, adventure; cause, matter; conduct, behaviour, practice; verse, metre.

वृत्तकर्षित a. distressed for subsistence.

वृत्तकाय a. round-bellied (leech).

वृत्तज्ञ a. knowing the conduct of (gen.).

वृत्तवन्त् a. round; also = seq.

वृत्तशालिन्, **°सपन्न**, & **°स्थ** a. well behaved, virtuous.

वृत्तान्त m. occurrence, adventures; report, story, tale.

वृत्ति f. turning, rolling; being, existence, livelihood, maintenance (acc. w. **कृ** or **कल्प्** & instr. live on or by); mode of being or acting, conduct, behaviour, esp. good conduct or respectful behaviour towards (gen. or —°); devotion to or pursuit of (loc. or —°); usage, practice, rule; nature, character, style (d.); action, activity, function or force of a word; commentary on a Sūtra.

वृत्तिन् a. occupied with, living by (—°).

वृत्तिमन्त् a. the same; acting like.

वृत्तौजस् a. displaying strength.

वृत्त्यर्थम् adv. for the sake of subsistence.

वृत्र m. coverer, besetter, encloser, N. of a demon, the chief enemy of Indra; n. (m.) i.g. foe or host of foes.

वृत्रतर m. a worse foe or Vṛtra.

वृत्रतुर् a. overcoming foes or Vṛtra.

वृत्रतूर्य n. abstr. to prec.

वृत्रपुत्रा f. Vṛtra's mother.

वृत्ररिपु m. Vṛtra's foe, E. of Indra.

वृत्रविद्विष् & **°वैरिन्** f. the same.

वृत्रहं a. slaying foes or Vṛtra.

वृत्रहत्य n, **वृत्रहथ** m. abstr. to prec.

वृत्रहन्, f. **°घ्नी** = **वृत्रहं**; m. E. of Indra.

वृत्रहन्त m. = prec. m.

वृत्रारि m. = **वृत्ररिपु.**

वृथक् adv. = seq.

वृथा adv. at will, at pleasure; freely, gaily, at random; in vain, for nothing, falsely, wrongly (often °—).

वृथाट्या f. useless travel.

वृथोत्पन्न a. begotten in vain.

वृद्ध a. grown up, adult, large, tall, strong, intense, great, high, important, aged, old, skilful, clever, distinguished or eminent by (instr. or —°); glad, cheerful, haughty, arrogant; subject to Vṛddhi (g.).

वृद्धकोल m. an old boar.

वृद्धगर्ग m. the elder Garga.

वृद्धचाणक्य m. the elder Cāṇakya.

वृद्धता f., **°त्व** n. old age.

वृद्धभाव m. the same.

वृद्धमहस् a. high-potent.

वृद्धयोषित् f. an old woman.

वृद्धरङ्क m. an old beggar.*

वृद्धवयस् & **°शवस्** a. very strong or mighty.

वृद्धविट m. an old bon-vivant.*
वृद्धशर्मन् m. N. of a king.
वृद्धशाकल्य m. the elder Çākalya.
वृद्धसृगाल m. an old jackal.
वृद्धसेवा f. reverence for the aged.
वृद्धसेविन् a. honouring the aged.
वृद्धायु a. vital, vigorous.
वृद्धि f. growth, increase; swelling, rising, ascending; thriving, prosperity, happiness; delight, enthusiasm, inspiration; gain, profit, interest (on money lent); the highest gradation of a vowel (cf. **गुण**).
वृद्धिकर, f. **ई** causing increase.
वृद्धिजीवक & **°जीवन** a. living by usury.
वृद्धिद a. the same.
वृद्धिमन्त् a. increasing, strong, mighty.
वृद्धिश्राद्ध n. a kind of funeral meal.
वृद्धोक्ष m. an old bull.
वृद्धोपसेविन् a. = **वृद्धसेविन्**.
1**वृध्**, **वर्धति**, **°ते**, pp. **वृद्ध** (q.v.) A. make to grow, elevate, strengthen, cheer, gladden, rouse, inspire; M.(A.) grow, thrive, increase in (acc.); spread, expand, lengthen (days); be blessed or fortunate (± **दिष्ट्या**). C. **वर्धयति**, **°ते** A. elevate, rear, bring up, promote, further, make great or strong; delight, cheer, inspire (M. intr. or refl.). — **अति** grow beyond. **अनु** grow after another or in proportion with (acc.); grow or increase gradually. **अभि** grow up, grow stronger or greater, thrive or increase in (instr.), spread, expand, grow beyond (acc.), surpass. **आ** A. cause to grow, M. grow, increase. **परि** grow up, increase, get stronger or mightier. C. cause to swell (the sea); rear up, foster; gladden, delight. **प्र** A. elevate, exalt, inspire; M. (A.) grow on or up, thrive, be animated or inspired. C. strengthen, augment, lengthen, bring up, promote, further, exalt. **अतिप्र** grow beyond (acc.), surpass, exceed. **संप्र** grow, increase, augment, thrive. **वि** grow, increase, swell, thrive, be blessed or fortunate; rise, originate. **संवि** thrive. **सम्** A. grant, fulfil (a wish); grow, increase. C. make to grow or thrive, bring up, rear, nourish, feed, strengthen, promote, cherish, embellish. — Cf. **अतिप्रवृद्ध**, **अतिवृद्ध**, **प्रवृद्ध** (sic!), **विवृद्ध**, **संवृद्ध**.
2**वृध्** a. pleased, merry, inspired; gladdening, increasing, strengthening.
वृध a. = prec.; m. comforter, promoter, friend.
वृधसान a. growing or rejoicing.
वृधस्नु a. cheerful, merry.
वृधीक a. a match for (gen.).
वृधे dat. inf. to 1**वृध्**.
वृन्त m. a cert. creeping animal or a kind of plant; n. leaf-stalk.
वृन्तक (adj. —°), f. **वृन्तिका** = prec. n.
वृन्द n. heap, multitude, herd, troop, band; **वृन्दैस्** & **वृन्दशस्** in groups or in large numbers.
वृन्दार m. a god.
वृन्दारक, f. **°रिका** being at the head of, the best or finest among (loc. or —°).
वृन्दावन n. N. of a sacred grove.
वृन्दिन् a. containing plenty of (—°).
वृश or **वृष** m. N. of a man.
वृश्चिक m. scorpion.
वृष्, **वर्षति**, **°ते**, pp. **वृष्ट** (q.v.) rain (either pers. w. Parjanya, Indra, etc. as subj., or impers.), pour down, shed or cover with (instr.); loc. **वर्षति** while it is raining. C. **वर्षयति** cause to rain or let fall down as rain; sprinkle or cover with (instr.). — **अभि** rain, pour down; sprinkle or cover with (instr.). **अव** & **आ** the same. **प्र** begin to rain, pour or shower down; sprinkle or cover with (instr.). **प्रति**, **वि** C., & **सम्** = prec. w. instr.
वृष m. man, husband, male of animals, esp. bull (old only —°), w. **गवाम्** the first of the dice; i.g. chief or best of (gen. or —°); E. of Çiva, Viṣṇu, etc., N. of sev. men.
वृषक m. a cert. plant, N. of a king.
†**वृषकर्मन्** a. acting like a man (hero) or like a bull.

वृषक्रतु a. manly-minded.
वृषखादि a. wearing big bracelets or rings.
वृषण m. scrotum, du. the testicles.
वृषणश्व a. drawn by stallions.
वृषण्य्, °ण्यति be in rut.
वृषण्वन्त् a. yoked with or drawn by stallions.
वृषण्वसु a. having rich treasures.
वृषत्व & °त्वन n. manhood.
वृषदंश m. cat (lit. = seq.).
वृषदन्त्, f. °दती strong-toothed.
1वृषध्वज m. a flag with a bull.
2वृषध्वज a. having a bull for a sign; m. E. of Çiva.
वृषन् a. manly, potent, strong. m. man, stallion, bull, boar, E. of sev. gods, esp. of Indra; f. वृषणी mare.
वृषनाभि a. having strong naves.
वृषपर्वन् a. strong-jointed, E. of Viṣṇu etc.
वृषपाणि a. strong-hoofed.
वृषप्रयावन् a. moving on with stallions.
वृषप्सु a. looking strong.
वृषभ a. manly, potent, strong; m. bull, first or best of (gen. or —°), chief, lord etc.
वृषभकेतु & °ध्वज a. & m. = 2वृषध्वज.
वृषभयान n. ox-waggon.
वृषभषोडशा f. pl. (± गो) fifteen cows and a bull.
वृषभानु m. N. of Rādhā's father.
वृषभानुजा f. patron. of Rādhā, T. of a play.
वृषभैकसहस्रा f. pl. (w. गो) a thousand cows and a bull.
वृषभैकादशा f. pl. (w. गो) ten cows and a bull.
वृषमणस् & °मण्यु a. strong-minded, manly, courageous.
वृषयु a. ruttish, petulant.
वृषल or वृषल m. little man, low person, esp. a Çūdra (f. वृषली).
वृषलता f., °त्व n. the condition of a Çūdra.
वृषलवृत्ति a. who gains his subsistence from Çūdras.
वृषलीपति m. the husband of a Çūdra woman.
वृषव्रत a. bearing strong sway or ruling over men.
वृषव्रात a. forming a strong band (Maruts).
वृषसेन a. having a host of men; m. a man's name.
वृषस्य्, °स्यति desire the male, be in rut.
वृषाकपि m. strong ape or man-ape, a mythol. being; E. of the sun, of Indra, etc.
वृषाङ्क a. & m. = 2वृषध्वज.
वृषान्न n. nourishing food.
1वृषाय्, °यति cause (acc.) to rain.
2वृषाय्, °यते be or roar like a bull, show manly strength or courage, be lustful or eager; rush upon (acc., dat., or loc.).
वृषायुध् a. fighting men.
वृषारव m. a kind of animal.
वृष्ट a. (having) rained; loc. वृष्टे when it has rained.
वृष्टि or वृष्टि f. rain (lit. & fig.).
वृष्टिपात m. a shower of rain.
वृष्टिमन्त् or वृष्टिमन्त् a. rainy, raining.
वृष्टिवनि & °सनि a. causing or giving rain.
वृष्टिसंपात m. = वृष्टिपात.
वृष्णि or वृष्णि a. manly, potent, strong; m. ram, E. of Çiva etc., pl. N. of a princely race.
वृष्णिपाल m. shepherd.
वृष्ण्य a. = seq.; n. manliness, vigour.
वृष्ण्यावन्त् a. manly, vigorous.
वृष्य a. causing manliness; m. E. of Çiva, n. an aphrodisiac.
वे m. (nom. वेस्) = 1वि.
वेक्षण n. = अवेक्षण.
वेग m. jerk, wrench, shock; gush, flood; violence, haste, speed, quick motion; onset, eruption, burst, paroxysm, effect (of a poison); impulse, agitation.
वेगवन्त् a. swelling, undulating, rapid.
वेगित & वेगिन् a. the same.
वेगोदग्र a. of rapid effect (venom).
वेङ्क m. pl. N. of a people.
वेङ्कट m. N. of a mountain.
वेट् v. seq.
वेट्कार m. the exclamation Veṭ (r.).
वेण m. worker in reed (a cert. caste); f. आ N. of a river.
1वेणातट m. the bank of the river Veṇā.

2वेणातट m. pl. N. of a people.
वेणि or वेणी f. a braid of hair, hair twisted into a single braid (cf. एकवेणि).
वेणीसंहार m. T. of a play.
वेणु or वेणु m. reed, esp. bamboo-reed (poss. °मन्त् †); also = seq. sgl.
वेणुक m. flute, fife; pl. N. of a people.
वेणुदल n. split bamboo-reed.
वेणुमय, f. ई made of bamboo-reed.
वेणुयव m. pl. bamboo seed, f. ई an oblation of it.
वेणुयष्टि f. a bamboo staff.
वेणुविदल n. split bamboo; °वैदल a. made of it.
वेतण्ड m. elephant.
वेतन n. wages, price.
वेतनादान n. non-payment of wages.
वेत्तवे & वेत्तवै dat. inf. to 3विद्.
वेतस m., f. ई the ratan, a kind of large reed.
वेतसवृत्ति a. pliable, supple (cf. prec.).
वेताल m. a kind of goblins or vampires.
वेतालपञ्चविंशति & °का f. the 25 tales of the Vetāla (T. of sev. collections).
1वेत्तृ m. knower, witness.
2वेत्तृ m. husband.
वेत्र m. n. a kind of reed; n. also staff.
वेत्रधारा f. a female door-keeper (lit. staff-bearer).
वेत्रयष्टि & °लता f. a staff of reed or cane.
वेत्रवन्त् a. poss. to वेत्र; f. °वती = वेत्रधारा, N. of a river.
वेत्रासन n. seat or chair of cane.
वेत्रिन् m. staff-bearer, i.e. door-keeper.
1वेद m. knowledge, esp. sacred knowledge, the (triple) Veda.
2†वेद m. finding, obtaining.
3वेद m. a tuft of strong grass used to sweep, to kindle fire, etc.
4वेद m. N. of sev. men.
वेदज्ञ a. knowing the Veda.
वेदतत्त्व n. the true nature of the Veda.
वेदतत्त्वार्थ m. the true meaning of the Veda, °विद् a. knowing it.
वेदता f. possession, wealth.
वेददर्शिन् a. = वेदज्ञ.
1वेदन a. making known, announcing; (also f. आ) understanding, knowledge; f. आ (also n.) feeling, sensation, esp. pain, ache.
2वेदन a. finding, getting, procuring (—°); n. finding, acquiring, marrying (of both sexes), wealth, property.
वेदनिन्दक a. reviling the Veda.
वेदनिन्दा f. abstr. to prec.
वेदपारग a. having got to the end of the Veda, i.e. thoroughly versed in it.
वेदपुण्य n. merit acquired by the (study of the) Veda.
वेदप्रदान n. imparting or teaching the Veda.
वेदफल n. the fruit of the (study of the) Veda.
वेदबाह्य a. external to the Veda, not based on it.
वेदब्रह्मचर्य n. Veda-apprenticeship.
वेदयज्ञ m. a sacrifice prescribed by the Veda.
वेदयितृ m. knower, perceiver.
वेदरहस्य n. the secret of the Veda i.e. the Upanishad.
वेदवन्त् a. familiar with the Veda.
वेदविद् a. knowing the Veda; superl. °वित्तम.
वेदविद्या f. the knowledge of the Veda.
वेदविद्वंस् a. = वेदविद्.
वेदवेदाङ्गपारग a. having gone through the Veda and the Vedāngas, well read in both.
वेदवेदाङ्गविद् a. knowing the Veda and the Vedāngas.
वेदशास्त्र n. the doctrine of the Veda, °विद् a. knowing it.
1वेदस् n. knowledge.
2वेदस् n. wealth, property.
†वेदस v. सर्ववेदस.
वेदसंहिता f. a collection or redaction of the Veda.
वेदसंन्यासिक a. who has gone through and gives up the study and ritual of the Veda.
वेदाङ्ग n. a limb of the Veda, i.e. one of the 6 auxiliary works belonging to it.
वेदादि m. the beginning of the Veda, the sacred syllable Om (also n.).
वेदाधिगम m. the study of the Veda.
वेदाध्ययन n. the same.

वेदाध्याय & °यिन् a. who studies or has studied the Veda.

वेदानध्ययन n. neglecting the study of the Veda.

वेदानुवचन n. repeating or reciting the Veda.

वेदान्त m. the end of the Veda or of the Veda-study; N. of a philos. system.

वेदान्तकृत् m. the author of the Vedānta.

वेदान्तविद् m. a knower of the Vedānta.

वेदान्तसार m., °सूत्र n. T. of works.

वेदान्तिन् m. a follower of the Vedānta.

वेदाभ्यास m. the study of the Veda.

वेदार्थ m. the meaning of the Veda; °विद् a. knowing it.

वेदि or वेदी f. the sacrificial bed or altar (excavated in the ground and covered with grass or straw); i.g. support, pedestal, bench.

वेदिका f. the same.

वेदितव्य or °तव्य a. to be known.

वेदितृ or वेदितृ m. knower.

1वेदिन् a. knowing or making known (—°).

2वेदिन् a. marrying (—°).

वेदिपुरीष n. loose earth of the sacrificial bed.

वेदिषद् a. sitting in or on the altar.

वेदिष्ठ (superl.) procuring most (acc.).

वेदीयंस् (compar.) knowing or finding better than (abl.).

वेदुक a. obtaining (acc.).

वेदोक्त & वेदोदित a. taught or contained in the Veda.

वेदोपकरण n. supplement or subordinate science to the Veda.

वेद्धृ m. piercer, nom. also who will pierce or hit (fut.).

1वेद्य a. to be (being) known or learned; notorious, famous.

2वेद्य a. to be acquired or married.

वेद्या f. knowledge, as instr. really, indeed.

वेद्याकृति f. a kind of altar.

वेध m. piercing, opening.

वेधक m. piercer.

वेधन n. piercing, hitting.

वेधस् a. pious, devout, true, faithful, good, virtuous, honest, capable, clever, wise. m. worshipper, servant of the gods; author, creator, E. of Brahman (± प्रथम), of Prajāpati, Çiva, etc.

वेधस्या (instr.) f. worship.

वेधित v. व्यध्.

वेधिन् a. piercing, hitting (—°).

वेध्य a. to be pierced or perforated.

वेन्, वेनति long for, desire; be envious or jealous. — अनु strive to entice or win. अप & वि turn away disdainfully.

वेन, f. ई longing for, desirous of, loving; m. longing for, wish, desire (also f. आ), a man's name.

वेन्य a. desirable, lovely, N. of a man.

वेप् v. 1विप्.

वेप a. (f. ई) & m. trembling, shaking.

वेपथु m. tremor.

वेपथुभृत् & °मन्त् a. = seq. a.

वेपन a. & n. trembling, shaking.

वेपस् n. = prec. n.

वेपिष्ठ (superl.) most inspired.

वेम m. a loom.

वेमक m., ई f. weaver.

वेमन् n. loom or shuttle.

वेला f. end-point, limit; either boundary of the land and of the sea i.e. shore, coast; or point of time, hour, day-time; also right time, opportunity, last hour, hour of death; tide, flow (opp. ebb).

वेलाजल & वेलाम्भस् n. flow-water, flow (opp. ebb).

वेलासलिल n. the same.*

वेलाहीन a. untimely, premature.

वेल्ल्, वेल्लति, pp. वेल्लित move to and fro, tremble, reel, undulate. — उद्, वि, & सम् = S. — Cf. उद्वेल्लित.

वेल्लन n. waving, rolling.

वेविज a. rapid, quick.

1वेश m. settler, neighbour; dwelling, tent, house, esp. brothel.

2वेश v. 1वेष.

वेशत्व n. settlement, neighbourhood.

वेशन n. entering, entrance.

वेशन्त m., वेशन्ता & वेशन्ती f. pond.

वेश्याभाव m. the nature of a courtezan.

वेश्यावधू & °वनिता f. a courtezan.

वेश्यावास m. brothel.

वेशंस् m. settler, neighbour.
वेशान्ता f. pond.
वेशिन् a. entering (—°).
वेशी f. pin.
वेश्मन् n. dwelling, house, chamber.
वेश्य n. neighbourhood; bondage, dependence.
वेश्यस्त्री & वेश्याङ्गना f. = seq.
वेश्या f. whore, courtezan (intranda).
वेश्यापुत्र m. whoreson.
1वेष m. work, activity, attendance; dress, external appearance.
2वेष a. working, active.
वेषण or वेषण n., वेषणा f. waiting on, attendance, service.
वेषधारिन् a. having the dress or appearance of (—°).
वेषान्यत्व n. change of dress.
वेष्क m. a noose for strangling.
वेष्ट्, वेष्टते wind around (intr.), cling or stick to (loc.). C. वेष्टयति, °ते, pp. वेष्टित wind or tie round; wrap, envelop, cover, enclose, surround. — अनु C. wrap, cover; spread. अप C. strip off. अभि wrap, cover. आ spread or expand over (loc.); C. wrap, cover, clothe; twist (a string); enclose, confine. उद् unwind, unfasten, untwist, unseal. उप C. wind round, embrace. नि clutch, grasp, wrap. निस् strip off, bare. परि wind or put around; wrap, cover, enclose, surround. वि strip off; wrap, envelop. सम् roll or shrink together. C. wrap, envelop, cover; cause to roll or shrink together.
वेष्ट m. snare, noose, knot.
वेष्टन n. winding round, wrapping, covering, enveloping; wrapper, bandage; turban, diadem; enclosure, fence.
वेष्टुक a. clinging, sticking.
वेष्ट्य m. head-band.
वेसर m. a mule.
वेहत् f. a barren or miscarrying cow.
वै a particle emphasizing the preceding word or merely expletive.
वैकक्ष n. upper garment, mantle, also = seq.
वैकक्षक n. a garland of flowers hanging down from the shoulder.
वैकर्ण m. du. N. of two tribes.
वैकर्त m. a cert. part of the sacrificial victim.
वैकर्तन a. relating to or descended from the (god of the) sun; m. E. of Karṇa.
वैकल्पिक, f. ई optional, arbitrary.
वैकल्य n. infirmity, imperfection, deficiency, want, absence; despondency, perplexity.
वैकारिक, f. ई resting on or undergoing a change; n. = seq.
वैकार्य n. change, alteration.
वैकालिक n. evening meditation or meal.
वैकुण्ठ m. E. of Indra or Viṣṇu; m.n. Viṣṇu's heaven.
वैकृत a. produced by change, derived, secondary; altered, disfigured, ugly; unnatural, artificial. n. change, alteration, degeneration, unnatural condition or apparition; aversion, enmity.
वैकृत्य n. = prec. n.
वैक्लव n. confusion, agitation, distress.
वैक्लव्य n., °ता f. the same.
1वैखानस m. a class of Rishis & cert. stars; a Brahman of the third order, ascetic, hermit (f. °सी).
2वैखानस a. relating to hermits or ascetics, monastic.
वैगुण्य a. bad quality, fault, defect.
वैचित्त्य n. confusion or absence of mind.
वैचित्र्य n. variety, diversity.
वैजयन्त m. Indra's banner, also = f. ई banner, flag i.g.
वैजयन्तिका f. flag, banner; a kind of necklace.
वैजात्य n. unequality, heterogeneousness.
वैडूर्य n. (m.) the cat's eye (a kind of gem).
वैण m. = वेण.
वैणव, f. ई made of bamboo-reed; m. flute.
वैतस, f. ई made of reed, reed-like; °सी वृत्तिः f. flexibility, pliantness.
वैतान & °निक a. relating to the three sacred fires, sacrifiaial.
वैतानकुशल a. skilled in fire-rites.
वैतालिक m. a king's bard or praiser.
वैतालीय a. belonging to the Vetālas; n. N. of a metre.

वैदग्धी f., **°ग्ध्य** n. knowingness, cleverness, skill at (loc. or —°).

वैदर्भ, f. **ई** relating to the Vidarbhas, a prince or princess of the Vidarbhas, pl. the Vidarbhas.

वैदिक, f. **ई** Vedic, scriptural, sacred.

वैदिश m. a prince of Vidiçā, pl. its inhabitants.

वैदूर्य v. **वैडूर्य**.

वैदेशिक (f. **ई**) & **°श्य** coming from abroad, foreign.

वैदेह, f. **ई** living in or coming from Videha; m. **वैदेह** (± **राजा**) a king of Videha (f. **°ही** a cow from Videha, E. of Sītā); pl. N. of a people & a mixed caste (also **वैदेहक**).

वैद्य a. learned; m. physician, doctor.

वैद्यनाथ m. chief of physicians, a man's name.

वैद्यराज m. king of physicians, E. of Dhanvantari.

वैद्याधर, f. **ई** relating to the Vidyādharas.

वैद्युत a. relating to lightning; flashing, glittering.

वैद्रुम a. consisting or made of corals.

वैधर्म्य n. unlawfulness, injustice; unequality, difference.

वैधव m. patr. of Budha (son of the moon).

वैधवेय m. the son of a widow.

वैधव्य n. widowhood.

वैधस, f. **ई** fatal, m. patr. of Hariçcandra.

वैधुर्य n. loneliness, absence, want.

वैधेय a. foolish, silly (lit. struck by Fate); m. fool, idiot.

वैनतेय a. descended from Vinatā, E. of Aruṇa & Garuḍa.

वैनयिक, f. **ई** relating to discipline or moral conduct.

वैनायक, f. **ई** belonging to Vināyaka i.e. Ganeça.

वैन्य m. patron. from Vena.

वैन्ध्य a. relating to the Vindhya.

वैपरीत्य n. inverted order, contrary.

वैपुल्य n. largeness, width, great extent.

वैफल्य n. fruitlessness, uselessness.

वैबुध, f. **ई** relating to the gods, divine.

वैभव n. might, power, high position, majesty, grandeur.

वैभाषिक a. optional, arbitrary.

वैभीत, **°तक**, & **°भीदक** a. coming from the Vibhītaka tree, made of its wood (dice).

वैभ्राज n. N. of a celestial grove.

वैमत्य n. dissension.

वैमनस्य n. dejectedness, uneasiness.

वैमल्य n. spotlessness, purity.

वैमात्र a. born of a different mother, w. **भ्रातृ** m. = seq.

वैमात्रक & **°त्रेय** m. step-brother.

वैमानिक, f. **ई** riding in a sky-chariot, i.e. celestial, divine.

वैमुख्य n. aversion, repugnance to (loc. or —°).

वैमूल्य n. difference of price.

वैयर्थ्य n. uselessness.

वैयाकरण m. grammarian.

वैयाघ्र a. coming from a tiger; n. a tiger's skin.

वैयास & **°सिक** a. coming from or composed by Vyāsa.

वैर a. hostile, revengeful; n. enmity, quarrel with (instr. ± **सह** or **सार्धम्** & —°).

वैरकर a. causing enmity or hatred.

वैरकारिन् a. beginning quarrel.

वैरकृत् a. hostile, malicious, quarrelsome.

वैरदेय n. enmity, revenge, punishment.

वैरयातना f. requital of enmity, retaliation.

वैरवन्त् a. hostile, inimical.

वैरस n. aversion, disgust.

वैरस्य n. the tasting bad or being repugnant, also = prec.

वैरहत्य n. killing men.

वैराग्य n. losing colour or turning pale; absence of passion, indifference, repugnance.

वैराज a. coming from Virāj or relating to the metre Virāj.

वैराट a. relating to or descended from Virāṭa.

वैराय्, **°यते** commence hostilities, becoming inimical to (**प्रति** or instr.).

वैरिक m. foe, enemy.*

वैरिता f., **°त्व** n. enmity, hostility.

वैरिन् a. inimical, m. enemy.

वैरी भू change into hatred.

वैरूप m. pl. N. of a class of the Añgiras.

वैरूप्य n. variety, difference; deformity.
वैरोचन a. belonging to or coming from the sun; m. E. of Viṣṇu, N. of a prince etc.
वैलक्षण्य n. diversity, unequality.
वैलक्ष्य n. sense of shame, embarrassment, perplexity.
वैवर्ण्य n. change of colour.
वैवस्वत, f. **ई** coming from the sun, relating to Yama or Manu; m. patron. of Yama or Manu.
वैवाह a. nuptial.
वैवाहिक, f. **ई** the same; n. wedding.
वैवाह्य a. & n. = prec.
वैशद्य n. clearness, purity.
वैशन्त, f. **ई** forming a pond, pond-like.
वैशंपायन m. N. of an ancient Rishi etc.
वैशस a. murderous, pernicious; n. murder, slaughter, war, destruction, horrible deed.
वैशाख m. a cert. month in summer, f. **ई** the full-moon day in it.
वैशारद, f. **ई** experienced, clever; n. = seq.
वैशारद्य n. abstr. to prec.
वैशाल, f. **ई** coming from Viçāla.
वैशिक, f. **ई** whorish.
वैशिष्ट्य n. particularity, superiority.
वैशेषिक, f. **ई** particular, specific, extraordinary. m. a follower of the Vaiçeshika doctrine; n. peculiarity, characteristic, N. of a philos. system.
वैशेष्य n. particularity, distinction, superiority.
1**वैश्य** m., **आ** f. a man & woman of the third caste; n. **वैश्य** condition of a V., dependence.
2**वैश्य** a. relating to a Vaiçya (v. prec.).
वैश्यता f., **°त्व** n., **°भाव** m. = prec. 1 n.
वैश्यपुत्र m. the son of a Vaiçya.
वैश्यवत् adv. like (of, to, in etc.) a Vaiçya.
वैश्याज & **°पुत्र** m. the son of a Vaiçya woman.
वैश्रवण m. patron. of Kubera.
वैश्व a. consecrated to the Viçve Devās, n. E. of a lunar mansion.
वैश्वकर्मण, f. **ई** belonging or consecrated to Viçvakarman.
वैश्वदेव (f. **ई**) & **°देविक** a. = **वैश्व** adj.
वैश्वरूप a. manifold, various; n. the universe.
वैश्वरूप्य a. = prec. adj.; n. variety, difference.

1**वैश्वानर**, f. **ई** belonging to or consisting of all men, universal, complete, omnipresent or omnipotent; m. fire or the god of fire, the sun, also = **विराज्** (ph.).
2**वैश्वानर** a. consecrated to Agni V.
वैश्वामित्र, f. **ई** relating to or descended from Viçvāmitra.
वैषम्य n. unevenness, unequality, difference, dissension, disproportion, difficulty, pain, distress, injustice, unkindness.
वैषुवत a. being in the middle (of the year etc.), central; n. centre.
वैष्णव, f. **ई** belonging or devoted to Viṣṇu; m. a worshipper of Viṣṇu (f. **ई**), n. E. of a lunar mansion.
वैष्णव्य a. relating to Viṣṇu.
वैसादृश्य n. unequality, difference.
वैस्पष्ट्य n. clearness, distinctness.
वैस्वर्य n. loss of voice or language.
वैहग (f. **ई**) & **वैहंग** a. bird-like.
वैहायस, f. **ई** being in the open air or in the sky. m. a dweller in the sky or in heaven; n. the sky.
वैह्वल्य n. exhaustion, weakness.
वोडु m. a kind of snake.
वोढव्य a. to be carried, drawn, borne, married, undertaken, accomplished.
वोढृ or **वोढृ** a. carrying, drawing, leading, bringing. m. horse or ox of draught (± **रथस्य** or **हलस्य**); carrier, charioteer, offerer, husband.
वोपदेव m. N. of an author.
वौषट् a sacrificial exclamation.
व्यंस a. having the shoulders apart, i.e. broad-shouldered; m. N. of a demon.
व्यंसन n. fraud, deceit.
व्यंसयितव्य a. to be deceived.
व्यक्त a. adorned, fair, manifest, clear, n. adv.; abstr. **°ता** f.
व्यक्ति f. appearance, manifestation, distinctness, variety, individual.
व्यग्र a. having no certain point or aim, unconcentrated, distracted, perplexed, bewildered; quite occupied with, eagerly engaged in (instr., loc., or —°). Abstr. **°ता** f., **°त्व** n.

1व्यङ्ग a. spotted; m. spot, stain (lit. & fig.).
2व्यङ्ग a. limbless, mutilated, crippled; abstr. °ता† f.
व्यङ्गय्, °यति, pp. व्यङ्गित rob of a limb, mutilate, maim, cripple.
व्यङ्गारे (loc.) when there is no coal burning.
व्यङ्गिन् a. = 2व्यङ्ग.
व्यङ्ग्य a. clear, distinct; implicit (rh.), abstr. °ता f., °त्व n.
व्यच्, विव्यक्ति extend around, embrace, encompass. — सम् = S.
व्यचस् n. compass, extent, space.
व्यचस्वन्त् a. capacious, extensive, large.
व्यचिष्ठ (superl.) extending far and wide.
व्यजन n. fanning; a fan (also °क n.).
व्यञ्जक a. manifesting, betraying (gen. or —°); abstr. °त्व n.
व्यञ्जन a. = prec. a. — f. आ indirect indication, insinuation (rh.). n. manifestation, betrayal, indirect or implicit expression, suggestion; mark, sign (esp. of gender or of puberty), characteristic, attribute, the insignia of a prince, ornament i.g., condiment, sauce, juice; consonant, syllable.
व्यति m. horse, steed.
व्यतिकर m. mixing, confusing; contact, union; confusion, disaster, accident.
व्यतिकरवन्त् a. mixed, altered, different.
व्यतिकरित a. mixed or joined with (instr. or —°).
व्यतिक्रम m. passing, getting a start; transgression, violation, disregard, omission, also = seq.
व्यतिक्रमण & °क्रान्त n., °क्रान्ति f. offence, injury.
व्यतिमिश्र a. mixed, confounded.
व्यतिरिक्त a. reaching beyond (acc.), excessive, abundant; richer or superior in (instr. or —°), increased by (—°); haughty, arrogant.
व्यतिरेक m. separateness, exclusion, exception, negation, contrast, opposite of (—°).
व्यतिषक्त a. mixed, joined, connected.
व्यतिहार m. barter, exchange; mutuality, reciprocity.
व्यतीत a. gone, dead; passed over (act. & pass.).
व्यत्यय m. change, inverted order.
व्यत्यस्त a. inverted, crossed.
व्यत्यास m. transposition, change, reverse.
व्यथ्, व्यथते (°ति), pp. व्यथित (q.v.) waver, reel, stagger, come to fall, go wrong, fail; tremble, be afraid or pained. C. व्यथयति cause to waver etc., bring to fall, make afraid or uneasy, distress, pain. — प्र, संप्र, वि, & सम् = S.
व्यथन a. exciting, disturbing; n. wavering, agitation, uneasiness.
व्यथयितृ m. harasser (acc.).
व्यथा f. failure, disappointment, misfortune, loss, adversity, uneasiness, sorrow, distress.
†व्यथि v. सव्यथि.
व्यथित a. wavering, agitated, disturbed, distressed; n. agitation, pain, harm.
व्यथिस् a. wavering, reeling, sneaking, crooked, mischievous, secret.
व्यद्वर m., व्यद्वरी f. a gnawing animal.
व्यध्, विध्यति (°ते), pp. विद्ध (q.v.) pierce, hit, wound, hurt, harm, injure, affect or afflict with (instr.). C. वेधयति pierce, hit, व्याधयति cause to pierce etc. - अति & व्यति pierce, perforate. अनु pierce or wound (after another); intertwine, set or fill with (instr.). अप hurl or throw away, give up, neglect. अभि wound, hit. अव precipitate into (loc.) or from (abl.). आ throw, bore or break through; scare, drive away, also = व्या & समा wave, swing, brandish. नि throw down, overthrow; shoot at, hit, pierce. निस् wound, kill, slay. परा hurl off, wound, hit. परि shoot at. प्र hurl, throw, shoot, perforate, wound. प्रति shoot, hit. वि pierce, shoot. सम् shoot. — Cf. अनुविद्ध, अपविद्ध, आविद्ध, प्रविद्ध, व्यपविद्ध.
व्यध m. piercing, hitting, perforation.
व्यधन a. & n. piercing, perforating.
व्यधिकरण a. relating to another subject; n. incongruency (g.).
व्यध्व m. half the way; loc. व्यध्वे or व्यूध्वे adv. midway.
व्यूध्वन् a. being midway or swerving from the way.

व्यध्वर a. piercing, boring (cf. व्यद्वर).
व्यून्त a. separated, remote.
1व्यन्तर n. interval, indistinctness.
2व्यन्तर m. a class of supernatural beings.
व्यन्तराम् adv. indifferently, moderately.
व्यपदेश m. designation, appellation, name, esp. family-name; pretext, pretence.
व्यपदेशवन्त् a. having a designation or name.
व्यपदेशिन् a. = prec.; —° designating, appealing or conforming one's self to.
व्यपनय m., °न n. taking off, removing.
व्यपनुत्ति f. pushing away, removal.
व्यपयान n. retreat, flight.
व्यपरोपण n. tearing out, removing, destroying.
व्यपविद्ध a. thrown asunder or away, scattered, broken, pierced, hit.
व्यपाय m. cessation, end; absence, want.
व्यपाश्रय m. seat, place, refuge, support; adj. —° resorting to, trusting in.
व्यपेक्षा f. regard, consideration; expectation, supposition.
व्यपेत a. separated, ceased, vanished.
व्यपोह m. removal, expulsion; negation, denial.
व्यभिचार m. going asunder or astray, failure; offence, going beyond, transgressing, sin, crime, esp. adultery (of a wife).
व्यभिचारिन् a. going asunder or astray, infidel, adulterous; going beyond, transgressing (—°).
व्यभ्र a. cloudless; loc. when the sky is clear.
व्यय्, °यति, °ते waste, squander, expend.
व्यय m. going asunder, perishing, disappearance, loss, destruction, waste, prodigality, expense, money.
व्ययकरण or °क m. pay-master.
व्ययकर्मन् n. a pay-master's office.
व्ययकृत a. expended, disbursed.
व्ययगुण a. prodigal, dissipated.
व्ययन n. going away, parting; waste, expense.
व्यर्थ a. useless, vain (n. adv.); unmeaning, contradictory; destitute of wealth or money, i.g. destitute of (instr.).
व्यर्थता f., °त्व n. uselessness or senselessness.
व्यर्धुक a. being deprived of (instr.).
व्यलीक a. false, deceitful; n. adv., as subst. falsehood, untruth, deceit, offence, pain, grief.
व्युल्कशा f. N. of a plant.
†व्यवच्छेद m. getting rid of (—°), separation, distinction, interruption, exclusion.
व्यवच्छेद्य a. to be excluded.
व्यवधान n. lying or stepping between, intercession, mediation, separation, distinction, interruption; also = seq.
व्यवधि m. covering, cover, veil.
व्यवसाय m. exertion, resolution, purpose, intention to (loc., प्रति, or —°).
व्यवसायवन्त् & °सायिन् a. determined, resolute.
व्यवसायात्मक, f. °त्मिका of a resolute or constant nature.
व्यवसित n., °सिति f. determination, resolve.
व्यवस्था f. distinctness, particularity; constancy, stability; state, position; decision, rule.
व्यवस्थान n. remaining, persevering, constancy; state, condition.
व्यवस्थित a. being in a state or position, situated, standing or being in, resting or dependent on, sticking to (loc. or —°); settled, fixed, limited, constant; existing, appearing as (nom., instr., ger., adv., or —°).
व्यवस्थिति f. distinctness, particularity, constancy, perseverance in (loc.), fixedness, decision.
व्यवहर्तव्य a. to be used or employed; to be acted or proceeded (n. impers.).
व्यवहर्तृ a. occupied or dealing with (instr.); m. judge.
व्यवहार m. procedure, conduct, way of acting; intercourse with (सह); usage, custom, activity, occupation, dealing with or in (loc. or —°); business, commerce, trade; legal dispute, lawsuit, litigation, contract, stipulation, administration of justice.
व्यवहारक m. man of business.
व्यवहारतन्त्र n. judicial relation.
व्यवहारदर्शन n. judicial investigation, trial.
व्यवहारपद n., °मार्ग m. case in law.
व्यवहारवन्त् a. dealing in (—°); m. man of business.

व्यवहारविधि m. judicial procedure, code of law.

व्यवहारस्थान n case in law.

व्यवहारस्थिति f. judicial procedure.

व्यवहारार्थिन् a. having a lawsuit, accuser.

व्यवहारिन् a. proceeding with, dealing in (—°); m. man of business, merchant.

व्यवहार्य a. to be dealt or communicated with.

व्यवहित a. separated, interrupted, hindered, disturbed.

व्यवहृति f. procedure, mode of acting, intercourse, commerce, lawsuit.

व्यवाय m. intervention, separation by inserting, penetration, coition.

व्यवायिन् a. intervening etc. (v. prec.).

व्यश्व a. horseless; m. N. of an ancient Rishi.

व्यष्टि f. acquisition, succession; individual (ph.).

व्यष्टिसमष्टिता f. the being individuality or totality (ph.).

व्यसन n. moving hither and thither, activity, industry, propensity or devotion to, zeal for (loc. or —°); passion, whim, hobby, evil habit, vice; ill luck, adversity, calamity.

व्यसनिन् a. active, exerting one's self; intently attached to, fond of (loc. or —°); having evil passions, vicious, wicked; unlucky, unfortunate. Abstr. °निता f., °त्व n.

व्यसि a. swordless.

व्यसु a. breathless, lifeless, dead; abstr. °त्व n.

व्यस्त a. torn asunder, shaken, tossed; divided, separated; separate, single, several, various; **व्यस्ते काले** sometimes, now and then.

व्यस्तकेश, f. ई having dishevelled hair.

व्यस्थक a. boneless.

व्या, **व्ययति**, °ते, pp. **वीत** (q.v.) wrap, veil, envelop; M. refl. — **अप** unveil, uncover; M. extricate one's self i.e. deny. **अपि** cover. **आ** wrap round (acc.), hide one's self in (loc.). **उप** hang about (esp. the sacred cord over the left shoulder). **नि** wind or hang about. **परि** wrap around; M. wind something as cover round one's self. **सम्** A. roll up, envelop; veil in (instr.), M. refl. – Cf. **उपवीत**, **निवीत**, **परिवीत**, **संवीत**.

व्याकरण n. putting asunder, separation; explanation, manifestation; analysis, grammar.

व्याकुल a. thoroughly filled with or full of (instr. or —°); quite intent upon or occupied with (—°); confused, disarranged, perplexed, bewildered. Abstr. °ता f., °त्व n.

व्याकुलय्, °यति confuse, disarrange; pp. **व्याकुलित** = prec.

व्याकुली कृ = prec., °भू P.

व्याकृति f. separation, analysis, explanation.

व्याकोश a. expanded, blossomed, open.

व्याक्रोश m. abusing, reviling.

व्याक्षेप m. = prec.; also distraction, absence of mind.

व्याक्षेपिन् a. dispelling, driving away.

व्याख्या f. explanation, commentary.

व्याख्यातव्य a. to be explained.

व्याख्यातृ m. explainer.

व्याख्यान, f. ई explaining, reminding of (gen.) n. explanation, recitation, story, tale.

व्याख्यानय्, °यति explain, relate.*

व्याघात m. stroke, blow, shot; agitation, confusion; shock, defeat; obstacle, hindrance.

व्याघारण n. sprinkling about (r.).

व्याघ्र m. tiger, first or best of (—°); f. **व्याघ्री** tigress. — Abstr. °ता† f., °त्व† n.

व्याघ्रचर्मन् n. a tiger's skin.

व्याघ्रलोमन् n. a tiger's hair.

व्याघ्र्य a. a tiger's or tiger-like.

व्याज m. (n.) deceit, fraud, false semblance, pretext, pretence; °— & instr. adv.; adj. —° having the mere semblance of, only appearing as.

व्याजनिन्दा f. ironical censure.

व्याजमय, f. ई feigned, simulated.

व्याजय्, °यति cheat, deceive.

व्याजसुप्त a. & n. feigning to sleep.

व्याजस्तुति f. ironical praise.

व्याड m. beast of prey.

व्याडि & **व्याळि** m. patron. of sev. men.

व्यात्त a. torn asunder, opened; n. the opened mouth, the jaws.

व्यात्तानन a. open-mouthed.

व्यादान n. tearing asunder, opening.

व्यादेश m. hint, direction.

व्याध & °क m. hunter, abstr. °ता; p. °धिन्.

व्याधि m. disease; °त a. ill, sick.

1व्याधिन् a. piercing, perforating.

2व्याधिन् v. व्याध.

व्याधिबहुल a. frequently visited by illness.

व्याधी f. care, sorrow.

व्याध्यार्त a. visited by illness.

व्यान m. breath, esp. the vital air diffused through the whole body.

व्यानदा a. giving breath.

व्यानम्र a. bent.

व्यानशि a. pervading.

व्यानोदान m. du. the Vyāna and Udāna.

व्यापक a. pervading, spread or diffused everywhere; contained in, inherent. Abstr. °ता f., °त्व n.

व्यापत्ति f. going amiss, ill luck, adversity, misfortune, ruin, death.

व्यापद् f. = prec., also misdeed.

व्यापाद m. ruin, death.

व्यापादन n. destroying, killing.

व्यापार m. occupation, business, exertion, concern.

व्यापारिन् a. occupied with (—°).

व्यापित a. = व्याप्त (—°).

व्यापित्व n. abstr. to seq.

व्यापिन् a. spreading, extending; reaching through, filling, containing (—°).

व्यापीत a. quite yellow.

व्यापृत a. active, busy, occupied with or in (—°, अर्थम् or हेतोस्).

व्यापृति f. occupation, activity.

व्याप्त a. pervaded or penetrated by, filled with (—°); acquired, won.

व्याप्ति f. obtaining, reaching, penetrating, filling, containing; universal pervasion, general rule.

व्याप्तिमन्त् a. stretching, all-pervading, general.

व्याप्य a. that wherein something is contained or inherent; abstr. °त्व n.

व्याभुग्न a. bent, curved.

व्याम m. a fathom (lit. stretch-out).

व्यामिश्र a. mixed, mingled or joined with (instr. or —°), manifold, various.

व्यामूढ a. bewildered, perplexed, confused.

व्यामोह m. unconsciousness, bewilderment, error, uncertainty.

व्यायत a. torn asunder, stretched out, long; strong, vigorous, abstr. °त्व n.

व्यायाम m. exertion, bodily exercise, struggle, fight; a fathom (cf. व्याम).

व्यायामभूमि & °शाला f. place or hall for gymnastic exercise.

व्यायुक a. running away.

व्यायुध a. weaponless, unarmed.

व्यायोग m. a kind of drama.

व्याल a. mischievous, malicious. m. a malicious elephant, beast of prey, snake (f. व्याली).

व्यालग्राह (& °हिन्*) m. snake-catcher.

व्यालमृग m. beast of prey.

व्यालम्ब & °लम्बिन् a. hanging down, pendulous.

व्यालोल a. trembling, waving, unsteady.

व्यावर्तक, f. °र्तिका excluding, removing; abstr. °ता f., °त्व n.

व्यावर्तन, f. ई = prec.; n. turning.

व्यावहारिक, f. ई relating to practice or business; common, real (opp. ideal); judicial; n. intercourse, commerce, settled usage or law.

व्यावृत् f. distinction, prevalence, superiority.

व्यावृत्त a. turned away (lit. & fig.), liberated from or rid of (abl. or —°); opened, divided, different from, incompatible with (—°); ceased, perished, at an end.

व्यावृत्ति f. turning away, getting rid or being deprived of (abl.); exclusion, removal; separation, distinction, difference; conclusion, end.

व्यास m. separation, division; extension, diffusion, prolixity; N. of a celebrated Rishi and author.

व्यासङ्ग m. attachment, adherence, desire of, delight in, passion for (loc. or —°).

व्यासेध m. hindrance, disturbance, interruption.

व्याहरण n. pronouncing, uttering.

व्याहार m. utterance, talk, conversation; singing (of birds).

व्याहारिन् a. talking, speaking, singing; resounding with (—°).

व्याहित a. indisposed, unwell, sick.
व्याहृत a. uttered, spoken, communicated; n. talk, speech, singing (of birds).
व्याहृति f. utterance, word, (sacred) exclamation (also **°ती** f.).
व्युच्छित्ति f., **°च्छेद** m. interruption, disturbance.
व्युच्य n. impers. to be objected or contested.
व्युत or **व्यूत** a. plaited, twisted, woven, variegated.
व्युत्क्रम m. transgression, offence; inverted order.
व्युत्थान n. awakening, rising.
व्युत्थित a. gone asunder, split; diverging, differing; roused, excited; (± **धर्मात्**) forgetful of one's duty, disloyal.
व्युत्पत्ति f. origin, growth, development.
व्युत्पन्न a. developed, derived (g.); taught, educated, versed in (instr.).
व्युद् & **°क** a. waterless, dry.
व्युदास m. letting go, giving up, removing, excluding.
व्युन्दन n. wetting, moistening.
व्युपरम m. coming to rest, cessation, end.
व्युपशम m. ceasing, desisting.
व्युष् f. dawn, daybreak.
व्युषित & **व्युष्ट** a. shone up, grown bright; loc. **व्युषिते** at daybreak.
व्युष्टि f. shining up, growing bright, dawning; reward for (gen., loc., or —°), requital, retaliation; grace, beauty.
व्युष्टिमन्त् a. fetching reward or endowed with beauty.
व्यूढ a. spread, expanded, broad, large.
व्यूढा f. led-away, married.
व्यूढोरस्क a. broad-breasted.
व्यूह m. shifting, dislocation, distribution, disposition, arrangement, military array; totality, a whole or complex; host, troop, multitude; detailed explanation or description.
व्यूहन a. & n. placing apart, separating; n. also shifting, change, development.
व्यृद्ध a. deprived of (instr.), failed, idle, vain.
व्यृद्धि f. exclusion, loss, failure, ill-luck, want.

व्येनस् a. guiltless, sinless.
व्योकस् a. dwelling far asunder.
व्योमग a. moving in the sky, flying; m. such a being.
व्योमगामिन्, **°चर**, & **°चारिन्** a. = prec.
व्योमन् n. heaven, sky, air; instr. **व्योममार्गेण** & **°वर्त्मना** through the air.
व्योमसद् a. dwelling in the sky.
व्योमस्पृश् a. touching the sky.
व्योष a. burning, hot.
व्रज्, **व्रजति** (**°ते**), pp. **व्रजित** proceed, march, go (± **पद्याम्** on foot), go to (acc., r. loc. or *dat.), go for i.e. to fetch (acc.), *be going to (infin., dat., or adj. in **अक**); attack, approach (a woman); go from, leave (abl.), pass away (time), get into a state or condition (acc.). With **अधस्** go down i.e. be digested; w. **पुनर्** return to life; w. **सह** agree, make peace. C. **व्राजयति** drive. — **अति** pass beyond, roam through. **अनु** go along, accompany, follow; visit, go to or into (acc.). **अप** go away. **अभि** go to or through. **आ** come near, approach; come back, return (± **पुनर्**); go to, arrive at (acc.). **प्रत्या** & **समा** come back, return. **उद्** leave home. **प्रत्युद्** go to meet. **उप** come near, go to, follow. **प्रत्युप** march against, attack. **परि** walk about, circumambulate; roam, wander (esp. as a religious mendicant). **प्र** march forth, go to, wander (= prec.). **अभिप्र** march forth towards or to meet. **सम्** travel. **अनुसम्** go after, follow. **उपसम्** enter (acc.). — Cf. **प्रव्रजित**.
व्रज m. (n.) fold, shed, stable, station of herds; herd, flock, troop, multitude; N. of a region.
व्रजन n. wandering, way, road.
व्रजनाथ m. lord of the folds, E. of Kṛṣṇa.
व्रजसुन्दरी & **°स्त्री** f. sheperdess.
व्रजाङ्गना f. the same.
व्रजिन् a. being in a stable.
व्रज्य a. belonging to a fold.
व्रज्या f. going, motion; group, class.
व्रण m. (n.) wound, sore; fracture, scar, rent.
व्रणन n. piercing, perforating.

व्रणय्, °यति, pp. व्रणित wound.
व्रणयुक्त & व्रणवन्त् a. wounded.
व्रणविरोपण a. & n. healing wounds.
व्रणितहृदय a. having a wounded heart.
व्रणिन् & व्रणिल a. wounded, sore.
व्रत n. will, decree, command, statute, order; dominion, province, sphere; wont activity or occupation; conduct, way of life; choice, determination, resolution, vow; holy work, religious observance; duty, obedience, service.
व्रतग्रहण n. making a vow i.e. becoming a monk or ascetic.
व्रतचर्या f. the practice of religious vows, esp. r. studentship; devotion, piety i.g.
व्रतचारिन् a. performing vows, fulfilling the duties of (—°).
व्रतति f. creeping plant, creeper.
व्रतपति m. the lord of vows or devotion.
व्रतपा a. maintaining ordinances or sacred duties.
व्रतपारण n. conclusion of a vow, esp. of fasting, breakfast.
व्रतभृत् a. maintaining the holy work.
व्रतमीमांसा f. examination of observances.
व्रतरुचि a. fond of vows or religious observances, devout, pious.
व्रतलोप m., °न n. breach or violation of a vow or observance.
व्रतवन्त् a. observing a vow or religious duty.
व्रतसंपादन n. performance of a vow or religious observance.
व्रतस्थ & °स्थित a. observing a vow or religious duty.
व्रतादान n. = व्रतग्रहण.
व्रतादेश m., °न n. instruction in the performance of vows.
व्रतिन् a. = व्रतवन्त्, also observing, honouring, behaving like (—°).
व्रतेश m. = व्रतपति, E. of Çiva.
1व्रत्य a. obedient, faithful (gen.).
2व्रत्य a. belonging to or fit for a vow or religious observance; m. partaker of it.
†व्रद्, व्रदते become soft or weak.
व्रन्दिन् a. softening, weakening (tr. or intr.).
व्रयस् n. overwhelming power.
व्रश्च्, वृश्चति, pp. वृक्ण hew down, fell (a tree), cut to pieces. — अपि hew off or asunder. अव cut off, sever. आ sever, separate, estrange or alienate from (dat. or loc.). नि hew down, fell. परि cut, mutilate. प्र cut or split off. वि cut or split asunder. सम् hew or cut in pieces.
व्रश्चन a. & n. hewing, felling, cutting.
व्रा f. troop, band.
व्राज m. host, multitude.
व्राण a. shut up, confined.
व्रात m. heap, troop, multitude, community, corporation.
व्रातीन a. belonging to a wandering band, vagrant.
व्रातपति m. lord of a host or band.
व्रात्य m. vagrant, tramp, outcast; abstr. °ता† f.
†व्राध् (व्राधते) stir up.
व्रिश् f. finger.
व्रीड्, व्रीडते, pp. व्रीडित be ashamed or embarrassed.
व्रीड m., आ f. shame, bashfulness.
व्रीडावन्त् a. ashamed, bashful, modest.
व्रीहि m. rice, pl. grains of rice.
व्रीहिन् a. planted with rice (field).
व्रीहिमन्त् a. mixed with rice or = prec.
व्रीहिमय a. made of rice.
व्रीहियव m. du. pl. & °यव n. sgl. rice and barley.
व्रीह्यपूप m. rice-cake.
व्रीह्युर्वरा f. field of rice.
व्रुड्, pp. व्रुडित sink.
†व्लग्, w. अभि pursue, overtake.
व्ली, व्लीनाति or व्लिनाति crush, fell; P. व्लीयते shrink, decay.
व्लेष्क v. ब्लेष्क.

श

शंयु a. benevolent, auspicious.

शंयोस् = शं योस् (v. 5शंम्).

शंवन्त् a. salutary.

शंस्, शंसति (°ते), pp. शस्त (q.v.) & शंशित say in a loud and solemn voice, recite, praise, vow, unfold, betray, announce, communicate, declare, foretell, prophesy. C. शंसयति cause to recite; announce, foretell. — अति recite beyond (2 acc. or instr. & acc.); omit in reciting. अनु recite or praise (after another). अभि accuse, defame; praise, commend. आ M.(A.) hope or trust in, strive after (loc., acc., dat., or infin.), try to master (acc.), suppose, expect, fear; wish, desire (acc. or — & — infin.), beg for (acc.); praise, commend, recite, announce, foretell. समा A. adjudge to (dat.); M. hope or trust in (acc.). उद् call upon, invoke. प्र tell forth, proclaim aloud; stir up, excite; praise, extol, recommend to (gen.). वि recite, divide in reciting. सम् recite (together). उपसम् recite in addition. — Cf. अभिशस्त, प्रशस्त.

शंस m. solemn utterance, invocation, summons, vow, praise, blessing, curse; f. शंसा praise, eulogy, communication, message.

शंसथ m. conversation.

शंसन n. recitation, utterance, confession, communication.

शंसिनीय a. to be praised.

शंसित a. praised, praiseworthy.

शंसितृ m. reciter.

शंसिन् a. reciting, uttering, telling, communicating, prophesying (—°).

शंस्तव्य a. to be recited.

शंस्तृ m. = शंसितृ.

शंस्य a. to be recited; praiseworthy, glorious.

शक्, शक्नोति, pp. शक्त (q.v.) & शकित be able, P. शक्यते impers. it is possible to (inf.) or pers. he is able to be, he can or may be (infin. w. pass. mg); be serviceable or helpful to (dat.), make another partake of (gen.). D. शिक्षति (q.v.). — अनु be equal in (acc.). आ assist (dat.), help a pers. (dat.) to (gen.), invite to (acc.). उप help, impart. परि master, overpower. प्र be able to (infin.). सम् be able to (infin.), w. न not be equal to or a match for (loc. or instr.).

1शंक n. dung, f. शंका a kind of bird or beast.

2शक m. pl. N. of a people.

शककाल m. the Caka-era (78 A.D.).

शकट n. (m.) cart, waggon (also शकटी f.) a cert. form of military array (± व्यूह m.)

शकटसार्थ m. a train of carts.

शकटिका f. a small cart.

शकटिन् m. the owner of a waggon.

शकधूम m. the smoke of dung.

शंकन् or शकन् n. dung (cf. शंकृत्).

शकपिण्ड m. a lump of dung.

शकमय a. produced in dung.

शकंभर a. carrying dung.

शंकर n. = seq. m. n.

शंकल m. n. chip, splint, potsherd; piece morsel, fragment; n. a half (esp. of an egg-shell).

शकलय्, °यति, pp. शकलित break or cut to pieces, reduce to fragments, divide. — वि = S.

शकली कृ = prec.; °भू P.

शकार m. the sound श; (d.) the brother of a king's concubine (who pronounces श instead of स or ष).

शकुन m. bird (esp. of large birds & such as give an omen).

शकुनज्ञ a. knowing omens.

शकुनज्ञान n. the knowledge of omens.

शकुनि m. = शकुन, N. of a serpent-demon etc., f. शकुनी a female bird.

शकुनिका f. = prec. f., a woman's name.

शकुनिलुब्धक m. a bird-catcher.*

शकुन्त m. bird, esp. a cert. bird of prey.

शकुन्तक m., °न्तिका f. a little bird.

शकुन्तला f. N. of an Apsaras, the heroine of a celebrated drama.
शकुन्ति m. bird.
शकुर a. tame (of beasts).
शकुल m., °ली f. a kind of fish.
शकृत् n. dung (cf. शकन्).
शकृत्पिण्ड m. a lump of dung.
शकेध m. dung-fire.
शक्त a. able, capable, competent (instr., gen., dat., loc., acc. w. प्रति, infin., or —°); strong, mighty, important, rich, opulent.
शक्तृ m. bearer, sufferer.
1 शक्ति f. ability, power, capacity of (infin., loc., gen., or —°); the triple power of a king; the energy or active power of a deity, esp. of Çiva; the power of a word i.e. its meaning or function; the productive power of a poet, i.e. his fancy or imagination; help, assistance, gift, donation.
2 शक्ति or शक्ती f. spear, lance.
3 शक्ति m. N. of a Rishi.
शक्तिकर a. giving strength.
शक्तिज्ञ a. knowing (one's own) power.
शक्तितस् adv. according to ability or power.
शक्तिद्वयवन्त् a. endowed with twofold power.
शक्तिधर a. carrying a spear, E. of Skanda.
शक्तिनाथ m. E. of Çiva.
1 शक्तिमन्त् a. having ability or power, able to, capable of (infin. or loc.).
2 शक्तिमन्त् a. armed with a spear.
शक्तीवन्त् a. powerful or helpful.
शक्मन् n. ability; enterprise, work.
शक्य a. possible, feasible, practicable (infin. w. pass. mg; n. impers., but also with a subject of any gender or number). Abstr. °ता f., °त्व n.
शक्र a. powerful, mighty, strong; m. E. of Indra.
शक्रतेजस् a. having the splendour or might of Indra.
शक्रदिश् f. Indra's region, i.e. the east.
शक्रप्रस्थ n. N. of a town = इन्द्रप्रस्थ.
शक्रभक्ष s. N. of a kind of hemp, a medic. plant (lit. Indra's food).
शक्रलोक m. Indra's world.
शक्रायुध n. Indra's weapon, i.e. the rainbow.
शक्रावतार s. Indra's descent, N. of a sacred bathing-place.
शक्राशन n. = शक्रभक्ष.
शक्रासन n. Indra's throne.
शक्वन्, f. शक्वरी capable, clever. m. artificer, f. N. of a metre & a cert. class of verses or songs.
शक्वर m. bull.
शग्म a. helpful, benevolent, kind, friendly.
शङ्क्, शङ्कते (°ति), pp. शङ्कित (q.v.) doubt, hesitate, be anxious or suspicious, be afraid of (acc. or abl.); suppose, expect, believe. C. शङ्कयति make anxious about (loc.). — अति suspect strongly or falsely. अभि distrust, doubt, hesitate at (acc. or gen.). आ be doubtful or afraid, distrust (acc.); suppose, think to be (इति or 2 acc.). उप suspect, accuse of (instr.). परि be anxious or doubtful, distrust, suspect, disbelieve (acc.); suppose, expect, think to be (2 acc.). वि be anxious or afraid of (acc. or abl.), distrust, doubt, suspect (acc.); think to be (2 acc.). सम् suspect. — Cf. अतिशङ्कित, अभिशङ्कित, उपशङ्कित (add.), परिशङ्कित, विशङ्कित.
शङ्कनीय a. to be suspected, feared, or supposed; n. impers.
शंकर, f. ई causing welfare or happiness; m. E. of Rudra-Çiva, a man's name.
शंकरगृह n. a temple of Çiva.*
शंकरविजय m. T. of a work.
शंकराचार्य m. N. of a celebrated scholar.
शंकरालय m. Çiva's residence (mount Kailāsa).
शङ्का f. hesitation, doubt, suspicion, fear of (abl., loc., प्रति, or —°); supposition, conjecture, the taking for (—°).
शङ्काभियोग m. accusation on (mere) suspicion (j.).
शङ्कितव्य a. = शङ्कनीय.
शङ्किन् a. fearing, afraid of, timid or suspicious like (—°); conjecturing, supposing.
शङ्कु m. a pointed peg or wooden nail, stake, pike, beam, arrow, spear, sting (lit. & fig.), N. of a serpent-demon etc.

शङ्कुकर्ण a. spike-eared (also °र्णिन्); m. N. of a Dānava etc.

शङ्कुमुख, f. ई having a pointed mouth.

शंकृत् a. beneficent.

शङ्क्य a. = शङ्कनीय.

शङ्ख m. n. conch-shell (used to blow upon or as ornament); m. the temporal bone, temple, one of the treasures of Kubera, N. of an Asura, etc.

शङ्खचक्रपाणि a. holding a conch and a discus (Viṣṇu).

शङ्खध्मं m. shell-blower.

शङ्खभृत् m. E. of Viṣṇu (holding a conch).

शङ्खध्वनि m. the sound of a conch or horn.

शङ्खपुष्पिका & °पुष्पी f. N. of a plant.

शङ्खमेखल m. N. of an ancient sage.

शङ्खान्तर n. forehead (cf. भुजान्तर).

शङ्खिन् a. having a shell or shells; f. °नी mother of pearl.

शंगं v. शंगु.

शंगयं, f. शंगयी beneficial to the household.

शंगवी (f.) & शंगु a. beneficial to cattle.

शंचिष्ठ a. most helpful.

शंची f. might or help, personif. as the wife of Indra.

शचीतीर्थ n. N. of a sacred bathing-place.

शचीपति m. lord of might or husband of Çacī (Indra).

शचीवन्त् & †शचीवसु a. rich in help.

शठ a. false, wicked; abstr. °त्व n.

शठधी, °बुद्धि, & °मति a. wicked-minded, malignant, mischievous.

शण m. a kind of hemp.

शणतान्तव, f. ई made of hempen string.

शणमय, f. ई hempen.

शणरज्जु f. a hempen rope.

शणशुल्ब n. a hempen string.

शणसूत्र n. a hempen thread.

शणसूत्रमय, f. ई of hempen thread.

शण्ड m. N. of the Purohita of the Asuras.

शण्डामर्क m. du. Çaṇḍa and Marka.

शण्डिल m. N. of a man, pl. his family.

शत्, शातयति, °ते cut in pieces, cause to fall off, break or throw down, destroy. — अप hurl away. व्यव scatter, dispense, remove. नि hew down, defeat (an army). प्र break, pluck. वि hew down, crush, disperse, chase away. सम् crush, destroy.

शतं n. (m.) hundred, also as expression of a large or infinite number (adj. f. —°).

शतक, f. शतिका consisting of hundred or the hundredth; n. a hundred.

शतकुम्भ m. N. of a mountain; f. आ N. of a river.

शतकृत्वस् adv. a hundred times.

शतकोटि m. Indra's thunderbolt (lit. having a hundred edges).

शतक्रतु a. having a hundred forces; m. E. of Indra.

शतखण्ड a. consisting of a hundred pieces; °ण्डं कृ break in a hundred pieces.*

शतगु a. possessed of a hundred cows.

शतगुण & °गुणित a. hundredfold.

शतग्विन् a. = prec.

शतघण्टा f. N. of a spear.

शतघ्नी v. शतहन्.

शतचक्र a. having a hundred wheels.

शतचर्मन् a. made of a hundred skins.

शतजित् a. vanquishing hundreds; m. E. of Viṣṇu, a man's name.

शततमं, f. आ & ई a. the hundredth.

शतद & शतदा a. giving a hundred.

शतदण्ड s. a fine of one hundred, °ण्डार्ह a. worthy of such a fine.

शतदन्त् a. having a hundred teeth (comb).

शतदल n. = शतपत्त्र n.

शतदातु a. hundredfold.

शतदाय or शतदाय a. giving a hundred.

शतदावन् a. = prec.

शतद्युम्न m. a man's name.

शतद्रु or °द्रू f. N. of a river.

शतद्वार a. hundred-gated.

शतधन्य a. worth a hundred.

शतधा adv. in a hundred parts or ways.

शतनीथ a. having a hundred arts or stratagems.

शतपति m. lord of a hundred.

शतपत्त्र a. having a hundred feathers or leaves; m. wood-pecker, n. a lotus-flower.

शतपथ a. having a hundred paths, many-sided; m. & °ब्राह्मण n. T. of a Brāhmaṇa.

शतंपद् (°पाद्), f. **शतपदी** a. having a hundred feet.

शतंपर्वन् a. having a hundred knots or joints.

शतबलि m. a cert. fish; N. of a monkey.

शतबुद्धि a. having hundredfold understanding; m. N. of a fish.

शतभाग m. the hundredth part.

शतभुजि a. hundredfold.

शतमख m. = **शतयज्ञ**.

शतंमन्यु a. having hundredfold wrath.

शतंमान a. hundredfold; m. n. a weight of a hundred Mānas in gold or silver.

शतमुख a. having a hundred openings or issues; m. N. of an Asura etc.

शतंमूति a. granting a hundred aids.

†**शतमूर्धन्** a. having a hundred heads.

शतंमूल a. having a hundred roots.

शतयज्ञ m. E. of Indra (lit. receiving a hundred sacrifice.)

***शतयष्टिक** m. a necklace consisting of a hundred strings.

शतरात्र m. n. a festival of a hundred days (nights).

शतंवन्त् a. containing or possessing a hundred, hundredfold.

शतवर्ष & °**वर्षिन्** a. a hundred years old.

शतंवाज a. giving a hundred forces.

शतंविचक्षण a. having a hundredfold appearance.

शतंवीर्य a. containing a hundred forces.

शतशंस् adv. by hundreds or hundredfoldly.

शतशाख, f. **आ** & **ई** having a hundred branches.

शतंशारद a. containing or granting a hundred autumns or years; n. such a period.

शतशीर्ष & **शतंशीर्षन्** a. having a hundred heads.

शतशृङ्ग a. having a hundred horns; m. N. of a mountain.

शतसंख्य a. numbering a hundred.

शतसनि a. winning or procuring a hundred.

शतसहस्र n. sgl. & pl. a hundred thousand.

शतसहस्रधा adv. in a hundred thousand pieces.

शतसा a. = **शतसनि**.

शतसाहस्र, f. **ई** hundred thousand-fold.

शतसाहस्रिक a. consisting of a hundred thousand.

शतसुख n. hundredfold luck.

शतसेय n. hundredfold gain.

शतस्विन् a. possessed of a hundred.

शतहन्, f. °**घ्नी** killing a hundred; f. °**घ्नी** a cert. weapon.

शतंहिम a. lasting for a hundred winters or years.

शतह्रद m. N. of an Asura; f. **आ** lightning.

शताङ्ग a. hundredfold (lit. -limbed).

शतात्मन् a. having or granting a hundred lives.

शताधिक a. hundred and one (lit. more than a hundred).

शतानीक a. having a hundred fronts or points.

शताब्द a. consisting of a hundred years.

शतायु a. lasting for a hundred years or hundred years old.

शतायुध a. having a hundred weapons.

शतायुस्, f. **शतायुषी** = **शतायु**.

शतार्घ a. worth a hundred.

शतार्ध n. half a hundred, fifty.

शतार्ह a. = **शतार्घ**.

शतावरी f. a cert. climbing plant.

शताश्रि a. having a hundred angles or edges.

शताश्व a. consisting of a hundred horses.

शतिक a. the hundredth or consisting of a hundred.

शतिन् a. hundredfold or possessing a hundred.

शतेन्द्रिय a. having a hundred senses.

शतेश m. the lord of a hundred (villages).

शतोति a. granting hundredfold help.

शतोदर a. having a hundred bellies (Çiva).

शतौदना f. a cert. ceremony.

शत्य a. consisting of a hundred.

शंत्रि m. N. of a man.

शत्रु m. rival, adversary, enemy, esp. the immediate neighbour of a prince as his natural enemy.

शत्रुघ्न a. slaying foes; m. a man's name.

शत्रुजित् & **शत्रुंजय** a. conquering foes.

शत्रुता f., °**त्व** n. rivalry, enmity.

शत्रूतूर्य n. overcoming foes.

शत्रुनन्दन a. gladdening foes.

शत्रुतप a. tormenting foes.
शत्रुंदम a. subduing foes.
शत्रुबाधन a. fighting foes.
शत्रुमर्दन a. crushing foes.
शत्रुसाह a. overwhelming foes.
शत्रुसेविन् a. serving an enemy.
शत्रुहं & शत्रुहन् a. = शत्रुघ्न adj.
शत्रूय्, pp. शत्रूयन्त् be hostile.
शत्रूषह् (°षाह्) a. overwhelming foes.
1शद्, only I. शाशदुस् etc., pp. शाशदान distinguish one's self, prevail.
2†शद्, perf. शशाद, pp. शन्न fall, decay. — व्यव fall off or asunder. परि fall by the side.
शद m. fall (—°); produce (of land).
शद्वला f. N. of a river.
शनकैस् adv. quietly, gently, gradually.
शनि m. the planet Saturn.
शनैश्चर a. moving slowly; m. = prec.
शनैस् or शनैस् (instr. adv.) = शनकैस्; often repeated, compar. शनैस्तराम्.
शंतनु a. beneficial to the body or person (abstr. शंतनुत्वं); m. N. of an ancient king etc.
शंतम (superl.) most auspicious or salutary.
शंताति a. beneficent; f. benefice.
शन्तिवं a. kind, peaceful.
शन्त्वं n. benefice, kindness.
शन्न a. fallen out or off; n. downfall.
शप्, शपति, °ते (शप्यति), pp. शप्त (q.v.) & शपित curse, execrate, revile, scold, blame; M.(A.) curse one's self if, i.e. assert with an oath that not (यदि), swear by (instr.), conjure (acc. or dat.); implore, entreat for (acc.) by (instr.). C. शापयति cause to swear, conjure by (instr.). — अभि curse, blame, accuse; C. conjure. परि curse, blame, revile. प्रति curse in return. सम् curse.
शपथ m. curse, oath, ordeal.
शपथ्य a. consisting in a curse.
शपन n. cursing.
शप्त a. cursed, conjured; n. curse, oath.
शप्तृ m. curser, swearer.
शफ m. hoof, claw.
शफर m., ई f. a small kind of carp.
शफवन्त् a. having hoofs or claws.
शबर् m. pl. N. of a people.
शबल a. variegated, brindled; mingled or joined with (—°); altered, disfigured. m. N. of a serpent-demon; f. शबली the Wonder-cow (myth.).
शबलता f., °त्व n. variety, alternation.
शब्द m. sound, cry, noise, call, word, speech, the sacred syllable Om, name, term, title. शब्दं कृ or दा raise the voice, call aloud; शब्देन by word i.e. explicitly.
शब्दकर्मक & °कर्मन् a. meaning sound (g.).
शब्दकल्पद्रुम m. T. of a dictionary.
शब्दत्व n. the being sound.
शब्दपति m. lord only by name.
शब्दब्रह्मन् n. the sacred scriptures (lit. the Word-Brahman).
शब्दभाज् a. having the title of (—°).
शब्दमय, f. ई made up of sound or sounds, sounding; consisting or formed of the word (—°).
शब्दय्, °यति, pp. शब्दित (q.v.) give forth sounds, call aloud, cry, talk, prate, call, name, invoke, communicate, teach. — अनु, अभि, & परि relate, communicate, talk over. सम् exclaim, mention, quote.
शब्दवन्त् a. sounding, n. adv. loudly.
शब्दविद्या f. grammar (the science of sounds or words).
शब्दवेध m. the shooting at the mere sound (without seeing the aim); adj. °धिन्, abstr. °धित्व n.
शब्दशासन & °शास्त्र n. = शब्दविद्या.
शब्दापय्, °यति & °ते call near, call, name. (P. be called*).
शब्दाय्, °यते & °ति sound, cry.
शब्दार्थ m. the meaning of sounds or of a word; du. word and sense.
शब्दित a. called, named, invoked, communicated, taught; n. crying.
शब्दिन् a. noisy, resounding with (—°).
1शम्, शमति, शम्यति, pp. शमित labour, work; make ready, prepare (r.). — Cf. शशमान.
2शम्, शाम्यति, °ते (शमति), pp. शान्त (q.v.)

be quiet, still, or content; be allayed or extinguished; cease, desist, stop. C. शमयति (शामयति) quiet, still, pacify, allay, extinguish, subdue, destroy, kill. — अभि cease, stop. समव C. pacify, still. उप cease, stop, be allayed or extinguished. C. tranquillize, pacify, cool, allay. व्युप & समुप cease, leave off. नि & परि C. appease, allay. प्र become calm or tranquil, be extinguished, stop, cease. C. appease, quench, allay, subdue, kill, destroy. (प्रति C. appease, allay*). सम् become thoroughly calm or pacified, make peace with (instr. ± सह), be allayed or extinguished, stop (tr. & intr.). C. mitigate, calm, soothe, allay, extinguish, finish, kill, destroy. — Cf. अभ्युपशान्त, अवशान्त, उपशान्त, प्रशान्त, संशान्त.

3शम् (शम्नीते) harm.

4शम्, शमयति & शामयति w. नि note, perceive, hear, learn. — अनुनि, समनुनि, अभिनि, उपनि, प्रणि, विनि, संनि = S.

5शं indecl. (± योस्) blessing, welfare, prosperity, happiness.

1शंम a. tame, domestic.

2शम m. peace of mind.

शमथ m. quiet, tranquillity, rest, calm, peace; cessation, extinction.

शमन a. (f. ई) & n. tranquillizing, stilling, allaying; n. also killing, destroying.

शमपर a. devoted to quietism or peace of mind.

शमप्रधान a. the same.

शमप्राप्त a. come to rest.

शमयितृ m. calmer, quieter; slayer.

शंमल n. stain, spot, fault, blemish.

शमवन्त् a. quiet, peaceable.

शमशम a. always quiet.

शमात्मक a. quiet-minded.

1शमाय्, °यंते effort one's self, be active or zealous.

2शमाय्, °यति seek for peace of mind; °यंते bring to rest i.e. kill.

1शंमि n. endeavour, effort.

2शमि m. a man's name.

1शमितृ m. dissector (of the sacrificial animal), killer, slaughterer, cook.

2शमितृ a. = seq.

शमिन् a. calm, tranquil.

शमिष्ठ (superl.) most active or busy.

1शंमी f. = 1शंमि.

2शमी f. N. of a tree.

शमीक m. a man's name.

शमीगर्भ a. grown or resting in a Çamī-tree; m. the holy fig-tree.

शमीधान्य n. Çamī-grains, pod-grain i.g.

शमीपर्ण n. Çamī-leaf.

शमीमय, f. ई made of Çamī-wood.

शमीशाखा f. Çamī-branch.

शमीसुमनस् f. Çamī-flower; °नोमाला f. garland of Çamī-flowers.

शंम्ब m. a cert. weapon of Indra.

शंम्बर m. N. of a demon slain by Indra, in l.l. also an enemy of the god of love.

शम्बरघ्न & °दारण m. slayer of Çambara (the god of love).

शम्बरवृत्रहन् m. slayer of Çambara and Vṛtra (Indra).

शम्बरसिद्धि m. N. of a juggler.

शम्बरहत्य n. the slaying of Çambara.

शम्बरहन् m. slayer of Çambara (Indra).

शम्बल n. provender for a journey (cf. संबल).

शम्बा कृ plough up and down.

शम्बिन् m. ferry-man.

शम्बु m. N. of a man.

शम्बूक m. conch-shell, snail, a cert. animal.

शम्भल m. N. of a place; f. ई bawd, procuress.

शंभव a. = शंभु a.

शंभविष्ठ superl. to prec. or seq. a.

शंभु & शंभू a. causing happiness or welfare, helpful, friendly; m. E. of Çiva, Brahman, etc.

शंभुकान्ता f. Çambhu's wife i.e. Gaurī.

शंम्या f. staff, peg, prop, stay; a cert. measure of length.

शम्यापात m. a Çamyā-throw (cf. prec.).

शम्याप्रास m., °प्रासन n. the same.

शय a. lying, sleeping, being in (—°). m. sleep; couch, bed (also शया f.).

शयथ m. couch, lair, abode.

शयध्यै dat. inf. to शी.

शयन a. & n. resting, sleeping; n. also couch, bed.

शयनगृह n., °भूमि f. bed-room.

शयनवासस् a. garment to sleep in.

शयनस्थ a. being on a couch.

शयनीय a. fit or suitable for sleep or rest; n. impers. (it is) to be rested or slept, as subst. coach, bed.

शयनीयगृह n., °वास m. bed-chamber.

शयालु a. sleepy, slothful, sluggish.

*शयित n. the place where a pers. (gen.) has lain or slept.

शयितव्य n. (impers.) it is to be rested or slept.

शयु a. lying, resting.

शयुत्रा adv. on or to the couch.

शय्या f. couch, bed; rest, sleep.

शय्यागृह n. bed-room.

1शर m. reed, arrow.

2शर m. sour cream.

3शर (°—) water.

शरकाण्ड s. reed-stalk.

शरकार m. arrow-maker.

शरक्षेप m. an arrow's throw or flight.

शरगुल्म m. a thicket of reeds.

शरगोचर m. an arrow's reach or flight.

शरच्चन्द्र m. the autumnal moon; °चन्द्रिका f. the autumnal moon-shine.

शरजन्मन् m. E. of Skanda (the reed-born).

शरजाल n. a thick shower of arrows.

शरज्ज्योत्स्ना f. the autumnal moon-shine.

1शरण n. falling asunder, decay.

2शरण a. protecting, guarding; n. protection, refuge or place of refuge, shelter, shed, hut, dwelling, abode; °णं गम् have recourse to (gen. or acc.).

शरणागत a. come for refuge, seeking protection.

शरणार्थिन् & शरणैषिन् a. seeking protection.

शरणालय m. place of refuge.

शरणि f. obstinacy, pertinacity.

शरण्य a. affording or seeking protection, refuge, or help; abstr. °ता f.

शरतल्प m. a couch made of arrows.

शरत्काल m. the autumnal season.

शरत्पद्म n. an autumnal lotus-flower.

शरत्पर्वन् n. a full-moon night in autumn.

शरत्पर्वशशिन् m. the full moon in autumn.

शरत्समय m. the autumnal season.

शरद् f. autumn, pl. also = year.

शरदण्ड m. reed-stalk.

शरदिज a. born or produced in autumn, autumnal.

शरद्वधू f. autumn conceived as a woman.

शरद्वन्त् a. advanced in years (autumns), aged.

शरधि m. receptacle for arrows, quiver.

शरन्मेघ m. an autumnal cloud.

शरपञ्जर n. = शरतल्प.

शरबन्ध m. a thick shower of arrows.

शरबर्हिस् n. reed-straw.

शरभ m. a kind of deer, later a fabulous eight-legged animal; E. of Viṣṇu, N. of an Asura etc.

शरभङ्ग m. N. of a Rishi.

शरभृष्टि f. reed-point.

शरमय, f. ई consisting or made of reeds.

शरवण n. a thicket of reeds.

1शरवर्ष m. a shower of arrows.

2शरवर्ष n. rain (of water).

1शरवर्षिन् a. raining arrows.

2शरवर्षिन् a. raining (water).

शरव्य n. aim, abstr. °ता f.; °व्या f. arrow-shot or hail of arrows.

शरशयन n. = शरतल्प.

शरस् n. cream, the scum on boiled milk.

शरस्तम्ब m. a thicket of reeds.

शराटि or °टी f. a kind of heron.

शरारु a. harming, noxious.

शराव m. n. a flat earthenware dish; also a measure for grain.

शरावर m. a quiver; n. shield or coat of mail (also °वरण n.).

शरावसंपात m. the appearance of dishes (at a meal); °ते वृत्ते when this is past, i.e. after meals.

शरावाप m. bow or quiver (arrow-scatterer).

शरास m., °न n. bow (arrow-thrower).

शरासार m. a shower of arrows.

शरास्य n. the same.

शरिन् a. having arrows.

शरीर n. (m.) the body, also = person; abstr. °ता† f., °त्व† n.

शरीरक n. a (small or inferior) body.
शरीरकर्तृ & °कृत् m. father (body-maker).
शरीरकर्षण n. tormenting the body.
शरीरग्रहण n. taking a bodily form.
शरीरज a. sprung from or belonging to the body, bodily; m. embryo, son, love or the god of love.
शरीरत्याग m. the sacrifice of life (lit. giving up the body).
शरीरदण्ड m. corporal punishment.
शरीरदेश m. region or part of the body.
शरीरधातु m. chief part or element of the body (blood, flesh, etc.).
शरीरधृक् a. bearing a body; m. living creature.
शरीरपात & °भेद m. death (lit. falling or breaking down of the body).
शरीरयष्टि f. a slender body.
शरीरयात्रा f. bodily subsistence.
शरीरयोगज a. sprung from bodily contact.
शरीरवन्त् a. having a body, bodily, solid, firm; m. a living creature.
शरीरवृत्ति f. = शरीरयात्रा.
शरीररत्न n. a jewel of a body.*
शरीरशुश्रूषा f. care of the body, personal attendance.
शरीरशोषण n. emaciation of the body.
शरीरसाद m. bodily exhaustion.
शरीरस्थ a. being in the body.
शरीराकार m. bodily shape.
शरीरान्त m. the hair (lit. end) of the body.
शरीरान्तकर m. destroyer of bodies.
शरीराभ्यधिक a. dearer than one's own person or body (friend).
शरीरार्ध m. the half of the body.
शरीरावयव m. a part of the body.
शरीरिन् a. having a body or having (—°) for body; m. living creature, man, soul
शरु f. (m.) spear or arrow.
शरुमन्त् a. armed with a spear or arrows.
शरौघ m. shower of arrows.
शर्कर a. consisting of gravel or grit; m. pebble, also = f. शर्करा gravel, grit, brown sugar.
शर्कराम्बु n. sugar-water.
शर्करोदक n. the same.
शर्कु m. N. of an evil demon.
शर्कोट m. a cert. snake.
शर्ध्, **शर्धति** fart (only w. अव & वि); be defiant or strong.
1**शर्ध** a. defiant, strong.
2**शर्ध** m. troop, host.
शर्धनीति a. leading the host (of the Maruts) or acting boldly.
1**शर्धस्** (only compar. शर्धस्तर) = 1शर्ध.
2**शर्धस्** n. = 2शर्ध.
†**शर्धिस्** (only —°) defiant, strong.
शर्ध्य s. a cert. part of a waggon.
शर्मक m. pl. N. of a people.
शर्मकारिन् & °कृत् a. causing welfare or happiness.
†**शर्मण्य** a. protecting.
शर्मन् n. cover, protection, shelter, refuge, comfort, welfare, joy, bliss (often —° in Brahman-names).
शर्मय्, only शर्मयन्त् protecting.
शर्मवन्त् a. containing the word शर्मन्.
शर्मिन् a. joyful, happy.
शर्मिष्ठा f. N. of sev. women, esp. of the wife of Yayāti.
शर्य m. arrow, dart; f. आ reed, arrow, pl. matting of reed (on the Soma-strainer).
*__शर्यण__ a. thicket of reeds; m. pl. N. of a region in Kurukṣetra.
शर्यणावन्त् m. pond, lake (cf. prec.), fig. of the Soma-vat.
शर्यहन् m. archer (killer with arrows).
शर्यात & **शर्याति** m. names of men.
शर्व m. N. of a god killing with arrows, in l. l. = Rudra-Çiva.
शर्वपत्नी f. Çarva's wife i.e. Pārvatī.
शर्वपर्वत m. Çarva's mountain, i.e. Kailāsa.
(*__शर्वर__ a. spotted); f. शर्वरी pl. the spotted deer (of the Maruts); sgl. the (starred) night.
शर्वाचल m. = शर्वपर्वत.
शर्वाणी f. N. of the wife of Çarva or Çiva.
1**शल्**, **शलति**, w. उद् leap, jump, rise. — Cf. उच्छलन्त्, उच्छलित.
2**शल्** an exclamation.
शल m. staff, quill of a porcupine (as a measure of length.

शलकर m. N. of a serpent-demon.
शलभ m. grasshopper, moth, night-butterfly; abstr. **°ता** f., **°त्व** n.
शलल n., **°ली** f. quill of a porcupine or bristle of a hog.
शललित a. furnished with squills.
(**शलाक** m.) & **शलाका** f. chip, splinter, stalk, rod, stick, peg, pin; finger, toe; quill of the porcupine.
शलाकिका f. small chip etc. (v. prec.).
शलाटु m. n. the unripe fruit of a tree.
शलातुर s. N. of the birth-place of Pāṇini.
शलुन m. a cert. insect.
शल्क m. n. chip, piece, bit; n. scale of a fish.
शल्य m. n. the point of a spear or an arrow, i.g. thorn, sting (lit. & fig.); blemish, fault, obstacle; m. also = seq.
शल्यक m. porcupine.
शल्यकर्तृ m. arrow-maker.
शल्यकर्तृ & **°कृन्त** m. surgeon.
शल्यवन्त् a. who has the arrow-point (either the killed deer or the killing hunter).
शल्लक m., **ई** f. a porcupine, f. also N. of a tree.
शव m. n. dead body, corpse.
शवकर्मन् n. funeral act, burial.
शवदह्या f. cremation of a body.
शवधर a. carrying a dead body.
शवर्त m. a. cert. worm (cf. **श्ववर्त**).
शववाह & **°क** m. corpse-carrier.
शवशिरस् n. scull.
शवशिरोध्वज m. a flag or emblem consisting of a scull; adj. carrying such a flag.
शवस् n. superiority, power, strength, heroism; instr. strongly, mightily.
शवसान a. superior, powerful, heroic.
†**शवसावन्त्** & **शवसिन्** a. the same.
शवसी f. powerful, mighty (Indra's mother).
शवस्पृश् a. who touches a corpse.
शवाग्नि m. funeral fire.
शवान्न n. funeral food.
शविष्ठ (superl.) most mighty or strong.
शवीर a. powerful, mighty.
शवोद्वह m. remover of corpses.
शव्य n. funeral.

शश्, **शशति** leap.
शश m. hare (seen also in the spot of the moon).
शशक m. hare, rabbit.
शशकविषाण n. a hare's horn (= impossibility).
शशधर m. the moon (hare-holder).
शशबिन्दु m. N. of a prince.
शशभृत् m. = **शशधर**.
शशमान a. active, busy, zealous, devout, pious.
शशय a. inexhaustible, incessant.
शशयु a. desiring or pursuing hares.
शशलक्षण m. the moon (hare-marked).
शशलक्ष्मन् n. the hare-mark; m. = prec.
शशलाञ्छन m. = prec. m.
शशविषाण n. = **शशकविषाण**.
शशशृङ्ग n. the same.
शशाङ्क m. = **शशलक्षण**.
शशाङ्कलेखा f. the lunar crescent (lit. moon-streak).
शशाङ्कवदना f. a moon-faced woman.
शशिकला f. a digit or sickle of the moon.
शशिन् m. the moon (hare-marked).
शशिप्रभ a. moon-like.
शशिमुखी f. = **शशाङ्कवदना**.
शशिमौलि m. E. of Çiva (moon-crested).
शशिलेखा f. = **शशाङ्कलेखा**.
शशिवदना f. = **शशाङ्कवदना**.
शशिशेखर m. = **शशिमौलि**.
शशिसंनिभ a. = **शशिप्रभ**.
शशीयंस् (compar.) more numerous, richer.
शश्वधा adv. constantly, always.
शश्वन्त्, f. **शश्वती** (**शश्वती**) ever repeating or renewing itself, frequent, numerous, all, every. — n. **शश्वत्** adv. again and again, always, frequently, once more; indeed, of course; **शश्वत्—शश्वत्** no sooner—than.
शष्कुलि & **°ली** f. the orifice of the ear or auditory passage; also a kind of food or meal.
शष्प n. (young) grass, p. **वन्त्**†.
शष्प्य a. grassy.
शस्, **शसति**, **शस्ति**, & **शास्ति**, pp. **शस्त** cut to pieces, slaughter. — **वि** = S.
शसन n., **शसा** f. slaughter, killing.

1शस्त a. recited, praised, commended, praiseworthy, auspicious, happy, cheerful, beautiful; n. praise, commendation.
2शस्त a. cut to pieces, slaughtered.
3शस्त n. a kind of girdle.
शस्तृ m. cutter, killer.
शस्ति f. praise or praiser.
1शस्त्र n. a kind of recitation (r.).
2शस्त्र n. knife, dagger (also f. शस्त्री & शस्त्रिका); sword, weapon i.g.
शस्त्रकलि m. sword-fight.
शस्त्रन्यास m. the laying down of arms.
शस्त्रपत्त्र n. blade of a knife or sword.
शस्त्रपाणि & °पाणिन् a. having a sword in hand.
शस्त्रपात m. the (fall or) cut of a knife.
शस्त्रप्रहार m. the stroke of a sword.
शस्त्रभृत् a. bearing a sword; m. warrior.
शस्त्रवन्त् a. armed with a sword.
शस्त्रविक्रयिन् m. dealer in weapons.
शस्त्रवृत्ति a. living by the trade of arms.
शस्त्रसंपात m. flying or discharge of missiles.
शस्त्रास्त्रभृत् a. carrying arms for striking and throwing; abstr. °त्त्व n.
शस्त्रिका & शस्त्री v. 2शस्त्र.
शस्त्रिन् a. = शस्त्रवन्त्.
शस्मन् n. praise, eulogy.
शस्य a. to be recited or praised; n. recitation.
शा, शिशाति, शिशीते, श्यति, pp. शात & शित (q.v.) sharpen, whet; excite, make eager, strengthen, promote; communicate, impart; present with, help to (acc. of pers., instr., dat., or gen. of thing). — अति strike at. अव rid of (acc.). आ help to, cause to partake of (loc.). नि sharpen, whet; offer, present; lay down, spread. सम् sharpen, whet; excite, make eager or ready for (dat.). — Cf. निशित, संशित.
1शाक m. help, assistance.
2शाक a. helpful; m. helper, assistant.
3शाक n. eatable herb, vegetable food.
4शाक a. belonging to the Çakas or to their kings; m. n. = seq.
शाककाल m. the Çaka-era (78 A.D.).
शाकटायन & शाकपूणि m. names of grammarians.
शाकल m. n. = शकल; m. pl. the adherents of Çākalya, a. relating to them.
शाकलहोम m. a cert. oblation; °मीय a. relating to it.
शाकल्य m. N. of an ancient teacher.
शाकवाट m., °वाटिका f. a garden of vegetables.
शाकिन् & शाकिन a. powerful, mighty.
शाकुन, f. ई relating to birds, bird-like; m. bird-catcher.
शाकुनि & °क m. = prec. m.
शाकुनिकलुब्धक m. the same.*
शाकुन्तल m. the son of Çakuntalā (Bharata); n. the play or the tale about Ç.
शाक्त m. teacher; worshipper of the Çakti or energy (of Çiva).
शाक्तीक m. spearman.
शाक्मन् n. help, aid.
शाक्य m. pl. N. of a warrior race, sgl. a man of this race, also = seq.
शाक्यभिक्षु m. a Buddhist mendicant.
शाक्यमुनि m. the saint of the Çākyas, i.e. Buddha.
शाक्यश्रमण (& °क*) m. = शाक्यभिक्षु.
शाक्र, f. ई belonging to Çakra (Indra).
शाक्वर, f. ई strong, mighty.
शाखा f. (adj. —° f. आ & ई) branch (lit. & fig.); limb, arm, leg, finger; ramification, subdivision, species, sort, branch of a Veda, i.e. Vedic school.
शाखाङ्ग n. limb of the body.
शाखान्तग a. having finished one Çākhā (r.).
शाखाबाहु m. an arm (-like) branch.
शाखाभेद m. pl. divisions and subdivisions.
शाखामय (f. ई*) consisting of branches.
शाखामृग m. ape (branch-animal).
शाखिन् a. having branches or schools (Veda); m. tree.
शाखीय a. belonging to the school of (—°).
शांकर, f. ई relating to Çiva or Çaṁkarācārya.
1शाङ्खायन m. N. of a teacher and author, pl. his race.
2शाङ्खायन, f. ई belonging to Çāṅkhāyana.
शाङ्खिक m. shell-blower.
शाङ्ख्य a. made of shells.
†शाचि m. pl. grains, grit.

†शाचिगु & शाचिपूजन m. E. of Indra.
शाट m., ई f., शाटक m. n. cloth, scarf.
शाट्यायन m. N. of an ancient teacher and legislator; pl. his followers (also °निन्).
शाठ्य n. falsehood, villany; p. °वन्त्.
1शाण, f. ई hempen; m. & f. ई a hempen garment.
2शाण m., आ f. grind- or touchstone.
3शाण m., आ f. a cert. weight.
शाणोपल m. grindstone.
शाण्ड m. a man's name.
शाण्डिल a. belonging to or descending from Çāṇḍilya, m. pl. his descendants.
शाण्डिल्य m. N. of sev. teachers.
1शात a. sharpened, whetted; thin, slender.
2शात m. the falling out (of hair, nails etc.).
शातकुम्भ n. gold (lit. coming from the river Çatakumbhā).
शातकुम्भमय (f. ई) & °कुम्भीय a. golden.
शातकौम्भ (f. ई) & °कौम्भमय a. = prec.
शातन a. (f. ई) & n. causing to fall, cutting off, destroying.
शातह्रद a. of lightning.
शातिन् m. cutter, hewer (—°).
शातोदर, f. ई thin-bellied, abstr. °त्व n.
शात्रव a. inimical; m. enemy.
शाद m. falling, dropping (—°); grass. f. शादा brick.
शादन n. falling out.
शाद्वल a. grassy, verdant, green; n. a grassy spot.
शाद्वलवन्त् & °लिन् a. = prec. a.
शान्त a. appeased, still, tranquil, calm, quiet, gentle, meek, soft; extinguished, ceased, dead. m. & f. आ a man's & woman's name; n. = seq.
शान्तता f., °त्व n. tranquillity, absence of passion.
शांतनव m. patron. of Bhīṣma.
शांतनु m. N. of an ancient king (= शंतनु).
शान्तमनस् a. of tranquil mind.
शान्तय्, °यति calm, pacify.
शान्तरजस् a. dustless or passionless (lit. having the dust or the quality of passion allayed).
शान्तरूप a. of calm appearance.
शान्तात्मन् a. calm-minded, composed.
शान्ति f. tranquillity, peace of mind; averting of an evil omen, expiation; welfare, bliss; stopping, ceasing, extinction (of fire), destruction, end, death.
शान्तिक & शान्तिकर्मन् n. any act for averting bad consequences.
शान्तिद a. causing bliss or happiness.
शान्तिपात्र & °भाजन n. vessel for the propitiatory water.
शान्तिसलिल & शान्त्युदक n. propitiatory water.
शान्तिहोम m. propitiatory oblation.
शान्त्वय् v. सान्त्वय्.
1शाप m. curse.
2शाप m. float, drift (concr.).
शापप्रदान n. the utterance of a curse.
शापमोच m. = prec. or deliverance from a c.
शापाम्बु & शापोदक n. curse-water (by applying which a pers. is cursed).
शाब v. 1शाव.
शाबर m. N. of a plant & a teacher, f. ई the language of the Çabaras.
शाबरिका f. a kind of leech.
शाबल्य n. medley, compound, f. °ल्या female jester or singer.
शाब्द, f. ई relating to sounds or words, esp. based upon the sacred word i.e. the Veda; m. philologist, grammarian.
शाब्दिक a. uttering a sound or familiar with sounds (words); m. = prec. m.
शामित्र a. relating to the slayer or cutter of the sacrificial victim; m. the fire for cooking the sacrif. flesh; n. a place for slaying cattle or = seq.
शामित्रकर्मन् n. the office of the slayer of the sacrificial animal.
शामील, f. ई made of Çamī-wood.
शामुल्य & शामूल n. a woolen shirt.
शाम्बर, f. ई relating to Çambara; n. jugglery, sorcery.
शाम्बरिक m. juggler, sorcerer.
शांभव, f. ई relating to Çambhu (Çiva).
शाम्य a. aiming at peae, peaceable; n. & °ता f. peace, tranquillity.
शाय a. lying, sleeping (—°).

शायक, f. °यिका = prec.; *f. also mode of lying or one's turn to lie.

शायिन् a. lying, resting, sleeping (mostly —°).

शार, f. आ mottled, spotted; m. a stone or piece used at sev. games (also f. ई).

शारङ्ग s. bow*; f. °ङ्गी the female of a cert. bird.

शारद, f. शारदी or शारदी autumnal.

शारदीन & **शारदीय** a. the same.

शारद्य n. autumn-corn.

शारद्वत m. a man's name.

शारि m. = शार m.; f. a kind of crow.

शारिक m., आ f. = prec. m. & f.

शारीर, f. ई made of bone; corporeal, of the body. n. bodily constitution, excrement.

शारीरक a. corporeal.

शारीरकमीमांसा f., °लक्षण n., °विद्या f. titles of works.

शार्ग m. a cert. bird.

शार्ङ्ग a. made of horn or coming from the Çṛṅga-tree. m. a cert. bird (f. ई); n. bow (esp. that of Viṣṇu).

शार्ङ्गक m., °ङ्गिका f. = prec. m. & f.

शार्ङ्गधनुर्धर m. E. of Viṣṇu-Kṛṣṇa.

शार्ङ्गधन्वन् & °धन्विन् m. = prec.

शार्ङ्गधर m. the same; N. of an author, °पद्धति f. his work.

शार्ङ्गधरपाणि & °भृत् m. E. of Viṣṇu-Kṛṣṇa.

शार्ङ्गरव m. N. of a man.

शार्ङ्गिन् m. = शार्ङ्गधनुर्धर.

शार्दूल m. tiger (f. ई); best among (—°).

शार्दूलचर्मन् n. a tiger's skin.

शार्दूललोमन् n. a tiger's hair.

शार्दूलविक्रीडित n. tiger's play, N. of a metre.

शार्यात m., ई f. patron. names.

शार्व, f. ई relating to Çarva (Çiva); w. दिश् f. the north-east.

शार्वर a. nocturnal; f. ई night.

शार्वरिक a. = prec. adj.

1**शाल** m. a kind of timber tree, tree i.g., wall, fence; f. शाला (q.v.).

2**शाल** a. being in a hut, house, room, hall etc.

3**शाल** m. a kind of fish.

शालग्राम m. N. of a sacred village.

शालङ्कायन m. N. of a Rishi, pl. his race.

शालपोत m. a young Çāla-tree.

शालभ a. moth-like; °विधि m. such a way of acting (cf. पतंगवृत्ति).

शालभञ्जिका & °भञ्जी f. statue.

शाला f. hut, house, hall, room, stable (—° also शाल n.).

शालार्क m. a bunch of chips or fagots; fagot-fire.

शालाग्नि m. domestic fire.

शालातुरीय a. native of Çalātura, m. E. of Pāṇini.

शालापति m. householder.

शालामुखीय a. being in the front of a house (fire).

शालावंश m. the chief post of a hut.

शालावृक m. cat (cf. सालावृक).

शालाश्रय (abstr. °त्व n.) & °सद् a. dwelling in a house.

शालास्तम्भ m. post or pillar of a house.

शालि m. sgl. & pl. rice.

शालिकण m. grain of rice.

शालिकेदार m., °क्षेत्र n. field of rice.

शालिगोप m., ई f. guardian of a rice-field.

शालिचूर्ण n. rice-flower, ground rice.

शालिन् a. possessing, full of, rich in, eminent by (—°); f. °नी a field of rice.

शालिभवन n., °भू f. a field of rice.

शालिवाहन m. N. of a king.

शालिहोत्र m. E. of the horse (lit. receiving rice-oblations); N. of an author on hippology, n. his work.

शालीन a. having a fixed abode, domestic; modest, bashful, ashamed; n. adv., as subst. modesty, humbleness.

शालीनता f. = prec. n.

शालीनत्व n. abstr. to शालीन in all mgs.

शालु n. a cert. fruit.

शालुड m. N. of an evil demon.

शालूक n. an esculent lotus-root.

शालूर m. frog.

शालेय, f. ई grown with rice.

शाल्मलि (adj. —°) = seq.

शाल्मलि m. f., °ली f. the silk-cotton tree; the latter also N. of a river & a bell.

शाल्मलीफलक s. a board of Çālmalī-wood.

शाल्यन्न n. boiled rice, rice-gruel.

शाल्योदन m. n. the same.

शाल्व m. pl. N. of a people.

1शाव m. the young of an animal.

2शाव a. relating to a dead body, cadaverous, dead.

शावक m. = 1शाव.

शावाशौच n. impurity on account of a dead body.

शाश & शाशक a. relating to a hare, leporine.

शाश्वत, f. ई constant, perpetual, uninterrupted, eternal; n. = seq.

शाश्वतत्व n. constancy, eternity.

1शास्, शास्ति, शास्ते (शासति, °ते), pp. शिष्ट (q.v.), शास्त, & शासित chasten, punish, correct, rule, govern, manage, direct, instruct, teach, order, command, announce, proclaim, foretell, avow, confess. — अनु teach, instruct, order, command (2 acc.); direct, indicate; rule, govern (± राज्यम् or स्वराज्यम्); chastise, punish. अभ्यनु indicate, designate. समनु teach, impart (2 acc.); w. राज्यम् rule, bear sway. अभि indicate, direct, rule. आ M.(A.) wish, pray or hope for (acc.); expect from (abl.); ± आशिषम् & आशिषस् make supplication, utter wishes for (dat. or loc.). उद् direct upwards (to the gods). प्र instruct, teach, direct, order, command; dispose of, decide (acc. ± अधि); rule, govern (± राज्यम्). संप्र w. राज्यम् bear sway, reign. वि give various instructions about (acc.). सम् direct, bid, invite. — Cf. अनुशिष्ट.

2शास् f. command or commander.

1शास m. order, command.

2शास m. punisher, ruler.

3शास m. knife.

शासक m. teacher, instructor.

शासन a. (f. ई) & n. chastising, punishing, instructing, teaching; n. also chastisement, punishment, discipline, government, order, command, edict, precept. — शासनं कृ, °ने वृत् or स्था obey the orders of (gen. or —°).

शासनधर m. messenger, envoy (bearer of commands).

शासनवाहक, °हारक & °हारिन् m. the same.

शासनीय a. to be taught or instructed.

शासहस्त a. holding a knife in the hand.

शासितृ m. chastiser, punisher, governor, teacher.

शासितव्य a. to be taught or prescribed.

शासिन् a. punishing, instructing, commanding, ruling (—°).

शासुस् n. direction, order.

शास्ति f. punishment, order, command.

शास्तृ m. = शासितृ.

शास्त्र n. instruction, precept, rule, theory, a scientific or canonical work.

शास्त्रकार & °कृत् m. the author of a Çāstra work (cf. prec.).

शास्त्रचिन्तक m. a learned man.

शास्त्रज्ञ a. versed in science.

शास्त्रतस् adv. according to precept or law.

शास्त्रदृष्ट a. mentioned or stated in a Çāstra work, according to precept or rule.

शास्त्रबुद्धि f. scholarship.

शास्त्रमति a. having a learned mind; m. a scholar.

शास्त्रवाद m. statement of the Çāstras.

शास्त्रवादिन् m. teacher (of sciences).

शास्त्रविद् a. = शास्त्रज्ञ.

शास्त्रिन् a. learned; m. a scholar or learned man.

शास्त्रीय a. scriptural, theoretical.

शास्य a. to be punished, directed, or ruled.

शि v. शा.

शिंश m. a kind of tree.

शिंशप m., शिंशपा f. a cert. tree.

शिंशुमार m. a porpoise.

शिक्य n. strap, carrying-girth; a balance suspended by strings.

शिक्व, शिक्वन्, & शिक्वस् a. able, clever.

शिच्, शिंचति, °ते, pp. शिचित (q.v.) strive to be able, try, practise, learn (mostly M.); be willing to help (dat.), to give or impart (acc.), or to present with (instr.). C. शिचयति (°ते) cause a person to learn a thing, teach, instruct (2 acc., or acc. of pers. & loc. of th. or infin.; also gen. of pers. & acc. of th.). — अनु learn, C. teach. अभि C. teach. आ cause to partake of (gen.), wish to present with (instr.). उप

attract, entice, invite; try, practise, learn (mostly M.). प्रति allure, invite. वि distribute. सम् C. teach.

शिक्षक a. teaching; m. teacher.

शिक्षण n. teaching, instruction in (loc.).

शिक्षणीय a. to be taught or to be instructed in (acc.).

शिक्षा f. ability, cleverness, skill, art, knowledge, instruction; esp. the science of the grammatical elements.

शिक्षानर a. befriending men.

शिक्षावन्त् a. rich in knowledge, instructive.

शिक्षित a. learnt or learned, taught, instructed in (acc., loc., or —°).

शिक्षितुकाम m. beginner (lit. willing to learn).*

शिक्षु a. communicative, helpful.

शिक्षेण्य a. instructive.

शिख m. N. of a serpent-demon; f. शिखा (q.v.).

शिखण्ड & °क† m. a tuft of hair or a peacock's tail.

शिखण्डिन् a. poss. to prec.; m. peacock, N. of a man, the son of Drupada, born as a female (शिखण्डिनी), f. °नी also a pea-hen.

शिखण्डिमन्त् a. rich in peacocks.

शिखर a. peaked; m. n. peak, top, summit.

शिखरिन् a. peaked, pointed, crested; m. mountain; f. °णी N. of a metre.

शिखा f. tuft or braid of hair, a peacock's crest, flame, ray of light, top, point, summit, end.

शिखाजट a. wearing a lock on the top of the head.

शिखादामन् n. garland worn on the head.

शिखाभरण n. ornament of the head, diadem.

शिखामणि m. crest-gem; best of (—°).

शिखालम्बिन् a. hanging down from the crest.

शिखावन्त् a. flaming, burning; pointed.

शिखावल m. peacock.

शिखिन् a. wearing a tuft of hair or a crest; m. peacock, fire or the god of fire, f. शिखिनी pea-hen.

शिग्रु m. pl. N. of a people; sgl. the horse-radish tree.

शिग्रुक m. = prec. sgl.

शिच् f. (nom. शिक्) = शिक्य, also net.

†**शिञ्ज्, शिङ्क्ते**, pp. शिञ्जित (q.v.) twang, tinkle. — वि warble. सम् = S. — Cf. आशिञ्जित.

शिञ्जा f. tinkling, humming.

शिञ्जार m. N. of a man.

शिञ्जित a. & n. twanging, tinkling, humming.

शिञ्जिनी f. bow-string (the twanging one).

शित a. whetted, sharp, thin.

शितधार a. sharp-edged.

शितामन् m. a cert. part of the sacrificial victim.

†**शिति** a. white or black (blue).

शितिकक्ष a. white-shouldered.

सितिकण्ठ a. white- or black-necked; m. a cert. bird or prey, a peacock, E. of Çiva, N. of a serpent-demon & sev. men.

शितिकण्ठक a. blue-necked.

शितिङ्ग a. whitish.

शितिपक्ष a. white-winged.

शितिपद् (°पाद्) a. white-footed.

शितिपाद a. the same.

शितिपृष्ठ a. white-backed.

शितिबाहु or °बाहु a. having white fore-legs.

शितिभ्रु a. white-browed.

शितिमांस n. fat (white flesh).

शितिरत्न n. sapphire (blue gem).

शितिवार & °वाल a. white-tailed.

शितिवासस् a. clad in dark.

शितोदर, f. ई thin-bellied.

शित्यंस a. white-shouldered.

शित्योष्ठ a. white-lipped.

शिथिर a. loose, slack, soft, tender.

शिथिल a. loose, flaccid, languid, trembling, feeble.

शिथिलता f. looseness, laxity.

शिथिलय्, °यति, pp. शिथिलित loosen, relax.

शिथिलसमाधि a. of relaxed attention, absent in thought.

शिथिली कृ = शिथिलय्, °भू intr.

शिनि m. a man's name.

शिपि v. seq.

शिपित a. superfluous.

शिपिविष्ट a. the same, bald. m. E. of Viṣṇu & Çiva.

शिप्रवन्त् a. full-cheeked.

शिप्रा f. du. the cheeks or those parts of a helmet that cover them.

शिप्रिणीवन्त् & **शिप्रिन्** a. = **शिप्रवन्त्**.

शिफा f. a fibrous or thin root; a lash with a rod.

शिबि m. N. of a king, pl. his people.

शिबिक m. = prec.; f. **आ** litter, palanquin, the weapon of Kubera.

शिबिर n. royal camp or tent.

शिभ्र a. wanton, lustful.

शिम्, **शिम्यति** = 1**शम्**.

शिम m. distributer of the sacrificial meat.

शिमी f. endeavour, effort.

शिमीवन्त् a. effective, pervading, strong.

शिम्ब m. legume, pod; °**ल** m. small pod.

शिम्बि f. = **शिम्ब**.

शिम्यु or **शिम्यु** m. pl. N. of a people.

शिर् (—°) crushing, afflicting.

शिरःकपाल n. (head-)scull, p. °**लिन्**.

शिरःकम्प m. shaking of the head; a. °**म्पिन्**.

शिरःकर्ण n. sgl. head and ear.

शिरःपट्ट m. head-band.

शिरश्छेद m., °**न** n. cutting of a head.

शिरःशूल n. violent head-ache.

शिरःशेष a. having only the head left; m. E. of Rāhu.

शिरस् n. head, top, point, summit, fore-part, front; **युद्धस्य** van. — Instr. w. **कृ**, **धृ**, etc. bear on the head i.e. esteem highly, honour, respect.

शिरसिज & °**रुह** m. the hair of the head (lit. head-growing).

शिरस्क (adj. —°) = **शिरस्**.

शिरस्तस् adv. from or at the head.

शिरस्त्र n. helmet (head-protector).

शिरस्त्राण n. the same.

शिरःस्नात a. who has bathed his head.

शिरीष m. N. of a tree, n. its blossom.

शिरोग्रीव n. sgl. head and neck.

शिरोघात m. blow on the head.

शिरोज n. pl. the hair of the head.

शिरोदामन् n. head-band.

शिरोदुःख n. head-ache.

शिरोधर m., **आ** f. the neck (head-bearer).

शिरोधरणीय & °**धार्य** a. to be borne on the head i.e. to be honoured or respected.

शिरोधूनन n. shaking of the head.

शिरोभाग m. head-end, top.

शिरोऽभिताप m. head-ache.

शिरोभूषण n. ornament for the head.

शिरोमणि m. crest-jewel; the crown, i.e. the first or chief of (gen or —°).

शिरोमुख n. sgl. head and face.

शिरोरत्न n. crest-gem, ornament for the head.

शिरोरुज् & °**रुजा** f. head-ache.

शिरोरुह m. hear or horn (head-born).

शिरोवेदना f. head-ache.

शिरोहृत्कमल n. du. the lotus of the head and heart (poet.).

शिल m. an ear of corn left on the field & the gleaning of it.

शिलवृत्ति a. who lives by gleaning.

शिला f. stone, rock.

शिलागृह n. a house made of stone or in a rock.

शिलाचय m. heap of stones, mountain.

शिलातल n. a flat stone (or grind-stone*).

शिलापट्ट & °**क** m. a slab or seat of stone.

शिलामय, f. **ई** made of stone, stony.

शिलावर्षिन् a. raining stones.

शिलावेश्मन् n. cave in a rock, rocky recess.

शिलास्तम्भ m. a stony pillar.

शिलिन् m. N. of a serpent-demon.

शिली भू become stone or as hard as stone.

शिलीन्ध्र n. a mushroom.

शिलीपद = **श्लीपद**.

शिलीमुख m. arrow, bee; N. of a hare.

शिलोच्चय m. = **शिलाचय**.

शिलोञ्छ m., °**न** n. gleaning; m. du. & n. sgl. gleaning and gathering grains.

1**शिलोञ्छवृत्ति** f. subsistence by gleaning.

2**शिलोञ्छवृत्ति** a. = seq.

शिलोञ्छिन् a. who lives by gleaning.

1**शिल्प** a. many-coloured, variegated.

2**शिल्प** n. variegation, decoration, ornament, art, craft; f. **शिल्पी** = seq.

शिल्पकारिका & °**कारी** f. a female artist.

शिल्पवन्त् m. artist.

शिल्पिदारिका f. female artist.*

शिल्पिन् a. knowing an art; m. & f. °**नी** artist, artisan.

शिल्पोपजीविन् m. = prec. m. (living by an art).

शिवं a. kind, friendly, mild, gracious, lovely, auspicious, fortunate. m. N. of a god (at first euphemistically = Rudra), jackal (mostly f. आ); du. Çiva and his wife. f. शिवा Çiva's energy, personif. as his wife. n. (m.) luck, happiness, bliss; शिवंम्, शिवेंन & शिवेंभिस् adv.

शिवक्षेत्र n. a field or place consecrated to Çiva, N. of a cert. district.

शिवताति a. causing welfare; f. welfare.

शिवदत्त & शिवदास m. names of men.

शिवदिश् f. Çiva's region (the north-east).

शिवपुर n., °पुरी f. N. of sev. towns & villages.

शिवपुराण n. T. of a Purāṇa.

शिवप्रिया f. Çiva's wife.

शिवभक्त m. a worshipper of Çiva.

शिवभक्ति f. worship of Çiva.

शिवभूति m. N. of a minister.

शिवमय, f. ई thoroughly devoted to Çiva.

शिवमार्ग m. final emancipation (lit. Çiva's path).

शिवयोषित् f. Çiva's wife.

शिवरूपिन् a. having the form of Çiva.

शिवलिङ्ग n. the phallus of Çiva.

शिवलोक m. Çiva's world.

शिवशर्मन् m. N. of a man.

शिवंसंकल्प a. bearing good will; m. E. of cert. verses.

शिवसुन्दरी f. Çiva's wife.

शिवसूत्र n. pl. N. of cert. grammatical & philosophical aphorisms.

शिवादेशक m. fortune-teller, astrologer.

शिवाभिमर्शन a. gently touching.

शिवायतन n. a temple of Çiva.

शिवालय m. Çiva's abode (a temple or mount Kailāsa).

शिवि, शिविक, शिविर v. शिबि etc.

शिवेतर a. malignant, unkind.

शिशान् (only शिश्ना) = शिश्न.

शिशयं a. communicative, liberal.

शिशयिषु a. wishing to lie down, sleepy.

शिशिर m. n. the cool or dewy season, i.g. hoar, frost, dew; as adj. cool, chilly.

शिशिरकर & °किरण m. the moon (having cold rays).

शिशिरदीधिति & °मयूख m. the same.

शिशिरय्, °यति to cool (trans.).

शिशिरांशु a. having cold rays; m. the moon.

शिशिरात्यय m. spring (end of the dewy season).

शिशिरर्तु & शिशिरसमय m. the cool season of the year.

शिशिरात्यय m. spring (end of the cool season).

शिशिरी w. कृ = शिशिरय्.

शिशु & शिशुक m. young, child.

शिशुकाल m. childlood.

शिशुकृच्छ्र n. a kind of penance.

शिशुचान्द्रायण n. the lunar penance of children.

शिशुजन m. sgl. (coll.) children.

शिशुता f., °त्व n. childhood.

शिशुनाग m. a young snake.

शिशुपाल m. N. of a king slain by Kṛṣṇa.

शिशुपालवध m. the slaying of Çiçupāla, T. of an epic poem by Māgha.

शिशुभाव m. childhood, childishness.

शिशुमन्त् a. having children or young.

शिशुमार m. the Gangetic porpoise (lit. child-killing) & a constellation conceived in the form of this animal and as an apparition of Viṣṇu.

शिशूल m. a little child.

शिश्न m. n. tail or the membrum virile.

शिश्नथ m. piercing, perforation.

शिश्नदेव m. pl. a class of tailed demons or false gods.

शिष्, शिनष्टि, शिंषति, pp. शिष्ट (q.v.) leave; P. शिष्यते be left, remain, w. न want, be missing. C. शेषयति, °ते leave, spare. — अति leave remaining; P. remain. अप leave out. अव leave remaining (also C.); P. be left, remain. उद् & परि the same. वि leave apart i.e. separate, distinguish, characterize. P. be distinguished by (instr.), differ from (abl.); be eminent among (gen. or loc.), be better or more excellent than (abl. or instr.). C. distinguish, characterize; pick out, prefer; exceed, surpass (acc.). प्रवि increase, augment. — Cf. अतिशिष्ट, अवशिष्ट, उच्छिष्ट, परिशिष्ट (sic!), विशिष्ट, संशिष्ट.

1शिष्ट a. ordered, commanded (pers. & th.);

taught, learned, wise. m. a wise or a good man; n. precept, rule, instruction.

2शिष्ट a. left, remaining; n. rest, remainder.

शिष्टप्रयोग m. the use or practice of learned men.

शिष्टभक्ष m. the eating of leavings.

शिष्टसभा f. an assembly of learned men.

शिष्टागम m. the tradition of learned men.

1शिष्टाचार m. the conduct of well-bred men.

2शिष्टाचार a. behaving like well-bred men.

शिष्टादिष्ट a. approved by wise men.

1शिष्टि f. punishment, command, instruction.

2†शिष्टि f. help, aid.

शिष्य a. to be taught or instructed; m. scholar, pupil (f. आ); abstr. °ता f.

शिष्यक m. = prec. m.

शिष्यरूपिन् a. having the form or appearance of a scholar.

1शी, शीयते fall, cease, perish.

2शी, शेते & शयते (°ति), pp. शयित (q.v.) lie, sleep, rest. C. शाययति, °ते cause to lie down or go to sleep, lay down, put on or in (loc.). D. शिशयिषते wish to sleep. -- अति sleep or go to rest before another (acc.); also = C. surpass, excel. व्यति reach beyond, surpass (acc.). अधि lie in or on, mount, enter (acc., r. loc.). अनु lie on or in (acc. or loc.), lie down after another (acc.); rue, repent. अभि lie upon (acc.). आ lie in or on (acc.). अन्वा stretch, extend. प्रत्या lie before or in front of (acc.). उप lie by or on (acc. or loc.). परि lie about, surround, encompass; be at or in (acc.). प्र lie down upon (acc.). सम् be undecided or in doubt, despair of (loc.); A. disagree about (acc.). — Cf. अतिशयित, संशयित.

3शी (—°) lying, resting.

शीक्, शीकते, pp. शीकित drip.

शीकर m. thin or drizzling rain; °कण m. drop.

शीकरिन् a. drizzling, sprinkling.

शीघ्र a. quick, speedy; शीघ्रम् & शीघ्रेण adv.

शीघ्रकारिन् & °कृत् a. acting quickly.

शीघ्रकृत्य a. to be done quickly.

शीघ्रग & °गामिन् a. going quickly, hastening, swift.

शीघ्रचार a. = prec., मण्डल° whirling around.

शीघ्रता f., °त्व n. quickness, speed.

शीघ्रपाणि a. quick-handed (the wind).

शीघ्रपातिन् a. flying swiftly.

शीघ्रपायिन् a. drinking or sucking swiftly.

शीघ्रयान n. & a. (also °यायिन्) going quickly.

शीघ्रवाहिन् a. riding or driving fast.

शीघ्रवेग m. moving on quickly.

शीघ्र्य a. speedy.

शीत a. cold, cool; n. cold, frost.

शीतक, f. शीतिका = prec. adj.

1शीतकर a. cooling.

2शीतकर m. the moon (cold-rayed).

शीतकिरण m. = prec. 2.

शीतकृच्छ्र n. a kind of penance.

शीतक्रिया f. cooling, refreshing.

शीतगु m. = 2शीतकर.

शीतता f., °त्व n. coldness, cold.

शीतदीधिति & °द्युति m. = 2शीतकर.

शीतपाणि & °भानु m. the same.

शीतपूतना f. N. of a female demon.

शीतमय a. cold, cool.

शीतमयूख & °मरीचि m. = 2शीतकर.

शीतय्, °यति to cool.

शीतरश्मि a. cold-rayed (abstr. °त्व n.); m. the moon.

शीतरुच्, °रुचि, & °रोचिस् m. = prec. m.

शीतज्वर m. n. du. cold and hot fever.

शीतल a. cold, cool (lit. & fig.); n. = seq.

शीतलता f., °त्व n. coldness, cold.

शीतलय्, °यति to cool.

शीतलस्पर्श a. cold to the touch.

शीतलाय्, °यते become cool.*

शीतली कृ to cool; °भू be or become cool (lit. & fig.).

शीतवह a. flowing cold (river).

शीतसंस्पर्श m. the touch (or sense) of cold.

शीतह्रद a. cool as a pond.

शीतांशु a. cold-rayed; m. the moon (also °मन्त् m.).

शीताद्रि m. snow-mountain (Himālaya).

शीताधिवास a. living in cool places or cooling.

शीतार्त a. pained with cold.

शीतालु a. suffering from cold, freezing.

†शीतिकावन्त्, f. °वती cool.

शीतेषु m. the cold arrow (a cert. myth. weapon).
शीतोष्ण a. cold and hot; n. sgl. & pl. cold and heat.
शीतोष्णकिरण m. du. moon and sun.
शीत्कृ make Çīt (cf. seq.).
शीत्कार m. the sound Çīt (expresses pleasurable sensations).
शीत्कृत n., °ति f. making Çīt (cf. prec.).
शीन a. coagulated, congealed; n. ice.
शीपाल s. N. of a plant.
शीफर a. charming.
शीभम् adv. quickly.
शीभर a. = शीफर.
शीभ्य a. moving quickly.
शीर a. sharp, pointed; m. boa.
शीरशोचिस् a. having piercing rays (Agni).
शीरि or शीरी f. a vein.
शीर्ण a. crushed, broken, torn, withered, faded, shriveled, decayed, rotten; abstr. °त्व† n.
शीर्णि & शीर्ति f. breaking, breach.
†शीर्य a. fragile, delible.
शीर्ष n. (adj. —° f. आ & ई) head; point, upper part.
शीर्षक n. head; a kind of fine (j.).
शीर्षकपाल n. (head-) scull.
शीर्षक्ति f. head-ache; p. °क्तिमन्त्.
शीर्षच्छिन्न a. beheaded.
शीर्षच्छेद m. decapitation.
शीर्षच्छेद्य a. to be beheaded.
शीर्षणी f. the head-end of a couch.
शीर्षण्य a. being at the head (lit. & fig.); n. = prec.
शीर्षण्वन्त् a. having a head.
शीर्षतस् adv. from or at the head, overhead.
शीर्षत्राण n. helmet (head-protector).
शीर्षन् n. head.
शीर्षपट्टक m., °बन्धना f. head-band.
शीर्षभिद्य n. cleaving a head.
शीर्षवेदना f. head-ache.*
शीर्षशोक & शीर्षामय m. the same.
शीर्षहार्य a. portable on the head.
शील n. character, nature, custom, habit, behaviour, conduct, esp. good or moral conduct, virtue (often adj. —°); abstr. °ता f., °त्व n.
शीलतस् adv. by character or nature.
शीलत्याग m. giving up honesty or virtue.
शीलन n. practice, exercise, study, repeated mention.
शीलभङ्ग m. = शीलत्याग (lit. breach of h.).
शीलय्, °यति, pp. शीलित (q.v.) practise, exercise, use or enjoy frequently, cherish, like. — परि = S.
शीलवन्त् a. of good character or conduct; having the nature or conduct of (—°).
1शीलवृत्त n. sgl. du. honesty and good conduct.
2शीलवृत्त a. well-conducted, moral.
शीलवेल a. (a sea) whose shores are virtues.*
शीलादित्य m. N. of sev. kings.
शीलित a. prepared, ready made.
शीलिन् a. = शीलवन्त्.
शीवन् a. lying, resting (—°).
शुक m. parrot, a man's name (abstr. °ता† f., °त्व† n.); f. शुकी female parrot or the myth. mother of parrots.
शुकदेव m. E. of Kṛṣṇa.
शुकबभ्रु a. reddish as a parrot.
शुकरूप a. having the colour or shape of a parrot.
शुकसप्तति f. the seventy stories of the parrot, T. of a work.
शुकहरि & °हरित a. green as a parrot.
शुक्त a. sour, acid; harsh, rough (words); n. sour drink or harsh speech.
शुक्तक a. sourish; n. sour eructation.
शुक्ति & °का f. pearl-oyster or oyster-shell.
शुक्तिज n. pearl (oyster-born).
शुक्र a. clear, bright, pure, white. — m. fire or the god of fire, the planet Venus, a cert. cup of Soma (± ग्रह), N. of sev. men. — n. brightness, purity; water, Soma, juice i.g., semen virile.
शुक्रज a. born of (one's own) seed (son).
शुक्रज्योतिस् a. shining bright.
शुक्रप & शुक्रपूतपा a. drinking clear or purified (Soma).
शुक्रवन्त् a. containing clear juice.
शुक्रवर्ण a. bright-coloured, light.

शुक्रवासस् a. clad in white.
शुक्रिय a. = शुक्रवन्त्; n. brightness.
शुक्ल a. = शुक्र; m. (± पक्ष) = शुक्लपक्ष, spawl, phlegm, snot; n. brightness, light; the white part of the eye.
शुक्लकृष्ण a. light and dark; n. du. a light and dark half.
शुक्लकेश a. white-haired.
शुक्लदन्त् a. white-toothed.
शुक्लपक्ष m. the light half of a month.
शुक्लरूप a. white-coloured.
शुक्लवत्सा f. a cow having a white calf.
शुक्लवस्त्र & °वासस् a. clad in white.
शुक्लवृत्त & शुक्लाचार a. of pure or moral conduct, virtuous, honest.
शुक्लापाङ्ग m. a peacock (having white eye-corners).
शुक्लाम्बर a. wearing white garments.
शुक्लिमन् m. whiteness, brightness.
शुक्ली कृ & भू make & be white.
शुङ्ग m. N. of a dynasty of kings; n. the sheath or calyx of a young bud (also शुङ्गा f.); effect; f. शुङ्गा & ई also N. of the mother of Garuḍa.
1शुच्, शोचति, °ते (शुच्यति & शोचिति) flame, light, shine, glow, burn; suffer burning pain; grieve at, mourn (acc. ± प्रति, loc., or instr.). C. शोचयति inflame, burn (lit. & fig. = afflict); grieve at, mourn, regret (acc.). I. शोशुचन् etc. flame brightly. — अनु grieve for (acc.), mourn with (acc.); C. = समनु bewail, deplore. अप I. flame away, remove by flaming. अभि burn, torment (also C. & I.); grieve, mourn. आ flame hither, bring by flaming. उद् flame up. नि be burning hot. निस् flame forth. परि feel grief or sorrow, mourn (absol. or tr. w. acc.). C. torment, afflict, bewail, deplore. प्र shine forth (also I.). अनुप्र bewail, deplore. प्रति flame against (acc.). सम् flame together; lament, regret (also C.).
2शुच् a. flaming, lighting, beaming (—°); f. flame, heat, sorrow, grief, pain, distress.
शुच a. clear, pure; f. शुचा grief, sorrow.
शुचय्, only pp. शुचयन्त् flaming, beaming.
शुचि a. flaming, beaming (lit. & fig.); light, bright, clear, pure; holy, virtuous, honest. m. purity, honesty, fire or a cert. fire, a cert. month in summer & summer i.g., the sun, a man's name.
शुचिचरित a. of pure or good conduct.
शुचिजन्मन् a. light-born.
शुचिता f., °त्व n. clearness, purity, honesty.
शुचिदन्त् a. bright-toothed.
शुचिपा a. drinking clear Soma.
शुचिप्रतीक a. clear-faced.
शुचिभ्राजस् a. shining bright.
शुचिवर्ण a. bright-coloured.
शुचिव्रत a. intent on purity, pure, holy.
शुचिषद् a. dwelling in light or virtue.
†शुचिष्मन्त् a. shining, resplendent.
शुचिस्मित a. sweetly smiling.
शुची कृ purify, °भू P.
शुच्यक्ष, f. ई clear-eyed.
शुज्, only शूशुजान strutting.
शुण्ठ a. white or small (bull or cow).
शुण्ठाकर्ण a. short-eared.
शुण्ठि or शुण्ठी f. dry ginger.
शुण्डा f. the trunk of an elephant (also °दण्ड m.).
शुण्डार m. the trunk of a young elephant.
शुण्डिक m. pl. N. of a people.
शुण्डिन् m. distiller or seller of spirituous liquors.
शुतुद्री f. N. of a river.
शुद्ध a. pure, clean, stainless, faultless; true, fair, simple; mere, whole, complete; tried, examined. m. = शुद्धपक्ष.
शुद्धकर्मन् a. acting honestly, virtuous.
शुद्धचैतन्य n. pure intelligence (ph.).
शुद्धता f., °त्व n. purity, honesty.
शुद्धदन्त् a. clear-toothed.
शुद्धदन्त, f. ई the same.
शुद्धधी a. pure-hearted.
शुद्धपक्ष m. = शुक्लपक्ष.
शुद्धबुद्धि a. pure-minded, innocent.
1शुद्धभाव a. = prec.
2शुद्धभाव m. a pure mind, innocence.
शुद्धमति a. = शुद्धबुद्धि.
शुद्धवंश्य a. of pure race.

शुद्धवध m. the simple or mere pain of death.
शुद्धवन्त् a. containing the word शुद्ध, f. °वती pl. N. of cert. verses.
शुद्धवाल a. bright-tailed.
शुद्धवेष a. dressed in clean garments.
शुद्धशील a. of a pure character or nature.
शुद्धसत्त्व & °स्वभाव a. the same.
शुद्धहस्त a. pure-handed.
शुद्धहृदय a. pure-hearted.
शुद्धात्मन् a. of a pure mind or nature.
शुद्धान्त m. harem, seraglio (lit. pure or sacred interior); pl. a king's wives and concubines.
शुद्धान्तचर & °चारिन् m. servant of a harem.
शुद्धाभ a. of pure light.
शुद्धाशय a. pure-minded.
शुद्धि f. purification, purity (lit. & fig.), justification, acquittal, justness, genuineness, paying off, clearing (of debts), clearness, truth, certainty.
शुद्धितम (superl.) the purest.
शुद्धिमन्त् a. pure, guiltless.
शुद्धोदन m. N. of Buddha's father.
शुध् or शुन्ध्, pp. शुद्ध (q.v.), शुन्धति, °ते purify, M. mostly intr. or refl.; शुध्यति (°ते) become pure or clear, be justified or excused. C. शोधयति purify (also शुन्धयति); mend, correct; wash or clear off, remove (what is impure or noxious); pay back, restore; examine, try; acquit, justify; make clear, explain. — परि (शुध्यति, °ते) become pure or clean, clear or justify one's self. C. pay back, restore; examine, try, explain. वि (शुध्यति, °ते) become thoroughly clean or pure. C. clear, purify, purge, justify, mend, correct, improve. सम् C. cleanse, purify; pay back, restore; mend, improve. — Cf. परिशुद्ध, विशुद्ध, संशुद्ध.
शुन a. grown, thriven, prosperous, fortunate; n. success, luck, prosperity; as adv. luckily, successfully.
शुनःपुच्छ m. N. of a man.
शुनक m. young dog, dog i.g., a man's name.
शुनंवन्त् & शुनावन्त् a. having a share (plough).
शुनकसदृश a. dog-like, impudent.*
शुनःशेप or शुनःशेफ m. N. of a man.
शुनासीर m. du. N. of two Vedic gods presiding over agriculture (Share and Plough); sgl. E. of Indra.
शुनी v. श्वन्.
शुनोलाङ्गूल m. N. of a man.
शुन्ध् v. शुध्.
शुन्धन a. (f. ई) & n. purifying.
शुन्ध्यु or शुन्ध्यू (f. ऊ) pure, clear, bright.
शुप्ति f. shoulder.
1शुभ् or शुम्भ्, शुम्भते glide along, move onward. — प्र = S.
2शुभ् f. gliding along, onward progress or course.
3शुभ् or शुम्भ्, शोभते (°ति); शुम्भति, शुम्भते (the nasalized forms more frequent in the Veda, the strong forms in l. l.) A. adorn, embellish, prepare, make ready; M. adorn one's self, or make one's self ready, look beautiful, make a show, shine, glitter (w. इव & यथा also look like, appear or seem to be). With न be unpleasant, look ugly. C. शोभयति (cf. also 2शुभय्) adorn, embellish, cause to shine. — अति look very beautiful, w. न displease. अभि M. lay round or put on for ornament, also = समभि shine, make a show; C. = S.C. उप, परि, प्रति, वि C. = S.C. सम् M. be beautiful or as beautiful as (instr.). C. adorn, embellish.
4शुभ् f. beauty, ornament, splendour.
शुभ a. fair, beautiful, pleasant, agreeable, fortunate, auspicious, good, right, true, pure. n. charm, beauty, grace, welfare, luck, bliss (also pl.); anything pleasant or good.
शुभंया & °यावन् a. lightly gliding along.
शुभंयु a. fond of ornaments; pretty, fair.
शुभकर & शुभंकर a. causing welfare.
शुभदत्त m. N. of a man.
शुभदर्शन a. looking beautiful.
शुभदिन n. a lucky day.
1शुभमङ्गल n. welfare, bliss.
2शुभमङ्गल a. blessed, fortunate.

शुभमय, f. ई splendid, beautiful.
1शुभय्, only शुभंयन्त् lightly moving along.
2शुभय्, शुभंयति adorn; M. refl.
शुभलक्षण a. having lucky marks.
शुभलग्न n. a lucky moment.
शुभव्रत a. of good conduct or character, virtuous, honest.
शुभशंसिन् a. foretelling good luck.
शुभसमन्वित a. pleasant, charming.
शुभस्पति m. du. the two lords of beauty or of speed.
शुभाङ्ग a. fair-limbed (Çiva); f. ई a woman's name.
शुभाचार a. of good conduct, virtuous.
शुभात्मक a. well-minded, benevolent.
शुभाय्, °यते shine, beam.
शुभार्थिन् a. wishing welfare or bliss.
शुभावह a. causing welfare or bliss.
शुभाशिस् f. blessing, benediction.
शुभाशीर्वचन n., °र्वाद m. the utterance of a benediction.
शुभाशुभ a. agreeable and (or) disagreeable, pleasant and (or) unpleasant, fortunate and (or) infortunate, good and (or) bad. n. weal and (or) woe, luck and (or) ill luck, something good and (or) bad etc.
शुभे dat. inf. to शुभ्.
शुभेतर a. bad, wicked (different from good).
शुभोदर्क a. having or causing happy results, auspicious, fortunate; abstr. °ता f.
शुभ्र a. beautiful, shining, white, pure, clear (also of sounds).
†शुभ्रखादि a. having beautiful rings or bracelets.
शुभ्रता f., °त्व n. white colour.
शुभ्रदन्त, f. ई white-toothed.
शुभ्रयाम a. having a shining chariot.
†शुभ्रयावन् a. moving on with shining (steeds).
शुभ्रंशुस्तम a. very shining or bright.
शुभ्रावन्त् & शुभ्रि a. bright, clear, fine.
शुम्वन् a. speedy, fleet.
शुम्बल n. straw or chaff.
शुम्भ् v. 1 & 3शुभ्.
शुम्भ m. N. of an Asura.
शुम्भन, f. ई purifying.
शुम्भनिशुम्भ m. du. Çumbha and Niçumbha.*
शुरुध् f. comfort, strength.
शुल्क m. price, toll, tax, duty; nuptial fee; contest-prize.
शुल्कद m. the giver of the nuptial fee.
शुल्ब n. string, cord.
शुशुक्कन & °क्कनि a. shining, radiant.
शुशुलूक m., °लूका f. cert. birds.
शुश्रू f. mother.
शुश्रूषक a. obeying, serving (gen. or —°).
शुश्रूषण n. desire to hear; obedience, homage, respect, service, kindness to (gen., dat., loc., or —°).
शुश्रूषा f. = prec.
शुश्रूषित a. to be obeyed or waited on; n. impers.
शुश्रूषिन् a. obeying, serving (—°).
शुश्रूषु a. wishing to hear or learn; obedient, devoted to (gen. or —°).
शुश्रूषेण्य a. to be willingly heard or attended to.
शुश्रूष्य a. = शुश्रूषितव्य.
1शुष्, शुष्यति (°ते) dry, wither, fade. C. शोषयति (°ते) make dry, dry up, parch, emaciate, afflict, destroy. अनु dry by slow degrees or after another. उद्, समुद्, उप, परि, वि, सम् dry or shrink in; C. make dry, dry up.
2शुष्, शुषति blow, hiss (of a snake). — आ hiss, whistle, yell; gasp, exert one's self, endeavour to attain or accomplish.
शुष्क a. dry, hard (w. गिर् f. hard speech); useless, vain; n. = seq.
शुष्ककाष्ठ n. pl. dry wood.
शुष्कता f., °त्व n. dryness.
शुष्कतोय a. whose water is dried up (river).
शुष्कदृति m. a dry (empty) bag.
शुष्कभृङ्गार m. N. of an ancient teacher.
शुष्कमुख a. whose mouth is dry.
शुष्कवन्त् a. dry, parched.
शुष्कवैर n. groundless enmity; a. °रिन्.
शुष्काग्र a. having a dry point.
शुष्कान्न n. dry food.
शुष्काप a. = शुष्कतोय; s. a dry pond.
शुष्कार्द्र a. dry and wet.
शुष्कास्य a. = शुष्कमुख.

शुष्ण m. N. of a demon slain by Indra.
शुष्णहत्य n. the slaying of Çuṣṇa (cf. prec.).
शुष्म a. whistling, splashing, sputtering (water, fire, etc.), fragrant; bold, impetuous. m. whistling etc., exhalation, fragrance; impetuosity, violence, fury; strength, power, vigour, vital energy.
शुष्मदं a. giving strength etc. (cf. prec.).
शुष्मन् m. fire; n. strength, courage, vigour.
शुष्मयं a. boldening, strengthening.
शुष्मवन्त् a. fiery, passionate.
शुष्मिन् a. = शुष्म a.
1†शू (only pf. stem शूशु in शूशुवत् etc.) prevail, be superior or victorious.
2शू v. श्वा.
शूक m. n. awn or beard (of corn); m. a kind of corn; n. sting (lit. & fig.).
शूकर m. = सूकर.
शूकार m. scaring (by making Çū).
शूकृत n. = prec.; a. scared, urged on.
शूघन a. swift.
शूद्र m., आ or ई f. a man and woman of the fourth caste.
शूद्रक m. N. of sev. kings, esp. of the supposed author of the Mṛcchakaṭikā.
शूद्रकृत a. made by a Çūdra.
शूद्रगमन n. sexual relation to a Çūdra.
शूद्रघ्न a. killing a Çūdra.
शूद्रजन m. a Çūdra(-person).
शूद्रजन्मन् a. descending from a Çūdra; m. a Çūdra.
शूद्रता f., °त्व n. state or condition of a Çūdra.
शूद्रयाजक a. sacrificing for a Çūdra.
शूद्रयोनि f. the womb of a Çūdra woman.
शूद्रराज्य n. the realm of a Çūdra.
शूद्रवृत्ति f. the occupation of a Çūdra.
शूद्रशिष्य m. the pupil of a Çūdra.
शूद्रसेवन m. serving Çūdras.
शूद्रहत्या f. abstr. to seq.
शूद्रहन् a. killing a Çūdra.
शूद्रान्न n. food from a Çūdra.
शूद्रावेदिन् a. marrying a Çūdra woman.
शूद्री भू become a Çūdra.
शूद्रोच्छिष्ट a. left by a Çūdra (water).
1शून a. swollen; abstr. °त्व n.
2शून n. emptiness, absence, want.
शूना v. सूना.
शून्य a. empty, void, desert, unoccupied, vacant; wanted, missing, absent, wandering or absent in mind; lonely, solitary; deprived of, free from (instr. or —°); unreal, vain. n. void, desert, solitude, vacuum, blank, absence of (—°); nought, a cypher; as adv. without, except (—°). — Loc. w. रु howl in a desert, cry in vain.
शून्यगेह n. an empty house.
शून्यचित्त a. empty-hearted, absent in mind, unsuspicious, harmless.
शून्यता f., °त्व n. emptiness, voidness, inanity; desert, loneliness; absence or wandering of mind; absence or want of (—°).
शून्यपाल m. a substitute.
शून्यमनस् & °हृदय (abstr. °त्व n.*) = शून्यचित्त.
शून्यी कृ make empty, leave; P. °भू.
शूर a. bold, valiant, mighty; m. warrior, hero, a man's name.
शूरण a. impetuous, fiery (horse).
शूरता f., °त्व n. boldness, heroism.
शूरदेव m. N. of a prince.
शूरपत्नी f. having a warlike lord or husband.
शूरपुत्र f. having a warlike son.
शूरपुर n. N. of a city.
शूरमानिन् a. thinking one's self a hero.
शूरवर्मन् m. a man's name.
शूरवीर a. having warlike men.
शूरसाति f (only loc.) fight, batte (lit. gain or reward of men).
शूरसेन m. pl. N. of a people; sgl. the country or a prince (f. ई princess) of the Ç.
शूर्प n. a winnowing basket.
शूर्पणखा (or °खी) f. N. of Rāvaṇa's sister.
शूर्पारक m. pl. N. of a people & country.
शूल m. n. spit, esp. turn spit (for roasting); pike, spear, esp. that of Çiva; any sharp or acute pain; pain, woe i.g.; m. & f. आ a stake for impaling criminals.
शूलधर a. holding a spear (Çiva).
शूलधारिन् & °धृक् a. the same.
शूलपाणि a. holding a spear in the hand; m. E. of Rudra-Çiva.

शूलभृत् a. = शूलधर.
शूलहस्त a. = शूलपाणि.
शूला w. कृ roast on the spit.
1शूलाग्र n. the point of a stake.
2शूलाग्र a. pointed like a stake.
शूलिन् a. having a spear; m. E. of Rudra-Çiva.
शूल्य a. relating to a spit (cf. seq.).
शूल्यमांस n. meat roasted on a spit.
शूल्यमांसभूयिष्ठ a. consisting chiefly of meat roasted on a spit (food).*
शूष a. whistling, yelling, tinkling, snorting; fierce, bold. m. sound, song; breath, vital energy (also शूंष).
शूष्य a. sounding, shouting.
शृ, शृणाति (शृणति), pp. शीर्ण (q.v.) crush, break, tear, hurt, kill. P. शीर्यते (°ति) be crushed or broken etc., go asunder, fall out or off, wither, moulder, decay, perish. — अपि break off. अव break down (tr.); P. be shattered, vanish. नि break off. निस् break asunder. परा break, crush. परि P. fly into pieces, burst. प्र break off or asunder. वि P. be broken or scattered, fall into pieces, perish. सम् break, crush, destroy; P. break down, be scattered or dispersed. — Cf. अवशीर्ण, विशीर्ण.
शृगाल v. सृगाल.
शृङ्खल s., आ f. chain, fetter.
शृङ्खलय्, °यति to chain or fetter.
शृङ्खलाकलाप m. chain or fetter (-band).*
शृङ्खलादामन् n., °पाश m. the same.
शृङ्घाणिका f. snot.
शृङ्ग n. (adj. —° f. आ & ई) horn (of every kind), tusk of an elephant, syringe, peak of a mountain, turret of a temple or palace; top, point i.g., also fig. the best of its kind.
शृङ्गक (adj. —° f. शृङ्गिका) horn, syringe.
शृङ्गगिरि m. N. of a mountain.
शृङ्गपुर n. N. of a town.
शृङ्गवन्त् a. horned, peaked (mountain).
†शृङ्गवृष् m. N. of a man.
शृङ्गवेर m. N. of a serpent-demon; n. ginger (fresh or dry).
शृङ्गाट & °क s. triangle, a triangular place or a place where three roads meet.
शृङ्गान्तर n. front (of an animal).
शृङ्गाय्, °यते butt with the horns.
शृङ्गार a. fair, beautiful; m. ornament, fine dress, love, sexual passion, a man's name.
शृङ्गारतिलक n. T. of sev. works.
शृङ्गारवन्त् a. erotic; f. °वती a woman's name.
शृङ्गारित a. adorned, embellished.
शृङ्गारिन् a. the same; enamoured or erotic.
शृङ्गारीय्, °यति wish for love.
शृङ्गिन् a. = शृङ्गवन्त्; m. horned beast or mountain.
शृङ्गेरिपुर n. N. of a town.
शृङ्खाणिका f. = शृङ्घाणिका.
शृत a. boiled, roasted; n. anything boiled, esp. boiled milk; abstr. शृतत्व the being cooked.
शृतकाम a. liking boiled milk.
शृतपा a. drinking what is boiled.
शृध्या f. boldness, daring.
शेखर m. peak, point, summit, head, crest, garland, crown, diadem; the chief or best of (—°).
शेप m. penis or tail.
शेपस् n. penis.
शेफ m. = prec., scrotum; du. the testicles.
शेफस् n. penis.
शेफालिका & °ली f. a kind of plant.
शेमुषी f. intelligence, intention, purpose.
शेलु m. N. of a plant.
शेव a. kind, dear.
शेवधि m. jewel, treasure or treasury.
शेवल a. slimy.
शेवार m. treasury.
शेवृध (शेवृध) a. kind, dear; m. a cert. snake.
†शेवृधक m. = prec. m.
शेव्य a. = prec. adj.
शेष a. remaining, left from (—°, esp. after a pp.), pl. all the other(s). m. n. rest, surplus or remainder of (loc., gen., or —°); end, supplement, anything secondary or accidental (adj. —° having only a rest of — left, or of which only — is left); loc. शेषे for the rest i.e. in other cases, else. —

m. N. of a serpent-demon, a Prajāpati, etc.; f. आ pl. flowers left from an offering, sgl. such a garland.

शेषतस् adv. otherwise, else.

शेषता f. abstr. to any comp. adj. ending in शेष.

शेषत्व n., शेषभाव m. the being rest or left.

शेषभुज् a. eating leavings.

1शेषभूत a. being left, remaining.

2शेषभूत a. (for शेषाभूत) being (as it were) a garland of flowers.

शेषभोजिन् a. = शेषभुज्.

शेषवन्त् a. being left or spared, alive.

शेषस् n. offspring, posterity.

शेषिन् a. having something secondary, s. the essential matter.

शेषी भू be left, remain.

शेष्य a. to be left aside.

शैक्य a. damasked; m. a cert. weapon.

शैक्यायस् & °मय a. made of damasked steel.

शैक्ष m. beginning student, beginner.

शैख m. the offspring of an outcast Brahman.

शैखिन a. coming from a peacock.

शैघ्र & शैघ्र्य n. swiftness, speed.

शैत्य n. coldness, cold.

शैथिल्य n. looseness, laxity, slackness, remissness, decrease, diminution.

शैनेय m. patron. from शिनि.

शैबल & शैबाल v. शैवल & शैवाल.

शैब्य a. relating to the Çibis; m. a descendant of Çibi or a king of the Çibis.

शैल, f. ई stony, stone-like; m. (adj. —° f. आ) rock, mountain, abstr. °ता f., °त्व n.

शैलकन्या f. the mountain-daughter i.e. Pārvatī.

शैलकम्पिन् a. shaking mountains.

शैलकूट s. peak of a mountain.

शैलगुरु a. heavy as a mountain; m. the father of mountains, Himālaya.

शैलज a. born or produced in mountains; rocky, stony.

शैलतनया f. = शैलकन्या.

शैलदुहितृ & °पुत्री f. the same.

शैलपुर n. N. of a city.

शैलप्रतिमा f. stony image of a god.*

शैलप्रस्थ s. table-land.

शैलमय, f. ई stony, of stone.

शैलमृग m. wild goat (mountain-deer).

शैलराज् & °राज m. the king of mountains i.e. Himālaya.

शैलशिखर n., °शेखर m., & °शृङ्ग n. mountain-top.

शैलसार a. hard as stone.

शैलसुता f. = शैलकन्या.

शैलाग्र n. mountain-top.

शैलाधिराज m. = शैलराज्.

शैलालि, शैलिन, & शैलिनि m. names of teachers.

शैली f. usage, custom.

शैलूष m. actor, dancer (f. °षी).

शैलेन्द्र m. = शैलराज्.

शैलेय m. n. benzoin or storax.

शैव, f. ई relating to Çiva, Çiva's; m. a worshipper of Ç.

शैवल s. a cert. water-plant; m. pl. N. of a people.

शैवलवन्त्, °लिन्, & °ल्य poss. to prec. s.

शैवाल n. = शैवल.

शैव्य v. शैब्य.

शैशव a. childish; n. childhood or childishness.

शैशिर, f. ई relating to the cool season.

1शोक a. glowing.

2शोक m. heat, flame; pain, distress, sorrow, grief at (gen. or —°).

शोकज a. grief-born (water = tears).

शोकतर a. overcoming sorrow.

शोकपरायण a. wholly given up to grief.

शोकपात्रात्मन् a. = prec. (lit. whose soul is a receptacle for sorrow).*

शोकमय a. full of sorrow.

शोकवन्त् a. sorrowful, sad.

शोकवर्तव्य a. obnoxious to (lit. to be veiled or darkened by) sorrow.*

शोकविनाशन a. destroying sorrow.

†शोकस् s. heat, flame.

शोकातिग a. overcoming sorrow.

शोकातुर a. sick with grief.

शोकान्तर a. sorrowless.

शोकार्त a. visited by sorrow.

शोकार्ति f. affliction (cf. prec.).

शोकावेश m. a fit or paroxysm of grief.

शोचनीय a. to be lamented (n. impers.); abstr. °ता f.

शोचिं f. flame, heat.
शोचितव्य a. = शोचनीय.
शोचिष्केश a. flame-haired.
शोचिष्ठ (superl.) most or bright flaming.
शोचिष्मन्त् a. glowing, flaming.
शोचिस् n. flame, beam, heat, glow.
शोच्य a. = शोचनीय.
शोण a. red, deep-red; m. redness, N. of a river.
शोणकर्ण a. red-eared (horse).
शोणता f. redness.
शोणहय & शोणाश्व a. having red horses (Droṇa).
शोणाधर a. red-lipped.
शोणित n. blood; abstr. °त्व n.
शोणितोत्पादक m. spiller of blood.
शोणिमन् m. redness.
शोथ m. swelling, tumefaction.
शोधक a. cleaning, purifying.
शोधन a. & n. = prec.; n. also means of purification; justification, inquiry, examination.
शोधनक m. officer in a law-court (lit. purifier).
शोधनीय a. to be cleansed or purified, to be paid off.
शोधिन् a. purifying.
शोध्य a. to be cleansed or purified, corrected or improved.
शोफ m. tumor, sore; p. °फिन्.
शोभ m. N. of a man; f. शोभा beauty, splendour, colour, semblance.
शोभक, f. °भिका splendid, beautiful.
शोभथ m. splendour.
शोभन, f. आ (& ई) beautiful, splendid, fair, good; eminent, distinguished by (instr. or —°); auspicious, fortunate. f. आ a fair woman; n. ornament, luck, welfare, (moral) good.
शोभनीय a. splendid, beautiful.
शोभसे dat. infin. to 3शुभ्.
शोभित & शोभिन् a. splendid, adorned or shining with (—°).
शोभिष्ठ (superl.) most beautiful or swift.
1शोष a. drying up, parching, removing, destroying; m. exsiccation, drought, consumption.
2शोष m. breath, vital energy.
शोषण, f. ई = 1शोष a.; n. exsiccation, drought.
शोषिन् a. drying (tr. & intr.), consumptive.
शौक्ल्य n. whiteness, clearness.
शौक्लेय m. metron. of Garuḍa; hawk or falcon.
शौच n. cleanness, purification by (—°), purity, honesty.
शौचकल्प m. mode of purification.
शौचपर a. fond of purity.
शौचप्रेप्सु a. seeking purity.
शौचवन्त् a. clean, pure.
शौटीर a. manly, proud, haughty; n., °र्य n. & °ता f. as abstr.
शौण्ड a. fond of spirituous liquor, addicted to drinking; i.g. given or devoted to, fond of, versed in, familiar with (—°).
शौण्डिक m. distiller or vender of spirituous liquors.
शौण्डिकागार & °कापण s. tavern (cf. prec.).*
शौण्डीर a. = शौटीर a.; n., °र्य n., & °ता f. as abstr.
शौद्र a. relating to a Çūdra, born of a Ç. woman.
शौन, f. ई belonging to a dog.
शौनक m. patron. of a celebrated grammarian; pl. his descendants or followers, f. ई his work.
शौनःशेप n. the story of Çunaḥçepa.
शौरसेन a. relating to the Çūrasenas, f. ई their language.
शौरि m. patron. of Kṛṣṇa etc.
शौर्य n. heroism, courage, valour.
शौर्यकर्मन् n. an heroic deed.
शौर्यवन्त् a. heroic, bold.
शौल m. a cert. part of a plough.
शौल्किक m. custom-officer.
शौव a. relating to dogs, doggish.
शौवस्तिक a. to-morrow's; abstr. °त्व n.
श्चन्द्, only I. चनिश्चदत् shine, glance.
†श्चन्द्र (only —°) shining.
1श्चुत्, later श्च्युत्, श्चोतति & श्च्योतति drip (tr. & intr.); C. श्चोतयति only trans. — अभि C. cause to drip or trickle; besprinkle. अव & व्यव drip, drop or fall down. नि M. ooze, trickle down. प्र drip forth (tr.

& intr.); C. cause to drip or flow. वि drip out. — Cf. आश्चुतित.

2श्चुत् & श्च्युत् (—°) dripping (trans.).

श्नथ् (श्नथिति), pp. श्नथित pierce, perforate; C. = S. — अप push back, repel. नि & परिनि strike down.

श्नथन a. piercing.

श्नथितृ m. piercer.

श्नप्त n. mouth-corner.

श्नुष्टि f. a small heap or weight (of rice etc.).

श्मशा f. ditch, channel.

श्मशान n. cemetery (for burning or burying the dead), place of execution; funeral rite.

श्मशानगोचर a. employed in burial-grounds.

श्मशाननिलय a. dwelling on burial-grounds (Çiva).

श्मशानपाल m. guardian of a cemetery.

श्मशानवाट m. enclosure of a cemetery.

श्मशानवासिन् a. = श्मशाननिलय.

श्मशानवीथी f. a row of trees or green walk on a cemetery.*

श्मशानसुमनस् n. flower from a burial-ground.

श्मश्रु n. beard, esp. moustaches.

श्मश्रुकर m. barber.

श्मश्रुकर्मन् n. shaving of the beard.

श्मश्रुण a. bearded.

श्मश्रुधर & °धारिन् a. wearing a beard.

श्मश्रुल & श्मश्रुवन्त् a. bearded.

श्मश्रुवर्धक m. shaver of beards.

श्या, श्यायति, pp. शीत, शीन, & श्यान (q.v.) freeze, coagulate (tr.); P. शीयते intr. — आ M. dry (intr.). — Cf. आश्यान.

श्यान a. dried, dry.

श्यापर्ण m. N. of a man, pl. his family.

श्याम a. black, dark-coloured. m. a black bull, a man's name; f. आ a young woman with particular marks, a cert. bird, N. of sev. plants, a woman's name.

श्यामक a. dark-coloured; m. a man's name; f. °मिका blackness, impurity.

श्यामता f., °त्व n. blackness, darkness.

श्याममुख a. dark-faced (cloud).

श्यामल & °क a. dark-coloured.

श्यामलित a. the same.

श्यामलिमन् m. darkness, blackness.

श्यामली कृ to colour dark.

श्यामवर्ण a. dark-coloured, abstr. °त्व n.

श्यामशबल m. du. the dark and the brindled (Yama's dogs).

श्यामाक m. a kind of millet, a. श्यामाक prepared of it.

श्यामाय्, °यते, pp. श्यामायित become dark.

श्यामावदात a. blackish-white.

श्यामित a. dark-coloured.

श्यामी कृ & भू colour & become dark.

श्याल v. स्याल.

1श्याव a. dark-brown, brown; m. a brown horse, f. आ & श्यावी a brown mare.

2श्याव m. N. of a man.

श्यावदन्त् a. brown- or black-toothed.

श्यावदन्त & °क a. = prec., abstr. °दन्तता f.

श्यावाक्ष a. dark-eyed.

श्यावाश्व a. having brown horses; m. a man's name.

श्याव्या f. darkness.

श्येत, f. श्येनी reddish-white.

श्येताक्ष, f. ई having reddish-white eyes.

श्येन m. eagle, falcon, hawk; a form of military array, N. of a man; f. श्येनी the mythol. mother of eagles etc.

श्येनजीविन् m. falconer.

श्येनजूत a. swift as an eagle.

श्येनपत्त्र n. an eagle's feather.

श्येनपत्वन् a. flying with (i.e. by the help of) eagles.

श्येनभृत a. brought by the eagle.

श्येनहृत & श्येनाभृत a. the same.

श्येनी v. श्येत.

श्रण्, C. श्राणयति w. वि grant, give, pay off.

श्रथ्, श्रथ्नाति, श्रथ्नीते, & (—°) शृन्थति become loose, give way; make loose or weak, M. untie. C. श्रथयति slacken, release, give room; M. become loose, give way. — अनु dissolve, M. scatter about. C. let go or in peace. वि M. & C. loosen, untie, release, remove, destroy.

श्रथर्य्, °र्यति become loose or slack.

†श्रथाय् (only imper. श्रथाय or श्रथय), w. अव & उद् loosen, untie (from below or above); w. वि = prec.

श्रद् indecl. w. कृ assure, warrant; w. धा

have faith or trust in (dat., in l. l. also gen. of pers. or th. & loc. of th.); believe a thing (acc.), think—to be (2 acc.); expect a thing (acc.) from (abl.); agree with, approve of (acc.); absol. be trustful or confident; receive willingly, welcome, like; wish, desire (acc. or inf.). With न distrust or disapprove.

श्रद्दधानता f. faith, belief, devotion.

श्रद्दधानवन्त् a. faithful, devout.

श्रद्धा a. trusting, faithful (dat.). — f. **आ** trust, faith, belief in (loc. or —°); fidelity, sincerity (also personif.); wish, desire, longing for (loc., acc. w. **प्रति**, infin., or —°); curiosity, whim, appetite.

श्रद्धादेव a. trusting in (a) god.

श्रद्धान n. faith.

श्रद्धामनस् a. faithful, believing.

श्रद्धामनस्या (f. instr. adv.) faithfully.

श्रद्धामय a. consisting or full of faith.

श्रद्धालु, **श्रद्धावन्त्**, & **श्रद्धिन्** a. faithful, believing.

श्रद्धिव a. credible.

श्रद्धेय a. the same; abstr. °त्व† n.

श्रपण n. cooking-fire; cooking.

श्रपय् v. **श्रा**.

श्रपयितृ m. cook.

श्रभ् v. **श्रम्भ्**.

श्रम्, **श्राम्यति**, **श्रमति**, °ते, pp. **श्रान्त** (q.v.) be weary, take pains, exert or castigate one's self. C. **श्रमयति** or **श्रामयति** weary, tire, bring down, subdue. — **अभि** weary, tire. **उप** rest, repose. **परि** take great pains, torment one's self. **वि** rest, recreate one's self; pause, cease; rely upon, trust in (loc.). C. cause to rest or repose; bring to rest i.e. appease, quench, finish. — Cf. **परिविश्रान्त**, **परिश्रान्त**, **विश्रान्त**, **संश्रान्त**.

श्रम m. weariness, exhaustion, exertion, labour, toil, effort at (loc. or —°).

श्रमकर a. causing fatigue.

श्रमघ्न & **श्रमच्छिद्** a. removing fatigue.

श्रमजल n. sweat (toil-water).

श्रमण m., **आ** & **ई** f. ascetic, mendicant; n. toil, exertion.

श्रमणक m., °**णिका** f. = prec. m. & f.

श्रमणाय्, °**यते** become a religious mendicant.

श्रमनुद् a. = **श्रमघ्न**.

श्रमयु a. exerting one's self.

श्रमवारि & **श्रमाम्बु** n. = **श्रमजल**.

श्रमार्त a. oppressed by fatigue.

श्रम्भ्, **श्रम्भते** w. **वि** trust, confide, place confidence in (loc.). C. loose, untie; comfort, encourage. — Cf. **विश्रब्ध**.

श्रयण n. leaning on, clinging to; refuge, shelter.

श्रव a. sounding; m. hearing, ear.

श्रवएष m. desire to praise.

1**श्रवण** n. hearing, learning; fame, (good) reputation; ear (also m.).

2**श्रवण** a. lame; m. (& f. **आ**) N. of a lunar mansion.

श्रवणकातरता f. shyness to hear.

श्रवणगोचर m. range of hearing.

श्रवणपथ m. the same; ear.

श्रवणपरुष a. harsh to the ear.

श्रवणमूल n. root of the ear.

श्रवणविषय m. = **श्रवणगोचर**.

श्रवणसुख or °**सुभग** a. pleasant to hear.

श्रवणहारिन् a. charming the ear.

श्रवणीय a. to be heard, worth hearing.

श्रवस् n. sound, call; loud praise, fame, glory, worth, eminence; zeal, eagerness, ambition; contest and its prize.

श्रवस्य्, °**स्यति** be eager to praise or move on quickly.

श्रवस्य a. eager, quick; active, ambitious; n. glorious deed, glory. f. °**स्या** ambition, zeal, haste; as instr. adv. quickly, fast.

श्रवस्यु a. desirous of glory, ambitious, eager, active, rash.

श्रवाय्य a. glorious, praiseworthy.

श्रविष्ठा f. N. of a lunar mansion.

श्रव्य a. = **श्रवणीय**.

श्रा, pp. **श्रात** & **शृत** (q.v.), C. **श्रपयति** (°ते) roast, boil, cook i.g. — Cf. **आशृत**, **प्रशृत** (add.).

श्रात a. cooked, roasted.

1**श्राद्ध** n. oblation to the Manes, funeral meal.

2**श्राद्ध**, f. **ई** faithful, pious; relating to a Çrāddha (cf. prec.).

श्राद्धकर्मन् n., °कल्प m. (celebration of) a Çrāddha or funeral meal.
श्राद्धकाल m. the time for a funeral meal.
श्राद्धदिन n. the day for a funeral meal.
श्राद्धदेव m. the god of the funeral oblation (Manu or Yama Vaivasvata, also Vivasvant etc.).
श्राद्धभुज् m. partaker of a funeral meal.
श्राद्धभोजन n. abstr. to prec.
श्राद्धमित्र a. seeking to win friends by funeral meals.
श्राद्धाह n. = श्राद्धदिन.
श्राद्धाह्निक a. performing Çrāddhas every day.
श्राद्धिक a. relating to a funeral meal.
श्राद्धिन् a. giving or partaking of funeral meals.
श्रान्त a. tired, worn out, exhausted; n. weariness, exhaustion, self-castigation, ascetism.
श्रान्ति f. weariness, fatigue.
श्रापिन् a. cooking (—°).
श्राय a. endowed with (loc.).
श्राव m. N. of a man.
श्रावक a. listening to (—°); audible far and wide. m. hearer, pupil, follower, esp. of Buddha.
1श्रावण a. perceived by the ear, audible; n. causing to be heard, communicating, announcing.
2श्रावण, f. ई relating to the lunar mansion Çravaṇa; m. a cert. month in the rainy season.
श्रावणीय a. to be announced or heard.
श्रावयत्पति a. making the mighty famous.
श्रावयत्सखि a. making the friend famous.
श्रावयितव्य a. to be communicated or informed of (acc.).
श्रावस्त m. N. of a king, f. ई N. of a city.
श्रावितृ m. hearer.
श्राविन् a. hearing or audible (—°).
श्राव्य a. audible, also = श्रावयितव्य.
श्रि, श्रयति, °ते, pp. श्रित (q.v.) A. trans. lean, lay against or on, turn or transfer to, spread (esp. light) over (loc.); M.P.(A.) intr. lean or rest upon, lie or be situated in or on, join one's self with (acc. or loc.); M.(A.) resort to, strive after (acc.); get entrance, befall (acc. or loc.); incur, undergo, get into a state or condition. — अधि A. spread over (acc. or loc.); put on (loc., esp. on the fire ± अग्नौ); lie or sit down upon (acc.). प्रत्यधि A. place near (the fire). समधि A. (± अग्नौ) place over the fire. अप M. lean, rest. अभि bring near; resort to (acc.). आ A. fix on (loc.); touch, befall (acc.). A.M. cling to, lean or rest upon (acc.); resort or have recourse to, seek protection from, come to, arrive at; undergo, incur, get; partake of, choose, take to (acc.). अपा A. (trans.) lean against, hang on (loc.); A.M. (intr.) lean or rest upon, have recourse to, take to, choose, seize, occupy. व्यपा approach for protection; take to, use, employ. उपा & समुपा lean against, resort to, rest or depend on (acc.). समा the same + take to, indulge in (acc.); seize, occupy. उद् A. lift, raise; M. arise, stand upright. C. उच्छ्रापयति lift, raise, increase, enhance. अभ्युद् M. rise, get up. प्रत्युद् rise against (acc.). समुद् lift, raise. उप A. (trans.) lean against (loc.); M. lean or rest upon (acc.); A.M. join, meet (acc.). परि lay about; enclose, fence, surround. प्र lean forward or against; join with, add to (loc.). वि A. put asunder, open, expand; M. refl. सम् A. put together, mix, mingle, join (M. refl.); M.(A.) betake one's self to, seek protection from, depend on, take to, partake of. अभिसम् seek help from or in; take to, partake of, use, employ (acc.). उपसम् go to meet, join, attend, depend on (acc.). — Cf. अधिश्रित, अभ्युच्छ्रित, आश्रित, उच्छ्रित, प्रश्रित, प्रोच्छ्रित (add.), संश्रित, समाश्रित, समुच्छ्रित.
श्रित् (—°) come to, being in.
श्रित a. clinging to, resting, seated, or placed upon, being or contained in (loc., r. acc. or —°), fled or resorted to, got into a state or condition (acc. or —°); pass. approached, applied to, occupied, chosen.
श्रिति f. way, path.
श्रियसे dat. inf. to make a show.

श्रिया f. welfare, bliss.
श्रियावास m. abode of welfare or bliss.
श्रियावासिन् a. dwelling with Çrī (Çiva).
श्रिष्, श्रेषति join, connect (cf. श्लिष्).
1श्री, श्रीणाति, श्रीणीते, pp. श्रीत mix, mingle with (instr.). — अभि & सम् = S.
2श्री f. mixture.
3श्री (nom. श्रीस्) f. beauty, splendour, ornament; comfort, satisfaction, welfare, bliss; wealth, treasure; high rank, glory, majesty, royalty & its insignia. Often personif. as the goddess of beauty, welfare, & royal splendour. Used also as honorific prefix to proper names = the famous, glorious, or mighty. — Du. श्रियौ beauty and welfare; dat. श्रियै or श्रियै as infin. or adv. pleasantly, prettily, gloriously.
श्रीक (adj. —°) beauty, highness.
श्रीकण्ठ m. a kind of bird; E. of Çiva & of Bhavabūti, N. of sev. men.
श्रीकर & °करण a. causing welfare or splendour.
श्रीकाम a. desirous of splendour.
श्रीकृच्छ्र m. a kind of penance.
श्रीखण्ड s. sandal-wood or the sandal-tree.
श्रीखण्डचर्चा f. anointing with sandal.
श्रीखण्डदास m. N. of a man.*
श्रीगिरि m. N. of a mountain.
श्रीद m. causing welfare; m. E. of Kubera.
श्रीदत्त m. a man's name.
श्रीदर्शन m. N. of a man.
श्रीधर m. E. of Viṣṇu (bearer of fortune.)
श्रीनगर n. N. of a town.
श्रीनाथ m. E. of Viṣṇu (husband of Çrī).
श्रीनिधि & °निवास m. the same (receptacle or abode of Çrī).
श्रीपति m. = श्रीनाथ.
श्रीपद्म m. E. of Kṛṣṇa.
श्रीपर्ण n. N. of a plant; also lotus-flower.*
श्रीपर्वत m. N. of sev. mountains.
श्रीफल m. N. of a plant, n. its fruit.
श्रीफलकृच्छ्र m. a kind of penance.
श्रीभक्ष m. auspicious food (Madhuparka).
श्रीभर्तृ m. = श्रीनाथ.
श्रीमत्ता f. beauty, splendour.
श्रीमनस् a. well-minded or disposed.
श्रीमन्त् a. beautiful, splendid, rich, fortunate.
श्रीमय a. quite full of Çrī (Viṣṇu).
श्रीयशस् n. pl. distinction and glory.
श्रीवत्स m. a curl of hair of a cert. form on the breast of Viṣṇu.
श्रीवह a. causing welfare; m. N. of a serpent-demon.
श्रीवास m. a kind of resin.
श्रीवृक्ष m. the holy fig-tree.
*श्रीवेष्ट m. a kind of resin.
श्रीश m. = श्रीनाथ.
श्रीशैल m. N. of sev. mountains.
*श्रीसंज्ञ n. cloves.
श्रीहर्ष & °हर्षदेव m. N. of a royal author.
श्रु, शृणोति, शृणुते, pp. श्रुत (q.v.) hear, learn (acc.) from (gen., abl., instr., & मुखात् or सकाशात्); hear—to be (2 acc.); listen or give ear to (acc. of th. or gen. of pers.); hear a teacher i.e. learn, study. M.P. be heard of, be known as or to be (2 nom.); be studied, taught, or read. C. श्रवयति & श्रावयति (°ते) cause a person to hear, i.e. address, inform of, communicate to, tell (acc. of thing & acc., gen., or dat. of pers.); let hear i.e. proclaim, announce, recite. D. शुश्रूषते (°ति) wish or like to hear i.e. attend to, obey, wait on, serve (acc.). — अति M. be heard of i.e. be celebrated above (all). अनु hear or learn (again); C. relate, tell (2 acc.); D.M. obey. अभि hear, learn—to be (2 acc.). C. cause to hear, speak to, address (acc.). आ listen to (acc. of th., gen. or dat. of pers.); hear, learn; promise. C. proclaim, make known; address, invoke, summon. अभ्या C. address. उप listen to (acc. or gen.), hear, learn from (मुखात् or सकाशात्), hear that—is (2 acc.). समुप hear, listen to (acc. or gen.), learn from (abl.). परि hear, learn, understand that—is (2 acc.). प्र M. be heard; become known or famous. प्रति listen or give ear; say yes, promise. C. answer. वि hear, learn; P. be heard of, become known or famous. C. let hear, announce, proclaim, tell; make known or famous, make resound. सम् hear (मुखात्), listen

to (acc.); accede to the request of, make a promise to (loc. or dat.). C. let hear, announce, proclaim; make resound. अभिसम् hear, learn. प्रतिसम् make a promise to (gen.). — Cf. अभिविश्रुत, अभिश्रुत, आश्रुत, परिश्रुत, विश्रुत.

श्रुत् (—°) hearing.

श्रुत a. heard, learnt, mentioned, stated, named, known as, famous, celebrated; n. hearing, learning, lore, tradition, (sacred) knowledge.

श्रुतकर्मन् m. N. of a hero (lit. of celebrated deeds).

श्रुतकाम a. desirous of learning.

श्रुतकीर्ति m. N. of a hero (of celebrated fame).

श्रुततस् adv. by hearsay.

श्रुतधर a. having a god memory (lit. keeping what is heard).

श्रुतपूर्व a. heard (of) before, known by hearsay.

श्रुतबोध m. T. of a treatise on metres.

श्रुतवन्त् a. having heard; learned, scientific.

श्रुतवृत्त n. du. learning and virtue.

श्रुतवृत्ताढ्य & °त्तोपपन्न a. endowed with learning and virtue.

श्रुतशील n. du. learning and character; poss. °वन्त्.

श्रुतशीलसंपन्न a. endowed with learning and character.

श्रुतश्रवस् m. a man's name.

1श्रुतसेन a. having a famous army.

2श्रुतसेन m. N. of a serpent-demon etc.

श्रुतामघ a. having famous treasures.

श्रुतायु & °युस् m. N. of sev. men.

श्रुति f. hearing, ear, sound, noise, report, hearsay, news, tidings, (sacred) utterance or prescription, revelation, sacred text, holy writ, the Veda; appellation, title.

श्रुतिकटु a. sounding harsh.

श्रुतिगोचर a. being within hearing.

श्रुतितस् adv. in the way of revelation; with regard or according to (sacred) prescription.

श्रुतिद्वैध n. conflict or contradiction of two sacred texts.

श्रुतिपथ m. range of hearing; °पथं गम, प्राप्, etc. come within hearing.

श्रुतिमन्त् a. having ears or possessing knowledge.

श्रुतिमहन्त् a. great in knowledge.

श्रुतिमार्ग m. = श्रुतिपथ.

श्रुतिशिरस् n. a chief passage of the holy scriptures.

श्रुतिशीलवन्त् v. श्रुतशीलवन्त्.

श्रुत्कर्ण a. having ears to hear.

श्रुत्य a. worth hearing.

श्रुत्युक्त a. said or taught in the sacred scriptures.

श्रुष् (श्रोषति, °ते) ± आ hear. — Cf. श्रोषमाण.

श्रुष्टि or श्रुष्टि a. obedient, ready; f. obedience, readiness, instr. श्रुष्टी readily, quickly. श्रुष्टिं कृ obey, follow.

श्रुष्टिमन्त् & श्रुष्टीवन् (f. °वरी) obedient, officious, zealous.

श्रूयमाणत्व n. the being heard.

श्रेणि or श्रेणी f. line, row, range, troop, multitude, swarm (of bees); company, guild (of artisans etc.).

श्रेणिमन्त् a. having many followers.

श्रेणिशस् adv. in rows or lines.

श्रेणीधर्म m. law of a guild.

श्रेणीबन्ध m. forming a row or line.

श्रेमन् m. distinction, superiority.

श्रेयस् (compar.) fairer, more beautiful or excellent, better than (न, esp. श्रेयस्—न better or rather—than); distinguished, excellent; dear, beloved; auspicious, fortunate. n. the better or good, i.e. (greater) welfare or prosperity.

श्रेयस्कर, f. ई making better or causing happiness.

श्रेयस्काम a. desiring felicity.

श्रेयस्त्व n. superiority, preeminence.

श्रेयोमय a. excellent.

श्रेयोऽर्थिन् a. = श्रेयस्काम.

श्रेष्ठ (superl.) the fairest, most excellent or best of (gen., loc., or —°), best in or with regard to (loc. or —°); better than (abl. or gen.); most auspicious or fortunate. n. the best.

श्रेष्ठतम & श्रेष्ठतर (superl. & compar.) fairest or best, fairer or better (than all).

श्रेष्ठता f., °त्व n. supremacy, eminence.
श्रेष्ठवर्चस् a. most powerful or glorious.
श्रेष्ठान्वय a. of excellent family.
श्रेष्ठिन् m. a man of high rank or the chief of a corporation.
श्रैष्ठ्य n. supremacy, precedence, first rank or place among (gen. or —°).
श्रोण a. lame.
श्रोणि or श्रोणी f. (adj. —° f. ई) buttock, hip (poss. श्रोणिमन्त्).
श्रोतव्य a. to be heard (n. impers.) or worth hearing.
श्रोतृ or श्रोतृ m. hearing (also as fut. auditurus).
श्रोत्र n. ear, hearing.
श्रोत्रतस् adv. on the ear.
श्रोत्रपद्वी f. range (path) of the ears.
श्रोत्रपरंपरा f. hearsay.
श्रोत्रपालि f., °पुट m. ear-lap.
श्रोत्रपेय a. worth hearing (lit. to be drunk with the ear).
श्रोत्रमय a. whose nature is hearing.
श्रोत्रमार्ग m. = श्रोत्रपद्वी.
श्रोत्रमूल n. the root of the ear.
श्रोत्रवन्त् a. having ears or the sense of hearing.
श्रोत्रसंवाद m. agreement (remembrance) of the ear.
श्रोत्रहीन & श्रोत्रापेत a. deaf.
श्रोत्रिय a. learned (in sacred tradition); m. a Brahman versed in sacred lore.
श्रोत्रियस्व n. property of a Çrotriya (cf. prec.).
श्रोषमाण a. obedient, trustful.
श्रौत, f. ई (आ) relating to the ears, based upon sound or words (w. उपमा f. an explicit comparison); relating to sacred tradition, Vedic.
श्रौतसूत्र n. a Sūtra work based upon sacred tradition.
श्रौत्र, f. ई relating to the ear.
श्रौषट् a sacrificial exclamation.
श्रौष्टि a. obedient.
श्लक्ष्ण a. slippery, smooth, even, soft, tender.
श्लथ् (only pp. श्लथन्त्) become loose or unfastened; C. श्लाथयति loose, relax. — आ & वि (श्लथते) = S.
श्लथ a. loose, slack, remiss, weak.
श्लथशिल a. covered with a loose stone (well).
श्लथसंधि a. having weak joints; abstr. °ता f.
श्लथाङ्ग a. slack-limbed, abstr. °ता f.
श्लथाय्, °यते become loose or relaxed.
श्लाघ्, श्लाघते (°ति) trust, have confidence in (dat.), speak confidently, brag, boast of (instr. or loc.); praise, extol. C. श्लाघयति comfort, console, praise, extol. — सम् brag, boast of (instr.).
श्लाघन a. & n. (or f. आ) bragging, boasting, praising.
श्लाघनीय a. to be praised, praiseworthy, honourable.
श्लाघा f. brag, boast, praise, glory.
श्लाघिन् a. boasting or proud of (—°), haughty, arrogant; famous, celebrated; praising, extolling.
श्लाघ्य a. = श्लाघनीय; abstr. °ता f.
श्लाघ्यपद n. honourable position.
श्लाघ्ययौवना f. a woman in the (splendid) blossom of youth.
श्लाघ्यान्वय a. of a honourable family.
श्लिष्, श्लिष्यति, °ते, pp. श्लिष्ट (q.v.) adhere, cling or stick to (loc., r. acc.); clasp, embrace; melt or join together (tr. & intr.). C. श्लेषयति join, close. — आ stick or cling to (loc. or acc.); approach, touch, clasp, embrace. C. fasten on (loc.), embrace, encircle. उपा clasp, grasp. समा cling to (acc.), embrace. C. join, unite. उप cling to (acc.), step near (± समीपम्). C. bring or draw near, join with (सह). वि get loose or unfastened; fall asunder or aside, miss the aim; also = C. disjoin, separate from, deprive of (abl.). सम् cleave or stick to (acc.), step near, approach, clasp, embrace; bring into immediate contact with (instr.). C. join, connect, put together, bring into contact with (instr. or loc.), transfer to (loc.). अभिसम् cling together (अन्योऽन्यम्); C. join tight or closely. उपसम् connect, unite. — Cf. आश्लिष्ट, उपश्लिष्ट (sic!), विश्लिष्ट, संश्लिष्ट.
श्लिष्ट a. hanging on, cleaving or sticking to (loc. or —°); joined, closed, limited or

confined (to itself); (holding) clasped or embraced.

श्लिष्टरूपक n. a kind of metaphor.

श्लीपद n. elephantiasis, p. °दिन्.

श्लेष m. clinging or sticking to (loc.); union, junction; embrace, sexual intercourse (also **आ** f.); sev. figures of rhetoric.

श्लेषोपमा f. a kind of comparison (rh.).

श्लेष्मण a. slimy, slippery.

श्लेष्मन् m. adhesive substance, slime, phlegm; n. band, string.

श्लेष्मातक m., **ई** f. N. of a tree.

श्लोक m. sound, noise, report, fame; strophe, stanza, esp. the epic Çloka.

श्लोकबद्ध a. composed in Çlokas.

श्लोकिन् & **श्लोक्य** a. noisy; renowned, famous.

श्लोण a. lame, abstr. **श्लोण्य** n.

श्वःकाल m. the day of to-morrow.

श्वक्रीडिन् a. breeding or keeping (lit. sporting with) dogs.

श्वगर्दभ n. sgl. dogs and asses.

श्वघ्निन् m. a gambler by profession.

श्वजाघनी f. a dog's tail.

श्वञ्च्, **श्वञ्चते** open (intr.) for (dat.), receive with open arms. C. **श्वञ्चयति** cause to open or burst. — **उद्** = S.

श्वदृति m. a dog's skin.

श्वन् m., **शुनी** f. dog, bitch.

श्वनिन् a. keeping dogs.

श्वनी m. leader of dogs.

श्वपच & **श्वपाक** m. a degraded class of men (lit. cooking dogs).

श्वपति m. lord or owner of dogs.

श्वपद् m. a beast of prey.

श्वपद n. a dog's foot (as a brand-mark).

श्वपुच्छ n. a dog's tail.

श्वभक्ष & °**क्ष्य** a. eating dog's flesh.

श्वभ्र m. n. fissure of the earth, pit, hole; m. hell, a man's name.

श्वभ्रीय्, °**यति** regard as a hole.

श्वमांस n. dog's flesh; °**भोजिन्** a. eating it.

श्वयथ & **श्वयथु** m. swelling.

श्वयातु m. a kind of demons or evil spirits.

श्ववन्त् a. having or keeping dogs.

श्ववर्त m. a cert. worm.

श्ववाल m. dog's hair.

श्वविष्ठा f. dog's dung.

1**श्ववृत्ति** f. a dog's life (service).

2**श्ववृत्ति** a. living by dogs.

श्ववृत्तिन् a. = prec.

श्वशुर m. father-in-law; du. father and mother-in-law.

श्वशुर्य m. husband's or wife's brother, brother-in-law.

श्वश्रू f. mother-in-law.

श्वश्रूस्नुषा f. du. the mother-in-law and the other wives of the father-in-law.

श्वःश्व n. procrastination (lit. to-morrow to-morrow).

1**श्वस्**, **श्वसिति**, **श्वसति**, °**ते**, pp. **श्वस्त** & **श्वसित** (q.v.) blow, bluster, hiss, whistle, snort, breathe, sigh. I. only **शाश्वसत्** snorting. — **अभि** blow hither, hiss, whistle, groan. **आ**, **पर्या**, **प्रत्या**, & **समा** get breath, recover, become quiet. C. quiet, comfort. **उद्** hiss, pant, gasp, groan, sigh; breathe upwards or out; stop or pause from (abl.), recover; heave (intr.), get loose, open, expand. C. cause to take breath, refresh, lift up; tear, rend asunder, interrupt, disturb. **प्रोद्** pant, breathe heavily. **समुद्** take breath, recover; rise, spring up. C. lift, swell (tr.). **नि** & **विनि** hiss, pant, sigh. **निस्** hiss, pant, breathe out or in, sigh. **विनिस्** hiss, pant, snort; heave a sigh. **प्र** blow forth or in, exhale or inhale. C. cause to breathe; quiet, comfort. **अभिप्र** blow forth upon (acc.). **वि** have confidence, be fearless, trust in (loc., gen., or acc.). C. inspire confidence (acc.). **अतिवि** have (too) great confidence in (loc. or acc.). **अभिवि** C. inspire confidence. **परिवि** C. quiet, comfort. — Cf. **उच्छ्वसित**, **निश्वसित**, **परिविश्वस्त** (add.), **विश्वस्त**, **समुच्छ्वसित**.

2**श्वस्** adv. to-morrow, next day; **श्वः श्वस्** from day to day, daily.

श्वसथ m. blowing, hissing, snorting.

श्वसन a. blowing, hissing, snorting, breathing deep. m. wind or the god of wind; n. hissing (of a serpent), breathing, esp. deep breath, sigh.

श्वसित a. having got breath or life; n. breath.

श्वस्तन a. of to-morrow; n. & f. ई the to-morrow or next day.
श्वःसुत्या f. the day before the Sutyā ceremony.
श्वहत a. killed by a dog.
श्वा, श्वयति, pp. शून (q.v.) swell. P. शूयते the same. — उद्, प्र, वि, & सम् = S. — Cf. उच्छून, संशून.
श्वाग्र n. a dog's tail.
श्वाजिन n. a dog's hide.
श्वात्त a. savoury, well-tasted; n. such food or drink.
श्वात्र्य a. = prec. adj.
श्वान m., ई f. dog, bitch.
श्वान्त a. peaceful, quiet, confident.
श्वापद् & °पद m. beast of prey.
श्वाविध् f. porcupine.
श्वाशुर, f. ई belonging to the father-in-law.
श्वास m. hissing, snorting; breath, esp. breathing in; aspiration (g.); sighing, sigh.
श्वासिन् a. hissing, panting.
श्विक्न m. pl. N. of a people.
श्वित् (श्वेतते) be bright, shine. — अव shine down. वि = S.
श्वितीचि, श्वित्न & श्वित्न्य a. whitish.
श्वित्यञ्च्, f. श्वितीची the same.
श्वित्र a. whitish, white, leprous. m. a cert. (domestic) white animal; n. white leprosy.
श्वित्रिन् a. having white leprosy.
श्वेत a. white, bright. m. white horse, N. of a serpent-demon etc.
श्वेतकाक m. a white crow (fig.); °काकीय a. quite uncommon, extraordinary.
श्वेतकेतु m. a man's name.
श्वेतच्छत्त्र n. a white umbrella, p. °त्त्रिन्.
श्वेतद्वीप m. n. N. of a sacred place & a myth. island.
श्वेतना f. dawning, dawn.
श्वेतपक्ष a. white-winged.
1श्वेतपुष्प n. a white flower.
2श्वेतपुष्प, f. ई having white flower.
श्वेतभानु a. having white rays; m. the moon.
श्वेतवत्सा f. having a white calf.
श्वेतवाह & °न a. guiding white horses; m. E. of Arjuna etc.
श्वेतांशु m. = श्वेतभानु.
श्वेताम्बर a. clad in white; m. a Jaina sect.
श्वेताय्, °यते become white.
श्वेतार्चिस् m. = श्वेतभानु.
1श्वेताश्व m. white horse.
2श्वेताश्व a. drawn by white horses (chariot); m. E. of Arjuna (guider of white horses).
श्वेताश्वतर m. N. of a teacher, pl. his school.
श्वेताश्वतरोपनिषद् f. T. of an Upanishad.
श्वेतिमन् m. whiteness, white colour.
श्वेत्य a. white, light.
श्वैक्न m. a prince of the Çviknas.
श्वैतरी f. whitish or having much milk.
श्वैत्य n. whiteness.
श्वैत्र्य n. white leprosy.
श्वोभाव m. abstr. to seq.
श्वोभाविन् & श्वोभूत a. being to-morrow.
श्वोवसीय n. future welfare.
श्वोवसीयस, f. ई granting future welfare.
श्वोवस्यस a. = prec.
श्वोविजयिन् a. who shall vanquish to-morrow.

ष

ष (–°) = षष्.
षट्क a. consisting of six; n. hectade.
षट्कर्ण a. heard by six ears (secret).
1षट्कर्मन् n. the six (allowed) occupations (of a Brahman) or the six magical arts.
2षट्कर्मन् a. following the six (allowed) occupations; m. a Brahman.
षट्कर्मवन्त् m. = prec. m.
षट्कृत्वस् adv. six times.
षट्चरण a. six-footed; m. a bee.
षट्तय a. consisting of six, sixfold.
षट्त्रिंश, f. ई the thirty-sixth.
षट्त्रिंशत् f. thirty-six.
षट्त्रिंशाब्दिक a. thirty-six years old.
षट्त्व n. the number six.
षट्पञ्चाशत् f. fifty-six.
षट्पत्त्र a. six-leaved.

षट्पद् (°पाद्), f. **षट्पदी** having six feet or containing six verses.
षट्पद a. = prec. adj.; also having (taken) six steps; m. insect, bee.
षट्पाद् a. six-footed; m. bee.
षट्शत n. one hundred and six; f. °**ती**† 600.
षट्शस् adv. sixfoldly.
षट्सप्त pl. six or seven.
षट्सहस्र a. numbering six thousand.
षडंश m. one sixth; adj. sixfold.
षडंह्रि m. = **षडङ्घ्रि**.
षडक्ष a. six-eyed.
षडक्षर, f. **ई** containing six syllables.
1**षडङ्ग** n. the six limbs or appendages of the Veda, i.e. the six Vedāṅgas.
2**षडङ्ग** a. having six limbs or six Vedāṅgas.
षडङ्गविद् a. knowing the six Vedāṅgas.
षडङ्घ्रि m. bee (lit. six-footed).
षडर (**षळर**) a. having six spokes.
षडर्च n. the number of six verses.
षडश्व a. drawn by six horses.
षडह m. a period of six days.
षडहोरात्र s. six days and nights.
1**षडानन** s. six mouths (only °—).
2**षडानन** a. having six mouths (Skanda).
षडुत्तर a. greater by six.
षडून a. less by six.
षडृच m. n. = **षडर्च**.
षड्गव m. n. six bulls or cows.
1**षड्गुण** m. the six qualities (ph.).
2**षड्गुण** a. sixfold.
षड्गुरुशिष्य m. N. of an author.
षड्ढा adv. in six ways or parts.
1**षड्दर्शन** n. the six philosophical systems.
2**षड्दर्शन** a. familiar with the six philosophical systems.
षड्धा adv. = **षड्ढा**.
षड्भाग m. a sixth part (esp. of the produce of the soil, due to the king).
षड्भागभाज् a. obtaining a sixth part.
षड्भुज a. six-armed.
षड्रात्र m. a period or a festival of six days.
षड्वक्त्र a. = 2**षडानन**.
षड्वर्ग m. six-group, aggregate of six things.
षड्विंश, f. **ई** the twenty-sixth.
षड्विंशत् & **षड्विंशति** f. twenty-six.
षड्विंशब्राह्मण n. T. of a Brāhmaṇa.
षड्विध a. sixfold, of six kinds.
षड्विधान a. forming an arrangement of six.
षण्ड m. group of trees (only —°); heap, multitude i.g.
षण्डिक m. a man's name.
षण्ढ, f. **ई** impotent; m. eunuch or hermaphrodite.
षण्ढय्, °**यति** emasculate.
षण्णवति f. ninety-six.
षण्मास s., °**सी** f. six-months.
षण्मासनिचय m. a quantity (of food) sufficient for six months.
षण्मासिक a. happening every six months, half-yearly.
षण्मास्य a. = prec.; n. six months.
षण्मुख a. six-faced or six-mouthed (Çiva & Skanda).
षत्व n. the transition of **स** into **ष** (g.).
षष् pl. (nom. **षट्**) six; **षट्** also as adv. six times.
षष्टि f. sixty.
षष्टिक n. the number sixty, sixty.
षष्टिधा adv. in sixty ways or parts.
षष्टिवर्षिन् a. sixty years old.
षष्टिहायन a. the same.
षष्ठ, f. **ई** the sixth; ± **काल** m. the sixth hour of the day & the sixth meal-time. f. **षष्ठी** the sixth day of a half-month; the sixth case (g.).
1**षष्ठभक्त** n. the sixth repast.
2**षष्ठभक्त** a. eating only the sixth repast.
षष्ठम, f. **ई** the sixth.
षष्ठांश m. = **षड्भाग**.
षष्ठांशवृत्ति a. living on the sixth part (king; cf. **षड्भाग**).
षष्ठान्नकाल a. = 2**षष्ठभक्त**; abstr. °**ता** f.
षष्ठ्य m. a sixth-part.
षाडव m. comfits with fruits.
षाड्गुण्य n. the six measures of royal policy.
षाण्मासिक, f. **ई** six-monthly.
षाण्मास्य a. the same.
षिड्ग m. libertine, gallant.
षोडश, f. **ई** the sixteenth; n. a sixteenth part.
षोडशधा adv. in sixteen parts or ways.

षोडशन् a. pl. sixteen.

षोडशम a. the sixteenth.

षोडशांश m. a sixteenth part.

षोडशिन् a. consisting of sixteen, sixteenfold.

षोढा adv. sixfoldly.

ष्ठिव् or **ष्ठीव्**, **ष्ठीवति**, pp. **ष्ठ्यूत** spew, spit. — **अभि** bespit. **नि** spit out. **अभिनि** & **अवनि** spit out upon (acc.). **विनि**, **निस्**, **प्र** spit out. **प्रति** bespit.

ष्ठीव a. spitting (—°).

ष्ठीवन a. & n. spewing, spitting; n. also spittle, saliva.

ष्ठीवि & **ष्ठीविन्** a. spitting.

स

1**स** pron.-stem of 3^d pers. (only nom. sgl. m. & f. **सः**, **सा** & loc. **सस्मिन्**, supplying the forms of **त**, q.v.).

2**स** (°— in adj. & adv., opp. **अ** priv.) accompanied by, furnished with, having.

3**स** (°—) one, the same.

सऋण a. having debts, indebted.

सऋषिक a. with the Rishis.

संयत् a. coherent, continual, uninterrupted. f. contract, agreement; fight, battle.

संयत a. held together, held in, restrained, checked, controlled, arranged, kept in order, limited, restricted; bound together, tied up (hair); fettered, confined, captive, prisoner.

संयताहार a. moderate in diet.

संयतेन्द्रिय a. whose senses are restrained, self-controlled; abstr. **°ता** f.

संयत्त a. met (as foes); concentrated, careful, prepared, ready.

संयन्तृ m. restrainer, subduer.

संयम m. restraint, check, control, esp. self-control; suppression, destruction, tying up or together, fettering; closing (of the eyes).

संयमधन a. possessing much self-control.

संयमन a. (f. **ई**) & n. restraining, checking, controlling, subduing; n. also tying up, fettering, drawing in (reins); band, fetter.

संयमित n. suppression (of the voice).

संयमिन् a. exercising self-control; tied up (hair).

संयाज्य n. participation in a sacrifice; f. **°ज्या** N. of cert. sacrif. texts.

संयान n. the going, driving, riding etc. (together); setting out, journey; vehicle, waggon.

संयास m. ardour, eagerness, zeal.

संयुक्त a. joined, united, married with (instr.); endowed or furnished with (instr. or —°). belonging or relating to (—°).

संयुग n. union, junction; fight, war.

संयुज् a. connected, related, kin.

संयुत a. bound, attached, joined or connected with (instr. ± **सह** or —°), consisting of (instr.), relating to (—°).

संयोग m. conjunction, connection, coherence; contact (ph.); relation, friendship, alliance; matrimony, sexual intercourse with (**सह**); a conjunct consonant (g.).

संयोगिन् a. being in contact or immediate connection with (instr. or —°); conjunct (g.).

संयोजन n. joining or uniting with (instr. or loc.).

सरक्त a. reddened, feeling love; charming, ravishing.

संरक्ष m. guardian or guard.

संरक्षक, **°क्षिका** f. guardian.

संरक्षण n. guarding, protecting from (gen. or —°).

संरक्षणीय & **°रक्ष्य** a. to be guarded (against).

संरब्ध a. hand in hand, close joined or connected with (instr.); excited, enraged, angry; increased, augmented, swelling, swollen.

संरम्भ m. taking hold of; rashness, eagerness, zeal, impetuosity, agitation, fury, wrath, violence, high degree.

संरम्भिन् a. eager for (—°), rash, angry.

संराग m. redness, passion.

संराधन, f. **ई** satisfying, propitiating.
संराध्य a. to be acquired or won.
संराव m., **°ण** n. shout, cry, yell.
संरुद्ध a. stopped, detained, checked, restrained; obstructed, impeded; surrounded by, covered or filled with (instr. or —°).
संरुषित a. enraged, wrathful.
संरूढ a. grown, grown together i.e. cicatrized, healed; come forth, arisen, appeared; deeply rooted, firm.
संरोदन n. weeping, howling.
संरोध m. obstruction, hindrance, suppression; confinement, siege.
संरोधन n. keeping back, hindering, suppressing, imprisoning.
संरोध्य a. to be imprisoned or confined.
संरोपण a. & n. causing to grow (together); healing or planting.
संरोह m. growing over or together, healing (intr.); growing up, appearing.
संरोहण a. & n. = **संरोपण**.
संरोहिन् a. growing in (—°).
संलक्ष्य a. perceivable, visible.
संलग्न a. stuck in or attached to, closely connected with (loc. or —°).
संलपन n. chattering, talking.
संलय m., **संलयन** n. cowering, lying or sitting down.
संलाप m. talk, chat, conversation with (instr. ± **सह** or gen.) about (—°).
संलीन a. stuck or clung to, hidden or cowering in (loc. or —°).
संलुलित a. mixed or mingled with (—°); disordered, disarranged.
1**संवत्** f. side, stretch, streak.
2**संवत्** abbrev. for **संवत्सरे** in the year (of Vikrama's era, 56 B.C.).
संवत्सम् adv. for a year.
संवत्सर m. (n.) year.
संवत्सरतम, f. **ई** coming next year.
संवत्सरनिरोध m. imprisonment for a year; abl. **°तस्**.
संवत्सरभृत a. borne or maintained for a year (fire).
संवत्सरवासिन् a. staying for a year (with the teacher).
संवत्सरसहस्र n. a thousand years.
संवत्सरायुष a. one year old.
संवत्सरीण & **°रीय** a. yearly, annual.
संवदन n. talk, conversation.
संवनन, f. **ई** a. propitiating, conciliating, winning over; n. means of propitiating or charming, gain, acquisition (of a treasure).
संवर a. keeping off; m. weir, dam.
1**संवरण**, f. **ई** enclosing, containing. n. enclosed place (for sacrifice etc.), cover, envelope; closing, hiding, concealing; feint, pretence.
2**संवरण** n. choosing (for husband).
संवर्ग a. & m. grasping, clutching.
संवर्गम् ger. by grasping or clutching.
संवर्णन n. description, tale.
संवर्त m. rolling up; anything rolled or kneaded, lump, clod, ball, heap, mass, thick cloud; a cert. period of time, the destruction of the world.
संवर्तक a. rolling up, destroying; m. such a fire, destruction of the world.
संवर्धन a. & n. increasing, augmenting; n. also growing, breeding (of a child); thriving, prospering.
संवल s. provender for a journey (cf. **शम्बल**).
संवलन n., **°ना** f. meeting (as friends or foes).
संवलित a. met, come together; mixed or joined with (instr. or —°).
संवसन n. meeting- or dwelling-place.
संवसु m. house-mate.
संवाच् f. colloquy.
संवाद m. speaking together, conversation with (instr. ± **सह**, loc., or —°); agreement, correspondence, sameness.
संवादिन् a. talking, conversing; agreeing with, corresponding to (gen. or —°).
संवार्य a. to be covered or concealed; n. a secret.
संवास m. dwelling together, living with (instr. ± **सह** or —°); cohabitation (also sex.); (common) dwelling-place.
1**संवासिन्** a. clothed in (—°).
2**संवासिन्** a. dwelling together, house-mate; inhabiting (—°).

संवाह m. driving-park; market-place; stroking with the hand (cf. seq.).

संवाहक, f. **°हिका** stroking or rubbing with the hand; m. a shampooer.

संवाहन n. driving, driving out, moving along (clouds etc.); bearing, carrying (also **°ना** f.); stroking or rubbing with the hand, shampooing.

संविग्न a. agitated, flurried, terrified.

संविज्ञान n. perceiving, understanding, knowing.

संवित्ति f. perception, knowledge, understanding.

1**संविद्** f. consciousness, feeling, perception; consent, agreement with (instr. ± **सह** or gen.) about (—°); appointment, rendezvous; plan, design; conversation, talk about (—°); news, tidings; custom, usage; name.

2**संविद्** f. acquisition, possession.

संविदान a. joined, united.

संविदित a. known, learnt, agreed.

संविद्य n. possession.

संविध् & **°धा** f. arrangement, contrivance.

संविधान (& **°क***) n., **°धि** m. the same.

संविभाग m. sharing with others; letting partake of, presenting with, distributing (—°); portion, share.

संवीत a. covered, wrapped, enveloped, veiled, clothed, armed; n. clothing.

संवृज् a. snatching.

1**संवृत्** a. covering.

2**संवृत्** f. bestriding; approach, assault.

संवृत a. covered, veiled in, protected, surrounded, or accompanied by, filled with (instr. or —°); concealed, kept secret; checked, restrained, suppressed; careful, cautious.

संवृतसंवार्य a. concealing secrets.

संवृति f. covering up, concealment, secrecy.

संवृत्त a. approached, arrived, met, happened, past, fulfilled; become (nom. or dat.).

संवृत्ति f. common occupation with (—°).

संवृद्ध a. grown up, increased, thriven, flourishing, blooming.

संवृद्धि f. growth, power, might.

संवेग m. agitation, flurry; intensity, high degree.

संवेद n. perception, sensation.

संवेदन n. perception, consciousness; telling, announcing.

संवेश m. entering, lying down, sleeping; room, chamber.

संवेशन, f. **ई** causing to lie down; n. lying, sleeping, sexual intercourse.

संव्यवहार m. intercourse; occupation or dealing with (instr. or —°).

संव्याध m. fight, contest.

संव्यान n. cloth, cover, mantle.

संव्रश्चम् (ger.) by cutting in pieces or dismembering.

संशप्त a. cursed.

संशप्तक m. pl. conspirators.

संशब्दन n. mentioning, naming.

संशम m. tranquillizing, satisfying.

संशमन a. (f. **ई**) & n. appeasing, calming

संशय m. doubt, hesitation, uncertainty about (loc., acc. w. **प्रति**, or —°); danger for (gen., loc., or —°).

संशयकर, f. **ई** causing danger, compromising (—°).

संशयात्मन् a. of doubtful or irresolute mind.

संशयालु a. doubtful, sceptic.

संशयावह a. causing danger.

संशयित a. doubtful, uncertain (pers. & th.); n. as abstr.

संशयोपमा f. a kind of comparison (rh.).

संशर m. breaking down, tearing asunder.

संशान्त a. thoroughly appeased or extinguished; ceased, gone, dead.

संशान्ति f. extinction.

संशासन n. direction, instruction.

संशित a. whetted, sharp, pointed (lit. & fig.); ready, resolute; fixed, settled.

संशितवाच् a. speaking pointedly.

संशितव्रत a. strictly keeping a vow.

संशिति f. sharpening.

संशिष्ट a. left, remained.

संशिस् f. invitation, summons.

संशीलन n. practising, exercising; frequent intercourse with (instr.).

संशुद्ध a. cleaned, purified; paid, restored; tried, approved.
संशुद्धि f. cleanness, purity.
संशुष्क a. dry, emaciated.
संशून a. swollen.
संशोधन a. (f. **ई**) & n. purifying.
संशोष m. drying up (intr.).
संशोषण a. & n. drying up (tr. & intr.).
संशोषिन् a. drying, draining.
संश्रय m. connection, relation, attachment, union, alliance, league; refuge, shelter, abode, dwelling-place; the resorting or having recourse to (loc. or —°); abl. in consequence or by means of (—°). Adj. —° connected with, living or being in (also **°यिन्**), relating to, intent upon.
संश्रयिन् a. resorted or fled to; dwelling or being in (—°); m. servant, subject.
संश्रव m., **°ण** n. hearing, loc. within hearing.
संश्रान्त a. wearied, exhausted.
संश्रित a. joined or connected with (instr. or —°); (being) leaned on or resorted to; belonging or relating to (loc. or —°); being, dwelling, living in or on (acc., loc., & —°); contained in (—°).
संश्रुत a. heard, learnt, read in (loc.); agreed, promised.
संश्लिष् a. (nom. **°श्लिट्**) entwined, coherent.
संश्लिष्ट a. sticking close to, firmly united with (acc., instr. ± **सह**, or —°); blended together; indistinct, neutral.
संश्लेष m. junction, connection, union, immediate contact with (instr.); embrace.
संश्लेषण a. (f. **ई**) & n. cementing, uniting firmly or closely; n. also cleaving or sticking to, cement, tie, band.
संश्लेषिन् a. uniting, connecting.
संसक्त a. hanging, sticking to, fixed or bent on, devoted to, occupied with (loc. or —°); met, engaged in battle; joined, connected, or furnished with (—°); contiguous, close, dense; lasting, continual, uninterrupted.
संसक्ति f. immediate touch or contact.
संसङ्ग m. connection, adj. **°ङ्गिन्**.
संसद् f. assembly, community, company, multitude; law-court, court of a prince.
संसमक a. put together.
संसरण n. walking about, wandering, esp. from one existence into another.
संसर्ग a. mixing, running together. m. mixture, union, connection, contact with (gen., instr., or —°); attachment, esp. to external objects, sensuality; dealing or intercourse (also sexual) with (gen., instr. ± **सह**, loc., or —°); participation (adj. —° having partaken of); living together, association, community of goods.
संसर्गिन् a. being in connection or contact with, partaking of (—°).
संसर्जन n. meeting, joining with (instr.).
संसर्प or **संसर्प** a. sneaking, gliding.
संसर्पण n. ascending (of a mountain); gliding, sneaking, stealing upon (an enemy).
संसर्पमाणक a. creeping.
संसर्पिन् a. moving on slowly; reaching or stretching to (—°).
संसहस्र a. accompanied by a thousand.
†**संसाद** m. company.
संसाधन n. preparing, arranging, contriving.
संसाध्य a. to be brought about, won, acquired, subdued.
संसार m. wandering, esp. from one existence into another, metempsychosis, transmigration, the cycle of existence; life i.g.
संसारगमन n. the course of transmigration.
संसारमार्ग m. the path of life.
संसारान्त m. the end of life.
संसारार्णव m. the ocean of mundane existence.
संसारिन् a. stretching far, comprising (intelligence); attached to mundane existence.
संसिच् a. shedding or pouring together.
संसिद्ध a. accomplished, attained, arranged, prepared; perfect, happy, emancipated.
संसिद्धि f. accomplishment, perfection, success, result.
संसुद् f. tasting, enjoying; dat. as infin.
संसुप्त a. sleeping, asleep.
संसूचन n. showing, betraying, uttering.
संसूद s. the palate.
संसृज् f. meeting.
संसृप् f. pl. E. of ten deitis (Agni etc.).

संसृष्ट a. collected, united, associated (as partners etc.), mixed or mingled with (instr. or —°); n. connection with, relation to (loc.).

संसृष्टि f. union, conjunction.

संसेवन n. using, employing, serving, worshipping (—°).

संसेवा f. frequenting, worshipping; use, employment; inclination to, fondness of (—°).

संसेव्य a. to be frequented, served, honoured, worshipped, used, employed.

संस्करण n. arranging, preparing, cremating (a dead body).

संस्कर्तृ m. arranger, preparer, consecrator, performer of a ceremony.

संस्कार m. preparing, arranging; cultivation, education; purification, sacrament, consecration, any rite or ceremony, esp. funeral obsequies; impression (ph.).

संस्कार्य a. to be connected or initiated.

संस्कृत a. put together, composed, prepared, arranged; consecrated, initiated, married; adorned, polished, cultivated, Sanskritic; n. arrangement, preparation; the Sanskrit language.

संस्कृतात्मन् a. having received the sacraments (lit. whose mind is prepared).

संस्कृति f. = seq. + consecration, initiation.

संस्क्रिया f. arranging, preparing, forming.

संस्तब्ध a. stiff, immovable.

संस्तम्भ m. pertinacy, resistance.

संस्तम्भन n. abstr. to seq.

संस्तम्भयितृ & **°म्भिन्** a. stopping, restraining.

संस्तर m. a bed or couch of leaves or straw; cover, veil; scattering or scattered mass; spreading, sacrificial act (± यज्ञ°).

संस्तरण n. straw; strewing, scattering.

संस्तव m., **°न** n. (common) praise or song.

संस्तार m. bed or couch of straw.

संस्तीर्ण & **संस्तृत** a. strewed, scattered.

संस्तुत a. praised or sung (together); equal to, passing for (instr. or —°); acquainted, familiar; n. plan, intention.

संस्तुति f. praise, eulogy.

संस्तुभ्, f. **संस्तोभ** m. shouting.

संस्त्यान a. stiffened, coagulated; n. stiffening, coagulation.

संस्त्याय m. heap, assemblage; house, habitation.

संस्थ a. standing, abiding, being or contained in (loc. or —°); belonging to, resting or dependent on, partaking or possessed of (—°); lasting, continuing. — m. **संस्थे** (only loc.) amidst or in presence of (gen.). f. **संस्था** staying, remaining with (—°); shape, form, esp. the ground-form of a sacrifice; manifestation, appearance, likeness (often adj. —°); fixed order, rule, nature, character; conclusion, end, death.

संस्थान n. standing, staying or abiding in (loc.); standing firm, duration, continuance; existence, being, life; dwelling-place, abode; public place in a city; shape, form, appearance; nature, character; conclusion, end.

संस्थानक m. N. of a prince.

संस्थापन n. fixing, establishing, settling; f. **आ** supporting, comforting.

संस्थित a. standing or having stood (in battle); being in or on (loc., उपरि, or —°); abiding, staying, lasting; resting or depending on, familiar with (loc.); perfect, finished; dead, deceased.

संस्थिति f. being together, union with or staying among (loc.), standing, sitting, etc. on (loc. or —°); position, situation; duration, continuance, perseverance; existence, possibility; shape, form, fixed order, rule; nature, character; conclusion, end, death.

संस्पर्धा f. contest, rivalry, jealousy, envy.

संस्पर्धिन् a. vying with (—°); jealous, envious.

संस्पर्श m. touch, contact.

संस्पर्शज a. produced by contact.

संस्पर्शन a. touching (—°); n. as subst.

संस्पर्शिन् & **संस्पृश्** a. = prec. a. (—°).

संस्पृष्ट a. touched, brought in close contact with (instr. or —°), adjoining, contiguous; touched or visited by (instr.).

संस्फीत a. perfect, complete.

संस्फोट m. striking or clashing together.

संस्मरण n. remembrance, recollection of (gen.).

संस्मरणीय & **°स्मर्तव्य** a. to be remembered, memorable.

संस्मृत a. remembered, thought of, prescribed, named, called.

संस्मृति f. = **संस्मरण**.

संस्मेर a. smiling.

संस्यन्दिन् a. flowing together.

संस्रव m. flowing together, conflux, flood; dregs, remains.

संस्राव m. = prec.

†**संस्रावण** a. flowing together.

संस्राव्य a. run together, mingled.

संस्वार m. sounding together.

संस्वेद m. sweat, perspiration.

संहत् f. layer, stratum.

संहत a. struck together, closely joined, well knit, hard, solid, compact, strong, intense; abstr. **°ता** f., **°त्व** n.

संहति f. striking or clasping together, closing tight (intr.); union or conjunction with (instr.); seam, suture; compactness, firmness, solidity, esp. of the body; bulk, heap, mass, plenty, abundance.

संहनन a. compact, firm, solid; n. striking together, compactness, firmness (lit. & fig.), solidity, a firm or solid stature, body i g.

संहनु a. beating the jaws together.

संहरण n. grasping, seizing, gathering, binding up (the hair), arranging; fetching back (of a shot arrow by magic); destroying.

संहर्तव्य a. to be brought together; to be arranged or repaired; to be removed or destroyed.

संहर्तृ m. destroyer.

संहर्ष m. bristling of the hair of the body, thrill of delight, rapture, joy; also = seq. n.

संहर्षण, f. **ई** causing the erection of the hair of the body, gladdening; n. ardour, emulation, jealousy.

संहर्षिन् a. gladdening (—°).

संहात m. succinctness, conciseness.

संहार m. drawing together, contraction, abridgment, compendium, collection; gathering etc. = **संहरण**; conclusion, end (d.).

संहारिन् a. destroying (—°).

संहार्य a. to be gathered or collected, to be avoided or removed; transportable, corruptible.

संहित a. put together, connected or endowed with, pertaining to (—°); allied with i.e. friendly to (instr. ± **सह**). f. **आ** connection, junction, esp. the euphonic junction of letters and words; any methodical collection of texts or verses.

संहितापाठ m. the continuous text of the Veda (cf. prec.).

संहृति f. destruction of the world; conclusion, end i.g.

संहृष्ट a. stiff, erected, bristling; thrilled, rejoiced, merry, gay.

संहोत्र n. community of sacrifice.

संह्राद m. loud sound, call, or cry; m. crier, N. of an Asura etc.

संह्रादन a. sounding loud.

संह्रादि m. N. of a Rākṣasa.

संह्रादिन् a. sounding loud; m. N. of a Rākṣasa.

संह्लादिन् a. refreshing, comforting.

संह्वयन n. calling or shouting together.

सक demin. to 1**स**.

सकण्टक a. thorny or having bristled hair.

सकम्प a. trembling, tremulous; n. adv.

सकरुण a. querulous, whining, pitiful, compassionate; n. adv.

सकर्ण & **°क** a. having ears, hearing.

सकर्मक a. having results or consequences; having an object, transitive (g.).

सकल a. having parts, divisible, material; all, whole, entire; n. everything.

सकलकलुष m. N. of a region in a wood.*

सकलजन m. every person, everybody.

सकलरूपक n. a complete metaphor (rh.).

सकलुष a. stained, obscured.*

सकललोक m. = **सकलजन**.

सकलविद्यामय a. containing all knowledge.

सकलिक a. furnished with blossoms.

सकलेन्दु m. the full moon.

सकल्प a. along with the Kalpa (part of the Veda).

सकषाय a. passionate.

सकष्टम् adv. unfortunately.
सकाकोल a. along with the hell Kākola.
सकातर a. depressed, sad.
सकाम a. satisfying wishes or having a wish satisfied; content, willing; enamoured.
सकार m. the sound स.
सकाश m. presence; acc. towards, to; loc. before, near, at; abl. & °तस् from; lit. to, in, & from the presence of (gen. or —°).
सकिंकर a. accompanied by servants.
सकुलज a. born of the same family with (gen.).
सकुल्य m. kinsman, relative.
सकूति a. desirous, enamoured.
सकृत् adv. at once, suddenly; once (semel or olim); ever (w. neg. never); once for all, evermore.
सकृत्सू a. bringing forth at once.
सकृत्स्नायिन् a. bathing once.
सकृद्विभात a. appeared at once.
सकृन्मद्वत् adv. once.
सकृपणम् adv. querulously, whiningly.
सकृपम् a. compassionately.
सकेत a. having one intention.
सकेश a. together with the hair or containing hair (food).
सकोप a. wrathful, angry; n. adv.
सकौतुक a. curious of, expectant (—°).
सकौतूहलम् adv. expectantly.
सक्त a. hanging on, sticking in or to, connected with (loc. or —°); committed or entrusted to (—°); intent upon, attached or devoted to, occupied with (loc., acc. w. प्रति, or —°); n., °ता† f., °त्व n. = seq.
सक्ति f. clinging together, attachment to (loc. or —°), esp. to wordly things.
सक्तु m. coarsely ground parched grains, grits, esp. of barley.
सक्तुहोम m. an oblation of grits.
सक्तुश्री a. mixed with grits.
सक्थ (adj. —°, f. ई) = seq.
सक्थन् & सक्थि n., सक्थी f. the thigh.
सक्मन् n. intercourse.
सक्म्य n. peculiarity, nature.
सक्रतु a. unanimous, harmonious with (instr.).
सक्रुध्, सक्रोध (n. adv.), & सक्रोधन a. angry.
†सक्ष & सक्षण a. overwhelming.
1सक्षणि a. the same (acc.).
2सक्षणि a. belonging to (gen.), joined with (instr.); m. companion, owner.
सक्षित् a. dwelling or lying together.
सक्षीर a. milky, lactescent (plant).
सख (a. —°) = सखि; also united with, accompanied by (f. आ).
सखड्ग a. (armed) with a sword.
सखि m. friend, comrade, attendant.
सखिता f., °त्व, & °त्वन n. friendship, fellowship, intimacy.
सखिपूर्व n., °भाव m. = prec.
सखिवन्त् a. having followers.
सखिविद् a. winning friends.
सखी f. female friend or companion.
सखीगण m. (number of female) friends.
सखीजन a. female friend, confidante (also coll.).
सखीस्नेह m. love for a (female) friend.*
सखीय्, only °यन्त् desirous of friendship.
सखेदम् adv. sorrowfully.
सख्य n. friendship, fellowship, relationship.
सगण a. having troops or followers, surrounded by (instr.); m. E. of Çiva.
सगद्गद a. spoken in a faltering voice; n. adv.
सगद्गदगिर् a. stammering words.
सगन्ध a. having a smell, smelling like or of (instr. or —°); related, kindred. m. kinsman, friend.
सगन्धिन् a. smelling like (—°).
सगर m. the atmosphere; N. of a myth. king,
सगर्भ a. with child, pregnant.
सगर्व a. arrogant, proud of (loc. or —°); n. adv.
सगु a. with cows.
सगुडा f. a kind of perfume.*
सगुण a. furnished with a rope or string, having attributes, qualities, or virtues.
सगृह a. with the house i.e. with kith and kin.
सगोत्र a. of the same family with (gen. or —°); related, of kin.
सगौरवम् adv. with dignity.
सग्धि f. a common meal.
सग्रह a. containing crocodiles (river); having

(i.e. seized by) the demon Graha, eclipsed (moon); along with a ladleful or cupful (r.).

सघ्, सघ्नोति be equal to or a match for; undergo, incur.

संघन् m. vulture.

सघन a. thick, dense; cloudy.

सघृण a. pitiful, compassionate.

सघृत a. mixed with ghee.

संघोष a. pl. shouting together.

संकट a. narrow, strait; thick, dense; difficult, hard. n. narrow path, difficult passage, difficulty, danger, distress, pain.

संकथन n., **°कथा** f. talk, discourse, conversation with (instr. ± **सह** or —°).

संकर m. mixture, confusion; esp. mixture of two figures of speech, or m. of caste by intermarriage.

संकरापात्रकृत्या f. pl. deeds which make unworthy or degrade to a mixed caste.

संकरिन् a. having illicit intercourse with (—°).

संकरीकरण n. degradation to a mixed caste.

संकर्तम् ger. by cutting in pieces.

संकर्ष m. drawing together, vicinity.

संकर्षण m. the Plougher (Halāyudha).

संकलन n. putting or keeping together.

संकलुष s. defilement, pollution.

संकल्प m. decision of the mind, persuasion; intention, purpose; wish, desire.

संकल्पक a. deciding (right); wishing.

संकल्पज a. sprung from a certain idea; also = seq. a. & m.

संकल्पजन्मन् a. sprung from desire; m. love or the god of love.

संकल्पन n., **°ना** f. wishing, desiring.

संकल्पनीय a. to be wished for or desired.

संकल्पभव & **°योनि** a. & m. = **संकल्पजन्मन्**.

संकल्पवन्त् a. who has to decide.

1**संकसुक** a. splitting, crumbling (trans.).

2**संकसुक** a. crumbling off, decaying; irresolute.

संङ्का f. combat, fight.

संकार m. sweepings, dust.

संकालन n. the carrying out and burning of a dead body.

संकाश m. appearance; adj. —° appearing like, similar to.

संकीर्ण a. mixed, confounded, covered or filled with (—°); n. & **°ता** f. confusion.

संकीर्णचारिन् a. moving about confusedly.

संकीर्णयोनि a. of mixed origin.

संकीर्तन n. mentioning, praising.

संकुचित a. contracted, wrinkled, shut, bent.

संकुल a. full of, swarming with, accompanied by, rich in (instr. or —°); thick, dense, intensive; confused, distressed. n. throng, pressure, pain, distress.

संकुलित (a. —°) = prec. a.

संकुली w. **कृ** assemble, gather; confound, disarrange.

संकृति a. arranging, restoring. m. a man's name; f. a kind of metre.

संक्लृप्त a. arranged, prepared, ready.

संक्लृप्ति f. will, wish.

संकेत & **°क** m. agreement, consent, appointment, rendezvous, token, signal.

संकेतकेतन n. place appointed for meeting (a lover).

संकेतकगृहक s. the same.*

संकेतस्थ a. coming to a rendezvous.

संकेतस्थान n. = **संकेतकेतन**.

संकेतोद्यान n. a garden for a rendezvous.

संकोच m. shrinking, contraction, decrease.

1**संकोचन** n. the same.

2**संकोचन**, f. **ई** contracting, astringent.

संक्रन्द m. roaring, wailing, lamenting, (shout of) war.

संक्रन्दन a. crying, roaring; n. fight, war.

संक्रम m. going or coming together, meeting; way, course; bridge, path, stairs; (the falling or shooting of stars*).

संक्रमण n. occurrence, taking place; passage or entrance into (loc. or —°), esp. into another world, death.

संक्रान्त a. come together, met; transferred, passed over from (abl.), to (—°).

संक्रान्ति f. passage or entrance into; transfer, transition.

संक्राम m. passing, elapsing.

संक्रामण n. carrying over.

संक्रीड m. play, sport.

संक्रोश m. clamour, shout, esp. of indignation.

संक्लेद m. making or becoming wet; wetness by (—°).
संक्लेश m. pain, woe.
संक्षय m. perishing, disappearance, destruction.
संक्षर & संक्षार m. flowing together.
संक्षालन n. water for washing or rinsing.
संक्षिप्त a. thrown together, compressed, narrow, small, short; abridged, concise.
संक्षेप m. throwing together, either destroying or abridging, compressing, esp. succinct or concise exposition, recapitulation.
संक्षेपक & °प्तृ m. destroyer (cf. prec.).
संक्षेपतस् a. succinctly, briefly.
संक्षोभ m. shock, jerk, wrench; disturbance, agitation.
संख्य n. fight, war.
संख्या f. reckoning up, numbering; number (also g.), numeral; appellation, name.
संख्याता f. a kind of riddle.
संख्यातिग a. innumerable.
संख्यान n. appearing, springing up; reckoning up, numbering, calculation.
संख्यानामन् & °पद n., °शब्द m. numeral.
संख्येय a. to be reckoned up, numerable.
1सङ्ग m. (adj. —° f. आ & ई) sticking to, hanging upon, contact with (loc. or —°); meeting, encounter; near relation to, intercourse (also sexual) with (gen., instr. ± सह, loc., or —°); attachment or devotion to, propensity for, desire of (loc. or —°).
2संग m. hostile encounter.
संगणना f. summing up, enumeration.
संगत a. come together, met, united; fit, proper, suitable to (—°). — n. meeting, union, alliance, intercourse, connection, stipulation.
संगतार्थ a. having a suitable meaning, intelligible.
संगति f. meeting, encountering (gen. or —°), betaking one's self to (loc.); association, alliance, intercourse (also sexual) with (instr. ± सह or समम्, loc., gen., or —°); happening, taking place; chance, accident; fitness, propriety; connection or coherence with, relation to (instr. or —°).
संगथ m. meeting, central point.
संगम m. coming together, meeting (as friends or foes), union (also sexual), association, intercourse with (instr. ± सह, gen., or —°); contact, relation, connection.
संगमन, f. ई assembling, gathering (trans.); n. meeting, contact or union with (instr. or —°).
संगमनीय a. effecting union; w. मणि m. = seq.
संगममणि m. the jewel of union (myth.).
संगमिन् a. having intercourse with (—°).
संगर m. agreement, promise; fight, contest with (instr.), about (gen.).
संगरण n. transacting, agreeing.
संगव m. the time when cows come together to be milked; morning or forenoon.
सङ्गवन्त् a. attached to (loc.).
सङ्गवर्जित a. free from wordly ties, unworldly.
संगविनी f. place for driving together and milking cows.
सङ्गिन् a. sticking to or in, hanging on, coming into contact with (—°); devoted to, intent upon, occupied with (loc., gen., or —°).
संगिर् f. agreement, promise.
संगिर a. devouring.
संगीत & °क n. song of many voices, concert, symphony.
संगीतकगृह n. concert-hall.
संगीतकपद n. place or situation at a theatre or concert.*
संगीतरत्नाकर m. T. of a musical work.
संगीतविद्या f. the art (science) of singing.
संगीतवेश्मन् n., °शाला f. concert-hall.
संगीतसहायिनी f. a female that accompanies another in singing.*
संगीतसारसंग्रह m. T. of a musical work.
संगीति f. N. of a metre.
संगुप्त a. kept, guarded; concealed, hidden.
संगुप्ति f. keeping, concealing.
संगृभीतृ m. restrainer, ruler (acc.).
संगृहीतृ m. tamer of horses, charioteer; ruler i.g.
संगोपन a. & n. concealing.
संग्रथित a. strung or tied together.
संग्रन्थन n. connecting, contriving.
संग्रसन n. devouring.

संग्रह m. seizing, grasping, laying hold on, keeping, winning, acquiring, taking (also to wife), enjoying, fetching back (of a shot arrow by magic), gathering, assembling, collection; enumeration, sum, totality; restraining, directing, government, concr. ruler, governor, arranger; short exposition, compendium of (—°); attracting, winning over, kindness.

संग्रहण a. seizing, grasping. n. seizing, getting, acquiring, collecting, enumerating; checking, restraining; attracting, conciliating, seducing, committing adultery (± स्त्री°).

संग्रहिन् m. collector, procurer.

संग्रहीतृ m. tamer of horses, charioteer; who wins over (acc.).

संग्राम m. popular assembly, host, troop; hostile encounter, fight, war, contest with (instr. ± समम्, सह, or सार्धम्, & —°).

संग्रामजित् a. victorious in battle.

संग्रामतूर्य n. battle-drum.

संग्रामभूमि f. field of battle.

संग्राममूर्धन् m. front of battle.

संग्रामशिरस् & **संग्रामाग्र** n. = संग्राममूर्धन्.

संग्रामिन् a. engaged in battle.

संग्राहक, f. **ई** contracting, comprehending, short.

संग्राहिन् a. collecting, gathering; attracting, winning (—°).

संग्राह्य a. to be embraced, attracted, or won.

संघ m. band, company, crowd.

संघचारिन् a. walking by troops.

संघटन n., **आ** f. combination, union.

संघट्ट m., **°न** n. collision, friction, encounter; union, conjunction.

संघर्ष m. friction (also **°ण** n.); emulation, contest, jealousy at (acc. w. प्रति or —°).

संघर्षिन् a. jealous, envious, emulous of (—°).

संघवृत्ति f. union, alliance.

संघशस् adv. by troops, in numbers.

संघात m. (n.) stroke, blow, hurt; shutting (of a door); collision, contest, fight; close union, aggregate, complex, collection, heap, mass; composition of words or formation of compounds (g.).

सच्, **सचते** (°ति), **सिषक्ति**, **सश्चि** (°ते) be united, have intercourse with, deal with, be possessed of or obnoxious to (instr.); belong, be attached or devoted to, attend on, accompany, follow, pursue, visit (acc.); help to (dat.); stay or be in (loc.). — **अनु** go after, follow, pursue; stick to (acc.). **अप** withdraw, escape. **अभि** seek, turn towards (acc.). **आ** & **उप** seek, look for (acc.). **नि** be closely connected with (instr.) **प्र** pursue. **प्रति** pursue with vengeance. **सम्** be united or connected with (instr.).

सचकितम् adv. tremblingly, timidly.

सचक्र a. furnished with wheels.

सचक्रिन् m. carrier, charioteer.

सचक्षुष & **सचक्षुस्** a. having eyes, seeing.

सचथ m. companionship, attendance.

सचथ्य a. helpful, ready; n. = prec.

सचध्यै dat. inf. to सच्.

सचन a. = सचथ्य adj.

सचनस् a. unanimous, harmonious with (instr.).

सचनस्य्, **°स्यते** show tenderness or care.

सचराचर a. together with movable and immovable things, n. adv.

सचस्य्, **°स्यते** receive care.

सचा adv. near, at hand; along, together; along with, in presence of, near, at, in (loc.).

सचाभू a. accompanied by; m. companion, friend.

सचि adv. together, at once.

सचित् a. thinking or = seq.

सचित्त a. having one (the same) thought.

सचित्र a. having (or together with) pictures.

सचिन्त a. thoughtful, n. adv.

सचिन्ताकुलम् adv. = prec. adv.

सचिव m. attendant, assistant, esp. counsellor or minister of a king; adj. —° supported by, furnished with.

सचिवता f., **°त्व** n. the office of a minister.

सचिविद् a. intimate, familiar.

सचेतन a. conscious, sensible.

सचेतस् a. having the same mind, unanimous; also = prec.

सचेल & **सचैल** a. having clothes, clothed.

सच्चन्द्रिका f. beautiful moon-shine.

1**सच्चरित** n. good or virtuous conduct.

2**सच्चरित** a. well-conducted, virtuous.

सच्चरित्र n., सच्चर्या f. = prec. 1.
सच्चित्तिशंसिन् a. indicating a good heart or suggesting good thoughts.*
1सच्चिदानन्द n. pl. existence, thought, and joy (ph.).
2सच्चिदानन्द a. consisting of existence, thought, and joy (ph.).
सच्चिदानन्दमय a. the same.
सच्चिन्मय a. consisting of existence and thought.
सच्छदिस् a. covered.
संच्छन्द a. consisting of equal metres.
संच्छन्दस् & °न्दस्य† a. the same.
सच्छल a. deceitful.
सच्छाय a. affording shade; coloured, of the same colour with (—°).
सच्छास्त्र n. good doctrine, p. °वन्त्.
सच्छील n. a good character.
सच्छेद a. interrupted.
सज् v. सञ्ज्.
सजन a. visited or inhabited by men; loc. among or with men.
संजन्य a. belonging to a friend or relation.
सजल a. containing water, wet.
सजलपृषत a. sprinkling water (wind).
सजागर a. awake, not sleeping.
सजात a. kindred; m. a kinsman or countryman, p. °वन्त्.
सजाति & °तीय a. belonging to the caste etc., homogeneous, similar.
सजात्य a. kindred; n. common origin, relationship.
सजाय a. having a wife, married.
सजार a. along with the lover.
सजाल a. maned.
सजित्वन्, f. °त्वरी victorious, superior.
सजीव a. animated, alive.
सजुष् (सजुस् & सजूर्) adv. together, moreover; along with (instr.).
सजोष a. unanimous, harmonious, equally disposed, being or acting along with (instr.).
सजोषण n. common amusement.
सजोषस् a. = सजोष; n. adv. together.
सज्ज a. having the string on, i.e. strung or put on the string (bow and arrow); i.g. ready, prepared (pers. & th.); abstr. °ता f., °त्व n.

सज्जकर्मन् n. stringing a bow (cf. prec.).
1सज्जन a. hanging down from (—°).
2सज्जन m. a good man.
सज्जय्, °यति, pp. सज्जित furnish with the string (a bow); prepare, make ready i.g.
सज्जी कृ = prec.; भू get ready for (dat.).
सज्य a. furnished with a string, strung (bow); put on the string (arrow).
सज्यकर्मन् & सज्यी कृ = सज्जकर्मन् & सज्जी कृ.
सज्योतिस् adv. according to the light (as long as the sun or stars give light).
सज्वर a. having fever.
सञ्च s. book for writing.
सञ्चक s. stamp or casting mould.
संचकान a. satisfied with (instr.).
संचय m. heaping up, gathering, heap, store, wealth, collection, multitude.
संचयन n. collecting.
संचयवन्त् a. wealthy, rich.
संचयिन् a. = prec. or abundant, copious.
संचर a. wandering together, happening at the same time, belonging to or partaking of (—°); m. way, road, passage.
संचरण, f. ई trodden, frequented (way). n. passing through, crossing (the sea); moving from (abl.), in (loc. or —°), by (—°).
संचरिष्णु a. moving, wandering.
संचर्वण n. chewing.
संचल a., °न n. trembling, quaking.
संचार m. wandering, roaming, riding, driving moving i.g.; going through, passage (also concr.); way, path.
संचारक m. guide.
संचारण n. leading to or in.
संचारणीय a. to be gone through, to be transferred to (loc.).
संचारपथ m. walk (concr.).
संचारिन् a. wandering, walking about, moving; movable, transmitted, hereditary (disease); being in, occupied with (—°); accessory, incidental. m. fellow (-traveller), companion (f. °णी).
संचित a. heaped up, accumulated, dense (forest), filled or endowed with (—°).
संचिति f. piling, gathering.
संचिन्तन n. pondering, reflecting.

संचिन्त्य a. to be thought of or considered.
संचूर्णन n. grinding down.
संचृत् f. fastening together, joining.
संचेय a. to be piled up or gathered.
संचोदन n. impelling, urging on.
संछन्न a. covered, veiled, hidden, unknown.
संछेत्तव्य a. to be removed (cf. seq.).
संछेत्तृ m. cleaver i.e. remover (of a doubt).
सञ्ज् or **सज्**, **सजति**, **°ते**, pp. **सक्त** (q.v.) A. trans. hang on or together; M. intr. hang on (acc.), cleave or stick to (loc.); P. **सज्यते** hang on (loc.), **सज्जते** (**°ति**) be hung on or attached to (loc.); cleave, stick; lag, tarry; be intent upon or devoted to (loc.). C. **सञ्जयति** attach, connect with (loc.); **सज्जयति** fix on, attach to (loc.); copulate i.e. prostitute. — **व्यति** mix or join mutually. **अनु** hang or stick with (instr.), add; P. **अनुषज्जते** hang on, adhere or cling to (acc. or loc.), devote one's self to or occupy one's self with (loc.). **अभि** utter a curse; lay a claim upon (loc.). **अव** A. hang or fasten upon, commit or transfer to (loc.). P. **अवसज्यते** be hung or fastened; **अवसज्जते** cling or attach one's self to. **आ** hang or suspend on (loc.); impose upon, transfer to (loc.); lean on, cling to (acc.), follow close to a person's (acc.) heels (also **आसज्जते**). C. suspend, cause a pers. (intr.) to hang or put on (loc.); appoint to (loc.). **व्या** get engaged in a quarrel or fight. **समा** hang on or round; lay (a change) on, commit or transfer to (loc.). **नि** M. hang round (one's self) or down. **प्र** A. attach (one's self) to (loc.); hang, stick, or furnish with (instr.); approach as an enemy, engage in a quarrel with (loc.); (cause to) happen, occur, or result. P. (in both forms) cling or stick to, be occupied with (loc.). **संप्र** (**सज्यते**, **°ति**), be attached to (loc.). **वि** A. hang on, suspend; P. (**षज्जते**) be devoted or attached to (loc.), esp. to the world or to a beloved person; be followed close by (instr.). **सम्** (**सज्जते**, **°ति**) stick, adhere, cling to (loc.); get into a quarrel or fight with (instr.), attack, assail (acc.); stop, falter (voice); flow together, join; be engaged, commence (fight). — Cf. **अतिषक्त**, **अनुषक्त**, **आषक्त**, **निषक्त**, **प्रसक्त**, **विषक्त**, **व्यतिषक्त**, **व्यासक्त** (add.), **संसक्त**.
सञ्जन n. attaching, fastening, putting together.
संजनन a. (f. **ई**) & n. producing, causing, effecting; n. also springing forth, growth.
संजय a. victorious; m. victory, a kind of military array, a man's name.
संजल्प m., **°ल्पित** n. talking together, conversation.
संजात a. born, produced, arisen, **°लज्ज** a. ashamed, embarrassed.
संजित् m. winner, conqueror.
संजिति f. gain, complete victory.
संजिजीवयिषु a. wishing to animate.
संजिजीविषु a. wishing to live
संजिहीर्षु a. wishing to destroy.
संजीव a. & m. reviving (tr. & intr.).
संजीवक, f. **°विका** animating; m. N. of a bull.
संजीवन, f. **ई** animating; m. a cert. hell; n. living or coming to life again.
संजीविन् a. animating, rendering alive.
संजुष्ट a. visited or inhabited by, filled with (instr. or —°).
संज्ञ & **संज्ञक**, f. **°ज्ञिका** (adj. —°) named, termed.
संज्ञता f. abstr. to **संज्ञा** consciousness.
संज्ञपन n. making unanimous or = seq.
संज्ञप्ति f. suffocation of the sacrif. animal.
संज्ञा f. mutual understanding, agreement, harmony; signal, gesticulation with the hand etc. (—°); consciousness, perception, idea; designation, name, technic term (cf. **संज्ञ** etc.); N. of Tvaṣṭṛ's daughter.
संज्ञातरूप a. of known appearance.
संज्ञाति f. unanimity, agreement.
संज्ञान a. causing unanimity or concord, f. such a ceremony. n. unanimity, harmony, agreement with (loc. or instr.), mutual or right understanding.
संज्ञार्थम् adv. to give an idea.
संज्ञित a. made known, produced, called, termed (—°).

संज्ञिन् a. conscious; having the name (—°).
संज्वर m. heat, fever, agitation.
संज्वलन n. fire-wood, fuel.
सटा f. braid of hair, mane, the bristles of a boar; multitude, abundance; light, splendour.
सटाल a. maned.
सटालु s. = **शलाटु** q.v.
सडिण्डिमम् adv. by the sound of a drum.
संत् v. **संन्त्**.
संत m. n. a cert. vessel or dish.
सतत (adj. °—) continual; n. & °— adv. continually, incessantly, always, ever; w. **न** never.
सततग & °**गति** m. the wind (lit. = °**यायिन्**).
सततधृति a. showing a constant will.
सततयायिन् a. ever-moving.
सततयुक्त a. constantly devoted.
सतति a. coherent, uninterrupted.
सतत्त्व n. the real or true nature; °**तस्** adv. in truth, really.
संतनु a. embodied, along with the body.
सतस् adv. equally.
1**सतीन** (—°) truly, really.
2**सतीन** m. a kind of pease.
(***सतीर्थ** &) **सतीर्थ्य** m. fellow-student (lit. having the same teacher).
सतूर्य a. accompanied by music; n. adv.
सतृण a. grassy; °— & n. adv. along with grass.
सतृणाभ्यवहारिन् a. eating all, even grass, i.e. making no difference, uncritical, insipid (poet).
सतृष्णम् adv. with desire, impatiently.
संतेजस् a. along with fire, splendour, or power.
संतोक a. along with the offspring.
सतोबृहन्त् a. equally high or great; f. °**हती** N. of a metre.
सतोमघवन् a. equally liberal.
सतोमहन्त् a. equally great.
सतोवीर a. equally heroic or valiant.
सत्कथा f. a fine story.
सत्करण n. the cremation of a dead body (lit. good action).
सत्कर्तव्य a. to be treated well.
सत्कर्तृ m. benefactor.
1**सत्कर्मन्** n. a good action.
2**सत्कर्मन्** a. doing good actions.
सत्कवि m. a good or true poet; abstr. °**त्व** n.
सत्कार m. good treatment or service, esp. good reception of a guest, hospitality; burning of a dead body.
सत्कार्य a. to be honoured (by a kind reception or funeral obsequies).
1**सत्कीर्ति** f. a good renown.
2**सत्कीर्ति** a. having a good renown.
1**सत्कुल** n. a good or noble race.
2**सत्कुल** a. sprung from a noble race.
सत्कुलीन a. = prec. 2.
सत्कृ make good, put in order, arrange, prepare, adorn, receive kindly (esp. a guest), treat well, honour (esp. the dead by burning). — **अभि** = S. **प्रति** honour in return.
सत्कृति f. = **सत्कार**.
सत्क्रिया f. putting in order, preparing; also = **सत्कार**, i.g. ceremony, festival of (—°).
सत्क्षेत्र n. a good field.
सत्त a. sitting, seated.
संत्तम (superl.) the best, first among or chief (gen. or —°).
संत्तृ m. sitter, esp. at a sacrifice.
सत्ता f. existence, being.
सत्ति f. setting in, beginning.
सत्त्र n. sacrificial session or any meritorious action of equal worth; alms-house, hospital.
सत्त्रराज् m. king of the Sattra (cf. prec.).
सत्त्रसद् m. Sattra-fellow.
सत्त्रसद्य n. Sattra-fellowship.
सत्त्रायण n. a sacrificial session lasting several years.
सत्त्रिन् m. the performer or partaker of a sacrificial session or of an action of equal merit.
सत्त्रिय or **सत्त्रीय** a. belonging to a Sattra.
सत्त्व n. being, existence, reality, nature, character; firmness, resolution, energy, courage; goodness (ph.); spiritual or intellectual being, spirit or vital breath; real being, thing, object; (also m.) living or sentient being, esp. animal, beast; phantom, spectre, imp, goblin.

सत्त्वकर्तृ m. creator of beings.
सत्त्वधामन् n. the splendour of goodness (ph.); °धर m. the bearer of it, i.e. Viṣṇu.
सत्त्वमय a. consisting of goodness (ph.).
सत्त्वराशि m. a paragon (lit. heap) of firmness or courage.
सत्त्वलक्षणा f. pregnant, with child, lit. marked by a (new) being.
सत्त्ववन्त् & सत्त्वशालिन् a. having a (strong) character; energetic, resolute, courageous.
सत्त्वशब्द m. a concrete, lit. word for a being (g.).
सत्त्वस्थ a. having character or courage; adhering to goodness (ph.).
सत्त्वोत्कर्ष m. extraordinary generosity.
सत्पति m. strong chief or hero; good lord or husband.
1सत्पुत्र m. a good son.
2सत्पुत्र a. having a good son.
सत्पुरुष m. a good or excellent man.
सत्प्रतिग्रह m. acceptance of a gift from good men.
सत्य a. real, true, genuine; serious, valid, effective, sincere, faithful, honest, good. m. E. of Kṛṣṇa, N. of a genius etc. f. आ E. of Durgā, N. of a daughter of Dharma etc. n. the real or true, reality, truth; true character, sincerity, faithfulness; vow, promise, oath; also adv. really, truly, indeed, yes, very well; of course, it is true (also यत्सत्यम्)—yet (तु, किं तु or तथापि). Instr. सत्येन according to truth; तेन सत्येन (± यथा) as truly as this, by this truth, on this account or for this reason.
1सत्यकर्मन् n. truthfulness.
2†सत्यकर्मन् a. practising truth.
सत्यकाम a. loving truth; m. a man's name.
सत्यगिर् a. whose word is true.
सत्यंकार m. promise, contract; earnest-money.
सत्यजित् a. truly conquering.
सत्यजिति f. a true victory.
सत्यज्ञ a. knowing truth.
सत्यतस् adv. in truth.
सत्यता f. reality, truth.
सत्यतात् & °ताति f., सत्यत्व n. = prec.
सत्यदर्शिन् & °दृश् a. seeing right.
1सत्यधर्म m. the law of truth.
2सत्यधर्म a. following the law of truth.
सत्यधर्मन् a. = prec. 2.
सत्यधृति a. adhering to truth.
सत्यनामन्, f. °म्नी having the true or right name; abstr. °मता f.
सत्यपराक्रम a. of true valour or power.
सत्यपुष्टि f. real prosperity.
सत्यप्रतिज्ञ a. faithful to a promise, keeping one's word.
सत्यप्रसव & °वस् a. whose impulse is true or right.
सत्यभामा f. N. of a wife of Kṛṣṇa.
सत्यभाषण n. truth-speaking.
सत्यभूय n. the being true, truth.
सत्यमन्त्र a. whose word is true.
सत्यमन्मन् a. whose thoughts are true or right.
सत्यमय, f. ई a. consisting in truth.
सत्यमुग्र a. truly powerful.
सत्यमूल a. based upon truth.
सत्ययज् a. worshipping truly or successfully.
सत्ययज्ञ m. N. of a man.
सत्ययोनि a. having a firm abode.
†सत्यराजन् m. true or eternal king.
सत्यराधस् a. having or bestowing real blessings.
सत्यलोक m. the world of truth.
सत्यवचन n. & a. truth-speaking.
सत्यवतीपुत्र m. Satyavatī's son, i.e. Vyāsa.
सत्यवदन n., °शील a. = सत्यवचन n. & a.
सत्यवन्त् a. true, veracious; m. & f. °वती a man's & woman's name.
सत्यवाक m. = सत्यवदन.
सत्यवाक्य n. & adj. = सत्यवचन.
सत्यवाच् f. & adj. the same.
सत्यवाचक a. = prec. adj.
सत्यवाद m. truth-speaking, promise, vow.
सत्यवादिन् a. truth-speaking, truthful; abstr. °वादिता f. & °त्व n.
सत्यविक्रम a. of real valour or strength.
1सत्यव्रत n. a vow of truthfulness.
2सत्यव्रत a. having i.e. keeping a vow of truthfulness.
सत्यशवस् a. really strong or fierce.
सत्यशील & °शीलिन् a. practising truth or veracity.

सत्यंशुष्म a. truly courageous or fierce.
सत्यंश्रवस् n. true glory; m. a man's name.
†सत्यश्रुत् a. hearing truth.
सत्यसंकल्प a. of firm resolution.
सत्यसंगर a. true to a promise or agreement.
†सत्यसत्वन् m. a true champion; adj. having good champions.
सत्यसंध a. = सत्यसंगर.
सत्यसव & °सवस् a. = सत्यप्रसव.
सत्यात्मक & °त्मन् a. whose nature is truth.
सत्यानृते n. du. truth and falsehood (fig. = commerce).
सत्यालापिन् a. truth-speaking, veracious.*
सत्योक्ति f. true speech.
सत्यौजस् a. truly powerful.
सत्रा adv. at once, together; along with (instr.); at all, by all means; thoroughly, much too.
सत्राजित् a. thoroughly victorious.
सत्राच् (f. सत्राची) a. united, common.
सत्रासह (°साह) a. all-conquering, irresistible.
सत्राहन् & °हन् a. all-destroying.
सत्वक् a. having skin or bark.
सत्वच् & सत्वचस् a. the same.
सत्वन् & सत्वन m. hero, warrior.
सत्वर a. hastening, quick; n. adv.
सत्संग m. intercourse with good people.
सत्संगति f., °संविधान n. the same.
1सद्, सीदति (°ते), pp. सत्त & सन्न (q.v.) sit, seat one's self (esp. for a sacrifice) on, at, or in (acc. or loc.); lie down, around or in wait for (acc.); sink beneath a burden, feel ill, become feeble, tired or languid, be overcome, fall into trouble, distress, or despair; decay, vanish. C. सादयति cause to sit down; set or place in, at, or on (loc.); afflict, distress, bring down, ruin, destroy. — अति die. अनु sit down after another. अव stand opposite, threaten, menace (acc.). अव descend upon (acc.); sink down, fall away, grow lean or feeble, get into trouble or distress, despair, perish. C. sink (trans.), depress, bring down, afflict, pain, overcome, destroy. आ sit upon or near (acc. or loc.), preside over (acc.); waylay, watch; get to, arrive at, approach (as friend or foe), meet with, find, hit, gain, obtain. C. cause to sit down upon, set or place in (loc. or acc.), appoint to (infin.); cause, produce; approach, come near (acc.), encounter, meet with; overtake, attack, assail; get or fall into (acc.); gain, obtain; visit, befall; use, apply. अध्या sit down upon (acc.). अभ्या the same; reach, attain. उपा sit down upon (acc.). C. approach, obtain, receive. न्या sit down near, in, or upon (loc. or acc.). प्रत्या be near or imminent. समा get to, reach, attain; come near, approach (loc. or acc.); meet, encounter; attack, assail. C. = S. उद् withdraw from (acc.), escape (gen.); disappear, perish. C. put aside, remove, extinguish, destroy; smear, anoint. उपोद् & प्रत्युद् betake one's self to (acc.). समुद् C. destroy, ruin. उप sit upon (acc.) or near; approach (as foe, pupil, or supplicant). C. put down or beside; get, obtain. अभ्युप C. get to, attain. प्रत्युप sit down near (acc.). समुप betake one's self to, reach, attain (acc.). नि (षीदति) sit or lie down, take one's seat (r.), be seated upon (loc.), perform by sitting i.e. celebrate (a Sattra); sink, perish. C. cause to sit or kneel down; constitute, appoint (2 acc.). अधिनि settle down in (loc.). अभिनि settle down about or near (acc.). उपनि approach, set about (acc.). परिनि sit or stay around. विनि sit down separately. संनि sit down (together). परि (षीदति) sit down about, surround, invest, besiege. प्र decay, decline, fall into the power of (acc.); become clear (lit. & fig.), cheer up; be soothed or appeased; pardon, forgive, be gracious or favourable, deign to (infin.), succeed or speed well. C. clear, brighten up, gladden, soothe, appease, make favourable, beg pardon, ask for or to (infin., dat., or loc., अर्थे or अर्थम्). अभिप्र settle down. C. propitiate, gladden, ask. संप्र cheer up, be gracious or favourable. C. propitiate, make favourable. वि (षीदति

be perplexed or dejected, despair, despond. C. vex, grieve, bring into despair. सम् sit together with (instr.) upon (acc.); M. settle down, shrink, perish, be dejected or distressed. C. set down (together); meet, join (acc.); depress, make sad. — Cf. अवसन्न, आसन्न, आसाद्य, उत्सन्न, उपसन्न, निषण्ण, निषत्त, प्रत्यासन्न (add.), प्रसत्त, प्रसन्न, विषण्ण, संसन्न, समासन्न, समासाद्य.

2सद् a. sitting or dwelling in (—°); m. leaping upon, covering (a female).

सद a. = prec. adj.; m. fruit; n. a cert. part of the sacrif. animal.

सदक्ष a. endowed with reason.

सदक्षिण a. along with presents.

सदंदि adv. commonly, usually.

सदधन् a. (mixed) with sour milk.*

सदन, f. ई causing settlement or stay. n. seat, place, abode, home, house (adj. —° living in); settling down, coming to rest.

सदनासद् a. sitting down on the seat.

सदंदि a. lasting, continual; lit. binding for ever (illness).

सदम् adv. always, ever.

सदय a. merciful, soft, tender, gentle; °— & n. adv.

सदर्प a. haughty, defying; n. adv.

1सदश्व m. a good horse.

2सदश्व a. having or drawn by good horses; m. a man's name.

सदस् n. seat, place, dwelling, abode; meeting, assembly.

सदसत्फल (°—) good and evil results.

सदसदात्मक, f. °त्मिका whose nature is at once to be and not to be.

सदसद्भाव m. reality and unreality, truth and falsehood.

सदसन्त् a. being and not being, true and false, good and bad; n. subst. what is being and not being etc.

सदसस्पति & सदस्पति m. lord of the seat i.e. of the assembly (met for a sacred purpose).

सदस्य m. partaker of an assembly, esp. of a Sattra-sacrifice.

सदा adv. always, ever, w. neg. never.

1सदागति f. constancy.

2सदागति a. being in constant motion; m. wind or the god of wind.

1सदाचार m. good conduct or observance.

2सदाचार a. well-conducted, virtuous.

सदाचारवन्त् & °रिन् a. = prec. 2.

1सदान a. having gifts.

2सदान a. ruttish (elephant).

सदानन a. fair-faced.

1सदानन्द m. eternal joy.

2सदानन्द a. feeling or granting eternal joy.

सदानीरा f. N. of a river.

सदान्वा f. N. of cert. female demons.

सदापृण a. always munificent.

सदाफल a. always bearing fruit.

सदाम a. along with the band or string.

सदामत्त & सदामद a. always wanton or ruttish.

सदार a. having a wife, married; together with a wife.

सदावृध a. always delighting.

सदाशिव a. always kind or friendly.

सदासह a. everlasting.

सदासा a. always winning or alwas abounding.

सदासुख n. eternal bliss.

सदिवस् adv. instantly, at once.

सदीनम् adv. miserably, lamentably.

सदुःख a. sad, unhappy.

सदूर्व a. covered with Dūrvā-grass.

सदृश, सदृश् (nom. सदृङ् & सदृक्), & सदृश a. similar, like, same; abstr. सदृशत्व n.

सदृशक्षम a. of equal patience.

सदृशविनिमय m. confounding or exchanging equal things.

सदृष्टिक्षेपम् or °विक्षेपम् adv. with an ogling (lit. eye-throw).

सदेव a. accompanied or protected by the gods.

सदेवमनुष्य a. along with gods and men.

सदोगत a. gone to or being in an assembly; pl. assembled, met.

सदोगृह n. assembly-room; नृपस्य court of a prince.

सदोद्यम a. ever-zealous.

1सदोष a. along with the night.

2सदोष a. faulty, vicious, wrong.

सद्गति f. good condition or the path of the good.

1सद्गुण m. good quality, virtue.

2सद्गुण a. having good qualities, virtuous.

सद्गुरु m. a good teacher.

सद्धर्म m. the good law.

सद्धर्मपुण्डरीक n. the lotus of the good law, T. of a work.

सद्भाव m. actual existence, reality; truth, honesty; kindness, affection.

सद्भूत a. (being) true.

सद्भृत्य m. a good servant.

1सद्मन् m. sitter, dweller.

2सद्मन् n. seat, place (esp. for a sacrifice); dwelling-place, building, house, temple; du. heaven and earth.

सद्यऊति a. helping quickly or daily.

सद्यःकृत्त a. just cut.

सद्यःक्री a. bought on the same day (Soma).

सद्यःपातिन् a. quickly dropping, frail.

सद्यःप्रसूता f. having just brought forth (a child etc.).

सद्यःफल a. quickly bearing fruits or consequences.

सद्यःशौच n. present or immediate purification (r.).

सद्यस् adv. on the same day, in one day, daily; immediately, recently, directly, at once, suddenly, quickly.

सद्यःसुत्या f. Soma-pressing on the same day.

सद्योअर्थ a. quickling reaching the goal.

सद्योजात a. newly born; f. आ having just brought forth.

सद्योजू a. quickly impelled.

सद्योभव a. having just begun, quite fresh.

सद्योमांस n. fresh meat.

सद्योमृत a. just died.

सद्रत्न n. a true jewel or pearl.

सद्रव्य a. along with the money.

1सद्वंश m. a god stem or (and) family.

2सद्वंश a. sprung from a good family.

सद्वचस् n. a fine speech.

सद्वत्सल a. kind to the good.

†सद्वन् a. sitting.

सद्वार्त्ता f. good news.

सद्विगर्हित a. blamed by the good or wise.

सद्विद्य a. having true knowledge.

सद्विद्या f. true knowledge or learning.

सद्वृक्ष m. a good tree.

1सद्वृत्त n. a fine roundness or good conduct.

2सद्वृत्त a. well-conducted.

सद्वृत्ति f. & n. good conduct, virtue.

सद्वैद्य m. a good physician.

†सध (°—) = सह.

1सधन n. common wealth.

2सधन a. wealthy (abstr. °ता f.) or along with the wealth.

सधमद् (°माद्) m. boon-companion, fellow, friend.

सधमाद m. compotation, banquet, feast; fellowship.

सधमादिन् m. = सधमद्.

सधमाद्य a. festive, convivial; m. boon-companion, comrade; n. banquet, feast.

1सधर्म m. equal nature, similarity.

2सधर्म a. equal, similar; honest, virtuous.

सधर्मचारिणी f. wife, lit. performing the same duties (scil. as the husband).

सधर्मत्व n. similarity, likeness.

सधर्मन् & °र्मिन् a. equal, similar, resembling (gen., instr., or —°).

†सधवीर a. united with men or heroes.

1सधस्तुति f. united praise, as instr. adv. along with united praise.

2†सधस्तुति a. receiving united praise.

सधस्तुत्य n. = prec. 1.

सधस्थ a. being here, present; n. place (of union); seat, abode, home; space i.g.

संधिस् n. aim or goal (of a motion), point or place (of rest).

संधी a. furnished with intelligence.

संधूम a. veiled in smoke.

सध्री adv. towards one goal (central point).

सध्रीचीन a. directed towards one goal, joined, united; right, just (instr. adv.).

सध्र्यञ्च्, f. सध्रीची a. having the same direction, converging; right, just; n. सध्र्यक् jointly, together; in the right way or manner.

सन्, सनोति (संनति), pp. सात win, conquer, acquire; receive as a present, possess, enjoy; win for another, procure, grant, bestow. D. सिषासति wish to acquire, strive after; wish to present or bestow. — आ win. प्र M. win = be successful. सम् gain, acquire. — Cf. अभिषात.

1सन a. old, ancient; N. of a Rishi etc.

2†सन m. gain, acquisition; offering, handing over.

सनक a. ancient, old; abl. from of old.

सनग m. N. of a teacher.

सनज a. old, ancient.

सनजा & °जा a. the same.

सनता adv. from of old, ever; w. neg. never.

सनत्कुमार m. the eternal youth, N. of a Rishi.

सनत्न, f. ई = सनातन.

सनद्रयि a. bestowing wealth.

सनद्वाज a. winning or granting wealth.

†सनन n. winning, acquiring.

सनय a. old, ancient.

†सनस् & सना adv. of old, always.

सनाजुर a. weak from age.

सनात् adv. from of old, always, for ever.

सनातन, f. ई eternal, everlasting; m. N. of a Rishi etc.

सनाथ a. having a master or protector; well protected by (instr. or —°); occupied by, connected or endowed with (instr. or —°).

सनाथता f. protectorship.

सनाथी कृ take into protection.

सनाभि a. connected by the same nave (spokes) or navel, nearly related, kindred; like, resembling.

सनाभ्य m. a near relative.

सनाम a. having one name with (gen.).

सनामन्, f. °म्नी = prec. or similar, like.

सनायु a. wishing for gain or reward.

सनारु m. N. of a teacher.

सनाल a. furnished with a stalk.

सनि m. f. gain, reward, gift, alms; acc. w. इ go begging.

सनिकार a. degrading (punishment).

सनिगडचरण a. having a chain on the foot, abstr. °त्व n.*

सनिति f. acquisition.

सनितुर adv. beside, except, without (w. preceding acc.).

सनितृ or सनितृ a. winning or granting.

सनित्र n. gift, donation.

सनित्व a. to be gained.

सनित्वन् m. gain or gift.

सनिद्र a. asleep.

सनिन्द a. reproachful; n. adv.

सनिमन्त a. rich in gifts.

सनिमेष a. winking, closing (eye).

सनियम a. performing a cert. observance or duty.

सनिर्वेद a. indifferent, indolent, despondent; n. adv.

सनिश्वासम् & सनिःश्वासम् adv. with a sigh.

सनिष्ठ (superl.) winning most.

सनिष्णु a. desirous to gain or make booty.

सनीड (सनीळ) a. having a common nest or origin; intimately united.

सनीयंस् (compar.) existing from of old; lasting many years.

सनुतर adv. aside, far off, away from (abl.). With यु & धा keep off, remove.

सनुतर & सनुत्य a. clandestine, unperceived.

सनुची f. gaining, procuring.

सनूपुर a having anklets on the feet.*

1सनेमि a. having fellies (wheel).

2सनेमि adv. from of old, for ever.

सनोजा a. existing from of old, eternal.

सन्त्, f. सती existing, being (often otiose), present, happening; belonging to (gen.); living, lasting; real, genuine, true, honest, good. m. pl. the living or the good, wise, noble etc. f. सती a virtuous wife, female i.g., also = भवती your honour, you; N. of Viçvāmitra's wife etc. — n. सत् the being or existent, existence, the real world, anything good or useful. As adv. well, fitly; सत्कृ v. s. v.

संतत a. overspread, covered with (instr. or —°); held together, uninterrupted, continuous; °— & n. adv.

संतति f. continuation, propagation; offspring, posterity; causal connection, uninterrupted line or mass of (—°).

संतनि a. propagating, continuing, forming an uninterrupted line; s. संतनि sound, music, संतनि a cert. oblation.

संतपन a. warming; n. becoming warm.

संतप्त a. hot, melted, vexed, distressed; n. pain, grief.*
संतमस n. (general) darkness.
संतरण a. leading over or through; n. crossing, passing over (lit. & fig.).
संतरम् or **संतराम्** adv. closer together.
संतरुत्र a. carrying across, sufficient.
संतर्जन a. & n. threatening, scolding.
संतर्पक a., °**ण** a. & n. refreshing, strengthening.
संतर्प्य a. to be refreshed or strengthened.
संताडन n. beating, crushing.
संतान m. continuity, uninterrupted series; sinew or nerve (of an animal); ramification, connection; transition (in reciting etc.); propagation of one's race or family, offspring, p. **वन्त्**†.
संताप m. heat, pain, sorrow, distress, repentance, penance.
संतापकारिन् a. causing sorrow.
संतापन a. tormenting, afflicting.
संतापहर (& °**हारक***) destroying heat or pain.
संताप्य a. to be kindled.
संतार m. crossing, passing (gen. or —°).
संतुष्ट a. well pleased, delighted with (instr. or —°).
संतुष्टि f. contentment, satisfaction.
संतृप्ति f. satiating, satisfying.
संतेजन a. sharpening (fig.).
संतोर्दिन् a. stinging, thrusting.
संतोष m. = **संतुष्टि** (p. °**षवन्त्** & °**षिन्**); acc. w. **कृ** be satisfied.
संतोषण n. satisfying, gladdening.
संतोषणीय a. to be satisfied.
†**सन्त्य** a. granting gifts.
संत्यक्त a. destitute of, wanting (instr. or —°).
संत्यज्य (ger.) letting aside, with exception of (acc.).
संत्याग m. quitting, abandoning, a. °**गिन्**.
संत्राण n. protection, rescue.
संत्रास m. terror, fear of (abl. or **तस्**).
संत्रासन n. frightening.
संत्वरा f. haste, speed.
संदंश m. biting or pinching together (the (lips); junction, union i.g.; crotchet, tongs, or any instrument of that kind.
संदर्दि a. seizing.
संदर्प m. arrogance, boasting of (—°).
संदर्भ m. stringing together, interweaving, wreathing (a garland); artificial arrangement or mixture; musical or literary composition.
संदर्श m. sight, appearance.
संदर्शन n. seeing, perceiving, sight, view, appearance; coming together with, meeting (instr. ± **सह**); showing, exhibition.
संदष्ट a. bitten, pressed (together).
संदातृ m. binder, fetterer.
संदान n. band, fetter; the region beneath the knee (of an elephant).
संदानित a. bound, fettered, surrounded.
1**संदाय** m. bridle, leash.
2**संदाय** a. (only —°) = seq.
संदायिन् a. granting.
संदिग्ध a. smeared or covered with (instr. or —°), confounded with (instr. or —°); indistinct, dubious, precarious; doubtful, uncertain. Abstr. **त्व** n.
संदिग्धबुद्धि a. of uncertain mind, doubtful.
संदित a. bound (together), detained, immovable.
संदिह् f. heap, mound, wall.
संदीपक a. inflaming.
संदीपन a. & n. kindling, inflaming (l. & f.).
संदीप्त a. flaming, glowing, burning (l. & f.).
संदुष्ट a. wicked, bad, hostile to (gen.).
संदूषण a. (f. **ई**) & n. marring, defiling.
संदृब्ध a. strung together; arranged, composed.
संदृश् f. sight, view, appearance; dat. infin. to behold.
संदृष्ट a. seen, foreseen, anticipated; permitted, allowed.
संदृष्टि f. sight, appearance.
संदेघ m. conglutination, mass, clod (fig. = the human body).
संदेश m. direction, commission, message.
संदेशहर & °**हारिन्** m. the bringer of a commission; messenger, envoy.
संदेशार्थ m. the contents of a message.
संदेश्य or °**देष्टव्य** a. to be directed or instructed.
संदेह m. = **सदेघ**; doubt, uncertainty about (gen., loc., or —°), danger.
संदेहपद a. subject to doubt, uncertain.

संदोह m. milking; abundance, plenty.
संदोहन a. milking, yielding.
संद्रष्टव्य a. to be seen.
संद्रष्टृ a. who sees or beholds.
संध n. junction, union.
संधय्, °यति, pp. **संधित** (q.v.) put together, join with (instr.); be reconciled, make peace. — Cf. **अतिसंधित**, **अनुसंधित**, & **अभिसंधित** (add.).
संधर्तृ m. who holds together.
संधा f. agreement, covenant, promise; limit, boundary, term.
संधातव्य a. to be joined or allied with.
संधातृ a. who puts together.
संधान a. & n. putting together; n. also joining, fixing (an arrow on the bow-string); mixing, compounding; joint, commissure, point of contact, meeting, assembling; propitiation, reconciliation, league, alliance, treaty, peace with (instr. ± **सह**); also = **संधि** (g.).
संधानीय a. = **संधातव्य**.
सधायिन् a. fixing an arrow, taking aim.
संधारण a. & n. holding together, supporting; n. also bearing (in the womb), restraining, keeping back; f. **आ** posture, attitude; thought, reflection.
संधार्य a. to be borne, kept, observed, restrained.
संधि m. putting together, junction, connection; union or intercourse with (instr.); compact, agreement, alliance, peace between (gen.), with (instr. ± **सह**); joint, commissure, suture, fold; anything that joins or lies between, as dawn, dusk, twilight (between day and night), wall (between two rooms), also interval, pause, opening, hole, breach, gap; euphonic combination of words and sentences (g.).
संधिच्छेदन n. house-breaking.
संधित a. put together, joined, fixed on the bow-string (arrow); allied.
संधित्सु a. wishing to make peace.
संधिदूषण n. breach of peace.
संधिन् m. a minister for alliances; f. °**नी** a cow in heat.
संधिनीक्षीर n. the milk of a cow in heat.
संधिबन्ध m. cement, plaster (also = seq.*).
***संधिबन्धन** n. join-band, i.e. tendon, nerve.*
संधिविग्रह s. peace and war; °**क** m. minister for p. & w.
संधिविपर्यय m. du. peace and its opposite (war).
संधिवेला f. time of twilight.
संधुक्षण a. & n. kindling, inflaming (l. & f.).
संधृति f. holding together.
संधेय a. to be put together; to be propitiated or won over.
संध्य a. lying on the point of contact or transition, relating to the euphonic combination. — f. **संध्या** time of junction or transition, morning or evening twilight (also = **संध्याकार्य**); the twilight at the beginning or end of a Yuga; N. of a river.
संध्यक्षर n. compound vowel, diphthong.
संध्यांश & °**क** m. the twilight of a Yuga.
संध्याकार्य n. morning or evening devotion.
संध्याकाल m. twilight-time.
संध्यापयोद m. rain-cloud in the evening.
संध्याबलि m. a twilight-oblation.
संध्यासमय m. = **संध्याकाल**.
संध्यभ्र n. = **संध्यापयोद**.
संध्याय्, °यते be like the twilight.
संध्यावन्दन n. morning or evening prayer.
संध्याविधि m. = **संध्याकार्य**.
संध्याशङ्ख m. a conch (or horn) blown in the hour of twilight.
संध्यासमय m. = **संध्याकाल**.
सन्न a. set down; sitting, resting; sunk, low (sound), languished, exhausted, extinguished, perished, dead.
संनख a. with joined or closed nails; w. **मुष्टि** m. a closed fistful.
संनत a. bent, curved; stooping, bowing to (gen.); depressed, deepened, straightened; du. yielding to or harmonizing with each other.
संनति f. depression (lit. & fig.), humility, modesty, kindness, favour, complaisance.
संनतिमन्त् a. humble, modest.
संनद्ध a. bound together or round, fastened,

put on; girt, armed, prepared, ready; swollen, exuberant.

सन्नमुसले (loc.) when the pestle is at rest.

संनय a. bringing together; m. assembly.

संनहन n. binding together, girding; arming, preparing; band, string, armour, mail.

संनाद m. sound, din, cry.

संनादन a. making resound, filling with noise.

संनाह m. = **संनहन**.

सन्नि f. despair, despondency; p. **॰मन्त्**.

संनिकर्ष m. drawing together or near, approach; contact with, relation to (—°); nearness, proximity.

संनिकाश m. appearance, likeness (only adj. —°).

संनिकृष्ट a. brought together, near; n. proximity.

संनिग्रह m. punishment, chastisement.

संनिचय m. piling up, collecting; heap, mass, plenty, provision.

संनिधातृ m. concealer or receiver of stolen goods; an officer who introduces people at court.

संनिधान n. nearness, neighbourhood, presence, existence.

संनिधायिन् a. approached, near, present.*

संनिधि m. juxtaposition, approximation, nearness etc. = prec. Loc. in presence of, coram; acc. towards, near (gen. or —°).

संनिपात m. encounter, meeting (of friends or foes); contact, union; heap, mass, aggregate; sexual intercourse.

संनिपातन n. causing to fall together.

संनिपात्य a. to be hurled upon (loc.).

संनिभ (—°) resembling, like.

संन्निमित्त n. a good omen; adv. for a good sake.

संनियच्छन n. taming, guiding (of horses).

संनियन्तृ m. restrainer, chastiser.

संनियोग m. direction, commission, precept.

संनिरोद्धव्य a. to be confined.

संनिवर्तन n. turning back.

संनिवाप m. collecting, piling up (fire).

संनिवारण n. keeping back.

संनिवार्य a. to be kept back.

संनिवास m. dwelling together or common dwelling.

संनिविष्ट a. seated, encamped; stopping, resting; contained in, dependent on (loc. or —°).

संनिवृत्त a. turned or come back; stopped, ceased.

संनिवेश m. sitting down, settlement, foundation (of a city); abode, dwelling-place; arrangement, preparation; state, condition; shape, form, appearance.

संनिवेशन n. abode, dwelling-place; arrangement, construction.

संनिवेश्य a. to be put or fixed in (loc.).

संनिश्चय m. settled opinion.

संनिहित a. placed near or together, present, at hand, fixed or situated in (—°).

सन्नी कृ appease, satisfy.

संन्यसन n. abandonment of the world.

संन्यास m. deposit, trust, stake (at a play); convention, agreement; relinquishment, resignation, abandonment of the world.

संन्यासिन् a. renouncing, resigning (—°); absol. who has abandoned the world.

सन्मङ्गल n. a right or correct ceremony etc.

सन्मणि m. a true jewel.

सन्मन्त्र m. a good word or verse.

सन्मात्र a. only (merely) being.

सन्मार्ग m. the right path (fig.).

सन्मित्र n. a good friend.

संन्यंस् (compar.) older (cf. **संनोयंस्**).

1**सप्**, **सपति**, **॰ते** follow after, be attached or devoted to, serve (acc.). C.M. & **अभि** M. = S.

2**सप्** (**साप्**) following, serving (—°).

सप m. penis.

1**सपक्ष** m. partisan, adherent, friend; partaker, companion. Abstr. **॰ता** f., **॰त्व** n.

2**सपक्ष** & **॰क** a. winged, feathered (arrow); befriended.

सपङ्कज a. adorned with lotus-flowers.

सपत्र m. arrow (feathered).

सपत्न m. rival, foe; abstr. **॰ता**† f., **॰त्व**† n.

सपत्नक्षयण (f. **ई**) & **॰क्षित्** destroying rivals.

सपत्नजित् & **॰तुर्** a. = seq.

सपत्नसाह्, f. **ई** overwhelming rivals.

सपत्नहन्, f. **॰घ्नी** slaying foes.

सपत्नी f. having the same lord or husband, fellow-wife or mistress; also = seq.

सपत्नीक a. along with a wife (wives).

सपत्नीजन m. the fellow-wives.

सपदि adv. instantly, quickly.

सपद्म & **°क** a. furnished with lotus-flowers.

सपरिक्रम a. along with a train.

सपरिच्छद a. along with a train or chattles.

सपरिजन a. along with attendants or followers.

सपरितोषम् a. with satisfaction.

सपरिबाध a. obstructed, limited.*

सपरिबृंहण a. along with the supplements (Veda).

सपरिवाह a. overflowing.

सपरिव्यय a. along with the condiments (food).

सपरिषत्क a. along with a train.

सपरिहारम् adv. with reserve or hesitation.*

सपर्य्, **°र्यति** serve, worship, pay homage or devotion to (acc.); like, accept gladly. — **वि** worship here and there.

सपर्या f. worship, homage.

सपर्याण a. saddled.

सपर्यु a. doing homage, serving.

सपर्येण्य a. to be honoured.

सपलाश a. having leaves (branch).

सपवित्र a. together with (purifying) sacrificial grass.

सपशु a. having cattle or along with the c.

सपात्र a. along with the vessels.

सपाद a. increased by a quarter.

सपादवन्दनम् adv. respectfully, differentially.*

सपाल a. attended by a herdsman.

सपिण्ड related (in the sixth, orig. only in the third generation); lit. sharing the funeral cake.

सपिण्डन & **सपिण्डीकरण** n. investing a person with the rights of a Sapiṇḍa (v. prec.).

सपितृक a. along with the father(s.).

सपित्व n. union, company.

1**सपीति** f. compotation.

2**सपीति** m. boon-companion (who drinks together).

सपुत्र a. having a son or along with the son (also **°क**).

सपुरुष a. along with the men.

सपुरोहित a. along with the house-priest.

सपुलक a. having the hair of the body erect, enraptured.

सपुष्प a. having flowers, blooming.

सप्तक a. containing seven; m. a week; m. n. a collection of seven, heptade (adj. —° f. **सप्तिका**).

सप्तकृत्वस् adv. seven times.

सप्तगण a. consisting of seven troops (the Maruts).

सप्तगु a. having seven cows.

सप्तगुण a. sevenfold.

सप्तचक्र a. having seven wheels.

सप्तचत्वारिंशत् f. forty-seven.

सप्तच्छद m. N. of a plant (lit. having seven leaves).

सप्तच्छिद्र a. having seven holes (flute).

सप्तजिह्व a. seven-tongued; m. fire.

सप्तजिह्वानन a. having a seven-tongued face (fire).

सप्ततन्तु a. having seven threads.

सप्ततन्त्र, f. **ई** having seven strings (lute).

सप्ततय, f. **ई** consisting of seven parts.

सप्तति f. seventy.

सप्तथ, f. **ई** the seventh.

सप्तदश, f. **ई** the seventeenth or containing seventeen.

सप्तदशधा adv. seventeenfold.

सप्तदशन् a. pl. seventeen.

सप्तद्वारावकीर्ण a. scattered at the seven gates (fig. = worldly, mundane).

1**सप्तद्वीप** (°—) the seven islands, i.e. the earth.

2**सप्तद्वीप**, f. **आ** consisting of seven islands (the earth).

सप्तद्वीपवन्त् a. = prec. a.; f. **°वती** the earth.

सप्तधा adv. in seven parts, seven times.

सप्तधातु a. consisting of seven, sevenfold.

सप्तन् a. pl. seven (used also to express an indefinite plurality).

सप्तपत्त्र a. having seven leaves; m. = **सप्तच्छद** m.

सप्तपद् & **°पद** (f. **°पदी** & **आ**) making seven steps (to close an alliance, a marriage, etc.).

सप्तपर्ण m. = **सप्तच्छद** m.

सप्तपुत्र a. having seven sons.

सप्तबुध्न a. having seven bottoms.

सप्तभूमि & °भौम a. having seven storeys.
सप्तम, f. ई the seventh. f. ई the seventh day in the halfmonth; the seventh case & his endings (g.).
सप्तरश्मि a. seven-stringed or -tongued.
सप्तरात्र n. seven days (lit. nights), week.
सप्तर्च a. containing seven verses; n. such a hymn.
सप्तर्षि m. pl. the seven sages or the seven stars of the Great Bear.
सप्तवध्रि a. fettered with seven thongs (the soul); m. N. of a man.
सप्तवर्ग m. a group of seven.
सप्तवर्ष & °वार्षिका (f. ई) seven years old.
सप्तविंश a. the twenty-seventh.
सप्तविंशत् & सप्तविंशति f. twenty-seven.
सप्तविध a. sevenfold.
सप्तवृष a. having seven bulls.
सप्तशत (only —°) & f. ई seven hundred.
सप्तशतक n. T. of a collection of erotic stanzas.
सप्तसफ a. seven-hoofed.
सप्तशिरस् a. seven-headed.
सप्तशीर्ष & सप्तशीर्षन् (f. °शीर्ष्णी) = prec.
सप्तसप्ति a. having seven horses; m. the sun.
सप्तस्वसृ a. having seven sisters.
सप्तहन् a. slaying seven.
सप्तहोतृ a. having seven priests (Agni).
सप्ताक्षर, f. ई seven-syllabled.
सप्ताङ्ग a. having seven members or parts.
सप्तार्चिस् a. seven-rayed; m. fire or the god of fire.
सप्ताश्व m. = सप्तसप्ति.
सप्तास्य a. seven-mouthed.
सप्ताह m. seven days.
सप्ति m. horse, esp. runner.
सप्तिन् a. containing seven.
सप्तीवन्त् a. drawn by runners.
सप्त्य n. running-place for horses.
सप्रज & सप्रजस् a. having offspring.
सप्रज्ञ a. endowed with reason.
सप्रणय a. affectionate, tender, n. adv.
सप्रणव a. together with the sacred syllable Om.
सप्रणामम् adv. with a bow.
सप्रतिबन्ध a. hindered, complicate.
सप्रत्यभिज्ञम् adv. with recognition.
सप्रत्यय a. sure, trustful or trustworthy.
सप्रत्याधान a. along with the receptacle.
सप्रत्याशम् adv. confidently, hopefully.
सप्रथस् or संप्रथस् a. diffused, spreading wide.
सप्रभ a. of like splendour or appearance with (—°).
सप्रभाव m. having might or strength.
सप्रमोदनम् & °दम् adv. merrily.
सप्रश्रयम् adv. respectfully.
सप्रसव a. having descendants.
सप्रहासम् adv. with a laughter.
सप्राण a. having breath, living.
सप्सर a. timid, reverential.
सफ m. N. of sev. men.
सफल a. having fruits or testicles; having reward, profit, or success.
सफलय्, °यति make profitable or lucrative, draw advantage from, enjoy.
सफली कृ the same, भू P.
सफलोदर्क a. bearing fruits (for the future).
सफेन a. foamy, frothy.
सबन्धु a. being of the same family, related; having a relative or friend.
सबर्दुघ, f. आ yielding milk easily or quickly.
सबर्दुह् (nom. धुक्) & सबर्धु f. the same.
सबल a. strong, mighty; along with the army.
सबलवाहन a. with army and train.
सबलात्कारम् adv. with force, forcibly.*
सबहुमानम् adv. with consideration, respectfully.
सबाध् a. pressed, afflicted.
सबाध a. disadvantageous to (gen.).
सबाधस् a. pressed, adv. urgently.
सबाष्प a. shedding tears; adv. with tears.
सबाह्यान्तःकरण a. with the external and internal organs; w. आत्मन् m. the whole self.
सब्रह्मचारिन् m., °णी f. fellow-student.
सभक्तिकम् adv. respectfully.
सभक्ष m. commensal.
सभय a. timid, afraid of (—°); n. adv.
सभरस् a. harmonious, harmonizing with (instr.).
सभस्मन् a. mingled or smeared with ashes.
सभा f. house or hall for public meetings, esp. gambling-house, council-chamber,

court of justice, court or palace of a prince; place of refuge, asylum; assembly, society, esp. good society.

सभागत a. appeared in court (j).

सभाजन n. service, honour, courtesy.

सभाजय्, °यति, °ते serve, honour, worship, praise.

सभापति m. president of an assembly.

सभापाल m. the same.

सभामण्डप s. assembly-hall.

सभार्य a. having a wife, with one's wife.

सभावन्त् a. fit for a council or assembly.

सभासद् m. member of (lit. sitter in) a council or society; assessor, judge.

सभासाह् a. ruling an assembly.

सभिक m. keeper of a gaming-house.

सभृत्य a. along with the servant(s).

सभेय a. fit for a (good) society, decent, courteous, polite.

सभ्य a. being in or relating to an assembly, also = prec. m. assessor, judge; a cert. fire (r.).

सभ्येतर a. indecent (language).

सभ्रूक्षेपम् adv. with a frown.

सभ्रूभङ्ग n. knitting the brows; n. adv.

सभ्रूभेदम् adv. with a frown.

सभ्रूविलासम् adv. with a play of the brows.

सम् adv. along with, together (mostly °—).

1**सम** pron. any, every.

2**सम** a. even, smooth, parallel; like, equal to (instr., gen., or —°) or in (instr., तस्, loc., or —°); (always) the same, unaltered; common, mediocre; indifferent, neutral; harmless, good, honest, fair, convenient, easy. n. & °— adv. equally, like, along, together, precisely, exactly, fairly; n. as subst. plain, evenness, balance, compensation, right measure or proportion, indifference, equanimity.

3†**सम** n. (—°) = **समा** year.

समक a. like, equal.

समकक्ष a. of the same weight or importance; f. आ = °ता f., °त्व n. as abstr.

समकाल (°—) & **समकालम्** adv. at the same time, simultaneously.

समक्ष a. being before the eyes, visible; °क्षम्, °क्षात्, °क्षतस्, & °क्षे visibly, publicly, before the eyes or in presence of (dat., gen., or —°).

समक्षदर्शन n. autopsy, ocular evidence.

समग्र, f. **समग्रा** whole, complete, full, entire, all; n. everything; °— wholly.

समग्रवर्तिन् a. wholly turned on (—°).

समग्रधन a. with the whole property.

समग्रेन्दु m. the full moon.

1**समङ्क** m. hook, cramp (fig. = pain).

2**समङ्क** a. bearing the same mark.

समङ्ग & °**ङ्गिन्**† a. having all limbs complete.

समचित्त a. equanimous, indifferent; abstr. °त्व n.

समचेतस् a. = prec. adj.

समज a. E. of Indra.

समज्या f. meeting-place, meeting.

समञ्चन n. bending in, contracting.

समञ्जन a. fitting together; n. rubbing in, anointing.

समञ्जस a. all right, perfect.

समता f., **समत्व** n. abstr. to 2**सम**.

समतिक्रम m. omission.

समतुला f. equal value.

समत्सर a. envious, jealous, grudging.

समद् f. fight, contest.

समद a. intoxicated, excited, ruttish.

1**समदन** n. = **समद्**.

2**समदन** a. enamoured, in love.

समदर्शन a. similar, like (—°); also = seq.

समदर्शिन् a. looking (at all) equally i.e. impartially.

समदुःख a. sharing another's woe, compassionate.

समदुःखसुख a. sharing another's woe and joy.

समदृष्टि a. = **समदर्शिन्**, f. as abstr.

समदेश m. smooth or level ground.

समद्युति a. of equal splendour with (—°).

समद्वन् a. fighting, warlike.

समधा adv. in like manner, equally as (instr.).

समधिक a. having a surplus, — and more; excessive, abundant. °— in adj. more— than (abl.), comp. °**तरम्** adv. more, in a higher degree.

समधुर a. carrying the same burden with (gen.).

समधृत a. weighed together, equalled in weight.

संमन n. meeting, encounter, intercourse, assembly, embrace; contest, fight.

समनगा a. going to an assembly.

समनन्तर a. immediately adjoining, nearest to (abl. or gen.); n. (& °—) immediately behind or after (abl., gen., or —°).

संमनस् & °**नस्क**† a. unanimous.

समना adv. in one point, together; at once, simultaneously; equally, in like manner.

समनीक n. front of battle.

समनुव्रत a. obedient, devoted to (acc.).

संमन्त a. adjoining, neighbouring, all, complete. f. **आ** pl. neighbourhood. n. **संमन्तम्** near, close to (instr.). **समन्तेन** all around, w. neg. nowhere. °—, **समन्तम्**, °**न्तात्**, & °**न्ततस्** all around, everywhere; completely, thoroughly.

संमन्तिकम् adv. in close contact.

समन्त्र & °**क** a. accompanied by mantras.

समन्मथ a. enamoured, in love.

समन्य a. fit for a festival, festive.

संमन्यु (**समन्यु**) a. unanimous, harmonious; wrathful, angry, dejected, sad.

समन्वय m. close connection.

समबुद्धि a. equanimous, indifferent.

समन्वित a. accompanied by, joined or connected with, full or possessed of (instr. or —°).

समभितस् adv. towards (acc.).

समभिधा f. appellation, name (only adj. —°).

समभिभाषण n. conversation with (instr. or —°).

समभिव्याहार m. intercourse with (gen.).

समभिहार m. repetition.

समभूमि f. = **समदेश**.

समभ्यर्थयितृ m. petitioner, suppliant.

समभ्याश m. nearness, presence.

समभ्युन्नत a. ascended, risen.

सममति a. even-minded, equanimous.

समय m. meeting or place of meeting, intercourse with (instr.), agreement, convention, contract, obligation, condition; trial, ordeal, (a fixed) point of time, i.g. time, season, occasion; case, occurrence, circumstance; rule, norm, doctrine; custom, usage.

समयक्रिया f., °**धर्म** m. stipulated obligation, contract, agreement.

समयपूर्वम् adv. after a previous agreement.*

समयभेदिन् & °**व्यभिचारिन्** a. breaking an agreement.

समयविद्या f. astrology.

समया (instr. adv.) in the middle of, betwixt (acc., r. instr.); near, close to (acc., instr., or *gen.); half (°—); throughout, w. **भू** lie between.

समयाचार m. conventional conduct.

समयाध्युषित a. half-risen (sun).

समयाध्वम् adv. mid-way.

समयाविषित a. half risen or set (sun).

समयोचित a. suitable to circumstances; n. adv.

समर m., **समरण** n. encounter, fight.

समरकर्मन् n. the same.

समरचिति, °**भू**, & °**भूमि** f. field of battle.

समरमूर्धन् m., °**शिरस्** n. = **समराग्र**.

समरसीमन् s. field of battle.

समराग्र n. the front or van of battle.

समराङ्गण or °**ङ्गन** n. field of battle.

समरेख a. straight-lined, straight.

समरोपाय m. stratagem.

समर्घ a. cheap.

समर्च a. having the same number of verses.

समर्चन n., °**ना** f. honouring, worshipping.

समर्थ a. corresponding, suitable, fit for (gen. or —°); a match for (gen.); able to, capable of (infin., loc., dat., or —°); having the same sense or meaning (g.).

समर्थता f., °**त्व** n. ability, capability.

समर्थन n. consideration, deliberation (also f. **आ**), confirmation, corroboration, justification; f. **आ** persuasion, invitation, also = prec.

समर्थय् v. **अर्थय्**.

समर्थनीय & °**र्थ्य** a. to be (being) confirmed or justified.

समर्धन, f. **ई** causing to prosper.

समर्धक a. prospering, thriving.

समर्पण n. putting, placing, handing over, imparting, committing, entrusting.

समर्पणीय a. to be placed or bestowed.

समर्पयितव्य & **समर्प्य** a. = prec.
समर्पितृ m. bestower.
समर्य्, only **सयर्यन्त्** pugnacious, warlike.
1**समर्य** n. conflux, multitude, mass, assembly, tumult, broil.
2**समर्य** a. frequented by people or accompanied by followers.
समर्यजित् a. victorious in battle.
समर्याद a. limited, n. adv. exactly.
समल a. stained, soiled, troubled.
समलोष्टकाञ्चन & **°ष्टाश्मकाञ्चन** a. to whom a clod, (a stone), and a piece of gold are all the same.
समवतार m. a sacred bathing-place.
समवत्त n. a gathered piece.
समवत्तधान a. containing gathered pieces.
समवर्ण a. of the same colour or caste.
समवर्तिन् a. being at an equal distance or behaving in an equal manner.
समवस्था f., **°न** n. state, condition.
समवस्थित a. standing, immovable, ready, prepared.
समवस्रव m. flowing off, discharge.
समवहार m. abundance, multitude.
समवहास्य a. ridiculous, abstr. **°ता** f.
समवाय m. meeting with, joining (gen. or —°); congress, assembly; union, connection, mixture, aggregate; intimate cohesion, inherence, adj. **°यिन्** (ph.).
समविषम n. even and uneven ground.*
समवृत्त n. an equal metre (containing four equal verses).
समवृत्ति a. (always) acting in the same way.
समवेक्षण n. viewing, inspecting.
समवेत a. come to (acc.), joined, united, all.
समवेष m. an equal dress.
समशस् adv. together, simultaneously.
समशील & **°लिन्** a. of like nature.
समश्नुव, f. **ई** reaching, grasping.
समष्टि f. reaching, attaining; aggregate, totality, abstr. **°ता** f.
समसंस्थित a. = **समस्थ**.
समसर्वगुण a. equally endowed with all virtues.
समस्त a. joined, composed, whole, entire, all.
समस्तधातृ m. the bearer of the universe (Viṣṇu).
समस्तव्यस्तरूपक n. a kind of metaphor (rh.).
समस्थ a. being in lucky (lit. even) circumstances.
समस्था f. conjunction, union, staying together.
समह adv. in any manner, somehow.
समा f. half-year, season, year.
1**समांश** m. an equal portion or share.
2**समांश** a. receiving an equal share.
समांशक & **°शिन्** a. the same.
समांस a. fleshy, animal-(food).
समाकर्षण n. drawing near, attracting.
समाकुल a. crowded, filled with, abundant in (instr. or —°); disturbed, perplexed, confused.
समाक्रन्दन n. calling, shouting.
समाक्रमण n. stepping into, entering.
समाख्या f. designation, name.
समाख्यान n. = prec., communication, report, tale.
समागम m. coming together, meeting, union, intercourse (also sexual) with (gen., instr. ± **सह**, or —°); assembly, company.
समागमन n. meeting, union, (sexual) intercourse.
समाघात m. collision.
समाचार m. proceeding, conduct, behaviour, custom, usage, manner.
समाचेष्टित n. deportment, behaviour.
समाज m. assembly, company, meeting, heap, multitude.
समाज्ञा f designation, name.
समादान n. receiving, accepting, undergoing.
समादेय a. to be received or accepted.
समादेश m. direction, injunction.
समाधातव्य a. to be settled or composed.
समाधान n. placing, setting up (esp. the sacred fire), arranging, settling, composing, making up, propitiating, reconciling; attention, meditation, devotion.
समाधानरूपक n. a kind of metaphor (rh.).
समाधि m. putting together, conjunction, union, a whole; performation, accomplishment, arrangement, reconcilement; attention, meditation, devotion.
समाधित a. conciliated.
समाधिमन्त् a. full of attention or devotion.

समाधिस्थ a. abiding in contemplation.

समाधेय a. to be put in order; to be directed or instructed; to be conceded or admitted.

1**समान**, f. **ई** & **आ** like, same, similiar, homogeneous, equal to (instr., gen., or —°), common, universal, all; °— & n. adv. equally, like (instr. or — °).

2**समान** m. one of the vital airs.

समानकाल & **°कालीन** a. of the same time or duration.

समानगुण a. of the same (good) qualities.

समानगोत्र a. of the same family.

समानजन m. a person of the same quality or position.

समानजन्मन् a. of the same origin or age.

समानजाति & **°जातीय** a. of the same kind, kindred.

समानतस् adv. equally or commonly.

समानता f. likeness, sameness with (gen. or —°).

समानत्र adv. on the same spot.

समानत्व n. likeness to (instr.).

समानदेवत & **°दैवत्य** a. consecrated to the same deity.

समानधर्मन् a. like, similar to (instr.).

समानपक्ष m. the same half-month.

समानप्रतिपत्ति a. of the same insight or penetration, (equally) sensible.

समानप्रभृति a. having the same beginning.

समानप्रेमन् a. equally loving.

समानबन्धु a. of the same family.

समानबर्हिस् a. having the same sacrificial bed.

समानयन n. bringing together or near.

समानयोजन a. harnessed alike.

समानयोनि a. having the same origin.

समानराग a. seized by the same passion.

समानरुचि a. having the same taste, abstr. **°ता** f.

समानरूप a. of the same colour or form.

समानवर्चस् a. having the same strength or energy.

समानवर्चस a. having the same splendour.

समानवर्ण a. having the same colour.

समानविद्य a. having the same science, abstr. **°ता** f.

समानशब्दा f. a kind of riddle.

समानसुखदुःख a. having the same joys and sorrows, abstr. **°ता** f.

समानाक्षर n. monophthong (opp. **संध्यक्षर**).

1**समानाधिकरण** n. grammatical congruence (in case).

2**समानाधिकरण** a. coordinate, having the same government or subject with (instr. or —°); abstr. **°ता** f., **°त्व** n.

समानार्थ a. having the same purpose or meaning with (instr. or —°); abstr. **°ता** f., **°त्व** n.

समानार्षेय a. descended from the same Rishi.

समानिचय a. having provisions for a year.

समानोदक a. distantly related (cf. **सपिण्ड**); abstr. **°भाव** m.

समानोदर्क a. having the same end.

समानोदर्य a. born from the same womb; m. such a brother.

समानोपमा f. a kind of comparison (rh.).

1**संमान्त** m. confiner, borderer.

2**समान्त** m. the end of the year.

समान्या adv. commonly, equally.

समापक a. finishing, supplying.

समापत्ति f. meeting, encountering; incident, chance; reaching, attaining, becoming (—°).

समापन a. & n. accomplishing, performing; f. **आ** the highest degree.

समापिन् a. finishing.

समाप्त a. finished, complete, perfect.

संमाप्ति f. attainment, acquisition, accomplishment, end, close.

समाप्तिक a. who has finished his studies, also = **समापिन्**.

समाप्य a. to be got, obtained, accomplished, closed.

समाप्लव & **°प्लाव** m. bathing, bath.

समाभाषण n. talk, conversation with (—°).

समाम m. length, adj. **°म्यु**.

समाम्नात a. remembered, mentioned, enumerated; n. mention, enumeration.

समाम्नाय m. enumeration, collection, literary composition, the sacred writings i.e. the Veda.

समायत्त a. based or dependent on (loc.).

समायुक्त a. arranged, pepared, entrusted;

met, come into contact (as friends or foes); joined, connected, endowed, or furnished with (instr. or —°).

समायुत a. put or brought together; consisting of or connected with (—°).

समायोग m. junction, connection, contact with (instr. ± सह or —°); arrangement, preparation; instr. by means or in consequence of (—°).

समारम्भ m. enterprise, beginning.

समारम्भण n. grasping, seizing.

समाराधन n. propitiating, winning.

समारुरुक्षु a. wishing to ascend.

समारूढ a. mounted, entered (act. & pass.); grown, increased; healed.

समारोप m., °ण n. placing in, transferring to (loc.); stringing (of a bow).

समारोहण n. mounting, rising, growing.

समार्थक a. having the same meaning.

समार्ष a. = समानार्षेय.

समालक्ष्य a. visible, perceivable.

समालभन n. unguent, °हस्त bearing unguent.

समालम्भ m. seizing, killing (a victim for sacrifice).

समालम्भन & °हस्त = समालभन & °हस्त.

समालम्भम् ger. by seizing.

समालम्भिन् a. killing (—°).

समालाप m. talk, conversation.

समालिङ्गन n. an embrace.

समालोक m., °न n. sight, view.

समावच्छस् adv. equally.

समावद्वीर्य a. equally strong.

समावन्त् a. equal, so great or so much (many); n. adv. so much.

समावर्त m., °न n. return (cf. समावृत्त).

समावह a. bringing, causing (—°).

समावाप m. mixing up the fires (r.).

समावाय m. = समवाय.

समाविग्न a. terrified, astounded.

समाविष्ट a. seized or overcome by, filled or endowed with (instr. or —°); instructed in (instr.) by (instr.).

समावृत्त a. returned (esp. from the teacher's house), come back from (—°); finished.

समावेश m. entering, meeting, coincidence, coexistence.

समावेशन n. entering, cohabitation.

समाश m. common meal, repast.

समाशिर् a. mixed.

समाश्रय m. connection, junction with or relation to (—°); refuge, shelter, dwelling-place; adj. —° living or situated in, relating or belonging to.

समाश्रित a. leaning or resting on, resorted to, entered or being in (acc., loc., or —°), got to, arrived at (acc.); devoted to, intent upon (acc. or —°); relating or belonging to (—°); pass. resorted to, sought, chosen; visited or afflicted by (instr. or —°).

समाश्लेष m., °ण n. an embrace.

समाश्वस्त a. recovered, comforted, confident.

समाश्वास m. breathing up, relief, comfort.

समाश्वासन n. comforting.

समास m. putting together, conjunction, composition, a compound word; condensation, abridgment. Instr. on the whole, also = abl., °तस् & °— summarily, succinctly.

समासक्त a. attached to, fixed on (loc.); relating to, occupied with (loc. or —°).

समासन्न a. near, proximate.

समासाद्य ger. according to, by means or on account of (acc.).

समासान्त m. suffix added at the end of a compound (g.).

समासोक्ति f. a kind of succint or compendiary expression (rh.).

समास्थित a. standing or sitting upon (acc., loc., or —°); remaining in (loc.); having incurred or got to (—°).

समास्या f. sitting together with (instr. or —°).

समाहर्तृ m. collector.

समाहार m. seizure, drawing back, abstraction; collection, aggregation.

समाहित a. put or fixed on, connected or linked with (instr. or —°); caused, produced, made, rendered; careful, concentrated, intent upon (loc. or —°); settled, proved, agreed; finished, concluded.

समाहितमति a. of collected mind, attentive.

समाहितिका f. a woman's name.

समाह्वय m. provoking, challenging, betting (esp. at animal-fights).

समाह्वातृ m. summoner to (dat.).
समाह्वान n. calling near, also = **समाह्वय**.
समित् f. encounter, combat.
1**संमित** a. united, joined with (instr. or —°).
2**संमित** a. equal in measure.
संमिति f. meeting, assembly, union, league; encounter, battle.
समितिंजय a. winning battles, E. of Yama & Viṣṇu.
समितिशोभन a. shining or excelling in battle.
समित्काष्ठ n. pl. fagots, fuel.
समित्पाणि a. holding fuel in the hands.
समित्पूल m. a bundle of fagots.
समित्र a. together with friends.
समिथ n. encounter, war, battle.
समिदाधान n. the placing of fuel (on the sacred fire).
समिद्धोम m. a libation poured out on burning wood).
समिद्धाग्नि a. whose fire is kindled.
समिद्धार a. fetching fuel.
समिद्धि f. burning, flaming.
समिद्वन्त् a. having fuel or containing the word **समिध्**.
समिध् a. flaming. — f. log of wood, fuel; kindling, flaming.
समिन्धन n. kindling; f. log of wood, fuel.
समिष् f. missile, spear.
संमिष्टि f. a complete sacrifice.
समिल्लता f. a creeping plant serving for fuel.
समीक n. encounter, fight, war.
समीकरण n. abstr. to seq. w. **कृ**; also assimilation, digestion.
समी कृ make even or equal to (instr.); °**भू** pass. or refl.
समीक्षण a. causing to see, showing; n. looking at, observing.
समीक्षा f. getting aware, sight, look, view, opinion.
समीक्षितव्य & °**क्ष्य** a. to be found out.
समीचीन a. converging, turned to one centre, being or staying together, joined, complete, fit, right; abstr. °**ता**† f., °**त्व**† n.
समीप a. near (in sp. & f.). — n. nearness, neibhbourhood, presence; acc. towards, to, loc. near, close to, in the presence of, before, towards, to, °**तस्** from (also abl. in **आत्**), near etc. = loc. (gen. or —°). Abstr. °**ता** f., °**त्व** n.
समीपग a. going or being near (gen. or —°).
समीपज a. produced or growing near.
समीपदेश m. neighbouring place, neighbourhood.
समीपवर्तिन् & °**स्थ** a. = **समीपग**.
समीर m. wind, air (also in the body).
समीरण a. setting in motion, exciting; m. = prec., also the god of the wind.
संमीषित a. stretched.
समीहा f. endeavour, wish, desire.
समीहित a. wished; n. = prec.
समुक्षण n. sprinkling.
समुचित a. used to (—°); fit, proper for (gen. or —°).
समुच्चय m. heap, mass, multitude, a whole or aggregate; addition, copulative relation (g.).
समुच्चयन n. collecting, putting together.
समुच्चयोपमा f. a kind of comparison (rh.).
समुच्छित्ति f., °**च्छेद** m., °**च्छेदन** n. destruction.
समुच्छ्रय m. erection, elevation, eminence, height (lit. & fig.).
समुच्छ्रित a. lifted up, raised, high (lit. & fig.).
समुच्छ्वसित a. & n. fetching breath.
समुज्ज्वल a. shining, resplendent.
समुत a. sewn together.
समुत्क a. longing for (—°).
समुत्कर्ष m. prominence, superiority.
समुत्त्रस्त a. alarmed, terrified.
समुत्थ a. rising, risen, existing, appearing, produced or occasioned by (abl. or —°).
समुत्थान n. rising, reviving, swelling, increasing; activity, undertaking, beginning, enterprise (w. **संभूय** cooperation, partnership); healing, cure.
समुत्थानव्यय m. the expenses of a cure.
समुत्थित a. risen, raised, high; sprung or produced from (abl.), appeared, grown (wings); ready or prepared for (loc. or infin.).
समुत्पत्ति f. rising, origin.
समुत्पन्न a. born, produced, begotten by (abl.) with (loc.); come, arrived.
समुत्पतन n. flying up together.

समुत्पाद m. rising, origin.
समुत्पाद्य a. to be caused or produced.
समुत्फुल्ल a. opened wide (eyes).
समुत्सर्ग m. ejection, discharge.
समुत्सारण n. scaring, driving away or asunder.
समुत्सुक a. agitated, uneasy, anxious, longing for (infin. or —°); abstr. °ता f., °त्व n.
समुत्सुकय्, °यति cause to long for.
समुत्सेध m. height, elevation.
समुद् a. rejoiced, joyful.
समुंदन्त a. reaching up to the brim.
समुदय m. (n.) coming together, meeting, gathering, combination, aggregate (w. कृ collect, assemble); revenue, income, success, prosperity.
समुदाचार m. presenting, offering (—°); good or correct behaviour (p. °वन्त्); intercourse with (instr.).
समुदाय m. union, combination, aggregate.
समुदीरण n. getting in motion.
समुदीर्ण a. roused, excited.
†समुद्ग m. tip, point (only —°); a small round box (also °क m.).
समुद्गम m. rising, mounting.
समुद्दण्ड a. lifted up (arm).
समुद्दिश्य ger. (lit. pointing to, aiming at) towards, against, concerning, for the sake or in honour of (acc.).
समुद्देश m. exposition, doctrine; place, standpoint.
समुद्धत a. raised (dust), swollen (water), lifted up, high, intensive, haughty, arrogant.
समुद्धरण n. drawing up or out, removing.
समुद्धर्तृ m. who lifts up or draws out; deliverer, redeemer.
समुद्धार m. = prec.; also salvation or destruction.
समुद्बन्धन n. hanging.
समुद्भव m. rising, origin, revival; adj. —° sprung from.
समुद्भूत a. sprung up, produced, risen; being, existing.
समुद्भूति f. rising, appearance.
समुद्भेद m. expansion, development.
समुद्यम m. lifting up, raising; effort, exertion, zeal for (loc., dat., or —°).
समुद्योग m. use, employment; energy, zeal, readiness.
1समुद्र m. the gathering of the waters above and under the firmament, either the sky as the aerial ocean, or ocean, sea i.g. (there are 3, 4, or 7 enumerated); fig. a large Soma-vat.
2समुद्र a. sealed.
समुद्रग a. going to the sea; f. आ river.
समुद्रगृह & °क n. a kind of bathing room.
समुद्रज a. born or produced in the sea.
समुद्रज्येष्ठ a. having the Ocean as chief.
समुद्रतस् adv. from the sea.
समुद्रतीर n. sea-shore.
समुद्रदत्त m. a man's name.
समुद्रनेमि a. encircled by the ocean.
समुद्रपत्नी f. river (wife of the ocean).
समुद्रमालिन् a. garlanded i.e. surrounded by the ocean.
समुद्रयात्रा f., °यान n. sea-voyage.
समुद्रयायिन् m. sea-farer, sea-trader.
समुद्रयोषित् & °वल्लभा f. = समुद्रपत्नी.
समुद्ररशन a. sea-girt (the earth).
समुद्रवसन a. sea-clad (the earth).
समुद्रवासिन् a. living on the sea-coast.
समुद्रवेला f. ocean-tide, flow (opp. ebb).
समुद्रव्यवहारिन् a. sea-faring.
1समुद्रान्त m. sea-shore.
2समुद्रान्त a. reaching up to or falling into the sea (the earth or a river).
समुद्राय्, °यते be like the sea.
समुद्रार्थ a. tending towards the sea.
समुद्रिय or °द्र्य a. marine, oceanic.
समुद्वाह m. marriage, wedding.
समुन्नति f. rising, elevation, height, rank, dignity.
समुन्नत a. lifted up, risen; prominent, projecting; high, sublime.
समुन्मूलन n. uprooting, destroying.
समुपचित a. abundant, plentiful.
समुपस्थित a. come near, approached, come to (acc.), sitting or lying on (loc.); risen, appeared, arrived, fallen to one's (acc. or gen.) share; imminent, future, ready for (acc. or gen.); fixed upon, undertaken.
समुपहव m. an invitation with others.

समुपानयन n. bringing near.

समुपार्जन n. acquiring, attaining.

समुपेत a. met, assembled, arrived; connected or provided with (instr.).

समुपेप्सु a. striving after (acc.).

समुल्लम्बित a. hanging, pendulous.

संमूल a. having roots, living, verdant; along with the root, complete, entire, °— & n. adv.

समूलकाषम् adv., w. **कष्** extirpate root and branch.

समूह m. heap, collection, multitude, aggregate, a whole or totality.

समूहन a. & n. sweeping together, collecting; f. **ई** broom.

संमृति f. encounter, collision, fight.

संमृद्ध a. achieved, perfect, complete; endowed with, possessed of (instr., abl. or —°); prosperous, wealthy, copious, abundant.

संमृद्धि f. thriving, success, prosperity, perfection, happiness, wealth, abundance.

समृद्धिन् a. prosperous, blessed, rich in (—°).

समृध् f. success, luck.

समृध a. perfect, complete.

समेत a. come to, got at (acc.); met, assembled; joined or connected with, possessed of (instr. or —°).

समेद्धृ m kindler.

संमेध a. vigorous, lively.

समेधन n. thriving, increase, growth.

संमोकस् a. dwelling together, closely connected or furnished with.

समोह m. = **समूह**.

संपत्ति f. agreement, harmony; completion, fulfilment; becoming, transition into; happening, falling to one's share; success, prosperity, fortune; wealth, plenty, abundance.

संपद् f. falling together, coinciding, agreeing; success, gain, acquisition; increase, growth; existence, abundance, high degree (adj. —° furnished with); right proportion, state, or condition; prosperity, happiness; wealth, beauty.

संपन्न a. born, produced, being, existing (°—); become a (—°); fallen to one's share; turned out well, accomplished, perfect; dainty, sweet; possessed of, endowed with (instr. or —°).

संपन्नक्षीरा f. giving sweet milk (cow).

संपन्नदन्त a. having (grown) teeth.

संपराय m. death; war, fight.

संपरिग्रह m. acceptation; property.

संपर्क m. junction, union, contact or intercourse with (instr. ± **सह**, gen., or —°) or between (—°).

संपवन n. purification.

संपा f. compotation.

संपात m. flying, flight, quick motion; encounter, collision, gathering, meeting; place of meeting or contact; happening, arising, occurrence; residue, leavings (esp. of a fluid or an offering).

संपाति m. N. of a fabulous bird.

संपातिन् a. falling down; flying together.

संपादक a. causing, producing, accomplishing, procuring.

संपादन, f. **ई** = prec.; n. as subst.

संपादयितृ, f. °**त्री** manager, accomplisher, provider.

संपादितत्व n. the being effected or accomplished.

संपाद्य a. to be effected or accomplished.

संपारण a. reaching or leading to the end; n. accomplishing.

संपारिन् a. crossing (ship).

संपिब a. swallowing.

संपीड m. pression (also °**न** n.); f. **आ** pain, torment.

संपुट & °**क** m., **संपुटिका** f. a round box.

संपुष्टि f. thriving, prosperity.

संपूजन n., °**पूजा** f. honouring.

संपूज्य a. to be honoured.

संपूर्ण a. full, replete, filled or richly furnished with (instr., gen., or —°); whole, entire, abundant; finished, accomplished.

संपूर्णपुच्छ a. spreading the tail (pea-hen).*

संपृक्त a. joined, united, combined, filled with (instr., r. loc.; or —°).

संपृण a. filling.

संप्रणेतृ m. leader, chief, manager.

संप्रतापन n. heating, a cert. hell.
संप्रति adv. just opposite (acc.); even, exactly, now, this moment.
संप्रतिपत्ति f. gain, acquisition; right conception or understanding; admission, assent.
संप्रतिष्ठा f. support, maintenance; perseverance, duration; rank, dignity.
संप्रतिष्ठित a. fixed, established, based upon (—°); being, existing.
संप्रतीक्ष्य a. to be expected.
संप्रत्ति f. & °**कर्मन्**† n. delivering over.
संप्रत्यय m. agreement, appointment; conviction, belief, confidence in (—°); notion, idea.
संप्रदातृ m. giver, offerer.
संप्रदान n. giving, presenting, handing over, tradition, bestowal, gift, oblation; the recipient (g.).
संप्रदाय m. bestower; oral tradition.
संप्रदायम् ger. giving, bestowing.
संप्रधारण n., °**णा** f. deliberation.
संप्रमुक्ति f. letting loose.
संप्रमोद m. great joy, exultation.
संप्रमोह m. perplexity (of mind).
संप्रयुक्त a. yoked, harnessed; impelled, urged on; joined, mixed, or endowed with (instr. or —°); brought into contact with (instr.); occupied with (—°); dependent on (loc.); quite intent upon an object.
संप्रयोग m. fastening, joining; union, connection, contact with (instr. ± **सह** or —°); marriage, sexual intercourse with (—°); usage, practice, employment, application.
संप्रलाप m. talk, chatter.
संप्रवृत्त a. finished, past.
संप्रवेश m. entering, entrance.
संप्रश्न m. question, inquiry after (—°).
संप्रसन्न a. appeased, tranquil, propitiated, gracious, favourable.
संप्रसाद m. perfect calm or peace of mind; serenity, grace, favour.
संप्रसारण n. the drawing asunder; the change of a semi vowel into the corresponding vowel (g.).
संप्रहर्ष m. great joy.
संप्रहार m. war, battle, fight with (instr. ± **सह** or —°); stroke, blow.
संप्रहास m. laughter, joy, mockery.
संप्राप्त a. met, (having) reached or obtained; arrived, come, descended from (abl.); perceived, learnt.
संप्राप्ति f. arrival at (—°); beginning, appearance; attainment, acquisition.
संप्रिय a. loving each other, agreeing well with (instr.); n. satisfaction.
संप्रीत a. delighted, pleased, glad.
संप्रीति f. joy, comfort, delight in, love of (loc. or —°); friendship with (instr. ± **सह**).
संप्रेप्सु a. striving after, longing for (acc.).
संप्रेरण n. inciting, bidding, command.
संप्रेषण n. sending away, dismission.
संप्रैष m. summons, direction (r.).
संप्रोक्षण n. besprinkling, consecrating; f. **ई** consecrated water.
संप्लव m. flowing together, flood, submersion, swelling (of the sea); destruction, ruin, end.
संप्लुत a. flowed together; having bathed in (—°); flooded, filled, or covered with (instr. or —°).
संफुल्ल a. full-blown, blossomed.
संफेट m. quarrel, altercation (rh.).
संबद्ध a. joined, united, coherent; connected or mixed with, full of (instr. or —°); contained in (—°); being, existing (°—).
संबन्ध m. collection; connection, relationship or fellowship of any kind (instr. ± **सह**, loc., or —°); also concr. a relation, friend, comrade, ally, etc.
संबन्धन n. connection, coherence.
संबन्धिता f., °**त्व** n. abstr. to seq.
संबन्धिन् a. joined or connected with, belonging or relating to (gen. or —°); partaking or possessed of (—°); related by blood or marriage; m. relative, kinsman.
संबन्धिबान्धव m. pl. kinsmen and relatives.
संबन्धु m. relative, kinsman.
सम्बल v. **शम्बल** & **संवल**.
संबाध m. throng, crowd; pressure, distress; a. narrow, crowded with (instr.).

संबुद्ध a. intelligent (lit. wide awake); clever, wise.

संबुद्धि f. calling to; the vocative case & its endings (g.).

संबोध m. understanding, intelligence.

संबोधन a. awakening; n. perceiving, understanding, reminding, also = **संबुद्धि**.

संबोध्य a. to be enlightened or brought to reason, to be be taught or instructed.

संभक्त a. partaking of, endowed with (gen.).

संभक्ष m. devourer.

संभग्न a. broken, crushed, routed (foe); frustrated, destroyed.

संभर a. bringing together or near.

संभरण n. bringing or putting together, bringing about, performing; multitude, collection.

संभर्तृ m. match-maker (who brings together).

संभव (संभव) m. being together, union, cohabitation; finding room or being contained in (loc.); birth, origin, source; cause, motive; happening, rising, appearance; being, existence, possibility. Often adj. originating in, sprung from, caused by, appearing in or at (—°).

संभवन n. becoming, existing.

संभविन् a. possible.

संभार m. bringing together or near; preparation, provision, materials, necessaries; possession, property; plenty, abundance, high degree.

संभार्य a. to be brought together, to be composed or prepared.

संभावना f. (°न n.) collecting, procuring; meeting with (gen.); honour, reverence, consideration, high opinion on (loc.); conjecture, supposition.

संभावनागुण m. a quite particular honour.

संभावनीय a. to be honoured, honourable; to be supposed, probable, likely.

संभावयितव्य a. = prec.

संभावित n. conjecture, supposition.

संभाव्य a. to be honoured or well treated; to be regarded as (nom.); to be (being) supposed or expected; fit, proper.

संभाष m., °षण & °षित n. talk, conversation.

संभाषिन् a. talking, conversing.

संभाष्य a. to be addressed or talked to.

संभिन्न a. cleft, split, broken, destroyed; contracted, brought into contact, tight.

संभीत a. afraid of (gen.).

संभूत a. born or produced from (abl. or —°); made or composed of (instr. or —°); become, being, existing; °— furnished with.

संभूति f. rising, birth, origin, growth.

संभूय ger. (by) joining together or making partnership.

संभृत a. put together, heaped up, collected; loaden, covered, or furnished with (instr. or —°); carried, borne (in the womb); augmented, increased, nourished; gained, acquired; caused, effected.

संभृति f. equipment, preparation.

संभृत्य a. = **संभार्य**.

संभेद m. piercing, splitting, separating, alienating; kind, species; mixture, junction, contact with (—°).

संभेदन n. breaking through.

संभेद्य a. to be pierced or joined.

संभोग m. possession, enjoyment, esp. carnal enjoyment, sexual union.

संभोगवन्त् & °गिन् a. poss. to prec.

संभोग्य a. to be (being) enjoyed or used; abstr. °ता f.

संभोज m. food.

संभोजन n., ई f. eating together, common meal.

संभोज्य a. to be enjoyed or eaten; with whom it is allowed to eat.

संभ्रम m. confusion, agitation, haste, hurry; zeal, assiduity; error, mistake.

संभ्रान्त a. confused, perplexed, agitated.

संभ्रान्ति f. confusion, bewilderment, hurry.

संमग्न a. immersed, sunk into (—°).

संमत a. esteemed, honoured, approved; agreeing with, corresponding to (—°); considered as, taken for (nom.). — n. opinion, agreement, honour, respect.

संमति f. opinion, assent, approval, respect, esteem.

संमत्त a. excited, intoxicated, ruttish.

संमद् m. delight, joy at (—°).
संमदिन् a. gladdening.
संमनस् a. unanimous, agreeing.
संमयन n. erecting (the sacrificial post).
संमर्द m. pressing, pounding, crushing; meeting, encounter with (—°).
संमर्शन n. smearing, anointing.
संमा f. equality in weight or number.
संमातृ (**संमातृ**) a. having the same mother.
संमान m. honour, respect.
संमानन n., °ना f. the same.
संमाननीय & °मान्य a. to be honoured.
संमार्ग m. wiping, cleansing; broom, brush.
संमार्जक a. sweeping.
संमार्जन n. wiping off, sweeping, cleansing; also = f. ई broom or brush.
संमित a. meted out, of the same measure, equal in length, breadth, etc.; corresponding, fit; looking like, passing for (instr. or —°); furnished with, consisting of (instr. or —°), destined for (—°).
संमिश्र a. mixed, mingled, furnished or endowed with (instr. or —°).
संमिश्ल a. mixed or united with (instr. or —°).
संमीलन n. shutting, closing, esp. of the eyes.
संमीलित a. shut, closed (cf. prec.).
संमुख, f. ई (आ) facing, fronting, directed towards, fig. inclined to, propitious, favourable (gen., loc., or —°). n. **संमुखम्** adv. towards, in front of, before (gen.); °— & loc. opposite, in front, before the eyes.
संमुखी कृ put in front or before one's eyes; **भू** refl.
संमुखीन a. facing, confronting; abstr. °त्व n. also presence.
संमुग्ध a. strayed, erring; perplexed, bewildered; confused (pers. & th.).
संमूढ a. perplexed, bewildered, mad, insane, foolish, stupid; abstr. °ता f., °त्व n.
संमूर्छित a. stupefied; strengthened, increased; full of (—°).
संमृष्ट a. washed, swept, cleaned.
संमेघ m. the cloudy season.
संमेलन n. meeting, mixture.
संमोह m. loss of consciousness, stupefaction, bewilderment, perplexity.
संमोहक a. stupefying, perplexing, fascinating.
संमोहन, f. ई the same; n. as subst.
सम्यक् v. **सम्यञ्च्**.
सम्यक्ता f., °क्त्व n. rightness, justness, correctness.
सम्यक्पालन n. right protection.
सम्यक्संकल्प m. right purpose.
1**सम्यग्दर्शन** n. right insight or perception.
2**सम्यग्दर्शन** a. seeing right (cf. prec.).
सम्यग्दर्शिन् & °ग्दृश् a. the same.
सम्यग्बोध m. right understanding.
सम्यग्वान्त a. having well spit or vomited (leech).
सम्यग्विजयिन् a. thoroughly victorious.
सम्यग्वृत्ति a. of right conduct or practice.
सम्यग्व्यवसित a. well resolved.
सम्यञ्च्, f. **समीची** or **समीची** turned to one point or against each other, universus or adversus; whole, entire, all; correct, right, true. n. **सम्यक्** adv. towards one point, together, truly, correctly, exactly, duly, thoroughly; w. neg. not at all.
सम्राज् m. lord of the universe, sovereign ruler (f. **सम्राज्ञी**); E. of Varuṇa, Indra, etc.
सयत्न a. taking pains, trying to, engaged in (infin.).
सयत्व n. fastening, conjunction.
सयन n. binding.
सयावक a. dyed with lac.
सयावन्, f. °वरी going along with (instr.).
सयुक्त्व n. the being joined.
सयुग्वन् & **सयुज्** a. joined, united, associated; m. attendant, companion.
संयोनि a. having the same (or along with the) source or origin; abstr. °ता† f. or °त्व† n.
सयौवन a. youthful.
सर a. fluid, liquid; (f. ई) running, moving, going (—°). f. **सरा** brook, **सरी** waterfall.
सरक n. cup, pot.
सरघ् s., **सरघा** f. bee.
सरट m. lizard, chameleon.
सरण a. & n. running.
सरणि f. way, path.

सरण्यु a. speedy, quick; f. ऊ N. of a daughter of Tvaṣṭṛ.
1सरथ a. along with the chariot.
2सरथम् adv. together (on one chariot) with (instr.).
सरथिन् a. riding in the same chariot.
सरन्ध्र a. having a hole (holes).
सरभस a. impetuous, passionate, rash; °— & n. adv.
सरमा f. the bitch of Indra or of the gods.
सरमात्मज m. dog (son of Saramā).
सरमापुत्र & °सुत m. the same.
सरयु (सरयू) f. N. of a river.
सरल a. straight, direct, candid, honest; m. & f. आ names of trees.
*सरलद्रव m. the resin of the Sarala tree.
सरश्मि a. shining, radiant.
सरस् n. trough, bucket; pool, pond, lake.
सरस a. juicy, moist, humid, fresh, new, tasty, pleasant, charming, passionate, enamoured; n. adv. with rapture.
सरसिज a. born in ponds; n. a lotus.
सरसिजमुखी & °जाक्षी f. a lotus-faced (-eyed) woman.
सरसिरुह n. a lotus.
सरसी f. pool, lake.
सरसीज & °रुह n. a lotus.
सरसीरुहाक्ष & °रुहेक्षण a. lotus-eyed.
सरस्य a. belonging to pools or lakes.
सरस्वतीकण्ठाभरण n. the necklace of Sarasvatī, T. of a rhet. work.
सरस्वन्त् a. rich in waters. — m. N. of the ruler of the aerial waters or of a consort to Sarasvatī, also = ocean, sea. f. °ती a land rich in waters, N. & E. of sev. rivers, N. of the goddess of speech and learning; speech, voice, eloquence i.g.
सरहस्य a. with the mysteries i.e. Upanishads.
सराग a. coloured, reddened; pleasant, charming; passionate, enamoured; n. adv.
सराजक & °जन् a. along with the king.
सराति a. equally liberal or gracious.
सरित् f. stream, river.
सरित्पति m. the ocean (lord of streams).
सरिन् a. hastening (to help).
सरिर n. the heaving flood.
सरीमन् a. current, draught (of the wind).
सरीसृप a. crawling, creeping; m. n. a creeping animal.
सरु m. = शरु.
सरुच् a. of high splendour or dignity.
सरुज् a. suffering (the same) pain or sickness; ill, diseased.
सरुज a. causing or suffering pain, unwell; abstr. °त्व n.
सरुष् a. angry.
सरूप a. of the same shape or form with (gen. or —°); like, similar; shaped, formed, embodied; beautiful, handsome.
सरेतस् a. containing (its) seed.
सरोग a. sick, diseased; abstr. °ता f.
सरोज a. & n. = सरसिज.
सरोजदृश् & °नयना f. a lotus-eyed woman.
सरोजनेत्र a. lotus-eyed.
सरोजिनी f. a multitude or a pond of lotuses.
सरोरुह n. = सरसिरुह.
सरोरुहदृश् & °रुहाक्षी f. = सरोजदृश्.
सरोरुहिणी f. = सरोजिनी.
सरोवर n. a beautiful lake.
सरोष a. angry, n. adv.
सरोषस्मितम् adv. with an angry smile.
सर्ग m. shot (lit. & fig.), jet or gush (of water etc.); letting loose, pouring out; a herd let loose from the stall, i.g. swarm, host, multitude; creation, creature, begetting, offspring, child; origin, nature, character; purpose, resolution; chapter of an epic poem.
सर्गकर्तृ & °कृत् m. creator.
सर्गतक्त & °प्रतक्त a. moving along as if shot off.
सर्गबन्ध m. a literary composition in Sargas i.e. an epic poem.
सर्ज्, सर्जति creak.
†सर्ज m. turner, twister (cf. रज्जुसर्ज); N. of a tree & its resin.
सर्जन n. cession, abandonment; creation.
सर्जरस m. a kind of resin.
सर्णीक n. E. of the water.
सर्तवे & सर्तवै dat. infin. to सृ.
सर्तृ m. courser, horse.

सर्प, f. **ई** crawling, creeping. m. & f. **सर्पी** snake, adder, a serpent-demon.
सर्पण n. crawling, sneaking, slow motion.
सर्पता f., **°त्व** n. abstr. to **सर्प**.
सर्पदष्ट n. the bite of a serpent.
सर्पमुद्रक n. a seal showing a serpent.*
सर्पराज m. serpent-king.
सर्पराज्ञी f. serpent-queen.
सर्परूपिन् a. shaped like a serpent.*
सर्पविद् a. familiar with serpents.
सर्पविद्या f., **°वेद** m. serpent-science.
सर्वविनाश m. destruction of serpents.
सर्पविवर m. n. a serpent's hole.
सर्पसत्त्र n. serpent-sacrifice.
सर्पारि m. a peacock or Garuḍa (enemy of serpents).
सर्पि m. N. of a man.
सर्पिन् a. creeping, gliding.
सर्पिरन्न a. eating ghee.
सर्पिरासुति a. sipping ghee.
सर्पिष्मन्त् & **सर्पिष्वन्त्** a. having ghee or made of ghee.
सर्पिस् n. clarified butter, ghee (= **घृत**).
सर्पी w. **भू** become a serpent.
सर्पेश्वर m. lord of serpents.
सर्म m. flowing.
सर्व a. whole, entire, all; m. sgl. everyone, pl. all (w. **अपि** all together); n. sgl. everything. — With a neg. not every, not every one or everything, no, nothing.
सर्वंसह a. bearing or enduring all; f. **आ** the earth.
1**सर्वकर्मन्** n. pl. work of all kind.
2**सर्वकर्मन्** a. containing all work.
1**सर्वकाम** m. pl. all wishes.
2**सर्वकाम** a. wishing everything, also = **सर्वकामिक**.
सर्वकामदुघ & **°दुह्** a. yielding (lit. milking) all wishes.
सर्वकामिक & **°कामिन्** a. fulfilling all wishes or having all wishes fulfilled.
सर्वकाल (°—) & **सर्वकालम्** adv. at all times, always.
सर्वग & **°गत** a. going everywhere, all-pervading, omnipresent, universal.
1**सर्वगण** m. the full number.
2**सर्वगण** or **सर्वगण** a. having or forming a full number.
1**सर्वगन्ध** m. pl. all kinds of perfumes.
2**सर्वगन्ध** a. containing all perfumes.
सर्वगन्धवह a. conveying all perfumes.
सर्वंकष a. very harsh or cruel (lit. all-grazing or all-injuring).
सर्वचरु m. N. of a man.
सर्वजन m. everyone, anybody.
सर्वजन्मन् a. of all kinds.
सर्वजित् a. all-conquering, all-surpassing.
सर्वज्ञ a. all-knowing, all-wise; abstr. **°ता** f., **°त्व** n.
सर्वज्ञातृ a. = prec.; abstr. **°त्व** n.
सर्वज्ञानमय a. containing all knowledge.
सर्वत a. all-sided.
सर्वतनु or **°तनू** a. complete of body or person.
सर्वतस् adv. from or on all sides; everywhere, wholly, entirely; as prep. *around (acc.).
सर्वता f. wholeness, totality.
सर्वताति f. wholeness, completeness, integrity; loc. **°ताता** on the whole, at all.
सर्वतेजोमय, f. **ई** containing all splendour or power.
सर्वतोदिशम् adv. in or from every direction.
सर्वतोभद्र a. quite pleasant or charming.
सर्वतोमुख, f. **ई** (having the face) turned everywhere; all-sided, complete, perfect.
सर्वतोवृत्त a. omnipresent, ubiquitous.
सर्वत्याग m. complete resignation.
सर्वत्र adv. everywhere, always, by all means; w. neg. in no case, by no means.
सर्वत्रग & **°गत** a. = **सर्वग**.
सर्वत्व n. wholeness, completeness.
सर्वथा adv. in all ways, by all means, at all; entirely, thoroughly.
सर्वद m. all-giving.
सर्वदमन a. all-subduing, m. E. of Bharata.
सर्वदर्शन & **°दर्शिन्** a. all-seeing.
सर्वदा adv. always, for ever.
सर्वदेवतामय, f. **ई** a. containing all deities.
सर्वदेवत्य a. belonging or consecrated to all gods.
सर्वदेवमय, f. **ई** comprising or representing all gods.

सर्वद्रष्टृ m. all-seer.
सर्वधर्ममय a. containing all laws.
सर्वधर्मविद् a. knowing all duties.
सर्वधा a. all-refreshing, all-comforting.
सर्वनर m. every man, anybody.
1सर्वनामन् n. pronoun.
2सर्वनामन् a. having all names.
सर्वनाश m. total destruction or ruin.
सर्वनियन्तृ m. all-subduer, abstr. °त्व n.
सर्वपति & °प्रभु m. lord of the universe.
सर्वप्रायश्चित्त, f. ई expiating or redressing all; n. general expiation or atonement.
सर्वप्रायश्चित्ति f. = prec. n.
सर्वभक्ष & °क्षिन् a. eating all kinds of food; omnivorous.
सर्वभाव m. the whole heart or soul; °— & instr. with all the heart.
सर्वभूत a. being everywhere, ubiquitous; n. pl. all beings.
सर्वभूतकृत् m. the maker of all things or beings.
सर्वभूतगुहाशय a. dwelling in the heart of all beings.
सर्वभूतमय, f. ई containing all beings.
सर्वभूतस्थित a. dwelling in all beings.
सर्वभूतात्मन् & °तान्तरात्मन् m. the (inner) soul of all beings.
सर्वभृत् a. all-sustaining.
सर्वभोग्य a. affording all enjoyments.
सर्वमङ्गल a. all-auspicious; f. आ E. of Durgā and Lakṣmī.
सर्वमनोरम a. charming or delighting all.
सर्वमय, f. ई all-containing, general.
सर्वमांसाद् m. the eater of every flesh.
सर्वमेध m. all-sacrifice (r.).
सर्वयत्न m. all pains or cares; instr. adv.
सर्वयोनि f. the source of all.
1सर्वरस m. fluids or juices of every kind (pl. or —°); every taste or flavour; pl. dainty things of all kind.
2सर्वरस a. containing all fluids etc.
सर्वराज् m. all-king.
सर्वराज्य n. universal sovereignty.
सर्वरात्र s. the whole night.
सर्वरूप or सर्वरूप a. of all colours or shapes.
सर्वर्तुक a. fit for every season.
सर्वलोक m. the universe; all people, every one (also pl. & —°).
सर्वलोकविद् a. knowing all worlds.
सर्ववर्ण a. of all colours.
सर्वविक्रयिन् a. selling all (sorts of things).
सर्ववित् a. all-knowing.
सर्वविद्य a. = prec.; f. आ all knowledge.
सर्ववीर a. with all men or all-heroic.
सर्ववेदस् a. having complete possession.
सर्ववेदस a. who after a sacrifice gives all his property to the priests (also °सिन्), or (a sacrifice) whereat all is given away (also सर्ववेदसदक्षिण); m. (± क्रतु) such a sacrifice. n. the whole property.
सर्वव्यापद् f. complete disappointment or general calamity.
सर्वव्यापिन् a. all-pervading, universal.
1सर्वव्रत n. all-vow.
2सर्वव्रत a. all-vowing.
सर्वशक्ति f. the whole strength; instr. with all strength.
सर्वशरीर n. the all-body (ph.).
सर्वशस् adv. wholly, entirely, altogether; by all means, anyhow; always, everywhere.
सर्वशास a ruling all.
सर्वशीघ्र a. swiftest of all.
सर्वशून्य a. completely empty; abstr. °ता f., °त्व n. complete emptiness, nihilism (ph.).
सर्वश्रेष्ठ a. the best of all.
सर्वश्वेत a. all white.
सर्वसंस्थ a. omnipresent or causing the death of all.
सर्वसंहार & °रिन् a. all-destroying.
सर्वसमता f. sameness towards all, equanimity.
सर्वसह a. all-bearing, patient.
सर्वसाधु adv. very well (exclamation).
सर्वसिद्धार्थ a. having every object attained, quite happy.
सर्वसेन a. leading the whole host.
सर्वस्तेनकृत् m. stealer of all things.
सर्वस्व n. the whole property; the whole substance of anything, entireness, totality.
सर्वहर a. seizing or taking all; m. E. of Yama.
सर्वहरण n., °हार m. abstr. to prec. adj.

सर्वहुत् & सर्वहुत a. what is all (at once) sacrificed.
सर्वहृद् n. the whole heart; instr. °हृदा with all the heart.
1सर्वाङ्ग n. (adj. —° f. ई) the whole body; pl. all limbs or members.
2सर्वाङ्ग, f. ई having all limbs or members; perfect, complete; n. adv.
सर्वाङ्गिक a. relating to or destined for the whole body (ornament).*
सर्वाङ्गीण a. covering or pervading the whole body.
सर्वाजीव a. yielding all subsistence.
1सर्वात्मन् m. the whole person or essence; the universal spirit (ph.), instr. with all the heart, thoroughly, perfectly.
2सर्वात्मन् or सर्वात्मन् a. perfect of person or nature.
सर्वात्मभूति f. the welfare of all beings (personif. as a deity).
सर्वानवद्याङ्ग, f. ई having a faultless body, perfectly beautiful.
सर्वानुक्रम m. a general index (esp. to the Veda).
सर्वानुक्रमणिका & °क्रमणी f. = prec.
सर्वानुभू a. perceiving all.
सर्वाप्ति f. the attainment of all.
सर्वाभाव m. absence of all.
सर्वाभिसंधक a. deceiving all people.
सर्वाभिसार m. general attack.
सर्वायु a. having or giving all life.
सर्वायुष & सर्वायुस् n. the whole life.
1सर्वार्थ m. pl. all things or every kind of thing.
2सर्वार्थ a. fit or useful for all.
सर्वार्थसाधक, f. °धिका effecting all things.
सर्वार्थसिद्ध a. = सर्वसिद्धार्थ.
सर्वावन्त् a. containing all, complete, entire.
सर्वावस्थम् adv. in all positions, on all sides.
सर्वावास & °सिन् a. abiding everywhere.
सर्वाशिन् a. eating all things; abstr. °शित्व n.
सर्वाश्चर्यमय, f. ई containing all wonders.
सर्वाह्ण m. the whole day.
सर्वेश m. the lord of all.
सर्वेश्वर m. the same, abstr. °त्व n.
सर्वोच्छित्ति f., °च्छेदन n. total destruction.
सर्वोपरम m. the ceasing or coming to rest of all; abstr. °त्व n.
सर्वौषध a. consisting of all herbs; n. = seq.
सर्वौषधि f. sgl. pl. all (sorts of) herbs.
सर्षप m. mustard or mustard-seed, also a small weight; °मात्र a. having the measure or weight of a mustard-seed.
सर्षपतैल n., °स्नेह m. mustard-oil.
सलक्षण & सलक्ष्मन् a. having the same marks or characteristics, similar, like.
सलज्ज & °ज्जित a. ashamed, embarrassed; n. adv.
सललितम् adv. playfully.*
†सलवि v. अपसलवि & प्रसलवि.
सलावृकी f. she-wolf or some other beast of prey.
सलिल a. waving, flowing, inconstant; n. flood, stream, water.
सलिलकर्मन् n., °क्रिया f. libation of water.
सलिलगर्गरी f. water-jar.*
सलिलज a. born or produced in water; s. such a being, m. shell.
सलिलद m. presenter of water (an office), or = seq.
सलिलधर m. cloud (water-bearer).
सलिलनिधि m. the ocean (water-receptacle).
सलिलपति m. lord of the water, i.e. Varuṇa.
सलिलसरक s. a mug with water.
सलिलार्णव m. the (water-)sea.
सलिलाशय m. water-receptacle, pond, lake.
सलिलोत्थित a. risen from the ocean.
सलोल a. sporting, playful; n. adv.
सलोक & सलोक्य a. being in the same world with (gen. or instr.).
सलोकता f. abstr. to prec.
सलोप्त्र a. with the theft or booty.*
सलोभ a. covetous, avaricious.
सलोमन् a. running with the hair or grain, congruent (opp. विलोमन्).
सल्लकी v. शल्लकी sub शल्लक.
सल्लोक m. pl. good people.
1सव m. pressing, esp. of Soma.
2सव m. bidder, impeller, impulse, command, enlivening, vivifying, N. of cert. sacrificial rites.
1सवन n. the pressing out or extracting of

the Soma juice, (performed three times a day), the juice itself & its libation, festival or sacrifice i.g., pl. the three day-times i.e. morning, midday & evening (cf. above).
2सवन n. bidding, impelling, setting in motion.
3सवन a. along with the woods.
सवनकर्मन् n. libation.
सवनीय a. belonging to a Soma-libation or to a sacrifice i.g.
सवयस् a. of like strength or age; m. & f. comrade, friend.
सवयस & °यस्क a. of the same age.
सवर्ण a. of the same colour or caste; similar, like, homogeneous (gen. or —°). Abstr. (°ता† f.*), °त्व† n.
सवासस् a. clothed, with the clothes.
सवासिन् a. dwelling together.
सविकल्प & °क a. admitting of difference or variety, differenced.
सविकार a. along with (its) changes.
सविक्लवम् adv. sadly, timidly.
सविज्ञान a. endowed or along with (detailed) knowledge.
सवितृ m. impeller, enlivener, N. of a god, often identif. with Sūrya.
सवितर्क a. thoughtful; n. adv.
सवित्त a. with the property or wealth.
सवित्री f. mother, female producer.
सविद्युत् a. accompanied by lightning (thunder).
सविद्युत n. thunderstorm.
सविध a. of the same kind, near, proximate; n. proximity.
सविधी कृ bring near; °भू come near.
सविनय a. well-bred, modest, polite; n. adv.
सविमर्श a. deliberating, thoughtful; n. adv.
सविलक्षम् adv. bashfully.
सविलक्षस्मितम् adv. with a bashful smile.
सविशेष a. having distinguishing qualities, extraordinary, uncommon; having discrimination, discriminating; °— & n. adv. distinctly, peculiarly.
सविशेषकौतूहलम् adv. in a peculiarly festive or solemn manner.*
सविशेषण a. having peculiar characteristics or attributes; °रूपक n. a kind of metaphor (ph.).
सविश्रम्भ a. confidential (prec. & th.).
सविष a. venomous, poisoned.
सविषाद a. amazed, perplexed; n. adv.
सविस्तर a. diffuse, detailed; n. adv.
सविस्मय a. astonished, surprised; n. adv.
सवीमन् n. impulse, direction (only loc.).
सवीर a. with the followers.
सवीर्य a. having (like) strength.
सवृत्ति a. with a maintenance or salary.*
सवृध् a. increasing; rejoicing together.
सवृषण a. with (the) testicles.
सवेग a. (equally) impetuous or violent; n. adv.
सवेताल a. containing a Vetāla (corpse).
सवेदस् a. having common or like possession.
सवेपथु a. trembling, quaking.
सवेष्टन a. turbaned (head).*
सवैक्लव्यम् adv. with perplexity or depression.
सवैर a. hostile, inimical.
सवैराग्यम् adv. with indifference.
सवैलक्ष्य a. ashamed, abashed, embarrassed; n. adv.
सवैलक्ष्यस्मितम् adv. with a bashful smile.
सव्य a. left (not right); °—, सव्यम्, °व्येन, °व्या, & °व्ये adv. from or on the left. m. the left arm, hand, or foot; n. the sacred thread (worn over the left shoulder).
सव्यतस् adv. from or on the left side.
सव्यथ a. sorrowful, sad.
सव्यपेक्ष a. requiring, presupposing, based upon (—°).
सव्यष्ठृ & °ष्ठा m. the charioteer standing on the left.
सव्यसाचिन् a. clever with the left hand (as well as with the right); m. E. of Arjuna.
सव्याज a. deceitful, false; n. adv.
सव्याधि a. ill, sick.
सव्यापार a. employed, based.
सव्यावृत् & °वृत्त a. turning & turned to the left.
सव्याहृतिप्रणवक a. with the (three sacred) utterances and the syllable Om.
सव्येतर a. right (opposite of left).
सव्येष्ठ m. = सव्यष्ठा.
सव्रण a. wounded, sore.
सव्रत a. harmonious, fitting together.
सव्रीड a. ashamed, bashful; n. adv.

सशङ्क a. afraid, timid; n. adv.
सशत्रु a. having enemies.
सशपथम् adv. with an oath.*
सशब्द a. having or making sound or noise; noisy, loud; n. adv.
सशयन, f. **ई** lying together, neighbouring.
सशर a. furnished with an arrow (bow) or along with the arrow.
सशरचापहस्त a. holding a bow with an arrow in the hand.
सशल्क a. furnished with bark or scales; m. a kind of fish.
सशल्य a. wounded or tormented (by an arrow-point).
सशाद्वल a. covered with grass.
सशिरःकम्पम् adv. shaking the head.
सशिरस् & **°स्क** a. with the head.
सशिष्य a. with the pupils.
सशीर्षन् a. having a head.
सशुच् a. sorrowful, sad.
सशृङ्गार a. decorated, dressed.
सशृङ्गारकम् a. passionately, tenderly.*
सशेष a. having or leaving a rest, not quite emptied or finished.
सशोक a. afflicted, sad; n. adv.
सश्च्, **सश्चति** v. **सच्**; pp. **सश्चत्** pursuer, enemy.
सश्रद्ध a. open-hearted.
सश्रीक a. beautiful, splendid; abstr. **°ता** f., (**°त्व** n.*).
सश्लाघम् adv. boastfully.
सश्लेष a. equivocal, ambiguous.
सश्वास a. breathing.
सष्टुभ् f. a cert. metre.
सस्, **सस्ति**, **संसस्ति** or **ससंस्ति** slumber, be lazy or slothful.
सस s. herb, grass.
ससंरम्भ a. wrathful, angry.
ससंशय a. doubtful, uncertain (subj. & obj.).
ससखीका & **ससखीजना** f. along with the (female) friends.
ससंकेत a. privy to a mystery.
ससचिव a. with the minister.
ससंज्ञ a. conscious, sensible.
ससत्त्व a. courageous, bold; containing living creatures; f. **आ** pregnant.
ससत्विन् or **संसत्विन्** m. companion at a festival.
ससंतान a. with the offspring.
ससंध्य a. along with the morning twilight.
ससंध्यांश a. along with the evening twilight.
ससभ्य a. with the assessor or judges.
ससंभ्रम a. excited, agitated; n. adv.
ससहाय a. along with companions or accomplices.
ससाक्षिक a. having or before witnesses; n. adv.
ससागर a. with the seas (the earth).
ससाध्वस a. frightened, alarmed.
ससाध्वीक a. along with Arundhātī (lit. the good wife).
ससार a. solid, firm.
ससारथि a. with the charioteer.
ससार्थ a. with a caravan.
ससितोत्पलमालिन् a. crowned with white lotus-flowers.
ससीत a. together with Sītā.
ससुगन्ध a. perfumed, sweet-scented.
ससुत a. with the sons or children.
1**ससुर** a. with the gods.
2**ससुर** a. with liquor, intoxicated.
ससुवर्ण a. with gold, dressed in gold.
ससूत a. with the charioteer.
ससैन्य a. with an army.
ससोम a. with Soma; abstr. **°त्व**† n.
ससौरभ a. fragrant.
सस्त्रीक a. along with the wife or having a wife, married.
सस्थूण a. along with the pillar.
सस्नि a. procuring, granting, bestowing; winning, acquiring.
सस्नेह a. oily, greasy; affectionate, tender.
सस्पृह a. desiring, longing for (loc. or infin.); n. adv.
सस्मय a. haughty, arrogant.
सस्मित a. smiling, n. adv.
सस्मेरम् adv. = prec. adv.
सस्य n. standing crop, produce of the field, seed, grain, fruit; poss. **°वन्त्**†.
सस्यक्षेत्र n. field of grain.
सस्यपाल m. watcher of the standing crop.
सस्यपूर्ण a. rich in grain.

सस्यप्रद् a. yielding crops, fertile.
सस्यमालिन् a. = prec. (wreathed with grain).
सस्यरचक m. = सस्यपाल.
†सस्याद् a. eating grain.
सस्यान्ते (loc.) when the grain is at en end.
सस्यावाप m. sowing (seed).
सस्र, सस्रि, सस्रुत्, & सस्रोतस् a. flowing.
सस्वन a. sounding, loud.
सस्वर् adv. secretly; prep. without (abl.).
सस्वर a. sounding like (instr. or —°); loud, n. adv.; accented.
सस्वर्ता adv. = सस्वर्.
सस्वाहाकार a. accompanied by the sound Svāhā.
सस्वेद a. sweating, perspiring.
1सह्, सहते (°ति), pp. साढ & सोढ overpower, win (battles), be victorious; be capable of or able to (infin. or loc.); master, withstand, suppress; bear, suffer, endure. C. साहयति (mostly —°) cause to endure, make supportable*. D. सीक्षते wish to overcome. — अभि overwhelm, subdue; violate (a woman); bear, suffer, pardon. उद् hold out, endure; be able to or capable of (infin , प्रति, loc., or dat.). C. urge on, impel to (loc.). अभ्युद् be a match for (acc.), be able to (infin.), incline to (dat.). प्रोद् C. encourage, excite, impel. समुद् be able to (infin.); C. = prec. C. निस् overpower. प्र vanquish, master, check, restrain; bear, endure; be able to (infin.). संप्र master, restrain, control, bear, suffer. प्रति resist, overcome. वि (षहते) overcome, sustain, withstand, resist, bear, suffer; be able to (infin.). सम् be a match for, withstand, overcome. – Cf. प्रसह्य.
2सह् (साह्) overpowering, bearing, enduring (—°).
1सह adv. together, in common, along with (mostly °— or as prep. w. instr.).
2सह a. powerful; overcoming, vanquishing (—°); bearing, withstanding, enduring, a match for (gen. or —°); capable of, able to (infin. or —°).
सहकर्तृ m. assistant.
सहकार m. assistance, cooperation; a kind of Mango, n. its blossom or juice.
सहकारिता f., °त्व n. abstr. to seq.
सहकारिन् a. working together, assisting; m. coadjutor, assistant.
सहखट्वासन n. sitting together on a bed.
†सहगु a. with cows.
सहगोप a. with the herd.
सहचर a. going or belonging together, similar, like. m. companion, comrade; f. ई wife, mistress.
सहचार m. going together, harmony, agreement.
सहचारित्व n. abstr. to seq.
सहचारिन्, f. °णी = सहचर, ई.
सहज a. born at the same time or together with (gen.); innate, inherent, natural.
सहजन्य m., आ f. N. of a Yakṣa & an Apsaras.
सहजा a. born or produced at the same time.
सहजात a. = prec., innate, inherent.
सहजानि a. with the wife.
सहजीविन् a. living together.
सहजेन्द्र m. N. of a man.
सहता f. bearing, endurance, equality (—°).
1सहत्व n. communion.
2सहत्व n. endurance, allowance (—°).
सहदण्ड a. with the army.
सहदानु a. with the Dānu(s).
सहदार a. with the wife.
सहदेव a. with the gods; m. N. of a Pāṇḍava etc.
सहदेवत a. with the deities.
सहधर्म m. community of duty.
सहधर्मचर, f. ई fulfilling the same duties or laws; f. (such) a wife.
सहधर्मचरण n. abstr. to prec.
सहधर्मचारिन्, f. °णी = सहधर्मचर.
सहन a. overpowering, mighty, strong; n. patient endurance.
सहनिर्वाप m. a common relation.
सहनिवासिता f. dwelling together.
सहनीय a. to be endured or pardoned.
सहन्तम (superl.) overpowering most, mightiest or strongest.
सहन्त्य a. overpowering, mighty, strong.
सहपत्नि & °पत्नीक a. with the wife.

सहंपत्नी a. with the husband.
सहपांसुक्रीडन n. playing together with sand.
सहपान n. compotation.
सहपिण्डक्रिया f. the common offering of the funeral cake.
सहपुत्र a. with the son(s).
सहपुरुष & सहंपूरुष a. with the men.
सहप्रयायिन् & °प्रस्थायिन् a. setting out together.
सहंभक्ष a. enjoying together.
सहभस्मन् a. with the ashes.
सहभाव m. communion, connection.
सहभुज् a. eating together with (—°).
सहभू a. appearing together with (—°); inborn, natural.
सहभोजन n. eating together or in company; common enjoyment of (gen.).
सहभोजिन् m. commensal.
सहंमूर & °मूल a. along with the root.
सहय a. with horses.
सहयज्ञ a. with the sacrifice.
सहंयशस् a. glorious, splendid.
सहयायिन् a. going along with, m. fellow-traveller.
सहयुज् a. yoked or harnessed together.
सहर्ष a. joyful, merry, n. adv.
सहंर्षभ a. with the bull.
सहर्षसाध्वसम् adv. cheerfully and timidly.
सहर्षाकूतम् adv. cheerfully and emphatically.
सहंवत्स a. with the calf.
सहवसति f. dwelling together.
सहवह् (वाह्) a. drawing together (horses).
सहवास m. = सहवसति; a. °वासिन्.
सहवाहन a. with the team, carriage etc.
सहंवीर a. with men.
सहव्रत a. having the same vows or duties; f. आ = सहधर्मचरी.
सहशय्या f., °शेय्य n. lying together.
संहस् a. powerful, victorious. n. power, might, victory; instr. sgl. & pl. strongly, violently, suddenly, at once.
सहसान a. powerful, mighty.
†सहसावन् & †सहसिन् a. = prec. (only voc.).
सहस्कृत् a. giving power or strength.
संहस्कृत a. strenghtened, excited.

सहस्त a. having hands; °तालम् adv. clapping the hands.
सहस्थ & °स्थित a. standing by, present; m. companion.
सहस्व a. strong, mighty.
सहंस्र n. (m.) a thousand (used also for any very large number).
1सहस्रक n. = prec.; adj. (—° f. °स्रिका) being or amounting to a thousand.
2सहस्रक a. thousand-headed.
सहस्रकर m. the sun (thousand-rayed).
सहस्रकिरण m. = prec.
सहस्रकृत्वस् adv. a thousand times.
सहस्रगु a. possessing a thousand cows; also = सहस्रकर.
सहस्रगुण & °गुणित a thousandfold.
सहंस्रचक्षस् a. thousand-eyed.
†सहस्रचक्षु & °चक्षुस् a. = prec.
सहस्रचरण a. thousand-footed (Viṣṇu).
सहस्रजित् a. vanquishing or conquering a thousand.
सहस्रणी m. chief of a thousand (or thousands).
सहंस्रणीति a. having a thousand ways.
सहंस्रणीथ a. knowing a thousand songs or = prec.
सहस्रतमं, f. ई the thousandth.
सहस्रद a. giving a thousand (cows).
सहंस्रदक्षिण a. (a sacrificer) giving or (a sacrifice) whereat are given a thousand (cows) as a fee.
सहस्रदा a. = सहस्रद.
सहंस्रदान & °दावन् a. giving a thousand (gifts).
सहस्रदीधिति m. = सहस्रकर.
सहस्रदृश् a. thousand-eyed (Indra).
सहंस्रद्वार & °द्वार† a. thousand-gated.
सहस्रधा adv. in a thousand ways or parts.
संहस्रधामन् a. having thousandfold might or splendour; m. the sun.
सहस्रधायस् a. nourishing or supporting thousands.
सहंस्रधार a. flowing in a thousand streams.
सहस्रनयन a. thousand-eyed; m. E. of Indra.
सहंस्रनामन्, f. °नाम्नी thousand-named.
सहंस्रनिर्णिज् a. having a thousand ornaments.
सहस्रनेत्र a. = सहस्रनयन.

सहस्रपति m. the chief of a thousand (villages).
सहस्रपद् (°पाद्) a. thousand-footed; m. N. of a Rishi.
सहस्रपर्ण, f. ई having a thousand leaves or feathers.
सहस्रपृष्ठ a. thousand-backed.
1सहस्रपोष m., °पोषा f., °पोष्य n. thousandfold prosperity.
2सहस्रपोष & °षिन् poss. to prec.
सहस्रबाहु a. having a thousand arms.
सहस्रभर a. conquering a thousand.
सहस्रभर्णस् a. thousandfold.
सहस्रभृष्टि a. thousand-edged.
सहस्रमुष्क a. having a thousand testicles.
सहस्रमूति a. helping in a thousand ways.
सहस्रमूर्धन् a. thousand-headed.
सहस्रंभर a. bringing a thousand.
सहस्रयज्ञ m. a sacrifice of a thousand (animals).
सहस्ररश्मि m. = सहस्रकर.
सहस्ररेतस् a. containing thousandfold seed.
सहस्रलोचन a. = सहस्रनयन.
सहस्रवक्त्र a. thousand-mouthed.
सहस्रवन्त् a. thousandfold.
सहस्रवर्चस् a. of infinite splendour.
सहस्रवल्शि & °वल्श a. thousand-branched.
सहस्रवाज a. having a thousand forces.
सहस्रवीर a. sufficient for a thousand men.
सहस्रवीर्य a. having a thousand forces.
सहस्रशतदक्षिण a. whereat a hundred thousand (cows) are given as a fee (sacrifice).
सहस्रशस् adv. by thousands.
सहस्रशिरस् & °शिरस a. thousand-headed.
सहस्रशीर्ष & सहस्रशीर्षन् a. = prec.
सहस्रशृङ्ग a. thousand-horned.
सहस्रशोकस् a. sparkling with a thousand flames.
सहस्रसंख्य a. amounting to a thousand.
सहस्रसनि & °सा a. winning or bestowing a thousand.
सहस्रसाव m. a thousandfold pressing (of Soma).
सहस्रहन् a. slaying a thousand.
†सहस्रहस्त a. thousand-handed.
सहस्रांशु m. = सहस्रकर.
सहस्राक्ष a. & m. = सहस्रनयन.

सहस्राधिपति m. the chief of a thousand (men or villages).
सहस्रामघ a. having a thousand treasures or gifts.
सहस्रायु a. living a thousand years.
सहस्रायुस् m. = prec.; m. N. of a man.
सहस्रार्घ & सहस्रार्घ a. worth a thousand.
सहस्रार्चिस् m. = सहस्रकर.
सहस्रार्ह a. = सहस्रार्घ.
सहस्राह s. a thousand days.
सहस्राह्न्य n. a thousand journeys.
सहस्रिन् a. thousandfold; winning, bestowing, containing etc. a thousand.
सहस्रिय & °स्रीय a. (giving) thousandfold.
सहस्रोति a. = सहस्रमूति.
सहस्वन्त् a. powerful, mighty; n. adv.
सहाध्ययन n. fellowship in study.
सहाध्यायिन् m. fellow-student.
सहाय m. companion, comrade, attendant; adj. —° accompanied or supported by.
सहायता f., °त्व n. abstr. to prec.
सहायन n. going along with, company.
सहायवन्त् a. having a companion or attendant; accompanied or attended by, furnished with (—°).
सहायार्थम् a. to be companion(s).
सहायिन् m. = सहाय; f. °नी female companion or friend.
सहावन् a. overpowering, strong.
सहावन्त् or सहावन्त् a. the same.
सहास a. laughing or smiling; n. adv.
सहासन n., सहास्था f. sitting together.
सहित a. united, joined (pl. ± सर्वे all); accompanied by, endowed or furnished with (instr. or —°); n. adv. together.
सहितव्य a. to be borne or endured.
सहिरण्य a. (furnished) with gold.
†सहिष्ठ (superl.) mightiest.
सहिष्णु a. bearing, enduring (acc., gen., or —°); patient, forbearing.
सहीयंस् (compar.) mightier, superior; most mighty or strong.
सहुरि a. powerful, superior, victorious.
सहूति f. common invocation.
संहृदय a. with the heart; hearty, affectionate.

सहेतु & **°क** a. having a cause, reason, or motive.
सहेन्द्र a. along with Indra.
सहेल a. playful, careless; n. adv.
सहोक्ति f. talking together or at the same time; a kind of comparison (rh.).
सहोजा a. produced by power, strong.
सहोजित् a. victorious by power.
1**सहोढ** a. having stolen goods.
2**सहोढ** a. married at the same time; born of a woman pregnant at marriage.
सहोत्थायिन् a. rising together, fellow-insurgent.
सहोदर, f. **आ** & **ई** born from the same womb; a brother or sister of whole blood.
सहोदा a. bestowing strength.
सहोभरि a. nourishing strength.
सहोवन् a. powerful, mighty.
सहोवृध् a. enjoying power.
सहोषित a. who has lived with another.
सहौजस् a. endowed with power or strength.
†**सह्य** a. to be borne or endured, tolerable, resistible (abstr. **°ता** f.); N. of a mountain.
सह्यवासिन् a. inhabiting the mountain Sahya; f. **°नी** E. of Durgā.*
सह्यंस = **संहीयंस्**.
सह्यकर्मन् n. assistance, help.
सह्यु & **सह्वन्** a. powerful, mighty.
1**सा** v. **सन्**.
2**सा** or **सि**, **स्यति**, **°ते** (only —°), **सिनाति** (**सिनोति**), pp. **सित** (q.v.) bind. C. **साययति** (only —°). — **अभि** fetter, destroy. **अव** unbind or unharness (the horses), turn in, stop, stay; go home or to rest; cease, finish, end; fix or insist upon (acc.); decide, ascertain. **अध्यव** cease, stop, finish; fix upon (acc.), choose; resolve, venture, undertake (acc., loc., or infin.); suppose, conjecture; regard as, take for (2 acc.). C. settle, determine. **अन्वव** stick or resort to, strive after, long for (acc.). **उदव** set out (esp. from the place of sacrifice), conclude, finish; move off to (loc.). **उपाव** settle down near (acc.). **निरव** C. furnish or satisfy with (instr.). **पर्यव** result, amount to or end in (loc. or acc. w. **प्रति**). **व्यव** dwell separately; be at variance, differ; be persuaded or convinced of (acc.), regard as, take for (2 acc.); decide, determine; settle, ascertain, resolve upon, undertake to (acc., dat., or infin.). **समव** decide for, fix upon (acc.). **उद्** fetter, catch. **वि** make loose, untie, unyoke, open, set free. — Cf. **अतिषित** (add.), **अध्यवसित**, **अवसित**, **उत्सित**, **पर्यवसित**, 1**प्रसित**, **व्यवसित**.
सांयुग, f. **ई** relating to war or battle; w. **भु** f. field of battle.
सांयुगीन a. warlike, valiant.
सांराविण n. general shout or cry.
सांवत्सर (f. **ई**) & **°रिक** a year old, lasting a year, yearly, annual; m. astrologer.
सांविद्य n. agreement.
सांशंसिक a. being recited together.
सांशयिक, f. **ई** doubtful, uncertain.
सांसारिक a. worldly, mundane.
सांस्पर्शक n. contact.
सांहत्य n. union, connection.
साकंयुज् a. joined together, united.
साकंवृत् a. rolling together (wheels).
साकंवृध् a. growing together.
साकंजं a. born together.
साकम् adv. with each other, at once, together, along with (instr.).
साकमुच् a. sprinkling or splashing together.
साकल्य n. wholeness, totality.
साकाङ्क्ष a. having a wish or desire; incomplete, correlative (g.).
साकूत a. intentional, significant; n. adv.
साकेत n. E. of the city Ayodhyā; m. pl. its inhabitants.
साक्षत a. filled with unhusked grain.
साक्षर a. having i.e. marked with letters (ring); eloquent, abstr. **°ता** f.
साक्षात् adv. with or before the eyes, i.e. plainly, actually, exactly, immediately, directly, in person. With **भू** appear in person; w. **कृ** take a view of, put before the eyes, witness, notice, call to mind.
साक्षात्कार m. abstr. to prec. w. **कृ**.
साक्षात्कृति & **°क्रिया** f. the same.

साक्षिक (adj. —°) = साक्षिन्; n. before, coram (—°).
साक्षिता f., °त्व n. abstr. to seq.
साक्षिन् m. on-looker, observer, eye-witness, witness i.g.
साक्षिप्रश्न m. examination of witnesses (j.).
साक्षिमन्त् a. having a witness.
साक्षी कृ call to witness.
साक्षेप a. containing an objection or limitation, reproachful, ironical, n. adv.
साक्ष्य a. visible for (—°); n. the being witness, testimony, evidence.
साख्य n. association, party; friendship, affection.
1सागर m. the ocean (said to have been dug by Sagara's sons); pl. Sagara's sons.
2सागर, f. ई relating to the sea, maritime.
सागरक m. pl. N. of a people; f. °रिका a woman's name.
सागरग a. flowing to the sea; f. आ such a river (also °गमा f.).
सागरगामिन् a. = prec. a.
सागरदत्त m. a man's name.
सागरपर्यन्त a. bounded by the sea (earth).
सागरमेखल a. sea-girt (the earth).
सागरवासिन् a. dwelling on the sea-shore.
सागरशुक्ति f. sea-shell.
1सागरान्त m. sea-coast.
2सागरान्त a. reaching to the sea (earth).
सागराम्बर a. ocean-clothed; f. आ the earth.
सागरिकामय a. consisting or full of Sāgarikās.*
सागस् a. guilty of a crime.
साग्नि a. with the fire.
साग्निक a. having Agni with them, accompanied by Agni (gods).
सांग्र a. with the point.
सांकाश्य m. N. of a man, f. आ & n. of a town.
सांकृत्य m. a patron. name.
सांख्य a. relating to the number (g.); n. N. of a philosophical system, m. an adherent of it.
सांख्यकारिका f., °प्रवचन n. titles of works.
सांख्याचार्य m. E. of Viṣṇu.
सांख्ययोग m. an adherent of the Sāṁkhya and Yoga systems; n. the S. and Y.
सांख्यायन m. N. of a teacher, pl. his pupils.
साङ्ग or सांङ्ग a. having limbs or a body; with all parts or supplements (Veda); complete, finished.
सांगतिक m. an old acquaintance (concr.).
साङ्गुष्ठ a. with the thumb.
सांग्रामजित्य n. victory in war.
सांग्रामिक, f. ई relating to war, martial; n. booty.
1साचि a. crooked, oblique; °— adv.
2साचि a. following, accompanying.
साचिव्य n. companionship, attendance; the office of a counsellor or minister.
साची कृ bend or turn aside.
साच्य a. to be assisted or befriended.
सांजात्य n. community of class or tribe with (gen.); equality, likeness.
साञ्जलि a. suppliant, humble (cf. अञ्जलि).
सांजीवीपुत्र m. N. of a teacher.
साटोप a. thundering, growling (cloud); self-conceited, arrogant, n. adv.
साढृ m. conqueror.
साण्ड a. having testicles, potent.
सात a. gained, acquired; m. N. of a Yaksha.
सातत्य n. continuity, uninterruptedness.
सातवाह & °न m. N. of a king.
साति f. gain, acquisition, wealth, property; winning the prize, making booty.
सातिरेक a. excessive, intensive.
सातिशय a. excellent, best, better.
सांतु m. receptacle.
सात्त्विक, f. ई relating to or endowed with the quality of goodness (ph.); courageous, energetic, virtuous, brave.
सात्मता f. unity of essence with (gen., instr., or —°).
सात्मत्व n. abstr. to seq.
सात्मन् a. having a soul or with the soul.
सात्म्य n. = सात्मता.
सात्य a. whose nature is truth.
सात्यकि m. patron. of Yuyudhāna.
1सात्वत m. a prince of the Satvant, E. of Kṛṣṇa etc., N. of a mixed tribe.

2सात्वत, f. ई relating to the Satvant or Sātvata (Kṛṣṇa); m. a follower of Kṛṣṇa.

साद m. sitting on horseback, riding; sinking down, exhaustion, despondency, despair; loss, disappearance.

सादन a. causing to sink, wearying, exhausting; n. placing down, sinking; seat, place, home; dish.

सादन्य a. domestic.

सादयितव्य a. to be destroyed.

सादर a. having or paying respect, considerate, careful; devoted to or intent upon (—°); n. adv.

सादि & सादिन् m. rider (lit. sitter).

सादृश्य n. likeness, similarity.

साद्भुत a. surprised, wondering.

साद्य a. fit for riding; m. riding-horse.

1साध्, साधति, °ते come or lead straight (to the aim); succeed, be accomplished, give way, obey; direct, put in order, effect, accomplish, finish. C. साधयति, °ते = S. tr.; also get, procure, acquire, recover (a debt), win, subdue; pay (taxes); make, render (2 acc.); set out, go away. — उप C. subdue, conquer; prepare (food). परि = prec.; obtain, recover (money). प्र C. put in order, arrange, adorn, perform, accomplish, make one's own, acquire, win; find out, prove, demonstrate. सम् subdue, conquer, make one's own, win, acquire, get, obtain, procure, perform, accomplish, prepare (food); recover (money), dismiss (a guest).

2साध् v. यज्ञसाध्.

साध m. performance, accomplishment.

साधक, f. °धिका accomplishing, effecting (gen. or —°); helping, useful; m. assistant, worshipper, sorcerer.

साधदिष्टि a. whose sacrifice or prayer has effect.

साधन, f. ई & आ leading to the aim, effecting, producing, procuring (gen. or —°); effective, capable. – n. subduing, mastering, accomplishing, effecting; getting, acquiring, recovering (debts); proving, evincing, argument, evidence; means, expedient, requisite; military force; result, consequence. Abstr. °ता† f., °त्व† n.

साधनक्षम a. provable, demonstrable.

साधनाध्यक्ष m. inspector of the military force.

साधनीय a. to be accomplished, acquired, or proved; abstr. °त्व n.

साधर्म्य n. similarity, likeness.

साधान a. with the receptacle.

साधारण, f. ई & आ common to or with (gen., dat., instr. ± सह, or —°); general, universal; equal, like, similar (instr. or —°). n. community, common cause. — Abstr. °ता† f., °त्व† n.

साधारण्य n. universality, community (instr. ण्या adv. commonly, together); similarity, analogy.

साधिक a. with a surplus, —and more.

साधिदैवत a. having a tutelary deity in (instr.).

साधिन् a. accomplishing, performing (—°).

साधिष्ठ & साधीयंस् superl. & compar. to seq.

साधु, f. साध्वी straight, right, good, excellent, virtuous. — m. a good or honest man; f. साध्वी a. faithful or excellent wife; n. the good or right, as adv. well, right; bravo!

साधुकर्मन् a. acting well or properly.

साधुकारिन् & °कृत् a. = prec., skilful, clever.

साधुकृत्य n. compensation, advantage; f. आ good or proper way of acting.

साधुजन m. a good man (or woman*).

साधुतस् adv. from good people.

साधुता f., °त्व n., °भाव m. abstr. to साधु.

साधुया adv. straight, directly, regularly, well.

साधुवाद m. right expression, good renown, also = साधुशब्द.

साधुवादिन् a. speaking right or applauding.

साधुवाहिन् a. well drawing (a waggon).

साधुवृत्त a. beautifully round (arm) or well-conducted; n. good conduct.

साधुशब्द m. cry of good or bravo.

साधुशील a. having a good character; abstr. °त्व n.

साधुसंस्कृत a. well arranged or prepared.

साध्य a. to be subdued, mastered, or won; to be (being) contrived or managed; to be accomplished or fulfilled, proved or demonstrated; conquerable, practicable,

feasible, curable, attainable. m. pl. a class of deities. — Abstr. °ता† f., °त्व† n.
साध्यवन्त् a. containing what is to be proved.
साध्यवसाना & °सानिका f. a kind of elliptical expression (rh.).
साध्या adv. = साधुया.
साध्वर्य a. faithfully devoted.
साध्वस n. perplexity, perturbation, fear, terror, timidity, shyness.
साध्वसाधु a. good and (or) bad.
साध्वसाराधन n. a timid beginning.
साध्वाचार m. the conduct of the good or good conduct.
साध्वाचार a. well-conducted, virtuous.
साध्वीक (adj. —°) = साध्वी, v. साधु.
सानग m. N. of a Rishi.
सानन्द a. glad, happy, delighted with (—°); °— & n. adv.
सानसि a. lucrative or victorious.
सानाथ्य n. assistance, help.
सानु m. n. top, surface, ridge, back.
सानुक a. greedy for booty.
सानुकम्प a. compassionate; n. adv.
सानुकूल्य n. favour, help, aid.
सानुक्रोश a. compassionate; n. adv.
सानुग & सानुचर (f. ई) with attendants or followers.
सानुताप a. full of repentance.
सानुनय a. courteous, kind.
सानुप्रास a. containing alliteration.
सानुबन्ध a. having consequences; continual, uninterrupted.
सानुमन्त् a. poss. to सानु; m. mountain, f. °मती N. of an Apsaras.
सानुयात्र a. with a retinue.
सानुराग a. passionate, enamoured.
सानुशय a. regretful; n. adv.
सानुशयविघटित a. regretful and dispirited.
सांतपन a. warming, warm; m. n. (± कृच्छ्र) a kind of penance.
सान्तराल a. with the mixed castes.
सान्तर्दीप a. having a light in the interior.
सान्तर्हास a. with an inward laugh; n. adv.
सांतानिक, f. ई desirous of offspring.
सान्त्व n. sgl. & pl. kind or comforting words.
सान्त्वन n., °ना f. appeasing by kind words.
सान्त्वपूर्व a. appeasing, propitiating (speech); n. adv.
सान्त्वय्, °यति & °यते appease, pacify, comfort, conciliate. — अभि, उप, & परि = S.
सान्द्र a. thick, dense, violent, intense, soft, bland; crowded with, full of (instr. or —°).
सान्द्रस्पर्श a. soft to the touch.
सांध्य a. relating to conjunction or combination; relating to the evening twilight, vespertine.
सांनाय्य n. an oblation consisting of sweet and sour milk.
सांनाहिक a. calling to arms (drum) or = seq.
सांनाह्नक a. able to bear arms.
सांनिध्य n. proximity, presence.
सान्वय a. with family or descendants; belonging to the same family, related or of kin.
सापत्न a. coming from a rival or = सापत्य.
सापत्नक n. rivalry, esp. among the wives of the same man; enmity, hatred i.g.
सापत्य a. sprung from rivalry; born from a rival wife.
सापराध a. guilty or faulty.
सापवाद a. reproachful; n. adv.
सापिण्ड्य n. connection by (offering) the funeral cake, consanguinity.
सापेक्ष a. having regard or respect for (loc. or acc. w. प्रति); requiring, presupposing, dependent on (—°).
साप्त or साप्त n. the number seven.
साप्तपद a. belonging to the seven steps (cf. सप्तपद); true, sincere.
साप्तपदीन a. = prec.; n. friendship.
साप्तपुरुष & °पौरुष (f. ई) extending over seven generations.
साफल्य n. fruitfulness, profit, success.
साबाध a. distressed, unwell, sick.
साभिकाम a. loving, affectionate.
साभिज्ञान a. with a token of recognition; n. adv.
साभिप्राय a. having or showing a certain intention; determined, resolute.
साभिमान a. full of pride or arrogance.
साभिलाष a. full of desire; eager, greedy for (loc., acc. w. प्रति, or —°).
साभ्र a. cloudy.

साम n. equality.
सामक n. the original debt.
सामगं or **०गा** m. chanter of the Sāmaveda.
सामगान m. = prec., n. chant of the S.
सामगाय m., **०गीत** n. = prec. n.
सामग्री f., **०ग्र्य** n. totality, completeness.
सामतस् adv. concerning the Sāmans.
सामदण्ड m. du. conciliation and force.
सामध्वनि m. the sound of the chanting (of the Sāmaveda).
1**सामन्** n. acquisition, property, wealth.
2**सामन्** n. song, esp. sacred song, a Vedic stanza arranged for chanting; pl. the Sāmaveda.
3**सामन्** n. consolation, conciliation, mild speech, kindness.
सामन्त a. being all around, surrounding, neighbouring. m. neighbour, vassal; n. neighbourhood.
सामन्तवासिन् a. dwelling near, neighbouring.
साममय a. consisting of Sāmans.
सामयाचारिक a. relating to conventional or right practice or conduct.
सामयिक a. conventional.
सामर्थ्य n. adequacy, fitness, sufficient cause for or just claim on (loc. or —°); strength, power, efficacy, ability (infin., dat., loc., or —°); the meaning or function of a word. Abl. **०योगात्** according to circumstances, by reason or on account of (—°).
सामर्थ्यवन्त् a. able, capable.
सामर्थ्यहीन a. powerless, weak.
सामर्ष a. impatient, angry; n. adv.
सामवाद m. pl. kind words.
सामविद् a. knowing the Sāmaveda.
सामविप्र a. skilled in sacred songs.
सामवेद m. the Sāmaveda (cf. 2**सामन्**).
सामश्रवस् m. N. of a man.
सामाजिक m. assistant at an assembly, spectator.
सामात्य a. along with the relatives or ministers.
सामानाधिकरण्य n. grammatical congruency, coordination.
सामान्य a. like, similar, common to or with (instr. ± **सह** or —°); ordinary, vulgar; general, universal. n. equality, congruence, right proportion, normal condition, totality, universality. °—, instr., & abl. in general, generally, **सामान्यम्** adv. in common, together; in the manner of, like (—°).
सामासिक, f. **ई** relating to a compound word; concise, succinct, brief. m. n. a compound word.
सामि adv. incompletely, prematurely, partly, half.
सामिधेन a. relating to fuel and kindling; f. **ई** such a verse (r.).
सामिष a. with flesh.
सामीप्य a. neighbouring, m. neighbour, n. neighbourhood, nearness (in sp. & t.).
सामुद्र a. oceanic, marine; m. mariner, sailor, pl. N. of a people; n. sea-salt.
सामुद्रक (a. = prec. a.*); f. **०द्रिका** a kind of leech; n. sea-salt.
सामुद्रिक a. sea-faring; m. sea-farer.
सामृद्ध्य n. thriving, success.
सांपराय m. transmigration from this world into another; pain, distress; war, fight.
सांपरायिक, f. **ई** & **आ** relating to the other world, future; useful in the time of need; relating to war, martial.
सांप्रत a. seasonable, fit; existing, present; n. adv. now, presently.
सांप्रदायिक a. based on tradition, traditional.
साम्ब m. N. of a son of Kṛṣṇa.
सांबन्धिक n. relation by marriage.
सांमनस्य n. sameness of opinion, agreement.
सांमुख्य n. being in front or turned towards; inclination or affection for (—°).
सांमेघ्य n. the cloudy season.
साम्य n. equality, resemblance or likeness to (instr. ± **सह**, gen., loc., or —°); right or normal condition; equanimity, impartiality, justice.
साम्यता f. likeness, equality.
1**साम्राज्य** n. universal sovereignty.
2**साम्राज्य** m. universal sovereign.
साय n. turning in, going to rest; evening, **सायम्** adv. in the evening.
सायक a. suitable for hurling; m. n. missile, arrow.
सायंकाल m. evening, eventide.

सायंकालिक & **°कालीन** a. belonging to evening, vespertine.
सायण m. N. of a celebrated scholar.
सायणमाधव & **सायणाचार्य** m. the same.
सायन्तन, f. **ई** vespertine.
सायंदुग्ध a. milked in the evening.
सायंदोह m. the milking in the evening.
सायमशन n., **सायमाश** m. evening-meal, supper.
सायमाहुति f. evening-oblation.
सायंप्रातर् adv. in the evening and in the morning.
सायंप्रातर्होम m. du. morning and evening oblation.
सायास a. painful, troublesome.
सायाहन् n. (only **°हनि**) & **सायाह्न** m. evening.
सायुज्य n. community, intimate union with or absorption into (gen., loc., instr., or —°). Abstr. **°ता†** f., **°त्व†** n.
सायुध a. having weapons, armed.
1**सार** a. driving away, removing; m. course, way (only —°).
2**सार** m. n. the interior firm parts of a body; firmness, solidity, strength; property, wealth; substance or essence of anything; nectar; water.
सारघ a. coming from a bee; m. bee; n. honey.
सारङ्ग or **सारङ्ग**, f. **सारङ्गी** dappled; relating to the dappled antelope. m. a kind of antelope, sev. birds, a bee.
सारङ्गलोचना f. deer-eyed.
सारङ्गाक्षी f. the same.
सारण n. causing to go, dismissing.
सारणि f. small river, channel.
सारणिक m. traveller, merchant.
सारतस् adv. according to the value.
सारता f., **°त्व** n. firmness, solidity; value, worth; highest degree.
सारथि m. charioteer; abstr. **°त्व†** n.
सारथिद्वितीय a. accompanied by the charioteer.
सारथ्य n. the office of a charioteer.
सारफल्गु a. strong or weak, good or bad; abstr. **°ता** f., **°त्व** n.
सारभाण्ड n. jewel, treasure.
सारभाण्डगृहक s. treasury.
सारभूत a. & n. (being) the best or the chief matter.
सारमेय m. dog (son of Saramā); f. **ई** bitch.
सारल्य n. straightness, rectitude, honesty.
सारवत्ता f. firmness, hardness, solidity.
सारवन्त् a. firm, strong; valuable, precious.
सारस, f. **ई** relating to a pond or lake. m. a cert. aquatic bird (f. **ई**), a man's name.
सारसन n. girdle.
सारस्वत, f. **ई** coming from or relating to Sarasvatī; n. eloquence.
सारासार n. strongness or weakness, worth and worthlessness.
सारिक m., **आ** f. a kind of crow.
सारिन् a. hastening; following (—°).
सारिसृक्क, **°सृक्त**, & **°सृक्व** m. names of men.
सारूप्य n. likeness, resemblance.
सार्चि & **सार्चिस्** a. flaming, burning.
सार्थ a. having a commission or business, having a meaning or signification; successful, important, rich. — m. company of traders, caravan; troop, band, host, multitude i.g.
सार्थक a. useful, advantageous; having a sense or meaning, abstr. **°ता** f., **°त्व** n.
सार्थज a. born or reared in a caravan, tame (elephant).
सार्थपति m. chief or leader of a caravan.
सार्थपाल & **°वाह** m. the same.
सार्थिक a. travelling (with a caravan), accompanying (gen.); merchant, trader.
सार्द्र a. wet, moist, damp.
सार्ध a. with a half; n. **सार्धम्** adv. together, along with (instr. or —°).
सार्प a. relating to serpents; n. E. of a lunar mansion.
सार्व a. useful to all.
सार्वकामिक, f. **ई** granting all wishes.
सार्वकाल & **°कालिक** a. of all times.
सार्वधातुक a. applicable to the whole or complete form of the base (g.).
सार्वभौतिक a. including all beings.
सार्वभौम a. spread or ruling over the whole earth.
सार्वलौकिक a. spread all over the world.

सार्ववर्णिक a. relating to every caste or tribe.
सार्ववेदस v. **सर्ववेदस**.
सार्ष्ट a. of equal rank or value.
सार्ष्टि a. = prec., abstr. **°ता** f.
†**साल** m. = 1**शाल** (& f. **आ**).
सालक a. having curled hair.
सालकानन n. Sāla-wood & a face with curled hair.
सालक्तक a. dyed with lac.
सालस a. languid, lazy.
सालावृक m. a wolf or some other beast of prey.
सालोक्य n. the being in the same world with (gen., instr. w. **सह**, & —°); abstr. **°ता** f.
साव m. libation of Soma.
सावचारण a. with the application.
सावज्ञ a. disdainful, contemptuous; n. adv.
सावद्य a. faulty, defective.
सावधान a. attentive, careful, n. adv.; abstr. **°ता** f.
सावधि a. limited.
सावमान a. contemptible.
सावयव a. composed of parts, abstr. **°त्व** n.
सावरण a. locked up, concealed, secret.
सावलेप a. haughty, arrogant.
सावशेष a. having a remainder, unfinished, left, remaining; n. remainder, rest.
सावष्टम्भ a. full of self-confidence, resolute; n. adv.
साविक a. relating to the pressing of Soma.
सावित्र, f. **ई** descended from, belonging or consecrated to Savitṛ; f. **°त्री** (± **ऋच्**) a cert. verse to Savitṛ.
सावित्रीपतित & **सावित्रीपरिभ्रष्ट** a. = **पतित-सावित्रीक** (q.v.).
†**साविन्** a. preparing Soma (—°).
सावेगम् adv. with haste or agitation.
सावेश्य n. neighbourhood.
साशंसम् adv. with the expression of desire or hope.
साशङ्क a. afraid, suspicious.
साश्चर्य a. astonished, wondering, n. adv.; wonderful, marvellous.
साश्रु a. tearful, weeping; n. adv.
साश्रुलोचन a. with weeping eyes.
साष्टाङ्ग a. made with eight members (bow); reverential. n. & **°पातम्** adv. (lit. by falling down with eight members) reverentially, humbly.
सासहि a. victorious, conquering (acc.); able to bear (—°).
सासु a. living, alive.
सासूय a impatient, angry; n. adv.
†**सास्ना** f. dewlap.
सास्र a. = **साश्रु**.
साह a. powerful; overwhelming, resisting (—°).
साहंकार a. full of egoism, selfish.
साहचर्य n. being or standing together, being joined or united with (instr. or —°).
साहन्त्य a. = **संहन्त्य**.
साहस a. rash, inconsiderate. m. n. punishment, fine; n. violence, rashness, temerity.
साहसकरण n. a violent act.
साहसकर्मता f. committing rash or violent acts; rashness, temerity.*
साहसकारिन् a. acting violently or inconsiderately.
साहसिक, f. **ई** bold, rash, violent.
साहसोपन्यासिन् a. suggesting violent deeds.*
साहस्र, f. **ई** & **आ** amounting to or consisting of a thousand; n. a thousand.
साहस्रक, f. **°स्रिका** containing a thousand; n. a thousand.
साहस्रवन्त् a. = prec. adj.
साहस्रशस् adv. in a thousand ways.
साहस्रिक a. consisting of a thousand, the thousandth.
साहायक n. assistance, help.
साहाय्य & **°क** n. the same.
साहित्य n. conjunction, association; literary composition, poetry.
साहित्यदर्पण m. mirror of composition, T. of a work.
साह्न a. of a day's length or duration.
साह्य n. assistance, help.
साह्लाद a. cheerful, merry; n. adv.
साह्व (—°) called.
1**सि** v. 2**सा**.
2**सि** hurl, only pp. **प्रसित** (q.v.).
सिंह m. lion (f. **ई**); best or bravest among (—°); king, ruler (°— or —°). Abstr. **°ता**† f., **°त्व**† n.

सिंहग्रीव a. lion-necked.
सिंहचर्मन् n. a lion's hide.
सिंहतुण्ड m. a kind of fish.
सिंहदंष्ट्र a. lion-tusked; m. a kind of arrows.
सिंहदत्त m. N. of an Asura & a poet.
सिंहदेव m. N. of a prince.
सिंहद्वार् f., °द्वार n. palace-gate.
सिंहध्वनि & °नाद m. a lion's roar, war-cry.
सिंहपराक्रम m. N. of a man.
सिंहपुर n. N. of a town.
सिंहप्रणाद & °रव m. = सिंहध्वनि.
सिंहप्रतीक a. lion-faced.
सिंहर्षभ m. a noble lion.
सिंहल m. pl. the people of Ceylon; sgl. the island itself.
सिंहवर्मन् m. a man's name.
सिंहशाव & °शिशु m. a lion's whelp.
सिंहसंहनन a. lion-shaped, strong.
सिंहस्कन्ध a. lion-shouldered.
सिंहाय्, °यते be or act like a lion.
सिंहासन n. lion-seat i.e. throne.
सिंहिका f. N. of a daughter of Dakṣa & a Rākṣasī.
सिंही कृ change into a lion; °भू P.
सिकता f. sand, gravel, p. °वन्त्.
सिकतिल & सिकत्य a. sandy.
सिक्ति f. sprinkling, effusion.
सिक्थ m. n. boiled rice; n. wax.
1सिच्, सिञ्चति, °ते, pp. सिक्त pour out, sprinkle, scatter (also semen); pour in or upon (loc.), besprinkle with (instr.); cast (molten metal), form into (2 acc.). C. सेचयति sprinkle, water. — अनु pour in or on (loc.). अभि pour upon, sprinkle, bathe, consecrate (M. refl.); C. the same. समभि sprinkle, wet, consecrate. अव pour upon, sprinkle, water; C. also bleed (tr.). आ pour or fill into, discharge one's self (river), pour off or out. C. pour into or to. अवा & अभिपर्या pour into (loc.). समा & अभिसमा pour or shed together. उद् pour upon, fill up, overfill. P. overflow, be puffed up, be haughty or arrogant. उप pour upon, sprinkle. नि pour down or in; infuse, instil; water, irrigate. C. sprinkle, wet. निस् & परा pour or shake off, remove. परि pour around or upon; pour out or into another vessel. C. sprinkle, wet. प्र pour out or upon; fill (a vessel); wet, moisten. P. be wetted or refreshed; flow forth. C. pour in. वि spill, shed. सम् pour together, mingle; sprinkle, water. — Cf. उत्सिक्त.
2सिंच् f. hem of a garment.
सिचय m. garment, cloth.
सिञ्ज्, सिञ्जा, सिञ्जित v. शिञ्ज् etc.
1सित v. सा & सि.
2सित a. white, bright, clear, pure.
सितकमल n. a white lotus flower.
सितकर m. the moon (white-rayed).
सिततेजस् a. shining white.
सितदीधिति m. = सितकर.
सितपक्ष m. the light half of a month
सितपीत a. white and yellow.
सितमणि m. crystal (white stone).
सितमणिमय a. of crystal.
सितमनस् a. pure-hearted.
सितरक्त a. white and red.
सितश्मश्रु a. white-bearded.
सितांशु m. = सितकर.
सितातपत्र n. a white umbrella (emblem of royal dignity).
सितातपवारण n. the same.
सितापाङ्ग m. a peacock (lit. having white eye-corners).
सिताभ्र m. a white cloud; camphor.
सिताम्बर a. clothed in white.
सितासित a. white and black.
सितिमन् m. whiteness.
सितेतर a. black, dark, blue (lit. opposite of white).
सितोत्पल n. a white lotus flower.
सिद्ध a. hit (aim), attained; brought about, accomplished, prepared, ready; settled, established, known, valid; resulting, following; fallen to one's share, one's own; peculiar, particular; perfected or sanctified; thoroughly skilled in magical arts or endowed with supernatural powers. m. seer, fortune-teller, a great saint or one of the bleessed (a class of semi-divine beings). n. supernatural power, magic art.

सिद्धक्षेत्र n. the field of the blessed, N. of a place.
सिद्धपुर n. the city of the blessed.
सिद्धभूमि f. the region of the blessed.
सिद्धमन्त्र m. magic word, spell.
सिद्धयोग m. magic agency, charm.
सिद्धलक्ष a. hitting the mark.
सिद्धाङ्गना f. a female Siddha.
सिद्धाञ्जन n. magic unguent.
सिद्धसंघ m. a company of saints.
1**सिद्धादेश** m. the prophecy of a fortune-teller.
2**सिद्धादेश** m. fortune-teller, prophet.
सिद्धान्त m. established end or truth, dogma, axiom (often °— & —° in titles of books).
सिद्धान्तकौमुदी f., °**शिरोमणि** m. titles of books.
सिद्धाभीष्ट a. having attained the desired object; successful, satisfied.
सिद्धार्थ a. = prec. or leading to the goal, effective, powerful; m. E. of Buddha.
सिद्धार्थमानिन् a. thinking one's self successful.
सिद्धाश्रम m. the hermitage of the blessed.
सिद्धि f. hitting or reaching the aim, attainment of an object, performance, accomplishment, conclusion, result; success, prosperity, welfare; perfection, supernatural power.
सिद्धिकर (f. **ई**) & °**कारक** a. causing success or felicity.
सिद्धिकारिन् a. accomplishing (gen.).
सिद्धिक्षेत्र n. the seat of fortune or bliss, N. of a place.
सिद्धिद a. giving success.
सिद्धिदर्शिन् a. foreseeing success, prophet of good tidings.
सिद्धिमन्त् a. having success or possessing magical power.
सिद्धिमन्त्र & °**योग** m. = **सिद्धमन्त्र** & °**योग**.
सिद्धी कृ accomplish.*
सिद्धीश्वर m. the lord of magic arts, E. of Çiva.
सिद्धेश & °**श्वर** m. the lord of the blessed.
सिद्धौषध n. magic herb, panacea.
1**सिध्**, **सेधति**, °**ते** drive off, scare away. — **अप** & **अव** = S. **आ** C. **आसेधयति** cause to be arrested. **व्या** keep off, prevent. **उद्** drive aside. **नि** drive away, keep off, hinder, prevent, forbid. C. ward off, keep back, interdict, deny. **निस्** drive away. **प्र** A.M. drive on. **प्रति** drive away, ward off, seek to divert from (abl.); omit, suppress; prevent, forbid, refuse, deny. C. ward off, keep back, refuse, forbid, deny. **संप्रति** keep back. — Cf. **प्रतिषिद्ध**, **विप्रतिषिद्ध**.
2**सिध्**, **सिध्यति** (°**ते**), pp. **सिद्ध** (q.v.) reach an aim, hit the mark; succeed, be fulfilled or accomplished; result, follow, be valid, boot, avail; submit to, obey (gen.); reach the highest aim, become perfect or blessed. — **अभि** succeed, be accomplished or perfected; acquire, obtain. **प्र** succeed; result, follow. **सम्** succeed, be accomplished; become perfect or blessed. — Cf. **प्रसिद्ध**, **संसिद्ध**.
1**सिध्म** a. going straight (to the goal).
2**सिध्म** a. white-spotted or leprous.
सिध्मन् m. n. a kind of leprosy.
सिध्मल a. leprous.
सिध्र a. = 1**सिध्म**.
सिन n. supply, provision, p. °**वन्त्**.
सिनीवाली f. N. of a goddess presiding over conception and childbirth.
सिन्दुवार m. N. of a plant, n. its berry.
सिन्दूर n. red lead, minium.
सिन्धु m. f. stream, esp. the Indus, pl. m. the land on the Indus & its inhabitants; m. also flood, sea, ocean, water i.g., N. of a Gandharva etc.
सिन्धुज a. born on the Indus.
सिन्धुतस् adv. from the Indus-country.
सिन्धुनाथ m. the ocean (lit. = seq.).
†**सिन्धुपति** m. lord of the rivers.
1**सिन्धुमातृ** f. the mother of rivers.
2**सिन्धुमातृ** a. having the sea as mother.
सिन्धुराज m. = **सिन्धुनाथ**.
सिन्धुवार m. = **सिन्दुवार**.
सिप्रा f. N. of a river.
सिम a. all, every; **सिमा** adv. everywhere.
सिम्ब m. N. of a man.
सिमिसिमाय्, °**यते** prickle, bubble, quiver.

सिरा f. stream, channel; vein, artery.
सिराल a. having many or strong veins.
सिरी f. shuttle or female weaver.
सिलाची & सिलाञ्जाला f. names of plants.
*सिल्ह m. olibanum.
सिव्, सीव्यति, °ते, pp. स्यूत (q.v.) sew. — व्यति & आ sew together. उद् sew in. परि sew around, wrap in. प्र sew up. प्रति sew on. वि sew on in different places. सम् sew together.
सिषासतु or °सनि a. desiring to obtain.
सिषासु a. = prec. or = seq.
†सिष्णु a. desiring to give.
सिसृक्षा f. desire of creating.
सिसृक्षु a. desiring to create.
सीकर & °रिन् v. शीकर & °रिन्.
सीता f. furrow; N. of the daughter of Janaka and wife of Rāma (said to have sprung from a furrow).
सीताद्रव्य n. implement of husbandry.
1सीतायज्ञ m. a sacrifice offered to the furrow.
2सीतायज्ञ a. sacrificing to the furrow.
सीधु m. rum or any similar spirit; fig. = nectar.
सीधुपान n. drinking rum (cf. prec.).
सीम् (encl.) lays stress upon a prec. pronoun or preposition.
सीमन् m. parting of the hair on the head, boundary-line, frontier, (also सीमन्त m., p. °वन्त् †); vertex, zenith; the scrotum.
सीमन्तक, f. °न्तिका wearing the hair parted.
सीमन्तय्, °यति mark by a line, part (hair).
सीमन्तिन् a. = सीमन्तवन्त्; f. °नी a woman.
सीमन्तोन्नयन n. arranging the parting of the hair (of pregnant women).
सीमलिङ्ग n. boundary-mark.
सीमा f. boundary, limit.
सीमाज्ञान f. ignorance of boundaries.
सीमाधिप m. boundary-guard, marcher.
सीमान्त m. boundary, landmark.
सीमापाल m. = सीमाधिप.
सीमालिङ्ग n. = सीमलिङ्ग.
सीमावाद & °विवाद m. dispute about boundaries.
सीमावृक्ष m. tree serving as boundary-mark.
सीमासंधि f. the meeting of two boundaries.

सीर n. m. plough; m. plough-ox.
सीरवाह a. drawing the plough.
सीरा f. stream.
सीरिन् a. ploughing; m. plougher, E. of Balarāma.
सीवन n. sewing.
सीस & सीसक n. lead.
1सु, सुनोति, सुनुते, pp. सुत (q.v.) press out, extract, esp. the Soma. — अधि = S. अभि press out, prepare or win by extracting. आ & वि = S. सम् & अभिसम् press out together. — Cf. प्रसुत.
2सु (सू) adv. well, indeed (strengthening and assevering); often °— in adj., adv., & subst. = εὐ (opp. दुस्).
सुऊति f. good help or protection.
सुक m. = शुक.
सुकण्ठ, f. ई sweet-voiced (lit. -throated).
सुकथा f. a beautiful tale.
सुकन्या f. N. of a woman (beautiful girl).
सुकर a. practicable, easy to be done.
1सुकर्मन् n. a good work.
2सुकर्मन् a. able, capable; m. artist, architect.
सुकलत्र n. a good wife.
सुकल्प a. easy to be done.
सुकवि m. a good poet.
सुकविता f. good poetry.
सुकान्त a. very handsome, charming.
सुकाल & °लिन् m. pl. a cert. class of Manes.
1सुकीर्ति f. good praise, celebration.
2सुकीर्ति a. praiseworthy, glorious.
सुकुचा f. handsome-breasted.
सुकुमार, f. ई delicate; abstr. °ता f., °त्व n.
1सुकुल n. a good family.
2सुकुल a. of good family, well-born.
सुकृत् a. well-doing, righteous, pious; also = 2सुकर्मन्.
1सुकृत n. a good deed, virtue, (moral) merit; kindness, favour, service.
2सुकृत a. well made or done, good, right, fair.
1सुकृतकर्मन् n. a good or meritorious work.
2सुकृतकर्मन् a. doing good works, virtuous.
सुकृतकृत् a. = prec. 2.
सुकृति f. & a. = 1 & 2सुकृतकर्मन्.
सुकृतिन् a. acting well, virtuous, clever, wise, fortunate.

1सुकृत्य n. a good work, well-doing.
2सुकृत्य a. doing one's duty.
सुकृत्या f. cleverness or well-doing, virtue.
सुकृत्वन् a. doing well or right.
सुकेत a. well-meaning.
सुकेतु a. very bright.
सुकेश (f. ई) & सुकेशान्त a. fair-locked.
सुकोमल a. very soft or tender.
सुक्रतु a. able, clever, wise.
सुक्रुद्ध a. very angry.
†सुक्रतूय्, °यते show one's self wise.
सुक्रतूया f. wisdom, judgment.
सुक्षत्र a. ruling well or granting power.
सुक्षिति f. a good dwelling; shelter, refuge, security.
1सुक्षेत्र n. a good field.
2सुक्षेत्र a. having or granting good fields (dwellings).
सुक्षेम n. good security, time of peace.
सुख a. easy, pleasant, comfortable, happy; n. ease, comfort, pleasure, joy, bliss, as adv. = instr. (abl.), & °— easily, with pleasure, willingly, happily.
सुखग्राह्य a. easy to be seized or understood.
सुखघात्य a. easy to be killed.
सुखद a. causing happiness or joy.
सुखदुःख n. pl. weal or woe.
सुखदुःखसुहृद् m. friend in weal and woe.
सुखप्रतिबन्धिता f. prevention or interruption of happiness.
सुखप्रत्यर्थिता f. = prec.
1सुखप्रसव m. abstr. to seq.
2सुखप्रसव f. bringing forth happily.*
सुखमार्जन n. auspicious ablution.*
सुखय्, °यति, pp. सुखित (q.v.) make happy, gladden, delight.
सुखयितृ (& °तृक*) a. gladdening, delighting.
सुखवास m. a pleasant abode.
सुखशयित a. resting pleasantly.
सुखशयित n. a pleasant rest; °प्रच्छक, f. प्रच्छिका inquiring after it.*
सुखशय्या f. a comfortable couch or rest.
सुखश्रव & °श्रव्य a. pleasant to hear.
सुखसंयोग m. gain of (eternal) bliss.
सुखसंस्थ & °स्थित a. feeling at ease; happy, comfortable.
सुखसंग m. attachment to pleasure.
सुखसाध्य a. easily subdued or attained.
सुखसुप्त a. sleeping sweetly.
सुखसुप्ति f. a sweet sleep.
सुखसुप्तिका f. = prec.; °प्रश्न m. the question how (sweetly) a person has slept.
सुखस्थ a. = सुखसंस्थ.
सुखस्पर्श a. agreeable to the touch (abstr. °ता f.*).
सुखादि a. wearing beautiful bracelets.
सुखाभ्युदयिक a. bringing happiness.
सुखाय्, °यते be at ease or comfortable; be pleasant, do good.
सुखार्थ m. pleasant thing, pleasure, comfort.
सुखार्थिन् a. seeking for happiness.
सुखालोक a. pleasant-looking.
सुखावह a. bringing pleasure, delighting.
सुखासीन a. comfortable seated.
सुखासुख n. sgl. pleasure and pain.
सुखित a. joyful, happy.
सुखिता f., °त्व n. abstr. to seq.
सुखिन् a. comfortable, easy, prosperous, happy.
सुखोचित a. accustomed to ease.
सुखोदय a. having happiness or joy as result; promising happiness.
सुखोदर्क a. = prec.
सुखोद्य a. easily pronounceable.
सुखोपगम्य a. easily accessible.
सुखोपविष्ट a. = सुखासीन.
सुखोषित a. having passed the night (± रजनीम्) well; having had a pleasant abode.
सुग a. easily passed; easy to approach or attain. n. good access or progress.
सुगत a. going or running well; who has well fared or has had a good time. m. a Buddha or a Buddhistic teacher.
सुगति f. welfare, happiness.
1सुगन्ध m. odour, perfume.
2सुगन्ध a. sweet-smelling, odoriferous.
सुगन्धि or सुगन्धि a. = prec.
सुगन्धिक & सुगन्धिन् a. the same.
सुगन्धितेजन m. n. a kind of fragrant grass.

सुगभस्ति or सुगभस्ति a. clever with the arm.
सुगम a. easy of access or approach; accessible, plain, intelligible.
सुगभीर a. very deep.
सुगम्य a. easily accessible.
1सुगव m. a fine bull.
2सुगव a. having fine bulls (or cows).
सुगव्य n. possession of good cattle.
सुगातु m. good progress or condition.
सुगातुया f. (instr.) desire of welfare.
सुगात्र, f. ई a. handsome (-limbed).
सुगाध a. easily fordable.
सुगार्हपत्य m. a good householder (Agni).
सुगीत n. a fine song.
सुगीति f. N. of a metre.
सुगु a. having fine cows (or bulls).
सुगुण & °णिन् a. virtuous, excellent.
सुगुप्त n. well hidden or concealed; n. adv.
सुगुप्ति f. secret procedure; acc. w. आ-धा proceed secretly.
सुगुप्ती कृ hide well.
सुगुरु a. very heavy (guilt).
सुगूढ a. well concealed; n. secretly.
सुगृह a. having a good house.
सुगृहपति m. a good householder.
सुगृहीत a. held fast, conceived or learnt well; applied properly or auspiciously.
सुगृहीतनामधेय a. having an auspicious name.*
सुगेहिनी f. a dear or good housewife.
1सुगोपा m. a good protector.
2सुगोपा a. well protected.
सुग्म्य a. progressing well (lit. & fig.).
सुग्रह a. grasped or handled; easy to be obtained.
सुग्रीव m., ई f. a man's or woman's name (mythol.).
सुग्रीष्म m. a fine summer.
सुघन a. very dense (forest).
सुघोर a. very fearful or terrible.
सुघोष a. sounding loud or well; m. the conch-shell of Nakula.
सुघ्न m. easy killing.
सुचक्र a. having beautiful wheels; n. a fine waggon.
सुचक्षस् a. seeing well, clear-sighted.
सुचक्षुस् a. = prec. or fair-eyed.
सुचन्दन m. a fine sandal tree.
1सुचरित a. well done; n. good conduct or work, virtue.
2सुचरित a. well-conducted, virtuous.
सुचरितचरित a. = prec. 2.
सुचारु a. very pleasant or beautiful; abstr. °ता f.
सुचित्त a. well-minded.
सुचित्र a. manifold, various; distinguished.
सुचिर a. very long (time); °— & n. adv.
सुचेतन a. remarkable, distinguished.
सुचेतस् a. sensible or well-minded.
सुचेतु, only instr. °तुना adv. graciously, benevolently.
सुचेल a. well-clothed.
*सुचेलक m. a fine cloth.
सुच्छद a. having fine leaves.
सुच्छर्दिस् a. giving good shelter.
सुच्छाय a. affording good shade; well-shining, splendid, beautiful.
सुजन m. a good man.
सुजनता f., °त्व n. kindness, goodness.
सुजन्मन् a. = prec. or of noble birth.
सुजम्भ a. strong-jawed (Agni).
1सुजय m. a great victory, triumph.
2सुजय a. easily vanquished.
सुजल a. having good water.
सुजात or सुजात a. well born or made, beautiful, good, noble; abstr. °तता f.
सुजामि a. having many brothers and sisters or relatives.
सुजित n. an easy victory.
सुजिह्व a. having a beautiful voice (lit. tongue).
सुजीर्ण a. quite decayed or well digested.
सुजीव n. impers. (it is) easy to live.
1सुजीवित n. a happy life.
2सुजीवित a. living happily, enjoying life.
सुजुष्ट a. beloved, welcome.
सुजूर्णि a. burning, hot.
सुज्जक & सुज्जि m. N. of men.
सुज्ञ a. well knowing.
1सुज्ञान n. easy understanding or good knowledge.

2सुज्ञान a. having good knowledge or easily understood.
सुज्योतिस् or सुज्योतिस् a. shining bright, resplendent.
सुत् pressing out, extracting (—°).
1सुत expressed or extracted; m. the expressed Soma juice, a Soma libation.
2सुत m., आ f. son, daughter.
1सुतनु a. very thin or slender.
2सुतनु a. handsome-limbed; f. (voc. °नु) a fair woman.
सुतन्त्रि a. melodious.
सुतपस् a. heating, warming; practising great penance.
सुतपा a. drinking Soma.
सुतपेय n. drinking or a draught of Soma.
सुतप्त a. very hot, much burnt or tormented.
सुतर a. easily passed or attained.
सुतरण a. easily crossed (river).
सुतराम् adv. in a higher or in the highest degree; more, very much.
सुतर्मन् a. well carrying across (ship).
सुतल n. a cert. hell.
सुतष्ट a. well made.
सुतसोम a. who has expressed the Soma (sacrifice) or whereat the S. is expressed (sacrifice).
सुतादान n. the gift of a daughter.
सुतार a. very clear or loud.
सुतार्थिन् a. desirous of a son.
सुतावन्त् a. who has (extracted) Soma juice.
सुतिन् a. having a son (sons).
सुतीक्ष्ण a. very sharp (lit. & fig.); n. in a high degree, very much.
सुतीय्, °यति treat as a son.
1सुतीर्थ n. a good road; a very holy bathing-place or any object of high veneration.
2सुतीर्थ a. easily fordable or accessible.
सुतुक a. hasty, fleet.
सुतुमुल a. very noisy.
सुतेकर a. busy with the Soma.
सुतेजस् a. very sharp or bright.
सुतेजित a. well sharpened.
सुतेरण a. delighting in Soma.
सुतोष & °ण a. easily satisfied.
सुत्य (± अहन्) n. Soma-day.
सुत्रात a. well protected.
सुत्रात्र a. = prec. or well protecting.
सुत्रामन् a. well protecting; m. E. of Indra.
सुत्रावन् a. = prec. a.
सुत्वन् a. pressing Soma; m. N. of a man.
सुदंसस् a. performing wonderful deeds.
सुदक्ष a. very capable or clever.
सुदक्षिण a. = prec. or friendly, kind; f. आ N. of a woman.
सुदत्र a. granting good gifts.
1सुदन्त् m. a good tooth.
2सुदन्त्, f. सुदती having good teeth.
सुदन्त a. = prec. 2.
सुदर्श a. easily seen or of beautiful aspect, pleasant.
सुदर्शन a. = prec.; m. & f. आ a man's & woman's name; m. n. Viṣṇu's disc.
सुदा a. giving well or much; very munificent.
सुदान n. a rich gift.
सुदानु a. flowing or giving richly.
सुदामन् a. giving liberally; m. (*cloud), a man's name.
सुदारु n. good wood.
सुदारुण a. very violent or terrible.
सुदावन् a. = सुदामन् a.
सुदास् a devoutly worshipping; m. N. of a king.
सुदास m. pl. N. of a people.
सुदिन a. clear, bright; n. a clear or auspicious day; abstr. सुदिनता f., °त्व n.
सुदिव् a. shining well, very bright.
सुदिव n. a fine day.
सुदिवस n. = prec.
सुदिह a. well polished, sharp (tooth).
1सुदीति f. abstr. to seq.
2सुदीति a. shining, resplendent.
सुदीदिति & सुदीप्त a. = prec. a.
सुदीर्घ a. very long (t. & sp.).
सुदुःख a. very painful or difficult; n. adv., as subst. great pain.
सुदुःखित a. much grieved, unhappy.
सुदुघ a. yielding much (milk); f. आ a good milk-cow.
सुदुराचार a. very ill-conducted.

सुदुराधर्ष a. quite intolerable or inaccessible.
सुदुर्गम & °गम्य a. very difficult to be approached or passed.
सुदुर्जय a. very difficult to be conquered.
सुदुर्ज्ञेय a. very difficult to be known or understood.
सुदुर्दर्श & °दृश a. difficult to be beheld or observed.
सुदुर्धष a. = सुदुराधर्ष.
सुदुर्बल a. very feeble.
सुदुर्बुद्धि a. very foolish or stupid.
सुदुर्मनस् a. much afflicted.
सुदुर्लभ a. very difficult to be obtained.
सुदुर्विद् & °वेद a. very difficult to be understood.
सुदुश्चर a. very difficult to be attained or performed.
सुदुष्कर a. very difficult to be done.
सुदुष्ट a. very bad or wicked.
सुदुष्पार a. very difficult to be penetrated or investigated.
सुदुष्प्राप a. very difficult to be approached or attained.
सुदुस्तर or सुदुस्तार a. very difficult to be passed or overcome.
सुदुःसह a. quite intolerable or invincible.
सुदूर a. very distant; °— & n. adv.
सुदृढ a. very firm or strong; n. adv.
सुदृप्त a. very arrogant.
सुदृश्, f. सुदृशी a. clear-sighted or fair-eyed.
सुदृशीक a. looking beautiful.
सुदृश्य a. easily visible; also = prec.
सुदृष्ट a. well, easily, or kindly seen.
1सुदेव m. a true or good god.
2सुदेव a. having true or right gods; m. a man's name.
सुदेव्य n. the host of the good gods.
सुदेश m. a good place.
सुदेह m. a fine body.
सुदोघ = सुदुघ adj.
सुदोह & सुदोहन a. easy to be milked.
सुद्युत् a. shining beautifully.
सुद्युम्न & सुद्योत्मन् a. = prec.
सुद्रविणस् a. having great riches or treasures.
सुद्रु m. good wood, a strong beam.

सुद्विज a. well-toothed; °वदन a. having a mouth with good teeth.
सुधन a. very rich.
सुधन्वन् a. wielding a god bow; m. a man's name, pl. a cert. mixed tribe.
सुधर्म m. justice, righteousness.
सुधर्मन् a. practising justice, honest, virtuous.
1सुधा f. welfare, comfort.
2सुधा f. nectar or milk (lit. good drink); chalk, rough-cast.
सुधांशु m. the moon (nectar-rayed).
सुधाकर m. = prec.
सुधाकार m. white-washer.
सुधात a. well cleansed or purified.
सुधातु a. well founded or conditioned.
सुधाद्रव m. lime-wash.
सुधाधवल, °धावलित & °धौत a. white-washed.
सुधाधारा f., °पूर m. a stream of nectar.
सुधामय, f. ई consisting of nectar.
सुधामृत n. nectar.
1सुधार a. flowing largely.
2सुधार a. sharp-edged or pointed (arrow).
सुधारश्मि m. moon-beam.
1सुधारस m. juice of nectar, milk.
2सुधारस a. tasting like nectar.
सुधावर्ष n. rain of nectar, adj. °र्षिन्.
सुधासित a. white-washed.
सुधित a. = सुधातु, also well arranged or prepared, settled, established, ready; well-disposed, comfortable, propitious, kind.
1सुधी f. good understanding, intelligence.
2सुधी a. wise, clever, sensible, devout, pious.
सुधीर a. very firm or constant.
सुधुर् & सुधुर a. carrying the yoke or a burden well (horse).
सुधृत a. very constant.
सुधृति m. N. of a king.
सुधृष्टम (superl.) very courageous.
सुधौत a. well cleaned or polished.
सुनक्षत्र n. a good or auspicious star.
सुनन्द m., आ f. a man's & woman's name.
सुनय m. proper conduct, wisdom.
सुनयन a. handsome-eyed.
सुनस a. handsome-nosed.

†सुनाथ a. having a good protector.
सुनाभ & सुनाभि a. having a beautiful nave or centre.
सुनामन् a. well named; m. a man's name.
सुनास & °सिक a. = सुनस.
सुनिक्षिप्त a. well deposed with (loc.).*
सुनिद्र a. sleeping sound.
सुनिभृतम् adv. very secretly.
सुनियत a. well restrained or having much self-control.
सुनिर्मल a. very clean.
सुनिर्वृत a. very courageous, well-humoured.
1सुनिश्चय m. a firm resolution.
2सुनिश्चय a. quite sure or certain; n. adv.
सुनिश्चल a. quite immovable.
सुनिश्चित a. well determined or quite certain (pers. & th.).
सुनिष्क a. having beautiful chains or rings.
सुनिःष्ठित a. well arranged or accomplished, ready.
सुनीत a. well conducted; n. good conduct, prudence.
1सुनीति or सुनीति a. well conducting.
2सुनीति or सुनीति f. = सुनीत n.
सुनीथ a. well conducting or conducted; m. a man's name.
सुनीहार a. very misty.
सुनृप m. a good king.
1सुनौ f. a good ship.
2सुनौ a. having a good ship.
सुन्द m. N. of an Asura.
सुन्दर, f. ई beautiful, fair; m. a man's name; f. ई a (fair) woman.
सुन्दरंमन्य a. thinking one's self beautiful.
सुन्वन्त् m. the offerer of a Soma libation, a man's name.
सुपक्व a. well cooked or matured.
सुपक्ष a. having beautiful wings.
सुपङ्क s. good loam or clay.
सुपति m. a good husband.
सुपत्त्र a. well winged or = seq.
सुपत्त्रित & °त्त्रिन् a. well feathered (arrow).
सुपत्नी f. a having a good husband or lord.
सुपथ् m. good path (lit. & fig.).
सुपथ n. (m.) & सुपथ्य n. = prec.
सुपद्, f. सुपदी a. swift-footed.
सुपद n. a good word.
सुपरिश्रान्त a. quite exhausted.
सुपरीक्षित a. well examined or investigated.
सुपर्ण, f. ई a. well-winged. m. a cert. large bird (eagle, vulture etc., fig. of the sun); a cert. myth. bird (often identif. with Garuḍa).
सुपर्याप्त a. very spacious or comprehensive.
सुपर्वन् a. well-knotted (arrow).
सुपलाश a. having many leaves, leafy.
सुपाणि a. beautiful-handed; skilful, dexterous.
सुपार a. easy to be crossed or subdued; easily carrying across, helping, furthering.
सुपारक्षत्र a. having helpful power.
सुपिधान a. well shut up.
सुपिश् a. beautifully decorated.
सुपीत a. quite yellow.
सुपु or सुपू a. well purifying.
1सुपुत्र m. an excellent son.
2सुपुत्र a. having excellent sons.
सुपुष्प & सुपुष्पित a. having beautiful flowers.
सुपूजित a. much honoured.
सुपूत a. well purified.
सुपूर a. easy to be filled.
सुपूर्ण a. quite full; well filled or decorated with (instr.).
सुपूर्वाह्णे loc. early in the morning.
सुपृक्ष् a. rich in food or refreshments.
सुपेशस् a. beautifully ornamented, handsome.
सुप्त a. asleep, insensible, inactive; n. sleep.
सुप्तक n., °प्तिका f. = prec. n.
सुप्तपूर्व a. having slept before.
सुप्तप्रबुद्ध a. awake from sleep.
सुप्तासुप्त a. asleep and awake.
सुप्ति f. sleep.
सुप्तोत्थित a. arisen from sleep.
सुप्रकाश a. very bright or clear.
1सुप्रकेत a. very visible or conspicuous; also = seq.
2सुप्रकेत a. very attentive or considerate.
सुप्रक्षालित a. well washed.
सुप्रचेतस् a. very wise.
सुप्रच्छन्न a. well hidden.
सुप्रज & °जस् a. having many or good children.

सुप्रजस्त्व & °जास्त्वं n. abstr. to prec.
सुप्रज्ञ a. very wise.
1सुप्रंणीति f. a wise guidance.
2सुप्रंणीति a. wisely guiding.
सुंप्रतिगृहीत a. well grasped or seized.
सुप्रतिपूजित a. well honoured or worshipped.
सुप्रतिष्ठ a. standing firmly or having handsome feet; f. आ firm ground or position.
सुंप्रतिष्ठित = prec. a.; well grounded or situated.
सुप्रंतीक a. good-looking, beautiful.
सुप्रतुंर् a. (nom. °तूंस्) advancing victoriously.
सुप्रंतूर्ति a. = prec.
1सुप्रपाणं n. a good drinking place.
2सुप्रपाणं a. easy for drinking.
सुप्रभ a. good-looking, handsome, beautiful.
सुप्रभात n. a beautiful day-break or morning.
सुप्रयंस् a. receiving good refreshments.
सुप्रवाचनं a. worthy of much praise.
सुप्रसन्न a. very clear or bright; also = seq.
सुप्रसाद a. very gracious or kind.
सुप्रसू a. easily bringing forth.
सुप्रांच् a. easily turned in front.
सुप्राप & °प्य a. easy to be obtained.
सुप्रायणं a. easily accessible.
सुप्रावीं a. very zealous or helpful.
सुंप्रिय a. very dear.
सुंप्रीत a. well pleased, content with (loc.).
सुप्रैंतु a. easily accessible.
सुंप्सन् m. N. of a man.
सुंफल or सुफलं a. bearing good fruit.
सुबंन्धु (सुबन्धुं) a. closely connected, related; m. a good friend, N. of a poet etc.
सुबल m. N. of a myth. bird etc.
सुबहु a. very much (many); °शस् adv. very often.
सुबाल a. very foolish.
सुबाहुं a. handsome-armed; m. N. of a serpent-demon etc.
सुबीज n. good seed; a. having good seed.
1सुबुद्धि f. good understanding, wisdom.
2सुबुद्धि a. wise, clever.
सुबोध & °न (f. ई) a. easy to be understood.
सुब्रह्मण्यं a. very kind to Brahmans. m. a cert. priest, f. आ a cert. recitation performed by this priest, also the priest himself.
1सुंब्रह्मन् m. a good Brahman.
2सुब्रंह्मन् a. having good prayers or a good Brahman.
सुभंग a. lucky, well, comfortable; lovely, charming, beautiful; f. आ a beloved wife. Abstr. सुभगता f., °त्वं n.
सुभगंमन्य a. thinking one's self happy.
सुभट m. a (good) soldier.
सुभणित a. well spoken.*
सुंभद्र a. excellent, beautiful, auspicious, fortunate; m. & f. आ a man's & woman's name; n. good fortune.
सुभंर a. massy, compact, solid, large, abundant; easy to be borne or managed.
सुभागं a. wealthy, rich.
सुभाषित a. spoken or speaking well, eloquent; n. a fine speech or a good word.
सुभिक्ष a. having or offering food enough; n. abundance of food, good time.
सुभुज a. handsome-armed.
सुभूं a. of good birth or nature, strong, solid, powerful.
सुभूतं a. succeeded, turned out well; n. = seq.
सुंभूति f. welfare, happiness.
सुंभृत a. well borne or maintained; heavily loaden.
सुभृश a. very vehement; n. adv. very much.
1सुभ्रु or सुभ्रू f. lovely eyebrows.
2सुभ्रु or सुभ्रू f. a. lovely-browed.
सुंमख a. jocund, merry; n. joy, festival.
सुमङ्गंल, f. °ङ्गली or सुमङ्गला bringing good luck.
सुमज्जन n. a good bath.*
सुमंत् adv. together, withal; along with (instr.).
1सुमतिं f. benevolence, favour; devotion, prayer.
2सुमति a. wise, intelligent; m. & f. (also °ती) a man's & woman's name.
सुमधुर a. very sweet or charming; n. adv.
सुमध्य & °म a. having a beautiful middle or waist, slender.
सुमंनस् a. well-disposed, kind; cheerful, glad; f. (only pl.) & n. flower.

सुमनस्य्, only °स्यमान = prec. a.
सुमनोदामन् n. a garland of flowers.*
सुमन्तु a. easily knowable or well known.
सुमन्त्र a. well advised; m. a man's name.
सुमन्त्रित a. = prec. adj.; n. impers.
1सुमन्मन् n. pl. good wishes.
2सुमन्मन् a. full of devotion or good wishes.
सुमहन्त् a. very large or great.
†सुमहस् a. excellent.
सुमहाकक्ष a. containing very large courts or halls.
सुमहातपस् a. very ascetic or devout.
सुमहातेजस् a. rich in splendour or dignity.
सुमहात्मन् & °मनस् a. very magnanimous.
सुमहाबल a. very strong or powerful.
सुमहामुनि m. an excellent sage.
सुमातृ a. having a beautiful mother.
सुमाय a. abounding in arts or stratagems.
सुमारुत n. the beautiful host of the Maruts.
1सुमित a. well measured.
2सुमित a. well fixed or founded.
सुमित्र a. good friend; m. & f. आ a man's & woman's name.
सुमित्र्य = prec. a.
1सुमुख n. a beautiful mouth.
2सुमुख, f. ई (आ) a. handsome-faced, cheerful, friendly, kind; disposed or willing to (—°); N. of a serpent-demon, an Asura, a king, etc.
सुमृडीक (°ळीक) a. merciful, gracious; n. mercy, favour.
सुमृत a. stone-dead.*
सुमेक a. firmly established.
सुमेध a. pithy, strong.
सुमेधस् a. intelligent, wise.
सुमेरु m. N. of a mountain.
सुम्न a. benevolent, gracious; n. grace, favour; devotion, prayer, hymn.
सुम्नय् & सुम्नाय्, only °यन्त् a. gracious, favourable.
सुम्नयु & सुम्नायु a. = prec. a. or devout, pious.
सुम्नावरी a. causing favour or satisfaction.
सुम्निन् a. gracious, favourable.
सुम्न्य a. deserving favour.
सुह्म m. pl. N. of a people.
सुयज् a. sacrificing well; f. = seq.

1सुयज्ञ m. a good sacrifice.
2सुयज्ञ a. performing or receiving a good sacrifice; m. N. of sev. men.
सुयत a. well restrained.
सुयन्तु a. easily guided.
सुयन्त्रित a. well bound or restrained; possessing perfect self-control.
सुयम a. = prec.
सुयवस a. having good pasturage; n. good pasturage.
सुयशस् a. very famous.
सुयाम a. well guiding.
सुयुज् a. well yoked (waggon or horses).
सुयुद्ध n. a good or honest fight.
सुयोधन m. older N. of Duryodhana.
सुर m., ई f. god, goddess.
सुरकार्मुक n. the gods' bow, i.e. the rainbow.
सुरकुल n. house of the gods; temple.
सुरक्षित a. well guarded or protected.
सुरक्षिन् m. a good protector.
सुरगज m. elephant of the gods.
सुरगण m. sgl. & pl. the host of gods.
सुरगृह n. = सुरकुल.
सुरङ्ग m. the orange tree; f. आ = सुरुङ्गा.
सुरचाप m. = सुरकार्मुक.
सुरण a. gay, merry; n. joy, pleasure.
सुरत n. great delight, esp. amorous pleasure, sexual intercourse.
सुरत्न a. rich in treasures.
1सुरथ m. a fine chariot.
2सुरथ a. having a fine chariot; m. charioteer, a man's name.
सुरद्विप m. = सुरगज.
सुरद्विष् m. god-hater, demon.
सुरधनुस् n. = सुरकार्मुक.
सुरपति m. lord of the gods (Indra or Çiva).
सुरपतिचाप m, °धनुस् n. Indra's bow, the rainbow.
सुरभय्, °यति, pp. सुरभित render fragrant, perfume.
सुरभि (f. इ or ई) sweet-smelling, fragrant, lovely, charming. m. the spring; f. °भि or °भी N. of a myth. cow, cow i.g.; n. any sweet-smelling substance, perfume.
सुरभिकन्दर m. N. of a mountain.

सुरभिगन्ध m. fragrance.
सुरभिगन्धि & °न्धिन् a. sweet-smelling, fragrant.
सुरभित a. = prec.
सुरभिन् (comp. °भिन्तर) & सुरभिमन्त् a. the same.
सुरभिष्ठम (superl.) most fragrant or lovely.
सुरभिमास & °समय m. the season of spring.
सुरभी कृ = सुरभय्.
सुरमणीय & सुरम्य a. very charming.
सुरयुवति & °योषित् f. a celestial woman, nymph, Apsaras.
सुरराज्, °राज, & °राजन् m. = सुरपति.
सुरर्षि m. a divine sage.
सुरलोक m. the world of the gods, heaven.
सुरवधू & °वनिता f. = सरयुवति.
सुरश्मि a. having beautiful rays.
सुरश्रेष्ठ m. the best of the gods (Indra, Viṣṇu, Çiva etc.).
सुरस a. well-flavoured, juicy, savoury, sweet, lovely; f. आ N. of a daughter of Dakṣa etc.
सुरसख m. friend of the gods.
सुरसंघ m. a company of gods.
सुरसरित् f. the river of the gods (Gaṅgā).
सुरसुत m. the son of a god.
सुरसुन्दरी & °स्त्री f. = सुरयुवति.
सुरा f. spirituous, liquor, wine.
सुराङ्गना f. = सुरयुवति.
सुराजीविन् m. tavern-keeper, distiller (lit. living by spirituous liquor).
सुराति a. granting good gifts.
सुराधस् a. bestowing or receiving good gifts; liberal or wealthy.
सुराधिप m. sovereign of the gods (Indra).
सुराध्वज m. sign of a distiller (liquor-sign).
सुराप m., आ f. & ई f. spirit-drinker.
1सुरापाण (or न) a. = prec. m.
2सुरापाण (or न) n. the drinking of spirit.
सुराभाजन n. a vessel for spirituous liquor.
सुरामत्त a. drunk in liquor.
सुरामूल्य n. drink-money, gratification.
सुरारि m. = सुरद्विष्.
सुरालय m. abode of the gods, heaven or temple.
सुरावन्त् a. having liquor.
सुराष्ट्र a. having a good government; m. N. of a country, pl. N. of a people.
सुरासव m. n. an intoxicating decoction.
सुरासुर m. pl. the gods and the Asuras.
सुरुक्म a. shining beautifully.
सुरुङ्गा f. a subterraneous passage, mine, breach.
1सुरुच् f. splendour, brightness.
2सुरुच् a. radiant, bright.
सुरुचिर a. = prec., splendid, beautiful.
सुरूप a. handsome-figured, beautiful. Abstr. °ता† f.
सुरूपकृत्नु a. working beautiful works.
सुरेख a. handsome, pretty; f. आ a beautiful line, N. of a woman.
सुरेतस् a. rich in seed, potent.
सुरेन्द्र m. lord of gods (Indra).
सुरेश & °श्वर m. = prec. (also E. of other gods).
सुरोत्तम a. the most excellent of the gods (Indra).
सुरोपम a. god-like.
सुरोमन् m. N. of a serpent-demon (fine-haired).
सुरोष a. very angry.
1सुलक्षण n. a good mark or charateristic.
2सुलक्षण a. having lucky marks.
सुलक्षित a. well examined or remarked.
सुलभ a. easy to be obtained, frequent, common. Abstr. °त्व n.
सुलभकोप a. easily irascible.*
सुलभावकाश a. easily gaining entrance into (—°).
सुलभेतर a. opp. to सुलभ.
सुललित a. graceful, pretty; n. adv.
सुलोचन a. fair-eyed.
सुवज्र a. having a strong thunderbolt.
सुवदन a. handsome-faced; f. आ a beautiful woman, N. of a metre.
सुवर्चस् a. full of splendour or vigour, fiery, glorious, strong, a man's name.
सुवर्चस or °सिन् a. = prec. adj.
सुवर्ण a. of a beautiful colour or appearance, glittering, golden; belonging to a good caste. n. gold, riches; m. (n.) a cert. weight of gold.

सुवर्णकटक n. a golden bracelet.*
सुवर्णकर्तृ & °कार m. gold-worker, goldsmith.
सुवर्णकारान्न n. the foot of a goldsmith.
सुवर्णचौर m. a stealer of gold.
सुवर्णचौरिका f. gold-stealing.*
सुवर्णपिञ्जर a. as yellow as gold.
सुवर्णबिन्दु m. N. of a sanctuary.
सुवर्णभाण्ड (& °क*) n. jewel-box.
सुवर्णभाण्डागार s. treasury.*
सुवर्णमय, f. ई made of gold, golden.
सुवर्णयूथिका f. a kind of jasmine.*
सुवर्णरजत a. of gold and silver.
सुवर्णशकटिका f. a toy-cart made of gold.*
1सुवर्मन् n. good armour.
2सुवर्मन् a. having good armour.
1सुवर्ष m. a good rain.
2सुवर्ष a. raining abundantly.
1सुवसन n. a good dwelling.
2सुवसन a. well clothed or clothing.
सुवसन्त m. a fine spring.
सुवस्त्र a. well clothed.
सुवाच् & सुवाचस् a. speaking well.
सुवान्त a. having well vomited (leech).
सुवासस् a. well dressed or decorated.
सुवासिनी f. a woman married or single who lives in her father's house.
सुवास्तु f. N. of a river.
सुविग्रह a. having a beautiful body.
सुविज्ञान a. very wise or = seq.
सुविज्ञेय a. easily discernible.
सुवित a. accessible, passable; proceeding well. n. good progress, welfare, happiness.
1सुवित्त n. good wealth.
2सुवित्त a. wealthy.
सुविदग्ध a. very knowing or cunning.*
सुविदत्र a. kindly noticing, benevolent, gracious; n. grace, favour, kindness.
सुविदत्रिय a. = prec. a.
सुविदित a. well known.
सुविद्या f. good knowledge.
सुविद्वंस् a. knowing, wise.
सुविध a. of a good kind.
सुविधि m. a good manner or way.
सुविपुल a. very large or great.

सुविभक्त a. well divided or proportioned, regular.
सुविरूढ a. well grown or fixed (root).
सुविश्रब्ध a. confident, cheerful, n. adv.
1सुविस्तर m. great extent, prolixity.
2सुविस्तर a. very extensive or diffuse, very strong or mighty; n. adv.
सुविहित a. well done or arranged; well provided with (instr.).
सुविहितप्रयोग m. well arranged performance (of a play); abstr. °ता f.*
सुवीर a. manly or having many men (heroes).
सुवीर्य n. manliness, heroism; abundance of men or heroes.
1सुवृक्ति f. excellent praise or hymn.
2सुवृक्ति a. well praising or praised.
सुवृक्ष m. a beautiful tree.
सुवृत् a. well rolling (waggon).
सुवृत्त a. well rounded or well behaved; n. impers. well done (w. instr.).
सुवृत्ति f. good conduct.
सुवृध a. jocund, merry.
सुवृष्ट n., सुवृष्टि f. a good rain.
1सुवेद a. having good knowledge.
2सुवेद a. easy to be gained.
सुवेदन a. = prec.
सुवेन, f. ई desirous, longing.
सुवेम a. sitting at a good loom.
सुवेल m. N. of a mountain.
1सुवेष m. a beautiful dress.
2सुवेष a. beautifully dressed.
सुवेषनिलय a. = prec. (lit. dwelling in fine clothes).*
सुव्यक्त a. very clear or manifest; n. adv.
सुव्रत a. ruling well; religious, pious, virtuous; m. & f. आ a man's & woman's name.
सुशंस & सुशंसिन् a. well-wishing, blessing.
सुशब्द a. well sounding (flute).*
सुशमि or °मी adv. accurately, carefully.
सुशरण a. affording a good refuge.
सुशर्मन् a. = prec.; n. good refuge.
सुशस्ति a. worthy of praise; f. good praise or recitation.
सुशान्त a. quite extinguished or appeased, very quiet or placid.

सुशिक्षित a. well learned or taught.
सुशिप्र or सुशिंप्र a. having beautiful cheeks or jaws.
सुशिश्वि a. well growing (in the womb).
सुशिष्टि f. good aid.
सुशिष्य m. a good scholar.*
सुशीत a. very cold.
सुशीतल a. = prec.; n. as subst.
सुशील n. a good character; a. of good character.
सुशीलवन्त् & °लिन् = prec. a.
सुशुक्वन् & सुशुक्वनि a. shining brightly.
सुशेव & सुशेवस् a. very gracious or kind.
सुश्चन्द्र a. beautifully shining.
सुश्रवस् a. well hearing or much heard of, famous, celebrated.
सुश्री & सुश्रीक a. splendid, beautiful.
सुश्रुत् a. hearing well or = seq. a.
सुश्रुत a. well heard or much heard of i.e. very famous or celebrated; m. N. of an ancient medical author.
सुश्रुति f. a good hearing (ear).
सुश्रोणि, f. ई having beautiful hips.
सुश्रोतु a. willingly hearing.
सुश्लक्ष्ण a. very smooth.
सुश्लिष्ट a. close, tight; exactly fitting, well tallying.
सुश्लोक a. well sounding or of good renown, celebrated.
सुश्लोक्य n. a well sounding speech.
सुषखि a. good friend.
सुषण & सुषणन a. easy to be obtained.
सुषद a. easy, comfortable (to sit in or ride on).
1सुषम a. beautiful, splendid; f. आ beauty.
2सुषम n. a good year.
सुषह a. easy to be mastered or won.
सुषा a. easily obtaining or procuring.
सुषारथि m. a good charioteer.
सुषिर a. hollow; n. hole, cavity.
सुषिरता f., °त्व n. abstr. to prec. adj.
सुषुत a. well extracted or prepared (Soma).
सुषुति f. good birth or procreation.
सुषुप्त a. fast asleep; n. = seq. f.
सुषुप्ति f. deep sleep, °वत् adv. as in deep sleep.
सुषुप्सा f. desire to sleep, sleepiness.
सुषुप्सु a. wishing to sleep, sleepy.
सुषुम्ण (म्न) a. very gracious or favourable; f. आ a cert. artery on the neck.
1सुषू a. very exciting or well extracted.
2सुषू f. easily bringing forth (children).
सुषूमा f. = prec.
सुषेण a. having a good missile; m. N. of a Gandharva etc., f. आ N. of a princess.
सुषोम m., आ f. a cert. Soma-vessel; f. also N. of a river.
सुष्टु & सुष्टुत a. highly praised.
सुष्टुति f. right or high praise.
सुष्टुभ् a. shrilling, shouting.
सुष्ठु adv. well, all right, very much, indeed.
सुष्वय् (सष्वयति, °ते) run, flow.
सुष्वि a. pressing or offering Soma.
सुसंयत a. well restrained or governed; having self-control.
सुसंरब्ध a. holding fast; much excited or enraged.
सुसंविग्न a. much agitated.
सुसंवीत a. well dressed or armed; richly furnished with (—°).
सुसंवृत a. well covered or dressed; well hidden or secret; well surrounded by or furnished with (instr.).
सुसंशित a. well sharpened, very sharp (lit. & fig.).
सुसंस्कृत a. well arranged or prepared; well perfected or completed.
सुसंहत a. well joined or knit, compact, solid, firm.
सुसंगता f. a woman's name.
सुसंगृहीत a. well kept or restrained.
सुसत्कृत a. well made or prepared, hospitably received, highly honoured.
सुसत्त्व a. resolute, courageous.
सुसदृश, f. ई very like or similar.
सुसंदृश् a. pleasant to look at.
सुसमाहित a. well loaden (waggon); well arranged or decorated; very fit or suitable, very intent, entirely concentrated upon one thing.
सुसमिद्ध a. well kindled or lighted.

सुसमीहित a. very much wished for, welcome.*
सुसमृद्ध a. thoroughly perfect; very copious or abundant; very rich or wealthy.
सुसंपन्न a. well thriven, richly furnished, (high grown*).
सुसंपिष्ट a. wholly crushed.
सुसंभ्रान्त a. wholly confounded.
सुसंर्तु f. N. of a river.
सुसर्व a. entirely complete.
सुसहाय & °**वन्त्** a. having good assistants.
सुसायं n. a good evening.
सुसित a. entirely white, snow-white.
सुसिद्धार्थ a. thoroughly successful or satisfied.
सुसीम a. having the hair well parted or divided, fair-haired (woman).
सुसुख a. very pleasant or comfortable; n. adv.
सुसुखिन् a. very happy or comfortable.
सुस्त्री f. a good or faithful wife.
सुस्थ a. being well or comfortable.
सुस्थकल्प a. quite well or comfortable.*
सुस्थित a. well-established; also = **सुस्थ**.
सुस्थिति f. a beautiful place.
सुस्थिर a. well-established, firm, constant.
सुस्निग्ध a. very lovely or tender.
सुस्वर a. sounding well or loud; n. adv.
सुस्वागत n. a hearty welcome.
सुस्वादु a. well-tasted, sweet; °**तोय** a. containing sweet water.
सुहन a. easy to be beaten or killed.
सुहव a. well invoked or invoking; n. good invocation.
सुहव्य a. fit for a good invocation.
सुहस्त a. having beautiful or skilful hands.
सुहस्त्य a. clever with the hands.
सुहित a. very fit, agreeable, or useful, wholly satisfied or satiated.
सुहुत a. rightly sacrificed or adored; n. right sacrifice.
सुहृज्जन m. a friend or friends.
सुहृत्ता f., °**त्त्व** n. friendship.
सुहृद् m. f. friendly, friend; m. also ally.
सुहृदय a. good-hearted; superl. °**तम**.
सुहृद्वध m. slaying a friend.
सुहोतृ & **सुहोतृ** m. a good sacrificer.
सुहोत्र m. a man's name.
सह्म m. pl. N. of a people.
1**सू**, **सूते**, **सौति**, **सुवति**, °**ते** (**सूयते**, °**ति**), pp. **सूत** & **सुत** (q.v.) generate, beget, bring forth, enliven, impel, set in motion. — **अप** sent or drive away. **अभि** consecrate for (acc.), endow with (instr.). **आ** hurt upon (dat.), send, bestow, procure. **निस्** & **परा** drive away, remove. **प्र** bring forth, produce, impel, set in motion, cause, bid. **संप्र** & **सम्** beget, bring forth, produce. — Cf. **प्रसूत**.
2**सू** m. f. begetter, father or mother; a. —° begetting, producing.
सूकर m. hog, pig (Sū-maker); f. °**री** sow.
सूक्त a. well spoken or recited; n. good recitation (also **सूक्त**), Vedic hymn.
सूक्तवाक m. the recitation of a verse or hymn.
सूक्तवाच् or **सूक्तवाच्** a. reciting a verse or hymn.
सूक्ति f. a good speech or word.
सूक्ष्म a. fine, small, minute, subtile, intangible, inconceivable, atomic; abstr. °**ता** f., °**त्व** n.
सूक्ष्मदर्शिता f. abstr. to seq.
सूक्ष्मदर्शिन् a. sharp-sighted, sagacious.
सूक्ष्मदृष्टि f. sharp sight, penetration.
सूक्ष्मपाद a. having little feet; abstr. °**त्व** n.
सूक्ष्मभूत n. subtile element (ph.).
सूक्ष्ममति & °**मन्त्** a. sagacious.
सूक्ष्मविषय m. subtile object (ph.).
सूक्ष्मशरीर n. the subtile body (ph.).
सूचक, f. **सूचिका** indicating, betraying (gen. or —°); m. informer, denouncer, N. of a man.
सूचन (f. **ई**) n. (& f. **आ**) indicating, announcing, manifesting.
सूचनीय a. to be indicated.
सूचय्, °**यति**, pp. **सूचित** indicate, show, manifest, betray. — **अभि**, **आ**, **उप**, **प्र**, & **सम्** = S.
सूचयितव्य a. to be found out.
सूचि or **सूची** f. needle, sting, any pointed object i.g., pointer i e. index (in books); a kind of military array.
सूचिभेद्य & **सूचीभेद्य** a. very thick or dense (lit. to be pierced with a needle).

सूचिन् m. informer, denouncer.
सूचीक m. a stinging insect.
1सूचीमुख n. point of a needle.
2सूचीमुख, f. ई needle-mouthed, pointed; m. a kind of insect or bird.
सूच्चैस् adv. very loud.
सूच्य a. to be indicated.
सूच्यग्र n. point of a needle.
सूत m. charioteer, a kind of herald or bard; abstr. °ता f., °त्व n.
सूतक n. bird, production; impurity from birth etc. — m. n. quicksilver; f. सूतिका a woman recently delivered.
सूतकान्न & °न्नाद्य n. food from any impure person (cf. prec.).
सूतज, °तनय, & °पुत्र m. the son of a charioteer, E. of Karṇa.
1सूति f. pressing out the Soma or the place for it.
2सूति f. birth, production, origin, offspring, progeny.
सूतिकान्न n. food from a woman recently delivered.
सूतु f. gestation, pregnancy.
सूत्र n. thread, cord, esp. the sacred cord worn by the first three classes; string, wire; line, brief rule or a book of such rules.
सूत्रकर्तृ m. the author of a Sūtra work.
सूत्रकार & °कृत् m. the same.
सूत्रधार m. thread-holder, carpenter or stage-manager, director (f. °री).
सूत्रभृत् m. = prec. (d.).
सूत्रय्, °यति, pp. सूत्रित put together, arrange, make into a Sūtra. — आ & समा bring about, perform, compose. वि drive away, remove.
सूत्रात्मन् m. the thread-soul (ph.).
सूत्रिन् a. furnished with strings; m. stage-manager, director.
सूनी f. genitals (of the cow).
सूद्, सूदयति, °ते lead straight on, keep a-going; put in order, arrange, bring about; finish, kill, destroy. — अभि, नि, विनि, & संनि finish, kill, destroy.
सूद m. receptacle of water, well; mud of a dried pool; a kind of soup; cook, abstr. °ता† f., °त्व† n.
सूदकर्मन् n. the art of cooking.
सूदन, f. आ & ई leading well, putting in order; finishing, destroying (n. as subst.).
सूदयित्नु & सूदिन् a. streaming, flowing over.
सूदशाला f. kitchen.
सूद्य a. belonging to a pool.
सून n. flower; f. आ a kind of plaited basket or dish; slaughter-bench or house, butchery; the killing of a living creature.
सूनर, f. ई beautiful, pleasant, charming, joyous.
सूनाचक्रध्वजवन्त् m. pl. butchers, oilmanufacturers, and distillers (or venders) of spirituous liquors.
सूनादोष m. the guilt of killing animals.
सूनापरिचर a. flying round a butchery (vulture).*
सूनास्थ a. kept in slaughter-house (meat).
सूनिक & सूनिन् m. butcher, flesh-seller.
सूनु m. son, offspring; p. सूनुमन्त्.
सूनृत a. joyous, friendly, kind; hearty i.e. true (speech). — f. आ joy, mirth, jubilation; friendliness, heartiness, truth (opp. अनृत).
†(सूनृतावन्), f. °वरी joyous.
सूनृतावन्त् a. = prec.
सूप m. soup, broth.
सूपकर्तृ m. a cook (soup-maker).
सूपकार & °कृत् m. the same.
सूपचर, °चरण, & °चार a. easily accessible.
सूपरस m. the taste of soup.
सूपवञ्चन a. easily tottered to.
सूपाय m. a good means or expedient.
सूपायन a. easily accessible.
सूभर्व a. well fed.
सूयवस a. & n. = सूयवस.
सूयवसिन् & °स्यु a. having & wishing for good pasturage.
सूर m. the sun.
सूरचक्षस् a. radiant as the sun.
सूरसुत m. the planet Saturn (son of the sun).*

सूरि m. impeller, inciter; sacrifice-master (= यजमान q.v.); chief, lord i.g.; a great scholar or sage.

सूर्क्ष्, सूर्क्षति heed, care for (acc. or gen.).

सूर्क्ष्य a. to be heeded or cared for.

सूर्त a. trodden.

सूर्मि or सूर्मी f. channel (for water); a tubular vessel serving as a candle-stick.

सूर्म्य a. being in tubes or channels.

सूर्य m. the sun or its deity; f. सूर्या the Sun personified as a female, a cert. hymn of the Rigveda.

सूर्यकर m. a sun-beam.

सूर्यकान्त m. the sun-stone (lit. -beloved, a fabulous gem, cf. चन्द्रकान्त).

सूर्यज & °तनय m. the planet Saturn (son of the sun).

सूर्यज्योतिस् a. = seq. 2.

1सूर्यतेजस् n. the heat of the sun.

2सूर्यतेजस् a. radiant or hot as the sun.

सूर्यत्वच् & °त्वचस् a. whose skin or external appearance is as bright as the sun.

सूर्यपाद m. sun-beam.

सूर्यपुत्र m. E. of the Açvins, Yama, & the planet Saturn (cf. सूर्यज); f. ई E. of the Yamunā.

सूर्यप्रभ a. bright as the sun.

सूर्यबिम्ब & °मण्डल n. the orb of the sun.

1सूर्यरश्मि m. a ray of the sun.

2सूर्यरश्मि a. sun-rayed.

सूर्यवंश m. the solar race (of kings); °श्य a. belonging to it.

सूर्यवन्त् a. sunny, solar.

सूर्यवर्चस् a. radiant or glorious as the sun.

†सूर्यवर्ण a. sun-coloured.

सूर्यवार m. Sunday.

सूर्यसम a. sun-like.

सूर्यसिद्धान्त m. T. of an astronomical work.

सूर्याचन्द्रमस् m. du. sun and moon.

सूर्यातप m. the heat of the sun.

सूर्यामास् m. du. sun and moon.

सूर्यास्त m. sunset.

सूर्योढ a. brought by the (setting) sun; m. (± अतिथि) an evening guest.

सूर्योदय m., °न n. sunrise.

सूवरी f. a bringing forth (children).

सृ, सिसर्ति, सरति, °ते, pp. सृत (—° act. & pass.), & सूर्त (q.v.) run, glide, flow, hasten, speed (w. वाजम् & आजिम् run a race); go to, pass over (acc.). C. सारयति cause to run or flow, (liquify, melt*), set in motion; M. सारयते begin to flow. D. सिसीर्षति wish to run. I. सरीसर्ति run hither and thither. — अनु flow or run towards, go along or after, follow, conform one's self to (acc.). C. bid follow, pursue. अप glide down from (abl.); roll back (पश्चात्, waggon); go off, cease, pass away. C. remove, take off or out. व्यप go asunder, withdraw. अपि flow upon (acc.). अभि run or flow near, approach (as friend or foe); visit (esp. of lovers). C. lead to, bring together with (acc.); M. (follow, persecute*), give an appointment or make a love-visit. समव descend; withdraw from (abl.); (C. put to flight*). आ run near, come; attack (acc.). उद् run away. C. drive away or asunder, cast off, remove, dismiss, give up. प्रोद् go off; C. drive away. समुद् send away, dismiss. उप come near, approach, visit (cf. अभि); resort to (acc.). निस् flow out, come forth, appear. C. turn out, expel, remove. अभिनिस् & विनिस् = prec. परा run away. परि flow or run aronnd, circumambulate (acc.), spread everywhere. प्र go forth, spread, appear, begin (also P.), set out, go towards (acc.), pass away. C. stretch forth or out, expose, divulge. विप्र extend farther. संप्र C. stretch out, draw asunder. प्रति rush against (acc.); go back, return. C. bring back, remove, replace. वि run asunder, spread (M. w. तन्वम् open or unveil itself); part with (instr.); come from (abl. or तस्), rush against (acc.). C. send forth. प्रवि rush forth; run away, escape. सम् flow together, go about, roam, wander (esp. from one existence to another). C. cause to wander or to be return bring together, introduce, fix in (loc.); put off, defer. अभिसम् stream together. — Cf. अनुसृत, अनुसृत्य, अभिसृत, प्रविसृत (add.), प्रसृत, विसृत.

सृक m. missile, lance.

सृकवन्त्, सृकायिन्, सृकावन्त्, & सृकाविन् poss. to prec.

सृकाहस्त a. holding a lance in the hand.

सृक्क & सृक्कन् m. n. the corner of the mouth.

सृक्कि n., सृक्किणी f. the same.

सृगवन्त्, सृगायिन् & सृगावन्त् a. = सृकवन्त् etc.

सृगाल m., °ली & °लिका f. jackal.

सृङ्का f. way, path.

1सृज्, सृजति, °ते, सर्जति, pp. सृष्ट (q.v.) let loose, hurl, throw, pour out, emit, send forth; create, produce, beget, make; procure, bestow; use, employ. C. सर्जयति, °ते. D. सिसृक्षति, °ते wish to let loose, M.(A.) wish to create. — अति hurl off, let loose, give up, dismiss, give leave (acc.); deliver, free from (2 acc.); yield, grant, bestow; M. create beyond or as something higher. अनु let loose, dismiss, pour out; deliver, grant, bestow; create after (acc.). अपि add to, mingle with (loc.). अभि hurl upon (acc.), let loose, give free, deliver, abandon, promise, grant, bestow. अव shoot off, pour out, let flow, give up (प्राणान्), deliver over, grant, bsstow; send away, dismiss (M. abdicate); remit, pardon; place in, fix on (loc.). अभ्यव dismiss, send forth to (acc.), let loose, let go (the reins). उपाव shoot off, admit (esp. the calf to the cow), give over to (acc.). व्यव hurl upon (gen.), set down, send away, dismiss; hang or fix on (loc.). समव hurl upon (loc.), let loose, let go, abandon, omit. आ shoot hither, pour in or out, admit (esp. to copulation). समा hang, fasten to (loc.), entrust to (loc.). उद् cast, hurl, pour out, shed, take off, lay down, depose, place in (loc.); stretch out, expand, open, set free, send forth, dismiss, give up; relinquish, abandon, despise, repudiate, renounce, resign; omit, pass over; entrust, commit; produce, create. समुद् hurl, send forth, utter, throw down, cast away, take off; dismiss, set free, let go, relinquish, abandon, expose; deliver up, hand over. उप hurl, cast, let flow, pour upon; send or bring to (acc. or dat.); admit, add, augment; affect or visit with (instr.), vex, plague. निस् pour out, let flow, set free, dismiss, deliver from (abl.), separate, remove. प्र let run or flow, open, set free, indulge, give up, resign, quit, abandon. प्रति hurl against (lit. & fig.), send back. वि throw, shoot, hurl (lit. & fig.), pour out, send forth, dismiss, emit, utter; let loose, set free, deliver from (abl.); cast away, relinquish, abandon; despise, repudiate, renounce, resign, M. cease from (abl.); yield, grant, bestow; create, produce. C. hurl, send forth, emit, utter, set free, leave alone, spare avoid, shun; abandon, expose; yield, grant, bestow, hand over (loc.); create, produce. अनुवि, अभिवि, & प्रतिवि shoot at (acc.). सम् shoot or throw with (instr.); bring together, mix, unite (M.P. refl.); endow or furnish with (instr.); create. — Cf. उपसृष्ट, निसृष्ट, संसृष्ट.

2सृज् (—°) letting loose, emitting, hurling, casting; creating, producing.

सृजय m. a kind of bird.

सृञ्जय m. a man's name.

सृणि m. an elephant-driver's hook; f. सृणी or सृणी sickle, poss. सृण्य.

सृत् running, hastening (—°).

सृत a. & n. running.

सृति f. road, path, way, course, wandering (esp. of the soul).

†सृत्य n. running, flowing.

सृत्वन्, f. सृत्वरी running, hastening.

सृप्, सर्पति, °ते, pp. सृप्त (q.v.) creep, crawl, glide. C. सर्पयति & D. सिसृप्सति only —°; I. सरीसृप्यते creep to and fro. — अति glide along or over (acc.). अधि & समधि glide over (acc.). अनु glide after or along, approach (acc.). समनु approach. अप & व्यप move off, recede. अभि steal upon (acc.). अव glide down (of the setting sun); steal upon, cover gradually (acc.). अन्वव glide after. उपाव, पर्याव, & प्रत्यव approach gently. व्यव creep into (acc.). आ creep near. उपोदा creep forth. उद् creep out or up, rise (lit. & fig.); move gently on. D. wish to rise. उपोद् & व्युद् creep forth. समुद् arise, appear, begin. उप go gently to, steal upon, creep or fall into (acc.); move on, come near, approach (also sexually). समुप approach. निस् & विनिस् creep out. परि go round, roam through. प्र creep near or into, steal upon (acc.), move on, break forth, spread, proceed. प्रति creep back or into. वि move about or along (acc.); move asunder, dispense, spread, expand. सम् creep along or into (acc.); move onward, approach. अनुसम् creep after. उपसम् creep near, steal upon (acc.).

सृप्त a. crept out of (abl.) or into (loc.); *n. the spot where some one has crept.

सृप्र a. slippery, fatty, smooth.

सृबिन्द m. N. of a demon.

सृम m. N. of an Asura.

सृमर m. a kind of animal.

सृष्ट a. let loose, hurled, cast, created, produced; joined or connected with (—∘); covered with, full of (instr.), resolute on (loc. or dat.).

सृष्टि f. letting loose, emission, creation (abstr. & concr.), production; nature, character; spending, liberality.

सृष्टिकृत् m. creator.

सेक m. sprinkling, watering, out-pouring, effusion, gush.

सेक्तृ m. who sprinkles or impregnates.

सेचन a. & n. pouring out, sprinkling.

सेचनघट m. watering pot.

सेतु a. binding, fettering; m. band, fetter; dam, weir, bridge, boundary, barrier, limit.

सेतुबन्ध m. the building of a dam or bridge, T. of a poem in Prākrit.

सेतृ m. who binds or fetters.

सेदि f. weariness, dejectedness.

†सेध a. driving, scaring.

सेधा f. hedge-hog, porcupine.

सेनजित् a. defeating armies; m. N. of a son of Kṛṣṇa etc.

1सेना f. missile, weapon.

2†सेना f. line of battle, army.

सेनाग्र n. the front of an army.

सेनाङ्ग n. a component part of an army.

सेनाचर, ∘जीव, or ∘जोविन् m. soldier.

सेनाजू a. swift as an arrow.

सेनानी m. leader or chief of an army.

सेनापति m. chief of an army, general.

सेनापत्य v. = सैनापत्य.

सेनामुख n. the front of an army.

सेनावाह m. leader of an army.

सेन्द्र a. along with Indra.

सेन्द्रचाप a. with a rainbow.

सेन्द्रिय a. having (with) the organs of sense.

सेन्य a. caused by a weapon (death); m. spearman, warrior.

सेर्ष्य a. jealous, envious.

सेलग m. robber, waylayer.

सेव्, सेवते (∘ति), pp. सेवित stay by (acc. or loc.), inhabit, frequent, visit; serve, revere, worship; attend upon, devote one's self to (acc.); practise, use, employ, enjoy (also sexually). C. सेवयति serve, worship. — अनु stay or dwell in; wait on, reverence. आ = S. समा devote one's self to (acc.), practise, use, employ. उप = S. अभ्युप worship, revere. नि (षेवते) stay in, have intercourse with (loc.); inhabit, visit, frequent, etc. = S. परि (षेवते & सेवते) visit, follow, obey, revere; practise, like. सम् be together, stay at or with, dwell in, frequent, visit etc. = S. — Cf. निषेवित.

सेवक (—∘) inhabiting, serving, revering, practising; m. inhabitant etc.

1सेवन n. sewing; seam, suture.

2सेवन n. following, serving, revering, practising, frequenting, using, employing (mostly —∘).

सेवनीय a. to be followed etc. (v. prec.).

सेवा f. visit, service, attendance, worship, devotion to, use, practice, employment; sexual intercourse with (gen. or —∘).

सेवादक्ष a. clever in service.

सेवाधर्म m. the duty or rule of service.
1सेवितव्य a. to be sewn.
2सेवितव्य a. to be inhabited, practised, honoured, served, taken care of.
सेवितृ a. & m. serving, worshipping, practising; servant etc.
सेविन् a. serving, following, revering, inhabiting, enjoying carnally, practising, using, employing.
सेव्य a. to be served etc. (v. prec.).
सैञ्ज m. a cert. dry substance & a cert. organ in the belly.
सैंह, f. ई relating to a lion, leonine.
सैकत, f. ई sandy, consisting or made of sand. n. (a. —° f. आ) sandy soil, sandbank, poss. °तिन्.
सैकावलि, f. ई furnished with an ornament consisting of a single string of pearls.
सैनान्य & सैनापत्य n. commandership.
सैनिक a. belonging to an army; m. soldier, warrior.
सैन्दूरी कृ dye with minium.
सैन्धव, f. ई belonging to the sea or to the Indus; m. pl. the inhabitants of the country near the Indus, m. n. a kind of rock-salt (found in this country).
सैन्धवखिल्य & °घन m. a lump of salt.
सैन्य a. relating to an army; m. soldier, n. army (also m.), camp.
सैरन्ध्र m., ई f. a kind of domestic servant, a mixed tribe or caste.
सैरावन्त् a. furnished with provender.
सैरिभ m. a buffalo.
सैर्य m. a cert. plant & a cert insect.
सैस & सैसक a. leaden.
सोच्छ्वास a. taking breath; adv.
सोढव्य a. to be borne.
सोढृ m. who bears or endures.
सोतु m. pressing or pouring out the Soma.
सोतृ or सोतृ m. who presses out the Soma.
सोत्क a. longing, regretful.
सोत्कण्ठ a. = prec., n. adv.
सोत्व a. to be pressed out.
सोत्प्रास a. ironical, sarcastic; n. adv.
सोत्सव a. festive, joyous, w. दिन n. a festival day.
सोत्साह a. energetic, resolute; n. adv.
सोत्सुक a. full of desire or longing for (loc., acc. w. प्रति, or —°).
सोत्सेक a. haughty, arrogant.
सोत्सेध a. high, elevated.
सोदक a. with water, containing water.
सोदर, f. ई born from the same womb; m. (± भ्रातृ) & f. ई such a brother and sister.
सोदरस्नेह m. brotherly love.
सोदर्य, f. आ = सोदर, f. ई.
सोदर्यस्नेह m. = सोदरस्नेह.
सोद्योग a. zealous, energetic.
सोद्वेग a. agitated, restless; n. adv.
सोन्माद a. mad, insane.
सोपकरण a. with the implement
सोपकार a. beneficial.
सोपचार a. polite, deferential; n. adv.
सोपस्वेद a. moistened, wet.
सोपहास a. laughing, sarcastic.
सोपाक m. a cert. mixed caste.
सोपान n. stairs, a ladder; abstr. °त्व n.
सोपानत्क a. having sandals or shoes.
सोपानह् a. (nom. °नत्) the same.
सोभरि m. N. of an ancient poet.
सोभरीयु a. longing for Sobhari (v. prec.).
सोम m. the Soma (plant or juice, often personified as a god); the moon or the god of the moon.
सोमक m. N. of a Rishi etc.; pl. N. of a people. f. सोमिका N. of a crow.
सोमकाम a. desirous of Soma.
सोमतीर्थ n. N. of a place of pilgrimage.
सोमदत्त m. a man's name.
सोमदेव m. the god of the moon; N. of an author etc.
सोमधान a. holding or containing Soma.
सोमन् m. who presses or offers the Soma.
सोमप a. Soma-drinking.
सोमपति m. lord of the Soma or of the moon.
सोमपर्ण n. Soma-leaf.
सोमपर्वन् n. Soma-time.
सोमपा a. = सोमप; superl. °तम.
सोमपात्र n. Soma-vessel.
1सोमपान n. abstr. to seq.
2सोमपान a. Soma-drinking.

सोमपायिन् & °पावन् a. = prec.
सोमपाल m. Soma-keeper.
सोमपीति f. a drinking of Soma (only dat.).
सोमपीथ m., °पेय n. = prec.
सोमपीथिन् a. partaking of a draught of Soma.
सोमपृष्ठ a. bearing Soma on the back.
सोमप्रभ a. radiant as the moon; m. & f. आ a man's & woman's name.
सोमभृत् a. bringing Soma.
सोममद (°माद्) a. drunk with Soma.
सोममद m. abstr. to prec.
सोमयज्ञ & °याग m. a Soma-sacrifice.
सोमयाजिन् a. offering Soma.
सोमरक्ष m. keeper of the Soma.
सोमराजन्, f. °ज्ञी having Soma as king.
सोमरात m. N. of a man.
1सोमरूप n. a form of Soma.
2सोमरूप a. Soma-formed.
सोमलिप्त a. smeared with Soma.
सोमवंश m. the lunar race of kings.
सोमवंशीय & °वंश्य a. belonging to the lunar race.
सोमवन्त् a. having or containing Soma
सोमवर्चस् a. glorious as Soma.
सोमवामिन् a. vomiting Soma.
सोमविक्रयिन् m. seller of Soma.
†सोमवृद्ध a. gladdened by Soma.
सोमशित a. excited by Soma.
सोमश्रवस् m. a man's name.
सोमश्रेष्ठ a. having Soma as chief.
सोमसखि a. having Soma as friend.
सोमसलिल a. Soma-water.
सोमसव m. Soma-pressing.
सोमसवन a. wherefrom Soma is pressed.
सोमसुत् a. pressing Soma.
सोमसुति & सोमसुत्या f. pressing of Soma.
सोमसुत्वन् a. = सोमसुत्.
सोमहार & °रिन्† a. robbing Soma.
सोमांशु m. Soma-stem or moon-beam.
सोमाद् a. eating Soma.
सोमापूषन् m. du. Soma and Pūṣan.
सोमाभिषिक्त a. sprinkled with Soma.
सोमारुद्र m. du. Soma and Rudra.
सोमार्थिन् a. desiring Soma.
सोमावती f. containing Soma.
सोमाहुति f. Soma-sacrifice.
सोमिन् a. having or offering Soma.
सोमेज्य f. Soma-sacrifice.
सोम्य a. having to do with Soma, consisting of Soma etc.; m. Soma-offerer.
सोष a. mixed with alkaline earth.
सोष्णीष a. turbaned.
सोष्मता f. heat, warmth.
सोष्मन् a. hot, warm.
सौकर, f. ई relating to a hog.
सौकर्य n. easiness of performance, facility.
(सौकुमार* &) सौकुमार्य n. tenderness, delicacy.
सौकृत्य n. well-doing.
सौक्ष्म्य n. minuteness, subtility.
सौख्य n. welfare, comfort, joy, bliss.
सौगत, f. ई Buddhistic; m. a Buddhist.
सौगन्धिक a. sweet-scented, fragrant; n. a white (or blue) water-lily.
सौगन्ध्य n. odour, perfume.
सौजन्य n. goodness, benevolence.
सौति m. E. of Lomaharṣaṇa (patron. from सूत).
1सौत्य a. relating to Soma-pressing.
2सौत्य a. relating to a charioteer, n. his office.
सौत्र a. consisting of threads or belonging to a Sūtra.
सौत्रामण, f. ई belonging to Indra; f. ई a cert. ceremony.
सौदर्य a. brotherly; n. brotherly relation.
सौदामनी or °मिनी (± विद्युत्) f. lightning; N. of sev. women.
सौदास m. a patron. name.
सौध n. a plastered or whitewashed mansion; any great house or palace.
सौधन्वन m. son of Sudhanvan, pl. E. of the Ribhus.
सौधर्म्य n. honesty.
सौन m. butcher; n. (± मांस) butcher's meat.
सौनिक m. butcher or hunter.
सौन्दर्य n. beauty, splendour, nobility.
सौपर्ण (सौपर्ण), f. ई relating to the falcon etc.
सौप्तिक a. relating to sleep, nocturnal; n. = seq.
सौप्तिकवध m. nocturnal attack on (—°).
सौप्रजास्त्व n. possession of good offspring.

सैबल m., **ई** f. son & daughter of Subala (Çakuni & Gāndhārī).

सौबलेय m., **ई** f. = prec.

सौभ n. N. of a mythical city.

सौभग n. happiness, loveliness, beauty.

सौभगत्व n. condition of happiness.

सौभद्र m. metron. of Abhimanyu.

सौभाग्य n. = **सौभग**.

सौभाग्यदेवता f. an auspicious or tutelary deity.

सौभ्रात्र n. good brotherhood, fraternity.

सौम a. relating to Soma.

सौमदत्ति m. patron. from Somadatta.

सौमनस, f. **ई** relating to flowers, flowery; n. pleasure, satisfaction, cheerfulness (also m.), benevolence, kindness, favour.

सौमनस्य a. causing pleasure or satisfaction; n. cheerfulness, mirth.

सौमिक, f. **ई** relating to Soma.

सौमित्र m. metron. of Lakṣmaṇa; n. friendship.

सौमित्रि m. = prec.; du. L. & Çatrughna.

सौमिल or **सौमिल्ल** m. N. of a poet.

सौमी (cf. **सौम्य**) f. moonshine.

सौमुख्य n. mirth, joy.

सौम्य or **सौम्य** (f. **सौमी** & **सौम्या**) relating or consecrated to Soma, consisting of S., i.g. Soma-; Soma- or moon-like, auspicious, gentle, dear (esp. voc. **सौम्य** my dear); m. pl. a class of Manes.

सौम्यता f., **॰त्व** n. gentleness, mildness.

सौम्यदर्शन a. of gentle aspect.

सौम्यनामन्, f. **॰म्नी** having a lovely name.

सौम्यरूप a. friendly, mild towards (gen.).

सौम्यवपुस् & **सौम्याकृति** a. of a pleasant form.

सौयवसि m. a patron. name.

1**सौर** a. consisting of spirituous liquor.

2**सौर**, f. **ई** relating to the sun, solar; m. a worshipper of the sun.

सौरभ a. sweet-smelling; f. **ई** a cow (daughter of Surabhi); n. odour, fragrance.

सौरभेय m., **ई** f. bull, cow.

सौरभ्य n. odour, fragrance.

सौराज्य n. good government, p. **॰वन्त्**.

सौराष्ट्र & **॰क** a. coming from Surāṣṭra; m. pl. the inhabitants of Surāṣṭra.

सौरिक a. relating to spirituous liquor.

सौर्य (f. **सौरी** & **सौर्या**) a. belonging to the sun.

सौर्व a. celestial.

सौवर a. relating to sound.

सौवर्ण, f. **ई** & **आ** golden.

सौवश्व्य n. horse-race or = **स्वश्व्य**.

(***सौविद** &) **॰दल्ल** m. guardian of a harem.

सौविष्टकृत, f. **ई** relating or consecrated to (Agni) Sviṣṭakṛt.

सौवीर & **॰क** m. pl. N. of a people.

सौव्रत्य n. faith, devotion.

सौशब्द्य n. the correct formation of grammatical forms.

सौशाम्य n. peace, conciliation.

सौशील्य n. goodness of nature or character.

सौश्रवस a. having a good renown; n. loud praise, glory, contest.

सौषुम्ण n. a cert. sun-beam.

सौष्ठव n. good condition, excellence.

सौहार्द & **सौहार्द्य** n. affection, friendship.

सौहित्य n. satiety, satisfaction; kindness, friendliness.

सौहृद a. coming from a friend, a friend's; m. a friend; n. = seq.

सौहृद्य n. friendship, affection.

स्कन्द्, **स्कन्दति**, **॰ते**, pp. **स्कन्न** leap, spring, spurt; drop, be spilled, fall; leap upon i.e. cover, impregnate. C. **स्कन्दयति** pour out, spill; omit, neglect. I. **कनिष्कन्** leaping (of frogs). — **अति** (**स्क** & **ष्क**) leap upon or over, fall down. **अभि** (**स्क** & **ष्क**) leap upon (for copulation). **अव** spring or spurt down; spring towards or upon, attack, overpower. **अभ्यव** spring down, in, or out; meet with, encounter. **समव** S. & C. assail. **आ** leap, resort to, depend on (acc.); also = **समा** attack, assail. **परि** (**स्क** & **ष्क**) leap about (also I. **चनिष्कदत्**); spill, scatter. **प्र** spring forth, down, upon (acc.); spurt, drop, fall; attack, assail. **सम्** drop or spring off. — Cf. **परिस्कन्न**.

†**स्कन्द** m. hopper, jumper; aggressor, assailant; N. of the god of war.

स्कन्दन m. the being spilt.

स्कन्दपुत्र m. son of Skanda i.e. thief.

स्कन्दपुराण n. T. of a Purāṇa.

स्कन्दित n. leaping upon, impregnation.

स्कन्धं m. shoulder, stem or trunk of a tree; section, chapter of a book, mass, multitude, a whole or aggregate.

स्कन्धदेश m. the region of the shoulder.

स्कन्धवन्त् a. having a stem (stems).

स्कन्धशिरस् n. shoulder-blade.

स्कंन्धस् n. ramification, branches or top of a tree.

स्कन्धावार m. head-quarters (lit. the stem's i.e. the king's guard).

स्कन्धिन् a. having a (strong) stem.

स्कंन्ध्य a. relating to the shoulders.

स्कभाय्, °यंति v. स्कभ्.

स्कंभीयंस् (compar.) supporting well.

स्कभ् or **स्कम्भ्**, स्कभ्नाति or स्कभ्नोति, pp. स्कभितं prop, support, fix; stop, restrain, obstruct. C. स्कभायंति = S. — आ fix in or at (loc.). उप hold up by supports. प्रति hold stand against; lean upon (acc.). वि (ष्क) fix, establish; C. the same. — Cf. प्रतिष्कंभे (add.).

स्कम्भं m. prop, support, pillar.

स्कम्भंदेष्ण a. whose gifts are firm (like pillars).

स्कंम्भन n., स्कम्भनिं & °नी (nom. °नीस्) = स्कम्भं.

स्कु, स्कौति, स्कुनोति, स्कुनाति stir (tr.), rake up (fire), pick (teeth). I. चोष्कूयंते rake together, accumulate.

†**स्कृधोयु** v. अस्कृधोयु.

स्खल्, स्खलंति, °ते, pp. स्खलित (q.v.) stumble, totter, waver, stammer, folter, eor, fail. C. स्खलयति cause to falter (voice). परि, प्र, & वि = S.

स्खल m. stumbling, tottering.

स्खलन & °लित n. the same; blunder, fault, error, loss.

स्तन्, स्तनति, mostly स्तनयति, pp. स्तनित (q.v.) thunder, roar, sound. — अभि, निस्, & प्र = S.

स्तंन m. the breast of a woman.

स्तनकोटि f. nipple (breast-point).

स्तनग्रह m. (a child's) taking of the breast.

स्तनतट m. n. bosom (slope of the breasts).

स्तनंथ or **स्तनंथु** m. roaring of the lion.

स्तनंधय, f. ई breast-sucking, a suckling.

स्तनप & °पायिन् a. = prec.

स्तनपान n. the sucking of the breast.

स्तनभर m. a thick (lit. weight of a) breast.

स्तनमध्य n. the room between the breasts.

स्तनंयद्म a. rushing along with thunder.

स्तनयित्नु m. thunder.

स्तनांशुक n. covering of the bosom.

स्तनान्तर n. = स्तनमध्य.

स्तनाभोग m. a full (lit. fulness of a) breast.

स्तनावरण n. covering of the bosom.

स्तनित a. thundering; n. thunder.

स्तनोत्तरीय n. covering of the bosom.

स्तन्य n. (m.) the milk in a woman's breast.

स्तन्यत्याग m. leaving off the mother's milk, weaning.

स्तबक m. bunch, esp. of flowers.

स्तब्ध a. stiff, rigid, immovable, n. adv. Abstr. °ता f., °त्व f.

स्तब्धकर्ण m. N. of a lion (stiff-eared).

स्तब्धलोचन a. having immovable i.e. unwinking eyes.

स्तब्धी कृ make rigid or stiff.

स्तब्धीभाव m. rigidity, immobility.

स्तम्ब & °क m. bunch, esp. grass-bunch.

स्तम्बजं a. bushy, tufty.

स्तम्बशंस् adv. by bunches.

स्तम्बमित्र m. N. of a man.

स्तम्बिंन् a. bushy.

स्तम्बेरम m. elephant (delighting in grass-bunches).

स्तभ् or **स्तम्भ्**, स्तभ्नाति, स्तभ्नोति, स्तम्भते (°ति), pp. स्तभितं & स्तब्ध (q.v.) prop, support, uphold, make firm or steady; M. become firm or rigid. C. स्तम्भायंति & स्तम्भयति, °ते = S., the latter also = make stiff or lame, paralyze, stun, obstruct, suppress. — अव (ष्ट) fix, fasten, prop, support, intr. lean upon (acc.); seize, take prisoner, obstruct, shut up. पर्यव (ष्ट) surround. समव (ष्ट) raise up (fig.); lean upon (acc.). उद् (त्त) prop up, fix, establish. C. lift up, raise (lit. & fig.); excite, impel. उप erect, uphold, support. प्रति (ष्ट) hold against, M. intr. वि (ष्ट) fix, establish, raise (lit. & fig.), make firm, stiff, or immovable, stop, obstruct; lean upon (acc.).

C. stop, hold back. सम् confirm, strengthen, make stiff or rigid, stop, suppress. C. the same. अभिसम्, परिसम् & प्रतिसम् confirm, strengthen. — Cf. अवष्टब्ध, उत्तब्ध & उत्तभित, प्रस्तब्ध, विष्टब्ध & विष्टभित, संस्तब्ध.

स्तम्भ m. post, column, prop, support (lit. & fig.); fixedness, stiffness, immobility; obstruction, hindrance, suppression; arrogance, haughtiness.

स्तम्भक a. stopping, restraining.

स्तम्भन (f. ई) & n. laming, paralyzing, fixing, stopping, restraining.

स्तम्भभञ्जक m. N. of an elephant (pillar-breaker).*

स्तम्भिन् a. having posts or columns; fixing, stopping; haughty, arrogant.

स्तम्भी भू become (as immovable as) a post.

स्तर m. stratum, layer.

स्तरण n. strewing, scattering.

स्तरी f. (nom. °रीस्) barren, not bearing, esp. a cow or heifer.

स्तरीमन् m. strewing, scattering (only loc.).

स्तर्य a. to be thrown down.

स्तव & स्तवथ m. praise, hymn, song.

स्तवन n. praising, celebrating.

स्तवान् (nom. sgl.) thundering or mighty.

स्तवितृ m. praiser.

स्तव्य a. to be praised.

स्तायु m. thief.

स्ताव m. praise; °क a. & m. praising, praiser.

स्ति m. pl. servants, dependants.

†स्तिघ्, स्तिघ्नोति, स्तिघ्नुते proceed, stride. — अति mount, ascend. प्र rise.

स्तिपा a. house-protecting.

स्तिम्, only pp. स्तिमित stiff, motionless, inactive; n. adv. or as abstr. (also °ता f., °त्व n.).

स्तिया f. standing or stagnant water.

स्तोम a. lazy, slow.

स्तीर्ण a. spread, scattered, strewed.

स्तीर्णबर्हिस् a. whose sacrificial straw is strewed.

स्तु, स्तौति, स्तुते, स्तवते (स्तवीति, स्तुवते, °ति), pp. स्तुत (q.v.) praise, extol, celebrate, sing, chant. C. स्तवयति praise, स्तावयते cause to praise. D. तुष्टूषति wish to praise. — अनु (ष्टौति), अभि (ष्टौति), उप, & परि (ष्टौति) = S. प्र praise; put forward, commence, begin; also = प्रस्तावयति mention. वि sing praises. सम् sing or praise (together). अभिसम् & परिसम् praise, extol. — Cf. प्रस्तुत, विष्टुत, संस्तुत.

(स्तुक m. &) स्तुका f. lock or tuft of wool or hair; poss. स्तुकाविन्.

स्तुत् & स्तुति f. praise, eulogy.

स्तुत a. praised; n. praise or = seq.

स्तुतिगीतक n. song of praise.

स्तुत्य a. to be praised, praiseworthy.

स्तुप m. tuft of hair, top-knot.

1स्तुभ्, स्तोभति (°ते) utter a sound, shout, exult, warble, etc. — अनु follow in shouting. अभि add by shouting. व्यव separate by sounds. परि shout around. प्र incite by shouting. प्रति shout in return, re-echo.

2स्तुभ् f. shout, exultation.

स्तुभ्वन् a. shouting, exulting.

स्तूप m. top, esp. of the head, tuft of hair; heap or pile of earth, a Buddhist tomb.

1स्तृ, स्तृणाति, स्तृणीते, स्तृणोति, स्तृणुते (स्तरति), pp. स्तीर्ण & स्तृत (q.v.) strew (esp. the sacrificial straw), spread out; strew over, cover; throw down, overthrow. D. तुस्तूर्षते wish to throw down. — अभि, अव, & समव strew, cover. आ strew, spread, expand; cover, smear. समा strew over. उप lay or pour over, (± आज्यम्) form a coating with the sacrificial butter, cover or wrap with (instr.), strew, expand; (± आज्यम्) pour the sacrificial butter over. नि throw down. परि strew around, cover, spread, expand. प्र strew, scatter, spread out. वि spread or stretch out, expand, diffuse; also = C. विस्तारयति amplify on (acc.). सम् spread or expand (together), strew, cover. — Cf. आस्तीर्ण & आस्तृत, उपस्तीर्ण, प्रस्तीर्ण, विस्तीर्ण & विस्तृत, संस्तीर्ण & संस्तृत.

2स्तृ (instr. pl. स्तृभिस्) star.

स्तृति f. spreading, covering.

स्तृत्य a. to be thrown down.

स्तृह्, स्तृहति crush.

स्तेन m. thief, robber; f. आ.
स्तेनय्, °यति steal, rob.
स्तेय n. theft, robbery.
स्तेयकृत् a. stealing, stealer of (—°).
स्तेयिन् m. thief, robber.
स्तैन्य n. theft, robbery.
स्तैमित्य n. lameness, fixedness, immobility.
स्तोक m. drop; adj. small, insignificant, °— & n. a little; *स्तोकेन & °कात् in comp. w. a pp. hardly, just. Abstr. °ता† f., °त्व† n.
स्तोकक m. E. of the bird Cātaka (who lives on rain-drops).
स्तोकशस् adv. drop by drop, sparingly.
स्तोकीय & स्तोक्य a. relating to drops (of ghee).
स्तोतव्य a. to be praised.
स्तोतृ m. praiser, worshipper.
स्तोत्र n. praise, hymn; a cert. kind of recitations (r.).
स्तोत्रिय or स्तोत्रीय a. relating to a Stotra.
स्तोभ m. shout, trill; p. °वन्त्.
स्तोम m. praise, song of praise.
स्तोममय a. consisting of Stomas.
स्तोमवर्धन a. increasing (or delighting in) praise.
स्तोमवाहस् a. offering or receiving praise.
स्तोम्य a. worthy of or relating to a song of praise.
स्तौल a. heavy, tardly, dull.
स्त्या, स्त्यायते, pp. स्त्यान (q.v.) coagulate, stiffen, thicken, strengthen (intr.). — Cf. संस्त्यान.
स्त्यान a. coagulate, stiff, rigid.
स्त्री f. woman, wife, female (also of animals); a feminine or the feminine gender (g.).
स्त्रीक (—°) woman, wife.
स्त्रीकटि or °टी f. a woman's hip.
स्त्रीकाम a. desirous of women or of female children.
स्त्रीकार्य n. the service of women.
स्त्रीक्षीर n. mother's milk.
स्त्रीगमन n. intercourse with women.
स्त्रीघातक & °घ्न a. murdering a (his) wife.
स्त्रीजन m. womankind.
स्त्रीजननी f. bringing forth (only) females.
स्त्रीजित a. ruled by a (his) wife.
स्त्रीत्व n. womanhood or the fem. gender (g.).
स्त्रीद्विष् & °द्वेषिन् a. hating woman, misogynist.
स्त्रीधन n. a wife's (peculiar) property.
स्त्रीधर्म m. the duty of or laws for woman; coition.
स्त्रीपुंधर्म m. the laws for man and wife.
स्त्रीपुंस m. du. man and wife.
स्त्रीपूर्व & °क a. having formerly been a woman.
स्त्रीप्रत्यय m. suffix forming feminines.
स्त्रीप्रसू f. = स्त्रीजननी.
स्त्रीबालघातिन् m. a slayer of women and children.
स्त्रीभव & °भाव m. the state or condition of a woman, womanhood.
स्त्रीमय, f. ई womanly, womanish.
स्त्रीय्, °यति desire a woman.
स्त्रीरत्न n. a jewel of a woman, E. of Lakṣmī.
1स्त्रीलिङ्ग n. the female organ or the feminine gender (g.).
2स्त्रीलिङ्ग a. having the characteristics of a female; feminine (g.), abstr. °त्व n.
स्त्रीवश & °वश्य a. ruled by a woman.
स्त्रीविवाह m. marriage (with a woman).
स्त्रीविषय m. cohabitation.
स्त्रीसख m. a friend of women.
स्त्रीषू f. = स्त्रीजननी.
स्त्रीसङ्ग m. intercourse with women.
स्त्रीसंग्रहण n. seduction or violation of a woman.
स्त्रीसंबन्ध m. matrimonial connection with a woman.
स्त्रीसंभोग m. the (carnal) enjoyment of a woman.
स्त्रीहत्या f. the murder of a woman.
स्त्रीहन्तृ m. the murderer of a woman.
स्त्रीहुत n. sacrifice offered by a woman.
स्त्रैण, f. ई female, feminine, fond of women; n. womanhood, womankind, a multitude of women.
*स्त्रैणगर्भ m. embryo.
स्त्रैषूय n. birth of a female.
स्त्र्याजीव m. subsisting on (the earnings or the prostitution of) a woman.
स्थ (ष्ठ) standing, living, being in, occupied with, devoted to (—°).

स्थग्, स्थगयति, pp. स्थगित cover, hide, conceal.

स्थगन n. covering, hiding.

स्थगु or स्थडु m. hunch.

स्थण्डिल a. levelled piece of ground prepared for a sacrifice, place, spot, ground i.g.

स्थण्डिलशय्या & °शायिका f. abstr. to seq.

स्थण्डिलशायिन् a. lying on the bare ground.

स्थपति m. chief or governor of a district; architect.

स्थपुट a. rugged, uneven, hump-backed; n. a hump.

स्थपुटगत a. belonging to a hump (flesh).

स्थल n. raised or dry ground, land (opp. water), earth, ground, place, spot; स्थली f. mound, eminence (also स्थला), ground, spot.

स्थलकमल n., °लिनी f. the flowering shrub.

स्थलग & °चर a. land-going, living on dry land.

स्थलज a. land-born, terrestrial.

स्थलस्थ a. standing (being) on dry ground.

स्थलारूढ a. alighted on the ground.

स्थली v. स्थल.

स्थलोद्देवता f. a local divinity.

स्थलीय्, °यति take for dry land.

स्थलीशायिन् a. lying on the bare ground.

स्थविमन् m. the thick end, the broad side.

स्थविर, f. आ & ई thick, broad, firm, massy, sturdy; full-grown, old, venerable.

स्थविष्ठ (superl.) thickest, grossest.

स्थवीयंस् (compar.) thicker, grosser, sturdier.

स्थशस् adv. according to the place.

1स्था, तिष्ठति, °ते, pp. स्थित (q.v.) stand, stay, stop, remain, wait; stand by (loc.), declare for (dat.); hold out or bear up against (gen. ± पुरस्); continue in a condition or action (nom., esp. of a pp.; ger., instr. or loc.), exist, be present; belong to (dat. or gen.); serve for (dat.); be turned to, rest on, abide in (loc.); enter, mount, ascend (acc.); spring or arise from (gen. or abl.); cease, desist from (abl.); remain unmentioned, be left aside (esp. imper.). C. स्थापयति, °ते cause to stand, stop, arrest, restrain; put, place, set in (loc. r. acc., w. वशे subdue), appoint to (loc. or अर्थम्, r. acc.); commit, entrust to (loc. or हस्ते); found, erect, build, establish; fix, settle, determine; make, render (2 acc.). D. तिष्ठासति wish to remain in (instr.). — अति rise over; rule, master (acc.). अधि stand upon, mount, ascend; stay, abide, be fixed or situated in (loc. or acc.); be founded or based upon (loc.); use, employ, show, betray; also = prec. समधि direct, guide, rule, manage, carry on. अनु stand still after or together with (loc. or acc.); stay, abide, sit down upon (acc.); follow, obey, conform one's self to, imitate, help, assist; carry on, practise, commit, perform, do. अन्तर् bar the way, obstruct, arrest. अप stand aloof, forsake (abl.). अपि stand in the way of (acc.). अभि set the foot upon, rise over, step towards or against (acc.), withstand, overcome. अव M.(A.) stand off, withdraw; be deprived of, miss (abl.); go down, descend; enter, come to (acc. or loc.); fall to one's (dat.) share; stop, stand still; abide or remain in (loc.); continue doing or being (ger., nom., or instr.); exist, be present; begin, undertake, determine. C. cause to stand, stop, restrain; let stand, leave behind; put, place, lay etc. in or on (loc.); establish, fix, settle; strengthen, comfort. पर्यव M. become strong or firm; penetrate, pervade. C. excite, comfort. प्रत्यव M. come back, return (w. पुनर्); resist, oppose. C. w. आत्मानम् compose one's self. व्यव M. be separated, part from (abl.); stop, stay, remain; prepare for (dat.); be valid, pass for, appear as (nom.). समव C. stop, arrest; fasten, strengthen. आ stand on (loc.); mount, ascend; step into, enter; take one's place at, resort to (acc.); get to, partake of, enjoy (acc.); undergo, incur; take, choose, use, employ. M. accede to, acknowledge; stand by, set a value upon (loc.). C. cause to ascend or enter, introduce; cause to stay, keep back; put, place, lay; bring near, procure; fix in, fasten to (loc.). अन्वा enter, ascend, attain (after one another). उपा go to, have intercourse with (acc.); attend to, observe. समुपा step near; attend to, practise. समा ascend, resort to, enter, stop, stay; prepare for, set about, take to, choose, use, employ, practise, execute. उद् stand up, rise (esp. from a sacrificial acts, i.e. finish, close), awake, appear, sprout, grow. M. raise one's self to, prepare for (dat. or loc.). C. cause to stand up, raise, scare up, awaken (from sleep or death); lift up, erect, establish; pull or draw out; send off, expel, incite, instigate, urge on, encourage. D. wish to rise. अनूद् rise after, follow. अभ्युद् rise towards, go to meet (acc.); begin, undertake. उपोद् rise before or to meet, approach, go to (acc.). प्रोद् spring up, rise, appear. प्रत्युद् rise up to meet (acc.). व्युद् rise up in different directions; turn from, give up (abl.); forget one's duty (M.). C. call in question, disagree about (acc.); alienate, remove, depose. समुद् rise (together), come out of, spring from (abl.); appear, become visible; go about to work, prepare for (loc. or infin.). C. cause or bid to rise, lift up, rouse, awaken. उप stand by, near, opposite, or round (acc.); come near, approach, resort to, attend on, serve, worship; present with (instr.); be present or at hand, be to one's disposal or fall to one's (acc. or gen.) share. C. cause to stand near or opposite (acc.); fetch, bring near. अनूप step near (after one another), approach (acc.). अभ्युप worship. C. bring near. पर्युप stand around (acc.); attend with (instr.). प्रत्युप M. stand opposite, attend on (acc.). समुप stand near, approach, fall to one's lot (acc.). नि C. fix in (loc.). परिनि C. teach thoroughly (gen. of pers.). निस् grow forth, rise from (abl.); bring to an end, accomplish, prepare, make ready. C. drive out; prepare, make ready. परि stand around or in the way; obstruct, hinder; be left, remain. प्र A.(M.) rise, stand upright, stand before (acc.); M. be up or awake, (A.) set out to go, depart from (abl.), betake one's self to (acc. ± प्रति or loc.). C. send out, dismiss, banish, put away. अतिप्र rise above (acc.), be prominent. अनुप्र set out after (acc.), follow; C. send after. अभिप्र go out in pursuit of, have in view (acc. ± प्रति), prevail over (acc.). C. drive out (cattle). विप्र M.(A.) rise or set out (in various directions); go asunder, spread, expand. संप्र M. stand or step together (before the altar); set out to go, betake one's self to (acc. or loc.). प्रति stand, stay, remain; stand still or firm, be established or founded upon (loc.); get a place or foothold, thrive, prosper; withstand, resist; spread over (acc.). C. set up, erect, fix, support; place in or upon, appoint to (loc.); present, offer, entrust or commit to (loc.). अनुप्रति get on, thrive or prosper after (acc.). संप्रति apply to (loc.). वि M.(A.) stand apart, go asunder, be spread in or over (acc.); part with or be separated from (abl.); stand firm, not budge. C. spread, extend. अनुवि & अभिवि M. spread over, pervade (acc.). सम् M.(A.) stand by, remain with (loc., w. वाक्ये obey); stand still, stop, stay; meet (as foes); come to an end or to perfection; succeed, prosper; perish, die. C. lift up, raise, strengthen, comfort (w. आत्मानम् compose one's self); fix, erect, build, establish, settle; bring on or in (loc.); check, restrain; get through, finish, kill. अनुसम् go along, pursue. M. be finished later. अभिसम् stand still or end with (acc.). C. cause to stand still or to end with. — Cf. अधिष्ठित, अनुष्ठित, अनुसंस्थित, अभिष्ठित, अभ्युत्थित, अभ्युपस्थित, अवस्थित, आस्थित, उत्थित, उपस्थित, उपास्थित, निष्ठित, निःष्ठित (sic!), परिनिष्ठित, परिष्ठित, परिस्थित, पर्यवस्थित (add.), पर्युपस्थित, प्रतिष्ठित, प्रत्युपस्थित, प्रस्थित, प्रोत्थित, विष्ठित, व्यवस्थित, व्युत्थित, संस्थित, समवस्थित, समास्थित, समुत्थित, समुपस्थित, संप्रतिष्ठित.

2स्था (nom. m. n. स्थास्) standing (often —°), immovable (opp. जंगत्).

स्थाणवीय a. belonging to Çiva (cf. seq.).

स्थाणु a. standing, firm, immovable; m. trunk or stem of a tree, post, pillar, E. of Çiva.

स्थाणुभूत a. (being) immovable as the trunk of a tree.

स्थाणूच्छेद् a. who roots out the trunks of trees.

स्थातव्य n. imp. (it is) to be stood or remained.

1स्थातृ a. standing, stationary.

2स्थातृ m. guide (of horses).

स्थात्र n. station, place.

स्थान n. standing, remaining, abiding, not budging; continuation, duration; state. condition, position, rank, dignity; shape, form, appearance; sphere, domain, province; abode, place, seat, home, stead (loc. w. gen. or —° instead of); proper place or time, occasion or object for (gen. or —°); place of articulation, organ (g.); the (4) stamina of a kingdom (treasury etc.).

स्थानक m. N. of a man. n. position, attitude; rank, dignity; place, spot.

स्थानपति & °पाल m. protector of a place or region.

स्थानभङ्ग m. ruin of a place.

स्थानभ्रंश m. loss of a place.

स्थानभ्रष्ट a. removed from one's place.

स्थानयोग m. pl. the various places or modes for keeping goods.

स्थानविद् a. knowing a place (places).

स्थानस्थ & °स्थित a. standing (being) at one's place.

स्थानान्तर n. another place.

स्थानासन n. du. standing and sitting down.

स्थानासेध m. confinement to a certain place, imprisonment.

स्थानिन् a. having the first or the right place; m. the primitive element (g.).

स्थानीय a. being in or instead of (—°).

स्थानेश्वर m. = स्थानपति.

स्थापक m. erector (of an image), establisher, founder; a cert. person of the stage-business.

स्थापत्य n. the office of a स्थपति.

स्थापन a. establishing, fixing, settling, founding; n. & f. आ the act of establishing etc.

स्थापनीय a. to be fixed or kept.

स्थाप्य a. to be established, fixed, placed in (loc. or acc.), kept, confined, restrained.

1स्थामन् n. standing-place, stand; stability, strength, power.

2स्थामन् n. neighing of a horse.

स्थायिता f., °त्व n. duration.

स्थायिन् a. standing, abiding, being in, at, or on (—°), present; steady, constant, faithful, true.

स्थायुक a. standing, staying in (—°); constant, durable.

स्थारश्मन् a. having firm reins.

स्थाल n. plate, dish, vessel, tooth-hole; f. स्थाली (earthen) pot, kettle.

स्थालीपाक m. a kind of cooked offering.

स्थावर a. standing, immovable, firm, lasting, constant; vegetable, belonging to the vegetable world. m. mountain; m. n. sgl. & pl. the vegetable kingdom; n. immovable property.

स्थावरक m. N. of a servant.

स्थावरजङ्गम n. the immovable and movable.

स्थावरता f. condition of being a plant.

स्थावरत्व n. immobility.

स्थाविर & °विर्य n. old age.

स्थासक s. perfume or unguent.

स्थास्नु a. stationary, immovable, firm, constant.

स्थित a. standing, abiding, remaining; continuing, keeping on (nom., loc., instr., ger., or adv.); turned to, intent upon, occupied with (loc. or —°); fixed, settled, determined, firm, valid; present, existing; left, ceased, stopped. n. the act or manner of standing.

स्थितधी a. steady-minded.

स्थितप्रज्ञ a. firm in judgment.

स्थितवन्त् a. standing, having one's place.

स्थिति f. standing, stopping, staying, remaining in or with (loc. or —°); abode, place; situation, rank, dignity; devotion to or occupation with (loc.); stability, duration; firmness, constancy, existence, occurrence; state, condition; conduct, procedure;

axiom, maxime, rule, custom, usage, boundary, limit; rectitude, virtue.

स्थितिमन्त् a. firm, stable, steady, constant, virtuous.

स्थिर a. hard, solid, firm, strong, lasting, durable, steadfast, constant, resolute, faithful, sure.

स्थिरचित्त a. firm-minded, constant.

स्थिरता f., °त्व n. hardness, firmness, stability, constancy.

स्थिरधन्वन् a. armed with a strong bow.

स्थिरपीत a. enjoying strong protection.

स्थिरप्रतिबन्ध a. firm in resistance.

स्थिरबुद्धि a. steady-minded, resolute.

स्थिरमति a. = prec.; f. firmness, resoluteness.

स्थिरयौवन a. ever youthful; n. eternal youth.

स्थिरसंस्कारता f. perfect accomplishment.

स्थिरसौहृद a. constant in friendship.

स्थिरारम्भ a. firm in undertaking, persevering.

स्थिरी कृ confirm, strengthen; °भू P.

स्थिरीकरण n. confirmation, corroboration.

स्थूण m. a man's name; f. स्थूणा post, pillar.

स्थूर a. thick, broad, massy, big, large; m. the lowe rpart of the thigh (also °क†); du. the ankles or buttocks.

स्थूरि a. drawn by one horse; n. such a waggon.

स्थूल a. = स्थूर, also coarse, gross, material (opp. सूक्ष्म); stupid, dull; n. = स्थूलशरीर.

स्थूलकेश m. N. of a Rishi.

स्थूलता f., °त्व n. abstr. to स्थूल.

स्थूलप्रपञ्च m. the material world (ph.).

स्थूलभूत n. a grosser element (ph.).

स्थूलभोग n. the enjoyment of grosser things (ph.).

स्थूलमध्य a. thick in the middle.

स्थूललक्ष & °लक्ष्य a. munificent, liberal.

स्थूलविषय m. material object.

स्थूलशरीर n. the material body (ph.).

स्थूलशिरस् a. large-headed; m. N. of a Rishi etc.

*स्थूलशाट & °क m., °शाटी f. coarse cloth.

स्थूलसूक्ष्म a. gross and subtle.

स्थूलसूक्ष्मप्रपञ्च m. the gross and the subtle world.

स्थूलसूक्ष्मशरीर n. the gross and the subtle body.

स्थूलहस्त m. an elephant's trunk.

*स्थूलान्त्र n. the langer intestine, the rectum.

स्थेमन् m. firmness, stability, duration.

स्थेय n. imp. (it is) to be stood or remained, to be acted or behaved; m. judge, umpire.

स्थेयंस् (compar.) very firm or constant.

स्थैर्य n. firmness, solidity, steadiness, constancy, calmness; p. °वन्त्.

स्थौललक्ष्य n. munificence, liberality.

स्थौल्य n. thickness, coarseness, bulk, size.

स्नपन, f. ई used for bathing (water etc.); n. bathing, ablution.

स्ना, स्नाति (स्नायते), pp. स्नात (q.v.) bathe, perform ablution (esp. at the end of religious studentship or of a vow), smear or anoint one's self with (instr.). C. स्नपयति or स्नापयति cause to bathe, wet, dip in (loc.). — उद् step out of the water. नि be steeped or absorbed in (loc.). प्र go into the water; C. bathe in (acc.). सम् C. bathe (tr.), wash. — Cf. निष्णात.

स्नात a. bathed, washed, purified by ablution; steeped i.e. versed in, familiar with (loc. or —°).

स्नातक m. a Brahman who has finished his religious studentship (lit. one who has performed his ablution).

स्नातलिप्त a. bathed and anointed.

स्नातानुलिप्त a. the same.

स्नान n. bathing, ablution (cf. prec.).

स्नानगृह n. bathing-room.

स्नात्व a. fit for bathing.

स्नानवस्त्र n. bathing-dress.

स्नानवेश्मन् n., °शाला f. bathing-room.

स्नानशाटी f. bathing-drawers.

स्नानशील a. used to or fond of bathing.

स्नानाम्बु n. water for bathing or washing.

स्नानिन् a. bathing, being in a bath.

स्नानीय a. fit or suitable for bathing.

स्नानीयवस्त्र n. = स्नानवस्त्र.

स्नानोत्तीर्ण a. risen from a bath.

स्नानोदक n. = स्नानाम्बु.

स्नानोपकरण n. implements for bathing.

स्नापक m. (a servant) who bathes (his master).

स्नापन n. bathing, washing.
स्नायिन् a. bathing, performing ablution.
स्नायु f. n. sinew, also = seq.
स्नायुबन्ध m. sinew-band, i.e. bowstring.
स्नायुमय, f. **ई** made of tendons.
स्नायुयुत a. held together by tendons.
स्नावन् or **स्नावन्** n. band, sinew, bowstring.
स्निग्ध a. supple, oily, greasy, sticky, smooth; bland, soft, kind, affectionate, faithful, loyal; abstr. **°ता** f., **°त्व** n.
स्निग्धभिन्नाञ्जन n. = **स्निग्धाञ्जन**.
स्निग्धमुद्ग m. a kind of bean.
स्निग्धशीतरूक्ष a. slippery, cool, or rough; abstr. **°त्व** n.
स्निग्धाञ्जन n. collyrium mixed with oil.
1**स्निह्, स्निह्यति, °ते**, pp. **स्निग्ध** (q.v.) be supple, greasy, or moist; stick to, be fixed upon (loc.), have affection for, be fond of (loc. or gen.). C. **स्नेहयति** make greasy, supple, or submissive. **उप** (also **स्निह्यते**) become supple or moist. C. conciliate, win over. — Cf. **प्रस्निग्ध**.
2**स्निह्** f. (nom. **स्निक्**) wetness, moisture.
स्निहिति or **स्नीहिति** f. the same.
स्नीहन् m. or **स्नीहा** f. wetness of the nose.
1**स्नु, स्नौति**, pp. **स्नुत** distil, drop, flow (esp. of the mother's breast or milk). — **प्र** = S.
2**स्नु** (—°) v. **घृतस्नु**.
3**स्नु** n. surface, top (= **सानु**).
स्नुषा f. daughter-in-law.
स्नुषाग a. having sexual intercourse with the daughter-in-law.
स्नुही f. the milk-hedge plant.
स्नूहन् m. wetness of the nose.
स्नेय n. imp. (it is) to be bathed.
स्नेह m. stickiness; oil, grease, a fluid of the body; attachment, love, friendship for (loc., gen., or —°).
स्नेहकुम्भ or **°घट** m. a pot with oil.
स्नेहगुरु a. heavy(-hearted) from love for (gen.).*
स्नेहन a. (f. **ई**) & n. lubricating, anointing; feeling affection.
स्नेहभूमि m. object of love.
स्नेहमय, f. **ई** consisting or full of affection.
स्नेहल a. affectionate, tender.
स्नेहवन्त् a. oily, greasy; also = prec.
स्नेहसंयुक्त a. mixed with oil or grease.
स्नेहसंज्वरवन्त् a. full of ardent love.
स्नेहाकूत n. feeling of love.
स्नेहाङ्कन n. a mark of affection.
स्नेहिन् a. liking, fond of (—°).
स्पन्द्, स्पन्दते, °ति, pp. **स्पन्दित** (q.v.) quiver, throb, quake, kick (of animals), budge. C. **स्पन्दयति (°ते)** make quiver. — **आ, परि, प्र, वि, सम्** quiver, shake.
स्पन्द m. quivering, throbbing, motion i.g.
स्पन्दन a. kicking (cow); m. a kind of tree; n. = prec.
स्पन्दित a. & n. quivering, moving.
स्पन्दिन् a. quivering.
स्पन्द्या f. thread, string.
स्परण, f. **ई** rescuing, delivering.
स्पर्धा f. contest, emulation with (instr. ± **सह**, gen., or —°) about (instr.).
स्पर्धावन्त् & **स्पर्धिन्** a. rivalling, emulous.
स्पर्ध्य a. desirable, precious.
स्पर्श a. touching, penetrating (—°); m. touch, contact; perception of touch, feeling, sensation. Abstr. **°ता**† f., **°त्व**† n.
स्पर्शक्षम a. tangible.
स्पर्शगुण a. having the quality of touch.
स्पर्शन n. touching, feeling, sensation.
स्पर्शनीय & **स्पर्शयितव्य** a. to be (being) touched or felt.
स्पर्शवन्त् a. having tangibility, palpable.
स्पर्शानुकूल a. grateful to the touch.
स्पर्शिन् a. touching, entering, penetrating (—°).
1**स्पश्** (**पश्**), pp. **स्पष्ट** (q.v.) see, behold, look at. C. **स्पाशयति** mark, notice, show. — Cf. **अनुस्पष्ट, विस्पष्ट**.
2**स्पश्** m. (nom. **स्पट्**) spy, guardian.
स्पश m. the same.
स्पष्ट a. visible, discernible, distinct, manifest, clear; n. adv.
स्पष्टार्थ a. clear in meaning, intelligible; n. adv.
स्पष्टी कृ a. make distinct or clear.
स्पार्ह a. desirable, enviable.
स्पार्हवीर a. consisting in enviable heroes.
स्पूर्ध् = 1**स्पृध्**.
स्पृ, स्पृणोति, स्पृणुते (**स्पृणाति**), pp. **स्पृत** loosen, free from (abl.), rescue, save, attract, win.

C. स्पार्ंयति the same. — अप free from (abl.), alienate. अव deliver. आ attract, win. निस् free from (abl.). वि tear asunder, separate.

1स्पृध्, स्पर्धते (°ति) contend, emulate, strive (instr. ± सह or acc. of pers. & loc. of th.). — अधि, प्र, प्रति, वि, & सम् = S.

2स्पृध् f. contest; rival, foe.

†स्पृध्य v. मिथ(:)स्पृध्य.

1स्पृश्, स्पृशति (°ते), pp. स्पृष्ट (q.v.) touch (acc. or loc.) esp. अपस्, उदकम् etc. touch water, also अद्भिस् wash or sprinkle with water (r.); feel, perceive (by touching); reach up to (loc. or acc.); attain, obtain, incur, suffer. C. स्पर्शयति (°ते) cause or make to touch (2 acc.), bring into immediate contact with (loc. or instr.); present to, bestow on (dat.). — अधि touch (superficially). अनु touch, fill with (instr.). अभि touch, visit, afflict. आ touch slightly. उद् reach up to (acc.). उप touch, stroke, caress; w. अपस् etc. = S. (also ± instr. of the water & ± acc. of the touched parts of the body). समुप touch (esp. water or with water; cf. S.), bathe in (loc.). परि touch, stroke. सम् touch, bring in contact with (instr.); reach to, attain, visit, befall; ± अपस् etc. wash, bathe (r.). — Cf. उपस्पृष्ट, संस्पृष्ट.

2स्पृश् (nom. स्पृक्) & स्पृश a. touching, reaching (—°).

स्पृश्य a. to be touched or felt.

स्पृष्ट a. touched, felt, visited by or afflicted with (instr. or —°).

स्पृष्टमैथुन a. defiled by sexual intercourse.

स्पृष्टि & स्पृष्टिका f. touch, contact.

स्पृष्टिन् a. who has touched.

स्पृह्, स्पृहयति, °ते be eager; strive after or long for (dat., gen., or acc.), envy (dat., gen. or loc.). — सम् desire ardently (acc.

स्पृहण n. desire, longing for (—°).

स्पृहणीय a. desirable, enviable, attractive, charming; abstr. °ता f., °त्व n.

स्पृहयाय्य a. worthy to be striven after or contested.

स्पृहयालु a. longing for, delighting in (dat. or loc.), wishing to (infin.); jealous, envious.

स्पृहा f. desire, longing for, delight in (gen., loc., or —°); envy.

स्पृहावन्त् a. longing for, delighting in (loc.).

स्फटिक m. rock-crystal.

स्फटिकमणि m. (& °शिला f.*) the same.

स्फटिकमय, f. ई made of crystal, crystalline.

स्फर्, C. स्फारयति, pp. स्फारित (q.v.) open widely, spread, expand, divulge, w. धनुस् etc. bend the bow, shoot off. — वि = S. — Cf. विस्फारित.

स्फल्, C. स्फालयति, w. आ strike or hurl against (acc. or loc.), w. सम् crush.

स्फाटिक, f. आ & ई crystalline; n. crystal.

स्फाति f. fattening, breeding (of cattle).

स्फातिमन्त् a. fat.

स्फाय्, स्फायते, pp. स्फीत (q.v.) grow, fat, swell, increase. C. स्फावयति fatten, enlarge, augment. — आ grow, increase. वि swell. — Cf. संस्फीत.

स्फार a. extensive, wide, big, large, violent, abundant.

स्फारफुल्ल a. full blown.

स्फारी भू open, expand, swell, increase.

स्फावयितृ m. fattener.

स्फिगी & स्फिज् (nom. स्फिक्) f. buttock, hip.

स्फिर a. fat.

स्फीत a. fat, swollen, large, thick; thriving, prosperous; numerous, abundant; richly endowed with, full of (instr. or —°).

स्फुट्, स्फुटति & स्फोटति burst, split, expand, open, blossom. C. स्फोटयति burst or rend asunder, shake, toss. — आ C. cleave, crush, shake, toss. प्र fly open, burst; C. cleave. वि burst, split, fly open.

स्फुट a. open, blossomed, blown; clear, distinct, plain. Abstr. °ता f, °त्व n.

*स्फुटन n. splitting, bursting.

स्फुटय्, °यति make clear or manifest.

स्फुटाक्षर a. clear or distinct (-syllabled).

1स्फुटार्थ m. a clear meaning.

2स्फुटार्थ a. clear in meaning.

स्फुटी कृ & भू make (become) clear or manifest.

स्फुर्, स्फुरति, °ते, pp. स्फुरित jerk, dart, kick (tr. & intr.); quiver, tremble, glitter, sparkle, start into view, appear, arise. — अप snap away, withdraw quickly. अव & निस् hurl away. परि quiver, throb; glitter, shine; rise, appear. प्र kick or hurl away, shake, tremble, quiver etc. = prec. वि fly asunder; tremble, quiver = prec.

स्फुर a. & n. trembling, vibrating.

स्फुरण a. glittering, sparkling; n. the action of quivering, trembling, glittering, shining forth, appearing.

स्फुरित a. throbbing, trembling, palpitating, glittering, sparkling; risen, appeared; n. = prec. n.

स्फुल्, pp. स्फुलित sprung forth, appeared.

स्फुलिङ्ग & °क m. spark of fire; p. °ङ्गवन्त्.

स्फूर्ज्, स्फूर्जति, pp. स्फूर्जित rumble, roar, thunder; burst forth, appear. C. स्फूर्जयति crackle, rustle.— अभि & अव roar, thunder. वि rumble, snort; break forth, appear. — Cf. विस्फूर्जित.

स्फूर्ज & °क m. a cert. plant.

स्फूर्जथु m. thunder.

स्फूर्जित n. thundering, roaring.

स्फूर्ति f. appearance, manifestation.

स्फोट m. bursting, splitting, opening, cracking, roaring; also = seq.

स्फोटक m., °टिका f. swelling, boil, tumor.

स्फोटन a. & n. splitting, breaking.

स्फोटायन m. N. of a grammarian.

स्फ्यच m. wooden splinter (r.).

स्म enclitic and slightly asseverative, often pleonastic, is added to other particles, esp. ह & हि, to न & मा, to rel. & dem. pronouns, & to verbs, esp. to the present tense, which it gives the value of a past.

स्मत् adv. together, at once, simultaneously; prep. along with (°— & instr.).

स्मदभीशु a. having reins.

स्मदिभ m. N. of a man.

स्मदिष्ट a. charged with a commission.

स्मदूध्नी f. having a full udder.

स्मद्दिष्टि a. disciplined, trained, expert.

स्मय m. astonishment, wonder; arrogance, pride in (—°).

स्मयन n. smiling, a smile.

स्मयिन् a. smiling, laughing (—°).

स्मर m. remembrance, love or the god of love.

स्मरकथा f. love-discourse.

स्मरकार, f. ई awakening love.

स्मरण n. remembrance, memory, tradition.

स्मरणीय a. to be remembered.

स्मरदायिन् & °दीपन a. rousing love.

स्मरशासन m. Smara's chastiser, i.e. Çiva.

स्मरसख m. Smara's friend, i.e. Spring.

स्मरारि m. Smara's foe i.e. Çiva.

स्मरातुर a. love-sick.

स्मर्तव्य a. = स्मरणीय.

स्मार m. remembrance, longing.

स्मारण n. reminding, calling to mind.

स्मारम् (ger., always repeated) remembering, in rembrance of (acc.).

स्मारिन् a. remembering, recollecting (—°).

स्मार्त a. relating to memory, based on tradition.

स्मि, स्मयते, °ति, pp. स्मित (q.v.) smile, blush, be proud or arrogant. — अव blush down (of the dawn). उद् smile up (with pride). अभ्युद् & उप smile upon (acc.). प्र break out into a laugh. वि be astounded or surprised by (instr., loc., or abl.); be proud, boast of (intr.). — Cf. विस्मित.

स्मित a. smiling, expanded, blown; n. a smile.

स्मितपूर्व a. preceded by a smile.

स्मितोज्ज्वल a. shining with a smile (eye).

स्मृ, स्मरति, °ते, pp. स्मृत (q.v.) remember (gen. or acc.); recollect, call to mind; hand down, record, declare, teach (esp. P. स्मर्यते be recorded or declared as a law or custom, pass for (nom. or loc.). Caus. स्मारयति & स्मरयति cause to remember, remind (2 acc. or gen. of pers. & acc. of th.). — अनु remember, collect; confess. C. remind. अप lose conscience, forget. उप remember, call to mind (acc.). प्र remember or forget. प्रति remember; C. remind. वि forget; C. cause to forget (2 acc.). सम् remember (acc.); C. remind of (2 acc.). — Cf. अनुस्मृत, विस्मृत, संस्मृत.

स्मृत a. remembered, handed down by memory or tradition, taught, enjoined; passing for, named, called (nom. ± इति).

स्मृति f. remembrance, memory, tradition (opp.

श्रुति revelation); a class of works based on authoritative tradition.

स्मृतिकारिन् a. reviving a recollection.

स्मृतिपाठक m. a lawyer.

स्मृतिभू m. the god of love.

स्मृभिभ्रंश m. loss or failure of memory.

स्मृतिमन्त् a. having (a good) memory or (full) conscience; versed in law.

स्मृतिमय, f. **ई** based on tradition.

स्मृतिविभ्रम m. confusion of memory.

स्मृतिशास्त्र n. law-book.

स्मेर a. smiling, friendly; expanded, blown; full of (—°).

स्य pron.-st. of 3^d pers. (only nom. sgl., cf. त्य).

1**स्यद्**, **स्यन्द्**, **स्यन्दते**, °ति, pp. **स्यन्न** flow, run, drive (in a carriage), hasten. C. **स्यन्दयति** = S. — **अच्छ** flow or run to (acc.). **अनु** run towards or along. **अभि** the same, overflow. **अव** flow down. **आ** & **उप** run or flow towards (acc.). **नि** flow down. **प्र** flow, run; drive away (in a carriage). **परि** flow around. **वि** flow forth or over, flow abundantly. **सम्** flow or run together. -- Cf. **विष्यस**.

2**स्यद्** v. **रघुष्यद्**.

स्यद m. rapid course.

स्यन्तृ a. hastening on.

स्यन्द m. flowing.

स्यन्दन a. & n. flowing, running; m. carriage, chariot.

स्यन्दिन् a. flowing; letting flow.

स्यन्द्रा v. **स्यन्द्रा**.

स्यन्द्र a. rushing, quick.

स्याल m. the wife's brother, brother-in-law.

स्यू f. thread or needle.

स्यूत a. sewn, sewn on.

स्यूमन् n. band, thong, rein; suture (on the scull).

स्येदु m. phlegm.

स्योन a. soft, mild, tender; n. a soft couch or seat, comfort i.g.

स्योनकृत् a. preparing a soft couch.

स्योनशी a. resting on a soft couch.

स्रंस्, **स्रंसते** (°ति), pp. **स्रस्त** (q.v.) fall, drop or hang down, decay, perish. C. **स्रंसयति** cause to fall, loosen. — **अव** fall down. **व्यव** fall asunder. **वि** fall asunder, break down, drop; C. cause to drop, loosen. — C. **आस्रस्त**, **उत्स्रस्त**, **विस्रस्त**.

†**स्रंस** a. breaking, loosening.

स्रंसिन् a. getting loose, falling down, depending.

स्रक्ति f. corner.

स्रक्त्य m. a cert. plant.

स्रक्व s. corner of the mouth; mouth, jaws.

स्रग्दामन् n. a garland of flowers.

स्रग्धर a. wearing a garland; f. **आ** N. of a metre.

स्रग्विन् a. = prec. adj.

स्रज् f. wreath, garland (—° also **स्रज** & **स्रजस्**).

स्रव m. stream or gush of, adj. flowing with, out-pouring (—°).

स्रवण n., **स्रवथ** m. flowing, streaming.

स्रवत् & **स्रवन्ती** f. stream, river.

स्रवस् n. (—°) = **स्रव** m.

स्रवितवे & **स्रवितवै** dat. infin. to **स्रु**.

स्रवथ m. flowing, running.

स्रष्टृ m. maker, creator.

स्रस्त a. fallen, loosened.

स्रस्तमुक्त a. hanging loose down.

स्रस्तर m. straw, couch.

1**स्राम** a. lame.

2**स्राम** m. disease, sickness.

स्राव m. flow, oozing.

स्रावण a. & n. making flow.

स्राविन् a. flowing; making flow (—°).

1**स्रिध्**, **स्रेधति** do or go amiss, fail.

2**स्रिध्** f. foe or sinner.

स्रीव्, **स्रीव्यति** fail.

स्रु, **स्रवति** (°ते), pp. **स्रुत** flow, stream; flow with (instr. or acc.); drip, leak (vessel); flow or waste away, perish, be lost. C. **स्रावयति** & **स्रवयति** cause to flow, spill, shed. — **अति** flow over. **अधि** flow off (abl.). **अभि** flow hither. **अव** flow down; C. = **अन्वव** C. cause to flow down. **आ** & **उप** flow towards (acc.). **नि** flow down. **निस्** flow asunder or out, flow forth, rise from (abl). **परि** flow around or abundantly; run away, pass (time). **प्र** flow forth, stream from (abl.); let flow, discharge. अभिप्र & संप्र stream forth. वि stream forth, flow from (abl.); let flow, discharge; melt away, perish. सम् flow or run together.

स्रुक्क (a. —°) = स्रुच्.

स्रुग्दण्ड m. the handle of the Sruc.

स्रुघ्न m. N. of a town.

स्रुच् f. (nom. स्रुक्) a large sacrificial ladle.

स्रुच्य a. performed with the Sruc.

स्रुत् (—°) flowing with, discharging.

स्रुतजल a. dry (lit. having the water flowed off).

स्रुति f. flow, stream, gush; way, road.

स्रुत्य a. relating to a road.

स्रुव m. a small sacrificial ladle.

†स्रेमन् v. अस्रेमन्.

स्रोत (adj. —°) current, channel.

स्रोतस् n. current, stream, river, channel; aperture of the body (as eyes, ears, etc.); organ of sense.

स्रोतस्य a. flowing in streams.

स्रोतोवह् & °वहा f. river.

स्रोत्या f. flood, wave, stream.

स्रौच a. performed with the Sruc.

स्रौतोवह a. relating to a stream.

स्व (poss. refl.) one's own (often °—). m. n. one's self (in the obl. cases also used as a pronoun, cf. आत्मन्); m. & f. आ a kinsman or relation, a man or woman of one's own caste; n. property, wealth, riches.

स्वक (poss. refl.) = prec.; m relative, friend; n. wealth, property.

स्वकर्मन् n. one's own work, business, or duty.

स्वकर्मस्थ a. doing one's duty.

स्वकामिन् a. self-willing.

स्वकाल m. one's own time, loc. in time.

स्वकीय (poss. refl.) one's own; m. pl. relatives or friends.

1स्वकुल n. one's own family or race.

2स्वकुल a. belonging to one's own family.

स्वकुशलमय, f. ई relating to one's own welfare.

स्वकृत a. self-done; n. such an action.

1स्वक्ष a. having a beautiful axle; m. such a a waggon.

2स्वक्ष, f. ई fair-eyed.

स्वक्षत्र a. having self-rule, free.

स्वगत a. relating or belonging to one's self; n. adv. apart, aside.

स्वगा (indecl.) a sacrificial formula; w. कृ utter this exclamation.

1स्वगुण m. one's own virtue or merit; abl. °तस्.

2स्वगुण a. having virtues and merits of one's own.

स्वगूर्त a. delectable by its own nature.

स्वगृह n. one's own house.

स्वग्नि a. having a good Agni (fire).

स्वङ्ग a. fair-limbed.

स्वङ्गुरि a. having handsome or clever fingers.

स्वचक्षुस् n. one's own eye.

स्वचेतस् n. one's own idea.

स्वच्छ a. very clear, transparent, bright, pure; abstr. °ता f., °त्व n.

1स्वच्छन्द m. one's own will or choice, independence; °— & °तस् at will, spontaneously, freely.

2स्वच्छन्द a. independent, spontaneous, free, n. adv.

स्वच्छन्दचार & °चारिन् a. moving at will, independent.

स्वच्छन्दवनजात a. grown wild (lit. spontaneously) in the wood.

स्वज्, स्वजते, °ति, pp. स्वक्त embrace, encircle. — अभि, परि, अभिपरि, संपरि, & वि (ष्व), सम्, अभिसम् = S.

स्वज a. born from or belonging to one's self, one's own; m. a viper.

स्वजन m. one's own man, (coll.) people or kindred.

स्वजन्मन् & स्वजात a. produced or begotten by one's self.

स्वजा a. self-born.

स्वजाति f. one's own caste or race; a. belonging to it.

स्वजातीय & °जात्य a. = prec. adj.

स्वजित a. conquered by one's self.

स्वजेन्य a. = स्वजन्मन्.

स्वज्ञाति m. one's own kindred or kin.

स्वञ्च् & स्वञ्चस a. moving lightly, quick.

1स्वतन्त्र n. self-dependence, i.e. independence, freedom; also °ता f.

2स्वतन्त्र a. self-dependent, free.

स्वतन्त्रय्, °यति bring into dependance, call to obedience.

स्वतवस् a. (nom. °वान्) self-strong, conscious of one's own strength.

स्वतस् adv. = abl. of स्व a. & m.

स्वता f., °त्वं n. relation to one's self.

स्वतेजस् n. one's own splendour.

स्वद्, स्वदति, °ते (स्वादते), pp. स्वात्त (q.v.) A. sweeten, make savoury or agreeable; A.(P.) be sweet or savoury, please; relish, taste, eat, enjoy; delight in (loc.). C. स्वदयति make savoury, season, cook; make soft i.e. calm, propitiate; स्वादयति relish, taste, eat. — आ & समा (स्वादयति) relish, eat, enjoy.

स्वदित a. well eaten.

स्वदेश m. one's own place or land, home.

स्वधन n. one's own wealth or property.

स्वधर्म m. one's own right or duty.

स्वधर्मन् a. keeping to one's custom.

1स्वधा f. (one's own or peculiar) nature or condition (lit. self-position, spontaneity), habit, custom, rule; accustomed place, home; welfare, comfort, pleasure. Instr. sgl. & pl., स्वधामनु, अनु स्वधाम्, & स्वधा अनु willingly, freely, in wonted wise, merrily, wantonly.

2स्वधा f. sweet drink, esp. a libation to the Manes; the exclamation Svadhā (used on presenting or instead of this libation).

स्वधाकर a. offering a libation to the Manes or pronouncing the exclamation Svadhā.

स्वधाकार m. the exclamation Svadhā.

स्वधावन्, f. °वरी = seq.

1स्वधावन्त् a. keeping to one's habit or custom, constant, faithful, comfortable, blessed.

2स्वधावन्त् a. containing sweet drink or refreshment.

स्वधाविन् a. = prec.

स्वधित a. healthy, strong.

1स्वधिति m. f. axe, hatchet.

2स्वधिति f. a kind of large tree with hard wood.

स्वधितीवन्त् a. consisting of Svadhā-wood (cf. prec.).

स्वधीत a. well taught or instructed; n. good study.

स्वधीति a. studying well.

स्वध्वर a. sacrificing well; m. n. a good sacrifice.

स्वन्, स्वनति, °ते, pp. स्वनित (q.v.) sound, roar, cry, hum. C. स्वनयति = S. — अव cry or roar down. आ sound. परि (I. सनिष्वत्) clang. प्र roar. प्रति sound back, re-echo. वि roar, howl, sound.

1स्वन m. sound, roar, thunder, in l. l. any kind of sound or noise.

2स्वन m. roaring water.

स्वनवन्त् a. sounding, loud.

†स्वनस् & †स्वनि (—°) = 1स्वन.

स्वनित a. sounding; n. sound.

†स्वनीक a. fair-faced.

स्वनुगुप्त a. well hidden.

स्वनुष्ठित a. well performed.

स्वन्त a. ending well.

स्वप्, स्वपिति & स्वपति, °ते, pp. सुप्त (q.v.) sleep, fall asleep, lie down, repose, be dead. C. स्वापयति (स्वपयति) make sleep, bring to rest, kill. D. सुषुप्सति wish to sleep. — नि go to sleep, die; C. put to sleep, kill. प्र fall asleep, go to rest, sleep. C. put to sleep, lull to rest. — Cf. अवसुप्त, प्रसुप्त, विसुप्त, संसुप्त, संप्रसुप्त (add.).

स्वपक्ष m. one's own side or party, opinion or statement.

1स्वपत्य n. good offspring or a good work.

2स्वपत्य a. having good offspring or doing a good work.

स्वपद n. one's own abode, place, position, rank or dignity.

स्वपन a. sleepy; n. sleeping, sleep.

स्वपराह्णे (loc.) late in the afternoon.

स्वपस् a. working or worked well, skilful or skilfully made; m. artist.

स्वपस्य्, °स्यते work well, be active or busy.

स्वपस्यु a. active, industrious.

स्वपस्या f. (instr.) activity, cleverness.

†स्वपाक a. working well, skilful.

†स्वपिवात a. well meaning or much desired.

स्वपू f. besom.
स्वप्तव्य n. impers. to be slept.
स्वप्न m. sleep, dream.
†स्वप्नज् a. sleepy.
स्वप्नज a. dreamt (sleep-born).
स्वप्नधीगम्य a. perceptible by the intellect in sleep.
स्वप्नभाज् a. enjoying sleep.
स्वप्नया adv. in dreaming.
स्वप्नलब्ध a. attained in sleep.
स्वप्नवृत्त a. happened in a dream, dreamt.
स्वप्नस् a. wealthy, rich.
स्वप्नसंदर्शन n. sight or illusion of a dream.
स्वप्नान्त m. condition of sleeping or dreaming.
स्वप्नाय्, °यते be sleepy; be like a dream.
स्वप्न्य n. vision of a dream; स्वप्न्यया adv. in dreaming.
स्वप्रधान a. self-dependent; abstr. °ता f.
स्वबन्धु m. (one's own) relation or friend.
स्वभानु a. self-luminous.
स्वभाव m. birth-place; (one's own) inherent disposition or nature; °—, abl., & instr. by nature, naturally, spontaneously.
स्वभावज a. innate, natural.
स्वभावोक्त a. uttered spontaneously.
स्वभिष्टि a. granting or receiving good assistance.
स्वभीशु a. having beautiful reins.
स्वभू a. self-existing; m. Brahman; f. one's own country or home.
1स्वभूति f. one's own welfare.
2†स्वभूति a. self-existing.
स्वभूमि f. = स्वभू f.
स्वभ्यक्त a. well anointed.
स्वमहिमन् m. one's own greatness.
स्वमांस n. one's own flesh.
स्वमातृतस् adv. from (one's own) mother's side.
स्वयंवर a. self-choosing; कन्या (± भर्तृ)स्वयंवरा f. a maiden who thus chooses her husband. m. self-choice (esp. of a husband by a girl of the warrior caste).
स्वयंवरवधू f. a self-chosen wife.*
स्वयंवृत a. self-chosen (husband).
स्वयंशीर्ण a. self-fallen.
स्वयंश्रेष्ठ a. best etc. by nature.
स्वयंस्रंस् & °स्रस्त a. falling & fallen spontaneously.
स्वयंकृत or स्वयंकृत a. self-made; done by or for one's self; made one's own, adopted.
स्वयंखात a. self-dug.
स्वयंग्रह m., °ग्रहण n. the (violent) taking for one's self.
1स्वयंग्राह m. = prec.
2स्वयंग्राह a. taking freely or violently; °— & n. adv. voluntarily, spontaneously.
स्वयंज & °जात a. self-born.
स्वयंज्योतिस् a. self-shining.
स्वयत a. self-guided.
स्वयंत्यक्त a. self-abandoned.
स्वयंदत्त a. self-given (son).
स्वयंधारित a. self-worn (ornament).*
स्वयंनिर्दिष्ट a. self-marked.
स्वयम् (indecl.) self (applied to the gramm. or log. subject); often °— self-, spontaneously, voluntarily, naturally.
स्वयमनुष्ठान n. self-performance or practice of (loc.).
स्वयमर्जित a. self-acquired.
स्वयमागत a. come of one's own accord.
स्वयमाहृत a. self-fetched.
स्वयमुद्यत a. offered spontaneously.
स्वयंप्रकाश a. self-manifest.
स्वयंप्रकाशमान a. self-luminous; abstr. °त्व n.
स्वयंप्रभ a. self-shining.
स्वयंप्रशीर्ण a. self-fallen.
स्वयंप्रस्तुत a. self-praised.
स्वयंभग्न a. broken or fallen off spontaneously.
स्वयंभु m. E. of Brahman & Çiva (cf. स्वयंभू).
स्वयंभुव a. = seq. adj.
स्वयंभू a. self-existent; m. E. of Brahman.
स्वयंमृत a. died of one's self.
स्वयशस् a. self-glorious or majestic.
स्वयु a. self-dependent.
स्वयुक्त a. self-yoked.
स्वयुक्ति f. one's own team; one's own arrangement or disposition, instr. & °तस्† naturally, of course.
स्वयुग्वन् or °युज् m. an ally.
1स्वयोनि f. one's own womb, home, or place.
2स्वयोनि (f. also ई) related by blood.
1स्वर्, स्वरति sound, make resound; sing,

praise; shine, be bright. C. स्वरयति (P. स्वर्यते) pronounce with the Svarita accent. – अति let a sound die away. अभि chime in. अव resound. सम् & अभिसम् salute, invoke.

2स्वृर् n. the sun, sunlight, light i.g., the light space i.e. the sky or heaven.

स्वर or स्वर m. sound, voice, accent, musical tone or note.

स्वृरंकृत a. well prepared (sacrifice).

स्वरण a. sounding loud, clear-voiced.

स्वरपरिवर्त m. change of the voice.

स्वरभक्ति f. vowel-fracture (g.).

स्वरभेद m. loss or change of the voice.

स्वरयोग m. sound-combination, voice.

स्वरवन्त् a. sounding, loud, accented.

स्वरसंयोग m. = स्वरयोग; also song or playing on the lute.*

स्वरसंक्रम m. transition of sounds or notes.

स्वरसंपद् f. harmony (of the voice).

स्वरसंपन्न a. harmonious (voice).

स्वराज् a. self-ruling, independent; m. = seq.

स्वराजन् m., °राज्ञी f. sovereign.

स्वराज्य n. independent dominion, also = seq.

स्वराष्ट्र n. one's own kingdom.

स्वरि a. loud, noisy.

स्वरित a. sounded, accented, having the Sv. accent; m. n. the Svarita accent; abstr. °त्व n.

स्वरित्र a. having good oars.

स्वरु m. the sacrificial post or a slip of wood from it.

1स्वरुचि f. one's own wish or pleasure; instr. at will.

2स्वरुचि a. self-willed, wilful.

स्वरूप n. (one's own) form or shape, true nature, p. °वन्त् & °पिन्; (± शब्द° or शब्दस्य) the word in its peculiar form, the word itself (g.); °— & °तस् by nature, of one's self, really.

1स्वरोचिस् n. one's own splendour.

2स्वरोचिस् a. self-resplendent.

स्वर्क a. singing well.

स्वर्ग a. going or leading to light or heaven, heavenly; m. (± लोक) the heavenly world, heaven, paradise.

स्वर्गकाम a. desirous of heaven.

स्वर्गगति f. going to heaven.

स्वर्गगमन n. the same, dying.

स्वर्गगामिन् a. going to heaven.

स्वर्गच्युत a. descended from heaven.

स्वर्गजित् a. conquering heaven.

स्वर्गजीविन् a. dwelling in heaven.

स्वर्गत a. gone to heaven, died.

स्वर्गतरंगिणी f. the heavenly river, Gaṅgā.

स्वर्गतरु m. a tree growing in heaven.

स्वर्गति f., स्वर्गमन n. going to heaven, death.

स्वर्गद्वार n. the gate of heaven.

स्वर्गपुरी f. the heavenly city, Amarāvatī.

स्वर्गपति & °भर्तृ m. lord of heaven, Indra.

स्वर्गमार्ग m. the road to heaven.

स्वर्गयाण, f. ई going or leading to heaven.

स्वर्गराज्य n. the kingdom of heaven.

1स्वर्गलोक m. the heavenly world.

2स्वर्गलोक a. dwelling in heaven.

स्वर्गवन्त् a. partaking of heaven.

स्वर्गसद् m. a dweller in heaven.

स्वर्गसुख n. the joy of heaven.

स्वर्गस्त्री f. heavenly woman, Apsaras.

स्वर्गस्थ a. being in heaven, dead.

स्वर्गस्थित a. the same.

स्वर्गामिन् a. gone to or being in heaven, dying or dead.

स्वर्गाय्, °यते be like heaven.*

स्वर्गिन् a. partaking of heaven, dead; m. a god.

स्वर्गीय a. relating to heaven, heavenly.

स्वर्गौकस् m. a dweller in heaven, a god.

स्वर्ग्य a. helping to or partaking of heaven, heavenly, celestial.

स्वृर्चक्षस् a. radiant as the sun.

स्वृर्चनस् a. pleasing (like) heaven.

स्वर्चि a. shining beautifully.

स्वर्जित् a. conquering light or heaven; m. a kind of sacrifice.

स्वर्ण (= सुवर्ण) n. gold (also °क n.) or a cert. weight of gold (also m.).

स्वर्णकार & °कृत् m. goldsmith.

स्वर्णदी f. the heavenly river (Gaṅgā).

स्वृर्णर & स्वृर्णृ m. the lord or the space of light.

स्वर्णरेखा f. a streak of gold (on the touch-stone); N. of a woman.
स्वर्थ a. pursuing the right aim.
स्वर्द or **स्वर्दा** a. granting heaven or light.
स्वर्दृश् a. (nom. °दृंक्) looking to or like heaven.
स्वर्धन् m. a good partisan.
स्वर्नगरी f. = **स्वर्गपुरी**.
स्वर्पति m. lord of light, E. of Indra.
स्वर्भानव m. a kind of stone; f. **ई** N. of a daughter of Svarbhānu.
स्वर्भानु m. N. of a demon obscuring the sun and the moon, in l. l. = Rāhu.
स्वर्भानुशत्रु & **°सूदन** m. the sun (foe or destroyer of Rāhu).
स्वर्मीळ्ह n. or as adj. w. **आजि** m. the contest for light; contest, fight i.g.
स्वर्मणि m. the heavenly jewel, the sun.
स्वर्य (f. Ved. **स्वरी**) sounding, roaring, noisy.
स्वर्यात a. gone to heaven, dead.
स्वर्यु a. desirous of light.
1**स्वर्लोक** m. the heavenly world, E. of mount Meru.
2**स्वर्लोक** a. partaking of heaven, m. a god.
स्वर्वधू f. heavenly woman, Apsaras.
स्वर्वन्त् a. light, celestial.
स्वर्विद् a. winning or possessing the heavenly light.
स्वर्षा a. = prec.
स्वर्षाति f. abstr. to prec., contest, fight.
स्वलंकृत a. well adorned.
स्वलज्जा f. (one's own) shame.
स्वल्प a. very small or minute, insignificant; instr. for a very short time. Compar. **°तर** & **स्वल्पीयंस्**.
स्वल्पक, f. **स्वल्पिका** very small or short.
स्वल्पतस् adv. by (small) degrees, slowly.
स्वल्पवयस् a. young (short-lived).
स्वल्पस्मृति a. of short memory.
स्वल्पी भू be small, fall short.
स्ववत् adv. as one's own.
स्ववश a. subject to one's own will, independent, free; abstr. **°ता** f.
स्ववान् (nom.) having or affording good protection.
स्वविद्युत् a. self-shining.
स्वविषय m. one's own sphere, province, or country.
स्ववृत्ति f. one's own way of life or means of subsistence, self-dependence, independence.
स्वशक्ति f. one's own might or power.
स्वशोचिस् & **स्वश्चन्द्र** a. self-shining.
स्वश्व a. having good horses.
स्वश्व्य n. possession of good horses, horsemanship.
स्वसर n. fold, stable, wont place, nest, house, home.
स्वसित a. quite black.
स्वसृ f. sister, **स्वसृत्व** n. sisterhood.
स्वसृत् a. going one's own way, free.
स्वस्तर m. self-prepared straw (for sitting or lying on).
स्वस्ति f. welfare, blessing, happiness; the same form as adv. with luck, happily (also **स्वस्तिभिस्**), as subst. n. = f., **स्वस्त्यस्तु ते** hail to thee!
स्वस्तिक m. a kind of bard (calling hail!); N. of a serpent-demon etc.; any lucky or auspicious figure, esp. the figure of a cross, a dish of a cert. form, the crossing of the arms; a building shaped like a cross (also n.).
स्वस्तिकार m. bard, herald (cf. prec.); the exclamation **स्वस्ति**.
स्वस्तिगा a. leading to welfare.
स्वस्तिता f. condition of welfare.
स्वस्तिद or **°दा** a. bestowing welfare.
स्वस्तिमन्त् a. prosperous, happy, auspicious.
स्वस्तिवाच् f., **°वाचक** m. blessing, benediction.
स्वस्तिवाचन n. the invitation of a Brahman to pronounce a benediction and the offering of flowers, fruits, & sweetmeats connected with it.
स्वस्तिवाचनक & **°निक** a. offering flowers etc. (cf. prec.).*
स्वस्तिवाच्य a. to be called upon to pronounce a benediction; n. = **स्वस्तिवाचन**.
स्वस्त्ययन n. good progress, success, welfare, blessing, benediction; a. (f. **ई**) producing happiness.
स्वस्त्यात्रेय m. N. of an ancient sage.

स्वस्थ a. being in one's natural condition, healthy, well, comfortable; abstr. °ता f.
स्वस्थमानस a. in good spirits, cheerful.
1स्वस्थान n. one's own place, home.
2स्वस्थान a. being at one's own place.
स्वस्रीय m., °आ f. a sister's son and daughter.
स्वस्वभाव m. one's own nature.
स्वस्वरूप n. one's own character.
स्वःसुन्दरी & °स्त्री f. heavenly maid, Apsaras.
स्वहरण n. seizure of one's property.
स्वहस्त m. one's own hand.
स्वहस्तिका f. hoe, hatchet.
स्वहित a. good for or kind to one's self; n. one's own welfare.
स्वांशतस् adv. (created) from a part of one's own.
स्वाकृति a. well shaped, handsome.
स्वागत a. welcome (also lit. well come i.e. well acquired); n. welcome, salutation, °तो कृ make into a welcome.
स्वाङ्क m. one's own lap.
स्वाङ्ग n. one's own body.
स्वाचरण a. well-conducted.
स्वाचान्त a. who has well rinsed his mouth.
1स्वाचार m. good conduct.
2स्वाचार a. well-conducted (also °वन्त्).
स्वाच्छन्द्य n. independence, liberty; instr. willingly, of one's own accord.
स्वाजीव & °व्य a. yielding a good subsistence.
स्वातन्त्र्य n. self-dependence, free will; instr. spontaneously, freely.
स्वाति or °ती f. N. of a constellation.
स्वात्त a. made savoury, seasoned; tasted, eaten.
स्वात्मन् m. one's own self or nature.
स्वात्मवध m. suicide.
स्वाद m. taste, flavour, charm.
स्वादन a. making savoury, sweetening, seasoning; n. tasting, relishing.
स्वादनीय a. tasty, savoury.
†स्वादस् v. प्रस्वादस्.
1स्वादान n. taking one's due.
2स्वादान a. easy to be taken.
स्वादिमन् m. sweetness.
स्वादु, f. °द्वी tasting good, savoury, sweet, sweeter than (abl.); n. = seq.
स्वादुता f. sweetness, charm.
स्वादुमन् & स्वाद्मन् m., स्वाद्मन् n. the same.
स्वादुयुक्त a. connected with sweetness, sweet.
स्वाद्य a. being tasted, tasty.
स्वाधी a. meditative, attentive, careful, longing.
स्वाधीन a. self-dependent, free; under one's own control, subject to one's own will. Abstr. °ता f.
स्वाधीनकुशल a. having prosperity in one's own power.
स्वाधीनोपाय a. having an expedient in one's own power.
स्वाध्याय m. reading or repeating (to one's self), esp. study of the Veda.
स्वाध्यायवन्त् & °यिन् a. practising the study of the Veda.
स्वाध्यायार्थिन् a. intent upon the study of the Veda.
स्वान m. sound, noise.
स्वानिन् a. sounding, noisy.
स्वान्त m. one's own end or death, kingdom or country; n. the heart (as the dominion of the self).
स्वाप m. sleep, dream.
स्वापतेय n. one's own wealth or property.
स्वापन a. causing sleep.
स्वापि m. a good relation or friend.
स्वाभाविक, f. ई belonging to one's own nature, natural, peculiar, inherent.
स्वाभाव्य n. abstr. to prec.
स्वाभु a. abundant, ready, at hand.
स्वामिक (adj. —°) = स्वामिन्.
स्वामिता f., °त्व n. ownership, dominion over (gen. or —°).
स्वामिन् m. owner, proprietor, master, lord; f. °नी.
स्वामिपाल m. du. master and herdsman.
स्वामिभट्टारक m. a noble lord.*
स्वामिसेवा f. service of a master.
स्वाम्य n. ownership, dominion.
स्वायत्त a. subject to one's self, standing under one's own control; abstr. °त्व n.
1स्वायंभुव a. relating to Svayaṁbhū (Brahman) or Svāyaṁbhuva (v. seq.).
2स्वायंभुव m. patr. of the first Manu.

स्वायुध a. well armed.
स्वार m. sound, accent, esp. the Svarita.
स्वारक्ष्य a. easily protected or defended.
स्वाराज्य n. self-sovereignty, unlimited dominion.
स्वारुह a. grown form its own root, firmly rooted.
स्वारोचिष m. patron. of the second Manu.
स्वार्जित a. self-acquired.
1**स्वार्थ** m. one's own affair or cause, own or original meaning.
2**स्वार्थ** a. relating to one's own person, self-interested, egoistic; abstr. **°ता** f.
स्वार्थसाधन n. attainment of one's own ends; **°तत्पर** a. intent upon it.
स्वालक्षण्य n. true disposition, peculiarity.
स्वाविश a. easily accessible.
स्वाशु a. very swift.
स्वास a. sharp-mouthed (Agni) or sharp-edged (axe).
स्वासन n. a fine seat.
स्वासस्थ a. having or offering a good or comfortable seat.
स्वासीन a. comfortably seated.
स्वास्तीर्ण a. well spread, wide.
स्वास्थ्य n. comfort, ease.
स्वाहा an exclam. used in making oblations = hail to (dat.), or at the end of an invocation = Amen; as f. a personification of the daughter of Dakṣa and wife of Agni.
स्वाहाकार m. the utterance of the word Svāhā, also = **°कृति**.
स्वाहाकृ utter the word Svāhā, pp. **°कृत** consecrated with Svāhā.
स्वाहाकृति f. consecration with the word Svāhā.
स्वाहुत a. well invoked or worshipped.
स्वित्त n. = **सुवित्त** welfare, happiness.
1**स्विद्**, **स्वेदते**, **स्विद्यति**, **°ते**, pp. **स्विन्न** sweat, perspire. C. **स्वेदयति** cause to sweat, make warm, foment. — **प्र** begin to sweat, become moist. **सम्** C. = S.C.
2**स्विद्** (indecl.) lays stress upon an interr. pron. or makes it indefinite (**कः स्विद्** who then or whosoever, **क्व स्विद्** anywhere), often expletive. Follows **अपि**, **उत** (which it also precedes), & **आहो**. Often in disjunctive questions in both clauses, alone or with a pronoun or another particle.
स्विन्न a. perspired, sweated; seethed, boiled.
स्विषु a. having good arrows.
1**स्विष्ट** a. well beloved.
2**स्विष्ट** a. well or properly sacrificed; n. a good sacrifice.
स्विष्टकृत् a. offering good sacrifices, E. of Agni.
1**स्विष्टि** f. a good or successful sacrifice.
2**स्विष्टि** a. sacrificing well.
स्वीकरण n. making one's own, appropriating, taking to wife, admitting, assenting.
स्वीकार m. appropriation, reception, admission, assent.
स्वी कृ M.(A.) make one's own, appropriate, win, take (also to wife ± **भार्यार्थे**), admit, assent.
स्वीय a. one's own.
स्वेच्छम् adv. at will or pleasure.
स्वेच्छा f. one's own wish or will; °— & instr. = prec.
स्वेच्छाचारिन् a. acting according to one's own will, humorous, wayward.
स्वेच्छाभोजन n. eating one's fill.
स्वेद m. sweat; pl. drops of sweat.
स्वेदज a. produced by sweat or hot moisture.
स्वेदजल n. sweat; **°कण** m. & **°कणिका** f. drop of sweat.
स्वेदन a. & n. sweating or causing sweat.
स्वेदबिन्दु m. drop of sweat.
स्वेदयु a. sweating, perspiring.
स्वेदलेश m. drop of sweat.
स्वेदवारि & **स्वेदाम्बु** n. sweat-water.
स्वेदोद्गम m. outbreak of perspiration.
स्वेष्ट a. dear to one's self, nearest to one's heart.
स्वैर a. moving on gently or cautiously; n. adv. of one's own accord, spontaneously, freely, easily, carelessly (also °— & instr.); gently, slowly, cautiously; as subst. independence, free choice.
स्वैरकम् adv. straight out, directly.
स्वैरगति a. moving freely.
स्वैरचारिन् a. = prec. & seq.

स्वैरवर्तिन् & **°वृत्त** a. acting freely.

स्वैरिन् a. free, independent; wanton, unchaste (woman).

स्वैष m. own or free choice.

स्वौजस् a. very strong or powerful.

ह

1**ह** (encl.) to be sure, indeed (=older **घ**), often expletive, esp. at the end of a verse.

2**ह** (—°) killing, slaying.

हंस, f. **ई** goose, also applied to the swan, flamingo and like water-fowl; fig. the sun, the soul, du. the individual and universal soul.

हंसक m. little or miserable goose, goose i.g. (f. **हंसिका**); s. anklet.

हंसगति* & **°गामिनी** f. moving (gracefully) like a swan.

हंसचन्द्रांशु m. pl. sun- and moon-beams.

हंसतूल n. the down of a geese.

हंसपद n. goose-foot (as a mark), a cert. weight; m. pl. N. of a people.

हंसपदिका f. N. of a woman.

हंसमाला f. a flight of wild geese.

हंसमुख, f. **ई** shaped like the beak of a goose.

1**हंसयान** n. a team of geese.

2**हंसयान**, f. **ई** riding on a goose.

हंसराज m. a big gander (lit. a king of geese).

हंसवन्त् a. containing the word **हंस**; f. **°वती** a woman's name.

हंससाचि m. a kind of bird.

हंसावली f. = **हंसमाला**.

हंहो a. vocative particle.

हञ्जिका f. maid-servant.

हञ्जे ind. (used in addressing a maid-servant).*

हट्ट m. market.

हठ m. violence, force, obstinacy; °—, abl., & instr. adv. violently, forcibly, necessarily, absolutely, by all means.

हठकर्मन् n. violent act, violence.

हठकामुक m. a violent suitor.

हठिका f. tumult, dreadful noise.

हण्डिका f. pot.

हत a. smitten, beaten, struck, raised (dust); hit, pierced; wounded, hurt (lit. & fig.); visited or afflicted by (instr. or —°); cheated, deceived; killed, slain; ruined, lost; cursed, wretched, miserable. Often °— having lost, deprived or destitute of; the wretched or cursed—.

हतक a. smitten, slain; cursed, wretched, miserable.

हतच्छाय a. robbed of beauty or grace.

हतजीवन & **°जीवित** n. the cursed life.

हतत्विष् a. robbed of light or splendour.

हतविधि m. the cursed fate.

हतहृदय n. the cursed heart.

हतस्त्रीक a. having killed a woman.

हताश a. desperate or good for nothing (lit. having lost or killed hope).

हति f. striking, stroke, blow.

हत्नु a. deadly, pernicious.

हत्य n. (—°) & **हत्या** f. killing, slaughter.

हथ m. stroke, blow.

हद्, **हदति** cacare.

1**हन्**, **हन्ति**, **हते**, **जिघ्नते**, **°ति** (**हनति**), pp. **हत** (q.v.) smite, beat, strike, strike down, hew off, hit, pierce, hurt, injure, throw (a spear or an arrow) upon (gen. or dat.), slay, kill, destroy (**आत्मानमात्मना** one's self), suppress, give up, abandon. C. **घातयति** (q.v.). D. **जिघांसति** (**°ते**) wish to strike down or kill. I. **जङ्घन्ति** (**जङ्घन्यते**) tread upon (loc. or acc.) strike, slay, destroy; vex, afflict. — **अप** beat off or out, repel, destroy, unhusk (corn). **अभि** strike at, beat (drum), smite, afflict, visit, touch. D. wish to strike down. **अव** throw down, strike, hit; scare away, repel, keep off. **आ** strike at (loc. or dat., M. strike a part of one's own body); hit, beat, attack, assault. **अभ्या** hit, strike, wound, impede. **प्रत्या** ward off, repel. **व्या** strike, hit, impede, hinder, keep off. **समा** beat (together), strike at, hew down, kill.

उद् force up, raise; root up or out; dig or throw up; M. hang one's self. उप beat, strike, touch; stick on, fix, fasten; hit, hurt, afflict, damage, destroy. नि strike in or down, hurl upon (loc.); hit at, touch; attack, assail; slay, destroy, bring to nought. अभिनि spit, put on; strike at (acc.). प्रणि bring to nought, destroy (acc. or gen.). प्रतिनि strike against (acc.). विनि beat, strike down, kill, destroy. संनि strike at, attack, kill. निस् dash out or off, drive away, slay, destroy. परा strike off or down, overthrow; hit, touch. परि strike around, encompass; extinguish (fire). प्र beat, strike at (acc.), hew down, kill. अभिप्र, (*निप्र w. gen.), & विप्र overwhelm. प्रति strike against (gen.), strike at, attack (acc.); strike down, break; pierce, broach; beat back, repel, hinder; frustrate, destroy. वि strike apart, break down, destroy; spread, extend; tear or beat off, repel, resist, frustrate. सम् strike together, join or unite closely, conglomerate; strike or break down. P. thicken (intr.), become firm or solid. — Cf. अभिहत, आहत, उद्धत, विहत, संहत, समुद्धत.

2हन्, f. घ्नी (—°) killing, slayer.

हनन a. (f. ई) & n. striking down, killing, destroying.

हनीयंस् (compar.) slaying more or most.

हनु f. the jaw.

हनुमन्त् a. having strong jaws; m. N. of a monkey-chief, the son of the god of wind and the ally of Rāma.

हनुमन्नाटक n. T. of a drama.

हनूमन्त् m. = हनुमन्त् m.

हन्त interj. come! go to! well! often repeated or w. हा.

हन्तव्य a. to be killed.

हन्तु m. killing (हन्तुम्, हन्तवे, हन्तवै, & हन्तोस् infin. to हन्).

हन्तुकाम a. wishing to kill.

हन्तृ (gen.) & हन्तृ (acc.) slaying, slayer.

हन्त्व a. to be slain.

हन्मन् s. stroke, blow.

हम्भा f. bellowing of a cow or calves.

हम्भाय्, °यते bellow.

हय m. horse; f. हया & हयी mare.

हयकर्मन् n. horsemanship.

हयग्रीव a. horse-necked; m. a form of Viṣṇu.

हयज्ञ a. skilled in horses; °ता f. = seq.

हयतत्त्व n. horsemanship (cf. हयविद्या).

1हयमुख n. the face of a horse.

2हयमुख a. horse-faced; f. ई N. of a Rākṣasī.

हयमेध m. horse-sacrifice.

हयविद्या f., °शास्त्र n. the science of (training and managing) horses.

1हयशिरस् n. a horse's head; N. of a cert. myth. weapon.

2हयशिरस् a. having a horse's head; m. a form of Viṣṇu.

हयशीर्ष & °र्षन् a. & m. = prec.

हयहर्तृ m. stealer of a horse.

हयारोह m. rider on horseback.

हयिन् m. horseman.

हये a vocat. particle.

हर (only —°, f. आ, r. ई) carrying, bringing; taking, receiving, seizing, robbing; ravishing, charming; removing, destroying. m. seizer or destroyer, E. of Çiva, a man's name.

हरण a. (f. आ & ई) & n. carrying, conveying, taking, receiving, seizing, holding, robbing, removing, destroying; n. also offering (of a sacrifice), nuptial fee.

हरदत्त m. a man's name.

हरनेत्र n. Çiva's eye.

हरयाण m. N. of a man.

हरवृषभ m. Çiva's bull.

1हरस् n. grip; draught (in drinking, also = drink, beverage); vigour, energy, strength, power; poss. °हरस्वन्त् & हरस्विन्.

2हरस् n. anger, wrath.

हरसख m. Çiva's friend i.e. Kubera.

हरसूनु m. Çiva's son i.e. Skanda.

हरि a. fallow, yellowish, greenish. m. horse, esp. the steeds of Indra (2, but also 20–200), lion, ape, the sun, fire, wind, E. of Viṣṇu, Indra etc.

हरिकेश a. yellow-haired; N. of a Yakṣa etc.

हरिगिरि m. N. of a mountain.

हरिगोपक m. the cochineal insect.
हरिचन्दन m. n. a sort of yellow sandal tree or wood; one of the 5 trees of paradise.
हरिण a. fallow, pale, yellowish, green; m. a kind of antelope (f. °णी), ichneumon, N. of a serpent-demon etc.
हरिणाक्ष, f. ई deer-eyed.
हरिणी v. हरिण & हरित.
हरिणीदृश् & °नयना f. deer-eyed.
हरिणेक्षण a. = prec.
हरित् a. fallow, yellowish, greenish. m. a fallow horse, esp. of the Sun-god, emerald; f. a fallow mare; region, quarter of the sky.
हरित (f. आ, older हरिणी fallow, pale, yellow, green. m. N. of sev. men etc.; f. हरिता Dūrvā grass; n. gold, greens, any yellowish or greenish substance.
हरितकपिश a. yellowish brown.
हरितगोमय m. pl. fresh cow-dung.
हरितच्छद a. green-leaved.
हरितस्रज् a. having (forming) yellow or green garlands (tree); wound with a golden chain (horse).
हरिताल n. auripigment; °मय, f. ई made of it.
हरितधान्य n. green or unripe grain.
हरितयव m. pl. green (unripe) barley.
हरिताश्व a. having fallow horses (Sun).
हरित्वच् a. yellow-skinned.
हरित्वन्त् a. gold-coloured.
हरिदत्त m. N. of a Dānava & sev. men.
हरिदश्व a. = हरिताश्व, m. the sun.
हरिद्र m. the yellow sandal tree; f. आ turmeric, N. of a river.
हरिनेत्र a. yellow-eyed (Çiva).
हरिपिङ्ग & °पिङ्गल a. yellowish-brown.
हरिप्रबोध m. T. of a work.
†**हरिप्रिय** m. friend of the fallow steeds, i.e. Indra.
हरिमन् m. yellowness, a kind of disease.
हरिमन्त् a. = हरिवन्त्.
हरियोग a. yoked with the fallow steeds (Indra's chariot).
हरियोजन n. harnessing the fallow steeds.
हरिवंश m. Hari's i.e. Viṣṇu's (Kṛṣṇa's) race, T. of a poem.
हरिवन्त् a having fallow steeds (Indra).
हरिवर्पस् a. green-coloured.
हरिवाहन a. guiding the fallow steeds; m. E. of Indra.
हरिशर्मन् & °शिख m. names of sev. men.
हरिश्चन्द्र a. having a golden-coloured splendour; m. N. of sev. kings.
हरिश्मशारु & °श्मश्रु† a. golden-bearded.
हरिश्री a. shining or beautiful as gold.
हरिष्ठा a. guiding (lit. standing over) fallow steeds.
हरिसिंह m. N. of a king.
1**हरिहय** m. a horse of Indra.
2**हरिहय** a. having fallow horses (Indra).
हरिहर m. a deity consisting of Viṣṇu and Çiva conjoined; du. Viṣṇu and Çiva.
हरिहेति f. Viṣṇu's or Indra's weapon (discus or rainbow).
हरिहेतिमन्त् a. adorned with a rainbow.
हरीतक m., ई f. N. of a tree.
हरीश m. a monkey-prince.
हरेणु m. a kind of pease.
हर्तव्य a. to be seized, robbed, or taken.
हर्तृ m. bringer, taker, receiver, seizer, remover, destroyer.
हर्म्य n. stronghold, castle, mansion, palace, house, home.
हर्म्यतल & °पृष्ठ n. platform, balcony.
हर्म्यवलभी f., °स्थल & हर्म्याग्र n. the same.
हर्म्येष्ठा a. being in a house.
हर्य्, हर्यति, °ते be gratified or comfortable, delight in (loc.), be fond of, desire, like (acc.). — अभि love, long for. आ M. love, cherish. प्रति be fond of, long for, also = वि dislike, reject.
हर्यक्ष a. green-eyed; m. cat or ape.
हर्यत a. desirable, pleasant, dear.
1**हर्यश्व** m. & 2हर्यश्व a. = 1 & 2हरिहय.
हर्यश्वचाप m. Indra's bow i.e. the rainbow.
हर्ष m. joy, delight, rapture, glee; N. of a king etc.
हर्षक a. delighting (—°).
हर्षगर्भ a. joyful, merry.
हर्षचरित n. T. of a work.

†हर्षण a. & n. gladdening, exciting.
हर्षदेव m. king Harsha.
हर्षदोहल s. amorous desire.*
हर्षनाद, °निस्वन & °निःस्वन m. shout of joy.
हर्षमय a. whose essence is joy (ph.).
हर्षवन्त् a. joyful; f. °वती N. of a princess & a city.
हर्षवर्धन m. N. of a king, pl. of a people.
हर्षवर्मन् m. N. of a prince.
हर्षशोक m. du. joy and sorrow.
हर्षाश्रु n. tear of joy.
†हर्षिन् a. rejoicing, delighting in (—°).
हर्षुमन्त् a. excited.
हर्षुल a. cheerful, merry.
हर्षोत्फुल्ललोचन a. opening the eyes wide in rapture.*
हर्ष्या (instr. adv.) in impatient agitation.
हल m. n. plough (also as a weapon).
हलधर & °भृत् m. plough-holder, plougher (E. of Balarāma).
हलमार्ग m. furrow.
हलमुख n. plough-share.
हलहला exclam. of applause.
हला a. vocat. particle used in addressing a female friend.*
हलायुध a. armed with a plough; m. E. of Baladeva, N. of sev. men.
हलाहल m. n. a cert. deadly poison.
हलिक्ष्ण m. a kind of lion (cf. हलीक्ष्ण).
हलिन् m. plougher, husbandman; (± राम) E. of Balarāma.
हलीक्ष्ण m. a cert. animal.
1हव m. sacrifice.
2हव a. calling; m. n. call, invocation.
1हवन n. sacrifice or = f. ई sacrif. ladle.
2हवन n. invocation.
हवनश्रुत् a. listening to an invocation.
हवनस्यद् a. hastening to an invocation.
हवस् n. invocation.
हविन् a. calling (for help).
हविरद् & हविरद a. eating oblations.
हविरद्य n. abstr. to prec.
हविराहुति f. a sacrificial offering.
हविरुच्छिष्ट n. the leavings of a sacrifice.
हविरुच्छिष्टभुज् a. eating the leavings of a sacrifice.
हविरुच्छिष्टाश & °शन a. = prec.
हविर्ग्रहणी f. the sacrificial shovel or ladle.
हविर्दा a. giving oblations.
हविर्दान n. gift of oblations.
हविर्धान n. a waggon on which Soma-plants and other offerings are put or a shed for such waggons, i.g. place of offering; p. °धानिन्.
हविर्भुज् a. eating oblations; m. fire or the god of fire, also Çiva or a good i.g.
हविर्मथि a. spoiling a sacrifice.
हविर्यज्ञ m. a sacrificial offering.
हविर्वह् (°र्वाह, nom. वाट्) carrying the sacrifice.
हविःशेष m. the leavings of a sacrifice; °भच a. eating them.
हविष्करण n. the preparation of a sacrifice.
हविष्कृत् a. preparing an oblation; m. the formula हविष्कृदेहि (r.).
हविष्कृत a. prepared as a sacrifice.
हविष्कृति f. = हविष्करण.
हविष्पङ्क्ति f. five (lit. a pentad of) sacrificial objects, grains, milk etc.
हविष्पति m. lord of a sacrifice.
हविष्पा a. drinking an oblation.
हविष्पात्र n. a vessel for oblations.
हविष्मन्त् a. having prepared the oblations or offering them; accompanied by oblations or containing them.
हविष्य a. fit for an oblation; m. n. sacrificial food.
हविष्यभुज् a. subsisting on sacrificial food.
हविष्याशिन् a. the same.
हविष्यान्न n. sacrificial food.
हविस् n. oblation or gift for the gods, esp. grain (parched, boiled, as porridge or as cake), Soma, milk, clarified butter, etc.
हवीमन् s. invocation.
हवै exclamation.
1हव्य n. oblation.
2हव्य (हव्य) a. to be invoked.
हव्यकव्य n. sgl. or du. an oblation to the gods and the Manes.
हव्यजुष्टि f. delight at offerings.
हव्यदाति a. & f. giving offerings.

हव्यवंह् (°वाह्, nom. °वाट्) bearing the oblations (to the gods); m. fire or the god of fire.
हव्यवाहं & °वाहनं a. & m. = prec.
हव्यसूंद्, °सूंद्, & °सूंदन a. affording oblations.
हव्यांद् & हंव्याद् a. eating oblations.
हव्याजुति f. a sacrificial offering.
1हस् interj. of laughter or mirth.
2हस्, हंसति (°ते), pp. हसित (q.v.) laugh, smile; laugh at (instr. or acc.), mock, ridicule, cut out. C. हासयति make laugh; mock, ridicule. — अप C. mock, deride. अव the same. उप smile; (also C.) laugh at, ridicule. परि sport or jest with (acc.); scoff, deride. प्र laugh out (± हासम्); laugh with (acc.); laugh at, ridicule. C. make laugh. संप्र laugh out; C. sport, jest. वि laugh out; mock, deride (acc., r. gen.). संवि laugh out, laugh.
हंस or हसं m. laughter, mirth.
हसन a. & n. laughing, joking; f. आ a laugh or smile.
हसनीय a. laughable, ridiculous.
हसामुदं a. laughing merrily.
हसित a. laughing out, laughing; n. impers. it was laughed by (instr.) at (प्रति); mocked, derided, outvied, surpassed. n. laughing, laughter.
हस्कर्तृ m. exciter or gratifier.
हस्कारं m. the laughing of the sky i.e. lightning (without thunder).
हंस्कृति f. loud mirth, laughter.
हंस्त m. hand (also as a measure of length), trunk (of an elephant), paw (of a tiger) etc., N. of sev. men & a lunar mansion; a. —° holding in the hand (cf. पाणिं); f. हंस्ता hand.
हस्तक m. hand, adj. —° (f. इका) = prec.
हस्तकमल n. a lotus carried in the hand.
हस्तकार्य a. to be done with the hand.
हंस्तकृत a. done with the hand.
हस्तग, °गत, & °गामिन् a. being in the hand or in the hands of (—°).
हस्तगृंह्य ger. taking by the hand.
हस्तग्रह m. taking the hand (of a girl), marriage.
हस्तग्राभं m. who marries or has married (cf. prec.).
हस्तग्राह m. who takes one's hand i.e. who is quite near, also = prec.; m. husband.
हस्तघ्नं m. hand-protector (cf. अङ्गुलित्र).
हस्तत्र s. the same.
हस्तदीप m. hand-lantern.
हस्तधारण f. = हस्तग्रह; also help, assistance.
हस्तपाद n. sgl. hands and feet.
हस्तप्रद a. offering a hand, helpful.
हस्तप्राप्त a. = हस्तग.
हस्तप्राप्य a. to be reached with the hand.
हस्तभ्रंशिन्* & °भ्रष्ट a. slipped from the hand.*
हंस्तवन्त् a. having hands; handy, clever.
हस्तसंज्ञा f. a sign with the hand.
हस्तस्थ a. being in the hand, held.
हस्ताग्र n. the extremity of the hand (i.e. finger) or of an elephant's trunk.
हस्ताङ्गुलि or °ली f. finger (of the hand).
हस्ताञ्जलि* s. hollowed hands (cf. अञ्जलिं).
हंस्तादान a. & n. seizing with the hand.
हस्ताभरण n. ornament for the hand.
हस्तालम्ब m., °न n. support for the hand, adj. —° leaning upon; (fig.) refuge, hope.
हस्तावलम्ब m., °न n. the same.
हस्तावाप m. hand-protector (cf. हस्तघ्नं).
हस्ताहस्ति adv. in close fight (lit. hand to hand).
हस्तिगवाश्व n. sgl. elephants, cows and horses.
हस्तिगोऽश्वोष्ट्रदमक m. a trainer of elephants, oxen, horses, or camels.
हस्तिंन् a. = हंस्तवन्त्; m. (± मृग) elephant (f. °नी), N. of an ancient king.
हस्तिचारिन् & °जीविन् m. elephant-driver.
हस्तिनापुर n. N. of a city.
हस्तिपं m. elephant-driver.
हस्तिपक, °पाल, & °पालक m. the same.
हस्तिराज m. elephant-king, a strong elephant or the leader of a herd of elephants.
हस्तिवर्चसं n. the strength of an elephant.
हस्तिशाला f. elephant-stable.
हस्तिशिक्षा f. the art of (training and keeping) elephants.
हस्तिस्नान n. the washing of an elephant.
हस्ती कृ hand over, deliver.*
हस्तेगृंह्य ger. taking by the hand.

हस्त्य a. being on or in the hand, done with the hand.
हस्त्यश्व n. sgl. elephants and horses.
हस्त्याजीव m. elephant-driver.
हस्त्यारोह m. elephant-rider or -driver.
हस्र a. laughing, smiling.
1हा, जिहीते, pp. हान (only —°) start up, go forth, move on; run away from, yield (dat.); rush upon (acc.), fly (arrow). — अति leap or pass over. अनु run after, follow, overtake, catch. अप run away. अभि catch, take. उद् start up, rise, run away, escape. अभ्युद् ascend with (acc.). प्रोद् rise, ascend. प्रत्युद् rise towards (acc.). समुद् rise, appear. नि descend, stoop. प्र start up or off. वि burst open, gape. C. (हापयति) open (tr.). सम् arise, stand up.
2हा, जहाति (जहति), pp. हीनं & जहित (q.v.) leave, forsake, abandon; emit, discharge, take off, cast aside, remove; give up, avoid, shun, lose. P.M. हीयते (हीयते, °ति) be left etc., remain behind, come short or be deprived of (abl. or instr.); come to harm, be a loser, fail (in a lawsuit etc.); decrease, wane, perish, be lost. C. हापयति, °ते neglect, omit, give up, miss, lose. D. जिहासति wish to leave etc. — अप leave, abandon; P.M. fall short, decrease. अव leave, relinquish, give up. P.M. remain behind, fall short or be deficient. नि P.M. fall short, fail, be deprived of (instr.). परि leave, desert, forsake, omit, neglect, overlook. P.M. be left etc., be deficient or wanting, decrease, wane, cease, vanish; fall short, fail; desist from, be deprived of (abl.). प्र leave, abandon, give up, resign. P.M. be left or omitted, cease, vanish, succumb, lose. विप्र leave, quit, resign. प्रति disregard; P.M. fail, lose. वि leave, desert, forsake, give up, lose, resign; cease, desist. P.M. stay behind, yield to (abl.); be diminished or lost. प्रवि & प्रतिवि give up, abandon. सम् leave (together); give up, resign. — Cf. अपहाय, निहीन (add.), परिहीण, प्रहीण, विहाय, विहीन, हित्वा.
3हा excl. of pain, astonishment, or joy, mostly w. vocative; w. acc. woe to! Often repeated or connected w. धिक्, हन्त etc.
हाकार m. the exclamation हा.
हाटक m. sgl. & pl. N. of a country & its inhabitants, n. gold; as adj. (f. ई) golden.
हाटकमय (f. ई) & °कीय a. golden.
हाटकेश, °केशान, & °केश्वर m. a cert. form of Çiva.
हातव्य a. to be left or given up.
हान n. leaving, giving up, wanting, ceasing.
हानि f. abandonment, relinquishment, want, privation, decrease, detriment, damage, loss, ruin.
हानिकर or °कृत् a. causing loss or damage.
1हायनं m. n. year (also f. ई); m. a kind of red rice.
2हायनं, f. ई yearly, annual.
हार्, हारति resemble a string of pearls.
हार, f. ई carrying, bringing, taking, seizing, ravishing, charming (—°). m. a string or garland of pearls (adj. —° f. आ); taking away, removing, deprivation, loss.
हारक, f. °रिका = prec. (adj. —°); m. thief, robber, also = seq.
हारयष्टि f. (adj. —° f. इ or ई) a string of pearls.
हारलता f. the same.
हारावली f. the same; T. of a dictionary.
हारिण a. belonging or relating to deer.
हारिद्र a. dyed with turmeric, yellow.
हारिद्रवं or हारिद्रव m. a cert. yellow bird.
1हारिन् a. conveying, bearing, bringing; carrying away, seizing, robbing, stealing, removing, destroying; ravishing, charming (—°).
2हारिन् a. having a string of pearls.
हारीत m. a kind of pigeon; m. N. of sev. men, esp. of a law-giver, pl. H.'s family or N. of a people.
हारुक a. seizing, consuming.
हार्द a. being in the heart; n. affection, love, p. °वन्त्†.
हार्दि m. n. heart; content, comfort.
हार्दिक्य m. a patron. name; n. friendship.
हार्दिन् a. feeling affection for (—°).

हार्दिवन् a. hearty or = seq.
हार्दन् a. heart-comforting.
हार्य a. to be taken away or stolen; ravishing, charming.
हाल m. N. of a king and poet.
हाला f. spirituous liquor, wine.
हालाहल m. a cert. deadly poison.
हालिक m. ploughman.
हाव m. calling, a call.
हास्, हासते go emulously; C. हासयति.
हास m. laughing, laughter, mirth, joy, derision.
हासक m. buffoon (who causes laughter).
हासन a. causing laughter, comical.
हासिन् a. laughing at or (shining) with (—°).
हास्तिक a. consisting of elephants; n. a herd or multitude of elephants.
हास्तिन a. belonging or relating to an elephant, so big or high.
हास्तिनपुर n. = हस्तिनापुर.
हास्य a. ridiculous; n. laughing, laughter, joke, हास्यार्थम् adv. for sport.
हास्यकर, °कार, or °कृत् a. causing laughter or mirth.
हास्यता f., °त्व n., °भाव m. ridiculousness.
हास्यार्णव m. sea of mirth, T. of a comedy.
हास्यास्पद n. an object of laughter; abstr. °त्व n.
हाहाकार m. the exclamation हाहा.
हाहाकृत & °भूत a. crying or sounding हाहा.
1हि, हिनोति, हिनुते, हिन्वति (हयति), pp. हित impel, urge on, set in motion, hurl, send forth (M. intr. hasten, speed); further, help to (dat.); get, procure. आ M. bring near. प्र (हिणोति) urge on, impel, hurl, cast, turn upon (dat. or loc.); call upon, summon; send out, dismiss, dispatch to (dat., gen. ± अन्तिकम् or पार्श्वम्, acc. ± प्रति), in order to (dat. or infin.); bring near, get, procure, furnish. अनुप्र send after. अभिप्र send hither. उपप्र send to (acc.). प्रतिप्र send or drive back. सम् send out; bring together, join, combine, compose.
2हि (indecl.) for, because, namely; surely, verily, indeed; well, pray (with an imper., conj., or optat.).
हिंस्, हिनस्ति, हिंस्ते, हिंसति, pp. हिंसित (q.v.) injure, hurt, harm, kill, destroy. C. हिंसयति the same. D. जिहिंसिषति wish to injure etc. — उप & वि = S.
हिंस a. harming, f. हिंसा abstr.
हिंसक a. = prec. adj.
हिंसन & हिंसित n. = हिंसा.
हिंसनीय & हिंस्य a. to be hurt or killed.
हिंसात्मक a. of an injurious nature.
हिंसाप्राय a. generally injurious.
हिंसारत a. delighting in mischief.
हिंस्र a. harming, malicious; m. a savage or cruel man, also = seq.
हिंस्रजन्तु & °पशु m. a beast of prey.
हिंस्राहिंस्र n. du. noxiousness or harmlessness.
हिक्क्, हिक्कति, pp. हिक्कित (v. seq.) sob.
हिक्का & हिक्किका f., हिक्कित n. sobbing.
हिङ् w. कृ utter the sound hiṅ (as a cow to her calf, also r.).
हिङ्कर्तृ m. who utters the sound hiṅ.
हिङ्कार m. the sound hiṅ.
हिङ्गु m. the plant Asa Fetida, n. its resin or juice.
हिङ्गुल & °क n. vermilion.
हिंगूज्ज्वला f. a kind of perfume.*
हिडिम्ब m., आ f. N. of a Rākṣasa & his sister.
हिण्ड्, हिण्डते w. आ roam.*
हित a. put, placed, laid; being in (loc.); arranged, constituted, regulated; fit, suitable, advantageous, salutary; useful, conducive to, good for (dat., gen., loc., or —°); kind, gracious, favourable. m. a good friend. f. आ v. sub voce. n. welfare, advantage, prize, good advice.
हितकर a. doing well.
हितकाम a. well-wishing.
हितकाम्या f. abstr. to prec.
हितकारक, °कारिन्, & °कृत् a. = हितकर.
हितप्रयस् a. who has prepared the sacrificial food or for whom it has been prepared.
हितप्रेप्सु a. desiring the good of (gen.).
हितबुद्धि a. well-minded; f. as abstr.

हितमित्र a. having good friends.
हितवचन n. a good word or advice.
हितवन्त् a. useful, conducive.
हिता f. E. of cert. veins or arteries; weir, dyke.
हितान्वेषिन् a. seeking the good of (gen.).
हिताभङ्ग m. destruction of a dyke.
हितार्थम् or °र्थाय adv. for the sake of (gen.).
हितार्थिन् a. seeking (one's own or another's) welfare.
हिताहित a. good and evil, n. advantage and disadvantage.
†हिति f. direction, arrangement (-- °).
हितेच्छा & हितेप्सा f. desire for (one's own or another's) welfare.
हितैषिन् a. well-wishing; abstr. °षिता f.
हितोपदेश m. salutary instruction, T. of a collection of fables.
हित्वन् a. rapid, quick.
हित्वा ger. leaving alone, neglecting; without, except.
हिन्ताल m. N. of a tree.
हिन्दु m. a Hindu; °स्थान n. Hindustan.
हिन्दोल m. a swing; den. °लय्, °यति.
हिन्व m. exciter, impeller.
1हिम m. the cold season, winter (also हिमा f.); n. snow, ice.
2हिम a. cold, cool.
हिमकर & °किरण m. the moon (cool-rayed).
हिमगर्भ a. having frost or snow (in the interior), cold.
हिमगिरि m. the snow-mountain, Himālaya.
हिमत्विष्, °दीधिति & °द्युति m. = हिमकर.
हिमपात m. snow-fall.
हिममयूख, °रश्मि, & °रुचि m. = हिमकर.
हिमवन्त् a. having frost or snow; m. snow-mountain, esp. Himālaya.
हिमवारि n. cold water.
*हिमवालुका f. camphor.
हिमशैल m. = हिमगिरि.
हिमसरस् n. a cool lake.
हिमस्रुति f. snow-fall.
हिमा f. v. 1हिम.
हिमांशु m. = हिमकर.
हिमागम m. approach of cold, winter.
हिमाचल m. = हिमगिरि.
हिमात्यय m. = हिमान्त.
हिमाद्रि m. = हिमगिरि.
हिमानी f. much or deep snow.
हिमान्त m. the end of winter.
हिमाम्भस् n. cold water.
हिमालय m. the Himālaya mountain (abode of snow).
हिमाहृति f. snow-fall.
हिमी w. कृ change into ice.
हिर m. band, stripe.
*हिरण n. gold, p. °णिन्.
हिरणमय, f. ई golden, gold-coloured.
हिरण्य n. gold, a gold coin or ornament; any precious metal, money.
हिरण्यकण्ठ, f. ई golden-necked.
हिरण्यकर्तृ m. worker in gold, goldsmith.
1हिरण्यकशिपु m. a golden mat or pillow.
2हिरण्यकशिपु a. poss. to prec.; m. N. of a Daitya.
हिरण्यकार m. = हिरण्यकर्तृ.
हिरण्यकेश, f. ई golden-haired or -maned.
हिरण्यकेश्य a. the same.
हिरण्यगर्भ m. golden womb or fetus, E. of Brahman.
हिरण्यचक्र a. having golden chariots.
हिरण्यजित् a. winning gold.
हिरण्यजिह्व a. golden-tongued.
1हिरण्यज्योतिस् n. splendour of gold.
2हिरण्यज्योतिस् a. shining as gold.
हिरण्यद or °दा a. granting gold.
हिरण्यदन्त a. golden-toothed.
हिरण्यनिर्णिज् a. adorned with gold.
हिरण्यनिधि m. a golden treasure.
†हिरण्यनेमि a. having golden rims.
हिरण्यपर्ण a. golden-winged or -leaved.
हिरण्यपाणि a. golden-handed.
हिरण्यपात्र n. a golden vessel.
हिरण्यपिण्ड m. a lump of gold.
हिरण्यबाहु a. golden-armed.
हिरण्यमय & हिरण्यय. f. ई golden.
हिरण्यमूर्धन् a. golden-headed.
हिरण्ययु a. fond of gold.
1हिरण्यरथ m. a golden chariot or a chariot full of gold.
2हिरण्यरथ a. riding in a golden chariot.
हिरण्यरूप a. golden-shaped. gold-like.

हिरण्यरेतस् m. fire (lit. whose seed is gold).
हिरण्यवक्षस् a. golden-breasted (the earth).
हिरण्यवन्त् a. abounding in or consisting of gold; n. abundance of gold.
हिरण्यवन्धुर a. having a golden seat or framework (chariot).
हिरण्यवर्ण a. golden-coloured, gold-like.
हिरण्यवर्तनि a. having a golden path.
हिरण्यवाशी f. a golden knife or hatchet.
†हिरण्यवाशीमन्त् (superl. °मत्तम) poss. to prec.
हिरण्यविमित n. a golden palace.
हिरण्यशिप्र a. having a golden helmet or visor.
हिरण्यशृङ्ग a. golden-horned.
हिरण्यश्मश्रु a. golden-bearded.
हिरण्यसंदृश् a. resembling gold.
1हिरण्यस्रज् f. a golden wreath, chain, etc.
2हिरण्यस्रज् a. poss. to prec.
हिरण्यहस्त a. golden-handed.
हिरण्याक्ष a. golden-eyed; m. N. of a Daitya.
हिरण्याभीशु a. having golden reins or traces (carriage).
†हिरि (°—) = हरि.
हिरिशिप्र a. golden-cheeked or having a golden helmet.
हिरिश्मश्रु a. golden-bearded.
हिरीमन्त् a. having bay horses.
हिरुक् adv. away, off, apart from (abl.), separately.
ही excl. of surprise or joy (often w. माणहे to express fear or depression*).
हीड् (हेडति, हेळते, हेलते), pp. होडित A. vex, afflict; M. be angry or hostile. C. pluck out.
हीडं (हीळ) m. plucker, puller, i.e. monisher.
हीन a. left, forsaken; excluded or shut out from, fallen short of (abl.); devoid or bereft of, free from, without (instr., abl., loc., °— or —°); inferior, less (opp. अधिक); low, base, mean; incomplete, deficient, wanting. Abstr. °ता† f., °त्व† n.
हीनकर्मन् a. given to low occupations or omitting the customary rites.
हीनक्रतु a. neglecting to sacrifice.
हीनक्रिय a. = हीनकर्मन्.
हीनज & °जाति a. low-born.
हीनपक्ष a. having no friends or adherents.
हीनबल a. deficient in strength, weak.
हीनवीर्य a. deficient in strength or courage.
हीनवृत्त a. of bad conduct.
हीनसेवा f. attendance on base people.
हीनांशु a. rayless, obscure.
हीनाङ्ग, f. आ & ई deficient in limbs or parts.
हीर & °क s. diamond.
हु, जुहोति, जुहुते, pp. हुत (q.v.) pour into the fire, cast into the fire, offer, sacrifice. C. हावयति cause to sacrifice or be sacrificed. D. जुहूषति wish to sacrifice. I. जोहवीति sacrifice repeatedly. — अधि sacrifice upon or over (loc.). अभि pour out the libation upon, make an oblation to (acc.). अव pour out upon (loc.). आ offer in (loc.), offer an oblation to (dat.), worship with oblations (acc.). उप offer in addition. प्र offer continually or successively. प्रति offer in return. सम् sacrifice (together).
हुंकार m. the sound hum (v. हुम्).
हुड m. ram; a cert. implement of war.
हुडु m. ram.
हुण्ड m. the same; pl. N. of a people.
हुत् (—°) offering, sacrificing.
हुत a. sacrificed or worshipped with a sacrifice; n. sacrifice, oblation.
हुतभाग a. partaking of a sacrifice.
हुतभुज् & °भोक्तृ m. fire or the fire-god (lit. oblation-eater).
हुतभोजन a. having oblations as food, m. = prec.
हुतवह m. fire or Agni (oblation-bearer).
हुतवहाय्, only °यमान resembling fire.*
हुतशेष m. the remainder of a sacrifice.
हुतहोम a. having offered oblations.
हुताग्नि a. having offered oblations in the fire.
हुताद् a. eating oblations.
हुताश & हुताशन m. = हुतभुज्.
हुताशनवन्त् a. furnished with fire.
हुताशिन् a. eating (only) oblations.
हुति f. oblation, sacrifice (only —°).
हुतोच्छिष्ट a. left from a sacrifice.

हुम् interj. w. कृ growl, grumble, speak roughly to (acc.).
हुरश्चित् a. plotting in the dark.
हुरस् adv. secretly, in the dark.
हुरुक् adv. = हिरुक्.
हुल = हुड.
हुलहुली or हुलुहुली f. howling.
हुवध्यै dat. inf. to हु.
†हुवन्य, °न्यति call, cry.
हुविष्क & हुष्क m. names of kings.
हूहू or हूहू m. N. of a Gandharva.
हु (ह्वा), ह्वयति, °ते, हवते, हुवते, °ति etc., pp. हूत call (अवसे or ऊतये for help), call upon, invoke, summon, invite, challenge (युद्धे to fight). C. ह्वाययति & D. जुहूषति (only —°). I. जोहवीति etc. call, invoke. — अति call over. अनु call again or back. अभि call near. अव call down or hither. आ call to or hither, invite, summon (r. & j.); utter, recite; M. challenge. C. cause to invite or challenge. I. call near, invoke. उपा M. invite, summon, challenge. प्रत्या answer a call. समा convoke, assemble, invite, challenge. उद् call forth, elicit. उप M. (A.) call upon, summon or invite to (acc., dat., or loc.); call encouragingly to, approve, praise. पर्युप & प्रत्युप call near. समुप convoke, assemble, invite; provoke, challenge. नि M. call down, in, or near. निस् call off. प्र invoke. प्रतिप्र call to (acc.). प्रति invoke. वि M. call hither and thither or emoulously, quarrel about (acc.); call off. सम् M. convoke.
हूंकृ & हूंकार m. = हुंकृ & हुंकार.
हूंकृति f. humming or snorting.
हूण m. pl. N. of a people
हूति f. calling, invoking; appellation, name.
हून m. = हूण.
हूम् = हुम्.
हूर्छ्, हूर्छति fall away; C. हूर्छयति cause to fall away. — अनु fall after (acc.). वि waddle, stagger, slip, fail.
हूहू m. = हूहू.
हृ, हरति, °ते (हर्ति, जिहर्ति), pp. हृत (q.v.) A. hold, carry, bring; offer, present (esp. बलिम्); hand over to (gen.); seize, steal, carry away, remove, turn off (face); M. (A.) take, receive (taxes), come into possession of (as heir); take to wife, marry; get hold or become master of; overpower, outdo, surpass; win over, captivate, charm; seize upon, take away, withdraw, retain, destroy, frustrate. C. हारयति cause to hold or carry (2 acc.), cause to be held, taken etc. by (instr.); get hold of, seize upon; permit to be carrried of, lose (esp. in game). D. जिहीर्षति wish to take away, desire, covet. — अति carry beyond (acc.). व्यति transpose mutually. अधि carry over (acc.). अनु imitate, resemble (acc. or gen.). अप carry away, take off, remove, separate from (abl.); seize, rob, steal; overpower, frustrate, destroy. अभि hand over, offer, present; C. place before, serve (food), put on (mail). अव draw in, move down, put off. अभ्यव throw down into (acc.), bring near, take, eat, enjoy. C. cause to throw or be thrown; attack, assail; eat, feed. व्यव move hither and thither; transpose, exchange; communicate or have intercourse with (instr. or loc.); meet, encounter (as foes), fight with (instr. ± सार्धम्); proceed, act, deal with (loc.); trade or traffic (loc., instr., or gen.); be active, work; be intent upon (acc.); *bet, play (w. gen. of stake); *manage, use, employ (acc.). P. be called or named. आ bring near, attract, fetch, get, procure, offer, present, give; receive, accept; take to wife, marry; eat, enjoy; take away, sever, remove, destroy, turn off, withdraw from (abl.); utter show, betray; name, call. C. cause to bring near etc., cause to pay (taxes etc., 2 acc.); procure, acquire; eat, enjoy; utter, manifest. D. be willing to procure or acquire. अन्वा repair, complete, supply. अभ्या offer, present. उदा bring near, fetch, bring out, say, tell, quote (esp. as an example), recite, enumerate, praise, commend; P. be called, mentioned, or quoted. अभ्युदा bring hither.

प्रभ्युदा answer; quote (as a counter example). समुदा say, tell, mention. उपा fetch, get, procure, offer, present, take hold of, win, acquire, undertake, accomplish. समुपा fetch, procure, offer, present, undertake, commence. उपन्या offer, present. पर्या hand over; turn, invert. प्रत्या draw back, withdraw, get back, recover; take up again, carry on, procecute; utter, tell, report. व्या bring out, utter, speak to or with (acc. or सह), sing (of birds). अनुव्या utter successively or in its turn, (answer by singing*); abuse, revile, curse. अभिव्या utter, pronounce, recite; bespeak, charm with words, conjure, curse. C. (cause to) utter or pronounce. प्रव्या utter, speak. समा bring together, gather, collect, assemble, combine, comprehend; draw back, withdraw, bring back, restore; captivate, charm. अनुसमा arrange or put in order (again). उद् take out or from (abl.), stretch out (पाणिम्); offer, present; lift up, raise, further, strengthen; set aside, select; choose, prefer; extricate, rescue, save; take away, cut off, sever (head), remove, destroy; except. C. (cause to) draw out or rescue. D. wish to save or relieve. अभ्युद् take or draw out (in addition), lay aside; rescue, save, recover; start, further, promote. समभ्युद्, प्रोद्, & प्रत्युद् draw out, lift up, rescue, relieve, promote, further. समुद् draw or take out, rescue, deliver from (abl.); deduct; remove, destroy; lift up etc. = prec. उप bring, fetch, proffer, present; M. accept, receive, gather, collect. C. proffer, serve (food). निस् take or carry out, extract, export (goods); M. remove, exclude or deliver from (abl.); get rid of (acc.); change or mix with (instr.). विनिस् draw out, extract, take (वृद्धिम् interest); remove, destroy. परि carry or move about; surround, gird (M. refl.); protect from (abl.); keep off, shun, avoid, beware, escape; save, spare, except. विपरि transpose, interchange. प्र stretch forth; fix in, hurl upon (loc.); offer, present; strike, hurt; attack, assail (acc., loc., dat., or gen.); M. fight, make war. अनुप्र throw into the fire. संप्र hurl, cast; attack, assail (acc. or loc.); M.(A.) engage in battle, fight hand to hand. प्रति throw, hold, or bring back; offer, present. M. take, eat. वि take apart, divide, separate; take or carry away; shed (tears); transpose, interchange; roam about, pass one's time (± acc.) pleasantly, enjoy one's self. सम् bring or draw together, contract, collect, gather; take away, rob; suppress, absorb, destroy. उपसम् draw together or in, gather, contract, absorb, suppress. प्रतिसम् draw together or back, take off, avert, absorb, suppress, destroy, annihilate. — Cf. अभिव्याहृत (sic!), उद्धृत, विहृत, व्याहृत.

हृच्छय a. lying in the heart; m. love or the god of love.

हृच्छयपीडित a. tormented by love.

हृच्छयवर्धन a. augmenting love.

हृच्छयाविष्ट a. penetrated by love; °चेतन a. enamoured, love-sick.

†हृच्छोक m. heart-grief.

हृणाय्, °यति be angry, pp. °यन्त्.

हृणीय्, °यते = prec.; pp. हृणीयमान.

हृत् (—°) bringing, taking, removing, destroying.

हृत a. held, carried, seized, taken etc.; often °— robbed or bereft of, without.

हृतदार a. robbed of one's wife.

हृतद्रव्य a. robbed of one's property.

हृतराज्य a. stripped of a kingdom.

हृतसर्वस्व a. bereft of everything, entirely ruined.

हृति f. taking away, robbing.

हृत्तस् adv. from or with the heart, willingly.

हृत्ताप m. heart-grief.

हृत्पङ्कज & हृत्पद्म n. the heart conceived as a lotus-flower.

हृत्स्थ a. being in the heart.

हृद् n. the heart, esp. as seat of the emotions and mental activity i.g.

हृदम्भोज n. = हृत्पङ्कज.

हृदय n. the heart, as an organ of the body

or as seat of the feelings, also the interior of the body i.g., the centre or essence of anything etc.

हृदयकम्पन a. heart-stirring, agitating; n. adv.

हृदयगत a. dwelling in one's heart.

हृदयग्राहिन् a. captivating the heart.

हृदयंगम a. going to the heart.

हृदयच्छिद् a. heart-piercing (lit. & fig.).

हृदयज्ञ a. knowing the heart or the essence of (—°).

हृदयदौर्बल्य n. weakness of heart.

हृदयप्रमाथिन् a. heart-disturbing.

हृदयप्रस्तर a. having a stone instead of the heart, cruel-hearted.*

हृदयप्रिय a. heart-dear, dearly beloved.

हृदयवल्लभ m. the beloved of the heart.

हृदयवृत्ति f. disposition or inclination of the heart.

हृदयशल्य m. a wound (lit. sting) in the heart.

हृदयशूल m. a spit for (roasting) the heart (of the sacrificial victim); also the action of roasting.

हृदयसंनिहित m., **आ** f. the inhabitant of a heart i.e. the beloved object.

हृदयस्थ a. resting in the heart (wish).

हृदयहारिन् a. ravishing or captivating the heart, charming, delightful.

हृदयामय m. sickness of heart.

हृदयाविध् a. heart-piercing.

हृदयेश m. lord of the heart, husband.

हृदयेशय a. resting in the heart.

हृदयेश्वर m. = **हृदयेश**.

हृदय्य a. = seq. (grief); beloved, dear.

हृदिस्थ a. being in the heart.

हृदिस्पृश् & **°स्पृश** a. heart-touching, affecting.

हृद्ग a. reaching to the heart (water).

हृद्गत a. = prec. or = **हृदिस्थ**.

हृद्य a. being in the heart, hearty, inner; dear to the heart, pleasant, agreeable.

हृद्रोग m. heart-disease or -grief.

हृष्, **हृष्यति**, **°ते** (**हर्षते**, **°ति**), pp. **हृष्ट** & **हृषित** (q.v.) be excited (with pleasure or fear), be delighted or amazed; bristle, stand on end (the hair). C. **हर्षयति**, **°ते** cause (the hair) to bristle or stand erect; excite, make impatient, rejoice (tr. & intr.). I. (**जर्हृषन्त** & **जर्हृषाण**) be very impatient or much excited. — **अनु** be excited or rejoice with (acc.). **अभि** & **समभि** C. gladden. **उद्** be excited, impatient, or glad. C. excite, gladden. **परि** & **संपरि** C. delight greatly, enrapture. **प्र** be merry, rejoice. **संप्र** the same; C. gladden. **प्रति** be glad in return. **सम्** be excited, rejoice, exult. C. gladden, delight. — Cf. **परिहृष्ट**, **प्रहृष्ट**, **प्रोद्धृषित** (add.), **संहृष्ट**.

हृषित a. standing on end, erect, stiff (hair); unwithered, fresh (flowers); enraptured, delighted.

हृषितस्रग्रजोहीन a. having unwithered garlands and free from dust.

हृषीक n. organ of sense.

हृषीकेश & **°श्वर** m. E. of Viṣṇu-Kṛṣṇa.

हृषीवन्त् a. enraptured, delighted, pleased.

हृष्ट a. standing on end, erect (hair); stiff, rigid; glad, merry.

हृष्टरोमन् a. having the hair bristling, thrilling (with delight or rapture).

हृष्टि f. joy, rapture.

हे a voc. particle.

हेड् v. **हीड्**.

हेड (**हेळ**) m. vexation, anger.

†**हेडन** (**हेळन**) & **हेडस्** (**हेळस्**) n. the same.

हेति f. (m.) weapon, missile, fire-flame (as Agni's weapon); stroke, wound.

हेतिमन्त् a. poss. to prec.

हेतु m. impulse, motive, cause, reason (gen., dat., loc., or —°), argument, proof; means (instr. —° by means of); condition; mode, manner, way; also concr. mover, impeller, esp. the agent of the causative (g.); adj. —° caused by. Abl. gen., instr.. dat., & loc. by reason, on account, or for the sake of (gen. or —°). Abstr. **°ता**† f., **°त्व**† n.

हेतुक (a. —° f. **ई**) causing or caused by.

हेतुमन्त् a. caused, causative (g.).

हेतुरूपक n. a kind of metaphor (rh.).

हेतुवाद m. statement of reasons, disputation.

हेतुवादिक & **°दिन्** m. sceptic.

हेतुविद्या f. & **हेतुशास्त्र** n. logic, dialectics.

हेतूपमा f. a kind of comparison (rh.).

हेतृ or **हेतृ** m. inciter.

हेत्वाभास m. a mere appearance of a reason or argument.
हेमक n. gold.
हेमकर्तृ m. goldsmith.
हेमकान्ति a. shining as gold.
हेमकार m. = हेमकर्तृ.
हेमकूट m. N. of a mountain (golden-peaked) and of a monkey.
हेमगिरि m. E. of mount Meru (the golden mountain).
हेमचन्द्र m. N. of a king & a celebrated scholar.
1हेमन् n. impulse.
2हेमन् n. gold.
3हेमन् (loc.) in winter (cf. seq.).
हेमन्त m. winter.
हेमपिङ्गल a. as yellow as gold.
हेममय, f. ई golden.
हेममालिन् a. having a golden garland, golden-crowned.
हेमरत्नमय, f. ई consisting of gold and gems.
हेमरत्नवन्त् a. the same.
हेमवन्त् a. golden or adorned with gold.
हेमवर्ण a. gold-coloured.
1हेमशृङ्ग n. a golden horn.
2हेमशृङ्ग m. N. of a mountain.
हेमसूत्र n. a golden thread (ornament).
हेमाङ्ग a. golden-limbed, golden.
हेमाद्रि m. = हेमगिरि; N. of an author.
हेमाभ a. gold-like.
हेमालंकार m. a golden ornament.
हेय a. to be left or abandoned.
हेरम्ब m. buffalo, E. of Ganeça.
हेल्, हेलते (cf. हीड्) be careless or fickle; C. हेलयति mock, deride, vex.
हेलन n. derision, contempt.
हेला f. wantonness, fickleness, levity, sport; °— & instr. easily, quickly, at once.
हेलावन्त् a. careless, easy.
हेष्, हेषति, °ते, pp. हेषित (q.v.) neigh. — अभि & प्रति neigh to.
हेषस् n. haste, speed, zeal, energy, strength, heat, splendour.
हेषस्वन्त् a. powerful, strong.
हेषा f., हेषित n. neighing.
हेषाय्, °यते neigh.
है a vocative particle.
हैडिम्ब a. relating to or descended from Hiḍimba; m. patr. of Ghaṭotkaca.
हैतुक, f. ई caused by, dependent on (—°); argumentative, rationalistic; m. rationalist, sceptic.
1हैम a. of snow or ice.
2हैम, f. ई golden.
हैमन (f. ई) & हैमन्त a. winterly, cold.
हैमन्तिक a. the same.
हैमवत, f. ई coming from or belonging to the Himālaya mountains; m. pl. N. of a people, f. ई patr. of Gaṅgā & Umā.
हैमी भू be golden, be turned into gold.
हैरण्य a. golden; containing or yielding gold.
हैरण्यक m. goldsmith.
हैरण्यगर्भ m. patr. of Manu & Vasiṣṭha.
हैहय m. pl. N. of a people.
हो a vocative particle.
होतृ m. offerer, priest, esp. chief priest, often applied to Agni.
होतव्य a. to be offered (n. impers.) or worshipped with offerings.
होतृक m. = होत्रक.
होतृत्व n. the office of the Hotṛ.
होतृप्रवर m. the choice of a Hotṛ.
होतृमन्त् a. having a Hotṛ.
होतृवर्य or °वूर्य n. the choice of a Hotṛ.
होतृषदन n. the seat of the Hotṛ.
होत्र n. sacrifice, oblation; the office of the Hotṛ.
होत्रक m. the assistant of the Hotṛ, also chief priest i.g.
होत्रवह (°वाह) a. carrying oblations.
1होत्रा f. the office of a priest, esp. of the Hotraka.
2होत्रा f. invocation.
होत्राविद् a. skilled in invocation.
होत्राशंसिन् m. pl. the assistants of the Hotṛ.
होत्रिय n. the office of the Hotṛ.
होत्रीय a. belonging to the Hotṛ or Hotraka.
होत्व a. to be sacrificed, fit for an oblation.
होम m. pouring or casting into the fire; oblation, sacrifice.
होमकर्मन् n. sacrificial act.
होमकाल m. the time for sacrifice.

होमतुरंग m. a horse for sacrifice.
होमधेनु f. a cow (that yields the milk) for sacrifice.
1होमन् n. oblation, sacrifice.
2होमन् n. calling, invocation.
होमभाण्ड n. a sacrificial vessel.
होमय्, °यति make oblations, sacrifice.
होमवन्त् a. making oblations.
होमवेला f. the time for offerings.
होमाग्नि & होमानल m. the sacrificial fire.
होमिन् a. sacrificing (--°).
होमीय & होम्य a. sacrificial.
होरा f. hour, horoscope, or = seq.
होराशास्त्र n. horoscopy.
हौत्र a. relating to the Hotṛ; n. his office.
हौम्य a. = होमीय.
ह्नु, ह्नुते (ह्नौति, ह्नवते, °ति) *hide from(dat.). — अप M. conceal from (abl.), refuse, deny; satisfy (dat.), apologize. नि M. make amends for (acc.) to (dat.), expiate; refuse, deny; hide, conceal (w. आत्मानम् refl.*). अपनि & विनि hide, conceal, deny. — Cf. निह्नुत.
ह्यस् adv. yesterday.
ह्यस्तन, f. ई yesterday's, hesternal.
1ह्रद m. noise, sound.
2ह्रद m. pool, lake.
ह्रदस्थ a. being in a pool.
ह्रदिन् a. abounding in water; f. °नी river.
ह्रद्य a. being in a pool or lake.
ह्रस्, ह्रसति, °ते (± निस्) become less or short; C. diminish.
ह्रसिष्ठ & ह्रसीयंस् superl. & comp. to seq.
ह्रस्व a. less, little, small, short.
ह्रस्वक a. very little.
ह्रस्वकर्ण m. Short-Ear, N. of a Rākṣasa.
ह्रस्वता f., °त्व n. littleness, shortness.
ह्रस्वबाहु a. short-armed; m. Short-Arm (an assumed name of Nala).
ह्राद्, ह्रादते sound, make a noise; C. ह्रादयति make resound. — नि & निस् C. = S.C., beat (a drum). सम् knock together (intr.). C. the same (tr.); sound loudly.
ह्राद m. noise, sound.
1ह्रादिन् a. sounding, loud.
2ह्रादिन् a. = ह्रदिन्.
ह्रादुनि or °नी f. hail-stones, hail.
ह्रादुनीवृत् a. clad in hail.
ह्रास m., °न n. shortening, decrease, diminution.
1ह्री, जिह्रेति, pp. ह्रीत (& ह्रीण) be ashamed or abashed. C. ह्रेपयति put to shame, confound. I. जेह्रीयते be greatly ashamed.
2ह्री f. shame, bashfulness.
ह्रीक (adj. —°) & ह्रीति f. the same.
ह्रीतमुख & °मुखिन् a. shame-faced.
ह्रीमन्त् a. ashamed, bashful, modest; abstr. °त्व n.
ह्रु, ह्रुणाति, pp. ह्रुत (q.v.), with वि cause to go wrong. — Cf. विह्रुत.
ह्रुत् f. cause of going wrong, stumbling-block.
ह्रुत a. crooked, bent.
ह्रेपण n. shame, embarrassment.
ह्रेष्, ह्रेषति, °ते, pp. ह्रेषित (v. seq.) neigh. C. ह्रेषयति cause to neigh.
ह्रेषा f., °षित n. neighing, whinnying.
ह्रेषिन् a. neighing.
ह्रेषुक m. a kind of shovel.
ल्हाद्, ल्हादते cool off, refresh one's self; C. ल्हादयति refresh, comfort. — आ C. = S.C. प्र refresh one's self. C. refresh.
ल्हाद m. refreshment, comfort.
ल्हादक a. cooling, refreshing.
ल्हादन a. & n. the same.
†ल्हादिकावती f. rich in cooling.
1ल्हादिन् a. = ल्हादन a.
2ल्हादिन् a. very loud.
ल्हादुक a. cool, fresh.
ल्हीक a. ashamed.
ह्वरस् n. crookedness, deceit; pl. the curves (a cert. part of the Soma-strainer).
ह्वल्, ह्वलति (°ते) go wrong, stagger, fail. C. ह्वलयति shake. — वि stagger, tremble. — Cf. विह्वलित (add.).
ह्वल a. staggering, trembling, f. आ as subst.
ह्वलन a. = prec. adj.
ह्वा v. ह्वे.
ह्वातव्य a. to be called.

ह्वान n. calling, call.
ह्वार m. serpent (the crooked).
ह्वार्य a. serpent-like; m. = prec.
ह्वाल m. failure.
†ह्वृ, ह्वरते (only —°), pp. ह्वृत go crookedly, bend over, fall. C. ह्वारयति cause to go crookedly (fig.), lead astray; M. deviate, go astray. — आ lead astray or into trouble. उप go crookedly. वि stagger, fall; C. overturn.

Additions and Corrections.

1अज m., add N. of a king.
अणिष्ठ etc. put after 2अणिमन्.
अतिरेक (accented).
अतिषित a. underbound.
अत्यादित्य a. excelling the sun.
अत्यारूढ a. risen too high, excessive, immoderate.
अध्यात्म a. (for m.).
अनघप्रसवा f. having happily brought forth.*
अनतिप्रौढ a. not full-grown.
अनार्य (accented).
अनिर्विण्णचेतस् v. निर्विण्ण.
अनुबद्ध a. bound, fettered, connected, coherent.
अन्तरागमन put after अन्तरा.
अपप्लुत a. retired, hidden.
अपावृत (accented).
अपीवृत a. covered, veiled, shut up.
अपेताश a. hopeless.
अप्रतिरूप (accented).
अभिनिम्रुक्त a. on whom the sun sets, i.e. whom the setting sun finds sleeping.
अभिपरिप्लुत a. filled with, full of (instr.).
अभिप्रवृत्त a. occupied in (loc.).
अभिमन्तृ (sic!).
अभ्युद्यत a. lifted up, offered, presented; risen, intent upon, prepared or ready for, going to (loc. or —°).
अभ्युन्नत a. raised, elevated.
अमृतभोजन a. eating ambrosia.
अम्बक n. eye (esp. Çiva's).
अयमितनख a. with uncut nails.
अरध्र a. wealthy, liberal.
अर्धिक a. measuring a half.
अवगतार्थ a. acquainted with the matter.*
अवबोधक a. awakening.
अवरुद्ध a. checked, stopped, imprisoned.
अवलीन a. sitting, cowering, hidden in (loc. or —°).
अविदासिन् a. not ceasing.
अश्वतर m., ई f. mule.
अष्टाङ्ग, dele a.
1अस्, under निस् read keep off.
असंप्राप्त (sic!)
असुनीति f. spirit-life or -world.
असुवृत्त a. of bad conduct.
असूर्त (sic!)
आपृत a. occupied, busy.
आमत्त a. intoxicated.
आम्नात a. remembered, taught, learnt.
आयस्त a. kindled, hot, eager, zealous.
आरब्ध. — आवृत्ति.
1आहाव m. bucket, trough.
2आहाव m. calling, invoking.
उच्छलितबाष्प a. shedding tears.*
उत्स्वप्नाय् put after उत्स्रस्त.
उद्वर्ग m. destroyer.
उपत्यका etc. read, foot.
उपमित a. compared, equal, like.
उपशङ्कित a. doubtful (pers. & th.).
उपश्लिष्ट. — उपावृत्त.
उपेक्षक a. regardless, indifferent.

उल्लम्बित a. hanging, pendulous.
उशमान a. disposing of, commanding (acc.).
ऊवध्य n. the contents of the stomach and the bowels.
ऋक्तस् (sic!)
ऋतानृत n. du. truth and untruth.
ओषधिपति (sic!)
कथन n. (not a.).
कररुध् a. stopping one's hand (ray).
1कृ etc., विप्र for पिप्र.
कृत्ति f. skin, hide.
क्रीड् etc., read सम्.
क्षुभ्, read, cf. विक्षोभ्योस्.
खिद्, C. also pursue.
गन्धगुण, read a. possessing the quality etc.
गात्रक n. body.
ग्रहीतृ put after ग्रहीतव्य.
घ्रातृ put after घ्राति.
चूर्णमुष्टि f. a handful of powder.
तर्कु. — तक्वन् & तक्ववी.
तन्त्रीस्वन m. tune etc.
तितउ. — तुवीमघ. — तूल.
त्वद्वर्जम् adv. except you.
दन्तान्तर n. the room between the tusks of an elephant.*
दयालु (unaccented). — 2दायक m.
दिवसमुख (sic!)
दिवास्वप्न m. sleep by day.
दीर्घोच्छ्वासम्. — दुर्हित.
द्रष्टुमनस् a. desirous of seeing.
द्विराज n. battle between two kings.
धूमलेखा f. column of smoke.
निरत put after निरञ्जन.
निर्बद्ध a. fixed upon, clung to; pressed hard, urged.
निलीन a. stuck or clung to, seated on, hidden in (loc. or —°).
निषण्ण. — निःष्ठित.
निहीन a. mean, low.
पद्मव्याकोश n. (for a.).
परिलुब्ध a. greedy after (—°) *
परिविश्वस्त a. confident, fearless, unsuspecting.
पर्यवस्थित a. standing there, stationed; contained in, occupied with, devoted to (loc.).
पर्याण n. saddle.
पर्यावृत a. covered, veiled.
प्रगल्भ. — प्रघास v. वरुण°.
प्रतिलग्न a. sticking in (—°).*
प्रतिषिद्धवाम a. greedy after what is forbidden.*
प्रतिष्कभे dat. inf. to hold against.
प्रत्यासन्न a. approached, near, neighbouring (gen. or —°); imminent, impending; closely connected or related.
प्रत्युक्त. — प्रभु.
प्रलम्बित a. hanging down.
प्रविसृत a. violent, intensive.
प्रवृद्ध (sic!) add, exalted, inspired.
प्रस्थित dele, to sacrifice.
प्रीतिमन्त्, dele, having Prīti.
प्रोच्छ्रित a. lifted up, lofty, high.
प्रोद्धृषित a. bristling, erect.
बाष्पस्तबक s. flood (lit. cluster) of tears.*
भोजन as subst. n.
मणिस्रज् f. — महीध्र.
मातरिश्वन् also = 1वायु.
माधवाचार्य (sic!)
मिद्, मेद्यति etc.
मिश्रविष्कम्भक m. a kind of interlude (d.).
मुकुट m. n. — मुख्यार्थ.
मुष्टिहन् a. — मृध m. n.
मेढ्र. — मोघता f. vainness etc.
मोमुघ. — मोरट.
यत्कारणम् (sic!)
यथेष्टासन a. sitting at ease.
यन्तृ put after यन्तव्य.
1-3यातृ put after यातुहन्.
यूथ, read, herd (for heat). — योग्य.
यौन a. (& n.).
रक्षाधिकृत (sic!)
रमट (after रम). — रोपण.
लय a. dulling etc. — लिखन n.
लोकदुःख n. worldly sorrows.
लोकपितामह m. E. of Brahman.
वधजीविन् a. living etc.
वध्यचिह्न n. sign of death.
वाजिरूपधर a. — विटङ्क s.
विधुर a. — विविधागम a.
श्वाची add, N. of an Apsaras.
विष्कम्भक (sic!)

विहस्त etc. read trunk for tusk, & add °स्ती कृ make handless or awkward.*

विह्वलित a. = विह्वल.

वीडुपवि a. strong-wheeled.

वीडुपाणि a. strong-hoofed.

वीडुङ्ग (sic!)

2वृ, add प्रति M. choose in return for (abl.).

वृचहन्तृ (sic!)

व्यासक्त a. attached to, intent on, occupied with (loc. or —°).

व्रज् add प्र approach or entreat for (2 acc.).*

शय्यागत a. lying on a bed.

शार्ङ्गहस्त a. bow in hand.

शुल्कस्थान n. toll-office.

श्वःसुत्या f. read, to-morrow's preparation for the S. ceremony.

संयतमुख, f. ई silent.

संयतात्मन् a. self-controlled.

संयाति m. a man's name.

संयाव m. a sort of cake.

संप्रसुप्त a. asleep, sleeping.

सुपरिज्ञात a. well known.

सुवर्णरज्जु f. a gold thread.

सुश्लिष्ट etc. add, well closed.*

हस्तिहिरण्य n. sgl. elephants and gold.

LaVergne, TN USA
09 September 2010
196493LV00003B/2/P

9 781108 007306